Essentials *of* Investments

The McGraw-Hill/Irwin Series in Finance, Insurance, and Real Estate

Stephen A. Ross
Franco Modigliani Professor of Finance
and Economics
Sloan School of Management
Massachusetts Institute of Technology
Consulting Editor

FINANCIAL MANAGEMENT

Block, Hirt, and Danielsen
Foundations of Financial Management
Sixteenth Edition

Brealey, Myers, and Allen
Principles of Corporate Finance
Twelfth Edition

Brealey, Myers, and Allen
**Principles of Corporate Finance,
Concise**
Second Edition

Brealey, Myers, and Marcus
Fundamentals of Corporate Finance
Eighth Edition

Brooks
FinGame Online 5.0

Bruner
**Case Studies in Finance: Managing
for Corporate Value Creation**
Sixth Edition

Cornett, Adair, and Nofsinger
Finance: Applications and Theory
Third Edition

Cornett, Adair, and Nofsinger
M: Finance
Third Edition

DeMello
Cases in Finance
Second Edition

Grinblatt (editor)
**Stephen A. Ross, Mentor: Influence
through Generations**

Grinblatt and Titman
**Financial Markets and Corporate
Strategy**
Second Edition

Higgins
Analysis for Financial Management
Eleventh Edition

Ross, Westerfield, Jaffe, and Jordan
Corporate Finance
Eleventh Edition

Ross, Westerfield, Jaffe, and Jordan
**Corporate Finance: Core Principles
and Applications**
Fourth Edition

Ross, Westerfield, and Jordan
Essentials of Corporate Finance
Ninth Edition

Ross, Westerfield, and Jordan
Fundamentals of Corporate Finance
Eleventh Edition

Shefrin
**Behavioral Corporate Finance:
Decisions That Create Value**

INVESTMENTS

Bodie, Kane, and Marcus
Essentials of Investments
Tenth Edition

Bodie, Kane, and Marcus
Investments
Tenth Edition

Hirt and Block
**Fundamentals of Investment
Management**
Tenth Edition

Jordan and Miller
**Fundamentals of Investments:
Valuation and Management**
Seventh Edition

Stewart, Piros, and Heisler
**Running Money: Professional
Portfolio Management**

Sundaram and Das
Derivatives: Principles and Practice
Second Edition

FINANCIAL INSTITUTIONS
AND MARKETS

Rose and Hudgins
**Bank Management and Financial
Services**
Ninth Edition

Rose and Marquis
Financial Institutions and Markets
Eleventh Edition

Saunders and Cornett
**Financial Institutions Management:
A Risk Management Approach**
Eighth Edition

Saunders and Cornett
Financial Markets and Institutions
Sixth Edition

INTERNATIONAL FINANCE

Eun and Resnick
International Financial Management
Seventh Edition

REAL ESTATE

Brueggeman and Fisher
Real Estate Finance and Investments
Fifteenth Edition

Ling and Archer
**Real Estate Principles: A Value
Approach**
Fourth Edition

FINANCIAL PLANNING AND
INSURANCE

Allen, Melone, Rosenbloom, and
Mahoney
**Retirement Plans: 401(k)s, IRAs,
and Other Deferred Compensation
Approaches**
Eleventh Edition

Altfest
Personal Financial Planning
Second Edition

Kapoor, Dlabay, and Hughes
**Focus on Personal Finance:
An Active Approach to Help You
Develop Successful Financial Skills**
Fifth Edition

Kapoor, Dlabay, and Hughes
Personal Finance
Eleventh Edition

Walker and Walker
**Personal Finance: Building Your
Future**
Second Edition

Essentials *of* Investments

Tenth Edition

ZVI BODIE
Boston University

ALEX KANE
University of California, San Diego

ALAN J. MARCUS
Boston College

McGraw Hill Education

ESSENTIALS OF INVESTMENTS
Published by McGraw-Hill Education, 2 Penn Plaza, New York, NY 10121. Copyright © 2017 by McGraw-Hill Education.
All rights reserved. Printed in the United States of America. No part of this publication may be reproduced or distributed
in any form or by any means, or stored in a database or retrieval system, without the prior written consent of McGraw-Hill
Education, including, but not limited to, in any network or other electronic storage or transmission, or broadcast for distance
learning.

Some ancillaries, including electronic and print components, may not be available to customers outside the United States.

This book is printed on acid-free paper.

2 3 4 5 6 7 8 9 LWI 21 20 19 18

ISBN 978-1-259-25504-5
MHID 1-259-25504-2

All credits appearing on page or at the end of the book are considered to be an extension of the copyright page.

The Internet addresses listed in the text were accurate at the time of publication. The inclusion of a website does not
indicate an endorsement by the authors or McGraw-Hill Education, and McGraw-Hill Education does not guarantee the
accuracy of the information presented at these sites.

mheducation.com/highered

About the Authors

Zvi Bodie
Boston University

Zvi Bodie is Professor of Finance and Economics at Boston University School of Management. He holds a PhD from the Massachusetts Institute of Technology and has served on the finance faculty at Harvard Business School and MIT's Sloan School of Management. Professor Bodie has published widely on pension finance and investment strategy in leading professional journals. His books include *Foundations of Pension Finance, Pensions in the U.S. Economy, Issues in Pension Economics,* and *Financial Aspects of the U.S. Pension System.* Professor Bodie is a member of the Pension Research Council of the Wharton School, University of Pennsylvania. His latest book is *Worry-Free Investing: A Safe Approach to Achieving Your Lifetime Financial Goals.*

Alex Kane
University of California, San Diego

Alex Kane is Professor of Finance and Economics at the Graduate School of International Relations and Pacific Studies at the University of California, San Diego. He holds a PhD from the Stern School of Business of New York University and has been Visiting Professor at the Faculty of Economics, University of Tokyo; Graduate School of Business, Harvard; Kennedy School of Government, Harvard; and Research Associate, National Bureau of Economic Research. An author of many articles in finance and management journals, Professor Kane's research is mainly in corporate finance, portfolio management, and capital markets.

Alan J. Marcus
Boston College

Alan Marcus is the Mario J. Gabelli Professor of Finance in the Carroll School of Management at Boston College. He received his PhD from MIT, has been a Visiting Professor at MIT's Sloan School of Management and Athens Laboratory of Business Administration, and has served as a Research Fellow at the National Bureau of Economic Research, where he participated in both the Pension Economics and the Financial Markets and Monetary Economics Groups. Professor Marcus also spent two years at the Federal Home Loan Mortgage Corporation (Freddie Mac), where he helped to develop mortgage pricing and credit risk models. Professor Marcus has published widely in the fields of capital markets and portfolio theory. He currently serves on the Research Foundation Advisory Board of the CFA Institute.

Brief Contents

Part ONE
ELEMENTS OF INVESTMENTS   1

1   Investments: Background and Issues   2

2   Asset Classes and Financial Instruments   26

3   Securities Markets   54

4   Mutual Funds and Other Investment Companies   84

Part TWO
PORTFOLIO THEORY   109

5   Risk and Return: Past and Prologue   110

6   Efficient Diversification   147

7   Capital Asset Pricing and Arbitrage Pricing Theory   192

8   The Efficient Market Hypothesis   232

9   Behavioral Finance and Technical Analysis   264

Part THREE
DEBT SECURITIES   289

10   Bond Prices and Yields   290

11   Managing Bond Portfolios   334

Part FOUR
SECURITY ANALYSIS   369

12   Macroeconomic and Industry Analysis   370

13   Equity Valuation   402

14   Financial Statement Analysis   443

Part FIVE
DERIVATIVE MARKETS   483

15   Options Markets   484

16   Option Valuation   519

17   Futures Markets and Risk Management   557

Part SIX
ACTIVE INVESTMENT MANAGEMENT   591

18   Portfolio Performance Evaluation   592

19   Globalization and International Investing   625

20   Hedge Funds   661

21   Taxes, Inflation, and Investment Strategy   684

22   Investors and the Investment Process   706

Appendixes

A   References   728

B   References to CFA Questions   734

Index   I-1

Contents

Part ONE
ELEMENTS OF INVESTMENTS 1

1 Investments: Background and Issues 2

1.1 Real Assets Versus Financial Assets 3
1.2 Financial Assets 5
1.3 Financial Markets and the Economy 6
The Informational Role of Financial Markets 6
Consumption Timing 6
Allocation of Risk 7
Separation of Ownership and Management 7
Corporate Governance and Corporate Ethics 8
1.4 The Investment Process 9
1.5 Markets Are Competitive 10
The Risk-Return Trade-Off 10
Efficient Markets 11
1.6 The Players 11
Financial Intermediaries 12
Investment Bankers 14
Venture Capital and Private Equity 15
1.7 The Financial Crisis of 2008 15
Antecedents of the Crisis 15
Changes in Housing Finance 17
Mortgage Derivatives 19
Credit Default Swaps 19
The Rise of Systemic Risk 20
The Shoe Drops 20
The Dodd-Frank Reform Act 21
1.8 Outline of the Text 22

End of Chapter Material 22–25

2 Asset Classes and Financial Instruments 26

2.1 The Money Market 27
Treasury Bills 27
Certificates of Deposit 28
Commercial Paper 28
Bankers' Acceptances 29

Eurodollars 29
Repos and Reverses 29
Brokers' Calls 29
Federal Funds 29
The LIBOR Market 30
Yields on Money Market Instruments 30
2.2 The Bond Market 32
Treasury Notes and Bonds 32
Inflation-Protected Treasury Bonds 33
Federal Agency Debt 33
International Bonds 33
Municipal Bonds 34
Corporate Bonds 36
Mortgages and Mortgage-Backed Securities 36
2.3 Equity Securities 38
Common Stock as Ownership Shares 38
Characteristics of Common Stock 39
Stock Market Listings 39
Preferred Stock 40
Depositary Receipts 40
2.4 Stock and Bond Market Indexes 40
Stock Market Indexes 40
Dow Jones Averages 40
Standard & Poor's Indexes 42
Other U.S. Market Value Indexes 44
Equally Weighted Indexes 44
Foreign and International Stock Market Indexes 45
Bond Market Indicators 45
2.5 Derivative Markets 46
Options 46
Futures Contracts 47

End of Chapter Material 48–53

3 Securities Markets 54

3.1 How Firms Issue Securities 55
Privately Held Firms 55
Publicly Traded Companies 56
Shelf Registration 56
Initial Public Offerings 57

3.2 How Securities are Traded   57
    Types of Markets 58
    Types of Orders 59
    Trading Mechanisms 61
3.3 The Rise of Electronic Trading 62
3.4 U.S. Markets 64
    NASDAQ 64
    The New York Stock Exchange 65
    ECNs 65
3.5 New Trading Strategies 65
    Algorithmic Trading 66
    High-Frequency Trading 66
    Dark Pools 67
    Bond Trading 68
3.6 Globalization of Stock Markets 68
3.7 Trading Costs 69
3.8 Buying on Margin 70
3.9 Short Sales 72
3.10 Regulation of Securities Markets 75
    Self-Regulation 76
    The Sarbanes-Oxley Act 77
    Insider Trading 78

    End of Chapter Material   78–83

4 Mutual Funds and Other Investment Companies 84

4.1 Investment Companies 85
4.2 Types of Investment Companies 85
    Unit Investment Trusts 86
    Managed Investment Companies 86
    Other Investment Organizations 87
4.3 Mutual Funds 88
    Investment Policies 88
    How Funds Are Sold 90
4.4 Costs of Investing in Mutual Funds 91
    Fee Structures 91
    Fees and Mutual Fund Returns 93
4.5 Taxation of Mutual Fund Income 94
4.6 Exchange-Traded Funds 95
4.7 Mutual Fund Investment Performance: a First Look 98
4.8 Information on Mutual Funds 101

    End of Chapter Material   103–108

Part TWO
PORTFOLIO THEORY   109

5 Risk and Return: Past and Prologue 110

5.1 Rates of Return 111
    Measuring Investment Returns over Multiple Periods 111
    Conventions for Annualizing Rates of Return 113
5.2 Inflation and the Real Rate of Interest 114
    The Equilibrium Nominal Rate of Interest 115
5.3 Risk and Risk Premiums 116
    Scenario Analysis and Probability Distributions 116
    The Normal Distribution 118
    Normality over Time 120
    Deviation from Normality and Value at Risk 121
    Using Time Series of Return 122
    Risk Premiums and Risk Aversion 123
    The Sharpe Ratio 125
5.4 The Historical Record 125
    History of U.S. Interest Rates, Inflation, and Real Interest Rates 125
    World and U.S. Risky Stock and Bond Portfolios 127
5.5 Asset Allocation across Risky and Risk-Free Portfolios 133
    The Risk-Free Asset 133
    Portfolio Expected Return and Risk 134
    The Capital Allocation Line 135
    Risk Aversion and Capital Allocation 136
5.6 Passive Strategies and the Capital Market Line 137
    Historical Evidence on the Capital Market Line 137
    Costs and Benefits of Passive Investing 138

    End of Chapter Material   139–146

6 Efficient Diversification 147

6.1 Diversification and Portfolio Risk 148
6.2 Asset Allocation with Two Risky Assets 149
    Covariance and Correlation 150
    Using Historical Data 153
    The Three Rules of Two-Risky-Assets Portfolios 154
    The Risk-Return Trade-Off with Two-Risky-Assets Portfolios 155
    The Mean-Variance Criterion 157
6.3 The Optimal Risky Portfolio with a Risk-Free Asset 159
6.4 Efficient Diversification with Many Risky Assets 163
    The Efficient Frontier of Risky Assets 163
    Choosing the Optimal Risky Portfolio 165
    The Preferred Complete Portfolio and a Separation Property 165
    Constructing the Optimal Risky Portfolio: An Illustration 166

6.5 A Single-Index Stock Market 168

Statistical and Graphical Representation of the Single-Index Model 170

Diversification in a Single-Index Security Market 172

Using Security Analysis with the Index Model 174

6.6 Risk of Long-Term Investments 176

Risk and Return with Alternative Long-Term Investments 176

Why the Unending Confusion? 179

End of Chapter Material 179–191

7 Capital Asset Pricing and Arbitrage Pricing Theory 192

7.1 The Capital Asset Pricing Model 193

The Model: Assumptions and Implications 193

Why All Investors Would Hold the Market Portfolio 194

The Passive Strategy Is Efficient 195

The Risk Premium of the Market Portfolio 196

Expected Returns on Individual Securities 197

The Security Market Line 198

Applications of the CAPM 199

7.2 The CAPM and Index Models 200

The Index Model, Realized Returns, and the Mean–Beta Equation 201

Estimating the Index Model 201

Predicting Betas 208

7.3 The CAPM and the Real World 208

7.4 Multifactor Models and the CAPM 210

The Fama-French Three-Factor Model 211

Multifactor Models and the Validity of the CAPM 214

7.5 Arbitrage Pricing Theory 214

Well-Diversified Portfolios and the APT 215

The APT and the CAPM 218

Multifactor Generalization of the APT and CAPM 218

End of Chapter Material 220–231

8 The Efficient Market Hypothesis 232

8.1 Random Walks and the Efficient Market Hypothesis 233

Competition as the Source of Efficiency 235

Versions of the Efficient Market Hypothesis 236

8.2 Implications of the EMH 237

Technical Analysis 237

Fundamental Analysis 238

Active versus Passive Portfolio Management 239

The Role of Portfolio Management in an Efficient Market 240

Resource Allocation 240

8.3 Are Markets Efficient? 241

The Issues 241

Weak-Form Tests: Patterns in Stock Returns 243

Predictors of Broad Market Returns 244

Semistrong Tests: Market Anomalies 244

Strong-Form Tests: Inside Information 249

Interpreting the Anomalies 249

8.4 Mutual Fund and Analyst Performance 252

Stock Market Analysts 252

Mutual Fund Managers 252

So, Are Markets Efficient? 256

End of Chapter Material 256–263

9 Behavioral Finance and Technical Analysis 264

9.1 The Behavioral Critique 265

Information Processing 266

Behavioral Biases 267

Limits to Arbitrage 269

Limits to Arbitrage and the Law of One Price 270

Bubbles and Behavioral Economics 272

Evaluating the Behavioral Critique 273

9.2 Technical Analysis and Behavioral Finance 274

Trends and Corrections 274

Sentiment Indicators 279

A Warning 280

End of Chapter Material 281–288

Part THREE

DEBT SECURITIES 289

10 Bond Prices and Yields 290

10.1 Bond Characteristics 291

Treasury Bonds and Notes 291

Corporate Bonds 293

Preferred Stock 294

Other Domestic Issuers 295

International Bonds 295

Innovation in the Bond Market 295

10.2 Bond Pricing 297

Bond Pricing between Coupon Dates 300

Bond Pricing in Excel 301

10.3 Bond Yields 302
   Yield to Maturity 302
   Yield to Call 304
   Realized Compound Return versus Yield to Maturity 306
10.4 Bond Prices over Time 308
   Yield to Maturity versus Holding-Period Return 309
   Zero-Coupon Bonds and Treasury STRIPS 310
   After-Tax Returns 310
10.5 Default Risk and Bond Pricing 312
   Junk Bonds 312
   Determinants of Bond Safety 312
   Bond Indentures 314
   Yield to Maturity and Default Risk 315
   Credit Default Swaps 317
10.6 The Yield Curve 319
   The Expectations Theory 319
   The Liquidity Preference Theory 322
   A Synthesis 323

   End of Chapter Material 324–333

11 Managing Bond Portfolios 334

11.1 Interest Rate Risk 335
   Interest Rate Sensitivity 335
   Duration 337
   What Determines Duration? 341
11.2 Passive Bond Management 343
   Immunization 343
   Cash Flow Matching and Dedication 349
11.3 Convexity 350
   Why Do Investors Like Convexity? 352
11.4 Active Bond Management 354
   Sources of Potential Profit 354
   Horizon Analysis 355
   An Example of a Fixed-Income Investment Strategy 355

   End of Chapter Material 356–368

Part FOUR
SECURITY ANALYSIS 369

12 Macroeconomic and Industry Analysis 370

12.1 The Global Economy 371

12.2 The Domestic Macroeconomy 373
   Gross Domestic Product 374
   Employment 374
   Inflation 374
   Interest Rates 374
   Budget Deficit 374
   Sentiment 374
12.3 Interest Rates 375
12.4 Demand and Supply Shocks 376
12.5 Federal Government Policy 377
   Fiscal Policy 377
   Monetary Policy 377
   Supply-Side Policies 378
12.6 Business Cycles 379
   The Business Cycle 379
   Economic Indicators 381
   Other Indicators 384
12.7 Industry Analysis 384
   Defining an Industry 385
   Sensitivity to the Business Cycle 387
   Sector Rotation 388
   Industry Life Cycles 389
   Industry Structure and Performance 392

   End of Chapter Material 393–401

13 Equity Valuation 402

13.1 Valuation by Comparables 403
   Limitations of Book Value 404
13.2 Intrinsic Value Versus Market Price 404
13.3 Dividend Discount Models 406
   The Constant-Growth DDM 407
   Stock Prices and Investment Opportunities 409
   Life Cycles and Multistage Growth Models 412
   Multistage Growth Models 416
13.4 Price–Earnings Ratios 417
   The Price–Earnings Ratio and Growth Opportunities 417
   P/E Ratios and Stock Risk 421
   Pitfalls in P/E Analysis 421
   Combining P/E Analysis and the DDM 424
   Other Comparative Valuation Ratios 424
13.5 Free Cash Flow Valuation Approaches 425
   Comparing the Valuation Models 428
   The Problem with DCF Models 429
13.6 The Aggregate Stock Market 429

   End of Chapter Material 431–442

14 Financial Statement Analysis 443

14.1 The Major Financial Statements 444

The Income Statement 444

The Balance Sheet 445

The Statement of Cash Flows 445

14.2 Measuring Firm Performance 448

14.3 Profitability Measures 448

Return on Assets 449

Return on Capital 449

Return on Equity 449

Financial Leverage and ROE 449

Economic Value Added 451

14.4 Ratio Analysis 452

Decomposition of ROE 452

Turnover and Asset Utilization 454

Liquidity Ratios 457

Market Price Ratios 458

Choosing a Benchmark 459

14.5 An Illustration of Financial Statement Analysis 460

14.6 Comparability Problems 463

Inventory Valuation 464

Depreciation 464

Inflation and Interest Expense 465

Fair Value Accounting 465

Quality of Earnings and Accounting Practices 466

International Accounting Conventions 468

14.7 Value Investing: The Graham Technique 469

End of Chapter Material 470–482

Part FIVE
DERIVATIVE MARKETS 483

15 Options Markets 484

15.1 The Option Contract 485

Options Trading 486

American and European Options 487

The Option Clearing Corporation 488

Other Listed Options 488

15.2 Values of Options at Expiration 489

Call Options 489

Put Options 490

Options versus Stock Investments 492

Option Strategies 494

15.3 Optionlike Securities 502

Callable Bonds 502

Convertible Securities 503

Warrants 505

Collateralized Loans 506

Leveraged Equity and Risky Debt 506

15.4 Exotic Options 507

Asian Options 508

Currency-Translated Options 508

Digital Options 508

End of Chapter Material 508–518

16 Option Valuation 519

16.1 Option Valuation: Introduction 520

Intrinsic and Time Values 520

Determinants of Option Values 520

16.2 Binomial Option Pricing 522

Two-State Option Pricing 522

Generalizing the Two-State Approach 525

Making the Valuation Model Practical 526

16.3 Black-Scholes Option Valuation 529

The Black-Scholes Formula 530

The Put-Call Parity Relationship 536

Put Option Valuation 539

16.4 Using the Black-Scholes Formula 539

Hedge Ratios and the Black-Scholes Formula 539

Portfolio Insurance 541

Option Pricing and the Crisis of 2008–2009 544

16.5 Empirical Evidence 545

End of Chapter Material 546–556

17 Futures Markets and Risk Management 557

17.1 The Futures Contract 558

The Basics of Futures Contracts 558

Existing Contracts 561

17.2 Trading Mechanics 563

The Clearinghouse and Open Interest 563

Marking to Market and the Margin Account 565

Cash versus Actual Delivery 567

Regulations 567

Taxation 567

17.3 Futures Market Strategies 568

Hedging and Speculation 568

Basis Risk and Hedging 570

17.4 Futures Prices 571

Spot-Futures Parity 571

Spreads 575

17.5 Financial Futures 576

Stock-Index Futures 576

Creating Synthetic Stock Positions 577

Index Arbitrage 577

Foreign Exchange Futures 578

Interest Rate Futures 578

17.6 Swaps 581

  Swaps and Balance Sheet Restructuring 582

  The Swap Dealer 582

  End of Chapter Material   583–590

Part SIX

ACTIVE INVESTMENT MANAGEMENT   591

18 Portfolio Performance Evaluation 592

18.1 Risk-Adjusted Returns 593

  Investment Clients, Service Providers, and Objectives of Performance Evaluation 593

  Comparison Groups 593

  Basic Performance-Evaluation Statistics 594

  Performance Evaluation of Entire-Wealth Portfolios Using the Sharpe Ratio and M-Square 595

  Performance Evaluation of Fund of Funds Using the Treynor Measure 597

  Performance Evaluation of a Portfolio Added to the Benchmark Using the Information Ratio 598

  The Relation of Alpha to Performance Measures 598

  Performance Evaluation with a Multi-Index Model 600

18.2 Style Analysis 601

18.3 Morningstar's Risk-Adjusted Rating 603

18.4 Risk Adjustments with Changing Portfolio Composition 605

  Performance Manipulation 606

18.5 Performance Attribution Procedures 606

  Asset Allocation Decisions 608

  Sector and Security Selection Decisions 609

  Summing Up Component Contributions 610

18.6 Market Timing 612

  Valuing Market Timing as an Option 613

  The Value of Imperfect Forecasting 614

  Measurement of Market-Timing Performance 615

  End of Chapter Material   616–624

19 Globalization and International Investing 625

19.1 Global Markets for Equities 626

  Developed Countries 626

  Emerging Markets 626

  Market Capitalization and GDP 629

  Home-Country Bias 630

19.2 Risk Factors in International Investing 630

  Exchange Rate Risk 630

  Imperfect Exchange Rate Risk Hedging 635

  Political Risk 635

19.3 International Investing: Risk, Return, and Benefits from Diversification 639

  Risk and Return: Summary Statistics 639

  Are Investments in Emerging Markets Riskier? 642

  Are Average Returns Higher in Emerging Markets? 644

  Is Exchange Rate Risk Important in International Portfolios? 645

  Benefits from International Diversification 647

  Misleading Representation of Diversification Benefits 649

  Realistic Benefits from International Diversification 649

  Are Benefits from International Diversification Preserved in Bear Markets? 650

  Active Management and International Diversification 651

19.4 International Investing and Performance Attribution 653

  Constructing a Benchmark Portfolio of Foreign Assets 653

  Performance Attribution 653

  End of Chapter Material   656–660

20 Hedge Funds 661

20.1 Hedge Funds Versus Mutual Funds 662

20.2 Hedge Fund Strategies 663

  Directional and Nondirectional Strategies 663

  Statistical Arbitrage 665

20.3 Portable Alpha 665

  An Example of a Pure Play 666

20.4 Style Analysis for Hedge Funds 668

20.5 Performance Measurement for Hedge Funds 669

  Liquidity and Hedge Fund Performance 670

  Hedge Fund Performance and Survivorship Bias 672

  Hedge Fund Performance and Changing Factor Loadings 673

  Tail Events and Hedge Fund Performance 674

20.6 Fee Structure in Hedge Funds 676

  End of Chapter Material   679–683

21 Taxes, Inflation, and Investment Strategy 684

21.1 Saving for the Long Run 685
    A Hypothetical Household 685
    The Retirement Annuity 685

21.2 Accounting for Inflation 686
    A Real Savings Plan 686
    An Alternative Savings Plan 688

21.3 Accounting for Taxes 689

21.4 The Economics of Tax Shelters 690
    A Benchmark Tax Shelter 691
    The Effect of the Progressive Nature of the Tax Code 692

21.5 A Menu of Tax Shelters 694
    Defined Benefit Plans 694
    Employee Defined Contribution Plans 694
    Individual Retirement Accounts 695
    Roth Accounts with the Progressive Tax Code 695
    Risky Investments and Capital Gains as Tax Shelters 697
    Sheltered versus Unsheltered Savings 697

21.6 Social Security 699

21.7 Large Purchases 700

21.8 Home Ownership: The Rent-Versus-Buy Decision 701

21.9 Uncertain Longevity and Other Contingencies 701

21.10 Matrimony, Bequest, and Intergenerational Transfers 702

    End of Chapter Material 703–705

22 Investors and the Investment Process 706

22.1 The Investment Management Process 707

22.2 Investor Objectives 709
    Individual Investors 709
    Professional Investors 710
    Life Insurance Companies 712
    Non-Life-Insurance Companies 713
    Banks 713
    Endowment Funds 713

22.3 Investor Constraints 714
    Liquidity 714
    Investment Horizon 715
    Regulations 715
    Tax Considerations 715
    Unique Needs 715

22.4 Investment Policies 717
    Top-Down Policies for Institutional Investors 718
    Active versus Passive Policies 719

22.5 Monitoring and Revising Investment Portfolios 721

    End of Chapter Material 721–727

Appendixes

A   References   728

B   References to CFA Questions   734

Index   I-1

A Note from the Authors . . .

The past three decades witnessed rapid and profound change in the investment industry as well as a financial crisis of historic magnitude. The vast expansion of financial markets during this period was due in part to innovations in securitization and credit enhancement that gave birth to new trading strategies. These strategies were in turn made feasible by developments in communication and information technology, as well as by advances in the theory of investments.

Yet the crisis was also rooted in the cracks of these developments. Many of the innovations in security design facilitated high leverage and an exaggerated notion of the efficacy of risk transfer strategies. This engendered complacency about risk that was coupled with relaxation of regulation as well as reduced transparency that masked the precarious condition of many big players in the system.

Of necessity, our text has evolved along with financial markets. We devote considerable attention to recent breathtaking changes in market structure and trading technology. At the same time, however, many basic *principles* of investments remain important. We continue to organize the book around one basic theme—that security markets are nearly efficient, meaning that you should expect to find few obvious bargains in these markets. Given what we know about securities, their prices usually appropriately reflect their risk and return attributes; free lunches are few and far apart in markets as competitive as these. This starting point remains a powerful approach to security valuation. While the degree of market efficiency is and will always be a matter of debate, this first principle of valuation, specifically that in the absence of private information prices are the best guide to value, is still valid. Greater emphasis on risk analysis is the lesson woven into the text.

This text also places greater emphasis on *asset allocation* than most other books. We prefer this emphasis for two important reasons. First, it corresponds to the procedure that most individuals actually follow when building an investment portfolio. Typically, you start with all of your money in a bank account, only then considering how much to invest in something riskier that might offer a higher expected return. The logical step at this point is to consider other risky asset classes, such as stock, bonds, or real estate. This is an asset allocation decision. Second, in most cases the asset allocation choice is far more important than specific security-selection decisions in determining overall investment performance. Asset allocation is the primary determinant of the risk-return profile of the investment portfolio, and so it deserves primary attention in a study of investment policy.

Our book also focuses on investment analysis, which allows us to present the practical applications of investment theory and to convey insights of practical value. We provide a systematic collection of Excel spreadsheets that give you tools to explore concepts more deeply. These spreadsheets are available as part of the Connect resources for this text and provide a taste of the sophisticated analytic tools available to professional investors.

In our efforts to link theory to practice, we also have attempted to make our approach consistent with that of the CFA Institute. The Institute administers an education and certification program to candidates seeking designation as a Chartered Financial Analyst (CFA). The CFA curriculum represents the consensus of a committee of distinguished scholars and practitioners regarding the core of knowledge required by the investment professional. We continue to include questions from previous CFA exams in our end-of-chapter problems as well as CFA-style questions derived from the Kaplan-Schweser CFA preparation courses.

This text will introduce you to the major issues of concern to all investors. It can give you the skills to conduct a sophisticated assessment of current issues and debates covered by both the popular media and more specialized finance journals. Whether you plan to become an investment professional or simply a sophisticated individual investor, you will find these skills essential.

Zvi Bodie
Alex Kane
Alan J. Marcus

Organization of the Tenth Edition

Essentials of Investments, Tenth Edition, is intended as a textbook on investment analysis most applicable for a student's first course in investments. The chapters are written in a modular format to give instructors the flexibility to either omit certain chapters or rearrange their order. The highlights in the margins describe updates and important features in this edition.

This part lays out the general framework for the investment process in a nontechnical manner. We discuss the major players in the financial markets and provide an overview of security types and trading mechanisms. These chapters make it possible for instructors to assign term projects analyzing securities early in the course.

Includes sections on securitization, the roots of the financial crisis, and the fallout from the crisis.

Extensive coverage of the rise of electronic markets, algorithmic and high-speed trading, and changes in market structure.

Greater coverage of innovations in exchange-traded funds.

This part contains the core of modern portfolio theory. For courses emphasizing security analysis, this part may be skipped without loss of continuity.

All data are updated and available on the web through the Connect resources. The data are used in new treatments of risk management and tail risk.

Introduces simple in-chapter spreadsheets that can be used to compute investment opportunity sets and the index model.

Introduces single-factor as well as multifactor models.

Updated with more coverage of anomalies over time.

Contains extensive treatment of behavioral finance and provides an introduction to technical analysis.

Part ONE
ELEMENTS OF INVESTMENTS   1

1   Investments: Background and Issues   2

2   Asset Classes and Financial Instruments   26

3   Securities Markets   54

4   Mutual Funds and Other Investment Companies   84

Part TWO
PORTFOLIO THEORY   109

5   Risk and Return: Past and Prologue   110

6   Efficient Diversification   147

7   Capital Asset Pricing and Arbitrage Pricing Theory   192

8   The Efficient Market Hypothesis   232

9   Behavioral Finance and Technical Analysis   264

Part THREE
DEBT SECURITIES   289

| 10 | Bond Prices and Yields | 290 |
| 11 | Managing Bond Portfolios | 334 |

Part FOUR
SECURITY ANALYSIS   369

12	Macroeconomic and Industry Analysis	370
13	Equity Valuation	402
14	Financial Statement Analysis	443

Part FIVE
DERIVATIVE MARKETS   483

15	Options Markets	484
16	Option Valuation	519
17	Futures Markets and Risk Management	557

Part SIX
ACTIVE INVESTMENT MANAGEMENT   591

18	Portfolio Performance Evaluation	592
19	Globalization and International Investing	625
20	Hedge Funds	661
21	Taxes, Inflation, and Investment Strategy	684
22	Investors and the Investment Process	706

This is the first of three parts on security valuation.

Includes material on sovereign credit default swaps.

Contains spreadsheet material on duration and convexity.

This part is presented in a "top-down" manner, starting with the broad macroeconomic environment before moving to more specific analysis.

Discusses how international political developments such as the euro crisis can have major impacts on economic prospects.

Contains free cash flow equity valuation models as well as a discussion of the pitfalls of discounted cash flow models.

Includes a top-down rationale for how ratio analysis can be organized to guide one's analysis of firm performance.

This part highlights how these markets have become crucial and integral to the financial universe and are major sources of innovation.

Offers thorough introduction to option payoffs, strategies, and securities with embedded options.

Extensive introduction to risk-neutral valuation methods and their implementation in the binomial option-pricing model.

This part unifies material on active management and is ideal for a closing-semester unit on applying theory to actual portfolio management.

Rigorous development of performance evaluation methods.

Provides evidence on international correlation and the benefits of diversification.

Updated assessment of hedge fund performance and the exposure of hedge funds to "black swans."

Employs extensive spreadsheet analysis of the interaction of taxes and inflation on long-term financial strategies.

Modeled after the CFA Institute curriculum, also includes guidelines on "How to Become a Chartered Financial Analyst."

Pedagogical Features

Learning Objectives

Each chapter begins with a summary of the chapter learning objectives, providing students with an overview of the concepts they should understand after reading the chapter. The end-of-chapter problems and CFA questions are tagged with the corresponding learning objective.

Learning Objectives

LO 3-1 Describe how firms issue securities to the public.

LO 3-2 Identify various types of orders investors can submit to their brokers.

LO 3-3 Describe trading practices in dealer markets, specialist-directed stock exchanges, and electronic communication networks.

LO 3-4 Compare the mechanics and investment implications of buying on margin and short-selling.

Chapter Overview

Each chapter begins with a brief narrative to explain the concepts that will be covered in more depth. Relevant websites related to chapter material can be found in Connect. These sites make it easy for students to research topics further and retrieve financial data and information.

> You learned in Chapter 1 that the process of building an investment portfolio usually begins by deciding how much money to allocate to broad classes of assets, such as safe money market securities or bank accounts, longer-term bonds, stocks, or even asset classes such as real estate or precious metals. This process is called *asset allocation*. Within each class the investor then selects specific assets from a more detailed menu. This is called *security selection*.
>
> short-term, marketable, liquid, low-risk debt securities. Money market instruments sometimes are called *cash equivalents*, or just *cash* for short. Capital markets, in contrast, include longer-term and riskier securities. Securities in the capital market are much more diverse than those found within the money market. For this reason, we will subdivide the capital market into three segments: longer-term debt markets, equity markets, and derivative markets in which options and futures trade.

Key Terms in the Margin

Key terms are indicated in color and defined in the margin the first time the term is used. A full list of key terms is included in the end-of-chapter materials.

Publicly Traded Companies

initial public offering (IPO)
First public sale of stock by a formerly private company.

When a private firm decides that it wishes to raise capital from a wide range of investors, it may decide to *go public*. This means that it will sell its securities to the general public and allow those investors to freely trade those shares in established securities markets. The first issue of shares to the general public is called the firm's **initial public offering (IPO)**. Later, the firm may go back to the public and issue additional shares. A *seasoned equity offering* is the sale of additional shares in firms that already are publicly traded. For example, a sale by Apple of new shares of stock would be considered a seasoned new issue.

Numbered Equations

Key equations are called out in the text and identified by equation numbers. These key formulas are listed at the end of each chapter. Equations that are frequently used are also featured on the text's end sheets for convenient reference.

One way of comparing bonds is to determine the interest rate on taxable bonds that would be necessary to provide an after-tax return equal to that of municipals. To derive this value, we set after-tax yields equal and solve for the *equivalent taxable yield* of the tax-exempt bond. This is the rate a taxable bond would need to offer in order to match the after-tax yield on the tax-free municipal.

$$r(1 - t) = r_m \tag{2.1}$$

or

$$r = \frac{r_m}{1 - t} \tag{2.2}$$

Thus, the equivalent taxable yield is simply the tax-free rate divided by $1 - t$. Table 2.2 presents equivalent taxable yields for several municipal yields and tax rates.

On the Market Front Boxes

Current articles from financial publications such as *The Wall Street Journal* are featured as boxed readings. Each box is referred to within the narrative of the text, and its real-world relevance to the chapter material is clearly defined.

CONCEPT check 2.5

Reconsider companies XYZ and ABC from Concept Check Question 2.4. Calculate the percentage change in the market value–weighted index. Compare that to the rate of return of a portfolio that holds $500 of ABC stock for every $100 of XYZ stock (i.e., an index portfolio).

Concept Checks

These self-test questions in the body of the chapter enable students to determine whether the preceding material has been understood and then reinforce understanding before students read further. Detailed Solutions to the Concept Checks are found at the end of each chapter.

EXAMPLE 2.4

Value-Weighted Indexes

To illustrate how value-weighted indexes are computed, look again at Table 2.3. The final value of all outstanding stock in our two-stock universe is $690 million. The initial value was $600 million. Therefore, if the initial level of a market value–weighted index of stocks ABC and XYZ were set equal to an arbitrarily chosen starting value such as 100, the index value at year-end would be $100 \times (690/600) = 115$. The increase in the index would reflect the 15% return earned on a portfolio consisting of those two stocks held in proportion to outstanding market values.

Unlike the price-weighted index, the value-weighted index gives more weight to ABC. Whereas the price-weighted index fell because it was dominated by higher-price XYZ, the value-weighted index rose because it gave more weight to ABC, the stock with the higher total market value.

Note also from Tables 2.3 and 2.4 that market value–weighted indexes are unaffected by stock splits. The total market value of the outstanding XYZ stock increases from $100 million to $110 million regardless of the stock split, thereby rendering the split irrelevant to the performance of the index.

Numbered Examples

Numbered and titled examples are integrated in each chapter. Using the worked-out solutions to these examples as models, students can learn how to solve specific problems step-by-step as well as gain insight into general principles by seeing how they are applied to answer concrete questions.

Excel Integration

Excel Applications

Since many courses now require students to perform analyses in spreadsheet format, Excel has been integrated throughout the book. It is used in examples as well as in this chapter feature which shows students how to create and manipulate spreadsheets to solve specific problems. This feature starts with an example presented in the chapter, briefly discusses how a spreadsheet can be valuable for investigating the topic, shows a sample spreadsheet, and asks students to apply the data to answer questions. These applications also direct the student to the web to work with an interactive version of the spreadsheet. The spreadsheet files are available for download in Connect; available spreadsheets are denoted by an icon. As extra guidance, the spreadsheets include a comment feature that documents both inputs and outputs. Solutions for these exercises are located on the password-protected instructor site only, so instructors can assign these exercises either for homework or just for practice.

Excel application spreadsheets are available for the following:

Chapter 3: Buying on Margin; Short Sales
Chapter 7: Estimating the Index Model
Chapter 11: Immunization; Convexity
Chapter 15: Options, Stock, and Lending; Straddles and Spreads
Chapter 17: Parity and Spreads
Chapter 18: Performance Measures; Performance Attribution
Chapter 19: International Portfolios

Spreadsheet exhibit templates are also available for the following:

Chapter 5: Spreadsheet 5.1
Chapter 6: Spreadsheets 6.1–6.6
Chapter 10: Spreadsheets 10.1 & 10.2
Chapter 11: Spreadsheets 11.1 & 11.2
Chapter 13: Spreadsheets 13.1 & 13.2
Chapter 16: Spreadsheet 16.1
Chapter 21: Spreadsheets 21.1–21.10

EXCEL APPLICATIONS

Buying on Margin

This spreadsheet is available in Connect

The Excel spreadsheet model below makes it easy to analyze the impacts of different margin levels and the volatility of stock prices. It also allows you to compare return on investment for a margin trade with a trade using no borrowed funds.

	A	B	C	D	E	F	G	H
1								
2			Action or Formula	Ending	Return on		Ending	Return with
3			for Column B	St Price	Investment		St Price	No Margin
4	Initial Equity Investment	$10,000.00	Enter data		−42.00%			−19.00%
5	Amount Borrowed	$10,000.00	(B4/B10)−B4	$20.00	−122.00%		$20.00	−59.00%
6	Initial Stock Price	$50.00	Enter data	25.00	−102.00%		25.00	−49.00%
7	Shares Purchased	400	(B4/B10)/B6	30.00	−82.00%		30.00	−39.00%
8	Ending Stock Price	$40.00	Enter data	35.00	−62.00%		35.00	−29.00%
9	Cash Dividends During Hold Per.	$0.50	Enter data	40.00	−42.00%		40.00	−19.00%
10	Initial Margin Percentage	50.00%	Enter data	45.00	−22.00%		45.00	−9.00%
11	Maintenance Margin Percentage	30.00%	Enter data	50.00	−2.00%		50.00	1.00%
12				55.00	18.00%		55.00	11.00%
13	Rate on Margin Loan	8.00%	Enter data	60.00	38.00%		60.00	21.00%
14	Holding Period in Months	6	Enter data	65.00	58.00%		65.00	31.00%
15				70.00	78.00%		70.00	41.00%
16	Return on Investment			75.00	98.00%		75.00	51.00%
17	Capital Gain on Stock	−$4,000.00	B7*(B8−B6)	80.00	118.00%		80.00	61.00%
18	Dividends	$200.00	B7*B9					
19	Interest on Margin Loan	$400.00	B5*(B14/12)*B13					
20	Net Income	−$4,200.00	B17+B18−B19				LEGEND:	
21	Initial Investment	$10,000.00	B4				Enter data	
22	Return on Investment	−42.00%	B20/B21				Value calculated	

Excel Questions

1. Suppose you buy 100 shares of stock initially selling for $50, borrowing 25% of the necessary funds from your broker; that is, the initial margin on your purchase is 25%. You pay an interest rate of 8% on margin loans.
   a. How much of your own money do you invest? How much do you borrow from your broker?
   b. What will be your rate of return for the following stock prices at the end of a one-year holding period? (i) $40, (ii) $50, (iii) $60.

End-of-Chapter Features

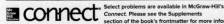

Select problems are available in McGraw-Hill's *Connect*. Please see the Supplements section of the book's frontmatter for more information.

PROBLEM SETS

1. In forming a portfolio of two risky assets, what must be true of the correlation coefficient between their returns if there are to be gains from diversification? Explain. *(LO 6-1)*
2. When adding a risky asset to a portfolio of many risky assets, which property of the

15. You can find a spreadsheet containing the historic returns presented in Table 5.2 in Connect. (Look for the Chapter 5 material.) Copy the data for the last 20 years into a new spreadsheet. Analyze the risk-return trade-off that would have characterized portfolios constructed from large stocks and long-term Treasury bonds over the last 20 years. What was the average rate of return and standard deviation of each asset? What was the correlation coefficient of their annual returns? What would have been the average return and standard deviation of portfolios with differing weights in the two assets?

Templates and spreadsheets are available in Connect

KAPLAN SCHWESER

10. A market order has: *(LO 3-2)*
   a. Price uncertainty but not execution uncertainty.
   b. Both price uncertainty and execution uncertainty.
   c. Execution uncertainty but not price uncertainty.

KAPLAN SCHWESER

11. Where would an illiquid security in a developing country *most likely* trade? *(LO 3-3)*
   a. Broker markets.
   b. Electronic crossing networks.
   c. Electronic limit-order markets.

CFA® PROBLEMS

CFA Problems

1. The following multiple-choice problems are based on questions that appeared in past CFA examinations.
   a. A bond with a call feature: *(LO 10-4)*
      (1) Is attractive because the immediate receipt of principal plus premium produces a high return.
      (2) Is more apt to be called when interest rates are high because the interest saving will be greater.
      (3) Will usually have a higher yield to maturity than a similar noncallable bond.
      (4) None of the above.

WEB *master*

1. Go to **finance.yahoo.com,** and enter the ticker symbol DIS (for Walt Disney Co.) in the *Look Up* box. Now click on *SEC Filings* and look for the link to Disney's most recent annual report (its 10-K). Financial tables are available from the *Summary* link, and Disney's full annual report may be obtained from the *EDGAR* link. Locate the company's Consolidated Balance Sheets and answer these questions:
   a. How much preferred stock is Disney authorized to issue? How much has been issued?
   b. How much common stock is Disney authorized to issue? How many shares are currently outstanding?
   c. Search for the term "Financing Activities." What is the total amount of borrowing listed for Disney? How much of this is medium-term notes?
   d. What other types of debt does Disney have outstanding?

Problem Sets
We strongly believe that practice in solving problems is a critical part of learning investments, so we provide a good variety. We have arranged questions by level of difficulty.

Excel Problems
Select end-of-chapter questions require the use of Excel. These problems are denoted with an icon. Templates and spreadsheets are available in Connect.

Kaplan-Schweser Problems
Each chapter contains select CFA-style questions derived from the Kaplan-Schweser CFA preparation courses. These questions are tagged with an icon for easy reference.

CFA Problems
We provide several questions from past CFA exams in applicable chapters. These questions represent the kinds of questions that professionals in the field believe are relevant to the practicing money manager. Appendix B, at the back of the book, lists each CFA question and the level and year of the CFA Exam it was included in, for easy reference when studying for the exam.

Web Master Exercises
These exercises are a great way to allow students to test their skills on the Internet. Each exercise consists of an activity related to practical problems and real-world scenarios.

MCGRAW-HILL *CONNECT*

Less Managing. More Teaching. Greater Learning.

McGraw-Hill *Connect* is an online assignment and assessment solution that connects students with the tools and resources they'll need to achieve success.

McGraw-Hill *Connect* helps prepare students for their future by enabling faster learning, more efficient studying, and higher retention of knowledge.

McGraw-Hill *Connect* Features

Connect offers a number of powerful tools and features to make managing assignments easier, so faculty can spend more time teaching. With *Connect*, students can engage with their coursework anytime and anywhere, making the learning process more accessible and efficient. *Connect* offers you the features described below.

Simple Assignment Management

With *Connect*, creating assignments is easier than ever, so you can spend more time teaching and less time managing. The assignment management function enables you to:

- Create and deliver assignments easily with selectable end-of-chapter questions and test bank items.
- Streamline lesson planning, student progress reporting, and assignment grading to make classroom management more efficient than ever.
- Go paperless with the eBook and online submission and grading of student assignments.

Smart Grading

When it comes to studying, time is precious. *Connect* helps students learn more efficiently by providing feedback and practice material when they need it, where they need it. When it comes to teaching, your time also is precious. The grading function enables you to:

- Have assignments scored automatically, giving students immediate feedback on their work and side-by-side comparisons with correct answers.
- Access and review each response; manually change grades or leave comments for students to review.
- Reinforce classroom concepts with practice tests and instant quizzes.

Instructor Library

The *Connect* Instructor Library is your repository for additional resources to improve student engagement in and out of class. You can select and use any asset that enhances your lecture.

This library contains information about the book and the authors, as well as all of the instructor supplements for this text, including:

- **Instructor's Manual** Revised by Nicholas Racculia, St. Vincent College, this instructional tool provides an integrated learning approach revised for this edition. Each chapter includes a Chapter Overview, Learning Objectives, and Presentation of Material that outlines and organizes the material around the PowerPoint Presentation.
- **Solutions Manual** The Solutions Manual, carefully revised by the authors with assistance from Marc-Anthony Isaacs, contains solutions to all basic, intermediate, and challenge problems found at the end of each chapter.
- **Test Bank** Prepared by Lynn Leary-Myers, University of Utah, and Matthew Will, University of Indianapolis, the Test Bank contains more than 1,200 questions and includes over 300 new questions. Each question is ranked by level of difficulty (easy, medium, hard) and tagged with the learning objective, the topic, AACSB, and Bloom's Taxonomy, which allows greater flexibility in creating a test. The Test Bank is assignable within Connect and available as a Word file or within EZ Test Online.
- **PowerPoint Presentations** These presentation slides, developed by Nicholas Racculia, contain figures and tables from the text, key points, and summaries in a visually stimulating collection of slides. These slides follow the order of the chapters, but if you have PowerPoint software, you may customize the program to fit your lecture.

Diagnostic and Adaptive Learning of Concepts: LearnSmart and SmartBook

LEARNSMART® Students want to make the best use of their study time. The LearnSmart adaptive self-study technology within *Connect* provides students with a seamless combination of practice, assessment, and remediation for every concept in the textbook. LearnSmart's intelligent software adapts to every student response and automatically delivers concepts that advance students' understanding while reducing time devoted to the concepts already mastered. The result for every student is the fastest path to mastery of the chapter concepts. LearnSmart:

- Applies an intelligent concept engine to identify the relationships between concepts and to serve new concepts to each student only when he or she is ready.
- Adapts automatically to each student, so students spend less time on the topics they understand and practice more those they have yet to master.
- Provides continual reinforcement and remediation, but gives only as much guidance as students need.
- Integrates diagnostics as part of the learning experience.
- Enables you to assess which concepts students have efficiently learned on their own, thus freeing class time for more applications and discussion.

SMARTBOOK® SmartBook®, powered by LearnSmart, is the first and only adaptive reading experience designed to change the way students read and learn. It creates a personalized reading experience by highlighting the most impactful concepts a student needs to learn at that moment in time. As a student engages with SmartBook, the reading experience continuously adapts by highlighting content based on what the student knows and doesn't know. This ensures that the focus is on the content he or she needs to learn, while simultaneously promoting long-term retention of material. Use SmartBook's real-time reports to quickly identify the concepts that require more attention from individual students—or the entire class. The end result? Students are more engaged with course content, can better prioritize their time, and come to class ready to participate.

Student Study Center

The *Connect* Student Study Center is the place for students to access additional resources. The Student Study Center:

- Offers students quick access to lectures, course materials, eBooks, and more.
- Provides instant practice material and study questions, easily accessible with LearnSmart and SmartBook.
- Gives students access to the Excel templates and files that accompany the text.

Student Progress Tracking

Connect keeps instructors informed about how each student, section, and class is performing, allowing for more productive use of lecture and office hours. The progress-tracking function enables you to:

- View scored work immediately and track individual or group performance with assignment and grade reports.
- Access an instant view of student or class performance relative to learning objectives.

Lecture Capture through Tegrity Campus

For an additional charge, Lecture Capture offers new ways for students to focus on the in-class discussion, knowing they can revisit important topics later. This can be delivered through Connect or separately. See below for more details.

For more information about Connect, go to connect.mheducation.com or contact your local McGraw-Hill sales representative.

TEGRITY CAMPUS: LECTURES 24/7

Tegrity Campus is a service that makes class time available 24/7 by automatically capturing every lecture in a searchable format for students to review when they study and complete assignments. With a simple one-click start-and-stop process, you capture all computer screens and corresponding audio. Students can replay any part of any class with easy-to-use browser-based viewing on a PC or Mac.

Educators know that the more students can see, hear, and experience class resources, the better they learn. In fact, studies prove it. With Tegrity Campus, students quickly recall key moments by using Tegrity Campus's unique search feature. This search helps students efficiently find what they need, when they need it, across an entire semester of class recordings. Help turn all your students' study time into learning moments immediately supported by your lecture.

To learn more about Tegrity, watch a 2-minute Flash demo at **http://tegritycampus.mhhe.com**.

Assurance of Learning Ready

Many educational institutions today are focused on the notion of *assurance of learning,* an important element of many accreditation standards. *Essentials of Investments,* Tenth Edition, is designed specifically to support your assurance-of-learning initiatives with a simple, yet powerful, solution.

Each chapter in the book begins with a list of numbered learning objectives, which also appear in the end-of-chapter problems. Every Test Bank question for *Essentials of Investments* maps to a specific chapter learning objective in the textbook. Each Test Bank question also identifies the topic area, level of difficulty, Bloom's Taxonomy level, and AACSB skill area. You can use our Test Bank software, *EZ Test Online,* or *Connect* to easily search for learning objectives that directly relate to the learning objectives for your course. You can then use the reporting features of *EZ Test* to aggregate student results in similar fashion, making the collection and presentation of assurance-of-learning data simple and easy.

AACSB Statement

McGraw-Hill/Irwin is a proud corporate member of AACSB International. Understanding the importance and value of AACSB accreditation, *Essentials of Investments,* Tenth Edition, recognizes the curricula guidelines detailed in the AACSB standards for business accreditation by connecting selected questions in the Test Bank to the general knowledge and skill guidelines in the AACSB standards.

The statements contained in *Essentials of Investments,* Tenth Edition, are provided only as a guide for the users of this textbook. The AACSB leaves content coverage and assessment within the purview of individual schools, the mission of the school, and the faculty. While *Essentials of Investments,* Tenth Edition, and the teaching package make no claim of any specific AACSB qualification or evaluation, we have labeled selected questions according to the six general knowledge and skills areas.

McGraw-Hill Customer Care Contact Information

At McGraw-Hill, we understand that getting the most from new technology can be challenging. That's why our services don't stop after you purchase our products. You can e-mail our Product Specialists 24 hours a day to get product-training online. Or you can search our knowledge bank of Frequently Asked Questions on our support website. For Customer Support, call **800-331-5094** or visit www.mhhe.com/support. One of our Technical Support Analysts will be able to assist you in a timely fashion.

Acknowledgments

We received help from many people as we prepared this book. An insightful group of reviewers commented on this and previous editions of this text. Their comments and suggestions improved the exposition of the material considerably. These reviewers all deserve special thanks for their contributions.

Anna Agapova *Florida Atlantic University, Boca Raton*

Sandro C. Andrade *University of Miami*

Bala Arshanapalli *Indiana University Northwest*

Rasha Ashraf *Georgia State University*

Anand Bhattacharya *Arizona State University, Tempe*

Randall S. Billingsley *Virginia Polytechnic Institute and State University*

Howard Bohnen *St. Cloud State University*

Paul Bolster *Northeastern University*

Lyle Bowlin *University of Northern Iowa*

Brian Boyer *Brigham Young University*

Nicole Boyson *Northeastern University*

Ben Branch *University of Massachussets, Amherst*

Thor W. Bruce *University of Miami*

Timothy Burch *University of Miama, Coral Gables*

Alyce R. Campbell *University of Oregon*

Mark Castelino *Rutgers University*

Greg Chaudoin *Loyola University*

Ji Chen *University of Colorado, Denver*

Joseph Chen *University of California, Davis*

Mustafa Chowdhury *Louisiana State University*

Ron Christner *Loyola University, New Orleans*

Shane Corwin *University of Notre Dame*

Brent Dalrymple *University of Central Florida*

Praveen Das *University of Louisiana, Lafayette*

Diane Del Guercio *University of Oregon*

David C. Distad *University of California at Berkeley*

Gary R. Dokes *University of San Diego*

James Dow *California State University, Northridge*

Robert Dubil *University of Utah, Salt Lake City*

John Earl *University of Richmond*

Jeff Edwards *Portland Community College*

Peter D. Ekman *Kansas State University*

John Elder *Colorado State University*

Richard Elliott *University of Utah, Salt Lake City*

James Falter *Franklin University*

Philip Fanara *Howard University*

Joseph Farinella *University of North Carolina, Wilmington*

Greg Feigel *University of Texas, Arlington*

James F. Feller *Middle Tennessee State University*

James Forjan *York College*

Beverly Frickel *University of Nebraska, Kearney*

Ken Froewiss *New York University*

Phillip Ghazanfari *California State University, Pomona*

Eric Girard *Siena College*

Richard A. Grayson *University of Georgia*

Richard D. Gritta *University of Portland*

Anthony Yanxiang Gu *SUNY Geneseo*

Deborah Gunthorpe *University of Tennessee*

Weiyu Guo *University of Nebraska, Omaha*

Pamela Hall *Western Washington University*

Thomas Hamilton *St. Mary's University*

Bing Han *University of Texas, Austin*

Yvette Harman *Miami University of Ohio*

Gay Hatfield *University of Mississippi*

Larry C. Holland *Oklahoma State University*

Harris Hordon *New Jersey City University*

Stephen Huffman *University of Wisconsin, Oshkosh*

Ron E. Hutchins *Eastern Michigan University*

David Ikenberry *University of Illinois, Urbana-Champaign*

A. Can (John) Inci *Florida State University*

Victoria Javine *University of Southern Alabama*

Nancy Jay *Mercer University*

Richard Johnson *Colorado State University*

Douglas Kahl *University of Akron*

Richard J. Kish *Lehigh University*

Tom Krueger *University of Wisconsin, La Crosse*

Donald Kummer *University of Missouri, St. Louis*

Merouane Lakehal-Ayat *St. John Fisher College*

Reinhold P. Lamb *University of North Florida*

Angeline Lavin *University of South Dakota*

Hongbok Lee *Western Illinois University*

Kartono Liano *Mississippi State University*

Jim Locke *Northern Virginia Community College*

John Loughlin *St. Louis University*

David Louton *Bryant College*

David Loy *Illinois State University*

Christian Lundblad *Indiana University*

Robert A. Lutz *University of Utah*
Laurian Casson Lytle *University of Wisconsin, Whitewater*
Leo Mahoney *Bryant College*
Herman Manakyan *Salisbury State University*
Steven V. Mann *University of South Carolina*
Jeffrey A. Manzi *Ohio University*
James Marchand *Westminster College*
Robert J. Martel *Bentley College*
Linda J. Martin *Arizona State University*
Stanley A. Martin *University of Colorado, Boulder*
Thomas Mertens *New York University*
Edward Miller *University of New Orleans*
Michael Milligan *California State University, Fullerton*
Rosemary Minyard *Pfeiffer University*
Walter Morales *Louisiana State University*
Mbodja Mougoue *Wayne State University*
Shabnam Mousavi *Georgia State University*
Majed Muhtaseb *California State Polytechnic University*
Deborah Murphy *University of Tennessee, Knoxville*
Mike Murray *Winona State University*
C. R. Narayanaswamy *Georgia Institute of Technology*
Walt Nelson *Missouri State University*
Karyn Neuhauser *SUNY, Plattsburgh*
Mike Nugent *SUNY Stonybrook*
Raj Padmaraj *Bowling Green University*
Elisabeta Pana *Illinois Wesleyan University*
John C. Park *Frostburg State University*
Percy Poon *University of Nevada, Las Vegas*
Robert B. Porter *University of Florida*
Dev Prasad *University of Massachusetts, Lowell*
Rose Prasad *Central Michigan University*
Elias A. Raad *Ithaca College*
Murli Rajan *University of Scranton*
Kumoli Ramakrishnan *University of South Dakota*
Rathin Rathinasamy *Ball State University*
Craig Rennie *University of Arkansas*
Cecilia Ricci *Montclair University*
Craig Ruff *Georgia State University*
Tom Sanders *University of Miami*
Jeff Sandri *University of Colorado, Boulder*
David Schirm *John Carroll University*
Chi Sheh *University of Houston*
Ravi Shukla *Syracuse University*
Allen B. Snively, Jr. *Indiana University*
Andrew Spieler *Hofstra University*
Kim Staking *Colorado State University*
Edwin Stuart *Southeastern Oklahoma State University*
George S. Swales *Southwest Missouri State University*
Paul Swanson *University of Cincinnati*
Bruce Swensen *Adelphi University*
Glenn Tanner *University of Hawaii*

John L. Teall *Pace University*
Anne Macy Terry *West Texas A&M University*
Donald J. Thompson *Georgia State University*
Steven Thorley *Brigham Young University*
James Tipton *Baylor University*
Steven Todd *DePaul University*
Michael Toyne *Northeastern State University*
William Trainor *Western Kentucky University*
Andrey Ukhov *Indiana University, Bloomington*
Cevdet Uruk *University of Memphis*
Joseph Vu *DePaul University*
Jessica Wachter *New York University*
Joe Walker *University of Alabama at Birmingham*
Richard Warr *North Carolina State University*
William Welch *Florida International University*
Russel Wermers *University of Maryland*
Andrew L. Whitaker *North Central College*
Howard Whitney *Franklin University*
Alayna Williamson *University of Utah, Salt Lake City*
Michael E. Williams *University of Texas at Austin*
Michael Willoughby *University of California, San Diego*
Tony Wingler *University of North Carolina*
Annie Wong *Western Connecticut State University*
David Wright *University of Wisconsin, Parkside*
Richard H. Yanow *North Adams State College*
Tarek Zaher *Indiana State University*
Allan Zebedee *San Diego State University*
Zhong-guo Zhou *California State University, Northridge*
Thomas J. Zwirlein *University of Colorado, Colorado Springs*

For granting us permission to include many of their examination questions in the text, we are grateful to the CFA Institute.

A special thanks goes to the talented experts who help us develop and review the instructor materials and online content in Connect and LearnSmart, including Vincent Muscolino, Anna Kovalenko, James Forjan, Hyuna Park, John Farlin, Marc-Anthony Isaacs, Nicholas Racculia, and Dongmei Li.

Much credit is also due to the development and production team of McGraw-Hill Education: Noelle Bathurst, Senior Product Developer; Chuck Synovec, Executive Brand Manager; Kathryn Wright, Core Project Manager; Kristin Bradley, Assessment Project Manager; Melissa Caughlin, Senior Marketing Manager; Dave O'Donnell, Marketing Specialist; and Matt Diamond, Designer.

Finally, once again, our most important debts are to Judy, Hava, and Sheryl for their unflagging support.

Zvi Bodie
Alex Kane
Alan J. Marcus

Elements of Investments

Chapters in This Part

1 Investments: Background and Issues

2 Asset Classes and Financial Instruments

3 Securities Markets

4 Mutual Funds and Other Investment Companies

Even a cursory glance at *The Wall Street Journal* reveals a bewildering collection of securities, markets, and financial institutions. But although it may appear so, the financial environment is not chaotic: There is rhyme and reason behind the vast array of financial instruments and the markets in which they trade.

These introductory chapters provide a bird's-eye view of the investing environment. We will give you a tour of the major types of markets in which securities trade, the trading process, and the major players in these arenas. You will see that both markets and securities have evolved to meet the changing and complex needs of different participants in the financial system.

Markets innovate and compete with each other for traders' business just as vigorously as competitors in other industries. The competition between NASDAQ, the New York Stock Exchange (NYSE), and several other electronic and non-U.S. exchanges is fierce and public.

Trading practices can mean big money to investors. The explosive growth of online electronic trading has saved them many millions of dollars in trading costs. On the other hand, some worry that lightning-fast electronic trading has put the stability of security markets at risk. All agree, however, that these advances will continue to change the face of the investments industry, and Wall Street firms are scrambling to formulate strategies that respond to these changes.

These chapters will give you a good foundation with which to understand the basic types of securities and financial markets as well as how trading in those markets is conducted.

1

Investments: Background and Issues

Learning Objectives

LO 1-1 Define an investment.

LO 1-2 Distinguish between real assets and financial assets.

LO 1-3 Explain the economic functions of financial markets and how various securities are related to the governance of the corporation.

LO 1-4 Describe the major steps in the construction of an investment portfolio.

LO 1-5 Identify different types of financial markets and the major participants in each of those markets.

LO 1-6 Explain the causes and consequences of the financial crisis of 2008.

investment

Commitment of current resources in the expectation of deriving greater resources in the future.

An **investment** is the *current* commitment of money or other resources in the expectation of reaping *future* benefits. For example, an individual might purchase shares of stock anticipating that the future proceeds from the shares will justify both the time that her money is tied up as well as the risk of the investment. The time you will spend studying this text (not to mention its cost) also is an investment. You are forgoing either current leisure or the income you could be earning at a job in the expectation that your future career will be sufficiently enhanced to justify this commitment of time and effort. While these two investments differ in many ways, they share one key attribute that is central to all investments: You sacrifice something of value now, expecting to benefit from that sacrifice later.

This text can help you become an informed practitioner of investments. We will focus on investments in securities such as stocks, bonds, or options and futures contracts, but much of what we discuss will be useful in the analysis of any type of investment. The text will provide you with background in the organization of various securities markets, will survey the valuation and risk management principles useful in particular markets, such as those for bonds or stocks, and will introduce you to the principles of portfolio construction.

Broadly speaking, this chapter addresses three topics that will provide a useful perspective for the material that is to come later. First, before delving into the topic of "investments," we consider the role of financial assets in the economy. We discuss the relationship between securities and the "real" assets that actually produce goods and services for consumers, and we consider why financial assets are important to the functioning of a developed economy. Given this background, we then take a first look at the types of decisions that confront investors as they assemble a portfolio of assets. These investment decisions are made in an environment where higher returns usually can be obtained only at the price of greater risk and in which it is rare to find assets that are so mispriced as to be obvious bargains. These themes—the risk-return trade-off and the efficient pricing of financial assets—are central to the investment process, so it is worth pausing for a brief discussion of their implications as we begin the text. These implications will be fleshed out in much greater detail in later chapters.

We provide an overview of the organization of security markets as well as the various players that participate in those markets. Together, these introductions should give you a feel for who the major participants are in the securities markets as well as the setting in which they act. Finally, we discuss the financial crisis that began playing out in 2007 and peaked in 2008. The crisis dramatically illustrated the connections between the financial system and the "real" side of the economy. We look at the origins of the crisis and the lessons that may be drawn about systemic risk. We close the chapter with an overview of the remainder of the text.

1.1 REAL ASSETS VERSUS FINANCIAL ASSETS

The material wealth of a society is ultimately determined by the productive capacity of its economy, that is, the goods and services its members can create. This capacity is a function of the **real assets** of the economy: the land, buildings, equipment, and knowledge that can be used to produce goods and services.

real assets
Assets used to produce goods and services.

In contrast to such real assets are **financial assets** such as stocks and bonds. Such securities are no more than sheets of paper or, more likely, computer entries and do not directly contribute to the productive capacity of the economy. Instead, these assets are the means by which individuals in well-developed economies hold their claims on real assets. Financial assets are claims to the income generated by real assets (or claims on income from the government). If we cannot own our own auto plant (a real asset), we can still buy shares in Honda or Toyota (financial assets) and, thereby, share in the income derived from the production of automobiles.

financial assets
Claims on real assets or the income generated by them.

While real assets generate net income to the economy, financial assets simply define the allocation of income or wealth among investors. Individuals can choose between consuming their wealth today or investing for the future. If they choose to invest, they may place their wealth in financial assets by purchasing various securities. When investors buy these securities from companies, the firms use the money so raised to pay for real assets, such as plant, equipment, technology, or inventory. So investors' returns on securities ultimately come from the income produced by the real assets that were financed by the issuance of those securities.

The distinction between real and financial assets is apparent when we compare the balance sheet of U.S. households, shown in Table 1.1, with the composition of national wealth in the United States, shown in Table 1.2. Household wealth includes financial assets such as bank accounts, corporate stock, or bonds. However, debt securities, which are financial assets of the households that hold them, are *liabilities* of the issuers of those securities. For example, a bond that you treat as an asset because it gives you a claim on interest income and repayment of principal from Toyota is a liability of Toyota, which is obligated to make these payments to

TABLE 1.1	Balance sheet of U.S. households					

Assets	$ Billion	% Total	Liabilities and Net Worth	$ Billion	% Total
Real assets					
Real estate	$22,820	23.9%	Mortgages	$ 9,551	10.0%
Consumer durables	5,041	5.3	Consumer credit	3,104	3.2
Other	468	0.5	Bank and other loans	493	0.5
Total real assets	$28,330	29.6%	Security credit	352	0.4
			Other	286	0.3
			Total liabilities	$13,785	14.4%
Financial assets					
Deposits	$ 9,783	10.2%			
Life insurance reserves	1,257	1.3			
Pension reserves	19,766	20.7			
Corporate equity	13,502	14.1			
Equity in noncorp. business	8,869	9.3			
Mutual fund shares	7,059	7.4			
Debt securities	5,263	5.5			
Other	1,720	1.8			
Total financial assets	$67,219	70.4%	Net worth	81,764	85.6
Total	$95,549	100.0%		$95,549	100.0%

Note: Column sums may differ from total because of rounding error.

Source: *Flow of Funds Accounts of the United States,* Board of Governors of the Federal Reserve System, June 2014.

TABLE 1.2	Domestic net worth

Assets	$ Billion
Commercial real estate	$20,092
Residential real estate	22,820
Equipment & intellectual property	7,404
Inventories	2,514
Consumer durables	5,041
Total	$57,873

Note: Column sums may differ from total because of rounding error.

Source: *Flow of Funds Accounts of the United States,* Board of Governors of the Federal Reserve System, June 2014.

you. Your asset is Toyota's liability. Therefore, when we aggregate over all balance sheets, these claims cancel out, leaving only real assets as the net wealth of the economy. National wealth consists of structures, equipment, inventories of goods, and land.[1]

[1]You might wonder why real assets held by households in Table 1.1 amount to $28,330 billion, while total real assets in the domestic economy (Table 1.2) are far larger, at $57,873 billion. A big part of the difference reflects the fact that real assets held by firms, for example, property, plant, and equipment, are included as *financial* assets of the household sector, specifically through the value of corporate equity and other stock market investments. Similarly, Table 1.2 includes assets of noncorporate businesses. Finally, there are some differences in valuation methods. For example, equity and stock investments in Table 1.1 are measured by market value, whereas plant and equipment in Table 1.2 are valued at replacement cost.

We will focus almost exclusively on financial assets. But you shouldn't lose sight of the fact that the successes or failures of the financial assets we choose to purchase ultimately depend on the performance of the underlying real assets.

Are the following assets real or financial?

a. Patents   *b.* Lease obligations   *c.* Customer goodwill

d. A college education *e.* A $5 bill

1.2 FINANCIAL ASSETS

It is common to distinguish among three broad types of financial assets: debt, equity, and derivatives. **Fixed-income** or **debt securities** promise either a fixed stream of income or a stream of income that is determined according to a specified formula. For example, a corporate bond typically would promise that the bondholder will receive a fixed amount of interest each year. Other so-called floating-rate bonds promise payments that depend on current interest rates. For example, a bond may pay an interest rate that is fixed at two percentage points above the rate paid on U.S. Treasury bills. Unless the borrower is declared bankrupt, the payments on these securities are either fixed or determined by formula. For this reason, the investment performance of debt securities typically is least closely tied to the financial condition of the issuer.

Nevertheless, debt securities come in a tremendous variety of maturities and payment provisions. At one extreme, the *money market* refers to fixed-income securities that are short term, highly marketable, and generally of very low risk. Examples of money market securities are U.S. Treasury bills and bank certificates of deposit (CDs). In contrast, the fixed-income [...] es such as Treasury bonds, as well as bonds issued [...] palities, and corporations. These bonds range from [...] ample, Treasury securities) to relatively risky (for [...] ey also are designed with extremely diverse provi- [...] vestor and protection against the bankruptcy of the [...] urities in Chapter 2 and undertake a more detailed [...] Three.

[...] or **equity,** in a firm represents an ownership share [...] romised any particular payment. They receive any [...] ted ownership in the real assets of the firm. If the [...] crease; if not, it will decrease. The performance of [...] y to the success of the firm and its real assets. For [...] iskier than investments in debt securities. Equity [...] of Part Four.

[...] ions and futures contracts provide payoffs that are [...] ch as bond or stock prices. For example, a call [...] out to be worthless if Intel's share price remains [...] as $35 a share, but it can be quite valuable if the [...] ve securities are so named because their values [...] ample, the value of the call option will depend on [...] ivative securities are futures and swap contracts.

[...] of the investment environment. One use of deriv- [...] sks or transfer them to other parties. This is done

[...] en exercise price on or before the option's expiration date. If [...] ight to buy for $35 will turn out to be valueless. If the share [...] the option can be exercised to obtain the share for only $35.

fixed-income (debt) securities
Pay a specified cash flow over a specific period.

equity
An ownership share in a corporation.

derivative securities
Securities providing payoffs that depend on the values of other assets.

successfully every day, and the use of these securities for risk management is so commonplace that the multitrillion-dollar market in derivative assets is routinely taken for granted. Derivatives also can be used to take highly speculative positions, however. Every so often, one of these positions blows up, resulting in well-publicized losses of hundreds of millions of dollars. While these losses attract considerable attention, they do not negate the potential use of such securities as risk management tools. Derivatives will continue to play an important role in portfolio construction and the financial system. We will return to this topic later in the text.

Investors and corporations regularly encounter other financial markets as well. Firms engaged in international trade regularly transfer money back and forth between dollars and other currencies. Well more than a trillion dollars of currency is traded each day in the market for foreign exchange, primarily through a network of the largest international banks.

Investors also might invest directly in some real assets. For example, dozens of commodities are traded on exchanges such as the New York Mercantile Exchange or the Chicago Board of Trade. You can buy or sell corn, wheat, natural gas, gold, silver, and so on.

Commodity and derivative markets allow firms to adjust their exposure to various business risks. For example, a construction firm may lock in the price of copper by buying copper futures contracts, thus eliminating the risk of a sudden jump in the price of its raw materials. Wherever there is uncertainty, investors may be interested in trading, either to speculate or to lay off their risks, and a market may arise to meet that demand.

1.3   FINANCIAL MARKETS AND THE ECONOMY

We stated earlier that real assets determine the wealth of an economy, while financial assets merely represent claims on real assets. Nevertheless, financial assets and the markets in which they trade play several crucial roles in developed economies. Financial assets allow us to make the most of the economy's real assets.

The Informational Role of Financial Markets

Stock prices reflect investors' collective assessment of a firm's current performance and future prospects. When the market is more optimistic about the firm, its share price will rise. That higher price makes it easier for the firm to raise capital and therefore encourages investment. In this manner, stock prices play a major role in the allocation of capital in market economies, directing capital to the firms and applications with the greatest perceived potential.

Do capital markets actually channel resources to the most efficient use? At times, they appear to fail miserably. Companies or whole industries can be "hot" for a period of time (think about the dot-com bubble that peaked in 2000), attract a large flow of investor capital, and then fail after only a few years. The process seems highly wasteful.

But we need to be careful about our standard of efficiency. No one knows with certainty which ventures will succeed and which will fail. It is therefore unreasonable to expect that markets will never make mistakes. The stock market encourages allocation of capital to those firms that appear *at the time* to have the best prospects. Many smart, well-trained, and well-paid professionals analyze the prospects of firms whose shares trade on the stock market. Stock prices reflect their collective judgment.

You may well be skeptical about resource allocation through markets. But if you are, then take a moment to think about the alternatives. Would a central planner make fewer mistakes? Would you prefer that Congress make these decisions? To paraphrase Winston Churchill's comment about democracy, markets may be the worst way to allocate capital except for all the others that have been tried.

Consumption Timing

Some individuals in an economy are earning more than they currently wish to spend. Others, for example, retirees, spend more than they currently earn. How can you shift your purchasing power from high-earnings periods to low-earnings periods of life? One way is to "store" your wealth in financial assets. In high-earnings periods, you can invest your savings in financial assets such as stocks and bonds. In low-earnings periods, you can sell these assets to provide funds for your consumption needs. By so doing, you can "shift" your consumption over the course of your lifetime, thereby allocating your consumption to periods that provide the greatest satisfaction. Thus, financial markets allow individuals to separate decisions concerning current consumption from constraints that otherwise would be imposed by current earnings.

Allocation of Risk

Virtually all real assets involve some risk. When Toyota builds its auto plants, for example, it cannot know for sure what cash flows those plants will generate. Financial markets and the diverse financial instruments traded in those markets allow investors with the greatest taste for risk to bear that risk, while other, less risk-tolerant individuals can, to a greater extent, stay on the sidelines. For example, if Toyota raises the funds to build its auto plant by selling both stocks and bonds to the public, the more optimistic or risk-tolerant investors can buy shares of stock in Toyota, while the more conservative ones can buy Toyota bonds. Because the bonds promise to provide a fixed payment, the stockholders bear most of the business risk but reap potentially higher rewards. Thus, capital markets allow the risk that is inherent to all investments to be borne by the investors most willing to bear that risk.

This allocation of risk also benefits the firms that need to raise capital to finance their investments. When investors are able to select security types with the risk-return characteristics that best suit their preferences, each security can be sold for the best possible price. This facilitates the process of building the economy's stock of real assets.

Separation of Ownership and Management

Many businesses are owned and managed by the same individual. This simple organization is well suited to small businesses and, in fact, was the most common form of business organization before the Industrial Revolution. Today, however, with global markets and large-scale production, the size and capital requirements of firms have skyrocketed. For example, in 2013 General Electric listed on its balance sheet almost $70 billion of property, plant, and equipment, and total assets in excess of $650 billion. Corporations of such size simply cannot exist as owner-operated firms. GE actually has over 500,000 stockholders with an ownership stake in the firm proportional to their holdings of shares.

Such a large group of individuals obviously cannot actively participate in the day-to-day management of the firm. Instead, they elect a board of directors that in turn hires and supervises the management of the firm. This structure means that the owners and managers of the firm are different parties. This gives the firm a stability that the owner-managed firm cannot achieve. For example, if some stockholders decide they no longer wish to hold shares in the firm, they can sell their shares to other investors, with no impact on the management of the firm. Thus, financial assets and the ability to buy and sell those assets in the financial markets allow for easy separation of ownership and management.

How can all of the disparate owners of the firm, ranging from large pension funds holding hundreds of thousands of shares to small investors who may hold only a single share, agree on the objectives of the firm? Again, the financial markets provide some guidance. All may agree that the firm's management should pursue strategies that enhance the value of their shares. Such policies will make all shareholders wealthier and allow them all to better pursue their personal goals, whatever those goals might be.

Do managers really attempt to maximize firm value? It is easy to see how they might be tempted to engage in activities not in the best interest of shareholders. For example, they might engage in empire building or avoid risky projects to protect their own jobs or overconsume luxuries such as corporate jets, reasoning that the cost of such perquisites is largely borne by the shareholders. These potential conflicts of interest are called **agency problems** because managers, who are hired as agents of the shareholders, may pursue their own interests instead.

agency problems

Conflicts of interest between managers and stockholders.

Several mechanisms have evolved to mitigate potential agency problems. First, compensation plans tie the income of managers to the success of the firm. A major part of the total compensation of top executives is typically in the form of shares or stock options, which means that the managers will not do well unless the stock price increases, benefiting shareholders. (Of course, we've learned that overuse of options can create its own agency problem. Options can create an incentive for managers to manipulate information to prop up a stock price temporarily, giving them a chance to cash out before the price returns to a level reflective of the firm's true prospects. More on this shortly.) Second, while boards of directors have sometimes been portrayed as defenders of top management, they can, and in recent years increasingly have, forced out management teams that are underperforming. Third, outsiders such as security analysts and large institutional investors such as mutual funds or pension funds monitor the firm closely and make the life of poor performers at the least uncomfortable. Such large investors today hold about half of the stock in publicly listed firms in the United States.

Finally, bad performers are subject to the threat of takeover. If the board of directors is lax in monitoring management, unhappy shareholders in principle can elect a different board. They can do this by launching a *proxy contest* in which they seek to obtain enough proxies (i.e., rights to vote the shares of other shareholders) to take control of the firm and vote in another board. However, this threat is usually minimal. Shareholders who attempt such a fight have to use their own funds, while management can defend itself using corporate coffers. Most proxy fights fail. The real takeover threat is from other firms. If one firm observes another underperforming, it can acquire the underperforming business and replace management with its own team. The stock price should rise to reflect the prospects of improved performance, which provides incentive for firms to engage in such takeover activity.

EXAMPLE 1.1	In February 2008, Microsoft offered to buy Yahoo! by paying its current shareholders $31 for each of their shares, a considerable premium to its closing price of $19.18 on the day before the offer. Yahoo!'s management rejected that offer and a better one at $33 a share; Yahoo!'s CEO Jerry Yang held out for $37 per share, a price that Yahoo! had not reached in over two years. Billionaire investor Carl Icahn was outraged, arguing that management was protecting its own position at the expense of shareholder value. Icahn notified Yahoo! that he had been asked to "lead a proxy fight to attempt to remove the current board and to establish a new board which would attempt to negotiate a successful merger with Microsoft."[3] To that end, he had purchased approximately 59 million shares of Yahoo! and formed a 10-person slate to stand for election against the current board. Despite this challenge, Yahoo!'s management held firm in its refusal of Microsoft's offer, and with the support of the board, Yang managed to fend off both Microsoft and Icahn. In July, Icahn agreed to end the proxy fight in return for three seats on the board to be held by his allies. But the 11-person board was still dominated by current Yahoo! management. Yahoo!'s share price, which had risen to $29 a share during the Microsoft negotiations, fell back to around $21 a share. Given the difficulty that a well-known billionaire faced in defeating a determined management, it is no wonder that proxy contests are rare. Historically, about three of four proxy fights go down to defeat.
Carl Icahn's Proxy Fight with Yahoo!	

Corporate Governance and Corporate Ethics

We've argued that securities markets can play an important role in facilitating the deployment of capital resources to their most productive uses. But market signals will help to allocate capital efficiently only if investors are acting on accurate information. We say that markets need to be *transparent* for investors to make informed decisions. If firms can mislead the public about their prospects, then much can go wrong.

Despite the many mechanisms to align incentives of shareholders and managers, the three years from 2000 through 2002 were filled with a seemingly unending series of scandals that collectively signaled a crisis in corporate governance and ethics. For example, the

---

[3]Open letter from Carl Icahn to Board of Directors of Yahoo!, May 15, 2008, published in press release from ICAHN CAPITAL LP.

telecom firm WorldCom overstated its profits by at least $3.8 billion by improperly classifying expenses as investments. When the true picture emerged, it resulted in the largest bankruptcy in U.S. history, at least until Lehman Brothers smashed that record in 2008. The next-largest U.S. bankruptcy was Enron, which used its now notorious "special purpose entities" to move debt off its own books and similarly present a misleading picture of its financial status. Unfortunately, these firms had plenty of company. Other firms such as Rite Aid, HealthSouth, Global Crossing, and Qwest Communications also manipulated and misstated their accounts to the tune of billions of dollars. And the scandals were hardly limited to the U.S. Parmalat, the Italian dairy firm, claimed to have a $4.8 billion bank account that turned out not to exist. These episodes suggest that agency and incentive problems are far from solved.

Other scandals of that period included systematically misleading and overly optimistic research reports put out by stock market analysts (their favorable analysis was traded for the promise of future investment banking business, and analysts were commonly compensated not for their accuracy or insight but for their role in garnering investment banking business for their firms) and allocations of initial public offerings to corporate executives as a quid pro quo for personal favors or the promise to direct future business back to the manager of the IPO.

What about the auditors who were supposed to be the watchdogs of the firms? Here too, incentives were skewed. Recent changes in business practice made the consulting businesses of these firms more lucrative than the auditing function. For example, Enron's (now defunct) auditor Arthur Andersen earned more money consulting for Enron than auditing it; given its incentive to protect its consulting profits, it should not be surprising that it, and other auditors, were overly lenient in their auditing work.

In 2002, in response to the spate of ethics scandals, Congress passed the Sarbanes-Oxley Act to tighten the rules of corporate governance. For example, the act requires corporations to have more independent directors, that is, more directors who are not themselves managers (or affiliated with managers). The act also requires each CFO to personally vouch for the corporation's accounting statements, creates an oversight board to oversee the auditing of public companies, and prohibits auditors from providing various other services to clients.

Ultimately, a firm's reputation for integrity is key to building long-term relationships with its customers and is therefore one of its most valuable assets. Indeed, the motto of the London Stock Exchange is "My word is my bond." Every so often firms forget this lesson, but in the end, investments in reputation are in fact good business practice.

1.4 THE INVESTMENT PROCESS

An investor's *portfolio* is simply his collection of investment assets. Once the portfolio is established, it is updated or "rebalanced" by selling existing securities and using the proceeds to buy new securities, by investing additional funds to increase the overall size of the portfolio, or by selling securities to decrease the size of the portfolio.

Investment assets can be categorized into broad asset classes, such as stocks, bonds, real estate, commodities, and so on. Investors make two types of decisions in constructing their portfolios. The **asset allocation** decision is the choice among these broad asset classes, while the **security selection** decision is the choice of which particular securities to hold *within* each asset class.

"Top-down" portfolio construction starts with asset allocation. For example, an individual who currently holds all of his money in a bank account would first decide what proportion of the overall portfolio ought to be moved into stocks, bonds, and so on. In this way, the broad features of the portfolio are established. For example, while the average annual return on the common stock of large firms since 1926 has been about 11.5% per year, the average return on U.S. Treasury bills has been less than 4%. On the other hand, stocks are far riskier, with annual returns (as measured by the Standard & Poor's 500 Index) that have ranged as low as −46% and as high as 55%. In contrast, T-bill returns are effectively risk-free: You know what

asset allocation

Allocation of an investment portfolio across broad asset classes.

security selection

Choice of specific securities within each asset class.

interest rate you will earn when you buy the bills. Therefore, the decision to allocate your investments to the stock market or to the money market where Treasury bills are traded will have great ramifications for both the risk and the return of your portfolio. A top-down investor first makes this and other crucial asset allocation decisions before turning to the decision of the particular securities to be held in each asset class.

security analysis

Analysis of the value of securities.

Security analysis involves the valuation of particular securities that might be included in the portfolio. For example, an investor might ask whether Merck or Pfizer is more attractively priced. Both bonds and stocks must be evaluated for investment attractiveness, but valuation is far more difficult for stocks because a stock's performance usually is far more sensitive to the condition of the issuing firm.

In contrast to top-down portfolio management is the "bottom-up" strategy. In this process, the portfolio is constructed from the securities that seem attractively priced without as much concern for the resultant asset allocation. Such a technique can result in unintended bets on one or another sector of the economy. For example, it might turn out that the portfolio ends up with a very heavy representation of firms in one industry, from one part of the country, or with exposure to one source of uncertainty. However, a bottom-up strategy does focus the portfolio on the assets that seem to offer the most attractive investment opportunities.

1.5   MARKETS ARE COMPETITIVE

Financial markets are highly competitive. Thousands of well-backed analysts constantly scour securities markets searching for the best buys. This competition means that we should expect to find few, if any, "free lunches," securities that are so underpriced that they represent obvious bargains. There are several implications of this no-free-lunch proposition. Let's examine two.

The Risk-Return Trade-Off

Investors invest for anticipated future returns, but those returns rarely can be predicted precisely. There will almost always be risk associated with investments. Actual or realized returns will almost always deviate from the expected return anticipated at the start of the investment period. For example, in 1931 (the worst calendar year for the market since 1926), the stock market lost 46% of its value. In 1933 (the best year), the stock market gained 55%. You can be sure that investors did not anticipate such extreme performance at the start of either of these years.

Naturally, if all else could be held equal, investors would prefer investments with the highest expected return.[4] However, the no-free-lunch rule tells us that all else cannot be held equal. If you want higher expected returns, you will have to pay a price in terms of accepting higher investment risk. If higher expected return can be achieved without bearing extra risk, there will be a rush to buy the high-return assets, with the result that their prices will be driven up. Individuals considering investing in the asset at the now-higher price will find the investment less attractive. The asset will be considered attractive and its price will continue to rise until its expected return is no more than commensurate with risk. At this point, investors can anticipate a "fair" return relative to the asset's risk, but no more. Similarly, if returns were independent of risk, there would be a rush to sell high-risk assets. Their prices would fall (improving their expected future rates of return) until they eventually were attractive enough to be included again in investor portfolios. We conclude that there should be a **risk-return trade-off** in the securities markets, with higher-risk assets priced to offer higher expected returns than lower-risk assets.

risk-return trade-off

Assets with higher expected returns entail greater risk.

Of course, this discussion leaves several important questions unanswered. How should one measure the risk of an asset? What should be the quantitative trade-off between risk (properly

---

[4]The "expected" return is not the return investors believe they necessarily will earn, or even their most likely return. It is instead the result of averaging across all possible outcomes, recognizing that some outcomes are more likely than others. It is the average rate of return across possible economic scenarios.

measured) and expected return? One would think that risk would have something to do with the volatility of an asset's returns, but this guess turns out to be only partly correct. When we mix assets into diversified portfolios, we need to consider the interplay among assets and the effect of diversification on the risk of the entire portfolio. *Diversification* means that many assets are held in the portfolio so that the exposure to any particular asset is limited. The effect of diversification on portfolio risk, the implications for the proper measurement of risk, and the risk-return relationship are the topics of Part Two. These topics are the subject of what has come to be known as *modern portfolio theory*. The development of this theory brought two of its pioneers, Harry Markowitz and William Sharpe, Nobel Prizes.

Efficient Markets

Another implication of the no-free-lunch proposition is that we should rarely expect to find bargains in the security markets. We will spend all of Chapter 8 examining the theory and evidence concerning the hypothesis that financial markets process all available information about securities quickly and efficiently, that is, that the security price usually reflects all the information available to investors concerning the value of the security. According to this hypothesis, as new information about a security becomes available, the price of the security quickly adjusts so that at any time, the security price equals the market consensus estimate of the value of the security. If this were so, there would be neither underpriced nor overpriced securities.

One interesting implication of this "efficient market hypothesis" concerns the choice between active and passive investment-management strategies. **Passive management** calls for holding highly diversified portfolios without spending effort or other resources attempting to improve investment performance through security analysis. **Active management** is the attempt to improve performance either by identifying mispriced securities or by timing the performance of broad asset classes—for example, increasing one's commitment to stocks when one is bullish on the stock market. If markets are efficient and prices reflect all relevant information, perhaps it is better to follow passive strategies instead of spending resources in a futile attempt to outguess your competitors in the financial markets.

If the efficient market hypothesis were taken to the extreme, there would be no point in active security analysis; only fools would commit resources to actively analyze securities. Without ongoing security analysis, however, prices eventually would depart from "correct" values, creating new incentives for experts to move in. Therefore, in Chapter 9, we examine challenges to the efficient market hypothesis. Even in environments as competitive as the financial markets, we may observe only *near*-efficiency, and profit opportunities may exist for especially insightful and creative investors. This motivates our discussion of active portfolio management in Part Six. More importantly, our discussions of security analysis and portfolio construction generally must account for the likelihood of nearly efficient markets.

passive management

Buying and holding a diversified portfolio without attempting to identify mispriced securities.

active management

Attempting to identify mispriced securities or to forecast broad market trends.

1.6 THE PLAYERS

From a bird's-eye view, there would appear to be three major players in the financial markets:

1. Firms are net demanders of capital. They raise capital now to pay for investments in plant and equipment. The income generated by those real assets provides the returns to investors who purchase the securities issued by the firm.
2. Households typically are suppliers of capital. They purchase the securities issued by firms that need to raise funds.
3. Governments can be borrowers or lenders, depending on the relationship between tax revenue and government expenditures. Since World War II, the U.S. government typically has run budget deficits, meaning that its tax receipts have been less than its expenditures. The government, therefore, has had to borrow funds to cover its budget deficit. Issuance of Treasury bills, notes, and bonds is the major way that the government borrows funds from the public. In contrast, in the latter part of the 1990s, the government enjoyed a budget surplus and was able to retire some outstanding debt.

Corporations and governments do not sell all or even most of their securities directly to individuals. For example, about half of all stock is held by large financial institutions such as pension funds, mutual funds, insurance companies, and banks. These financial institutions stand between the security issuer (the firm) and the ultimate owner of the security (the individual investor). For this reason, they are called *financial intermediaries.* Similarly, corporations do not directly market their securities to the public. Instead, they hire agents, called investment bankers, to represent them to the investing public. Let's examine the roles of these intermediaries.

Financial Intermediaries

Households want desirable investments for their savings, yet the small (financial) size of most households makes direct investment difficult. A small investor seeking to lend money to businesses that need to finance investments doesn't advertise in the local newspaper to find a willing and desirable borrower. Moreover, an individual lender would not be able to diversify across borrowers to reduce risk. Finally, an individual lender is not equipped to assess and monitor the credit risk of borrowers.

financial intermediaries

Institutions that "connect" borrowers and lenders by accepting funds from lenders and loaning funds to borrowers.

For these reasons, **financial intermediaries** have evolved to bring together the suppliers of capital (investors) with the demanders of capital (primarily corporations and the federal government). These financial intermediaries include banks, investment companies, insurance companies, and credit unions. Financial intermediaries issue their own securities to raise funds to purchase the securities of other corporations.

For example, a bank raises funds by borrowing (taking deposits) and lending that money to other borrowers. The spread between the interest rates paid to depositors and the rates charged to borrowers is the source of the bank's profit. In this way, lenders and borrowers do not need to contact each other directly. Instead, each goes to the bank, which acts as an intermediary between the two. The problem of matching lenders with borrowers is solved when each comes independently to the common intermediary.

Financial intermediaries are distinguished from other businesses in that both their assets and their liabilities are overwhelmingly financial. Table 1.3 presents the aggregated balance sheet of commercial banks, one of the largest sectors of financial intermediaries. Notice that the balance sheet includes only very small amounts of real assets. Compare Table 1.3 to the aggregated balance sheet of the nonfinancial corporate sector in Table 1.4, for which real assets are about half of all assets. The contrast arises because intermediaries simply move funds from one sector to another. In fact, the primary social function of such intermediaries is to channel household savings to the business sector.

Other examples of financial intermediaries are investment companies, insurance companies, and credit unions. All these firms offer similar advantages in their intermediary role. First, by pooling the resources of many small investors, they are able to lend considerable sums to large borrowers. Second, by lending to many borrowers, intermediaries achieve significant diversification, so they can accept loans that individually might be too risky. Third, intermediaries build expertise through the volume of business they do and can use economies of scale and scope to assess and monitor risk.

investment companies

Firms managing funds for investors. An investment company may manage several mutual funds.

Investment companies, which pool and manage the money of many investors, also arise out of economies of scale. Here, the problem is that most household portfolios are not large enough to be spread among a wide variety of securities. It is very expensive in terms of brokerage fees and research costs to purchase one or two shares of many different firms. Mutual funds have the advantage of large-scale trading and portfolio management, while participating investors are assigned a prorated share of the total funds according to the size of their investment. This system gives small investors advantages they are willing to pay for via a management fee to the mutual fund operator.

Investment companies also can design portfolios specifically for large investors with particular goals. In contrast, mutual funds are sold in the retail market, and their investment philosophies are differentiated mainly by strategies that are likely to attract a large number of clients.

TABLE 1.3   Balance sheet of FDIC-insured commercial banks and savings institutions

Assets	$ Billion	% Total	Liabilities and Net Worth	$ Billion	% Total
Real assets			Liabilities		
Equipment and premises	$ 120.7	0.8%	Deposits	$11,490.3	75.8%
Other real estate	27.9	0.2	Debt and other borrowed funds	888.2	5.9
Total real assets	$ 148.6	1.0%	Federal funds and repurchase agreements	366.7	2.4
			Other	703.2	4.6
			Total liabilities	$13,448.4	88.7%
Financial assets					
Cash	$ 1,843.1	12.2%			
Investment securities	3,113.1	20.5			
Loans and leases	8,111.2	53.5			
Other financial assets	870.3	5.7			
Total financial assets	$13,937.7	91.9%			
Other assets					
Intangible assets	$ 365.6	2.4%			
Other	712.7	4.7			
Total other assets	$ 1,078.3	7.1%	Net worth	1,716.2	11.3
Total	$15,164.6	100.0%		$15,164.6	100.0%

Note: Column sums may differ from total because of rounding error.

Source: Federal Deposit Insurance Corporation, **www.fdic.gov**, September 2014.

TABLE 1.4   Balance sheet of U.S. nonfinancial corporations

Assets	$ Billion	% Total	Liabilities and Net Worth	$ Billion	% Total
Real assets			Liabilities		
Equipment & intellectual property	$ 6,200	17.7%	Bonds and mortgages	$ 7,905	22.6%
Real estate	10,166	29.0	Bank loans	654	1.9
Inventories	2,203	6.3	Other loans	1,072	3.1
Total real assets	$18,569	53.1%	Trade debt	1,996	5.7
			Other	4,275	12.2
			Total liabilities	$15,902	45.4%
Financial assets					
Deposits and cash	$ 1,040	3.0%			
Marketable securities	838	2.4			
Trade and consumer credit	2,581	7.4			
Other	11,969	34.2			
Total financial assets	$16,428	46.9%	Net worth	19,094	54.6
Total	$34,997	100.0%		$34,997	100.0%

Note: Column sums may differ from total because of rounding error.

Source: *Flow of Funds Accounts of the United States*, Board of Governors of the Federal Reserve System, June 2014.

Like mutual funds, *hedge funds* also pool and invest the money of many clients. But they are open only to institutional investors such as pension funds, endowment funds, or wealthy individuals. They are more likely to pursue complex and higher-risk strategies. They typically

On the MARKET FRONT

SEPARATING COMMERCIAL BANKING FROM THE INVESTMENT BANKING INDUSTRY

Until 1999, the Glass-Steagall Act prohibited banks from both accepting deposits and underwriting securities. In other words, it forced a separation of the investment and commercial banking industries. But when Glass-Steagall was repealed, many large commercial banks began to transform themselves into "universal banks" that could offer a full range of commercial and investment banking services. In some cases, commercial banks started their own investment banking divisions from scratch, but more commonly they expanded through merger. For example, Chase Manhattan acquired J. P. Morgan to form JPMorgan Chase. Similarly, Citigroup acquired Salomon Smith Barney to offer wealth management, brokerage, investment banking, and asset management services to its clients. Most of Europe had never forced the separation of commercial and investment banking, so their giant banks such as Credit Suisse, Deutsche Bank, HSBC, and UBS had long been universal banks. Until 2008, however, the stand-alone investment banking sector in the U.S. remained large and apparently vibrant, including such storied names as Goldman Sachs, Morgan Stanley, Merrill Lynch, and Lehman Brothers.

But the industry was shaken to its core in 2008, when several investment banks were beset by enormous losses on their holdings of mortgage-backed securities. In March, on the verge of insolvency, Bear Stearns was merged into JPMorgan Chase. On September 14, 2008, Merrill Lynch, also suffering steep mortgage-related losses, negotiated an agreement to be acquired by Bank of America. The next day, Lehman Brothers entered into the largest bankruptcy in U.S. history, having failed to find an acquirer who was able and willing to rescue it from its steep losses. The next week, the only two remaining major independent investment banks, Goldman Sachs and Morgan Stanley, decided to convert from investment banks to traditional bank holding companies. In so doing, they became subject to the supervision of national bank regulators such as the Federal Reserve and the far tighter rules for capital adequacy that govern commercial banks.[5] The firms decided that the greater stability they would enjoy as commercial banks, particularly the ability to fund their operations through bank deposits and access to emergency borrowing from the Fed, justified the conversion. These mergers and conversions marked the effective end of the independent investment banking industry—but not of investment banking. Those services now will be supplied by the large universal banks.

Today, the debate about the separation between commercial and investment banking that seemed to have ended with the repeal of Glass-Steagall has come back to life. The Dodd-Frank Wall Street Reform and Consumer Protection Act places new restrictions on bank activities. For example, the Volcker Rule, named after former chairman of the Federal Reserve Paul Volcker, prohibits banks from "proprietary trading," that is, trading securities for their own accounts, and restricts their investments in hedge funds or private equity funds. The rule is meant to limit the risk that banks can take on. While the Volcker Rule is far less restrictive than Glass-Steagall had been, both are motivated by the belief that banks enjoying federal guarantees should be subject to limits on the sorts of activities in which they can engage. Proprietary trading is a core activity for investment banks, so limitations on this activity for commercial banks would reintroduce a separation between their business models.

---

keep a portion of trading profits as part of their fees, whereas mutual funds charge a fixed percentage of assets under management.

Economies of scale also explain the proliferation of analytic services available to investors. Newsletters, databases, and brokerage house research services all engage in research to be sold to a large client base. This setup arises naturally. Investors clearly want information, but with small portfolios to manage, they do not find it economical to personally gather all of it. Hence, a profit opportunity emerges: A firm can perform this service for many clients and charge for it.

Investment Bankers

Just as economies of scale and specialization create profit opportunities for financial intermediaries, so too do these economies create niches for firms that perform specialized services for businesses. Firms raise much of their capital by selling securities such as stocks and bonds to the public. Because these firms do not do so frequently, however, **investment bankers** that specialize in such activities can offer their services at a cost below that of maintaining an in-house security issuance division.

Investment bankers advise an issuing corporation on the prices it can charge for the securities issued, appropriate interest rates, and so forth. Ultimately, the investment banking firm

investment bankers

Firms specializing in the sale of new securities to the public, typically by underwriting the issue.

---

[5]For example, a typical leverage ratio (total assets divided by bank capital) at commercial banks in 2008 was about 10 to 1. In contrast, leverage at investment banks reached 30 to 1. Such leverage increased profits when times were good but provided an inadequate buffer against losses and left the banks exposed to failure when their investment portfolios were shaken by large losses.

handles the marketing of the security in the **primary market,** where new issues of securities are offered to the public. In this role, the banks are called *underwriters.* Later, investors can trade previously issued securities among themselves in the so-called **secondary market.**

For most of the last century, investment banks and commercial banks in the U.S. were separated by law. While those regulations were effectively eliminated in 1999, until 2008 the industry known as "Wall Street" still comprised large, independent investment banks such as Goldman Sachs, Merrill Lynch, or Lehman Brothers. But that stand-alone model came to an abrupt end in September 2008, when all the remaining major U.S. investment banks were absorbed into commercial banks, declared bankruptcy, or reorganized as commercial banks. The nearby box presents a brief introduction to these events.

primary market

A market in which new issues of securities are offered to the public.

secondary market

Previously issued securities are traded among investors.

Venture Capital and Private Equity

While large firms can raise funds directly from the stock and bond markets with help from their investment bankers, smaller and younger firms that have not yet issued securities to the public do not have that option. Start-up companies rely instead on bank loans and investors who are willing to invest in them in return for an ownership stake in the firm. The equity investment in these young companies is called **venture capital (VC).** Sources of venture capital are dedicated venture capital funds, wealthy individuals known as *angel investors,* and institutions such as pension funds.

Most venture capital funds are set up as limited partnerships. A management company starts with its own money and raises additional capital from limited partners such as pension funds. That capital may then be invested in a variety of start-up companies. The management company usually sits on the start-up company's board of directors, helps recruit senior managers, and provides business advice. It charges a fee to the VC fund for overseeing the investments. After some period of time, for example, 10 years, the fund is liquidated and proceeds are distributed to the investors.

Venture capital investors commonly take an active role in the management of a start-up firm. Other active investors may engage in similar hands-on management but focus instead on firms that are in distress or firms that may be bought up, "improved," and sold for a profit. Collectively, these investments in firms that do not trade on public stock exchanges are known as **private equity** investments.

venture capital (VC)

Money invested to finance a new firm.

private equity

Investments in companies that are not traded on a stock exchange.

1.7 THE FINANCIAL CRISIS OF 2008

This chapter has laid out the broad outlines of the financial system, as well as some of the links between the financial side of the economy and the "real" side, in which goods and services are produced. The financial crisis of 2008 illustrated in a painful way the intimate ties between these two sectors. We present in this section a capsule summary of the crisis, attempting to draw some lessons about the role of the financial system as well as the causes and consequences of what has become known as *systemic risk.* Some of these issues are complicated; we consider them briefly here but will return to them in greater detail later in the text once we have more context for analysis.

Antecedents of the Crisis

In early 2007, most observers thought it inconceivable that within two years the world financial system would be facing its worse crisis since the Great Depression. At the time, the economy seemed to be marching from strength to strength. The last significant macroeconomic threat had been from the collapse of the high-tech bubble in 2000–2002. But the Federal Reserve responded to an emerging recession by aggressively reducing interest rates. Figure 1.1 shows that Treasury bill rates dropped drastically between 2001 and 2004, and the LIBOR rate (LIBOR is an acronym for the London Interbank Offer Rate), which is the interest

FIGURE 1.1

Short-term LIBOR and Treasury bill rates and the TED spread

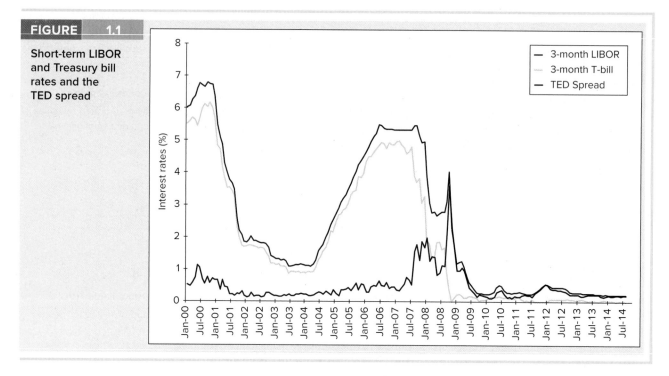

rate at which major money-center banks lend to each other, fell in tandem.[6] These actions appeared to have been successful, and the recession was short-lived and mild.

By mid-decade the economy was once again apparently healthy. While the stock market had declined substantially between 2001 and 2002, Figure 1.2 shows that it reversed direction just as dramatically beginning in 2003, fully recovering all of its post-tech-meltdown losses within a few years. Of equal importance, the banking sector seemed healthy. The spread between the LIBOR rate (at which banks borrow from each other) and the Treasury bill rate (at which the U.S. government borrows), a common measure of credit risk in the banking sector (often referred to as the *TED spread*),[7] was only around .25% in early 2007 (see the dark blue

FIGURE 1.2

Cumulative value of a $1 investment in the S&P 500 Index

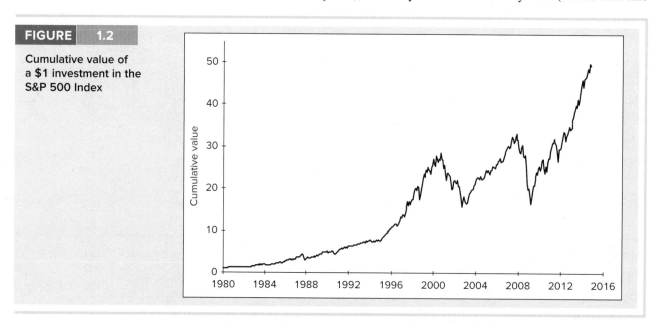

[6]The London Interbank Offer Rate is a rate charged in an interbank lending market outside the U.S. (largely centered in London). The rate is typically quoted for three-month loans.

[7]*TED* stands for "Treasury-Eurodollar spread." The Eurodollar rate in this spread is, in fact, LIBOR.

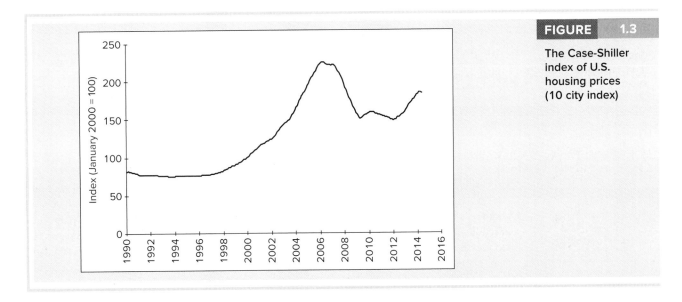

FIGURE 1.3

The Case-Shiller index of U.S. housing prices (10 city index)

line in Figure 1.1), suggesting that fears of default or "counterparty" risk in the banking sector were extremely low.

The combination of dramatically reduced interest rates and an apparently stable economy fed a historic boom in the housing market. Figure 1.3 shows that U.S. housing prices began rising noticeably in the late 1990s and accelerated dramatically after 2001 as interest rates plummeted. In the 10 years beginning 1997, average prices in the U.S. approximately tripled.

But confidence in the power of macroeconomic policy to reduce risk, the impressive recovery of the economy from the high-tech implosion, and particularly the housing price boom following the aggressive reduction in interest rates may have sown the seeds for the debacle that played out in 2008. On the one hand, the Fed's policy of reducing interest rates had resulted in low yields on a wide variety of investments, and investors were hungry for higher-yielding alternatives. On the other hand, low volatility and bright macroeconomic prospects encouraged greater tolerance for risk in the search for these higher-yielding investments. Nowhere was this more evident than in the exploding market for securitized mortgages. The U.S. housing and mortgage finance markets were at the center of a gathering storm.

Changes in Housing Finance

Prior to 1970, most mortgage loans would come from a local lender such as a neighborhood savings bank or credit union. A homeowner would borrow funds for a home purchase and repay it over a long period, commonly 30 years. A typical thrift institution would have as its major asset a portfolio of these long-term home loans, while its major liability would be the accounts of its depositors. This landscape began to change in the 1970s when Fannie Mae (FNMA, or Federal National Mortgage Association) and Freddie Mac (FHLMC, or Federal Home Loan Mortgage Corporation) began buying large quantities of mortgage loans from originators and bundling them into pools that could be traded like any other financial asset. These pools, which were essentially claims on the underlying mortgages, were soon dubbed "mortgage-backed securities," and the process was called **securitization.** Fannie and Freddie quickly became the behemoths of the mortgage market, between them buying more than half of all mortgages originated by the private sector.

Figure 1.4 illustrates how cash flows passed from the original borrower to the ultimate investor in a mortgage-backed security. The loan originator, for example, the savings and loan, might make a $100,000 loan to a homeowner. The homeowner would repay principal and interest (P&I) on the loan over 30 years. But then the originator would sell the mortgage

securitization

Pooling loans into standardized securities backed by those loans, which can then be traded like any other security.

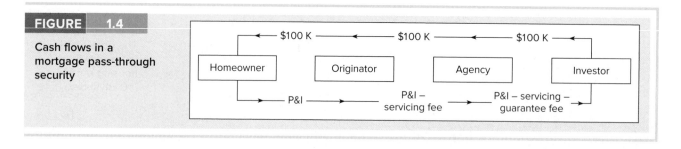

FIGURE 1.4

Cash flows in a mortgage pass-through security

to Freddie Mac or Fannie Mae and recover the cost of the loan. The originator could continue to service the loan (e.g., collect monthly payments from the homeowner) for a small servicing fee, but the loan payments net of that fee would be passed along to the agency. In turn, Freddie or Fannie would pool the loans into mortgage-backed securities and sell the securities to investors such as pension funds or mutual funds. The agency (Fannie or Freddie) typically would guarantee the credit or default risk of the loans included in each pool, for which it would retain a guarantee fee before passing along the rest of the cash flow to the ultimate investor. Because the mortgage cash flows were passed along from the homeowner to the lender, to Fannie or Freddie, and finally to the investor, the mortgage-backed securities were also called *pass-throughs.*

Until the last decade, the vast majority of the mortgages that had been securitized into pass-throughs were held or guaranteed by Freddie Mac or Fannie Mae. These were low-risk *conforming* mortgages, meaning that eligible loans for agency securitization couldn't be too big and homeowners had to meet underwriting criteria establishing their ability to repay the loan. For example, the ratio of loan amount to house value could be no more than 80%.

Conforming loans were pooled almost entirely through Freddie Mac and Fannie Mae, but once the securitization model took hold, it created an opening for a new product: securitization by private firms of *nonconforming* "subprime" loans with higher default risk. One important difference between the government-agency pass-throughs and these so-called private-label pass-throughs was that the investor in the private-label pool would bear the risk that homeowners might default on their loans. Thus, originating mortgage brokers had little incentive to perform due diligence on the loan *as long as the loans could be sold to an investor.* These investors, of course, had no direct contact with the borrowers and could not perform detailed underwriting concerning loan quality. Instead, they relied on borrowers' credit scores, which steadily came to replace conventional underwriting.

A strong trend toward low-documentation and then no-documentation loans entailing little verification of a borrower's ability to carry a loan soon emerged. Other subprime underwriting standards also quickly deteriorated. For example, allowed leverage on home loans (as measured by the loan-to-value ratio) rose dramatically. By 2006, the majority of subprime borrowers purchased houses by borrowing the *entire* purchase price! When housing prices began falling, these highly leveraged loans were quickly "underwater," meaning that the house was worth less than the loan balance, and many homeowners decided to "walk away" or abandon their homes—and their loans.

Adjustable rate mortgages (ARMs) also grew in popularity, quickly becoming the standard in the subprime market. These loans offered borrowers low initial or "teaser" interest rates, but these rates eventually would reset to current market interest yields, for example, the Treasury bill rate plus 3%. While many of these borrowers had "maxed out" their borrowing capacity at the teaser rate, as soon as the loan rate was reset, their monthly payments would soar, especially if market interest rates had increased.

Despite these obvious risks, the ongoing increase in housing prices over the last decade seemed to have lulled many investors into complacency, with a widespread belief that continually rising home prices would bail out poorly performing loans. But starting in 2004, the ability of refinancing to save a loan began to diminish. First, higher interest rates put payment pressure on homeowners who had taken out adjustable rate mortgages. Second, as Figure 1.3 shows, housing prices peaked by 2006, so homeowners' ability to refinance a loan using built-up equity in the house declined. Mortgage default rates began to surge in 2007, as did losses on mortgage-backed securities. The crisis was ready to shift into high gear.

Mortgage Derivatives

One might ask: Who was willing to buy all of these risky subprime mortgages? Securitization, restructuring, and credit enhancement provide a big part of the answer. New risk-shifting tools enabled investment banks to carve out AAA-rated securities from original-issue "junk" loans. Collateralized debt obligations, or CDOs, were among the most important and eventually damaging of these innovations.

CDOs were designed to concentrate the credit (i.e., default) risk of a bundle of loans on one class of investors, leaving the other investors in the pool relatively protected from that risk. The idea was to prioritize claims on loan repayments by dividing the pool into senior versus junior slices called *tranches*. The senior tranches had first claim on repayments from the entire pool. Junior tranches would be paid only after the senior ones had received their cut. For example, if a pool was divided into two tranches, with 70% of the pool allocated to the senior tranche and 30% allocated to the junior one, the senior investors would be repaid in full as long as 70% or more of the loans in the pool performed, that is, as long as the default rate on the pool remained below 30%. Even with pools composed of risky subprime loans, default rates above 30% seemed extremely unlikely, and thus senior tranches were commonly granted the highest (i.e., AAA) rating by the major credit rating agencies, Moody's, Standard & Poor's, and Fitch. Large amounts of AAA-rated securities were thus carved out of pools of low-rated mortgages. (We will describe CDOs in more detail in Chapter 10.)

Of course, we know now that these ratings were wrong. The senior-subordinated structure of CDOs provided far less protection to senior tranches than investors anticipated. When housing prices across the entire country began to fall in unison, defaults in all regions increased and the hoped-for benefits from diversifying loans geographically never materialized.

Why had the rating agencies so dramatically underestimated credit risk in these subprime securities? First, default probabilities had been estimated using historical data from an unrepresentative period characterized by a housing boom and an uncommonly prosperous economy. Moreover, the ratings analysts had extrapolated historical default experience to a new sort of borrower pool—one without down payments, with exploding payment loans, and with low- or no-documentation loans (often called *liar loans*). Past default experience was largely irrelevant given these profound changes in the market. Moreover, there was excessive optimism about the power of cross-regional diversification to minimize risk.

Finally, there were apparent agency problems. The ratings agencies were paid to provide ratings by the issuers of the securities—not the purchasers. They faced pressure from the issuers, who could shop around for the most favorable treatment, to provide generous ratings.

When Freddie Mac and Fannie Mae pooled conforming mortgages into securities, they guaranteed the underlying mortgage loans against homeowner defaults. In contrast, there were no guarantees on the mortgages pooled into subprime mortgage–backed securities, so investors would bear credit risk. Were either of these arrangements necessarily a better way to manage and allocate default risk?

CONCEPT check **1.2**

Credit Default Swaps

In parallel to the CDO market, the market in *credit default swaps* also exploded in this period. A credit default swap, or CDS, is in essence an insurance contract against the default of one or more borrowers. (We will describe these in more detail in Chapter 10.) The purchaser of the swap pays an annual premium (like an insurance premium) for the protection from credit risk. Credit default swaps became an alternative method of credit enhancement, seemingly allowing investors to buy subprime loans and insure their safety. But, in practice, some swap issuers ramped up their exposure to credit risk to unsupportable levels, without sufficient capital to back those obligations. For example, the large insurance company AIG alone sold more than $400 billion of CDS contracts on subprime mortgages.

The Rise of Systemic Risk

By 2007, the financial system displayed several troubling features. Many large banks and related financial institutions had adopted an apparently profitable financing scheme: borrowing short term at low interest rates to finance holdings in higher-yielding, long-term, illiquid[8] assets and treating the interest rate differential between their assets and liabilities as economic profit. But this business model was precarious: By relying primarily on short-term loans for their funding, these firms needed to constantly refinance their positions (i.e., borrow additional funds as the loans matured), or else face the necessity of quickly selling off their less liquid asset portfolios, which would be difficult in times of financial stress. Moreover, these institutions were highly leveraged and had little capital as a buffer against losses. Large investment banks on Wall Street in particular had sharply increased leverage, which added to an underappreciated vulnerability to refunding requirements—especially if the value of their asset portfolios came into question. Even small portfolio losses could drive their net worth negative, at which point no one would be willing to extend them loans.

Another source of fragility was widespread investor reliance on credit protection through products like CDOs. Many of the assets underlying these pools were illiquid, hard to value, and highly dependent on forecasts of future performance of other loans. In a widespread downturn, with rating downgrades, these assets would prove difficult to sell.

The steady displacement of formal exchange trading by informal "over-the-counter" markets created other problems. In formal exchanges such as futures or options markets, participants must put up collateral called *margin* to guarantee their ability to make good on their obligations. Prices are computed each day, and gains or losses are continually added to or subtracted from each trader's margin account. If a margin account runs low after a series of losses, the investor can be required to either contribute more collateral or close out the position before actual insolvency ensues. Positions, and thus exposures to losses, are transparent to other traders. In contrast, the over-the-counter markets where CDS contracts trade are effectively private contracts between two parties with less public disclosure of positions and less opportunity to recognize either cumulative gains or losses over time or the resultant credit exposure of each trading partner.

This new financial model was brimming with **systemic risk,** a potential breakdown of the financial system when problems in one market spill over and disrupt others. When lenders such as banks have limited capital, and are afraid of further losses, they may rationally choose to hoard their capital instead of lending it out to customers such as small firms, thereby exacerbating funding problems for their customary borrowers.

systemic risk

Risk of breakdown in the financial system, particularly due to spillover effects from one market into others.

The Shoe Drops

By fall of 2007, housing prices were in decline (Figure 1.3), mortgage delinquencies increased, and the stock market entered its own free fall (Figure 1.2). Many investment banks, which had large investments in mortgages, also began to totter.

The crisis peaked in September 2008. On September 7, the giant federal mortgage agencies Fannie Mae and Freddie Mac, both of which had taken large positions in subprime mortgage–backed securities, were put into conservatorship. (We will have more to say on their travails in Chapter 2.) The failure of these two mainstays of the U.S. housing and mortgage finance industries threw financial markets into a panic. By the second week of

---

[8]*Liquidity* refers to the speed and the ease with which investors can realize the cash value of an investment. Illiquid assets, for example, real estate, can be hard to sell quickly, and a quick sale may require a substantial discount from the price at which the asset could be sold in an unrushed situation.

September, it was clear that both Lehman Brothers and Merrill Lynch were on the verge of bankruptcy. On September 14, Merrill Lynch was sold to Bank of America. The next day, Lehman Brothers, which was denied equivalent treatment, filed for bankruptcy protection. Two days later, on September 17, the government reluctantly lent $85 billion to AIG, reasoning that its failure would have been highly destabilizing to the banking industry, which was holding massive amounts of its credit guarantees (i.e., CDS contracts). The next day, the Treasury unveiled its first proposal to spend $700 billion to purchase "toxic" mortgage-backed securities.

A particularly devastating fallout of the Lehman bankruptcy was on the "money market" for short-term lending. Lehman had borrowed considerable funds by issuing very short-term unsecured debt called *commercial paper.* Among the major customers in the commercial paper were money market mutual funds, which invest in short-term, high-quality debt of commercial borrowers. When Lehman faltered, fear spread that these funds were exposed to losses on their large investments in commercial paper, and money market fund customers across the country rushed to withdraw their funds. In turn, the funds rushed out of commercial paper into safer and more liquid Treasury bills, essentially shutting down short-term financing markets.

The freezing up of credit markets was the end of any dwindling possibility that the financial crisis could be contained to Wall Street. Larger companies that had relied on the commercial paper market were now unable to raise short-term funds. Banks similarly found it difficult to raise funds. (Look back to Figure 1.1, where you will see that the TED spread, a measure of bank insolvency fears, skyrocketed in 2008.) With banks unwilling or unable to extend credit to their customers, thousands of small businesses that relied on bank lines of credit also became unable to finance their normal business operations. Capital-starved companies were forced to scale back their own operations precipitously. The unemployment rate rose rapidly, and the economy was in its worst recession in decades. The turmoil in the financial markets had spilled over into the real economy, and Main Street had joined Wall Street in a bout of protracted misery.

The Dodd-Frank Reform Act

The crisis engendered many calls for reform of Wall Street. These eventually led to the passage in 2010 of the Dodd-Frank Wall Street Reform and Consumer Protection Act, which proposed several mechanisms to mitigate systemic risk.

The act calls for stricter rules for bank capital, liquidity, and risk management practices, especially as banks become larger and their potential failure would be more threatening to other institutions. With more capital supporting banks, the potential for one insolvency to trigger another could be contained. In addition, when banks have more capital, they have less incentive to ramp up risk, as potential losses will come at their own expense and not the FDIC's.

Dodd-Frank also mandates increased transparency, especially in derivative markets. For example, one suggestion was to standardize CDS contracts so they can trade in centralized exchanges where prices can be determined in a deep market and gains or losses can be settled on a daily basis. Margin requirements, enforced daily, prevent CDS participants from taking on greater positions than they can handle, and exchange trading facilitates analysis of the exposure of firms to losses in these markets.

The act also attempts to limit the risky activities in which banks can engage. The so-called Volcker Rule, named after former chairman of the Federal Reserve Paul Volcker, limits a bank's ability to trade for its own account and to own or invest in a hedge fund or private equity fund.

The law also addresses shortcomings of the regulatory system that became apparent in 2008. The U.S. has several financial regulators with overlapping responsibility, and some institutions were accused of "regulator shopping," seeking to be supervised by the most lenient regulator. Dodd-Frank seeks to unify and clarify lines of regulatory authority and responsibility in one or a smaller number of government agencies.

The act addresses incentive issues. Among these are proposals to force employee compensation to reflect longer-term performance. The act requires public companies to set "claw-back provisions" to take back executive compensation if it was based on inaccurate financial statements. The motivation is to discourage excessive risk taking by large financial institutions in which big bets can be wagered with the attitude that a successful outcome will result in a big bonus while a bad outcome will be borne by the company, or worse, the taxpayer.

The incentives of the bond rating agencies are also a sore point. Few are happy with a system that has the ratings agencies paid by the firms they rate. The act creates an Office of Credit Ratings within the Securities and Exchange Commission to oversee the credit rating agencies.

It is still too early to know which, if any, of these reforms will stick. The implementation of Dodd-Frank is still subject to considerable interpretation by regulators, and the act is still under attack by some members of Congress. But the crisis surely has made clear the essential role of the financial system in the functioning of the real economy.

1.8 OUTLINE OF THE TEXT

The text has six parts, which are fairly independent and may be studied in a variety of sequences. Part One is an introduction to financial markets, instruments, and trading of securities. This part also describes the mutual fund industry.

Part Two is a fairly detailed presentation of "modern portfolio theory." This part of the text treats the effect of diversification on portfolio risk, the efficient diversification of investor portfolios, the choice of portfolios that strike an attractive balance between risk and return, and the trade-off between risk and expected return. This part also treats the efficient market hypothesis as well as behavioral critiques of theories based on investor rationality.

Parts Three through Five cover security analysis and valuation. Part Three is devoted to debt markets and Part Four to equity markets. Part Five covers derivative assets, such as options and futures contracts.

Part Six is an introduction to active investment management. It shows how different investors' objectives and constraints can lead to a variety of investment policies. This part discusses the role of active management in nearly efficient markets, considers how one should evaluate the performance of managers who pursue active strategies, and takes a close look at hedge funds. It also shows how the principles of portfolio construction can be extended to the international setting.

SUMMARY

- Real assets create wealth. Financial assets represent claims to parts or all of that wealth. Financial assets determine how the ownership of real assets is distributed among investors.
- Financial assets can be categorized as fixed-income (debt), equity, or derivative instruments. Top-down portfolio construction techniques start with the asset allocation decision—the allocation of funds across broad asset classes—and then progress to more specific security-selection decisions.
- Competition in financial markets leads to a risk-return trade-off, in which securities that offer higher expected rates of return also impose greater risks on investors. The presence of risk, however, implies that actual returns can differ considerably from expected returns at the beginning of the investment period. Competition among security analysts also results in financial markets that are nearly informationally efficient, meaning that prices reflect all available information concerning the value of the security. Passive investment strategies may make sense in nearly efficient markets.
- Financial intermediaries pool investor funds and invest them. Their services are in demand because small investors cannot efficiently gather information, diversify, and

monitor portfolios. The financial intermediary, in contrast, is a large investor that can take advantage of scale economies.

- Investment banking brings efficiency to corporate fund raising. Investment bankers develop expertise in pricing new issues and in marketing them to investors. By the end of 2008, all the major stand-alone U.S. investment banks had been absorbed into commercial banks or had reorganized themselves into bank holding companies. In Europe, where universal banking had never been prohibited, large banks had long maintained both commercial and investment banking divisions.
- The financial crisis of 2008 showed the importance of systemic risk. Systemic risk can be limited by transparency that allows traders and investors to assess the risk of their counterparties, capital requirements to prevent trading participants from being brought down by potential losses, frequent settlement of gains or losses to prevent losses from accumulating beyond an institution's ability to bear them, incentives to discourage excessive risk taking, and accurate and unbiased analysis by those charged with evaluating security risk.

KEY TERMS

active management, 11
agency problems, 7
asset allocation, 9
derivative securities, 5
equity, 5
financial assets, 3
financial intermediaries, 12
fixed-income (debt)
   securities, 5
investment, 2
investment bankers, 14
investment companies, 12
passive management, 11
primary market, 15
private equity, 15
real assets, 3
risk-return trade-off, 10
secondary market, 15
securitization, 17
security analysis, 10
security selection, 9
systemic risk, 20
venture capital (VC), 15

PROBLEM SETS

Select problems are available in McGraw-Hill's Connect. Please see the Supplements section of the book's frontmatter for more information.

1. What are the differences between equity and fixed-income securities? *(LO 1-5)*
2. What is the difference between a primary asset and a derivative asset? *(LO 1-1)*
3. What is the difference between asset allocation and security selection? *(LO 1-4)*
4. What are agency problems? What are some approaches to solving them? *(LO 1-3)*
5. What are the differences between real and financial assets? *(LO 1-2)*
6. How does investment banking differ from commercial banking? *(LO 1-5)*
7. For each transaction, identify the real and/or financial assets that trade hands. Are any financial assets created or destroyed in the transaction? *(LO 1-2)*
   a. Toyota takes out a bank loan to finance the construction of a new factory.
   b. Toyota pays off its loan.
   c. Toyota uses $10 million of cash on hand to purchase additional inventory of spare auto parts.
8. Suppose that in a wave of pessimism, housing prices fall by 10% across the entire economy. *(LO 1-2)*
   a. Has the stock of real assets of the economy changed?
   b. Are individuals less wealthy?
   c. Can you reconcile your answers to (a) and (b)?

9. Lanni Products is a start-up computer software development firm. It currently owns computer equipment worth $30,000 and has cash on hand of $20,000 contributed by Lanni's owners. For each of the following transactions, identify the real and/or financial assets that trade hands. Are any financial assets created or destroyed in the transaction? *(LO 1-2)*

   a. Lanni takes out a bank loan. It receives $50,000 in cash and signs a note promising to pay back the loan over three years.

   b. Lanni uses the cash from the bank plus $20,000 of its own funds to finance the development of new financial planning software.

   c. Lanni sells the software product to Microsoft, which will market it to the public under the Microsoft name. Lanni accepts payment in the form of 2,500 shares of Microsoft stock.

   d. Lanni sells the shares of stock for $50 per share and uses part of the proceeds to pay off the bank loan.

10. Reconsider Lanni Products from Problem 9.   *(LO 1-2)*

    a. Prepare its balance sheet just after it gets the bank loan. What is the ratio of real assets to total assets?

    b. Prepare the balance sheet after Lanni spends the $70,000 to develop its software product. What is the ratio of real assets to total assets?

    c. Prepare the balance sheet after Lanni accepts the payment of shares from Microsoft. What is the ratio of real assets to total assets?

11. What reforms to the financial system might reduce its exposure to systemic risk? *(LO 1-6)*

12. Examine the balance sheet of commercial banks in Table 1.3.   *(LO 1-2)*

    a. What is the ratio of real assets to total assets?

    b. What is that ratio for nonfinancial firms (Table 1.4)?

    c. Why should this difference be expected?

13. Why do financial assets show up as a component of household wealth, but not of national wealth? Why do financial assets still matter for the material well-being of an economy?   *(LO 1-2)*

14. Discuss the advantages and disadvantages of the following forms of managerial compensation in terms of mitigating agency problems, that is, potential conflicts of interest between managers and shareholders.   *(LO 1-3)*

    a. A fixed salary.

    b. Stock in the firm that must be held for five years.

    c. A salary linked to the firm's profits.

15. Oversight by large institutional investors or creditors is one mechanism to reduce agency problems. Why don't individual investors in the firm have the same incentive to keep an eye on management?   *(LO 1-3)*

16. Wall Street firms have traditionally compensated their traders with a share of the trading profits that they generated. How might this practice have affected traders' willingness to assume risk? What is the agency problem this practice engendered?   *(LO 1-3)*

17. Why would you expect securitization to take place only in highly developed capital markets?   *(LO 1-6)*

18. What would you expect to be the relationship between securitization and the role of financial intermediaries in the economy? For example, what happens to the role of local banks in providing capital for mortgage loans when national markets in mortgage-backed securities become highly developed?   *(LO 1-6)*

19. Give an example of three financial intermediaries, and explain how they act as a bridge between small investors and large capital markets or corporations.   *(LO 1-5)*

20. Firms raise capital from investors by issuing shares in the primary markets. Does this imply that corporate financial managers can ignore trading of previously issued shares in the secondary market?   *(LO 1-4)*

21. The average rate of return on investments in large stocks has outpaced that on investments in Treasury bills by about 7% since 1926. Why, then, does anyone invest in Treasury bills? *(LO 1-1)*

22. You see an advertisement for a book that claims to show how you can make $1 million with no risk and with no money down. Will you buy the book? *(LO 1-1)*

---

1. Log on to **finance.yahoo.com** and enter the ticker symbol "RRD" in the *Get Quotes* box to find information about R.R. Donnelley & Sons.
   a. Click on company *Profile*. What is Donnelly's main line of business?
   b. Now go to *Key Statistics*. How many shares of the company's stock are outstanding? What is the total market value of the firm? What were its profits in the most recent fiscal year?
   c. Look up *Major Holders* of the company's stock. What fraction of total shares is held by insiders?
   d. Now go to *Analyst Opinion*. What is the average price target (i.e., the predicted stock price of the Donnelly shares) of the analysts covering this firm? How does that compare to the price at which the stock is currently trading?
   e. Look at the company's *Balance Sheet*. What were its total assets at the end of the most recent fiscal year?

2. Visit the website of the Securities and Exchange Commission, **www.sec.gov.** What is the mission of the SEC? What information and advice does the SEC offer to beginning investors?

3. Now visit the website of the NASD, **www.finra.org.** What is its mission? What information and advice does it offer to beginners?

4. Now visit the website of the IOSCO, **www.iosco.org.** What is its mission? What information and advice does it offer to beginners?

1.1 a. Real
    b. Financial
    c. Real
    d. Real
    e. Financial

1.2 The central issue is the incentive to monitor the quality of loans both when originated and over time. Freddie and Fannie clearly had incentive to monitor the quality of conforming loans that they had guaranteed, and their ongoing relationships with mortgage originators gave them opportunities to evaluate track records over extended periods of time. In the subprime mortgage market, the ultimate investors in the securities (or the CDOs backed by those securities), who were bearing the credit risk, should not have been willing to invest in loans with a disproportional likelihood of default. If they properly understood their exposure to default risk, then the (correspondingly low) prices they would have been willing to pay for these securities would have imposed discipline on the mortgage originators and servicers. The fact that they were willing to hold such large positions in these risky securities suggests that they did not appreciate the extent of their exposure. Maybe they were led astray by overly optimistic projections for housing prices or by biased assessments from the credit reporting agencies. While in principle either arrangement for default risk could have provided the appropriate discipline on the mortgage originators, in practice the informational advantages of Freddie and Fannie probably made them the better "recipients" of default risk. The lesson is that information and transparency are some of the preconditions for well-functioning markets.

Asset Classes and Financial Instruments

Learning Objectives

LO 2-1 Distinguish among the major assets that trade in money markets and in capital markets.

LO 2-2 Describe the construction of stock market indexes.

LO 2-3 Calculate the profit or loss on investments in options and futures contracts.

You learned in Chapter 1 that the process of building an investment portfolio usually begins by deciding how much money to allocate to broad classes of assets, such as safe money market securities or bank accounts, longer-term bonds, stocks, or even asset classes such as real estate or precious metals. This process is called *asset allocation*. Within each class the investor then selects specific assets from a more detailed menu. This is called *security selection*.

Each broad asset class contains many specific security types, and the many variations on a theme can be overwhelming. Our goal in this chapter is to introduce you to the important features of broad classes of securities. Toward this end, we organize our tour of financial instruments according to asset class.

Financial markets are traditionally segmented into money markets and capital markets. Money market instruments include short-term, marketable, liquid, low-risk debt securities. Money market instruments sometimes are called *cash equivalents,* or just *cash* for short. Capital markets, in contrast, include longer-term and riskier securities. Securities in the capital market are much more diverse than those found within the money market. For this reason, we will subdivide the capital market into three segments: longer-term debt markets, equity markets, and derivative markets in which options and futures trade.

We first describe money market instruments. We then move on to debt and equity securities. We explain the structure of various stock market indexes in this chapter because market benchmark portfolios play an important role in portfolio construction and evaluation. Finally, we survey the derivative security markets for options and futures contracts. A selection of the markets, instruments, and indexes covered in this chapter appears in Table 2.1.

2.1   THE MONEY MARKET

The **money market** is a subsector of the debt market. It consists of very short-term debt securities that are highly marketable. Many of these securities trade in large denominations and so are out of the reach of individual investors. Money market mutual funds, however, are easily accessible to small investors. These mutual funds pool the resources of many investors and purchase a wide variety of money market securities on their behalf.

money markets

Include short-term, highly liquid, and relatively low-risk debt instruments.

Treasury Bills

U.S. **Treasury bills** (T-bills, or just bills, for short) are the most marketable of all money market instruments. T-bills represent the simplest form of borrowing. The government raises money by selling bills to the public. Investors buy the bills at a discount from the stated maturity value. At the bill's maturity, the holder receives the face value of the bill from the government. The difference between the purchase price and the ultimate maturity value represents the investor's earnings.

Treasury bills

Short-term government securities issued at a discount from face value and returning the face amount at maturity.

T-bills are issued with initial maturities of 4, 13, 26, or 52 weeks. Individuals can purchase them directly from the Treasury or on the secondary market from a government securities dealer. T-bills are highly liquid; that is, they are easily converted to cash and sold at low transaction cost and with little price risk. Unlike most other money market instruments, which sell in minimum denominations of $100,000, T-bills sell in minimum denominations of only $100, although $10,000 denominations are far more common. While the income earned on T-bills is taxable at the federal level, it is exempt from all state and local taxes, another characteristic distinguishing T-bills from other money market instruments.

Figure 2.1 is a partial listing of T-bills from *The Wall Street Journal Online* (look for the *Market Data* tab and then *Money Rates* under *Additional Data*). Rather than providing prices of each bill, the financial press reports yields based on those prices. You will see yields corresponding to both bid and asked prices. The *asked price* is the price you would have to pay to buy a T-bill from a securities dealer. The *bid price* is the slightly lower price you would receive if you wanted to sell a bill to a dealer. The *bid–asked spread* is the difference in these prices, which is the dealer's source of profit.

The first two yields in Figure 2.1 are reported using the *bank-discount method*. This means that the bill's discount from its maturity, or face, value is "annualized" based on a 360-day year and then reported as a percentage of face value. For example, for the highlighted bill maturing on March 12, 2015, days to maturity are 177 and the yield under the column labeled "ASKED" is given as .040%. This means that a dealer was willing to sell the bill at a discount from face value of .040% $\times$ (177/360) = .0197%. So a bill with $10,000 face value

TABLE 2.1	Financial markets and indexes	
The money market	**The bond market**
Treasury bills	Treasury bonds and notes
Certificates of deposit	Federal agency debt
Commercial paper	Municipal bonds
Bankers' acceptances	Corporate bonds
Eurodollars	Mortgage-backed securities
Repos and reverses	**Equity markets**
Federal funds	Common stocks
Brokers' calls	Preferred stocks
Indexes	**Derivative markets**
Dow Jones averages	Options
Standard & Poor's indexes	Futures and forwards
Bond market indicators	Swaps
International indexes	

FIGURE   2.1

Treasury bill listings

Source: *The Wall Street Journal Online*, September 16, 2014.

Treasury Bills

MATURITY	DAYS TO MATURITY	BID	ASKED	CHG	ASKED YIELD
Nov 28 14	73	0.010	0.005	−0.005	0.005
Jan 02 15	108	0.015	0.010	0.000	0.010
Mar 12 15	177	0.045	0.040	0.000	0.041
May 28 15	254	0.045	0.040	−0.005	0.041
Jul 23 15	310	0.080	0.075	0.000	0.076

could be purchased for $10,000 \times (1 - .000197) = \$9,998.033$. Similarly, on the basis of the bid yield of .045%, a dealer would be willing to purchase the bill for $10,000 \times (1 - .00045 \times 177/360) = \$9,997.788$. Notice that prices and yields are inversely related, so the higher bid *yield* reported in Figure 2.1 implies a lower bid *price*.

The bank discount method for computing yields has a long tradition, but it is flawed for at least two reasons. First, it assumes that the year has only 360 days. Second, it computes the yield as a fraction of face value rather than of the price the investor paid to acquire the bill.[1] An investor who buys the bill for the asked price and holds it until maturity will see her investment grow over 177 days by a multiple of $\$10,000/\$9,998.033 = 1.000197$, for a gain of .0197%. Annualizing this gain using a 365-day year results in a yield of $.0197\% \times 365/177 = .041\%$, which is the value reported in the last column, under "asked yield." This last value is called the Treasury bill's *bond-equivalent yield*.

Certificates of Deposit

certificate of deposit

A bank time deposit.

A **certificate of deposit** (CD) is a time deposit with a bank. Time deposits may not be withdrawn on demand. The bank pays interest and principal to the depositor only at the end of the fixed term of the CD. CDs issued in denominations larger than $100,000 are usually negotiable, however; that is, they can be sold to another investor if the owner needs to cash in the certificate before its maturity date. Short-term CDs are highly marketable, although the market significantly thins out for maturities of three months or more. CDs are treated as bank deposits by the Federal Deposit Insurance Corporation, so they are insured for up to $250,000 in the event of a bank insolvency.

Commercial Paper

The typical corporation is a net borrower of both long-term funds (for capital investments) and short-term funds (for working capital). Large, well-known companies often issue their own short-term unsecured debt notes directly to the public, rather than borrowing from banks. These notes

commercial paper

Short-term unsecured debt issued by large corporations.

are called **commercial paper** (CP). Sometimes, CP is backed by a bank line of credit, which gives the borrower access to cash that can be used if needed to pay off the paper at maturity.

CP maturities range up to 270 days; longer maturities require registration with the Securities and Exchange Commission and so are almost never issued. CP most commonly is issued with maturities of less than one or two months in denominations of multiples of $100,000. Therefore, small investors can invest in commercial paper only indirectly, through money market mutual funds.

CP is considered to be a fairly safe asset, given that a firm's condition presumably can be monitored and predicted over a term as short as one month. CP trades in secondary markets and so is quite liquid. Most issues are rated by at least one agency such as Standard & Poor's. The yield on CP depends on its time to maturity and credit rating.

While most CP historically was issued by nonfinancial firms, in recent years there was a sharp increase in so-called *asset-backed commercial paper* issued by financial firms such as banks. This short-term CP typically was used to raise funds for the institution to invest in other assets, most notoriously, subprime mortgages. These assets in turn were used as collateral for

---

[1] Both of these "errors" were dictated by computational simplicity in the days before computers. It is easier to compute percentage discounts from a round number such as face value than from purchase price. It is also easier to annualize using a 360-day year, since 360 is an even multiple of so many numbers.

the CP—hence the label "asset-backed." This practice led to many difficulties starting in the summer of 2007 when those subprime mortgages began defaulting. The banks found themselves unable to issue new CP to refinance their positions as the old paper matured.

Bankers' Acceptances

A **bankers' acceptance** starts as an order to a bank by a bank's customer to pay a sum of money at a future date, typically within six months. At this stage, it is like a postdated check. When the bank endorses the order for payment as "accepted," it assumes responsibility for ultimate payment to the holder of the acceptance. At this point, the acceptance may be traded in secondary markets much like any other claim on the bank. Bankers' acceptances are considered very safe assets, as they allow traders to substitute the bank's credit standing for their own. They are used widely in foreign trade where the creditworthiness of one trader is unknown to the trading partner. Acceptances sell at a discount from the face value of the payment order, just as T-bills sell at a discount from par value.

> **bankers' acceptance**
> An order to a bank by a customer to pay a sum of money at a future date.

Eurodollars

Eurodollars are dollar-denominated deposits at foreign banks or foreign branches of American banks. By locating outside the United States, these banks escape regulation by the Federal Reserve Board. Despite the tag "Euro," these accounts need not be in European banks, although that is where the practice of accepting dollar-denominated deposits outside the United States began.

Most Eurodollar deposits are for large sums, and most are time deposits of less than six months' maturity. A variation on the Eurodollar time deposit is the Eurodollar certificate of deposit, which resembles a domestic bank CD except it is the liability of a non-U.S. branch of a bank, typically a London branch. The advantage of Eurodollar CDs over Eurodollar time deposits is that the holder can sell the asset to realize its cash value before maturity. Eurodollar CDs are considered less liquid and riskier than domestic CDs, however, and so offer higher yields. Firms also issue Eurodollar bonds, that is, dollar-denominated bonds outside the U.S., although such bonds are not a money market investment by virtue of their long maturities.

> **Eurodollars**
> Dollar-denominated deposits at foreign banks or foreign branches of American banks.

Repos and Reverses

Dealers in government securities use **repurchase agreements,** also called repos (RPs), as a form of short-term, usually overnight, borrowing. The dealer sells securities to an investor on an overnight basis, with an agreement to buy back those securities the next day at a slightly higher price. The increase in the price is the overnight interest. The dealer thus takes out a one-day loan from the investor. The securities serve as collateral for the loan.

A *term repo* is essentially an identical transaction, except the term of the implicit loan can be 30 days or more. Repos are considered very safe in terms of credit risk because the loans are collateralized by the securities. A *reverse repo* is the mirror image of a repo. Here, the dealer finds an investor holding government securities and buys them with an agreement to resell them at a specified higher price on a future date.

> **repurchase agreements (repos)**
> Short-term sales of securities with an agreement to repurchase the securities at a higher price.

Brokers' Calls

Individuals who buy stocks on margin borrow part of the funds to pay for the stocks from their broker. The broker in turn may borrow the funds from a bank, agreeing to repay the bank immediately (on call) if the bank requests it. The rate paid on such loans is usually about one percentage point higher than the rate on short-term T-bills.

Federal Funds

Just as most of us maintain deposits at banks, banks maintain deposits of their own at the Federal Reserve Bank, or the Fed. Each member bank of the Federal Reserve System is required to maintain a minimum balance in a reserve account with the Fed. The required balance depends on the total deposits of the bank's customers. Funds in the bank's reserve account are called **Federal funds** or *Fed funds.* At any time, some banks have more funds than required at the Fed. Other banks, primarily big New York and other financial center banks, tend to have a

> **Federal funds**
> Funds in the accounts of commercial banks at the Federal Reserve Bank.

On the MARKET FRONT

THE LIBOR SCANDALS

LIBOR was designed initially as a survey of interbank lending rates but soon became a key determinant of short-term interest rates with far-reaching significance. Around $350 trillion of derivative contracts have payoffs tied to it, and several trillion dollars of loans and bonds with floating interest rates linked to LIBOR are currently outstanding. LIBOR is quoted for loans in several currencies, such as the dollar, yen, euro, and U.K. pound, and for maturities ranging from a day to a year, although three months is the most common.

However, LIBOR is not a rate at which actual transactions occur; instead, it is just a survey of "estimated" borrowing rates, and this has made it vulnerable to manipulation. Several large banks are asked to report the rate at which they *believe* they can borrow in the interbank market. Outliers are trimmed from the sample of responses, and LIBOR is calculated as the average of the mid-range estimates.

Over time, several problems surfaced. First, it appeared that many banks understated the rates at which they claimed they could borrow in an effort to make themselves look financially stronger. Other surveys that asked for estimates of the rates at which *other* banks could borrow resulted in higher values. Moreover, LIBOR did not seem to reflect current market conditions. A majority of LIBOR submissions were unchanged from day to day even when other interest rates fluctuated, and LIBOR spreads showed surprisingly low correlation with other measures of credit risk such as spreads on credit default swaps. Even worse, once the market came under scrutiny, it emerged that participating banks were colluding to manipulate their LIBOR submissions to enhance profits on their derivatives trades. Traders used emails and instant messages to tell each other whether they wanted to see higher or lower submissions. Members of this informal cartel essentially set up a "favor bank" to help each other move the survey average up or down depending on their trading positions.

To date, around $4 billion in fines have been paid: UBS paid $1.52 billion, Rabobank $1.07 billion, Royal Bank of Scotland $612 million, Barclays $454 million, and Lloyds $370 million. Other banks remain under investigation. But government fines may be only the tip of the iceberg. Private lawsuits are also possible, as anyone trading a LIBOR derivative against these banks or anyone who participated in a loan with an interest rate tied to LIBOR can claim to have been harmed.

Several reforms have been suggested and some have been implemented. The British Bankers Association, which until recently ran the LIBOR survey, yielded responsibility for LIBOR to British regulators. LIBOR quotes in less active currencies and maturities, where collusion is easier, have been eliminated. More substantive proposals would replace the survey rate with one based on actual, verifiable transactions—that is, real loans among banks.

---

shortage of Federal funds. In the Federal funds market, banks with excess funds lend to those with a shortage. These loans, which are usually overnight transactions, are arranged at a rate of interest called the *Federal funds rate.*

Although the Fed funds market arose primarily as a way for banks to transfer balances to meet reserve requirements, today the market has evolved to the point that many large banks use Federal funds in a straightforward way as one component of their total sources of funding. Therefore, the Fed funds rate is simply the rate of interest on very short-term loans among financial institutions. While most investors cannot participate in this market, the Fed funds rate commands great interest as a key barometer of monetary policy.

The LIBOR Market

LIBOR

Lending rate among banks in the London market.

The **London Interbank Offer Rate (LIBOR)** is the rate at which large banks in London are willing to lend money among themselves. This rate has become the premier short-term interest rate quoted in the European money market and serves as a reference rate for a wide range of transactions. A corporation might borrow at a rate equal to LIBOR plus two percentage points, for example. Like the Fed funds rate, LIBOR is a statistic widely followed by investors.

LIBOR interest rates may be tied to currencies other than the U.S. dollar. For example, LIBOR rates are widely quoted for transactions denominated in British pounds, yen, euros, and so on. There is also a similar rate called EURIBOR (European Interbank Offer Rate) at which banks in the euro zone are willing to lend euros among themselves.

LIBOR is a key reference rate in the money market, and many trillions of dollars of loans and derivative assets are tied to it. Therefore, the 2012 scandal involving the fixing of LIBOR deeply shook these markets. The nearby box discusses those events.

Yields on Money Market Instruments

Although most money market securities are of low risk, they are not risk-free. The securities of the money market promise yields greater than those on default-free T-bills, at least in part because of their greater relative risk. Investors who require more liquidity also will accept

On the MARKET FRONT

MONEY MARKET FUNDS AND THE FINANCIAL CRISIS OF 2008

Money market funds are mutual funds that invest in the short-term debt instruments that comprise the money market. In 2008, these funds had investments totaling about $3.4 trillion. They are required to hold only short-maturity debt of the highest quality: The average maturity of their holdings must be maintained at less than three months. Their biggest investments tend to be in commercial paper, but they also hold sizable fractions of their portfolios in certificates of deposit, repurchase agreements, and Treasury securities. Because of this very conservative investment profile, money market funds typically experience extremely low price risk. Investors for their part usually acquire check-writing privileges with their funds and often use them as a close substitute for a bank account. This is feasible because the funds almost always maintain share value at $1 and pass along all investment earnings to their investors as interest.

Until 2008, only one fund had "broken the buck," that is, suffered losses large enough to force value per share below $1. But when Lehman Brothers filed for bankruptcy protection on September 15, 2008, several funds that had invested heavily in its commercial paper suffered large losses. The next day, Reserve Primary Fund, the oldest money market fund, broke the buck when its value per share fell to only $.97.

The realization that money market funds were at risk in the credit crisis led to a wave of investor redemptions similar to a run on a bank. Only three days after the Lehman bankruptcy, Putnam's Prime Money Market Fund announced that it was liquidating due to heavy redemptions. Fearing further outflows, the U.S. Treasury announced that it would make federal insurance available to money market funds willing to pay an insurance fee. This program would thus be similar to FDIC bank insurance. With the federal insurance in place, the outflows were quelled.

However, the turmoil in Wall Street's money market funds had already spilled over into "Main Street." Fearing further investor redemptions, money market funds had become afraid to commit funds even over short periods, and their demand for commercial paper had effectively dried up. Firms throughout the economy had come to depend on those markets as a major source of short-term finance to fund expenditures ranging from salaries to inventories. Further break-down in the money markets would have had an immediate crippling effect on the broad economy.

To end the panic and stabilize the money markets, the federal government decided to guarantee investments in money market funds. The guarantee did in fact calm investors and end the run, but it put the government on the hook for a potential liability of up to $3 trillion—the assets held in money market funds at the time.

In 2014, U.S. regulators approved a series of reforms to reduce the risks of runs on these funds. Institutional money market funds (those servicing institutions rather than private investors) will be required to "float" the prices of their shares based on the value of their assets rather than maintain a fixed $1 value per share. This limits the incentive during a crisis for investors to compete to be the first to withdraw funds while share prices are maintained at a nonsustainable level of $1. In addition, funds will have the authority to either limit redemptions or impose redemption fees of up to 2% if a fund's assets fall by more than 30%. Finally, the rules call for enhanced transparency, with greater disclosure of assets' values, portfolio composition, and liquidity. These reforms will go into effect in 2016.

---

lower yields on securities, such as T-bills, that can be more quickly and cheaply sold for cash. Figure 2.2 shows that bank CDs, for example, consistently have paid a risk premium over T-bills. Moreover, as Figure 2.2 shows, that premium increases with economic crises such as the energy price shocks associated with the Organization of Petroleum Exporting Countries

FIGURE 2.2

Spread between three-month CD and T-bill rates

(OPEC) disturbances, the failure of Penn Square Bank, the stock market crash in 1987, the collapse of Long Term Capital Management in 1998, and the financial crisis resulting from the breakdown of the subprime mortgage market beginning in 2007. If you look back to Figure 1.1 in Chapter 1, you'll see that the TED spread, the difference between the LIBOR rate and the Treasury bill rate, also peaked during the financial crisis.

Money market funds are mutual funds that invest in money market instruments and have become major sources of funding to that sector. The nearby box discusses the fallout of the financial crisis of 2008 on those funds.

2.2   THE BOND MARKET

The bond market is composed of longer-term borrowing or debt instruments than those that trade in the money market. This market includes Treasury notes and bonds, corporate bonds, municipal bonds, mortgage securities, and federal agency debt.

These instruments are sometimes said to comprise the *fixed-income capital market,* because most of them promise either a fixed stream of income or stream of income that is determined according to a specified formula. In practice, these formulas can result in a flow of income that is far from fixed. Therefore, the term "fixed income" is probably not fully appropriate. It is simpler and more straightforward to call these securities either debt instruments or bonds.

Treasury Notes and Bonds

Treasury notes or bonds

Debt obligations of the federal government with original maturities of one year or more.

The U.S. government borrows funds in large part by selling **Treasury notes** and **bonds.** T-notes are issued with original maturities ranging up to 10 years, while T-bonds are issued with maturities ranging from 10 to 30 years. Both bonds and notes may be issued in increments of $100 but far more commonly trade in denominations of $1,000. Both bonds and notes make semiannual interest payments called *coupon payments,* so named because in pre-computer days, investors would literally clip a coupon attached to the bond and present it to receive the interest payment.

Figure 2.3 is an excerpt from a listing of Treasury issues. The highlighted bond matures in May 2017. The coupon income or interest paid by the bond is 4.5% of par value, meaning that for a $1,000 face value bond, $45 in annual interest payments will be made in two semiannual installments of $22.50 each.

The bid price of the highlighted bond is 109.3516. (This is the decimal version of 109 45/128. The minimum *tick size,* or price increment in the Treasury bond market, is generally 1/128 of a point.) Although bonds are typically traded in denominations of $1,000 par value, prices are quoted as a percentage of par. Thus, the bid price should be interpreted as 109.3516% of par, or $1,093.516 for the $1,000 par value bond. Similarly, the ask price at which the bond could be sold to a dealer is 109.375% of par, or $1,093.75. The .0234 change means that the asked price on this day increased by .0234% of par value (equivalently, by 3/128 of a point) from the previous day's close. Finally, the yield to maturity based on the asked price is .927%.

FIGURE 2.3						
Listing of Treasury issues	**MATURITY**	**COUPON**	**BID**	**ASKED**	**CHG**	**ASKED YLD TO MATURITY**
Source: Compiled from data from *The Wall Street Journal Online,* September 16, 2014.	2015 Feb 15	4.000	101.6250	101.6328	−0.0078	0.046
	2017 May 15	4.500	109.3516	109.3750	0.0234	0.927
	2020 Feb 15	3.625	108.8906	108.9375	0.0938	1.880
	2025 Feb 15	7.625	146.1719	146.2500	0.2031	2.541
	2030 May 15	6.250	141.3125	141.3906	0.2734	2.934
	2036 Feb 15	4.500	121.3359	121.4141	0.2578	3.121
	2044 Aug 15	3.125	95.9297	95.9922	0.1875	3.338

The *yield to maturity* reported in the last column is a measure of the annualized rate of return to an investor who buys the bond for the asked price and holds it until maturity. It accounts for both coupon income as well as the difference between the purchase price of the bond and its final value of $1,000 at maturity. We discuss the yield to maturity in detail in Chapter 10.

What were the bid price, asked price, and yield to maturity of the 3.625% February 2020 Treasury bond displayed in Figure 2.3? What was its asked price the previous day?

CONCEPT check 2.1

Inflation-Protected Treasury Bonds

The best place to start building an investment portfolio is at the least risky end of the spectrum. Around the world, governments of many countries, including the U.S., have issued bonds that are linked to an index of the cost of living in order to provide their citizens with an effective way to hedge inflation risk.

In the United States, inflation-protected Treasury bonds are called *TIPS* (Treasury Inflation Protected Securities). The principal amount on these bonds is adjusted in proportion to increases in the Consumer Price Index. Therefore, they provide a constant stream of income in real (inflation-adjusted) dollars, and the real interest rates you earn on these securities are risk-free if you hold them to maturity. We return to TIPS bonds in more detail in Chapter 10.

Federal Agency Debt

Some government agencies issue their own securities to finance their activities. These agencies usually are formed for public policy reasons to channel credit to a particular sector of the economy that Congress believes is not receiving adequate credit through normal private sources.

The major mortgage-related agencies are the Federal Home Loan Bank (FHLB), the Federal National Mortgage Association (FNMA, or Fannie Mae), the Government National Mortgage Association (GNMA, or Ginnie Mae), and the Federal Home Loan Mortgage Corporation (FHLMC, or Freddie Mac).

Although the debt of federal agencies was never explicitly insured by the federal government, it had long been assumed that the government would assist an agency nearing default. Those beliefs were validated when Fannie Mae and Freddie Mac encountered severe financial distress in September 2008. With both firms on the brink of insolvency, the government stepped in and put them both into conservatorship, assigned the Federal Housing Finance Agency to run the firms, but did in fact agree to make good on the firm's bonds. (Turn back to Chapter 1 for more discussion of the Fannie and Freddie failures.)

International Bonds

Many firms borrow abroad and many investors buy bonds from foreign issuers. In addition to national capital markets, there is a thriving international capital market, largely centered in London.

A *Eurobond* is a bond denominated in a currency other than that of the country in which it is issued. For example, a dollar-denominated bond sold in Britain would be called a *Eurodollar bond.* Similarly, investors might speak of Euroyen bonds, yen-denominated bonds sold outside Japan. Since the European currency is called the *euro,* the term *Eurobond* may be confusing. It is best to think of them simply as international bonds.

In contrast to bonds that are issued in foreign currencies, many firms issue bonds in foreign countries but in the currency of the investor. For example, a Yankee bond is a dollar-denominated bond sold in the U.S. by a non-U.S. issuer. Similarly, Samurai bonds are yen-denominated bonds sold in Japan by non-Japanese issuers.

Municipal Bonds

municipal bonds

Tax-exempt bonds issued by
state and local governments.

Municipal bonds ("munis") are issued by state and local governments. They are similar to Treasury and corporate bonds, except their interest income is exempt from federal income taxation. The interest income also is usually exempt from state and local taxation in the issuing state. Capital gains taxes, however, must be paid on munis if the bonds mature or are sold for more than the investor's purchase price.

There are basically two types of municipal bonds. *General obligation bonds* are backed by the "full faith and credit" (i.e., the taxing power) of the issuer, while *revenue bonds* are issued to finance particular projects and are backed either by the revenues from that project or by the municipal agency operating the project. Typical issuers of revenue bonds are airports, hospitals, and turnpike or port authorities. Revenue bonds are riskier in terms of default than general obligation bonds.

An *industrial development bond* is a revenue bond that is issued to finance commercial enterprises, such as the construction of a factory that can be operated by a private firm. In effect, this device gives the firm access to the municipality's ability to borrow at tax-exempt rates, and the federal government limits the amount of these bonds that may be issued.[2] Figure 2.4 plots outstanding amounts of industrial revenue bonds as well as general obligation municipal bonds.

Like Treasury bonds, municipal bonds vary widely in maturity. A good deal of the debt issued is in the form of short-term *tax anticipation notes* that raise funds to pay for expenses before actual collection of taxes. Other municipal debt may be long term and used to fund large capital investments. Maturities range up to 30 years.

The key feature of municipal bonds is their tax-exempt status. Because investors pay neither federal nor state taxes on the interest proceeds, they are willing to accept lower yields on these securities.

An investor choosing between taxable and tax-exempt bonds needs to compare after-tax returns on each bond. An exact comparison requires the computation of after-tax rates of return with explicit recognition of taxes on income and realized capital gains. In practice, there is a simpler rule of thumb. If we let t denote the investor's combined federal plus local marginal tax rate and r denote the total before-tax rate of return available on taxable bonds,

**Outstanding tax-exempt
debt**

Source: *Flow of Funds Accounts
of the U.S.*, Board of Governors
of the Federal Reserve System,
June 2014.

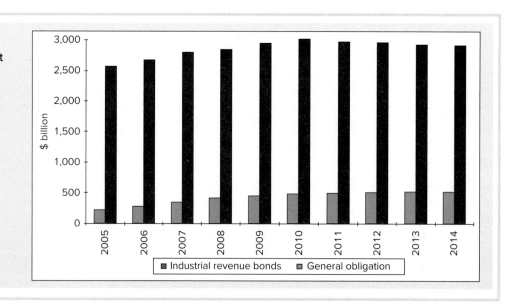

---

[2]A warning, however. Although interest on industrial development bonds usually is exempt from federal tax, it can be subject to the alternative minimum tax if the bonds are used to finance projects of for-profit companies.

TABLE 2.2	Equivalent taxable yields corresponding to various tax-exempt yields				
	Tax-Exempt Yield				
Marginal Tax Rate	**1%**	**2%**	**3%**	**4%**	**5%**
20%	1.25%	2.50%	3.75%	5.00%	6.25%
30	1.43	2.86	4.29	5.71	7.15
40	1.67	3.33	5.00	6.67	8.33
50	2.00	4.00	6.00	8.00	10.00

then $r(1 - t)$ is the after-tax rate available on those securities.[3] If this value exceeds the rate on municipal bonds, r_m, the investor does better holding the taxable bonds. Otherwise, the tax-exempt municipals provide higher after-tax returns.

One way of comparing bonds is to determine the interest rate on taxable bonds that would be necessary to provide an after-tax return equal to that of municipals. To derive this value, we set after-tax yields equal and solve for the *equivalent taxable yield* of the tax-exempt bond. This is the rate a taxable bond would need to offer in order to match the after-tax yield on the tax-free municipal.

$$r(1 - t) = r_m \tag{2.1}$$

or

$$r = \frac{r_m}{1 - t} \tag{2.2}$$

Thus, the equivalent taxable yield is simply the tax-free rate divided by $1 - t$. Table 2.2 presents equivalent taxable yields for several municipal yields and tax rates.

This table frequently appears in the marketing literature for tax-exempt mutual bond funds because it demonstrates to high-tax-bracket investors that municipal bonds offer highly attractive equivalent taxable yields. Each entry is calculated from Equation 2.2. If the equivalent taxable yield exceeds the actual yields offered on taxable bonds, after taxes the investor is better off holding municipal bonds. The equivalent taxable interest rate increases with the investor's tax bracket; the higher the bracket, the more valuable the tax-exempt feature of municipals. Thus, high-bracket individuals tend to hold municipals.

We also can use Equation 2.1 or 2.2 to find the tax bracket at which investors are indifferent between taxable and tax-exempt bonds. The cutoff tax bracket is given by solving Equation 2.1 for the tax bracket at which after-tax yields are equal. Doing so, we find

$$t = 1 - \frac{r_m}{r} \tag{2.3}$$

Thus, the yield ratio r_m/r is a key determinant of the attractiveness of municipal bonds. The higher the yield ratio, the lower the cutoff tax bracket, and the more individuals will prefer to hold municipal debt.

Figure 2.5 plots the ratio of 20-year municipal debt yields to the yield on Baa-rated corporate debt. The default risk on these bonds may be roughly comparable in many periods but certainly will fluctuate over time. For example, the sharp run-up in the ratio starting in 2011 probably reflects increased concern at the time about the precarious financial condition of several states and municipalities, leading to higher credit spreads on their bonds.

---

[3]An approximation to the combined federal plus local tax rate is just the sum of the two rates. For example, if your federal tax rate is 28% and your state rate is 5%, your combined tax rate would be approximately 33%. A more precise approach would recognize that state taxes are deductible at the federal level. You owe federal taxes only on income net of state taxes. Therefore, for every dollar of income, your after-tax proceeds would be $(1 - t_{federal}) \times (1 - t_{state})$. In our example, your after-tax proceeds on each dollar earned would be $(1 - .28) \times (1 - .05) = .684$, which implies a combined tax rate of $1 - .684 = .316$, or 31.6%.

Ratio of yields on
municipal debt to
corporate Baa-rated
debt

Source: **www.federalreserve.gov/
releases/h15/data.htm.**

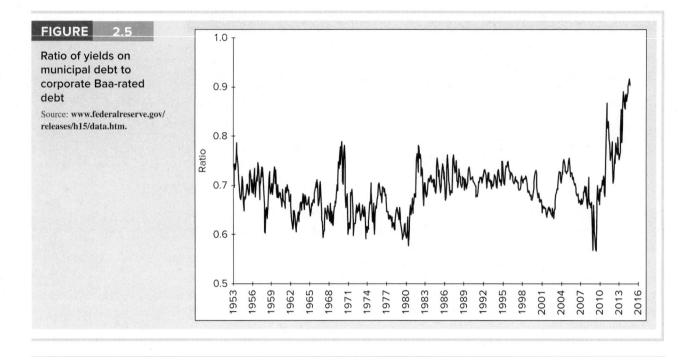

EXAMPLE 2.1

*Taxable versus
Tax-Exempt Yields*

Figure 2.5 shows that for most of the last 30 years (until 2011), the ratio of tax-exempt to taxable yields fluctuated around .75. What does this imply about the cutoff tax bracket above which tax-exempt bonds provide higher after-tax yields? Equation 2.3 shows that an investor whose combined tax bracket (federal plus local) exceeds $1 - .75 = .25$, or 25%, will derive a greater after-tax yield from municipals. As we pointed out, however, it is difficult to control precisely for differences in the risks of these bonds, so the cutoff tax bracket must be taken as approximate.

**CONCEPT
check** **2.2**

Suppose your tax bracket is 28%. Would you prefer to earn a 6% taxable return or a 4% tax-free yield? What is the equivalent taxable yield of the 4% tax-free yield?

Corporate Bonds

corporate bonds

Long-term debt issued by
private corporations typically
paying semiannual coupons
and returning the face value
of the bond at maturity.

Corporate bonds are the means by which private firms borrow money directly from the public. These bonds are structured much like Treasury issues in that they typically pay semiannual coupons over their lives and return the face value to the bondholder at maturity. Where they differ most importantly from Treasury bonds is in risk.

Default risk is a real consideration in the purchase of corporate bonds. We treat this issue in considerable detail in Chapter 10. For now, we distinguish only among secured bonds, which have specific collateral backing them in the event of firm bankruptcy; unsecured bonds, called *debentures,* which have no collateral; and subordinated debentures, which have a lower priority claim to the firm's assets in the event of bankruptcy.

Corporate bonds sometimes come with options attached. *Callable bonds* give the firm the option to repurchase the bond from the holder at a stipulated call price. *Convertible bonds* give the bondholder the option to convert each bond into a stipulated number of shares of stock. These options are treated in more detail in Part Three.

Mortgages and Mortgage-Backed Securities

Because of the explosion in mortgage-backed securities, almost anyone can invest in a portfolio of mortgage loans, and these securities have become a major component of the fixed-income market.

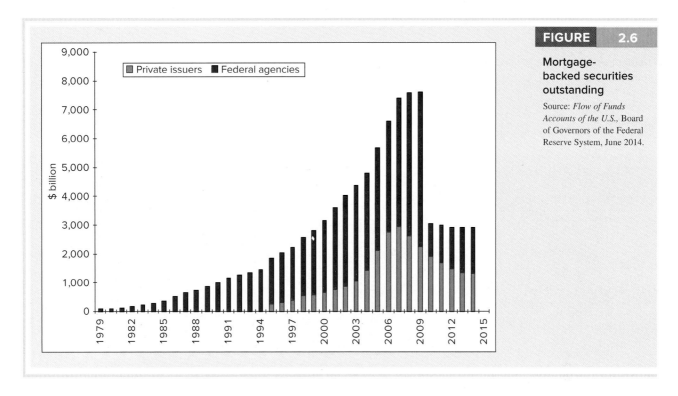

FIGURE 2.6

Mortgage-backed securities outstanding

Source: *Flow of Funds Accounts of the U.S.,* Board of Governors of the Federal Reserve System, June 2014.

As described in Chapter 1, a *mortgage-backed security* is either an ownership claim in a pool of mortgages or an obligation that is secured by such a pool. Most pass-throughs traditionally comprised *conforming mortgages,* which meant that the loans had to satisfy certain underwriting guidelines (standards for the creditworthiness of the borrower) before they could be purchased by Fannie Mae or Freddie Mac. In the years leading up to the financial crisis, however, a large amount of *subprime mortgages,* that is, riskier loans made to financially weaker borrowers, were bundled and sold by "private-label" issuers. Figure 2.6 illustrates the explosive growth of these securities, at least until the crisis.

In an effort to make housing more affordable to low-income households, the government-sponsored enterprises were encouraged to buy subprime mortgage securities. These loans turned out to be disastrous, with trillion-dollar losses spread among banks, hedge funds, and other investors, as well as Freddie and Fannie, which lost billions of dollars on the subprime mortgages they had purchased. You can see from Figure 2.6 that, starting in 2007, the market in private-label mortgage pass-throughs began to shrink rapidly. Agency pass-throughs shrank even more precipitously following an agreement for Freddie and Fannie to wind down purchases of mortgages for new pass-throughs. At the same time, existing pass-throughs shrank as healthy loans were paid off and delinquent loans were removed from outstanding pools.

Despite these troubles, few believe that securitization itself will cease, although it is certain that practices in this market will be far more conservative than in previous years, particularly with respect to the credit standards that must be met by the ultimate borrower. Indeed, securitization has become an increasingly common staple of many credit markets. For example, it is now common for car loans, student loans, home equity loans, credit card loans, and even debt of private firms to be bundled into pass-through securities that can be traded in the capital market. Figure 2.7 documents the rapid growth of nonmortgage asset-backed securities. The market expanded more than fivefold in the decade ending 2007. After the financial crisis, it contracted considerably as the perceived risks of credit card and home equity loans skyrocketed, but the asset-backed market is still substantial.

FIGURE   2.7

Asset-backed securities outstanding

Source: Securities Industry & Financial Markets Association, **www.sifma.org.**

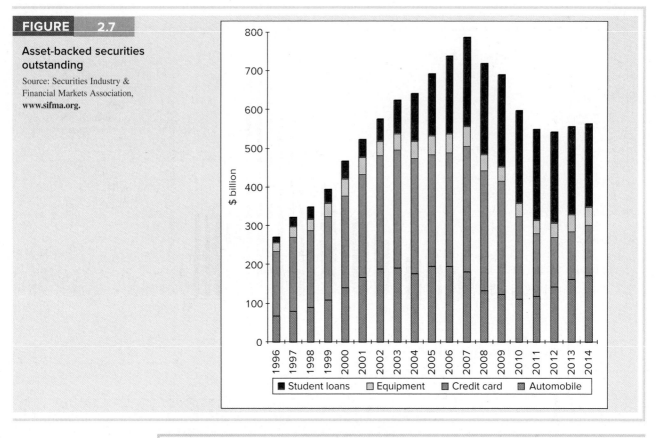

2.3   EQUITY SECURITIES

Common Stock as Ownership Shares

common stocks

Ownership shares in a publicly held corporation. Shareholders have voting rights and may receive dividends.

Common stocks, also known as equity securities, or equities, represent ownership shares in a corporation. Each share of common stock entitles its owners to one vote on any matters of corporate governance put to a vote at the corporation's annual meeting and to a share in the financial benefits of ownership (e.g., the right to any dividends that the corporation may choose to distribute).[4]

A corporation is controlled by a board of directors elected by the shareholders. The board, which meets only a few times each year, selects managers who run the corporation on a day-to-day basis. Managers have the authority to make most business decisions without the board's approval. The board's mandate is to oversee management to ensure that it acts in the best interests of shareholders.

The members of the board are elected at the annual meeting. Shareholders who do not attend the annual meeting can vote by proxy, empowering another party to vote in their name. Management usually solicits the proxies of shareholders and normally gets a vast majority of these proxy votes. Thus, management usually has considerable discretion to run the firm as it sees fit, without daily oversight from the equityholders who actually own the firm.

We noted in Chapter 1 that such separation of ownership and control can give rise to "agency problems," in which managers pursue goals not in the best interests of shareholders. However, there are several mechanisms designed to alleviate these agency problems. Among these are compensation schemes that link the success of the manager to that of the firm; oversight by the board of directors as well as outsiders such as security analysts, creditors, or large institutional investors; the threat of a proxy contest in which unhappy shareholders attempt to replace the current management team; or the threat of a takeover by another firm.

The common stock of most large corporations can be bought or sold freely on one or more of the stock markets. A corporation whose stock is not publicly traded is said to be *private*. In most privately held corporations, the owners of the firm also take an active role in its management. Takeovers generally are not an issue.

[4]Sometimes a corporation issues two classes of common stock, one bearing the right to vote, the other not. Because of their restricted rights, the nonvoting stocks sell for a lower price, reflecting the value of control.

Characteristics of Common Stock

The two most important characteristics of common stock as an investment are its residual claim and its limited liability features.

Residual claim means stockholders are the last in line of all those who have a claim on the assets and income of the corporation. In a liquidation of the firm's assets, the shareholders have claim to what is left after paying all other claimants, such as the tax authorities, employees, suppliers, bondholders, and other creditors. In a going concern, shareholders have claim to the part of operating income left after interest and income taxes have been paid. Management either can pay this residual as cash dividends to shareholders or reinvest it in the business to increase the value of the shares.

Limited liability means that the most shareholders can lose in event of the failure of the corporation is their original investment. Shareholders are not like owners of unincorporated businesses, whose creditors can lay claim to the personal assets of the owner—such as houses, cars, and furniture. In the event of the firm's bankruptcy, corporate stockholders at worst have worthless stock. They are not personally liable for the firm's obligations: Their liability is limited.

a. If you buy 100 shares of IBM common stock, to what are you entitled? b. What is the most money you can make over the next year? c. If you pay \$190 per share, what is the most money you could lose over the year?	**CONCEPT** **2.3** check

Stock Market Listings

Figure 2.8 presents key trading data for a small sample of stocks traded on the New York Stock Exchange. The NYSE is one of several markets in which investors may buy or sell shares of stock. We will examine issues of trading in these markets in the next chapter.

To interpret Figure 2.8, consider the listing for General Electric, the last listed stock. The table provides the ticker symbol (GE), the closing price of the stock (\$26.21), and its change (+0.29) from the previous trading day. Over 27 million shares of GE traded on this day. The table also provides the highest and lowest price at which GE has traded in the last 52 weeks. The .88 value in the DIV column means that the last quarterly dividend payment was \$.22 per share, which is consistent with annual dividend payments of \$.22 × 4 = \$.88. This corresponds to a dividend yield (i.e., annual dividend per dollar paid for the stock) of .88/26.21 = .0336, or 3.36%.

The dividend yield is only part of the return on a stock investment. It ignores prospective *capital gains* (i.e., price increases) or losses. Shares in low-dividend firms presumably offer greater prospects for capital gains, or investors would not be willing to hold these stocks in their portfolios. If you scan Figure 2.8, you will see that dividend yields vary widely across companies.

The P/E ratio, or price-to-earnings ratio, is the ratio of the current stock price to last year's earnings. The P/E ratio tells us how much stock purchasers must pay per dollar of earnings the firm generates for each share. For GE, the ratio of price to earnings is 18.23. The P/E ratio also varies widely across firms. Where the dividend yield and P/E ratio are not reported in Figure 2.8, the firms have zero dividends, or zero or negative earnings. We shall have much to say about P/E ratios in Part Four. Finally, we see that GE's stock price has decreased by 6.49% since the beginning of the year.

G	SYMBOL	CLOSE	NET CHG	VOLUME	52 WEEK HIGH	52 WEEK LOW	DIV	YIELD	PE	YTD % CHG
Gap	GPS	44.12	0.09	2,696,353	46.84	36.13	0.88	1.99	15.99	12.90
Gartner	IT	76.36	0.02	372,214	76.82	56.57	....	....	36.71	7.47
GasLog	GLOG	24.91	1.11	1,291,997	32.44	14.02	0.48	1.93	40.84	45.76
GasLog Partners	GLOP	31.59	1.24	34,738	37.39	25.50	....	....	0.04	20.99
GATX	GMT	64.10	0.83	259,151	69.87	45.27	1.32	2.06	14.54	22.87
Gazit-Globe	GZT	12.61	0.26	7,478	14.07	12.12	....	....	1.69	−5.97
GenCorp	GY	17.31	−0.01	451,629	19.77	15.01	....	....	7.58	−3.94
Generac Holdings	GNRC	42.72	−0.53	651,462	62.50	39.01	....	....	15.82	−24.58
General Cable	BGC	20.47	−0.16	983,060	34.61	20.21	0.72	3.52	....dd	−30.40
General Dynamics	GD	127.75	0.90	1,244,284	128.34	83.61	2.48	1.94	19.30	33.70
General Electric	GE	26.21	0.29	27,026,512	28.09	23.50	0.88	3.36	18.23	−6.49

FIGURE 2.8

Listing of stocks traded on the New York Stock Exchange

Source: Compiled from data from *The Wall Street Journal Online*, September 17, 2014.

Note: dd means that P/E cannot be computed because earnings were negative.

Preferred Stock

Preferred stock has features similar to both equity and debt. Like a bond, it promises to pay to its holder a fixed stream of income each year. In this sense, preferred stock is similar to an infinite-maturity bond, that is, a perpetuity. It also resembles a bond in that it does not give the holder voting power regarding the firm's management.

Preferred stock is an equity investment, however. The firm retains discretion to make the dividend payments to the preferred stockholders: It has no contractual obligation to pay those dividends. Instead, preferred dividends are usually *cumulative;* that is, unpaid dividends cumulate and must be paid in full before any dividends may be paid to holders of common stock. In contrast, the firm does have a contractual obligation to make timely interest payments on the debt. Failure to make these payments sets off corporate bankruptcy proceedings.

Preferred stock also differs from bonds in terms of its tax treatment for the firm. Because preferred stock payments are treated as dividends rather than as interest on debt, they are not tax-deductible expenses for the firm. This disadvantage is largely offset by the fact that corporations may exclude 70% of dividends received from domestic corporations in the computation of their taxable income. Preferred stocks, therefore, make desirable fixed-income investments for some corporations.

Even though preferred stock ranks after bonds in terms of the priority of its claim to the assets of the firm in the event of corporate bankruptcy, preferred stock often sells at lower yields than corporate bonds. Presumably this reflects the value of the 70% dividend exclusion, because the higher risk of preferred stock would tend to result in higher yields than those offered by bonds. Individual investors, who cannot use the exclusion, generally will find preferred stock yields unattractive relative to those on other available assets.

Corporations issue preferred stock in variations similar to those of corporate bonds. Preferred stock can be callable by the issuing firm, in which case it is said to be *redeemable*. It also can be convertible into common stock at some specified conversion ratio. A relatively recent innovation is adjustable-rate preferred stock, which, like adjustable-rate bonds, ties the dividend rate to current market interest rates.

Depositary Receipts

American Depositary Receipts (ADRs) are certificates traded in U.S. markets that represent ownership in shares of a foreign company. Each ADR may correspond to ownership of a fraction of a foreign share, one share, or several shares of the foreign corporation. ADRs were created to make it easier for foreign firms to satisfy U.S. security registration requirements. They are the most common way for U.S. investors to invest in and trade the shares of foreign corporations.

2.4 STOCK AND BOND MARKET INDEXES

Stock Market Indexes

The daily performance of the Dow Jones Industrial Average is a staple portion of the evening news report. While the Dow is the best-known measure of the performance of the stock market, it is only one of several indicators. Other more broadly based indexes are computed and published daily. In addition, several indexes of bond market performance are widely available.

The ever-increasing role of international trade and investments has made indexes of foreign financial markets part of the general news. Thus, foreign stock exchange indexes such as the Nikkei Average of Tokyo or the *Financial Times* index of London have become household names.

Dow Jones Averages

The Dow Jones Industrial Average (DJIA) of 30 large, "blue-chip" corporations has been computed since 1896. Its long history probably accounts for its preeminence in the public mind. (The average covered only 20 stocks until 1928.)

TABLE 2.3	Data to construct stock price indexes				
Stock	**Initial Price**	**Final Price**	**Shares (millions)**	**Initial Value of Outstanding Stock ($ million)**	**Final Value of Outstanding Stock ($ million)**
ABC	$ 25	$30	20	$500	$600
XYZ	100	90	1	100	90
Total				$600	$690

Originally, the DJIA was calculated as the average price of the stocks included in the index. So, if there were 30 stocks in the index, one would add up the prices of the 30 stocks and divide by 30. The percentage change in the DJIA would then be the percentage change in the average price of the 30 shares.

This procedure means that the percentage change in the DJIA measures the return (excluding any dividends paid) on a portfolio that invests one share in each of the 30 stocks in the index. The value of such a portfolio (holding one share of each stock in the index) is the sum of the 30 prices. Because the percentage change in the *average* of the 30 prices is the same as the percentage change in the *sum* of the 30 prices, the index and the portfolio have the same percentage change each day.

The Dow measures the return (excluding dividends) on a portfolio that holds one share of each stock. The amount of money invested in each company in that portfolio is therefore proportional to the company's share price, so the Dow is called a **price-weighted average.**

price-weighted average
An average computed by adding the prices of the stocks and dividing by a "divisor."

Consider the data in Table 2.3 for a hypothetical two-stock version of the Dow Jones Average. Let's compare the changes in the value of the portfolio holding one share of each firm and the price-weighted index. Stock ABC starts at $25 a share and increases to $30. Stock XYZ starts at $100, but falls to $90.

Portfolio: Initial value = $25 + $100 = $125
Final value = $30 + $90 = $120
Percentage change in portfolio value = −5/125 = −.04 = −4%

Index: Initial index value = (25 + 100)/2 = 62.5
Final index value = (30 + 90)/2 = 60
Percentage change in index = −2.5/62.5 = −.04 = −4%

The portfolio and the index have identical 4% declines in value.

Notice that price-weighted averages give higher-priced shares more weight in determining the performance of the index. For example, although ABC increased by 20% while XYZ fell by only 10%, the index dropped in value. This is because the 20% increase in ABC represented a smaller dollar price gain ($5 per share) than the 10% decrease in XYZ ($10 per share). The "Dow portfolio" has four times as much invested in XYZ as in ABC because XYZ's price is four times that of ABC. Therefore, XYZ dominates the average. We conclude that a high-price stock can dominate a price-weighted average.

EXAMPLE 2.2

Price-Weighted Average

You might wonder why the DJIA is (in mid-2015) at a level of about 18,000 if it is supposed to be the average price of the 30 stocks in the index. The DJIA no longer equals the average price of the 30 stocks because the averaging procedure is adjusted whenever a stock splits or pays a stock dividend of more than 10% or when one company in the group of 30 industrial firms is replaced by another. When these events occur, the divisor used to compute the "average price" is adjusted so as to leave the index unaffected by the event.

TABLE 2.4	Data to construct stock price indexes after stock split				
Stock	**Initial Price**	**Final Price**	**Shares (millions)**	**Initial Value of Outstanding Stock ($ million)**	**Final Value of Outstanding Stock ($ million)**
ABC	$25	$30	20	$500	$600
XYZ	50	45	2	100	90
Total				$600	$690

EXAMPLE 2.3

Splits and Price-Weighted Averages

Suppose firm XYZ from Example 2.2 were to split two for one so that its share price fell to $50. We would not want the average to fall, as that would incorrectly indicate a fall in the general level of market prices. Following a split, the divisor must be reduced to a value that leaves the average unaffected. Table 2.4 illustrates this point. The initial share price of XYZ, which was $100 in Table 2.3, falls to $50 if the stock splits at the beginning of the period. Notice that the number of shares outstanding doubles, leaving the market value of the total shares unaffected.

We find the new divisor as follows: The index value before the stock split was 125/2 = 62.5. We must find a new divisor, d, that leaves the index unchanged after XYZ splits and its price falls to $50. Therefore we solve for d in the following equation:

$$\frac{\text{Price of ABC} + \text{Price of XYZ}}{d} = \frac{25 + 50}{d} = 62.5$$

which implies that the divisor must fall from its original value of 2.0 to a new value of 1.20.

Because the split changes the price of stock XYZ, it also changes the relative weights of the two stocks in the price-weighted average. Therefore, the return of the index is affected by the split.

At period-end, ABC will sell for $30, while XYZ will sell for $45, representing the same negative 10% return it was assumed to earn in Table 2.3. The new value of the price-weighted average is (30 + 45)/1.20 = 62.5. The index is unchanged, so the rate of return is zero, greater than the −4% return that would have resulted in the absence of a split. The relative weight of XYZ, which is the poorer-performing stock, is reduced by a split because its price is lower; so the performance of the average is higher. This example illustrates that the implicit weighting scheme of a price-weighted average is somewhat arbitrary, being determined by the prices rather than by the outstanding market values (price per share times number of shares) of the shares in the average.

In the same way that the divisor is updated for stock splits, if one firm is dropped from the average and another firm with a different price is added, the divisor has to be updated to leave the average unchanged by the substitution. By mid-2015, the divisor for the Dow Jones Industrial Average had fallen to a value of about .150.

Because the Dow Jones averages are based on small numbers of firms, care must be taken to ensure that they are representative of the broad market. As a result, the composition of the average is changed every so often to reflect changes in the economy. Table 2.5 presents the composition of the Dow industrials in 1928 as well as its composition in 2015. The table presents striking evidence of the changes in the U.S. economy in the last century. Many of the "bluest of the blue chip" companies in 1928 no longer exist, and the industries that were the backbone of the economy in 1928 have given way to ones that could not have been imagined at the time.

CONCEPT check 2.4

Suppose XYZ's final price in Table 2.3 increases to $110, while ABC falls to $20. Find the percentage change in the price-weighted average of these two stocks. Compare that to the percentage return of a portfolio that holds one share in each company.

Standard & Poor's Indexes

The Standard & Poor's Composite 500 (S&P 500) stock index represents an improvement over the Dow Jones averages in two ways. First, it is a more broadly based index of 500 firms.

TABLE 2.5   Companies included in the Dow Jones Industrial Average: 1928 and 2015

Dow Industrials in 1928	Current Dow Companies	Ticker Symbol	Industry	Year Added to Index
Wright Aeronautical	3M	MMM	Diversified industrials	1976
Allied Chemical	American Express	AXP	Consumer finance	1982
North American	AT&T	T	Telecommunications	1999
Victor Talking Machine	Boeing	BA	Aerospace and defense	1987
International Nickel	Caterpillar	CAT	Construction	1991
International Harvester	Chevron	CVX	Oil and gas	2008
Westinghouse	Cisco Systems	CSCO	Computer equipment	2009
Texas Gulf Sulphur	Coca-Cola	KO	Beverages	1987
General Electric	DuPont	DD	Chemicals	1935
American Tobacco	ExxonMobil	XOM	Oil and gas	1928
Texas Corp	General Electric	GE	Diversified industrials	1907
Standard Oil (NJ)	Goldman Sachs	GS	Investment banking	2013
Sears Roebuck	Home Depot	HD	Home improvement retailers	1999
General Motors	Intel	INTC	Semiconductors	1999
Chrysler	IBM	IBM	Computer services	1979
Atlantic Refining	Johnson & Johnson	JNJ	Pharmaceuticals	1997
Paramount Publix	JPMorgan Chase	JPM	Banking	1991
Bethlehem Steel	McDonald's	MCD	Restaurants	1985
General Railway Signal	Merck	MRK	Pharmaceuticals	1979
Mack Trucks	Microsoft	MSFT	Software	1999
Union Carbide	Nike	NKE	Apparel	2013
American Smelting	Pfizer	PFE	Pharmaceuticals	2004
American Can	Procter & Gamble	PG	Household products	1932
Postum Inc	Travelers	TRV	Insurance	2009
Nash Motors	United Health Group	UNH	Health insurance	2012
American Sugar	United Technologies	UTX	Aerospace	1939
Goodrich	Verizon	VZ	Telecommunications	2004
Radio Corp	Visa	V	Electronic payments	2013
Woolworth	Wal-Mart	WMT	Retailers	1997
U.S. Steel	Walt Disney	DIS	Broadcasting and entertainment	1991

Second, it is a **market value–weighted index.** In the case of the firms XYZ and ABC in Example 2.2, the S&P 500 would give ABC five times the weight given to XYZ because the market value of its outstanding equity is five times larger, $500 million versus $100 million.

The S&P 500 is computed by calculating the total market value of the 500 firms in the index and the total market value of those firms on the previous day of trading.[5] The percentage increase in the total market value from one day to the next represents the increase in the index. The rate of return of the index equals the rate of return that would be earned by an investor holding a portfolio of all 500 firms in the index in proportion to their market value, except that the index does not reflect cash dividends paid by those firms.

market value-weighted index

Index return equals the weighted average of the returns of each component security, with weights proportional to outstanding market value.

[5]Actually, most indexes today use a modified version of market value weights. Rather than weighting by total market value, they weight by the market value of "free float," that is, by the value of shares that are freely tradable among investors. For example, this procedure does not count shares held by founding families or governments, which are effectively not available for investors to purchase. The distinction is more important in Japan and Europe, where a higher fraction of shares are held in such nontraded portfolios.

To illustrate how value-weighted indexes are computed, look again at Table 2.3. The final value of all outstanding stock in our two-stock universe is $690 million. The initial value was $600 million. Therefore, if the initial level of a market value–weighted index of stocks ABC and XYZ were set equal to an arbitrarily chosen starting value such as 100, the index value at year-end would be $100 \times (690/600) = 115$. The increase in the index would reflect the 15% return earned on a portfolio consisting of those two stocks held in proportion to outstanding market values.

Unlike the price-weighted index, the value-weighted index gives more weight to ABC. Whereas the price-weighted index fell because it was dominated by higher-price XYZ, the value-weighted index rose because it gave more weight to ABC, the stock with the higher total market value.

Note also from Tables 2.3 and 2.4 that market value–weighted indexes are unaffected by stock splits. The total market value of the outstanding XYZ stock increases from $100 million to $110 million regardless of the stock split, thereby rendering the split irrelevant to the performance of the index.

A nice feature of both market value–weighted and price-weighted indexes is that they reflect the returns to straightforward portfolio strategies. If one were to buy each share in the index in proportion to its outstanding market value, the value-weighted index would perfectly track capital gains on the underlying portfolio. Similarly, a price-weighted index tracks the returns on a portfolio composed of equal shares of each firm.

Investors today can easily buy market indexes for their portfolios. One way is to purchase shares in mutual funds that hold shares in proportion to their representation in the S&P 500 as well as other stock indexes. These *index funds* yield a return equal to that of the particular index and so provide a low-cost passive investment strategy for equity investors. Another approach is to purchase an *exchange-traded fund,* or ETF, which is a portfolio of shares that can be bought or sold as a unit, just as a single share would be traded. Available ETFs range from portfolios that track extremely broad global market indexes all the way to narrow industry indexes. We discuss both mutual funds and ETFs in detail in Chapter 4.

Reconsider companies XYZ and ABC from Concept Check Question 2.4. Calculate the percentage change in the market value–weighted index. Compare that to the rate of return of a portfolio that holds $500 of ABC stock for every $100 of XYZ stock (i.e., an index portfolio).

Other U.S. Market Value Indexes

The New York Stock Exchange publishes a market value–weighted composite index of all NYSE-listed stocks, in addition to subindexes for industrial, utility, transportation, and financial stocks. These indexes are even more broadly based than the S&P 500. The National Association of Securities Dealers publishes an index of more than 3,000 firms traded on the NASDAQ market.

The ultimate U.S. equity index so far computed is the Wilshire 5000 Index of the market value of essentially all actively traded stocks in the U.S. Despite its name, the index actually includes more than 5,000 stocks. The performance of many of these indexes appears daily in *The Wall Street Journal.*

Equally Weighted Indexes

Market performance is sometimes measured by an equally weighted average of the returns of each stock in an index. Such an averaging technique, by placing equal weight on each return, corresponds to a portfolio strategy that places equal dollar values in each stock. This is in contrast to both price weighting, which requires equal numbers of shares of each stock, and market value weighting, which requires investments in proportion to outstanding value.

equally weighted index

An index computed from a simple average of returns.

Unlike price- or market value–weighted indexes, **equally weighted indexes** do not correspond to buy-and-hold portfolio strategies. Suppose you start with equal dollar investments in the two stocks of Table 2.3, ABC and XYZ. Because ABC increases in value by 20% over the year, while XYZ decreases by 10%, your portfolio is no longer equally weighted but is now more heavily invested in ABC. To reset the portfolio to equal weights, you would need to rebalance: Sell some ABC stock and/or purchase more XYZ stock. Such rebalancing would be necessary to align the return on your portfolio with that on the equally weighted index.

Foreign and International Stock Market Indexes

Development in financial markets worldwide includes the construction of indexes for these markets. Among these are the Nikkei (Japan), FTSE (U.K., pronounced "footsie"), DAX (Germany), Hang Seng (Hong Kong), and TSX (Toronto). A leader in the construction of international indexes has been MSCI (Morgan Stanley Capital International), which computes over 50 country indexes and several regional indexes. Table 2.6 presents many of the indexes computed by MSCI.

Bond Market Indicators

Just as stock market indexes provide guidance concerning the performance of the overall stock market, several bond market indicators measure the performance of various categories of bonds. The three most well-known groups of indexes are those of Merrill Lynch, Barclays (formerly Lehman Brothers), and Salomon Smith Barney (now part of Citigroup). Figure 2.9 presents the components of the bond market in 2014.

TABLE 2.6 MSCI stock indexes

Regional Indexes		Countries	
Developed Markets	**Emerging Markets**	**Developed Markets**	**Emerging Markets**
EAFE (Europe, Australasia, Far East)	Emerging Markets (EM)	Australia	Brazil
EASEA (EAFE excluding Japan)	EM Asia	Austria	Chile
Europe	EM Far East	Belgium	China
EMU	EM Latin America	Canada	Colombia
Far East	EM Eastern Europe	Denmark	Czech Republic
Kokusai (World excluding Japan)	EM Europe	Finland	Egypt
Nordic Countries	EM Europe & Middle East	France	Hungary
North America		Germany	India
Pacific		Greece	Indonesia
World		Hong Kong	Korea
G7 countries		Ireland	Malaysia
World excluding U.S.		Israel	Mexico
		Italy	Peru
		Japan	Philippines
		Netherlands	Poland
		New Zealand	Russia
		Norway	South Africa
		Portugal	Taiwan
		Singapore	Thailand
		Spain	Turkey
		Sweden	
		Switzerland	
		U.K.	
		U.S.	

Source: MSCI, **www.msci.com.**

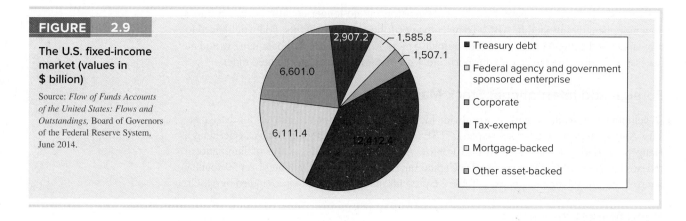

FIGURE   2.9

The U.S. fixed-income market (values in $ billion)

Source: *Flow of Funds Accounts of the United States: Flows and Outstandings,* Board of Governors of the Federal Reserve System, June 2014.

The major problem with these indexes is that true rates of return on many bonds are difficult to compute because bonds trade infrequently, which makes it hard to get reliable, up-to-date prices. In practice, some prices must be estimated from bond-valuation models. These so-called matrix prices may differ from true market values.

2.5   DERIVATIVE MARKETS

Futures and options contracts provide payoffs that depend on the values of other variables, such as commodity prices, bond and stock prices, interest rates, or market index values. For this reason, these instruments sometimes are called **derivative assets:** Their values *derive from* the values of other assets. We discuss derivative assets in detail in Part Five.

Options

derivative asset

A security with a payoff that depends on the prices of other securities.

A **call option** gives its holder the right to purchase an asset for a specified price, called the *exercise* or *strike price,* on or before some specified expiration date. An October call option on Apple stock with exercise price $100, for example, entitles its owner to purchase Apple stock for a price of $100 at any time up to and including the option's expiration date in October. Each option contract is for the purchase of 100 shares, with quotations made on a per share basis. The holder of the call need not exercise the option; it will make sense to exercise only if the market value of the asset that may be purchased exceeds the exercise price.

call option

The right to buy an asset at a specified price on or before a specified expiration date.

When the market price exceeds the exercise price, the option holder may "call away" the asset for the exercise price and reap a benefit equal to the difference between the stock price and the exercise price. Otherwise, the option will be left unexercised. If not exercised before the expiration date, the option expires and no longer has value. Calls, therefore, provide greater profits when stock prices increase and so represent bullish investment vehicles.

put option

The right to sell an asset at a specified exercise price on or before a specified expiration date.

In contrast, a **put option** gives its holder the right to sell an asset for a specified exercise price on or before a specified expiration date. An October put on Apple with exercise price $100 entitles its owner to sell Apple stock to the put writer at a price of $100 at any time before expiration in October even if the market price of Apple is lower than $100. Whereas profits on call options increase when the asset increases in value, profits on put options increase when the asset value falls. The put is exercised only if its holder can deliver an asset worth less than the exercise price in return for the exercise price.

Figure 2.10 is an excerpt of options quotations for Apple. The price of Apple shares on this date was $101.05. The first two columns give the expiration month and exercise (or strike) price for each option. We have included listings for call and put options with exercise prices $95 through $105 per share and with expiration dates in September and October of 2014.

The next columns provide the prices of each option. For example, the October 2014 expiration call with an exercise price of $100 sold for $2.62. Each option *contract* (on 100 shares) therefore cost $262.

FIGURE 2.10

Option trading in Apple (AAPL), September 17, 2014

Source: www.cboe.com, September 17, 2014.

Apple (AAPL)		Underlying stock price = $101.05	
Expiration	Strike	Call	Put
September	95	6.20	0.21
October	95	6.35	0.33
September	100	2.20	1.18
October	100	2.62	1.55
September	105	0.36	4.35
October	105	0.66	4.75

Notice that the prices of call options decrease as the exercise price increases. For example, the October expiration call with exercise price $105 cost only $.66. This makes sense, because the right to purchase a share at a higher price is less valuable. Conversely, put prices increase with the exercise price. The right to sell Apple at a price of $100 in October costs $1.55 while the right to sell at $105 cost $4.75.

Option prices also increase with time until expiration. Clearly, one would rather have the right to buy Apple for $100 at any time until October rather than at any time until September. Not surprisingly, this shows up in a higher price for the October expiration options. For example, the call with exercise price $100 expiring in September sold for only $2.20 compared to $2.62 for the October call.

What would be the profit or loss per share of stock to an investor who bought the October 2014 expiration Apple call option with exercise price $100, if the stock price at the expiration of the option is $110? What about a purchaser of the put option with the same exercise price and expiration?

CONCEPT check 2.6

Futures Contracts

A **futures contract** calls for delivery of an asset (or, in some cases, its cash value) at a specified delivery or maturity date, for an agreed-upon price, called the *futures price,* to be paid at contract maturity. The long position is held by the trader who commits to purchasing the commodity on the delivery date. The trader who takes the short position commits to delivering the commodity at contract maturity.

futures contract

Obliges traders to purchase or sell an asset at an agreed-upon price at a specified future date.

Figure 2.11 illustrates the listing of the corn futures contract on the Chicago Board of Trade for September 17, 2014. Each contract calls for delivery of 5,000 bushels of corn. Each row details prices for contracts expiring on various dates. The first row is for the nearest term or "front" contract, with maturity in December 2014. The most recent price was $3.4175 per bushel. (The numbers after each apostrophe denote eighths of a cent.) That price is down $.02 from yesterday's close. The next columns show the contract's opening price that day as well as the high and low price. Volume is the number of contracts trading that day; open interest is the number of outstanding contracts.

The trader holding the long position profits from price increases. Suppose that at expiration, corn is selling for $3.6175 per bushel. The long position trader who entered the contract at the futures price of $3.4175 on September 17 would pay that previously agreed-upon price for each bushel of corn, which at contract maturity would be worth $3.6175.

Because each contract calls for delivery of 5,000 bushels, the profit to the long position, ignoring brokerage fees, would equal 5,000 × ($3.6175 − $3.4175) = $1,000. Conversely, the short position must deliver 5,000 bushels for the previously agreed-upon futures price. The short position's loss equals the long position's profit.

FIGURE   2.11

Corn futures prices in the Chicago Board of Trade, September 17, 2014

Source: Data from *The Wall Street Journal Online,* September 17, 2014.
Note: Numbers after apostrophes denote eighths of a cent.

MONTH	LAST	CHG	OPEN	HIGH	LOW	VOLUME	OPEN INT
Dec '14	341'6	−2'0	343'2	344'2	339'2	74580	796121
Mar '15	354'0	−1'4	355'4	356'0	351'0	19416	201794
May '15	362'4	−1'6	364'0	364'2	359'4	6153	51800
Jul '15	369'6	−1'4	371'2	371'2	366'6	5171	76051
Sep '15	377'2	−2'0	378'0	378'0	375'0	1791	20972
Dec '15	388'2	−1'6	389'4	390'0	385'4	3876	99741

The *right* to purchase an asset at an agreed-upon price versus the *obligation* to purchase it distinguishes a call option from a long position in a futures contract. A futures contract *obliges* the long position to purchase the asset at the futures price; the call option merely *conveys the right* to purchase the asset at the exercise price. The purchase will be made only if the asset is ultimately worth more than the exercise price.

Clearly, the holder of a call has a better position than the holder of a long position on a futures contract with a futures price equal to the option's exercise price. This advantage, of course, comes only at a price. Call options must be purchased; futures investments are entered into without cost. The purchase price of an option is called the *premium.* It represents the compensation the purchaser of the call must pay for the ability to exercise the option only when it is advantageous to do so. Similarly, the difference between a put option and a short futures position is the right, as opposed to the obligation, to sell an asset at an agreed-upon price.

SUMMARY

- Money market securities are very short-term debt obligations. They are usually highly marketable and have relatively low credit risk. Their low maturities and low credit risk ensure minimal capital gains or losses. These securities often trade in large denominations, but they may be purchased indirectly through money market funds.
- Much of U.S. government borrowing is in the form of Treasury bonds and notes. These are coupon-paying bonds usually issued at or near par value. Treasury bonds are similar in design to coupon-paying corporate bonds.
- Municipal bonds are distinguished largely by their tax-exempt status. Interest payments (but not capital gains) on these securities are exempt from income taxes.
- Mortgage pass-through securities are pools of mortgages sold in one package. Owners of pass-throughs receive all principal and interest payments made by the borrower. The firm that originally issued the mortgage merely services the mortgage, simply "passing through" the payments to the purchasers of the mortgage. Payments of interest and principal on government agency pass-through securities are guaranteed, but payments on private-label mortgage pools are not.
- Common stock is an ownership share in a corporation. Each share entitles its owner to one vote on matters of corporate governance and to a prorated share of the dividends paid to shareholders. Stock, or equity, owners are the residual claimants on the income earned by the firm.
- Preferred stock usually pays a fixed stream of dividends for the life of the firm: It is a perpetuity. A firm's failure to pay the dividend due on preferred stock, however, does not set off corporate bankruptcy. Instead, unpaid dividends simply cumulate. Varieties of preferred stock include convertible and adjustable-rate issues.
- Many stock market indexes measure the performance of the overall market. The Dow Jones averages, the oldest and best-known indicators, are price-weighted indexes. Today, many broad-based, market value–weighted indexes are computed daily. These include the Standard & Poor's Composite 500 stock index, the NYSE index, the NASDAQ index, the Wilshire 5000 Index, and several international indexes, including the Nikkei, FTSE, and DAX.

- A call option is a right to purchase an asset at a stipulated exercise price on or before an expiration date. A put option is the right to sell an asset at some exercise price. Calls increase in value, while puts decrease in value, as the price of the underlying asset increases.
- A futures contract is an obligation to buy or sell an asset at a stipulated futures price on a maturity date. The long position, which commits to purchasing, gains if the asset value increases, while the short position, which commits to delivering the asset, loses.

KEY TERMS

bankers' acceptance, 29	Federal funds, 29	price-weighted average, 41
call option, 46	futures contract, 47	put option, 46
certificate of deposit, 28	London Interbank Offer	repurchase agreements, 29
commercial paper, 28	Rate (LIBOR), 30	Treasury bills, 27
common stocks, 38	market value–weighted	Treasury bonds, 32
corporate bonds, 36	index, 43	Treasury notes, 32
derivative asset, 46	money markets, 27	
equally weighted index, 44	municipal bonds, 34	
Eurodollars, 29	preferred stock, 40	

KEY FORMULAS

Equivalent taxable yield: $\dfrac{r_{\text{muni}}}{1 - \text{tax rate}}$ where r_{muni} is the rate on tax-free municipal debt

Cutoff tax rate (for indifference to taxable versus tax-free bonds): $1 - \dfrac{r_{\text{muni}}}{r_{\text{taxable}}}$

PROBLEM SETS

 Select problems are available in McGraw-Hill's *Connect*. Please see the Supplements section of the book's frontmatter for more information.

1. What are the key differences between common stock, preferred stock, and corporate bonds? *(LO 2-1)*

2. Why do most professionals consider the Wilshire 5000 a better index of the performance of the broad stock market than the Dow Jones Industrial Average? *(LO 2-2)*

3. What features of money market securities distinguish them from other fixed-income securities? *(LO 2-1)*

4. What are the major components of the money market? *(LO 2-1)*

5. Describe alternative ways that an investor may add positions in international equity to his or her portfolio. *(LO 2-1)*

6. Why are high-tax-bracket investors more inclined to invest in municipal bonds than are low-bracket investors? *(LO 2-1)*

7. What is meant by the LIBOR rate? The Federal funds rate? *(LO 2-1)*

8. How does a municipal revenue bond differ from a general obligation bond? Which would you expect to have a lower yield to maturity? *(LO 2-1)*

9. Why are corporations more apt to hold preferred stock than are other potential investors? *(LO 2-1)*

10. What is meant by limited liability? *(LO 2-1)*

11. Which of the following **correctly** describes a repurchase agreement? *(LO 2-1)*
    a. The sale of a security with a commitment to repurchase the same security at a specified future date and a designated price.
    b. The sale of a security with a commitment to repurchase the same security at a future date left unspecified, at a designated price.
    c. The purchase of a security with a commitment to purchase more of the same security at a specified future date.

12. Why are money market securities sometimes referred to as "cash equivalents"? *(LO 2-1)*

13. A municipal bond carries a coupon rate of 6¾% and is trading at par. What would be the equivalent taxable yield of this bond to a taxpayer in a 35% tax bracket?   *(LO 2-1)*

14. Suppose that short-term municipal bonds currently offer yields of 4%, while comparable taxable bonds pay 5%. Which gives you the higher after-tax yield if your tax bracket is: *(LO 2-1)*
    a. Zero
    b. 10%
    c. 20%
    d. 30%

15. An investor is in a 30% combined federal plus state tax bracket. If corporate bonds offer 9% yields, what must municipals offer for the investor to prefer them to corporate bonds?   *(LO 2-1)*

16. Find the equivalent taxable yield of the municipal bond in Problem 14 for tax brackets of: *(LO 2-1)*
    a. Zero
    b. 10%
    c. 20%
    d. 30%

17. Turn back to Figure 2.3 and look at the Treasury bond maturing in February 2036. *(LO 2-1)*
    a. How much would you have to pay to purchase one of these bonds?
    b. What is its coupon rate?
    c. What is the current yield (i.e., coupon income as a fraction of bond price) of the bond?

18. Turn to Figure 2.8 and look at the listing for General Dynamics.   *(LO 2-1)*
    a. What was the firm's closing price yesterday?
    b. How many shares could you buy for $5,000?
    c. What would be your annual dividend income from those shares?
    d. What must be General Dynamics' earnings per share?

19. Consider the three stocks in the following table. P_t represents price at time t, and Q_t represents shares outstanding at time t. Stock C splits two-for-one in the last period.   *(LO 2-2)*

	P_0	Q_0	P_1	Q_1	P_2	Q_2
A	90	100	95	100	95	100
B	50	200	45	200	45	200
C	100	200	110	200	55	400

   a. Calculate the rate of return on a price-weighted index of the three stocks for the first period ($t = 0$ to $t = 1$).
   b. What must happen to the divisor for the price-weighted index in year 2?
   c. Calculate the rate of return of the price-weighted index for the second period ($t = 1$ to $t = 2$).

20. Using the data in the previous problem, calculate the first-period rates of return on the following indexes of the three stocks: *(LO 2-2)*
    a. A market value–weighted index
    b. An equally weighted index

21. What problems would confront a mutual fund trying to create an index fund tied to an equally weighted index of a broad stock market?   *(LO 2-2)*

22. What would happen to the divisor of the Dow Jones Industrial Average if FedEx, with a current price of around $180 per share, replaced AT&T (with a current value of about $34 per share)? *(LO 2-2)*

23. A T-bill with face value $10,000 and 87 days to maturity is selling at a bank discount ask yield of 3.4%. *(LO 2-1)*
    a. What is the price of the bill?
    b. What is its bond equivalent yield?

24. Which security should sell at a greater price? *(LO 2-3)*
    a. A 10-year Treasury bond with a 9% coupon rate or a 10-year T-bond with a 10% coupon.
    b. A three-month expiration call option with an exercise price of $40 or a three-month call on the same stock with an exercise price of $35.
    c. A put option on a stock selling at $50 or a put option on another stock selling at $60. (All other relevant features of the stocks and options are assumed to be identical.)

25. Look at the futures listings for corn in Figure 2.11. *(LO 2-3)*
    a. Suppose you buy one contract for December 2015 delivery. If the contract closes in December at a price of $3.95 per bushel, what will be your profit or loss? (Each contract calls for delivery of 5,000 bushels.)
    b. How many December 2015 maturity contracts are outstanding?

26. Turn back to Figure 2.10 and look at the Apple options. Suppose you buy an October expiration call option with exercise price $100. *(LO 2-3)*
    a. If the stock price in October is $102, will you exercise your call? What are the profit and rate of return on your position?
    b. What if you had bought the October call with exercise price $95?
    c. What if you had bought an October put with exercise price $100?

27. What options position is associated with: *(LO 2-3)*
    a. The right to buy an asset at a specified price?
    b. The right to sell an asset at a specified price?
    c. The obligation to buy an asset at a specified price?
    d. The obligation to sell an asset at a specified price?

28. Why do call options with exercise prices higher than the price of the underlying stock sell for positive prices? *(LO 2-3)*

29. Both a call and a put currently are traded on stock XYZ; both have strike prices of $50 and maturities of six months. *(LO 2-3)*
    a. What will be the profit to an investor who buys the call for $4 in the following scenarios for stock prices in six months? (*i*) $40; (*ii*) $45; (*iii*) $50; (*iv*) $55; (*v*) $60.
    b. What will be the profit in each scenario to an investor who buys the put for $6?

30. What would you expect to happen to the spread between yields on commercial paper and Treasury bills if the economy were to enter a steep recession? *(LO 2-1)*

31. Examine the stocks listed in Figure 2.8. For how many of these stocks is the 52-week high price at least 40% greater than the 52-week low price? What do you conclude about the volatility of prices on individual stocks? *(LO 2-1)*

32. Find the after-tax return to a corporation that buys a share of preferred stock at $40, sells it at year-end at $40, and receives a $4 year-end dividend. The firm is in the 30% tax bracket. *(LO 2-1)*

Challenge

33. Explain the difference between a put option and a short position in a futures contract. *(LO 2-3)*

34. Explain the difference between a call option and a long position in a futures contract. *(LO 2-3)*

CFA Problem

1. Preferred stock yields often are lower than yields on bonds of the same quality because of: *(LO 2-1)*
   a. Marketability
   b. Risk
   c. Taxation
   d. Call protection

WEB *master*

1. Go to **finance.yahoo.com,** and enter the ticker symbol DIS (for Walt Disney Co.) in the *Look Up* box. Now click on *SEC Filings* and look for the link to Disney's most recent annual report (its 10-K). Financial tables are available from the *Summary* link, and Disney's full annual report may be obtained from the *EDGAR* link. Locate the company's Consolidated Balance Sheets and answer these questions:
   a. How much preferred stock is Disney authorized to issue? How much has been issued?
   b. How much common stock is Disney authorized to issue? How many shares are currently outstanding?
   c. Search for the term "Financing Activities." What is the total amount of borrowing listed for Disney? How much of this is medium-term notes?
   d. What other types of debt does Disney have outstanding?

2. Not all stock market indexes are created equal. Different methods are used to calculate various indexes, and different indexes will yield different assessments of "market performance." Using one of the following data sources, retrieve the stock price for five different firms on the first and last trading days of the previous month.

   www.nasdaq.com—Get a quote; then select *Charts* and specify one month. When the chart appears, click on a data point to display the underlying data.

   www.bloomberg.com—Get a quote; then plot the chart; next, use the moving line to see the closing price today and one month ago.

   finance.yahoo.com—Get a quote; then click on *Historical Data* and specify a date range.

   a. Compute the monthly return on a price-weighted index of the five stocks.
   b. Compute the monthly return on a value-weighted index of the five stocks.
   c. Compare the two returns and explain their differences. Explain how you would interpret each measure.

SOLUTIONS TO CONCEPT *checks*

2.1 The bid price of the bond is 108.8906% of par, or $1,088.906. The asked price is 108.9375 or $1089.375. This asked price corresponds to a yield of 1.880%. The ask price increased .0938 from its level yesterday, so the ask price then must have been 108.8437, or $1,088.437.

2.2 A 6% taxable return is equivalent to an after-tax return of 6(1 − .28) = 4.32%. Therefore, you would be better off in the taxable bond. The equivalent taxable yield of the tax-free bond is 4/(1 − .28) = 5.55%. So a taxable bond would have to pay a 5.55% yield to provide the same after-tax return as a tax-free bond offering a 4% yield.

2.3 *a.* You are entitled to a prorated share of IBM's dividend payments and to vote in any of IBM's stockholder meetings.
   b. Your potential gain is unlimited because IBM's stock price has no upper bound.
   c. Your outlay was $190 × 100 = $19,000. Because of limited liability, this is the most you can lose.

2.4 The price-weighted index increases from 62.50 [=(100 + 25)/2] to 65 [=(110 + 20)/2], a gain of 4%. An investment of one share in each company requires an outlay of $125 that would increase in value to $130, for a return of 4% (=5/125), which equals the return to the price-weighted index.

2.5 The market value–weighted index return is calculated by computing the increase in the value of the stock portfolio. The portfolio of the two stocks starts with an initial value of $100 million + $500 million = $600 million and falls in value to $110 million + $400 million = $510 million, a loss of 90/600 = .15, or 15%. The index portfolio return is a weighted average of the returns on each stock with weights of ⅙ on XYZ and ⅚ on ABC (weights proportional to relative investments). Because the return on XYZ is 10%, while that on ABC is −20%, the index portfolio return is (⅙) 10 + (⅚)(−20) = −15%, equal to the return on the market value–weighted index.

2.6 The payoff to the call option is $110 − $100 = $10. The call cost $2.62. The profit is $10 − $2.62 = $7.38 per share. The put will pay off zero—it expires worthless since the stock price exceeds the exercise price. The loss is the cost of the put, $1.55.

3

Securities Markets

Learning Objectives

LO 3-1   Describe how firms issue securities to the public.

LO 3-2   Identify various types of orders investors can submit to their brokers.

LO 3-3   Describe trading practices in dealer markets, specialist-directed stock exchanges, and electronic communication networks.

LO 3-4   Compare the mechanics and investment implications of buying on margin and short-selling.

This chapter will provide you with a broad introduction to the many venues and procedures available for trading securities in the United States and international markets. We will see that trading mechanisms range from direct negotiation among market participants to fully automated computer crossing of trade orders.

The first time a security trades is when it is issued to the public. Therefore, we begin with a look at how securities are first marketed to the public by investment bankers, the midwives of securities. We turn next to a broad survey of how already-issued securities may be traded among investors, focusing on the differences between dealer markets, electronic markets, and specialist markets. With this background, we then turn to specific trading arenas such as the New York Stock Exchange, NASDAQ, and several all-electronic markets. We compare the mechanics of trade execution and the impact of cross-market integration of trading.

We then turn to the essentials of some specific types of transactions, such as buying on margin and short-selling stocks. We close the chapter with a look at some important aspects of the regulations governing security trading, including insider trading laws, circuit breakers, and the role of security markets as self-regulating organizations.

3.1 HOW FIRMS ISSUE SECURITIES

Firms regularly need to raise new capital to help pay for their many investment projects. Broadly speaking, they can raise funds either by borrowing money or by selling shares in the firm. Investment bankers are generally hired to manage the sale of these securities in what is called a **primary market** for newly issued securities. Once these securities are issued, however, investors might well wish to trade them among themselves. For example, you may decide to raise cash by selling some of your shares in Apple to another investor. This transaction would have no impact on the total outstanding number of Apple shares. Trades in existing securities take place in the **secondary market.**

Shares of *publicly listed* firms trade continually on well-known markets such as the New York Stock Exchange or the NASDAQ Stock Market. There, any investor can choose to buy shares for his or her portfolio. These companies are also called *publicly traded, publicly owned,* or just *public companies.* Other firms, however, are *private corporations,* whose shares are held by small numbers of managers and investors. While ownership stakes in the firm are still determined in proportion to share ownership, those shares do not trade in public exchanges. Some private firms are relatively young companies that have not yet chosen to make their shares generally available to the public, others may be more established firms that are still largely owned by the company's founders or families, and others may simply have decided that private organization is preferable.

> **primary market**
> Market for new issues of securities.

> **secondary market**
> Market for already-existing securities.

Privately Held Firms

A privately held company is owned by a relatively small number of shareholders. Privately held firms have fewer obligations to release financial statements and other information to the public. This saves money and frees the firm from disclosing information that might be helpful to its competitors. Some firms also believe that eliminating requirements for quarterly earnings announcements gives them more flexibility to pursue long-term goals free of shareholder pressure.

When private firms wish to raise funds, they sell shares directly to a small number of institutional or wealthy investors in a **private placement.** Rule 144A of the SEC allows them to make these placements without preparing the extensive and costly registration statements required of a public company. While this is attractive, shares in privately held firms do not trade in secondary markets such as a stock exchange, and this greatly reduces their liquidity and presumably reduces the prices that investors will pay for them. *Liquidity* has many specific meanings, but generally speaking, it refers to the ability to trade an asset at a fair price on short notice. Investors demand price concessions to buy illiquid securities.

> **private placement**
> Primary offerings in which shares are sold directly to a small group of institutional or wealthy investors.

Until recently, privately held firms were allowed to have only up to 499 shareholders. This limited their ability to raise large amounts of capital from a wide base of investors. Thus, almost all of the largest companies in the U.S. have been public corporations.

As firms increasingly chafed against the informational requirements of going public, federal regulators came under pressure to loosen the constraints entailed by private ownership. The JOBS (Jumpstart Our Business Startups) Act, which was signed into law in 2012, increased the number of shareholders that a company may have before being required to register its common stock with the SEC and file public reports from 500 to 2,000. It also loosened rules limiting the degree to which private firms could market their shares to the public.

Trading in private corporations also evolved in recent years. To get around the maximum-investor restriction, middlemen formed partnerships to buy shares in private companies; the partnership counts as only one investor, even though many individuals may participate in it.

Very recently, some firms have set up computer networks to enable holders of private-company stock to trade among themselves. However, unlike the public stock markets regulated by the SEC, these networks require little disclosure of financial information and provide correspondingly little oversight of the operations of the market. Skeptics worry that investors in these markets cannot obtain a clear view of the firm, the interest among other investors in the firm, or the process by which trades in the firm's shares are executed.

Publicly Traded Companies

When a private firm decides that it wishes to raise capital from a wide range of investors, it may decide to *go public*. This means that it will sell its securities to the general public and allow those investors to freely trade those shares in established securities markets. The first issue of shares to the general public is called the firm's **initial public offering (IPO).** Later, the firm may go back to the public and issue additional shares. A *seasoned equity offering* is the sale of additional shares in firms that already are publicly traded. For example, a sale by Apple of new shares of stock would be considered a seasoned new issue.

Public offerings of both stocks and bonds typically are marketed by investment bankers who in this role are called **underwriters.** More than one investment banker usually markets the securities. A lead firm forms an underwriting syndicate of other investment bankers to share the responsibility for the stock issue.

Investment bankers advise the firm regarding the terms on which it should attempt to sell the securities. A preliminary registration statement must be filed with the Securities and Exchange Commission (SEC), describing the issue and the prospects of the company. When the statement is in final form, and approved by the SEC, it is called the **prospectus.** At this point, the price at which the securities will be offered to the public is announced.

In a typical underwriting arrangement, the investment bankers purchase the securities from the issuing company and then resell them to the public. The issuing firm sells the securities to the underwriting syndicate for the public offering price less a spread that serves as compensation to the underwriters. This procedure is called a *firm commitment*. In addition to the spread, the investment banker also may receive shares of common stock or other securities of the firm. Figure 3.1 depicts the relationships among the firm issuing the security, the lead underwriter, the underwriting syndicate, and the public.

Shelf Registration

An important innovation in the issuing of securities was introduced in 1982 when the SEC approved Rule 415, which allows firms to register securities and gradually sell them to the public for two years following the initial registration. Because the securities are already registered, they can be sold on short notice, with little additional paperwork. Moreover, they can be sold in small amounts without incurring substantial flotation costs. The securities are "on the shelf," ready to be issued, which has given rise to the term *shelf registration*.

CONCEPT **check**	**3.1**	Why does it make sense for shelf registration to be limited in time?

FIGURE **3.1**	
Relationship among a firm issuing securities, the underwriters, and the public	

Initial Public Offerings

Investment bankers manage the issuance of new securities to the public. Once the SEC has commented on the registration statement and a preliminary prospectus has been distributed to interested investors, the investment bankers organize *road shows* in which they travel around the country to publicize the imminent offering. These road shows serve two purposes. First, they generate interest among potential investors and provide information about the offering. Second, they provide information to the issuing firm and its underwriters about the price at which they will be able to market the securities. Large investors communicate their interest in purchasing shares of the IPO to the underwriters; these indications of interest are called a *book* and the process of polling potential investors is called *bookbuilding*. The book provides valuable information to the issuing firm because institutional investors often will have useful insights about both the market demand for the security as well as the prospects of the firm and its competitors. It is common for investment bankers to revise both their initial estimates of the offering price of a security and the number of shares offered based on feedback from the investing community.

Why do investors truthfully reveal their interest in an offering to the investment banker? Might they be better off expressing little interest, in the hope that this will drive down the offering price? Truth is the better policy in this case because truth telling is rewarded. Shares of IPOs are allocated across investors in part based on the strength of each investor's expressed interest in the offering. If a firm wishes to get a large allocation when it is optimistic about the security, it needs to reveal its optimism. In turn, the underwriter needs to offer the security at a bargain price to these investors to induce them to participate in bookbuilding and share their information. Thus, IPOs commonly are underpriced compared to the price at which they could be marketed. Such underpricing is reflected in price jumps that occur on the date when the shares are first traded in public security markets. The September 2014 IPO of the giant Chinese e-commerce firm Alibaba was a typical example of underpricing. The company issued about 320 million shares to the public at a price of $68. The stock price closed that day at $93.89, a bit more than 38% above the offering price.

While the explicit costs of an IPO tend to be around 7% of the funds raised, such underpricing should be viewed as another cost of the issue. For example, if Alibaba had sold its shares for the $93.89 that investors obviously were willing to pay for them, its IPO would have raised 38% more money than it actually did. The money "left on the table" in this case far exceeded the explicit cost of the stock issue. Nevertheless, underpricing seems to be a universal phenomenon. For example, Figure 3.2 presents average first-day returns on IPOs of stocks across the world. The results consistently indicate that IPOs are marketed to investors at attractive prices.

Pricing of IPOs is not trivial and not all IPOs turn out to be underpriced. Some do poorly after issue. Facebook's 2012 IPO was a notable disappointment. Within a week of its IPO, Facebook's share price was 15% below the $38 offer price, and five months later, its shares were selling at about half the offer price. (In the end, however, those who held onto their shares profited; by late 2014, the share price was near double the IPO offer price.)

Interestingly, despite their typically attractive first-day returns, IPOs have been poor long-term investments. Ritter calculates the returns to a hypothetical investor who bought equal amounts of each U.S. IPO between 1980 and 2011 and held each position for three years. That portfolio would have underperformed the broad U.S. stock market on average by 18.7% for three-year holding periods and underperformed "style-matched" portfolios of firms with comparable size and ratio of book value to market value by 7.0%.[1]

Other IPOs cannot even be fully sold to the market. Underwriters left with unmarketable securities are forced to sell them at a loss on the secondary market. Therefore, the investment banker bears the price risk of an underwritten issue.

3.2   HOW SECURITIES ARE TRADED

Financial markets develop to meet the needs of particular traders. Consider what would happen if organized markets did not exist. Any household wishing to invest in some type of financial asset would have to find others wishing to sell. Soon, venues where interested traders

---

[1]Professor Jay Ritter's website contains a wealth of information and data about IPOs: **http://bear.warrington.ufl .edu/ritter/ipodata.htm.**

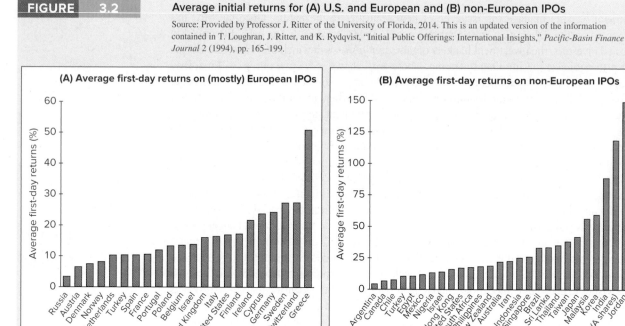

Source: Provided by Professor J. Ritter of the University of Florida, 2014. This is an updated version of the information contained in T. Loughran, J. Ritter, and K. Rydqvist, "Initial Public Offerings: International Insights," *Pacific-Basin Finance Journal* 2 (1994), pp. 165–199.

FIGURE 3.2   Average initial returns for (A) U.S. and European and (B) non-European IPOs

could meet would become popular. Eventually, financial markets would emerge from these meeting places. Thus, a pub in old London called Lloyd's launched the maritime insurance industry. A Manhattan curb on Wall Street became synonymous with the financial world.

Types of Markets

We can differentiate four types of markets: direct search markets, brokered markets, dealer markets, and auction markets.

DIRECT SEARCH MARKETS   A *direct search market* is the least organized market. Buyers and sellers must seek each other out directly. An example of a transaction in such a market is the sale of a used refrigerator where the seller advertises for buyers on Craigslist. Such markets are characterized by sporadic participation and nonstandard goods. It would not pay for most people or firms to specialize in such markets.

BROKERED MARKETS   The next level of organization is a *brokered market*. In markets where trading in a good is active, brokers find it profitable to offer search services to buyers and sellers. A good example is the real estate market, where economies of scale in searches for available homes and for prospective buyers make it worthwhile for participants to pay brokers to conduct the searches. Brokers in particular markets develop specialized knowledge on valuing assets traded in that market.

The *primary market,* where new issues of securities are offered to the public, is an example of a brokered market. In the primary market, investment bankers who market a firm's securities to the public act as brokers; they seek investors to purchase securities directly from the issuing corporation.

dealer markets

Markets in which traders specializing in particular assets buy and sell for their own accounts.

DEALER MARKETS   When trading activity in a particular type of asset increases, **dealer markets** arise. Dealers specialize in various assets, purchase these assets for their own accounts, and later sell them for a profit from their inventory. The spreads between dealers' buy (or "bid") prices and sell (or "ask") prices are a source of profit. Dealer markets save traders on search costs because market participants can easily look up the prices at which they can buy from or sell to dealers. A fair amount of market activity is required before dealing in a market is an attractive source of income. Most bonds trade in over-the-counter dealer markets.

AUCTION MARKETS The most integrated market is an **auction market,** in which all traders converge at one place (either physically or "electronically") to buy or sell an asset. The New York Stock Exchange (NYSE) is an example of an auction market. An advantage of auction markets over dealer markets is that one need not search across dealers to find the best price for a good. If all participants converge, they can arrive at mutually agreeable prices and save the bid–ask spread.

auction market
A market where all traders meet at one place to buy or sell an asset.

Notice that both over-the-counter dealer markets and stock exchanges are secondary markets. They are organized for investors to trade existing securities among themselves.

> Many assets trade in more than one type of market. What types of markets do the following trade in?
> a. Used cars
> b. Paintings
> c. Rare coins

CONCEPT check 3.2

Types of Orders

Before comparing alternative trading practices and competing security markets, it is helpful to begin with an overview of the types of trades an investor might wish to have executed in these markets. Broadly speaking, there are two types of orders: market orders and orders contingent on price.

MARKET ORDERS Market orders are buy or sell orders that are to be executed immediately at current market prices. For example, our investor might call her broker and ask for the market price of Facebook. The broker might report back that the best **bid price** is $76.40 and the best **ask price** is $76.42, meaning that the investor would need to pay $76.42 to purchase a share and could receive $76.40 a share if she wished to sell some of her own holdings of Facebook. The **bid–ask spread** in this case is $.02. So an order to buy 100 shares "at market" would result in purchase at $76.42, and an order to "sell at market" would be executed at $76.40.

This simple scenario is subject to a few potential complications. First, posted price quotes actually represent commitments to trade up to a specified number of shares. If the market order is for more than this number of shares, the order may be filled at multiple prices. For example, if the asked price is good for orders up to 1,000 shares, and the investor wishes to purchase 1,500 shares, it may be necessary to pay a slightly higher price for the last 500 shares. Figure 3.3 shows the average *depth* of the markets for shares of stock (i.e., the total number of shares offered for trading at the best bid and ask prices). Notice that depth is considerably higher for the large stocks in the S&P 500 than for the smaller stocks that constitute the Russell 2000 index. Depth is considered another component of liquidity. Second, another trader may beat our investor to the quote, meaning that her order would then be executed at a worse price. Finally, the best price quote may change before her order arrives, again causing execution at a different price than the one at the moment of the order.

bid price
The price at which a dealer or other trader is willing to purchase a security.

ask price
The price at which a dealer or other trader will sell a security.

bid–ask spread
The difference between the bid and asked prices.

PRICE-CONTINGENT ORDERS Investors also may place orders specifying prices at which they are willing to buy or sell a security. A **limit buy order** may instruct the broker to buy some number of shares if and when they may be obtained at or below a stipulated price. Conversely, a **limit sell** instructs the broker to sell if and when the stock price rises *above* a specified limit. A collection of limit orders waiting to be executed is called a *limit order book*.

limit buy (sell) order
An order specifying a price at which an investor is willing to buy or sell a security.

FIGURE 3.3

Average market depth for large (S&P 500) and small (Russell 2000) firms

Source: Adapted from James J. Angel, Lawrence E. Harris, and Chester Spatt, "Equity Trading in the 21st Century," *Quarterly Journal of Finance* 1 (2011), pp. 1–53; Knight Capital Group.

FIGURE 3.4

A portion of the limit order book for Facebook on the BATS market, September 22, 2014

Facebook, Inc. (FB) - NasdaqGS

76.37 ↓1.54(1.98%) 3:13PM EDT - Nasdaq Real Time Price

Order Book

Top of Book

Bid		Ask	
Price	Size	Price	Size
76.40	600	76.42	400
76.39	900	76.43	600
76.38	817	76.44	700
76.37	964	76.45	1,300
76.36	710	76.46	764

Figure 3.4 is a portion of the limit order book for shares in Facebook taken from the BATS exchange (one of several electronic exchanges; more on these shortly). Notice that the best orders are at the top of the list: the offers to buy at the highest price and to sell at the lowest price. The buy and sell orders at the top of the list—$76.40 and $76.42—are called the *inside quotes;* they are the highest buy and lowest sell orders. For Facebook, the inside spread at this time was only 2 cents. However, that order sizes at the inside quotes can be fairly small. Therefore, investors interested in larger trades face an *effective* spread greater than the nominal one since they cannot execute their entire trades at the inside price quotes.

stop order

Trade is not to be executed unless stock hits a price limit.

Stop orders are similar to limit orders in that the trade is not to be executed unless the stock hits a price limit. For *stop-loss orders,* the stock is to be *sold* if its price falls *below* a stipulated level. As the name suggests, the order lets the stock be sold to stop further losses from accumulating. Similarly, *stop-buy orders* specify that a stock should be bought when its price rises above a limit. These trades often accompany *short sales* (sales of securities you don't own but have borrowed from your broker) and are used to limit potential losses from the short position. Short sales are discussed in greater detail later in this chapter. Figure 3.5 organizes these types of trades in a convenient matrix.

FIGURE 3.5

Price-contingent orders

CONCEPT
c h e c k   3.3

What type of trading order might you give to your broker in each of the following circumstances?
  a. You want to buy shares of Intel to diversify your portfolio. You believe the share price is approximately at the "fair" value, and you want the trade done quickly and cheaply.
  b. You want to buy shares of Intel but believe that the current stock price is too high given the firm's prospects. If the shares could be obtained at a price 5% lower than the current value, you would like to purchase shares for your portfolio.
  c. You plan to purchase a condominium sometime in the next month or so and will sell your shares of Intel to provide the funds for your down payment. While you believe that Intel share price is going to rise over the next few weeks, if you are wrong and the share price drops suddenly, you will not be able to afford the purchase. Therefore, you want to hold on to the shares for as long as possible but still protect yourself against the risk of a big loss.

Trading Mechanisms

An investor who wishes to buy or sell shares will place an order with a brokerage firm. The broker charges a commission for arranging the trade on the client's behalf. Brokers have several avenues by which they can execute that trade, that is, find a buyer or seller and arrange for the shares to be exchanged.

Broadly speaking, there are three trading systems employed in the United States: over-the-counter dealer markets, electronic communication networks, and specialist markets. The best-known markets such as NASDAQ or the New York Stock Exchange actually use a variety of trading procedures, so before delving into these markets, it is useful to understand the basic operation of each type of trading system.

DEALER MARKETS   Roughly 35,000 securities trade on the **over-the-counter (OTC) market.** Thousands of brokers register with the SEC as security dealers. Dealers quote prices at which they are willing to buy or sell securities. A broker then executes a trade by contacting a dealer listing an attractive quote.

Before 1971, all OTC quotations were recorded manually and published daily on so-called pink sheets. In 1971, the National Association of Securities Dealers introduced its Automatic Quotations System, or NASDAQ, to link brokers and dealers in a computer network where price quotes could be displayed and revised. Dealers could use the network to display the bid price at which they were willing to purchase a security and the ask price at which they were willing to sell. The difference in these prices, the bid–ask spread, was the source of the dealer's profit. Brokers representing clients could examine quotes over the computer network, contact the dealer with the best quote, and execute a trade.

As originally organized, NASDAQ was more of a price quotation system than a trading system. While brokers could survey bid and ask prices across the network of dealers in the search for the best trading opportunity, actual trades required direct negotiation (often over the

over-the-counter (OTC) market

An informal network of brokers and dealers who negotiate sales of securities.

phone) between the investor's broker and the dealer in the security. However, as we will see, NASDAQ has progressed far beyond a pure price quotation system. While dealers still post bid and ask prices over the network, what is now called the **NASDAQ Stock Market** allows for electronic execution of trades at quoted prices without the need for direct negotiation, and the vast majority of trades are executed electronically.

ELECTRONIC COMMUNICATION NETWORKS (ECNs)   **Electronic communication networks** allow participants to post market and limit orders over computer networks. The limit order book is available to all participants. An example of such an order book from BATS, one of the leading ECNs, appears in Figure 3.4. Orders that can be "crossed," that is, matched against another order, are done so automatically without requiring the intervention of a broker. For example, an order to buy a share at a price of $76 or lower will be immediately executed if there is an outstanding asked price of $76. Therefore, ECNs are true trading systems, not merely price quotation systems.

ECNs offer several attractions. Direct crossing of trades without using a broker-dealer system eliminates the bid–ask spread that otherwise would be incurred. Instead, trades are automatically crossed at a modest cost, typically less than a penny per share. ECNs are attractive as well because of the speed with which a trade can be executed. Finally, these systems offer investors considerable anonymity in their trades.

SPECIALIST MARKETS   Specialist systems have been largely replaced by electronic communication networks, but as recently as two decades ago, they were still the dominant form of market organization for trading in stocks. In these systems, exchanges such as the NYSE assign responsibility for managing the trading in each security to a **specialist.** Brokers wishing to buy or sell shares for their clients direct the trade to the specialist's post on the floor of the exchange. While each security is assigned to only one specialist, each specialist firm makes a market in many securities. The specialist maintains the limit order book of all outstanding unexecuted limit orders. When orders can be executed at market prices, the specialist executes or "crosses" the trade. The highest outstanding bid price and the lowest outstanding ask price "win" the trade.

Specialists are also mandated to maintain a "fair and orderly" market when the book of limit buy and sell orders is so thin that the spread between the highest bid price and lowest ask price becomes too wide. In this case, the specialist firm would be expected to offer to buy and sell shares from its own inventory at a narrower bid–ask spread. In this role, the specialist serves as a dealer in the stock and provides liquidity to other traders. In this context, liquidity providers are those who stand willing to buy securities from or sell securities to other traders.

3.3   THE RISE OF ELECTRONIC TRADING

When first established, NASDAQ was primarily an over-the-counter dealer market and the NYSE was a specialist market. But today both are primarily electronic markets. These changes were driven by an interaction of new technologies and new regulations. New regulations allowed brokers to compete for business, broke the hold that dealers once had on information about best-available bid and ask prices, forced integration of markets, and allowed securities to trade in ever-smaller price increments (called *tick sizes*). Technology made it possible for traders to rapidly compare prices across markets and direct their trades to the markets with the best prices. The resulting competition drove down the cost of trade execution to a tiny fraction of its value just a few decades ago.

In 1975, fixed commissions on the NYSE were eliminated, which freed brokers to compete for business by lowering their fees. In that year also, Congress amended the Securities Exchange Act to create the National Market System to at least partially centralize trading across exchanges and enhance competition among different market makers. The idea was to implement centralized reporting of transactions as well as a centralized price quotation system to give traders a broader view of trading opportunities across markets.

The aftermath of a 1994 scandal at NASDAQ turned out to be a major impetus in the further evolution and integration of markets. NASDAQ dealers were found to be colluding to maintain

---

NASDAQ Stock Market

The computer-linked price quotation and trade execution system.

electronic communication networks (ECNs)

Computer networks that allow direct trading without the need for market makers.

specialist

A trader who makes a market in the shares of one or more firms and who maintains a "fair and orderly market" by dealing personally in the market.

wide bid–ask spreads. For example, if a stock was listed at $30 bid–$30½ ask, a retail client who wished to buy shares from a dealer would pay $30½ while a client who wished to sell shares would receive only $30. The dealer would pocket the ½-point spread as profit. Other traders may have been willing to step in with better prices (e.g., they may have been willing to buy shares for $30⅛ or sell them for $30⅜), but those better quotes were not made available to the public, enabling dealers to profit from artificially wide spreads at the public's expense. When these practices came to light, an antitrust lawsuit was brought against NASDAQ.

In response to the scandal, the SEC instituted new order-handling rules. Published dealer quotes now had to reflect limit orders of customers, allowing them to effectively compete with dealers to capture trades. As part of the antitrust settlement, NASDAQ agreed to integrate quotes from ECNs into its public display, enabling the electronic exchanges to also compete for trades. Shortly after this settlement, the SEC adopted Regulation ATS (Alternative Trading Systems), giving ECNs the right to register as stock exchanges. Not surprisingly, they captured an ever-larger market share, and in the wake of this new competition, bid–ask spreads narrowed.

Even more dramatic narrowing of trading costs came in 1997, when the SEC allowed the minimum tick size to fall from one-eighth of a dollar to one-sixteenth. Not long after, in 2001, "decimalization" allowed the tick size to fall to 1 cent. Bid–ask spreads again fell dramatically. Figure 3.6 shows estimates of the "effective spread" (the cost of a transaction) during three distinct time periods defined by the minimum tick size. Notice how dramatically effective spread falls along with the minimum tick size.

Technology was also changing trading practices. The first ECN, Instinet, was established in 1969. By the 1990s, exchanges around the world were rapidly adopting fully electronic trading systems. Europe led the way in this evolution, but eventually American exchanges followed suit. The National Association of Securities Dealers (NASD) spun off the NASDAQ Stock Market as a separate entity in 2000, which quickly evolved into a centralized limit-order matching system—effectively a large ECN. The NYSE acquired the electronic Archipelago Exchange in 2006 and renamed it NYSE Arca.

In 2005, the SEC adopted Regulation NMS (National Market System), which was fully implemented in 2007. The goal was to link exchanges electronically, thereby creating in effect one integrated electronic market. The regulation required exchanges to honor quotes of other

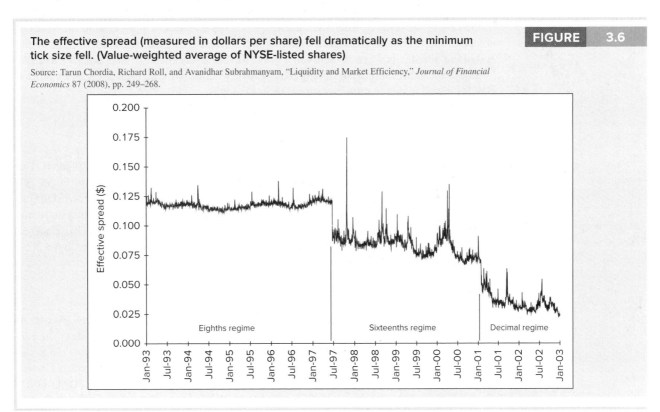

The effective spread (measured in dollars per share) fell dramatically as the minimum tick size fell. (Value-weighted average of NYSE-listed shares)

FIGURE 3.6

Source: Tarun Chordia, Richard Roll, and Avanidhar Subrahmanyam, "Liquidity and Market Efficiency," *Journal of Financial Economics* 87 (2008), pp. 249–268.

FIGURE 3.7

Market share of trading in NYSE-listed shares

Source: James J. Angel, Lawrence E. Harris, and Chester Spatt, "Equity Trading in the 21st Century," *Quarterly Journal of Finance* 1 (2011), pp. 1–53.

exchanges when they could be executed automatically. An exchange that could not handle a quote electronically would be labeled a "slow market" under Reg NMS and could be ignored by other market participants. The NYSE, which was still devoted to the specialist system, was particularly at risk of being passed over, and in response to this pressure, it moved aggressively toward automated execution of trades. Electronic trading networks and the integration of markets in the wake of Reg NMS made it much easier for exchanges around the world to compete; the NYSE lost its effective monopoly in trading its own listed stocks, and by the end of the decade, its share in the trading of NYSE-listed stocks fell from about 75% to 25%.

While specialists still exist, trading today is overwhelmingly electronic, at least for stocks. Bonds are still traded in more traditional dealer markets.

3.4 U.S. MARKETS

The NYSE and the NASDAQ Stock Market remain the best-known U.S. stock markets. But electronic communication networks have steadily increased their market share. Figure 3.7 shows the comparative trading volume of NYSE-listed shares on the NYSE and NASDAQ as well as on the major ECNs, namely, BATS, NYSE Arca, and Direct Edge. Since this study was published, BATS and Direct Edge merged, creating one of the world's largest stock exchanges, called BATS Global Markets. The "Other" category, which recently has risen above 30%, includes so-called dark pools, which we will discuss shortly.

NASDAQ

The NASDAQ Stock Market lists around 3,000 firms. It has steadily introduced ever-more sophisticated trading platforms, which today handle the great majority of its trades. The current version, called the NASDAQ Market Center, consolidates NASDAQ's previous electronic markets into one integrated system. NASDAQ merged in 2007 with OMX, a Swedish-Finnish company that controls seven Nordic and Baltic stock exchanges, to form NASDAQ OMX Group. In addition to maintaining the NASDAQ Stock Market, it also maintains several stock markets in Europe as well as an options and futures exchange in the U.S.

NASDAQ has three levels of subscribers. The highest, level 3 subscribers, are registered market makers. These are firms that make a market in securities, maintain inventories of securities, and post bid and ask prices at which they are willing to buy or sell shares. Level 3 subscribers can enter and change bid–ask quotes continually and have the fastest execution of trades. They profit from the spread between bid and ask prices.

Level 2 subscribers receive all bid and ask quotes but cannot enter their own quotes. They can see which market makers are offering the best prices. These subscribers tend to be brokerage firms that execute trades for clients but do not actively deal in stocks for their own account.

Level 1 subscribers receive only inside quotes (i.e., the best bid and ask prices) but do not see how many shares are being offered. These subscribers tend to be investors who are not actively buying or selling but want information on current prices.

The New York Stock Exchange

The NYSE is the largest U.S. **stock exchange** as measured by the market value of listed firms. In 2006, the NYSE merged with the Archipelago Exchange to form a publicly held company called the NYSE Group, and then in 2007, it merged with the European exchange Euronext to form NYSE Euronext. The firm acquired the American Stock Exchange in 2008, which was renamed NYSE Amex and focuses on small firms. More than 3 billion shares trade daily on the NYSE. NYSE Arca is the firm's electronic communications network. In 2013, NYSE Euronext was acquired by Intercontinental Exchange (ICE), whose main business to date had been energy-futures trading. ICE has retained the NYSE Euronext name.

stock exchanges
Secondary markets where already-issued securities are bought and sold by members.

The NYSE was long committed to its specialist trading system, which relied heavily on human participation in trade execution. It began its transition to electronic trading for smaller trades in 1976 with the introduction of its DOT (Designated Order Turnaround) and later SuperDOT systems, which could route orders directly to the specialist. In 2000, the exchange launched Direct+, which could automatically cross smaller trades (up to 1,099 shares) without human intervention, and in 2004, it began eliminating the size restrictions on Direct+ trades. The change of emphasis dramatically accelerated in 2006 with the introduction of the NYSE Hybrid Market, which allowed brokers to send orders either for immediate electronic execution or to the specialist, who could seek price improvement from another trader. The Hybrid system allowed the NYSE to qualify as a fast market for the purposes of Regulation NMS but still offer the advantages of human intervention for more complicated trades. In contrast, NYSE's Arca marketplace is fully electronic.

ECNs

Over time, more fully automated markets have gained market share at the expense of less automated ones, in particular, the NYSE. Some of the biggest ECNs today are NASDAQ, BATS, and NYSE Arca. Brokers that have an affiliation with an ECN have computer access and can enter orders in the limit order book. As orders are received, the system determines whether there is a matching order, and if so, the trade is immediately crossed.

Originally, ECNs were open only to other traders using the same system. But following the implementation of Reg NMS, ECNs began listing limit orders on other networks. Traders could use their computer systems to sift through the limit order books of many ECNs and instantaneously route orders to the market with the best prices. Those cross-market links have become the impetus for one of the more popular strategies of so-called high-frequency traders, which seek to profit from even small, transitory discrepancies in prices across markets. Speed is obviously of the essence here, and ECNs compete in terms of the speed they can offer. **Latency** refers to the time it takes to accept, process, and deliver a trading order. BATS, for example, advertises (in 2015) average latency times of less than 200 microseconds, that is, .0002 second.

latency
The time it takes to accept, process, and deliver a trading order.

3.5 NEW TRADING STRATEGIES

The marriage of electronic trading mechanisms with computer technology has had far-ranging impacts on trading strategies and tools. *Algorithmic trading* delegates trading decisions to computer programs. *High-frequency trading* is a special class of algorithmic trading in which computer programs initiate orders in tiny fractions of a second, far faster than any human could process the information driving the trade. Much of the market liquidity that once was provided by brokers making a market in a security has been displaced by these high-frequency traders. But when high-frequency traders abandon the market, as in the so-called flash crash of 2010, liquidity can likewise evaporate in a flash. *Dark pools* are trading venues that preserve anonymity but also affect market liquidity. We will address these emerging issues later in this section.

Algorithmic Trading

algorithmic trading

The use of computer programs to make rapid trading decisions.

Algorithmic trading is the use of computer programs to make trading decisions. Well more than half of all equity volume in the U.S. is believed to be initiated by computer algorithms. Many of these trades exploit very small discrepancies in security prices and entail numerous and rapid cross-market price comparisons that are well suited to computer analysis. These strategies would not have been feasible before decimalization of the minimum tick size.

Some algorithmic trades attempt to exploit very short-term trends (as short as a few seconds) as new information about a firm or, more controversially, about the intentions of other traders, becomes available. Others use versions of *pairs trading* in which normal price relations between pairs (or larger groups) of stocks seem temporarily disrupted and offer small profit opportunities as they move back into alignment. Still others attempt to exploit discrepancies between stock prices and prices of stock-index futures contracts.

Some algorithmic trading involves activities akin to traditional market making. The traders seek to profit from the bid–ask spread by buying a stock at the bid price and rapidly selling it at the ask price before the price can change. While this mimics the role of a market maker who provides liquidity to other traders in the stock, these algorithmic traders are not registered market makers and so do not have an affirmative obligation to maintain both bid and ask quotes. If they abandon a market during a period of turbulence, the shock to market liquidity can be disruptive. This seems to have been a problem during the flash crash of May 6, 2010, when the stock market encountered extreme volatility, with the Dow Jones average falling by 1,000 points before recovering around 600 points in intraday trading. The nearby box discusses this amazing and troubling episode.

High-Frequency Trading

high-frequency trading

A subset of algorithmic trading that relies on computer programs to make very rapid trading decisions.

It is easy to see that many algorithmic trading strategies require extremely rapid trade initiation and execution. **High-frequency trading** is a subset of algorithmic trading that relies on computer programs to make extremely rapid decisions. High-frequency traders compete for trades that offer very small profits. But if those opportunities are numerous enough, they can accumulate to big money.

We pointed out that one high-frequency strategy entails a sort of market making, attempting to profit from the bid–ask spread. Another relies on cross-market arbitrage, in which even tiny price discrepancies across markets allow the firm to buy a security at one price and simultaneously sell it at a slightly higher price. The competitive advantage in these strategies lies with the firms that are quickest to identify and execute these profit opportunities. There is a tremendous premium on being the first to "hit" a bid or ask price.

Trade execution times for high-frequency traders are now measured in milliseconds, even microseconds. This has induced trading firms to "co-locate" their trading centers next to the computer systems of the electronic exchanges. When execution or latency periods are less than a millisecond, the extra time it takes for a trade order to travel from a remote location to a New York exchange would be enough to make it nearly impossible to win the trade.

To understand why co-location has become a key issue, consider this calculation: Even light can travel only 186 miles in one millisecond, so an order originating in Chicago transmitted at the speed of light would take almost five milliseconds to reach New York. That order could not possibly compete with one launched from a co-located facility.

In some ways, co-location is a new version of an old phenomenon. Think about why, even before the advent of the telephone, so many brokerage firms originally located their

On the MARKET FRONT

THE FLASH CRASH OF MAY 2010

At 2:42 New York time on May 6, 2010, the Dow Jones Industrial Average was already down about 300 points for the day. The market was demonstrating concerns about the European debt crisis, and nerves were on edge. Then, in the next five minutes, the Dow dropped an *additional* 600 points. And only 20 minutes after that, it had recovered most of those 600 points. Besides the staggering intraday volatility of the broad market, trading in individual shares and ETFs was even more disrupted. The iShares Russell 1000 Value Fund temporarily fell from $59 a share to 8 cents. Shares in the large consulting company Accenture, which had just sold for $38, traded at 1 cent only a minute or two later. At the other extreme, price quotes for Apple and Hewlett-Packard momentarily increased to over $100,000. These markets were clearly broken.

The causes of the flash crash are still debated. An SEC report issued after the trade points to a $4 billion sale of market index futures contracts by a mutual fund (believed to be Waddell & Reed Financial). As market prices began to tumble, many algorithmic trading programs withdrew from the markets, and those that remained became net sellers, further pushing down equity prices. As more and more of these algorithmic traders shut down, liquidity in these markets evaporated: Buyers for many stocks simply disappeared.

Finally, trading was halted for a short period. When it resumed, buyers decided to take advantage of many severely depressed stock prices, and the market rebounded almost as quickly as it had crashed. Given the intraday turbulence and the clearly distorted prices at which some trades had been executed, the NYSE and NASDAQ decided to cancel all trades that were executed more than 60% away from a "reference price" close to the opening price of the day. Almost 70% of those canceled trades involved ETFs.

The SEC has since approved experimentation with new circuit breakers to halt trading for five minutes in large stocks that rise or fall by more than 10% in a five-minute period. The idea is to prevent trading algorithms from moving share prices quickly before human traders have a chance to determine whether those prices are moving in response to fundamental information.

The flash crash highlighted the fragility of markets in the face of huge variation in trading volume created by algorithmic traders. The potential for these high-frequency traders to withdraw from markets in periods of turbulence remains a concern, and many observers are not convinced that we are protected from future flash crashes.

---

headquarters in New York: They were "co-locating" with the NYSE so that their brokers could bring trades (on foot!) to the exchange quickly and efficiently. Today, trades are transmitted electronically, but competition among traders for fast execution means that the need to be near the market (now embodied in computer servers) remains.

Dark Pools

Many large traders seek anonymity. They fear that if others see them executing a buy or a sell program, their intentions will become public and prices will move against them. Very large trades (called **blocks,** usually defined as a trade of more than 10,000 shares) were traditionally brought to "block houses," brokerage firms specializing in matching block buyers and sellers. Part of the expertise of block brokers was in identifying traders who might be interested in a large purchase or sale if given an offer. These brokers discreetly arranged large trades out of the public eye, and so avoided moving prices against their clients.

Block trading today has been displaced to a great extent by **dark pools,** trading systems in which participants can buy or sell large blocks of securities without showing their hand. Not only are buyers and sellers in dark pools hidden from the public, but even trades may not be reported, or if they are reported, they may be lumped with other trades to obscure information about particular participants.

Dark pools are somewhat controversial because they contribute to the fragmentation of markets. When many orders are removed from the consolidated limit order book, there are fewer orders left to absorb fluctuations in demand for the security, and the public price may no longer be "fair" in the sense that it reflects all the potentially available information about security demand.

Another approach to dealing with large trades is to split them into many small trades, each of which can be executed on electronic markets, attempting to hide the fact that the total number of shares ultimately to be bought or sold is large. This trend has led to rapid decline in average trade size, which today is less than 300 shares.

blocks

Large transactions in which at least 10,000 shares of stock are bought or sold.

dark pools

Electronic trading networks where participants can anonymously buy or sell large blocks of securities.

Bond Trading

In 2006, the NYSE obtained regulatory approval to expand its bond trading system to include the debt issues of any NYSE-listed firm. In the past, each bond needed to be registered before listing; such a requirement was too onerous to justify listing most bonds. In conjunction with these new listings, the NYSE has expanded its electronic bond-trading platform, which is now called NYSE Bonds, and is the largest centralized bond market of any U.S. exchange.

Nevertheless, the vast majority of bond trading occurs in the OTC market among bond dealers, even for bonds that are actually listed on the NYSE. This market is a network of bond dealers such as Merrill Lynch (now part of Bank of America), Salomon Smith Barney (a division of Citigroup), and Goldman Sachs that is linked by a computer quotation system. However, because these dealers do not carry extensive inventories of the wide range of bonds that have been issued to the public, they cannot necessarily offer to sell bonds from their inventory to clients or even buy bonds for their own inventory. They may instead work to locate an investor who wishes to take the opposite side of a trade. In practice, however, the corporate bond market often is quite "thin," in that there may be few investors interested in trading a bond at any particular time. As a result, the bond market is subject to a type of liquidity risk, for it can be difficult to sell one's holdings quickly if the need arises.

3.6   GLOBALIZATION OF STOCK MARKETS

Figure 3.8 shows that the NYSE Euronext is by far the largest equity market, as measured by the total market value of listed firms. All major stock markets today are effectively electronic.

Securities markets have come under increasing pressure in recent years to make international alliances or mergers. Much of this pressure is due to the impact of electronic trading. To a growing extent, traders view stock markets as networks that link them to other traders, and there are increasingly fewer limits on the securities around the world that they can trade. Against this background, it becomes more important for exchanges to provide the cheapest and most efficient mechanism by which trades can be executed and cleared. This argues for global alliances that can facilitate the nuts and bolts of cross-border trading and can benefit from economies of scale. Exchanges feel that they eventually need to offer 24-hour global markets. Finally, companies want to be able to go beyond national borders when they wish to raise capital.

These pressures have resulted in a broad trend toward market consolidation. Many mergers have been "local," that is, involving exchanges operating in the same continent. In the U.S., the NYSE merged with the Archipelago ECN in 2006, and in 2008 acquired the American Stock Exchange. NASDAQ acquired Instinet (which operated the other major ECN, INET) in 2005 and the Boston Stock Exchange in 2007. In the derivatives market, the Chicago Mercantile Exchange acquired the Chicago Board of Trade in 2007. In Europe, Euronext was formed by the merger of the Paris, Brussels, Lisbon, and Amsterdam exchanges and shortly thereafter purchased LIFFE, the derivatives exchange based in London. The LSE merged in 2007 with Borsa Italiana, which operates the Milan exchange. In 2013, the Tokyo Stock Exchange merged with the Osaka exchange, creating the world's third-largest exchange, measured by market capitalization of traded shares.

There has also been a wave of intercontinental consolidation. The NYSE Group and Euronext merged in 2007, and that international firm was acquired by ICE in 2013. Germany's Deutsche Börse and the NYSE Euronext agreed to merge in late 2011. The merged firm would have been able to support trading in virtually every type of investment. However, in early 2012, the proposed merger ran into trouble when European Union antitrust regulators recommended that the combination be blocked. Still, the attempt at the merger indicates the thrust of market pressures, and other combinations continue to develop. The NYSE and the Tokyo stock exchange have linked their networks to give customers of each access to both markets. In 2007, the NASDAQ Stock Market merged with OMX, which operates seven Nordic and Baltic stock exchanges, to form NASDAQ OMX Group. In 2008, Euronext took over International Securities Exchange (ISE), to form a major options exchange.

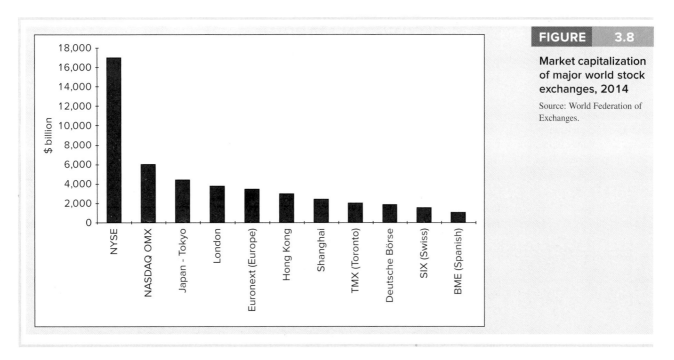

FIGURE **3.8**

Market capitalization of major world stock exchanges, 2014

Source: World Federation of Exchanges.

3.7 TRADING COSTS

Part of the cost of trading a security is obvious and explicit. Your broker must be paid a commission. Individuals may choose from two kinds of brokers: full-service or discount brokers. Full-service brokers who provide a variety of services often are referred to as account executives or financial consultants.

Besides carrying out the basic services of executing orders, holding securities for safekeeping, extending margin loans, and facilitating short sales, brokers routinely provide information and advice relating to investment alternatives.

Full-service brokers usually depend on a research staff that prepares analyses and forecasts of general economic as well as industry and company conditions and often makes specific buy or sell recommendations. Some customers take the ultimate leap of faith and allow a full-service broker to make buy and sell decisions for them by establishing a *discretionary account*. In this account, the broker can buy and sell prespecified securities whenever deemed fit. (The broker cannot withdraw any funds, though.) This action requires an unusual degree of trust on the part of the customer, for an unscrupulous broker can "churn" an account, that is, trade securities excessively with the sole purpose of generating commissions.

Discount brokers, on the other hand, provide "no-frills" services. They buy and sell securities, hold them for safekeeping, offer margin loans, facilitate short sales, and that is all. The only information they provide about the securities they handle is price quotations. Discount brokerage services have become increasingly available in recent years. Many banks, thrift institutions, and mutual fund management companies now offer such services to the investing public as part of a general trend toward the creation of one-stop "financial supermarkets." Stock trading fees have fallen steadily over the last decade, and discount brokerage firms such as Schwab, E*Trade, or Ameritrade now offer commissions below $10.

In addition to the explicit part of trading costs—the broker's commission—there is an implicit part—the dealer's bid–ask spread. Sometimes the broker is a dealer in the security being traded and charges no commission but instead collects the fee entirely in the form of the bid–ask spread. Another implicit cost of trading that some observers would distinguish is the price concession an investor may be forced to make for trading in quantities greater than those associated with the posted bid or asked prices.

3.8   BUYING ON MARGIN

When purchasing securities, investors have easy access to a source of debt financing called *broker's call loans*. The act of taking advantage of broker's call loans is called *buying on margin*.

Purchasing stocks on margin means the investor borrows part of the purchase price of the stock from a broker. The **margin** in the account is the portion of the purchase price contributed by the investor; the remainder is borrowed from the broker. The brokers in turn borrow money from banks at the call money rate to finance these purchases; they then charge their clients that rate (defined in Chapter 2), plus a service charge for the loan. All securities purchased on margin must be maintained with the brokerage firm in street name, for the securities are collateral for the loan.

The Board of Governors of the Federal Reserve System limits the extent to which stock purchases can be financed using margin loans. The current initial margin requirement is 50%, meaning that at least 50% of the purchase price must be paid for in cash, with the rest borrowed.

margin

Describes securities purchased with money borrowed in part from a broker. The margin is the net worth of the investor's account.

EXAMPLE 3.1

Margin

The percentage margin is defined as the ratio of the net worth, or the "equity value," of the account to the market value of the securities. To demonstrate, suppose an investor initially pays $6,000 toward the purchase of $10,000 worth of stock (100 shares at $100 per share), borrowing the remaining $4,000 from a broker. The initial balance sheet looks like this:

Assets		Liabilities and Owners' Equity	
Value of stock	$10,000	Loan from broker	$4,000
		Equity	$6,000

The initial percentage margin is

$$\text{Margin} = \frac{\text{Equity in account}}{\text{Value of stock}} = \frac{\$6,000}{\$10,000} = .60, \text{ or } 60\%$$

If the price declines to $70 per share, the account balance becomes:

Assets		Liabilities and Owners' Equity	
Value of stock	$7,000	Loan from broker	$4,000
		Equity	$3,000

The assets in the account fall by the full decrease in the stock value, as does the equity. The percentage margin is now

$$\text{Margin} = \frac{\text{Equity in account}}{\text{Value of stock}} = \frac{\$3,000}{\$7,000} = .43, \text{ or } 43\%$$

If the stock value in Example 3.1 were to fall below $4,000, owners' equity would become negative, meaning the value of the stock is no longer sufficient collateral to cover the loan from the broker. To guard against this possibility, the broker sets a *maintenance margin*. If the percentage margin falls below the maintenance level, the broker will issue a *margin call,* which requires the investor to add new cash or securities to the margin account. If the investor does not act, the broker may sell securities from the account to pay off enough of the loan to restore the percentage margin to an acceptable level.

EXAMPLE 3.2

Maintenance Margin

Suppose the maintenance margin is 30%. How far could the stock price fall before the investor would get a margin call?

Let P be the price of the stock. The value of the investor's 100 shares is then $100P$, and the equity in the account is $100P - \$4,000$. The percentage margin is $(100P - \$4,000)/100P$. The price at which the percentage margin equals the maintenance margin of .3 is found by solving the equation

(continued)

EXAMPLE 3.2

$$\frac{100P - 4,000}{100P} = .3$$

which implies that $P = \$57.14$. If the price of the stock were to fall below $57.14 per share, the investor would get a margin call.

Maintenance Margin (concluded)

Suppose the maintenance margin in Example 3.2 is 40%. How far can the stock price fall before the investor gets a margin call?

CONCEPT check 3.4

Why do investors buy securities on margin? They do so when they wish to invest an amount greater than their own money allows. Thus, they can achieve greater upside potential, but they also expose themselves to greater downside risk.

To see how, let's suppose an investor is bullish on Fincorp stock, which is selling for $100 per share. An investor with $10,000 to invest expects the share price to rise by 30% during the next year. Ignoring any dividends, the expected rate of return would be 30% if the investor invested $10,000 to buy 100 shares.

But now assume the investor borrows another $10,000 from the broker and invests it in Fincorp, too. The total investment would be $20,000 (for 200 shares). Assuming an interest rate on the margin loan of 9% per year, what will the investor's rate of return be now (again ignoring dividends) if the stock goes up 30% by year's end?

The 200 shares will be worth $26,000. Paying off $10,900 of principal and interest on the margin loan leaves $15,100 (i.e., $26,000 − $10,900). The rate of return in this case will be

$$\frac{\$15,100 - \$10,000}{\$10,000} = 51\%$$

The investor has parlayed a 30% rise in the stock's price into a 51% rate of return on the $10,000 investment.

Doing so, however, magnifies the downside risk. Suppose that, instead of going up by 30%, the stock price drops by 30% to $70 per share. In that case, the 200 shares will be worth $14,000, and the investor is left with $3,100 after paying off the $10,900 of principal and interest on the loan. The result is a disastrous return of

$$\frac{\$3,100 - \$10,000}{\$10,000} = -69\%$$

Table 3.1 summarizes the possible results of these hypothetical transactions. If there is no change in the stock price, the investor loses 9%, the cost of the loan.

TABLE 3.1 Illustration of buying stock on margin

Change in Stock Price	End-of-Year Value of Shares	Repayment of Principal and Interest*	Investor's Rate of Return
30% increase	$26,000	$10,900	51%
No change	20,000	10,900	−9
30% decrease	14,000	10,900	−69

*Assuming the investor buys $20,000 worth of stock by borrowing $10,000 at an interest rate of 9% per year.

Buying on Margin

The Excel spreadsheet model below makes it easy to analyze the impacts of different margin levels and the volatility of stock prices. It also allows you to compare return on investment for a margin trade with a trade using no borrowed funds.

	A	B	C	D	E	F	G	H
1								
2			Action or Formula	Ending	Return on		Ending	Return with
3			for Column B	St Price	Investment		St Price	No Margin
4	Initial Equity Investment	$10,000.00	Enter data		−42.00%			−19.00%
5	Amount Borrowed	$10,000.00	(B4/B10)−B4	$20.00	−122.00%		$20.00	−59.00%
6	Initial Stock Price	$50.00	Enter data	25.00	−102.00%		25.00	−49.00%
7	Shares Purchased	400	(B4/B10)/B6	30.00	−82.00%		30.00	−39.00%
8	Ending Stock Price	$40.00	Enter data	35.00	−62.00%		35.00	−29.00%
9	Cash Dividends During Hold Per.	$0.50	Enter data	40.00	−42.00%		40.00	−19.00%
10	Initial Margin Percentage	50.00%	Enter data	45.00	−22.00%		45.00	−9.00%
11	Maintenance Margin Percentage	30.00%	Enter data	50.00	−2.00%		50.00	1.00%
12				55.00	18.00%		55.00	11.00%
13	Rate on Margin Loan	8.00%	Enter data	60.00	38.00%		60.00	21.00%
14	Holding Period in Months	6	Enter data	65.00	58.00%		65.00	31.00%
15				70.00	78.00%		70.00	41.00%
16	**Return on Investment**			75.00	98.00%		75.00	51.00%
17	Capital Gain on Stock	−$4,000.00	B7*(B8−B6)	80.00	118.00%		80.00	61.00%
18	Dividends	$200.00	B7*B9					
19	Interest on Margin Loan	$400.00	B5*(B14/12)*B13					
20	Net Income	−$4,200.00	B17+B18−B19			LEGEND:		
21	Initial Investment	$10,000.00	B4			Enter data		
22	Return on Investment	−42.00%	B20/B21			Value calculated		

Excel Questions

1. Suppose you buy 100 shares of stock initially selling for $50, borrowing 25% of the necessary funds from your broker; that is, the initial margin on your purchase is 25%. You pay an interest rate of 8% on margin loans.
   a. How much of your own money do you invest? How much do you borrow from your broker?
   b. What will be your rate of return for the following stock prices at the end of a one-year holding period? (i) $40, (ii) $50, (iii) $60.

2. Repeat Question 1 assuming your initial margin was 50%. How does margin affect the risk and return of your position?

CONCEPT check   3.5

Suppose that in the Fincorp example above, the investor borrows only $5,000 at the same interest rate of 9% per year. What will the rate of return be if the stock price goes up by 30%? If it goes down by 30%? If it remains unchanged?

3.9 SHORT SALES

Normally, an investor would first buy a stock and later sell it. With a short sale, the order is reversed. First, you sell and then you buy the shares. In both cases, you begin and end with no shares.

short sale

The sale of shares not owned by the investor but borrowed through a broker and later purchased to replace the loan.

A **short sale** allows investors to profit from a decline in a security's price. An investor borrows a share of stock from a broker and sells it. Later, the short-seller must purchase a share of the same stock in order to replace the share that was borrowed.[2] This is called *covering the short position.* Table 3.2 compares stock purchases to short sales.

[2] *Naked short-selling* is a variant on conventional short-selling. In a naked short, a trader sells shares that have not yet been borrowed, assuming that the shares can be acquired and delivered whenever the short sale needs to be closed out.

This Excel spreadsheet model was built using Example 3.3 for Dot Bomb. The model allows you to analyze the effects of returns, margin calls, and different levels of initial and maintenance margins. The model also includes a sensitivity analysis for ending stock price and return on investment.

This spreadsheet is available in Connect

	A	B	C	D	E
1					
2			Action or Formula	Ending	Return on
3			for Column B	St Price	Investment
4	Initial Investment	$50,000.00	Enter data		60.00%
5	Initial Stock Price	$100.00	Enter data	$170.00	−140.00%
6	Number of Shares Sold Short	1,000	(B4/B9)/B5	160.00	−120.00%
7	Ending Stock Price	$70.00	Enter data	150.00	−100.00%
8	Cash Dividends Per Share	$0.00	Enter data	140.00	−80.00%
9	Initial Margin Percentage	50.00%	Enter data	130.00	−60.00%
10	Maintenance Margin Percentage	30.00%	Enter data	120.00	−40.00%
11				110.00	−20.00%
12	**Return on Short Sale**			100.00	0.00%
13	Capital Gain on Stock	$30,000.00	B6*(B5−B7)	90.00	20.00%
14	Dividends Paid	$0.00	B8*B6	80.00	40.00%
15	Net Income	$30,000.00	B13−B14	70.00	60.00%
16	Initial Investment	$50,000.00	B4	60.00	80.00%
17	Return on Investment	60.00%	B15/B16	50.00	100.00%
18				40.00	120.00%
19	**Margin Positions**			30.00	140.00%
20	Margin Based on Ending Price	114.29%	(B4+(B5*B6)−B14−(B6*B7))/(B6*B7)	20.00	160.00%
21				10.00	180.00%
22	Price for Margin Call	$115.38	(B4+(B5*B6)−B14)/(B6*(1+B10))		
23				LEGEND:	
24				Enter data	
25				Value calculated	

Excel Questions

1. Suppose you sell short 100 shares of stock initially selling for $100 a share. Your initial margin requirement is 50% of the value of the stock sold. You receive no interest on the funds placed in your margin account.
   a. How much do you need to contribute to your margin account?
   b. What will be your rate of return for the following stock prices at the end of a one-year holding period (assume the stock pays no dividends)? (i) $90; (ii) $100; (iii) $110.

2. Repeat Question 1 (*b*) but now assume that the stock pays dividends of $2 per share at year-end. What is the relationship between the total rate of return on the stock and the return to your short position?

TABLE 3.2	Cash flows from purchasing versus short-selling shares of stock

Purchase of Stock

Time	Action	Cash Flow*
0	Buy share	−Initial price
1	Receive dividend, sell share	Ending price + Dividend

Profit = (Ending price + Dividend) − Initial price

Short Sale of Stock

Time	Action	Cash Flow*
0	Borrow share; sell it	+Initial price
1	Repay dividend and buy share to replace the share originally borrowed	−(Ending price + Dividend)

Profit = Initial price − (Ending price + Dividend)

*Note: A negative cash flow implies a cash *outflow*.

The short-seller anticipates the stock price will fall, so that the share can be purchased later at a lower price than it initially sold for; if so, the short-seller will reap a profit. Short-sellers must not only replace the shares but also pay the lender of the security any dividends paid during the short sale.

In practice, the shares loaned out for a short sale are typically provided by the short-seller's brokerage firm, which holds a wide variety of securities of its other investors in street name (i.e., the broker holds the shares registered in its own name on behalf of the client). The owner of the shares need not know that the shares have been lent to the short-seller. If the owner wishes to sell the shares, the brokerage firm will simply borrow shares from another investor. Therefore, the short sale may have an indefinite term. However, if the brokerage firm cannot locate new shares to replace the ones sold, the short-seller will need to repay the loan immediately by purchasing shares in the market and turning them over to the brokerage house to close out the loan.

Finally, exchange rules require that proceeds from a short sale must be kept on account with the broker. The short-seller cannot invest these funds to generate income, although large or institutional investors typically will receive some income from the proceeds of a short sale being held with the broker. Short-sellers also are required to post margin (cash or collateral) with the broker to cover losses should the stock price rise during the short sale.

EXAMPLE 3.3

Short Sales

To illustrate the mechanics of short-selling, suppose you are bearish (pessimistic) on Dot Bomb stock, and its market price is $100 per share. You tell your broker to sell short 1,000 shares. The broker borrows 1,000 shares either from another customer's account or from another broker.

The $100,000 cash proceeds from the short sale are credited to your account. Suppose the broker has a 50% margin requirement on short sales. This means you must have other cash or securities in your account worth at least $50,000 that can serve as margin on the short sale.

Let's say that you have $50,000 in Treasury bills. Your account with the broker after the short sale will then be:

Assets		Liabilities and Owners' Equity	
Cash	$100,000	Short position in Dot Bomb stock (1,000 shares owed)	$100,000
T-bills	50,000	Equity	50,000

Your initial percentage margin is the ratio of the equity in the account, $50,000, to the current value of the shares you have borrowed and eventually must return, $100,000:

$$\text{Percentage margin} = \frac{\text{Equity}}{\text{Value of stock owed}} = \frac{\$50,000}{\$100,000} = .50$$

Suppose you are right and Dot Bomb falls to $70 per share. You can now close out your position at a profit. To cover the short sale, you buy 1,000 shares to replace the ones you borrowed. Because the shares now sell for $70, the purchase costs only $70,000.[3] Because your account was credited for $100,000 when the shares were borrowed and sold, your profit is $30,000: The profit equals the decline in the share price times the number of shares sold short.

Like investors who purchase stock on margin, a short-seller must be concerned about margin calls. If the stock price rises, the margin in the account will fall; if margin falls to the maintenance level, the short-seller will receive a margin call.

---

[3]Notice that when buying on margin, you borrow a given amount of dollars from your broker, so the amount of the loan is independent of the share price. In contrast, when short-selling, you borrow a given number of *shares*, which must be returned. Therefore, when the price of the shares changes, the value of the loan also changes.

EXAMPLE 3.4

*Margin Calls on Short
Positions*

Suppose the broker has a maintenance margin of 30% on short sales. This means the equity in your account must be at least 30% of the value of your short position at all times. How much can the price of Dot Bomb stock rise before you get a margin call?

Let P be the price of Dot Bomb stock. Then the value of the shares you must pay back is $1,000P$, and the equity in your account is $\$150,000 - 1,000P$. Your short position margin ratio is equity/value of stock $= (150,000 - 1,000P)/1,000P$. The critical value of P is thus

$$\frac{\text{Equity}}{\text{Value of shares owed}} = \frac{150,000 - 1,000P}{1,000P} = .3$$

which implies that $P = \$115.38$ per share. If Dot Bomb stock should *rise* above $\$115.38$ per share, you will get a margin call, and you will either have to put up additional cash or cover your short position by buying shares to replace the ones borrowed.

a. Construct the balance sheet if Dot Bomb goes up to $110.
b. If the short position maintenance margin in Example 3.4 is 40%, how far can the stock price rise before the investor gets a margin call?

You can see now why stop-buy orders often accompany short sales. Imagine that you short-sell Dot Bomb when it is selling at $100 per share. If the share price falls, you will profit from the short sale. On the other hand, if the share price rises, let's say to $130, you will lose $30 per share. But suppose that when you initiate the short sale, you also enter a stop-buy order at $120. The stop-buy will be executed if the share price surpasses $120, thereby limiting your losses to $20 per share. (If the stock price drops, the stop-buy will never be executed.) The stop-buy order thus provides protection to the short-seller if the share price moves up.

Short-selling periodically comes under attack, particularly during times of financial stress when share prices fall. The last few years have been no exception to this rule, and the nearby box examines the controversy surrounding short sales in greater detail.

3.10 REGULATION OF SECURITIES MARKETS

Trading in securities markets in the United States is regulated by a myriad of laws. The major governing legislation includes the Securities Act of 1933 and the Securities Exchange Act of 1934. The 1933 act requires full disclosure of relevant information relating to the issue of new securities. This is the act that requires registration of new securities and issuance of a prospectus that details the financial prospects of the firm. SEC approval of a prospectus or financial report is not an endorsement of the security as a good investment. The SEC cares only that the relevant facts are disclosed; investors must make their own evaluation of the security's value.

The 1934 act established the Securities and Exchange Commission to administer the provisions of the 1933 act. It also extended the disclosure principle of the 1933 act by requiring periodic disclosure of relevant financial information by firms with already-issued securities on secondary exchanges.

The 1934 act also empowers the SEC to register and regulate securities exchanges, OTC trading, brokers, and dealers. While the SEC is the administrative agency responsible for broad oversight of the securities markets, it shares responsibility with other regulatory agencies. The Commodity Futures Trading Commission (CFTC) regulates trading in futures markets, while the Federal Reserve has broad responsibility for the health of the U.S. financial system. In this role, the Fed sets margin requirements on stocks and stock options and regulates bank lending to securities markets participants.

The Securities Investor Protection Act of 1970 established the Securities Investor Protection Corporation (SIPC) to protect investors from losses if their brokerage firms fail. Just as the Federal Deposit Insurance Corporation provides depositors with federal protection against

SHORT-SELLING COMES UNDER FIRE—AGAIN

Short-selling has long been viewed with suspicion, if not outright hostility. England banned short sales for a good part of the eighteenth century. Napoleon called short-sellers enemies of the state. In the U.S., short-selling was widely viewed as contributing to the market crash of 1929, and in 2008, short-sellers were blamed for the collapse of the investment banks Bear Stearns and Lehman Brothers. With share prices of other financial firms tumbling in September 2008, the SEC instituted a temporary ban on short-selling for about 800 of those firms. Similarly, the Financial Services Authority, the financial regulator in the U.K., prohibited short sales on about 30 financial companies, and Australia banned shorting altogether.

The motivation for these bans is that short sales put downward pressure on share prices that in some cases may be unwarranted: Stories abound of investors who first put on a short sale and then spread negative rumors about the firm to drive down its price. More often, however, shorting is an innocent bet that a share price is too high and is due to fall. Nevertheless, during the market stresses of late 2008, the widespread feeling was that even if short positions were legitimate, regulators should do what they could to prop up the affected institutions.

Hostility to short-selling may well stem from confusion between bad news and the bearer of that news. Short-selling allows investors whose analysis indicates a firm is overpriced to take action on that belief—and to profit if they are correct. Rather than *causing* the stock price to fall, shorts may simply be *anticipating* a decline in the stock price. Their sales simply force the market to reflect the deteriorating prospects of troubled firms sooner than it might have otherwise. In other words, short-selling is part of the process by which the full range of information and opinion—pessimistic as well as optimistic—is brought to bear on stock prices.

For example, short-sellers took large (negative) positions in firms such as WorldCom, Enron, and Tyco even before these firms were exposed by regulators. In fact, one might argue that these emerging short positions helped regulators identify the previously undetected scandals. And in the end, Lehman and Bear Stearns were brought down by their very real losses on their mortgage-related investments—not by unfounded rumors.

Academic research supports the conjecture that short sales contribute to efficient "price discovery." For example, the greater the demand for shorting a stock, the lower its future returns tend to be; moreover, firms that attack short-sellers with threats of legal action or bad publicity tend to have especially poor future returns.[4] Short-sale bans may in the end be nothing more than an understandable, but nevertheless misguided, impulse to "shoot the messenger."

---

bank failure, the SIPC ensures that investors will receive securities held for their account in street name by a failed brokerage firm up to a limit of $500,000 per customer. The SIPC is financed by levying an "insurance premium" on its participating, or member, brokerage firms.

Security trading is also subject to state laws, known generally as *blue sky laws* because they are intended to give investors a clearer view of investment prospects. State laws to outlaw fraud in security sales existed before the Securities Act of 1933. Varying state laws were somewhat unified when many states adopted portions of the Uniform Securities Act, which was enacted in 1956.

Self-Regulation

In addition to government regulation, there is considerable self-regulation of the securities market. The most important overseer in this regard is the Financial Industry Regulatory Authority (FINRA), which is the largest nongovernmental regulator of all securities firms in the United States. FINRA was formed in 2007 through the consolidation of the National Association of Securities Dealers (NASD) with the self-regulatory arm of the New York Stock Exchange. It describes its broad mission as the fostering of investor protection and market integrity. It examines securities firms, writes and enforces rules concerning trading practices, and administers a dispute resolution forum for investors and registered firms.

There is also self-regulation among the community of investment professionals. For example, the CFA Institute has developed standards of professional conduct that govern the behavior of members with the Chartered Financial Analysts designation, commonly referred to as CFAs. The nearby box presents a brief outline of those principles.

---

[4]See, for example, C. Jones and O. A. Lamont, "Short Sale Constraints and Stock Returns," *Journal of Financial Economics,* November 2002, pp. 207–239, or O. A. Lamont, "Go Down Fighting: Short Sellers vs. Firms," *Review of Asset Pricing Studies* (2), 2012, pp. 1–30.

On the MARKET FRONT

EXCERPTS FROM CFA INSTITUTE STANDARDS OF PROFESSIONAL CONDUCT

I. Professionalism

- Knowledge of law. Members must understand knowledge of and comply with all applicable laws, rules, and regulations including the Code of Ethics and Standards of Professional Conduct.
- Independence and objectivity. Members shall maintain independence and objectivity in their professional activities.
- Misrepresentation. Members must not knowingly misrepresent investment analysis, recommendations, or other professional activities.

II. Integrity of Capital Markets

- Non-public information. Members must not exploit material non-public information.
- Market manipulation. Members shall not attempt to distort prices or trading volume with the intent to mislead market participants.

III. Duties to Clients

- Loyalty, prudence, and care. Members must place their clients' interests before their own and act with reasonable care on their behalf.
- Fair dealing. Members shall deal fairly and objectively with clients when making investment recommendations or taking actions.
- Suitability. Members shall make a reasonable inquiry into a client's financial situation, investment experience, and investment objectives prior to making appropriate investment recommendations.
- Performance presentation. Members shall attempt to ensure that investment performance is presented fairly, accurately, and completely.

- Confidentiality. Members must keep information about clients confidential unless the client permits disclosure.

IV. Duties to Employers

- Loyalty. Members must act for the benefit of their employer.
- Compensation. Members must not accept compensation from sources that would create a conflict of interest with their employer's interests without written consent from all involved parties.
- Supervisors. Members must make reasonable efforts to detect and prevent violation of applicable laws and regulations by anyone subject to their supervision.

V. Investment Analysis and Recommendations

- Diligence. Members must exercise diligence and have reasonable basis for investment analysis, recommendations, or actions.
- Communication. Members must distinguish fact from opinion in their presentation of analysis and disclose general principles of investment processes used in analysis.

VI. Conflicts of Interest

- Disclosure of conflicts. Members must disclose all matters that reasonably could be expected to impair their objectivity or interfere with their other duties.
- Priority of transactions. Transactions for clients and employers must have priority over transactions for the benefit of a member.

VII. Responsibilities as Member of CFA Institute

- Conduct. Members must not engage in conduct that compromises the reputation or integrity of the CFA Institute or CFA designation.

SOURCE: Excerpts from "Code of Ethics and Standards of Professional Conduct," *Standards of Practice Handbook*, 10th Ed. © 2010, CFA Institute.

The Sarbanes-Oxley Act

The scandals of 2000–2002 centered largely on three broad practices: allocations of shares in initial public offerings, tainted securities research and recommendations put out to the public, and, probably most important, misleading financial statements and accounting practices. The Sarbanes-Oxley Act, often called SOX, was passed by Congress in 2002 in response to these problems. Among the key reforms are:

- Creation of the Public Company Accounting Oversight Board to oversee the auditing of public companies.
- Rules requiring independent financial experts to serve on audit committees of a firm's board of directors.
- CEOs and CFOs must now personally certify that their firms' financial reports "fairly represent, in all material respects, the operations and financial condition of the company," and are subject to personal penalties if those reports turn out to be misleading. Following the letter of GAAP rules may still be necessary, but it is no longer sufficient accounting practice.
- Auditors may no longer provide several other services to their clients. This is intended to prevent potential profits on consulting work from influencing the quality of their audit.
- The board of directors must be composed of independent directors and hold regular meetings of directors in which company management is not present (and therefore cannot impede or influence the discussion).

More recently, there has been a fair amount of push-back on Sarbanes-Oxley. Many observers believe that the compliance costs associated with the law are too onerous, especially for smaller firms, and that heavy-handed regulatory oversight is giving foreign locales an undue advantage over the United States when firms decide where to list their securities. Moreover, the efficacy of single-country regulation is being tested in the face of increasing globalization and the ease with which funds can move across national borders.

One of the most contentious issues in regulation has to do with "rules" versus "principles." Rules-based regulation attempts to lay out specifically what practices are or are not allowed. This has generally been the American approach, particularly at the SEC. In contrast, principles-based regulation relies on a less explicitly defined set of understandings about risk taking, the goals of regulation, and the sorts of financial practices considered allowable. This has been the dominant approach in the U.K. and seems to be the more popular model for regulators throughout the world.

Insider Trading

inside information

Nonpublic knowledge about a corporation possessed by corporate officers, major owners, or other individuals with privileged access to information about the firm.

Regulations also prohibit insider trading. It is illegal for anyone to transact in securities to profit from **inside information,** that is, private information held by officers, directors, or major stockholders that has not yet been divulged to the public. But the definition of insiders can be ambiguous. While it is obvious that the chief financial officer of a firm is an insider, it is less clear whether the firm's biggest supplier can be considered an insider. Yet a supplier may deduce the firm's near-term prospects from significant changes in orders. This gives the supplier a unique form of private information, yet the supplier is not technically an insider. These ambiguities plague security analysts, whose job is to uncover as much information as possible concerning the firm's expected prospects. The distinction between legal private information and illegal inside information can be fuzzy. (We return to this issue in Chapter 12.)

The SEC requires officers, directors, and major stockholders to report all transactions in their firm's stock. A compendium of insider trades is published monthly in the SEC's *Official Summary of Securities Transactions and Holdings.* The idea is to inform the public of any implicit vote of confidence or no confidence made by insiders.

Insiders *do* exploit their knowledge. Three forms of evidence support this conclusion. First, there have been well-publicized convictions of principals in insider trading schemes.

Second, there is considerable evidence of "leakage" of useful information to some traders before any public announcement of that information. For example, share prices of firms announcing dividend increases (which the market interprets as good news concerning the firm's prospects) commonly increase in value a few days *before* the public announcement of the increase. Clearly, some investors are acting on the good news before it is released to the public. Share prices still rise substantially on the day of the public release of good news, however, indicating that insiders, or their associates, have not fully bid up the price of the stock to the level commensurate with the news.

A third form of evidence on insider trading has to do with returns earned on trades by insiders. Researchers have examined the SEC's summary of insider trading to measure the performance of insiders. In one of the best known of these studies, Jaffe (1974) examined the abnormal return of stocks over the months following purchases or sales by insiders. For months in which insider purchasers of a stock exceeded insider sellers of the stock by three or more, the stock had an abnormal return in the following eight months of about 5%. Moreover, when insider sellers exceeded insider buyers, the stock tended to perform poorly.

SUMMARY

- Firms issue securities to raise the capital necessary to finance their investments. Investment bankers market these securities to the public on the primary market. Investment bankers generally act as underwriters who purchase the securities from the firm and resell them to the public at a markup. Before the securities may be sold to the public, the firm must publish an SEC-approved prospectus that provides information on the firm's prospects.
- Already-issued securities are traded on the secondary market, that is, in organized stock markets, or, primarily for bonds, on the over-the-counter market. Brokerage firms holding

licenses to trade on an exchange sell their services to individuals, charging commissions for executing trades on their behalf.

- Trading may take place in dealer markets, via electronic communication networks, or in specialist markets. In dealer markets, security dealers post bid and ask prices at which they are willing to trade. Brokers for individuals execute trades at the best available prices. In electronic markets, the existing book of limit orders provides the terms at which trades can be executed. Mutually agreeable offers to buy or sell securities are automatically crossed by the computer system operating the market. In specialist markets, the specialist acts to maintain an orderly market with price continuity. Specialists maintain a limit order book but also sell from or buy for their own inventories of stock.

- NASDAQ was traditionally a dealer market in which a network of dealers negotiated directly over sales of securities. The NYSE was traditionally a specialist market. In recent years, however, both exchanges dramatically increased their commitment to electronic and automated trading. The overwhelming majority of trades today are electronic.

- Buying on margin means borrowing money from a broker in order to buy more securities than can be purchased with one's own money alone. By buying securities on a margin, an investor magnifies both the upside potential and the downside risk. If the equity in a margin account falls below the required maintenance level, the investor will get a margin call from the broker.

- Short-selling is the practice of selling securities that the seller does not own. The short-seller borrows the securities sold through a broker and may be required to cover the short position at any time on demand. The cash proceeds of a short sale are kept in escrow by the broker, and the broker usually requires that the short-seller deposit additional cash or securities to serve as margin (collateral) for the short sale.

- Securities trading is regulated by the Securities and Exchange Commission, by other government agencies, and through self-regulation of the exchanges. Many of the important regulations have to do with full disclosure of relevant information concerning the securities in question. Insider trading rules also prohibit traders from attempting to profit from inside information.

KEY TERMS

algorithmic trading, 66
ask price, 59
auction market, 59
bid–ask spread, 59
bid price, 59
blocks, 67
dark pools, 67
dealer markets, 58
electronic communication networks (ECNs), 62
high-frequency trading, 66
initial public offering (IPO), 56
inside information, 78
latency, 65
limit buy (sell) order, 59
margin, 70
NASDAQ Stock Market, 62
over-the-counter (OTC) market, 61
primary market, 55
private placement, 55
prospectus, 56
secondary market, 55
short sale, 72
specialist, 62
stock exchanges, 65
stop order, 60
underwriters, 56

PROBLEM SETS

Select problems are available in McGraw-Hill's *Connect*. Please see the Supplements section of the book's frontmatter for more information.

1. What is the difference between an IPO (initial public offering) and an SEO (seasoned equity offering)? *(LO 3-1)*
2. What are some different components of the effective costs of buying or selling shares of stock? *(LO 3-3)*

3. What is the difference between a primary and secondary market?   *(LO 3-3)*

4. How do security dealers earn their profits?   *(LO 3-3)*

5. In what circumstances are private placements more likely to be used than public offerings?   *(LO 3-1)*

6. What are the differences between a stop-loss order, a limit sell order, and a market order?   *(LO 3-3)*

7. Why have average trade sizes declined in recent years?   *(LO 3-3)*

8. What is the role of an underwriter? A prospectus?   *(LO 3-1)*

9. How do margin trades magnify both the upside potential and downside risk of an investment portfolio?   *(LO 3-4)*

10. A market order has: *(LO 3-2)*
    a. Price uncertainty but not execution uncertainty.
    b. Both price uncertainty and execution uncertainty.
    c. Execution uncertainty but not price uncertainty.

11. Where would an illiquid security in a developing country *most likely* trade?   *(LO 3-3)*
    a. Broker markets.
    b. Electronic crossing networks.
    c. Electronic limit-order markets.

12. Suppose you short-sell 100 shares of IBX, now selling at $200 per share.   *(LO 3-4)*
    a. What is your maximum possible loss?
    b. What happens to the maximum loss if you simultaneously place a stop-buy order at $210?

13. Call one full-service broker and one discount broker and find out the transaction costs of implementing the following strategies: *(LO 3-3)*
    a. Buying 100 shares of IBM now and selling them six months from now.
    b. Investing an equivalent amount in six-month at-the-money call options on IBM stock now and selling them six months from now.

14. DRK, Inc., has just sold 100,000 shares in an initial public offering. The underwriter's explicit fees were $60,000. The offering price for the shares was $40, but immediately upon issue, the share price jumped to $44.   *(LO 3-1)*
    a. What is your best guess as to the total cost to DRK of the equity issue?
    b. Is the entire cost of the underwriting a source of profit to the underwriters?

15. Dée Trader opens a brokerage account and purchases 300 shares of Internet Dreams at $40 per share. She borrows $4,000 from her broker to help pay for the purchase. The interest rate on the loan is 8%.   *(LO 3-4)*
    a. What is the margin in Dée's account when she first purchases the stock?
    b. If the share price falls to $30 per share by the end of the year, what is the remaining margin in her account? If the maintenance margin requirement is 30%, will she receive a margin call?
    c. What is the rate of return on her investment?

16. Old Economy Traders opened an account to short-sell 1,000 shares of Internet Dreams from the previous question. The initial margin requirement was 50%. (The margin account pays no interest.) A year later, the price of Internet Dreams has risen from $40 to $50, and the stock has paid a dividend of $2 per share.   *(LO 3-4)*
    a. What is the remaining margin in the account?
    b. If the maintenance margin requirement is 30%, will Old Economy receive a margin call?
    c. What is the rate of return on the investment?

17. Consider the following limit order book for a share of stock. The last trade in the stock occurred at a price of $50.   *(LO 3-3)*

Limit Buy Orders		Limit Sell Orders	
Price	Shares	Price	Shares
$49.75	500	$50.25	100
49.50	800	51.50	100
49.25	500	54.75	300
49.00	200	58.25	100
48.50	600		

a. If a market buy order for 100 shares comes in, at what price will it be filled?

b. At what price would the next market buy order be filled?

c. If you were a security dealer, would you want to increase or decrease your inventory of this stock?

18. You are bullish on Telecom stock. The current market price is $50 per share, and you have $5,000 of your own to invest. You borrow an additional $5,000 from your broker at an interest rate of 8% per year and invest $10,000 in the stock. *(LO 3-4)*

a. What will be your rate of return if the price of Telecom stock goes up by 10% during the next year? (Ignore the expected dividend.)

b. How far does the price of Telecom stock have to fall for you to get a margin call if the maintenance margin is 30%? Assume the price fall happens immediately.

19. You are bearish on Telecom and decide to sell short 100 shares at the current market price of $50 per share. *(LO 3-4)*

a. How much in cash or securities must you put into your brokerage account if the broker's initial margin requirement is 50% of the value of the short position?

b. How high can the price of the stock go before you get a margin call if the maintenance margin is 30% of the value of the short position?

20. Here is some price information on Marriott:

	Bid	Asked
Marriott	$67.95	$68.05

You have placed a stop-loss order to sell at $68. What are you telling your broker? Given market prices, will your order be executed? *(LO 3-2)*

21. Here is some price information on Fincorp stock. Suppose first that Fincorp trades in a dealer market. *(LO 3-2)*

Bid	Asked
55.25	55.50

a. Suppose you have submitted an order to your broker to buy at market. At what price will your trade be executed?

b. Suppose you have submitted an order to sell at market. At what price will your trade be executed?

c. Suppose you have submitted a limit order to sell at $55.62. What will happen?

d. Suppose you have submitted a limit order to buy at $55.37. What will happen?

22. You've borrowed $20,000 on margin to buy shares in Ixnay, which is now selling at $40 per share. Your account starts at the initial margin requirement of 50%. The maintenance margin is 35%. Two days later, the stock price falls to $35 per share. *(LO 3-4)*

a. Will you receive a margin call?

b. How low can the price of Ixnay shares fall before you receive a margin call?

23. On January 1, you sold short one round lot (that is, 100 shares) of Snow's stock at $21 per share. On March 1, a dividend of $3 per share was paid. On April 1, you covered the short

✗

Templates and spreadsheets are available in Connect

✗

Templates and spreadsheets are available in Connect

sale by buying the stock at a price of $15 per share. You paid 50 cents per share in commissions for each transaction. What is the value of your account on April 1?   *(LO 3-4)*

Challenge

24. Suppose that XTel currently is selling at $40 per share. You buy 500 shares using $15,000 of your own money, borrowing the remainder of the purchase price from your broker. The rate on the margin loan is 8%.   *(LO 3-4)*
    a. What is the percentage increase in the net worth of your brokerage account if the price of XTel *immediately* changes to (i) $44; (ii) $40; (iii) $36? What is the relationship between your percentage return and the percentage change in the price of XTel?
    b. If the maintenance margin is 25%, how low can XTel's price fall before you get a margin call?
    c. How would your answer to (*b*) change if you had financed the initial purchase with only $10,000 of your own money?
    d. What is the rate of return on your margined position (assuming again that you invest $15,000 of your own money) if XTel is selling *after one year* at (i) $44; (ii) $40; (iii) $36? What is the relationship between your percentage return and the percentage change in the price of XTel? Assume that XTel pays no dividends.
    e. Continue to assume that a year has passed. How low can XTel's price fall before you get a margin call?

25. Suppose that you sell short 500 shares of XTel, currently selling for $40 per share, and give your broker $15,000 to establish your margin account.   *(LO 3-4)*
    a. If you earn no interest on the funds in your margin account, what will be your rate of return after one year if XTel stock is selling at (i) $44; (ii) $40; (iii) $36? Assume that XTel pays no dividends.
    b. If the maintenance margin is 25%, how high can XTel's price rise before you get a margin call?
    c. Redo parts (*a*) and (*b*), but now assume that XTel also has paid a year-end dividend of $1 per share. The prices in part (*a*) should be interpreted as ex-dividend, that is, prices after the dividend has been paid.

CFA Problems

1. If you place a stop-loss order to sell 100 shares of stock at $55 when the current price is $62, how much will you receive for each share if the price drops to $50?   *(LO 3-2)*
   a. $50
   b. $55
   c. $54.87
   d. Cannot tell from the information given
2. Specialists on the New York Stock Exchange traditionally did all of the following *except:*   *(LO 3-3)*
   a. Act as dealers for their own accounts.
   b. Execute limit orders.
   c. Help provide liquidity to the marketplace.
   d. Act as odd-lot dealers.

WEB *master*

Several factors must be considered when selecting a brokerage firm. There are also a wide range of services that claim to objectively evaluate these firms. However, many are actually sponsored by the brokerage firms themselves.

Go to the website **www.consumersearch.com/online-brokers/reviews** and read the information provided under "Ratings of Sources." Do a search for Barron's best online brokers survey. There you can find general information as well as details on offerings, costs, and so on. Suppose that you have $3,000 to invest and want to put it in a non-IRA account.

1. Are all of the brokerage firms suitable if you want to open a cash account? Are they all suitable if you want a margin account?

2. Choose two of the firms listed. Assume that you want to buy 200 shares of LLY stock using a market order. If the order is filled at $42 per share, how much will the commission be for the two firms if you place an online order?

3. Are there any maintenance fees associated with the account at either brokerage firm?

4. Now assume that you have a margin account and the balance is $3,000. Calculate the interest rate you would pay if you borrowed money to buy stock.

3.1 Limited-time shelf registration was introduced because of its favorable trade-off of saving issue costs versus providing disclosure. Allowing unlimited shelf registration would circumvent "blue sky" laws that ensure proper disclosure as the financial circumstances of the firm change over time.

3.2 *a.* Used cars trade in dealer markets (used-car lots or auto dealerships) and in direct search markets when individuals advertise in local newspapers or on websites.

   b. Paintings trade in broker markets when clients commission brokers to buy or sell art for them, in dealer markets at art galleries, and in auction markets.

   c. Rare coins trade in dealer markets, for example, in coin shops or shows, but they also trade in auctions and in direct search markets when individuals advertise they want to buy or sell coins.

3.3 *a.* You should give your broker a market order. It will be executed immediately and is the cheapest type of order in terms of brokerage fees.

   b. You should give your broker a limit buy order, which will be executed only if the shares can be obtained at a price about 5% below the current price.

   c. You should give your broker a stop-loss order, which will be executed if the share price starts falling. The limit or stop price should be close to the current price to avoid the possibility of large losses.

3.4 Solving

$$\frac{100P - \$4,000}{100P} = .4$$

yields $P = \$66.67$ per share.

3.5 The investor will purchase 150 shares, with a rate of return as follows:

Year-End Change in Price	Year-End Value of Shares	Repayment of Principal and Interest	Investor's Rate of Return
30%	$19,500	$5,450	40.5%
No change	15,000	5,450	−4.5
−30%	10,500	5,450	−49.5

3.6 *a.* Once Dot Bomb stock goes up to $110, your balance sheet will be:

Assets		Liabilities and Owners' Equity	
Cash	$100,000	Short position in Dot Bomb	$110,000
T-bills	50,000	Equity	40,000

   b. Solving

$$\frac{\$150,000 - 1,000P}{1,000P} = .4$$

yields $P = \$107.14$ per share.

Chapter 4

Mutual Funds and Other Investment Companies

Learning Objectives

LO 4-1 Cite advantages and disadvantages of investing with an investment company rather than buying securities directly.

LO 4-2 Contrast open-end mutual funds with closed-end funds, unit investment trusts, hedge funds, and exchange-traded funds.

LO 4-3 Define *net asset value* and measure the rate of return on a mutual fund.

LO 4-4 Classify mutual funds according to investment style.

LO 4-5 Demonstrate the impact of expenses and turnover on mutual fund investment performance.

C hapter 3 provided an introduction to the mechanics of trading securities and the structure of the markets in which securities trade. Increasingly, however, individual investors are choosing not to trade securities directly for their own accounts. Instead, they direct their funds to investment companies that purchase securities on their behalf. The most important of these financial intermediaries are mutual funds, which are currently owned by about one-half of U.S. households. Other types of investment companies, such as unit investment trusts and closed-end funds, also merit distinction.

We begin the chapter by describing and comparing the various types of investment companies available to investors—unit investment trusts, closed-end investment companies, and open-end investment companies, more commonly known as mutual funds. We devote most of our attention to mutual funds, examining the functions of such funds, their investment styles and policies, and the costs of investing in these funds.

Next, we take a first look at the investment performance of these funds. We consider the impact of expenses and turnover on net performance and examine the extent to which performance is consistent from one period to the next. In other words, will the mutual funds that were the best past performers be the best *future* performers? Finally, we discuss sources of information on mutual funds and consider in detail the information provided in the most comprehensive guide, Morningstar's *Mutual Fund Sourcebook*.

4.1 INVESTMENT COMPANIES

Investment companies are financial intermediaries that collect funds from individual investors and invest those funds in a potentially wide range of securities or other assets. Pooling of assets is the key idea behind investment companies. Each investor has a claim to the portfolio established by the investment company in proportion to the amount invested. These companies thus provide a mechanism for small investors to "team up" to obtain the benefits of large-scale investing.

investment companies
Financial intermediaries that invest the funds of individual investors in securities or other assets.

Investment companies perform several important functions for their investors:

1. *Record keeping and administration.* Investment companies issue periodic status reports, keeping track of capital gains distributions, dividends, investments, and redemptions, and they may reinvest dividend and interest income for shareholders.
2. *Diversification and divisibility.* By pooling their money, investment companies enable investors to hold fractional shares of many different securities. They can act as large investors even if any individual shareholder cannot.
3. *Professional management.* Investment companies can support full-time staffs of security analysts and portfolio managers who attempt to achieve superior investment results for their investors.
4. *Lower transaction costs.* Because they trade large blocks of securities, investment companies can achieve substantial savings on brokerage fees and commissions.

While all investment companies pool the assets of individual investors, they also need to divide claims to those assets among those investors. Investors buy shares in investment companies, and ownership is proportional to the number of shares purchased. The value of each share is called the **net asset value (NAV)**. Net asset value equals assets minus liabilities expressed on a per-share basis:

net asset value (NAV)
Assets minus liabilities expressed on a per-share basis.

$$\text{Net asset value} = \frac{\text{Market value of assets minus liabilities}}{\text{Shares outstanding}}$$

Consider a mutual fund that manages a portfolio of securities worth $120 million. Suppose the fund owes $4 million to its investment advisers and owes another $1 million for rent, wages due, and miscellaneous expenses. The fund has 5 million shares. Then

$$\text{Net asset value} = \frac{\$120 \text{ million} - \$5 \text{ million}}{5 \text{ million shares}} = \$23 \text{ per share}$$

> Consider these data from the September 2013 balance sheet of the Growth and Income mutual fund sponsored by the Vanguard Group. (All values are in millions.) What was the net asset value of the portfolio?
>
> | | |
> |---|---|
> | Assets: | $2,905.1 |
> | Liabilities: | $ 36.1 |
> | Shares: | 79.6 |

CONCEPT check 4.1

4.2 TYPES OF INVESTMENT COMPANIES

In the United States, investment companies are classified by the Investment Company Act of 1940 as either unit investment trusts or managed investment companies. The portfolios of unit investment trusts are essentially fixed and thus are called "unmanaged." In contrast, managed companies are so named because securities in their investment portfolios continually are bought and sold: The portfolios are managed. Managed companies are further classified as either closed-end or open-end. Open-end companies are what we commonly call *mutual funds.*

Unit Investment Trusts

Unit investment trusts are pools of money invested in a portfolio that is fixed for the life of the fund. To form a unit investment trust, a sponsor, typically a brokerage firm, buys a portfolio of securities which are deposited into a trust. It then sells to the public shares, or "units," in the trust, called *redeemable trust certificates.* All income and payments of principal from the portfolio are paid out by the fund's trustees (a bank or trust company) to the shareholders.

There is little active management of a unit investment trust because once established, the portfolio composition is fixed; hence these trusts are referred to as *unmanaged.* Trusts tend to invest in relatively uniform types of assets; for example, one trust may invest in municipal bonds, another in corporate bonds. The uniformity of the portfolio is consistent with the lack of active management. The trusts provide investors a vehicle to purchase a pool of one particular type of asset, which can be included in an overall portfolio as desired. The lack of active management of the portfolio implies that management fees can be lower than those of managed funds.

Sponsors of unit investment trusts earn their profit by selling shares in the trust at a premium to the cost of acquiring the underlying assets. For example, a trust that has purchased $5 million of assets may sell 5,000 shares to the public at a price of $1,030 per share, which (assuming the trust has no liabilities) represents a 3% premium over the net asset value of the securities held by the trust. The 3% premium is the trustee's fee for establishing the trust.

Investors who wish to liquidate their holdings of a unit investment trust may sell the shares back to the trustee for net asset value. The trustees can either sell enough securities from the asset portfolio to obtain the cash necessary to pay the investor, or they may instead sell the shares to a new investor (again at a slight premium to net asset value).

Unit investment trusts have steadily lost market share to mutual funds in recent years. Assets in such trusts declined from $105 billion in 1990 to only $87 billion in 2013.

Managed Investment Companies

There are two types of managed companies: closed-end and open-end. In both cases, the fund's board of directors, which is elected by shareholders, hires a management company to manage the portfolio for an annual fee that typically ranges from .2% to 1.5% of assets. In many cases the management company is the firm that organized the fund. For example, Fidelity Management and Research Corporation sponsors many Fidelity mutual funds and is responsible for managing the portfolios. It assesses a management fee on each Fidelity fund. In other cases, a mutual fund will hire an outside portfolio manager. For example, Vanguard has hired Wellington Management as the investment adviser for its Wellington Fund. Most management companies have contracts to manage several funds.

Open-end funds stand ready to redeem or issue shares at their net asset value (although both purchases and redemptions may involve sales charges). When investors in open-end funds wish to "cash out" their shares, they sell them back to the fund at NAV. In contrast, **closed-end funds** do not redeem or issue shares. Investors in closed-end funds who wish to cash out must sell their shares to other investors. Shares of closed-end funds are traded on organized exchanges and can be purchased through brokers just like other common stock; their prices therefore can differ from NAV.

Figure 4.1 is a listing of closed-end funds from *The Wall Street Journal Online.* The first column gives the fund's name and ticker symbol. The next two columns give the fund's most recent net asset value and closing share price. The premium or discount is the percentage difference between price and NAV: (Price − NAV)/NAV. Notice that there are more funds selling at discounts to NAV (indicated by negative differences) than premiums. Finally, the 52-week return based on the percentage change in share price plus dividend income is presented in the last column.

FUND	NAV	MKT PRICE	PREM/ DISC %	52 WEEK MARKET RETURN %	FUND	NAV	MKT PRICE	PREM/ DISC %	52 WEEK MARKET RETURN %
Central Securities Corp (CET)	27.97	23.12	−17.34	15.42	Gabelli Div & Inc Tr (GDV)	24.03	21.89	−8.91	14.43
Cohen & Steers CE Oppty (FOF)ᵃ	14.89	13.52	−9.20	18.98	Gabelli Equity Trust (GAB)	7.06	6.85	−2.97	10.92
Cornerstone Prog Return (CFP)	4.18	4.31	+2.99	4.99	General Amer Investors (GAM)	44.15	37.78	−14.43	15.35
Cornerstone Strat Value (CLM)	5.38	6.03	+12.08	3.52	Guggenheim Enh Eq Inc (GPM)	9.56	9.24	−3.35	22.08

FIGURE 4.1

Closed-end mutual funds

Source: Compiled from data obtained from *The Wall Street Journal Online*, September 22, 2014.

The common divergence of price from net asset value, often by wide margins, is a puzzle that has yet to be fully explained. To see why this is a puzzle, consider a closed-end fund that is selling at a discount from net asset value. If the fund were to sell all the assets in the portfolio, it would realize proceeds equal to net asset value. The difference between the market price of the fund and the fund's NAV would represent the per-share increase in the wealth of the fund's investors. Despite this apparent profit opportunity, sizable discounts seem to persist for long periods of time.

Moreover, several studies have shown that, on average, fund premiums or discounts tend to dissipate over time, so funds selling at a discount receive a boost to their rate of return as the discount shrinks. Pontiff (1995) estimates that a fund selling at a 20% discount would have an expected 12-month return more than 6% greater than funds selling at net asset value.

Interestingly, while many closed-end funds sell at a discount from net asset value, the prices of these funds when originally issued are often above NAV. This is a further puzzle, as it is hard to explain why investors would purchase these newly issued funds at a premium to NAV when the shares tend to fall to a discount shortly after issue.

In contrast to closed-end funds, the price of open-end funds cannot fall below NAV, because these funds stand ready to redeem shares at NAV. The offering price will exceed NAV, however, if the fund carries a **load.** A load is, in effect, a sales charge. Load funds are sold by securities brokers and directly by mutual fund groups.

load
A sales commission charged on a mutual fund.

Unlike closed-end funds, open-end mutual funds do not trade on organized exchanges. Instead, investors simply buy shares from and liquidate through the investment company at net asset value. Thus, the number of outstanding shares of these funds changes daily. In early 2014, about $280 billion of assets were held in closed-end funds.

Other Investment Organizations

Some intermediaries are not formally organized or regulated as investment companies but nevertheless serve similar functions. Among the more important are commingled funds, real estate investment trusts, and hedge funds.

COMMINGLED FUNDS Commingled funds are partnerships of investors that pool funds. The management firm that organizes the partnership, for example, a bank or insurance company, manages the funds for a fee. Typical partners in a commingled fund might be trust or retirement accounts that have portfolios much larger than those of most individual investors but are still too small to warrant managing on a separate basis.

Commingled funds are similar in form to open-end mutual funds. Instead of shares, though, the fund offers *units,* which are bought and sold at net asset value. A bank or insurance company may offer an array of different commingled funds, for example, a money market fund, a bond fund, and a common stock fund.

REAL ESTATE INVESTMENT TRUSTS (REITs) A REIT is similar to a closed-end fund. REITs invest in real estate or loans secured by real estate. Besides issuing shares, they raise capital by borrowing from banks and issuing bonds or mortgages. Most of them are highly leveraged, with a typical debt ratio of 70%.

There are two principal kinds of REITs. *Equity trusts* invest in real estate directly, whereas *mortgage trusts* invest primarily in mortgage and construction loans. REITs generally are established by banks, insurance companies, or mortgage companies, which then serve as investment managers to earn a fee.

hedge fund

A private investment pool, open to wealthy or institutional investors, that is largely exempt from SEC regulation and can pursue more speculative policies than mutual funds.

HEDGE FUNDS   Like mutual funds, **hedge funds** are vehicles that allow private investors to pool assets to be invested by a fund manager. Unlike mutual funds, however, hedge funds are commonly structured as private partnerships and thus are not subject to many SEC regulations. Typically they are open only to wealthy or institutional investors. Many require investors to agree to initial "lock-ups," that is, periods as long as several years in which investments cannot be withdrawn. Lock-ups allow hedge funds to invest in illiquid assets without worrying about meeting demands for redemption of funds. Moreover, since hedge funds are only lightly regulated, their managers can pursue other investment strategies that are not open to mutual fund managers, for example, heavy use of derivatives, short sales, and leverage.

Hedge funds by design are empowered to invest in a wide range of investments, with various funds focusing on derivatives, distressed firms, currency speculation, convertible bonds, emerging markets, merger arbitrage, and so on. Other funds may jump from one asset class to another as perceived investment opportunities shift.

Hedge funds enjoyed great growth in the last several years, with assets under management ballooning from about $50 billion in 1990 to about $3 trillion in 2015. We devote all of Chapter 20 to these funds.

4.3   MUTUAL FUNDS

Mutual fund is the common name for an open-end investment company. This is the dominant investment company in the U.S. today, accounting for about 88% of investment company assets. Assets under management in the U.S. mutual fund industry were nearly $15 trillion in early 2014. Roughly another $15 trillion was invested in mutual funds of non-U.S. sponsors.

Investment Policies

Each mutual fund has a specified investment policy, which is described in the fund's prospectus. For example, money market mutual funds hold the short-term, low-risk instruments of the money market (see Chapter 2 for a review of these securities), while bond funds hold fixed-income securities. Some funds have even more narrowly defined mandates. For example, some bond funds will hold primarily Treasury bonds, others primarily mortgage-backed securities.

Management companies manage a family, or "complex," of mutual funds. They organize an entire collection of funds and then collect a management fee for operating them. By managing a collection of funds under one umbrella, these companies make it easy for investors to allocate assets across market sectors and to switch assets across funds while still benefiting from centralized record keeping. Some of the most well-known management companies are Fidelity, Vanguard, and Dreyfus. Each offers an array of open-end mutual funds with different investment policies. In early 2014, there were nearly 8,000 mutual funds in the United States, which were offered by about 800 fund complexes.

Some of the more important fund types, classified by investment policy, are discussed next.

MONEY MARKET FUNDS   These funds invest in money market securities such as commercial paper, repurchase agreements, or certificates of deposit. The average maturity of these assets tends to be a bit more than one month. They usually offer check-writing features, and net asset value is fixed at $1 per share,[1] so that there are no tax implications such as capital gains or losses associated with redemption of shares.

---

[1]The box in Chapter 2 noted that money market funds are able to maintain NAV at $1 because they invest in short-maturity debt of the highest quality with minimal price risk. In rare circumstances, funds have experienced losses sufficient to drive NAV below $1. In September 2008, Reserve Primary Fund, the nation's oldest money market fund, "broke the buck" when it suffered losses on its holding of Lehman Brothers commercial paper, and its NAV fell to $.97.

EQUITY FUNDS Equity funds invest primarily in stock, although they may, at the portfolio manager's discretion, also hold fixed-income or other types of securities. Equity funds commonly will hold about 5% of total assets in money market securities to provide the liquidity necessary to meet potential redemption of shares.

Stock funds are traditionally classified by their emphasis on capital appreciation versus current income. Thus *income funds* tend to hold shares of firms with high dividend yields that provide high current income. *Growth funds* are willing to forgo current income, focusing instead on prospects for capital gains. While the classification of these funds is couched in terms of income versus capital gains, in practice the more relevant distinction concerns the level of risk these funds assume. Growth stocks—and therefore growth funds—are typically riskier and respond more dramatically to changes in economic conditions than do income funds.

SPECIALIZED SECTOR FUNDS Some equity funds, called *sector funds,* concentrate on a particular industry. For example, Fidelity markets dozens of "select funds," each of which invests in a specific industry such as biotechnology, utilities, energy, or telecommunications. Other funds specialize in securities of particular countries.

BOND FUNDS As the name suggests, these funds specialize in the fixed-income sector. Within that sector, however, there is considerable room for further specialization. For example, various funds will concentrate on corporate bonds, Treasury bonds, mortgage-backed securities, or municipal (tax-free) bonds. Indeed, some municipal bond funds invest only in bonds of a particular state (or even city!) in order to satisfy the investment desires of residents of that state who wish to avoid local as well as federal taxes on interest income. Many funds also specialize by maturity, ranging from short-term to intermediate to long-term, or by the credit risk of the issuer, ranging from very safe to high-yield or "junk" bonds.

INTERNATIONAL FUNDS Many funds have international focus. *Global funds* invest in securities worldwide, including the United States. In contrast, *international funds* invest in securities of firms located outside the U.S. *Regional funds* concentrate on a particular part of the world, and *emerging market funds* invest in companies of developing nations.

BALANCED FUNDS Some funds are designed to be candidates for an individual's entire investment portfolio. These *balanced funds* hold both equities and fixed-income securities in relatively stable proportions. *Life-cycle funds* are balanced funds in which the asset mix can range from aggressive (primarily marketed to younger investors) to conservative (directed at older investors). Static allocation life-cycle funds maintain a stable mix across stocks and bonds, while *targeted-maturity funds* gradually become more conservative as the investor ages.

Many balanced funds are in fact **funds of funds.** These are mutual funds that primarily invest in shares of other mutual funds. Balanced funds of funds invest in equity and bond funds in proportions suited to their investment goals.

funds of funds

Mutual funds that primarily invest in shares of other mutual funds.

ASSET ALLOCATION AND FLEXIBLE FUNDS These funds are similar to balanced funds in that they hold both stocks and bonds. However, asset allocation funds may dramatically vary the proportions allocated to each market in accord with the portfolio manager's forecast of the relative performance of each sector. Hence, these funds are engaged in market timing and are not designed to be low-risk investment vehicles.

INDEX FUNDS An index fund tries to match the performance of a broad market index. The fund buys shares in securities included in a particular index in proportion to the security's representation in that index. For example, the Vanguard 500 Index Fund is a mutual fund that replicates the composition of the Standard & Poor's 500 stock price index. Because the S&P 500 is a value-weighted index, the fund buys shares in each S&P 500 company in proportion to the market value of that company's outstanding equity. Investment in an index fund is a low-cost way for small investors to pursue a passive investment strategy—that is, to invest without engaging in security analysis. Nearly 20% of assets held in equity funds in 2014 were in index funds.

Of course, index funds can be tied to nonequity indexes as well. For example, Vanguard offers a bond index fund and a real estate index fund.

Table 4.1 breaks down the number of mutual funds by investment orientation. Sometimes the fund name describes its investment policy. For example, Vanguard's GNMA Fund invests in mortgage-backed securities, the Municipal Intermediate Fund invests in intermediate-term municipal bonds, and the High-Yield Corporate Bond Fund invests in large part in specula-tive grade, or "junk," bonds with high yields. However, names of common stock funds often reflect little or nothing about their investment policies. Examples are Vanguard's Windsor and Wellington funds.

How Funds Are Sold

Mutual funds are generally marketed to the public either directly by the fund underwriter or indi-rectly through brokers acting on behalf of the underwriter. Direct-marketed funds are sold through the mail, various offices of the fund, over the phone, or on the Internet. Investors contact the fund directly to purchase shares. For example, if you look at the financial pages of your local news-paper, you will see several advertisements for funds, along with toll-free phone numbers or web addresses that you can use to receive a fund's prospectus and an application to open an account.

About half of fund sales today are distributed through a sales force. Brokers or financial advisers receive a commission for selling shares to investors. (Ultimately, the commission

TABLE 4.1	U.S. mutual funds by investment classification		
	Assets ($ billion)	Percent of Total Assets	Number of Funds
Equity funds			
Capital appreciation focus	$ 1,725	11.5%	1,329
World/international	2,034	13.5	1,345
Total return	4,004	26.7	1,866
Total equity funds	$ 7,764	51.7%	4,540
Bond funds			
Investment grade	$ 1,451	9.7%	594
High yield	412	2.7	225
World	339	2.3	270
Government	239	1.6	214
Multisector	327	2.2	143
Single-state municipal	145	1.0	331
National municipal	353	2.4	229
Total bond funds	$ 3,265	21.7%	2,006
Hybrid (bond/stock) funds	$ 1,270	8.5%	606
Money market funds			
Taxable	$ 2,448	16.3%	382
Tax-exempt	271	1.8	173
Total money market funds	$ 2,718	18.1%	555
Total	$15,018	100.0%	7,707

Note: Column sums subject to rounding error.

Source: *2014 Mutual Fund Fact Book,* Investment Company Institute is paid by the investor. More on this shortly.) Investors who rely on their broker's advice to select their mutual funds should be aware that brokers may have a conflict of interest with regard to fund selection. This can arise from a practice called *revenue sharing,* in which fund companies pay the brokerage firm for preferential treatment when making investment recommendations.

Many funds also are sold through "financial supermarkets" that can sell shares in funds of many complexes. These programs allow customers to buy funds from many different fund groups. Instead of charging customers a sales commission, the supermarket splits management fees with the mutual fund company. Another advantage is unified record keeping for all funds purchased from the supermarket, even if the funds are offered by different complexes. On the other hand, many contend that these supermarkets result in higher expense ratios because mutual funds pass along the costs of participating in these programs in the form of higher management fees.

4.4 COSTS OF INVESTING IN MUTUAL FUNDS

Fee Structure

An individual investor choosing a mutual fund should consider not only the fund's stated investment policy and past performance, but also its management fees and other expenses. Comparative data on virtually all important aspects of mutual funds are available in Morningstar's *Mutual Fund Sourcebook,* which can be found in many academic and public libraries. You should be aware of four general classes of fees.

OPERATING EXPENSES   Operating expenses are the costs incurred by the mutual fund in operating the portfolio, including administrative expenses and advisory fees paid to the investment manager. These expenses, usually expressed as a percentage of total assets under management, may range from 0.2% to 2%. Shareholders do not receive an explicit bill for these operating expenses; however, the expenses periodically are deducted from the assets of the fund. Shareholders pay for these expenses through the reduced value of the portfolio.

The simple average of the expense ratio of all equity funds in the U.S. was 1.37% in 2013. But larger funds tend to have lower expense ratios (and investors place more of their assets in lower-cost funds), so the average expense ratio weighted by assets under management is considerably smaller, .74%. Not surprisingly, the average expense ratio of indexed funds (weighted by assets under management) is substantially lower, .12%, while that of actively managed funds is higher, .89%.

In addition to operating expenses, most funds assess fees to pay for marketing and distribution costs. These charges are used primarily to pay the brokers or financial advisers who sell the funds to the public. Investors can avoid these expenses by buying shares directly from the fund sponsor, but many investors are willing to incur these distribution fees in return for the advice they may receive from their broker.

FRONT-END LOAD   A front-end load is a commission or sales charge paid when you purchase the shares. These charges, which are used primarily to pay the brokers who sell the funds, may not exceed 8.5%, but in practice they are rarely higher than 6%. *Low-load funds* have loads that range up to 3% of invested funds. *No-load funds* have no front-end sales charges. About half of all funds today (measured by assets) are no load. Loads effectively reduce the amount of money invested. For example, each $1,000 paid for a fund with a 6% load results in a sales charge of $60 and fund investment of only $940. You need cumulative returns of 6.4% of your net investment (60/940 = .064) just to break even.

BACK-END LOAD   A back-end load is a redemption, or "exit," fee incurred when you sell your shares. Typically, funds that impose back-end loads start them at 5% or 6% and reduce them by one percentage point for every year the funds are left invested. Thus, an exit fee that starts at 6% would fall to 4% by the start of your third year. These charges are known more formally as "contingent deferred sales loads."

12b-1 fees

Annual fees charged by a mutual fund to pay for marketing and distribution costs.

12b-1 CHARGES   The Securities and Exchange Commission allows the managers of so-called 12b-1 funds to use fund assets to pay for distribution costs such as advertising, promotional literature including annual reports and prospectuses, and, most important, commissions paid to brokers who sell the fund to investors. These **12b-1 fees** are named after the SEC rule that permits use of these plans. Funds may use annual 12b-1 charges instead of, or in addition to, front-end loads to generate the fees with which to pay brokers. As with operating expenses, investors are not explicitly billed for 12b-1 charges. Instead, the fees are deducted from the assets of the fund. Therefore, 12b-1 fees (if any) must be added to operating expenses to obtain the true annual expense ratio of the fund. The SEC now requires that all funds include in the prospectus a consolidated expense table that summarizes all relevant fees. The 12b-1 fees are limited to 1% of a fund's average net assets per year.[2]

Many funds offer "classes" which represent ownership in the same portfolio of securities, but with different combinations of fees. Typical Class A shares have front-end loads and a small 12b-1 fee, often around .25%. Class C shares rely on larger 12b-1 fees, commonly 1%, and often charge a modest back-end load. Class C shares generally rely on 12b-1 fees and back-end loads. These shares usually will not convert to Class A shares. Class I shares are sold to institutional investors. These are sometimes called Class Y shares and carry no loads or 12b-1 fees.[3]

EXAMPLE 4.1

Fees for Various Classes (Dreyfus Equity Growth Fund)

Here are fees for different classes of the Dreyfus Equity Growth Fund in 2014. Notice the trade-off between the front-end loads and the 12b-1 charges.

	Class A	Class C	Class I
Front-end load	5.75%[a]	0	0
Back-end load	0	1%	0[b]
12b-1 fees[c]	0.25%	1.0	0
Expense ratio	1.1%	1.1%	1.1%

Notes:

[a]Depending on size of investment.

[b]Depending on years until holdings are sold.

[c]Including service fee of .25%.

Each investor must choose the best combination of fees. Obviously, pure no-load no-fee funds distributed directly by the mutual fund group are the cheapest alternative, and these will often make the most sense for knowledgeable investors. But as we noted earlier, many investors are willing to pay for financial advice, and the commissions paid to advisers who sell these funds are the most common form of payment. Alternatively, investors may choose to hire a fee-only financial manager who charges directly for services instead of collecting commissions. These advisers can help investors select portfolios of low- or no-load funds (as well as provide other financial advice). Independent financial planners have become increasingly important distribution channels for funds in recent years.

If you do buy a fund through a broker, the choice between paying a load and paying 12b-1 fees will depend primarily on your expected time horizon. Loads are paid only once for each purchase, whereas 12b-1 fees are paid annually. Thus, if you plan to hold your fund for a long time, a one-time load may be preferable to recurring 12b-1 charges.

---

[2]The maximum 12b-1 charge for the sale of the fund is .75%. However, an additional service fee of .25% of the fund's assets also is allowed for personal service and/or maintenance of shareholder accounts.

[3]Many funds used to market Class B shares as well. These relied on 12b-1 fees as well as a modest back-end load. If an investor held Class B shares for a long enough duration, typically 6–8 years, the shares would convert into Class A shares. However, Class B shares have become increasingly less common in recent years.

Fees and Mutual Fund Returns

The rate of return on an investment in a mutual fund is measured as the increase or decrease in net asset value plus income distributions such as dividends or distributions of capital gains expressed as a fraction of net asset value at the beginning of the investment period. If we denote the net asset value at the start and end of the period as NAV_0 and NAV_1, respectively, then

$$\text{Rate of return} = \frac{NAV_1 - NAV_0 + \text{Income and capital gain distributions}}{NAV_0}$$

For example, if a fund has an initial NAV of $20 at the start of the month, makes income distributions of $.15 and capital gain distributions of $.05, and ends the month with NAV of $20.10, the monthly rate of return is computed as

$$\text{Rate of return} = \frac{\$20.10 - \$20.00 + \$.15 + \$.05}{\$20.00}$$

$$= .015, \text{ or } 1.5\%$$

Notice that this measure of the rate of return ignores any commissions such as front-end loads paid to purchase the fund.

On the other hand, the rate of return is affected by the fund's expenses and 12b-1 fees. This is because such charges are periodically deducted from the portfolio, which reduces net asset value. Thus the investor's rate of return on the fund equals the gross return on the underlying portfolio minus the total expense ratio.

EXAMPLE 4.2

Expenses and Rates of Return

To see how expenses can affect rate of return, consider a fund with $100 million in assets at the start of the year and with 10 million shares outstanding. The fund invests in a portfolio of stocks that provides no income but increases in value by 10%. The expense ratio, including 12b-1 fees, is 1%. What is the rate of return for an investor in the fund?

The initial NAV equals $100 million/10 million shares = $10 per share. In the absence of expenses, fund assets would grow to $110 million and NAV would grow to $11 per share, for a 10% rate of return. However, the expense ratio of the fund is 1%. Therefore, $1 million will be deducted from the fund to pay these fees, leaving the portfolio worth only $109 million, and NAV equal to $10.90. The rate of return on the fund is only 9%, which equals the gross return on the underlying portfolio minus the total expense ratio.

Fees can have a big effect on performance. Table 4.2 considers an investor who starts with $10,000 and can choose between three funds that all earn an annual 12% return on investment before fees but have different fee structures. The table shows the cumulative amount in each fund after several investment horizons. Fund A has total operating expenses of .5%, no load, and no 12b-1 charges. This might represent a low-cost producer like Vanguard. Fund B has no load but has 1% management expenses and .5% in 12b-1 fees. This level of charges is fairly typical of actively managed equity funds. Finally, Fund C has 1% in management expenses, has no 12b-1 charges, but assesses an 8% front-end load on purchases.

Note the substantial return advantage of low-cost Fund A. Moreover, that differential is greater for longer investment horizons.

CONCEPT check   4.2

The Equity Fund sells Class A shares with a front-end load of 4% and Class B shares with 12b-1 fees of .5% annually as well as back-end load fees that start at 5% and fall by 1% for each full year the investor holds the portfolio (until the fifth year). Assume the rate of return on the fund portfolio net of operating expenses is 10% annually. What will be the value of a $10,000 investment in Class A and Class B shares if the shares are sold after (*a*) 1 year, (*b*) 4 years, (*c*) 10 years? Which fee structure provides higher net proceeds at the end of each investment horizon?

TABLE 4.2	Impact of costs on investment performance		
	Cumulative Proceeds (all dividends reinvested)		
	Fund A	**Fund B**	**Fund C**
Initial investment*	$10,000	$10,000	$ 9,200
5 years	17,234	16,474	15,502
10 years	29,699	27,141	26,123
15 years	51,183	44,713	44,018
20 years	88,206	73,662	74,173

Notes: Fund A is no-load with .5% expense ratio, Fund B is no-load with 1.5% total expense ratio, and Fund C has an 8% load on purchases and a 1% expense ratio. Gross return on all funds is 12% per year before expenses.

*After front-end load, if any.

Although expenses can have a big impact on net investment performance, it is sometimes difficult for the investor in a mutual fund to measure true expenses accurately. This is because of the common practice of paying for some expenses in **soft dollars.** A portfolio manager earns soft-dollar credits with a brokerage firm by directing the fund's trades to that broker. Based on those credits, the broker will pay for some of the mutual fund's expenses, such as databases, computer hardware, or stock-quotation systems. The soft-dollar arrangement means that the stockbroker effectively returns part of the trading commission to the fund. Purchases made with soft dollars are not included in the fund's expenses, so funds with extensive soft-dollar arrangements may report artificially low expense ratios to the public. However, the fund will have paid its brokers needlessly high commissions to obtain its soft-dollar "rebates." The impact of the higher trading commissions shows up in net investment performance rather than the reported expense ratio.

soft dollars

The value of research services that brokerage houses provide "free of charge" in exchange for the investment manager's business.

4.5   TAXATION OF MUTUAL FUND INCOME

Investment returns of mutual funds are granted "pass-through status" under the U.S. tax code, meaning that taxes are paid only by the investor in the mutual fund, not by the fund itself. The income is treated as passed through to the investor as long as the fund meets several requirements, most notably that the fund be sufficiently diversified and that virtually all income is distributed to shareholders.

A fund's short-term capital gains, long-term capital gains, and dividends are passed through to investors as though the investor earned the income directly.[4] The pass-through of investment income has one important disadvantage for individual investors. If you manage your own portfolio, you decide when to realize capital gains and losses on any security; therefore, you can time those realizations to efficiently manage your tax liabilities. When you invest through a mutual fund, however, the timing of the sale of securities from the portfolio is out of your control, which reduces your ability to engage in tax management.

turnover

The ratio of the trading activity of a portfolio to the assets of the portfolio.

A fund with a high portfolio turnover rate can be particularly "tax inefficient." **Turnover** is the ratio of the trading activity of a portfolio to the assets of the portfolio. It measures the fraction of the portfolio that is "replaced" each year. For example, a $100 million portfolio

[4]An interesting problem that an investor needs to be aware of derives from the fact that capital gains and dividends on mutual funds are typically paid out to shareholders once or twice a year. This means that an investor who has just purchased shares in a mutual fund can receive a capital gain distribution (and be taxed on that distribution) on transactions that occurred long before he or she purchased shares in the fund. This is particularly a concern late in the year when such distributions typically are made.

with $50 million in sales of some securities and purchases of other securities would have a turnover rate of 50%. High turnover means that capital gains or losses are being realized constantly, and therefore that the investor cannot time the realizations to manage his or her overall tax obligation. Turnover rates in equity funds in the last decade have typically been around 60% when weighted by assets under management. By contrast, a low-turnover fund such as an index fund may have turnover as low as 2%, which is both tax-efficient and economical with respect to trading costs.

SEC rules require funds to disclose the tax impact of portfolio turnover. Funds must include in their prospectus after-tax returns for the past 1-, 5-, and 10-year periods. Marketing literature that includes performance data also must include after-tax results. The after-tax returns are computed accounting for the impact of the taxable distributions of income and capital gains passed through to the investor, assuming the investor is in the maximum federal tax bracket.

4.6 EXCHANGE-TRADED FUNDS

Exchange-traded funds (ETFs) are offshoots of mutual funds first introduced in 1993 that allow investors to trade index portfolios just as they do shares of stock. The first ETF was the "Spider," a nickname for SPDR or Standard & Poor's Depository Receipt, which is a unit investment trust holding a portfolio matching the S&P 500 Index. Unlike mutual funds, which can be bought or sold only at the end of the day when NAV is calculated, investors could trade Spiders throughout the day, just like any other share of stock. Spiders gave rise to many similar products such as "Diamonds" (based on the Dow Jones Industrial Average, ticker DIA), Qubes (pronounced "cubes", based on the NASDAQ 100 Index, ticker QQQ), and WEBS (World Equity Benchmark Shares, which are shares in portfolios of foreign stock market indexes). By early 2014, about $1.7 trillion was invested in about 1,300 ETFs in five general classes: broad U.S. market indexes, narrow industry or "sector" portfolios, international indexes, commodities, and bond portfolios. Table 4.3, Panel A, presents some of the sponsors of ETFs; Panel B is a small sample of ETFs, which we include to give you a flavor of the sort of products available.

exchange-traded funds
Offshoots of mutual funds that allow investors to trade index portfolios.

Figure 4.2 shows the rapid growth in the ETF market since 1998. Until 2008, most ETFs were required to track specified indexes, and ETFs tracking broad indexes still dominate the industry. However, there are dozens of industry-sector ETFs, and as Figure 4.2 makes clear, commodity, bond, and international ETFs have grown especially dramatically in recent years. Figure 4.3 shows that ETFs have captured a significant portion of the assets under management in the investment company universe.

Barclay's Global Investors was long the market leader in the ETF market, using the product name iShares. Since Barclay's 2009 merger with BlackRock, iShares have operated under the BlackRock name. The firm sponsors ETFs for several dozen equity index funds, including many broad U.S. equity indexes, broad international and single-country funds, and U.S. and global industry sector funds. BlackRock also offers several bond ETFs and a few commodity funds such as ones for gold and silver. For more information on these funds, go to **www.iShares.com.**

TABLE 4.3   ETF sponsors and products

A. ETF Sponsors

Sponsor	Product Name
BlackRock	iShares
Merrill Lynch	HOLDRS (Holding Company Depository Receipts: "Holders")
StateStreet	Select Sector SPDRs (S&P Depository Receipts: "Spiders")
Vanguard	Vanguard ETFs

B. Sample of ETF Products

Name	Ticker	Index Tracked
Broad U.S. indexes		
Spiders	SPY	S&P 500
Diamonds	DIA	Dow Jones Industrials
Qubes	QQQ	NASDAQ 100
iShares Russell 2000	IWM	Russell 2000
Total Stock Market (Vanguard)	VTI	Wilshire 5000
Industry indexes		
Energy Select Spider	XLE	S&P 500 energy companies
iShares Energy Sector	IYE	Dow Jones energy companies
Oil Service HOLDRS	OIH	Portfolio of oil service firms
Financial Sector Spider	XLF	S&P 500 financial companies
iShares Financial Sector	IYF	Dow Jones financial companies
Vanguard Financials ETF	VFH	MSCI financials index
International indexes		
WEBS United Kingdom	EWU	MCSI U.K. Index
WEBS France	EWQ	MCSI France Index
WEBS Japan	EWJ	MCSI Japan Index

More recently, a variety of new ETF products have been devised. Among these are leveraged ETFs, with daily returns that are a targeted *multiple* of the returns on an index, and inverse ETFs, which move in the opposite direction to an index. A more recent innovation is actively managed ETFs that, like actively managed mutual funds, attempt to outperform passive indexes. However, until recently, these funds have had to report portfolio holdings on a daily basis, which makes it easy for competitors to take advantage of their buying and selling programs. This requirement has severely limited the growth of this segment of the market. In 2014, however, the SEC gave permission to Eaton Vance to offer an actively managed "nontransparent" ETF that is required to report its portfolio composition only once each quarter, the same frequency at which mutual funds disclose their portfolio holdings.

Other even more exotic variations are so-called synthetic ETFs such as exchange-traded notes (ETNs) or exchange-traded vehicles (ETVs). These are nominally debt securities, but with payoffs linked to the performance of an index. Often that index measures the performance of an illiquid and thinly traded asset class, so the ETF gives the investor the opportunity to add that asset class to his or her portfolio. However, rather than invest in those assets directly,

Assets in ETFs

Source: Investment Company Institute, *2010–2014 Investment Company Fact Books.* Washington, DC 2014.

FIGURE 4.2

FIGURE 4.3

Investment company assets under management, 2013 ($ billion)

Source: Investment Company Institute, *2014 Investment Company Fact Book.* Washington, DC 2014.

the ETF achieves this exposure by entering a "total return swap" with an investment bank in which the bank agrees to pay the ETF the return on the index in exchange for a relatively fixed fee. These have become controversial, as the ETF is then exposed to risk that in a period of financial stress, the investment bank will be unable to fulfill its obligation, leaving investors without the returns they were promised.

ETFs offer several advantages over conventional mutual funds. First, as we just noted, a mutual fund's net asset value is quoted—and therefore, investors can buy or sell their shares in the fund—only once a day. In contrast, ETFs trade continuously. Moreover, like other shares, but unlike mutual funds, ETFs can be sold short or purchased on margin.

ETFs also offer a potential tax advantage over mutual funds. When large numbers of mutual fund investors redeem their shares, the fund must sell securities to meet the redemptions. The sale can trigger capital gains taxes, which are passed through to and must be paid by the remaining shareholders. In contrast, when small investors wish to redeem their position in an ETF they simply sell their shares to other traders, with no need for the fund to sell any of the underlying portfolio. Moreover, when large traders wish to redeem their position in the ETF, redemptions are satisfied with shares of stock in the underlying portfolio. Again, a redemption does not trigger a stock sale by the fund sponsor.

The ability of large investors to redeem ETFs for a portfolio of stocks constituting the index, or to exchange a portfolio of stocks for shares in the corresponding ETF, ensures that the price of an ETF cannot depart for long from the NAV of that portfolio. Any meaningful discrepancy would offer arbitrage trading opportunities for these large traders, which would quickly eliminate the disparity.

ETFs are also cheaper than mutual funds. Investors who buy ETFs do so through brokers, rather than buying directly from the fund. Therefore, the fund saves the cost of marketing itself directly to small investors. This reduction in expenses translates into lower management fees. For example, the expense ratio on Vanguard's Total Stock Market mutual fund, which tracks an index of the entire U.S. equity market, is .17%, whereas the ratio on its Total Stock Market ETF is only .05%.

There are some disadvantages to ETFs, however. First, while mutual funds can be bought for NAV with no expense from no-load funds, ETFs must be purchased from brokers for a fee. Investors also incur a bid–ask spread when purchasing an ETF.

In addition, because ETFs trade as securities, their prices can depart from NAV, at least for short periods, and these price discrepancies can easily swamp the cost advantage that ETFs otherwise offer. While those discrepancies typically are quite small, they can spike unpredictably when markets are stressed. Chapter 3 briefly discussed the so-called flash crash of May 6, 2010, when the Dow Jones Industrial Average fell by 583 points in *seven minutes,* leaving it down nearly 1,000 points for the day. Remarkably, the index recovered more than 600 points in the next 10 minutes. In the wake of this incredible volatility, the stock exchanges canceled many trades that had gone off at what were viewed as distorted prices. Around one-fifth of all ETFs changed hands on that day at prices less than one-half of their closing price, and ETFs accounted for about two-thirds of all canceled trades.

At least two problems were exposed in this episode. First, when markets are not working properly, it can be hard to measure the net asset value of the ETF portfolio, especially for ETFs that track less liquid assets. And, reinforcing this problem, some ETFs may be supported by only a very small number of dealers. If they drop out of the market during a period of turmoil, prices may swing wildly.

4.7   MUTUAL FUND INVESTMENT PERFORMANCE: A FIRST LOOK

We noted earlier that one of the benefits of mutual funds for the individual investor is the ability to delegate management of the portfolio to investment professionals. The investor retains control over the broad features of the overall portfolio through the asset allocation decision: Each individual chooses the percentages of the portfolio to invest in bond funds versus equity funds versus money market funds, and so forth, but can leave the specific security selection decisions within each investment class to the managers of each fund. Shareholders hope that these portfolio managers can achieve better investment performance than they could obtain on their own.

What is the investment record of the mutual fund industry? This seemingly straightforward question is deceptively difficult to answer because we need a standard against which to evaluate performance. For example, we clearly would not want to compare the investment performance of an equity fund to the rate of return available in the money market. The vast differences in the risk of these two markets dictate that year-by-year as well as average performance will differ considerably. We would expect to find that equity funds outperform money market funds (on average) as compensation to investors for the extra risk incurred in equity markets. How can we determine whether mutual fund portfolio managers are performing up to par *given* the level of risk they incur? In other words, what is the proper benchmark against which investment performance ought to be evaluated?

Measuring portfolio risk properly and using such measures to choose an appropriate benchmark is far from straightforward. We devote all of Parts Two and Three of the text to issues surrounding the proper measurement of portfolio risk and the trade-off between risk and return. In this chapter, therefore, we will satisfy ourselves with a first look at the question of fund performance by using only very simple performance benchmarks and ignoring the more subtle issues of risk differences across funds. However, we will return to this topic in Chapter 8, where we take a closer look at mutual fund performance after adjusting for differences in the exposure of portfolios to various sources of risk.

Here, we will use as a benchmark for the performance of equity fund managers the rate of return on the Wilshire 5000 Index. Recall from Chapter 2 that this is a value-weighted index of more than 5,000 stocks that trade on the NYSE, NASDAQ, and Amex stock markets. It is the most inclusive index of the performance of U.S. equities. The performance of the Wilshire 5000 is a useful benchmark with which to evaluate professional managers because it corresponds to a simple passive investment strategy: Buy all the shares in the index in proportion to their outstanding market value. Moreover, this is a feasible strategy for even small investors, because the Vanguard Group offers an index fund (its Total Stock Market Index Fund) designed to replicate the performance of the Wilshire 5000 Index. Using the Wilshire 5000 Index as a benchmark, we may pose the problem of evaluating the performance of mutual fund portfolio managers this way: How does the typical performance of actively managed equity mutual funds compare to the performance of a passively managed portfolio that simply replicates the composition of a broad index of the stock market?

Casual comparisons of the performance of the Wilshire 5000 Index versus that of professionally managed mutual fund portfolios show disappointing results for most fund managers. Figure 4.4 shows that the average return on diversified equity funds was below the return on the Wilshire 5000 Index in 26 of the 43 years from 1971 to 2013. The average return on the index was 12.4%, which was .9% greater than that of the average mutual fund.[5]

This result may seem surprising. After all, it would not seem unreasonable to expect that professional money managers should be able to outperform a very simple rule such as "hold an indexed portfolio." As it turns out, however, there may be good reasons to expect such a result. We will explore them in detail in Chapter 8, where we discuss the efficient market hypothesis.

Of course, one might argue that there are good managers and bad managers, and that good managers can, in fact, consistently outperform the index. To test this notion, we examine whether managers with good performance in one year are likely to repeat that performance in a following year. Is superior performance in any particular year due to luck, and therefore random, or due to skill, and therefore consistent from year to year?

To answer this question, we can examine the performance of a large sample of equity mutual fund portfolios, divide the funds into two groups based on total investment return, and ask: "Do funds with investment returns in the top half of the sample in one period continue to perform well in the subsequent period?"

Table 4.4 presents such an analysis from a study by Malkiel (1995). The table shows the fraction of "winners" (i.e., top-half performers) in each year that turn out to be winners or losers in the following year. If performance were purely random from one period to the next, there would be entries of 50% in each cell of the table, as top- or bottom-half performers

---

[5]Of course, actual funds incur trading costs while indexes do not, so a fair comparison between the returns on actively managed funds versus those on a passive index should first reduce the return on the Wilshire 5000 by an estimate of such costs. Vanguard's Total Stock Market Index portfolio, which tracks the Wilshire 5000, charges an expense ratio of less than .10%, and, because it engages in little trading, incurs low trading costs. Therefore, it would be reasonable to reduce the returns on the index by about .15%. This reduction would not erase the difference in average performance.

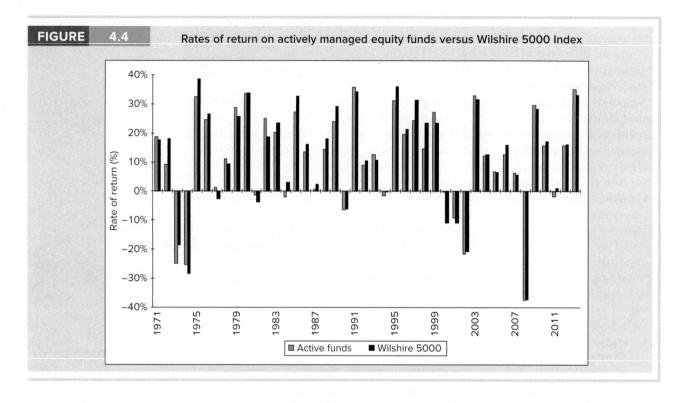

FIGURE	4.4	Rates of return on actively managed equity funds versus Wilshire 5000 Index

TABLE 4.4   Consistency of investment results

	Successive Period Performance	
Initial Period Performance	**Top Half**	**Bottom Half**
A. 1970s		
Top half	65.1%	34.9%
Bottom half	35.5%	64.5%
B. 1980s		
Top half	51.7%	48.3%
Bottom half	47.5%	52.5%

Source: Burton G. Malkiel, "Returns from Investing in Equity Mutual Funds 1971–1991," *Journal of Finance* 50 (June 1995), pp. 549–72.

would be equally likely to perform in either the top or bottom half of the sample in the following period. On the other hand, if performance were due entirely to skill, with no randomness, we would expect to see entries of 100% on the diagonals and entries of 0% on the off-diagonals: Top-half performers would all remain in the top half while bottom-half performers similarly would all remain in the bottom half. In fact, Panel A shows that 65.1% of initial top-half performers in the 1970s fall in the top half of the sample in the following period, while 64.5% of initial bottom-half performers fall in the bottom half in the following period. This evidence is consistent with the notion that at least part of a fund's performance is a function of skill as opposed to luck, so that relative performance tends to persist from one period to the next.[6]

[6]Another possibility is that performance consistency is due to variation in fee structure across funds. We return to this possibility in Chapter 8.

On the other hand, this relationship does not seem stable across different sample periods. While initial-year performance predicts subsequent-year performance in the 1970s (see Panel A), the pattern of persistence in performance virtually disappears in the 1980s (Panel B).

Other studies suggest that there is little performance persistence among professional managers, and if anything, bad performance is more likely to persist than good performance.[7] This makes some sense: It is easy to identify fund characteristics that will predictably lead to consistently poor investment performance, notably, high expense ratios and high turnover ratios with associated trading costs. It is far harder to identify the secrets of successful stock picking. (If it were easy, we would all be rich!) Thus, the consistency we do observe in fund performance may be due in large part to the poor performers. This suggests that the real value of past performance data is to avoid truly poor funds, even if identifying the future top performers is still a daunting task.

> Suppose you observe the investment performance of 400 portfolio managers and rank them by investment returns during the year. Twenty percent of all managers are truly skilled, and therefore always fall in the top half, but the others fall in the top half purely because of good luck. What fraction of these top-half managers would you expect to be top-half performers next year? Assume skilled managers always are top-half performers.

CONCEPT check 4.4

4.8 INFORMATION ON MUTUAL FUNDS

The first place to find information on a mutual fund is in its prospectus. The Securities and Exchange Commission requires that the prospectus describe the fund's investment objectives and policies in a concise "Statement of Investment Objectives" as well as in lengthy discussions of investment policies and risks. The fund's investment adviser and its portfolio manager also are described. The prospectus also presents the costs associated with purchasing shares in the fund in a fee table. Sales charges such as front-end and back-end loads as well as annual operating expenses such as management fees and 12b-1 fees are detailed in the fee table.

Funds provide information about themselves in two other sources. The Statement of Additional Information, or SAI, also known as Part B of the prospectus, includes a list of the securities in the portfolio at the end of the fiscal year, audited financial statements, a list of the directors and officers of the fund as well as their personal investments in the fund, and data on brokerage commissions paid by the fund. Unlike the fund prospectus, however, investors do not receive the SAI unless they specifically request it; one industry joke is that SAI stands for "something always ignored." The fund's annual report also includes portfolio composition and financial statements, as well as a discussion of the factors that influenced fund performance over the last reporting period.

With more than 8,000 mutual funds to choose from, it can be difficult to find and select the fund that is best suited for a particular need. Several publications now offer "encyclopedias" of mutual fund information to help in the search process. One prominent source is Morningstar's *Mutual Fund Sourcebook.* Morningstar's website, **www.morningstar.com,** is another excellent source of information, as is Yahoo!'s site, **finance.yahoo.com/funds.** The Investment Company Institute—the national association of mutual funds, closed-end funds, and unit investment trusts—publishes an annual *Directory of Mutual Funds* that includes information on fees as well as phone numbers to contact funds. To illustrate the range of information available about funds, we consider Morningstar's report on Wells Fargo Advantage Growth Fund, reproduced in Figure 4.5.

---

[7]See, for example, Mark M. Carhart, "On Persistence in Mutual Fund Performance," *Journal of Finance* 52 (1997), 57–82. Carhart's study also addresses survivorship bias, the tendency for better-performing funds to stay in business and thus remain in the sample. We return to his study in Chapter 8.

FIGURE 4.5 Morningstar report

Source: Morningstar Mutual Funds. © 2012 Morningstar, Inc.

Wells Fargo Advantage Growth Inv (USD)

	Morningstar Analyst Rtg™	Overall Morningstar Rtg™	Standard Index	Category Index	Morningstar Cat
	⬡ Bronze 01-03-2012	★★★★★	S&P 500 TR	Russell 1000	US OE Large Growth
		1,514 US OE Large Growth		Growth TR USD	

Performance 09-30-2012

Quarterly Returns	1st Qtr	2nd Qtr	3rd Qtr	4th Qtr	Total %
2010	6.54	−8.57	14.19	13.42	26.14
2011	12.89	1.33	−14.16	9.87	7.88
2012	19.35	−6.73	7.35	—	19.50

Trailing Returns	1 Yr	3 Yr	5 Yr	10 Yr	Incept
Load-adj Mthly	31.29	21.60	7.49	12.45	11.17
Std 09-30-2012	31.29	—	7.49	12.45	11.17
Total Return	31.29	21.60	7.49	12.45	11.17
+/− Std Index	1.09	8.40	6.43	4.43	—
+/− Cat Index	2.10	6.87	4.25	4.04	—
% Rank Cat	14	1	1	2	
No. in Cat	1678	1514	1311	867	
7-day Yield	—				

Performance Disclosure
The Overall Morningstar Rating is based on risk-adjusted returns, derived from a weighted average of the three-, five-, and 10-year (if applicable) Morningstar metrics.

The performance data quoted represents past performance and does not guarantee future results. The investment return and principal value of an investment will fluctuate; thus an investor's shares, when sold or redeemed, may be worth more or less than their original cost.

Current performance may be lower or higher than return data quoted herein. For performance data current to the most recent month-end, please call 800-222-8222 or visit www.wellsfargo.com/advantagefunds.

Fees and Expenses

Sales Charges
Front-End Load %	NA
Deferred load %	NA

Fund Expenses
Management Fees %	0.66
12b1 Expense %	NA
Gross Expense Ratio %	1.31

Risk and Return Profile

	3 Yr 1514 funds	5 Yr 1311 funds	10 Yr 867 funds
Morningstar Rating™	5★	5★	5★
Morningstar Risk	+Avg	Avg	+Avg
Morningstar Return	High	High	High

	3 Yr	5 Yr	10 Yr
Standard Deviation	18.25	20.76	17.38
Mean	21.60	7.49	12.45
Sharpe Ratio	1.16	0.42	0.66

MPT Statistics	Standard Index	Best Fit Index Morningstar Mid Growth TR USD
Alpha	6.36	6.19
Beta	1.10	0.95
R-Squared	87.72	94.65
12-Month Yield		—
30-day SEC Yield		—
Potential Cap Gains Exp		22.38%

Operations

Family:	Wells Fargo Advantage
Manager:	Multiple
Tenure:	10.4 Years
Objective:	Growth
Base Currency:	USD
Ticker:	SGROX
Minimum Initial Purchase:	$2,500
Min Auto Investment Plan:	$2,500
Minimum IRA Purchase:	$1,000
Purchase Constraints:	C
Incept:	12-31-1993
Type:	MF
Total Assets:	$10,859.15 mil

Investment Style: Equity, Stock %

Growth of $10,000
- ■ Wells Fargo Advantage Growth Inv 15,327
- Category Average 10,540
- Standard Index 13,682

	2001	2002	2003	2004	2005	2006	2007	2008	2009	2010	2011	09-12	History
Investment Style box	97	97	98	98	100	98	98	98	99	99	94	97	
	17.68	13.21	17.19	19.35	21.09	22.72	28.95	17.24	25.40	32.04	34.11	40.76	NAV/Price
	−34.39	−25.28	30.13	12.57	8.99	7.73	27.42	−40.45	47.33	26.14	7.88	19.50	Total Return %
	−22.51	−3.18	1.44	1.68	4.08	−8.07	21.93	−3.45	20.87	11.08	5.77	3.05	+/− Standard Index
	−13.97	2.60	0.38	6.27	3.73	−1.34	15.61	−2.01	10.12	9.43	5.24	2.70	+/− Category Index
	91	34	32	11	29	44	5	49	11	2	1	—	% Rank Cat
	1064	1234	1311	1400	1495	1642	1748	1809	1796	1718	1683	1715	No. of Funds in Cat

Portfolio Analysis 08-31-2012

Asset Allocation % 07-31-2012	Net %	Long %	Short %
Cash	2.90	2.90	0.00
US Stocks	92.23	92.23	0.00
Non-US Stocks	4.88	4.88	0.00
Bonds	0.00	0.00	0.00
Other/Not Clsfd	0.00	0.00	0.00
Total	100.00	100.00	0.00

Equity Style

Portfolio Statistics	Port Avg	Rel Index	Rel Cat
P/E Ratio TTM	22.9	1.50	1.25
P/C Ratio TTM	15.1	1.63	1.24
P/S Ratio TTM	4.4	2.01	1.38
Geo Avg Mkt Cap $mil	18892	0.32	0.35

Fixed-Income Style

Avg Eff Maturity	—
Avg Eff Duration	—
Avg Wtd Coupon	—
Avg Wtd Price	—

Credit Quality Breakdown— Bond %

AAA	—
AA	—
A	—
BBB	—
BB	—
B	—
Below B	—
NR/NA	—

Regional Exposure

	Stock %	Rel Std Index
Americas	97.5	0.98
Greater Europe	2.2	2.41
Greater Asia	0.3	—

Top Holdings 07-31-2012

Share Chg since 07-2012	Share Amount	Holdings: 100 Total Stocks, 0 Total Fixed-Income, 47% Turnover Ratio	% Net Assets
⊖	1 mil	Apple, Inc.	8.26
⊖	3 mil	Alexion Pharmaceuticals, Inc.	3.35
⊖	500,100	Google, Inc. Class A	3.08
⊕	7 mil	eBay Inc	3.07
⊕	4 mil	Kansas City Southern, Inc.	3.01
⊖	5 mil	Cognizant Technology Solutions Cor	2.64
⊖	3 mil	Whole Foods Market, Inc.	2.42
⊖	2 mil	Tractor Supply	2.18
⊖	8 mil	EMC Corporation	2.10
⊕	487,200	MasterCard Incorporated Class A	2.07
⊕	313,800	Priceline.com, Inc.	2.02
⊖	2 mil	Pioneer Natural Resources Company	1.95
⊖	5 mil	Rackspace Hosting, Inc.	1.94
⊕	1 mil	Mettler-Toledo International, Inc.	1.86
⊖	7 mil	CarMax, Inc.	1.80

Sector Weightings	Stocks %	Rel Std Index
↻ Cyclical	27.1	0.97
Basic Materials	1.0	0.34
Consumer Cyclical	20.8	2.14
Financial Services	5.3	0.40
Real Estate	0.0	0.00
W Sensitive	52.9	1.17
Communication Services	0.0	0.00
Energy	5.4	0.48
Industrials	13.1	1.21
Technology	34.4	1.85
→ Defensive	20.0	0.75
Consumer Defensive	7.1	0.62
Healthcare	12.9	1.09
Utilities	0.0	0.00

Performance Quartile (within category)

The table on the left, labeled "Performance," first shows the fund's quarterly returns in the last few years, and just below that, returns over longer periods. You can compare returns to both its "standard index," (the S&P 500) and its "category index" (the Russell 1000) in the rows labeled +/− Index, as well as its percentile rank within its comparison group or "category." Continuing down the left column, we see data on fees and expenses as well as several measures of the fund's risk and return characteristics. (We will discuss all of these measures in Part Two of the text.) The fund has provided good returns compared to risk, earning it the coveted Morningstar 5-star rating. Of course, we are all accustomed to the disclaimer that "past performance is not a reliable measure of future results," and this is true as well of Morningstar's star ratings. Consistent with this disclaimer, past results have little predictive power for future performance, as we saw in Table 4.4.

More data on the performance of the fund are provided in the graph near the top of the figure. The line graph compares the growth of $10,000 invested in the fund versus its two comparison indexes over the last 10 years. Below the graph are boxes for each year that depict the relative performance of the fund for that year. The shaded area on the box shows the quartile in which the fund's performance falls relative to other funds with the same objective. If the shaded band is at the top of the box, the firm was a top quartile performer in that period, and so on. The table below the bar charts presents historical data on the year-by-year performance of the fund.

Below the table, the "Portfolio Analysis" table shows the asset allocation of the fund, and then Morningstar's well-known style box. In this box, Morningstar evaluates style along two dimensions: One dimension is the size of the firms held in the portfolio as measured by the market value of outstanding equity; the other dimension is a value/growth measure. Morningstar defines *value stocks* as those with low ratios of market price per share to various measures of value. It puts stocks on a growth-value continuum based on the ratios of stock price to the firm's earnings, book value, sales, cash flow, and dividends. Value stocks are those with a low price relative to these measures of value. In contrast, *growth stocks* have high ratios, suggesting that investors in these firms must believe that the firm will experience rapid growth to justify the prices at which the stocks sell. The shaded box shows that the fund tends to hold larger firms (top row) and growth stocks (right column).

Finally, the tables in the right column provide information on the current composition of the portfolio. There you can find the fund's 15 "Top Holdings" as well as the weighting of the portfolio across various sectors of the economy.

SUMMARY

- Unit investment trusts, closed-end management companies, and open-end management companies are all classified and regulated as investment companies. Unit investment trusts are essentially unmanaged in the sense that the portfolio, once established, is fixed. Managed investment companies, in contrast, may change the composition of the portfolio as deemed fit by the portfolio manager. Closed-end funds are traded like other securities; they do not redeem shares for their investors. Open-end funds will redeem shares for net asset value at the request of the investor.
- Net asset value equals the market value of assets held by a fund minus the liabilities of the fund divided by the shares outstanding.
- Mutual funds free the individual from many of the administrative burdens of owning individual securities and offer professional management of the portfolio. They also offer advantages that are available only to large-scale investors, such as lower trading costs. On the other hand, funds are assessed management fees and incur other expenses, which reduce the investor's rate of return. Funds also eliminate some of the individual's control over the timing of capital gains realizations.
- Mutual funds often are categorized by investment policy. Major policy groups include money market funds; equity funds, which are further grouped according to emphasis on

income versus growth; fixed-income funds; balanced and income funds; asset allocation funds; index funds; and specialized sector funds.

- Costs of investing in mutual funds include front-end loads, which are sales charges; back-end loads, which are redemption fees or, more formally, contingent-deferred sales charges; fund operating expenses; and 12b-1 charges, which are recurring fees used to pay for the expenses of marketing the fund to the public.
- Income earned on mutual fund portfolios is not taxed at the level of the fund. Instead, as long as the fund meets certain requirements for pass-through status, the income is treated as being earned by the investors in the fund.
- The average rate of return of the average equity mutual fund in the last 40 years has been below that of a passive index fund holding a portfolio to replicate a broad-based index like the S&P 500 or Wilshire 5000. Some of the reasons for this disappointing record are the costs incurred by actively managed funds, such as the expense of conducting the research to guide stock-picking activities, and trading costs due to higher portfolio turnover. The record on the consistency of fund performance is mixed. In some sample periods, the better-performing funds continue to perform well in the following periods; in other sample periods they do not.

KEY TERMS

closed-end fund, 86	investment companies, 85	soft dollars, 94
exchange-traded funds, 95	load, 87	turnover, 94
funds of funds, 89	net asset value (NAV), 85	12b-1 fees, 92
hedge fund, 88	open-end fund, 86	unit investment trust, 86

PROBLEM SETS

 Select problems are available in McGraw-Hill's *Connect*. **Please see the Supplements section of the book's frontmatter for more information.**

1. What are the benefits to small investors of investing via mutual funds? What are the costs?   *(LO 4-1)*
2. Why can closed-end funds sell at prices that differ from net value while open-end funds do not?   *(LO 4-2)*
3. What is a 12b-1 fee?   *(LO 4-1)*
4. What are some differences between a unit investment trust and a closed-end fund?   *(LO 4-2)*
5. What are the advantages and disadvantages of exchange-traded funds versus mutual funds?   *(LO 4-2)*
6. What are some differences between hedge funds and mutual funds?   *(LO 4-2)*
7. Would you expect a typical open-end fixed-income mutual fund to have higher or lower operating expenses than a fixed-income unit investment trust? Why?   *(LO 4-2)*
8. Balanced funds and asset allocation funds invest in both the stock and bond markets. What is the difference between these types of funds?   *(LO 4-4)*
9. What are some comparative advantages of investing your assets in the following: *(LO 4-2)*
    a. Unit investment trusts.
    b. Open-end mutual funds.
    c. Individual stocks and bonds that you choose for yourself.

10. Open-end equity mutual funds find it necessary to keep a significant percentage of total investments, typically around 5% of the portfolio, in very liquid money market assets. Closed-end funds do not have to maintain such a position in "cash-equivalent" securities. What difference between open-end and closed-end funds might account for their differing policies? *(LO 4-2)*

11. An open-end fund has a net asset value of $10.70 per share. It is sold with a front-end load of 6%. What is the offering price? *(LO 4-3)*

12. If the offering price of an open-end fund is $12.30 per share and the fund is sold with a front-end load of 5%, what is its net asset value? *(LO 4-3)*

13. The composition of the Fingroup Fund portfolio is as follows:

Stock	Shares	Price
A	200,000	$35
B	300,000	40
C	400,000	20
D	600,000	25

The fund has not borrowed any funds, but its accrued management fee with the portfolio manager currently totals $30,000. There are 4 million shares outstanding. What is the net asset value of the fund? *(LO 4-3)*

14. Reconsider the Fingroup Fund in the previous problem. If during the year the portfolio manager sells all of the holdings of stock D and replaces it with 200,000 shares of stock E at $50 per share and 200,000 shares of stock F at $25 per share, what is the portfolio turnover rate? *(LO 4-5)*

15. The Closed Fund is a closed-end investment company with a portfolio currently worth $200 million. It has liabilities of $3 million and 5 million shares outstanding. *(LO 4-3)*
    a. What is the NAV of the fund?
    b. If the fund sells for $36 per share, what is its premium or discount as a percent of NAV?

16. Corporate Fund started the year with a net asset value of $12.50. By year-end, its NAV equaled $12.10. The fund paid year-end distributions of income and capital gains of $1.50. What was the rate of return to an investor in the fund? *(LO 4-3)*

17. A closed-end fund starts the year with a net asset value of $12. By year-end, NAV equals $12.10. At the beginning of the year, the fund is selling at a 2% premium to NAV. By the end of the year, the fund is selling at a 7% discount to NAV. The fund paid year-end distributions of income and capital gains of $1.50. *(LO 4-3)*
    a. What is the rate of return to an investor in the fund during the year?
    b. What would have been the rate of return to an investor who held the same securities as the fund manager during the year?

18. Loaded-Up Fund charges a 12b-1 fee of 1% and maintains an expense ratio of .75%. Economy Fund charges a front-end load of 2%, but has no 12b-1 fee and an expense ratio of .25%. Assume the rate of return on both funds' portfolios (before any fees) is 6% per year. How much will an investment in each fund grow to after: *(LO 4-5)*
    a. 1 year?
    b. 3 years?
    c. 10 years?

19. City Street Fund has a portfolio of $450 million and liabilities of $10 million. *(LO 4-3)*
    a. If there are 44 million shares outstanding, what is the net asset value?
    b. If a large investor redeems 1 million shares, what happens to the portfolio value, to shares outstanding, and to NAV?

20. a. Impressive Fund had excellent investment performance last year, with portfolio returns that placed it in the top 10% of all funds with the same investment policy. Do you expect it to be a top performer next year? Why or why not?

    b. Suppose instead that the fund was among the poorest performers in its comparison group. Would you be more or less likely to believe its relative performance will persist into the following year? Why?   *(LO 4-5)*

21. Consider a mutual fund with $200 million in assets at the start of the year and with 10 million shares outstanding. The fund invests in a portfolio of stocks that provides dividend income at the end of the year of $2 million. The stocks included in the fund's portfolio increase in price by 8%, but no securities are sold, and there are no capital gains distributions. The fund charges 12b-1 fees of 1%, which are deducted from portfolio assets at year-end.   *(LO 4-3)*

    a. What is the net asset value at the start and end of the year?

    b. What is the rate of return for an investor in the fund?

22. The New Fund had average daily assets of $2.2 billion in the past year. The fund sold $400 million and purchased $500 million worth of stock during the year. What was its turnover ratio?   *(LO 4-5)*

23. The New Fund (from Problem 22) had an expense ratio of 1.1%, and its management fee was .7%.   *(LO 4-5)*

    a. What were the total fees paid to the fund's investment managers during the year?

    b. What were the other administrative expenses?

24. You purchased 1,000 shares of the New Fund at a price of $20 per share at the beginning of the year. You paid a front-end load of 4%. The securities in which the fund invests increase in value by 12% during the year. The fund's expense ratio is 1.2%. What is your rate of return on the fund if you sell your shares at the end of the year?   *(LO 4-5)*

25. The Investments Fund sells Class A shares with a front-end load of 6% and Class B shares with 12b-1 fees of .5% annually as well as back-end load fees that start at 5% and fall by 1% for each full year the investor holds the portfolio (until the fifth year). Assume the portfolio rate of return net of operating expenses is 10% annually.   *(LO 4-5)*

    a. If you plan to sell the fund after four years, are Class A or Class B shares the better choice for you?

    b. What if you plan to sell after 15 years?

26. You are considering an investment in a mutual fund with a 4% load and an expense ratio of .5%. You can invest instead in a bank CD paying 6% interest.   *(LO 4-5)*

    a. If you plan to invest for two years, what annual rate of return must the fund portfolio earn for you to be better off in the fund than in the CD? Assume annual compounding of returns.

    b. How does your answer change if you plan to invest for six years? Why does your answer change?

    c. Now suppose that instead of a front-end load the fund assesses a 12b-1 fee of .75% per year.

        i. What annual rate of return must the fund portfolio earn for you to be better off in the fund than in the CD?

        ii. Does your answer in this case depend on your time horizon?

27. Suppose that every time a fund manager trades stock, transaction costs such as commissions and bid–ask spreads amount to .4% of the value of the trade. If the portfolio turnover rate is 50%, by how much is the total return of the portfolio reduced by trading costs?   *(LO 4-5)*

28. You expect a tax-free municipal bond portfolio to provide a rate of return of 4%. Management fees of the fund are .6%.   *(LO 4-4)*

    a. What fraction of portfolio income is given up to fees?

    b. If the management fees for an equity fund also are .6%, but you expect a portfolio return of 12%, what fraction of portfolio income is given up to fees?

c. Why might management fees be a bigger factor in your investment decision for bond funds than for stock funds? Can your conclusion help explain why unmanaged unit investment trusts tend to focus on the fixed-income market?

29. Why would it be challenging to properly compare the performance of an equity fund to a fixed-income mutual fund?   *(LO 4-4)*

Challenge

30. Suppose you observe the investment performance of 350 portfolio managers for five years and rank them by investment returns during each year. After five years, you find that 11 of the funds have investment returns that place the fund in the top half of the sample in each and every year of your sample. Such consistency of performance indicates to you that these must be the funds whose managers are in fact skilled, and you invest your money in these funds. Is your conclusion warranted?   *(LO 4-5)*

Go to **www.morningstar.com**. In the Morningstar Tools section, click on the link for the *Mutual Fund Screener*. Set the criteria you desire, then click on the *Show Results* tab. If you get no funds that meet all of your criteria, choose the criterion that is least important to you and relax that constraint. Continue the process until you have several funds to compare.

1. Examine all of the views available in the drop-down box menu (*Snapshot, Performance, Portfolio,* and *Nuts and Bolts*) to answer the following questions:
   - Which fund has the best expense ratio?
   - Which funds have the lowest Morningstar Risk rating?
   - Which fund has the best 3-year return? Which has the best 10-year return?
   - Which fund has the lowest turnover ratio? Which has the highest?
   - Which fund has the longest manager tenure? Which has the shortest?
   - Do you need to eliminate any of the funds from consideration due to a minimum initial investment that is higher than you are capable of making?

2. Based on what you know about the funds, which one do you think would be the best one for your investment?

3. Select up to five funds that are of the most interest to you. Click on the button that says *Score These Results*. Customize the criteria listed by indicating their importance to you. Examine the score results. Does the fund with the highest score match the choice you made in part 2?

4.1 NAV = ($2,905.1 − $36.1)/79.6 = $36.04

SOLUTIONS TO CONCEPT *checks*

4.2 The net investment in the Class A shares after the 4% commission is $9,600. If the fund earns a 10% return, the investment will grow after n years to $9,600 × $(1.10)^n$. The Class B shares have no front-end load. However, the net return to the investor after 12b-1 fees will be only 9.5%. In addition, there is a back-end load that reduces the sales proceeds by a percentage equal to (5 − years until sale) until the fifth year, when the back-end load expires.

Horizon	Class A Shares $9,600 × (1.10)^n$	Class B Shares $10,000 × (1.095)^n × (1 − percentage exit fee)$
1 year	$10,560.00	$10,000 × (1.095) × (1 − .04) = $10,512.00
4 years	$14,055.36	$10,000 × (1.095)^4 × (1 − .01) = $14,232.89
10 years	$24,899.93	$10,000 × (1.095)^{10}$ = $24,782.28

For a very short horizon such as one year, the Class A shares are the better choice. The front-end and back-end loads are equal, but the Class A shares don't have to pay the 12b-1 fees. For moderate horizons such as four years, the Class B shares dominate because the front-end load of the Class A shares is more costly than the 12b-1 fees and the now-smaller exit fee. For long horizons of 10 years or more, Class A again dominates. In this case, the one-time front-end load is less expensive than the continuing 12b-1 fees.

4.3 *a.* Turnover = $400,000 in trades per $1 million of portfolio value = 40%.

b. Realized capital gains are $10 \times 1,000 = \$10,000$ on FedEx and $5 \times 10,000 = \$50,000$ on Cisco. The tax owed on the capital gains is therefore $.15 \times \$60,000 = \$9,000$.

4.4 Twenty percent of the managers are skilled, which accounts for $.2 \times 400 = 80$ of those managers who appear in the top half. There are 120 slots left in the top half, and 320 other managers, so the probability of an unskilled manager "lucking into" the top half in any year is 120/320, or .375. Therefore, of the 120 lucky managers in the first year, we would expect $.375 \times 120 = 45$ to repeat as top-half performers next year. Thus, we should expect a total of $80 + 45 = 125$, or 62.5%, of the better initial performers to repeat their top-half performance.

Portfolio Theory

PART 2

Chapters in This Part

5 **Risk and Return: Past and Prologue**

6 **Efficient Diversification**

7 **Capital Asset Pricing and Arbitrage Pricing Theory**

8 **The Efficient Market Hypothesis**

9 **Behavioral Finance and Technical Analysis**

The last 90 years witnessed the Great Depression, seven additional recessions of varying severity, and the deep recession that began in 2007. Yet even with these downturns, a dollar invested in a broad portfolio of stocks over this period still grew to a value almost 200 times greater than a dollar invested (and reinvested) in safe assets such as Treasury bills. Why then would anyone invest in a safe asset? Because investors are risk averse, and risk is as important to them as the expected value of returns. Chapter 5, the first of five in Part Two, provides the tools needed to interpret the history of rates of return, and the lessons that history offers for how investors might go about constructing portfolios using both safe and risky assets.

Deciding the proportion an investor desires to put at risk must be augmented by a decision of how to construct an efficient portfolio of risky assets. Chapter 6 lays out modern portfolio theory (MPT), which involves the construction of the risky portfolio. It aims to accomplish efficient diversification across asset classes like bonds and stocks and across individual securities within these asset classes.

This analysis quickly leads to other questions. For example, how should one measure the risk of an individual asset held as part of a diversified portfolio? You may be surprised at the answer. Once we have an acceptable measure of risk, what precisely should be the relation between risk and return? And what is the minimally acceptable rate of return for an investment to be considered attractive? These questions also are addressed in this part of the text. Chapter 7 introduces the Capital Asset Pricing Model (CAPM) and Arbitrage Pricing Theory (APT), as well as index and multi-index models, all mainstays of applied financial economics. These models link risk with the return investors can reasonably expect on various securities.

Next, we come to one of the most controversial topics in investment management, the question of whether portfolio managers—amateur or professional—can outperform simple investment strategies such as "buy a market index fund." The evidence in Chapter 8 will at least make you pause before pursuing active strategies. You will come to appreciate how good active managers must be to outperform passive strategies. Finally, Chapter 9 on behavioral finance is concerned with lessons from psychology that have been proposed to explain irrational investor behavior that leads to observed anomalies in patterns of asset returns.

5

Risk and Return: Past and Prologue

Learning Objectives

LO 5-1 Compute various measures of return on multi-year investments.

LO 5-2 Use either historical data on the past performance of stocks and bonds or forward-looking scenario analysis to characterize the risk and return features of these investments.

LO 5-3 Determine the expected return and risk of portfolios that are constructed by combining risky assets with risk-free investments in Treasury bills.

LO 5-4 Use the Sharpe ratio to evaluate the performance of a portfolio and provide a guide for capital allocation.

What constitutes a satisfactory investment portfolio? Until the early 1970s, a reasonable answer would have been a federally insured bank savings account (a risk-free asset) plus a risky portfolio of U.S. stocks. Nowadays, investors have access to a vast array of assets and can easily construct portfolios that include foreign stocks and bonds, real estate, precious metals, and collectibles. Even more complex strategies may include futures, options, and other derivatives to insure portfolios against specified risks.

Clearly every individual security must be judged on its contributions to both the expected return and the risk of the entire portfolio. We begin with an examination of various conventions for measuring and reporting rates of return. Next, we turn to the historical performance of several broadly diversified portfolios.

We then consider the simplest form of risk control, capital allocation: choosing the fraction of the portfolio invested in virtually risk-free securities versus risky securities. We show how to calculate the performance one may expect from various allocations and contemplate the mix that would best suit different investors. With this background, we can evaluate a passive strategy that will serve as a benchmark for the active strategies considered in the next chapter.

5.1 RATES OF RETURN

A key measure of investors' success is the rate at which their funds have grown during the investment period. The total **holding-period return (HPR)** of a share of stock depends on the increase (or decrease) in the price of the share over the investment period as well as on any dividend income the share has provided. The rate of return is defined as dollars earned over the investment period (price appreciation plus dividends) per dollar invested:

holding-period return (HPR)

Rate of return over a given investment period.

$$\text{HPR} = \frac{\text{Ending price} - \text{Beginning price} + \text{Cash dividend}}{\text{Beginning price}} \qquad \text{(5.1)}$$

This definition assumes that the dividend is paid at the end of the holding period. When dividends are received earlier, the definition ignores reinvestment income between the receipt of the dividend and the end of the holding period. The percentage return from dividends, cash dividends/beginning price, is called the *dividend yield,* and so the dividend yield plus the capital gains yield equals the HPR.

This definition of holding return is easy to modify for other types of investments. For example, the HPR on a bond would use the same formula, with interest or coupon payments taking the place of dividends.

EXAMPLE 5.1
Holding-Period Return

The price of a share of an indexed stock is currently $100, and your time horizon is one year. You expect the cash dividend during the year to be $4, so your expected dividend yield is 4%.

Your HPR will depend on the price one year from now. Suppose your best guess is that it will be $110 per share. Then your expected *capital gain* will be $10, so your capital gains yield will be $10/$100 = .10, or 10%. The HPR is the sum of the dividend yield plus the capital gains yield, 4% + 10% = 14%.

$$\text{HPR} = \frac{\$110 - \$100 + \$4}{\$100} = .14, \text{ or } 14\%$$

Measuring Investment Returns over Multiple Periods

The HPR is a simple and unambiguous measure of investment return over a single period. But often you will be interested in average returns over longer periods of time. For example, you might want to measure how well a mutual fund has performed over the preceding five-year period. In this case, return measurement is ambiguous.

Consider a fund that starts with $1 million under management. It receives additional funds from new and existing shareholders and also redeems shares of existing shareholders so that net cash inflow can be positive or negative. The fund's quarterly results are given in Table 5.1, with negative numbers in parentheses.

The numbers indicate that when the firm does well (i.e., achieves a high HPR), it attracts new funds; otherwise it may suffer a net outflow. For example, the 10% return in the first quarter by itself increased assets under management by .10 × $1 million = $100,000; it also elicited new investments of $100,000, thus bringing assets under management to $1.2 million by the end of the quarter. An even better HPR in the second quarter elicited a larger net inflow, and the second quarter ended with $2 million under management. However, HPR in the third quarter was negative, and net inflows were negative.

How would we characterize fund performance over the year, given that the fund experienced both cash inflows and outflows? There are several candidate measures of performance, each with its own advantages and shortcomings: the *arithmetic average, geometric average,* and *dollar-weighted return.* These measures may vary considerably, so it is important to understand their differences.

ARITHMETIC AVERAGE The **arithmetic average** of the quarterly returns is just the sum of the quarterly returns divided by the number of quarters: (10 + 25 − 20 + 20)/4 = 8.75%.

arithmetic average

The sum of returns in each period divided by the number of periods.

TABLE 5.1	Quarterly cash flows and rates of return of a mutual fund			
	1st Quarter	**2nd Quarter**	**3rd Quarter**	**4th Quarter**
Assets under management at start of quarter ($ million)	1.0	1.2	2.0	0.8
Holding-period return (%)	10.0	25.0	(20.0)	20.0
Total assets before net inflows	1.1	1.5	1.6	0.96
Net inflow ($ million)*	0.1	0.5	(0.8)	0.6
Assets under management at end of quarter ($ million)	1.2	2.0	0.8	1.56

*New investment less redemptions and distributions, all assumed to occur at the end of each quarter.

Because this statistic ignores compounding, it does not represent an equivalent, single quarterly rate for the year. However, without information beyond the historical sample, the arithmetic average is the best forecast of performance for the next quarter.

geometric average

The single per-period return that gives the same cumulative performance as the sequence of actual returns.

GEOMETRIC AVERAGE   The **geometric average** of the quarterly returns is equal to the single per-period return that would give the same cumulative performance as the sequence of actual returns. We calculate the geometric average by compounding the actual period-by-period returns and then finding the single per-period rate that will compound to the same final value. In our example, the geometric average quarterly return, r_G, is defined by:

$$(1 + .10) \times (1 + .25) \times (1 - .20) \times (1 + .20) = (1 + r_G)^4$$

The left-hand side of this equation is the compounded year-end value of a $1 investment earning the four quarterly returns. The right-hand side is the compounded value of a $1 investment earning r_G *each* quarter. We solve for r_G:

$$r_G = [(1 + .10) \times (1 + .25) \times (1 - .20) \times (1 + .20)]^{1/4} - 1 = .0719, \text{ or } 7.19\% \quad \text{(5.2)}$$

The geometric return is also called a *time-weighted average return* because it ignores the quarter-to-quarter variation in funds under management. In fact, an investor will obtain a larger cumulative return when high returns are earned in periods when larger sums have been invested and low returns are earned when less money is at risk. In Table 5.1, the higher returns (25% and 20%) were achieved in quarters 2 and 4, when the fund managed $1,200,000 and $800,000, respectively. The lower returns (−20% and 10%) occurred when the fund managed $2,000,000 and $1,000,000, respectively. In this case, better returns were earned when *less* money was under management—an unfavorable combination.

Published data on past returns earned by mutual funds actually are *required* to be time-weighted returns. The rationale for this practice is that since the fund manager does not have full control over the amount of assets under management, we should not weight returns in one period more heavily than those in other periods when assessing "typical" past performance.

DOLLAR-WEIGHTED RETURN   To account for varying amounts under management, we treat the fund cash flows as we would a capital budgeting problem in corporate finance and compute the portfolio manager's internal rate of return (IRR). The initial value of $1 million and the net cash inflows are treated as the cash flows associated with an investment "project." The year-end "liquidation value" of the portfolio is the final cash flow of the project. In our example, the investor's net cash flows are as follows:

	Quarter				
	0	**1**	**2**	**3**	**4**
Net cash flow ($ million)	−1.0	−.1	−.5	.8	−.6 + 1.56 = .96

The entry for time 0 reflects the starting contribution of $1 million; the negative entries for times 1 and 2 are additional net inflows in those quarters, whereas the positive value for quarter 3 signifies a withdrawal of funds. Finally, the entry for time 4 represents the sum of the final (negative) cash inflow plus the value of the portfolio at the end of the fourth quarter. The latter is the value for which the portfolio could have been liquidated at year-end.

The **dollar-weighted average return** is the internal rate of return of the project. The IRR is the interest rate that sets the present value of the cash flows realized on the portfolio (including the $1.56 million for which the portfolio can be liquidated at the end of the year) equal to the initial cost of establishing the portfolio. It therefore is the interest rate that satisfies the following equation:

dollar-weighted average return

The internal rate of return on an investment.

$$0 = -1.0 + \frac{-.1}{1 + IRR} + \frac{-.5}{(1 + IRR)^2} + \frac{.8}{(1 + IRR)^3} + \frac{.96}{(1 + IRR)^4} \qquad \textbf{(5.3)}$$

The solution to Equation 5.3 is IRR = 0.0338 = 3.38%. The dollar-weighted return in this example is smaller than the time-weighted return of 7.19% because, as we noted, the portfolio returns were higher when less money was under management. The difference between the dollar- and time-weighted average return in this case is quite large.

CONCEPT check   5.1

A fund begins with $10 million and reports the following monthly results (with negative figures in parentheses):

	Month		
	1	**2**	**3**
Net inflows (end of month, $ million)	3	5	0
HPR (%)	2	8	(4)

Compute the arithmetic, time-weighted, and dollar-weighted average monthly returns.

Conventions for Annualizing Rates of Return

We've seen that there are several ways to compute average rates of return. There also is some variation in how the mutual fund in our example might annualize its quarterly returns.

Returns on assets with regular cash flows, such as mortgages (with monthly payments) and bonds (with semiannual coupons), usually are quoted as annual percentage rates, or APRs, which annualize per-period rates using a simple interest approach, ignoring compound interest:

$$APR = \text{Per-period rate} \times \text{Periods per year}$$

However, because it ignores compounding, the APR does not equal the rate at which your invested funds actually grow. The latter is called the *effective annual rate* (EAR). When there are n compounding periods in the year, we first recover the rate per period as APR/n and then compound that rate for the number of periods in a year. For example, $n = 12$ for monthly payment mortgages and $n = 2$ for bonds making payments semiannually.

$$1 + EAR = (1 + \text{Rate per period})^n = \left(1 + \frac{APR}{n}\right)^n \tag{5.4}$$

Because the rate earned each period is APR/n, after one year (when n periods have passed), your cumulative return is $(1 + APR/n)^n$. Note that one needs to know the holding period when given an APR in order to convert it to an effective rate.

Rearranging Equation 5.4, we can also find APR given EAR:[1]

$$APR = [(1 + EAR)^{1/n} - 1] \times n$$

EAR diverges from APR by greater amounts as n becomes larger (we compound cash flows more frequently). In the limit, we can envision continuous compounding when n becomes extremely large in Equation 5.4. With continuous compounding, the APR is related to EAR by

$$1 + EAR = e^{APR} \tag{5.5A}$$

or, equivalently,

$$APR = \ln(1 + EAR) = r_{cc} \tag{5.5B}$$

As Equation 5.5B shows, we will use the notation r_{cc} when we want to highlight that we are using continuously compounded rates. We will return to continuous compounding later in the chapter.

EXAMPLE 5.2

Annualizing Treasury-Bill Returns

Suppose you buy a $10,000 face value Treasury bill maturing in six months for $9,900. On the bill's maturity date you collect the face value. Because there are no other interest payments, the holding-period return for this six-month investment is

$$HPR = \frac{\text{Cash income} + \text{Price change}}{\text{Initial price}} = \frac{0 + \$100}{\$9,900} = .0101 = 1.01\%$$

The APR on this investment is therefore $1.01\% \times 2 = 2.02\%$. The effective annual rate is higher:

$$1 + EAR = (1.0101)^2 = 1.0203$$

which implies that EAR = .0203 = 2.03%.

A warning: Terminology on the street can be loose. Occasionally, *annual percentage yield* or *APY* and even *APR* are used interchangeably with effective annual rate, and this can lead to confusion. To avoid error, you must be alert to context.

The difficulties in interpreting rates of return over time do not end here. Two thorny issues remain: the uncertainty surrounding the investment in question and the effect of inflation.

5.2   INFLATION AND THE REAL RATE OF INTEREST

A 10% annual rate of return means that your investment is worth 10% more at the end of the year than at the beginning. This does not necessarily mean, however, that you can buy 10% more goods and services with that money, for it is possible that in the course of the year prices

---

[1]The Excel function "EFFECT" will convert APR to EAR, while "NOMINAL" will do the reverse.

of goods also have increased. If prices have changed, the increase in your purchasing power will not match the increase in your dollar wealth.

At any time, the prices of some goods may rise while the prices of others may fall; the *general* trend in prices is measured by changes in the consumer price index (CPI). The CPI measures the cost of purchasing a representative bundle of goods, the "consumption basket" of a typical urban family of four. The **inflation rate** is measured by the rate of increase of the CPI.

inflation rate

The rate at which prices are rising, measured as the rate of increase of the CPI.

Suppose the rate of inflation (the percentage change in the CPI, denoted by i) for the last year amounted to $i = 6\%$. The purchasing power of money is thus reduced by 6%. Therefore, part of your investment earnings are offset by the reduction in purchasing power. With a 10% interest rate, after you net out the 6% reduction in the purchasing power of money, you are left with a net increase in purchasing power of about 4%. Thus, we need to distinguish between a **nominal interest rate**—the growth rate of money—and a **real interest rate**—the growth rate of purchasing power. If we call R the nominal rate, r the real rate, and i the inflation rate, then we conclude

nominal interest rate

The interest rate in terms of nominal (not adjusted for purchasing power) dollars.

$$r \approx R - i \qquad \text{(5.6)}$$

In words, the real rate of interest is the nominal rate reduced by the rate of inflation.

In fact, the exact relationship between the real and nominal interest rates is given by

real interest rate

The excess of the interest rate over the inflation rate. The growth rate of purchasing power derived from an investment.

$$1 + r = \frac{1 + R}{1 + i} \qquad \text{(5.7)}$$

In words, the growth factor of your purchasing power, $1 + r$, equals the growth factor of your money, $1 + R$, divided by the new price level that is $1 + i$ times its value in the previous period. The exact relationship can be rearranged to

$$r = \frac{R - i}{1 + i} \qquad \text{(5.8)}$$

which shows that the approximate rule overstates the real rate by the factor $1 + i$.[2]

If the interest rate on a one-year CD is 8%, and you expect inflation to be 5% over the coming year, then using the approximation given in Equation 5.6, you expect the real rate to be $r = 8\% - 5\% = 3\%$. Using the exact formula given in Equation 5.8, the real rate is $r = \frac{.08 - .05}{1 + .05} = .0286$, or 2.86%.

Therefore, the approximation rule overstates the expected real rate by only .14 percentage points. The approximation rule of Equation 5.7 is more accurate for small inflation rates and is perfectly exact for continuously compounded rates.

EXAMPLE 5.3

Real versus Nominal Rates

The Equilibrium Nominal Rate of Interest

We've seen that the real rate of return is approximately the nominal rate minus the inflation rate. Because investors should be concerned with real returns—the increase in their purchasing power—they will demand higher nominal rates of return in the face of expected inflation.

Irving Fisher (1930) argued that the nominal rate ought to increase one-for-one with increases in the expected inflation rate. Using $E(i)$ to denote the current expected inflation over the coming period, the *Fisher equation* is

$$R = r + E(i) \qquad \text{(5.9)}$$

---

[2]Notice that for continuously compounded rates, Equation 5.7 is perfectly accurate. Because $\ln(x/y) = \ln(x) - \ln(y)$, the continuously compounded real rate of return, r_{cc}, can be derived from the annual rates as

$$r_{cc} = \ln(1 + r) = \ln\left(\frac{1 + R}{1 + i}\right) = \ln(1 + R) - \ln(1 + i) = R_{cc} - i_{cc}$$

Suppose the real rate of interest is 2%, and expected inflation is 4%, so that the nominal interest rate is about 6%. If expected inflation rises to 5%, the nominal interest rate should climb to roughly 7%. The increase in the nominal rate offsets the increase in expected inflation, giving investors an unchanged growth of purchasing power at a 2% rate.

CONCEPT
check **5.2**

a. Suppose the real interest rate is 3% per year, and the expected inflation rate is 8%. What is the nominal interest rate?

b. Suppose the expected inflation rate rises to 10%, but the real rate is unchanged. What happens to the nominal interest rate?

The Fed is normally concerned with price stability, that is, keeping inflation both moderate and predictable. When it is successful, T-bill rates tend to follow anticipated inflation, thereby resulting in a stable real rate, just as Fisher hypothesized. The Fisher equation is more prone to fail in extreme and, more importantly, unanticipated economic conditions. For example, in the face of a booming economy, when inflation substantially exceeds expectations, nominal rates can lag and real rates will fall to unusually low, even negative, levels. At the other end, when the economy tanks and inflation falls rapidly, if interest rates lag behind, real rates will rise to abnormally high levels. In even more extreme downturns such as the Great Depression, inflation can be negative, with the general level of prices actually falling; nominal rates, however, cannot sink below zero, meaning that the real rate can be extremely high. Hence, the empirical validity of the Fisher equation may be quite sensitive to boom and bust episodes within any particular period.

5.3   RISK AND RISK PREMIUMS

Any investment involves some degree of uncertainty about future holding-period returns, and in many cases that uncertainty is considerable. Sources of investment risk range from macroeconomic fluctuations, to the changing fortunes of various industries, to asset-specific unexpected developments. Analysis of these multiple sources of risk is presented in Part Four, "Security Analysis."

Scenario Analysis and Probability Distributions

scenario analysis

Process of devising a list of possible economic scenarios and specifying the likelihood of each one, as well as the HPR that will be realized in each case.

probability distribution

List of possible outcomes with associated probabilities.

expected return

The mean value of the distribution of HPR.

When we attempt to quantify risk, we begin with the question: What HPRs are possible, and how likely are they? A good way to approach this question is to devise a list of possible economic outcomes, or *scenarios,* and specify both the likelihood (probability) of each scenario and the HPR the asset will realize in that scenario. Therefore, this approach is called **scenario analysis.** The list of possible HPRs with associated probabilities is the **probability distribution** of HPRs. Consider an investment in a broad portfolio of stocks, say, an index fund, which we will refer to as the "stock market." A very simple scenario analysis for the stock market (assuming only four possible scenarios) is illustrated in Spreadsheet 5.1.

The probability distribution lets us derive measurements for both the reward and the risk of the investment. The reward from the investment is its **expected return,** which you can think of as the average HPR you would earn if you were to repeat an investment in the asset many times. The expected return also is called the *mean of the distribution* of HPRs and often is referred to as the *mean return.*

To compute the expected return from the data provided, we label scenarios by s and denote the HPR in each scenario as $r(s)$, with probability $p(s)$. The expected return, denoted $E(r)$, is then the weighted average of returns in all possible scenarios, $s = 1, \ldots, S,$ with weights equal to the probability of that particular scenario.

$$E(r) = \sum_{s=1}^{S} p(s)r(s)$$ **(5.10)**

SPREADSHEET 5.1

Scenario analysis for the stock market

	A	B	C	D	E	F
1				Column B x Column C	Deviation from Mean Return	Column B x Squared Deviation
2	Scenario	Probability	HPR (%)			
3	1. Severe recession	0.05	−37	−1.85	−47.00	110.45
4	2. Mild recession	0.25	−11	−2.75	−21.00	110.25
5	3. Normal growth	0.40	14	5.60	4.00	6.40
6	4. Boom	0.30	30	9.00	20.00	120.00
7	Column sums:		Expected return =	10.00	Variance =	347.10
8			Square root of variance = Standard deviation (%) =			18.63

This spreadsheet is available in Connect

Each entry in column D of Spreadsheet 5.1 corresponds to one of the products in the summation in Equation 5.10. The value in cell D7, which is the sum of these products, is therefore the expected return. Therefore, $E(r) = 10\%$.

Because there is risk to the investment, the actual return may be (a lot) more or less than 10%. If a "boom" materializes, the return will be better, 30%, but in a severe recession the return will be a disappointing −37%. How can we quantify this uncertainty?

The "surprise" return in any scenario is the difference between the actual return and the expected return. For example, in a boom (scenario 4) the surprise is $r(4) - E(r) = 30\% - 10\% = 20\%$. In a severe recession (scenario 1), the surprise is $r(1) - E(r) = -37\% - 10\% = -47\%$.

Uncertainty surrounding the investment is a function of both the magnitudes and the probabilities of the possible surprises. To summarize risk with a single number, we define the **variance** as the expected value of the *squared* deviation from the mean (the expected squared "surprise" across scenarios).

$$\text{Var}(r) \equiv \sigma^2 = \sum_{s=1}^{S} p(s)[r(s) - E(r)]^2 \tag{5.11}$$

variance

The expected value of the squared deviation from the mean.

We square the deviations because otherwise, negative deviations would offset positive deviations with the result that the expected deviation from the mean return would necessarily be zero. Squared deviations are necessarily positive. Squaring (which is a nonlinear transformation) exaggerates large (positive or negative) deviations and deemphasizes small deviations.

Another result of squaring deviations is that the variance has a dimension of percent squared. To give the measure of risk the same dimension as expected return (%), we use the **standard deviation,** defined as the square root of the variance:

$$SD(r) \equiv \sigma = \sqrt{\text{Var}(r)} \tag{5.12}$$

standard deviation

The square root of the variance.

Applying Equation 5.10 to the data in Spreadsheet 5.1, we find that the expected rate of return on the stock index fund is

$$E(r) = .05 \times (-37) + .25 \times (-11) + .40 \times 14 + .30 \times 30 = 10\%$$

We use Equation 5.11 to find the variance. First we take the difference between the holding-period return in each scenario and the mean return, then we square that difference, and finally we multiply by the probability of each scenario. The sum of the probability-weighted squared deviations is the variance.

$$\sigma^2 = .05(-37 - 10)^2 + .25(-11 - 10)^2 + .40(14 - 10)^2 + .30(30 - 10)^2 = 347.10$$

and so the standard deviation is

$$\sigma = \sqrt{347.10} = 18.63\%$$

Column F of Spreadsheet 5.1 replicates these calculations. Each entry in that column is the squared deviation from the mean multiplied by the probability of that scenario. The sum of the probability-weighted squared deviations that appears in cell F7 is the variance, and the square root of that value is the standard deviation (in cell F8).

EXAMPLE 5.4

Expected Return and Standard Deviation

The Normal Distribution

The normal distribution is central to the theory *and* practice of investments. Its familiar bell-shaped plot is symmetric, with identical values for all three standard measures of "typical" results: the mean (the expected value discussed earlier), the median (the value above and below which we expect 50% of the observations), and the mode (the most likely value).

Figure 5.1 illustrates a normal distribution with a mean of 10% and standard deviation (SD) of 20%. Notice that the probabilities are highest for outcomes near the mean and are significantly lower for outcomes far from the mean. But what do we mean by an outcome "far" from the mean? A return 15% below the mean would hardly be noteworthy if typical volatility were high, for example, if the standard deviation of returns were 20%, but that same outcome would be highly unusual if the standard deviation were only 5%. For this reason, it is often useful to think about deviations from the mean in terms of how many standard deviations they represent. If the standard deviation is 20%, that 15% negative surprise would be only three-fourths of a standard deviation, unfortunate perhaps but not uncommon. But if the standard deviation were only 5%, a 15% deviation would be a "three-sigma event," and quite rare.

We can transform any normally distributed return, r_i, into a "standard deviation score," by first subtracting the mean return (to obtain the distance from the mean or the return "surprise") and then dividing by the standard deviation (which enables us to measure distance from the mean in units of standard deviations).

$$sr_i = \frac{r_i - E(r_i)}{\sigma_i} \tag{5.13A}$$

This standardized return, which we have denoted sr_i, is normally distributed with a mean of zero and a standard deviation of 1. We therefore say that sr_i is a "standard normal" variable.

Conversely, we can start with a standard normal return, sr_i, and recover the original return by multiplying by the standard deviation and adding back the mean return:

$$r_i = E(r_i) + sr_i \times \sigma_i \tag{5.13B}$$

In fact, this is how we drew Figure 5.1. Start with a standard normal (mean = 0 and SD = 1); next, multiply the distance from the mean by the assumed standard deviation of 20%; finally, recenter the mean away from zero by adding 10%. This gives us a normal variable with mean 10% and standard deviation 20%.

FIGURE   5.1

The normal distribution with mean return 10% and standard deviation 20%

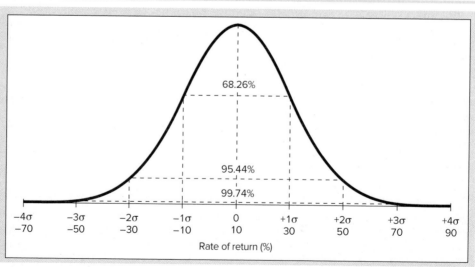

Figure 5.1 shows that when returns are normally distributed, roughly two-thirds (more precisely, 68.26%) of the observations fall within one standard deviation of the mean, that is, the probability that any observation in a sample of returns would be no more than one standard deviation away from the mean is 68.26%. Deviations from the mean of more than two SDs are even rarer: 95.44% of the observations are expected to lie within this range. Finally, only 2.6 out of 1,000 observations are expected to deviate from the mean by three or more SDs.

Two special properties of the normal distribution lead to critical simplifications of investment management when returns are normally distributed:

1. The return on a portfolio comprising two or more assets whose returns are normally distributed also will be normally distributed.
2. The normal distribution is completely described by its mean and standard deviation. No other statistic is needed to learn about the behavior of normally distributed returns.

These two properties in turn imply this far-reaching conclusion:

3. The standard deviation is the appropriate measure of risk for a portfolio of assets with normally distributed returns. In this case, no other statistic can improve the risk assessment conveyed by the standard deviation of a portfolio.

Suppose you worry about large investment losses in worst-case scenarios for your portfolio. You might ask: "How much would I lose in a fairly extreme outcome, for example, if my return were in the fifth percentile of the distribution?" You can expect your investment experience to be worse than this value only 5% of the time and better 95% of the time. In investments parlance, this cutoff is called the **value at risk** (denoted by **VaR,** to distinguish it from Var, the common notation for variance). A loss-averse investor might desire to limit portfolio VaR, that is, limit the loss corresponding to a probability of 5%.

value at risk (VaR)

Measure of downside risk. The worst loss that will be suffered with a given probability, often 5%.

For normally distributed returns, VaR can be derived from the mean and standard deviation of the distribution. We calculate it using Excel's standard normal function = NORMSINV(0.05). This function computes the fifth percentile of a normal distribution with a mean of zero and a variance of 1, which turns out to be −1.64485. In other words, a value that is 1.64485 standard deviations below the mean would correspond to a VaR of 5%.

$$\text{VaR} = E(r) + (-1.64485)\sigma \qquad (5.14)$$

We can also obtain this value directly from Excel's *nonstandard* normal distribution function = NORMINV (.05, $E(r)$, σ).

When faced with a sample of actual returns that may not be normally distributed, we must estimate the VaR directly. The 5% VaR is the fifth-percentile rate of return. For a sample of 100 returns this is straightforward: If the rates are ordered from high to low, count the fifth observation from the bottom.

Calculating the 5% VaR for samples where 5% of the observations don't make an integer requires interpolation. Suppose we have 72 monthly observations so that 5% of the sample is 3.6 observations. We approximate the VaR by going .6 of the distance from the third to the fourth rate from the bottom. Suppose these rates are −42% and −37%. The interpolated value for VaR is then −42 + .6(42 − 37) = −39%.

In practice, analysts sometimes compare the historical sample VaR to the VaR implied by a normal distribution with the same mean and SD as the sample rates. The difference between these VaR values indicates the deviation of the observed rates from normality.

CONCEPT check 5.3

a. The current value of a stock portfolio is $23 million. A financial analyst summarizes the uncertainty about next year's holding-period return using the scenario analysis in the following spreadsheet. What are the annual holding-period returns of the portfolio in each

(continued)

(concluded)

scenario? Calculate the expected holding-period return, the standard deviation of returns, and the 5% VaR. What is the VaR of a portfolio with normally distributed returns with the same mean and standard deviation as this stock?

	A	B	C	D	E
1	Business Conditions	Scenario, s	Probability, p	End-of-Year Value ($ million)	Annual Dividend ($ million)
2	High growth	1	0.30	35	4.40
3	Normal growth	2	0.45	27	4.00
4	No growth	3	0.20	15	4.00
5	Recession	4	0.05	8	2.00

b. Suppose that the worst three rates of return in a sample of 36 monthly observations are 17%, −5%, and 2%. Estimate the 5% VaR.

Normality over Time

The fact that portfolios of normally distributed assets also are normally distributed greatly simplifies analysis of risk because standard deviation, a simple-to-calculate number, is the appropriate risk measure for normally distributed portfolios.

But even if returns are normal for any particular time period, will they also be normal for other holding periods? Suppose that monthly rates are normally distributed with a mean of 1%. The expected annual rate of return is then $1.01^{12} - 1$. Can this annual rate, which is a nonlinear function of the monthly return, also be normally distributed? Unfortunately, the answer is no. Similarly, why would monthly rates be normally distributed when a monthly rate is $(1 + \text{daily rate})^{30} - 1$? Indeed, they are not. So, do we really get to enjoy the simplifications offered by the normal distribution?

Despite these potential complications, when returns over very short time periods (e.g., an hour or even a day) are normally distributed, then HPRs up to holding periods as long as a month will be *nearly* normal, so we can treat them as if they are normal. Longer-term, for example, annual, HPRs will indeed deviate more substantially from normality, but even here, if we expressed those HPRs as continuously compounded rates, they will remain normally distributed. The practical implication is this: Use continuously compounded rates in all work where normality plays a crucial role, as in estimating VaR from actual returns.

To see why relatively short-term rates are still nearly normal, consider these calculations: Suppose that rates are normally distributed over an infinitesimally short period. Beyond that, compounding takes them adrift from normality. But for short holding periods those deviations will be very small. Suppose that the continuously compounded rate of return in a particular year was .12 (i.e., 12%; we must work with decimals when using continuously compounded rates). Then the effective annual rate (using Equation 5.5A) was $e^{.12} - 1 = .1275$. So the difference between the effective annual rate and continuously compounded rate is meaningful, .75%, or 75 basis points. On a monthly basis, however, the equivalent continuously compounded return was 1%, implying a monthly effective rate of $e^{.01} - 1 = .01005$. The difference between effective and continuously compounded rates here is trivial, only one-half of a basis point. For shorter periods the difference will be smaller still. Therefore, when continuously compounded rates are normal, rates over periods up to a month are so close to continuously compounded values that we can treat them as if they are effectively normal.

Another important aspect of (normal) continuously compounded rates over time is this: Just as the total continuously compounded rate grows in direct proportion to the length of the investment period, so does the variance (*not* the standard deviation) of the total continuously compounded return. Hence, for an asset with annual continuously compounded SD of .20 (20%), the variance is $.20^2 = .04$, and the quarterly variance is .01, implying a quarterly standard deviation of .10, or 10%. (Verify that the monthly standard deviation is 5.77%.) Because variance grows in direct proportion to time, the standard deviation grows in proportion to the square root of time.

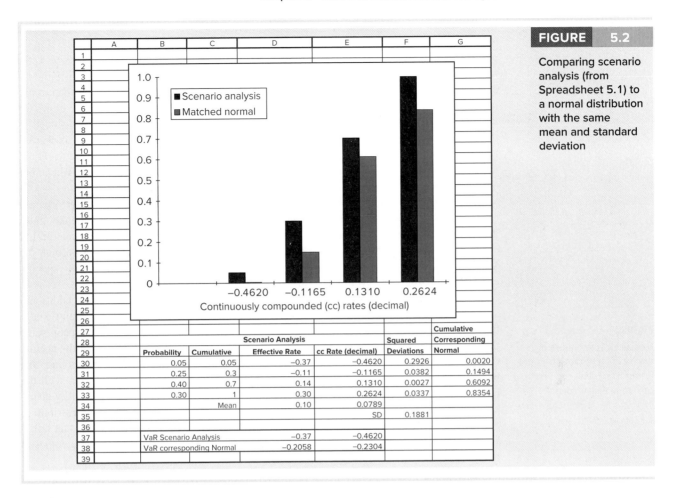

FIGURE   5.2

Comparing scenario analysis (from Spreadsheet 5.1) to a normal distribution with the same mean and standard deviation

			Scenario Analysis			Squared	Cumulative Corresponding
	Probability	Cumulative	Effective Rate	cc Rate (decimal)	Deviations	Normal
	0.05	0.05	−0.37	−0.4620	0.2926	0.0020
	0.25	0.3	−0.11	−0.1165	0.0382	0.1494
	0.40	0.7	0.14	0.1310	0.0027	0.6092
	0.30	1	0.30	0.2624	0.0337	0.8354
		Mean	0.10	0.0789		
				SD	0.1881	
	VaR Scenario Analysis		−0.37	−0.4620		
	VaR corresponding Normal		−0.2058	−0.2304		

Deviation from Normality and Value at Risk

The scenario analysis laid out in Spreadsheet 5.1 offers insight about the issue of normality in practice. While a four-scenario analysis is quite simplistic, even this simple example can shed light on how practical analysis might take shape.[3]

How can the returns specified in the scenario analysis in Spreadsheet 5.1 be judged against the normal distribution? As prescribed above, we first convert the effective rates in each scenario to continuously compounded rates using Equation 5.5. Obviously, it is naive to believe that this simple analysis specifies the probabilities of all possible rates. But while we cannot explicitly pin down probabilities of rates other than those given in the table, we can get a good sense of the entire spectrum of potential outcomes by examining the distribution of the assumed scenario rates, as well as their mean and standard deviation.

Figure 5.2 shows the known points from the cumulative distribution of the scenario analysis next to the corresponding points from a "matched normal distribution" (a normal distribution with the same mean and standard deviation). Below the graph, we see a table of the actual distributions. The mean in cell D34 is computed from the formula =SUMPRODUCT($B$30:$B$33, D30:D33), where the probability cells B30:B33 are fixed to allow copying to the right.[4] Similarly,

---

[3]You may wonder: Is the fact that the probability of the worst-case scenario is .05 in Spreadsheet 5.1 just a lucky happenstance given our interest in the 5% VaR? The answer is no. Given investor concern about VaR, it is fair (in fact, necessary) to demand of analysts that their scenario analysis explicitly take a stand on the rate of return corresponding to the probability of the VaR of interest, here .05.

[4]The Excel function SUMPRODUCT multiplies each term in the first column specified (in this case, the probabilities in column B) with the corresponding terms in the second column specified (in this case, the returns in column D), and then adds up those products. This gives us the expected rate of return across scenarios.

the SD in cell F35 is computed from =SUMPRODUCT($B30:$B33, F30:F33)^0.5. The 5% VaR of the normal distribution in cell E38 is computed from =NORMINV(0.05, E34, F35).

VaR values appear in cells D37 and D38. The VaR from the scenario analysis, −37%, is far worse than the VaR corresponding to the matched normal distribution, −20.58%. This immediately suggests that the scenario analysis entails a higher probability of extreme losses than would be consistent with a normal distribution. On the other hand, the normal distribution allows for the possibility of extremely large returns, beyond the maximum return of 30% envisioned in the scenario analysis. We conclude that the scenario analysis has a distribution that is skewed to the left compared to the normal. It has a longer left tail (larger losses) and a shorter right tail (smaller gains). It makes up for this negative attribute with a larger probability of positive, but not extremely large, gains (14% and 30%).

This example shows when and why the VaR is an important statistic. When returns are normal, knowing just the mean and standard deviation allows us to fully describe the entire distribution. In that case, we do not need to estimate VaR explicitly—we can calculate it exactly from the properties of the normal distribution. But when returns are not normal, the VaR conveys important additional information beyond mean and standard deviation, specifically, the probability of severe losses arising from deviations from normality.[5]

Because risk is largely driven by the likelihood of extreme negative returns, two additional statistics are used to indicate whether a portfolio's probability distribution differs significantly from normality with respect to potential extreme values. The first is **kurtosis,** which compares the frequency of extreme values to that of the normal distribution. The kurtosis of the normal distribution is zero, so positive values indicate higher frequency of extreme values than this benchmark. A negative value suggests that extreme values are less frequent than with the normal distribution. Kurtosis sometimes is called "fat tail risk," as plots of probability distributions with higher likelihood of extreme events will be higher than the normal distribution at both ends or "tails" of the distribution; in other words, the distributions exhibit "fat tails." Similarly, exposure to extreme events is often called *tail risk,* because these are outcomes in the far reaches or "tail" of the probability distribution.

The second statistic is the **skew,** which measures the asymmetry of the distribution. Skew takes on a value of zero if, like the normal, the distribution is symmetric. Negative skew suggests that extreme negative values are more frequent than extreme positive ones. Nonzero values for kurtosis and skew indicate that special attention should be paid to the VaR, in addition to the use of standard deviation as measure of portfolio risk.

Using Time Series of Returns

Scenario analysis postulates a probability distribution of future returns. But where do the probabilities and rates of return come from? In large part, they come from observing a sample history of returns. Suppose we observe a 10-year time series of monthly returns on a diversified portfolio of stocks. We can interpret each of the 120 observations as one potential "scenario" offered to us by history. Adding judgment to this history, we can develop a scenario analysis of future returns.

As a first step, we estimate the expected return, standard deviation, and VaR for the sample history. We assume that each of the 120 returns represents one independent draw from the historical probability distribution. Hence, each return is assigned an equal probability of $1/120 = .0083$. When you use such equal probabilities in Equation 5.10, you obtain the simple average of the observations, often used to estimate the mean return.

As mentioned earlier, the same principle applies to VaR. We sort the returns from high to low. The bottom six observations comprise the lower 5% of the distribution. The sixth observation from the bottom is just at the fifth percentile, and so would be the 5% VaR for the historical sample.

kurtosis

Measure of the fatness of the tails of a probability distribution relative to that of a normal distribution. Indicates likelihood of extreme outcomes.

skew

Measure of the asymmetry of a probability distribution.

---

[5]The financial crisis of 2008–2009 demonstrated that bank portfolio returns are far from normally distributed, with exposure to unlikely but catastrophic returns in extreme market meltdowns. The international Basel accord on bank regulation requires banks to monitor portfolio VaR to better control risk.

Estimating variance from Equation 5.11 requires a minor modification. Remember that variance is the expected value of squared deviations from the mean return. But the true mean is not observable; we *estimate* it using the sample average. If we compute variance as the average of squared deviations from the sample average, we will slightly underestimate it because this procedure ignores the fact that the average necessarily includes some estimation error. The necessary correction turns out to be simple: With a sample of n observations, we divide the sum of the squared deviations from the sample average by $n - 1$ instead of n. Thus, the estimates of variance and standard deviation from a time series of returns, r_t, are

$$\bar{r}_t = \frac{1}{n}\Sigma r_t; \quad \text{Var}(r_t) = \frac{1}{n-1}\Sigma(r_t - \bar{r}_t)^2; \quad \text{SD}(r_t) = \sqrt{\text{Var}(r_t)} \qquad \textbf{(5.15)}$$

EXAMPLE 5.5

Historical Means and Standard Deviations

To illustrate how to calculate average returns and standard deviations from historical data, let's compute these statistics for the returns on the S&P 500 portfolio using five years of data from the following table. The average return over this period is 16.7%, computed by dividing the sum of column (1), below, by the number of observations. In column (2), we take the deviation of each year's return from the 16.7% average return. In column (3), we calculate the squared deviation. The variance is, from Equation 5.15, the sum of the five squared deviations divided by (5 − 1). The standard deviation is the square root of the variance. If you input the column of rates into a spreadsheet, the AVERAGE and STDEV functions will give you the statistics directly.

Year	(1) Rate of Return	(2) Deviation from Average Return	(3) Squared Deviation
1	16.9%	0.2%	0.0
2	31.3	14.6	213.2
3	−3.2	−19.9	396.0
4	30.7	14.0	196.0
5	7.7	−9.0	81.0
Total	83.4%		886.2

Average rate of return = 83.4/5 = 16.7

Variance = $\frac{1}{5-1}$ × 886.2 = 221.6

Standard deviation = $\sqrt{221.6}$ = 14.9%

Risk Premiums and Risk Aversion

How much, if anything, would you invest in the index stock fund described in Spreadsheet 5.1? First, you must ask how much of an expected reward is offered to compensate for the risk involved in stocks.

We measure the "reward" as the difference between the expected HPR on the index fund and the **risk-free rate,** the rate you can earn on Treasury bills. We call this difference the **risk premium.** If the risk-free rate in the example is 4% per year, and the expected index fund return is 10%, then the risk premium on stocks is 6% per year.

The rate of return on Treasury bills also varies over time. However, we know the rate of return on T-bills *at the beginning* of the holding period, while we can't know the return we will earn on risky assets until the end of the holding period. Therefore, to study the risk premium on risky assets we compile a series of **excess returns,** that is, returns in excess of the T-bill rate in each period. A reasonable forecast of an asset's risk premium is the average of its historical excess returns.

risk-free rate
The rate of return that can be earned with certainty.

risk premium
An expected return in excess of that on risk-free securities.

excess return
Rate of return in excess of the risk-free rate.

risk aversion

Reluctance to accept risk.

The degree to which investors are willing to commit funds to stocks depends on **risk aversion.** It seems obvious that investors are risk averse in the sense that, without a positive risk premium, they would not be willing to invest in stocks. In theory then, there must always be a positive risk premium on all risky assets in order to induce risk-averse investors to hold the existing supply of these assets.

A positive risk premium distinguishes speculation from gambling. Investors taking on risk to earn a risk premium are speculating. Speculation is undertaken *despite* the risk because of a favorable risk-return trade-off. In contrast, gambling is the assumption of risk for no purpose beyond the enjoyment of the risk itself. Gamblers take on risk even without a risk premium.[6]

To determine an investor's optimal portfolio strategy, we need to quantify his degree of risk aversion. To do so, we look at how he is willing to trade off risk against expected return. An obvious benchmark is the risk-free asset, which has neither volatility nor risk premium: It pays a certain rate of return, r_f. Risk-averse investors will not hold risky assets without the prospect of earning some premium above the risk-free rate. An individual's degree of risk aversion can be inferred by contrasting the risk premium on the investor's entire wealth (the complete portfolio, C), $E(r_C) - r_f$, against the variance of the portfolio return, σ_C^2. We assume normality here, so variance adequately measures risk. The risk premium and volatility of the *individual* assets in the complete wealth portfolio are of no concern to the investor here. All that counts is the bottom line: *complete portfolio* risk premium versus *complete portfolio* risk.

A natural way to proceed is to measure risk aversion by the risk premium necessary to compensate an investor for investing his entire wealth in a portfolio, say Q, with a variance, σ_Q^2. This approach relies on the principle of *revealed preference:* We infer preferences from the choices individuals are willing to make. We will measure risk aversion by the risk premium offered by the complete portfolio per unit of variance. This ratio measures the compensation that an investor has apparently required (per unit of variance) to be induced to hold this portfolio. For example, if we were to observe that the entire wealth of an investor is held in a portfolio with annual risk premium of .10 (10%) and variance of .0256 (SD = 16%), we would infer this investor's degree of risk aversion as:

$$A = \frac{E(r_Q) - r_f}{\sigma_Q^2} = \frac{0.10}{0.0256} = 3.91 \tag{5.16}$$

price of risk

The ratio of portfolio risk premium to variance.

We call the ratio of a portfolio's risk premium to its variance the **price of risk.**[7] Later in the section, we turn the question around and ask how an investor with a given degree of risk aversion, say, $A = 3.91$, should allocate wealth between the risky and risk-free assets.

To get an idea of the level of the risk aversion exhibited by investors in U.S. capital markets, we can look at a representative portfolio held by these investors. Assume that all short-term borrowing offsets lending; that is, average net borrowing and lending are zero. In that case, the average investor holds a complete portfolio represented by a stock-market index;[8] call it M. A common proxy for the market index is the S&P 500. Using a long-term series of historical returns on the S&P 500 to estimate investors' expectations about mean and variance, we can recast Equation 5.16 with these stock market data to obtain an estimate of average risk aversion:

$$\bar{A} = \frac{\text{Average}(r_M) - r_f}{\text{Sample } \sigma_M^2} \approx \frac{0.08}{0.04} = 2 \tag{5.17}$$

The price of risk of the market index portfolio, which reflects the risk aversion of the average investor, is sometimes called the *market price of risk.* Conventional wisdom holds that plausible estimates for the value of A lie in the range of $1.5 - 4$.

---

[6]Sometimes a gamble might *seem* like speculation to the participants. If two investors differ in their forecasts of the future, they might take opposite positions in a security, and both may have an expectation of earning a positive risk premium. In such cases, only one party can, in fact, be correct.

[7]Notice that when we use variance rather than SD, the price of risk of a portfolio does not depend on the holding period. The reason is that variance is proportional to the holding period. Since portfolio return and risk premium also are proportional to the holding period, the portfolio pays the same price of risk for any holding period.

[8]In practice, a broad market index such as the S&P 500 often is taken as representative of the entire market.

The Sharpe Ratio

Risk aversion implies that investors will accept a lower reward (as measured by their portfolio risk premium) in exchange for a sufficient reduction in standard deviation. A statistic commonly used to rank portfolios in terms of this risk-return trade-off is the **Sharpe ratio,** defined as

$$S = \frac{\text{Portfolio risk premium}}{\text{Standard deviation of portfolio excess return}} = \frac{E(r_P) - r_f}{\sigma_P} \qquad \textbf{(5.18)}$$

Sharpe ratio

Ratio of portfolio risk premium to standard deviation.

A risk-free asset would have a risk premium of zero and a standard deviation of zero. Therefore, the Sharpe ratio of a risky portfolio quantifies the incremental reward (the increase in risk premium) for each increase of 1% in the portfolio standard deviation. For example, the Sharpe ratio of a portfolio with an annual risk premium of 8% and standard deviation of 20% is 8/20 = 0.4. A higher Sharpe ratio indicates a better reward per unit of SD, in other words, a more efficient portfolio. Portfolio analysis in terms of mean and standard deviation (or variance) of excess returns is called **mean-variance analysis.**

mean-variance analysis

Ranking portfolios by their Sharpe ratios.

A warning: We will see in the next chapter that while standard deviation and VaR of returns are useful risk measures for diversified portfolios, these are not useful ways to think about the risk of individual securities. Therefore, the Sharpe ratio is a valid statistic *only* for ranking portfolios; it is *not* useful for comparing individual assets. For now, we examine the historical Sharpe ratios of broadly diversified portfolios that reflect the performance of some important asset classes.

---

a. A respected analyst forecasts that the return of the S&P 500 Index portfolio over the coming year will be 10%. The one-year T-bill rate is 5%. Examination of recent returns of the S&P 500 Index suggests that the standard deviation of returns will be 18%. What does this information suggest about the degree of risk aversion of the average investor, assuming that the average portfolio resembles the S&P 500?

b. What is the Sharpe ratio of the portfolio in (a)?

CONCEPT check 5.4

5.4 THE HISTORICAL RECORD

History of U.S. Interest Rates, Inflation, and Real Interest Rates

Figure 5.3 plots nominal interest rates, inflation rates, and real rates in the U.S. between 1926 and 2013. The Fisher relation is clearly erratic: In periods of economic stability, when inflation is around its long-term average of 3%, T-bill rates generally track inflation. In periods of extreme high or low inflation, however, nominal (T-bill) rates seem to lag, and real rates therefore go to extremes. Nevertheless, it appears that fluctuations in the real rates have moderated considerably in the last 30 years, presumably due to better monetary control by the Fed as well as more accurate investor anticipation of inflation.

Table 5.2 quantifies what we see in the figure. The geometric mean of the historical T-bill rate was 3.50%, implying that a $1 investment at the beginning of 1926 would have grown to $20.56 by the end of 2013 (88 years later). But adjusted for inflation, the geometric mean of the real T-bill rate was only 0.51%, implying that your purchasing power would have grown after 88 years by only 57%, from $1 to $1.57.

Despite numerous recessions in the latter part of the sample, culminating in the Great Recession of 2008–2009, the geometric means of all three rates for the 58 years since 1956 are higher. Investing for 88 years at the higher real rate that characterized the more recent part of the sample, 0.92%, your purchasing power would have increased by the start of 2014 to $2.24 (instead of $1.57). Of course, this is still paltry compared to the nominal growth in wealth corresponding to the higher nominal rate (4.76%). Such is the insidious effect of even moderate inflation.

FIGURE **5.3**

Interest rates, inflation, and real interest rates, 1926–2013

Source: T-bills: Prof. Kenneth French, **http://mba.tuck.dart mouth.edu/pages/faculty/ken .french/data_library.html;** Inflation: Bureau of Labor Statistics, **www.bls.gov;** Real rate: authors' calculations.

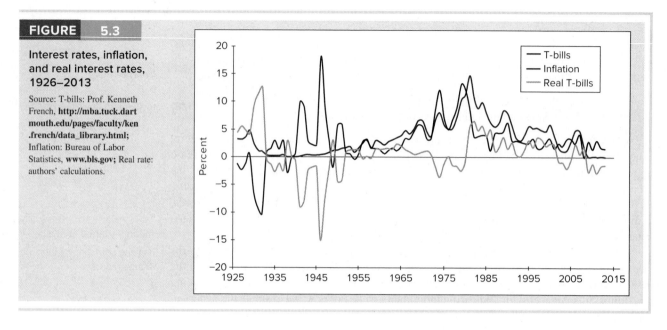

Notice that the lowest real rate (in 1946) occurs in the year of highest inflation, and the highest real rate (in 1932) occurs when inflation is at its lowest (deflation is highest).

The standard deviation of the T-bill rate actually does not represent short-term investment risk. After all, investors know the rate they will earn on their bills in advance. Rather, the standard deviation reflects changes over time in nominal rates demanded by investors. There is little evidence that this rate has become less volatile. But there is an indication that the volatility of inflation and real rates have markedly declined, suggesting the Fed has become more effective in moderating economic business cycles.

A related aspect of the data provides additional insight into inflation and the Fisher equation. If investors can anticipate inflation well, then the nominal T-bill rate will track the rate

| **TABLE 5.2** | Annual rate of return statistics for U.S. T-bills, inflation, and real T-bill returns, 1926–2013 |

	T-Bill Rate	**Inflation Rate**	**Real T-Bill Rate**
Geometric average (%)	3.50	2.97	0.51
58 years since 1956	4.76	3.81	0.92
Arithmetic average (%)	3.54	3.05	0.59
Lowest rate*	−0.02 (1938)	−10.27 (1932)	−15.05 (1946)
Highest rate	14.71 (1981)	18.13 (1946)	12.52 (1932)
Standard deviation	3.11	4.10	3.85
58 years since 1956	3.04	2.85	2.21
Correlation with inflation rate			
1926–2013	0.41		−0.72
1926–1955	−0.30		−0.98
1956–1985	0.72		−0.48
1986–2013	0.53		0.01

*Negative yields on bills should be impossible, as one can always hold cash (with a zero yield) as an alternative. In the 1930s, however, Treasury securities were exempt from personal property taxes in some states and were required as collateral in some transactions. These advantages drove up their price above par value, resulting in a slightly negative yield in 1938.

Source: T-bills: Professor Kenneth French website: http://mba.tuck.dartmouth.edu/pages/faculty/ken.french/data_library.html

Inflation data: Bureau of Labor Statistics

of inflation closely, resulting in high correlation between the two. Because nominal rates will rise with anticipated inflation rates, the real rate will be largely unaffected and therefore uncorrelated with either of them, instead fluctuating randomly with variation in demand and supply of capital. Conversely, if investors were wholly unable to predict future inflation, the nominal T-bill rate would be uncorrelated with inflation. In this case, any surprise in inflation would reduce the real rate by an equal amount, and the real rate would be highly *negatively* correlated with inflation. Table 5.2 shows that the correlation between T-bill and inflation rates has gone from a negative value prior to 1955 to a positive since then. Consistent with this pattern, the correlation between the real T-bill rate and the inflation rate was highly negative before 1955, but since then has been almost precisely zero. These changes signal the greater predictability of inflation in recent decades, which is good news for financial markets.

Inflation-indexed bonds called Treasury Inflation-Protected Securities (TIPS) were introduced in the U.S. in 1997. These are bonds of 5- to 30-year original maturities with coupons and principal that increase at the rate of inflation. (We discuss these bonds in more detail in Chapter 10.) The difference between nominal rates on conventional T-bonds and the rates on equal-maturity TIPS provides a measure of expected inflation (often called *break-even inflation*) over that maturity.

World and U.S. Risky Stock and Bond Portfolios

We begin our examination of risk with the return history of five risky asset classes. These include three well-diversified stock portfolios—world large stocks, U.S. large stocks, and U.S. small stocks—as well as two long-term bond portfolios—world and U.S. Treasury bonds. The 88 annual observations for each of the five time series of returns span the period 1926–2013.

Until 1969, the "World Portfolio" of stocks was constructed from a diversified sample of large capitalization stocks of 16 developed countries weighted in proportion to gross domestic product. Since 1970 this portfolio has been diversified across 24 developed countries (almost 6,000 stocks) with weights determined by the relative capitalization of each market. "Large Stocks" is the Standard & Poor's market value–weighted portfolio of 500 U.S. common stocks selected from the largest market capitalization stocks. "Small U.S. Stocks" are the smallest 20% of all stocks trading on the NYSE, NASDAQ , and Amex (currently about 1,000 stocks).

The World Portfolio of bonds was constructed from the same set of countries as the World Portfolio of stocks, using long-term government bonds from each country. Until 1996, "Long-Term T-Bonds" were represented by U.S. government bonds with at least a 20-year maturity and approximately current-level coupon rate.[9] Since 1996, this bond series has been measured by the Barclay's Long-Term Treasury Bond Index.

Figure 5.4 provides one view of the hierarchy of risk. Here we plot the year-by-year returns on U.S. large stocks, long-term Treasury bonds, and T-bills. Risk is reflected by wider swings of returns from year to year. Small stocks are the most risky, followed by large stocks and then long-term bonds. At the same time, the higher average return offered by riskier assets is evident, consistent with investor risk aversion. T-bill returns are by far the least volatile. That is, changes in interest rates are of a smaller order than fluctuations in returns on risky assets.

Another view of return history is presented in Figure 5.5, Panel A, which shows histograms of the continuously compounded annual returns of the five risky portfolios and of Treasury bills. The higher risk of large stocks, and even more so, of small stocks is reflected in their wider dispersion of returns.

To better assess the normality of these risky returns, Panel B presents histograms of the 1,058 *monthly* excess returns, expressed as continuously compounded rates,[10] on U.S. small and large stocks. The bell-shaped curves in both Panels A and B are "matched" normal distributions, constructed with the same mean and variance as the historical sample. Deviations from normality are suggested by the higher frequency of extreme (or tail) outcomes, the lower

---

[9]The importance of the coupon rate when comparing returns on bonds is discussed in Part Three.

[10]Testing for normality requires us to use continuously compounded rates from Equation 5.5, $\ln(1 + \text{annual rate})$, and to compute excess returns by subtracting the continuously compounded rate of return on T-bills.

**Rates of return on
stocks, bonds, and bills**

Source: Prepared from the same
annual data used to construct
Table 5.3.

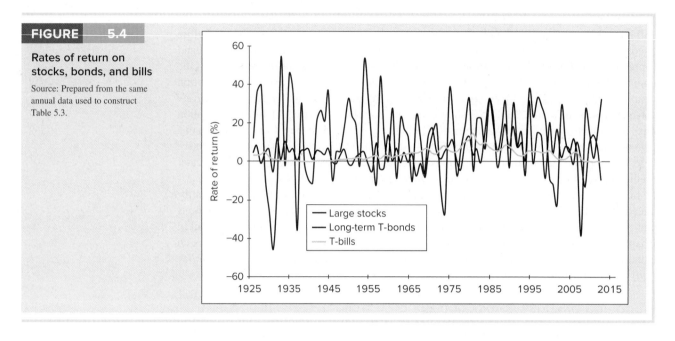

incidence of midrange positive or negative returns (compared to the "shoulders" of the normal distribution), and finally, the higher incidence of returns in the vicinity of the mean.

Table 5.3 presents statistics on the return history of the five portfolios over the 88-year period.[11] We start with the geometric averages of total returns in the top panel of the table. This is the equivalent, constant annual rate of return earned over the period.

To appreciate the power of compounding, consider the growth of invested funds in each of these asset classes. Investing $1 in each at the beginning of 1926 would have yielded the following growth of invested funds by the end of 2013:

	Government Bonds		Stocks		
	World	U.S.	World	U.S. Large	U.S. Small
Geometric average (%)	5.37	5.07	8.24	9.88	11.82
Growth of $1 (nominal value)	100	77	1,060	3,982	18,629

Obviously, even small differences in rates of return compound to large dollar values over time.

The *geometric* average of total return is backward looking. It measures the single compound rate of growth that was *actually* earned over a period. Only part of that return is attributable to risk. The component that is a reward for bearing risk is the *increment* to the safe rate, which we measure by the excess return over the one-month T-bill rate.[12] Therefore, portfolio risk should be measured from the volatility of *excess* returns.

Observe the high standard deviations of excess returns in Table 5.3. For large stock portfolios, the annual SD of excess returns over the 88-year period was nearly 20% (and a lot higher for small stocks). This represents a high level of risk. The average return in "bad years" (years with returns below the 88-year average) was −11.4%, around 20% (or one standard deviation) less than the 88-year average of 9.4%; the return in "good years" was about one standard deviation, or 21%, above the average return. The dispersion of returns for small stocks, with a standard deviation of 37.3%, is even higher. Investments in long-term bond portfolios also entail high risk.

The fat tails we observed in the histograms of Figure 5.5 tell us that we should devote some attention to risk measures that focus on extreme events, for example, VaR (value at risk).

[11]Year-by-year returns are available in Connect or through your course instructor.

[12]Notice that excess returns do not need to be adjusted for inflation because they are returns over and above the *nominal* risk-free rate.

Frequency distribution of annual and monthly returns

Source: Prepared from the same data used to construct Table 5.3.
Note: Bell shaped curves are the matched normal distribution, constructed with the same mean and standard deviation as the
historical sample.

FIGURE 5.5

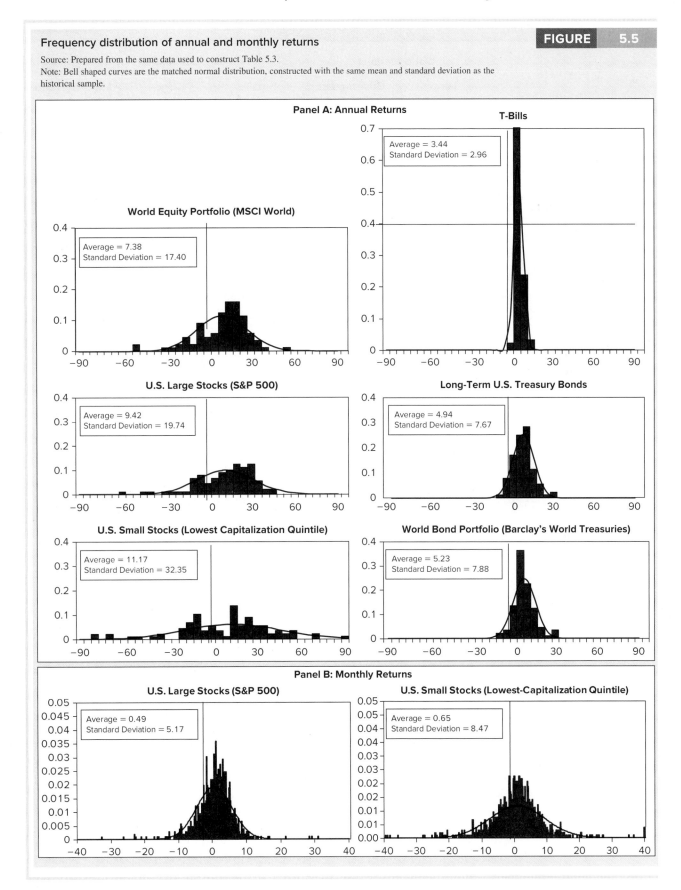

TABLE 5.3   Statistics for asset-class index portfolios, 1926–2013 (annual rates in U.S. dollars, %)

	World Markets		U.S. Markets		
	Large Stocks	Government Bonds	Small Stocks	Large Stocks	U.S. Long-Term Treasuries
A. Total Returns (%)					
Geometric average	8.24	5.37	11.82	9.88	5.07
Lowest return	−39.94 (1931)	−13.50 (1946)	−54.27 (1937)	−45.56 (1931)	−13.82 (2009)
Highest return	70.81 (1933)	34.12 (1985)	159.05 (1933)	54.56 (1933)	32.68 (1985)
B. Risk (Measured Using Excess Returns)					
Standard deviation	18.89	8.44	37.29	20.52	8.01
Value at risk (VaR) 5%	−25.88	−10.67	−48.33	−31.96	−11.51
C. Deviation from Normality*					
VaR assuming normality	−22.54	−10.43	−36.96	−23.51	−10.23
Actual VaR minus normal	−3.34	−0.24	−11.37	−8.46	−1.28
Skew	−0.09	0.68	0.83	−0.31	0.39
Kurtosis	1.08	1.39	1.97	−0.05	0.53
D. Returns in Excess of One-Month T-Bill Rates					
Average excess return	6.32	2.16	13.94	8.34	1.83
Standard error	2.01	0.90	3.97	2.19	0.85
E. Sharpe Ratios for 1926–2013 and Three Subperiods					
Entire period	0.33	0.26	0.37	0.41	0.23
1926–1955	0.43	0.22	0.40	0.46	0.59
1956–1985	0.19	0.05	0.38	0.28	−0.11
1986–2013	0.35	0.52	0.37	0.48	0.41
F. Correlations of Excess Returns					
With inflation	−0.13	−0.27	−0.02	−0.06	−0.17
With T-bill rates	−0.25	−0.16	−0.22	−0.17	−0.12

Note: Colored entries indicate measures of tail risk that exceed values consistent with a normal distribution.

Sources: World portfolio of Equities: 1926–1969 Dimson, Marsh and Staunton (Equity Premia Around the World); 1970–2013 Bloomberg—MSCI World in US$; World bonds: 1926–1987 Dimson, Marsh, and Staunton (ibid); 1988–2013 Bloomberg: Barclay's Global Treasuries in U.S.$.; Small Stocks: Kenneth French Data Library, Lowest Quantile; Large stocks: Center for Research in Security Price (CRSP), S&P 500; Long-Term Treasury bonds: Bloomberg: Barclay's U.S. Long-Term Treasury index; T-bills: Kenneth French Data Library, monthly rollover of 30-day T-bills; Inflation data: Economagic—Bureau of Labor Statistics cpiu dec2dec.

Table 5.3, Panel B, documents that the threat of extreme returns is real: in each of the 5% of the worst-return years, the excess return on small stocks was less than −48%. Even for Treasury bonds, excess return was less than −10% in each of the 5% worst years. This degree of extreme poor performance is greater than the VaR of normal distributions with the same means and standard deviations. The colored entries in Panel C indicate measures of tail risk that exceed values consistent with a normal distribution. All three stock portfolios show *actual* losses in the 5% worst years that are greater than would be expected from normal distributions.

Deviation from normality is also evident in the skew and kurtosis statistics shown in Panel C. These measures are derived by raising deviations from the mean to even higher powers than variance. Just as variance is the average value of *squared* deviations from the average, skew is the average value of those deviations raised to the *third* power (expressed as a multiple of the third power of standard deviation). Similarly, kurtosis is calculated from the average value of deviations raised to the *fourth* power (expressed as a multiple of the fourth power of standard deviation). Because they raise deviations to higher powers than variance, they are highly sensitive to extreme outcomes and therefore are considered measures of "tail risk," that is, outcomes in the tail of the probability distribution.

Because skew raises deviations to the third power (an odd exponent), negative deviations remain negative; therefore, negative values of skew indicate a risk of extreme *bad* outcomes. In contrast, kurtosis takes deviations to an even power, which makes all outcomes positive. Therefore, it measures the tendency to observe extreme outcomes in *either* end of the probability distribution, positive or negative. It is therefore a measure of "fat tails," that is, exposure to extreme good or bad results. The expected value of this statistic for a normally distributed variable is 3. Therefore, it is common to express kurtosis by first subtracting 3, making a value of zero consistent with normality and higher values indicative of fat tails.

Because they are very sensitive to one or two extreme outcomes, skew and kurtosis estimates are statistically reliable only in large samples. Nevertheless, the history we have calls for caution. For example, while the skew of U.S. small stocks is positive (and therefore, is not a worry for investors), the kurtosis of small stocks is 1.97, indicating the risk of fat tails beyond the risk implicit in the already high SD of 37.29%. As a whole, the tail risk measures in Table 5.3 suggest that SD alone can provide too narrow a view of stock risk.

Identifying the reward one can expect from bearing the risk quantified in Table 5.3 begins by comparing the average excess returns provided by each asset class. These are shown in Panel D. The *arithmetic* average excess return is forward looking: It provides the best statistical estimate of the expected excess return in the next period.[13] Bear in mind that this forecast of future returns comes with some imprecision, which we measure using the standard error. The standard error (which equals $SD/\sqrt{n}$) measures the likely sampling variation in the estimate of mean excess return due to year-by-year variability in returns. We find that even with a fairly long 88-year history, the standard error of the average excess return of the stock portfolios is large, between 2% and 4% for the different stock portfolios. Nevertheless, these standard errors are all less than half the average excess return, implying that we can discern a significant *risk premium* even through all the noise.

But are these risk premiums fair compensation for the degree of risk posed by the investments? This central question has generated enormous volumes of theoretical and empirical research. To answer it, we must first determine what an appropriate reward-risk relationship should be. We will defer that discussion until the next section; here we just point out that the differences between the historical average excess returns on the five portfolios are significant.[14]

The potential import of the risk premium can be illustrated with a simple example. Consider two investors with $1 million as of December 31, 2000. One invests for a decade in the small-stock portfolio, and the other in T-bills. Suppose both investors reinvest all income from their portfolios and liquidate their investments on December 31, 2010. We can find the annual rates of return for this period from the spreadsheet of returns available in Connect or through your course instructor. We compute a "wealth index" for each investment by compounding wealth at the end of each year by the return earned in the following year. For example, we calculate the value of the wealth index for small stocks as of 2003 by multiplying the value as of 2002 (1.1404) by 1 plus the rate of return earned in 2003 (measured in decimals), that is, by 1 + .7475, to obtain 1.9928.	**EXAMPLE 5.6** *The Risk Premium and Growth of Wealth*

(continued)

---

[13]In practice, forecasts may be augmented with judgment (prior beliefs) based on theoretical considerations.

[14]Formal statistical tests for the significance of the difference between returns on portfolios depend on the correlation between them. In this case, despite the high volatility of returns, the difference in average excess returns between small and large U.S. stocks, 5.61%, is statistically significant. In part, this is because of the large difference between their average returns but is also due to the high correlation between them, .79.

EXAMPLE 5.6

*The Risk Premium
and Growth of Wealth
(concluded)*

Year	Small Stocks		T-Bills	
	Return (%)	Wealth Index	Return (%)	Wealth Index
2000		1		1
2001	29.25	1.2925	3.86	1.0386
2002	−11.77	1.1404	1.63	1.0555
2003	74.75	1.9928	1.02	1.0663
2004	14.36	2.2790	1.19	1.0790
2005	3.26	2.3533	2.98	1.1111
2006	17.69	2.7696	4.81	1.1646
2007	−8.26	2.5408	4.67	1.2190
2008	−39.83	1.5288	1.64	1.2390
2009	36.33	2.0842	0.05	1.2396
2010	29.71	2.7034	0.08	1.2406

The final value of each portfolio as of December 31, 2010, equals its initial value ($1 million) multiplied by the wealth index at the end of the period:

Date	Small Stocks	T-Bills
December 31, 2000	$1,000,000	$1,000,000
December 31, 2010	$2,703,420	$1,240,572

The difference in total return is dramatic. Even with its devastating 2008 return, the value of the small-stock portfolio after 10 years is 118% more than that of the T-bill portfolio.

We can also calculate the geometric average return of each portfolio over this period. For T-bills, the geometric average over the 10-year period is computed from:

$$(1 + r_G)^{10} = 1.2406$$

$$1 + r_G = 1.2406^{1/10} = 1.0218$$

$$r_G = 2.18\%$$

Similarly, the geometric average for small stocks is 10.46%. The difference in geometric average reflects the difference in cumulative wealth provided by the small-stock portfolio over this period.

Turning to investment performance, recall that the Sharpe ratios shown in Panel E (the ratio of average excess return to SD) should be applied only to portfolios that are candidates for the entire risky investment. As we shall see in the next chapter, none of the five portfolios in Table 5.3 is sufficiently diversified for this purpose, yet the stock portfolios come closest to meeting this criterion. Sharpe ratios for the entire 88-year period are larger for the stock than for the bond portfolios, indicating that bond-only portfolios are flatly inadequate candidates for the overall investment portfolio. The Sharpe ratio for large U.S. stocks implies that diversified stock portfolios have yielded an incremental average excess return of about 0.4% for every 1% of SD. The ratio is a bit smaller for non-U.S. and smaller stocks.

CONCEPT check 5.5

Compute the average excess return on large-company stocks (over the T-bill rate), the standard deviation, and the Sharpe ratio for the years 1926–1934. You will need to obtain data from the spreadsheet available in Connect or through your course instructor. Look for Chapter 5 material.

5.5   ASSET ALLOCATION ACROSS RISKY AND RISK-FREE PORTFOLIOS

History shows that long-term bonds have been riskier investments than investments in Treasury bills and that stock investments have been riskier still. At the same time, the riskier investments have offered higher average returns. But investors do not make all-or-nothing choices from these investment classes. They normally include securities from all asset classes in their portfolios.

A simple strategy to control portfolio risk is to specify the fraction of the portfolio invested in broad asset classes such as stocks, bonds, and safe assets. This aspect of portfolio management is called **asset allocation** and plays an important role in the determination of portfolio performance. Consider this statement by John Bogle, made when he was the chairman of the Vanguard Group of Investment Companies:

> The most fundamental decision of investing is the allocation of your assets: How much should you own in stock? How much should you own in bonds? How much should you own in cash reserves? . . . That decision [has been shown to account] for an astonishing 94% of the differences in total returns achieved by institutionally managed pension funds. . . . There is no reason to believe that the same relationship does not also hold true for individual investors.[15]

asset allocation

Portfolio choice among broad investment classes.

The most basic form of asset allocation classifies all assets as either risky or risk free. The fraction of the portfolio placed in risky assets is called the **capital allocation to risky assets** and speaks directly to investor risk aversion.

To focus on the capital allocation decision, we think about an investor who allocates funds between T-bills and a portfolio of risky assets. We can envision the risky portfolio, *P*, as a mutual fund or ETF (exchange-traded fund) that includes a bundle of risky assets in desired, fixed proportions. Thus, when we shift wealth into and out of *P*, we do not change the relative proportion of the various securities within the risky portfolio. We put off until the next chapter the question of how to best construct the risky portfolio. We call the overall portfolio composed of the risk-free asset and the risky portfolio the **complete portfolio** that includes the investor's entire wealth.

capital allocation to risky assets

The choice between risky and risk-free assets.

complete portfolio

The entire portfolio including risky and risk-free assets.

The Risk-Free Asset

The power to tax and to control the money supply lets the government, and only the government, issue default-free (Treasury) bonds. The default-free guarantee by itself is not sufficient to make the bonds risk-free in real terms, since inflation affects the purchasing power of the proceeds from the bonds. The only risk-free asset in real terms would be a price-indexed government bond such as TIPS. Even then, a default-free, perfectly indexed bond offers a guaranteed real rate to an investor only if the maturity of the bond is identical to the investor's desired holding period. These qualifications notwithstanding, it is common to view Treasury bills as *the* risk-free asset. Any inflation uncertainty over the course of a few weeks, or even months, is negligible compared to the uncertainty of stock market returns.[16]

---

[15]John C. Bogle, *Bogle on Mutual Funds* (Burr Ridge, IL: Irwin Professional Publishing, 1994), p. 235.

[16]In the wake of the euro crisis as well as the credit downgrade of the United States in the summer of 2011, one clearly needs to consider whether (or when) sovereign debt can be treated as risk-free. Governments that issue debt in their home currency can in principle always repay that debt, if need be by printing more money in that currency. This strategy, however, can lead to runaway inflation, so the real return on that debt would hardly be risk-free. Moreover, the cost of possible hyperinflation can be so great that they might justifiably conclude that default is the lesser of the two evils. Governments that issue debt in currencies they do not control (e.g., euro-denominated Greek debt) cannot fall back on the printing press, even under extreme duress, so default in that situation is certainly possible. For this reason, analysts focus on measures of sovereign fiscal health such as the ratio of indebtedness to GDP. As is also true of corporate debt, longer-term debt issues are riskier, as they allow more time for credit conditions to deteriorate before the loan is paid off.

In practice, most investors treat a broader range of money market instruments as effectively risk-free assets. All the money market instruments are virtually immune to interest rate risk (unexpected fluctuations in the price of a bond due to changes in market interest rates) because of their short maturities, and all are fairly safe in terms of default or credit risk.

Money market mutual funds hold, for the most part, three types of securities: Treasury bills, bank certificates of deposit (CDs), and commercial paper. The instruments differ slightly in their default risk. The yields to maturity on CDs and commercial paper for identical maturities are always slightly higher than those of T-bills. A history of this yield spread for 90-day CDs is shown in Figure 2.2 in Chapter 2.

Money market funds have changed their relative holdings of these securities over time, but by and large, the risk of CDs and commercial paper is minuscule compared to that of long-term bonds. Hence, we treat money market funds, as well as T-bills, as representing the most easily accessible risk-free asset for most investors.

Portfolio Expected Return and Risk

Consider the hierarchy of decisions an investor must make in a capital allocation framework. The properties of the risky portfolio are summarized by expected return and risk, as measured by standard deviation. The risk-free asset has a standard deviation of zero: Its rate of return is known. The investor must decide on the fraction of the *complete* portfolio that will be allocated to the risky portfolio. To make this determination, one must first determine the expected return and risk corresponding to any possible allocation. This is the technical part of the allocation decision. Given the trade-off between risk and return, which is common to all investors, each individual can choose his or her preferred allocation between the risky portfolio and the risk-free asset. This choice depends on personal preferences, specifically risk aversion. We begin with the risk-return trade-off.

Because the composition of the risky portfolio, P, already has been determined, the only concern here is with the proportion of the investment budget (y) to be allocated to it. The remaining proportion $(1 - y)$ is to be invested in the risk-free asset, which has a rate of return denoted r_f.

We denote the *actual* risky rate of return by r_P, the *expected* rate of return on P by $E(r_P)$, and its standard deviation by σ_P. In our numerical example, $E(r_P) = 15\%$, $\sigma_P = 22\%$, and $r_f = 7\%$. Thus, the risk premium on the risky asset is $E(r_P) - r_f = 8\%$.

Let's start with two extreme cases. If you invest all of your funds in the risky asset, that is, $y = 1$, the expected return on your complete portfolio will be 15% and the standard deviation will be 22%. This combination of risk and return is plotted as point P in Figure 5.6. At the other extreme, you might put all of your funds into the risk-free asset, that is, $y = 0$. In this case, you would earn a riskless return of 7%. (This choice is plotted as point F in Figure 5.6.)

Now consider more moderate choices. For example, if you allocate equal amounts of your *complete portfolio, C,* to the risky and risk-free assets, that is, you choose $y = .5$, the expected return on the complete portfolio will be the average of $E(r_P)$ and r_f. Therefore, $E(r_C) = .5 \times 7\% + .5 \times 15\% = 11\%$. The risk premium of the complete portfolio is therefore $11\% - 7\% = 4\%$, which is half of the risk premium of P. The standard deviation of the portfolio also is one-half of P's, that is, 11%. When you reduce the fraction of the complete portfolio allocated to the risky asset by half, you reduce both the risk and risk premium by half.

To generalize, the risk premium of the complete portfolio, C, will equal the risk premium of the risky asset times the fraction of the portfolio invested in the risky asset.

$$E(r_C) - r_f = y[E(r_P) - r_f] \tag{5.19}$$

The standard deviation of the complete portfolio will equal the standard deviation of the risky asset times the fraction of the portfolio invested in the risky asset.

$$\sigma_C = y\sigma_P \tag{5.20}$$

In sum, both the risk premium and the standard deviation of the complete portfolio increase in proportion to the investment in the risky portfolio. Therefore, the points that describe the risk

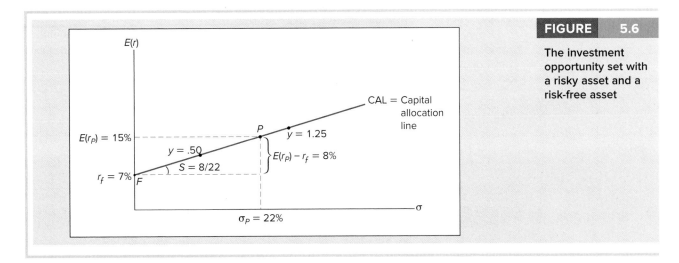

FIGURE   **5.6**

The investment opportunity set with a risky asset and a risk-free asset

and return of the complete portfolio for various capital allocations, y, all plot on the straight line connecting F and P, as shown in Figure 5.6, with an intercept of r_f and slope (rise/run) equal to the familiar Sharpe ratio of P:

$$S = \frac{E(r_P) - r_f}{\sigma_P} = \frac{15 - 7}{22} = .36 \qquad \textbf{(5.21)}$$

What are the expected return, risk premium, standard deviation, and ratio of risk premium to standard deviation for a complete portfolio with $y = .75$?

The Capital Allocation Line

The line plotted in Figure 5.6 depicts the risk-return combinations available by varying capital allocation, that is, by choosing different values of y. For this reason it is called the **capital allocation line (CAL).** The slope, S, of the CAL equals the increase in expected return that an investor can obtain per unit of additional standard deviation, or equivalently, extra return per extra risk. This is the Sharpe ratio, after William Sharpe who first suggested its use. It is obvious why the Sharpe ratio is sometimes called the *reward-to-volatility ratio.*

Notice that the Sharpe ratio is the same for risky portfolio P and the complete portfolio that mixes P and the risk-free asset.

capital allocation line (CAL)
Plot of risk-return combinations available by varying portfolio allocation between a risk-free asset and a risky portfolio.

	Expected Return	Risk Premium	Standard Deviation	Sharpe Ratio
Portfolio P:	15%	8%	22%	$\frac{8}{22} = 0.36$
Portfolio C:	11%	4%	11%	$\frac{4}{11} = 0.36$

In fact, the Sharpe ratio is the same for all complete portfolios that plot on the capital allocation line. While the risk-return combinations differ according to the investor's choice of y, the *ratio* of reward to risk is constant.

What about points on the CAL to the right of portfolio P in the investment opportunity set? You can construct complete portfolios to the right of point P by borrowing, that is, by choosing $y > 1$. This means that you borrow a proportion of $y - 1$ and invest both the borrowed funds and your own wealth in the risky portfolio P. If you can borrow at the risk-free rate, $r_f = 7\%$, then your rate of return will be $r_C = -(y - 1)r_f + y\, r_P = r_f + y(r_P - r_f)$. This complete portfolio has risk premium of $y[E(r_P) - r_f]$ and $SD = y\, \sigma_P$. Verify that your Sharpe ratio equals that of any other portfolio on the same CAL.

EXAMPLE 5.7	

Levered Complete Portfolios

Suppose the investment budget is $300,000, and an investor borrows an additional $120,000, investing the $420,000 in the risky asset. This is a levered position in the risky asset, which is financed in part by borrowing. In that case

$$y = \frac{420{,}000}{300{,}000} = 1.4$$

and $1 - y = 1 - 1.4 = -.4$, reflecting a short position in the risk-free asset, or a borrowing position. Rather than lending at a 7% interest rate, the investor borrows at 7%. With weights of $-.4$ in the risk-free asset and 1.4 in the risky portfolio, the portfolio rate of return is

$$E(r_C) = (-.4) \times 7\% + 1.4 \times 15\% = 18.2$$

Another way to find this portfolio rate of return is as follows: You expect to earn $63,000 (15% of $420,000) and pay $8,400 (7% of $120,000) in interest on the loan. Simple subtraction yields an expected profit of $54,600, which is 18.2% of your investment budget of $300,000. Therefore, $E(r_C) = 18.2\%$.

Your portfolio still exhibits the same reward-to-volatility or Sharpe ratio:

$$\sigma_C = 1.4 \times 22 = 30.8$$

$$S = \frac{E(r_C) - r_f}{\sigma_C} = \frac{11.2}{30.8} = .36$$

As you might have expected, the levered portfolio has both a higher expected return and a higher standard deviation than an unlevered position in the risky asset.

Risk Aversion and Capital Allocation

We have developed the CAL, the graph of all feasible risk-return combinations available from allocating the complete portfolio between a risky portfolio and a risk-free asset. The investor confronting the CAL now must choose one optimal combination from the set of feasible choices. This choice entails a trade-off between risk and return. Individual investors with different levels of risk aversion, given an identical capital allocation line, will choose different positions in the risky asset. Specifically, the more risk-averse investors will choose to hold *less* of the risky asset and *more* of the risk-free asset.

How can we find the best allocation between the risky portfolio and risk-free asset? Recall from Equation 5.16 that a particular investor's degree of risk aversion (A) measures the price of risk she demands from the complete portfolio in which her entire wealth is invested. The compensation for risk demanded by the investor must be compared to the price of risk offered by the risky portfolio, P. We can find the investor's preferred capital allocation, y, by dividing the risky portfolio's price of risk by the investor's risk aversion, her *required* price of risk:

$$y = \frac{\text{Available risk premium to variance ratio}}{\text{Required risk premium to variance ratio}} = \frac{[E(r_P) - r_f]/\sigma_P^2}{A} = \frac{[E(r_P) - r_f]}{A\sigma_P^2} \quad \textbf{(5.22)}$$

Notice that when the price of risk of the available risky portfolio exactly matches the investor's degree of risk aversion, her entire wealth will be invested in it ($y = 1$).

What would the investor of Equation 5.16 (with $A = 3.91$) do when faced with the market index portfolio of Equation 5.17 (with price of risk $= 2$)? Equation 5.22 tells us that this investor would invest $y = 2/3.91 = 0.51$ (51%) in the market index portfolio and a proportion $1 - y = 0.49$ in the risk-free asset.

Graphically, more risk-averse investors will choose portfolios near point F on the capital allocation line plotted in Figure 5.6. More risk-tolerant investors will choose points closer to P, with higher expected return and higher risk. The most risk-tolerant investors will choose portfolios to the right of point *P*. These levered portfolios provide even higher expected returns, but even greater risk.

The investor's asset allocation choice also will depend on the trade-off between risk and return. When the Sharpe ratio is higher, investors will take on riskier positions. Suppose an investor reevaluates the probability distribution of the risky portfolio and now perceives a greater expected return without an accompanying increase in the standard deviation. This amounts to an increase in the Sharpe ratio or, equivalently, an increase in the slope of the CAL. As a result, this investor will choose a higher *y*, that is, a greater position in the risky portfolio.

One role of a professional financial adviser is to present investment opportunity alternatives to clients, obtain an assessment of the client's risk tolerance, and help determine the appropriate complete portfolio.[17]

5.6   PASSIVE STRATEGIES AND THE CAPITAL MARKET LINE

A **passive strategy** is based on the premise that securities are fairly priced, and it avoids the costs involved in undertaking security analysis. Such a strategy might at first blush appear to be naive. However, we will see in Chapter 8 that intense competition among professional money managers might indeed force security prices to levels at which further security analysis is unlikely to turn up significant profit opportunities. Passive investment strategies may make sense for many investors.

passive strategy

Investment policy that avoids security analysis.

To avoid the costs of acquiring information on any individual stock or group of stocks, we may follow a "neutral" diversification approach. Select a diversified portfolio of common stocks that mirrors the corporate sector of the broad economy. This results in a value-weighted portfolio, which, for example, invests a proportion in GE stock that equals the ratio of GE's market value to the market value of all listed stocks.

Such strategies are called *indexing*. The investor chooses a portfolio of all the stocks in a broad market index such as the S&P 500. The rate of return on the portfolio then replicates the return on the index. Indexing has become a popular strategy for passive investors. We call the capital allocation line provided by one-month T-bills and a broad index of common stocks the **capital market line (CML).** That is, a passive strategy using the broad stock market index as the risky portfolio generates an investment opportunity set that is represented by the CML.

capital market line (CML)

The capital allocation line using the market index portfolio as the risky asset.

Historical Evidence on the Capital Market Line

Table 5.4 is a small cut-and-paste from Table 5.3, which concentrates on S&P 500 data, a popular choice for a broad stock-market index. As we discussed earlier, the large standard deviation of its rate of return implies that we cannot reject the hypothesis that the entire 88-year period is characterized by the same Sharpe ratio. Using this history as a guide, investors might reasonably forecast a risk premium of around 8% coupled with a standard deviation of approximately 20%, resulting in a Sharpe ratio of .4.

To hold a complete portfolio with these risk-return characteristics, the "average" investor (who chooses $y = 1$) must have a coefficient of risk aversion of $.08/.20^2 = 2$. But that average investor would need some courage. As the VaR figures in Table 5.4 indicate, history suggests a probability of 5% of an annual loss on a market index portfolio exceeding 25%. This substantial risk, together with differences in risk aversion across individuals, might explain the large differences we observe in portfolio positions across investors.

Finally, notice the instability of the excess returns on the S&P 500 across the 30-year subperiods in Table 5.4. The great variability in excess returns raises the question of whether

---

[17]"Risk tolerance" is simply the flip side of "risk aversion." Either term is a reasonable way to describe attitudes toward risk. We generally find it easier to talk about risk *aversion,* but practitioners often use the term risk *tolerance.*

TRIUMPH OF THE OPTIMISTS

As a whole, the last eight decades have been very kind to U.S. equity investors. Even accounting for miserable 2008 returns, stock investments have outperformed investments in safe Treasury bills by more than 7% per year. The real rate of return averaged more than 6%, implying an expected doubling of the real value of the investment portfolio about every 12 years!

Is this experience representative? A book by three professors at the London Business School, Elroy Dimson, Paul Marsh, and Mike Staunton, extends the U.S. evidence to other countries and to longer time periods. Their conclusion is given in the book's title, *Triumph of the Optimists*[*]: In every country in their study (which included markets in North America, Europe, Asia, and Africa), the investment optimists—those who bet on the economy by investing in stocks rather than bonds or bills—were vindicated. Over the long haul, stocks beat bonds everywhere.

On the other hand, the equity risk premium is probably not as large as the post-1926 evidence from Table 5.3 would seem to indicate. First, results from the first 25 years of the last century (which included the first World War) were less favorable to stocks. Second, U.S. returns have been better than those of most other countries, and so a more representative value for the historical risk premium may be lower than the U.S. experience. Finally, the sample that is amenable to historical analysis suffers from a self-selection problem. Only those markets that have survived to be studied can be included in the analysis. This leaves out countries such as Russia or China, whose markets were shut down during communist rule, and whose results if included would surely bring down the average historical performance of equity investments. Nevertheless, there is powerful evidence of a risk premium that shows its force everywhere the authors looked.

[*]Elroy Dimson, Paul Marsh, Mike Staunton, *Triumph of the Optimists: 101 Years of Global Investment Returns* (Princeton, NJ: Princeton University Press, 2002).

---

the 8% historical average really is a reasonable estimate of the risk premium looking into the future. It also suggests that different investors may come to different conclusions about future excess returns, another reason for capital allocations to vary.

In fact, there has been considerable debate among financial economists about the "true" equity risk premium, with an emerging consensus that the historical average may be an unrealistically high estimate of the future risk premium. This argument is based on several factors: the use of longer time periods in which equity returns are examined; a broad range of countries rather than just the U.S. in which excess returns are computed (Dimson, Marsh, and Staunton, 2001); direct surveys of financial executives about their expectations for stock market returns (Graham and Harvey, 2001); and inferences from stock market data about investor expectations (Jagannathan, McGrattan, and Scherbina, 2000; Fama and French, 2002). The box above discusses some of this evidence.

Costs and Benefits of Passive Investing

The fact that an individual's capital allocation decision is hard does not imply that its implementation needs to be complex. A passive strategy is simple and inexpensive to implement: Choose a broad index fund or ETF and divide your savings between it and a money market fund. To justify spending your own time and effort or paying a professional to pursue an active

TABLE 5.4	Excess return statistics for the S&P 500			
	Excess Return (%)			
	Average	**Std Dev**	**Sharpe Ratio**	**5% VaR**
1926–2013	8.34	20.23	0.41	−25.88
1926–1955	11.67	25.40	0.46	NA*
1956–1985	5.01	17.58	0.28	NA*
1986–2013	8.33	17.73	0.47	NA*

*Too few observations for meaningful calculation.

strategy requires some evidence that those activities are likely to be profitable. As we shall see later in the text, this is much harder to come by than you might expect!

To choose an active strategy, an investor must be convinced that the benefits outweigh the cost, and the cost can be quite large. As a benchmark, annual expense ratios for index funds are around 20 and 50 basis points for U.S. and international stocks, respectively. The cost of utilizing a money market fund is smaller still, and T-bills can be purchased at no cost.

Here is a very cursory idea of the cost of active strategies: The annual expense ratio of an active stock mutual fund averages around 1% of invested assets, and mutual funds that invest in more exotic assets such as real estate or precious metals can be more expensive still. A hedge fund will cost you 1% to 2% of invested assets plus 10% or more of any returns above the risk-free rate. If you are wealthy and seek more dedicated portfolio management, costs will be even higher.

Because of the power of compounding, an extra 1% of annual costs can have large consequences for the future value of your portfolio. With a risk-free rate of 2% and a risk premium of 8%, you might expect your wealth to grow by a factor of $1.10^{30} = 17.45$ over a 30-year investment horizon. If fees are 1%, then your net return is reduced to 9%, and your wealth grows by a factor of only $1.09^{30} = 13.26$ over that same horizon. That seemingly small management fee reduces your final wealth by about one-quarter.

The potential benefits of active strategies are discussed in detail in Chapter 8. The news is generally not that good for active investors. However, the factors that keep the active management industry going are (1) the large potential of enrichment from successful investments—the same power of compounding works in your favor if you can add even a few basis points to total return, (2) the difficulty in assessing performance (discussed in Chapter 18), and (3) uninformed investors who are willing to pay for professional money management. There is no question that some money managers can outperform passive strategies. The problem is (1) how do you identify them and (2) do their fees outstrip their potential. Whatever the choice one makes, one thing is clear: The CML using the passive market index is not an obviously inferior choice.

SUMMARY

- Investors face a trade-off between risk and expected return. Historical data confirm our intuition that assets with low degrees of risk should provide lower returns on average than do those of higher risk.
- Shifting funds from the risky portfolio to the risk-free asset is the simplest way to reduce risk. Another method involves diversification of the risky portfolio. We take up diversification in later chapters.
- U.S. T-bills provide a perfectly risk-free asset in nominal terms only. Nevertheless, the standard deviation of real rates on short-term T-bills is small compared to that of assets such as long-term bonds and common stocks, so for the purpose of our analysis, we consider T-bills the risk-free asset. Besides T-bills, money market funds hold short-term, safe obligations such as commercial paper and CDs. These entail some default risk but relatively little compared to most other risky assets. For convenience, we often refer to money market funds as risk-free assets.
- A risky investment portfolio (referred to here as the risky asset) can be characterized by its Sharpe, or reward-to-volatility ratio. This ratio is the slope of the capital allocation line (CAL), the line connecting the risk-free asset to the risky asset. All combinations of the risky and risk-free asset lie on this line. Investors would prefer a steeper-sloping CAL, because that means higher expected returns for any level of risk.
- An investor's preferred choice among the portfolios on the capital allocation line will depend on risk aversion. Risk-averse investors will weight their complete portfolios more heavily toward Treasury bills. Risk-tolerant investors will hold higher proportions of their complete portfolios in the risky asset.
- The capital market line is the capital allocation line that results from using a passive investment strategy that treats a market index portfolio, such as the Standard & Poor's 500, as the risky asset. Passive strategies are low-cost ways of obtaining well-diversified portfolios with performance that will reflect that of the broad stock market.

KEY TERMS

arithmetic average, 111
asset allocation, 133
capital allocation to risky
    assets, 133
capital allocation line
    (CAL), 135
capital market line (CML), 137
complete portfolio, 133
dollar-weighted average
    return, 113
excess return, 123

expected return, 116
geometric average, 112
holding-period return
    (HPR), 111
inflation rate, 115
kurtosis, 122
mean-variance analysis, 125
nominal interest rate, 115
passive strategy, 137
price of risk, 124
probability distribution, 116

real interest rate, 115
risk aversion, 124
risk-free rate, 123
risk premium, 123
scenario analysis, 116
Sharpe (or reward-to-
    volatility) ratio, 125
skew, 122
standard deviation, 117
value at risk (VaR), 119
variance, 117

KEY FORMULAS

Arithmetic average of n returns: $(r_1 + r_2 + \ldots + r_n)/n$

Geometric average of n returns: $[(1 + r_1)(1 + r_2) \ldots (1 + r_n)]^{1/n} - 1$

Continuously compounded rate of return, r_{cc}: $\ln(1 + \text{Effective annual rate})$

Real rate of return: $\dfrac{1 + \text{Nominal return}}{1 + \text{Inflation rate}} - 1$

Real rate of return (continuous compounding): $r_{\text{nominal}} - \text{Inflation rate}$

Expected return: $\Sigma\ [\text{prob(Scenario)} \times \text{Return in scenario}]$

Variance: $\Sigma\ [\text{prob(Scenario)} \times (\text{Deviation from mean in scenario})^2]$

Standard deviation: $\sqrt{\text{Variance}}$

Sharpe ratio: $\dfrac{\text{Portfolio risk premium}}{\text{Standard deviation of excess return}} = \dfrac{E(r_P) - r_f}{\sigma_P}$

Optimal capital allocation to the risky asset, y: $\dfrac{E(r_P) - r_f}{A\sigma_P^2}$

PROBLEM SETS

 Select problems are available in McGraw-Hill's *Connect*. Please see the Supplements section of the book's frontmatter for more information.

1. Suppose you've estimated that the fifth-percentile value at risk of a portfolio is -30%. Now you wish to estimate the portfolio's first-percentile VaR (the value below which lie 1% of the returns). Will the 1% VaR be greater or less than -30%?   *(LO 5-2)*

2. To estimate the Sharpe ratio of a portfolio from a history of asset returns, we use the difference between the simple (arithmetic) average rate of return and the T-bill rate. Why not use the geometric average?   *(LO 5-4)*

3. When estimating a Sharpe ratio, would it make sense to use the average excess real return that accounts for inflation?   *(LO 5-4)*

4. You've just decided upon your capital allocation for the next year, when you realize that you've underestimated both the expected return and the standard deviation of your risky portfolio by 4%. Will you increase, decrease, or leave unchanged your allocation to risk-free T-bills?   *(LO 5-4)*

5. Suppose your expectations regarding the stock market are as follows:

State of the Economy	Probability	HPR
Boom	0.3	44%
Normal growth	0.4	14
Recession	0.3	−16

Use Equations 5.10–5.12 to compute the mean and standard deviation of the HPR on stocks.   *(LO 5-4)*

6. The stock of Business Adventures sells for $40 a share. Its likely dividend payout and end-of-year price depend on the state of the economy by the end of the year as follows: *(LO 5-2)*

	Dividend	Stock Price
Boom	$2.00	$50
Normal economy	1.00	43
Recession	0.50	34

    a. Calculate the expected holding-period return and standard deviation of the holding-period return. All three scenarios are equally likely.

    b. Calculate the expected return and standard deviation of a portfolio invested half in Business Adventures and half in Treasury bills. The return on bills is 4%.

7. XYZ stock price and dividend history are as follows:

Year	Beginning-of-Year Price	Dividend Paid at Year-End
2010	$100	$4
2011	$110	$4
2012	$ 90	$4
2013	$ 95	$4

An investor buys three shares of XYZ at the beginning of 2010, buys another two shares at the beginning of 2011, sells one share at the beginning of 2012, and sells all four remaining shares at the beginning of 2013.   *(LO 5-1)*

    a. What are the arithmetic and geometric average time-weighted rates of return for the investor?

    b. What is the dollar-weighted rate of return? (*Hint:* Carefully prepare a chart of cash flows for the *four* dates corresponding to the turns of the year for January 1, 2010, to January 1, 2013. If your calculator cannot calculate internal rate of return, you will have to use a spreadsheet or trial and error.)

8. *a.* Suppose you forecast that the standard deviation of the market return will be 20% in the coming year. If the measure of risk aversion in Equation 5.17 is $A = 4$, what would be a reasonable guess for the expected market risk premium?

    b. What value of A is consistent with a risk premium of 9%?

    c. What will happen to the risk premium if investors become more risk tolerant?   *(LO 5-4)*

9. Using the historical risk premiums as your guide, what is your estimate of the expected annual HPR on the S&P 500 stock portfolio if the current risk-free interest rate is 5%?   *(LO 5-3)*

10. What has been the historical average *real* rate of return on stocks, Treasury bonds, and Treasury bills?   *(LO 5-2)*

11. Consider a risky portfolio. The end-of-year cash flow derived from the portfolio will be either $50,000 or $150,000, with equal probabilities of .5. The alternative riskless investment in T-bills pays 5%.   *(LO 5-3)*

    a. If you require a risk premium of 10%, how much will you be willing to pay for the portfolio?

    b. Suppose the portfolio can be purchased for the amount you found in (*a*). What will the expected rate of return on the portfolio be?

  c. Now suppose you require a risk premium of 15%. What is the price you will be will-
     ing to pay now?
  d. Comparing your answers to (a) and (c), what do you conclude about the relationship
     between the required risk premium on a portfolio and the price at which the portfolio
     will sell?

**For Problems 12–16, assume that you manage a risky portfolio with an expected rate of return
of 17% and a standard deviation of 27%. The T-bill rate is 7%.**

12. Your client chooses to invest 70% of a portfolio in your fund and 30% in a T-bill money
    market fund.   *(LO 5-3)*
  a. What is the expected return and standard deviation of your client's portfolio?
  b. Suppose your risky portfolio includes the following investments in the given
     proportions:

Stock A	27%
Stock B	33%
Stock C	40%

     What are the investment proportions of your client's overall portfolio, including the
     position in T-bills?
  c. What is the Sharpe ratio (S) of your risky portfolio and your client's overall portfolio?
  d. Draw the CAL of your portfolio on an expected return/standard deviation diagram.
     What is the slope of the CAL? Show the position of your client on your fund's CAL.

13. Suppose the same client in the previous problem decides to invest in your risky portfolio
    a proportion (y) of his total investment budget so that his overall portfolio will have an
    expected rate of return of 15%.   *(LO 5-3)*
  a. What is the proportion y?
  b. What are your client's investment proportions in your three stocks and the T-bill fund?
  c. What is the standard deviation of the rate of return on your client's portfolio?

14. Suppose the same client as in the previous problem prefers to invest in your portfolio a
    proportion (y) that maximizes the expected return on the overall portfolio subject to the
    constraint that the overall portfolio's standard deviation will not exceed 20%.   *(LO 5-3)*
  a. What is the investment proportion, y?
  b. What is the expected rate of return on the overall portfolio?

15. You estimate that a passive portfolio invested to mimic the S&P 500 stock index yields
    an expected rate of return of 13% with a standard deviation of 25%. Draw the CML and
    your fund's CAL on an expected return/standard deviation diagram.   *(LO 5-4)*
  a. What is the slope of the CML?
  b. Characterize in one short paragraph the advantage of your fund over the passive fund.

16. Your client (see previous problem) wonders whether to switch the 70% that is invested
    in your fund to the passive portfolio.   *(LO 5-4)*
  a. Explain to your client the disadvantage of the switch.
  b. Show your client the maximum fee you could charge (as a percent of the investment
     in your fund deducted at the end of the year) that would still leave him at least as well
     off investing in your fund as in the passive one. (*Hint:* The fee will lower the slope of
     your client's CAL by reducing the expected return net of the fee.)

17. What do you think would happen to the expected return on stocks if investors perceived
    an increase in the volatility of stocks?   *(LO 5-4)*

18. You manage an equity fund with an expected risk premium of 10% and a standard devia-
    tion of 14%. The rate on Treasury bills is 6%. Your client chooses to invest $60,000 of
    her portfolio in your equity fund and $40,000 in a T-bill money market fund. What is the
    expected return and standard deviation of return on your client's portfolio?   *(LO 5-3)*

19. What is the reward-to-volatility ratio for the *equity fund* in the previous problem? *(LO 5-4)*

For Problems 20–22, download the spreadsheet containing the data used to prepare Table 5.3, "Rates of return, 1926–2013," from Connect.

Templates and spreadsheets are available in Connect

20. Calculate the same subperiod means and standard deviations for small stocks as Table 5.4 of the text provides for large stocks.   *(LO 5-2)*
    a. Have small stocks provided better reward-to-volatility (Sharpe) ratios than large stocks?
    b. Do small stocks show a similar higher standard deviation in the earliest subperiod as Table 5.4 documents for large stocks?

21. Convert the nominal returns on both large and small stocks to real rates. Reproduce Table 5.4 using real rates instead of excess returns. Compare the results to those of Table 5.4.   *(LO 5-1)*

22. Repeat the previous problem for small stocks and compare with the results for nominal rates.   *(LO 5-1)*

Challenge

23. Download the annual returns on the combined NYSE/NASDAQ/AMEX markets as well as the S&P 500 from Connect. For both indexes, calculate: *(LO 5-2)*

Templates and spreadsheets are available in Connect

    a. Average return.
    b. Standard deviation of return.
    c. Skew of return.
    d. Kurtosis of return.
    e. The 5% value at risk.
    f. Based on your answers to parts (b)–(e), compare the risk of the two indexes.

CFA Problems

1. A portfolio of nondividend-paying stocks earned a geometric mean return of 5% between January 1, 2005, and December 31, 2011. The arithmetic mean return for the same period was 6%. If the market value of the portfolio at the beginning of 2005 was $100,000, what was the market value of the portfolio at the end of 2011?   *(LO 5-1)*

2. Which of the following statements about the standard deviation is/are *true?* A standard deviation: *(LO 5-2)*
    a. Is the square root of the variance.
    b. Is denominated in the same units as the original data.
    c. Can be a positive or a negative number.

3. Which of the following statements reflects the importance of the asset allocation decision to the investment process? The asset allocation decision: *(LO 5-3)*
    a. Helps the investor decide on realistic investment goals.
    b. Identifies the specific securities to include in a portfolio.
    c. Determines most of the portfolio's returns and volatility over time.
    d. Creates a standard by which to establish an appropriate investment time horizon.

Use the following data in answering CFA Questions 4–6.

Investment	Expected Return, $E(r)$	Standard Deviation, σ
1	0.12	0.30
2	0.15	0.50
3	0.21	0.16
4	0.24	0.21

Suppose investor "satisfaction" with a portfolio increases with expected return and decreases with variance according to the following "utility" formula: $U = E(r) - \frac{1}{2} A\sigma^2$ where $A = 4$.

4. Based on the formula for investor satisfaction or "utility," which investment would you select if you were risk averse with $A = 4$? *(LO 5-4)*

5. Based on the formula above, which investment would you select if you were risk neutral, with $A = 0$? *(LO 5-4)*

6. The variable (A) in the utility formula represents the: *(LO 5-4)*
   a. Investor's return requirement.
   b. Investor's aversion to risk.
   c. Certainty equivalent rate of the portfolio.
   d. Preference for one unit of return per four units of risk.

Use the following scenario analysis for stocks X and Y to answer CFA Questions 7 through 9.

	Bear Market	Normal Market	Bull Market
Probability	0.2	0.5	0.3
Stock X	−20%	18%	50%
Stock Y	−15%	20%	10%

7. What are the expected returns for stocks X and Y? *(LO 5-2)*

8. What are the standard deviations of returns on stocks X and Y? *(LO 5-2)*

9. Assume that of your $10,000 portfolio, you invest $9,000 in stock X and $1,000 in stock Y. What is the expected return on your portfolio? *(LO 5-3)*

10. Probabilities for three states of the economy and probabilities for the returns on a particular stock in each state are shown in the table below.

State of Economy	Probability of Economic State	Stock Performance	Probability of Stock Performance in Given Economic State
Good	0.3	Good	0.6
		Neutral	0.3
		Poor	0.1
Neutral	0.5	Good	0.4
		Neutral	0.3
		Poor	0.3
Poor	0.2	Good	0.2
		Neutral	0.3
		Poor	0.5

What is the probability that the economy will be neutral *and* the stock will experience poor performance? *(LO 5-2)*

11. An analyst estimates that a stock has the following probabilities of return depending on the state of the economy. What is the expected return of the stock? *(LO 5-2)*

State of Economy	Probability	Return
Good	0.1	15%
Normal	0.6	13
Poor	0.3	7

1. Use data from **finance.yahoo.com** to answer the following questions.
   a. Select the Company tab and enter the ticker symbol for Adobe, ADBE. Click on the *Profile* tab to see an overview of the company.
   b. What is the latest price reported in the *Summary* section? What is the 12-month target price? Calculate the expected holding-period return based on these prices.
   c. Use the *Historical Prices* section to answer the question "How much would I have today if I invested $10,000 in ADBE five years ago?" Using this information, calculate the five-year holding-period return on Adobe's stock.

2. From the *Historical Prices* tab, download Adobe's dividend-adjusted stock price for the last 24 months into an Excel spreadsheet. Calculate the monthly rate of return for each month, the average return, and the standard deviation of returns over that period.

3. Calculating the real rate of return is an important part of evaluating an investment's performance. To do this, you need to know the nominal return on your investment and the rate of inflation during the corresponding period. To estimate the expected real rate of return before you make an investment, you can use the promised yield and the expected inflation rate.
   a. Go to **www.bankrate.com** and click on the *CDs and Investments* tab. Using *Compare CDs & Investment Rates* box, find the average one-year CD rate from banks across the nation (these will be nominal rates).
   b. Use the St. Louis Federal Reserve's website at **research.stlouisfed.org/fred2** as a source for data about expected inflation. Search for "MICH inflation," which will provide you with the University of Michigan Inflation Expectation data series (MICH). Click on the *View Data* link and find the latest available data point. What is the expected inflation rate for the next year?
   c. On the basis of your answers to parts *(a)* and *(b)*, calculate the expected real rate of return on a one-year CD investment.
   d. What does the result tell you about real interest rates? Are they positive or negative, and what does this mean?

5.1 *a.* The arithmetic average is $(2 + 8 - 4)/3 = 2\%$ per month.
    b. The time-weighted (geometric) average is
    $[(1 + .02) \times (1 + .08) \times (1 - .04)]^{1/3} - 1 = .0188 = 1.88\%$ per month.
    c. We compute the dollar-weighted average (IRR) from the cash flow sequence (in $ millions):

	Month		
	1	**2**	**3**
Assets under management at beginning of month	10.0	13.2	19.256
Investment profits during month (HPR × Assets)	0.2	1.056	(0.77)
Net inflows during month	3.0	5.0	0.0
Assets under management at end of month	13.2	19.256	18.486

	Time			
	0	**1**	**2**	**3**
Net cash flow*	−10	−3.0	−5.0	+18.486

*Time 0 is today. Time 1 is the end of the first month. Time 3 is the end of the third month, when net cash flow equals the ending value (potential liquidation value) of the portfolio.

The IRR of the sequence of net cash flows is 1.17% per month.
The dollar-weighted average is less than the time-weighted average because the negative return was realized when the fund had the most money under management.

5.2 *a.* Solving:

$$1 + R = (1 + r)(1 + i) = (1.03)(1.08) = 1.1124$$
$$R = 11.24\%$$

b. Solving:

$$1 + R = (1.03)(1.10) = 1.133$$
$$R = 13.3\%$$

5.3 *a.* Computing the HPR for each scenario, we convert the price and dividend data to rate-of-return data:

Scenario	Prob	Ending Value ($ million)	Dividend ($ million)	HPR	HPR × Prob	Deviation: HPR-mean	Prob × Dev'n Squared
1	0.30	$35	$4.40	0.713	0.214	0.406	0.049
2	0.45	27	4.00	0.348	0.157	0.040	0.001
3	0.20	15	4.00	−0.174	−0.035	−0.481	0.046
4	0.05	8	2.00	−0.565	−0.028	−0.873	0.038
Sum:					0.307		0.135

Expected HPR = .307 = 30.7%.

Variance = .135.

Standard deviation = $\sqrt{.135}$ = .367 = 36.7%.

5% VaR = −56.5%.

For the corresponding normal distribution, VaR would be 30.7% − 1.64485 × 36.7% = −29.67%.

b. With 36 returns, 5% of the sample would be .05 × 36 = 1.8 observations. The worst return is −17%, and the second-worst is −5%. Using interpolation, we estimate the fifth-percentile return as:

$$-17\% + .8[-5\% - (-17\%)] = -7.4\%$$

5.4 *a.* If the average investor chooses the S&P 500 portfolio, then the implied degree of risk aversion is given by Equation 5.17:

$$A = \frac{.10 - .05}{.18^2} = 1.54$$

b. $S = \dfrac{10 - 5}{18} = .28$

5.5 The mean excess return for the period 1926–1934 is 3.56% (below the historical average), and the standard deviation (using $n - 1$ degrees of freedom) is 32.55% (above the historical average). These results reflect the severe downturn of the great crash and the unusually high volatility of stock returns in this period.

5.6 $E(r) = 7 + .75 \times 8\% = 13\%$

$\sigma = .75 \times 22\% = 16.5\%$

Risk premium = 13 − 7 = 6%

$$S = \frac{\text{Risk premium}}{\text{Standard deviation}} = \frac{13 - 7}{16.5} = .36$$

Efficient Diversification

Learning Objectives

LO 6-1 Show how covariance and correlation affect the power of diversification to reduce portfolio risk.

LO 6-2 Calculate mean, variance, and covariance using either historical data or scenario analysis.

LO 6-3 Construct efficient portfolios and use the Sharpe ratio to evaluate portfolio efficiency.

LO 6-4 Calculate the composition of the optimal risky portfolio.

LO 6-5 Use index models to analyze the risk and return characteristics of securities and portfolios.

LO 6-6 Understand the effect of investment horizon on portfolio risk.

I n this chapter we describe how investors can construct the best possible risky portfolio. The key concept is efficient diversification.

The notion of diversification is age-old. The adage "Don't put all your eggs in one basket" obviously predates formal economic theory. However, a rigorous model showing how to make the most of the power of diversification was not devised until 1952, a feat for which Harry Markowitz won the Nobel Prize in Economics. This chapter is largely developed from his work, as well as from later insights that built on his work.

We start with a bird's-eye view of how diversification reduces the variability of portfolio returns. We then turn to the construction of optimal risky portfolios. We follow a top-down approach, starting with asset allocation across a small set of broad asset classes, such as stocks, bonds, and money market securities. Then we show how the principles of optimal asset allocation can easily be generalized to solve the problem of security selection among many risky assets. We discuss the efficient set of risky portfolios and show how it leads to the best capital allocation. Finally, we show how index models of security returns can simplify the search for efficient portfolios and the interpretation of the risk characteristics of individual securities.

The last section examines the common fallacy that long-term investment horizons mitigate the impact of asset risk. We show that the common belief in "time diversification" is in fact an illusion.

6.1 DIVERSIFICATION AND PORTFOLIO RISK

Suppose you have in your risky portfolio only one stock, say, Dana Computer Corporation. What are the sources of risk affecting this "portfolio"?

We can identify two broad sources of uncertainty. The first is the risk from general economic conditions, such as business cycles, inflation, interest rates, exchange rates, and so forth. None of these macroeconomic factors can be predicted with certainty, and all affect Dana stock. Then you must add firm-specific influences, such as Dana's success in R&D, its management style and philosophy, and so on. Firm-specific factors are those that affect Dana without noticeably affecting other firms.

Now consider adding another security to the risky portfolio. If you invest half of your risky portfolio in ExxonMobil, leaving the other half in Dana, what happens to portfolio risk? Because the firm-specific influences on the two stocks differ (statistically speaking, the influences are uncorrelated), this strategy should reduce portfolio risk. For example, when oil prices fall, hurting ExxonMobil, computer prices might rise, helping Dana. The two effects are offsetting, which stabilizes portfolio return.

But why stop at only two stocks? Diversifying into many more securities continues to reduce exposure to firm-specific factors, so portfolio volatility should continue to fall. Ultimately, however, there is no way to avoid all risk. To the extent that virtually all securities are affected by common (risky) macroeconomic factors, we cannot eliminate exposure to general economic risk, no matter how many stocks we hold.

Figure 6.1 illustrates these concepts. When all risk is firm-specific, as in Figure 6.1A, diversification can reduce risk to low levels. With all risk sources independent, and with investment spread across many securities, exposure to any particular source of risk is negligible. This is an application of the law of large numbers. The reduction of risk to very low levels because of independent risk sources is called the *insurance principle*.

market risk,
systematic risk,
nondiversifiable risk

Risk factors common to the whole economy.

When a common source of risk affects all firms, however, even extensive diversification cannot eliminate all risk. In Figure 6.1B, portfolio standard deviation falls as the number of securities increases, but it is not reduced to zero. The risk that remains even after diversification is called **market risk,** risk that is attributable to marketwide risk sources. Equivalent terms are **systematic risk** or **nondiversifiable risk.** The risk that *can* be eliminated by diversification is called **unique risk, firm-specific risk, nonsystematic risk,** or **diversifiable risk.**

unique risk,
firm-specific risk,
nonsystematic risk,
diversifiable risk

Risk that can be eliminated by diversification.

This analysis is borne out by empirical studies. Figure 6.2 shows the effect of portfolio diversification, using data on NYSE stocks. The figure shows the average standard deviations of equally weighted portfolios constructed by selecting stocks at random as a function of the number of stocks in the portfolio. On average, portfolio risk does fall with diversification, but

---

FIGURE 6.1

Portfolio risk as a function of the number of stocks in the portfolio

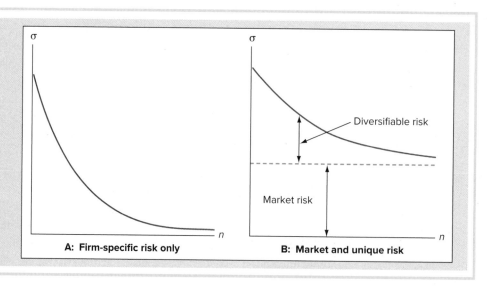

A: Firm-specific risk only   B: Market and unique risk

On the MARKET FRONT

DANGEROUS 401(K) PLANS

For many individuals, the 401(k) plan is the major source of retirement savings. The employee puts aside a given percentage of wages, in the process, sheltering it from current taxation. In addition, the employer commonly matches some fraction of that contribution. So if the employee places, let's say, 8% of his or her salary in the 401(k) plan, the employer might contribute an additional 4% of salary, or even more. In many plans, the savings are invested in shares of the company stock. As part owners of the firm, employees might be encouraged to work even smarter and harder, making everyone better off. It sounds like a win-win arrangement; what could go wrong with it? Plenty, it turns out.

The problem is that once you start concentrating your portfolio in your company stock, you increase risk in two ways. First,

focusing your investments in any single company rather than a diversified portfolio almost never makes sense. A single stock typically has more than double the volatility of a diversified portfolio. So when you load up your 401(k) plan with the stock of one company, you are taking on much greater volatility than is necessary, and much of that volatility does not even translate to higher average returns.

Second, when you invest in your own company, you are doubling down on your exposure to that single firm. If your company implodes, you can lose your source of income at the same time that your investment portfolio is decimated. Just ask the employees of Lehman Brothers, whose 401(k) plans entailed massive positions in the company stock; when the company failed, the employees' 401(k) plans were wiped out along with their jobs.

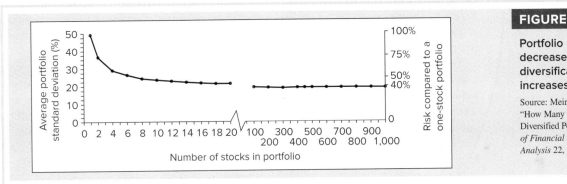

FIGURE 6.2

Portfolio risk decreases as diversification increases

Source: Meir Statman, "How Many Stocks Make a Diversified Portfolio?" *Journal of Financial and Quantitative Analysis* 22, September 1987.

the power of diversification to reduce risk is limited by common sources of risk. The nearby box, "Dangerous 401(k) Plans," highlights the dangers of neglecting diversification.

In light of this discussion, it is worth pointing out that general macroeconomic conditions in the U.S. do not move in lockstep with those in other countries. International diversification may further reduce portfolio risk, but here too, global economic and political factors affecting all countries to various degrees will limit the extent of risk reduction.

6.2 ASSET ALLOCATION WITH TWO RISKY ASSETS

In the last chapter we examined the capital allocation decision, how much of the portfolio to place in risk-free securities versus in a risky portfolio. Of course, investors need to choose the precise composition of the risky portfolio. In a top-down process, the first step would be an asset allocation decision. Most investment professionals recognize that the asset allocation decision must take precedence over the choice of particular stocks.

We turn first to asset allocation between only two risky assets, which we will assume are a bond fund and a stock fund. Once we understand the portfolios of two risky assets,

	A	B	C	D	E	F
1			Stock Fund		Bond Fund	
2	Scenario	Probability	Rate of Return	Col B × Col C	Rate of Return	Col B × Col E
3	Severe recession	0.05	−37	−1.9	−9	−0.45
4	Mild recession	0.25	−11	−2.8	15	3.8
5	Normal growth	0.40	14	5.6	8	3.2
6	Boom	0.30	30	9.0	−5	−1.5
7	Expected or Mean Return:			SUM: 10.0		SUM: 5.0

we will reintroduce the choice of the risk-free asset. This will complete the asset allocation problem across the three key asset classes: stocks, bonds, and T-bills. Constructing
efficient portfolios of many risky securities is a straightforward extension of this asset
allocation exercise.

Covariance and Correlation

To optimally construct a portfolio from risky assets, we need to understand how the uncertainties of asset returns interact. A key determinant of portfolio risk is the extent to which the
returns on the two assets vary either in tandem or in opposition. Portfolio risk depends on the
covariance between the returns of the assets in the portfolio. We can see why using a simple
scenario analysis.

The scenario analysis in Spreadsheet 6.1 posits four possible scenarios for the economy:
a severe recession, a mild recession, normal growth, and a boom. The performance of stocks
follows the broad economy, returning, respectively, −37%, −11%, 14%, and 30% in the four
scenarios. In contrast, bonds perform best in a mild recession, returning 15% (since falling
interest rates create capital gains), and in the normal growth scenario, where their return is
8%. They suffer from defaults in severe recession, resulting in a negative return, −9%, and
from inflation in the boom scenario, where their return is −5%. Notice that bonds outperform
stocks in both the mild and severe recession scenarios. In both normal growth and boom scenarios, stocks outperform bonds.

The expected return on each fund equals the probability-weighted average of the outcomes
in the four scenarios. The last row of Spreadsheet 6.1 shows that the expected return of the
stock fund is 10% and that of the bond fund is 5%. The variance is the probability-weighted
average of the squared deviation of actual return from the expected return; the standard deviation is the square root of the variance. These values are computed in Spreadsheet 6.2.

	A	B	C	D	E	F	G	H	I	J
1			Stock Fund				Bond Fund			
2				Deviation				Deviation		
3			Rate	from		Column B	Rate	from		Column B
4			of	Expected	Squared	×	of	Expected	Squared	×
5	Scenario	Prob.	Return	Return	Deviation	Column E	Return	Return	Deviation	Column I
6	Severe recession	0.05	−37	−47	2209	110.45	−9	−14	196	9.80
7	Mild recession	0.25	−11	−21	441	110.25	15	10	100	25.00
8	Normal growth	0.40	14	4	16	6.40	8	3	9	3.60
9	Boom	0.30	30	20	400	120.00	−5	−10	100	30.00
10					Variance = SUM	347.10			Variance:	68.40
11				Standard deviation = SQRT(Variance)		18.63			Std. Dev.:	8.27

SPREADSHEET 6.3

Performance of a portfolio invested in the stock and bond funds

	A	B	C	D	E	F	G
1			Portfolio invested 40% in stock fund and 60% in bond fund				
2			Rate	Column B	Deviation from		Column B
3			of	×	Expected	Squared	×
4	Scenario	Probability	Return	Column C	Return	Deviation	Column F
5	Severe recession	0.05	−20.2	−1.01	−27.2	739.84	36.99
6	Mild recession	0.25	4.6	1.15	−2.4	5.76	1.44
7	Normal growth	0.40	10.4	4.16	3.4	11.56	4.62
8	Boom	0.30	9.0	2.70	2.0	4.00	1.20
9		Expected return:		7.00		Variance:	44.26
10						Standard deviation:	6.65

Χ

Spreadsheets are
available in Connect

What about the risk and return characteristics of a portfolio made up from the stock and bond funds? The portfolio return is the weighted average of the returns on each fund with weights equal to the proportion of the portfolio invested in each fund. Suppose we form a portfolio with 40% in stocks and 60% in bonds. Then the portfolio return in each scenario is the weighted average of the returns on the two funds. For example

$$\text{Portfolio return in mild recession} = .40 \times (-11\%) + .60 \times 15\% = 4.6\%$$

which appears in cell C6 of Spreadsheet 6.3.

Spreadsheet 6.3 shows the rate of return of the portfolio in each scenario. Notice that both funds suffer in a severe downturn and, therefore, the portfolio also experiences a substantial loss of 20.2%. This is a manifestation of systematic risk affecting a broad spectrum of securities. Declines of more than 25% in the S&P 500 Index have occurred five times in the past 88 years (1930, 1931, 1937, 1974, and 2008), roughly once every 18 years. Avoiding losses in these extreme outcomes would require one to devote a large allocation of the portfolio to risk-free (and correspondingly low return) investments or (expensive) portfolio insurance (which we will discuss in Chapter 16). Extreme events such as severe recessions make for the large standard deviation of stocks, 18.63%, and even of bonds, 8.27%. Still, the overall standard deviation of the diversified portfolio, 6.65%, is considerably smaller than that of stocks and even smaller than that of bonds.

The low risk of the portfolio is due to the inverse relationship between the performances of the stock and bond funds. In a mild recession, stocks fare poorly, but this is offset by the large positive return of the bond fund. Conversely, in the boom scenario, bond prices fall, but stocks do very well. Notice that while the portfolio's expected return is just the weighted average of the expected return of the two assets, *the portfolio standard deviation is actually lower than that of either component fund.*

Portfolio risk is reduced most when the returns of the two assets most reliably offset each other. The natural question investors should ask, therefore, is how one can measure the tendency of the returns on two assets to vary either in tandem or in opposition to each other. The statistics that provide this measure are the covariance and the correlation coefficient.

The covariance is calculated in a manner similar to the variance. Instead of multiplying the difference of an asset return from its expected value by itself (i.e., squaring it), we multiply it by the deviation of the *other* asset return from *its* expectation. The sign and magnitude of this product are determined by whether deviations from the mean move together (i.e., are both positive or negative in the same scenarios) and whether they are small or large at the same time.

We start in Spreadsheet 6.4 with the deviation of the return on each fund from its expected value. For each scenario, we multiply the deviation of the stock fund return from its mean by the deviation of the bond fund. The product will be positive if both asset returns exceed their respective means or if both fall short of their respective means. The product will be negative if one asset exceeds its mean return when the other falls short. Spreadsheet 6.4 shows that

SPREADSHEET 6.4

Covariance between the returns of the stock and bond funds

Spreadsheets are
available in Connect

	A	B	C	D	E	F
1			Deviation from Mean Return		Covariance	
2	Scenario	Probability	Stock Fund	Bond Fund	Product of Dev	Col B × Col E
3	Severe recession	0.05	−47	−14	658	32.9
4	Mild recession	0.25	−21	10	−210	−52.5
5	Normal growth	0.40	4	3	12	4.8
6	Boom	0.30	20	−10	−200	−60.0
7					Covariance =	SUM: −74.8
8	Correlation coefficient = Covariance/(StdDev(stocks)*StdDev(bonds)) =					−0.49

the stock fund return in a mild recession falls short of its expected value by 21%, while the bond fund return exceeds its mean by 10%. Therefore, the product of the two deviations is $-21 \times 10 = -210$, as reported in column E. The product of deviations is negative if one asset performs well when the other is performing poorly. It is positive if both assets perform well or poorly in the same scenarios.

The probability-weighted average of the products is called *covariance* and measures the *average* tendency of the asset returns to vary in tandem, that is, to co-vary. The formula for the covariance of the returns on the stock and bond funds is given in Equation 6.1. Each particular scenario in this equation is labeled or "indexed" by i. In general, i ranges from scenario 1 to n (the total number of scenarios; here, $n = 4$). The probability of each scenario is denoted $p(i)$.

$$\text{Cov}(r_S, r_B) = \sum_{i=1}^{n} p(i)[r_S(i) - E(r_S)][r_B(i) - E(r_B)] \tag{6.1}$$

The covariance of the stock and bond funds is computed in the next-to-last line of Spreadsheet 6.4 using Equation 6.1. The negative value for the covariance indicates that the two assets, on average, vary inversely; when one performs well, the other tends to perform poorly.

Like variance, the unit of covariance is percent square, which is why it is difficult to interpret its magnitude. For instance, does the covariance of −74.8 in cell F7 indicate that the inverse relationship between the returns on stock and bond funds is strong? It's hard to say. An easier statistic to interpret is the *correlation coefficient,* which is the covariance divided by the product of the standard deviations of the returns on each fund. We denote the correlation coefficient by the Greek letter rho, ρ.

$$\text{Correlation coefficient} = \rho_{SB} = \frac{\text{Cov}(r_S, r_B)}{\sigma_S \sigma_B} = \frac{-74.8}{18.63 \times 8.27} = -.49 \tag{6.2}$$

Correlation is a pure number and can range from −1 to +1. A correlation of −1 indicates that one asset's return varies perfectly inversely with the other's. If you were to do a linear regression of one asset's return on the other, the slope coefficient would be negative and the R-square of the regression would be 100%, indicating a perfect fit. The R-square is the square of the correlation coefficient and tells you the fraction of the variance of one return explained by the other. With a correlation of −1, you could predict 100% of the variability of one asset's return if you knew the return on the other asset. Conversely, a correlation of +1 would indicate perfect positive correlation and also would imply an R-square of 100%. A correlation of zero indicates that the returns on the two assets are unrelated. The correlation coefficient of $\rho_{SB} = -.49$ in Equation 6.2 confirms the tendency of the returns on the stock and bond funds to vary inversely. In fact, a fraction of $(-.49)^2 = .24$ of the variance of stocks can be explained by the returns on bonds.

Equation 6.2 shows that whenever the covariance is called for in a calculation we can replace it with the following expression using the correlation coefficient:

$$\text{Cov}(r_S, r_B) = \rho_{SB}\sigma_S\sigma_B \tag{6.3}$$

We are now in a position to derive the risk and return features of portfolios of risky assets.

Suppose the rates of return of the bond portfolio in the four scenarios of Spreadsheet 6.1 are −10% in a severe recession, 10% in a mild recession, 7% in a normal period, and 2% in a boom. The stock returns in the four scenarios are −37%, −11%, 14%, and 30%. What are the covariance and correlation coefficient between the rates of return on the two portfolios?

Using Historical Data

We've seen that portfolio risk and return depend on the means and variances of the component securities, as well as on the covariance between their returns. One way to obtain these inputs is a scenario analysis as in Spreadsheets 6.1–6.4. A common alternative approach to produce these inputs is to make use of historical data. The idea is that variability and covariability change slowly over time. Thus, if we estimate these statistics from recent data, our estimates will provide useful predictions for the near future—perhaps next month or next quarter.

In this approach, we use realized returns to estimate variances and covariances. Means cannot be as precisely estimated from past returns. We discuss mean returns in great detail later. The estimate of variance is the average value of the squared deviations around the sample average; the estimate of the covariance is the average value of the cross-product of deviations. Notice that, as in scenario analysis, the focus for risk is on deviations of returns from their average value. Instead of using mean returns based on the scenario analysis, we use average returns during the sample period. We can illustrate this approach with a simple example.

EXAMPLE 6.1

Using Historical Data to Estimate Means, Standard Deviations, Covariance, and Correlation

Consider the 10 annual returns for the two mutual funds presented in the following spreadsheet. Although this sample period is far shorter than most analysts would use, for the sake of illustration we will pretend that it is adequate to estimate mean returns and relevant risk statistics with acceptable precision. In practice, analysts would use higher-frequency data (e.g., monthly or even daily data) to estimate risk coefficients and would, as well, supplement historical data with fundamental analysis to forecast future returns.

The spreadsheet starts with the raw return data in columns B and C. We use standard Excel functions to obtain average returns, standard deviation, covariance, and correlation (see rows 18–21). We also confirm (in cell F14) that covariance is the average value of the product of each asset's deviation from its mean return.

The average returns and standard deviations in this spreadsheet are similar to those of our previous scenario analysis. However, the correlation between stock and bond returns in this example is low but positive, which is more consistent with historical experience than the strongly negative correlation of −.49 implied by our scenario analysis.

	A	B	C	D	E	F
1		|← Rates of Return →|		|← Deviations from Average Returns →|		Products of
2	Year	Stock Fund	Bond Fund	Stock Fund	Bond Fund	Deviations
3	2006	30.17	5.08	20.17	0.08	1.53
4	2007	32.97	7.52	22.97	2.52	57.78
5	2008	21.04	−8.82	11.04	−13.82	−152.56
6	2009	−8.10	5.27	−18.10	0.27	−4.82
7	2010	−12.89	12.20	−22.89	7.20	−164.75
8	2011	−28.53	−7.79	−38.53	−12.79	493.00
9	2012	22.49	6.38	12.49	1.38	17.18
10	2013	12.58	12.40	2.58	7.40	19.05
11	2014	14.81	17.29	4.81	12.29	59.05
12	2015	15.50	0.51	5.50	−4.49	−24.70
13						
14	Average	10.00	5.00	Covariance = Average product of deviations:		30.08
15	SD	19.00	8.00	Correlation = Covariance/(SD stocks*SD bonds):		0.20
16						
17	**Excel formulas**					
18	Average	=average(B3:B12)				
19	Std deviation	=stdevp(B3:B12)				
20	Covariance	=covar(B3:B12,C3:C12)				
21	Correlation	=correl(B3:B12,C3:C12)				
22						
23						

Two comments on Example 6.1 are in order. First, you may recall from a statistics class and from Chapter 5 that when variance is estimated from a sample of n observed returns, it is common to divide the squared deviations by $n - 1$ rather than by n. This is because we take deviations from an estimated average return rather than the true (but unknown) expected return; this procedure is said to adjust for a "lost degree of freedom." In Excel, the function STDEVP computes standard deviation dividing by n, while the function STDEV uses $n - 1$. Excel's covariance and correlation functions both use n. In Example 6.1, we ignored this fine point, and divided by n throughout. In any event, the correction for the lost degree of freedom is negligible when there are plentiful observations. For example, with 60 returns (e.g., five years of monthly data), the difference between dividing by 60 or 59 will affect variance or covariance by a factor of only 1.017.

Second, we repeat the warning about the statistical reliability of historical estimates. Estimates of variance and covariance from past data are generally reliable forecasts (at least for the short term). However, averages of past returns typically provide highly noisy (i.e., imprecise) forecasts of future expected returns. In this example, we use past averages from small samples because our objective is to demonstrate the methodology. In practice, professional investors spend most of their resources on macroeconomic and security analysis to improve their estimates of mean returns.

CONCEPT
check   **6.2**

The following tables present returns on various pairs of stocks in several periods. In part A, we show you a scatter diagram of the returns on the first pair of stocks. Draw (or prepare in Excel) similar scatter diagrams for cases B through E. Match up your diagrams (A–E) to the following list of correlation coefficients by choosing the correlation that best describes the relationship between the returns on the two stocks: $\rho = -1, 0, .2, .5, 1.0$.

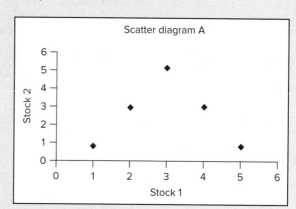

A.

% Return	
Stock 1	**Stock 2**
5	1
1	1
4	3
2	3
3	5

B.

% Return	
Stock 1	**Stock 2**
1	1
2	2
3	3
4	4
5	5

C.

% Return	
Stock 1	**Stock 2**
1	5
2	4
3	3
4	2
5	1

D.

% Return	
Stock 1	**Stock 2**
5	5
1	3
4	3
2	0
3	5

E.

% Return	
Stock 1	**Stock 2**
5	4
1	3
4	1
2	0
3	5

The Three Rules of Two-Risky-Asset Portfolios

Suppose a proportion denoted by w_B is invested in the bond fund and the remainder $1 - w_B$, denoted by w_S, is invested in the stock fund. The properties of the portfolio are determined by the following three rules governing combinations of random variables:

Rule 1: The rate of return on a portfolio is the weighted average of returns on the component securities, with the investment proportions as weights.

$$r_P = w_B r_B + w_S r_S \qquad\qquad (6.4)$$

Rule 2: The expected *rate of return on a portfolio is the weighted average of the* expected *returns on the component securities, with the portfolio proportions as weights.*

$$E(r_P) = w_B E(r_B) + w_S E(r_S) \qquad\qquad (6.5)$$

Rules 1 and 2 say that a portfolio's actual return and its mean return are linear functions of the component security returns and portfolio weights. This is not so for portfolio variance, as the third rule shows.

Rule 3: The variance of the rate of return on a two-risky-asset portfolio is

$$\sigma_P^2 = (w_B \sigma_B)^2 + (w_S \sigma_S)^2 + 2(w_B \sigma_B)(w_S \sigma_S)\rho_{BS} \qquad\qquad (6.6)$$

where ρ_{BS} is the correlation coefficient between the returns on the stock and bond funds. Notice that using Equation 6.3, we may replace the last term in Equation 6.6 with $2w_B w_S Cov(r_B, r_S)$.

The variance of a portfolio is the *sum* of the contributions of the component security variances *plus* a term that involves the correlation coefficient (and hence, covariance) between the returns on the component securities. We know from the last section why this last term arises. When the correlation between the component securities is small or negative, there will be a greater tendency for returns on the two assets to offset each other. This will reduce portfolio risk. Equation 6.6 tells us that portfolio variance is lower when the correlation coefficient is lower.

The formula describing portfolio variance is more complicated than that describing portfolio return. This complication has a virtue, however: a tremendous potential for gains from diversification.

The Risk-Return Trade-Off with Two-Risky-Assets Portfolios

We can assess the benefit from diversification by using Rules 2 and 3 to compare the risk and expected return of a better-diversified portfolio to a less diversified benchmark. Suppose an investor estimates the following input data:

$$E(r_B) = 5\%; \ \sigma_B = 8\%; \ E(r_S) = 10\%; \ \sigma_S = 19\%; \ \rho_{BS} = .2$$

Currently, all funds are invested in the bond fund, but the invester ponders a portfolio invested 40% in stock and 60% in bonds. Using Rule 2, the expected return of this portfolio is

$$E(r_P) = .4 \times 10\% + .6 \times 5\% = 7\%$$

which represents an increase of 2% compared to a bond-only investment. Using Rule 3, the portfolio standard deviation is

$$\sigma = \sqrt{(.4 \times 19)^2 + (.6 \times 8)^2 + 2(.4 \times 19) \times (.6 \times 8) \times .2} = 9.76\%$$

which is less than the weighted average of the component standard deviations: $.4 \times 19 + .6 \times 8 = 12.40\%$. The difference of 2.64% reflects the benefits of diversification. This benefit is cost-free in the sense that diversification allows us to experience the full contribution of the stock's higher expected return, while keeping the portfolio standard deviation below the average of the component standard deviations.

Suppose we invest 85% in bonds and only 15% in stocks. We can construct a portfolio with an expected return higher than bonds $(.85 \times 5) + (.15 \times 10) = 5.75\%$ and, at the same time, a standard deviation less than bonds. Using Equation 6.6 again, we find that the portfolio variance is

$$(.85 \times 8)^2 + (.15 \times 19)^2 + 2(.85 \times 8)(.15 \times 19) \times .2 = 62.1$$

and, accordingly, the portfolio standard deviation is $\sqrt{62.1} = 7.88\%$, which is less than the standard deviation of either bonds or stocks alone. Taking on a more volatile asset (stocks) actually reduces portfolio risk! Such is the power of diversification.

We can find investment proportions that will reduce portfolio risk even further. The risk-minimizing proportions are 90.7% in bonds and 9.3% in stocks.[1] With these proportions, the portfolio standard deviation will be 7.80%, and the portfolio's expected return will be 5.47%.

Is this portfolio preferable to the one considered in Example 6.2, with 15% in the stock fund? That depends on investor preferences, because the portfolio with the lower variance also has a lower expected return.

What the analyst can and must do is show investors the entire **investment opportunity set.** This is the set of all attainable combinations of risk and return offered by portfolios formed using the available assets in differing proportions. We find the investment opportunity set using Spreadsheet 6.5. Columns A and B set out several different proportions for investments in the stock

investment opportunity set

Set of available portfolio risk-return combinations.

SPREADSHEET   6.5

The investment opportunity set with the stock and bond funds

Spreadsheets are available in Connect

	A	B	C	D	E
1			**Input Data**		
2	$E(r_S)$	$E(r_B)$	σ_S	σ_B	ρ_{BS}
3	10	5	19	8	0.2
4	Portfolio Weights		Expected Return, $E(r_p)$		Std Dev
5	$w_S = 1 - w_B$	w_B	Col A*A3 + Col B*B3		(Equation 6.6)
6	−0.2	1.2	4.0		9.59
7	−0.1	1.1	4.5		8.62
8	0.0	1.0	5.0		8.00
9	0.0932	0.9068	5.5		7.804
10	0.1	0.9	5.5		7.81
11	0.2	0.8	6.0		8.07
12	0.3	0.7	6.5		8.75
13	0.4	0.6	7.0		9.77
14	0.5	0.5	7.5		11.02
15	0.6	0.4	8.0		12.44
16	0.7	0.3	8.5		13.98
17	0.8	0.2	9.0		15.60
18	0.9	0.1	9.5		17.28
19	1.0	0.0	10.0		19.00
20	1.1	−0.1	10.5		20.75
21	1.2	−0.2	11.0		22.53
22	Notes:				
23	1. Negative weights indicate short positions.				
24	2. The weights of the minimum-variance portfolio are computed using the formula in Footnote 1.				

[1]The minimum-variance portfolio minimizes the variance (and hence standard deviation) of returns, regardless of the expected return. The formula for the weight in bonds is $w_B = \dfrac{\sigma_S^2 - \sigma_B \sigma_S \rho_{BS}}{\sigma_S^2 + \sigma_B^2 - 2\sigma_B \sigma_S \rho_{BS}}$, and the weight in stocks is $w_S = 1 - w_B$. Notice that when correlation is zero, the variance-minimizing weight simplifies to the ratio of stock variance to the sum of the variances of stocks and bonds: $w_B = \dfrac{\sigma_S^2}{\sigma_S^2 + \sigma_B^2}$.

FIGURE 6.3

The investment opportunity set with the stock and bond funds

and bond funds. The next columns present the portfolio expected return and standard deviation corresponding to each allocation. These risk-return combinations are plotted in Figure 6.3.

The Mean-Variance Criterion

Investors desire portfolios that lie to the "northwest" in Figure 6.3. These are portfolios with high expected returns (toward the "north" of the figure) and low volatility (to the "west"). These preferences mean that we can compare portfolios using a *mean-variance criterion* in the following way: Portfolio A is said to dominate portfolio B if all investors prefer A over B. This will be the case if it has higher mean return and lower variance or standard deviation:

$$E(r_A) \geq E(r_B) \quad \text{and} \quad \sigma_A \leq \sigma_B$$

Graphically, when we plot the expected return and standard deviation of each portfolio in Figure 6.3, portfolio A will lie to the northwest of B. Given a choice between portfolios A and B, *all* investors would choose A. For example, the stock fund in Figure 6.3 dominates portfolio Z; the stock fund has higher expected return and lower volatility.

Portfolios that lie below the minimum-variance portfolio in the figure can therefore be rejected out of hand as inefficient. Any portfolio on the downward-sloping portion of the curve (including the bond fund) is "dominated" by the portfolio that lies directly above it on the upward-sloping portion of the curve since that portfolio has higher expected return and equal standard deviation. The best choice among the portfolios on the upward-sloping portion of the curve is not as obvious, because in this region higher expected return is accompanied by greater risk. We will discuss the best choice when we introduce the risk-free asset to the portfolio decision.

So far we have assumed a correlation of .2 between stock and bond returns. We know that low correlations aid diversification and that a higher correlation coefficient results in a reduced effect of diversification. What are the implications of perfect positive correlation between bonds and stocks?

A correlation coefficient of 1 simplifies Equation 6.6 for portfolio variance. Looking at it again, you will see that substitution of $\rho_{BS} = 1$ allows us to "complete the square" of the quantities $w_B\sigma_B$ and $w_S\sigma_S$ to obtain

$$\sigma_P^2 = w_B^2\sigma_B^2 + w_S^2\sigma_S^2 + 2w_B\sigma_B w_S\sigma_S = (w_B\sigma_B + w_S\sigma_S)^2$$

$$\sigma_P = w_B\sigma_B + w_S\sigma_S$$

The portfolio standard deviation is a weighted average of the component security standard deviations only in the special case of perfect positive correlation. In this circumstance, there are no gains to be had from diversification. Both the portfolio mean and the standard deviation are simple weighted averages. Figure 6.4 shows the opportunity set with perfect positive correlation—a straight line through the component securities. No portfolio can be discarded

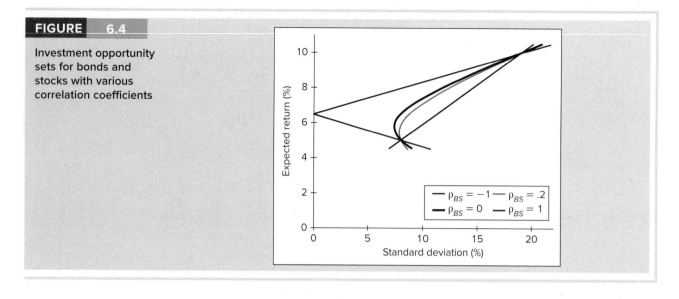

FIGURE   6.4

Investment opportunity sets for bonds and stocks with various correlation coefficients

as inefficient in this case, and the choice among portfolios depends only on risk aversion. Diversification in the case of perfect positive correlation is not effective.

Perfect positive correlation is the *only* case in which there is no benefit from diversification. Whenever $\rho < 1$, the portfolio standard deviation is less than the weighted average of the standard deviations of the component securities. Therefore, *there are benefits to diversification whenever asset returns are less than perfectly positively correlated.*

Our analysis has ranged from very attractive diversification benefits ($\rho_{BS} < 0$) to no benefits at all ($\rho_{BS} = 1$). For ρ_{BS} within this range, the benefits will be somewhere in between.

A realistic correlation coefficient between stocks and bonds based on historical experience is actually around .20. The expected returns and standard deviations that we have so far assumed also reflect historical experience, which is why we include a graph for $\rho_{BS} = .2$ in Figure 6.4. Spreadsheet 6.6 enumerates some of the points on the various opportunity sets in Figure 6.4. As the figure illustrates, $\rho_{BS} = .2$ is a lot better for diversification than perfect positive correlation and a bit worse than zero correlation.

Negative correlation between a pair of assets is also possible. When correlation is negative, there will be even greater diversification benefits. Again, let us start with the extreme. With perfect negative correlation, we substitute $\rho_{BS} = -1$ in Equation 6.6 and simplify it by completing the square:

$$\sigma_P^2 = (w_B\sigma_B - w_S\sigma_S)^2$$

and, therefore,

$$\sigma_P = \text{ABS}[w_B\sigma_B - w_S\sigma_S] \qquad \textbf{(6.7)}$$

The right-hand side of Equation 6.7 denotes the absolute value of $w_B\sigma_B - w_S\sigma_S$. The solution involves the absolute value because standard deviation cannot be negative.

With perfect negative correlation, the benefits from diversification stretch to the limit. Equation 6.7 yields the proportions that will reduce the portfolio standard deviation all the way to zero.[2] With our data, this will happen when $w_B = 70.37\%$. While exposing us to zero risk, investing 29.63% in stocks (rather than placing all funds in bonds) will still increase the portfolio expected return from 5% to 6.48%. Of course, we can hardly expect results this attractive in reality.

---

[2]The proportion in bonds that will drive the standard deviation to zero when $\rho = -1$ is

$$w_B = \frac{\sigma_S}{\sigma_B + \sigma_S}$$

Compare this formula to the formula in footnote 1 for the variance-minimizing proportions when $\rho = 0$.

SPREADSHEET 6.6

Investment opportunity set for stocks and bonds with various correlation coefficients

	A	B	C	D	E	F	G
1		**Input Data**					
2	$E(r_S)$	$E(r_B)$	σ_S	σ_B			
3	10	5	19	8			
4							
5	Weights in Stocks	Portfolio Expected Return	Portfolio Standard Deviation[1] for Given Correlation, ρ				
6	w_S	$E(r_P) = $ Col A*A3 + (1 − Col A)*B3	−1	0	0.2	0.5	1
7	−0.1	4.5	10.70	9.00	8.62	8.02	6.90
8	0.0	5.0	8.00	8.00	8.00	8.00	8.00
9	0.1	5.5	5.30	7.45	7.81	8.31	9.10
10	0.2	6.0	2.60	7.44	8.07	8.93	10.20
11	0.3	6.5	0.10	7.99	8.75	9.79	11.30
12	0.4	7.0	2.80	8.99	9.77	10.83	12.40
13	0.6	8.0	8.20	11.84	12.44	13.29	14.60
14	0.8	9.0	13.60	15.28	15.60	16.06	16.80
15	1.0	10.0	19.00	19.00	19.00	19.00	19.00
16	1.1	10.5	21.70	20.92	20.75	20.51	20.10
17			Minimum-Variance Portfolio[2,3,4,5]				
18	$w_S(\min) = (\sigma_B{}^2 - \sigma_B\sigma_S\rho)/(\sigma_S{}^2 + \sigma_B{}^2 - 2*\sigma_B\sigma_S\rho) =$		0.2963	0.1506	0.0923	−0.0440	−0.7273
19	$E(r_P) - w_S(\min)*A3 + (1 - w_S(\min))*B3 =$		6.48	5.75	5.46	4.78	1.36
20		$\sigma_P =$	0.00	7.37	7.80	7.97	0.00

Notes:

1. $\sigma_P = $ SQRT[(Col A*C3)^2 + ((1 − Col A)*D3)^2 + 2*Col A*C3*(1 − Col A)*D3*ρ]

2. The standard deviation is calculated from Equation 6.6 using the weights of the minimum-variance portfolio:

$$\sigma_P = \text{SQRT}[(w_S(\min)*C3)^2 + ((1 - w_S(\min))*D3)^2 + 2*w_S(\min)*C3*(1 - w_S(\min))*D3*\rho]$$

3. As the correlation coefficient grows, the minimum-variance portfolio requires a smaller position in stocks (even a negative position for higher correlations), and the performance of this portfolio becomes less attractive.

4. Notice that with correlation of .5 or higher, minimum variance is achieved with a short position in stocks. The standard deviation is lower than that of bonds, but the mean is lower as well.

5. With perfect positive correlation (column G), you can drive the standard deviation to zero by taking a large, short position in stocks. The mean return is then as low as 1.36%.

𝕏

Spreadsheets are available in Connect

Suppose that for some reason you are *required* to invest 50% of your portfolio in bonds and 50% in stocks. Use the data on mean returns and standard deviations in Spreadsheet 6.5 to answer the following questions.

CONCEPT check 6.3

   a. If the standard deviation of your portfolio is 10%, what must be the correlation coefficient between stock and bond returns?
   b. What is the expected rate of return on your portfolio?
   c. Now suppose that the correlation between stock and bond returns is .22 instead of the value you found in part (*a*) but that you are free to choose whatever portfolio proportions you desire. Are you likely to be better or worse off than you were in part (*a*)?

6.3 THE OPTIMAL RISKY PORTFOLIO WITH A RISK-FREE ASSET

Now we can expand the asset allocation problem to include a risk-free asset. Let us continue to use the input data from Spreadsheet 6.5. Suppose then that we are still confined to the risky bond and stock funds but now can also invest in T-bills yielding 3%. When we add the risk-free asset to a stock-plus-bond risky portfolio, the resulting opportunity set is the straight line that we called the CAL (capital allocation line) in Chapter 5. We now consider various CALs constructed from risk-free bills and a variety of possible risky portfolios, each formed by combining the stock and bond funds in alternative proportions.

We start in Figure 6.5 with the opportunity set of risky assets constructed only from the bond and stock funds. The lowest-variance risky portfolio is labeled MIN (denoting the *minimum-variance portfolio*). CAL$_{\text{MIN}}$ is drawn through it and shows the risk-return trade-off with various positions in T-bills and portfolio MIN. It is immediately evident from the figure that we could do better (i.e., obtain a higher Sharpe ratio) by using portfolio *A* instead of MIN as the risky portfolio. CAL$_A$ dominates CAL$_{\text{MIN}}$, offering a higher expected return for any level of volatility. Spreadsheet 6.6 (see bottom panel of column E) shows that portfolio MIN's expected return is 5.46% and its standard deviation (SD) is 7.80%. Portfolio *A* (row 10 in Spreadsheet 6.6) offers an expected return of 6% with an SD of 8.07%.

The slope of the CAL that uses a risky portfolio, *P*, is the Sharpe ratio of that portfolio, that is, the ratio of its expected excess return to its standard deviation:

$$S_P = \frac{E(r_P) - r_f}{\sigma_P} \tag{6.8}$$

With a T-bill rate of 3% we obtain the Sharpe ratio of the two portfolios:

$$S_{\text{MIN}} = \frac{5.46 - 3}{7.80} = .32 \quad S_A = \frac{6 - 3}{8.07} = .37 \tag{6.9}$$

The higher ratio for portfolio *A* compared to MIN measures the improvement it offers in the risk-return trade-off.

But why stop at portfolio *A*? We can continue to ratchet the CAL upward until it reaches the ultimate point of tangency with the investment opportunity set. This must yield the CAL with the highest feasible Sharpe ratio. Therefore, the tangency portfolio (*O*) in Figure 6.6 is the **optimal risky portfolio** to mix with T-bills, which may be defined as the risky portfolio that generates the steepest CAL.

Figure 6.6 clearly shows the improvement in the risk-return trade-off obtained with CAL$_O$. With the exception of the optimal portfolio *O*, any portfolio formed by combining just the stock and bond funds has lower expected return than a portfolio on CAL$_O$ with the same standard deviation.

To find the composition of the optimal risky portfolio, *O*, we search for weights in the stock and bond funds that maximize the portfolio's Sharpe ratio. With only two risky assets, we can solve for the optimal portfolio weights using the following formula:[3]

$$w_B = \frac{[E(r_B) - r_f]\sigma_S^2 - [E(r_S) - r_f]\sigma_B\sigma_S\rho_{BS}}{[E(r_B) - r_f]\sigma_S^2 + [E(r_S) - r_f]\sigma_B^2 - [E(r_B) - r_f + E(r_S) - r_f]\sigma_B\sigma_S\rho_{BS}}$$

$$w_S = 1 - w_B \tag{6.10}$$

optimal risky portfolio

The best combination of risky assets to be mixed with safe assets to form the complete portfolio.

[3]Equation 6.10, providing the weights that maximize the Sharpe ratio, can be obtained using calculus: Write the Sharpe ratio of a portfolio formed from the stock and bond funds as a function of w_B and $w_S = 1 - w_B$, as well as the expected returns, standard deviations, and correlation coefficient of the two funds. Setting the derivative of the Sharpe ratio with respect to w_B equal to zero produces an equation that can be solved for the optimal w_B.

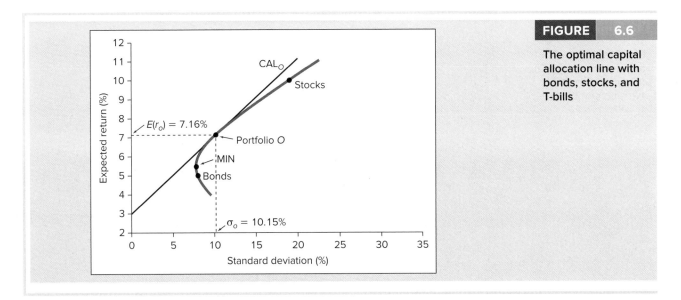

Using the risk premiums (expected excess return over the risk-free rate) of the stock and bond funds, their standard deviations, and the correlation between their returns in Equation 6.10, we find that the weights of the optimal portfolio are $w_B(O) = .568$ and $w_S(O) = .432$. Using these weights, Equations 6.5, 6.6, and 6.8 imply that $E(r_O) = 7.16\%$, $\sigma_O = 10.15\%$, and therefore the Sharpe ratio of the optimal portfolio (the slope of its CAL) is

$$S_O = \frac{E(r_O) - r_f}{\sigma_O} = \frac{7.16 - 3}{10.15} = .41$$

This Sharpe ratio is significantly higher than those provided by either the bond or stock portfolios alone.

In the last chapter we saw that the preferred *complete* portfolio formed from a risky portfolio and a risk-free asset depends on risk aversion. More risk-averse investors prefer low-risk portfolios despite the lower expected return, while more risk-tolerant investors choose higher-risk, higher-return portfolios. Both investors, however, will choose portfolio O as their risky portfolio since it provides highest return per unit of risk, that is, the steepest capital allocation line. Investors will differ only in their allocation of investment funds between portfolio O and the risk-free asset.

Figure 6.7 shows one possible choice for the preferred complete portfolio, C. The investor places 55% of wealth in portfolio O and 45% in Treasury bills. The rate of return and volatility of the portfolio are

$$E(r_C) = 3 + .55 \times (7.16 - 3) = 5.29\%$$

$$\sigma_C = .55 \times 10.15 = 5.58\%$$

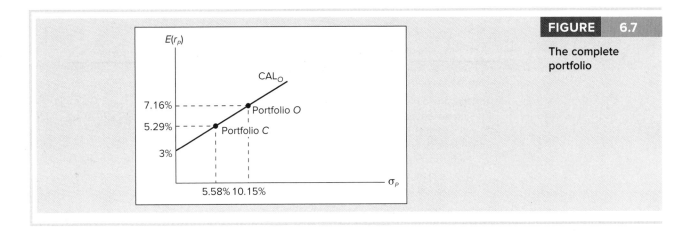

FIGURE 6.7

The complete portfolio

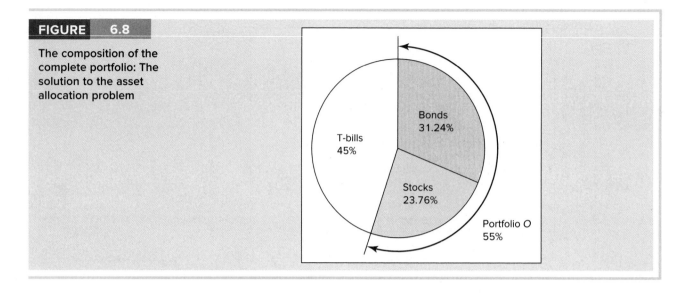

FIGURE 6.8

The composition of the complete portfolio: The solution to the asset allocation problem

Because portfolio *O* is a mix of the bond fund and stock fund with weights of 56.8% and 43.2%, the overall asset allocation of the *complete* portfolio is as follows:

Weight in risk-free asset		45.00%
Weight in bond fund	0.568 × 55% =	31.24
Weight in stock fund	0.432 × 55% =	23.76
Total		100.00%

Figure 6.8 depicts the overall asset allocation. The allocation reflects considerations of both efficient diversification (the construction of the optimal risky portfolio, *O*) and risk aversion (the allocation of funds between the risk-free asset and the risky portfolio *O* to form the complete portfolio, *C*).

CONCEPT check 6.4

A universe of securities includes a risky stock (*X*), a stock-index fund (*M*), and T-bills. The data for the universe are:

	Expected Return	Standard Deviation
X	15%	50%
M	10	20
T-bills	5	0

The correlation coefficient between *X* and *M* is −.2.

  a. Draw the opportunity set of securities *X* and *M*.
  b. Find the optimal risky portfolio (*O*), its expected return, standard deviation, and Sharpe ratio. Compare with the Sharpe ratios of *X* and *M*, each taken individually.
  c. Find the slope of the CAL generated by T-bills and portfolio *O*.
  d. Suppose an investor places 2/9 (i.e., 22.22%) of the complete portfolio in the risky portfolio *O* and the remainder in T-bills. Calculate the composition of the complete portfolio, its expected return, SD, and Sharpe ratio.

6.4 EFFICIENT DIVERSIFICATION WITH MANY RISKY ASSETS

We extend the two-risky-assets portfolio methodology to many risky assets in three steps. First, we generalize the two-risky-asset opportunity set to allow for many assets. Next we determine the optimal risky portfolio that supports the steepest CAL, that is, maximizes the Sharpe ratio. Finally, we choose a complete portfolio on CAL_O based on risk aversion by mixing the risk-free asset with the optimal risky portfolio.

The Efficient Frontier of Risky Assets

To get a sense of how additional risky assets can improve investment opportunities, look at Figure 6.9. Points *A, B,* and *C* represent the expected returns and standard deviations of three stocks. The curve passing through *A* and *B* shows the risk-return combinations of portfolios formed from those two stocks. Similarly, the curve passing through *B* and *C* shows portfolios formed from those two stocks. Now observe point *E* on the *AB* curve and point *F* on the *BC* curve. These points represent two portfolios chosen from the set of *AB* and *BC* combinations. The curve that passes through *E* and *F* in turn represents portfolios constructed from portfolios *E* and *F*. Since *E* and *F* are themselves constructed from *A, B,* and *C,* this curve shows some of the portfolios constructed from these *three* stocks. Notice that curve *EF* extends the investment opportunity set to the northwest, which is the desired direction.

Now we can continue to take other points (each representing portfolios) from these three curves and further combine them into new portfolios, thus shifting the opportunity set even farther to the northwest. You can see that this process would work even better with more stocks. Moreover, the boundary or "envelope" of all the curves thus developed will lie quite away from the individual stocks in the northwesterly direction, as shown in Figure 6.10.

The analytical technique to derive the efficient set of risky assets was developed by Harry Markowitz in 1951 and ultimately earned him the Nobel Prize in Economics. We sketch his approach here.

First, we determine the risk-return opportunity set. The aim is to construct the northwesternmost portfolios in terms of expected return and standard deviation from the universe of securities. The inputs are the expected returns and standard deviations of each asset in the universe, along with the correlation coefficients between each pair of assets. These data come from security analysis, to be discussed in Part Four. The graph that connects all the northwesternmost portfolios is called the **efficient frontier** of risky assets. It represents the set of portfolios that offers the highest possible expected rate of return for each level of portfolio standard deviation. These portfolios may be viewed as efficiently diversified. One such frontier is shown in Figure 6.10.

efficient frontier

Graph representing a set of portfolios that maximizes expected return at each level of portfolio risk.

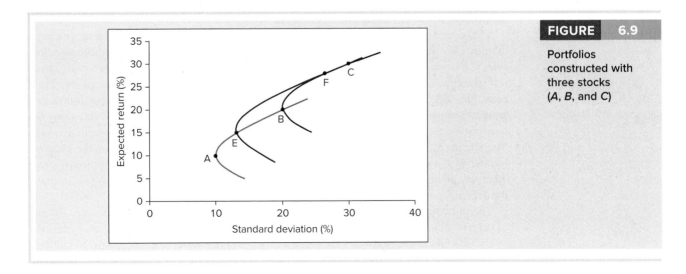

FIGURE 6.9

Portfolios constructed with three stocks (*A, B,* and *C*)

FIGURE   **6.10**

The efficient frontier
of risky assets and
individual assets

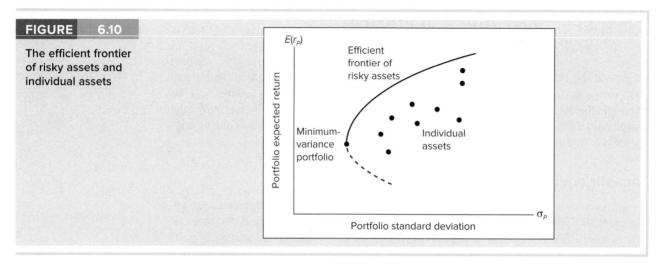

There are three equivalent ways to produce the efficient frontier. We will sketch each in a way that allows you to participate and gain insight into the logic and mechanics of the efficient frontier: Take a pencil and paper and draw the graph as you follow along with our discussion. For each method, first draw the horizontal axis for portfolio standard deviation and the vertical axis for risk premium. We focus on the risk premium (expected excess returns), R, rather than total returns, r, so that the risk-free asset will lie at the origin (with zero SD and zero risk premium). We begin with the minimum-variance portfolio—mark it as point G (for *global* minimum variance). Imagine that G's coordinates are .10 (SD = 10%) and .03 (risk premium = 3%); this is your first point on the efficient frontier. Later, we add detail about how to find these coordinates.

The three ways to draw the efficient frontier are (1) maximize the risk premium for any level of SD; (2) minimize the SD for any level of risk premium; and (3) maximize the Sharpe ratio for any level of SD (or risk premium).

For the first method, maximizing the risk premium for any level of SD, draw a few vertical lines to the right of G (there can be no portfolio with SD less than G's). Choose the vertical line drawn at SD = 12%; we therefore search for the portfolio with the highest possible expected return consistent with an SD of 12%. So we give the computer an assignment to maximize the risk premium subject to two constraints: (i) The portfolio weights sum to 1 (this is called the *feasibility* constraint, since any legitimate portfolio must have weights that sum to 1), and (ii) the portfolio SD must match the constraint value, $\sigma = .12$. The optimization software searches over all portfolios with $\sigma = .12$ and finds the highest feasible portfolio on the vertical line drawn at $\sigma = .12$; this is the portfolio with the highest risk premium. Assume that for this portfolio $R = .04$. You now have your second point on the efficient frontier. Do the same for other vertical lines to the right of .12, and when you "connect the dots," you will have drawn a frontier like that in Figure 6.10.

The second method is to minimize the SD for any level of risk premium. Here, you need to draw a few horizontal lines above G (portfolios lying below G are inefficient because they offer a *lower* risk premium and *higher* variance than G). Draw the first horizontal line at $R = .04$. Now the computer's assignment is to minimize the SD subject to the usual feasibility constraint. But in this method, we replace the constraint on SD by one on the portfolio's risk premium ($R = .04$). Now the computer seeks the portfolio that is farthest to the left along the horizontal line—this is the portfolio with the lowest SD consistent with a risk premium of 4%. You already know that this portfolio must be at $\sigma = .12$, since the first point on the efficient frontier that you found using method 1 was $(\sigma, R) = (.12, .04)$. Repeat this approach using other risk premiums, and you will find other points along the efficient frontier. Again, connect the dots and you will have the frontier of Figure 6.10.

The third approach to forming the efficient frontier, maximizing the Sharpe ratio for any SD or risk premium, is easiest to visualize by revisiting Figure 6.5. Observe that each portfolio on the efficient frontier provides the highest Sharpe ratio, the slope of a ray from the risk-free rate, for any choice of SD or expected return. Let's start by specifying the SD constraint, achieved by using the vertical lines to the right of *G.* To each line, we draw rays from the origin at ever-increasing slopes, and we assign the computer to find the *feasible* portfolio with the highest slope. This is similar to sliding up the vertical line to find the highest risk premium. We must find the same frontier as that found with either of the first two methods. Similarly, we could instead specify a risk-premium constraint and construct rays from the origin to horizontal lines. We assign the computer to find the *feasible* portfolio with the highest slope to the given horizontal line. This is similar to sliding to the left on horizontal lines in method 2.

We started the efficient frontier from the minimum-variance portfolio, *G. G* is found with a program that minimizes SD subject *only* to the feasibility constraint. This portfolio has the lowest SD for *any* risk premium, which is why it is called the "global" minimum-variance portfolio. By the same principle, the optimal portfolio, *O,* will maximize the Sharpe ratio globally, subject only to the feasibility constraint. Any *individual* asset ends up inside the efficient frontier, because single-asset portfolios are inefficient—they are not efficiently diversified.

Various constraints may preclude a particular investor from choosing portfolios on the efficient frontier, however. If an institution is prohibited by law from taking short positions in any asset, the portfolio manager must add constraints to the computer-optimization program that rule out negative (short) positions.

Some clients may want to ensure a minimum level of expected dividend yield. In this case, input data must include a set of expected dividend yields. The optimization program is made to include a constraint to ensure that the expected *portfolio* dividend yield will equal or exceed the desired level. Another common constraint forbids investments in companies engaged in "undesirable social activity." This constraint implies that portfolio weights in these companies must equal zero.

In principle, portfolio managers can tailor an efficient frontier to meet any particular objective. Of course, satisfying constraints carries a price tag. An efficient frontier subject to additional constraints will offer a lower Sharpe ratio. Clients should be aware of this cost and may want to think twice about constraints that are not mandated by law.

Deriving the efficient frontier and graphing it with any number of assets and any set of constraints is quite straightforward. For a not-too-large number of assets, the efficient frontier can be computed and graphed even with a spreadsheet program.

Our spreadsheet program, available in Connect or through your course instructor, can easily incorporate restrictions against short sales imposed on some portfolio managers. To impose this restriction, the program simply requires that each weight in the optimal portfolio be greater than or equal to zero. One way to see whether the short-sale constraint actually matters is to find the efficient portfolio without it. If one or more of the weights in the optimal portfolio turn out negative, we know the short-sale restrictions will result in a different efficient frontier with a less attractive risk-return trade-off.

Choosing the Optimal Risky Portfolio

The second step of the optimization plan involves the risk-free asset. Using the current risk-free rate, we search for the capital allocation line with the highest Sharpe ratio (the steepest slope), as shown in Figures 6.5 and 6.6.

The CAL formed from the optimal risky portfolio (*O*) will be tangent to the efficient frontier of risky assets discussed above. This CAL dominates all feasible CALs. Portfolio *O,* therefore, is the optimal risky portfolio. Because we know that an investor will choose a point on the CAL that mixes the *optimal* risky portfolio with T-bills, there is actually no need to either provide access to or derive the entire efficient frontier. Therefore, rather than solving for the entire efficient frontier, we can proceed directly to determining the optimal portfolio. This requires maximizing the Sharpe ratio subject only to the feasibility constraint. The "global" maximum-Sharpe-ratio portfolio is the optimal portfolio *O.* The ray from the origin to *O* and beyond is the optimal CAL.

The Preferred Complete Portfolio and a Separation Property

Finally, in the third step, each investor chooses the appropriate mix between the optimal risky portfolio (*O*) and T-bills, exactly as in Figure 6.7.

A portfolio manager will offer the same risky portfolio (O) to all clients, no matter what their degrees of risk aversion. Risk aversion comes into play only when clients select their desired point on the CAL. Regardless of risk aversion, all clients will use portfolio O as the optimal risky investment vehicle.

This result is called a **separation property,** introduced by James Tobin (1958), the 1983 Nobel Laureate for Economics: Its name reflects the fact that portfolio choice can be separated into two independent tasks. The first task, to determine the optimal risky portfolio (O), is purely technical. Given the input data, the best risky portfolio is the same for all clients regardless of risk aversion. The second task, construction of the complete portfolio from bills and portfolio O, is personal and depends on risk aversion. Here the client is the decision maker.

In practice, optimal risky portfolios for different clients may vary because of constraints on short sales, dividend yield, tax considerations, or other client preferences. Our analysis, though, suggests that a few portfolios may be sufficient to serve the demands of a wide range of investors. We see here the theoretical basis of the mutual fund industry. If the optimal portfolio is the same for all clients, professional management is more efficient and less costly. One management firm can serve many clients with relatively small incremental administrative costs.

The (computerized) optimization technique is the easiest part of portfolio construction. When different managers use different input data, they will develop different efficient frontiers and offer different "optimal" portfolios. Therefore, the real arena of the competition among portfolio managers is in the sophisticated security analysis that produces the input estimates. The rule of GIGO (garbage in–garbage out) applies fully to portfolio selection. If the quality of security analysis is poor, a passive portfolio such as a market-index fund will yield better results than an active portfolio tilted toward *seemingly* favorable securities.

Constructing the Optimal Risky Portfolio: An Illustration

To illustrate how the optimal risky portfolio might be constructed, suppose an analyst wished to construct an efficiently diversified global portfolio using the stock market indices of six countries. The top panel of Table 6.1 shows the input list. The values for standard deviations and the correlation matrix are estimated from recent historical data, while forecasts of risk premiums are generated from fundamental analysis. Examination of the table shows the U.S. index portfolio has the highest Sharpe ratio. China and Japan have the lowest, and the correlation of France and Germany with the U.S. is high. Given these data, one might be tempted to conclude that, *perhaps,* U.S. investors may not benefit much from international diversification during this period. But even in this sample period, we will see that diversification is beneficial.

Panel B shows the efficient frontier developed as follows: First we generate the global minimum-variance portfolio G by minimizing the SD with just the feasibility constraint, and then we find portfolio O by maximizing the Sharpe ratio subject only to the same constraint. To fill out the curve, we choose more risk premiums; for each, we maximize the Sharpe ratio subject to the feasibility constraint as well as the appropriate risk-premium constraint. In all, we have 13 points to draw the graph in Figure 6.11, one of which is the global maximum-Sharpe-ratio portfolio, O.

The results are quite striking. Observe that the SD of the global minimum-variance portfolio of 10.94% is far lower than that of the lowest-variance country (the U.K.), which has an SD of 14.93%. G is formed by taking short positions in Germany and France, as well as a large position in the relatively low-risk U.K. Moreover, the Sharpe ratio of this portfolio is higher than that of all countries but the U.S! Still, even this portfolio will be rejected in favor of the highest Sharpe-ratio portfolio.

Portfolio O attains a Sharpe ratio of .4477, compared to the U.S. ratio of .4013, a significant improvement that can be verified from the CAL shown in Panel C. The points in Panel C are selected to have the same SD as those on the efficient frontier portfolios, so the risk premium for each equals the SD times the Sharpe ratio of portfolio O.[4] Notice that portfolio (9) on the CAL has the same risk premium as the U.S., 6%, but an SD of 13.41%, fully 1.5% less

---

[4]Since the Sharpe ratio is S = risk premium/SD, we can rearrange to show that SD = risk premium/S_O. The CAL has the same slope everywhere, equal to the Sharpe ratio of portfolio O that supports it.

TABLE 6.1 Efficient frontiers for international diversification with and without short sales and CAL with short sales

A. Input List

Excess Returns

	Mean	SD	Sharpe Ratio	INPUT LIST
U.S.	0.0600	0.1495	0.4013	Expected excess returns from fundamental analysis.
U.K.	0.0530	0.1493	0.3551	Standard deviations and correlation matrix constructed
FRANCE	0.0680	0.2008	0.3386	from historical returns.
GERMANY	0.0800	0.2270	0.3525	
JAPAN	0.0450	0.1878	0.2397	
CHINA	0.0730	0.3004	0.2430	

Correlation Matrix

	U.S.	U.K.	France	Germany	Japan	China
U.S.	1					
U.K.	0.83	1				
FRANCE	0.83	0.92	1			
GERMANY	0.85	0.88	0.96	1		
JAPAN	0.43	0.44	0.47	0.43	1	
CHINA	0.16	0.28	0.26	0.29	0.14	1

B. Efficient Frontier: Short Sales Allowed

Portfolio:	(1)	(2)	G	(4)	(5)	(6)	(7)	O	(9)	(10)	(11)	(12)	(13)
Risk premium	0.0325	0.0375	0.0410	0.0425	0.0450	0.0500	0.0550	0.058474	0.0600	0.0650	0.0700	0.0800	0.0850
SD	0.1147	0.1103	0.1094	0.1095	0.1106	0.1154	0.1234	0.130601	0.1341	0.1469	0.1612	0.1933	0.2104
Slope (Sharpe)	0.2832	0.3400	0.3749	0.3880	0.4070	0.4334	0.4457	0.447733	0.4474	0.4425	0.4341	0.4140	0.4040
Portfolio weights													
U.S.	0.5948	0.6268	0.6476	0.6569	0.6724	0.7033	0.7342	0.755643	0.7651	0.7960	0.8269	0.8887	0.9196
U.K.	1.0667	0.8878	0.7681	0.7155	0.6279	0.4527	0.2775	0.155808	0.1023	−0.0728	−0.2480	−0.5984	−0.7736
FRANCE	−0.1014	−0.1308	−0.1618	−0.1727	−0.1908	−0.2272	−0.2635	−0.2888	−0.2999	−0.3362	−0.3725	−0.4452	−0.4816
GERMANY	−0.8424	−0.6702	−0.5431	−0.4901	−0.4019	−0.2253	−0.0487	0.0740	0.1278	0.3044	0.4810	0.8341	1.0107
JAPAN	0.2158	0.1985	0.1866	0.1815	0.1729	0.1558	0.1386	0.126709	0.1215	0.1043	0.0872	0.0529	0.0357
CHINA	0.0664	0.0879	0.1025	0.1089	0.1195	0.1407	0.1619	0.176649	0.1831	0.2043	0.2256	0.2680	0.2892

C. Capital Allocation Line (CAL) with Short Sales

Risk premium	0.0000	0.0494	0.0490	0.0490	0.0495	0.0517	0.0553	0.0585	0.0600	0.0658	0.0722	0.0865	0.1343
SD	0.0000	0.1103	0.1094	0.1095	0.1106	0.1154	0.1234	0.1306	0.1341	0.1469	0.1612	0.1933	0.3000

D. Efficient Frontier: No Short Sales

Portfolio	(1)	(2)	(3)	(4)	(5)	Min Var	(7)	(8)	Optimum	(10)	(11)	(12)	(13)
Risk premium	0.0450	0.0475	0.0490	0.0510	0.0535	0.0560	0.0573	0.0590	0.0607	0.0650	0.07	0.0750	0.0800
SD	0.1878	0.1555	0.1435	0.1372	0.1330	0.131648	0.1321	0.1337	0.1367	0.1493	0.1675332	0.1893	0.2270
Slope (Sharpe)	0.2397	0.3055	0.3414	0.3718	0.4022	0.425089	0.4339	0.4411	0.4439	0.4353	0.4178277	0.3963	0.3525
Portfolio weights													
U.S.	0.0000	0.0000	0.0000	0.0671	0.2375	0.4052	0.4964	0.6122	0.7067	0.6367	0.4223	0.1680	0.0000
U.K.	0.0000	0.3125	0.5000	0.5465	0.3967	0.2491	0.1689	0.0670	0.0000	0.0000	0.0000	0.0000	0.0000
FRANCE	0.0000	0.0000	0.0000	0.0000	0.0000	0.0000	0.0000	0.0000	0.0000	0.0000	0.0000	0.0000	0.0000
GERMANY	0.0000	0.0000	0.0000	0.0000	0.0000	0.0000	0.0000	0.0000	0.0000	0.1324	0.3558	0.5976	1.0000
JAPAN	1.0000	0.6875	0.5000	0.3642	0.3029	0.2424	0.2096	0.1679	0.1114	0.0232	0.0000	0.0000	0.0000
CHINA	0.0000	0.0000	0.0000	0.0222	0.0630	0.1032	0.1251	0.1529	0.1819	0.2077	0.2219	0.2343	0.0000

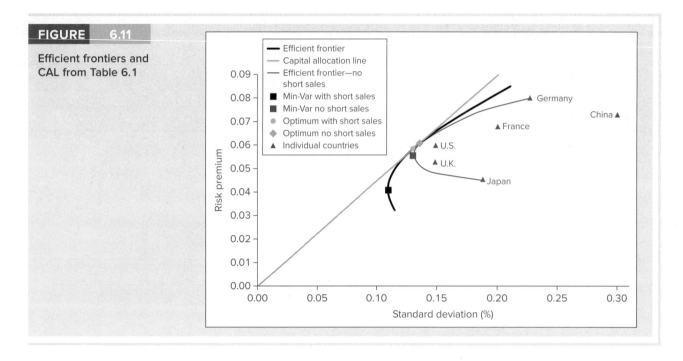

FIGURE 6.11

Efficient frontiers and CAL from Table 6.1

than the 14.95% SD of the U.S. All this is achieved while still investing 76% of the portfolio in the U.S., although it does require a large short position in France (−29.99%).

Many institutional investors are prohibited from taking short positions, and individuals may be averse to large short positions because the unlimited upward potential of stock prices implies unlimited potential losses on short sales. Panel D shows the efficient frontier when an additional constraint is applied to each portfolio, namely, that all weights must be nonnegative.

Take a look at the two frontiers in Figure 6.11. The no-short-sale frontier is clearly inferior on both ends. This is because both very low-return and very high-return frontier portfolios will typically entail short positions. At the low-return/low-volatility end of the frontier, portfolios have short positions in stocks with a high correlation and low risk premium that reduce variance at low cost to expected return. At the other (high expected return) end of the frontier, we find short positions in low-risk-premium stocks in favor of larger positions in high-risk-premium stocks. At the same time, the no-short-sale frontier is restricted to begin with the lowest-risk-premium country (Japan) and end with the highest (Germany). Without short sales, we cannot achieve lower or higher risk premiums than are offered by these portfolios. Intermediate-return portfolios on each frontier, including the optimal portfolio, *O,* are not far apart. Thus, even under the no-short-sale constraint, the Sharpe ratio (.4439) is still higher than that of the U.S. The no-short-sale CAL can match the U.S. risk premium of 6% with an SD of only 13.52%, still 1.4% less than the SD of the U.S.

CONCEPT check 6.5

Two portfolio managers work for competing investment management houses. Each employs security analysts to prepare input data for the construction of the optimal portfolio. When all is completed, the efficient frontier obtained by manager A dominates that of manager B in that A's optimal risky portfolio lies northwest of B's. Is the more attractive efficient frontier asserted by manager A evidence that she really employs better security analysts?

6.5 A SINGLE-INDEX STOCK MARKET

index model

Model that relates stock returns to returns on both a broad market index and firm-specific factors.

We started this chapter with the distinction between systematic and firm-specific risk. Systematic risk is macroeconomic, affecting all securities, while firm-specific risk factors affect only one particular firm or, at most, a cluster of firms. **Index models** are statistical models designed to estimate these two components of risk for a particular security or portfolio. The first to use an index model to explain the benefits of diversification was another Nobel Prize winner, William F. Sharpe (1963). We will introduce his major work (the capital asset pricing model) in the next chapter.

The popularity of index models is due to their practicality. To construct the efficient frontier from a universe of 100 securities, we would need to estimate 100 expected returns, 100 variances, and $100 \times 99/2 = 4{,}950$ covariances. And a universe of 100 securities is actually quite small. A universe of 1,000 securities would require estimates of $1{,}000 \times 999/2 = 499{,}500$ covariances, as well as 1,000 expected returns and variances. Assuming that one common factor is responsible for all the covariability of stock returns, with all other variability due to firm-specific factors, dramatically simplifies the analysis.

Let us use R_i to denote the **excess return** on a security, that is, the rate of return in excess of the risk-free rate: $R_i = r_i - r_f$. Then we can express the distinction between macroeconomic and firm-specific factors by decomposing this excess return in some holding period into three components:[5]

excess return

Rate of return in excess of the risk-free rate.

$$R_i = \beta_i R_M + e_i + \alpha_i \qquad \textbf{(6.11)}$$

The first two terms on the right-hand side of Equation 6.11 reflect the impact of two sources of uncertainty. R_M is the excess return on a broad market index (the S&P 500 is commonly used for this purpose), so variation in this term reflects the influence of economywide or macroeconomic events that generally affect all stocks to greater or lesser degrees. The security's **beta,** β_i, is the typical response of that particular stock's excess return to changes in the market index's excess return. As such, beta measures a stock's comparative sensitivity to macroeconomic news. A value greater than 1 would indicate a stock with greater sensitivity to the economy than the average stock. These are known as *cyclical stocks*. Betas less than 1 indicate below-average sensitivity and therefore are known as *defensive stocks*. Recall that the risk attributable to the stock's exposure to uncertain market returns is called market or *systematic* risk, because it relates to the uncertainty that pervades the whole economic system.

beta

The sensitivity of a security's returns to the market factor.

The term e_i in Equation 6.11 represents the impact of **firm-specific** or **residual risk.** The expected value of e_i is zero, as the impact of unexpected events must average out to zero. Both residual risk and systematic risk contribute to the total volatility of returns.

firm-specific or **residual risk**

Component of return variance that is independent of the market factor.

The term α_i in Equation 6.11 is not a risk measure. Instead, α_i represents the expected return on the stock *beyond* any return induced by movements in the market index. This term is called the security **alpha.** A positive alpha is attractive to investors and suggests an underpriced security: Among securities with identical sensitivity (beta) to the market index, securities with higher alpha values will offer higher expected returns. Conversely, stocks with negative alphas are apparently overpriced; for any value of beta, they offer lower expected returns.

alpha

A stock's expected return beyond that induced by the market index; its expected excess return when the market's excess return is zero.

In sum, the index model separates the realized rate of return on a security into macro (systematic) and micro (firm-specific) components. The excess rate of return on each security is the sum of three components:

	Symbol
1. The component of return due to movements in the overall market (as represented by the index R_M); β_i is the security's responsiveness to the market.	$\beta_i R_M$
2. The component attributable to unexpected events that are relevant only to this security (firm-specific).	e_i
3. The stock's expected excess return if the market factor is neutral, that is, if the market-index excess return is zero.	α_i

[5]Equation 6.11 is surprisingly simple and would appear to require very strong assumptions about security market equilibrium. But, in fact, if rates of return are normally distributed, then returns will be linear in one or more indexes. Statistics theory tells us that, when rates of return on a set of securities are *joint-normally* distributed, then the rate of return on each asset is linear in one identical index as in Equation 6.11. When rates of return exhibit a multivariate normal distribution, we can use a multi-index generalization of Equation 6.11. Practitioners employ index models such as 6.11 extensively because of the ease of use as we just noted, but they would not do so unless empirical evidence supported them.

Because the firm-specific component of the stock return is uncorrelated with the market return, we can write the variance of the excess return of the stock as[6]

$$\text{Variance } (R_i) = \text{Variance } (\alpha_i + \beta_i R_M + e_i)$$
$$= \text{Variance } (\beta_i R_M) + \text{Variance } (e_i)$$
$$= \beta_i^2 \sigma_M^2 \qquad\qquad + \sigma^2(e_i)$$
$$= \text{Systematic risk } + \text{Firm-specific risk} \qquad \textbf{(6.12)}$$

Therefore, the total variance of the rate of return of each security is a sum of two components:

1. The variance attributable to the uncertainty of the entire market. This variance depends on both the variance of R_M, denoted σ_M^2, *and* the beta of the stock on R_M.
2. The variance of the firm-specific return, e_i, which is independent of market performance.

This single-index model is convenient. It relates security returns to a market index that investors follow. Moreover, as we soon shall see, its usefulness goes beyond mere convenience.

Statistical and Graphical Representation of the Single-Index Model

Equation 6.11, $R_i = \alpha_i + \beta_i R_M + e_i$, may be interpreted as a single-variable *regression equation* of R_i on the market excess return R_M. The excess return on the security (R_i) is the dependent variable that is to be explained by the regression. On the right-hand side of the equation are the intercept α_i; the regression (slope) coefficient beta, β_i, multiplying the independent (explanatory) variable R_M; and the residual (unexplained) return, e_i. We plot this regression in Figure 6.12, which shows a scatter diagram of 12 observations of Dana's excess return paired against the excess return of the market index.

The horizontal axis of the scatter diagram measures the explanatory variable, here the market excess return, R_M. The vertical axis measures the dependent variable, here Dana's excess return, R_D. Each point on the scatter diagram represents a sample pair of returns (R_M, R_D) observed over a particular holding period. Point *T,* for instance, describes a holding period when the excess return was 17% for the market index and 27% for Dana.

Regression analysis uses a sample of historical returns to estimate the coefficients (alpha and beta) of the index model. The algorithm finds the regression line, shown in Figure 6.12, that minimizes the sum of the squared deviations around it. Hence, we say the regression line "best fits" the data in the scatter diagram. The line is called the **security characteristic line (SCL).**

security characteristic line (SCL)

Plot of a security's *predicted* excess return from the excess return of the market.

The regression intercept (α_D) is measured from the origin to the intersection of the regression line with the vertical axis. Any point on the vertical axis represents zero market excess return, so the intercept gives us the *expected excess* return on Dana when market return is "neutral," that is, equal to the T-bill return. The intercept in Figure 6.12 is 4.5%.

The slope of the regression line, the ratio of rise to run, is called the *regression coefficient* or simply the beta. In Figure 6.12, Dana's beta is 1.4. A stock beta measures systematic risk since it predicts the response of the security to each extra 1% return on the market index.

The regression line does not represent *actual* returns; points on the scatter diagram almost never lie exactly on the regression line. Rather, the line represents average tendencies; it shows the *expectation* of R_D given the market excess return, R_M. The algebraic representation of the regression line is

$$E(R_D|R_M) = \alpha_D + \beta_D R_M \qquad \textbf{(6.13)}$$

which reads: The expectation of R_D given a value of R_M equals the intercept plus the slope coefficient times the value of R_M.

---

[6]The covariance between R_M and e is zero. Notice that because α_i is a constant, it has no bearing on the variance of R_i.

FIGURE   6.12

Scatter diagram for Dana Computer Corp.

Because the regression line represents expectations and these expectations may not be realized (as the scatter diagram shows), the *actual* returns also include a residual, e_i, reflecting the firm-specific component of return. This surprise (at point T, for example) is measured by the vertical distance between the point of the scatter diagram and the regression line. The expected return on Dana, given a market return of 17%, would have been $4.5\% + 1.4 \times 17\% = 28.3\%$. The actual return was only 27%, so point T falls below the regression line by 1.3%.

Equation 6.12 shows that the greater the beta of a security, that is, the greater the slope of the regression, the greater the systematic risk and total variance. Because the market index comprises all securities, the typical response to a market movement must be one for one. An "aggressive" investment will have a beta higher than 1; that is, the security has above-average market risk.[7] Conversely, securities with betas lower than 1 are called defensive.

A security may have a negative beta. Its regression line will then slope downward, meaning that, for more favorable macro events (higher R_M), we would expect a *lower* return, and vice versa. The latter means that when the macro economy goes bad (negative R_M) and securities with positive beta are expected to have negative excess returns, the negative-beta security will shine. The result is that a negative-beta security provides a hedge against systematic risk.

The dispersion of the scatter of actual returns about the regression line is determined by the residual variance $\sigma^2(e_D)$. The magnitude of firm-specific risk varies across securities. One way to measure the relative importance of systematic risk is to measure the ratio of systematic variance to total variance.

$$\rho^2 = \frac{\text{Systematic (or explained) variance}}{\text{Total variance}}$$

$$= \frac{\beta_D^2 \sigma_M^2}{\sigma_D^2} = \frac{\beta_D^2 \sigma_M^2}{\beta_D^2 \sigma_M^2 + \sigma^2(e_D)} \tag{6.14}$$

where ρ is the correlation coefficient between R_D and R_M. Its square measures the ratio of explained variance to total variance, that is, the proportion of total variance that can be attributed to market fluctuations. But if beta is negative, so is the correlation coefficient, an indication that the explanatory and dependent variables are expected to move in opposite directions.

---

[7]Note that only the *weighted* average of betas (using market values as weights) will be 1, since the stock market index is value-weighted. We know from Chapter 5 that the distribution of securities by market value is not symmetric: There are relatively few large corporations and many more smaller ones. As a result, the simple average of the betas of individual securities, when computed against a value-weighted index such as the S&P 500, will be greater than 1, pushed up by the tendency for stocks of low-capitalization companies to have betas greater than 1.

At the extreme, when the correlation coefficient is either 1 or −1, the security return is fully explained by the market return and there are no firm-specific effects. All the points of the scatter diagram will lie exactly on the line. This is called *perfect correlation* (either positive or negative); the return on the security is perfectly predictable from the market return. A large correlation coefficient (in absolute value terms) means systematic variance dominates the total variance; that is, firm-specific variance is relatively unimportant. When the correlation coefficient is small (in absolute value terms), the market factor plays a relatively unimportant part in explaining the variance of the asset, and firm-specific factors dominate.

CONCEPT
c h e c k   **6.6**

Interpret the eight scatter diagrams of Figure 6.13 in terms of systematic risk, diversifiable risk, and the intercept.

Example 6.3 illustrates how you can use a spreadsheet to estimate the single-index model from historical data.

Diversification in a Single-Index Security Market

Imagine a portfolio that is divided equally among securities whose returns follow the single-index model of Equation 6.11. What are the systematic and nonsystematic variances of this portfolio?

The beta of the portfolio is a simple average of the individual security betas; hence, the systematic variance equals $\beta_P^2 \sigma_M^2$. This is the level of market risk in Figure 6.1B. The market variance (σ_M^2) and the beta of the portfolio determine its market risk.

The systematic component of each security return, $\beta_i R_M$, is driven by the market factor and therefore is perfectly correlated with the systematic part of any other security's return. Hence, there are no diversification effects on systematic risk no matter how many securities are involved. As far as *market risk* goes, a single security has the same systematic risk as a diversified portfolio with the same beta. The number of securities makes no difference.

FIGURE   **6.13**

Various scatter diagrams

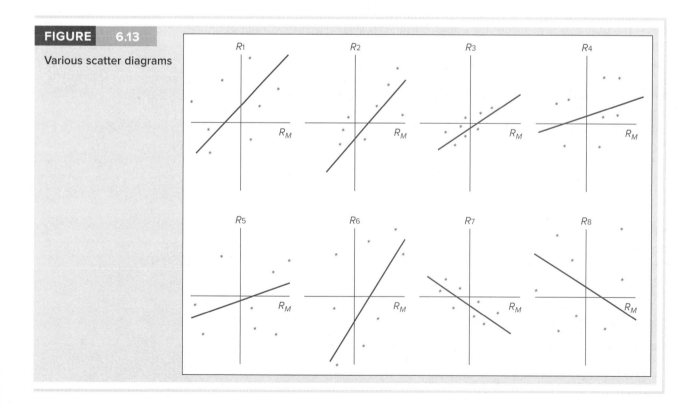

A direct way to calculate the slope and intercept of the characteristic lines for ABC and XYZ is from the variances and covariances. Here, we use the Data Analysis menu of Excel to obtain the covariance matrix in the following spreadsheet.

EXAMPLE 6.3

Estimating the Index Model Using Historical Data

The slope coefficient for ABC is given by the formula

$$\beta_{ABC} = \frac{Cov(R_{ABC}, R_{Market})}{Var(R_{Market})} = \frac{773.31}{669.01} = 1.156$$

The intercept for ABC is

$$\alpha_{ABC} = Average(R_{ABC}) - \beta_{ABC} \times Average(R_{Market})$$

$$= 15.20 - 1.156 \times 9.40 = 4.33$$

Therefore, the security characteristic line of ABC is given by

$$R_{ABC} = 4.33 + 1.156R_{Market}$$

This result also can be obtained by using the "Regression" command from Excel's Data Analysis menu, as we show at the bottom of the spreadsheet. The minor differences between the direct regression output and our calculations above are due to rounding error.

	A	B	C	D	E	F	G	H	I
2			**Annualized Rates of Return**				**Excess Returns**		
3	Week	ABC	XYZ	Mkt. Index	Risk free		ABC	XYZ	Market
4	1	65.13	−22.55	64.40	5.23		59.90	−27.78	59.17
5	2	51.84	31.44	24.00	4.76		47.08	26.68	19.24
6	3	−30.82	−6.45	9.15	6.22		−37.04	−12.67	2.93
7	4	−15.13	−51.14	−35.57	3.78		−18.91	−54.92	−39.35
8	5	70.63	33.78	11.59	4.43		66.20	29.35	7.16
9	6	107.82	32.95	23.13	3.78		104.04	29.17	19.35
10	7	−25.16	70.19	8.54	3.87		−29.03	66.32	4.67
11	8	50.48	27.63	25.87	4.15		46.33	23.48	21.72
12	9	−36.41	−48.79	−13.15	3.99		−40.40	−52.78	−17.14
13	10	−42.20	52.63	20.21	4.01		−46.21	48.62	16.20
14	Average:						**15.20**	**7.55**	**9.40**
15									
16	**COVARIANCE MATRIX**								
17		ABC	XYZ	Market					
18	ABC	3020.933							
19	XYZ	442.114	1766.923						
20	Market	773.306	396.789	669.010					
21									
22	**SUMMARY OUTPUT OF EXCEL REGRESSION**								
23									
24	Regression Statistics								
25	Multiple R	0.544							
26	R-Square	0.296							
27	Adj. R-Square	0.208							
28	Standard Error	48.918							
29	Observations	10.000							
30									
31									
32		Coefficients	Std. Error	t-Stat	p-value				
33	Intercept	4.336	16.564	0.262	0.800				
34	Market return	1.156	0.630	1.834	0.104				
35									

Note: This is the output provided by the Data Analysis tool in Excel. As a technical aside, we should point out that the covariance matrix produced by Excel does not adjust for degrees of freedom. In other words, it divides total squared deviations from the sample average (for variance) or total cross product of deviations from sample averages (for covariance) by total observations, despite the fact that sample averages are estimated parameters. This procedure does not affect regression coefficients, however, because in the formula for beta, both the numerator (i.e., the covariance) and denominator (i.e., the variance) are affected equally.

Notice that your forecast of R_G implies that Google's alpha is $\alpha_G = R_G - \beta_G R_M$. We use two key statistics, $\alpha_G/\sigma^2(e_G)$ and R_M/σ_M^2, to find the position of Google in the optimal risky portfolio in two steps. In step 1, we compute

$$w_G^0 = \frac{\alpha_G/\sigma^2(e_G)}{R_M/\sigma_M^2} \qquad (6.16)$$

In step 2, we adjust the value from Equation 6.16 for the beta of Google:

$$w_G^* = \frac{w_G^0}{1 + w_G^0(1 - \beta_G)} \qquad w_M^* = 1 - w_G^* \qquad (6.17)$$

The Sharpe ratio of this portfolio exceeds that of the passive portfolio M, S_M, according to

$$S_O^2 - S_M^2 = \left(\frac{\alpha_G}{\sigma(e_G)}\right)^2 \qquad (6.18)$$

The improvement over the passive benchmark is determined by the ratio $\alpha_G/\sigma(e_G)$, which is called Google's **information ratio.** This application of the index model is called the Treynor-Black model, after Fischer Black and Jack Treynor who proposed it in 1973.

information ratio

Ratio of alpha to the standard deviation of the residual.

The value of the Treynor-Black model becomes dramatic when you analyze more than one stock. To compute the optimal portfolio comprising the benchmark portfolio and more than two stocks, you would need to use the involved Markowitz methodology of Section 6.4. But with the Treynor-Black model, the task is straightforward. You can view Google in the previous discussion as your **active portfolio.** If instead of Google alone you analyze several stocks, a portfolio of these stocks would make up your active portfolio, which then would be mixed with the passive index. You would use the alpha, beta, and residual SD of the active portfolio in Equations 6.16–6.18 to obtain the weights of the optimal portfolio, O, and its Sharpe ratio. Thus, the only task left is to determine the exact composition of the active portfolio, as well as its alpha, beta, and residual standard deviation.

active portfolio

The portfolio formed by optimally combining analyzed stocks.

Suppose that in addition to analyzing Google, you analyze Dana's stock (D) and estimate its alpha, beta, and residual variance. You estimate the ratio for Google, $\alpha_G/\sigma^2(e_G)$, the corresponding ratio for Dana, and the sum of these ratios for all stocks in the active portfolio. Using Google and Dana,

$$\sum_i \alpha_i/\sigma^2(e_i) = \alpha_G/\sigma^2(e_G) + \alpha_D/\sigma^2(e_D) \qquad (6.19)$$

Treynor and Black showed that the optimal weight of Google and Dana in the active portfolio, A, should be

$$w_{GA} = \frac{\alpha_G/\sigma^2(e_G)}{\sum_i \alpha_i/\sigma^2(e_i)} \qquad w_{DA} = \frac{\alpha_D/\sigma^2(e_D)}{\sum_i \alpha_i/\sigma^2(e_i)} \qquad (6.20)$$

Notice that the active portfolio entails two offsetting considerations. On the one hand, a stock with a higher alpha value calls for a high weight to take advantage of its attractive expected return. On the other hand, a high residual variance leads us to temper our position in the stock to avoid bearing firm-specific risk.

The alpha and beta of the active portfolio are weighted averages of each component stock's alpha and beta, and the residual variance is the weighted sum of each stock's residual variance, using the squared portfolio weights:

$$\alpha_A = w_{GA}\alpha_{GA} + w_{DA}\alpha_{DA}; \quad \beta_A = w_{GA}\beta_{GA} + w_{DA}\beta_{DA}$$
$$\sigma^2(e_A) = w_{GA}^2\sigma^2(e_G) + w_{DA}^2\sigma^2(e_D) \qquad (6.21)$$

Given these parameters, we can now use Equations 6.16–6.18 to determine the weight of the active portfolio in the optimal portfolio and the Sharpe ratio it achieves.

EXAMPLE 6.4

The Treynor-Black Model

Suppose your benchmark portfolio is the S&P 500 Index. The input list in Panel A of Table 6.2 includes the data for the passive index as well as the two stocks, Google and Dana. Both stocks have positive alpha values, so you would expect the optimal portfolio to be tilted toward these stocks. However, the tilt will be limited to avoid excessive exposure to otherwise-diversifiable firm-specific risk. The optimal trade-off maximizes the Sharpe ratio. We use the Treynor-Black model to accomplish this task.

We begin in Panel B assuming that the *active portfolio* comprises solely Google, which has an information ratio of .115. This "portfolio" is then combined with the passive index to form the optimal risky portfolio as in Equations 6.16–6.18. The calculations in Table 6.2 show that the optimal portfolio achieves a Sharpe ratio of .20, compared with .16 for the passive benchmark. This optimal portfolio is invested 43.64% in Google and 56.36% in the passive benchmark.

In Panel C, we add Dana to the list of actively analyzed stocks. The optimal weights of each stock in the active portfolio are 55.53% in Google and 44.47% in Dana. This gives the active portfolio an information ratio of .14, which improves the Sharpe ratio of the optimal portfolio to .24. The optimal portfolio invests 91.73% in the active portfolio and 8.27% in the index. This large tilt is acceptable because the residual standard deviation of the active portfolio (6.28%) is far less than that of either stock. Finally, the optimal portfolio weight in Google is 50.94% and in Dana, 40.79%. Notice that the weight in Google is now *larger* than its weight without Dana! This, too, is a result of diversification within the active position that allows a larger tilt toward Google's large alpha.

6.6 RISK OF LONG-TERM INVESTMENTS

So far we have envisioned portfolio investment for one period. We have not made any explicit assumptions about the duration of that period, so one might take it to be of any length, and thus our analysis would seem to apply as well to long-term investments. Yet investors are frequently advised that stock investments for the long run are not as risky as it might appear from the statistics presented in this chapter and the previous one. To understand this widespread misconception, we must first understand what the alternative long-term investment strategies are.

Risk and Return with Alternative Long-Term Investments

We have not yet had much to say about the investor's time horizon. From the standpoint of risk and return,[9] does it matter whether an investor's horizon is long or short? A common misconception is that long-term investors should allocate a greater proportion of wealth into stocks simply because in some sense stocks are less risky over long-term horizons. The belief that stocks become less risky over longer horizons is based on a notion of "time diversification," that spreading your risky investments over many time periods offers a similar benefit in risk reduction as spreading an investment budget over many assets in a given period (the subject we have worked on throughout this chapter). That belief, however, is incorrect.

We can gain insight into risk in the long run by comparing one-year ("short-term") and two-year ("longer-term") *risky* investments. Imagine an investment opportunity set that is identical in each of the two years. It includes a risky portfolio with a normally distributed, continuously compounded, annual risk premium of R and variance of σ^2. The one-year Sharpe ratio is therefore $S_1 = R/\sigma$, and the one-year price of risk is $P_1 = R/\sigma^2$. Investors can allocate their portfolios between that risky portfolio and a risk-free asset with zero risk premium and variance.[10] As we learned from Table 5.2, we can safely assume that the stock portfolio returns are serially uncorrelated.

---

[9]An investor may choose a specific investment horizon for a number of reasons, such as the target retirement age. Other factors that we have not considered, for example, the magnitude of one's human capital (the value of future earning power) versus current financial wealth, also may affect investment horizon and portfolio allocations.

[10]The hierarchy of portfolio choice we developed for any given holding period is this: Construct a risky portfolio with the highest Sharpe ratio. Allocate the entire investment budget between this portfolio and the risk-free asset. The optimal weight in the risky portfolio is $y = P/A$, where P is the price of risk and A is the investor's risk aversion.

TABLE 6.2	Construction of optimal portfolios using the index model

Input List

	Benchmark Portfolio (S&P 500)	Active Portfolio	
		Google	Dana
A. Input Data			
Risk premium	0.7	2.20	1.74
Standard deviation	4.31	11.39	10.49
Sharpe ratio	0.16	not applicable	
Alpha		1.04	0.75
Beta		1.65	1.41
Residual standard deviation		9.01	8.55
Information ratio = alpha/residual SD		0.1154	0.0877
Alpha/residual variance		0.0128	0.0103

Portfolio Construction

B. Optimal Portfolio with Google Only in Active Portfolio

Performance data

Sharpe ratio = SQRT (index Sharpe^2 + Google information ratio^2)   0.20

Composition of optimal portfolio

w^0 = (alpha/residual variance)/(index risk premium/index variance)   0.3400

w^* = w^0/(1 + w^0(1 − beta))   0.5636   0.4364

C. Optimal Portfolio with Google and Dana in the Active Portfolio

			Active Portfolio (sum)
Composition of the active portfolio			
w^0 of stock (Equation 6.15)	0.3400	0.2723	0.6122
w^0/Sum w^0 of analyzed stocks	0.5553	0.4447	1.0000
Performance of the active portfolio			
alpha = weight in active portfolio × stock alpha	0.58	0.33	0.91
beta = weight in active portfolio × stock beta	0.92	0.63	1.54
Residual variance = square weight × stock residual variance	25.03	14.46	39.49
Residual SD = SQRT (active portfolio residual variance)			6.28
Information ratio = active portfolio alpha/residual SD			0.14
Performance of the optimal portfolio			
Sharpe ratio	0.24		

	Index	Active	
Composition of optimal portfolio			
w^0		0.6122	
w^*	0.0827	0.9173	

	Google	Dana
Weight of active portfolio × weight of stock in active portfolio	0.5094	0.4079

Spreadsheets are available in Connect

Of course, you cannot properly compare a one-year to a two-year investment without specifying what the one-year investor will do in the second year. To make the comparison meaningful, we compare the strategies of three investment companies that advertise three alternative two-year strategies: Company 1 calls its strategy "Two-In": Invest everything in the risky portfolio for two years. Company 2 touts its "One-In" strategy: In one year invest fully in the risk-free asset, and in the other year invest fully in the risky portfolio. Finally, Company 3 advocates a "Half-in-Two" strategy: In both years, invest half the budget in the risk-free asset and the other half in the risky portfolio. We must decide which strategy is best.

Recall that both the mean and variance of continuously compounded, serially uncorrelated returns (or excess returns) grow in proportion to the length of the holding period. We show the rate-of-return statistics for the three strategies in Table 6.3. The risk premium is zero for bills and R for the risky portfolio, so the first row of the table shows the accumulation of the investor's risk premium over two years using each strategy. Similarly, the second row shows the accumulation of the variance of the investor's wealth.

We see immediately that risk is *not* lower for longer-term investors. A two-year investment in stocks (the Two-In strategy) has twice the variance as the One-In strategy. This observation already should settle the debate of whether total risk in the long run is smaller—it clearly is not. Rather, it grows proportionally over time: The two-year investment in the risky portfolio has double the variance of the one-year investment.

While the One-In investment is less risky than the Two-In strategy, an even safer investment strategy that still offers the same risk premium as One-In is the Half-in-Two strategy, which invests half the wealth in stocks in *each* of the two years. This has only one-half the variance of One-In and only one-fourth the variance of Two-In. When less risk than Two-In is desired, spreading the risk evenly over time, rather than lumping all the risk into a concentrated period (as the One-In strategy does), is the best strategy. This is evident from the Sharpe ratios of each strategy (line 3 of the table): The Sharpe ratio of Half-in-Two exceeds that of One-In by a multiple of $\sqrt{2}$. Does this mean that Half-in-Two actually does offer a meaningful benefit of time diversification? Put differently, does Half-in-Two allow investors to prudently allocate greater portfolio shares to the risky portfolio? Surprisingly, the answer is no. Even this more limited notion of time diversification is faulty.

We will compare investors' optimal capital allocations under each of these strategies. However, we can dismiss the One-In strategy out of hand, as it clearly is dominated by the Half-in-Two strategy, which has equal risk premium with only half the variance. Therefore, we need only compare Two-In with Half-in-Two. We established earlier that an investor with a degree of risk aversion A will allocate a fraction of overall wealth to the risky portfolio equal

TABLE 6.3	Two-year risk premium, variance, Sharpe ratio, and price of risk for three strategies		
Strategy:	**Two-In[1]**	**One-In[2]**	**Half-in-Two[3]**
Risk premium	$R + R = 2R$	$0 + R = R$	$2 \times \frac{1}{2} R = R$
Variance	$\sigma^2 + \sigma^2 = 2\sigma^2$	$0 + \sigma^2 = \sigma^2$	$2 \times \frac{1}{4} \sigma^2 = \sigma^2/2$
Sharpe ratio[4]	$\dfrac{2R}{\sigma\sqrt{2}} = S_1\sqrt{2}$	$R/\sigma = S_1$	$\dfrac{R}{\sigma\sqrt{2}} = S_1\sqrt{2}$
Price of risk[5]	$R/\sigma^2 = P_1$	$R/\sigma^2 = P_1$	$\dfrac{R}{\sigma^2/2} = 2P_1$

[1]Two-In: Invest entirely in the risky portfolio for two years.

[2]One-In: Invest entirely in the risky portfolio for one year and in the risk-free asset in the other.

[3]Half-in-Two: Invest half the budget in the risky portfolio for two years.

[4]Sharpe ratio $= \dfrac{\text{Risk premium}}{\text{Standard deviation}}$

[5]Price of risk $= \dfrac{\text{Risk premium}}{\text{Variance}}$

to $y = \dfrac{\text{Price of risk}}{A}$. For Two-In, that fraction is $\dfrac{R/\sigma^2}{A}$, while for Half-in-Two, it is $\dfrac{2R/\sigma^2}{A}$. So the Half-in-Two strategy gets double the allocation as All-In; but remember that Half-in-Two is only half as heavily invested in the risky portfolio. These effects precisely cancel out: The higher risk and return of Two-In are precisely offset by the investor's reduced allocation to it. So the Half-in-Two strategy that *seems* to offer the benefit of time diversification does not in fact elicit a greater overall allocation to the risky portfolio.

Would it matter if we extended the horizon from two years to some greater value? With a horizon of T years, a "time diversification strategy" (we must now change our strategy from "Half in Two" to "1/T in T") puts at risk $1/T$ of the budget each year. The price of risk of the time-diversified strategy is TR/σ^2, compared to only R/σ^2 for the All-In strategy. Will this elicit greater investments in the risky portfolio as T increases? Once again, the telling point is that the time-diversified portfolio has better Sharpe ratio than the fully invested All-In portfolio: The Sharpe ratio for both strategies is now $S_1\sqrt{T}$. Any investor will invest with the time-diversified strategy T times the fraction he would with the All-In T-year strategy; the net effect is that these alternatives are for all practical purposes equivalent. The investor choosing between these two alternatives is simply sliding up or down the CAL. Despite its higher price of risk, the overall allocation to the risky portfolio is not higher for the time-diversified portfolio.

Why the Unending Confusion?

It is no secret that the vast majority of financial advisers believe that "stocks are less risky if held for the long run," and so advise their clients. Their reasoning is this: The risk premium grows at the rate of the horizon, T. The standard deviation grows at the slower rate of only $\sqrt{T}$. The fact that risk grows more slowly than the risk premium is evident from the Sharpe ratio, $S_1\sqrt{T}$, which grows with the investment horizon.

This story sounds compelling, and in fact it contains no mathematical error. However, it is only half the story. Time diversification seems to offer a better risk-return trade-off (a higher Sharpe ratio) if you compare the All-In to the "One-In" strategy that invests all in one year and nothing later. But the relevant alternative to All-In is 1/T in T. The long-term 1/T in T investment strategy falls on the same "time CAL" as the All-In strategy, since it uses the same risky portfolio for the entire horizon. When this strategy is on the menu, complete portfolio allocations will *not* shift toward risky investments even as the investor's horizon extends.

SUMMARY

- The expected rate of return of a portfolio is the weighted average of the component asset expected returns with the investment proportions as weights.
- The variance of a portfolio is a sum of the contributions of the component-security variances *plus* terms involving the covariance among assets.
- Even if correlations are positive, the portfolio standard deviation will be less than the weighted average of the component standard deviations, as long as the assets are not *perfectly* positively correlated. Thus, portfolio diversification is of value as long as assets are less than perfectly correlated.
- The contribution of an asset to portfolio variance depends on its correlation with the other assets in the portfolio, as well as on its own variance. An asset that is perfectly negatively correlated with a portfolio can be used to reduce the portfolio variance to zero. Thus, it can serve as a perfect hedge.
- The efficient frontier of risky assets is the graphical representation of the set of portfolios that maximizes portfolio expected return for a given level of portfolio standard deviation. Rational investors will choose a portfolio on the efficient frontier.

- A portfolio manager identifies the efficient frontier by first establishing estimates for the expected returns and standard deviations and determining the correlations among them. The input data are then fed into an optimization program that produces the investment proportions, expected returns, and standard deviations of the portfolios on the efficient frontier.
- In general, portfolio managers will identify different efficient portfolios because of differences in the methods and quality of security analysis. Managers compete on the quality of their security analysis relative to their management fees.
- If a risk-free asset is available and input data are identical, all investors will choose the same portfolio on the efficient frontier, the one that is tangent to the CAL. All investors with identical input data will hold the identical risky portfolio, differing only in how much each allocates to this optimal portfolio and to the risk-free asset. This result is characterized as the separation principle of portfolio selection.
- The single-index model expresses the excess return on a security as a function of the market excess return: $R_i = \alpha_i + \beta_i R_M + e_i$. This equation also can be interpreted as a regression of the security excess return on the market-index excess return. The regression line has intercept α_i and slope β_i and is called the security characteristic line.
- In a single-index model, the variance of the rate of return on a security or portfolio can be decomposed into systematic and firm-specific risk. The systematic component of variance equals β^2 times the variance of the market excess return. The firm-specific component is the variance of the residual term in the index-model equation.
- The beta of a portfolio is the weighted average of the betas of the component securities. A security with negative beta reduces the portfolio beta, thereby reducing exposure to market volatility. The unique risk of a portfolio approaches zero as the portfolio becomes more highly diversified.

KEY TERMS

active portfolio, 175	index model, 168	optimal risky portfolio, 160
alpha, 169	information ratio, 175	residual risk, 169
beta, 169	investment opportunity	security characteristic
diversifiable risk, 148	set, 156	line, 170
efficient frontier, 163	market risk, 148	separation property, 166
excess return, 169	nondiversifiable risk, 148	systematic risk, 148
firm-specific risk, 148	nonsystematic risk, 148	unique risk, 148

KEY FORMULAS

The expected rate of return on a portfolio: $E(r_P) = w_B E(r_B) + w_S E(r_S)$

The variance of the return on a portfolio: $\sigma_P^2 = (w_B \sigma_B)^2 + (w_S \sigma_S)^2 + 2(w_B \sigma_B)(w_S \sigma_S)\rho_{BS}$

The Sharpe ratio of a portfolio: $S_P = \dfrac{E(r_P) - r_f}{\sigma_P}$

Sharpe ratio maximizing portfolio weights with two risky assets (B and S) and a risk-free asset:

$$w_B = \frac{[E(r_B) - r_f]\sigma_S^2 - [E(r_S) - r_f]\sigma_B \sigma_S \rho_{BS}}{[E(r_B) - r_f]\sigma_S^2 + [E(r_S) - r_f]\sigma_B^2 - [E(r_B) - r_f + E(r_S) - r_f]\sigma_B \sigma_S \rho_{BS}}$$

$$w_S = 1 - w_B$$

The index-model equation: $R_i = \beta_i R_M + \alpha_i + e_i$

Decomposition of variance based on the index-model equation:

$$\text{Variance}(R_i) = \beta_i^2 \sigma_M^2 + \sigma^2(e_i)$$

Percent of security variance explained by the index return = the square of the correlation coefficient of the regression of the security on the market:

$$\rho^2 = \frac{\text{Systematic (or explained) variance}}{\text{Total variance}}$$

$$= \frac{\beta_i^2 \sigma_M^2}{\sigma_i^2} = \frac{\beta_i^2 \sigma_M^2}{\beta_i^2 \sigma_M^2 + \sigma^2(e_i)}$$

Optimal position in the active portfolio, A:

$$w_A^* = \frac{w_A^0}{1 + w_A^0(1 - \beta_A)}; \quad w_M^* = 1 - w_A^*$$

$$w_A^0 = \frac{\alpha_A/\sigma^2(e_A)}{R_M/\sigma_M^2}$$

Optimal weight of a security, G, in the active portfolio, A: $w_{GA} = \dfrac{\alpha_G/\sigma^2(e_G)}{\sum_i \alpha_i/\sigma^2(e_i)}$

 Select problems are available in McGraw-Hill's *Connect*. Please see the Supplements section of the book's frontmatter for more information.

PROBLEM SETS

1. In forming a portfolio of two risky assets, what must be true of the correlation coefficient between their returns if there are to be gains from diversification? Explain. *(LO 6-1)*

2. When adding a risky asset to a portfolio of many risky assets, which property of the asset is more important, its standard deviation or its covariance with the other assets? Explain. *(LO 6-1)*

3. A portfolio's expected return is 12%, its standard deviation is 20%, and the risk-free rate is 4%. Which of the following would make for the greatest increase in the portfolio's Sharpe ratio? *(LO 6-3)*
   a. An increase of 1% in expected return.
   b. A decrease of 1% in the risk-free rate.
   c. A decrease of 1% in its standard deviation.

4. An investor ponders various allocations to the optimal risky portfolio and risk-free T-bills to construct his complete portfolio. How would the Sharpe ratio of the complete portfolio be affected by this choice? *(LO 6-3)*

5. The standard deviation of the market-index portfolio is 20%. Stock A has a beta of 1.5 and a residual standard deviation of 30%. *(LO 6-5)*
   a. What would make for a larger increase in the stock's variance: an increase of .15 in its beta or an increase of 3% (from 30% to 33%) in its residual standard deviation?
   b. An investor who currently holds the market-index portfolio decides to reduce the portfolio allocation to the market index to 90% and to invest 10% in stock A. Which of the changes in (a) will have a greater impact on the portfolio's standard deviation?

6. Suppose that the returns on the stock fund presented in Spreadsheet 6.1 were −40%, −14%, 17%, and 33% in the four scenarios. *(LO 6-2)*
   a. Would you expect the mean return and variance of the stock fund to be more than, less than, or equal to the values computed in Spreadsheet 6.2? Why?

b. Calculate the new values of mean return and variance for the stock fund using a format similar to Spreadsheet 6.2. Confirm your intuition from part (a).

c. Calculate the new value of the covariance between the stock and bond funds using a format similar to Spreadsheet 6.4. Explain intuitively the change in the covariance.

7. Use the rate-of-return data for the stock and bond funds presented in Spreadsheet 6.1, but now assume that the probability of each scenario is as follows: severe recession: .10; mild recession: .20; normal growth: .35; boom: .35.   (LO 6-2)

a. Would you expect the mean return and variance of the stock fund to be more than, less than, or equal to the values computed in Spreadsheet 6.2? Why?

b. Calculate the new values of mean return and variance for the stock fund using a format similar to Spreadsheet 6.2. Confirm your intuition from part (a).

c. Calculate the new value of the covariance between the stock and bond funds using a format similar to Spreadsheet 6.4. Explain intuitively why the absolute value of the covariance has changed.

The following data apply to Problems 8–12.

A pension fund manager is considering three mutual funds. The first is a stock fund, the second is a long-term government and corporate bond fund, and the third is a T-bill money market fund that yields a sure rate of 5.5%. The probability distributions of the risky funds are:

	Expected Return	Standard Deviation
Stock fund (S)	15%	32%
Bond fund (B)	9	23

The correlation between the fund returns is .15.

8. Tabulate and draw the investment opportunity set of the two risky funds. Use investment proportions for the stock fund of 0% to 100% in increments of 20%. What expected return and standard deviation does your graph show for the minimum-variance portfolio?   (LO 6-2)

9. Draw a tangent from the risk-free rate to the opportunity set. What does your graph show for the expected return and standard deviation of the optimal risky portfolio?   (LO 6-3)

10. What is the Sharpe ratio of the best feasible CAL?   (LO 6-3)

11. Suppose now that your portfolio must yield an expected return of 12% and be efficient, that is, on the best feasible CAL.   (LO 6-4)

a. What is the standard deviation of your portfolio?

b. What is the proportion invested in the T-bill fund and each of the two risky funds?

12. If you were to use only the two risky funds and still require an expected return of 12%, what would be the investment proportions of your portfolio? Compare its standard deviation to that of the optimal portfolio in the previous problem. What do you conclude?   (LO 6-4)

13. Stocks offer an expected rate of return of 10% with a standard deviation of 20%, and gold offers an expected return of 5% with a standard deviation of 25%.   (LO 6-3)

a. In light of the apparent inferiority of gold to stocks with respect to both mean return and volatility, would anyone hold gold? If so, demonstrate graphically why one would do so.

b. How would you answer (a) if the correlation coefficient between gold and stocks were 1? Draw a graph illustrating why one would or would not hold gold. Could these expected returns, standard deviations, and correlation represent an equilibrium for the security market?

14. Suppose that many stocks are traded in the market and that it is possible to borrow at the risk-free rate, r_f. The characteristics of two of the stocks are as follows:

Stock	Expected Return	Standard Deviation
A	8%	40%
B	13	60
Correlation = −1		

Could the equilibrium r_f be greater than 10%? (*Hint:* Can a particular stock portfolio be substituted for the risk-free asset?) *(LO 6-3)*

15. You can find a spreadsheet containing the historic returns presented in Table 5.2 in Connect. (Look for the Chapter 5 material.) Copy the data for the last 20 years into a new spreadsheet. Analyze the risk-return trade-off that would have characterized portfolios constructed from large stocks and long-term Treasury bonds over the last 20 years. What was the average rate of return and standard deviation of each asset? What was the correlation coefficient of their annual returns? What would have been the average return and standard deviation of portfolios with differing weights in the two assets? For example, consider weights in stocks starting at zero and incrementing by .10 up to a weight of 1. What was the average return and standard deviation of the minimum-variance combination of stocks and bonds? *(LO 6-2)*

Templates and spreadsheets are available in Connect

16. Assume expected returns and standard deviations for all securities, as well as the risk-free rate for lending and borrowing, are known. Will investors arrive at the same optimal risky portfolio? Explain. *(LO 6-4)*

17. Your assistant gives you the following diagram as the efficient frontier of the group of stocks you asked him to analyze. The diagram looks a bit odd, but your assistant insists he double-checked his analysis. Would you trust him? Is it possible to get such a diagram? *(LO 6-4)*

18. What is the relationship of the portfolio standard deviation to the weighted average of the standard deviations of the component assets? *(LO 6-1)*

19. A project has a .7 chance of doubling your investment in a year and a .3 chance of halving your investment in a year. What is the standard deviation of the rate of return on this investment? *(LO 6-2)*

20. Investors expect the market rate of return this year to be 10%. The expected rate of return on a stock with a beta of 1.2 is currently 12%. If the market return this year turns out to be 8%, how would you revise your expectation of the rate of return on the stock? *(LO 6-5)*

21. The following figure shows plots of monthly rates of return and the stock market for two stocks. *(LO 6-5)*

    a. Which stock is riskier to an investor currently holding a diversified portfolio of common stock?

    b. Which stock is riskier to an undiversified investor who puts all of his funds in only one of these stocks?

Templates and spreadsheets are available in Connect

22. Log in to Connect and link to the material for Chapter 6, where you will find a spreadsheet containing monthly rates of return for Ford, the S&P 500, and T-bills over a recent five-year period. Set up a spreadsheet just like that of Example 6.3 and find the beta of Ford. *(LO 6-5)*

23. Here are rates of return for six months for Generic Risk, Inc. What is Generic's beta? (*Hint:* Find the answer by plotting the scatter diagram.) *(LO 6-5)*

Month	Market Return	Generic Return
1	0%	+2%
2	0	0
3	−1	0
4	−1	−2
5	+1	+4
6	+1	+2

Challenge

24. Log in to Connect to find rate-of-return data over a 60-month period for Google, the T-bill rate, and the S&P 500, which we will use as the market-index portfolio. *(LO 6-4)*

    a. Use these data and Excel's regression function to compute Google's excess return in each month as well as its alpha, beta, and residual standard deviation, $\sigma(e)$, over the entire period.

    b. What was the Sharpe ratio of the S&P 500 over this period?

    c. What was Google's information ratio over this period?

    d. If someone whose risky portfolio is currently invested in an index portfolio such as the S&P 500 wishes to take a position in Google based on the estimates from parts (*a*)–(*c*), what would be the optimal fraction of the risky portfolio to invest in Google? Use Equations 6.16 and 6.17.

    e. Based on Equation 6.18 and your answer to part (*d*), by how much would the Sharpe ratio of the optimal risky portfolio increase given the incremental position in Google?

25. Turn back to Table 6.3 and consider these three-year strategies: Three-In (fully invested in the risky portfolio in each of the three years); One-In (fully invested in the risky portfolio in one year, and in the risk-free asset in the other two); and Third-In-Three (one-third of the portfolio invested in the risky portfolio and the remainder in T-bills in each of the three years). *(LO 6-6)*

    a. Create a table like Table 6.3 for these three strategies.

    b. Which strategy has the lowest Sharpe ratio?

c. Which strategy provides the highest price of risk?

d. Suppose your risk aversion coefficient is $A = 2$, the expected return on the risky portfolio is 10%, the standard deviation of the risky portfolio is 20%, and the T-bill rate is 4%. If you were allocating your complete portfolio in any year between Three-In and T-bills, what fraction would you devote to Three-In?

e. If you were allocating your complete portfolio in any year between Third-In-Three and T-bills, what fraction would you devote to Third-In-Three?

f. Is there any difference in the complete portfolios that you find in parts (d) and (e)?

g. Is the rational allocation to the risky portfolio for a one-year investor any different than it is for a longer-term three-year investor? In other words, does "time diversification" imply that long-term investors should devote a higher fraction of their investment budget to the risky portfolio?

CFA Problems

1. A three-asset portfolio has the following characteristics:

Asset	Expected Return	Standard Deviation	Weight
X	15%	22%	0.50
Y	10	8	0.40
Z	6	3	0.10

What is the expected return on this three-asset portfolio? *(LO 6-1)*

2. George Stephenson's current portfolio of $2 million is invested as follows:

Summary of Stephenson's Current Portfolio				
	Value	Percent of Total	Expected Annual Return	Annual Standard Deviation
Short-term bonds	$ 200,000	10%	4.6%	1.6%
Domestic large-cap equities	600,000	30	12.4	19.5
Domestic small-cap equities	1,200,000	60	16.0	29.9
Total portfolio	$2,000,000	100%	13.8%	23.1%

Stephenson soon expects to receive an additional $2 million and plans to invest the entire amount in an index fund that best complements the current portfolio. Stephanie Coppa, CFA, is evaluating the four index funds shown in the following table for their ability to produce a portfolio that will meet two criteria relative to the current portfolio: (1) maintain or enhance expected return and (2) maintain or reduce volatility.

Each fund is invested in an asset class that is not substantially represented in the current portfolio.

Index Fund Characteristics			
Index Fund	Expected Annual Return	Expected Annual Standard Deviation	Correlation of Returns with Current Portfolio
Fund A	15%	25%	+0.80
Fund B	11	22	+0.60
Fund C	16	25	+0.90
Fund D	14	22	+0.65

State which fund Coppa should recommend to Stephenson. Justify your choice by describing how your chosen fund *best* meets both of Stephenson's criteria. No calculations are required.   *(LO 6-4)*

3. Abigail Grace has a $900,000 fully diversified portfolio. She subsequently inherits ABC Company common stock worth $100,000. Her financial adviser provided her with the following estimates: *(LO 6-5)*

	Risk and Return Characteristics	
	Expected Monthly Returns	Standard Deviation of Monthly Returns
Original Portfolio	0.67%	2.37%
ABC Company	1.25	2.95

The correlation coefficient of ABC stock returns with the original portfolio returns is .40.

a. The inheritance changes Grace's overall portfolio and she is deciding whether to keep the ABC stock. Assuming Grace keeps the ABC stock, calculate the:
   i. Expected return of her new portfolio which includes the ABC stock.
   ii. Covariance of ABC stock returns with the original portfolio returns.
   iii. Standard deviation of her new portfolio which includes the ABC stock.

b. If Grace sells the ABC stock, she will invest the proceeds in risk-free government securities yielding .42% monthly. Assuming Grace sells the ABC stock and replaces it with the government securities, calculate the:
   i. Expected return of her new portfolio which includes the government securities.
   ii. Covariance of the government security returns with the original portfolio returns.
   iii. Standard deviation of her new portfolio which includes the government securities.

c. Determine whether the beta of her new portfolio, which includes the government securities, will be higher or lower than the beta of her original portfolio.

d. Based on conversations with her husband, Grace is considering selling the $100,000 of ABC stock and acquiring $100,000 of XYZ Company common stock instead. XYZ stock has the same expected return and standard deviation as ABC stock. Her husband comments, "It doesn't matter whether you keep all of the ABC stock or replace it with $100,000 of XYZ stock." State whether her husband's comment is correct or incorrect. Justify your response.

e. In a recent discussion with her financial adviser, Grace commented, "If I just don't lose money in my portfolio, I will be satisfied." She went on to say, "I am more afraid of losing money than I am concerned about achieving high returns." Describe *one* weakness of using standard deviation of returns as a risk measure for Grace.

The following data apply to CFA Problems 4–6:

Hennessy & Associates manages a $30 million equity portfolio for the multimanager Wilstead Pension Fund. Jason Jones, financial vice president of Wilstead, noted that Hennessy had rather consistently achieved the best record among the Wilstead's six equity managers. Performance of the Hennessy portfolio had been clearly superior to that of the S&P 500 in four of the past five years. In the one less favorable year, the shortfall was trivial.

Hennessy is a "bottom-up" manager. The firm largely avoids any attempt to "time the market." It also focuses on selection of individual stocks, rather than the weighting of favored industries.

There is no apparent conformity of style among the six equity managers. The five managers, other than Hennessy, manage portfolios aggregating $250 million, made up of more than 150 individual issues.

Jones is convinced that Hennessy is able to apply superior skill to stock selection, but the favorable results are limited by the high degree of diversification in the portfolio. Over the years, the portfolio generally held 40–50 stocks, with about 2% to 3% of total funds committed to each issue. The reason Hennessy seemed to do well most years was that the firm was able to identify each year 10 or 12 issues that registered particularly large gains.

Based on this overview, Jones outlined the following plan to the Wilstead pension committee:

Let's tell Hennessy to limit the portfolio to no more than 20 stocks. Hennessy will double the commitments to the stocks that it really favors and eliminate the remainder. Except for this one new restriction, Hennessy should be free to manage the portfolio exactly as before.

All the members of the pension committee generally supported Jones's proposal, because all agreed that Hennessy had seemed to demonstrate superior skill in selecting stocks. Yet the proposal was a considerable departure from previous practice, and several committee members raised questions.

4. Answer the following: *(LO 6-1)*
   a. Will the limitation of 20 stocks likely increase or decrease the risk of the portfolio? Explain.
   b. Is there any way Hennessy could reduce the number of issues from 40 to 20 without significantly affecting risk? Explain.

5. One committee member was particularly enthusiastic concerning Jones's proposal. He suggested that Hennessy's performance might benefit further from reduction in the number of issues to 10. If the reduction to 20 could be expected to be advantageous, explain why reduction to 10 might be less likely to be advantageous. (Assume that Wilstead will evaluate the Hennessy portfolio independently of the other portfolios in the fund.) *(LO 6-1)*

6. Another committee member suggested that, rather than evaluate each managed portfolio independently of other portfolios, it might be better to consider the effects of a change in the Hennessy portfolio on the total fund. Explain how this broader point of view could affect the committee decision to limit the holdings in the Hennessy portfolio to either 10 or 20 issues. *(LO 6-1)*

7. Dudley Trudy, CFA, recently met with one of his clients. Trudy typically invests in a master list of 30 equities drawn from several industries. As the meeting concluded, the client made the following statement: "I trust your stock-picking ability and believe that you should invest my funds in your five best ideas. Why invest in 30 companies when you obviously have stronger opinions on a few of them?" Trudy plans to respond to his client within the context of Modern Portfolio Theory. *(LO 6-1)*
   a. Contrast the concepts of systematic risk and firm-specific risk, and give an example of each type of risk.
   b. Critique the client's suggestion. Discuss how both systematic and firm-specific risk change as the number of securities in a portfolio is increased.

---

1. Go to **finance.yahoo.com** and download five years of monthly closing prices for Eli Lilly (ticker = LLY), Alcoa (AA), and the S&P 500 Index (GSPC). Download the data into an Excel file and use the Adjusted-Close prices, which adjust for dividend payments, to calculate the monthly rate of return for each price series. Use an XY scatter plot chart with no line joining the points to plot Alcoa's returns against the S&P 500. Now select one of the data points, and right-click to obtain a shortcut menu allowing you to enter a trend line. This is Alcoa's characteristic line, and the slope is Alcoa's beta. Repeat this process for Lilly. What conclusions can you draw from each company's characteristic line?

2. Following the procedures in the previous question, find five years of monthly returns for Staples. Using the first two years of data, what is Staples' beta? What is the beta using the

WEB *master*

latest two years of data? How stable is the beta estimate? If you use all five years of data, how close is your estimate of beta to the estimate reported in Yahoo's *Key Statistics* section?

3. Following the procedures in the previous questions, find five years of monthly returns for the following firms: Genzyme Corporation, Sony, Cardinal Health, Inc., Black & Decker Corporation, and Kellogg Company. Copy the returns from these five firms into a single Excel workbook, with the returns for each company properly aligned. Use the full range of available data. Then do the following:

   a. Using the Excel functions for average (AVERAGE) and sample standard deviation (STDEV), calculate the average and the standard deviation of the returns for each of the firms.

   b. Using Excel's correlation function (CORREL), construct the correlation matrix for the five stocks based on their monthly returns for the entire period. What are the lowest and the highest individual pairs of correlation coefficients? (*Alternative:* You may use Excel's Data Analysis Tool to generate the correlation matrix.)

4. There are some free online tools that will calculate the optimal asset weights and draw the efficient frontier for the assets that you specify. One of the sites is **www.investorcraft .com/PortfolioTools/EfficientFrontier.aspx.**

   Go to this site and enter at least eight assets in the selection box. You can search for the companies by name or by symbol. Click on the *Next Step* button and select one of the time spans offered. Specify an appropriate risk-free rate, a minimum allowable asset weight of 0, and a maximum allowable asset weight of 100. Click on *Calculate* to get your results.

   a. What are the expected return and the standard deviation of the portfolio based on adjusted weights?

   b. How do they compare to those for the optimal portfolio and the minimum variance portfolio?

   c. Of the three portfolios shown, with which one would you feel most comfortable as an investor?

SOLUTIONS TO CONCEPT *checks*

6.1 Recalculation of Spreadsheets 6.1 and 6.4 shows that the covariance is now -5.80 and the correlation coefficient is $-.07$.

	A	B	C	D	E	F
1			Stock Fund		Bond Fund	
2	Scenario	Probability	Rate of Return	Col B × Col C	Rate of Return	Col B × Col E
3	Severe recession	0.05	−37.0	−1.9	−10	−0.5
4	Mild recession	0.25	−11.0	−2.8	10	2.5
5	Normal growth	0.40	14.0	5.6	7	2.8
6	Boom	0.30	30.0	9.0	2	0.6
7	Expected or Mean Return:		SUM:	10.0	SUM:	5.4
8						
9			Deviation from Mean Return		Covariance	
10	Scenario	Probability	Stock Fund	Bond Fund	Product of Dev	Col B × Col E
11	Severe recession	0.05	−47.0	−15.4	723.8	36.19
12	Mild recession	0.25	−21.0	4.6	−96.6	−24.15
13	Normal growth	0.40	4.0	1.6	6.4	2.56
14	Boom	0.30	20.0	−3.4	−68.0	−20.40
15		SD =	18.63	4.65	Covariance =	−5.80
16		Correlation coefficient = Covariance/(StdDev(stocks)*StdDev(bonds)) =				−0.07

6.2 The scatter diagrams for pairs B–E are shown below. Scatter diagram A (presented with the Concept Check) shows an exact mirror image between the pattern of points 1,2,3 versus 3,4,5. Therefore, the correlation coefficient is zero. Scatter diagram B shows perfect positive correlation (1). Similarly, C shows perfect negative correlation (−1). Now compare the scatters of D and E. Both show a general positive correlation, but scatter D is tighter. Therefore, D is associated with a correlation of about .5 (use a spreadsheet to show that the exact correlation is .54), and E is associated with a correlation of about .2 (show that the exact correlation coefficient is .23).

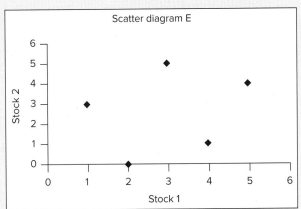

6.3 *a.* Using Equation 6.6 with the data $\sigma_B = 8$; $\sigma_S = 19$; $w_B = .5$; and $w_S = 1 - w_B = .5$, we obtain the equation

$$\sigma_P^2 = 10^2 = (w_B\sigma_B)^2 + (w_S\sigma_S)^2 + 2(w_B\sigma_B)(w_S\sigma_S)\rho_{BS}$$
$$= (.5 \times 8)^2 + (.5 \times 19)^2 + 2(.5 \times 8)(.5 \times 19)\rho_{BS}$$

which yields $\rho = -.0822$.

b. Using Equation 6.5 and the additional data $E(r_B) = 5\%$; $E(r_S) = 10\%$, we obtain

$$E(r_P) = w_B E(r_B) + w_S E(r_S) = (.5 \times 5) + (.5 \times 10) = 7.5\%$$

c. On the one hand, you should be happier with a correlation of .17 than with .22 since the lower correlation implies greater benefits from diversification and means that, for any level of expected return, there will be lower risk. On the other hand, the constraint that you must hold 50% of the portfolio in bonds represents a cost to you since it prevents you from choosing the risk-return trade-off most suited to your tastes. Unless you would choose to hold about 50% of the portfolio in bonds anyway, you are better off with the slightly higher correlation but with the ability to choose your own portfolio weights.

6.4 *a.* Implementing Equations 6.5 and 6.6, we generate data for the graph. See Spreadsheet 6.7 and Figure 6.14.

b. Implementing the formulas indicated in Spreadsheet 6.6, we generate the optimal risky portfolio (*O*) and the minimum-variance portfolio.

c. The slope of the CAL is equal to the risk premium of the optimal risky portfolio divided by its standard deviation $(11.28 - 5)/17.59 = .357$.

d. The mean of the complete portfolio is $.2222 \times 11.28 + .7778 \times 5 = 6.395\%$, and its standard deviation is $.2222 \times 17.58 = 3.91\%$. Sharpe ratio $= (6.395 - 5)/3.91 = .357$.

	A	B	C	D	E	F	G
5		Data	X	M	T-Bills		
6		Mean (%)	15	10	5		
7		Std. Dev. (%)	50	20	0		
8		Corr. Coeff. X and S		−0.20			
9		Portfolio Opportunity set					
10		Weight in X	Weight in S	Pf Mean (%)	Pf Std Dev (%)		
11		−1.00	2.00	5.00	70.00		
12		−0.90	1.90	5.50	64.44		
13		−0.80	1.80	6.00	58.92		
14		−0.70	1.70	6.50	53.45	=B13*$C$6+C13*$D$6	
15		−0.60	1.60	7.00	48.04		
16		−0.50	1.50	7.50	42.72		
17		−0.40	1.40	8.00	37.52		
18		−0.30	1.30	8.50	32.51	=(B15^2*$C$7^2	
19		−0.20	1.20	9.00	27.78	+C15^2*$D$7^2	
20		−0.10	1.10	9.50	23.52	+2*B15*C15	
21		0.00	1.00	10.00	20.00	*$C$7*$D$7*$D$8)^0.5	
22		0.10	0.90	10.50	17.69		
23		0.20	0.80	11.00	17.09		
24		0.30	0.70	11.50	18.36		
25		0.40	0.60	12.00	21.17		
26		0.50	0.50	12.50	25.00		
27		0.60	0.40	13.00	29.46		
28		0.70	0.30	13.50	34.31		
29		0.80	0.20	14.00	39.40		
30		0.90	0.10	14.50	44.64		
31		1.00	0.00	15.00	50.00		
32		1.10	−0.10	15.50	55.43		
33		1.20	−0.20	16.00	60.93		
34		1.30	−0.30	16.50	66.46		
35		1.40	−0.40	17.00	72.03		
36		1.50	−0.50	17.50	77.62		
37		1.60	−0.60	18.00	83.23		
38		1.70	−0.70	18.50	88.87		
39		1.80	−0.80	19.00	94.51		
40		1.90	−0.90	19.50	100.16		
41		2.00	−1.00	20.00	105.83		
42	Min. Var Pf	0.18	0.82	10.91	17.06		
43	Optimal Pf	0.26	0.74	11.28	17.59		
44							
45							
46		=((C6-E6)*D7^2-(D6-E6)*C7*D7*D8)/					
47		((C6-E6)*D7^2+(D6-E6)*C7^2-(C6-E6+D6-E6)*C7*D7*D8)					
48							
49							

The composition of the complete portfolio is

.2222 × .26 = .06 (i.e., 6%) in X

.2222 × .74 = .16 (i.e., 16%) in M

and 78% in T-bills.

6.5 Efficient frontiers derived by portfolio managers depend on forecasts of the rates of return on various securities and estimates of risk, that is, standard deviations and correlation coefficients. The forecasts themselves do not control outcomes. Thus, to prefer a manager with a rosier forecast (northwesterly frontier) is tantamount to rewarding the bearers of good news and punishing the bearers of bad news. What the investor wants is to reward bearers of *accurate* news. Investors should monitor forecasts of portfolio managers on a regular basis to develop a track record of their forecasting accuracy. Portfolio choices of the more accurate forecasters will, in the long run, outperform the field.

6.6 *a.* Beta, the slope coefficient of the security on the factor: Securities $R_1 - R_6$ have a positive beta. These securities move, on average, in the same direction as the market (R_M). R_1, R_2, R_6 have large betas, so they are "aggressive" in that they carry more systematic risk than R_3, R_4, R_5, which are "defensive." R_7 and R_8 have a negative beta. These are hedge assets that carry negative systematic risk.

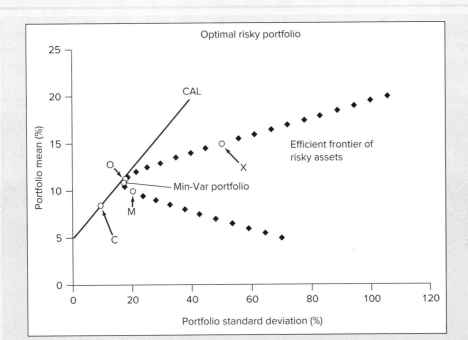

For Concept Check 6.4. Plot of mean return versus standard deviation using data from spreadsheet.

FIGURE 6.14

For Concept Check 6.4. Plot of mean return versus standard deviation using data from spreadsheet.

b. Intercept, the expected return when the market is neutral: The estimates show that R_1, R_4, R_8 have a positive intercept, while R_2, R_3, R_5, R_6, R_7 have negative intercepts. To the extent that one believes these intercepts will persist, a positive value is preferred.

c. Residual variance, the nonsystematic risk: R_2, R_3, R_7 have a relatively low residual variance. With sufficient diversification, residual risk eventually will be eliminated, and, hence, the difference in the residual variance is of little economic significance.

d. Total variance, the sum of systematic and nonsystematic risk: R_3 has a low beta and low residual variance, so its total variance will be low. R_1, R_6 have high betas and high residual variance, so their total variance will be high. But R_4 has a low beta and high residual variance, while R_2 has a high beta with a low residual variance. In sum, total variance often will misrepresent systematic risk, which is the part that matters.

6.7 a. To obtain the characteristic line of XYZ, we continue the spreadsheet of Example 6.3 and run a regression of the excess return of XYZ on the excess return of the market-index fund.

Summary Output	
Regression Statistics	
Multiple R	0.363
R-square	0.132
Adjusted R-square	0.023
Standard error	41.839
Observations	10

	Coefficients	Standard Error	t-Stat	p-Value	Lower 95%	Upper 95%
Intercept	3.930	14.98	0.262	0.800	−30.62	38.48
Market	0.582	0.528	1.103	0.302	−0.635	1.798

The regression output shows that the slope coefficient of XYZ is .582 and the intercept is 3.93%; hence the characteristic line is $R_{XYZ} = 3.93 + .582 R_{Market}$.

b. The beta coefficient of ABC is 1.156, greater than XYZ's .582, implying that ABC has greater systematic risk.

c. The regression of XYZ on the market index shows an R-square of .132. Hence the proportion of unexplained variance (nonsystematic risk) is .868, or 86.8%.

Capital Asset Pricing and Arbitrage Pricing Theory

Learning Objectives

LO 7-1 Use the implications of capital market theory to estimate security risk premiums.

LO 7-2 Construct and use the security market line.

LO 7-3 Specify and use a multifactor security market line.

LO 7-4 Take advantage of an arbitrage opportunity with a portfolio that includes mispriced securities.

LO 7-5 Use arbitrage pricing theory with more than one factor to identify mispriced securities.

The capital asset pricing model, almost always referred to as the CAPM, is a centerpiece of modern financial economics. It was first proposed by William F. Sharpe, who was awarded the 1990 Nobel Prize in Economics.

The CAPM predicts the relationship we should observe between the risk of an asset and its expected return. This relationship serves two vital functions.

First, it provides a benchmark rate of return for evaluating possible investments. For example, a security analyst might want to know whether the expected return she forecasts for a stock is more or less than its "fair" return given its risk. Second, the model helps us make an educated guess as to the expected return on assets that have not yet been traded in the marketplace. For example, how do we price an initial public offering of stock? How

will a major new investment project affect the return investors require on a company's stock? Although the CAPM does not fully withstand empirical tests, it is widely used because of the insight it offers and because its accuracy suffices for important applications.

The intuition behind the CAPM is readily generalized to allow for multiple sources of risk. Therefore, we turn next to multifactor models of risk and return, and we show how these result in richer descriptions of the risk-return relationship.

Finally, we consider an alternative derivation of the risk-return relationship known as arbitrage pricing theory (APT). Arbitrage is the exploitation of security mispricing to earn risk-free economic profits. The most basic principle of capital market theory is that prices ought to be aligned to eliminate risk-free profit opportunities. If actual prices allowed for such arbitrage, the resulting opportunities for profitable trading would lead to strong pressure on security prices that would persist until equilibrium is restored and the opportunities eliminated. We will see that this no-arbitrage principle leads to a risk-return relationship like that of the CAPM. Like the generalized version of the CAPM, the simple APT is easily extended to accommodate multiple sources of systematic risk.

7.1 THE CAPITAL ASSET PRICING MODEL

Historically, the CAPM was developed prior to the index model introduced in the previous chapter (Equation 6.11). The index model was widely adopted as a natural description of the stock market immediately on the heels of the CAPM because the CAPM implications so neatly match the intuition underlying the model. So it makes sense to use the index model to help understand the lessons of the CAPM.

The index model describes an empirical relationship between the excess return on an individual stock, R_i, and that of a broad market-index portfolio, R_M: $R_i = \beta_i R_M + \alpha_i + e_i$, where alpha is the expected firm-specific return and e_i is zero-mean "noise," or firm-specific risk. Therefore, the expected excess return on a stock, given (conditional on) the market excess return, R_M, is $E(R_i|R_M) = \beta_i R_M + \alpha_i$.

What does this mean to portfolio managers? Hunt for positive-alpha stocks, don't invest in negative-alpha stocks, and, better yet, sell short negative-alpha stocks if short sales are not prohibited. Investor demand for a positive-alpha stock will increase its price. As the price of a stock rises, other things being equal, its expected return falls, reducing and ultimately eliminating the very alpha that first created the excess demand. Conversely, the drop in demand for a negative-alpha stock will reduce its price, pushing its alpha back toward zero. In the end, such buying or selling pressure will leave most securities with zero alpha values most of the time. Put another way, unless and until your own analysis of a stock tells you otherwise, you should assume alpha is zero.

When alpha is zero, there is no reward from bearing firm-specific risk; the only way to earn a higher expected return than the T-bill rate is by bearing systematic risk. Recall the Treynor-Black model, in which the position in any active portfolio is zero if the alpha is zero. In that case, the best portfolio is the one that completely eliminates nonsystematic risk, and that portfolio is an indexed portfolio that mimics the broad market. This is the conclusion of the CAPM. But science demands more than a story like this. It requires a carefully set up model with explicit assumptions in which an outcome such as the one we describe will be the only possible result. Here goes.

The Model: Assumptions and Implications

The **capital asset pricing model (CAPM)** was developed by Treynor, Sharpe, Lintner, and Mossin in the early 1960s, and further refined later. The model predicts the relationship between the risk and equilibrium expected returns on risky assets. We begin by laying down the necessary, albeit unrealistic, assumptions that underlie the model. Thinking about an admittedly unrealistic world allows a relatively easy leap to the solution. With this accomplished, we can add realism to the environment, one step at a time, and see how the theory must be amended. This process allows us to develop a reasonably realistic model.

capital asset pricing model (CAPM)

A model that relates the required rate of return on a security to its systematic risk as measured by beta.

The conditions that lead to the CAPM ensure competitive security markets, where investors will choose identical efficient portfolios using the mean-variance criterion:

1. Markets for securities are perfectly competitive and equally profitable to all investors.
   1.A. No investor is sufficiently wealthy that his or her actions alone can affect market prices.
   1.B. All information relevant to security analysis is publicly available at no cost.

1.C. All securities are publicly owned and traded, and investors may trade all of them. Thus, all risky assets are in the investment universe.

1.D. There are no taxes on investment returns. Thus, all investors realize identical returns from securities.

1.E. Investors confront no transaction costs that inhibit their trading.

1.F. Lending and borrowing at a common risk-free rate are unlimited.

2. Investors are alike in every way except for initial wealth and risk aversion; hence, they all choose investment portfolios in the same manner.

2.A. Investors plan for the same (single-period) horizon.

2.B. Investors are rational, mean-variance optimizers.

2.C. Investors are efficient users of analytical methods, and by assumption 1.B they have access to all relevant information. Hence, they use the same inputs and consider identical portfolio opportunity sets. This assumption is often called *homogeneous expectations.*

Obviously, these assumptions ignore many real-world complexities. However, they lead to powerful insights into the nature of equilibrium in security markets.

Given these assumptions, we summarize the equilibrium that will prevail in this hypothetical world of securities and investors. We elaborate on these implications in the following sections.

market portfolio (*M*)

The portfolio for which each security is held in proportion to its total market value.

1. All investors will choose to hold the **market portfolio** (*M*), which includes all assets of the security universe. For simplicity, we shall refer to all assets as stocks. The proportion of each stock in the market portfolio equals the market value of the stock (price per share times the number of shares outstanding) divided by the total market value of all stocks.

2. The market portfolio will be on the efficient frontier. Moreover, it will be the optimal risky portfolio, the tangency point of the capital allocation line (CAL) to the efficient frontier. As a result, the capital market line (CML), the line from the risk-free rate through the market portfolio, *M,* is also the best attainable capital allocation line. All investors hold *M* as their optimal risky portfolio, differing only in the amount invested in it versus in the risk-free asset.

3. The risk premium on the market portfolio will be proportional to the variance of the market portfolio and investors' typical degree of risk aversion. Mathematically,

$$E(r_M) - r_f = \bar{A}\sigma_M^2 \tag{7.1}$$

where σ_M is the standard deviation of the return on the market portfolio and $\bar{A}$ represents the degree of risk aversion of the average investor.

4. The risk premium on individual assets will be proportional to the risk premium on the market portfolio (*M*) and to the *beta coefficient* of the security on the market portfolio. Beta measures the extent to which returns respond to the market portfolio. Formally, beta is the regression (slope) coefficient of the security return on the market return, representing sensitivity to fluctuations in the overall security market.

Why All Investors Would Hold the Market Portfolio

Given all our assumptions, it is easy to see why all investors hold identical risky portfolios. If all investors use mean-variance analysis (assumption 2.B), apply it to the same universe of securities (assumptions 1.C and 1.F) with an identical time horizon (assumption 2.A), use the same security analysis (assumption 2.C), and experience identical net returns from the same securities (assumptions 1.A, 1.D, and 1.E), they all must arrive at the same determination of the optimal risky portfolio.

With everyone choosing to hold the same risky portfolio, stocks will be represented in the aggregate risky portfolio in the same proportion as they are in each investor's (common) risky portfolio. If Google represents 1% in each common risky portfolio, Google will be 1% of the aggregate risky portfolio. This in fact is the market portfolio because the market is no more than the aggregate of all individual portfolios. Because each investor uses the market portfolio for the optimal risky portfolio, the CAL in this case is called the *capital market line,* or CML, as in Figure 7.1.

Suppose the optimal portfolio of our investors does not include the stock of some company, say, Southwest Airlines. When no investor is willing to hold Southwest stock, the demand is zero, and the stock price will take a free fall. As Southwest stock gets progressively cheaper, it begins to look more attractive, while all other stocks look (relatively) less attractive. Ultimately, Southwest will reach a price at which it is desirable to include it in the optimal stock portfolio, and investors will buy.

This price adjustment process guarantees that all stocks will be included in the optimal portfolio. The only issue is the price. At a given price level, investors will be willing to buy a stock; at another price, they will not. The bottom line is this: If all investors hold an *identical* risky portfolio, this portfolio must be the *market* portfolio.

The Passive Strategy Is Efficient

The CAPM implies that a passive strategy, using the CML as the optimal CAL, is a powerful alternative to an active strategy. The market portfolio proportions are a result of profit-oriented "buy" and "sell" orders that cease only when there is no more profit to be made. And in the simple world of the CAPM, all investors use precious resources in security analysis. A passive investor who takes a free ride by simply investing in the market portfolio benefits from the efficiency of that portfolio. In fact, an active investor who chooses any other portfolio will end on a CAL that is inferior to the CML used by passive investors.

We sometimes call this result a **mutual fund theorem** because it implies that only one mutual fund of risky assets—the market index fund—is sufficient to satisfy the investment demands of all investors. The mutual fund theorem is another incarnation of the separation property discussed in Chapter 6. Assuming all investors choose to hold a market-index mutual fund, we can separate portfolio selection into two components: (1) a technical side, in which an efficient mutual fund is created by professional management; and (2) a personal side, in which an investor's risk aversion determines the allocation of the complete portfolio between the mutual fund and the risk-free asset. Here, all investors agree that the mutual fund they would like to hold is invested in the market portfolio.

While investment managers in the real world generally construct risky portfolios that differ from the market index, we attribute this to the differences in their estimates of risk and expected return (in violation of assumption 2.C). Nevertheless, a passive investor may view the market index as a reasonable first approximation to an efficient risky portfolio.

mutual fund theorem

States that all investors desire the same portfolio of risky assets and can be satisfied by a single mutual fund composed of that portfolio.

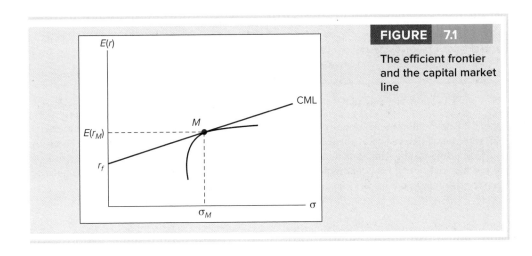

FIGURE 7.1

The efficient frontier and the capital market line

The logical inconsistency of the CAPM is this: If a passive strategy is costless *and* efficient, why would anyone follow an active strategy? But if no one does any security analysis, what brings about the efficiency of the market portfolio?

We have acknowledged from the outset that the CAPM simplifies the real world in its search for a tractable solution. Its applicability to the real world depends on whether its predictions are accurate enough. The model's use is some indication that its predictions are reasonable. We discuss this issue in Section 7.3 and in greater depth in Chapter 8.

CONCEPT check 7.1	If only some investors perform security analysis while all others hold the market portfolio (*M*), would the CML still be the efficient CAL for investors who do not engage in security analysis? Explain.

The Risk Premium of the Market Portfolio

In Chapter 5 we showed how individual investors decide how much to invest in the risky portfolio when they can include a risk-free asset in the investment budget. Returning now to the decision of how much to invest in the market portfolio *M* and how much in the risk-free asset, what can we deduce about the equilibrium risk premium of portfolio *M*?

We asserted earlier that the equilibrium risk premium of the market portfolio, $E(r_M) - r_f$, will be proportional to the degree of risk aversion of the average investor and to the risk of the market portfolio, σ_M^2. Now we can explain this result.

When investors purchase stocks, their demand drives up prices, thereby lowering expected rates of return and risk premiums. But when risk premiums fall, investors will move some of their funds from the risky market portfolio into the risk-free asset. In equilibrium, the risk premium on the market portfolio must be just high enough to induce investors to hold the available supply of stocks. If the risk premium is too high, there will be excess demand for securities, and prices will rise; if it is too low, investors will not hold enough stock to absorb the supply, and prices will fall. The *equilibrium* risk premium of the market portfolio is therefore proportional both to the risk of the market, as measured by the variance of its returns, and to the degree of risk aversion of the average investor, denoted by $\bar{A}$ in Equation 7.1.

EXAMPLE 7.1 *Market Risk, the Risk Premium, and Risk Aversion*	Suppose the risk-free rate is 5%, the average investor has a risk-aversion coefficient of $\bar{A} = 2$, and the standard deviation of the market portfolio is 20%. Then, from Equation 7.1, we estimate the equilibrium value of the market risk premium[1] as $2 \times .20^2 = .08$. So the expected rate of return on the market must be $$E(r_M) = r_f + \text{Equilibrium risk premium}$$ $$= .05 + .08 = .13 = 13\%$$ If investors were more risk averse, it would take a higher risk premium to induce them to hold shares. For example, if the average degree of risk aversion were 3, the market risk premium would be $3 \times .20^2 = .12$, or 12%, and the expected return would be 17%.

CONCEPT check 7.2	Historical data for the S&P 500 Index show an average excess return over Treasury bills of about 7.5% with standard deviation of about 20%. To the extent that these averages approximate investor expectations for the sample period, what must have been the coefficient of risk aversion of the average investor? If the coefficient of risk aversion were 3.5, what risk premium would have been consistent with the market's historical standard deviation?

[1]To use Equation 7.1, we must express returns in decimal form rather than as percentages.

Expected Returns on Individual Securities

The CAPM is built on the insight that the appropriate risk premium on an asset will be determined by its contribution to the risk of investors' overall portfolios. Portfolio risk is what matters to investors, and portfolio risk is what governs the risk premiums they demand.

We know that nonsystematic risk can be reduced to an arbitrarily low level through diversification (Chapter 6); therefore, investors do not require a risk premium as compensation for bearing nonsystematic risk. They need to be compensated only for bearing systematic risk, which cannot be diversified. We know also that the contribution of a single security to the risk of a large diversified portfolio depends only on the systematic risk of the security as measured by its beta, as we saw in Section 6.5. Therefore, it should not be surprising that the risk premium of an asset is proportional to its beta; a security with double the systematic risk of another must pay twice the risk premium. Thus, the ratio of risk premium to beta should be the same for any two securities or portfolios.

If we equate the ratio of risk premium to systematic risk for the market portfolio, which has a beta of 1, to the corresponding ratio for a particular stock, for example, Delta Air Lines, we find that

$$\frac{E(r_M) - r_f}{1} = \frac{E(r_D) - r_f}{\beta_D}$$

Rearranging results in the CAPM's **expected return–beta relationship**:

$$E(r_D) = r_f + \beta_D[E(r_M) - r_f] \tag{7.2}$$

In words, an asset's risk premium equals the asset's systematic risk measure (its beta) times the risk premium of the (benchmark) market portfolio. This expected return (or mean return)–beta relationship is the most familiar expression of the CAPM.

The mean–beta relationship of the CAPM makes a powerful economic statement. It implies, for example, that a security with a high variance but a relatively low beta of .5 will carry one-third the risk premium of a low-variance security with a beta of 1.5. Equation 7.2 quantifies the conclusion we reached in Chapter 6: Only systematic risk matters to investors who can diversify, and systematic risk is measured by beta.

expected return (mean return)–beta relationship

Implication of the CAPM that security risk premiums (expected excess returns) will be proportional to beta.

EXAMPLE 7.2

Expected Returns and Risk Premiums

Suppose the risk premium of the market portfolio is 8%, and we estimate the beta of Delta as $\beta_D = 1.2$. The risk premium predicted for the stock is therefore 1.2 times the market risk premium, or $1.2 \times 8\% = 9.6\%$. The expected rate of return on Delta is the risk-free rate plus the risk premium. For example, if the T-bill rate were 3%, the expected rate of return would be 3% + 9.6% = 12.6%, or, using Equation 7.2 directly,

$$E(r_D) = r_f + \beta_D[\text{Market risk premium}]$$

$$= 3\% + 1.2 \times 8\% = 12.6\%$$

If the estimate of Delta's beta were only 1.1, its required risk premium would fall to 8.8%. Similarly, if the market risk premium were only 6% and $\beta_D = 1.2$, Delta's risk premium would be only 7.2%.

The fact that many investors hold active portfolios that differ from the market portfolio does not necessarily invalidate the CAPM. Recall that reasonably well-diversified portfolios shed almost all firm-specific risk and are subject to only systematic risk. Even if one does not hold the precise market portfolio, a well-diversified portfolio will be so highly correlated with the market that a stock's beta relative to the market still will be a useful risk measure.

In fact, several researchers have shown that modified versions of the CAPM will hold despite differences among individuals that may cause them to hold different portfolios. A study by Brennan (1970) examines the impact of differences in investors' personal tax rates on market equilibrium. Another study by Mayers (1972) looks at the impact of nontraded assets such as human capital (earning power). Both find that while the market portfolio is no longer each investor's optimal risky portfolio, a modified version of the mean–beta relationship still holds.

If the mean–beta relationship holds for any individual asset, it must hold for any combination of assets. The beta of a portfolio is simply the weighted average of the betas of the stocks in the portfolio, using as weights the portfolio proportions. Thus, beta also predicts a portfolio's risk premium in accordance with Equation 7.2.

EXAMPLE 7.3

Portfolio Beta and Risk Premium

Consider the following portfolio:

Asset	Beta	Risk Premium	Portfolio Weight
Microsoft	1.2	9.0%	0.5
American Electric Power	0.8	6.0	0.3
Gold	0.0	0.0	0.2
Portfolio	0.84	?	1.0

If the market risk premium is 7.5%, the CAPM predicts that the risk premium on each stock is its beta times 7.5%, and the risk premium on the portfolio is .84 × 7.5% = 6.3%. This is the same result that is obtained by taking the weighted average of the risk premiums of the individual stocks. (Verify this for yourself.)

A word of caution: We often hear that a well-managed firm will provide a high rate of return. This is true when referring to the *firm's* accounting return on investments in plant and equipment. The CAPM, however, predicts returns on investments in the *securities* of the firm that trade in capital markets.

Say everyone knows a firm is well run. Its stock price will be bid up, and returns to stockholders at those high prices will not be extreme. Security *prices* reflect public information about a firm's prospects, but only the risk of the company (as measured by beta) should affect *expected returns*. In a rational market, investors receive high expected returns only if they bear systematic risk.

CONCEPT check 7.3

Suppose the risk premium on the market portfolio is estimated at 8% with a standard deviation of 22%. What is the risk premium on a portfolio invested 25% in GE with a beta of .8 and 75% in Delta with a beta of 1.2?

The Security Market Line

The expected return–beta relationship or equivalently, the mean-beta relationship, is a reward-risk equation. The beta of a security is the appropriate measure of its risk because beta is proportional to the variance the security contributes to the optimal risky portfolio.[2]

With approximately normal returns, we measure the risk of a portfolio by its standard deviation. Because the beta of a stock measures the stock's contribution to the standard deviation of the market portfolio, we expect the required risk premium to be a function of beta. The CAPM confirms this intuition, stating further that the security's risk premium is directly proportional to both the beta and the risk premium of the market portfolio; that is, the risk premium equals $\beta[E(r_M) - r_f]$.

security market line (SML)

Graphical representation of the expected return-beta relationship of the CAPM.

The mean–beta relationship is represented by the **security market line (SML)** in Figure 7.2. Its slope is the risk premium of the market portfolio. At the point where $\beta = 1$ (the beta of the market portfolio), we can read off the vertical axis the expected return on the market portfolio.

---

[2]The contribution of a security to portfolio variance equals the variance of the portfolio when the security is included minus the variance when the security is excluded, with the weights of all other securities increased proportionally to bring total weights to 1.

FIGURE 7.2

The security market
line and a positive-
alpha stock

It is useful to compare the SML to the capital market line. The CML graphs the risk premiums of efficient complete portfolios (made up of the market portfolio and the risk-free asset) as a function of portfolio standard deviation. This is appropriate because standard deviation is a valid measure of risk for portfolios that are candidates for an investor's complete portfolio.

The SML, in contrast, graphs *individual-asset* risk premiums as a function of asset risk (which we measure by beta). The relevant measure of risk for an individual asset (which is held as part of a well-diversified portfolio) is not the asset standard deviation but rather the asset beta. The SML is valid both for individual assets and portfolios.

The security market line provides a benchmark for evaluation of investment performance. The SML provides the required rate of return that will compensate investors for the beta risk of that investment, as well as for the time value of money.

Because the SML is the graphical representation of the mean–beta relationship, "fairly priced" assets plot exactly on the SML. The expected returns of such assets are commensurate with their risk. Whenever the CAPM holds, all securities must lie on the SML. Underpriced stocks plot above the SML: Given beta, their expected returns are greater than is indicated by the CAPM. Overpriced stocks plot below the SML. The difference between fair and actual expected rates of return on a stock is the **alpha,** denoted α. The expected return on a mispriced security is given by $E(r_s) = \alpha_s + r_f + \beta_s[E(r_M) - r_f]$.

alpha

The abnormal rate of return on a security in excess of what would be predicted by an equilibrium model such as the CAPM.

Suppose the return on the market is expected to be 14%, a stock has a beta of 1.2, and the T-bill rate is 6%. The SML would predict an expected return on the stock of

$$E(r) = r_f + \beta[E(r_M) - r_f]$$

$$= 6 + 1.2(14 - 6) = 15.6\%$$

If one believes the stock will provide instead a return of 17%, its implied alpha would be 1.4%, as shown in Figure 7.2. If instead the expected return were only 15%, the stock alpha would be negative, −.6%.

EXAMPLE 7.4

The Alpha of a Security

Applications of the CAPM

One place the CAPM may be used is in the investment management industry. The SML provides a benchmark to assess the *fair* expected return on any risky asset. Then an analyst calculates the return she actually expects. Notice that we depart here from the simple CAPM world in that active investors apply their own analysis to derive a private "input list." If a stock is perceived to be a good buy, or underpriced, it will provide a positive alpha, that is, an expected return in excess of the fair return stipulated by the SML.

The CAPM is also useful in capital budgeting decisions. When a firm is considering a new project, the SML provides the required return demanded of the project. This is the cutoff internal rate of return (IRR) or "hurdle rate" for the project.

EXAMPLE 7.5

The CAPM and Capital Budgeting

Suppose Silverado Springs Inc. is considering a new spring-water bottling plant. The business plan forecasts an internal rate of return of 14% on the investment. Research shows the beta of similar products is 1.3. Thus, if the risk-free rate is 4%, and the market risk premium is estimated at 8%, the hurdle rate for the project should be $4 + 1.3 \times 8 = 14.4\%$. Because the IRR is less than the risk-adjusted discount or hurdle rate, the project has a negative net present value and ought to be rejected.

Yet another use of the CAPM is in utility rate-making cases. Here the issue is the rate of return a regulated utility should be allowed to earn on its investment in plant and equipment.

EXAMPLE 7.6

The CAPM and Regulation

Suppose shareholder equity invested in a utility is $100 million, and the equity beta is .6. If the T-bill rate is 6%, and the market risk premium is 8%, then a fair annual profit will be $6 + (.6 \times 8) = 10.8\%$ of $100 million, or $10.8 million. Because regulators accept the CAPM, they will allow the utility to set prices at a level expected to generate these profits.

CONCEPT
check   **7.4**

a. Stock XYZ has an expected return of 12% and $\beta = 1$. Stock ABC is expected to return 13% with a beta of 1.5. The market's expected return is 11% and $r_f = 5\%$. According to the CAPM, which stock is a better buy? What is the alpha of each stock? Plot the SML and the two stocks. Show the alphas of each on the graph.

b. The risk-free rate is 8% and the expected return on the market portfolio is 16%. A firm considers a project with an estimated beta of 1.3. What is the required rate of return on the project? If the IRR of the project is 19%, what is the project alpha?

7.2   THE CAPM AND INDEX MODELS

The CAPM has two limitations: It relies on the theoretical market portfolio, which includes *all* assets (such as real estate, foreign stocks, etc.), and it applies to *expected* as opposed to actual returns. To implement the CAPM, we cast it in the form of an *index model* and use realized, not expected, returns.

An index model replaces the theoretical all-inclusive portfolio with a market index such as the S&P 500. The composition and rate of return of the index are unambiguous and widely published, and therefore provide a clear benchmark for performance evaluation.

Absent an index model representation, the CAPM revolves around the elusive "market portfolio." However, because many assets are not traded, investors would not have full access to the market portfolio even if they could exactly identify it. Thus, the theory behind the CAPM rests on a shaky real-world foundation. But, as in all science, a theory is legitimate if it predicts real-world outcomes with sufficient accuracy. In particular, the reliance on the market portfolio shouldn't faze us if the predictions are sufficiently accurate when the index portfolio is substituted for the CAPM market portfolio.

We can start with the central prediction of the CAPM: The market portfolio is mean-variance efficient. An index model can be used to test this hypothesis by verifying that an index designed to represent the full market is mean-variance efficient. To test mean-variance efficiency of an index, we must show that its Sharpe ratio is not surpassed by any other portfolio. We will examine tests of this question in the next chapter.

The CAPM predicts relationships among *expected* returns. However, all we can observe are realized (historical) holding-period returns, which in a particular holding period seldom, if ever, match initial expectations. For example, the S&P 500 returned -39% in 2008. Could such a large negative return possibly have been expected when investors could have invested in risk-free Treasury bills? In fact, this logic implies that any stock-index return less than T-bills must entail a negative departure from expectations. Because expectations must be realized on average, this means that more often than not, positive excess returns exceeded expectations.

The Index Model, Realized Returns, and the Mean–Beta Equation

To move from a model cast in expectations to a realized-return framework, we start with the single-index regression equation in realized excess returns, Equation 6.11:

$$r_{it} - r_{ft} = \alpha_i + \beta_i(r_{Mt} - r_{ft}) + e_{it} \tag{7.3}$$

where r_{it} is the holding-period return (HPR) on asset i in period t and α_i and β_i are the intercept and slope of the security characteristic line that relates asset i's realized excess return to the realized excess return of the index. We denote the index return by r_M to emphasize that the index is proxying for the market portfolio. The e_{it} measures firm-specific effects during holding period t; it is the deviation in that period of security i's realized HPR from the regression line, the forecast of return based on the index's actual HPR. We set the relationship in terms of *excess* returns (over r_{ft}), consistent with the CAPM's logic of risk premiums.

To compare the index model with the CAPM predictions about expected asset returns, we take expectations in Equation 7.3. Recall that the expectation of e_{it} is zero, so in terms of expectations, Equation 7.3 becomes

$$E(r_{it}) - r_{ft} = \alpha_i + \beta_i[E(r_{Mt}) - r_{ft}] \tag{7.4}$$

Comparing Equation 7.4 to Equation 7.2 reveals that the CAPM predicts $\alpha_i = 0$. Thus, we have converted the CAPM prediction about unobserved expectations of security returns relative to an unobserved market portfolio into a prediction about the intercept in a regression of observed variables: realized excess returns of a security relative to those of an observed index.

Operationalizing the CAPM in the form of an index model has a drawback, however. If intercepts of regressions of returns on an index differ substantially from zero, you will not be able to tell whether it is because you chose a bad index to proxy for the market or because the theory is not useful.

In actuality, some instances of persistent, positive significant alpha values have been identified; these will be discussed in Chapter 8. Among these are (1) small versus large stocks; (2) stocks of companies that have recently announced unexpectedly good earnings; (3) stocks with high ratios of book value to market value; and (4) stocks with "momentum" that have experienced recent advances in price. In general, however, future alphas are practically impossible to predict from past values. The result is that index models are widely used to operationalize capital asset pricing theory.

Estimating the Index Model

To illustrate how to estimate the index model, we will use actual data and apply the model to the stock of Google (G), in a manner similar to that followed by practitioners. Let us rewrite Equation 7.3 for Google, denoting Google's excess return as $R_G = r_G - r_f$ and denoting months using the subscript t.

$$R_{Gt} = \alpha_G + \beta_G R_{Mt} + e_{Gt}$$

The dependent variable in this regression equation is Google's excess return in each month, explained by the excess return on the market index in that month, R_{Mt}. The regression coefficients are intercept α_G and slope β_G.

The alpha of Google is the average of the firm-specific factors during the sample period; the zero-average surprise in each month is captured by the last term in the equation, e_{Gt}. This residual is the difference between Google's actual excess return and the excess return that would be predicted from the regression line:

$$\text{Residual} = \text{Actual excess return} - \text{Predicted excess return for Google}$$
$$e_{Gt} = R_{Gt} \qquad\qquad - (\alpha_G + \beta_G R_{Mt})$$

We are interested in estimating the intercept α_G and Google's beta as measured by the slope coefficient, β_G. We estimate Google's firm-specific risk by *residual standard deviation,* which is just the standard deviation of e_{Gt}.

We conduct the analysis in three steps: Collect and process relevant data; feed the data into a statistical program (here we use Excel) to estimate the regression Equation 7.3; and use the results to answer these questions about Google's stock: (*a*) What have we learned about the behavior of Google's returns, (*b*) what required rate of return is appropriate for investments with the same risk as Google's equity, and (*c*) how might we assess the performance of a port-folio manager who invested heavily in Google stock during this period?

COLLECTING AND PROCESSING DATA   We start with the monthly series of Google stock prices and the S&P 500 Index, adjusted for stock splits and dividends over the period January 2006–December 2010.[3] From these series we computed monthly holding-period returns on Google and the market index.

For the same period we compiled monthly rates of return on one-month T-bills.[4] With these three series of returns we generate monthly excess return on Google's stock and the market index. Some statistics for these returns are shown in Table 7.1. Notice that the monthly varia-tion in the T-bill return reported in Table 7.1 does not reflect risk, as investors knew the return on bills at the beginning of each month.

The period of January 2006–December 2010 includes the late stage of recovery from the mild 2001 recession, the severe recession that officially began in December 2007, as well as the first stage of the recovery that began in June 2009. Table 7.1 shows that the effect of the financial crisis was so severe that the monthly geometric average return of the market index, .107%, was less than that of T-bills, .180%. We noted in Chapter 5 that arithmetic averages exceed geometric averages, with the difference between them increasing with return volatility.[5] In this period, the monthly SD of the market index, 5.11%, was large enough that despite the market return's lower geometric average, its monthly arithmetic average, .239%, was greater than that of T-bills, .185%, resulting in a positive average excess return of .054% per month.

Google had a cumulative five-year return of 43.17%, a lot better than T-bills (11.65%) or the S&P 500 (6.60%). Its monthly standard deviation of 10.40%, about double that of the mar-ket, raises the question of how much of that volatility is systematic.

Google's returns over subperiods within these five years illustrate a common illusion. Observe that Google's prerecession increase between January 2006 and October 2007 was 70.42%. The subsequent financial crisis decline (November 2007–May 2009) and recovery (June 2009–December 2010) were of similar magnitudes of −40.99% and 42.36%, respec-tively, and you might think they should have just about canceled out. Yet the total five-year return was "only" 43.17%, around 27% less than the prerecession gain of 70.42%. Where did that 27% go? It went in the crisis: The decline and subsequent increase had a total impact on cumulative return of $(1 - .4099) \times (1 + .4236) = .8401$, resulting in a loss of about 16%.

---

[3]Returns are available from **finance.yahoo.com.** We need to use the price series adjusted for dividends and splits in order to obtain holding-period returns (HPRs). The unadjusted price series would tell us about capital gains alone rather than total returns.

[4]We downloaded these rates from Professor Kenneth French's website: **mba.tuck.dartmouth.edu/pages/faculty/ ken.french/data_library.html.**

[5]When returns are normally distributed, the relation between the arithmetic average return, r_A, and the geometric average return, r_G (expressed as decimals, not percentages), is arithmetic average = geometric average plus one-half variance of returns. This relation holds approximately when returns are not precisely normally distributed.

TABLE 7.1	Monthly return statistics: T-bills, S&P 500, and Google, January 2006–December 2010		
Statistic (%)	**T-bills**	**S&P 500**	**Google**
Average rate of return	0.184	0.239	1.125
Average excess return	–	0.054	0.941
Standard deviation*	0.177	5.11	10.40
Geometric average	0.180	0.107	0.600
Cumulative total 5-year return	11.65	6.60	43.17
Gain Jan 2006–Oct 2007	9.04	27.45	70.42
Gain Nov 2007–May 2009	2.29	−38.87	−40.99
Gain June 2009–Dec 2010	0.10	36.83	42.36

*The rate on T-bills is known in advance; hence SD does not reflect risk.

Apply that loss to the prerecession value of stock, and you obtain .8401 × (1 + .7042) = 1.43, just equal to the five-year cumulative return.

Why didn't the 40.99% loss and 42.36% gain roughly cancel out? In general, a large gain following a large loss has a muted impact on cumulative return because it acts on a diminished investment base, while a large loss following a large gain has an amplified impact because it acts on a greater investment base. The greater the fluctuations, the greater the impact on final investment value, which is why the spread between the geometric average (which reflects cumulative return) and the arithmetic average grows with stock volatility.

Figure 7.3, Panel A shows the monthly return on the securities during the sample period. The significantly higher volatility of Google is evident, and the graph suggests that its beta is greater than 1: When the market moves, Google tends to move in the same direction, but by greater amounts.

Figure 7.3, Panel B shows the evolution of cumulative returns. It illustrates the positive index returns in the early years of the sample, the steep decline during the recession, and the significant partial recovery of losses at the end of the sample period. Whereas Google outperforms T-bills, T-bills outperform the market index over the period, highlighting the worse-than-expected realizations in the capital market.

ESTIMATION RESULTS   We regressed Google's excess returns against those of the index using the Regression command from the Data Analysis menu of Excel.[6] The scatter diagram in Figure 7.4 shows the data points for each month as well as the regression line that best fits the data. As noted in the previous chapter, this is called the **security characteristic line (SCL),** because it describes the relevant characteristics of the stock. Figure 7.4 allows us to view the residuals, the deviation of Google's return each month from the prediction of the regression equation. By construction, these residuals *average* to zero, but in any particular month, the residual may be positive or negative.

The residuals for April 2008 (23.81%) and November 2008 (−10.97%) are labeled explicitly. The April 2008 point lies above the regression line, indicating that in this month, Google's return was better than predicted from the market return. The distance between the point and the regression line is Google's firm-specific return, which is the residual for April.

The standard deviation of the residuals indicates the accuracy of predictions from the regression line. If there is a lot of firm-specific risk, there will be a wide scatter of points around the line (a high residual standard deviation), indicating that the market return will not enable a precise forecast of Google's return.

security characteristic line (SCL)

A plot of a security's expected excess return over the risk-free rate as a function of the excess return on the market.

[6]Mac users can download a free data analysis tool kit called StatPlus from **www.AnalystSoft.com.**

FIGURE   7.3   Returns for T-bills, S&P 500 Index, and Google stock.

A: Monthly returns

B: Cumulative returns

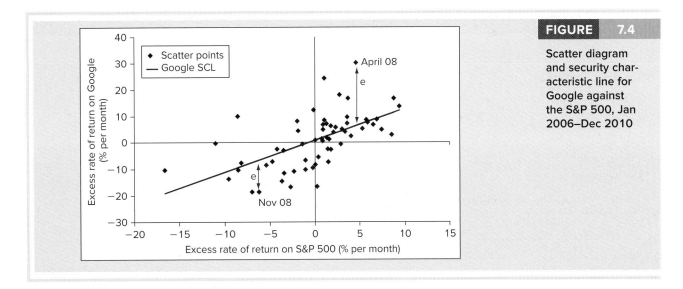

FIGURE 7.4

Scatter diagram and security characteristic line for Google against the S&P 500, Jan 2006–Dec 2010

Table 7.2 is the regression output from Excel. The first line shows that the correlation coefficient between the excess returns of Google and the index was .59. The more relevant statistic, however, is the *adjusted R-square* (.3497). It is the square of the correlation coefficient, adjusted downward for the number of coefficients or "degrees of freedom" used to estimate the regression line.[7] The adjusted R-square tells us that 34.97% of the variance of Google's excess returns is explained by the variation in the excess returns of the index, and hence the remainder, or 65.03%, of the variance is firm specific, or unexplained by market movements. The dominant contribution of firm-specific factors to variation in Google's returns is typical of individual stocks, reminding us why diversification can greatly reduce risk.

The standard deviation of the residuals is referred to in the output (below the adjusted R-square) as the "standard error" of the regression (8.46%). In roughly two-thirds of the months, the firm-specific component of Google's excess return was between ±8.46%. This wide spread is more evidence of Google's considerable firm-specific volatility.

Finally, the lower panel of the table shows the estimates of the regression intercept and slope (alpha = .88% and beta = 1.20). The positive alpha means that, measured by *realized* returns, Google stock was above the security market line (SML) for this period. But the next column shows considerable imprecision in this estimate as measured by its standard error, 1.09, considerably larger than the estimate itself. The *t*-statistic (the ratio of the estimate of alpha to its standard error) is only .801, indicating low statistical significance. This is reflected in the large *p*-value in the next column, .426, which indicates the probability that an estimate of alpha this large could have resulted from pure chance even if the true alpha were zero. The last two columns give the upper and lower bounds of the 95% confidence interval around the coefficient estimate. This confidence interval tells us that, with a probability of .95, the true alpha lies in the wide interval from −1.74 to 3.49. Thus, we cannot conclude from this particular sample, with any degree of confidence, that Google's true alpha was not zero, which would be the prediction of the CAPM.

The second line in the panel gives the estimate of Google's beta, which is 1.20. The standard error of this estimate is .215, resulting in a *t*-statistic of 5.58, and a practically zero *p*-value for the hypothesis that the true beta is in fact zero. In other words, the probability of observing an estimate this large if the true beta were zero is negligible. Another important

---

[7]The relationship between the adjusted R-square (R_A^2) and the unadjusted (R^2) with n observations and k independent variables (plus intercept) is $1 - R_A^2 = (1 - R^2)\dfrac{n-1}{n-k-1}$, and thus a greater k will result in a larger downward adjustment to R_A^2. While R^2 cannot fall when you add an additional independent variable to a regression, R_A^2 can actually fall, indicating that the explanatory power of the added variable is not enough to compensate for the extra degree of freedom it uses. The more "parsimonious" model (without the added variable) would be considered statistically superior.

TABLE 7.2	Security characteristic line for Google (S&P 500 used as market index), January 2006–December 2010

Linear Regression

Regression Statistics

R (correlation)	0.5914
R-square	0.3497
Adjusted R-square	0.3385
SE of regression	8.4585
Total number of observations	60

Regression Equation: Google (excess return) = 0.8751 + 1.2031 × S&P 500 (excess return)

	Coefficients	Standard Error	t-Statistic	p-Value	LCL	UCL
Intercept	0.8751	1.0920	0.8013	0.4262	21.7375	3.4877
S&P 500	1.2031	0.2154	5.5848	0.0000	0.6877	1.7185

LCL—Lower confidence interval (95%)
UCL—Upper confidence interval (95%)

question is whether Google's beta is significantly different from the average stock beta of 1. This hypothesis can be tested by computing the t-statistic:

$$t = \frac{\text{Estimated value} - \text{Hypothesis value}}{\text{Standard error of estimate}} = \frac{1.2031 - 1}{.2154} = .94$$

This value is considerably below the conventional threshold for statistical significance; we cannot say with confidence that Google's beta differs from 1. The 95% confidence interval for beta ranges from .69 to 1.72.

WHAT WE LEARN FROM THIS REGRESSION   The regression analysis reveals much about Google, but we must temper our conclusions by acknowledging that the tremendous volatility in stock market returns makes it difficult to derive strong statistical conclusions about the parameters of the index model, at least for individual stocks. With such noisy variables we must expect imprecise estimates; such is the reality of capital markets.

Despite these qualifications, we can safely say that Google is a cyclical stock. Its returns vary equally with or more than the overall market, as its beta is higher than the average value of 1, albeit not significantly so. Thus, we would expect Google's excess return to respond, on average, more than one-for-one with the market index. Without additional information, if we had to forecast the volatility of a portfolio that includes Google, we would use the beta estimate of 1.20 to compute the contribution of Google to portfolio variance.

Moreover, if we had to advise Google's management of the appropriate discount rate for a project that is similar in risk to its equity,[8] we would use this beta estimate in conjunction with the prevailing risk-free rate and our forecast of the expected excess return on the market index. Suppose the current T-bill rate is 2.75%, and our forecast for the market excess return is 5.5%. Then the required rate of return for an investment with the same risk as Google's equity would be

$$\text{Required rate} = \text{Risk-free rate} + \beta \times \text{Expected excess return of index}$$
$$= r_f + \beta(r_M - r_f) = 2.75 + 1.20 \times 5.5 = 9.35\%$$

[8]A word of caution: Remember that as a general rule, equity beta is greater than asset beta, because leverage increases the exposure of equity to business risk. The required rate of return on Google's *stock* would be appropriate for an investment with the same risk as Google's *equity*. In this instance, Google had virtually no debt so this issue may be moot, but this is not generally the case.

In light of the imprecision of both the market risk premium and Google's beta estimate, we would try to bring more information to bear on these estimates. For example, we would compute the betas of other firms in the industry, which ought to be similar to Google's, to sharpen our estimate of Google's systematic risk.

Finally, suppose we were asked to determine whether, given Google's positive alpha, a portfolio manager was correct in loading up a managed portfolio with Google stock over the period 2006–2010.

To answer this question, let's find the optimal position in Google that would have been prescribed by the Treynor-Black model of the previous chapter. Let us assume that the manager had an accurate estimate of Google's alpha and beta, as well as its residual standard deviation and correlation with the index (from Tables 7.1 and 7.2). We still need information about the manager's forecast for the index as we know it was *not* the actual return. Suppose the manager assumed a market-index risk premium of .6%/month (near the historical average) and correctly estimated the index standard deviation of 5.11%/month. Thus, the manager's input list would have included:

Security	Risk Premium (%)	Standard Deviation (%)	Correlation
Index	0.6	5.11	
Google	0.875 + 1.203 × 0.6 = 1.60	10.40	0.59

Using Equation 6.10 we calculate for the optimized portfolio (P):

$$w_M = .3911 \quad w_G = .6089 \quad E(R_P) = 1.21\% \quad \sigma_P = 7.69\%$$

Thus, it appears the manager would have been quite right to tilt the portfolio heavily toward Google during this period. This reflects its large positive alpha over the sample period.

We can also measure the improvement in portfolio performance. Using Equation 6.8, the Sharpe ratio of the index and the optimized portfolios based on expected returns are

$$S_M = .12 \quad S_P = .16$$

So the position in Google substantially increased the Sharpe ratio.

This exercise would not be complete without the next step, where we observe the performance of the proposed "optimal" portfolio. After all, analysts commonly use available data to construct portfolios for a future period. We put *optimal* in quotes because everyone in the profession knows that past alpha values do not predict future values. Hence, a portfolio formed solely, or even primarily, by extrapolating past alpha would never qualify as optimal. However, if we treat this alpha as though it came from security analysis, we can paint a picture of what might go on in the trenches of portfolio management.

Suppose we now observe 10 additional months of returns (January 2011–October 2011) for the S&P 500, Google, and T-bills. We test the proposed portfolio for three future periods following the data collection and analysis period: the next quarter, next semiannual period, and next 10 months. For each of these periods we compare the performance of the proposed portfolio to the passive index portfolio and to T-bills. The results are as follows:

Cumulative Returns (%) of Three Alternative Strategy Portfolios			
Portfolio	Proposed Google-S&P 500	Passive: S&P 500 Index	T-bills
2011 Q1	1.36	5.42	0.01
2011 First half	−7.35	5.01	0.01
January–October 2011	0.41	−0.35	0.01

We see that 2011 began as a good year for the market, with a half-year cumulative excess return of 5.01%. Up to this point, however, Google stock dropped and the proposed portfolio stumbled badly. Yet the next four months saw a complete reversal of fortune: The market stumbled badly, dragging its cumulative return into negative territory, while Google shined and propelled the proposed "optimal" portfolio into positive territory. It is clear that evaluating performance is fraught with enormous potential estimation error. Even a nonsense portfolio can have its day when volatility is so high. This basic fact of investment life makes portfolio performance evaluation hazardous, as we discuss in Chapter 18.

Predicting Betas

A single-index model may not be fully consistent with the CAPM and may not be a sufficiently accurate predictor of risk premiums. Still the concept of systematic versus diversifiable risk is useful. Systematic risk is approximated well by the regression equation beta and nonsystematic risk by the residual variance of the regression.

As an empirical rule, it appears that betas exhibit a statistical property called *mean reversion*. This suggests that high-β (that is, $\beta > 1$) securities tend to exhibit a lower β in the future, while low-β (that is, $\beta < 1$) securities exhibit a higher β in future periods. Researchers who desire predictions of future betas often adjust beta estimates from historical data to account for regression toward 1. For this reason, it is necessary to verify whether the estimates are already "adjusted betas."

A simple way to account for mean reversion is to forecast beta as a weighted average of the sample estimate with the value 1.

EXAMPLE 7.7

Forecast of Beta

Suppose that past data yield a beta estimate of .65. A common weighting scheme is ⅔ on the sample estimate and ⅓ on the value 1. Thus, the adjusted forecast of beta will be

$$\text{Adjusted beta} = \tfrac{2}{3} \times .65 + \tfrac{1}{3} \times 1 = .77$$

The final forecast of beta is in fact closer to 1 than the sample estimate.

A more sophisticated technique would base the weight of the sample beta on its statistical quality. A more precise estimate of beta will get a higher weight.

However, obtaining a precise statistical estimate of beta from past data on individual stocks is a formidable task, because the volatility of rates of return is so large. In particular, there is a lot of "noise" in the data due to firm-specific events. The problem is less severe with portfolios because diversification reduces firm-specific variance.

One might hope that more precise estimates of beta could be obtained by using a long time series of returns. Unfortunately, this is not a solution because betas change over time and old data can provide a misleading guide to current betas.

Two methods can help improve forecasts of beta. The first is an application of a technique that goes by the name of ARCH models.[9] ARCH models better predict variance and covariance using high-frequency (daily) historical data to identify persistent changes in variance and covariance. The second method involves an additional step where beta estimates from time series regressions are augmented by other information about the firm, for example, P/E ratios.

7.3 THE CAPM AND THE REAL WORLD

In many ways, portfolio theory and the CAPM have become accepted tools in the practitioner community. Many investment professionals think about the distinction between firm-specific and systematic risk and are comfortable with the use of beta to measure systematic risk. One

---

[9]*ARCH* stands for "autoregressive conditional heteroskedasticity." (The model was developed by Robert F. Engle, who received the 2003 Nobel Prize in Economics.) This is a fancy way of saying that the volatility (and covariance) of stocks changes over time in ways that can be at least partially predicted from past data.

extensive survey found that about three-quarters of financial managers use the CAPM when estimating the cost of capital.[10] In the money management industry, alpha is regularly computed. On the other hand, compensation of portfolio managers is rarely based on alpha or other appropriate risk-adjusted measures such as those addressed later in the text (see Chapter 18). What can we make of this?

Part of the problem clearly derives from the mixed success of the CAPM in explaining variation in rates of return across assets. Let's review some of the evidence on this score.

The CAPM was first published by Sharpe in 1964 and took the world of finance by storm. Early tests by Black, Jensen, and Scholes (1972) and Fama and MacBeth (1973) were partially supportive of the CAPM: Average returns were higher for higher-beta portfolios, but the reward for beta risk was less than predicted by the simple version of the CAPM.

While this sort of evidence against the CAPM remained largely within the ivory towers of academia, Roll's (1977) paper "A Critique of Capital Asset Pricing Tests" shook the practitioner world as well. Roll argued that the true market portfolio can never be observed. The usual stock market indexes used as proxies for the market portfolio ignore the large majority of investor wealth, for example, real estate, fixed income securities, foreign investments, and not least, the value of human capital. Without a good measure of the return on a broad measure of investor assets, the theory is *necessarily* untestable.

The publicity given the now classic "Roll's critique" resulted in popular articles such as "Is Beta Dead?" that effectively slowed the permeation of portfolio theory through the world of finance.[11] Although Roll is absolutely correct on theoretical grounds, more recent research suggests that the error introduced by using a broad market index as proxy for the true, unobserved market portfolio is perhaps not even the greatest problem of the CAPM. For example, Fama and French (1992) published a study that dealt the CAPM an even harsher blow. They found that in contradiction to the CAPM, certain characteristics of the firm, namely, size and the ratio of market to book value, were far more useful in predicting future returns than beta.

Fama and French and several others have published many follow-up studies on this topic. It seems clear from these studies (to which we will return in more detail later in the chapter) that beta does not tell the whole story of risk. There seem to be risk factors that affect security returns beyond beta's one-dimensional measurement of market sensitivity. In the next section, we introduce a theory of risk premiums that explicitly allows for multiple risk factors.

Liquidity, a different kind of risk factor, was ignored for a long time. Although first analyzed by Amihud and Mendelson as early as 1986, it is yet to be accurately measured and incorporated in portfolio management. Measuring liquidity and the premium commensurate with illiquidity is part of a larger field in financial economics, namely, market structure. We now know that trading mechanisms on stock exchanges can affect the liquidity of assets traded on these exchanges and thus significantly affect their market value.

Despite all these issues, beta is not dead. Research shows that when we use a more inclusive proxy for the market portfolio than the S&P 500 (specifically, an index that includes human capital) and allow for the fact that beta changes over time, the performance of beta in explaining security returns is enhanced (Jagannathan and Wang, 1996). We know that the CAPM is not a perfect model and that it will continue to be refined. Still, the logic of the model is compelling and captures the two key points made by all of its more sophisticated variants: first, the crucial distinction between diversifiable risk and systematic risk that cannot be avoided by diversification, and second, the fact that investors will demand a premium for bearing nondiversifiable risk. The CAPM therefore provides a useful framework for thinking rigorously about the relationship between security risk and return.

---

[10]See J. R. Graham and C. R. Harvey, "The Theory and Practice of Corporate Finance: Evidence from the Field," *Journal of Financial Economics* 61 (2001), pp. 187–243.

[11]A. Wallace, "Is Beta Dead?" *Institutional Investor* 14 (July 1980), pp. 22–30.

7.4   MULTIFACTOR MODELS AND THE CAPM

The index model allows us to decompose stock variance into systematic risk and firm-specific risk that can be diversified in large portfolios. In the index model, the return on the market portfolio summarized the aggregate impact of macro factors. In reality, however, systematic risk is not due to one source but instead derives from uncertainty in a number of economywide factors such as business-cycle risk, interest or inflation rate risk, energy price risk, and so on. It stands to reason that a more explicit representation of systematic risk, allowing stocks to exhibit different sensitivities to its various facets, would constitute a useful refinement of the single-factor model. We can expect that models that allow for several systematic factors—**multifactor models**—can provide better descriptions of security returns.

multifactor models

Models of security returns that respond to several systematic factors.

Let's illustrate with a two-factor model. Suppose the two most important macroeconomic sources of risk are the state of the business cycle reflected in returns on a broad market index such as the S&P 500 and unanticipated changes in interest rates captured by returns on a Treasury-bond portfolio. The return on any stock will respond both to sources of macro risk and to its own firm-specific influences. Therefore, we can expand the single-index model, Equation 7.3, describing the excess rate of return on stock i in some time period t as follows:

$$R_{it} = \alpha_i + \beta_{iM} R_{Mt} + \beta_{iTB} R_{TBt} + e_{it} \qquad (7.5)$$

where $\beta_{i\,TB}$ is the sensitivity of the stock's excess return to that of the T-bond portfolio and R_{TBt} is the excess return of the T-bond portfolio in month t.

How will the security market line of the CAPM generalize once we recognize multiple sources of systematic risk? Not surprisingly, a multifactor index model gives rise to a multi-factor security market line in which the risk premium is determined by the exposure to *each* systematic risk factor and by a risk premium associated with each of those factors. Such a multifactor CAPM was first presented by Merton (1973).

In the two-factor economy of Equation 7.5, the expected rate of return on a security would be the sum of three terms:

1. The risk-free rate of return.
2. The sensitivity to the market index (i.e., the market beta, β_{iM}) times the risk premium of the index, $[E(r_M) - r_f]$.
3. The sensitivity to interest rate risk (i.e., the T-bond beta, $\beta_{i\,TB}$) times the risk premium of the T-bond portfolio, $[E(r_{TB}) - r_f]$.

This assertion is expressed mathematically as a two-factor security market line for security *i:*

$$E(r_i) = r_f + \beta_{iM}[E(r_M) - r_f] + \beta_{iTB}[E(r_{TB}) - r_f] \qquad (7.6)$$

Equation 7.6 is an expansion of the simple security market line. Once we generalize the single-index SML to multiple risk sources, each with its own risk premium, the insights are similar.

EXAMPLE 7.8

A Two-Factor SML

Northeast Airlines has a market beta of 1.2 and a T-bond beta of .7. Suppose the risk premium of the market index is 6%, while that of the T-bond portfolio is 3%. Then the overall risk premium on Northeast stock is the sum of the risk premiums required as compensation for each source of systematic risk.

The portion of the risk premium attributable to market risk is the stock's exposure to that risk, 1.2, multiplied by the corresponding risk premium, 6%, or 1.2 × 6% = 7.2%. Similarly, the risk premium attributable to interest rate risk is .7 × 3% = 2.1%. The total risk premium is 7.2 + 2.1 = 9.3%. Therefore, if the risk-free rate is 4%, the expected return on the portfolio should be

4.0%	Risk-free rate
+ 7.2	+ Risk premium for exposure to market risk
+ 2.1	+ Risk premium for exposure to interest rate risk
13.3%	Total expected return

More concisely,

$$E(r) = 4\% + 1.2 \times 6\% + .7 \times 3\% = 13.3\%$$

The multifactor model clearly gives us a richer way to think about risk exposures and compensation for those exposures than the single-index model or the CAPM. But what are the relevant additional systematic factors?

Economic theory suggests factors that affect investor welfare in three possible ways: (1) factors that are correlated with prices of important consumption goods, such as housing or health care; (2) factors that are correlated with future investment opportunities, such as interest rates, return volatility, or risk premiums; and (3) factors that correlate with the general state of the economy, such as industrial production and employment. Alas, multifactor equations employing likely candidates for these theoretically plausible factors have not produced sufficient improvement over the explanatory power of the single-factor model. Instead, pioneering research by Eugene F. Fama and Kenneth French (1992) produced today's state-of-the-art approach to multifactor models.

The Fama-French Three-Factor Model

Fama and French proposed a three-factor model that has become a standard tool for empirical studies of asset returns. They add to the market-index portfolios formed on the basis of firm size and book-to-market ratio to explain average returns. These additional factors are motivated by the observations that average returns on stocks of small firms and firms with high ratios of book value of equity to market value of equity have been higher than predicted by the CAPM. This observation suggests that size and book-to-market (B/M) ratio may be *proxies* for exposures to sources of systematic risk not captured by beta and thus result in return premiums.

While a high book-to-market ratio can result from financial distress, which depresses market value relative to book value, for the most part, this group includes relatively mature firms. The latter derive a larger share of their market value from assets already in place, rather than growth opportunities. This group often is called *value stocks*. In contrast, low-B/M companies are viewed as *growth firms* whose market values derive from anticipated future cash flows, rather than from assets already in place. Considerable evidence (which we will review in the following chapter) suggests that value stocks trade at lower prices than growth stocks (or, equivalently, have offered a higher average rate of return); the differential is known as the *value premium*.

One mechanism by which a high book-to-market ratio may capture aspects of systematic risk is through the impact of large fixed assets. When the economy tanks, these assets cannot be used at full capacity, and a large share of their value may be lost. Therefore, a high B/M ratio, which can result from large investments in fixed assets, may imply higher systematic risk than indicated by historically estimated beta.

Firm size may also predict some aspects of risk. Shares of large firms may be less risky than those of small firms, other things being equal, because they are covered by more analysts, and there is more accurate information about them. With better-informed investors, prices will better reflect true value and be less susceptible to systematic as well as firm-specific fluctuations. With deeper pockets and greater debt capacity, large firms also can better withstand economic downturns. On both counts, stock in small firms will command higher risk premiums than indicated by beta alone.

Fama and French also pioneered a method to construct size and B/M factor portfolios to facilitate estimates of each factor's effect on stock returns. Their approach has since been used to construct other factor portfolios. To illustrate, we will follow the same general approach that we applied for Google earlier, but now using the more general model.

COLLECTING AND PROCESSING DATA To create portfolios that track the size and B/M factors, one can sort industrial firms by size (market capitalization or market "cap") and

TABLE 7.3	Statistics for monthly rates of return (%), January 2006–December 2010			
	Excess Return*		**Total Return**	
Security	**Average**	**Standard Deviation**	**Geometric Average**	**Cumulative Return**
T-bill	0	0	0.18	11.65
Market index†	0.26	5.44	0.30	19.51
SMB	0.34	2.46	0.31	20.70
HML	0.01	2.97	−0.03	−2.06
Google	0.94	10.40	0.60	43.17

*Total return for SMB and HML.

†Includes all NYSE, NASDAQ, and AMEX stocks.

by B/M ratio. The size premium is constructed as the difference in returns between small and large firms and is denoted by SMB ("small minus big"). Similarly, the B/M premium is calculated as the difference in returns between firms with a high versus low B/M ratio and is denoted HML ("high minus low").

Taking the difference in returns between two portfolios has an economic interpretation. The SMB return, for example, equals the return from a long position in small stocks, financed with a short position in the large stocks. Note that this is a portfolio that entails no *net* investment.[12]

Summary statistics for these portfolios in our sample period are reported in Table 7.3. We use a broad market index, the value-weighted return on all stocks traded on U.S. national exchanges (NYSE, Amex, and NASDAQ) to compute the excess return on the market portfolio.

The "returns" of the SMB and HML portfolios require careful interpretation. As noted above, these portfolios do not by themselves represent investment portfolios, as they entail zero net investment. Rather, they may be interpreted as side bets on whether one type of stock will beat another (e.g., small versus large ones for SMB).

To apply the FF three-factor portfolio to Google, we need to estimate Google's beta on each factor. To do so, we generalize regression Equation 7.3 of the single-index model and fit a multivariate regression:[13]

$$r_G - r_f = \alpha_G + \beta_M (r_M - r_f) + \beta_{HML} r_{HML} + \beta_{SMB} r_{SMB} + e_G \qquad (7.7)$$

To the extent that returns on the size (SMB) and book-to-market (HML) portfolios proxy for risk that is not fully captured by the market index, the beta coefficients on these portfolios represent exposure to systematic risks beyond the market-index beta.[14]

ESTIMATION RESULTS Both the single-index model (alternatively employing the S&P 500 Index and the broad market index) and the FF three-factor model are summarized in Table 7.4. The broad market index includes more than 4,000 stocks, while the S&P

[12]Interpreting the returns on the SMB and HML portfolios is a bit subtle because both portfolios are zero net investments, and therefore one cannot compute profit per dollar invested. For example, in the SMB portfolio, for every dollar held in small capitalization stocks, there is an offsetting short position in large capitalization stocks. The "return" for this portfolio is actually the profit on the overall position per dollar invested in the small-cap firms (or equivalently, per dollar shorted in the large-cap firms).

[13]The data for the factor portfolio are available from Kenneth French's website: **mba.tuck.dartmouth.edu/pages/faculty/ken.french/data_library.html.**

[14]When we estimate Equation 7.7, we must subtract the risk-free return from the market return but not from the returns on the SMB or HML portfolios. This is because the SMB and HML factors are *already* risk premiums, for size or book-to-market respectively. We subtract the risk-free rate from the market index return to similarly cast it as a risk premium.

TABLE 7.4	Regression statistics for alternative specifications:
	1. A Single index with S&P 500 as market proxy
	1. B Single index with broad market index (NYSE + NASDAQ + Amex)
	2. Fama-French three-factor model (broad market + SMB + HML)

Monthly returns January 2006–December 2010

Estimate	Single Index Specification		FF 3-Factor Specification with Broad Market Index
	S&P 500	**Broad Market Index**	
Correlation coefficient	0.59	0.61	0.70
Adjusted R-Square	0.34	0.36	0.47
Residual SD = Regression SE (%)	8.46	8.33	7.61
Alpha = Intercept (%)	0.88 (1.09)	0.64 (1.08)	0.62 (0.99)
Market beta	1.20 (0.21)	1.16 (0.20)	1.51 (0.21)
SMB (size) beta	–	–	−0.20 (0.44)
HML (book to market) beta	–	–	−1.33 (0.37)

Note: Standard errors in parenthesis.

500 includes only 500 of the largest U.S. stocks, in which list Google ranked fourteenth in January 2012.[15]

In this sample, the broad market index tracks Google's returns better than the S&P 500, and the three-factor model is a better specification than the one-factor model. This is reflected in three aspects of a successful specification: a higher adjusted R-square, a lower residual SD, and a smaller value of alpha. This outcome turns out to be typical, which makes a broader market index the choice of researchers and the FF model the current first-line empirical model of security returns.[16]

Google's market beta estimate is very different in the three-factor model (1.51 versus 1.20 or 1.16 in one-factor models). Moreover, this coefficient value implies high cyclicality and is significantly greater than 1: It exceeds 1 by 2.43 standard errors. The SMB beta is negative (−.20), as you would expect for a firm as large as Google, yet it is not significantly different from zero (standard error = .44). Google still exhibits a negative and significant book-to-market beta (coefficient = 1.33, standard error = .37), however, indicating that it is still a growth stock.

WHAT WE LEARN FROM THIS REGRESSION   While the FF three-factor model offers a richer and more accurate description of asset returns, applying this model requires two more forecasts of future returns, namely, for the SMB and HML portfolios. We have so far in this section been using a T-bill rate of 2.75% and a market risk premium of 5.5%. If we add to these values a forecast of 2.5% for the SMB premium and 4% for HML, the required rate for an investment with the same risk as Google's equity would be

$$E(r_G) = r_f + \beta_M[E(r_M) - r_f] + \beta_{SMB}E(r_{SMB}) + \beta_{HML}E(r_{HML})$$
$$2.75 + (1.51 \times 5.5) + (-.20 \times 2.5) + (-1.33 \times 4) = 5.24\%$$

[15]You may ask, "Why switch to another market index?" In Table 7.2 we were concerned with typical industry practice. When using the more sophisticated FF model, it is important to use a more representative index than the S&P 500, specifically one with greater representation of smaller and younger firms.

[16]The FF model is often augmented by an additional factor, usually *momentum,* which classifies stocks according to which ones have recently increased or recently decreased in price. Liquidity is also increasingly used as yet another additional factor.

which is considerably lower than the rate derived from cyclical considerations alone (i.e., single-beta models). Notice from this example that to obtain expected rates of return, the FF model requires, in addition to a forecast of the market-index return, a forecast of the returns of the SMB and HML portfolios, making the model more difficult to apply. This can be a critical issue. If such forecasts are difficult to devise, the single-factor model may be preferred even if it is less successful in explaining *past* returns.[17]

Multifactor Models and the Validity of the CAPM

The single-index CAPM fails empirical tests because its empirical representation, the single-index model, inadequately explains returns on too many securities. In short, too many statistically significant values of alpha (which should be zero) show up in single-index regressions. Despite this failure, it is still widely used in the industry.

Multifactor models such as the FF model may also be tested by the prevalence of significant alpha values. The three-factor model shows a material improvement over the single-index model in that regard. But the use of multi-index models comes at a price: They require forecasts of the additional factor returns. If forecasts of those additional factors are themselves subject to forecast error, these models will be less accurate than the theoretically inferior single-index model. Nevertheless, multifactor models have a definite appeal because it is clear that real-world risk is multifaceted.

Merton (1973) first showed that the CAPM could be extended to allow for multiple sources of systematic risk. His model results in a multifactor security market line like that of Equation 7.8 but with risk factors that relate to the extra-market sources of risk that investors wish to hedge. In this light, a reasonable interpretation of multivariate index models such as FF is that they constitute an application of the multifactor CAPM, rather than a rejection of the underlying logic of the simple model.

The original FF model has spawned a cottage industry generating new factor portfolios, including, but not limited to, momentum or liquidity factors. One expects that the marginal contributions of these additional factors will be smaller than those of the first two, SMB and HML. Still, the search for the ultimate version of the expected return-risk relationship is far from over.

7.5   ARBITRAGE PRICING THEORY

One reason for skepticism about the validity of the CAPM is the unrealistic nature of the assumptions needed to derive it. Most unappealing are assumptions 2.A–C, namely, that all investors are identical in every way but wealth and risk aversion. For this reason, as well as for its economic insights, the arbitrage pricing theory is of great interest. To understand this theory we begin with the concept of *arbitrage*.

Arbitrage is the act of exploiting mispricing of two or more securities to achieve risk-free profits. As a trivial example, consider a security that is priced differently in two markets. A long position in the cheaper market financed by a short position in the expensive market will lead to a sure profit. As investors avidly pursue this strategy, prices are forced back into alignment, so arbitrage opportunities vanish almost as quickly as they materialize.

The first to apply this concept to equilibrium security returns was Ross (1976), who developed the **arbitrage pricing theory (APT).** The APT depends on the observation that well-functioning capital markets preclude arbitrage opportunities. A violation of the APT's pricing relationships will cause extremely strong pressure to restore them even if only a limited number of investors become aware of the disequilibrium. Ross's accomplishment is to

arbitrage

Creation of riskless profits made possible by relative mispricing among securities.

arbitrage pricing theory (APT)

A theory of risk-return relationships derived from no-arbitrage considerations in large capital markets.

[17]This is a fairly common outcome: Theoretically inferior models with fewer explanatory variables often describe out-of-sample outcomes more accurately than models employing more explanatory variables. This reflects in part the tendency of some researchers to "data mine," that is, to search too aggressively for variables that help describe a sample but have no staying power out of sample. In addition, each explanatory variable of a model must be forecast to make a prediction, and each of those forecasts adds some uncertainty to the prediction.

derive the equilibrium rates of return that would prevail in a market where prices are aligned to eliminate arbitrage opportunities. The APT thus avoids the most objectionable assumptions of the CAPM.

Well-Diversified Portfolios and the APT

To illustrate how the APT works, we begin with a single-index market; generalization to multi-factor markets is straightforward. Suppose a portfolio, P, with beta of β_P, is believed to have a positive alpha. If we invest in P and add a short position in the broad market benchmark portfolio (with a beta of 1), we can hedge away the systematic risk of P and reduce overall beta to zero. We can then go even further and turn the positive-alpha, zero-beta position into a zero-net-investment position by adding an appropriate position in the risk-free asset. In all, we combine the positive-alpha P with both the benchmark and T-bills to create a costless, zero-beta "arbitrage portfolio," A, with a positive alpha. Table 7.5 shows how.

Table 7.5 shows that portfolio A with excess return $\alpha_P + e_P$ is still risky as long as the residual variance, σ_e^2 is positive. This shows that a zero-investment, zero-beta, positive-alpha portfolio is not necessarily an arbitrage opportunity; true arbitrage implies no risk. However, if P were highly diversified, its residual risk would be small. A portfolio with practically negligible residual risk is called a **well-diversified portfolio.** The difference in the scatter diagrams of any asset versus that of a well-diversified portfolio with the same beta is shown in Figure 7.5.

Portfolio A, when constructed from a *well-diversified portfolio,* is an **arbitrage portfolio.** An arbitrage portfolio is a money machine: It can generate risk-free profits with zero net investment. Therefore, investors who succeed in constructing one will scale it up as much as they can, financing with as much leverage and/or as many short positions as available.

well-diversified portfolio

A portfolio sufficiently diversified that nonsystematic risk is negligible.

arbitrage portfolio

A zero-net-investment, risk-free portfolio with a positive return.

EXAMPLE 7.9

Constructing an Arbitrage Portfolio

Suppose the benchmark, M, in Table 7.5 is the observed, broad market index. Imagine that on December 31, 2015, a portfolio manager possessed the following predictions based on security and macro analyses:

1. The risk-free rate on T-bills over the next year is estimated at 2.2%.

2. The return on the market benchmark is estimated at 5.0%.

3. A highly diversified portfolio P, is composed of large-capitalization stocks and is believed to be *underpriced.* Its expected return is forecast at 6.0%.

4. Portfolio P's beta against the benchmark is estimated at .95, which leads to the following calculation for its alpha: $6.0\% = 2.2\% + \alpha + .95(5.0\% - 2.2)$; $\alpha = 1.14\%$.

Therefore, we set $w_P = 1$, $w_M = -.95$, and $w_f = -.05$. Arbitrage portfolio A has no residual risk because it is well diversified, and it has no systematic risk because it has zero beta. Yet its alpha is positive: $\alpha_A = 1.14\%$.

TABLE 7.5 Steps to convert a well-diversified portfolio into an arbitrage portfolio

Portfolio Weight*	In Asset	Contribution to Excess Return
$w_P = 1$	Portfolio P	$w_P(\alpha_P + \beta_P R_M + e_P) = \alpha_P + \beta_P R_M + e_P$
$w_M = -\beta_P$	Benchmark	$w_M R_M = -\beta_P R_M$
$w_f = \beta_P - 1$	Risk-free asset	$w_f \times 0 = 0$
$\Sigma w = 0$	Portfolio A	$\alpha_P + e_P$

*When alpha is negative, you would reverse the signs of each portfolio weight to achieve a portfolio A with positive alpha and no net investment.

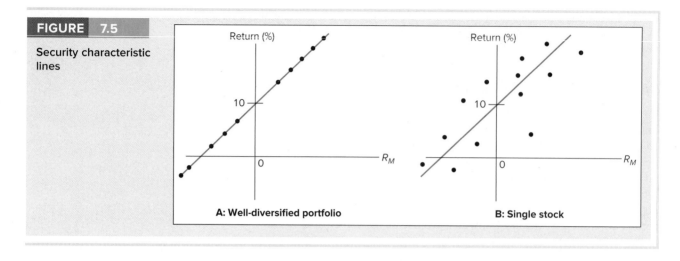

FIGURE 7.5

Security characteristic lines

A: Well-diversified portfolio

B: Single stock

Example 7.9 shows how to construct an arbitrage portfolio from a mispriced well-diversified portfolio. But it leaves us with an important question: How diversified must a portfolio be to be "well diversified"? For example, is even the highly diversified S&P 500 a well-diversified portfolio? Table 7.6 shows the weight of the 10 largest stocks in the S&P 500. While these firms are only 2% of the firms in the index, they account for almost 20% of the market capitalization, and their weights in the index are far from negligible. We will evaluate the S&P relative to a comprehensive market benchmark comprising all stocks traded on the NYSE, NASDAQ, and Amex markets.

We can estimate the residual risk of the S&P 500 relative to this comprehensive benchmark from a regression of its monthly returns against the benchmark over the prediction period (January 1, 2006, to December 31, 2010). The essential regression output is displayed in Table 7.7. Notice that the (annualized) standard deviation of the regression residuals, called the *standard error of the regression,* was 2.07%. Is this residual SD small enough for us to deem the S&P 500 "well diversified"?

To answer the question, we recognize that investors who consider an arbitrage strategy must invest their existing wealth *somewhere*. The risk of their alternative portfolio is therefore relevant to the discussion. Obviously, the lowest-risk investment would be to roll over T-bills. A measure of the risk of this strategy is the uncertainty of its real rate of return over the prediction period.[18] Table 7.8 suggests that the annual SD of the real rate from rolling over bills is in the range of .5%–1.5% per year depending on the sample period.

TABLE 7.6	Ten largest capitalization stocks in the S&P 500 and their weights in the index (February 2015)		
	Weight (%)		**Weight (%)**
Apple (AAPL)	4.05	Wells Fargo (WFC)	1.39
ExxonMobil (XOM)	2.04	General Electric (GE)	1.35
Microsoft (MSFT)	1.93	Procter & Gamble (PG)	1.24
Johnson & Johnson (JNJ)	1.52	JP Morgan Chase (JPM)	1.19
Berkshire Hathaway (BRK.B)	1.45	Pfizer (PFE)	1.17
Total for 10 largest firms	17.33		

[18]Obviously, five-year TIPS would carry a practically zero risk to the real rate. But we deal here with active portfolio managers who continuously rebalance their portfolios and must maintain considerable liquidity. For very short holding periods, TIPS would not be practical for these investors.

TABLE 7.7 Regression statistics of the S&P 500 portfolio on the benchmark portfolio, January 2006–December 2010

Linear Regression

Regression Statistics

R	0.9933	
R-square	0.9866	
Adjusted R-square	0.9864	**Annualized**
Regression SE	0.5968	2.067
Total number of observations	60	

S&P 500 = −0.1909 + 0.9337* Benchmark

	Coefficients	Standard Error	t-stat	p-level
Intercept	−0.1909	0.0771	−2.4752	0.0163
Benchmark	0.9337	0.0143	65.3434	0.0000

TABLE 7.8 Annual standard deviation of the real, inflation, and nominal rates

Period	Real Rate	Inflation Rate	Nominal Rate
1/1/2006–12/31/2010	1.46	1.46	0.61
1/1/1996–12/31/2000	0.57	0.54	0.17
1/1/1986–12/31/1990	0.86	0.83	0.37

Our question then comes down to this: What would be the marginal increase in risk from adding an arbitrage portfolio with an SD of about 2% per year to a portfolio with an SD of .5%–1.5% per year? Because the two rates are uncorrelated, the variance of the portfolio will be the sum of the variances. The SD of this complete portfolio minus the SD of the T-bill portfolio is the *marginal* risk of the S&P 500 in its use as an arbitrage portfolio. The following table shows some examples of the marginal risk of the arbitrage portfolio, first treating T-bills as the initial portfolio to which the arbitrage portfolio is added (with three assumptions for the SD of its real return) and then treating the comprehensive benchmark portfolio as the initial position, with an assumed SD = 20%.

SD of Real Rate on Initial Portfolio	SD of Total Portfolio	Marginal Risk
0.5% (T-bills)	$(.005^2 + .0207^2)^{1/2} = 2.13\%$	1.63%
1.0 (T-bills)	2.30	1.30
1.5 (T-bills)	2.56	1.06
20.0 (benchmark)	20.11	0.11

There is no widely accepted threshold for the acceptable marginal risk of an arbitrage portfolio in a practical application. Nevertheless, the marginal risk in the first three lines of the table, which is just about the same as the SD of the real rate on bills, may well be above the appropriate threshold. Moreover, an alpha of 2% per year in this example is not even decisively statistically significant. We learn from this exercise that well-diversified portfolios are not easy to construct, and arbitrage opportunities are likely few and far between. On the other hand, when the arbitrage portfolio is added to the risky benchmark portfolio, the marginal increase in overall standard deviation is minimal.

We are now ready to derive the APT. Our argument follows from Example 7.9. Investors, however few, will invest large amounts in any arbitrage portfolio they can identify. This will entail large-scale purchases of positive-alpha portfolios or large-scale shorting of negative-alpha portfolios. These actions will move the prices of component securities until alpha disappears. In the end, when alphas of all well-diversified portfolios are driven to zero, their return equations become

$$r_P = r_f + \beta_P(r_M - r_f) + e_P \tag{7.8}$$

Taking the expectations in Equation 7.8 results in the familiar CAPM mean–beta equation:

$$E(r_P) = r_f + \beta_P[E(r_M) - r_f] \tag{7.9}$$

For portfolios such as the S&P 500 that shed *most* residual risk, we can still expect buying and selling pressure to drive their alpha close to zero. If alphas of portfolios with very small residual risk are near zero, then even less diversified portfolios will tend to have small alpha values. Thus, the APT implies a hierarchy of certainty about alphas of portfolios, based on the degree of diversification.

The APT and the CAPM

Why did we need so many restrictive assumptions to derive the CAPM when the APT seems to arrive at the expected return–beta relationship with seemingly fewer and less objectionable assumptions? The answer is simple: Strictly speaking, the APT applies only to well-diversified portfolios. Absence of riskless arbitrage alone cannot guarantee that, in equilibrium, the expected return–beta relationship will hold for any and all assets.

With additional effort, however, one can use the APT to show that the relationship must hold approximately even for individual assets. The essence of the proof is that if the expected return–beta relationship were violated by many individual securities, it would be virtually impossible for all well-diversified portfolios to satisfy the relationship. So the relationship must *almost* surely hold true for individual securities.

We say "almost" because, according to the APT, there is no guarantee that *all* individual assets will lie on the SML. If only a few securities violated the SML, their effect on well-diversified portfolios could conceivably be negligible. In this sense, it is possible that the SML relationship is violated for some securities. If many securities violate the expected return–beta relationship, however, the relationship will no longer hold for well-diversified portfolios comprising these securities, and arbitrage opportunities will be available.

The APT serves many of the same functions as the CAPM. It gives us a benchmark for fair rates of return that can be used for capital budgeting, security valuation, or performance evaluation of managed portfolios. Moreover, the APT highlights the crucial distinction between nondiversifiable risk (systematic or factor risk) that requires a reward in the form of a risk premium and diversifiable risk that does not.

The bottom line is that neither of these theories dominates the other. The APT is more general in that it gets us to the expected return–beta relationship without requiring the most unrealistic assumptions of the CAPM, particularly homogeneous expectations and the reliance on the market portfolio. The latter improves the prospects for testing the APT. But the CAPM is more general in that it applies to all assets without reservation. The good news is that both theories agree on the expected return–beta relationship.

It is worth noting that because past tests of the mean–beta relationship examined the rates of return on highly diversified portfolios, they actually came closer to testing the APT than the CAPM. Thus, it appears that econometric concerns, too, favor the APT.

Multifactor Generalization of the APT and CAPM

So far, we've examined the APT in a one-factor world. In reality, there are several sources of systematic risk such as uncertainty in the business cycle, interest rates, energy prices, and so on. Presumably, exposure to any of these factors will affect a stock's appropriate expected return. We can use a multifactor version of the APT to accommodate these multiple sources of risk.

Expanding the single-factor model of Equation 7.8 to a two-factor model:

$$R_i = \alpha_i + \beta_{i1}R_{M1} + \beta_{i2}R_{M2} + e_i \qquad (7.10)$$

where R_{M1} and R_{M2} are the excess returns on portfolios that represent the two systematic factors. Factor 1 might be, for example, unanticipated changes in industrial production, while factor 2 might represent unanticipated changes in short-term interest rates. We assume again that there are many securities available with any combination of betas. This implies that we can form well-diversified **factor portfolios** with a beta of 1 on one factor and zero on all others. Thus, a factor portfolio with a beta of 1 on the first factor will have a rate of return of R_{M1}; a factor portfolio with a beta of 1 on the second factor will have a rate of return of R_{M2}; and so on. Factor portfolios can serve as the benchmark portfolios for a multifactor generalization of the security market line relationship.

factor portfolio

A well-diversified portfolio constructed to have a beta of 1 on one factor and a beta of zero on any other factor.

> **EXAMPLE 7.10**
>
> *Multifactor SML*
>
> Suppose the two factor portfolios, here called portfolios 1 and 2, have expected returns $E(r_1) = 10\%$ and $E(r_2) = 12\%$. Suppose further that the risk-free rate is 4%. The risk premium on the first factor portfolio is therefore 6%, while that on the second factor portfolio is 8%.
>
> Now consider an arbitrary well-diversified portfolio (P), with beta on the first factor, $\beta_{P1} = .5$, and on the second factor, $\beta_{P2} = .75$. The multifactor APT states that the portfolio risk premium must equal the sum of the risk premiums required as compensation to investors for each source of systematic risk. The risk premium attributable to risk factor 1 is the portfolio's exposure to factor 1, β_{P1}, times the risk premium earned on the first factor portfolio, $E(r_1) - r_f$. Therefore, the portion of portfolio P's risk premium that is compensation for its exposure to the first risk factor is $\beta_{P1}[E(r_1) - r_f] = .5(10\% - 4\%) = 3\%$, while the risk premium attributable to risk factor 2 is $\beta_{P2}[E(r_2) - r_f] = .75(12\% - 4\%) = 6\%$. The total risk premium on the portfolio, therefore, should be $3 + 6 = 9\%$, and the total return on the portfolio should be 13%.
>
> | | |
> |---|---|
> | 4% | Risk-free rate |
> | + 3% | Risk premium for exposure to factor 1 |
> | + 6% | Risk premium for exposure to factor 2 |
> | 13% | Total expected return |

Suppose portfolio P of Example 7.10 actually has an expected excess return of 11% and therefore a positive alpha of 2%. We can generalize the methodology of Table 7.5 to construct an arbitrage portfolio for this two-factor problem. Table 7.9 shows how. Because P is well diversified, e_P must be small, and the excess return on the zero-investment, zero-beta portfolio A is just $\alpha_P = 2\%$.

Here, too, extensive trading by arbitrageurs will eliminate completely alphas of well-diversified portfolios. We conclude that, in general, the APT hierarchy of possible alpha values, declining with the extent of portfolio diversification, applies to any multifactor market. In the absence of private information from security and macro analyses, investors and corporate officers must use the multifactor SML equation (with zero alpha) to determine the expected rates on securities and the required rates of return on the firm's projects.

> **CONCEPT check 7.6** Using the factor portfolios of Example 7.10, find the fair rate of return on a security with $\beta_1 = .2$ and $\beta_2 = 1.4$.

Estimating the Index Model

The spreadsheet below contains monthly returns for a small sample of stocks during the height of the financial crisis in 2008–2009. A related workbook (available within Connect) contains spreadsheets that show raw returns, risk premiums, and beta coefficients for the stocks in the Dow Jones Industrial Average. The security characteristic lines are estimated with five years of monthly returns.

	A	B	C	D	E	F
1	Rates of Return					
2	**Month**	**Ford**	**Honda**	**Toyota**	**S&P 500**	**T-bills**
3						
4	Dec-08	−18.34	23.02	−2.95	−8.31	0.09
5	Nov-08	−14.87	−25.44	3.71	0.97	0.02
6	Oct-08	22.83	−26.04	−17.07	−7.04	0.08
7	Sep-08	−57.88	−13.77	−11.32	−16.67	0.15
8	Aug-08	16.59	−29.61	−4.23	−9.54	0.12
9	Jul-08	−7.08	−4.92	4.11	1.40	0.15
10	Jun-08	−0.21	−11.01	−8.46	−1.07	0.17

Excel Questions

1. What were the betas of Ford, Toyota, and Honda?

2. In light of each firm's exposure to the financial crisis, does the value for Ford compared to Honda and Toyota make sense to you?

TABLE 7.9 Constructing an arbitrage portfolio with two systematic factors

Portfolio Weight	In Asset	Contribution to Excess Return
1	Portfolio P	$\alpha_P + \beta_{P1}R_1 + \beta_{P2}R_2 + e_P$
$-\beta_{P1} = -0.5$	Factor portfolio 1	$-\beta_{P1}R_1$
$-\beta_{P2} = -0.75$	Factor portfolio 2	$-\beta_{P2}R_2$
$\beta_{P1} + \beta_{P1} - 1 = 0.25$	Risk-free asset	0
Total = 1	Portfolio A	$\alpha_P + e_P = 2\% + e_P$

SUMMARY

- The CAPM assumes investors are rational, single-period planners who agree on a common input list from security analysis and seek mean-variance optimal portfolios.
- The CAPM assumes ideal security markets in the sense that (*a*) markets are large and investors are price takers, (*b*) there are no taxes or transaction costs, (*c*) all risky assets are publicly traded, and (*d*) any amount can be borrowed and lent at a fixed, risk-free rate. These assumptions mean that all investors will hold identical risky portfolios. The CAPM implies that, in equilibrium, the market portfolio is the unique mean-variance efficient tangency portfolio, which indicates that a passive strategy is efficient.
- The market portfolio is a value-weighted portfolio. Each security is held in a proportion equal to its market value divided by the total market value of all securities. The risk premium on the market portfolio is proportional to its variance, σ_M^2 and to the risk aversion of the average investor.

- The CAPM implies that the risk premium on any individual asset or portfolio is the product of the risk premium of the market portfolio and the asset's beta. The security market line shows the return demanded by investors as a function of the beta of their investment. This expected return is a benchmark for evaluating investment performance.

- In a single-index security market, once an index is specified, a security beta can be estimated from a regression of the security's excess return on the index's excess return. This regression line is called the security characteristic line (SCL). The intercept of the SCL, called alpha, represents the average excess return on the security when the index excess return is zero. The CAPM implies that alphas should be zero.

- The CAPM and the security market line can be used to establish benchmarks for evaluation of investment performance or to determine appropriate discount rates for capital budgeting applications. They are also used in regulatory proceedings concerning the "fair" rate of return for regulated industries.

- The CAPM is usually implemented as a single-factor model, with all systematic risk summarized by the return on a broad market index. However, multifactor generalizations of the basic model may be specified to accommodate multiple sources of systematic risk. In such multifactor extensions of the CAPM, the risk premium of any security is determined by its sensitivity to each systematic risk factor as well as the risk premium associated with that source of risk.

- There are two general approaches to finding extra-market systematic risk factors. One is characteristics based and looks for factors that are empirically associated with high average returns and so may be proxies for relevant measures of systematic risk. The other focuses on factors that are plausibly important sources of risk to wide segments of investors and may thus command risk premiums.

- An arbitrage opportunity arises when the disparity between two or more security prices enables investors to construct a zero net investment portfolio that will yield a sure profit. The presence of arbitrage opportunities and the resulting volume of trades will create pressure on security prices that will persist until prices reach levels that preclude arbitrage. Only a few investors need to become aware of arbitrage opportunities to trigger this process because of the large volume of trades in which they will engage.

- When securities are priced so that there are no arbitrage opportunities, the market satisfies the no-arbitrage condition. Price relationships that satisfy the no-arbitrage condition are important because we expect them to hold in real-world markets.

- Portfolios are called *well diversified* if they include a large number of securities in such proportions that the residual or diversifiable risk of the portfolio is negligible.

- In a single-factor security market, all well-diversified portfolios must satisfy the expected return–beta relationship of the SML in order to satisfy the no-arbitrage condition. If all well-diversified portfolios satisfy the expected return–beta relationship, then all but a small number of securities also must satisfy this relationship.

- The APT implies the same expected return–beta relationship as the CAPM yet does not require that all investors be mean-variance optimizers. The price of this generality is that the APT does not guarantee this relationship for all securities at all times.

- A multifactor APT generalizes the single-factor model to accommodate several sources of systematic risk.

---

alpha, 199
arbitrage, 214
arbitrage portfolio, 215
arbitrage pricing theory
  (APT), 214
capital asset pricing model
  (CAPM), 193

expected return–beta
  relationship, 197
factor portfolio, 219
market portfolio (*M*), 194
multifactor models, 210
mutual fund theorem, 195

security characteristic line
  (SCL), 203
security market line
  (SML), 198
well-diversified
  portfolio, 215

KEY TERMS

KEY FORMULAS

CAPM: Market portfolio risk premium is proportional to average risk aversion and market risk:

$$E(r_M) - r_f = \bar{A}\sigma_M^2$$

SML: Expected return as a function of systematic risk:

$$E(r_i) = r_f + \beta_i[E(r_M) - r_f]$$

The index model in realized returns:

$$r_{it} - r_{ft} = \alpha_i + \beta_i(r_{Mt} - r_{ft}) + e_{it}$$

The two-index model in realized excess returns:

$$R_{it} = \alpha_i + \beta_{iM}R_{Mt} + \beta_{iTB}R_{TBt} + e_{it}$$

The two-factor SML (where TB is the second factor):

$$E(r_i) = r_f + \beta_{iM}[E(r_M) - r_f] + \beta_{iTB}[E(r_{TB}) - r_f]$$

The Fama-French three-factor model in realized returns:

$$r_i - r_f = \alpha_i + \beta_M(r_M - r_f) + \beta_{HML}r_{HML} + \beta_{SMB}r_{SMB} + e_i$$

Instructions to construct arbitrage portfolios for single- and two-factor markets are shown in Tables 7.5 and 7.9.

PROBLEM SETS

 Select problems are available in McGraw-Hill's *Connect*. Please see the Supplements section of the book's frontmatter for more information.

1. Suppose investors believe that the standard deviation of the market-index portfolio has increased by 50%. What does the CAPM imply about the effect of this change on the required rate of return on Google's investment projects?   *(LO 7-1)*

2. Consider the statement: "If we can identify a portfolio that beats the S&P 500 Index portfolio, then we should reject the single-index CAPM." Do you agree or disagree? Explain.   *(LO 7-1)*

3. Are the following true or false? Explain.   *(LO 7-5)*
   a. Stocks with a beta of zero offer an expected rate of return of zero.
   b. The CAPM implies that investors require a higher return to hold highly volatile securities.
   c. You can construct a portfolio with a beta of .75 by investing .75 of the investment budget in T-bills and the remainder in the market portfolio.

4. Here are data on two companies. The T-bill rate is 4% and the market risk premium is 6%.

Company	$1 Discount Store	Everything $5
Forecast return	12%	11%
Standard deviation of returns	8%	10%
Beta	1.5	1.0

What would be the expected rate of return for each company, according to the capital asset pricing model (CAPM)?   *(LO 7-1)*

5. Characterize each company in the previous problem as underpriced, overpriced, or properly priced. *(LO 7-2)*

6. What is the expected rate of return for a stock that has a beta of 1 if the expected return on the market is 15%? *(LO 7-2)*
   a. 15%.
   b. More than 15%.
   c. Cannot be determined without the risk-free rate.

7. Kaskin, Inc., stock has a beta of 1.2 and Quinn, Inc., stock has a beta of .6. Which of the following statements is *most* accurate? *(LO 7-1)*
   a. The expected rate of return will be higher for the stock of Kaskin, Inc., than that of Quinn, Inc.
   b. The stock of Kaskin, Inc., has more total risk than Quinn, Inc.
   c. The stock of Quinn, Inc., has more systematic risk than that of Kaskin, Inc.

8. Which of the following statements is *true?* Explain. *(LO 7-1)*
   a. It is possible that the APT is valid and the CAPM is not.
   b. It is possible that the CAPM is valid and the APT is not.

9. What must be the beta of a portfolio with $E(r_P) = 20\%$, if $r_f = 5\%$ and $E(r_M) = 15\%$? *(LO 7-2)*

10. The market price of a security is $40. Its expected rate of return is 13%. The risk-free rate is 7%, and the market risk premium is 8%. What will the market price of the security be if its beta doubles (and all other variables remain unchanged)? Assume the stock is expected to pay a constant dividend in perpetuity. *(LO 7-2)*

11. You are a consultant to a large manufacturing corporation considering a project with the following net after-tax cash flows (in millions of dollars):

Years from Now	After-Tax CF
0	−20
1–9	10
10	20

    The project's beta is 1.7. Assuming $r_f = 9\%$ and $E(r_M) = 19\%$, what is the net present value of the project? What is the highest possible beta estimate for the project before its NPV becomes negative? *(LO 7-2)*

12. Consider the following table, which gives a security analyst's expected return on two stocks for two particular market returns: *(LO 7-2)*

Market Return	Aggressive Stock	Defensive Stock
5%	2%	3.5%
20	32	14

    a. What are the betas of the two stocks?
    b. What is the expected rate of return on each stock if the market return is equally likely to be 5% or 20%?
    c. If the T-bill rate is 8%, and the market return is equally likely to be 5% or 20%, draw the SML for this economy.
    d. Plot the two securities on the SML graph. What are the alphas of each?
    e. What hurdle rate should be used by the management of the aggressive firm for a project with the risk characteristics of the defensive firm's stock?

If the simple CAPM is valid, which of the situations in Problems 13–19 below are possible? Explain. Consider each situation independently.

13.

Portfolio	Expected Return	Beta
A	20%	1.4
B	25	1.2

(LO 7-1)

14.

Portfolio	Expected Return	Standard Deviation
A	30%	35%
B	40	25

(LO 7-1)

15.

Portfolio	Expected Return	Standard Deviation
Risk-free	10%	0%
Market	18	24
A	16	12

(LO 7-1)

16.

Portfolio	Expected Return	Standard Deviation
Risk-free	10%	0%
Market	18	24
A	20	22

(LO 7-1)

17.

Portfolio	Expected Return	Beta
Risk-free	10%	0
Market	18	1.0
A	16	1.5

(LO 7-1)

18.

Portfolio	Expected Return	Beta
Risk-free	10%	0
Market	18	1.0
A	16	0.9

(LO 7-1)

19.

Portfolio	Expected Return	Standard Deviation
Risk-free	10%	0%
Market	18	24
A	16	22

(LO 7-1)

Ⴘ

Templates and spreadsheets are available in Connect

20. Go to Connect and link to Chapter 7 materials, where you will find a spreadsheet with monthly returns for GM, Ford, and Toyota, the S&P 500, and Treasury bills. *(LO 7-1)*
    a. Estimate the index model for each firm over the full five-year period. Compare the betas of each firm.
    b. Now estimate the betas for each firm using only the first two years of the sample and then using only the last two years. How stable are the beta estimates obtained from these shorter subperiods?

In Problems 21–23 below, assume the risk-free rate is 8% and the expected rate of return on the market is 18%.

21. A share of stock is now selling for $100. It will pay a dividend of $9 per share at the end of the year. Its beta is 1. What do investors expect the stock to sell for at the end of the year? *(LO 7-2)*

22. I am buying a firm with an expected perpetual cash flow of $1,000 but am unsure of its risk. If I think the beta of the firm is zero, when the beta is really 1, how much *more* will I offer for the firm than it is truly worth? *(LO 7-2)*

23. A stock has an expected return of 6%. What is its beta? *(LO 7-2)*

24. Two investment advisers are comparing performance. One averaged a 19% return and the other a 16% return. However, the beta of the first adviser was 1.5, while that of the second was 1. *(LO 7-2)*
    a. Can you tell which adviser was a better selector of individual stocks (aside from the issue of general movements in the market)?
    b. If the T-bill rate were 6% and the market return during the period were 14%, which adviser would be the superior stock selector?
    c. What if the T-bill rate were 3% and the market return 15%?

25. Suppose the yield on short-term government securities (perceived to be risk-free) is about 4%. Suppose also that the expected return required by the market for a portfolio with a beta of 1 is 12%. According to the capital asset pricing model: *(LO 7-2)*
    a. What is the expected return on the market portfolio?
    b. What would be the expected return on a zero-beta stock?
    c. Suppose you consider buying a share of stock at a price of $40. The stock is expected to pay a dividend of $3 next year and to sell then for $41. The stock risk has been evaluated at $\beta = -.5$. Is the stock overpriced or underpriced?

26. Based on current dividend yields and expected capital gains, the expected rates of return on portfolios A and B are 11% and 14%, respectively. The beta of A is .8 while that of B is 1.5. The T-bill rate is currently 6%, while the expected rate of return of the S&P 500 Index is 12%. The standard deviation of portfolio A is 10% annually, while that of B is 31%, and that of the index is 20%. *(LO 7-2)*
    a. If you currently hold a market-index portfolio, would you choose to add either of these portfolios to your holdings? Explain.
    b. If instead you could invest *only* in bills and one of these portfolios, which would you choose?

27. Consider the following data for a one-factor economy. All portfolios are well diversified.

Portfolio	E(r)	Beta
A	10%	1.0
F	4	0

Suppose another portfolio E is well diversified with a beta of 2/3 and expected return of 9%. Would an arbitrage opportunity exist? If so, what would the arbitrage strategy be? *(LO 7-4)*

28. Assume both portfolios A and B are well diversified, that $E(r_A) = 14\%$ and $E(r_B) = 14.8\%$. If the economy has only one factor, and $\beta_A = 1$ while $\beta_B = 1.1$, what must be the risk-free rate?   *(LO 7-4)*

29. Assume a market index represents the common factor and all stocks in the economy have a beta of 1. Firm-specific returns all have a standard deviation of 30%.

    Suppose an analyst studies 20 stocks and finds that one-half have an alpha of 3%, and one-half have an alpha of −3%. The analyst then buys $1 million of an equally weighted portfolio of the positive-alpha stocks and sells short $1 million of an equally weighted portfolio of the negative-alpha stocks.   *(LO 7-4)*

    a. What is the expected profit (in dollars), and what is the standard deviation of the analyst's profit?

    b. How does your answer change if the analyst examines 50 stocks instead of 20? 100 stocks?

30. If the APT is to be a useful theory, the number of systematic factors in the economy must be small. Why?   *(LO 7-4)*

31. The APT itself does not provide information on the factors that one might expect to determine risk premiums. How should researchers decide which factors to investigate? Is industrial production a reasonable factor to test for a risk premium? Why or why not?   *(LO 7-3)*

32. Suppose two factors are identified for the U.S. economy: the growth rate of industrial production, IP, and the inflation rate, IR. IP is expected to be 4% and IR 6%. A stock with a beta of 1 on IP and .4 on IR currently is expected to provide a rate of return of 14%. If industrial production actually grows by 5%, while the inflation rate turns out to be 7%, what is your best guess for the rate of return on the stock?   *(LO 7-3)*

33. Suppose there are two independent economic factors, M_1 and M_2. The risk-free rate is 7%, and all stocks have independent firm-specific components with a standard deviation of 50%. Portfolios A and B are both well diversified.

Portfolio	Beta on M_1	Beta on M_2	Expected Return (%)
A	1.8	2.1	40
B	2.0	20.5	10

What is the expected return–beta relationship in this economy?   *(LO 7-5)*

Challenge

34. As a finance intern at Pork Products, Jennifer Wainwright's assignment is to come up with fresh insights concerning the firm's cost of capital. She decides that this would be a good opportunity to try out the new material on the APT that she learned last semester. As such, she decides that three promising factors would be (i) the return on a broad-based index such as the S&P 500; (ii) the level of interest rates, as represented by the yield to maturity on 10-year Treasury bonds; and (iii) the price of hogs, which are particularly important to her firm. Her plan is to find the beta of Pork Products against each of these factors and to estimate the risk premium associated with exposure to each factor. Comment on Jennifer's choice of factors. Which are most promising with respect to the likely impact on her firm's cost of capital? Can you suggest improvements to her specification?   *(LO 7-3)*

35. Suppose the market can be described by the following three sources of systematic risk. Each factor in the following table has a mean value of zero (so factor values represent realized surprises relative to prior expectations), and the risk premiums associated with each source of systematic risk are given in the last column.

Systematic Factor	Risk Premium
Industrial production, IP	6%
Interest rates, INT	2
Credit risk, CRED	4

The excess return, R, on a particular stock is described by the following equation that relates realized returns to surprises in the three systematic factors:

$$R = 6\% + 1.0 \text{ IP} + .5 \text{ INT} + .75 \text{ CRED} + e$$

Find the equilibrium expected excess return on this stock using the APT. Is the stock overpriced or underpriced? *(LO 7-3)*

CFA Problems

1. Which of the following statements about the security market line (SML) are *true?* *(LO 7-2)*
   a. The SML provides a benchmark for evaluating expected investment performance.
   b. The SML leads all investors to invest in the same portfolio of risky assets.
   c. The SML is a graphic representation of the relationship between expected return and beta.
   d. Properly valued assets plot exactly on the SML.

2. Karen Kay, a portfolio manager at Collins Asset Management, is using the capital asset pricing model for making recommendations to her clients. Her research department has developed the information shown in the following exhibit. *(LO 7-2)*

Forecasted Returns, Standard Deviations, and Betas			
	Forecasted Return	Standard Deviation	Beta
Stock X	14.0%	36%	0.8
Stock Y	17.0	25	1.5
Market index	14.0	15	1.0
Risk-free rate	5.0		

   a. Calculate expected return and alpha for each stock.
   b. Identify and justify which stock would be more appropriate for an investor who wants to:
      i. Add this stock to a well-diversified equity portfolio.
      ii. Hold this stock as a single-stock portfolio.

3. Joan McKay is a portfolio manager for a bank trust department. McKay meets with two clients, Kevin Murray and Lisa York, to review their investment objectives. Each client expresses an interest in changing his or her individual investment objectives. Both clients currently hold well-diversified portfolios of risky assets. *(LO 7-1)*
   a. Murray wants to increase the expected return of his portfolio. State what action McKay should take to achieve Murray's objective. Justify your response in the context of the capital market line.
   b. York wants to reduce the risk exposure of her portfolio but does not want to engage in borrowing or lending activities to do so. State what action McKay should take to achieve York's objective. Justify your response in the context of the security market line.

4. Jeffrey Bruner, CFA, uses the capital asset pricing model (CAPM) to help identify mispriced securities. A consultant suggests Bruner use arbitrage pricing theory (APT) instead. In comparing CAPM and APT, the consultant made the following arguments:
   a. Both the CAPM and APT require a mean-variance efficient market portfolio.
   b. The CAPM assumes that one specific factor explains security returns but APT does not.

   State whether each of the consultant's arguments is correct or incorrect. Indicate, for each incorrect argument, why the argument is incorrect. *(LO 7-5)*

5. The security market line depicts: *(LO 7-2)*
   a. A security's expected return as a function of its systematic risk.
   b. The market portfolio as the optimal portfolio of risky securities.

  c. The relationship between a security's return and the return on an index.

  d. The complete portfolio as a combination of the market portfolio and the risk-free asset.

6. According to CAPM, the expected rate of return of a portfolio with a beta of 1 and an alpha of 0 is: *(LO 7-2)*

  a. Between r_M and r_f.

  b. The risk-free rate, r_f.

  c. $\beta \, (r_M - r_f)$.

  d. The expected return on the market, r_M.

The following table (for CFA Problems 7 and 8) shows risk and return measures for two portfolios.

Portfolio	Average Annual Rate of Return	Standard Deviation	Beta
R	11%	10%	0.5
S&P 500	14%	12%	1.0

7. When plotting portfolio *R* on the preceding table relative to the SML, portfolio *R* lies: *(LO 7-2)*

  a. On the SML.

  b. Below the SML.

  c. Above the SML.

  d. Insufficient data given.

8. When plotting portfolio *R* relative to the capital market line, portfolio *R* lies: *(LO 7-2)*

  a. On the CML.

  b. Below the CML.

  c. Above the CML.

  d. Insufficient data given.

9. Briefly explain whether investors should expect a higher return from holding portfolio *A* versus portfolio *B* under capital asset pricing theory (CAPM). Assume that both portfolios are fully diversified. *(LO 7-2)*

	Portfolio A	Portfolio B
Systematic risk (beta)	1.0	1.0
Specific risk for each individual security	High	Low

10. Assume that both *X* and *Y* are well-diversified portfolios and the risk-free rate is 8%.

Portfolio	Expected Return	Beta
X	16%	1.00
Y	12%	0.25

In this situation you could conclude that portfolios *X* and *Y:* *(LO 7-4)*

  a. Are in equilibrium.

  b. Offer an arbitrage opportunity.

  c. Are both underpriced.

  d. Are both fairly priced.

11. According to the theory of arbitrage: *(LO 7-4)*
    a. High-beta stocks are consistently overpriced.
    b. Low-beta stocks are consistently overpriced.
    c. Positive alpha investment opportunities will quickly disappear.
    d. Rational investors will pursue arbitrage consistent with their risk tolerance.

12. A zero-investment well-diversified portfolio with a positive alpha could arise if: *(LO 7-5)*
    a. The expected return of the portfolio equals zero.
    b. The capital market line is tangent to the opportunity set.
    c. The law of one price remains unviolated.
    d. A risk-free arbitrage opportunity exists.

13. An investor takes as large a position as possible when an equilibrium price relationship is violated. This is an example of: *(LO 7-4)*
    a. A dominance argument.
    b. The mean-variance efficient frontier.
    c. Arbitrage activity.
    d. The capital asset pricing model.

14. In contrast to the capital asset pricing model, arbitrage pricing theory: *(LO 7-4)*
    a. Requires that markets be in equilibrium.
    b. Uses risk premiums based on micro variables.
    c. Specifies the number and identifies specific factors that determine expected returns.
    d. Does not require the restrictive assumptions concerning the market portfolio.

---

1. A firm's beta can be estimated from the slope of the characteristic line. The first step is to plot the return on the firm's stock (*y*-axis) versus the return on a broad market index (*x*-axis). Next, a regression line is estimated to find the slope.

    WEB *master*

    a. Go to **finance.yahoo.com,** enter the symbol for Alcoa, and click on *Get Quotes*. On the left-side menu, click on *Historical Prices;* then enter starting and ending dates that correspond to the most recent two years. Select the *Daily* option. Save the data to a spreadsheet.
    b. Repeat the process to get comparable data for the S&P 500 Index (symbol ∧GSPC). Download the data and copy it into the same spreadsheet as Alcoa with dates aligned.
    c. Sort the data from earliest to latest. Calculate the excess return on the stock and the return on the index for each day using the adjusted closing prices. (You can use four-week T-bill rates to calculate excess returns from the Federal Reserve website at **www.federalreserve.gov/releases/h15/data.htm.**)
    d. Prepare an *xy* scatter plot with no line inserted. Be sure that the firm's excess returns represent the *y*-variable and the market's excess returns represent the *x*-variable.
    e. Select one of the data points by pointing to it and clicking the left mouse button. While the point is selected, right-click to pull up a shortcut menu. Select *Add Trend-line,* choose the linear type, then click on the *Options* tab and select *Display Equation on Chart.* When you click on OK, the trendline and the equation appear. The trend-line represents the regression equation. What is Alcoa's beta?

2. In the previous question, you used 60 months of data to calculate the beta of Alcoa. Now compute the alpha of Alcoa in two consecutive periods. Estimate the index-model regression using the first 30 months of data. Now repeat the process using the second half of the sample. This will give you the alpha (intercept) and beta (slope) estimates for two consecutive time periods. How do the two alphas compare to the risk-free rate and to each other? Select 11 other firms and repeat the regressions to find the alphas for the first two-year period and the last two-year period.

3. Given your results for Question 2, investigate the extent to which beta in one period predicts beta in future periods and whether alpha in one period predicts alpha in future periods. Regress the beta of each firm in the second period (Y) against the beta in the first period (X). (If you estimated regressions for a dozen firms in Question 2, you will have 12 observations in this regression.) Do the same for the alphas of each firm. Use the coefficients you found to forecast the betas of the 12 firms for the next two-year period.

4. Our expectation is that beta in the first period predicts beta in the next period but that alpha in the first period has no power to predict alpha in the next period. (In other words, the regression coefficient on first-period beta will be statistically significant in explaining second-period beta, but the coefficient on alpha will not be.) Why does this prediction make sense? Is it borne out by the data?

5. *a.* Which of the stocks would you classify as defensive? Which would be classified as aggressive?
   b. Do the beta coefficients for the low-beta firms make sense given the industries in which these firms operate? Briefly explain.

SOLUTIONS TO
CONCEPT
checks

7.1 The CML would still represent efficient investments. We can characterize the entire population by two representative investors. One is the "uninformed" investor, who does not engage in security analysis and holds the market portfolio, while the other optimizes using the Markowitz algorithm with input from security analysis. The uninformed investor does not know what input the informed investor uses to make portfolio purchases. The uninformed investor knows, however, that if the other investor is informed, the market portfolio proportions will be optimal. Therefore, to depart from these proportions would constitute an uninformed bet, which will, on average, reduce the efficiency of diversification with no compensating improvement in expected returns.

7.2 Substituting the historical mean and standard deviation in Equation 7.1 yields a coefficient of risk aversion of

$$\bar{A} = \frac{E(r_M) - r_f}{\sigma_M^2} = \frac{.075}{.20^2} = 1.88$$

This relationship also tells us that for the historical standard deviation and a coefficient of risk aversion of 3.5, the risk premium would be

$$E(r_M) - r_f = \bar{A}\sigma_M^2 = 3.5 \times .20^2 = .14 = 14\%$$

7.3 $\beta_{Delta} = 1.2$, $\beta_{GE} = .8$. Therefore, given the investment proportions, the portfolio beta is

$$\beta_P = w_{Delta}\beta_{Delta} + w_{GE}\beta_{GE} = (.75 \times 1.2) + (.25 \times .8) = 1.1$$

and the risk premium of the portfolio will be

$$E(r_P) - r_f = \beta_P[E(r_M) - r_f] = 1.1 \times 8\% = 8.8\%$$

7.4 *a.* The alpha of a stock is its expected return in excess of that required by the CAPM.

$$\alpha = E(r) - \{r_f + \beta[E(r_M) - r_f]\}$$
$$\alpha_{XYZ} = 12 - [5 + 1.0(11 - 5)] = 1$$
$$\alpha_{ABC} = 13 - [5 + 1.5(11 - 5)] = -1\%$$

b. The project-specific required rate of return is determined by the project beta coupled with the market risk premium and the risk-free rate. The CAPM tells us that an acceptable expected rate of return for the project is

$$r_f + \beta[E(r_M) - r_f] = 8 + 1.3(16 - 8) = 18.4\%$$

which becomes the project's hurdle rate. If the IRR of the project is 19%, then it is desirable. Any project (of similar beta) with an IRR less than 18.4% should be rejected.

7.5 $E(r) = 4\% + 1.2 \times 4\% + .7 \times 2\% = 10.2\%$

7.6 Using Equation 7.11, the expected return is

$$4 + (0.2 \times 6) + (1.4 \times 8) = 16.4\%$$

The Efficient Market Hypothesis

Learning Objectives

LO 8-1 Demonstrate why security price changes should be essentially unpredictable in an efficient market.

LO 8-2 Cite evidence that supports and contradicts the efficient market hypothesis.

LO 8-3 Provide interpretations of various stock market "anomalies."

LO 8-4 Formulate investment strategies that make sense in informationally efficient markets.

One of the early applications of computers in economics in the 1950s was to analyze economic time series. Business-cycle theorists felt that tracing the evolution of several economic variables over time would clarify and predict the progress of the economy through boom and bust periods. A natural candidate for analysis was the behavior of stock market prices over time. On the assumption that stock prices reflect the prospects of the firm, recurrent patterns of peaks and troughs in economic performance ought to show up in those prices.

When Maurice Kendall (1953) examined this proposition, however, he found to his great surprise that he could identify no predictable patterns in stock prices. Prices seemed to evolve randomly. They were as likely to go up as they were to go down on any particular day, regardless of past performance. The data provided no way to predict price movements.

At first blush, Kendall's results were disturbing to some financial economists. They seemed to imply that the stock market is dominated by erratic market psychology, or "animal spirits"—that it follows no logical rules. In short, the results appeared to confirm the irrationality of the market. On further reflection, however, economists came to reverse their interpretation of Kendall's study.

It soon became apparent that random price movements indicated a well-functioning or efficient market, not an irrational one. In this chapter we explore the reasoning behind what may seem a surprising conclusion. We show how competition among analysts leads naturally to market efficiency, and we examine the implications of the efficient market hypothesis for investment policy. We also consider empirical evidence that supports and contradicts the notion of market efficiency.

8.1 RANDOM WALKS AND THE EFFICIENT MARKET HYPOTHESIS

Suppose Kendall had discovered that changes in stock prices can be reliably predicted. What a gold mine this would have been. If they could use Kendall's equations to predict stock prices, investors would reap unending profits simply by purchasing stocks that the computer model implied were about to increase in price and by selling those stocks about to fall in price.

A moment's reflection should be enough to convince yourself that this situation could not persist for long. For example, suppose that the model predicts with great confidence that XYZ stock price, currently at $100 per share, will rise dramatically in three days to $110. What would all investors with access to the model's prediction do today? Obviously, they would place a great wave of immediate buy orders to cash in on the forthcoming increase in stock price. No one holding XYZ, however, would be willing to sell. The net effect would be an *immediate* jump in the stock price to $110. The forecast of a future price increase will lead instead to an immediate price increase. In other words, the stock price will immediately reflect the "good news" implicit in the model's forecast.

This simple example illustrates why Kendall's attempt to find recurrent patterns in stock price movements was likely to fail. A forecast about favorable *future* performance leads instead to favorable *current* performance, as market participants all try to get in on the action before the price increase.

More generally, one might say that any information that could be used to predict stock performance should already be reflected in stock prices. As soon as there is any information indicating that a stock is underpriced and therefore offers a profit opportunity, investors flock to buy the stock and immediately bid up its price to a fair level, where only ordinary rates of return can be expected. These "ordinary rates" are simply rates of return commensurate with the risk of the stock.

However, if prices are bid immediately to fair levels, given all available information, it must be that they increase or decrease only in response to new information. New information, by definition, must be unpredictable; if it could be predicted, then the prediction would be part of today's information. Thus, stock prices that change in response to new (that is, previously unpredicted) information also must move unpredictably.

This is the essence of the argument that stock prices should follow a **random walk,** that is, that price changes should be random and unpredictable. Far from a proof of market irrationality, randomly evolving stock prices would be the necessary consequence of intelligent investors competing to discover relevant information on which to buy or sell stocks before the rest of the market becomes aware of that information.

random walk

The notion that stock price changes are random and unpredictable.

Don't confuse randomness in price *changes* with irrationality in the *level* of prices. If prices are determined rationally, then only new information will cause them to change. Therefore, a random walk would be the natural result of prices that always reflect all current knowledge. Indeed, if stock price movements were predictable, that would be damning evidence of stock market inefficiency, because the ability to predict prices would indicate that all available information was not already reflected in stock prices. Therefore, the notion that stocks already reflect all available information is referred to as the **efficient market hypothesis (EMH).**[1]

Figure 8.1 illustrates the response of stock prices to new information in an efficient market. The graph plots the price response of a sample of 194 firms that were targets of takeover attempts. In most takeovers, the acquiring firm pays a substantial premium over current market prices. Therefore, announcement of a takeover attempt should cause the stock price to jump. The figure shows that stock prices jump dramatically on the day the news becomes public. However, there is no further drift in prices *after* the announcement date, suggesting that prices reflect the new information, including the likely magnitude of the takeover premium, by the end of the trading day.

efficient market hypothesis (EMH)

The hypothesis that prices of securities fully reflect available information about securities.

---

[1]Market efficiency should not be confused with the idea of efficient portfolios introduced in Chapter 6. An informationally efficient *market* is one in which information is rapidly disseminated and reflected in prices. An efficient *portfolio* is one with the highest expected return for a given level of risk.

Cumulative abnormal returns before takeover attempts: Target companies

Source: Arthur Keown and John Pinkerton, "Merger Announcements and Insider Trading Activity," *Journal of Finance* 36 (September 1981), pp. 855–869. Updates courtesy of Jinghua Yan.

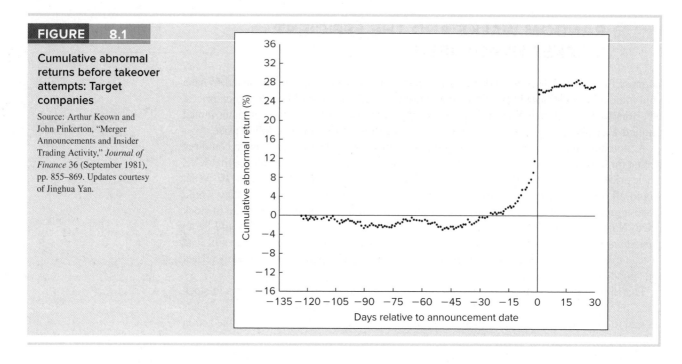

Even more dramatic evidence of rapid response to new information may be found in intra-day prices. For example, Patel and Wolfson (1984) show that most of the stock price response to corporate dividend or earnings announcements occurs within 10 minutes of the announcement. A nice illustration of such rapid adjustment is provided in a study by Busse and Green (2002), who track minute-by-minute stock prices of firms featured on CNBC's "Morning" or "Midday Call" segments.[2] Minute 0 in Figure 8.2 is the time at which the stock is mentioned on the midday show. The top line is the average price movement of stocks that receive positive reports, while the bottom line reports returns on stocks with negative reports. Notice that the top line levels off, indicating that the market has fully digested the news, within 5 minutes of the report. The bottom line levels off within about 12 minutes.

Stock price reaction to CNBC reports. The figure shows the reaction of stock prices to on-air stock reports during the "Midday Call" segment on CNBC. The chart plots cumulative returns beginning 15 minutes before the stock report.

Source: Reprinted from J. A. Busse and T. C. Green, "Market Efficiency in Real Time," *Journal of Financial Economics* 65 (2002), p. 422.

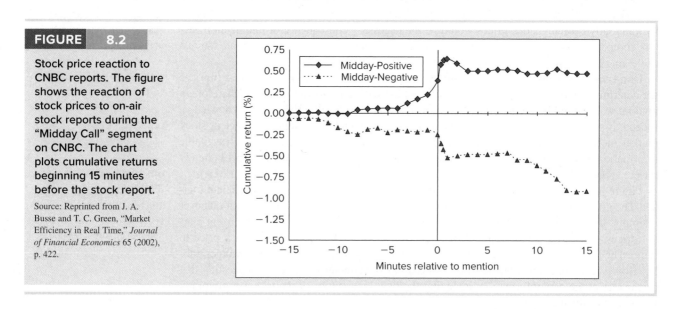

[2]You can find an intraday movie version of this figure at **www.bus.emory.edu/cgreen/cnbc.htm.**

Competition as the Source of Efficiency

Why should we expect stock prices to reflect "all available information"? After all, if you are willing to spend time and money on gathering information, it might seem reasonable that you could turn up something that has been overlooked by the rest of the investment community. When information is costly to uncover and analyze, one would expect investment analysis calling for such expenditures to result in an increased expected return.

This point has been stressed by Grossman and Stiglitz (1980). They argued that investors will have an incentive to spend time and resources to analyze and uncover new information only if such activity is likely to generate higher investment returns. Thus, in market equilibrium, efficient information-gathering activity should be fruitful. Moreover, it would not be surprising to find that the degree of efficiency differs across various markets. For example, emerging markets that are less intensively analyzed than U.S. markets or in which accounting disclosure requirements are less rigorous may be less efficient than U.S. markets. Small stocks which receive relatively little coverage by Wall Street analysts may be less efficiently priced than large ones. Therefore, while we would not go so far as to say that you absolutely cannot come up with new information, it makes sense to consider and respect your competition.

Consider an investment management fund currently managing a $5 billion portfolio. Suppose that the fund manager can devise a research program that could increase the portfolio rate of return by one-tenth of 1% per year, a seemingly modest amount. This program would increase the dollar return to the portfolio by $5 billion × .001, or $5 million. Therefore, the fund would be willing to spend up to $5 million per year on research to increase stock returns by a mere tenth of 1% per year. With such large rewards for such small increases in investment performance, it should not be surprising that professional portfolio managers are willing to spend large sums on industry analysts, computer support, and research effort, and therefore that price changes are, generally speaking, difficult to predict.

With so many well-backed analysts willing to spend considerable resources on research, easy pickings in the market will be rare. Moreover, the incremental rates of return on research activity may be so small that only managers of the largest portfolios will find them worth pursuing.

EXAMPLE 8.1

Rewards for Incremental Performance

Although it may not literally be true that "all" relevant information will be uncovered, it is virtually certain that there are many investigators hot on the trail of most leads that seem likely to improve investment performance. Competition among these many well-backed, highly paid, aggressive analysts ensures that, as a general rule, stock prices ought to reflect available information regarding their proper levels.

It is often said that the most precious commodity on Wall Street is information, and the competition for it is intense. Sometimes the quest for a competitive advantage can tip over into a search for illegal inside information. Recent years have witnessed several major insider trading cases. For example, in 2011, Raj Rajaratnam, the head of the Galleon Group hedge fund, which once managed $6.5 billion, was convicted for soliciting tips from a network of corporate insiders and traders. In 2014, another successful hedge fund, SAC Capital Advisors, paid $1.8 billion to settle an insider trading probe. While these firms clearly crossed the line separating legitimate and prohibited means to acquire information, that line is often murky. For example, a large industry of *expert-network* firms has emerged in the last decade to connect (for a fee) investors to industry experts who can provide a unique perspective on a company. As the nearby box discusses, this sort of arrangement can easily lead to insider trading and, in fact, was a key component of the case against SAP Capital.

MATCHMAKERS FOR THE INFORMATION AGE

The most precious commodity on Wall Street is information, and informed players can charge handsomely for providing it. An industry of so-called *expert-network providers* has emerged to sell access to experts with unique insights about a wide variety of firms and industries to investors who need that information to make decisions. These firms have been dubbed "matchmakers for the information age." Experts can range from doctors who help predict the release of blockbuster drugs to meteorologists who forecast weather that can affect commodity prices to business executives who can provide specialized insight about companies and industries.

But it's turned out that some of those experts have peddled prohibited inside information. In 2011, Winifred Jiau, a consultant for Primary Global Research, was convicted of selling information to the hedge fund SAC Capital Advisors. Several other employees of Primary Global also were charged with insider trading.

Expert firms are supposed to provide only public information, along with the expert's insights and perspective. But the temptation to hire experts with inside information and charge handsomely for access to them is obvious. The SEC has raised concerns about the boundary between legitimate and illegal services, and several hedge funds in 2011 shut down after raids searching for evidence of such illicit activity.

In the wake of increased scrutiny, compliance efforts of both buyers and sellers of expert information have mushroomed. The largest network firm is Gerson Lehrman Group, with a stable of 300,000 experts. It now maintains down-to-the-minute records of which of its experts talks to whom and the topics they have discussed.[3] These records could be turned over to authorities in the event of an insider trading investigation. And for their part, some hedge funds have simply ceased working with expert-network firms or have promulgated clearer rules for when their employees may talk with consultants.

Even with these safeguards, however, there remains room for trouble. For example, an investor may meet an expert through a legitimate network, and then the two may establish a consulting relationship on their own. The legal matchmaking becomes the precursor to the illegal selling of insider tips. Where there is a will to cheat, there usually will be a way.

Versions of the Efficient Market Hypothesis

It is common to distinguish among three versions of the EMH: the weak, semistrong, and strong forms of the hypothesis. These versions differ by their notions of what is meant by the term "all available information."

weak-form EMH

The assertion that stock prices already reflect all information contained in the history of past trading.

The **weak-form** hypothesis asserts that stock prices already reflect all information that can be derived by examining market trading data such as the history of past prices, trading volume, or short interest. This version of the hypothesis implies that trend analysis is fruitless. Past stock price data are publicly available and virtually costless to obtain. The weak-form hypothesis holds that if such data ever conveyed reliable signals about future performance, all investors already would have learned to exploit the signals. Ultimately, the signals lose their value as they become widely known because a buy signal, for instance, would result in an immediate price increase.

semistrong-form EMH

The assertion that stock prices already reflect all publicly available information.

The **semistrong-form** hypothesis states that all publicly available information regarding the prospects of a firm already must be reflected in the stock price. Such information includes, in addition to past prices, fundamental data on the firm's product line, quality of management, balance sheet composition, patents held, earning forecasts, and accounting practices. Again, if investors have access to such information from publicly available sources, one would expect it to be reflected in stock prices.

strong-form EMH

The assertion that stock prices reflect all relevant information, including inside information.

Finally, the **strong-form** version of the efficient market hypothesis states that stock prices reflect all information relevant to the firm, even including information available only to company insiders. This version of the hypothesis is quite extreme. Few would argue with the proposition that corporate officers have access to pertinent information long enough before public release to enable them to profit from trading on that information. Indeed, much of the activity of the Securities and Exchange Commission is directed toward preventing insiders from profiting by exploiting their privileged situation. Rule 10b-5 of the Security Exchange Act of 1934 sets limits on trading by corporate officers, directors, and substantial owners, requiring them to report trades to the SEC. These insiders, their relatives, and any associates who trade on information supplied by insiders are considered in violation of the law.

[3]"Expert Networks Are the Matchmakers for the Information Age," *The Economist*, June 16, 2011.

Defining insider trading is not always easy, however. After all, stock analysts are in the business of uncovering information not already widely known to market participants. As we saw in Chapter 3 and in the nearby box, the distinction between private and inside information is sometimes murky.

Notice one thing that all versions of the EMH have in common: They all assert that prices should reflect *available* information. We do not expect traders to be superhuman or market prices to always be right. We will always like more information about a company's prospects than will be available. Sometimes market prices will turn out in retrospect to have been outrageously high; at other times, absurdly low. The EMH asserts only that at the given time, using current information, we cannot be sure if today's prices will ultimately prove themselves to have been too high or too low. If markets are rational, however, we can expect them to be correct on average.

> **CONCEPT check 8.1**
>
> a. Suppose you observed that high-level managers make superior returns on investments in their company's stock. Would this be a violation of weak-form market efficiency? Would it be a violation of strong-form market efficiency?
>
> b. If the weak form of the efficient market hypothesis is valid, must the strong form also hold? Conversely, does strong-form efficiency imply weak-form efficiency?

8.2   IMPLICATIONS OF THE EMH

Technical Analysis

Technical analysis is essentially the search for recurrent and predictable patterns in stock prices. Although technicians recognize the value of information regarding future economic prospects of the firm, they believe that such information is not necessary for a successful trading strategy. This is because whatever the fundamental reason for a change in stock price, if the stock price responds slowly enough, the analyst will be able to identify a trend that can be exploited during the adjustment period. The key to successful technical analysis is a sluggish response of stock prices to fundamental supply-and-demand factors. This prerequisite, of course, is diametrically opposed to the notion of an efficient market.

Technical analysts are sometimes called *chartists* because they study records or charts of past stock prices, hoping to find patterns they can exploit to make a profit. As an example of technical analysis, consider the *relative strength* approach. The chartist compares stock performance over a recent period to performance of the market or other stocks in the same industry. A simple version of relative strength takes the ratio of the stock price to a market indicator such as the S&P 500 Index. If the ratio increases over time, the stock is said to exhibit relative strength because its price performance is better than that of the broad market. Such strength presumably may continue for a long enough period of time to offer profit opportunities.

One of the most commonly heard components of technical analysis is the notion of **resistance levels** or **support levels.** These values are said to be price levels above which it is difficult for stock prices to rise or below which it is unlikely for them to fall, and they are believed to be levels determined by market psychology.

technical analysis

Research on recurrent and predictable stock price patterns and on proxies for buy or sell pressure in the market.

resistance level

A price level above which it is supposedly unlikely for a stock or stock index to rise.

support level

A price level below which it is supposedly unlikely for a stock or stock index to fall.

> **EXAMPLE 8.2**
>
> *Resistance Levels*
>
> Consider stock XYZ, which traded for several months at a price of $72 and then declined to $65. If the stock eventually begins to increase in price, $72 is considered a resistance level (according to this theory) because investors who bought originally at $72 will be eager to sell their shares as soon as they can break even on their investment. Therefore, at prices near $72 a wave of selling pressure would exist. Such activity imparts a type of "memory" to the market that allows past price history to influence current stock prospects.

The efficient market hypothesis implies that technical analysis is without merit. The past history of prices and trading volume is publicly available at minimal cost. Therefore, any information that was ever available from analyzing past prices has already been reflected in stock prices. As investors compete to exploit their common knowledge of a stock's price history, they necessarily drive stock prices to levels where expected rates of return are exactly commensurate with risk. At those levels one cannot expect abnormal returns.

As an example of how this process works, consider what would happen if the market believed that a level of $72 truly were a resistance level for stock XYZ in Example 8.2. No one would be willing to purchase the stock at a price of $71.50, because it would have almost no room to increase in price but ample room to fall. However, if no one would buy it at $71.50, then $71.50 would become a resistance level. But then, using a similar analysis, no one would buy it at $71, or $70, and so on. The notion of a resistance level is a logical conundrum. Its simple resolution is the recognition that if the stock is ever to sell at $71.50, investors *must* believe that the price can as easily increase as fall. The fact that investors are willing to purchase (or even hold) the stock at $71.50 is evidence of their belief that they can earn a fair expected rate of return at that price.

CONCEPT
check   **8.2**

If everyone in the market believes in resistance levels, why do these beliefs not become self-fulfilling prophecies?

An interesting question is whether a technical rule that seems to work will continue to work in the future once it becomes widely recognized. A clever analyst may occasionally uncover a profitable trading rule, but the real test of efficient markets is whether the rule itself becomes reflected in stock prices once its value is discovered. Once a useful technical rule (or price pattern) is discovered, it ought to be invalidated when the mass of traders attempts to exploit it. In this sense, price patterns ought to be *self-destructing*.

Thus, the market dynamic is one of a continual search for profitable trading rules, followed by destruction by overuse of those rules found to be successful, followed by more search for yet-undiscovered rules. We return to the rationale for technical analysis as well as some of its methods in the next chapter.

Fundamental Analysis

fundamental analysis

Research on determinants of stock value, such as earnings and dividend prospects, expectations for future interest rates, and risk of the firm.

Fundamental analysis uses earnings and dividend prospects of the firm, expectations of future interest rates, and risk evaluation of the firm to determine proper stock prices. Ultimately, it represents an attempt to determine the present discounted value of all the payments a stockholder will receive from each share of stock. If that value exceeds the stock price, the fundamental analyst would recommend purchasing the stock.

Fundamental analysts usually start with a study of past earnings and an examination of company financial statements. They supplement this analysis with further detailed economic analysis, ordinarily including an evaluation of the quality of the firm's management, the firm's standing within its industry, and the prospects for the industry as a whole. The hope is to attain insight into future performance of the firm that is not yet recognized by the rest of the market. Chapters 12 through 14 provide a detailed discussion of the types of analyses that underlie fundamental analysis.

Once again, the efficient market hypothesis predicts that *most* fundamental analysis also is doomed to failure. If the analyst relies on publicly available earnings and industry information, his or her evaluation of the firm's prospects is not likely to be significantly more accurate than those of rival analysts. There are many well-informed, well-financed firms conducting such market research, and in the face of such competition it will be difficult to uncover data not also available to other analysts. Only analysts with a unique insight will be rewarded.

Fundamental analysis is much more difficult than merely identifying well-run firms with good prospects. Discovery of good firms does an investor no good in and of itself if the rest of the market also knows those firms are good. If the knowledge is already public, the investor will be forced to pay a high price for those firms and will not realize a superior rate of return.

The trick is not to identify firms that are good but to find firms that are *better* than everyone else's estimate. Similarly, troubled firms firms can be great bargains if their prospects are not quite as bad as their stock prices suggest.

This is why fundamental analysis is difficult. It is not enough to do a good analysis of a firm; you can make money only if your analysis is better than that of your competitors because the market price will already reflect all commonly recognized information.

Active versus Passive Portfolio Management

By now it is apparent that casual efforts to pick stocks are not likely to pay off. Competition among investors ensures that any easily implemented stock evaluation technique will be used widely enough so that any insights derived will be reflected in stock prices. Only serious analysis and uncommon techniques are likely to generate the *differential* insight necessary to yield trading profits.

Moreover, these techniques are economically feasible only for managers of large portfolios. If you have only $100,000 to invest, even a 1%-per-year improvement in performance generates only $1,000 per year, hardly enough to justify herculean efforts. The billion-dollar manager, however, reaps extra income of $10 million annually from the same 1% increment.

If small investors are not in a favored position to conduct active portfolio management, what are their choices? The small investor probably is better off investing in mutual funds or ETFs. By pooling resources in this way, small investors can gain from economies of scale.

More difficult decisions remain, though. Can investors be sure that even large funds have the ability or resources to uncover mispriced stocks? Furthermore, will any mispricing be sufficiently large to repay the costs entailed in active portfolio management?

Proponents of the efficient market hypothesis believe that active management is largely wasted effort and unlikely to justify the expenses incurred. Therefore, they advocate a **passive investment strategy** that makes no attempt to outsmart the market. A passive strategy aims only at establishing a well-diversified portfolio of securities without attempting to find under- or overvalued stocks. Passive management is usually characterized by a buy-and-hold strategy. Because the efficient market theory indicates that stock prices are at fair levels, given all available information, it makes no sense to buy and sell securities frequently, which generates large brokerage fees without increasing expected performance.

passive investment strategy

Buying a well-diversified portfolio without attempting to search out mispriced securities.

One common strategy for passive management is to create an **index fund,** which is a fund designed to replicate the performance of a broad-based index of stocks. For example, Vanguard's 500 Index Fund holds stocks in direct proportion to their weight in the Standard & Poor's 500 stock price index. The performance of the 500 Index Fund therefore replicates the performance of the S&P 500. Investors in this fund obtain broad diversification with relatively low management fees. The fees can be kept to a minimum because Vanguard does not need to pay analysts to assess stock prospects and does not incur transaction costs from high portfolio turnover. Indeed, while the typical annual expense ratio for an actively managed equity fund is almost 1% of assets, the expense ratio of the 500 Index Fund is only .17%. Today, Vanguard's 500 Index Fund is among the largest equity mutual funds with over $200 billion of assets in mid-2015. The share of equity funds held in indexed portfolios has been steadily rising, reaching more than 20% by 2015.

index fund

A mutual fund holding shares in proportion to their representation in a market index such as the S&P 500.

Indexing need not be limited to the S&P 500, however. For example, some of the funds offered by the Vanguard Group track the broader-based CRSP[4] index of the total U.S. equity market, the Barclays Capital U.S. Aggregate Bond Index, the CRSP index of small-capitalization U.S. companies, and the *Financial Times* indexes of the European and Pacific Basin equity markets. Several other mutual fund complexes offer indexed portfolios, but Vanguard dominates the retail market for indexed products. In 2015, Vanguard's bond index fund became the largest fixed-income mutual fund.

Exchange-traded funds (ETFs) are a close (and usually lower-expense) alternative to indexed mutual funds. As noted in Chapter 4, these are shares in diversified portfolios that

---

[4]CRSP is the Center for Research in Security Prices at the University of Chicago.

can be bought or sold just like shares of individual stock. ETFs matching several broad stock market indexes such as the S&P 500 or CRSP indexes and dozens of international and industry stock indexes are available to investors who want to hold a diversified sector of a market without attempting active security selection.

> **CONCEPT check 8.3**
>
> What would happen to market efficiency if *all* investors attempted to follow a passive strategy?

The Role of Portfolio Management in an Efficient Market

If the market is efficient, why not throw darts at *The Wall Street Journal* instead of trying rationally to choose a stock portfolio? This is a tempting conclusion to draw from the notion that security prices are fairly set, but it is far too facile. There is a role for rational portfolio management, even in perfectly efficient markets.

You have learned that a basic principle in portfolio selection is diversification. Even if all stocks are priced fairly, each still poses firm-specific risk that can be eliminated through diversification. Therefore, rational security selection, even in an efficient market, calls for the selection of a well-diversified portfolio providing the systematic risk level that the investor wants.

Rational investment policy also requires that tax considerations be reflected in security choice. High-tax-bracket investors generally will not want the same securities that low-bracket investors find favorable. At an obvious level, high-bracket investors find it advantageous to buy tax-exempt municipal bonds despite their relatively low pretax yields, whereas those same bonds are unattractive to low-tax-bracket investors. At a more subtle level, high-bracket investors might want to tilt their portfolios in the direction of capital gains as opposed to interest income, because capital gains are taxed less heavily and because the option to defer the realization of capital gains income is more valuable the higher the current tax bracket. Hence these investors may prefer stocks that yield low dividends yet offer greater expected capital gains income. They also will be more attracted to investment opportunities for which returns are sensitive to tax benefits, such as real estate ventures.

A third argument for rational portfolio management relates to the particular risk profile of the investor. For example, a Toyota executive whose annual bonus depends on Toyota's profits generally should not invest additional amounts in auto stocks. To the extent that his or her compensation already depends on Toyota's well-being, the executive is already overinvested in Toyota and should not exacerbate the lack of diversification. This lesson was learned with considerable pain in September 2008 by Lehman Brothers employees who were famously invested in their own firm when the company failed. Roughly 30% of the shares in the firm were owned by its 24,000 employees, and their losses on those shares were around $10 billion.

Investors of varying ages also might warrant different portfolio policies with regard to risk bearing. For example, older investors who are essentially living off savings might choose to avoid long-term bonds whose market values fluctuate dramatically with changes in interest rates (discussed in Part Four). Because these investors are living off accumulated savings, they require conservation of principal. In contrast, younger investors might be more inclined toward long-term inflation-indexed bonds. The steady flow of real income over long periods of time that is locked in with these bonds can be more important than preservation of principal to those with long life expectancies.

In conclusion, there is a role for portfolio management even in an efficient market. Investors' optimal positions will vary according to factors such as age, tax bracket, risk aversion, and employment. The role of the portfolio manager in an efficient market is to tailor the portfolio to these needs, rather than to beat the market.

Resource Allocation

We've focused so far on the investments implications of the efficient market hypothesis. Deviations from efficiency may offer profit opportunities to better-informed traders at the expense of less-informed traders.

However, deviations from informational efficiency would also result in a large cost that will be borne by all citizens, namely, inefficient resource allocation. Recall that in a capitalist economy, investments in *real* assets such as plant, equipment, and know-how are guided in large part by the prices of financial assets. For example, if the value of telecommunication capacity reflected in stock market prices exceeds the cost of installing such capacity, managers might justifiably conclude that telecom investments seem to have positive net present value. In this manner, capital market prices guide allocation of real resources.

If markets were inefficient and securities commonly mispriced, then resources would be systematically misallocated. Corporations with overpriced securities will be able to obtain capital too cheaply, and corporations with undervalued securities might forgo investment opportunities because the cost of raising capital will be too high. Therefore, inefficient capital markets would diminish one of the most potent benefits of a market economy. As an example of what can go wrong, consider the dot-com bubble of the late 1990s, which sent a strong but, as it turned out, wildly overoptimistic signal about prospects in Internet and telecommunication firms and ultimately led to substantial overinvestment in those industries.

Before writing off markets as a means to guide resource allocation, however, one has to be reasonable about what can be expected from market forecasts. In particular, you shouldn't confuse an efficient market, where all available information is reflected in prices, with a perfect-foresight market. As we said previously, "all available information" is still far from complete information, and generally rational market forecasts will sometimes be wrong; sometimes, in fact, they will be very wrong.

8.3   ARE MARKETS EFFICIENT?

The Issues

Not surprisingly, the efficient market hypothesis does not exactly arouse enthusiasm in the community of professional portfolio managers. It implies that a great deal of the activity of portfolio managers—the search for undervalued securities—is at best wasted effort, and quite probably harmful to clients because it costs money and leads to imperfectly diversified portfolios. Consequently, the EMH has never been widely accepted on Wall Street, and debate continues today on the degree to which security analysis can improve investment performance. Before discussing empirical tests of the hypothesis, we want to note three factors that together imply that the debate probably never will be settled: the *magnitude issue,* the *selection bias issue,* and the *lucky event issue.*

THE MAGNITUDE ISSUE   We noted that an investment manager overseeing a $5 billion portfolio who can improve performance by only .1% per year will increase investment earnings by .001 × $5 billion = $5 million annually. This manager clearly would be worth her salary! Yet can we, as observers, statistically measure her contribution? Probably not: A .1% contribution would be swamped by the yearly volatility of the market. Remember, the annual standard deviation of the well-diversified S&P 500 Index has been around 20%. Against these fluctuations a small increase in performance would be hard to detect.

All might agree that stock prices are very close to fair values and that only managers of large portfolios can earn enough trading profits to make the exploitation of minor mispricing worth the effort. According to this view, the actions of intelligent investment managers are the driving force behind the constant evolution of market prices to fair levels. Rather than ask the qualitative question, "Are markets efficient?" we should instead ask a more quantitative question: "How efficient are markets?"

THE SELECTION BIAS ISSUE   Suppose that you discover an investment scheme that could really make money. You have two choices: either publish your technique in *The Wall Street Journal* to win fleeting fame, or keep your technique secret and use it to earn millions of dollars. Most investors would choose the latter option, which presents us with a conundrum. Only investors who find that an investment scheme cannot generate abnormal returns will be willing to report their findings to the whole world. Hence opponents of the efficient

HOW TO GUARANTEE A SUCCESSFUL MARKET NEWSLETTER

Suppose you want to make your fortune publishing a market newsletter. You need first to convince potential subscribers that you have talent worth paying for. But what if you have no talent? The solution is simple: Start eight newsletters.

In year 1, let four of your newsletters predict an up-market and four a down-market. In year 2, let half of the originally optimistic group of newsletters continue to predict an up-market and the other half a down-market. Do the same for the originally pessimistic group. Continue in this manner to obtain the pattern of predictions in the table that follows (U = prediction of an up-market, D = prediction of a down-market).

After three years, no matter what has happened to the market, one of the newsletters would have had a perfect prediction record. This is because after three years there are $2^3 = 8$ outcomes for the market, and we have covered all eight possibilities with the eight newsletters. Now, we simply slough off the seven unsuccessful newsletters, and market the eighth newsletter based on its perfect track record. If we want to establish a newsletter with

a perfect track record over a four-year period, we need $2^4 = 16$ newsletters. A five-year period requires 32 newsletters, and so on.

After the fact, the one newsletter that was always right will attract attention for your uncanny foresight and investors will rush to pay large fees for its advice. Your fortune is made, and you have never even researched the market!

WARNING: This scheme is illegal! The point, however, is that with hundreds of market newsletters, you can find one that has stumbled onto an apparently remarkable string of successful predictions without any real degree of skill. After the fact, *someone's* prediction history can seem to imply great forecasting skill. This person is the one we will read about in *The Wall Street Journal;* the others will be forgotten.

Newsletter Predictions

Year	1	2	3	4	5	6	7	8
1	U	U	U	U	D	D	D	D
2	U	U	D	D	U	U	D	D
3	U	D	U	D	U	D	U	D

markets view of the world always can use evidence that various techniques do not provide investment rewards as proof that the techniques that do work simply are not being reported to the public. This is a problem in *selection bias;* the outcomes we are able to observe have been preselected in favor of failed attempts. Therefore, we cannot fairly evaluate the true ability of portfolio managers to generate winning stock market strategies.

THE LUCKY EVENT ISSUE In virtually any month it seems we read an article about some investor or investment company with a fantastic investment performance over the recent past. Surely the superior records of such investors disprove the efficient market hypothesis.

Yet this conclusion is far from obvious. As an analogy to the investment game, consider a contest to flip the most number of heads out of 50 trials using a fair coin. The expected outcome for any person is, of course, 50% heads and 50% tails. If 10,000 people, however, compete in this contest, it would not be surprising if at least one or two contestants flipped more than 75% heads. In fact, elementary statistics tells us that the expected number of contestants flipping 75% or more heads would be two. It would be silly, though, to crown these people the "head-flipping champions of the world." Obviously, they are simply the contestants who happened to get lucky on the day of the event. (See the nearby box.)

The analogy to efficient markets is clear. Under the hypothesis that any stock is fairly priced given all available information, any bet on a stock is simply a coin toss. There is equal likelihood of winning or losing the bet. However, if many investors using a variety of schemes make fair bets, statistically speaking, *some* of those investors will be lucky and win a great majority of the bets. For every big winner, there may be many big losers, but we never hear of these managers. The winners, though, turn up in *The Wall Street Journal* as the latest stock market gurus; then they can make a fortune publishing market newsletters.

Our point is that after the fact there will have been at least one successful investment scheme. A doubter will call the results luck; the successful investor will call it skill. The proper test would be to see whether the successful investors can repeat their performance in another period, yet this approach is rarely taken.

With these caveats in mind, we turn now to some of the empirical tests of the efficient market hypothesis.

Legg Mason's Value Trust, managed by Bill Miller, outperformed the S&P 500 in each of the 15 years ending in 2005. Is Miller's performance sufficient to dissuade you from a belief in efficient markets? If not, would *any* performance record be sufficient to dissuade you? Now consider that in the next 3 years, the fund dramatically underperformed the S&P 500; by the end of 2008, its cumulative 18-year performance was barely different from the index. Does this affect your opinion?

Weak-Form Tests: Patterns in Stock Returns

RETURNS OVER SHORT HORIZONS   Early tests of efficient markets were tests of the weak form. Could speculators find trends in past prices that would enable them to earn abnormal profits? This is essentially a test of the efficacy of technical analysis.

One way of discerning trends in stock prices is by measuring the *serial correlation* of stock market returns. Serial correlation refers to the tendency for stock returns to be related to past returns. Positive serial correlation means that positive returns tend to follow positive returns (a momentum type of property). Negative serial correlation means that positive returns tend to be followed by negative returns (a reversal or "correction" property). Both Conrad and Kaul (1988) and Lo and MacKinlay (1988) examine weekly returns of NYSE stocks and find positive serial correlation over short horizons. However, the correlation coefficients of weekly returns tend to be fairly small, at least for large stocks for which price data are the most reliably up to date. Thus, while these studies demonstrate weak price trends over short periods,[5] the evidence does not clearly suggest the existence of trading opportunities.

While broad market indexes demonstrate only weak serial correlation, there appears to be stronger momentum in performance across market sectors exhibiting the best and worst recent returns. In an investigation of intermediate-horizon stock price behavior (using 3- to 12-month holding periods), Jegadeesh and Titman (1993) found a **momentum effect** in which good or bad recent performance of particular stocks continues over time. They conclude that while the performance of individual stocks is highly unpredictable, *portfolios* of the best-performing stocks in the recent past appear to outperform other stocks with enough reliability to offer profit opportunities. Thus, it appears that there is evidence of short- to intermediate-horizon price momentum in both the aggregate market and cross-sectionally (i.e., across particular stocks).

momentum effect

The tendency of poorly performing stocks and well-performing stocks in one period to continue that abnormal performance in following periods.

RETURNS OVER LONG HORIZONS   Although short- to intermediate-horizon returns suggest momentum in stock market prices, studies of long-horizon returns (i.e., returns over multiyear periods) by Fama and French (1988) and Poterba and Summers (1988) indicate pronounced *negative* long-term serial correlation in the performance of the aggregate market. The latter result has given rise to a "fads hypothesis," which asserts that the stock market might overreact to relevant news. Such overreaction leads to positive serial correlation (momentum) over short time horizons. Subsequent correction of the overreaction leads to poor performance following good performance and vice versa. The corrections mean that a run of positive returns eventually will tend to be followed by negative returns, leading to negative serial correlation over longer horizons. These episodes of apparent overshooting followed by correction give the stock market the appearance of fluctuating around its fair value.

These long-horizon results are dramatic but still not conclusive. First, the study results need not be interpreted as evidence for stock market fads. An alternative interpretation of these results holds that they indicate only that the market risk premium varies over time. For example, when the risk premium and the required return on the market rise, stock prices will

---

[5]On the other hand, there is evidence that share prices of individual securities (as opposed to broad market indexes) are more prone to reversals than continuations at very short horizons. See, for example, B. Lehmann, "Fads, Martingales and Market Efficiency," *Quarterly Journal of Economics* 105 (February 1990), pp. 1–28; and N. Jegadeesh, "Evidence of Predictable Behavior of Security Returns," *Journal of Finance* 45 (September 1990), pp. 881–898. However, as Lehmann notes, this is probably best interpreted as due to liquidity problems after big movements in stock prices as market makers adjust their positions in the stock.

fall. When the market then rises (on average) at this higher rate of return, the data convey the impression of a stock price recovery. In this view, the apparent overshooting and correction are in fact no more than a rational response of market prices to changes in discount rates.

In addition to studies suggestive of overreaction in overall stock market returns over long horizons, many other studies suggest that over long horizons, extreme performance in particular securities also tends to reverse itself: The stocks that have performed best in the recent past seem to underperform the rest of the market in following periods, while the worst past performers tend to offer above-average future performance. De Bondt and Thaler (1985) and Chopra, Lakonishok, and Ritter (1992) find strong tendencies for poorly performing stocks in one period to experience sizable reversals over the subsequent period, while the best-performing stocks in a given period tend to follow with poor performance in the following period.

For example, the De Bondt and Thaler study found that if one were to rank-order the performance of stocks over a five-year period and then group stocks into portfolios based on investment performance, the base-period "loser" portfolio (defined as the 35 stocks with the worst investment performance) outperformed the "winner" portfolio (the top 35 stocks) by an average of 25% (cumulative return) in the following three-year period. This **reversal effect,** in which losers rebound and winners fade back, suggests that the stock market overreacts to relevant news. After the overreaction is recognized, extreme investment performance is reversed. This phenomenon would imply that a *contrarian* investment strategy—investing in recent losers and avoiding recent winners—should be profitable. Moreover, these returns seem pronounced enough to be exploited profitably.

Thus, it appears that there may be short-run momentum but long-run reversal patterns in price behavior both for the market as a whole and across sectors of the market. One interpretation of this pattern is that short-run overreaction (which causes momentum in prices) may lead to long-term reversals (when the market recognizes its past error).

reversal effect

The tendency of poorly performing stocks and well-performing stocks in one period to experience reversals in the following period.

Predictors of Broad Market Returns

Several studies have documented the ability of easily observed variables to predict market returns. For example, Fama and French (1988) showed that the return on the aggregate stock market tends to be higher when the dividend/price ratio, the dividend yield, is high. Campbell and Shiller (1988) found that the earnings yield can predict market returns. Keim and Stambaugh (1986) showed that bond market data such as the spread between yields on high- and low-grade corporate bonds also help predict broad market returns.

Again, the interpretation of these results is difficult. On the one hand, they may imply that abnormal stock returns can be predicted, in violation of the efficient market hypothesis. More probably, however, these variables are proxying for variation in the market risk premium. For example, given a level of dividends or earnings, stock prices will be lower and dividend and earnings yields will be higher when the risk premium (and therefore the expected market return) is higher. Thus, a high dividend or earnings yield will be associated with higher market returns. This does not indicate a violation of market efficiency. The predictability of market returns is due to predictability in the risk premium, not in risk-adjusted abnormal returns.

Fama and French (1989) showed that the yield spread between high- and low-grade bonds has greater predictive power for returns on low-grade bonds than for returns on high-grade bonds, and greater predictive power for stock returns than for bond returns, suggesting that the predictability in returns is in fact a risk premium rather than evidence of market inefficiency. Similarly, the fact that the dividend yield on stocks helps to predict bond market returns suggests that the yield captures a risk premium common to both markets rather than mispricing in the equity market.

Semistrong Tests: Market Anomalies

Fundamental analysis uses a much wider range of information to create portfolios than does technical analysis. Investigations of the efficacy of fundamental analysis ask whether publicly available information beyond the trading history of a security can be used to improve investment performance, and therefore they are tests of semistrong-form market efficiency. Surprisingly, several easily accessible statistics, for example a stock's price–earnings ratio or its market capitalization, seem to predict abnormal risk-adjusted returns. Findings such as these, which we will review in the following pages, are difficult to reconcile with the efficient market hypothesis and therefore are often referred to as efficient market **anomalies.**

A difficulty in interpreting these tests is that we usually need to adjust for portfolio risk before evaluating the success of an investment strategy. Many tests, for example, have used the CAPM to adjust for risk. However, we know that even if beta is a relevant descriptor of stock risk, the empirically measured quantitative trade-off between risk as measured by beta and expected return differs from the predictions of the CAPM. If we use the CAPM to adjust portfolio returns for risk, inappropriate adjustments may lead to the conclusion that various portfolio strategies can generate superior returns, when in fact it simply is the risk adjustment procedure that has failed.

Another way to put this is to note that tests of risk-adjusted returns are *joint tests* of the efficient market hypothesis *and* the risk adjustment procedure. If it appears that a portfolio strategy can generate superior returns, we must then choose between rejecting the EMH and rejecting the risk adjustment technique. Usually, the risk adjustment technique is based on more-questionable assumptions than is the EMH; by opting to reject the procedure, we are left with no conclusion about market efficiency.

An example of this issue is the discovery by Basu (1977, 1983) that portfolios of low price–earnings (P/E) ratio stocks have higher returns than do high P/E portfolios. The **P/E effect** holds up even if returns are adjusted for portfolio beta. Is this a confirmation that the market systematically misprices stocks according to P/E ratio? This would be an extremely surprising and, to us, disturbing conclusion, because analysis of P/E ratios is such a simple procedure. Although it may be possible to earn superior returns through unusual insight, it hardly seems plausible that such a simplistic technique is enough to generate abnormal returns.

Another interpretation of these results is that returns are not properly adjusted for risk. If two firms have the same expected earnings, the riskier stock will sell at a lower price and lower P/E ratio. Because of its higher risk, the low P/E stock also will have higher expected returns. Therefore, unless the CAPM beta fully adjusts for risk, P/E will act as a useful additional descriptor of risk and will be associated with abnormal returns if the CAPM is used to establish benchmark performance.

THE SMALL-FIRM EFFECT The so-called size or **small-firm effect,** originally documented by Banz (1981), is illustrated in Figure 8.3. It shows the historical performance of portfolios formed by dividing the NYSE stocks into 10 portfolios each year according to firm size (i.e., the total value of outstanding equity). Average annual returns between 1926 and 2013 are consistently higher on the small-firm portfolios. The difference in average annual return between portfolio 10 (with the largest firms) and portfolio 1 (with the smallest firms) is 8.0%. Of course, the smaller-firm portfolios tend to be riskier. But even when returns are adjusted for risk using the CAPM, there is still a consistent premium for the smaller-sized portfolios.

Imagine earning a premium of this size on a billion-dollar portfolio. Yet it is remarkable that following a simple (even simplistic) rule such as "invest in low-capitalization stocks" should enable an investor to earn excess returns. After all, any investor can measure firm size at little cost. One would not expect such minimal effort to yield such large rewards.

THE NEGLECTED-FIRM AND LIQUIDITY EFFECTS Arbel and Strebel (1983) gave another interpretation of the small-firm effect. Because they tend to be neglected by large institutional traders, information about smaller firms is less available. This information deficiency makes smaller firms riskier investments that command higher returns. "Brand-name" firms, after all, are subject to considerable monitoring from institutional investors, which promises high-quality information, and presumably investors do not purchase "generic" stocks without the prospect of greater returns.

---

anomalies

Patterns of returns that seem to contradict the efficient market hypothesis.

P/E effect

Portfolios of low P/E stocks have exhibited higher average risk-adjusted returns than high P/E stocks.

small-firm effect

Stocks of small firms have earned abnormal returns, primarily in the month of January.

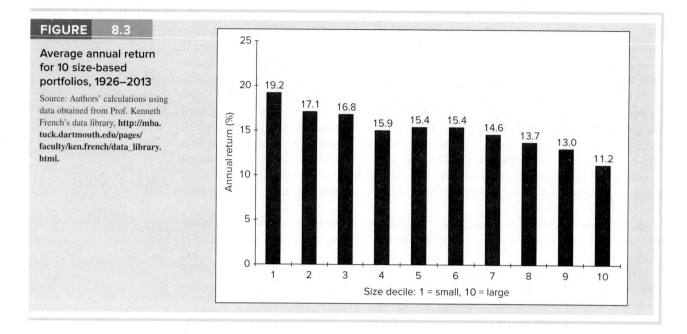

FIGURE 8.3

Average annual return for 10 size-based portfolios, 1926–2013

Source: Authors' calculations using data obtained from Prof. Kenneth French's data library, **http://mba.tuck.dartmouth.edu/pages/faculty/ken.french/data_library.html.**

neglected-firm effect

The tendency of investments in stock of less well-known firms to generate abnormal returns.

Merton (1987) provides a rationale for the **neglected firm effect.** He shows that neglected firms might be expected to earn higher equilibrium returns as compensation for the risk associated with limited information. In this sense the neglected-firm premium is not strictly a market inefficiency but is a type of risk premium.

Work by Amihud and Mendelson (1986, 1991) on the effect of liquidity on stock returns might be related to both the small-firm and neglected-firm effects. They argue that investors will demand a rate-of-return premium to invest in less liquid stocks that entail higher trading costs. In accord with their hypothesis, Amihud and Mendelson showed that these stocks show a strong tendency to exhibit abnormally high risk-adjusted rates of return. Because small and less-analyzed stocks as a rule are less liquid, the liquidity effect might be a partial explanation of their abnormal returns. However, exploiting these effects can be more difficult than it would appear. The high trading costs on small stocks can easily wipe out any apparent abnormal profit opportunity.

BOOK-TO-MARKET RATIOS   Fama and French (1992) showed that a powerful predictor of returns across securities is the ratio of the book value of the firm's equity to the market value of equity. Fama and French stratified firms into 10 groups according to book-to-market ratios and examined the average rate of return of each of the 10 groups. Figure 8.4 is an updated version of their results. The decile with the highest book-to-market ratio had an average annual return of 17.5%, while the lowest-ratio decile averaged only 11.0%. The dramatic dependence of returns on book-to-market ratio is independent of beta, suggesting either that high book-to-market ratio firms are relatively underpriced or that the book-to-market ratio is serving as a proxy for a risk factor that affects equilibrium expected returns.

book-to-market effect

The tendency for investments in shares of firms with high ratios of book value to market value to generate abnormal returns.

In fact, Fama and French found that after controlling for the size and **book-to-market effects,** beta seemed to have no power to explain average security returns.[6] This finding is an important challenge to the notion of rational markets because it seems to imply that a factor

[6]However, a study by S. P. Kothari, Jay Shanken, and Richard G. Sloan (1995) finds that when betas are estimated using annual rather than monthly returns, securities with high beta values do in fact have higher average returns. Moreover, the authors find a book-to-market effect that is attenuated compared to the results in Fama and French and furthermore is inconsistent across different samples of securities. They conclude that the empirical case for the importance of the book-to-market ratio may be somewhat weaker than the Fama and French study would suggest.

FIGURE 8.4

Average annual return as a function of the book-to-market ratio, 1926–2013

Source: Website of Prof. Kenneth French, **http://mba.tuck.dartmouth.edu/pages/faculty/ken.french/data_library.html.**

that should affect returns—systematic risk—seems not to matter, while a factor that should not matter—the book-to-market ratio—seems capable of predicting future returns. We will return to the interpretation of this anomaly.

POST-EARNINGS-ANNOUNCEMENT PRICE DRIFT

A fundamental principle of efficient markets is that any new information ought to be reflected in stock prices very rapidly. When good news is made public, for example, the stock price should jump immediately. A puzzling anomaly, therefore, is the apparently sluggish response of stock prices to firms' earnings announcements, as uncovered by Ball and Brown (1968). Their results were later confirmed and extended in many other papers.[7]

The "news content" of an earnings announcement can be evaluated by comparing the announcement of actual earnings to the value previously expected by market participants. The difference is the "earnings surprise." (Market expectations of earnings can be roughly measured by averaging the published earnings forecasts of Wall Street analysts or by applying trend analysis to past earnings.) Rendleman, Jones, and Latané (1982) provide an influential study of sluggish price response to earnings announcements. They calculate earnings surprises for a large sample of firms, rank the magnitude of the surprise, divide firms into 10 deciles based on the size of the surprise, and calculate abnormal returns for each decile. The abnormal return of each portfolio is the return adjusting for both the market return in that period and the portfolio beta. It measures return over and above what would be expected given market conditions in that period. Figure 8.5 plots cumulative abnormal returns by decile.

Their results are dramatic. The correlation between ranking by earnings surprise and abnormal returns across deciles is as predicted. There is a large abnormal return (a jump in cumulative abnormal return) on the earnings announcement day (time 0). The abnormal return is positive for positive-surprise firms and negative for negative-surprise firms.

The more remarkable, and interesting, result of the study concerns stock price movement *after* the announcement date. The cumulative abnormal returns of positive-surprise stocks continue to rise—in other words, exhibit momentum—even after the earnings information becomes public, while the negative-surprise firms continue to suffer negative abnormal returns. The market appears to adjust to the earnings information only gradually, resulting in a sustained period of abnormal returns.

[7]There is a voluminous literature on this phenomenon, often referred to as post-earnings-announcement price drift. See, for example, V. Bernard and J. Thomas, "Evidence That Stock Prices Do Not Fully Reflect the Implications of Current Earnings for Future Earnings," *Journal of Accounting and Economics* 13 (1990), pp. 305–340, or R. H. Battalio and R. Mendenhall, "Earnings Expectation, Investor Trade Size, and Anomalous Returns around Earnings Announcements," *Journal of Financial Economics* 77 (2005), pp. 289–319.

FIGURE   8.5

Cumulative abnormal returns in response to earnings announcements

Source: Reprinted from R. J. Rendleman Jr., C. P. Jones, and H. A. Latané, "Empirical Anomalies Based on Unexpected Earnings and the Importance of Risk Adjustments," *Journal of Financial Economics* 10 (1982), pp. 269–287.

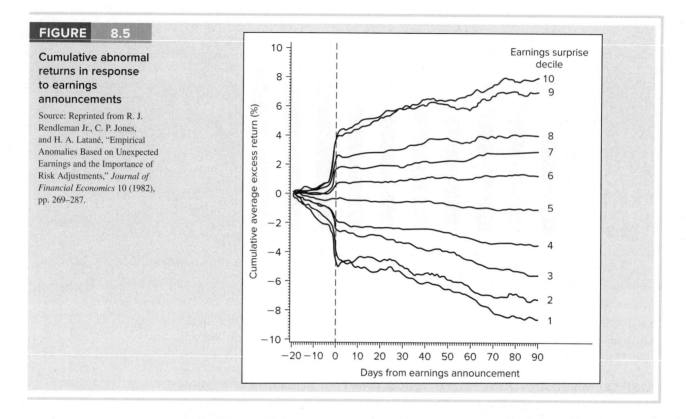

Evidently, one could have earned abnormal profits simply by waiting for earnings announcements and purchasing a stock portfolio of positive-earnings-surprise companies. These are precisely the types of predictable continuing trends that ought to be impossible in an efficient market.

BUBBLES AND MARKET EFFICIENCY   Every so often, it seems (at least in retrospect) that asset prices lose their grounding in reality. For example, in the tulip mania in seventeenth-century Holland, tulip prices peaked at several times the annual income of a skilled worker. This episode has become the symbol of a speculative "bubble" in which prices appear to depart from any semblance of intrinsic value. Less than a century later, the South Sea bubble in England became almost as famous. In this episode, the share price of the South Sea Company rose from £128 in January 1720 to £550 in May and peaked at around £1,000 in August—just before the bubble burst and the share price collapsed to £150 in September, leading to widespread bankruptcies among those who had borrowed to buy shares on credit. In fact, the company was a major lender of money to investors willing to buy (and thus bid up) its shares. This sequence may sound familiar to anyone who lived through the dot-com boom and bust of 1995–2002[8] or, more recently, the financial turmoil of 2008, with origins widely attributed to a collapsing housing price bubble (see Chapter 1).

It is hard to defend the position that security prices in these instances represented rational, unbiased assessments of intrinsic value. And, in fact, some economists, most notably Hyman Minsky, have suggested that bubbles arise naturally. During periods of stability and rising prices, investors extrapolate that stability into the future and become more willing to take on risk. Risk premiums shrink, leading to further increases in asset prices, and expectations become even more optimistic in a self-fulfilling cycle. But, in the end, pricing and risk taking become excessive and the bubble bursts. Ironically, the initial period of stability fosters behavior that ultimately results in instability.

[8]The dot-com boom gave rise to the term *irrational exuberance*. In this vein consider that one company, going public in the investment boom of 1720, described itself simply as "a company for carrying out an undertaking of great advantage, but nobody to know what it is."

But beware of jumping to the conclusion that asset prices may generally be thought of as arbitrary and obvious trading opportunities abundant. First, most bubbles become "obvious" only *after* they have burst. At the time, there is often a seemingly defensible rationale for the price run-up. In the dot-com boom, for example, many contemporary observers rationalized stock price gains as justified by the prospect of a new and more profitable economy, driven by technological advances. Even the irrationality of the tulip mania may have been overblown in its later retelling.[9] In addition, security valuation is intrinsically difficult. Given the considerable imprecision of estimates of intrinsic value, large bets on perceived mispricing may entail hubris.

Moreover, even if you suspect that prices are in fact "wrong," it can be difficult to take advantage of them. We explore these issues in more detail in the following chapter. For now, we can simply point out some impediments to making aggressive bets against an asset: the costs of short-selling overpriced securities as well as potential problems obtaining the securities to sell short and the possibility that, even if you are ultimately correct, the market may disagree and prices still can move dramatically against you in the short term, thus wiping out your portfolio.

Strong-Form Tests: Inside Information

It would not be surprising if insiders were able to make superior profits trading in their firm's stock. In other words, we do not expect markets to be strong-form efficient; we regulate and limit trades based on inside information. The ability of insiders to trade profitably in their own stock has been documented in studies by Jaffe (1974), Seyhun (1986), Givoly and Palmon (1985), and others. Jaffe's was one of the earlier studies that documented the tendency for stock prices to rise after insiders intensively bought shares and to fall after intensive insider sales.

Can other investors benefit by following insiders' trades? The Securities and Exchange Commission requires all insiders to register their trading activity, and it publishes these trades in an *Official Summary of Security Transactions and Holdings*. Since 2002, insiders must report large trades to the SEC within two business days. Once the *Official Summary* is published, the trades become public information. At that point, if markets are efficient, fully and immediately processing the information released in the *Official Summary* of trading, an investor should no longer be able to profit from following the pattern of those trades. Several Internet sites contain information on insider trading.

The study by Seyhun, which carefully tracked the public release dates of the *Official Summary,* found that following insider transactions would be to no avail. Although there is some tendency for stock prices to increase even after the *Official Summary* reports insider buying, the abnormal returns are not of sufficient magnitude to overcome transaction costs.

Interpreting the Anomalies

How should we interpret the ever-growing anomalies literature? Does it imply that markets are grossly inefficient, allowing for simplistic trading rules to offer large profit opportunities? Or are there other, more-subtle interpretations?

RISK PREMIUMS OR INEFFICIENCIES? The price–earnings, small-firm, market-to-book, momentum, and long-term reversal effects are currently among the most puzzling phenomena in empirical finance. There are several interpretations of these effects. First note that to some extent, some of these phenomena may be related. The feature that small firms, low-market-to-book firms, and recent "losers" seem to have in common is a stock price that has fallen considerably in recent months or years. Indeed, a firm can become a small firm or a low-market-to-book firm by suffering a sharp drop in price. These groups therefore may contain a relatively high proportion of distressed firms that have suffered recent difficulties.

[9]For interesting discussions of this possibility, see Peter Garber, *Famous First Bubbles: The Fundamentals of Early Manias* (Cambridge: MIT Press, 2000), and Anne Goldgar, *Tulipmania: Money, Honor, and Knowledge in the Dutch Golden Age* (Chicago: University of Chicago Press, 2007).

FIGURE	8.6

Return to style portfolio as a predictor of GDP growth. Average difference in the return on the style portfolio in years before good GDP growth versus in years before bad GDP growth. Positive value means the style portfolio does better in years prior to good macroeconomic performance. HML = high minus low portfolio, sorted on ratio of book-to-market value. SMB = small minus big portfolio, sorted on firm size.

Source: Reprinted from J. Liew and M. Vassalou, "Can Book-to-Market, Size, and Momentum Be Risk Factors That Predict Economic Growth?" *Journal of Financial Economics* 57 (2000), pp. 221–245.

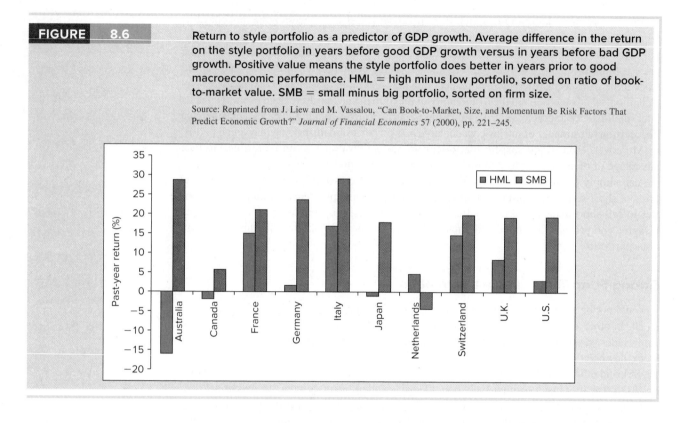

Fama and French (1993) argue that these effects can be explained as manifestations of risk premiums. Using their three-factor model, they show that stocks with higher "betas" (also known in this context as factor loadings) on size or market-to-book factors have higher average returns; they interpret these returns as evidence of a risk premium associated with the factor. This model does a much better job than the one-factor CAPM in explaining security returns. While size or book-to-market ratios per se are obviously not risk factors, they perhaps might act as proxies for more fundamental determinants of risk. Fama and French argue that these patterns of returns may therefore be consistent with an efficient market in which expected returns are consistent with risk. In this regard, it is worth noting that returns to "style portfolios," for example, the return on portfolios constructed based on the ratio of book-to-market value (specifically, the Fama-French high minus low book-to-market portfolio) or firm size (the return on the small minus big firm portfolio) do indeed seem to predict business cycles in many countries. Figure 8.6 shows that returns on these portfolios tend to have positive returns in years prior to rapid growth in gross domestic product.

The opposite interpretation is offered by Lakonishok, Shleifer, and Vishny (1995), who argue that these phenomena are evidence of inefficient markets, more specifically, of systematic errors in the forecasts of stock analysts. They believe that analysts extrapolate past performance too far into the future and therefore overprice firms with recent good performance and underprice firms with recent poor performance. Ultimately, when market participants recognize their errors, prices reverse. This explanation is consistent with the reversal effect and also, to a degree, with the small-firm and book-to-market effects because firms with sharp price drops may tend to be small or have high book-to-market ratios.

If Lakonishok, Shleifer, and Vishny are correct, we ought to find that analysts systematically err when forecasting returns of recent "winner" versus "loser" firms. A study by La Porta (1996) is consistent with this pattern. He finds that shares of firms for which analysts predict low growth rates of earnings actually perform better than those with high expected earnings growth. Analysts seem overly pessimistic about firms with low growth prospects and overly optimistic about firms with high growth prospects. When these too-extreme expectations are "corrected," the low-expected-growth firms outperform high-expected-growth firms.

ANOMALIES OR DATA MINING?   We have covered many of the so-called anomalies cited in the literature, but our list could go on and on. Some wonder whether these anomalies are really unexplained puzzles in financial markets or whether they instead are an artifact of data mining. After all, if one reruns the database of past returns over and over and examines stock returns along enough dimensions, simple chance will cause some criteria to *appear* to predict returns.

In this regard, it is noteworthy that some anomalies have not shown much staying power after being reported in the academic literature. For example, after the small-firm effect was published in the early 1980s, it promptly disappeared for much of the rest of the decade.

Still, even acknowledging the potential for data mining, a common thread seems to run through many of the anomalies we have considered, lending support to the notion that there is a real puzzle to explain. Value stocks—defined by low P/E ratio, high book-to-market ratio, or depressed prices relative to historic levels—seem to have provided higher average returns than "glamour" or growth stocks.

One way to address the problem of data mining is to find a data set that has not already been researched and see whether the relationship in question shows up in the new data. Such studies have revealed size, momentum, and book-to-market effects in other security markets around the world. While these phenomena may be a manifestation of a systematic risk premium, the precise nature of that risk is not fully understood.

ANOMALIES OVER TIME   We pointed out previously that while no market can be perfectly efficient, in well-functioning markets, anomalies ought to be self-destructing. As market participants learn of profitable trading strategies, their attempts to exploit them should move prices to levels at which abnormal profits are no longer available. Chordia, Subrahmanyam, and Tong (2012) look for this dynamic in the pattern of many of the anomalies discussed in this chapter. They focus on abnormal returns associated with several characteristics including size, book-to-market ratio, momentum, and turnover (which may be inversely related to the neglected firm effect). They break their sample at 1993 and show that the abnormal returns associated with these characteristics in the pre-1993 period largely disappear in the post-1993 period (with the notable exception of the book-to-market effect). Their interpretation is that the market has become more efficient as knowledge about these anomalies percolated through the investment community. Interestingly, they find that the attenuation of alphas is greatest in the most liquid stocks, where trading activity is least costly.

McLean and Pontiff (2015) provide further insight into this phenomenon. They identify more than 80 characteristics identified in the academic literature as associated with abnormal returns. Rather than using a common break point for all characteristics, they carefully track both the publication date of each finding as well as the date the paper was first posted to the Social Science Research Network. This allows them to break the sample for each finding at dates corresponding to when that particular finding became public. They conclude that the postpublication decay in abnormal return is about 35% (e.g., a 5% abnormal return prepublication falls on average to 3.25% after publication).[10] They show that trading volume and variance in stocks identified with anomalies increase, as does short interest in "overpriced" stocks. These patterns are consistent with informed participants attempting to exploit newly recognized mispricing. Moreover, the decay in alpha is most pronounced for stocks that are larger, more liquid, and with low idiosyncratic risk. These are precisely the stocks for which trading activity in pursuit of reliable abnormal returns is most feasible. Thus, while abnormal returns do not fully disappear, these results are consistent with a market groping its way toward greater efficiency over time.

[10]About a third of that decay occurs between the final date of the sample and the publication date, which the authors note may reflect the portion of apparent abnormal returns that actually are due to data mining. The remaining decay would then be attributable to the actions of sophisticated investors whose trades move anomalous prices back toward intrinsic value.

8.4   MUTUAL FUND AND ANALYST PERFORMANCE

We have documented some of the apparent chinks in the armor of efficient market proponents. For investors, the issue of market efficiency boils down to whether skilled investors can make consistent abnormal trading profits. The best test is to look at the performance of market professionals to see if they can generate performance superior to that of a passive index fund that buys and holds the market. We will look at two facets of professional performance: that of stock market analysts who recommend investment positions and that of mutual fund managers who actually manage portfolios.

Stock Market Analysts

Stock market analysts historically have worked for brokerage firms, which presents an immediate problem in interpreting the value of their advice: Analysts have tended to be overwhelmingly positive in their assessment of the prospects of firms.[11] For example, Barber, Lehavy, McNichols, and Trueman (2001) find that on a scale of 1 (strong buy) to 5 (strong sell), the average recommendation for 5,628 covered firms in 1996 was 2.04. As a result, one cannot take positive recommendations (e.g., to buy) at face value. Instead, we must look at either the relative enthusiasm of analyst recommendations compared to those for other firms or at the change in consensus recommendations.

Womack (1996) focuses on changes in analysts' recommendations and finds that positive changes are associated with increased stock prices of about 5% and negative changes result in average price decreases of 11%. One might wonder whether these price changes reflect the market's recognition of analysts' superior information or insight about firms or, instead, simply result from new buy or sell pressure brought on by the recommendations themselves. Womack argues that price impact seems to be permanent and, therefore, consistent with the hypothesis that analysts do in fact reveal new information. Jegadeesh, Kim, Krische, and Lee (2004) also find that changes in consensus recommendations are associated with price changes, but that the *level* of consensus recommendations is an inconsistent predictor of future stock performance.

Barber, Lehavy, McNichols, and Trueman (2001) focus on the level of consensus recommendations and show that firms with the most favorable recommendations outperform those with the least favorable recommendations. While their results seem impressive, the authors note that portfolio strategies based on analyst consensus recommendations would result in extremely heavy trading activity with associated costs that probably would wipe out the potential profits from the strategy.

In sum, the literature suggests that some value is added by analysts, but ambiguity remains. Are superior returns following analyst upgrades due to revelation of new information or due to changes in investor demand in response to the changed outlook? Also, are these results exploitable by investors who necessarily incur trading costs?

Mutual Fund Managers

As we pointed out in Chapter 4, casual evidence does not support the claim that professionally managed portfolios can consistently beat the market. Figure 4.4 in that chapter demonstrated that between 1972 and 2013 the returns of a passive portfolio indexed to the Wilshire 5000 typically would have been better than those of the average equity fund. On the other hand, there was some (admittedly inconsistent) evidence of persistence in performance, meaning that the better managers in one period tended to be better managers in following periods. Such a pattern would suggest that the better managers can with some consistency outperform their

---

[11]This problem may be less severe in the future; as noted in Chapter 3, one recent reform intended to mitigate the conflict of interest in having brokerage firms that sell stocks also provide investment advice is to separate analyst coverage from the other activities of the firm.

competitors, and it would be inconsistent with the notion that market prices already reflect all relevant information.

The analyses cited in Chapter 4 were based on total returns; they did not properly adjust returns for exposure to systematic risk factors. In this section we revisit the question of mutual fund performance, paying more attention to the benchmark against which performance ought to be evaluated.

As a first pass, we can examine the risk-adjusted returns (i.e., the alpha, or return in excess of required return based on beta and the market return in each period) of a large sample of mutual funds. But the market index may not be an adequate benchmark against which to evaluate mutual fund returns. Because mutual funds tend to maintain considerable holdings in equity of small firms, whereas the S&P 500 exclusively comprises large firms, mutual funds as a whole will tend to outperform the S&P when small firms outperform large ones and underperform when small firms fare worse. Thus, a better benchmark for the performance of funds would be an index that incorporates the stock market performance of smaller firms.

The importance of the benchmark can be illustrated by examining the returns on small stocks in various subperiods.[12] In the 20-year period between 1945 and 1964, for example, a small-stock index underperformed the S&P 500 by about 4% per year (i.e., the alpha of the small-stock index after adjusting for systematic risk was −4%). In the following 20-year period, between 1965 and 1984, small stocks outperformed the S&P 500 Index by 10%. Thus, if one were to examine mutual fund returns in the earlier period, they would tend to look poor, not necessarily because fund managers were poor stock pickers but simply because mutual funds as a group tended to hold more small stocks than were represented in the S&P 500. In the later period, funds would look better on a risk-adjusted basis relative to the S&P 500 because small stocks performed better. The "style choice," that is, the exposure to small stocks (which is an asset allocation decision) would dominate the evaluation of performance even though it has little to do with managers' stock-picking ability.[13]

The conventional performance benchmark today is a four-factor model, which employs the three Fama-French factors (the return on the market index, and returns to portfolios based on size and book-to-market ratio) augmented by a momentum factor (a portfolio constructed based on prior-year stock return). Alphas constructed using an expanded index model using these four factors control for a wide range of mutual fund–style choices that may affect average returns, for example, an inclination to growth versus value or small- versus large-capitalization stocks. Figure 8.7 shows a frequency distribution of four-factor alphas for U.S. domestic equity funds.[14] The results show that the distribution of alpha is roughly bell-shaped, with a slightly negative mean. On average, it does not appear that these funds outperform their style-adjusted benchmarks.

Consistent with Figure 8.7, Fama and French (2010) use the four-factor model to assess the performance of equity mutual funds and show that while they may exhibit positive alphas *before* fees, after the fees charged to their customers, alphas were negative. Likewise, Wermers (2000), who uses both style portfolios as well as the characteristics of the stocks held by mutual funds to control for performance, also finds positive gross alphas but negative net alphas after controlling for fees and risk.

Carhart (1997) reexamines the issue of consistency in mutual fund performance to see whether better performers in one period continue to outperform in later periods. He uses the four-factor extension described above and finds that after controlling for these factors, there is only minor persistence in relative performance across managers. Moreover, much of that persistence seems due to expenses and transactions costs rather than gross investment returns.

---

[12]This illustration and the statistics cited are based on E. J. Elton, M. J. Gruber, S. Das, and M. Hlavka, "Efficiency with Costly Information: A Reinterpretation of Evidence from Managed Portfolios," *Review of Financial Studies* 6 (1993), pp. 1–22.

[13]Remember that the asset allocation decision is usually in the hands of the individual investor. Investors allocate their investment portfolios to funds in asset classes they desire to hold, and they can reasonably expect only that mutual fund portfolio managers will choose stocks advantageously *within* those asset classes.

[14]We are grateful to Professor Richard Evans for these data.

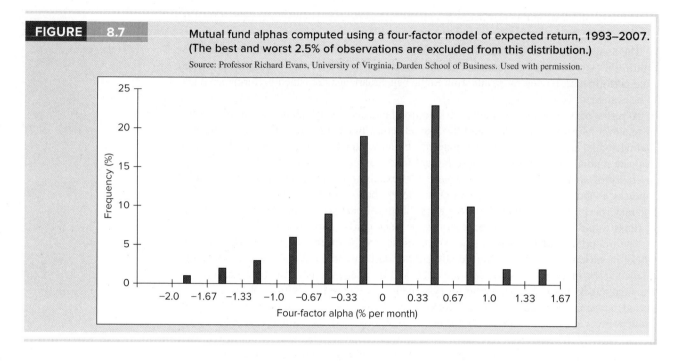

FIGURE 8.7   Mutual fund alphas computed using a four-factor model of expected return, 1993–2007. (The best and worst 2.5% of observations are excluded from this distribution.)
Source: Professor Richard Evans, University of Virginia, Darden School of Business. Used with permission.

Even allowing for expenses and turnover, some amount of performance persistence seems to be due to differences in investment strategy. Carhart finds, however, that the evidence of persistence is concentrated at the two extremes. Figure 8.8, from his study, documents performance persistence. Equity funds are ranked into 1 of 10 groups by performance in the formation year, and the performance of each group in the following years is plotted. It is clear that except for the best-performing top-decile group and the worst-performing 10th-decile group, performance in future periods is almost independent of earlier-year returns. Carhart's results suggest that there may be a small group of exceptional managers who can with some

FIGURE 8.8

Persistence of mutual fund performance. Performance over time of mutual fund groups ranked by initial-year performance

Source: Mark M. Carhart, "On Persistence in Mutual Fund Performance," *Journal of Finance* 52 (March 1997), pp. 57–82.

consistency outperform a passive strategy, but that for the majority of managers over- or underperformance in any period is largely a matter of chance.

Bollen and Busse (2004) find more evidence of performance persistence, at least over short horizons. They rank mutual fund performance using the four-factor model over a base quarter, assign funds into one of 10 deciles according to base-period alpha, and then look at performance in the following quarter. Figure 8.9 illustrates their results. The solid line is the average alpha of funds within each of the deciles in the base period (expressed on a quarterly basis). The steepness of that line reflects the considerable dispersion in performance in the ranking period. The dashed line is the average performance of the funds in each decile in the following quarter. The shallowness of this line indicates that most of the original performance differential disappears. Nevertheless, the plot is still clearly downward-sloping, so it appears that at least over a short horizon such as one quarter, there is some performance consistency. However, that persistence is probably too small a fraction of the original performance differential to justify performance chasing by mutual fund customers.

This pattern is actually consistent with the prediction of an influential paper by Berk and Green (2004). They argue that skilled mutual fund managers with abnormal performance will attract new funds until the additional costs and complexity of managing those extra funds drive alphas down to zero. Thus, skill will show up not in superior returns but rather in the amount of funds under management. Therefore, even if managers are skilled, alphas will be short-lived, as they seem to be in Figure 8.9.

Del Guercio and Reuter (2014) offer a finer interpretation of mutual fund performance than the Berk and Green hypothesis. They split mutual fund investors into those who buy funds directly for themselves versus those who purchase funds through brokers, reasoning that the direct-sold segment may be more financially literate while the broker-sold segment is less comfortable making financial decisions without professional advice. Consistent with this hypothesis, they show that direct-sold investors direct their assets to funds with positive alphas (consistent with the Berk-Green model), but broker-sold investors generally do not. This provides an incentive for direct-sold funds to invest relatively more in alpha-generating inputs such as talented portfolio managers or analysts than broker-sold funds. Moreover, they show that the after-fee performance of direct-sold funds is as good as that of index funds (again consistent with Berk-Green), while the performance of broker-sold funds is considerably worse. It thus appears that the average underperformance of actively managed mutual funds is driven largely by broker-sold funds, and that this underperformance may be interpreted as an implicit cost that less informed investors pay for the advice they get from their brokers.

In contrast to the extensive studies of equity fund managers, there have been few studies of the performance of bond fund managers. Blake, Elton, and Gruber (1993) examined the performance of fixed-income mutual funds. They found that, on average, bond funds

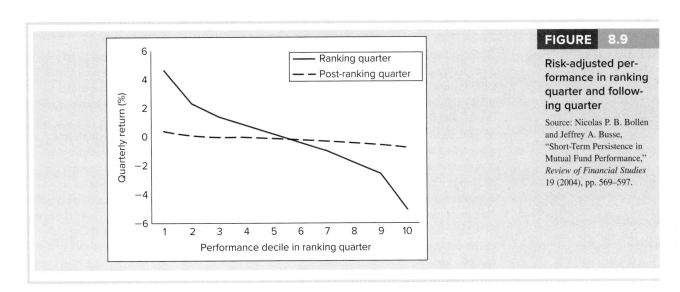

FIGURE 8.9

Risk-adjusted performance in ranking quarter and following quarter

Source: Nicolas P. B. Bollen and Jeffrey A. Busse, "Short-Term Persistence in Mutual Fund Performance," *Review of Financial Studies* 19 (2004), pp. 569–597.

underperform passive fixed-income indexes by an amount roughly equal to expenses and that there is no evidence that past performance can predict future performance. More recently, Chen, Ferson, and Peters (2010) find that, on average, bond mutual funds outperform passive bond indexes in terms of gross returns but underperform once the fees they charge their investors are subtracted, a result similar to those others have found for equity funds.

Thus, the evidence on the risk-adjusted performance of professional managers is mixed at best. We conclude that the performance of professional managers is broadly consistent with market efficiency. The amounts by which professional managers as a group beat or are beaten by the market fall within the margin of statistical uncertainty. In any event, it is quite clear that performance superior to passive strategies is far from routine. Studies show either that most managers cannot outperform passive strategies or that if there is a margin of superiority, it is small.

On the other hand, a small number of investment superstars—Peter Lynch (formerly of Fidelity's Magellan Fund), Warren Buffett (of Berkshire Hathaway), John Templeton (of Templeton Funds), and Mario Gabelli (of GAMCO), among them—have compiled career records that show a consistency of superior performance hard to reconcile with absolutely efficient markets. In a careful statistical analysis of mutual fund "stars," Kosowski, Timmerman, Wermers, and White (2006) conclude that the stock-picking ability of a minority of managers is sufficient to cover their costs and that their superior performance tends to persist over time. However, Nobel Prize–winner Paul Samuelson (1989) points out that the records of the vast majority of professional money managers offer convincing evidence that there are no easy strategies to guarantee success in the securities markets.

So, Are Markets Efficient?

There is a telling joke about two economists walking down the street. They spot a $20 bill on the sidewalk. One starts to pick it up, but the other one says, "Don't bother; if the bill were real someone would have picked it up already."

The lesson is clear. An overly doctrinaire belief in efficient markets can paralyze the investor and make it appear that no research effort can be justified. This extreme view is probably unwarranted. There are enough anomalies in the empirical evidence to justify the search for underpriced securities that clearly goes on.

The bulk of the evidence, however, suggests that any supposedly superior investment strategy should be taken with many grains of salt. The market is competitive *enough* that only differentially superior information or insight will earn money; the easy pickings have been picked. In the end it is likely that the margin of superiority that any professional manager can add is so slight that the statistician will not easily be able to detect it.

We conclude that markets are very efficient, but that rewards to the especially diligent, intelligent, or creative may in fact be waiting.

SUMMARY

- Statistical research has shown that to a close approximation stock prices seem to follow a random walk with no discernible predictable patterns that investors can exploit. Such findings are now taken to be evidence of market efficiency, that is, evidence that market prices reflect all currently available information. Only new information will move stock prices, and this information is equally likely to be good news or bad news.

- Market participants distinguish among three forms of the efficient market hypothesis. The weak form asserts that all information to be derived from past trading data already is reflected in stock prices. The semistrong form claims that all publicly available information is already reflected. The strong form, which generally is acknowledged to be extreme, asserts that all information, including insider information, is reflected in prices.

- Technical analysis focuses on stock price patterns and on proxies for buy or sell pressure in the market. Fundamental analysis focuses on the determinants of the underlying value of the firm, such as current profitability and growth prospects. Because both types of analysis are based on public information, neither should generate excess profits if markets are operating efficiently.

- Proponents of the efficient market hypothesis often advocate passive as opposed to active investment strategies. The policy of passive investors is to buy and hold a broad-based market index. They expend resources neither on market research nor on frequent purchase and sale of stocks. Passive strategies may be tailored to meet individual investor requirements.

- Empirical studies of technical analysis do not generally support the hypothesis that such analysis can generate superior trading profits. One notable exception to this conclusion is the apparent success of momentum-based strategies over intermediate-term horizons.

- Several anomalies regarding fundamental analysis have been uncovered. These include the P/E effect, the small-firm-in-January effect, the neglected-firm effect, post-earnings-announcement price drift, and the book-to-market effect. Whether these anomalies represent market inefficiency or poorly understood risk premiums is still a matter of debate.

- By and large, the performance record of professionally managed funds lends little credence to claims that most professionals can consistently beat the market.

KEY TERMS

anomalies,   245
book-to-market effect,   246
efficient market
   hypothesis,   233
fundamental analysis,   238
index fund,   239
momentum effect,   243

neglected-firm effect,   246
passive investment
   strategy,   239
P/E effect,   245
random walk,   233
resistance level,   237
reversal effect,   244

semistrong-form
   EMH,   236
small-firm effect,   245
strong-form EMH,   236
support level,   237
technical analysis,   237
weak-form EMH,   236

PROBLEM SETS

 Select problems are available in McGraw-Hill's *Connect.* Please see the Supplements section of the book's frontmatter for more information.

1. If markets are efficient, what should be the correlation coefficient between stock returns for two nonoverlapping time periods? *(LO 8-1)*

2. "If all securities are fairly priced, all must offer equal expected rates of return." Comment. *(LO 8-1)*

3. If prices are as likely to increase as decrease, why do investors earn positive returns from the market on average? *(LO 8-1)*

4. A successful firm like Microsoft has consistently generated large profits for years. Is this a violation of the EMH? *(LO 8-2)*

5. At a cocktail party, your co-worker tells you that he has beaten the market for each of the last three years. Suppose you believe him. Does this shake your belief in efficient markets? *(LO 8-2)*

6. Which of the following statements are *true* if the efficient market hypothesis holds? *(LO 8-1)*
   a. It implies that future events can be forecast with perfect accuracy.
   b. It implies that prices reflect all available information.
   c. It implies that security prices change for no discernible reason.
   d. It implies that prices do not fluctuate.

7. In an efficient market, professional portfolio management can offer all of the following benefits *except* which of the following? *(LO 8-4)*
   a. Low-cost diversification.
   b. A targeted risk level.
   c. Low-cost record keeping.
   d. A superior risk-return trade-off.

8. Which version of the efficient market hypothesis (weak, semistrong, or strong-form) focuses on the most inclusive set of information? *(LO 8-1)*

9. "Highly variable stock prices suggest that the market does not know how to price stocks." Respond. *(LO 8-1)*

10. Which of the following sources of market inefficiency would be most easily exploited? *(LO 8-4)*

    a. A stock price drops suddenly due to a large block sale by an institution.

    b. A stock is overpriced because traders are restricted from short sales.

    c. Stocks are overvalued because investors are exuberant over increased productivity in the economy.

11. Which of the following most appears to contradict the proposition that the stock market is *weakly* efficient? Explain. *(LO 8-3)*

    a. Over 25% of mutual funds outperform the market on average.

    b. Insiders earn abnormal trading profits.

    c. Every January, the stock market earns abnormal returns.

12. Suppose that, after conducting an analysis of past stock prices, you come up with the following observations. Which would appear to *contradict* the *weak form* of the efficient market hypothesis? Explain. *(LO 8-3)*

    a. The average rate of return is significantly greater than zero.

    b. The correlation between the return during a given week and the return during the following week is zero.

    c. One could have made superior returns by buying stock after a 10% rise in price and selling after a 10% fall.

    d. One could have made higher-than-average capital gains by holding stocks with low dividend yields.

13. Which of the following observations would provide evidence *against* the *semistrong form* of the efficient market theory? Explain. *(LO 8-3)*

    a. Mutual fund managers do not on average make superior returns.

    b. You cannot make superior profits by buying (or selling) stocks after the announcement of an abnormal rise in dividends.

    c. Low P/E stocks tend to have positive abnormal returns.

    d. In any year approximately 50% of pension funds outperform the market.

14. Steady Growth Industries has never missed a dividend payment in its 94-year history. Does this make it more attractive to you as a possible purchase for your stock portfolio? *(LO 8-4)*

15. Suppose you find that prices of stocks before large dividend increases show on average consistently positive abnormal returns. Is this a violation of the EMH? *(LO 8-3)*

16. "If the business cycle is predictable, and a stock has a positive beta, the stock's returns also must be predictable." Respond. *(LO 8-1)*

17. Which of the following phenomena would be either consistent with or a violation of the efficient market hypothesis? Explain briefly. *(LO 8-3)*

    a. Nearly half of all professionally managed mutual funds are able to outperform the S&P 500 in a typical year.

    b. Money managers who outperform the market (on a risk-adjusted basis) in one year are likely to outperform in the following year.

    c. Stock prices tend to be predictably more volatile in January than in other months.

    d. Stock prices of companies that announce increased earnings in January tend to outperform the market in February.

    e. Stocks that perform well in one week perform poorly in the following week.

18. Why are the following "effects" considered efficient market anomalies? Are there rational explanations for these effects? *(LO 8-2)*

    a. P/E effect

    b. Book-to-market effect

     c. Momentum effect

     d. Small-firm effect

19. Dollar-cost averaging means that you buy equal dollar amounts of a stock every period, for example, $500 per month. The strategy is based on the idea that when the stock price is low, your fixed monthly purchase will buy more shares, and when the price is high, fewer shares. Averaging over time, you will end up buying more shares when the stock is cheaper and fewer when it is relatively expensive. Therefore, by design, you will exhibit good market timing. Evaluate this strategy. *(LO 8-4)*

20. We know that the market should respond positively to good news and that good-news events such as the coming end of a recession can be predicted with at least some accuracy. Why, then, can we not predict that the market will go up as the economy recovers? *(LO 8-1)*

21. You know that firm XYZ is very poorly run. On a scale of 1 (worst) to 10 (best), you would give it a score of 3. The market consensus evaluation is that the management score is only 2. Should you buy or sell the stock? *(LO 8-4)*

22. Good News, Inc., just announced an increase in its annual earnings, yet its stock price fell. Is there a rational explanation for this phenomenon? *(LO 8-1)*

23. Shares of small firms with thinly traded stocks tend to show positive CAPM alphas. Is this a violation of the efficient market hypothesis? *(LO 8-3)*

Challenge

24. Examine the accompanying figure, which presents cumulative abnormal returns both before and after dates on which insiders buy or sell shares in their firms. How do you interpret this figure? What are we to make of the pattern of CARs before and after the event date? *(LO 8-3)*

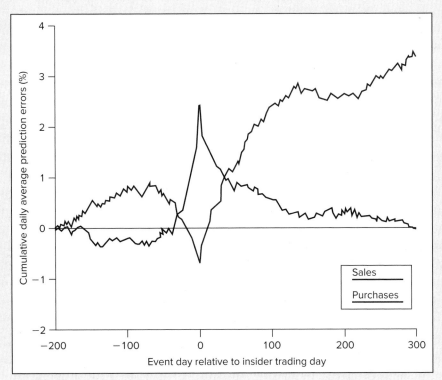

Source: Nejat H. Seyhun, "Insiders, Profits, Costs of Trading and Market Efficiency," *Journal of Financial Economics* 16 pp. 189–212.

25. Suppose that as the economy moves through a business cycle, risk premiums also change. For example, in a recession when people are concerned about their jobs, risk tolerance might be lower and risk premiums might be higher. In a booming economy, tolerance for risk might be higher and risk premiums lower. *(LO 8-3)*

    a. Would a predictably shifting risk premium such as described here be a violation of the efficient market hypothesis?

    b. How might a cycle of increasing and decreasing risk premiums create an appearance that stock prices "overreact," first falling excessively and then seeming to recover?

CFA Problems

1. The semistrong form of the efficient market hypothesis asserts that stock prices: *(LO 8-1)*

   a. Fully reflect all historical price information.
   b. Fully reflect all publicly available information.
   c. Fully reflect all relevant information including insider information.
   d. May be predictable.

2. Assume that a company announces an unexpectedly large cash dividend to its shareholders. In an efficient market *without* information leakage, one might expect: *(LO 8-1)*

   a. An abnormal price change at the announcement.
   b. An abnormal price increase before the announcement.
   c. An abnormal price decrease after the announcement.
   d. No abnormal price change before or after the announcement.

3. Which one of the following would provide evidence *against* the *semistrong form* of the efficient market theory? *(LO 8-3)*

   a. About 50% of pension funds outperform the market in any year.
   b. You cannot make abnormal profits by buying stocks after an announcement of strong earnings.
   c. Trend analysis is worthless in forecasting stock prices.
   d. Low P/E stocks tend to have positive abnormal returns over the long run.

4. According to the efficient market hypothesis: *(LO 8-3)*

   a. High-beta stocks are consistently overpriced.
   b. Low-beta stocks are consistently overpriced.
   c. Positive alphas on stocks will quickly disappear.
   d. Negative-alpha stocks consistently yield low returns for arbitrageurs.

5. A "random walk" occurs when: *(LO 8-1)*

   a. Stock price changes are random but predictable.
   b. Stock prices respond slowly to both new and old information.
   c. Future price changes are uncorrelated with past price changes.
   d. Past information is useful in predicting future prices.

6. A market anomaly refers to: *(LO 8-3)*

   a. An exogenous shock to the market that is sharp but not persistent.
   b. A price or volume event that is inconsistent with historical price or volume trends.
   c. A trading or pricing structure that interferes with efficient buying and selling of securities.
   d. Price behavior that differs from the behavior predicted by the efficient market hypothesis.

7. Some scholars contend that professional managers are incapable of outperforming the market. Others come to an opposite conclusion. Compare and contrast the assumptions about the stock market that support (*a*) passive portfolio management and (*b*) active portfolio management. *(LO 8-2)*

8. You are a portfolio manager meeting a client. During the conversation that follows your formal review of her account, your client asks the following question: *(LO 8-2)*

   My grandson, who is studying investments, tells me that one of the best ways to make money in the stock market is to buy the stocks of small-capitalization firms late in December and to sell the stocks one month later. What is he talking about?

   a. Identify the apparent market anomalies that would justify the proposed strategy.

   b. Explain why you believe such a strategy might or might not work in the future.

9. *a.* Briefly explain the concept of the efficient market hypothesis (EMH) and each of its three forms—weak, semistrong, and strong—and briefly discuss the degree to which existing empirical evidence supports each of the three forms of the EMH. *(LO 8-2)*

   b. Briefly discuss the implications of the efficient market hypothesis for investment policy as it applies to: *(LO 8-4)*

      i. Technical analysis in the form of charting.

      ii. Fundamental analysis.

   c. Briefly explain the roles or responsibilities of portfolio managers in an efficient market environment. *(LO 8-4)*

10. Growth and value can be defined in several ways. *Growth* usually conveys the idea of a portfolio emphasizing or including only companies believed to possess above-average future rates of per-share earnings growth. Low current yield, high price-to-book ratios, and high price-to-earnings ratios are typical characteristics of such portfolios. *Value* usually conveys the idea of portfolios emphasizing or including only issues currently showing low price-to-book ratios, low price-to-earnings ratios, above-average levels of dividend yield, and market prices believed to be below the issues' intrinsic values. *(LO 8-3)*

    a. Identify and provide reasons why, over an extended period of time, value-stock investing might outperform growth-stock investing.

    b. Explain why the outcome suggested in (*a*) should not be possible in a market widely regarded as being highly efficient.

11. Your investment client asks for information concerning the benefits of active portfolio management. She is particularly interested in the question of whether active managers can be expected to consistently exploit inefficiencies in the capital markets to produce above-average returns without assuming higher risk.

    The semistrong form of the efficient market hypothesis asserts that all publicly available information is rapidly and correctly reflected in securities prices. This implies that investors cannot expect to derive above-average profits from purchases made after information has become public because security prices already reflect the information's full effects. *(LO 8-2)*

    a. Identify and explain two examples of empirical evidence that tend to support the EMH implication stated above.

    b. Identify and explain two examples of empirical evidence that tend to refute the EMH implication stated above.

    c. Discuss reasons why an investor might choose not to index even if the markets were, in fact, semistrong-form efficient.

---

1. Use data from **finance.yahoo.com** to answer the following questions.

   a. Collect the following data for 25 firms of your choosing.

      i. Book-to-market ratio.

      ii. Price–earnings ratio.

      iii. Market capitalization (size).

      iv. Price–cash flow ratio (i.e, market capitalization/operating cash flow).

      v. Another criterion that interests you.

WEB *master*

You can find this information by choosing a company and then clicking on *Key Statistics*. Rank the firms based on each of the criteria separately, and divide the firms into five groups based on their ranking for each criterion. Calculate the average rate of return for each group of firms.

Do you confirm or reject any of the anomalies cited in this chapter? Can you uncover a new anomaly? Note: For your test to be valid, you must form your portfolios based on criteria observed at the *beginning* of the period when you form the stock groups. Why?

b. Use the price history from the *Historical Prices* tab to calculate the beta of each of the firms in part (*a*). Use this beta, the T-bill rate, and the return on the S&P 500 to calculate the risk-adjusted abnormal return of each stock group. Does any anomaly uncovered in the previous question persist after controlling for risk?

c. Now form stock groups that use two criteria simultaneously. For example, form a portfolio of stocks that are both in the lowest quintile of price–earnings ratio and in the highest quintile of book-to-market ratio. Does selecting stocks based on more than one characteristic improve your ability to devise portfolios with abnormal returns? Repeat the analysis by forming groups that meet three criteria simultaneously. Does this yield any further improvement in abnormal returns?

8.1 *a.* A high-level manager might well have private information about the firm. Her ability to trade profitably on that information is not surprising. This ability does not violate weak-form efficiency: The abnormal profits are not derived from an analysis of past price and trading data. If they were, this would indicate that there is valuable information that can be gleaned from such analysis. But this ability does violate strong-form efficiency. Apparently, there is some private information that is not already reflected in stock prices.

b. The information sets that pertain to the weak, semistrong, and strong form of the EMH can be described by the following illustration:

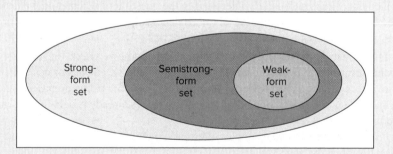

The weak-form information set includes only the history of prices and volumes. The semistrong-form set includes the weak form set *plus* all other publicly available information. In turn, the strong-form set includes the semistrong set *plus* insiders' information. It is illegal to act on this incremental information (insiders' private information). The direction of *valid* implication is

Strong-form EMH ⇒ Semistrong-form EMH ⇒ Weak-form EMH

The reverse direction implication is *not* valid. For example, stock prices may reflect all past price data (weak-form efficiency) but may not reflect relevant fundamental data (semistrong-form inefficiency).

8.2 The point we made in the preceding discussion is that the very fact that we observe stock prices near so-called resistance levels belies the assumption that the price can be a resistance level. If a stock is observed to sell *at any price,* then investors must believe that a fair rate of return can be earned if the stock is purchased at that price. It is logically impossible for a stock to have a resistance level *and* offer a fair rate of return at prices just below the resistance level. If we accept that prices are appropriate, we must reject any presumption concerning resistance levels.

8.3 If *everyone* follows a passive strategy, sooner or later prices will fail to reflect new information. At this point there are profit opportunities for active investors who uncover mispriced securities. As they buy and sell these assets, prices again will be driven to fair levels.

8.4 The answer depends on your prior beliefs about market efficiency. Miller's initial record was incredibly strong. On the other hand, with so many funds in existence, it is less surprising that *some* fund would appear to be consistently superior after the fact. Exceptional past performance of a small number of managers is possible by chance even in an efficient market. A better test is provided in "continuation studies." Are better performers in one period more likely to repeat that performance in later periods? Miller's record in the last three years fails the continuation or consistency criterion.

Behavioral Finance and Technical Analysis

Learning Objectives

LO 9-1 Describe several behavioral biases, and explain how they could lead to anomalies in stock market prices and returns.

LO 9-2 Explain why limits to arbitrage might allow anomalies due to behavioral biases to persist over time.

LO 9-3 Identify reasons why technical analysis may be profitable.

LO 9-4 Use indicators such as volume, put/call ratios, breadth, short interest, or confidence indexes to measure the "technical conditions" of the market.

The efficient market hypothesis makes two important predictions. First, it implies that security prices properly reflect whatever information is available to investors. A second implication follows immediately: Active traders will find it difficult to outperform passive strategies such as holding market indexes. To do so would require differential insight; this in a highly competitive market is very hard to come by.

Unfortunately, it is hard to devise measures of the "true" or intrinsic value of a security, and correspondingly difficult to test directly whether prices match those values. Therefore, most tests of market efficiency have focused on the performance of active trading strategies. These tests have been of two kinds. The anomalies literature has examined strategies that apparently *would* have provided

superior risk-adjusted returns (e.g., investing in stocks with momentum or in value rather than glamour stocks). Other tests have looked at the results of *actual* investments by asking whether professional managers have been able to beat the market.

Neither class of tests has proven fully conclusive. The anomalies literature suggests that several strategies would have provided superior returns. But there are questions as to whether some of these apparent anomalies reflect risk premiums not captured by simple models of risk and return, or even if they merely reflect data mining. Moreover, the apparent inability of the typical money manager to turn these anomalies into superior returns on actual portfolios casts additional doubt on their "reality."

A relatively new school of thought dubbed *behavioral finance* argues that the sprawling literature on trading strategies has missed a larger and more important point by overlooking the first implication of efficient markets—the correctness of security prices. This may be the more important implication because market economies rely on prices to allocate resources efficiently. The behavioral school argues that even if security prices are wrong, it still can be difficult to exploit them, and, therefore, that the failure to uncover obviously successful trading rules or traders cannot be taken as proof of market efficiency.

Whereas conventional theories presume that investors are rational, behavioral finance starts with the assumption that they are not. We will examine some of the information-processing and behavioral irrationalities uncovered by psychologists in other contexts and show how these tendencies applied to financial markets might result in some of the anomalies discussed in the previous chapter. We then consider the limitations of strategies designed to take advantage of behaviorally induced mispricing. If the limits to such arbitrage activity are severe, mispricing can survive even if some rational investors attempt to exploit it. We turn next to technical analysis and show how behavioral models give some support to techniques that clearly would be useless in efficient markets. We close the chapter with a brief survey of some of these technical strategies.

9.1 THE BEHAVIORAL CRITIQUE

The premise of **behavioral finance** is that conventional financial theory ignores how real people make decisions and that people make a difference.[1] A growing number of economists have come to interpret the anomalies literature as consistent with several "irrationalities" that seem to characterize individuals making complicated decisions. These irrationalities fall into two broad categories: first, that investors do not always process information correctly and therefore infer incorrect probability distributions about future rates of return; and second, that even given a probability distribution of returns, they often make inconsistent or systematically suboptimal decisions.

Of course, the existence of irrational investors would not by itself be sufficient to render capital markets inefficient. If such irrationalities did affect prices, then sharp-eyed arbitrageurs taking advantage of profit opportunities might be expected to push prices back to their proper values. Thus, the second leg of the behavioral critique is that in practice the actions of such arbitrageurs are limited and therefore insufficient to force prices to match intrinsic value.

This leg of the argument is important. Virtually everyone agrees that if prices are right (i.e., price = intrinsic value), then there are no easy profit opportunities. But the converse is not necessarily true. If behaviorists are correct about limits to arbitrage activity, then the absence of profit opportunities does not necessarily imply that markets are efficient. We've noted that most tests of the efficient market hypothesis have focused on the existence of profit opportunities, often as reflected in the performance of money managers. But their failure to systematically outperform passive investment strategies need not imply that markets are in fact efficient.

We will start our summary of the behavioral critique with the first leg of the argument, surveying a sample of the informational processing errors uncovered by psychologists in other areas. We next examine a few of the behavioral irrationalities that seem to characterize decision makers. Finally, we look at limits to arbitrage activity and conclude with a tentative assessment of the import of the behavioral debate.

behavioral finance

Models of financial markets that emphasize potential implications of psychological factors affecting investor behavior.

[1]The discussion in this section is based on an excellent survey article: Nicholas Barberis and Richard Thaler, "A Survey of Behavioral Finance," in the *Handbook of the Economics of Finance,* eds. G. M. Constantinides, M. Harris, and R. Stulz (Amsterdam: Elsevier, 2003).

Information Processing

Errors in information processing can lead investors to misestimate the true probabilities of possible events or associated rates of return. Several such biases have been uncovered. Here are four of the more important ones.

FORECASTING ERRORS   A series of experiments by Kahneman and Tversky (1972, 1973) indicates that people give too much weight to recent experience compared to prior beliefs when making forecasts (sometimes dubbed a *memory bias*) and tend to make forecasts that are too extreme given the uncertainty inherent in their information. De Bondt and Thaler (1990) argue that the P/E effect can be explained by earnings expectations that are too extreme. In this view, when forecasts of a firm's future earnings are high, perhaps due to favorable recent performance, they tend to be *too* high relative to the objective prospects of the firm. This results in a high initial P/E (due to the optimism built into the stock price) and poor subsequent performance when investors recognize their error. Thus, high P/E firms tend to be poor investments.

OVERCONFIDENCE   People tend to overestimate the precision of their beliefs or forecasts, and they tend to overestimate their abilities. In one famous survey, 90% of drivers in Sweden ranked themselves as better-than-average drivers. Such overconfidence may be responsible for the prevalence of active versus passive investment management—itself an anomaly to adherents of the efficient market hypothesis. Despite the growing popularity of indexing, only about 20% of the equity in the mutual fund industry is held in indexed accounts. The dominance of active management in the face of the typical underperformance of such strategies (consider the generally disappointing performance of actively managed mutual funds reviewed in Chapter 4 as well as in the previous chapter) is consistent with a tendency to overestimate ability.

An interesting example of overconfidence in financial markets is provided by Barber and Odean (2001), who compare trading activity and average returns in brokerage accounts of men and women. They find that men (in particular, single men) trade far more actively than women, consistent with the generally greater overconfidence among men well-documented in the psychology literature. They also find that trading activity is highly predictive of poor investment performance. The top 20% of accounts ranked by portfolio turnover had average returns seven percentage points lower than the 20% of the accounts with the lowest turnover rates. As they conclude, "Trading [and by implication, overconfidence] is hazardous to your wealth."

Overconfidence appears to be a widespread phenomenon, also showing up in many corporate finance contexts. For example, overconfident CEOs are more likely to overpay for target firms when making corporate acquisitions (Malmendier and Tate, 2008). Just as overconfidence can degrade portfolio investments, it also can lead such firms to make poor investments in real assets.

conservatism bias

Investors are too slow (too conservative) in updating their beliefs in response to recent evidence.

CONSERVATISM   A **conservatism bias** means that investors are too slow (too conservative) in updating their beliefs in response to new evidence. This means that they might initially underreact to news about a firm, so that prices will fully reflect new information only gradually. Such a bias would give rise to momentum in stock market returns.

representativeness bias

People are too prone to believe that a small sample is representative of a broad population and infer patterns too quickly.

SAMPLE-SIZE NEGLECT AND REPRESENTATIVENESS   The notion of **representativeness bias** holds that people commonly do not take into account the size of a sample, acting as if a small sample is just as representative of a population as a large one. They may therefore infer a pattern too quickly based on a small sample and extrapolate apparent trends too far into the future. It is easy to see how such a pattern would be consistent with overreaction and correction anomalies. A short-lived run of good earnings reports or high stock returns would lead such investors to revise their assessments of likely future performance and thus generate buying pressure that exaggerates the price run-up. Eventually, the gap between price and intrinsic value becomes glaring and the market corrects its initial error. Interestingly, stocks with the best recent performance suffer reversals precisely in the few days surrounding management earnings forecasts or actual earnings announcements, suggesting that the correction occurs just as investors learn that their initial beliefs were too extreme (Chopra, Lakonishok, and Ritter, 1992).

CONCEPT check **9.1**

We saw in the previous chapter that stocks seem to exhibit a pattern of short- to middle-term momentum, along with long-term reversals. How might this pattern arise from an interplay between the conservatism and representativeness biases?

Behavioral Biases

Even if information processing were perfect, many studies conclude that individuals would tend to make less-than-fully rational decisions using that information. These behavioral biases largely affect how investors frame questions of risk versus return, and therefore make risk-return trade-offs.

FRAMING   Decisions seem to be affected by how choices are **framed.** For example, an individual may reject a bet when it is posed in terms of the risk surrounding possible gains but may accept that same bet when described in terms of the risk surrounding potential losses. In other words, individuals may act risk averse in terms of gains but risk seeking in terms of losses. But in many cases, the choice of how to frame a risky venture—as involving gains or losses—can be arbitrary.

framing

Decisions are affected by how choices are posed, for example, as gains relative to a low baseline level or losses relative to a higher baseline.

EXAMPLE 9.1

Framing

Consider a coin toss with a payoff of $50 for tails. Now consider a gift of $50 that is bundled with a bet that imposes a loss of $50 if that coin toss comes up heads. In both cases, you end up with zero for heads and $50 for tails. But the former description frames the coin toss as posing a risky gain while the latter frames the coin toss in terms of risky losses. The difference in framing can lead to different attitudes toward the bet.

MENTAL ACCOUNTING   **Mental accounting** is a specific form of framing in which people segregate certain decisions. For example, an investor may take a lot of risk with one investment account but establish a very conservative position with another account that is dedicated to her child's education. Rationally, it might be better to view both accounts as part of the investor's overall portfolio with the risk-return profiles of each integrated into a unified framework. Nevertheless, Statman (2008) points out that a central distinction between conventional and behavioral finance theory is that the behavioral approach views investors as building their portfolios in "distinct mental account layers in a pyramid of assets," where each layer may be tied to particular goals and elicit different levels of risk aversion.

mental accounting

A specific form of framing in which people segregate certain decisions.

In another paper, Statman (1997) argues that mental accounting is consistent with some investors' irrational preference for stocks with high cash dividends (they feel free to spend dividend income, but would not "dip into capital" by selling a few shares of another stock with the same total rate of return) and with a tendency to ride losing stock positions for too long (because "behavioral investors" are reluctant to realize losses). In fact, investors are more likely to sell stocks with gains than those with losses, precisely contrary to a tax-minimization strategy (Shefrin and Statman, 1985; Odean, 1998).

Mental accounting effects also can help explain momentum in stock prices. The *house money effect* refers to gamblers' greater willingness to accept new bets if they currently are ahead. They think of (i.e., frame) the bet as being made with their "winnings account," that is, with the casino's and not with their own money, and thus are more willing to accept risk. Analogously, after a stock market run-up, individuals may view investments as largely funded out of a "capital gains account," become more tolerant of risk, discount future cash flows at a lower rate, and thus further push up prices.

REGRET AVOIDANCE   Psychologists have found that individuals who make decisions that turn out badly have more regret (blame themselves more) when that decision was more unconventional. For example, buying a blue-chip portfolio that turns down is not as painful as experiencing the same losses on an unknown start-up firm. Any losses on the blue-chip stocks can be more easily attributed to bad luck rather than bad decision making and cause less regret. De Bondt and Thaler (1987) argue that such **regret avoidance** is consistent with both the size and book-to-market effect. Higher-book-to-market firms tend to have depressed stock prices. These firms are "out of favor" and more likely to be in a financially precarious position. Similarly, smaller, less well-known firms are also less conventional investments. Such firms require more "courage" on the part of the investor, which increases the required rate of return. Mental accounting can add to this effect. If investors focus on the gains or losses of individual stocks, rather than on broad portfolios, they can become more risk averse concerning stocks with recent poor performance, discount their cash flows at a higher rate, and thereby create a value-stock risk premium.

regret avoidance

People blame themselves more for unconventional choices that turn out badly so they avoid regret by making conventional decisions.

> **CONCEPT check 9.2**   How might the P/E effect (discussed in the previous chapter) also be explained as a consequence of regret avoidance?

AFFECT   Conventional models of portfolio choice focus on asset risk and return. But behavioral finance focuses as well on *affect,* which is a feeling of "good" or "bad" that consumers may attach to a potential purchase or investors to a stock. For example, firms with reputations for socially responsible policies or attractive working conditions, or those producing popular products, may generate higher affect in public perception. If investors favor stocks with good affect, that might drive up prices and drive down average rates of return. Statman, Fisher, and Anginer (2008) look for evidence that affect influences security pricing. They find that stocks ranked high in *Fortune*'s survey of most admired companies (i.e., with high affect) tended to have lower average risk-adjusted returns than the least admired firms, suggesting that their prices have been bid up relative to their underlying profitability and, therefore, that their expected future returns are lower.

prospect theory

Behavioral theory that investor utility depends on gains or losses from investors' starting position, rather than on their levels of wealth.

PROSPECT THEORY   **Prospect theory** modifies the analytic description of rational risk-averse investors found in standard financial theory.[2] Figure 9.1, Panel A, illustrates the conventional description of a risk-averse investor. Higher wealth provides higher satisfaction or "utility," but at a diminishing rate (the curve flattens as the individual becomes wealthier). This gives rise to risk aversion: A gain of $1,000 increases utility by less than a loss of $1,000 reduces it; therefore, investors will reject risky prospects that don't offer a risk premium.

Figure 9.1, Panel B, shows a competing description of preferences characterized by "loss aversion." Utility depends not on the *level* of wealth, as in Panel A, but on *changes* in wealth from current levels. Moreover, to the left of zero (zero denotes no change from current wealth), the curve is convex rather than concave. This has several implications. Whereas many conventional utility functions imply that investors may become less risk averse as wealth increases, the function in Panel B always recenters on current wealth, thereby ruling out such decreases in risk aversion and possibly helping to explain high average historical equity risk premiums. Moreover, the convex curvature to the left of the origin in Panel B will induce investors to be risk seeking rather than risk averse when it comes to losses. Consistent with loss aversion, traders in the T-bond futures contract have been observed to assume significantly greater risk in afternoon sessions following morning sessions in which they have lost money (Coval and Shumway, 2005).

These are only a sample of many behavioral biases uncovered in the literature. Many have implications for investor behavior.

---

[2]Prospect theory originated with a highly influential paper about decision making under uncertainty by D. Kahneman and A. Tversky, "Prospect Theory: An Analysis of Decision under Risk," *Econometrica* 47 (1979), pp. 263–291.

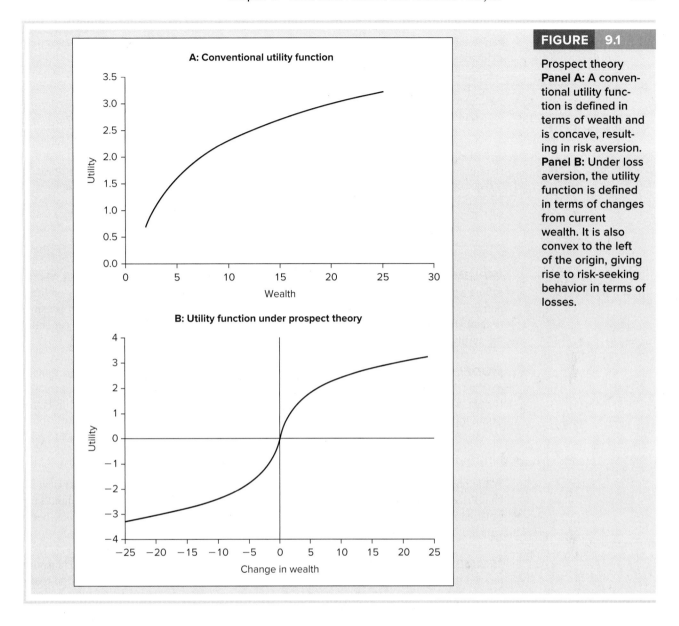

FIGURE 9.1

Prospect theory
Panel A: A conventional utility function is defined in terms of wealth and is concave, resulting in risk aversion. **Panel B:** Under loss aversion, the utility function is defined in terms of changes from current wealth. It is also convex to the left of the origin, giving rise to risk-seeking behavior in terms of losses.

Limits to Arbitrage

Behavioral biases would not matter for stock pricing if rational arbitrageurs could fully exploit the mistakes of behavioral investors. Trades of profit-seeking investors would correct any misalignment of prices. However, behavioral advocates argue that in practice, several factors limit the ability to profit from mispricing.[3]

FUNDAMENTAL RISK   Suppose that a share of IBM is underpriced. Buying it may present a profit opportunity, but it is hardly risk-free because the presumed market underpricing can get worse. While price eventually should converge to intrinsic value, this may not happen until after the trader's investment horizon. For example, the investor may be a mutual fund manager who may lose clients (not to mention a job!) if short-term performance is poor or a trader who may run through her capital if the market turns against her, even temporarily.

---

[3]Some of the more influential references on limits to arbitrage are J. B. DeLong, A. Schleifer, L. Summers, and R. Waldmann, "Noise Trader Risk in Financial Markets," *Journal of Political Economy* 98 (August 1990), pp. 704–738; and A. Schleifer and R. Vishny, "The Limits of Arbitrage," *Journal of Finance* 52 (March 1997), pp. 35–55.

A comment often attributed to the famous economist John Maynard Keynes is that "markets can remain irrational longer than you can remain solvent." The *fundamental risk* incurred in exploiting apparent profit opportunities presumably will limit the activity of traders.

EXAMPLE 9.2	Early in this decade, the NASDAQ index fluctuated at a level around 2,700. From that perspective, the value the index had reached in 2000, around 5,000, seemed obviously crazy. Surely some investors living through the Internet "bubble" of the late 1990s must have identified the index as grossly overvalued, suggesting a good selling opportunity. But this hardly would have been a risk-less arbitrage opportunity. Consider that NASDAQ may also have been overvalued in 1999 when it first crossed above 3,500. An investor in 1999 who believed that NASDAQ was overvalued at 3,500 and decided to sell it short would have suffered enormous losses as the index increased by another 1,500 points before finally peaking at 5,000. While the investor might have derived considerable satisfaction at eventually being proven right about the overpricing, by entering a year before the market "corrected," he might also have gone broke.
Fundamental Risk	

IMPLEMENTATION COSTS   Exploiting overpricing can be particularly difficult. Short-selling a security entails costs; short-sellers may have to return the borrowed security on little notice, rendering the horizon of the short sale uncertain; other investors such as many pension or mutual fund managers face strict limits on their discretion to short securities. This can limit the ability of arbitrage activity to force prices to fair value.

MODEL RISK   One always has to worry that an apparent profit opportunity is more apparent than real. Perhaps you are using a faulty model to value the security, and the price actually is right. Mispricing may make a position a good bet, but it is still a risky one, which limits the extent to which it will be pursued.

Limits to Arbitrage and the Law of One Price

While one can debate the implications of much of the anomalies literature, surely the Law of One Price (positing that effectively identical assets should have identical prices) should be satisfied in rational markets. Yet there are several instances where the law seems to have been violated. These instances are good case studies of the limits to arbitrage.

"SIAMESE TWIN" COMPANIES[4]   In 1907, Royal Dutch Petroleum and Shell Transport merged their operations into one firm. The two original companies, which continued to trade separately, agreed to split all profits from the joint company on a 60/40 basis. Shareholders of Royal Dutch receive 60% of the cash flow, and those of Shell receive 40%. One would therefore expect that Royal Dutch should sell for exactly 60/40 = 1.5 times the price of Shell. But this is not the case. Figure 9.2 shows that the relative value of the two firms has departed considerably from this "parity" ratio for extended periods of time.

Doesn't this mispricing give rise to an arbitrage opportunity? If Royal Dutch sells for more than 1.5 times Shell, why not buy relatively underpriced Shell and short-sell overpriced Royal? This seems like a reasonable strategy, but if you had followed it in February 1993 when Royal sold for about 10% more than its parity value, Figure 9.2 shows that you would have lost a lot of money as the premium widened to about 17% before finally reversing after 1999. As in Example 9.2, this opportunity posed fundamental risk.

EQUITY CARVE-OUTS   Several equity carve-outs also have violated the Law of One Price.[5] To illustrate, consider the case of 3Com, which in 1999 decided to spin off its Palm division. It first sold 5% of its stake in Palm in an IPO, announcing that it would distribute the

---

[4]This discussion is based on K. A. Froot and E. M. Dabora, "How Are Stock Prices Affected by the Location of Trade?" *Journal of Financial Economics* 53 (1999), pp. 189–216.

[5]O. A. Lamont and R. H. Thaler, "Can the Market Add and Subtract? Mispricing in Tech Carve-Outs," *Journal of Political Economy* 111 (2003), pp. 227–268.

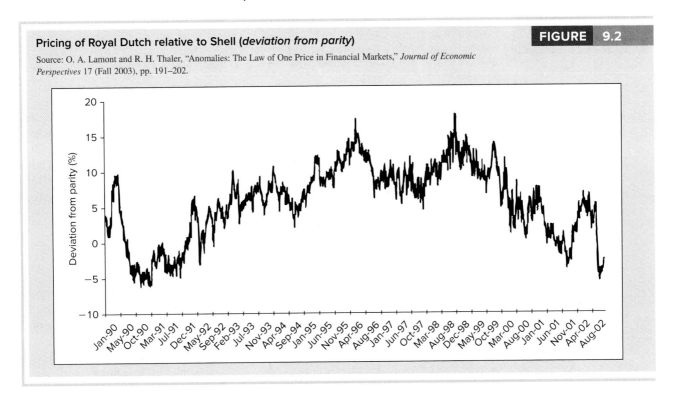

Pricing of Royal Dutch relative to Shell (*deviation from parity*)

Source: O. A. Lamont and R. H. Thaler, "Anomalies: The Law of One Price in Financial Markets," *Journal of Economic Perspectives* 17 (Fall 2003), pp. 191–202.

FIGURE 9.2

remaining 95% of its Palm shares to 3Com shareholders six months later in a spinoff. Each 3Com shareholder would receive 1.5 shares of Palm in the spinoff.

Once Palm shares began trading, but prior to the spinoff, the share price of 3Com should have been *at least* 1.5 times that of Palm. After all, each share of 3Com entitled its owner to 1.5 shares of Palm *plus* an ownership stake in a profitable company. Instead, Palm shares at the IPO actually sold for *more* than the 3Com shares. The *stub value* of 3Com (i.e., the value of each 3Com share net of the value of the claim to Palm represented by that share) could be computed as the price of 3Com minus 1.5 times the price of Palm. This calculation, however, implies that 3Com's stub value was negative, this despite the fact that it was a profitable company with cash assets alone of about $10 per share.

Again, an arbitrage strategy seems obvious. Why not buy 3Com and sell Palm? The limit to arbitrage in this case was the inability of investors to sell Palm short. Virtually all available shares in Palm were already borrowed and sold short, and the negative stub values persisted for more than two months.

CLOSED-END FUNDS We noted in Chapter 4 that closed-end funds often sell for substantial discounts or premiums from net asset value. This is "nearly" a violation of the Law of One Price because one would expect the value of the fund to equal the value of the shares it holds. We say nearly, because in practice, there are a few wedges between the value of the closed-end fund and its underlying assets. One is expenses. The fund incurs expenses that ultimately are paid for by investors, and these will reduce share price. On the other hand, if managers can invest fund assets to generate positive risk-adjusted returns, share price might exceed net asset value.

Lee, Shleifer, and Thaler (1991) argue that the patterns of discounts and premiums on closed-end funds are driven by changes in investor sentiment. They note that discounts on various funds move together and are correlated with the return on small stocks, suggesting that all are affected by common variation in sentiment. One might consider buying funds selling at a discount from net asset value and selling those trading at a premium, but discounts and premiums can widen, subjecting this strategy too to fundamental risk. Pontiff (1996) demonstrates that deviations of price from net asset value in closed-end funds tend to be higher in funds that are more difficult to arbitrage, for example, those with more idiosyncratic volatility.

Closed-end fund discounts are a good example of apparent anomalies that also may have rational explanations. Ross (2002) demonstrates that they can be reconciled with rational investors even if expenses or fund abnormal returns are modest. He shows that if a fund has a dividend yield of δ, an alpha (risk-adjusted abnormal return) of α, and expense ratio of ε, then using the constant-growth dividend discount model (see Chapter 13), the premium of the fund over its net asset value will be

$$\frac{\text{Price} - \text{NAV}}{\text{NAV}} = \frac{\alpha - \varepsilon}{\delta + \varepsilon - \alpha}$$

If the fund manager's performance more than compensates for expenses (i.e., if $\alpha > \varepsilon$), the fund will sell at a premium to NAV; otherwise it will sell at a discount. For example, suppose $\alpha = .015$, the expense ratio is $\varepsilon = .0125$, and the dividend yield is $\delta = .02$. Then the premium will be .14, or 14%. But if the market turns sour on the manager and revises its estimate of α downward to .005, that premium quickly turns into a discount of 43%.

This analysis might explain why the public is willing to purchase closed-end funds at a premium; if investors do not expect α to exceed ε, they won't purchase shares in the fund. But the fact that most premiums eventually turn into discounts indicates how difficult it is for management to fulfill these expectations.[6]

Bubbles and Behavioral Economics

In Example 9.2, we pointed out that the stock market run-up of the late 1990s, and even more spectacularly, the run-up of the technology-heavy NASDAQ market, seems in retrospect to have been an obvious bubble. In a six-year period beginning in 1995, the NASDAQ index increased by a factor of more than 6. Former Fed Chairman Alan Greenspan famously characterized the dot-com boom as an example of "irrational exuberance," and his assessment turned out to be correct: By October 2002, the index fell to less than one-fourth the peak value it had reached only two and a half years earlier. This episode seems to be a case in point for advocates of the behavioral school, exemplifying a market moved by irrational investor sentiment. Moreover, in accord with behavioral patterns, as the dot-com boom developed, it seemed to feed on itself, with investors increasingly confident of their investment prowess (overconfidence bias) and apparently willing to extrapolate short-term patterns into the distant future (representativeness bias).

Only five years later, another bubble, this time in housing prices, was under way. As in the dot-com bubble, expectations of continued price increases fueled speculative demand by purchasers. Shortly thereafter, of course, housing prices stalled and then fell. The bursting bubble set off the worst financial crisis in 75 years.

On the other hand, bubbles are a lot easier to identify as such once they are over. While they are going on, it is not as clear that prices are irrationally exuberant, and, indeed, many financial commentators at the time justified the dot-com boom as consistent with glowing forecasts for the "new economy." A simple example shows how hard it can be to tie down the fair value of stock investments.[7]

---

[6]We might ask why this logic of discounts and premiums does not apply to open-end mutual funds because they incur similar expense ratios. Because investors in these funds can redeem shares for NAV, the shares cannot sell at a discount to NAV. Expenses in open-end funds reduce returns in each period rather than being capitalized into price and inducing a discount.

[7]The following example is taken from R. A. Brealey, S. C. Myers, and F. Allen, *Principles of Corporate Finance*, 9th ed. (Burr Ridge, IL: McGraw-Hill/Irwin, 2008).

In 2000, near the peak of the dot-com boom, the dividends paid by the firms included in the S&P 500 totaled $154.6 million. If the discount rate for the index was 9.2% and the expected dividend growth rate was 8%, the value of these shares according to the constant-growth dividend discount model (see Chapter 13 for more on this model) would be

$$\text{Value} = \frac{\text{Dividend}}{\text{Discount rate} - \text{Growth rate}} = \frac{\$154.6}{.092 - .08} = \$12{,}883 \text{ million}$$

This was quite close to the actual total value of those firms at the time. But the estimate is highly sensitive to the input values, and even a small reassessment of their prospects would result in a big revision of price. Suppose the expected dividend growth rate fell to 7.4%. This would reduce the value of the index to

$$\text{Value} = \frac{\text{Dividend}}{\text{Discount rate} - \text{Growth rate}} = \frac{\$154.6}{.092 - .074} = \$8{,}589 \text{ million}$$

which was about the value to which the S&P 500 firms had fallen by October 2002. In light of this example, the run-up and crash of the 1990s seem easier to reconcile with rational behavior.

Still, other evidence seems to tag the dot-com boom as at least partially irrational. Consider, for example, the results of a study by Rau, Dimitrov, and Cooper (2001) documenting that firms adding ".com" to the end of their names during this period enjoyed a meaningful stock price increase. That doesn't sound like rational valuation.

Evaluating the Behavioral Critique

As investors, we are concerned with the existence of profit opportunities. The behavioral explanations of efficient market anomalies do not give guidance as to how to exploit any irrationality. For investors, the question is still whether there is money to be made from mispricing, and the behavioral literature is largely silent on this point.

However, as we have emphasized above, one of the important implications of the efficient market hypothesis is that security prices serve as reliable guides to the allocation of real assets. If prices are distorted, then capital markets will give misleading signals (and incentives) as to where the economy may best allocate resources. In this crucial dimension, the behavioral critique of the efficient market hypothesis is certainly important irrespective of any implication for investment strategies.

There is considerable debate among financial economists concerning the strength of the behavioral critique. Many believe that the behavioral approach is too unstructured, in effect allowing virtually any anomaly to be explained by some combination of irrationalities chosen from a laundry list of behavioral biases. While it is easy to "reverse engineer" a behavioral explanation for any particular anomaly, these critics would like to see a consistent or unified behavioral theory that can explain a *range* of anomalies.

More fundamentally, others are not convinced that the anomalies literature as a whole is a convincing indictment of the efficient market hypothesis. Fama (1998) reviews the anomalies literature and poses a challenge to the behavioral school. He notes that the anomalies are inconsistent in terms of their support for one type of irrationality versus another. For example, some papers document long-term corrections (consistent with overreaction), while others document long-term continuations of abnormal returns (consistent with underreaction). Moreover, the statistical significance of many of these results is hard to assess. Even small errors in choosing a benchmark against which to compare returns can cumulate to large apparent abnormalities in long-term returns.

The behavioral critique of full rationality in investor decision making is well taken, but the extent to which limited rationality affects asset pricing remains controversial. Whether or not investor irrationality affects asset prices, however, behavioral finance already makes important points about portfolio management. Investors who are aware of the potential pitfalls in information processing and decision making that seem to characterize their peers should be better able to avoid such errors. Ironically, the insights of behavioral finance may lead to some of the same policy conclusions embraced by efficient market advocates. For example, an easy way to avoid some behavioral minefields is to pursue passive, largely indexed portfolio strategies. It seems that only rare individuals can consistently beat passive strategies; this conclusion may hold true whether your fellow investors are behavioral or rational.

9.2   TECHNICAL ANALYSIS AND BEHAVIORAL FINANCE

Technical analysis attempts to exploit recurring and predictable patterns in stock prices to generate superior investment performance. Technicians do not deny the value of fundamental information but believe that prices only gradually close in on intrinsic value. As fundamentals shift, astute traders can exploit the adjustment to a new equilibrium.

For example, one of the best-documented behavioral tendencies is the *disposition effect,* which refers to the tendency of investors to hold on to losing investments. Behavioral investors seem reluctant to realize losses. Grinblatt and Han (2005) show that the disposition effect can lead to momentum in stock prices even if fundamental values follow a random walk. The fact that the demand of "disposition investors" for a company's shares depends on the price history of those shares means that prices close in on fundamental values only over time, consistent with the central motivation of technical analysis.

Behavioral biases may also be consistent with technical analysts' use of volume data. An important behavioral trait noted above is overconfidence, a systematic tendency to overestimate one's abilities. As traders become overconfident, they may trade more, inducing an association between trading volume and market returns (Gervais and Odean, 2001). Technical analysis thus uses volume data as well as price history to direct trading strategy.

Finally, technicians believe that market fundamentals can be perturbed by irrational or behavioral factors, sometimes labeled "sentiment variables." More or less random price fluctuations will accompany any underlying price trend, creating opportunities to exploit corrections as these fluctuations dissipate.

Trends and Corrections

Much of technical analysis seeks to uncover trends in market prices. This is in effect a search for momentum. Momentum can be absolute, in which case one searches for upward price trends, or relative, in which case the analyst looks to invest in one sector over another (or even take on a long-short position in the two sectors). Relative strength statistics (discussed later in this chapter) are designed to uncover these cross-sector potential opportunities.

MOMENTUM AND MOVING AVERAGES   While we all would like to buy shares in firms whose prices are trending upward, this begs the question of how to identify the underlying direction of prices, if in fact such trends actually exist. A primary tool for this purpose is the moving average.

The moving average of a stock price is the average price over a given interval, where that interval is updated as time passes. For example, a 50-day moving average traces the average price over the previous 50 days. The average is recomputed each day by dropping the oldest observation and adding the newest. Figure 9.3 is a moving-average chart for Adobe. Notice that the moving average (the blue curve) is a "smoothed" version of the original data series (the jagged red curve).

After a period in which prices have been falling, the moving average will be above the current price (because the moving average continues to "average in" the older and higher prices until they leave the sample period). In contrast, when prices have been rising, the moving average will be below the current price.

Breaking through the moving average from below, as at point *A* in Figure 9.3, is taken as a bullish signal, because it signifies a shift from a falling trend (with prices below the moving

Share price and 50-day moving average for Adobe (ADBE)

Source: Yahoo! Finance, **finance.yahoo.com**, November 11, 2014.

FIGURE 9.3

average) to a rising trend (with prices above the moving average). Conversely, when prices drop below the moving average, as at point *B,* analysts might conclude that market momentum has become negative.

Other techniques also are used to uncover potential momentum in stock prices. Two of the more famous ones are Elliott wave theory and Kondratieff waves. Both posit the existence of long-term trends in stock market prices that may be disturbed by shorter-term trends as well as daily fluctuations of little importance. Elliott wave theory superimposes long-term and short-term wave cycles in an attempt to describe the complicated pattern of actual price movements. Once the longer-term waves are identified, investors presumably can buy when the long-term direction of the market is positive. While there is considerable noise in the actual evolution of stock prices, by properly interpreting the wave cycles, one can, according to the theory, predict broad movements. Similarly, Kondratieff waves are named after a Russian economist who asserted that the macroeconomy (and therefore the stock market) moves in broad waves lasting between 48 and 60 years. Kondratieff's assertion is hard to evaluate empirically, however, because cycles that last about 50 years provide only two independent data points per century, which is hardly enough data to test the predictive power of the theory.

EXAMPLE 9.4

Moving Averages

Consider the price data in the following table. Each observation represents the closing level of the Dow Jones Industrial Average (DJIA) on the last trading day of the week. The five-week moving average for each week is the average of the DJIA over the previous five weeks. For example, the first entry, for week 5, is the average of the index value between weeks 1 and 5: 17,290, 17,380, 17,399, 17,379, and 17,450. The next entry is the average of the index values between weeks 2 and 6, and so on.

Figure 9.4 plots the level of the index and the five-week moving average. Notice that while the index itself moves up and down rather abruptly, the moving average is a relatively smooth series, because the impact of each week's price movement is averaged with that of the previous weeks. Week 16 is a bearish point according to the moving-average rule. The price series crosses from above the moving average to below it, signifying the beginning of a downward trend in stock prices.

(continued)

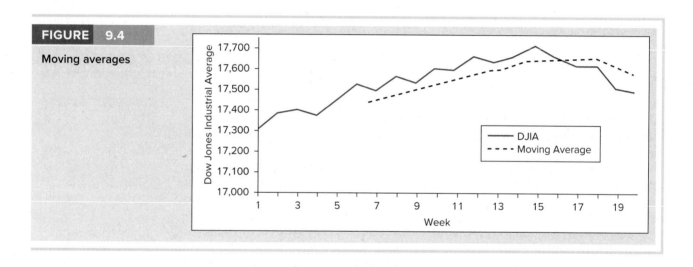

EXAMPLE 9.4

Moving Averages (concluded)

Week	DJIA	5-Week Moving Average	Week	DJIA	5-Week Moving Average
1	17,290		11	17,590	17,555
2	17,380		12	17,652	17,586
3	17,399		13	17,625	17,598
4	17,379		14	17,657	17,624
5	17,450	17,380	15	17,699	17,645
6	17,513	17,424	16	17,647	17,656
7	17,500	17,448	17	17,610	17,648
8	17,565	17,481	18	17,595	17,642
9	17,524	17,510	19	17,499	17,610
10	17,597	17,540	20	17,466	17,563

FIGURE 9.4

Moving averages

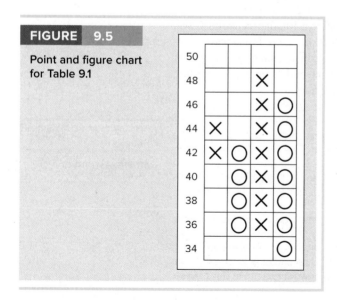

FIGURE 9.5

Point and figure chart for Table 9.1

POINT AND FIGURE CHARTS A variant on pure trend analysis is the *point and figure chart* depicted in Figure 9.5. This figure has no time dimension. It simply traces significant upward or downward movements in stock prices without regard to their timing. The data for Figure 9.5 come from Table 9.1.

Suppose, as in Table 9.1, that a stock's price is currently $40. If the price rises by at least $2, you put an X in the first column at $42 in Figure 9.5. Another increase of at least $2 calls for placement of another X in the first column, this time at the $44 level. If the stock then falls by at least $2, you start a new column and put an O next to $42. Each subsequent $2 price fall results in another O in the second column. When prices reverse yet again and head upward, you begin the third column with an X denoting each consecutive $2 price increase.

The single asterisks in Table 9.1 mark an event resulting in the placement of a new X or O in the chart. The daggers denote price movements that result in the start of a new column of Xs or Os.

TABLE 9.1	Stock price history		
Date	**Price**	**Date**	**Price**
January 2	$40.00	February 1	$40.00*
January 3	40.50	February 2	41.00
January 4	41.00	February 5	40.50
January 5	42.00*	February 6	42.00*
January 8	41.50	February 7	45.00*
January 9	42.50	February 8	44.50
January 10	43.00	February 9	46.00*
January 11	43.75	February 12	47.00
January 12	44.00*	February 13	48.00*
January 15	45.00	February 14	47.50
January 16	44.00	February 15	46.00†
January 17	41.50†	February 16	45.00
January 18	41.00	February 19	44.00*
January 19	40.00*	February 20	42.00*
January 22	39.00	February 21	41.00
January 23	39.50	February 22	40.00*
January 24	39.75	February 23	41.00
January 25	38.00*	February 26	40.50
January 26	35.00*	February 27	38.00*
January 29	36.00†	February 28	39.00
January 30	37.00	March 1	36.00*
January 31	39.00*	March 2	34.00*

*Indicates an event that has resulted in a stock price increase or decrease of at least $2.

†Denotes a price movement that has resulted in either an upward or a downward reversal in the stock price.

Sell signals are generated when the stock price *penetrates* previous lows, and buy signals occur when previous high prices are penetrated. A *congestion area* is a horizontal band of Xs and Os created by several price reversals. These regions correspond to support and resistance levels and are indicated in Figure 9.6, which is an actual chart with congestion and resistance levels marked.

One can devise point and figure charts using price increments other than $2, but it is customary in setting up a chart to require reasonably substantial price changes before marking pluses or minuses.

Draw a point and figure chart using the history in Table 9.1 with price increments of $3.   **CONCEPT** **9.4** **check**

BREADTH   The **breadth** of the market is a measure of the extent to which movement in a market index is reflected widely in the price movements of all the stocks in the market. The most common measure of breadth is the spread between the number of stocks that advance and decline in price. If advances outnumber declines by a wide margin, then the market is viewed as being stronger because the rally is widespread. These numbers are reported daily in *The Wall Street Journal* (see Figure 9.7).

breadth

The extent to which movements in broad market indexes are reflected widely in movements of individual stock prices.

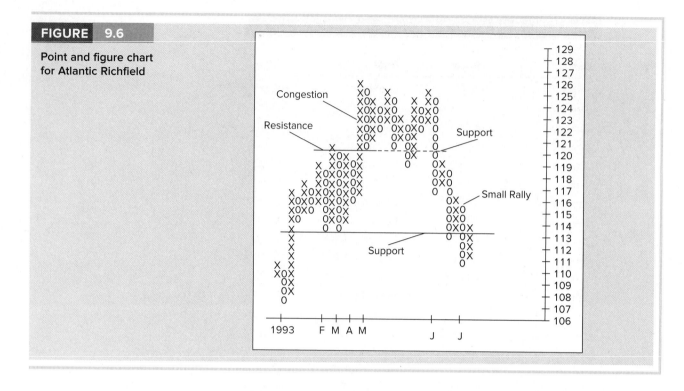

FIGURE 9.6

Point and figure chart for Atlantic Richfield

Some analysts cumulate breadth data each day as in Table 9.2. The cumulative breadth for each day is obtained by adding that day's net advances (or declines) to the previous day's total. The direction of the cumulated series is then used to discern broad market trends. Analysts might use a moving average of cumulative breadth to gauge broad trends.

relative strength

Recent performance of a given stock or industry compared to that of a broader market index.

RELATIVE STRENGTH   **Relative strength** measures the extent to which a security has outperformed or underperformed either the market as a whole or its particular industry. Relative strength is computed by calculating the ratio of the price of the security to a price index for the industry. For example, the relative strength of Toyota versus the auto industry would be measured by movements in the ratio of the price of Toyota divided by the level of an auto industry index. A rising ratio implies Toyota has been outperforming the rest of the industry. If relative strength can be assumed to persist over time, then this would be a signal to buy Toyota.

Similarly, the strength of an industry relative to the whole market can be computed by tracking the ratio of the industry price index to the market price index.

FIGURE 9.7

Market diary

Source: *The Wall Street Journal Online*, November 11, 2014.

Markets Diary Issues	NYSE	NASDAQ	NYSE MKT
Advances	1,602	1,264	186
Declines	1,534	1,421	185
Unchanged	124	129	23
Issues at			
New Highs	210	122	7
New Lows	38	52	10
Share Volume			
Total	2,920,523,915	1,636,186,210	88,729,633
Advancing	1,515,532,381	829,508,757	49,187,491
Declining	1,332,273,976	754,643,461	35,798,206

TABLE 9.2	Breadth			
Day	Advances	Declines	Net Advances	Cumulative Breadth
1	1,802	1,748	54	54
2	1,917	1,640	277	331
3	1,703	1,772	−69	262
4	1,512	2,122	−610	−348
5	1,633	2,004	−371	−719

Note: The sum of advances plus declines varies across days because some stock prices are unchanged.

Sentiment Indicators

Behavioral finance devotes considerable attention to market "sentiment," which may be interpreted as the general level of optimism among investors. Technical analysts have devised several measures of sentiment; we review a few of them.

TRIN STATISTIC Market volume is sometimes used to measure the strength of a market rise or fall. Increased investor participation in a market advance or retreat is viewed as a measure of the significance of the movement. Technicians consider market advances to be a more favorable omen of continued price increases when they are associated with increased trading volume. Similarly, market reversals are considered more bearish when associated with higher volume. The **trin statistic** is defined as

> **trin statistic**
> The ratio of average volume in declining issues to average volume in advancing issues.

$$\text{Trin} = \frac{\text{Volume declining/Number declining}}{\text{Volume advancing/Number advancing}}$$

Therefore, trin is the ratio of average trading volume in declining issues to average volume in advancing issues. Ratios above 1 are considered bearish because the falling stocks would then have higher average volume than the advancing stocks, indicating net selling pressure.

The Wall Street Journal Online provides the data necessary to compute trin in its Markets Diary section. Using the data in Figure 9.7, trin for the NYSE on this day was:

$$\text{Trin} = \frac{\$1,332,273,976/1,534}{\$1,515,532,381/1,602} = .918$$

Note, however, that for every buyer, there must be a seller of stock. Rising volume in a rising market should not necessarily indicate a larger imbalance of buyers versus sellers. For example, a trin statistic above 1, which is considered bearish, could equally well be interpreted as indicating that there is more *buying* activity in declining issues.

CONFIDENCE INDEX *Barron's* computes a confidence index using data from the bond market. The presumption is that actions of bond traders reveal trends that will emerge soon in the stock market.

The **confidence index** is the ratio of the average yield on 10 top-rated corporate bonds divided by the average yield on 10 intermediate-grade corporate bonds. The ratio will always be below 100% because higher-rated bonds will offer lower promised yields to maturity. When bond traders are optimistic about the economy, however, they might require smaller default premiums on lower-rated debt. Hence, the yield spread will narrow, and the confidence index will approach 100%. Therefore, higher values of the confidence index are bullish signals.

> **confidence index**
> Ratio of the yield of top-rated corporate bonds to the yield on intermediate-grade bonds.

CONCEPT check 9.5

Yields on lower-rated debt typically rise along with fears of recession. This reduces the confidence index. When these yields increase, should the stock market be expected to fall, or will it already have fallen?

short interest

The total number of shares currently sold short in the market.

SHORT INTEREST   **Short interest** is the total number of shares of stock currently sold short in the market. Some technicians interpret high levels of short interest as bullish, some as bearish. The bullish perspective is that, because all short sales must be covered (i.e., short-sellers eventually must purchase shares to return the ones they have borrowed), short interest represents latent future demand for the stocks. As short sales are covered, the demand created by the share purchase will force prices up.

The bearish interpretation of short interest is based on the fact that short-sellers tend to be larger, more sophisticated investors. Accordingly, increased short interest reflects bearish sentiment by those investors "in the know," which would be a negative signal of the market's prospects.

put/call ratio

Ratio of put options to call options outstanding on a stock.

PUT/CALL RATIO   Call options give investors the right to buy a stock at a fixed "exercise" price and therefore are a way of betting on stock price increases. Put options give the right to sell a stock at a fixed price and therefore are a way of betting on stock price decreases.[8] The ratio of outstanding put options to outstanding call options is called the **put/call ratio.** Because put options do well in falling markets while call options do well in rising markets, deviations of the ratio from historical norms are considered to be a signal of market sentiment and therefore predictive of market movements.

Interestingly, however, a change in the ratio can be given a bullish or a bearish interpretation. Many technicians see an increase in the ratio as bearish, as it indicates growing interest in put options as a hedge against market declines. Thus, a rising ratio is taken as a sign of broad investor pessimism and a coming market decline. Contrarian investors, however, believe that a good time to buy is when the rest of the market is bearish because stock prices are then unduly depressed. Therefore, they would take an increase in the put/call ratio as a signal of a buy opportunity.

A Warning

The search for patterns in stock market prices is nearly irresistible, and the ability of the human eye to discern apparent patterns is remarkable. Unfortunately, it is possible to perceive patterns that really don't exist. Consider Figure 9.8, which presents simulated and actual values of the Dow Jones Industrial Average during 1956 taken from a famous study by Harry Roberts (1959). In Figure 9.8, Panel B, it appears as though the market presents a classic head-and-shoulders pattern where the middle hump (the head) is flanked by two shoulders. When the price index "pierces the right shoulder"—a technical trigger point—it is believed to be heading lower, and it is time to sell your stocks. Figure 9.8, Panel A also looks like a "typical" stock market pattern.

Can you tell which of the two graphs is constructed from the real value of the Dow and which from the simulated data? Figure 9.8, Panel A is based on the real data. The graph in Panel B was generated using "returns" created by a random-number generator. These returns *by construction* were patternless, but the simulated price path that is plotted appears to follow a pattern much like that of Panel A.

Figure 9.9 shows the weekly price *changes* behind the two panels in Figure 9.8. Here the randomness in both series—the stock price as well as the simulated sequence—is obvious.

A problem related to the tendency to perceive patterns where they don't exist is data mining. After the fact, you can always find patterns and trading rules that would have generated enormous profits. If you test enough rules, some will have worked in the past. Unfortunately, picking a theory that would have worked after the fact carries no guarantee of future success.

In evaluating trading rules, you should always ask whether the rule would have seemed reasonable *before* you looked at the data. If not, you might be buying into the one arbitrary rule among many that happened to have worked in the recent past. The hard but crucial question is whether there is reason to believe that what worked in the past should continue to work in the future.

---

[8]Puts and calls were defined in Chapter 2, Section 2.5. They are discussed more fully in Chapter 15.

Actual and simulated levels for stock market prices of 52 weeks FIGURE 9.8

Note: Friday closing levels, December 30, 1955–December 28, 1956, Dow Jones Industrial Average.
Source: Harry Roberts, "Stock Market 'Patterns' and Financial Analysis: Methodological Suggestions," *Journal of Finance* 14 (March 1959), pp. 1–10.

Actual and simulated changes in weekly stock prices for 52 weeks FIGURE 9.9

Note: Changes from Friday to Friday (closing) January 6, 1956–December 28, 1956, Dow Jones Industrial Average.
Source: Harry Roberts, "Stock Market 'Patterns' and Financial Analysis: Methodological Suggestions," *Journal of Finance* 14 (March 1959), pp. 1–10.

SUMMARY

- Behavioral finance focuses on systematic irrationalities that characterize investor decision making. These "behavioral shortcomings" may be consistent with several efficient market anomalies.
- Among the information processing errors uncovered in the psychology literature are memory bias, overconfidence, conservatism, and representativeness. Behavioral tendencies include framing, mental accounting, regret avoidance, and loss aversion.
- Limits to arbitrage activity impede the ability of rational investors to exploit pricing errors induced by behavioral investors. For example, fundamental risk means that even

if a security is mispriced, it still can be risky to attempt to exploit the mispricing. This limits the actions of arbitrageurs who take positions in mispriced securities. Other limits to arbitrage are implementation costs, model risk, and costs to short-selling. Occasional failures of the Law of One Price suggest that limits to arbitrage are sometimes severe.

- The various limits to arbitrage mean that even if prices do not equal intrinsic value, it still may be difficult to exploit the mispricing. As a result, the failure of traders to beat the market may not be proof that markets are in fact efficient, with prices equal to intrinsic value.

- Technical analysis also uses volume data and sentiment indicators. These are broadly consistent with several behavioral models of investor activity. Technical analysis is the search for recurring and predictable patterns in stock prices. It is based on the premise that prices only gradually close in on intrinsic value. As fundamentals shift, astute traders can exploit the adjustment to a new equilibrium.

- Technical analysts try to uncover trends in stock prices and anticipate reversals of those trends. Moving averages, relative strength, and breadth are used in various trend-based strategies.

- Some sentiment indicators are the trin statistic, the confidence index, and the put/call ratio.

KEY TERMS

behavioral finance, 265	mental accounting, 267	representativeness bias, 266
breadth, 277	prospect theory, 268	short interest, 280
confidence index, 279	put/call ratio, 280	trin statistic, 279
conservatism bias, 266	regret avoidance, 268	
framing, 267	relative strength, 278	

PROBLEM SETS

 connect Select problems are available in McGraw-Hill's *Connect.* Please see the Supplements section of the book's frontmatter for more information.

1. Match each example to one of the following behavioral characteristics. *(LO 9-1)*

a. Investors are slow to update their beliefs when given new evidence.	i. Disposition effect
b. Investors are reluctant to bear losses due to their unconventional decisions.	ii. Representativeness bias
c. Investors exhibit less risk tolerance in their retirement accounts versus their other stock accounts.	iii. Regret avoidance
d. Investors are reluctant to sell stocks with "paper" losses.	iv. Conservatism bias
e. Investors disregard sample size when forming views about the future from the past.	v. Mental accounting

2. After reading about three successful investors in *The Wall Street Journal* you decide that active investing will also provide you with superior trading results. What sort of behavioral tendency are you exhibiting? *(LO 9-1)*

3. What do we mean by fundamental risk, and why may such risk allow behavioral biases to persist for long periods of time? *(LO 9-2)*

4. What are the strong points of the behavioral critique of the efficient market hypothesis? What are some problems with the critique? *(LO 9-2)*

5. What are some possible investment implications of the behavioral critique?   *(LO 9-1)*

6. Jill Davis tells her broker that she does not want to sell her stocks that are below the price she paid for them. She believes that if she just holds on to them a little longer, they will recover, at which time she will sell them. What behavioral characteristic does Davis have as the basis for her decision making?   *(LO 9-1)*
   a. Loss aversion
   b. Conservatism
   c. Representativeness

7. After Polly Shrum sells a stock, she avoids following it in the media. She is afraid that it may subsequently increase in price. What behavioral characteristic does Shrum have as the basis for her decision making?   *(LO 9-1)*
   a. Fear of regret
   b. Representativeness
   c. Mental accounting

8. All of the following actions are consistent with feelings of regret *except:*   *(LO 9-1)*
   a. Selling losers quickly.
   b. Hiring a full-service broker.
   c. Holding on to losers too long.

9. Which one of the following would be a bullish signal to a technical analyst using moving average rules?   *(LO 9-4)*
   a. A stock price crosses above its 52-week moving average.
   b. A stock price crosses below its 52-week moving average.
   c. The stock's moving average is increasing.
   d. The stock's moving average is decreasing.

10. What is meant by data mining, and why must technical analysts be careful not to engage in it?   *(LO 9-3)*

11. Even if prices follow a random walk, they still may not be informationally efficient. Explain why this may be true, and why it matters for the efficient allocation of capital in our economy.   *(LO 9-2)*

12. What is meant by "limits to arbitrage"? Give some examples of such limits.   *(LO 9-2)*

13. Following a shock to a firm's intrinsic value, the share price will slowly but surely approach that new intrinsic value. Is this view characteristic of a technical analyst or a believer in efficient markets? Explain.   *(LO 9-3)*

14. Use the data from *The Wall Street Journal* in Figure 9.7 to calculate the trin ratio for the NYSE. Is the trin ratio bullish or bearish?   *(LO 9-4)*

15. Calculate breadth for the NYSE using the data in Figure 9.7. Is the signal bullish or bearish?   *(LO 9-4)*

16. Collect data on the DJIA for a period covering a few months. Try to identify primary trends. Can you tell whether the market currently is in an upward or downward trend?   *(LO 9-4)*

17. Suppose Baa-rated bonds currently yield 7%, while Aa-rated bonds yield 5%. Now suppose that due to an increase in the expected inflation rate, the yields on both bonds increase by 1%.   *(LO 9-4)*
   a. What would happen to the confidence index?
   b. Would this be interpreted as bullish or bearish by a technical analyst?
   c. Does this make sense to you?

18. Table 9.3 presents price data for Computers, Inc., and a computer industry index. Does Computers, Inc., show relative strength over this period?   *(LO 9-4)*

19. Use the data in Table 9.3 to compute a five-day moving average for Computers, Inc. Can you identify any buy or sell signals?   *(LO 9-4)*

20. *a.* Construct a point and figure chart for Computers, Inc., using again the data in Table 9.3. Use $2 increments for your chart.

TABLE 9.3   Computers, Inc., stock price history

Trading Day	Computers, Inc.	Industry Index	Trading Day	Computers, Inc.	Industry Index
1	19.63	50.0	21	19.63	54.1
2	20.00	50.1	22	21.50	54.0
3	20.50	50.5	23	22.00	53.9
4	22.00	50.4	24	23.13	53.7
5	21.13	51.0	25	24.00	54.8
6	22.00	50.7	26	25.25	54.5
7	21.88	50.5	27	26.25	54.6
8	22.50	51.1	28	27.00	54.1
9	23.13	51.5	29	27.50	54.2
10	23.88	51.7	30	28.00	54.8
11	24.50	51.4	31	28.50	54.2
12	23.25	51.7	32	28.00	54.8
13	22.13	52.2	33	27.50	54.9
14	22.00	52.0	34	29.00	55.2
15	20.63	53.1	35	29.25	55.7
16	20.25	53.5	36	29.50	56.1
17	19.75	53.9	37	30.00	56.7
18	18.75	53.6	38	28.50	56.7
19	17.50	52.9	39	27.75	56.5
20	19.00	53.4	40	28.00	56.1

    b. Do the buy or sell signals derived from your chart correspond to those derived from the moving-average rule (see the previous problem)?   *(LO 9-4)*

21. Yesterday, the Dow Jones industrials gained 54 points. However, 1,704 issues declined in price while 1,367 advanced. Why might a technical analyst be concerned even though the market index rose on this day?   *(LO 9-4)*

22. Table 9.4 contains data on market advances and declines. Calculate cumulative breadth and decide whether this technical signal is bullish or bearish.   *(LO 9-4)*

23. If the trading volume in advancing shares on day 1 in the previous problem was 1.1 billion shares, while the volume in declining issues was .9 billion shares, what was the trin statistic for that day? Was trin bullish or bearish?   *(LO 9-4)*

24. Using the following data on bond yields, calculate the change in the confidence index from last year to this year. What besides a change in confidence might explain the pattern of yield changes?   *(LO 9-4)*

	This Year	Last Year
Yield on top-rated corporate bonds	8%	8.5%
Yield on intermediate-grade corporate bonds	10.5	10

Ӿ
Templates and
spreadsheets are available
in Connect

25. Log in to Connect and link to the material for Chapter 9, where you will find five years of weekly returns for the S&P 500.   *(LO 9-4)*

    a. Set up a spreadsheet to calculate the 26-week moving average of the index. Set the value of the index at the beginning of the sample period equal to 100. The index value in each week is then updated by multiplying the previous week's level by (1 + rate of return over previous week).

TABLE 9.4   Market advances and declines

Day	Advances	Declines	Day	Advances	Declines
1	906	704	6	970	702
2	653	986	7	1002	609
3	721	789	8	903	722
4	503	968	9	850	748
5	497	1095	10	766	766

b. Identify every instance in which the index crosses through its moving average from below. In how many of the weeks following a cross-through does the index increase? Decrease?

c. Identify every instance in which the index crosses through its moving average from above. In how many of the weeks following a cross-through does the index increase? Decrease?

d. How well does the moving-average rule perform in identifying buy or sell opportunities?

26. Log in to Connect and link to the material for Chapter 9, where you will find five years of weekly returns for the S&P 500 and Fidelity's Select Banking Fund (ticker FSRBX). *(LO 9-4)*

Templates and spreadsheets are available in Connect

a. Set up a spreadsheet to calculate the relative strength of the banking sector compared to the broad market. (*Hint:* As in the previous problem, set the initial value of the sector index and the S&P 500 Index equal to 100, and use each week's rate of return to update the level of each index.)

b. Identify every instance in which the relative strength ratio increases by at least 5% from its value five weeks earlier. In how many of the weeks immediately following a substantial increase in relative strength does the banking sector outperform the S&P 500? In how many of those weeks does the banking sector underperform the S&P 500?

c. Identify every instance in which the relative strength ratio decreases by at least 5% from its value five weeks earlier. In how many of the weeks immediately following a substantial decrease in relative strength does the banking sector underperform the S&P 500? In how many of those weeks does the banking sector outperform the S&P 500?

d. How well does the relative strength rule perform in identifying buy or sell opportunities?

Challenge

27. One apparent violation of the Law of One Price is the pervasive discrepancy between the prices and net asset values of closed-end mutual funds. Would you expect to observe greater discrepancies on diversified or less diversified funds? Why? *(LO 9-2)*

CFA Problems

1. Don Sampson begins a meeting with his financial adviser by outlining his investment philosophy as shown below:

Statement Number	Statement
1	Investments should offer strong return potential but with very limited risk. I prefer to be conservative and to minimize losses, even if I miss out on substantial growth opportunities.
2	All nongovernmental investments should be in industry-leading and financially strong companies.

continued

Statement Number	Statement
3	Income needs should be met entirely through interest income and cash dividends. All equity securities held should pay cash dividends.
4	Investment decisions should be based primarily on consensus forecasts of general economic conditions and company-specific growth.
5	If an investment falls below the purchase price, that security should be retained until it returns to its original cost. Conversely, I prefer to take quick profits on successful investments.
6	I will direct the purchase of investments, including derivative securities, periodically. These aggressive investments result from personal research and may not prove consistent with my investment policy. I have not kept records on the performance of similar past investments, but I have had some "big winners."

Select the statement from the table above that best illustrates each of the following behavioral finance concepts. Justify your selection. *(LO 9-1)*
   i. Mental accounting.
   ii. Overconfidence (illusion of control).
   iii. Reference dependence (framing).

2. Monty Frost's tax-deferred retirement account is invested entirely in equity securities. Because the international portion of his portfolio has performed poorly in the past, he has reduced his international equity exposure to 2%. Frost's investment adviser has recommended an increased international equity exposure. Frost responds with the following comments:
   a. Based on past poor performance, I want to sell all my remaining international equity securities once their market prices rise to equal their original cost.
   b. Most diversified international portfolios have had disappointing results over the past five years. During that time, however, the market in country XYZ has outperformed all other markets, even our own. If I do increase my international equity exposure, I would prefer that the entire exposure consist of securities from country XYZ.
   c. International investments are inherently more risky. Therefore, I prefer to purchase any international equity securities in my "speculative" account, my best chance at becoming rich. I do not want them in my retirement account, which has to protect me from poverty in my old age.

Frost's adviser is familiar with behavioral finance concepts but prefers a traditional or standard finance approach (modern portfolio theory) to investments.

   Indicate the behavioral finance concept that Frost most directly exhibits in each of his three comments. Explain how each of Frost's comments can be countered by using an argument from standard finance. *(LO 9-1)*

3. Louise and Christopher Maclin live in London, United Kingdom, and currently rent an apartment in the metropolitan area. During an initial discussion of the Maclins' financial plans, Christopher Maclin makes the following statements to the Maclins' financial adviser, Grant Webb:
   a. "I have used the Internet extensively to research the outlook for the housing market over the next five years, and I believe now is the best time to buy a house."
   b. "I do not want to sell any bond in my portfolio for a lower price than I paid for the bond."
   c. "I will not sell any of my company stock because I know my company and I believe it has excellent prospects for the future."

For each statement (*a*)–(*c*) identify the behavioral finance concept most directly exhibited. Explain how each behavioral finance concept is affecting the Maclins' investment decision making. *(LO 9-1)*

4. During an interview with her investment adviser, a retired investor made the following two statements:
   a. "I have been very pleased with the returns I've earned on Petrie stock over the past two years, and I am certain that it will be a superior performer in the future."

b. "I am pleased with the returns from the Petrie stock because I have specific uses for that money. For that reason, I certainly want my retirement fund to continue owning the Petrie stock."

Identify which principle of behavioral finance is most consistent with each of the investor's two statements. *(LO 9-1)*

5. Claire Pierce comments on her life circumstances and investment outlook:

I must support my parents who live overseas on Pogo Island. The Pogo Island economy has grown rapidly over the past two years with minimal inflation, and consensus forecasts call for a continuation of these favorable trends for the foreseeable future. Economic growth has resulted from the export of a natural resource used in an exciting new technology application.

I want to invest 10% of my portfolio in Pogo Island government bonds. I plan to purchase long-term bonds because my parents are likely to live more than 10 years. Experts uniformly do not foresee a resurgence of inflation on Pogo Island, so I am certain that the total returns produced by the bonds will cover my parents' spending needs for many years to come. There should be no exchange rate risk because the bonds are denominated in local currency. I want to buy the Pogo Island bonds but am not willing to distort my portfolio's long-term asset allocation to do so. The overall mix of stocks, bonds, and other investments should not change. Therefore, I am considering selling one of my U.S. bond funds to raise cash to buy the Pogo Island bonds. One possibility is my High Yield Bond Fund, which has declined 5% in value year to date. I am not excited about this fund's prospects; in fact I think it is likely to decline more, but there is a small probability that it could recover very quickly. So I have decided instead to sell my Core Bond Fund that has appreciated 5% this year. I expect this investment to continue to deliver attractive returns, but there is a small chance this year's gains might disappear quickly.

Once that shift is accomplished, my investments will be in great shape. The sole exception is my Small Company Fund, which has performed poorly. I plan to sell this investment as soon as the price increases to my original cost.

Identify three behavioral finance concepts illustrated in Pierce's comments and describe each of the three concepts. Discuss how an investor practicing standard or traditional finance would challenge each of the three concepts. *(LO 9-1)*

WEB *master*

1. Log on to **finance.yahoo.com** to find the monthly dividend-adjusted closing prices for the most recent four years for Abercrombie & Fitch (ANF). Also collect the closing level of the S&P 500 Index over the same period.
   a. Calculate the four-month moving average of both the stock and the S&P 500 over time. For each series, use Excel to plot the moving average against the actual level of the stock price or index. Examine the instances where the moving average and price series cross. Is the stock more or less likely to increase when the price crosses through the moving average? Does it matter whether the price crosses the moving average from above or below? How reliable would an investment rule based on moving averages be? Perform your analysis for both the stock price and the S&P 500.
   b. Calculate and plot the relative strength of the stock compared to the S&P 500 over the sample period. Find all instances in which relative strength of the stock increases by more than 10 percentage points (e.g., an increase in the relative strength index from .93 to 1.03) and all those instances in which relative strength of the stock decreases by more than 10 percentage points. Is the stock more or less likely to outperform the S&P in the following two months when relative strength has increased or to underperform when relative strength has decreased? In other words, does relative strength continue? How reliable would an investment rule based on relative strength be?
2. The Yahoo! Finance charting function allows you to specify comparisons between companies by choosing the *Technical Analysis* tab. Short interest ratios are found in the *Key Statistics* table. You can prepare charts of moving averages for any company by going to the *Interactive Charts* tab, choosing the *+Indicator* option, and specifying the type and

length of the moving average. Prepare charts of moving averages and obtain short interest ratios for GE and SWY. Prepare a one-year chart of the 50- and 200-day average price of GE, SWY, and the S&P 500 Index.

a. Which, if either, of the companies is priced above its 50- and 200-day averages?

b. Would you consider their charts as bullish or bearish? Why?

c. What are the short interest ratios for the two companies?

9.1 Conservatism implies that investors will at first respond too slowly to new information, leading to trends in prices. Representativeness can lead them to extrapolate trends too far into the future and overshoot intrinsic value. Eventually, when the pricing error is corrected, we observe a reversal.

9.2 Out-of-favor stocks will exhibit low prices relative to various proxies for intrinsic value such as earnings. Because of regret avoidance, these stocks will need to offer a more attractive rate of return to induce investors to hold them. Thus, low P/E stocks might on average offer higher rates of return.

9.3 At liquidation, price will equal NAV. This puts a limit on fundamental risk. Investors need only carry the position for a few months to profit from the elimination of the discount. Moreover, as the liquidation date approaches, the discount should dissipate. This greatly limits the risk that the discount can move against the investor. At the announcement of impending liquidation, the discount should immediately disappear, or at least shrink considerably.

9.4

9.5 By the time the news of the recession affects bond yields, it also ought to affect stock prices. The market should fall *before* the confidence index signals that the time is ripe to sell.

Debt Securities

Chapters in This Part

10 Bond Prices and Yields

11 Managing Bond Portfolios

Bond markets used to be a sedate arena for risk-averse investors who wanted worry-free investments with modest but stable returns. They are no longer so quiet. The fixed-income market was at the center of the financial crisis of 2008–2009, and the downgrade of U.S. Treasury debt by Standard & Poor's in 2011 triggered a massive one-day stock market decline of more than 6% when markets opened.

These markets are no longer free of risk. Interest rates in the last three decades have become more volatile than anyone in 1965 would have dreamed possible. Volatility means that investors have great opportunities for gain, but also for losses, and we have seen dramatic examples of both in recent years.

Long-Term Capital Management, at the time the world's most successful hedge fund, shocked Wall Street when it was felled by investment reversals in 1998, among them losses of more than $1 billion on its interest rate positions. But those losses seem almost quaint when compared to the devastation suffered in the market meltdown of 2008–2009. The beginning of that period was signaled by revelation of losses of $1 billion on mortgage bonds held by two Bear Stearns hedge funds in 2007. Over the course of the next two years, hundreds of billions were lost by investors in other mortgage-backed bonds and those who sold insurance on those securities. Of course, in many of these instances, there were traders on the other side of the transaction who did quite well. The bearish bets made by hedge fund manager John Paulson in 2007 made his funds more than $15 billion.

The chapters in Part Three provide an introduction to debt markets and securities. We will show you how to value such securities and why their values change with interest rates. We will see what features determine the sensitivity of bond prices to interest rates and how investors measure and manage interest rate risk.

Learning Objectives

LO 10-1 Explain the general terms of a bond contract and how bond prices are quoted in the financial press.

LO 10-2 Compute a bond's price given its yield to maturity, and compute its yield to maturity given its price.

LO 10-3 Calculate how bond prices will change over time for a given interest rate projection.

LO 10-4 Describe call, convertibility, and sinking fund provisions, and analyze how these provisions affect a bond's price and yield to maturity.

LO 10-5 Identify the determinants of bond safety and rating and how credit risk is reflected in bond yields and the prices of credit default swaps.

LO 10-6 Calculate several measures of bond return, and demonstrate how these measures may be affected by taxes.

LO 10-7 Analyze the factors likely to affect the shape of the yield curve at any time, and impute forward rates from the yield curve.

In the previous chapters on risk and return relationships, we have treated securities at a high level of abstraction. We have assumed implicitly that a prior, detailed analysis of each security already has been performed and that its risk and return features have been assessed.

We turn now to specific analyses of particular security markets. We examine valuation principles, determinants of risk and return, and portfolio strategies commonly used within and across the various markets.

We begin by analyzing debt securities. A debt security is a claim on a specified periodic stream of income. Debt securities are often called *fixed-income securities*, because they promise either a fixed stream of income or one determined according to a specified formula. These securities have the advantage of being relatively easy to understand because the payment formulas are specified in advance. Uncertainty about their cash flows is minimal as long as the issuer of the security is sufficiently creditworthy. That makes these securities a convenient starting point for our analysis of the universe of potential investment vehicles.

The bond is the basic debt security, and this chapter starts with an overview of bond markets, including Treasury, corporate, and international bonds. We turn next to bond pricing, showing how bond prices are set in accordance with market interest rates and why bond prices change with those rates. Given this background, we can compare the myriad measures of bond returns such as yield to maturity, yield to call, holding-period return, and realized compound rate of return. We show how bond prices evolve over time, discuss certain tax rules that apply to debt securities, and show how to calculate after-tax returns. Next, we consider the impact of default or credit risk on bond pricing and look at the determinants of credit risk and the default premium built into bond yields. Finally, we turn to the term structure of interest rates, the relationship between yield to maturity and time to maturity.

10.1 BOND CHARACTERISTICS

A **bond** is a security that is issued in connection with a borrowing arrangement. The borrower issues (i.e., sells) a bond to the lender for some amount of cash; the bond is in essence the "IOU" of the borrower. The arrangement obligates the issuer to make specified payments to the bondholder on specified dates. A typical coupon bond obligates the issuer to make semi-annual payments of interest, called *coupon payments,* to the bondholder for the life of the bond. These are called coupon payments because, in precomputer days, most bonds had coupons that investors would clip off and present to the issuer of the bond to claim the interest payment. When the bond matures, the issuer repays the debt by paying the bond's **par value** (or equivalently, its **face value**). The **coupon rate** of the bond determines the interest payment: The annual payment equals the coupon rate times the bond's par value. The coupon rate, maturity date, and par value of the bond are part of the *bond indenture,* which is the contract between the issuer and the bondholder.

To illustrate, a bond with a par value of $1,000 and a coupon rate of 8% might be sold to a buyer for $1,000. The issuer then pays the bondholder 8% of $1,000, or $80 per year, for the stated life of the bond, say, 30 years. The $80 payment typically comes in two semiannual installments of $40 each. At the end of the 30-year life of the bond, the issuer also pays the $1,000 par value to the bondholder.

Bonds usually are issued with coupon rates set just high enough to induce investors to pay par value to buy the bond. Sometimes, however, **zero-coupon bonds** are issued that make no coupon payments. In this case, investors receive par value at the maturity date but receive no interest payments until then: The bond has a coupon rate of zero. These bonds are issued at prices considerably below par value, and the investor's return comes solely from the difference between issue price and the payment of par value at maturity. We will return to these bonds below.

bond
A security that obligates the issuer to make specified payments to the holder over a period of time.

face value, par value
The payment to the bondholder at the maturity of the bond.

coupon rate
A bond's annual interest payment per dollar of par value.

zero-coupon bond
A bond paying no coupons that sells at a discount and provides only a payment of par value at maturity.

Treasury Bonds and Notes

Figure 10.1 is an excerpt from the listing of Treasury issues from the *The Wall Street Journal Online.* Treasury notes are issued with original maturities between 1 and 10 years, while Treasury bonds are issued with maturities ranging from 10 to 30 years. Both bonds and notes may be purchased directly from the Treasury in denominations of only $100, but denominations of $1,000 are far more common. Both make semiannual coupon payments.

The highlighted issue in Figure 10.1 matures in August 2023. Its coupon rate is 6.25%. Par value is $1,000; thus, the bond pays interest of $62.50 per year in two semiannual payments of $31.25. Payments are made in February and August of each year. Although bonds are typically

FIGURE   10.1

Prices and yields of
U.S. Treasury bonds on
August 15, 2014

Source: *The Wall Street Journal
Online,* August 15, 2014.

U.S. Treasury Quotes

Treasury note and bond data are representative over-the-counter quotations as of 3pm Eastern time.

MATURITY	Coupon	BID	ASKED	CHG	ASK YLD
10/15/2015	0.250	100.0938	100.1094	−0.0078	0.155
10/15/2016	0.625	100.1563	100.1953	0.0000	0.534
11/15/2018	9.000	131.8984	131.9297	0.0313	1.247
11/30/2018	1.375	99.8984	99.9297	0.0703	1.392
8/15/2023	6.250	132.9453	132.9922	0.4531	2.188
8/15/2026	6.750	144.3828	144.4609	0.6953	2.449
11/15/2027	6.125	139.7188	139.7969	0.7969	2.562
2/15/2031	5.375	134.5625	134.6406	0.9766	2.748
2/15/2036	4.500	125.0781	125.1563	1.1250	2.916
5/15/2044	3.375	104.7500	104.8125	1.2500	3.125

sold in denominations of $1,000 par value, the bid and ask prices[1] are quoted as a percentage of par value. Therefore, the ask price is 132.992% of par value, or $1,329.92. The minimum price increment, or tick size, in *The Wall Street Journal* listing is 1/128, so this bond may also be viewed as selling for $132\frac{127}{128}\%$ of par value.[2]

The last column, labeled "Ask Yld," is the bond's yield to maturity based on the ask price. The yield to maturity is often interpreted as a measure of the average rate of return to an investor who purchases the bond for the ask price and holds it until its maturity date. We will have much to say about yield to maturity below.

ACCRUED INTEREST AND QUOTED BOND PRICES   The bond prices that you see quoted in the financial pages are not actually the prices that investors pay for the bond. This is because the quoted price does not include the interest that accrues between coupon payment dates.

If a bond is purchased between coupon payments, the buyer must pay the seller for accrued interest, the prorated share of the upcoming semiannual coupon. For example, if 30 days have passed since the last coupon payment, and there are 182 days in the semiannual coupon period, the seller is entitled to a payment of accrued interest of $\frac{30}{182}$ of the semiannual coupon. The sale, or *invoice price* of the bond, which is the amount the buyer actually pays, would equal the stated price plus the accrued interest.

In general, the formula for the amount of accrued interest between two dates is

$$\text{Accrued interest} = \frac{\text{Annual coupon payment}}{2} \times \frac{\text{Days since last coupon payment}}{\text{Days separating coupon payments}}$$

EXAMPLE 10.1

Accrued Interest

Suppose that the coupon rate is 8%. Then the semiannual coupon payment is $40. Because 30 days have passed since the last coupon payment, the accrued interest on the bond is $40 × $\frac{30}{182}$ = $6.59. If the quoted price of the bond is $990, then the invoice price will be $990 + $6.59 = $996.59.

The practice of quoting bond prices net of accrued interest explains why the price of a maturing bond is listed at $1,000 rather than $1,000 plus one coupon payment. A purchaser of an 8% coupon bond one day before the bond's maturity would receive $1,040 on the following day and so should be willing to pay a total price of $1,040 for the bond. In fact, $40 of that total

[1]Recall that the bid price is the price at which you can sell the bond to a dealer. The ask price, which is slightly higher, is the price at which you can buy the bond from a dealer.

[2]Bonds traded on formal exchanges are subject to minimum tick sizes set by the exchange. For example, the minimum price increment, or tick size, on the two-year Treasury bond futures contract (traded on the Chicago Board of Trade) is 1/128, although longer-term T-bonds have larger tick sizes. Private traders can negotiate their own tick size. For example, you can find price quotes on Bloomberg screens with tick sizes as low as 1/256.

Listing of corporate bonds

FIGURE 10.2

Source: FINRA (Financial Industry Regulatory Authority), October 13, 2014.

ISSUER NAME	SYMBOL	COUPON	MATURITY	MOODY'S/S&P/ FITCH	HIGH	LOW	LAST	CHANGE	YIELD %
EXPRESS SCRIPTS HLDG CO	ESRX3954262	2.100%	02/12/2015	Baa3/BBB+/BBB	100.500	100.473	100.500	−0.0020	0.5435
GOLDMAN SACHS GROUP INC	GS.XV	6.750%	10/01/2037	Baa2/BBB+/A−	122.950	120.978	122.950	0.6710	5.0498
JPMORGAN CHASE & CO	JPM.SCH	3.150%	07/05/2016	A3/A/A+	103.882	103.638	103.746	−0.0340	0.9478
JPMORGAN CHASE & CO	JPM4091128	2.350%	01/28/2019	A3/A/A+	102.131	100.944	102.131	1.0853	1.8300
MEDTRONIC INC	MDT4099940	4.625%	03/15/2044	A2//	105.056	104.311	105.005	0.6930	4.3199
MORGAN STANLEY	MS4161029	4.350%	09/08/2026	Baa3/BBB+/BBB+	102.674	100.328	100.616	0.3800	4.2829

payment constitutes the accrued interest for the preceding half-year period. The bond price is quoted net of accrued interest and thus appears as $1,000.[3]

Corporate Bonds

Like the government, corporations borrow money by issuing bonds. Figure 10.2 is a sample of corporate bond listings. Although some bonds trade electronically on the NYSE Bonds platform, most bonds are traded over the counter in a network of bond dealers linked by a computer quotation system. In practice, the bond market can be quite "thin," in that there are few investors interested in trading a particular issue at any particular time.

The bond listings in Figure 10.2 include the coupon, maturity, price, and yield to maturity of each bond. The "Rating" column is the estimation of bond safety given by the three major bond rating agencies, Moody's, Standard & Poor's, and Fitch. Bonds with A ratings are safer than those rated B or below. As a general rule, safer bonds with higher ratings promise lower yields to maturity. We will return to this topic toward the end of the chapter.

CALL PROVISIONS ON CORPORATE BONDS   Some corporate bonds are issued with call provisions, allowing the issuer to repurchase the bond at a specified *call price* before the maturity date. For example, if a company issues a bond with a high coupon rate when market interest rates are high, and interest rates later fall, the firm might like to retire the high-coupon debt and issue new bonds at a lower coupon rate to reduce interest payments. The proceeds from the new bond issue are used to pay for the repurchase of the existing higher-coupon bonds at the call price. This is called *refunding*. **Callable bonds** typically come with a period of call protection, an initial time during which the bonds are not callable. Such bonds are referred to as *deferred* callable bonds.

callable bonds

Bonds that may be repurchased by the issuer at a specified call price during the call period.

The option to call the bond is valuable to the firm, allowing it to buy back the bonds and refinance at lower interest rates when market rates fall. Of course, the firm's benefit is the bondholder's burden. Holders of called bonds forfeit their bonds for the call price, thereby giving up the prospect of an attractive rate of interest on their original investment. To compensate investors for this risk, callable bonds are issued with higher coupons and promised yields to maturity than noncallable bonds.

Suppose that Verizon issues two bonds with identical coupon rates and maturity dates. One bond is callable, however, while the other is not. Which bond will sell at a higher price?

CONCEPT 10.1
c h e c k

[3]In contrast to bonds, stocks do not trade at flat prices with adjustments for "accrued dividends." Whoever owns the stock when it goes "ex-dividend" receives the entire dividend payment, and the stock price reflects the value of the upcoming dividend. The price therefore typically falls by about the amount of the dividend on the "ex day." There is no need to differentiate between reported and invoice prices for stocks.

convertible bond

A bond with an option allowing the bondholder to exchange the bond for a specified number of shares of common stock in the firm.

CONVERTIBLE BONDS   **Convertible bonds** give bondholders an option to exchange each bond for a specified number of shares of common stock of the firm. The *conversion ratio* gives the number of shares for which each bond may be exchanged. Suppose a convertible bond is issued at par value of $1,000 and is convertible into 40 shares of a firm's stock. The current stock price is $20 per share, so the option to convert is not profitable now. Should the stock price later rise to $30, however, each bond may be converted profitably into $1,200 worth of stock. The *market conversion value* is the current value of the shares for which the bonds may be exchanged. At the $20 stock price, for example, the bond's conversion value is $800. The *conversion premium* is the excess of the bond price over its conversion value. If the bond were selling currently for $950, its premium would be $150.

Convertible bondholders benefit from price appreciation of the company's stock. Not surprisingly, this benefit comes at a price; convertible bonds offer lower coupon rates and stated or promised yields to maturity than nonconvertible bonds. At the same time, the actual return on the convertible bond may exceed the stated yield to maturity if the option to convert becomes profitable.

We discuss convertible and callable bonds further in Chapter 15.

PUTTABLE BONDS   While the callable bond gives the issuer the option to extend or retire the bond at the call date, the *extendable* or **put bond** gives this option to the bondholder. If the bond's coupon rate exceeds current market yields, for instance, the bondholder will choose to extend the bond's life. If the bond's coupon rate is too low, it will be optimal not to extend; the bondholder instead reclaims principal, which can be invested at current yields.

put bond

A bond that the holder may choose either to exchange for par value at some date or to extend for a given number of years.

floating-rate bonds

Bonds with coupon rates periodically reset according to a specified market rate.

FLOATING-RATE BONDS   **Floating-rate bonds** make interest payments that are tied to some measure of current market rates. For example, the rate might be adjusted annually to the current T-bill rate plus 2%. If the one-year T-bill rate at the adjustment date is 4%, the bond's coupon rate over the next year would then be 6%. This arrangement means that the bond always pays approximately current market rates.

The major risk involved in floaters has to do with changing credit conditions. The yield spread is fixed over the life of the security, which may be many years. If the financial health of the firm deteriorates, then investors will demand a greater yield premium than is offered by the security. In this case, the price of the bond will fall. While the coupon rate on floaters adjusts to changes in the general level of market interest rates, it does not adjust to changes in the financial condition of the firm.

Preferred Stock

Although preferred stock strictly speaking is considered to be equity, it often is included in the fixed-income universe. This is because, like bonds, preferred stock promises to pay a specified stream of dividends. However, unlike bonds, the failure to pay the promised dividend does not result in corporate bankruptcy. Instead, the dividends owed simply cumulate, and the common stockholders may not receive any dividends until the preferred stockholders have been paid in full. In the event of bankruptcy, the claim of preferred stockholders to the firm's assets has lower priority than that of bondholders but higher priority than that of common stockholders.

Preferred stock commonly pays a fixed dividend. Therefore, it is in effect a perpetuity, providing a level cash flow indefinitely. In contrast, floating-rate preferred stock is much like floating-rate bonds. The dividend rate is linked to a measure of current market interest rates and is adjusted at regular intervals.

Unlike interest payments on bonds, dividends on preferred stock are not considered tax-deductible expenses to the firm. This reduces their attractiveness as a source of capital to issuing firms. On the other hand, there is an offsetting tax advantage to preferred stock. When one corporation buys the preferred stock of another corporation, it pays taxes on only 30% of the dividends received. For example, if the firm's tax bracket is 35%, and it receives $10,000 in preferred-dividend payments, it will pay taxes on only $3,000 of that income: Total taxes owed on the income will be .35 × $3,000 = $1,050. The firm's effective tax rate on preferred dividends is therefore only .30 × 35% = 10.5%. Given this tax rule, it is not surprising that most preferred stock is held by corporations.

Preferred stock rarely gives its holders full voting privileges in the firm. However, if the preferred dividend is skipped, the preferred stockholders will then be provided some voting power.

Other Domestic Issuers

There are, of course, several issuers of bonds in addition to the Treasury and private corporations. For example, state and local governments issue municipal bonds. The outstanding feature of these is that interest payments are tax-free. We examined municipal bonds, the value of the tax exemption, and the equivalent taxable yield of these bonds in Chapter 2.

Government agencies, such as the Federal Home Loan Bank Board, the Farm Credit agencies, and the mortgage pass-through agencies Ginnie Mae, Fannie Mae, and Freddie Mac also issue considerable amounts of bonds. These too were reviewed in Chapter 2.

International Bonds

International bonds are commonly divided into two categories: *foreign bonds* and *Eurobonds*. Foreign bonds are issued by a borrower from a country other than the one in which the bond is sold. The bond is denominated in the currency of the country in which it is marketed. For example, if a German firm sells a dollar-denominated bond in the U.S., the bond is considered a foreign bond. These bonds are given colorful names based on the countries in which they are marketed. For example, foreign bonds sold in the U.S. are called *Yankee bonds*. Like other bonds sold in the U.S., they are registered with the Securities and Exchange Commission. Yen-denominated bonds sold in Japan by non-Japanese issuers are called *Samurai bonds*. British-pound-denominated foreign bonds sold in the U.K. are called *bulldog bonds*.

In contrast to foreign bonds, Eurobonds are denominated in one currency, usually that of the issuer, but sold in other national markets. For example, the Eurodollar market refers to dollar-denominated bonds sold outside the U.S. (not just in Europe), although London is the largest market for Eurodollar bonds. Because the Eurodollar market falls outside U.S. jurisdiction, these bonds are not regulated by U.S. federal agencies. Similarly, Euroyen bonds are yen-denominated bonds selling outside Japan, Eurosterling bonds are pound-denominated Eurobonds selling outside the U.K., and so on.

Innovation in the Bond Market

Issuers constantly develop innovative bonds with unusual features; these issues illustrate that bond design can be extremely flexible. Here are examples of some novel bonds. They should give you a sense of the potential variety in security design.

INVERSE FLOATERS   These are similar to the floating-rate bonds we described earlier, except that the coupon rate on these bonds *falls* when the general level of interest rates rises. Investors in these bonds suffer doubly when rates rise. Not only does the present value of each dollar of cash flow from the bond fall as the discount rate rises but the level of those cash flows falls as well. (Of course, investors in these bonds benefit doubly when rates fall.)

ASSET-BACKED BONDS   Miramax has issued bonds with coupon rates tied to the financial performance of *Pulp Fiction* and other films. Domino's Pizza has issued bonds with payments backed by revenue from its pizza franchises. "David Bowie bonds" have been issued with payments tied to royalties on some of his albums. These are examples of asset-backed securities. The income from a specified group of assets is used to service the debt. More conventional asset-backed securities are mortgage-backed securities or securities backed by auto or credit card loans, as we discussed in Chapter 2.

TABLE 10.1	Principal and interest payments for a Treasury Inflation Protected Security					
Time	Inflation in Year Just Ended	Par Value	Coupon Payment	+ Principal Repayment	=	Total Payment
0		$1,000.00				
1	2%	1,020.00	$40.80	0		$ 40.80
2	3	1,050.60	42.02	0		42.02
3	1	1,061.11	42.44	$1,061.11		1,103.55

PAY-IN-KIND BONDS   Issuers of pay-in-kind bonds may choose to pay interest either in cash or in additional bonds. If the issuer is short on cash, it will likely choose to pay with new bonds rather than scarce cash.

CATASTROPHE BONDS   Oriental Land Co., which manages Tokyo Disneyland, has issued bonds with a final payment that depends on whether there has been an earthquake near the park. More recently, FIFA (the Fédération Internationale de Football Association) issued catastrophe bonds with payments that would have been halted if terrorism forced the cancellation of the 2006 World Cup. These bonds are a way to transfer "catastrophe risk" from insurance companies to the capital markets. Investors in these bonds receive compensation in the form of higher coupon rates for taking on the risk. But in the event of a catastrophe, the bondholders will lose all or part of their investments. "Disaster" can be defined either by total insured losses or by criteria such as wind speed in a hurricane or Richter level in an earthquake. Issuance of catastrophe bonds has grown in recent years as insurers have sought ways to spread their risks across a wider spectrum of the capital market.

INDEXED BONDS   Indexed bonds make payments that are tied to a general price index or the price of a particular commodity. For example, Mexico has issued bonds with payments that depend on the price of oil. Some bonds are indexed to the general price level. The United States Treasury started issuing such inflation-indexed bonds in January 1997. They are called Treasury Inflation Protected Securities (TIPS). By tying the par value of the bond to the general level of prices, coupon payments, as well as the final repayment of par value, on these bonds increase in direct proportion to the consumer price index. Therefore, the interest rate on these bonds is a risk-free real rate.

To illustrate how TIPS work, consider a newly issued bond with a three-year maturity, par value of $1,000, and a coupon rate of 4%. For simplicity, we will assume the bond makes annual coupon payments. Assume that inflation turns out to be 2%, 3%, and 1% in the next three years. Table 10.1 shows how the bond cash flows will be calculated. The first payment comes at the end of the first year, at $t = 1$. Because inflation over the year was 2%, the par value of the bond increases from $1,000 to $1,020; because the coupon rate is 4%, the coupon payment is 4% of this amount, or $40.80. Notice that principal value increases by the inflation rate, and because the coupon payments are 4% of principal, they too increase in proportion to the general price level. Therefore, the cash flows paid by the bond are fixed in *real* terms. When the bond matures, the investor receives a final coupon payment of $42.44 plus the (price-level-indexed) repayment of principal, $1,061.11.[4]

The *nominal* rate of return on the bond in the first year is

$$\text{Nominal return} = \frac{\text{Interest} + \text{Price appreciation}}{\text{Initial price}} = \frac{40.80 + 20}{1,000} = 6.08\%$$

---

[4]By the way, total nominal income (i.e., coupon plus that year's increase in principal) is treated as taxable income in each year.

The real rate of return is precisely the 4% real yield on the bond:

$$\text{Real return} = \frac{1 + \text{Nominal return}}{1 + \text{Inflation}} - 1 = \frac{1.0608}{1.02} - 1 = .04, \text{ or } 4\%$$

One can show in a similar manner (see Problem 19 in the end-of-chapter questions) that the rate of return in each of the three years is 4% as long as the real yield on the bond remains constant. If real yields do change, then there will be capital gains or losses on the bond. In mid-2015, the real yield on TIPS bonds with 20-year maturity was about .6%.

10.2 BOND PRICING

Because a bond's coupon and principal repayments all occur months or years in the future, the price an investor would be willing to pay for a claim to those payments depends on the value of dollars to be received in the future compared to dollars in hand today. This "present value" calculation depends in turn on market interest rates. As we saw in Chapter 5, the nominal risk-free interest rate equals the sum of (1) a real risk-free rate of return and (2) a premium above the real rate to compensate for expected inflation. In addition, because most bonds are not riskless, the discount rate will embody an additional premium that reflects bond-specific characteristics such as default risk, liquidity, tax attributes, call risk, and so on.

We simplify for now by assuming there is one interest rate that is appropriate for discounting cash flows of any maturity, but we can relax this assumption easily. In practice, there may be different discount rates for cash flows accruing in different periods. For the time being, however, we ignore this refinement.

To value a security, we discount its expected cash flows by the appropriate discount rate. The cash flows from a bond consist of coupon payments until the maturity date plus the final payment of par value. Therefore

Bond value = Present value of coupons + Present value of par value

If we call the maturity date T and call the discount rate r, the bond value can be written as

$$\text{Bond value} = \sum_{t=1}^{T} \frac{\text{Coupon}}{(1 + r)^t} + \frac{\text{Par value}}{(1 + r)^T} \qquad \textbf{(10.1)}$$

The summation sign in Equation 10.1 directs us to add the present value of each coupon payment; each coupon is discounted based on the time until it will be paid. The first term on the right-hand side of Equation 10.1 is the present value of an annuity. The second term is the present value of a single amount, the final payment of the bond's par value.

You may recall from an introductory finance class that the present value of a $1 annuity that lasts for T periods when the interest rate equals r is $\frac{1}{r}\left[1 - \frac{1}{(1+r)^T}\right]$. We call this expression the T-period *annuity factor* for an interest rate of r.[5] Similarly, we call $\frac{1}{(1+r)^T}$

[5]Here is a quick derivation of the formula for the present value of an annuity. An annuity lasting T periods can be viewed as an equivalent to a perpetuity whose first payment comes at the end of the current period *less* another perpetuity whose first payment doesn't come until the end of period $T + 1$. The immediate perpetuity net of the delayed perpetuity provides exactly T payments. We know that the value of a $1 per period perpetuity is $1/r. Therefore, the present value of the delayed perpetuity is $1/r discounted for T additional periods, or $\frac{1}{r} \times \frac{1}{(1+r)^T}$. The present value of the annuity is the present value of the first perpetuity minus the present value of the delayed perpetuity, or $\frac{1}{r}\left[1 - \frac{1}{(1+r)^T}\right]$.

the *PV factor,* that is, the present value of a single payment of $1 to be received in T periods. Therefore, we can write the price of the bond as

$$\text{Price} = \text{Coupon} \times \frac{1}{r}\left[1 - \frac{1}{(1+r)^T}\right] + \text{Par value} \times \frac{1}{(1+r)^T} \qquad \textbf{(10.2)}$$
$$= \text{Coupon} \times \text{Annuity factor}(r,\,T) + \text{Par value} \times \text{PV factor}(r,\,T)$$

EXAMPLE 10.2

Bond Pricing

We discussed earlier an 8% coupon, 30-year maturity bond with par value of $1,000 paying 60 semiannual coupon payments of $40 each. Suppose that the interest rate is 8% annually, or $r = 4\%$ per six-month period. Then the value of the bond can be written as

$$\text{Price} = \sum_{t=1}^{60}\frac{\$40}{(1.04)^t} + \frac{\$1{,}000}{(1.04)^{60}}$$
$$= \$40 \times \text{Annuity factor}(4\%,\,60) + \$1{,}000 \times \text{PV factor}(4\%,\,60)$$

It is easy to confirm that the present value of the bond's 60 semiannual coupon payments of $40 each is $904.94 and that the $1,000 final payment of par value has a present value of $95.06, for a total bond value of $1,000. You can calculate the value directly from Equation 10.2, perform these calculations on any financial calculator (see Example 10.3), use a spreadsheet (such as Spreadsheet 10.1), or a set of present value tables.

In this example, the coupon rate equals the market interest rate, and the bond price equals par value. If the interest rate were not equal to the bond's coupon rate, the bond would not sell at par value. For example, if the interest rate were to rise to 10% (5% per six months), the bond's price would fall by $189.29, to $810.71, as follows:

$$\$40 \times \text{Annuity factor (5\%, 60)} + \$1{,}000 \times \text{PV factor (5\%, 60)}$$
$$= \$757.17 + \$53.54 = \$810.71$$

At a higher interest rate, the present value of the payments to be received by the bondholder is lower. Therefore, bond prices fall as market interest rates rise. This illustrates a crucial general rule in bond valuation.[6]

Bond prices are tedious to calculate without a spreadsheet or financial calculator, but they are easy to calculate with either. Financial calculators designed with present value and future value formulas already programmed can greatly simplify calculations of the sort we just encountered in Example 10.2. The basic financial calculator uses five keys that correspond to the inputs for time-value-of-money problems such as bond pricing:

- *n* is the number of time periods. In the case of a bond, *n* equals the number of periods until the bond matures. If the bond makes semiannual payments, *n* is the number of half-year periods or, equivalently, the number of semiannual coupon payments. For example, if the bond has 10 years until maturity, you would enter 20 for *n* because each payment period is one-half year.
- *i* is the interest rate per period, expressed as a percentage (not as a decimal, which is required by spreadsheet programs). For example, if the interest rate is 6%, you would enter 6, not .06.
- *PV* is the present value. Many calculators require that PV be entered as a negative number, in recognition of the fact that purchase of the bond is a cash *outflow,* while the receipt of coupon payments and face value are cash *inflows.*
- *FV* is the future value or face value of the bond. In general, FV is interpreted as a one-time future payment of a cash flow, which, for bonds, is the face (i.e., par) value.

---

[6]Here is a trap to avoid: You should not confuse the bond's *coupon* rate, which determines the interest paid to the bondholder, with the market interest rate. Once a bond is issued, its coupon rate is fixed. When the *market* interest rate increases, investors discount any fixed payments at a higher discount rate, which means present value, and bond prices fall.

- *PMT* is the amount of any recurring payment. For coupon bonds, PMT is the coupon payment; for zero-coupon bonds, PMT will be zero.

Given any four of these inputs, the calculator will solve for the fifth.

EXAMPLE 10.3

Bond Pricing on a Financial Calculator

We can illustrate how to use a financial calculator with the bond in Example 10.2. To find its price when the annual market interest rate is 8%, you would enter these inputs (in any order):

n	60	The bond has a maturity of 30 years, so it makes 60 semiannual payments.
i	4	The *semiannual* interest rate is 4%.
FV	1,000	The bond will provide a one-time cash flow of $1,000 when it matures.
PMT	40	Each semiannual coupon payment is $40.

On most calculators, you now punch the "compute" key (labeled "*COMP*" or "*CPT*") and then enter PV to obtain the bond price, that is, the present value today of the bond's cash flows. If you do this, you should find a value of −1,000. The negative sign signifies that while the investor receives cash flows from the bond, the price paid to *buy* the bond is a cash *out*flow, or a negative cash flow.

If you want to find the value of the bond when the interest rate is 10% (the second part of Example 10.2), just enter 5% for the semiannual interest rate (type "5" and then "*i*"), and then when you compute PV, you will find that it is −810.71.

Figure 10.3 shows the price of the 30-year, 8% coupon bond for a range of interest rates including 8%, at which the bond sells at par, and 10%, at which it sells for $810.71. The negative slope illustrates the inverse relationship between prices and yields. The shape of the curve in Figure 10.3 implies that an increase in the interest rate results in a price decline that is smaller than the price gain resulting from a decrease of equal magnitude in the interest rate. This property of bond prices is called *convexity* because of the convex shape of the bond price curve. This curvature reflects the fact that progressive increases in the interest rate result in progressively smaller reductions in the bond price.[7] Therefore, the price curve becomes flatter at higher interest rates. We will return to convexity in the next chapter.

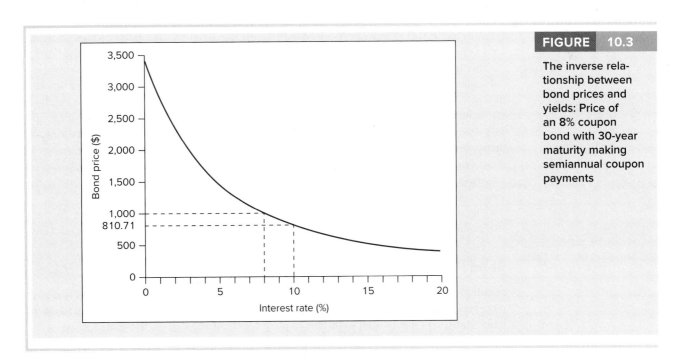

FIGURE 10.3

The inverse relationship between bond prices and yields: Price of an 8% coupon bond with 30-year maturity making semiannual coupon payments

---

[7]The progressively smaller impact of interest rate increases results largely from the fact that at higher rates the bond is worth less. Therefore, an additional increase in rates operates on a smaller initial base, resulting in a smaller price reduction.

TABLE 10.2 Bond prices at different interest rates (8% coupon bond, coupons paid semiannually)

Time to Maturity	Bond Price at Given Market Interest Rate				
	2%	4%	6%	8%	10%
1 year	$1,059.11	$1,038.83	$1,019.13	$1,000.00	$981.41
10 years	1,541.37	1,327.03	1,148.77	1,000.00	875.38
20 years	1,985.04	1,547.11	1,231.15	1,000.00	828.41
30 years	2,348.65	1,695.22	1,276.76	1,000.00	810.71

CONCEPT check 10.2

Calculate the price of the bond for a market interest rate of 3% per half-year. Compare the capital gains for the interest rate decline to the losses incurred when the rate increases to 5%.

Corporate bonds typically are issued at par value. This means the underwriters of the bond issue (the firms that market the bonds to the public for the issuing corporation) must choose a coupon rate that very closely approximates market yields. In a primary issue, the underwriters attempt to sell the newly issued bonds directly to their customers. If the coupon rate is inadequate, investors will not pay par value for the bonds.

After the bonds are issued, bondholders may buy or sell bonds in secondary markets. In these markets, bond prices fluctuate inversely with the market interest rate.

The inverse relationship between price and yield is a central feature of fixed-income securities. Interest rate fluctuations represent the main source of risk in the bond market, and we devote considerable attention in the next chapter to assessing the sensitivity of bond prices to market yields. For now, however, we simply highlight one key factor that determines that sensitivity, namely, the maturity of the bond.

As a general rule, keeping all other factors the same, the longer the maturity of the bond, the greater the sensitivity of its price to fluctuations in the interest rate. For example, consider Table 10.2, which presents the price of an 8% coupon bond at different market yields and times to maturity. For any departure of the interest rate from 8% (the rate at which the bond sells at par value), the change in the bond price is greater for longer times to maturity.

This makes sense. If you buy the bond at par with an 8% coupon rate, and market rates subsequently rise, then you suffer a loss: You have tied up your money earning 8% when alternative investments offer higher returns. This is reflected in a capital loss on the bond—a fall in its market price. The longer the period for which your money is tied up, the greater the loss and, correspondingly, the greater the drop in the bond price. In Table 10.2, the row for one-year maturity bonds shows little price sensitivity—that is, with only one year's earnings at stake, changes in interest rates are not too threatening. But for 30-year maturity bonds, interest rate swings have a large impact on bond prices. The force of discounting is greatest for the longest-term bonds.

This is why short-term Treasury securities such as T-bills are considered the safest. They are free not only of default risk but also largely of price risk attributable to interest rate volatility.

Bond Pricing between Coupon Dates

Equation 10.2 for bond prices assumes that the next coupon payment is in precisely one payment period, either a year for an annual payment bond or six months for a semiannual payment bond. But you probably want to be able to price bonds all 365 days of the year, not just on the one or two dates each year that it makes a coupon payment!

In principle, the fact that the bond is between coupon dates does not affect the pricing problem. The procedure is always the same: Compute the present value of each remaining payment and sum up. But if you are between coupon dates, there will be fractional periods remaining until each payment, and this does complicate the arithmetic computations.

Fortunately, bond pricing functions are included in many financial calculators and spreadsheet programs such as Excel. The spreadsheets allow you to enter today's date as well as the maturity date of the bond and so can provide prices for bonds at any date.

As we pointed out earlier, bond prices are typically quoted net of accrued interest. These prices, which appear in the financial press, are called *flat prices*. The actual *invoice price* that a buyer pays for the bond includes accrued interest. Thus,

$$\text{Invoice price} = \text{Flat price} + \text{Accrued interest}$$

When a bond pays its coupon, flat price equals invoice price because at that moment accrued interest reverts to zero. However, this will be the exceptional case, not the rule.

Excel pricing functions provide the flat price of the bond. To find the invoice price, we need to add accrued interest. Excel also provides functions that count the days since the last coupon payment and thus can be used to compute accrued interest. Spreadsheet 10.1 illustrates how to use these functions. The spreadsheet provides examples using bonds that have just paid a coupon and so have zero accrued interest, as well as a bond that is between coupon dates.

Bond Pricing in Excel

Excel asks you to input both the date you buy the bond (called the *settlement date*) and the maturity date of the bond.

The Excel function for bond price is

= PRICE (settlement date, maturity date, annual coupon rate, yield to maturity, redemption value as percent of par value, number of coupon payments per year)

For the 6.25% coupon August 2023 maturity bond highlighted in Figure 10.1, we would enter the values in Spreadsheet 10.1, Column B. Alternatively, we could simply enter the following function in Excel:

= PRICE(DATE(2014,8,15), DATE(2023,8,15), .0625, .02188, 100, 2)

The DATE function in Excel, which we use for both the settlement and maturity dates, uses the format DATE(year,month,day). The first date is August 15, 2014, when the bond may be purchased, and the second is August 15, 2023, when it matures.

Notice that the coupon rate and yield to maturity in Excel must be expressed as decimals, not percentages. In most cases, redemption value is 100 (i.e., 100% of par value), and the resulting price similarly is expressed as a percent of par value. Occasionally, however, you may encounter bonds that pay off at a premium or discount to par value. One example would be callable bonds, discussed shortly.

SPREADSHEET 10.1

Valuing bonds using a spreadsheet

	A	B	C	D	E	F	G
1		6.25% coupon bond,		6.125% coupon bond,		8% coupon bond,	
2		maturing August 15, 2023	Formula in column B	maturing November 2027		30-year maturity	
3							
4	Settlement date	8/15/2014	=DATE(2014,8,15)	8/15/2014		1/1/2000	
5	Maturity date	8/15/2023	=DATE(2023,8,15)	11/15/2027		1/1/2030	
6	Annual coupon rate	0.0625		0.06125		0.08	
7	Yield to maturity	0.02188		0.02562		0.1	
8	Redemption value (% of face value)	100		100		100	
9	Coupon payments per year	2		2		2	
10							
11							
12	Flat price (% of par)	133.0205	=PRICE(B4,B5,B6,B7,B8,B9)	139.8128		81.0707	
13	Days since last coupon	0	=COUPDAYBS(B4,B5,2,1)	92		0	
14	Days in coupon period	184	=COUPDAYS(B4,B5,2,1)	184		182	
15	Accrued interest	0	=(B13/B14)*B6*100/2	1.531		0	
16	**Invoice price**	133.0205	=B12+B15	141.3441		81.0707	

Spreadsheets are available in Connect

The value of the bond returned by the pricing function is 133.0205 (cell B12), which is within 3 cents of the price reported in *The Wall Street Journal*. (The yield to maturity is reported to only three decimal places, which induces some rounding error.) This bond has just paid a coupon. In other words, the settlement date is precisely at the beginning of the coupon period, so no adjustment for accrued interest is necessary.

To illustrate the procedure for bonds between coupon payments, let's apply the spreadsheet to the 6.125% coupon November 2027 bond which also appears in Figure 10.1. Using the entries in column D of the spreadsheet, we find in cell D12 that the (flat) price of the bond is 139.8128, which, except for minor rounding error, matches the price given in *The Wall Street Journal*.

What about the bond's invoice price? Rows 12 through 16 make the necessary adjustments. The function described in cell C13 counts the days since the last coupon. This day count is based on the bond's settlement date, maturity date, coupon period (1 = annual; 2 = semiannual), and day count convention (choice 1 uses actual days). The function described in cell C14 counts the total days in each coupon payment period. Therefore, the entries for accrued interest in row 15 are the semiannual coupon multiplied by the fraction of a coupon period that has elapsed since the last payment. Finally, the invoice prices in row 16 are the sum of flat price (which again is within a few cents of the reported price in *The Wall Street Journal*) plus accrued interest.

As a final example, suppose you wish to find the price of the bond in Example 10.2. It is a 30-year maturity bond with a coupon rate of 8% (paid semiannually). The market interest rate given in the latter part of the example is 10%. However, you are not given a specific settlement or maturity date. You can still use the PRICE function to value the bond. Simply choose an *arbitrary* settlement date (January 1, 2000, is convenient) and let the maturity date be 30 years hence. The appropriate inputs appear in column F of the spreadsheet, with the resulting price, 81.071% of face value, appearing in cell F16.

10.3   BOND YIELDS

Most bonds do not sell for par value. But ultimately, barring default, they will mature to par value. Therefore, we would like a measure of rate of return that accounts for current income as well as the price increase or decrease over the bond's life. The yield to maturity is the standard measure of the total rate of return. However, it is far from perfect, and we will explore several variations of this measure.

Yield to Maturity

yield to maturity (YTM)
The discount rate that makes the present value of a bond's payments equal to its price.

In practice, an investor considering the purchase of a bond is not quoted a promised rate of return. Instead, the investor must use the bond price, maturity date, and coupon payments to infer the return offered by the bond over its life. The **yield to maturity (YTM)** is defined as the discount rate that makes the present value of a bond's payments equal to its price. This rate is often viewed as a measure of the average rate of return that will be earned on a bond if it is bought now and held until maturity. To calculate the yield to maturity, we solve the bond price equation for the interest rate given the bond's price.

EXAMPLE 10.4

Yield to Maturity

Suppose an 8% coupon, 30-year bond is selling at $1,276.76. What average rate of return would be earned by an investor purchasing the bond at this price? We find the interest rate at which the present value of the remaining 60 semiannual payments equals the bond price. This is the rate consistent with the observed price of the bond. Therefore, we solve for r in the following equation:

$$\$1,276.76 = \sum_{t=1}^{60} \frac{\$40}{(1+r)^t} + \frac{\$1,000}{(1+r)^{60}}$$

or, equivalently,

$$1,276.76 = 40 \times \text{Annuity factor}(r, 60) + 1,000 \times \text{PV factor}(r, 60)$$

(continued)

EXAMPLE 10.4

Yield to Maturity (concluded)

These equations have only one unknown variable, the interest rate, *r*. You can use a financial calculator or spreadsheet to confirm that the solution is *r* = .03, or 3% per half-year.[8] This is the bond's yield to maturity.

The financial press reports yields on an annualized basis and annualizes the bond's semiannual yield using simple interest techniques, resulting in an annual percentage rate or APR. Yields annualized using simple interest are also called *bond equivalent yields*. Therefore, the semiannual yield would be doubled and reported in the newspaper as a bond equivalent yield of 6%. The *effective annual yield* of the bond, however, accounts for compound interest. If one earns 3% interest every six months, then after one year, each dollar invested grows with interest to $1 \times (1.03)^2 = 1.0609$, and the effective annual interest rate on the bond is 6.09%.

In Example 10.4, we asserted that a financial calculator or spreadsheet can be used to find the yield to maturity on the coupon bond. Here are two examples demonstrating how you can use these tools. Example 10.5 illustrates the use of financial calculators while Example 10.6 uses Excel.

EXAMPLE 10.5

Finding Yield to Maturity Using a Financial Calculator

Consider the yield to maturity problem in Example 10.4. On a financial calculator, we would enter the following inputs (in any order):

n	60	The bond has a maturity of 30 years, so it makes 60 semiannual payments.
PMT	40	Each semiannual coupon payment is $40.
PV	(−)1,276.76	The bond can be purchased for $1,276.76, which on some calculators must be entered as a negative number as it is a cash outflow.
FV	1,000	The bond will provide a one-time cash flow of $1,000 when it matures.

Given these inputs, you now use the calculator to find the interest rate at which $1,276.76 actually equals the present value of the 60 payments of $40 each plus the one-time payment of $1,000 at maturity. On some calculators, you first punch the "compute" key (labeled "*COMP*" or "*CPT*") and then enter *i* to have the interest rate computed. If you do so, you will find that *i* = 3, or 3% semiannually, as we claimed. (Notice that just as the cash flows are paid semiannually, the computed interest rate is a rate per semiannual time period.) The bond equivalent yield will be reported in the financial press as 6%.

Excel also contains built-in functions that you can use to find yield to maturity. The following example, along with Spreadsheet 10.2, illustrates.

EXAMPLE 10.6

Finding Yield to Maturity Using Excel

Excel's function for yield to maturity is

=YIELD(settlement date, maturity date, annual coupon rate, bond price, redemption value as percent of par value, number of coupon payments per year)

The bond price used in the function should be the reported, or "flat," price, without accrued interest. For example, to find the yield to maturity of the bond in Example 10.5, we would use column B of Spreadsheet 10.2. If the coupons were paid only annually, we would change the entry for payments per year to 1 (see cell D8), and the yield would fall slightly to 5.99%.

The bond's yield to maturity is the internal rate of return on an investment in the bond. The yield to maturity can be interpreted as the compound rate of return over the life of the bond under the assumption that all bond coupons can be reinvested at that yield.[9] Yield to maturity therefore is widely accepted as a proxy for average return.

---

[8]Without a financial calculator or spreadsheet, you still could solve the equation, but you would need to use a trial-and-error approach.

[9]If the reinvestment rate does not equal the bond's yield to maturity, the compound rate of return will differ from YTM. This is demonstrated below in Examples 10.7 and 10.8.

SPREADSHEET 10.2

Finding yield to maturity using a spreadsheet (30-year maturity bond, coupon rate = 8%, price = 100% of par)

𝕏

Spreadsheets are
available in Connect

	A	B	C	D
1		Semiannual coupons		Annual coupons
2				
3	Settlement date	1/1/2000		1/1/2000
4	Maturity date	1/1/2030		1/1/2030
5	Annual coupon rate	0.08		0.08
6	Bond price (flat)	127.676		127.676
7	Redemption value (% of face value)	100		100
8	Coupon payments per year	2		1
9				
10	**Yield to maturity (decimal)**	0.0600		0.0599
		The formula entered here is =YIELD(B3,B4,B5,B6,B7,B8)		

current yield

Annual coupon divided by
bond price.

Yield to maturity differs from the **current yield** of a bond, which is the bond's annual coupon payment divided by the bond price. For example, for the 8%, 30-year bond currently selling at $1,276.76, the current yield would be $80/$1,276.76 = .0627, or 6.27% per year. In contrast, recall that the effective annual yield to maturity is 6.09%. For this bond, which is selling at a premium over par value ($1,276 rather than $1,000), the coupon rate (8%) exceeds the current yield (6.27%), which exceeds the yield to maturity (6.09%). The coupon rate exceeds current yield because the coupon rate divides the coupon payments by par value ($1,000), which is less than the bond price ($1,276). In turn, the current yield exceeds yield to maturity because the yield to maturity accounts for the built-in capital loss on the bond; the bond bought today for $1,276 will eventually fall in value to $1,000 at maturity.

premium bonds

Bonds selling above par value.

This example illustrates a general rule: For **premium bonds** (bonds selling above par value), coupon rate is greater than current yield, which in turn is greater than yield to maturity. For **discount bonds** (bonds selling below par value), these relationships are reversed (see Concept Check 10.3).

discount bonds

Bonds selling below par value.

It is common to hear people talking loosely about the yield on a bond. In these cases, they almost always are referring to the yield to maturity.

CONCEPT check 10.3

What will be the relationship among coupon rate, current yield, and yield to maturity for bonds selling at discounts from par? Illustrate using the 30-year 8% (semiannual payment) coupon bond assuming it is selling at a yield to maturity of 10%.

Yield to Call

Yield to maturity is calculated on the assumption that the bond will be held until maturity. What if the bond is callable, however, and may be retired prior to the maturity date? How should we measure average rate of return for bonds subject to a call provision?

Figure 10.4 illustrates the risk of call to the bondholder. The colored line is the value of a "straight" (that is, noncallable) bond with par value of $1,000, an 8% coupon rate, and a 30-year time to maturity as a function of the market interest rate. If interest rates fall, the bond price, which equals the present value of the promised payments, can rise substantially. Now consider a bond that has the same coupon rate and maturity date but is callable at 110% of par value, or $1,100. When interest rates fall, the present value of the bond's *scheduled* payments rises, but the call provision allows the issuer to repurchase the bond at the call price. If the call price is less than the present value of the scheduled payments, the issuer can call the bond at the expense of the bondholder.

The dark line in Figure 10.4 is the value of the callable bond. At high market interest rates, the risk of call is negligible because the present value of scheduled payments is substantially less than the call price; therefore, the values of the straight and callable bonds converge. At

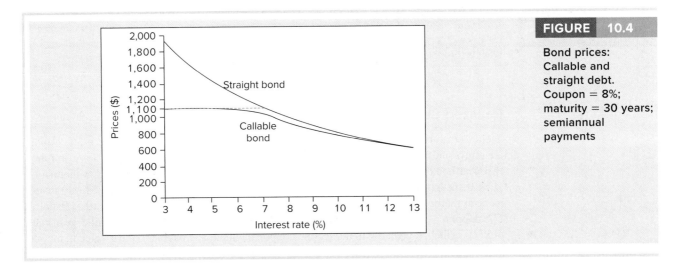

FIGURE 10.4

Bond prices: Callable and straight debt. Coupon = 8%; maturity = 30 years; semiannual payments

lower rates, however, the values of the bonds begin to diverge, with the difference reflecting the value of the firm's option to reclaim the callable bond at the call price. At very low market rates the present value of schedule payments significantly exceeds the call price, so the bond is called. Its value at this point is simply the call price, $1,100.

This analysis suggests that bond market analysts might be more interested in a bond's yield to call rather than its yield to maturity, especially if the bond is likely to be called. The yield to call is calculated just like the yield to maturity, except that the time until call replaces time until maturity and the call price replaces the par value. This computation is sometimes called "yield to first call," as it assumes the issuer will call the bond as soon as it may do so.

EXAMPLE 10.7

Yield to Call

Suppose the 8% coupon, 30-year maturity bond sells for $1,150 and is callable in 10 years at a call price of $1,100. Its yield to maturity and yield to call would be calculated using the following inputs:

	Yield to Call	Yield to Maturity
Coupon payment	$40	$40
Number of semiannual periods	20 periods	60 periods
Final payment	$1,100	$1,000
Price	$1,150	$1,150

Yield to call is then 6.64%. To confirm this on your calculator, input $n = 20$; PV = (−)1150; FV = 1100; PMT = 40; compute i as 3.32%, or 6.64% bond equivalent yield. In contrast, yield to maturity is 6.82%. To confirm, input $n = 60$; PV = (−)1150; FV = 1000; PMT = 40; compute i as 3.41%, or 6.82% bond equivalent yield. In Excel, you can calculate yield to call as =YIELD(DATE(2000,1,1), DATE(2010,1,1), .08, 115, 110, 2). Notice that redemption value is 110, that is, 110% of par value.

While most callable bonds are issued with an initial period of explicit call protection, an additional implicit form of call protection operates for bonds selling at deep discounts from their call prices. Even if interest rates fall a bit, deep-discount bonds still will sell below the call price and thus will not be subject to a call.

Premium bonds that might be selling near their call prices, however, are especially apt to be called if rates fall further. If interest rates fall, a callable premium bond is likely to provide a lower return than could be earned on a discount bond whose potential price appreciation is not limited by the likelihood of a call. Investors in premium bonds therefore may be more interested in the bond's yield to call than its yield to maturity, because it may appear to them that the bond will be retired at the call date.

CONCEPT
check   **10.4**

A 20-year maturity 9% coupon bond paying coupons semiannually is callable in five years at a call price of $1,050. The bond currently sells at a yield to maturity of 8% (bond equivalent yield). What is the yield to call?

Realized Compound Return versus Yield to Maturity

Yield to maturity will equal the rate of return realized over the life of the bond if all coupons are reinvested at an interest rate equal to the bond's yield to maturity. Consider for example, a two-year bond selling at par value paying a 10% coupon once a year. The yield to maturity is 10%. If the $100 coupon payment is reinvested at an interest rate of 10%, the $1,000 investment in the bond will grow after two years to $1,210, as illustrated in Figure 10.5, Panel A. The coupon paid in the first year is reinvested and grows with interest to a second-year value of $110, which, together with the second coupon payment and payment of par value in the second year, results in a total value of $1,210. To summarize, the initial value of the investment is $V_0 = \$1,000$. The final value in two years is $V_2 = \$1,210$. The compound rate of return, therefore, is calculated as follows.

$$V_0(1 + r)^2 = V_2$$
$$\$1,000\,(1 + r)^2 = \$1,210$$
$$r = .10 = 10\%$$

realized compound return

Compound rate of return on a bond with all coupons reinvested until maturity.

With a reinvestment rate equal to the 10% yield to maturity, the **realized compound return** equals yield to maturity.

But what if the reinvestment rate is not 10%? If the coupon can be invested at more than 10%, funds will grow to more than $1,210, and the realized compound return will exceed 10%. If the reinvestment rate is less than 10%, so will be the realized compound return. Consider the following example.

EXAMPLE 10.8

Realized Compound Return

If the interest rate earned on the first coupon is less than 10%, the final value of the investment will be less than $1,210, and the realized compound yield will be less than 10%. Suppose the interest rate at which the coupon can be invested is only 8%. The following calculations are illustrated in Panel B of Figure 10.5.

Future value of first coupon payment with interest earnings	$100 × 1.08 = $ 108
Cash payment in second year (final coupon plus par value)	1,100
Total value of investment with reinvested coupons	$ 1,208

The realized compound return is the compound rate of growth of invested funds, assuming that all coupon payments are reinvested. The investor purchased the bond for par at $1,000, and this investment grew to $1,208.

$$\$1,000(1 + r)^2 = \$1,208$$
$$r = .0991 = 9.91\%$$

Example 10.8 highlights the problem with conventional yield to maturity when reinvestment rates can change over time. However, in an economy with future interest rate uncertainty, the rates at which interim coupons will be reinvested are not yet known. Therefore, while realized compound return can be computed *after* the investment period ends, it cannot be computed in advance without a forecast of future reinvestment rates. This reduces much of the attraction of the realized return measure.

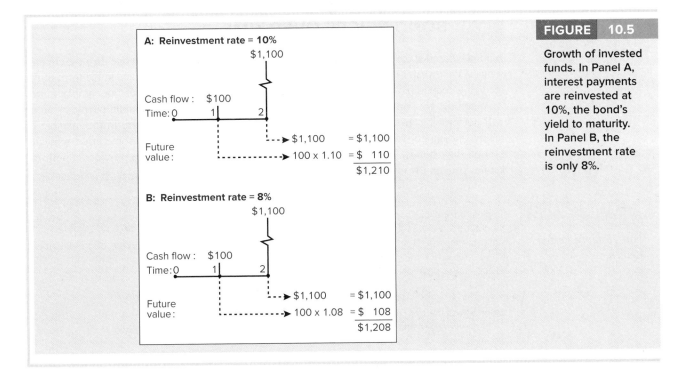

FIGURE **10.5**

Growth of invested funds. In Panel A, interest payments are reinvested at 10%, the bond's yield to maturity. In Panel B, the reinvestment rate is only 8%.

We also can calculate realized compound yield over holding periods greater than one period. This is called **horizon analysis** and is similar to the procedure in Example 10.8. The forecast of total return will depend on your forecasts of *both* the yield to maturity of the bond when you sell it *and* the rate at which you are able to reinvest coupon income. With a longer investment horizon, however, reinvested coupons will be a larger component of your final proceeds.

horizon analysis

Analysis of bond returns over a multiyear horizon, based on forecasts of the bond's yield to maturity and the reinvestment rate of coupons.

EXAMPLE 10.9

Horizon Analysis

Suppose you buy a 30-year, 7.5% (annual payment) coupon bond for $980 (when its yield to maturity is 7.67%) and you plan to hold it for 20 years. Your forecast is that the bond's yield to maturity will be 8% when it is sold and that the reinvestment rate on the coupons will be 6%. At the end of your investment horizon, the bond will have 10 years remaining until expiration, so the forecast sales price (using a yield to maturity of 8%) will be $966.45. The 20 coupon payments will grow with compound interest to $2,758.92. (This is the future value of a 20-year $75 annuity with an interest rate of 6%.)

Based on these forecasts, your $980 investment will grow in 20 years to $966.45 + $2,758.92 = $3,725.37. This corresponds to an annualized compound return of 6.90%:

$$\$980 \, (1 + r)^{20} = \$3,725.37$$

$$r = .0690 = 6.90\%$$

Examples 10.8 and 10.9 demonstrate that as interest rates change, bond investors are actually subject to two sources of offsetting risk. On the one hand, when rates rise, bond prices fall, which reduces the value of the portfolio. On the other hand, reinvested coupon income will compound more rapidly at those higher rates. This **reinvestment rate risk** will offset the impact of price risk. In the next chapter, we will explore this trade-off in more detail and will discover that by carefully tailoring their bond portfolios, investors can precisely balance these two effects for any given investment horizon.

reinvestment rate risk

Uncertainty surrounding the cumulative future value of reinvested bond coupon payments.

10.4 BOND PRICES OVER TIME

A bond will sell at par value when its coupon rate equals the market interest rate. In these circumstances, the investor receives fair compensation for the time value of money in the form of the recurring coupon payments. No further capital gain is necessary to provide fair compensation.

When the coupon rate is lower than the market interest rate, the coupon payments alone will not provide investors as high a return as they could earn elsewhere in the market. To receive a competitive return on such an investment, investors also need some price appreciation on their bonds. The bonds, therefore, must sell below par value to provide a "built-in" capital gain on the investment.

EXAMPLE 10.10

Fair Holding-Period Return

To illustrate built-in capital gains or losses, suppose a bond was issued several years ago when the interest rate was 7%. The bond's annual coupon rate was thus set at 7%. (We will suppose for simplicity that the bond pays its coupon annually.) Now, with three years left in the bond's life, the interest rate is 8% per year. The bond's fair market price is the present value of the remaining annual coupons plus payment of par value. That present value is[10]

$$\$70 \times \text{Annuity factor(8\%, 3)} + \$1,000 \times \text{PV factor(8\%, 3)} = \$974.23$$

which is less than par value.

In another year, after the next coupon is paid and remaining maturity falls to two years, the bond would sell at

$$\$70 \times \text{Annuity factor(8\%, 2)} + \$1,000 \times \text{PV factor(8\%, 2)} = \$982.17$$

thereby yielding a capital gain over the year of $7.94. If an investor had purchased the bond at $974.23, the total return over the year would equal the coupon payment plus capital gain, or $70 + $7.94 = $77.94. This represents a rate of return of $77.94/$974.23, or 8%, exactly the current rate of return available elsewhere in the market.

CONCEPT check 10.5

What will be the price of the bond in Example 10.10 in yet another year, when only one year remains until maturity? What is the rate of return to an investor who purchases the bond at $982.17 and sells it one year later?

When bond prices are set according to the present value formula, any discount from par value provides an anticipated capital gain that will augment a below-market coupon rate by just enough to provide a fair total rate of return. Conversely, if the coupon rate exceeds the market interest rate, the interest income by itself is greater than that available elsewhere in the market. Investors will bid up the price of these bonds above their par values. As the bonds approach maturity, they will fall in value because fewer of these above-market coupon payments remain. The resulting capital losses offset the large coupon payments so that the bondholder again receives only a competitive rate of return.

Problem 16 at the end of the chapter asks you to work through the case of the high-coupon bond. Figure 10.6 traces out the price paths (net of accrued interest) of two bonds, one with a coupon above the yield to maturity and another with a coupon below yield to maturity, as time to maturity approaches, at least for the case in which the market interest rate is constant. The low-coupon bond enjoys capital gains as price steadily approaches par value, while the high-coupon bond suffers capital losses.[11]

We use these examples to show that each bond offers investors the same total rate of return. Although the capital gains versus income components differ, the price of each bond is set to provide competitive rates, as we should expect in well-functioning capital markets. Security returns

[10]Using a calculator, enter $n = 3$, $i = 8$, PMT = 70, FV = 1000, and compute PV.

[11]If interest rates are volatile, the price path will be "jumpy," vibrating around the price path in Figure 10.6 and reflecting capital gains or losses as interest rates fluctuate. Ultimately, however, the price must reach par value at the maturity date, so, on average, the price of the premium bond will fall over time while that of the discount bond will rise.

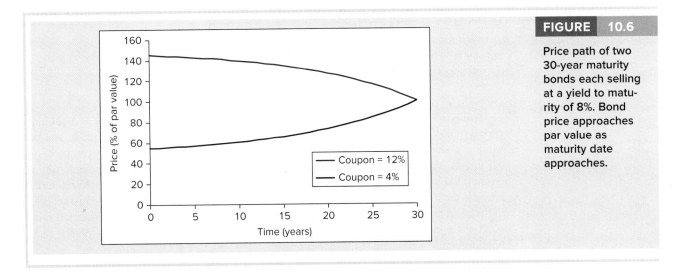

FIGURE 10.6

Price path of two 30-year maturity bonds each selling at a yield to maturity of 8%. Bond price approaches par value as maturity date approaches.

all should be comparable on an after-tax risk-adjusted basis. If they are not, investors will try to sell low-return securities, thereby driving down their prices until the total return at the now-lower price is competitive with other securities. Prices should continue to adjust until all securities are fairly priced in that expected returns are comparable (given appropriate risk and tax adjustments).

We see evidence of this price adjustment in Figure 10.1. Compare the two bonds maturing in November 2018. The November 30 maturity bond has a coupon rate of 1.375%, while the November 15 bond has a much higher coupon rate, 9%. But the higher coupon rate on that bond does not mean that it offers a higher return; instead, it sells at a higher price. The yields to maturity on the two bonds are nearly equal, both around 1.3%. This makes sense because investors should care about their total return, including both coupon income as well as price change. In the end, prices of similar-maturity bonds adjust until yields are pretty much equalized.

Of course, the yields across bonds in Figure 10.1 are not all equal. Clearly, longer-term bonds at this time offered higher promised yields, a common pattern, and one that reflects the relative risks of the bonds. We will explore the relationship between yield and time to maturity later in the chapter.

Yield to Maturity versus Holding-Period Return

In Example 10.10, the holding-period return and the yield to maturity were equal. The bond yield started and ended the year at 8%, and the bond's holding-period return also equaled 8%. This turns out to be a general result. When the yield to maturity is unchanged over the period, the rate of return on the bond will equal that yield. As we noted, this should not be surprising: The bond must offer a rate of return competitive with those available on other securities.

However, when yields fluctuate, so will a bond's rate of return. Unanticipated changes in market rates will result in unanticipated changes in bond returns, and, after the fact, a bond's holding-period return can be better or worse than the yield at which it initially sells. An increase in the bond's yield to maturity acts to reduce its price, which means that the holding-period return will be less than the initial yield. Conversely, a decline in yield to maturity results in a holding-period return greater than the initial yield.

Consider a 30-year bond paying an annual coupon of $80 and selling at par value of $1,000. The bond's initial yield to maturity is 8%. If the yield remains at 8% over the year, the bond price will remain at par, so the holding-period return also will be 8%. But if the yield falls below 8%, the bond price will increase. Suppose the yield falls and the price increases to $1,050. Then the holding-period return is greater than 8%:

$$\text{Holding-period return} = \frac{\$80 + (\$1,050 - \$1,000)}{\$1,000} = .13 \text{ or } 13\%$$

EXAMPLE 10.11

Yield to Maturity versus Holding-Period Return

Show that if the yield to maturity increases, then holding-period return is *less* than that initial yield. For example, suppose in Example 10.11 that by the end of the first year, the bond's yield to maturity is 8.5%. Find the one-year holding-period return and compare it to the bond's initial 8% yield to maturity.

Here is another way to think about the difference between yield to maturity and holding-period return. Yield to maturity depends only on the bond's coupon, *current* price, and par value at maturity. All of these values are observable today, so yield to maturity can be easily calculated. Yield to maturity is commonly interpreted as a measure of the *average* rate of return if the investment in the bond is held until the bond matures. In contrast, holding-period return is the rate of return over a particular investment period and depends on the market price of the bond at the end of that holding period; of course this price is *not* known today. Because bond prices over the holding period will respond to unanticipated changes in interest rates, holding-period return can at most be forecast.

Zero-Coupon Bonds and Treasury STRIPS

Original-issue discount bonds are less common than coupon bonds issued at par. These are bonds that are issued intentionally with low coupon rates that cause the bond to sell at a discount from par value. The most common example of this type of bond is the *zero-coupon bond,* which carries no coupons and provides all its return in the form of price appreciation. Zeros provide only one cash flow to their owners, on the maturity date of the bond.

U.S. Treasury bills are examples of short-term zero-coupon instruments. If the bill has face value of $10,000, the Treasury issues or sells it for some amount less than $10,000, agreeing to repay $10,000 at maturity. All of the investor's return comes in the form of price appreciation.

Longer-term zero-coupon bonds are commonly created from coupon-bearing notes and bonds. A broker who purchases a Treasury coupon bond may ask the Treasury to break down the cash flows into a series of independent securities, where each security is a claim to one of the payments of the original bond. For example, a 10-year coupon bond would be "stripped" of its 20 semiannual coupons and each coupon payment would be treated as a stand-alone zero-coupon bond. The maturities of these bonds would thus range from six months to 10 years. The final payment of principal would be treated as another stand-alone zero-coupon security. Each of the payments would then be treated as an independent security and assigned its own CUSIP number, the security identifier that allows for electronic trading over the Fed-wire system. The payments are still considered obligations of the U.S. Treasury. The Treasury program under which coupon stripping is performed is called STRIPS (Separate Trading of Registered Interest and Principal of Securities), and these zero-coupon securities are called *Treasury strips.*

What should happen to prices of zeros as time passes? On their maturity dates, zeros must sell for par value. Before maturity, however, they should sell at discounts from par, because of the time value of money. As time passes, price should approach par value. In fact, if the interest rate is constant, a zero's price will increase at exactly the rate of interest.

To illustrate, consider a zero with 30 years until maturity, and suppose the market interest rate is 10% per year. The price of the bond today is $1,000/(1.10)^{30} = \$57.31$. Next year, with only 29 years until maturity, if the yield to maturity is still 10%, the price will be $1,000/(1.10)^{29} = \$63.04$, a 10% increase over its previous-year value. Because the par value of the bond is now discounted for one less year, its price has increased by the one-year discount factor.

Figure 10.7 presents the price path of a 30-year zero-coupon bond for an annual market interest rate of 10%. The bond's price rises exponentially, not linearly, until its maturity.

After-Tax Returns

The tax authorities recognize that the "built-in" price appreciation on original-issue discount (OID) bonds such as zero-coupon bonds represents an implicit interest payment to the holder

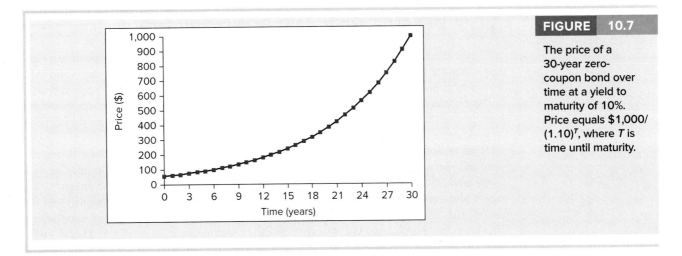

FIGURE 10.7

The price of a 30-year zero-coupon bond over time at a yield to maturity of 10%. Price equals $1,000/(1.10)^T$, where T is time until maturity.

of the security. The Internal Revenue Service (IRS), therefore, calculates a price appreciation schedule to impute taxable interest income for the built-in appreciation during a tax year, even if the asset is not sold or does not mature until a future year. Any additional gains or losses that arise from changes in market interest rates are treated as capital gains or losses if the OID bond is sold during the tax year.

EXAMPLE 10.12

Taxation of Original-Issue Discount Bonds

If the interest rate originally is 10%, the 30-year zero would be issued at a price of $\$1,000/1.10^{30} = \$57.31$. The following year, the IRS calculates what the bond price would be if its yield were still 10%. This is $\$1,000/1.10^{29} = \$63.04$. Therefore, the IRS imputes interest income of $\$63.04 - \$57.31 = \$5.73$. This amount is subject to tax. Notice that the imputed interest income is based on a "constant yield method" that ignores any changes in market interest rates.

If interest rates actually fall, let's say to 9.9%, the bond price will be $\$1,000/1.099^{29} = \$64.72$. If the bond is sold, then the difference between $64.72 and $63.04 will be treated as capital gains income and taxed at the capital gains tax rate. If the bond is not sold, then the price difference is an unrealized capital gain and does not result in taxes in that year. In either case, the investor must pay taxes on the $5.73 of imputed interest at the ordinary income tax rate.

The procedure illustrated in Example 10.12 applies as well to the taxation of other original-issue discount bonds, even if they are not zero-coupon bonds. Consider, as another example, a 30-year maturity bond that is issued with a coupon rate of 4% and a yield to maturity of 8%. For simplicity, we will assume that the bond pays coupons once annually. Because of the low coupon rate, the bond will be issued at a price far below par value, specifically at a price of $549.69. (Confirm this for yourself.) If the bond's yield to maturity is still 8%, then its price in one year will rise to $553.66. (Confirm this also.) This would provide a pretax holding-period return of exactly 8%:

$$\text{HPR} = \frac{\$40 + (\$553.66 - \$549.69)}{\$549.69} = .08$$

The increase in the bond price based on a constant yield, however, is treated as interest income, so the investor is required to pay taxes on imputed interest income of $553.66 − $549.69 = $3.97, as well as on the explicit coupon income of $40. If the bond's yield actually changes during the year, the difference between the bond's price and the "constant yield value" of $553.66 would be treated as capital gains income if the bond were sold at year-end.

CONCEPT check 10.7

Suppose that the yield to maturity of the 4% coupon, 30-year maturity bond falls to 7% by the end of the first year and that the investor sells the bond after the first year. If the investor's federal plus state tax rate on interest income is 38% and the combined tax rate on capital gains is 20%, what is the investor's after-tax rate of return?

10.5 DEFAULT RISK AND BOND PRICING

Although bonds generally *promise* a fixed flow of income, that income stream is not risk-less unless the investor can be sure the issuer will not default on the obligation. While U.S. government bonds may be treated as free of default risk, this is not true of corporate bonds. If the company goes bankrupt, the bondholders will not receive all the payments they have been promised. Therefore, the actual payments on these bonds are uncertain, for they depend to some degree on the ultimate financial status of the firm.

Bond default risk is measured by Moody's Investor Services, Standard & Poor's Corporation, and Fitch Investors Service, all of which provide financial information on firms as well as the credit risk of large corporate and municipal bond issues. International sovereign bonds, which also entail default risk, especially in emerging markets, also are commonly rated for default risk. Each rating firm assigns letter grades to reflect its assessment of bond safety. The top rating is AAA or Aaa. Moody's modifies each rating class with a 1, 2, or 3 suffix (e.g., Aaa1, Aaa2, Aaa3) to provide a finer gradation of ratings. The other agencies use a + or − modification.

Those rated BBB or above (S&P, Fitch) or Baa and above (Moody's) are considered **investment grade bonds,** while lower-rated bonds are classified as **speculative grade** or **junk bonds.** Certain regulated institutional investors such as insurance companies have not always been allowed to invest in speculative grade bonds.

Figure 10.8 provides definitions of each bond rating classification.

Junk Bonds

Junk bonds, also known as *high-yield bonds,* are nothing more than speculative grade (low-rated or unrated) bonds. Before 1977, almost all junk bonds were "fallen angels," that is, bonds issued by firms that originally had investment grade ratings but that had since been downgraded. In 1977, however, firms began to issue "original-issue junk."

Much of the credit for this innovation is given to Drexel Burnham Lambert, and especially its trader, Michael Milken. Drexel had long enjoyed a niche as a junk bond trader and had established a network of potential investors in junk bonds. Firms not able to muster an investment grade rating were happy to have Drexel (and other investment bankers) market their bonds directly to the public, as this opened up a new source of financing. Junk issues were a lower-cost financing alternative than borrowing from banks.

High-yield bonds gained considerable notoriety in the 1980s when they were used as financing vehicles in leveraged buyouts and hostile takeover attempts. Shortly thereafter, however, the legal difficulties of Drexel and Michael Milken in connection with Wall Street's insider trading scandals of the late 1980s tainted the junk bond market.

At the height of Drexel's difficulties, the high-yield bond market nearly dried up but eventually rebounded dramatically. However, the average credit quality of newly issued high-yield debt today is higher than the average quality in the boom years of the 1980s. Of course, junk bonds are more vulnerable to financial distress than investment grade bonds. During the financial crisis of 2008–2009, prices on these bonds fell dramatically, and their yields to maturity rose equally dramatically. The spread between yields on Treasury bonds and B-rated bonds widened from around 3% in early 2007 to an astonishing 19% by the start of 2009.

Determinants of Bond Safety

Bond rating agencies base their quality ratings largely on an analysis of the level and trend of some of the issuer's financial ratios. The key ratios used to evaluate safety are:

1. *Coverage ratios.* Ratios of company earnings to fixed costs. For example, the *times-interest-earned ratio* is the ratio of earnings before interest payments and taxes to interest obligations. The *fixed-charge coverage ratio* includes lease payments and sinking fund payments with interest obligations to arrive at the ratio of earnings to all fixed cash obligations. Low or falling coverage ratios signal possible cash flow difficulties.

---

investment grade bond

A bond rated BBB and above by Standard & Poor's or Baa and above by Moody's.

speculative grade or junk bond

A bond rated BB or lower by Standard & Poor's, Ba or lower by Moody's, or unrated.

FIGURE 10.8

Definitions of each bond rating class

Sources: From Stephen A. Ross, Randolph W. Westerfield, and Jeffrey F. Jaffe, *Corporate Finance*, 9th ed. © 2010, McGraw-Hill Publishing. Data from various editions of *Standard & Poor's Bond Guide* and *Moody's Bond Guide*.

	Bond Ratings			
	Very High Quality	High Quality	Speculative	Very Poor
Standard & Poor's	AAA AA	A BBB	BB B	CCC D
Moody's	Aaa Aa	A Baa	Ba B	Caa C

At times both Moody's and Standard & Poor's use adjustments to these ratings. S&P uses plus and minus signs: A+ is the strongest A rating and A− the weakest. Moody's uses a 1, 2, or 3 designation, with 1 indicating the strongest.

Moody's	S&P	
Aaa	AAA	Debt rated Aaa and AAA has the highest rating. Capacity to pay interest and principal is extremely strong.
Aa	AA	Debt rated Aa and AA has a very strong capacity to pay interest and repay principal. Together with the highest rating, this group comprises the high-grade bond class.
A	A	Debt rated A has a strong capacity to pay interest and repay principal, although it is somewhat more susceptible to the adverse effects of changes in circumstances and economic conditions than debt in higher-rated categories.
Baa	BBB	Debt rated Baa and BBB is regarded as having an adequate capacity to pay interest and repay principal. Whereas it normally exhibits adequate protection parameters, adverse economic conditions or changing circumstances are more likely to lead to a weakened capacity to pay interest and repay principal for debt in this category than in higher-rated categories. These bonds are medium grade obligations.
Ba B Caa Ca	B CCC CC	Debt rated in these categories is regarded, on balance, as predominantly speculative with respect to capacity to pay interest and repay principal in accordance with the terms of the obligation. BB and Ba indicate the lowest degree of speculation, and CC and Ca the highest degree of speculation. Although such debt will likely have some quality and protective characteristics, these are outweighed by large uncertainties or major risk exposures to adverse conditions. Some issues may be in default.
C	C	This rating is reserved for income bonds on which no interest is being paid.
D	D	Debt rated D is in default, and payment of interest and/or repayment of principal is in arrears.

2. *Leverage ratio (Debt-to-equity ratio).* A too-high leverage ratio indicates excessive indebtedness, signaling the possibility the firm will be unable to earn enough to satisfy the obligations on its bonds.

3. *Liquidity ratios.* The two common liquidity ratios are the *current ratio* (current assets/current liabilities) and the *quick ratio* (current assets excluding inventories/current liabilities). These ratios measure the firm's ability to pay bills coming due with its most liquid assets.

4. *Profitability ratios.* Measures of rates of return on assets or equity. Profitability ratios are indicators of a firm's overall performance. The *return on assets* (earnings before interest and taxes divided by total assets) or return on equity (net income/equity) are the most

popular of these measures. Firms with higher return on assets or equity should be better able to raise money in security markets because they offer prospects for better returns on the firm's investments.

5. *Cash flow-to-debt ratio.* This is the ratio of total cash flow to outstanding debt.

Standard & Poor's periodically computes median values of selected ratios for firms in several rating classes, which we present in Table 10.3. Of course, ratios must be evaluated in the context of industry standards, and analysts differ in the weights they place on particular ratios. Nevertheless, Table 10.3 demonstrates the tendency of ratios to improve along with the firm's rating class. And default rates vary dramatically with bond rating. Historically, only about 1% of industrial bonds originally rated AA or better at issuance had defaulted after 15 years. That ratio is around 7.5% for BBB-rated bonds and 40% for B-rated bonds. Credit risk clearly varies dramatically across rating classes.

Bond Indentures

indenture

The document defining the contract between the bond issuer and the bondholder.

In addition to specifying a payment schedule, the bond **indenture,** which is the contract between the issuer and the bondholder, also specifies a set of restrictions that protect the rights of the bondholders. Such restrictions include provisions relating to collateral, sinking funds, dividend policy, and further borrowing. The issuing firm agrees to these so-called protective covenants to market its bonds to investors concerned about the safety of the bond issue.

SINKING FUNDS   Bonds call for the payment of par value at the end of the bond's life. This payment constitutes a large cash commitment for the issuer. To help ensure that the commitment does not create a cash flow crisis, the firm may agree to establish a **sinking fund** to spread the payment burden over several years. The fund may operate in one of two ways:

sinking fund

A bond indenture that calls for the issuer to periodically repurchase some proportion of the outstanding bonds prior to maturity.

1. The firm may repurchase a fraction of the outstanding bonds in the open market each year.
2. The firm may purchase a fraction of outstanding bonds at a special call price associated with the sinking fund provision. The firm has an option to purchase the bonds at either the market price or the sinking fund price, whichever is lower. To allocate the burden of the sinking fund call fairly among bondholders, the bonds chosen for the call are selected at random based on serial number.[12]

The sinking fund call differs from a conventional call provision in two important ways. First, the firm can repurchase only a limited fraction of the bond issue at the sinking fund call

TABLE 10.3   Financial ratios and default risk by rating class, long-term debt

	Three-Year Medians						
	AAA	**AA**	**A**	**BBB**	**BB**	**B**	**CCC**
EBIT interest coverage multiple	23.8	19.5	8.0	4.7	2.5	1.2	0.4
EBITDA interest coverage multiple	25.5	24.6	10.2	6.5	3.5	1.9	0.9
Funds from operations/total debt (%)	203.3	79.9	48.0	35.9	22.4	11.5	5.0
Free operating cash flow/total debt (%)	127.6	44.5	25.0	17.3	8.3	2.8	(002.1)
Total debt/EBITDA multiple	0.4	0.9	1.6	2.2	3.5	5.3	7.9
Return on capital (%)	27.6	27.0	17.5	13.4	11.3	8.7	3.2
Total debt/total debt + equity (%)	12.4	28.3	37.5	42.5	53.7	75.9	113.5

Note: EBITDA is earnings before interest, taxes, depreciation, and amortization.

Source: *Corporate Rating Criteria,* Standard & Poor's, 2006.

---

[12]While it is uncommon, the sinking fund provision also may call for periodic payments to a trustee, with the payments invested so that the accumulated sum can be used for retirement of the entire issue at maturity.

price. At most, some indentures allow firms to use a *doubling option,* which allows repurchase of double the required number of bonds at the sinking fund call price. Second, while callable bonds generally have call prices above par value, the sinking fund call price usually is set at the bond's par value.

Although sinking funds ostensibly protect bondholders by making principal repayment more likely, they can hurt the investor. The firm will choose to buy back discount bonds (selling below par) at their market price, while exercising its option to buy back premium bonds (selling above par) at par. Therefore, if interest rates fall and bond prices rise, a firm will benefit from the sinking fund provision that enables it to repurchase its bonds at below-market prices. In these circumstances, the firm's gain is the bondholder's loss.

One bond issue that does not require a sinking fund is a *serial bond* issue in which the firm sells bonds with staggered maturity dates. As bonds mature sequentially, the principal repayment burden for the firm is spread over time just as it is with a sinking fund. Serial bonds do not include call provisions. Unlike sinking fund bonds, serial bonds do not confront security holders with the risk that a particular bond may be called for the sinking fund. The disadvantage of serial bonds, however, is that the bonds of each maturity date are different bonds, which reduces the liquidity of the issue. Trading these bonds, therefore, is more expensive.

SUBORDINATION OF FURTHER DEBT One of the factors determining bond safety is the total outstanding debt of the issuer. If you bought a bond today, you would be understandably distressed to see the firm tripling its outstanding debt tomorrow. Your bond would be riskier than it appeared when you bought it. To prevent firms from harming bondholders in this manner, **subordination clauses** restrict the amount of their additional borrowing. Additional debt might be required to be subordinated in priority to existing debt; that is, in the event of bankruptcy, *subordinated* or *junior* debtholders will not be paid unless and until the prior senior debt is fully paid off.

> **subordination clauses**
>
> Restrictions on additional borrowing that stipulate that senior bondholders will be paid first in the event of bankruptcy.

DIVIDEND RESTRICTIONS Covenants also limit the dividends firms may pay. These limitations protect the bondholders because they force the firm to retain assets rather than pay them out to stockholders. A typical restriction disallows payments of dividends if cumulative dividends paid since the firm's inception exceed cumulative retained earnings plus proceeds from sales of stock.

COLLATERAL Some bonds are issued with specific collateral behind them. **Collateral** is a particular asset that the bondholders receive if the firm defaults. If the collateral is property, the bond is called a *mortgage bond.* If the collateral takes the form of other securities held by the firm, the bond is a *collateral trust bond.* In the case of equipment, the bond is known as an *equipment obligation bond.* This last form of collateral is used most commonly by firms such as railroads, where the equipment is fairly standard and can be easily sold to another firm should the firm default.

> **collateral**
>
> A specific asset pledged against possible default on a bond.

Collateralized bonds generally are considered safer than general **debenture** bonds, which are unsecured, meaning they do not provide for specific collateral; credit risk of unsecured bonds depends on the general earning power of the firm. If the firm defaults, debenture owners become general creditors of the firm. Because they are safer, collateralized bonds generally offer lower yields than general debentures.

> **debenture**
>
> A bond not backed by specific collateral.

Figure 10.9 shows the terms of a bond issued by Mobil as described in *Moody's Industrial Manual.* The terms of the bond are typical and illustrate many of the indenture provisions we have mentioned. The bond is registered and listed on the NYSE. It was issued in 1991, but it was not callable until 2002. Although the call price started at 105.007% of par value, it falls gradually until it reaches par after 2020.

Yield to Maturity and Default Risk

Because corporate bonds are subject to default risk, we must distinguish between the bond's promised yield to maturity and its expected yield. The promised or stated yield will be realized

FIGURE   **10.9**

Callable bond issued by Mobil

Source: *Moody's Industrial Manual,* Moody's Investor Services, 1997.

Mobil Corp. debenture 8s, due 2032:

Rating — Aa2

AUTH — $250,000,000.
OUTSTG — Dec. 31, 1993. $250,000,000.
DATED — Oct. 30, 1991.
INTEREST — F&A 12.
TRUSTEE — Chemical Bank.
DENOMINATION — Fully registered, $1,000 and integral multiples thereof. Transferable and exchangeable without service charge.
CALLABLE — As a whole or in part, at any time, on or after Aug. 12, 2002, at the option of Co. on at least 30 but not more than 60 days' notice to each Aug. 11 as follows:

2003........105.007	2004........104.756	2005........104.506	2006........104.256
2007........104.005	2008........103.755	2009........103.505	2010........103.254
2011........103.004	2012........102.754	2013........102.503	2014........102.253
2015........102.003	2016........101.752	2017........101.502	2018........101.252
2019........101.001	2020........100.751	2021........100.501	2022........100.250

and thereafter at 100 plus accrued interest.
SECURITY — Not secured. Ranks equally with all other unsecured and unsubordinated indebtedness of Co. Co. nor any Affiliate will not incurr any indebtedness; provided that Co. will not create as security for any indebtedness for borrowed money, any mortgage, pledge, security interest or lien on any stock or indebtedness is directly owned by Co., without effectively providing that the debt securities shall be secured equally and ratably with such indebtedness, so long as such indebtedness shall be so secured.
INDENTURE MODIFICATION — Indenture may be modified, except as provided with, consent of $66\frac{2}{3}$% of debs. outstg.
RIGHTS ON DEFAULT — Trustee, or 25% of debs. outstg., may declare principal due and payable (30 days' grace for payment of interest).
LISTED — On New York Stock Exchange.
PURPOSE — Proceeds used for general corporate purposes.
OFFERED — ($250,000,000) at 99.51 plus accrued interest (proceeds to Co., 99.11) on Aug. 5, 1992 thru Merrill Lynch & Co., Donaldson, Lufkin & Jenerette Securities Corp., PaineWebber Inc., Prudential Securities Inc., Smith Barney, Harris Upham & Co. Inc. and associates.

only if the firm meets the obligations of the bond issue. Therefore, the stated yield is the *maximum possible* yield to maturity of the bond. The expected yield to maturity must take into account the possibility of a default.

For example, at the height of the financial crisis in October 2008, as Ford Motor Company struggled, its 6.625% coupon bonds due in 2028 were rated CCC and were selling at about 33% of par value, resulting in a yield to maturity of about 20%. Investors did not really believe the expected rate of return on these bonds was 20%. They recognized the distinct possibility that bondholders would not receive all the payments promised in the bond contract and that the yield based on *expected* cash flows was far less than the yield based on *promised* cash flows. As it turned out, of course, Ford weathered the storm, and investors who purchased its bonds made a very nice profit: In 2014, the bonds were selling at prices about 20% *above* par value.

EXAMPLE 10.13

Expected versus Promised Yield

Suppose a firm issued a 9% coupon bond 20 years ago. The bond now has 10 years left until its maturity date, but the firm is having financial difficulties. Investors believe that the firm will be able to make good on the remaining interest payments but that at the maturity date, the firm will be forced into bankruptcy and bondholders will receive only 70% of par value. The bond is selling at $750.

Yield to maturity (YTM) would then be calculated using the inputs shown in the following table.

	Expected YTM	Stated YTM
Coupon payment	$45	$45
Number of semiannual periods	20 periods	20 periods
Final payment	$700	$1,000
Price	$750	$750

The yield to maturity based on promised payments is 13.7%. Based on the expected payment of $700 at maturity, however, the yield would be only 11.6%. The stated yield to maturity is greater than the yield to maturity investors actually expect to receive.

Example 10.13 suggests that when a bond becomes more subject to default risk, its price will fall, and therefore its promised yield to maturity will rise. Therefore, the default premium, the spread between the stated yield to maturity and that on otherwise comparable Treasury bonds, will rise. However, its expected yield to maturity, which ultimately is tied to the systematic risk of the bond, will be far less affected. Let's continue the example.

Suppose that the condition of the firm in Example 10.13 deteriorates further, and investors now believe that the bond will pay off only 55% of face value at maturity. Investors now demand an expected yield to maturity of 12% (i.e., 6% semiannually), which is .4% higher than in Example 10.13. But the price of the bond will fall from $750 to $688 [*n* = 20; *i* = 6; FV = 550; PMT = $45]. At this price, the stated yield to maturity based on promised cash flows is 15.2%. While the expected yield to maturity has increased by .4%, the drop in price has caused the promised yield to maturity (and the default premium) to rise by 1.5%.

To compensate for the possibility of default, corporate bonds must offer a **default premium.** The default premium is the difference between the promised yield on a corporate bond and the yield of an otherwise identical government bond that is riskless in terms of default. If the firm remains solvent and actually pays the investor all of the promised cash flows, the investor will realize a higher yield to maturity than would be realized from the government bond. If, however, the firm goes bankrupt, the corporate bond is likely to provide a lower return than the government bond. The corporate bond has the potential for both better and worse performance than the default-free Treasury bond. In other words, it is riskier.

default premium

The increment to promised yield that compensates the investor for default risk.

The pattern of default premiums offered on risky bonds is sometimes called the *risk structure of interest rates.* The greater the default risk, the higher the default premium. Figure 10.10 shows spreads between yields to maturity of bonds of different risk classes since 1997. You can see here clear evidence of default-risk premiums on promised yields. Notice, for example, the incredible run-up of credit spreads during the crisis of 2008–2009.

Credit Default Swaps

A **credit default swap (CDS)** is in effect an insurance policy on the default risk of a bond or loan. To illustrate, the annual premium in early 2010 on a five-year Greek Sovereign CDS was about 3%, meaning that the CDS buyer would pay the seller an annual premium of $3 for each

credit default swap (CDS)

An insurance policy on the default risk of a corporate bond or loan.

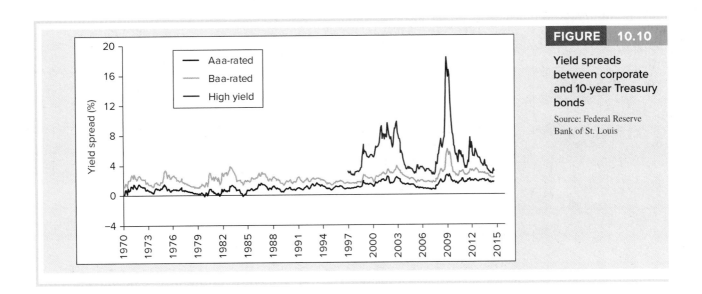

FIGURE 10.10

Yield spreads between corporate and 10-year Treasury bonds

Source: Federal Reserve Bank of St. Louis

$100 of bond principal. The seller collects these annual payments for the term of the contract, but must compensate the buyer for loss of bond value in the event of a default.[13]

As originally envisioned, credit default swaps were designed to allow lenders to buy protection against losses on sizable loans. The natural buyers of CDSs would then be large bondholders or banks that had made large loans and wished to enhance the creditworthiness of those loans. Even if the bond issuer had shaky credit standing, the "insured" debt would be as safe as the issuer of the CDS. An investor holding a bond with a BB rating could, in principle, raise the effective quality of the debt to AAA by buying a CDS on the issuer.

This insight suggests how CDS contracts should be priced. If a BB-rated bond bundled with insurance via a CDS is effectively equivalent to a AAA-rated bond, then the fair price of the swap ought to approximate the yield spread between AAA-rated and BB-rated bonds.[14] The risk structure of interest rates and CDS prices ought to be tightly aligned.

Figure 10.11 shows the prices of five-year CDS contracts on Greek government debt between 2009 and 2010 as well as the spread between yields on Greek and German government bonds. As expected, the credit spread and the CDS prices move almost in lockstep.

You can see in Figure 10.11 that both the credit spread and CDS price started to increase dramatically toward the end of 2009. As perceptions of Greece's credit risk increased, so did the price of insuring its debt. Ultimately, in what amounted to the largest-ever sovereign default, lenders agreed in 2012 to reduce Greece's debt by around $130 billion.

CDS contracts trade on corporate as well as on sovereign debt. While CDSs were conceived as a form of bond insurance, it wasn't long before investors realized that they could be used to speculate on the financial health of particular companies. For example, someone in August 2008 wishing to bet against the financial sector might have purchased CDS contracts on those firms and would have profited as CDS prices spiked in September. In fact, hedge fund manager John Paulson famously did just this. His bearish bets in 2007–2008 on commercial banks and Wall Street firms as well as on some riskier mortgage-backed securities made his funds more than $15 billion, bringing him a personal payoff of more than $3.7 billion.

The nearby box discusses the role of credit default swaps in the financial crisis of 2008–2009.

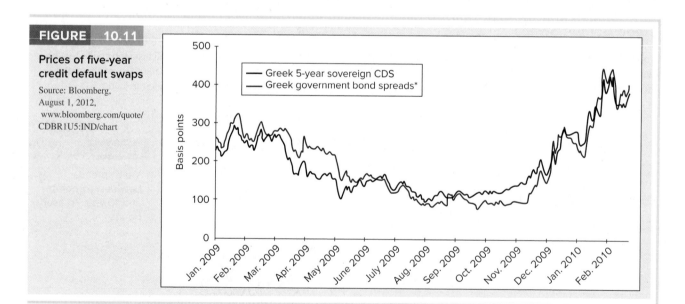

FIGURE   10.11

Prices of five-year credit default swaps

Source: Bloomberg, August 1, 2012, www.bloomberg.com/quote/CDBR1U5:IND/chart

---

[13]Actually, credit default swaps may pay off even short of an actual default. The contract specifies which particular "credit events" will trigger a payment. For example, restructuring (rewriting the terms of a firm's outstanding debt as an alternative to formal bankruptcy proceedings) may be defined as a triggering credit event.

[14]We say "approximately" because there are some differences between highly rated bonds and bonds synthetically enhanced with credit default swaps. For example, the term of the swap may not match the maturity of the bond. Tax treatment of coupon payments versus swap payments may differ, as may the liquidity of the bonds. Finally, some CDSs may entail one-time up-front payments as well as annual premiums.

CREDIT DEFAULT SWAPS, SYSTEMIC RISK, AND THE FINANCIAL CRISIS OF 2008–2009

The credit crisis of 2008–2009, when lending among banks and other financial institutions effectively seized up, was in large measure a crisis of transparency. The biggest problem was a widespread lack of confidence in the financial standing of counterparties to a trade. If one institution could not be confident that another would remain solvent, it would understandably be reluctant to offer it a loan. When doubt about the credit exposure of customers and trading partners spiked to levels not seen since the Great Depression, the market for loans dried up.

Credit default swaps were particularly cited for fostering doubts about counterparty reliability. By August 2008, $63 trillion of such swaps were reportedly outstanding. (By comparison, U.S. gross domestic product in 2008 was about $14 trillion.) As the subprime-mortgage market collapsed and the economy entered a deep recession, the potential obligations on these contracts ballooned to levels previously considered unimaginable and the ability of CDS sellers to honor their commitments was in doubt. For example, the huge insurance firm AIG alone had sold more than $400 billion of CDS contracts on subprime mortgages and other loans and was days from insolvency. But AIG's insolvency would have triggered the insolvency of other firms that had relied on its promise of protection against loan defaults. These in turn might have triggered further defaults. In the end, the government felt compelled to rescue AIG to prevent a chain reaction of insolvencies.

Counterparty risk and lax reporting requirements made it effectively impossible to tease out firms' exposures to credit risk. One problem was that CDS positions do not have to be accounted for on balance sheets. And the possibility of one default setting off a sequence of further defaults means that lenders may be exposed to the default of an institution with which they do not even directly trade. Such knock-on effects create *systemic risk,* in which the entire financial system can freeze up. With the ripple effects of bad debt extending in ever-widening circles, it can seem imprudent to lend to anyone.

In the aftermath of the credit crisis, the Dodd-Frank Act called for new regulation and reforms. Among its provisions is the creation of a central clearinghouse for credit derivatives such as CDS contracts. Such a system would foster transparency of positions, allow netting of offsetting positions, and require daily recognition of gains or losses on positions through a margin or collateral account. If losses were to mount, positions would have to be unwound before growing to unsustainable levels. Allowing traders to accurately assess counterparty risk, and limiting such risk through margin accounts and the extra backup of the clearinghouse, would go a long way in limiting systemic risk.

10.6 THE YIELD CURVE

Return to Figure 10.1 again, and you will see that while yields to maturity on bonds of similar maturities are reasonably close, yields do differ. Bonds with shorter maturities generally offer lower yields to maturity than longer-term bonds. The graphical relationship between the yield to maturity and the term to maturity is called the **yield curve.** The relationship also is called the **term structure of interest rates** because it relates yields to maturity to the term (maturity) of each bond. The yield curve may be found at several websites, for example, *The Wall Street Journal Online* or Yahoo! Finance. Four such sets of curves are reproduced in Figure 10.12. Figure 10.12 illustrates that a wide range of yield curves may be observed in practice. Panel A is an essentially flat yield curve. Panel B is an upward-sloping curve, and Panel C is a downward-sloping, or "inverted," yield curve. Finally, the yield curve in Panel D is hump-shaped, first rising and then falling. Rising yield curves are most commonly observed. We will see why momentarily.

Why should bonds of differing maturity offer different yields? The two most plausible possibilities have to do with expectations of future rates and risk premiums. We will consider each of these arguments in turn.

yield curve

A graph of yield to maturity as a function of term to maturity.

term structure of interest rates

The relationship between yields to maturity and terms to maturity across bonds.

The Expectations Theory

Suppose everyone in the market believes firmly that while the current one-year interest rate is 8%, the interest rate on one-year bonds next year will rise to 10%. What would this belief imply about the proper yield to maturity on two-year bonds issued today?

It is easy to see that an investor who buys the one-year bond and rolls the proceeds into another one-year bond in the following year will earn, on average, about 9% per year. This value is just the average of the 8% earned this year and the 10% expected for next year. More

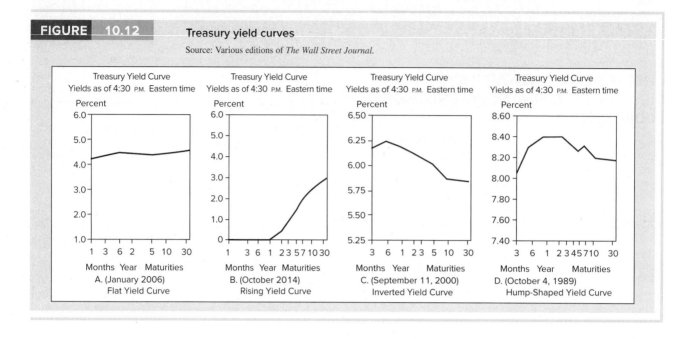

FIGURE   10.12   Treasury yield curves

Source: Various editions of *The Wall Street Journal*.

precisely, the investment will grow by a factor of 1.08 in the first year and 1.10 in the second year, for a total two-year growth factor of $1.08 \times 1.10 = 1.188$. This corresponds to an annual growth rate of 8.995% (because $1.08995^2 = 1.188$).

For investments in two-year bonds to be competitive with the strategy of rolling over one-year bonds, these two-year bonds also must offer an average annual return of 8.995% over the two-year holding period. This is illustrated in Figure 10.13. The current short-term rate of 8% and the expected value of next year's short-term rate are depicted above the time line. The two-year rate that provides the same expected two-year total return is below the time line. In this example, therefore, the yield curve will be upward-sloping; while one-year bonds offer an 8% yield to maturity, two-year bonds offer an 8.995% yield.

expectations hypothesis

The theory that yields to maturity are determined solely by expectations of future short-term interest rates.

This notion is the essence of the **expectations hypothesis** of the yield curve, which asserts that the slope of the yield curve is attributable to expectations of changes in short-term rates. Relatively high yields on long-term bonds reflect expectations of future increases in rates, while relatively low yields on long-term bonds (a downward-sloping or inverted yield curve) reflect expectations of falling short-term rates.

One of the implications of the expectations hypothesis is that expected holding-period returns on bonds of all maturities ought to be about equal. Even if the yield curve is upward-sloping (so that two-year bonds offer higher yields to maturity than one-year bonds), this does not necessarily mean investors expect higher rates of return on the two-year bonds. As we've seen, the higher initial yield to maturity on the two-year bond is necessary to compensate investors for the fact that interest rates the next year will be even higher. Over the two-year period, and indeed over any holding period, this theory predicts that holding-period returns will be equalized across bonds of all maturities.

FIGURE   10.13

Returns to two two-year investment strategies

Suppose we buy the one-year zero-coupon bond with a current yield to maturity of 8%. If its face value is $1,000, its price will be $925.93, providing an 8% rate of return over the coming year. Suppose instead that we buy the two-year zero-coupon bond at its yield of 8.995%. Its price today is $1,000/(1.08995)^2 = $841.76. After a year passes, the zero will have a remaining maturity of only one year; based on the forecast that the one-year yield next year will be 10%, it then will sell for $1,000/1.10 = $909.09. The expected rate of return over the year is thus ($909.09 − $841.76)/$841.76 = .08, or 8%, precisely the same return provided by the one-year bond. This makes sense: If risk considerations are ignored when pricing the two bonds, they ought to provide equal expected rates of return.

In fact, advocates of the expectations hypothesis commonly invert this analysis to *infer* the market's expectation of future short-term rates. They note that we do not directly observe the expectation of next year's rate, but we *can* observe yields on bonds of different maturities. Suppose, as in this example, we see that one-year bonds offer yields of 8% and two-year bonds offer yields of 8.995%. Each dollar invested in the two-year zero would grow after two years to $1 × 1.08995^2 = $1.188. A dollar invested in the one-year zero would grow by a factor of 1.08 in the first year and, then, if reinvested or "rolled over" into another one-year zero in the second year, would grow by an additional factor of $1 + r_2$. Final proceeds would be $1 × 1.08 × (1 + r_2)$.

The final proceeds of the rollover strategy depend on the interest rate that actually transpires in year 2. However, we can solve for the second-year interest rate that makes the expected payoff of these two strategies equal. This "break-even" value is called the **forward rate** for the second year, f_2, and is derived as follows:

$$1.08995^2 = 1.08 × (1 + f_2)$$

which implies that f_2 = .10, or 10%. Notice that the forward rate equals the market's expectation of the year-2 short rate. Hence, we conclude that if the expected total return of a long-term bond equals that of rolling over a short-term bond, the forward rate equals the expected short-term interest rate. This is why the theory is called the expectations hypothesis.

More generally, we obtain the forward rate by equating the return on an *n*-period zero-coupon bond with that of an (*n* − 1)-period zero-coupon bond rolled over into a one-year bond in year *n:*

$$(1 + y_n)^n = (1 + y_{n-1})^{n-1} (1 + f_n) \tag{10.3}$$

The actual total returns on the two *n*-year strategies will be equal if the short-term interest rate in year *n* turns out to equal f_n.

forward rate
The inferred short-term rate of interest for a future period that makes the expected total return of a long-term bond equal to that of rolling over short-term bonds.

Suppose that two-year maturity bonds offer yields to maturity of 6% and three-year bonds have yields of 7%. What is the forward rate for the third year? We could compare these two strategies as follows:

1. Buy a three-year bond. Total proceeds per dollar invested will be

$$\$1 × (1.07)^3 = \$1.2250$$

2. Buy a two-year bond. Reinvest all proceeds in a one-year bond in the third year, which will provide a return in that year of r_3. Total proceeds per dollar invested will be the result of two years' growth of invested funds at 6% plus the final year's growth at rate r_3:

$$\$1 × (1.06)^2 × (1 + r_3) = \$1.1236 × (1 + r_3)$$

The forward rate is the rate in year 3 that makes the total return on these strategies equal:

$$1.2250 = 1.1236 × (1 + f_3)$$

We conclude that the forward rate for the third year satisfies $(1 + f_3)$ = 1.0902, so that f_3 is 9.02%.

While the expectations hypothesis gives us a tool to infer expectations of future market interest rates from the yield curve, it tells us nothing of what underlying considerations generated those expectations. Ultimately, interest rates reflect investors' expectations of the state of the macroeconomy. Not surprisingly, then, forward rates and the yield curve have proven themselves to be useful inputs for economic forecasts. The slope of the yield curve is one of the more important components of the index of leading economic indicators used to predict the course of economic activity. Inverted yield curves in particular, which imply falling interest rates, turn out to be among the best indicators of a coming recession.

The Liquidity Preference Theory

The expectations hypothesis starts from the assertion that bonds are priced so that "buy and hold" investments in long-term bonds provide the same returns as rolling over a series of short-term bonds. However, the risks of long- and short-term bonds are not equivalent.

We have seen that longer-term bonds are subject to greater interest rate risk than short-term bonds. As a result, investors in long-term bonds might require a risk premium to compensate them for this risk. In this case, the yield curve will be upward-sloping even in the absence of any expectations of future increases in rates. The source of the upward slope in the yield curve is investor demand for higher expected returns on assets that are perceived as riskier.

liquidity preference theory

The theory that investors demand a risk premium on long-term bonds.

This viewpoint is called the **liquidity preference theory** of the term structure. Its name derives from the fact that shorter-term bonds have more "liquidity" than longer-term bonds, in the sense that they offer greater price certainty and trade in more active markets with lower bid–ask spreads. The preference of investors for greater liquidity makes them willing to hold these shorter-term bonds even if they do not offer expected returns as high as those of longer-term bonds.

liquidity premium

The extra expected return demanded by investors as compensation for the greater risk of longer-term bonds.

We can think of a **liquidity premium** as resulting from the extra compensation investors demand for holding longer-term bonds with greater price risk. We measure it as the spread between the forward rate of interest and the expected short rate:

$$f_n = E(r_n) + \text{Liquidity premium} \tag{10.4}$$

In the absence of a liquidity premium, the forward rate would equal the expectation of the future short rate. But, generally, we expect the forward rate to be higher to compensate investors for the lower liquidity of longer-term bonds.

Advocates of the liquidity preference theory also note that borrowers seem to prefer to issue long-term bonds. This allows them to lock in an interest rate on their borrowing for long periods, and thus they may be willing to pay higher yields on these issues. In sum, bond buyers demand higher rates on longer-term bonds, and bond issuers are willing to pay higher rates on those bonds. As a result, the yield curve generally slopes upward.

According to the liquidity preference theory, forward rates of interest will exceed the market's expectations of future interest rates. Even if rates are expected to remain unchanged, the yield curve will slope upward because of the liquidity premium. That upward slope would be mistakenly attributed to expectations of rising rates if one were to use the pure expectations hypothesis to interpret the yield curve.

EXAMPLE 10.17

Liquidity Premiums and the Yield Curve

Suppose that the short-term rate of interest is currently 8% and that investors expect it to remain at 8% next year. In the absence of a liquidity premium, with no expectation of a change in yields, the yield to maturity on two-year bonds also would be 8%, the yield curve would be flat, and the forward rate would be 8%. But what if investors demand a risk premium to invest in two-year rather than one-year bonds? If the liquidity premium is 1%, then the forward rate would be 8% + 1% = 9%, and the yield to maturity on the two-year bond would be determined by

$$(1 + y_2)^2 = 1.08 \times 1.09 = 1.1772$$

implying that $y_2 = .085 = 8.5\%$. Here, the yield curve is upward-sloping due solely to the liquidity premium embedded in the price of the longer-term bond.

Suppose that the expected value of the interest rate for year 3 remains at 8% but that the liquidity premium for that year is also 1%. What would be the yield to maturity on three-year zeros? What would this imply about the slope of the yield curve?

CONCEPT check 10.8

A Synthesis

Of course, we do not need to make an either/or choice between expectations and risk premiums. Both influence the yield curve, and both should be considered in interpreting it.

Figure 10.14 shows two possible yield curves. In Panel A, rates are expected to rise over time. This fact, together with a liquidity premium, makes the yield curve steeply upward-sloping. In Panel B, rates are expected to fall, which by itself would make the yield curve slope downward. However, the liquidity premium lends something of an upward slope. The net effect of these two opposing factors is a "hump-shaped" curve.

These two examples make it clear that the combination of varying expectations and liquidity premiums can result in a wide array of yield-curve profiles. For example, an upward-sloping curve does not in and of itself imply expectations of higher future interest rates, because the slope can result either from expectations or from risk premiums. A curve that is more steeply sloped than usual might signal expectations of higher rates, but even this inference is perilous.

Figure 10.15 presents yield spreads between 90-day T-bills and 10-year T-bonds since 1970. The figure shows that the yield curve is generally upward-sloping in that the longer-term bonds usually offer higher yields to maturity, despite the fact that rates could not have been expected to increase throughout the entire period. This tendency is the empirical basis for the liquidity premium doctrine that at least part of the upward slope in the yield curve must be due to a risk premium.

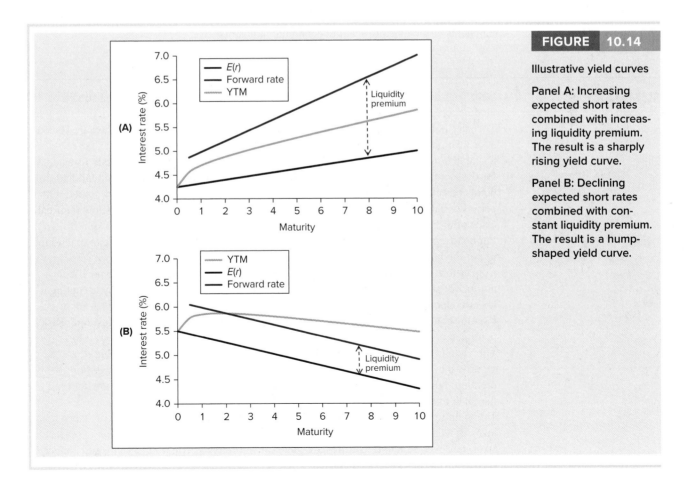

FIGURE 10.14

Illustrative yield curves

Panel A: Increasing expected short rates combined with increasing liquidity premium. The result is a sharply rising yield curve.

Panel B: Declining expected short rates combined with constant liquidity premium. The result is a hump-shaped yield curve.

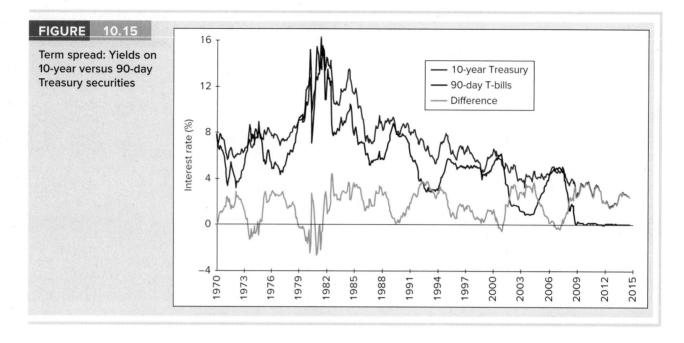

Because the yield curve normally has an upward slope due to risk premiums, a downward-sloping yield curve is taken as a strong indication that yields are more likely than not to fall. The prediction of declining interest rates is in turn often interpreted as a signal of a coming recession. Short-term rates exceeded long-term ones in each of the seven recessions since 1970. For this reason, it is not surprising that the slope of the yield curve is one of the key components of the index of leading economic indicators.

SUMMARY

- Debt securities are distinguished by their promise to pay a fixed or specified stream of income to their holders. The coupon bond is a typical debt security.
- Treasury notes and bonds have original maturities greater than one year. They are issued at or near par value, with their prices quoted net of accrued interest.
- Callable bonds should offer higher promised yields to maturity to compensate investors for the fact that they will not realize full capital gains should the interest rate fall and the bonds be called away from them at the stipulated call price. Bonds often are issued with a period of call protection. In addition, discount bonds selling significantly below their call price offer implicit call protection.
- Put bonds give the bondholder rather than the issuer the choice to terminate or extend the life of the bond.
- Convertible bonds may be exchanged, at the bondholder's discretion, for a specified number of shares of stock. Convertible bondholders "pay" for this option by accepting a lower coupon rate on the security.
- Floating-rate bonds pay a fixed premium over a referenced short-term interest rate. Risk is limited because the rate paid is tied to current market conditions.
- The yield to maturity is the single discount rate that equates the present value of a security's cash flows to its price. Bond prices and yields are inversely related. For premium bonds, the coupon rate is greater than the current yield, which is greater than the yield to maturity. These inequalities are reversed for discount bonds.
- The yield to maturity often is interpreted as an estimate of the average rate of return to an investor who purchases a bond and holds it until maturity. This interpretation is subject to error, however. Related measures are yield to call, realized compound yield, and expected (versus promised) yield to maturity.

- Treasury bills are U.S. government–issued zero-coupon bonds with original maturities of up to one year. Treasury STRIPS are longer-term default-free zero-coupon bonds. Prices of zero-coupon bonds rise exponentially over time, providing a rate of appreciation equal to the interest rate. The IRS treats this price appreciation as imputed taxable interest income to the investor.

- When bonds are subject to potential default, the stated yield to maturity is the maximum possible yield to maturity that can be realized by the bondholder. In the event of default, however, that promised yield will not be realized. To compensate bond investors for default risk, bonds must offer default premiums, that is, promised yields in excess of those offered by default-free government securities. If the firm remains healthy, its bonds will provide higher returns than government bonds. Otherwise, the returns may be lower.

- Bond safety often is measured using financial ratio analysis. Bond indentures offer safeguards to protect the claims of bondholders. Common indentures specify sinking fund requirements, collateralization, dividend restrictions, and subordination of future debt.

- Credit default swaps provide insurance against the default of a bond or loan. The swap buyer pays an annual premium to the swap seller but collects a payment equal to lost value if the loan later goes into default.

- The term structure of interest rates is the relationship between time to maturity and term to maturity. The yield curve is a graphical depiction of the term structure. The forward rate is the break-even interest rate that would equate the total return on a rollover strategy to that of a longer-term zero-coupon bond.

- The expectations hypothesis holds that forward interest rates are unbiased forecasts of future interest rates. The liquidity preference theory, however, argues that long-term bonds will carry a risk premium known as a liquidity premium. A positive liquidity premium can cause the yield curve to slope upward even if no increase in short rates is anticipated.

KEY TERMS

bond, 291	face value, 291	realized compound
callable bonds, 293	floating-rate bonds, 294	return, 306
collateral, 315	forward rate, 321	reinvestment rate risk, 307
convertible bonds, 294	horizon analysis, 307	sinking fund, 314
coupon rate, 291	indenture, 314	speculative grade or junk
credit default swap	investment grade	bond, 312
(CDS), 317	bonds, 312	subordination clauses, 315
current yield, 304	liquidity preference	term structure of interest
debenture, 315	theory, 322	rates, 319
default premium, 317	liquidity premium, 322	yield curve, 319
discount bonds, 304	par value, 291	yield to maturity
expectations	premium bonds, 304	(YTM), 302
hypothesis, 320	put bond, 294	zero-coupon bond, 291

KEY FORMULAS

Price of a coupon bond:

$$\text{Price} = \text{Coupon} \times \frac{1}{r}\left[1 - \frac{1}{(1+r)^T}\right] + \text{Par value} \times \frac{1}{(1+r)^T}$$

$$= \text{Coupon} \times \text{Annuity factor}(r, T) + \text{Par value} \times \text{PV factor}(r, T)$$

Forward rate of interest: $1 + f_n = \dfrac{(1 + y_n)^n}{(1 + y_{n-1})^{n-1}}$

Liquidity premium: Forward rate − Expected short rate

PROBLEM SETS

 Select problems are available in McGraw-Hill's *Connect*. Please see the Supplements section of the book's frontmatter for more information.

1. Define the following types of bonds: *(LO 10-1)*
   a. Catastrophe bond.
   b. Eurobond.
   c. Zero-coupon bond.
   d. Samurai bond.
   e. Junk bond.
   f. Convertible bond.
   g. Serial bond.
   h. Equipment obligation bond.
   i. Original-issue discount bond.
   j. Indexed bond.

2. What is the option embedded in a callable bond? A puttable bond? *(LO 10-1)*

3. What would be the likely effect on the yield to maturity of a bond resulting from: *(LO 10-5)*
   a. An increase in the issuing firm's times-interest-earned ratio?
   b. An increase in the issuing firm's debt-equity ratio?
   c. An increase in the issuing firm's quick ratio?

4. A coupon bond paying semiannual interest is reported as having an ask price of 117% of its $1,000 par value. If the last interest payment was made one month ago and the coupon rate is 6%, what is the invoice price of the bond? *(LO 10-1)*

5. A zero-coupon bond with face value $1,000 and maturity of five years sells for $746.22. What is its yield to maturity? What will happen to its yield to maturity if its price falls immediately to $730? *(LO 10-2)*

6. Why do bond prices go down when interest rates go up? Don't bond investors like to receive high interest rates? *(LO 10-2)*

7. Two bonds have identical times to maturity and coupon rates. One is callable at 105, the other at 110. Which should have the higher yield to maturity? Why? *(LO 10-4)*

8. Consider a bond with a 10% coupon and with yield to maturity = 8%. If the bond's YTM remains constant, then in one year will the bond price be higher, lower, or unchanged? Why? *(LO 10-2)*

9. A bond with an annual coupon rate of 4.8% sells for $970. What is the bond's current yield? *(LO 10-2)*

10. An investor believes that a bond may temporarily increase in credit risk. Which of the following would be the most liquid method of exploiting this? *(LO 10-5)*
    a. The purchase of a credit default swap.
    b. The sale of a credit default swap.
    c. The short sale of the bond.

11. Which of the following *most accurately* describes the behavior of credit default swaps? *(LO 10-5)*
    a. When credit risk increases, swap premiums increase.
    b. When credit and interest rate risk increases, swap premiums increase.
    c. When credit risk increases, swap premiums increase, but when interest rate risk increases, swap premiums decrease.

12. You buy an eight-year bond that has a 6% current yield and a 6% coupon (paid annually). In one year, promised yields to maturity have risen to 7%. What is your holding-period return? *(LO 10-3)*

13. The stated yield to maturity and realized compound yield to maturity of a (default-free) zero-coupon bond will always be equal. Why? *(LO 10-6)*

14. Which security has a higher *effective* annual interest rate?   *(LO 10-6)*
    a. A three-month T-bill with face value of $100,000 currently selling at $97,645.
    b. A coupon bond selling at par and paying a 10% coupon semiannually.

15. Treasury bonds paying an 8% coupon rate with *semiannual* payments currently sell at par value. What coupon rate would they have to pay in order to sell at par if they paid their coupons *annually?*   *(LO 10-2)*

16. Consider a bond paying a coupon rate of 10% per year semiannually when the market interest rate is only 4% per half-year. The bond has three years until maturity.   *(LO 10-6)*
    a. Find the bond's price today and six months from now after the next coupon is paid.
    b. What is the total rate of return on the bond?

17. A 20-year maturity bond with par value $1,000 makes semiannual coupon payments at a coupon rate of 8%. Find the bond equivalent and effective annual yield to maturity of the bond if the bond price is: *(LO 10-2)*
    a. $950
    b. $1,000
    c. $1,050

18. Redo the previous problem using the same data, but now assume that the bond makes its coupon payments annually. Why are the yields you compute lower in this case?   *(LO 10-2)*

19. Return to Table 10.1 and calculate both the real and nominal rates of return on the TIPS bond in the second and third years.   *(LO 10-6)*

20. Fill in the table below for the following zero-coupon bonds, all of which have par values of $1,000.   *(LO 10-2)*

Price	Maturity (years)	Yield to Maturity
$400	20	?
$500	20	?
$500	10	?
?	10	10%
?	10	8%
$400	?	8%

21. A bond has a par value of $1,000, a time to maturity of 10 years, and a coupon rate of 8% with interest paid annually. If the current market price is $800, what will be the approximate capital gain yield of this bond over the next year if its yield to maturity remains unchanged?   *(LO 10-3)*

22. A bond with a coupon rate of 7% makes semiannual coupon payments on January 15 and July 15 of each year. *The Wall Street Journal* reports the ask price for the bond on January 30 at 100.125. What is the invoice price of the bond? The coupon period has 182 days.   *(LO 10-1)*

23. A bond has a current yield of 9% and a yield to maturity of 10%. Is the bond selling above or below par value? Explain.   *(LO 10-2)*

24. Is the coupon rate of the bond in the previous problem more or less than 9%?   *(LO 10-2)*

25. Consider a bond with a settlement date of February 22, 2015, and a maturity date of March 15, 2023. The coupon rate is 5.5%. If the yield to maturity of the bond is 5.34% (bond equivalent yield, semiannual compounding), what is the list price of the bond on the settlement date? What is the accrued interest on the bond? What is the invoice price of the bond?   *(LO 10-1)*

Templates and spreadsheets are available in Connect

26. Now suppose the bond in the previous question is selling for 102. What is the bond's yield to maturity? What would the yield to maturity be at a price of 102 if the bond paid its coupons only once per year?   *(LO 10-2)*

Templates and spreadsheets are available in Connect

27. A 10-year bond of a firm in severe financial distress has a coupon rate of 14% and sells for $900. The firm is currently renegotiating the debt, and it appears that the lenders will allow the firm to reduce coupon payments on the bond to one-half the originally contracted amount. The firm can handle these lower payments. What are the stated and expected yields to maturity of the bonds? The bond makes its coupon payments annually.   *(LO 10-5)*

28. A two-year bond with par value $1,000 making annual coupon payments of $100 is priced at $1,000. What is the yield to maturity of the bond? What will be the realized compound yield to maturity if the one-year interest rate next year turns out to be (*a*) 8%, (*b*) 10%, (*c*) 12%?   *(LO 10-6)*

29. Suppose that today's date is April 15. A bond with a 10% coupon paid semiannually every January 15 and July 15 is quoted as selling at an ask price of 101.25. If you buy the bond from a dealer today, what price will you pay for it?   *(LO 10-1)*

30. Assume that two firms issue bonds with the following characteristics. Both bonds are issued at par.

	ABC Bonds	**XYZ Bonds**
Issue size	$1.2 billion	$150 million
Maturity	10 years*	20 years
Coupon	9%	10%
Collateral	First mortgage	General debenture
Callable	Not callable	In 10 years
Call price	None	110
Sinking fund	None	Starting in 5 years

*Bond is extendable at the discretion of the bondholder for an additional 10 years.

Ignoring credit quality, identify four features of these issues that might account for the lower coupon on the ABC debt. Explain.   *(LO 10-4)*

31. A large corporation issued both fixed- and floating-rate notes five years ago, with terms given in the following table: *(LO 10-4)*

	9% Coupon Notes	**Floating-Rate Note**
Issue size	$250 million	$280 million
Maturity	20 years	15 years
Current price (% of par)	93	98
Current coupon	9%	5%
Coupon adjusts	Fixed coupon	Every year
Coupon reset rule	—	1-year T-bill rate + 2%
Callable	10 years after issue	10 years after issue
Call price	106	102.50
Sinking fund	None	None
Yield to maturity	9.9%	—
Price range since issued	$85–$112	$97–$102

a. Why is the price range greater for the 9% coupon bond than the floating-rate note?
b. What factors could explain why the floating-rate note is not always sold at par value?
c. Why is the call price for the floating-rate note not of great importance to investors?
d. Is the probability of call for the fixed-rate note high or low?
e. If the firm were to issue a fixed-rate note with a 15-year maturity, callable after five years at 106, what coupon rate would it need to offer to issue the bond at par value?
f. Why is an entry for yield to maturity for the floating-rate note not appropriate?

32. A 30-year maturity, 8% coupon bond paying coupons semiannually is callable in five years at a call price of $1,100. The bond currently sells at a yield to maturity of 7% (3.5% per half-year). *(LO 10-4)*
    a. What is the yield to call?
    b. What is the yield to call if the call price is only $1,050?
    c. What is the yield to call if the call price is $1,100 but the bond can be called in two years instead of five years?

33. A newly issued 20-year maturity, zero-coupon bond is issued with a yield to maturity of 8% and face value $1,000. Find the imputed interest income in the first, second, and last year of the bond's life. *(LO 10-3)*

34. A newly issued 10-year maturity, 4% coupon bond making *annual* coupon payments is sold to the public at a price of $800. What will be an investor's taxable income from the bond over the coming year? The bond will not be sold at the end of the year. The bond is treated as an original-issue discount bond. *(LO 10-3)*

35. Masters Corp. issues two bonds with 20-year maturities. Both bonds are callable at $1,050. The first bond is issued at a deep discount with a coupon rate of 4% and a price of $580 to yield 8.4%. The second bond is issued at par value with a coupon rate of 8.75%. *(LO 10-2)*
    a. What is the yield to maturity of the par bond? Why is it higher than the yield of the discount bond?
    b. If you expect rates to fall substantially in the next two years, which bond would you prefer to hold?
    c. In what sense does the discount bond offer "implicit call protection"?

36. Under the expectations hypothesis, if the yield curve is upward-sloping, the market must expect an increase in short-term interest rates. True/false/uncertain? Why? *(LO 10-7)*

37. The yield curve is upward-sloping. Can you conclude that investors expect short-term interest rates to rise? Why or why not? *(LO 10-7)*

38. Assume you have a one-year investment horizon and are trying to choose among three bonds. All have the same degree of default risk and mature in 10 years. The first is a zero-coupon bond that pays $1,000 at maturity. The second has an 8% coupon rate and pays the $80 coupon once per year. The third has a 10% coupon rate and pays the $100 coupon once per year. *(LO 10-3)*
    a. If all three bonds are now priced to yield 8% to maturity, what are their prices?
    b. If you expect their yields to maturity to be 8% at the beginning of next year, what will their prices be then? What is your rate of return on each bond during the one-year holding period?

39. Under the liquidity preference theory, if inflation is expected to be falling over the next few years, long-term interest rates will be higher than short-term rates. True/false/uncertain? Why? *(LO 10-7)*

40. The current yield curve for default-free zero-coupon bonds is as follows:

Maturity (years)	YTM
1	10%
2	11
3	12

    a. What are the implied one-year forward rates? *(LO 10-7)*
    b. Assume that the pure expectations hypothesis of the term structure is correct. If market expectations are accurate, what will the pure yield curve (that is, the yields to maturity on one- and two-year zero-coupon bonds) be next year? *(LO 10-7)*
    c. If you purchase a two-year zero-coupon bond now, what is the expected total rate of return over the next year? What if you purchase a three-year zero-coupon bond? (*Hint:* Compute the current and expected future prices.) Ignore taxes. *(LO 10-6)*

41. The yield to maturity on one-year zero-coupon bonds is 8%. The yield to maturity on two-year zero-coupon bonds is 9%.   *(LO 10-7)*
    a. What is the forward rate of interest for the second year?
    b. If you believe in the expectations hypothesis, what is your best guess as to the expected value of the short-term interest rate next year?
    c. If you believe in the liquidity preference theory, is your best guess as to next year's short-term interest rate higher or lower than in (*b*)?

42. The following table contains spot rates and forward rates for three years. However, the labels got mixed up. Can you identify which row of the interest rates represents spot rates and which one the forward rates?   *(LO 10-7)*

Year:	1	2	3
Spot rates or forward rates?	10%	12%	14%
Spot rates or forward rates?	10%	14.0364%	18.1078%

Challenge

43. Consider the following $1,000 par value zero-coupon bonds:

Bond	Years until Maturity	Yield to Maturity
A	1	5%
B	2	6
C	3	6.5
D	4	7

According to the expectations hypothesis, what is the market's expectation of the yield curve one year from now? Specifically, what are the expected values of next year's yields on bonds with maturities of (*a*) 1 year; (*b*) 2 years; (*c*) 3 years?   *(LO 10-7)*

44. A newly issued bond pays its coupons once a year. Its coupon rate is 5%, its maturity is 20 years, and its yield to maturity is 8%.   *(LO 10-6)*
    a. Find the holding-period return for a one-year investment period if the bond is selling at a yield to maturity of 7% by the end of the year.
    b. If you sell the bond after one year when its yield is 7%, what taxes will you owe if the tax rate on interest income is 40% and the tax rate on capital gains income is 30%? The bond is subject to original-issue discount (OID) tax treatment.
    c. What is the after-tax holding-period return on the bond?
    d. Find the realized compound yield *before taxes* for a two-year holding period, assuming that (i) you sell the bond after two years, (ii) the bond yield is 7% at the end of the second year, and (iii) the coupon can be reinvested for one year at a 3% interest rate.
    e. Use the tax rates in part (*b*) to compute the *after-tax* two-year realized compound yield. Remember to take account of OID tax rules.

CFA Problems

1. The following multiple-choice problems are based on questions that appeared in past CFA examinations.
    a. A bond with a call feature: *(LO 10-4)*
        (1) Is attractive because the immediate receipt of principal plus premium produces a high return.
        (2) Is more apt to be called when interest rates are high because the interest saving will be greater.
        (3) Will usually have a higher yield to maturity than a similar noncallable bond.
        (4) None of the above.

b. In which *one* of the following cases is the bond selling at a discount?   *(LO 10-2)*
   (1) Coupon rate is greater than current yield, which is greater than yield to maturity.
   (2) Coupon rate, current yield, and yield to maturity are all the same.
   (3) Coupon rate is less than current yield, which is less than yield to maturity.
   (4) Coupon rate is less than current yield, which is greater than yield to maturity.

c. Consider a five-year bond with a 10% coupon selling at a yield to maturity of 8%. If interest rates remain constant, one year from now the price of this bond will be: *(LO 10-3)*
   (1) Higher
   (2) Lower
   (3) The same
   (4) Par

d. Which of the following statements is *true?*   *(LO 10-7)*
   (1) The expectations hypothesis indicates a flat yield curve if anticipated future short-term rates exceed current short-term rates.
   (2) The basic conclusion of the expectations hypothesis is that the long-term rate is equal to the anticipated short-term rate.
   (3) The liquidity hypothesis indicates that, all other things being equal, longer maturities will have higher yields.
   (4) The liquidity preference theory states that a rising yield curve necessarily implies that the market anticipates increases in interest rates.

2. On May 30, 2015, Janice Kerr is considering the newly issued 10-year AAA corporate bonds shown in the following exhibit: *(LO 10-3)*

Description	Coupon	Price	Callable	Call Price
Sentinal, due May 30, 2025	4.00%	100	Noncallable	NA
Colina, due May 30, 2025	4.20%	100	Currently callable	102

a. Suppose that market interest rates decline by 100 basis points (i.e., 1%). Contrast the effect of this decline on the price of each bond.

b. Should Kerr prefer the Colina over the Sentinal bond when rates are expected to rise or to fall?

c. What would be the effect, if any, of an increase in the *volatility* of interest rates on the prices of each bond?

3. A convertible bond has the following features. What is its conversion premium?   *(LO 10-4)*

Coupon	5.25%
Maturity	June 15, 2025
Market price of bond	$77.50
Market price of underlying common stock	$28.00
Annual dividend	$1.20
Conversion ratio	20.83 shares

4. *a.* Explain the impact on the offering yield of adding a call feature to a proposed bond issue.

   b. Explain the impact on the bond's expected life of adding a call feature to a proposed bond issue.

   c. Describe one advantage and one disadvantage of including callable bonds in a portfolio.   *(LO 10-4)*

5. Bonds of Zello Corporation with a par value of $1,000 sell for $960, mature in five years, and have a 7% annual coupon rate paid semiannually. *(LO 10-6)*
   a. Calculate the:
   (1) Current yield.
   (2) Yield to maturity.
   (3) Horizon yield (also called realized compound return) for an investor with a three-year holding period and a reinvestment rate of 6% over the period. At the end of three years the 7% coupon bonds with two years remaining will sell to yield 7%.
   b. Cite *one* major shortcoming for *each* of the following fixed-income yield measures:
   (1) Current yield.
   (2) Yield to maturity.
   (3) Horizon yield (also called realized compound return).

WEB *master*

1. Go to the website of Standard & Poor's at **www.standardandpoors.com.** Look for *Rating Services (Find a Rating)*. Find the ratings on bonds of at least 10 companies. Try to choose a sample with a wide range of ratings. Then go to a website such as **money.msn.com** or **finance.yahoo.com** and obtain, for each firm, as many of the financial ratios tabulated in Table 10.3 as you can find. What is the relationship between bond rating and these ratios? Can you tell from your sample which of these ratios are the more important determinants of bond rating?

2. The FINRA operates the TRACE (Trade Reporting and Compliance Engine) system, which reports over-the-counter secondary market trades of fixed-income securities. Go to the FINRA home page at **www.finra.org** and click on the link for *Industry Professionals*. Search (located at the top right) for the "TRACE Fact Book" and click the first link that appears. Find the detailed data tables and locate the table with information on issues, excluding convertible bonds (typically Table 1). For each of the last three years, calculate the following:
   a. The percentage of bonds that were publicly traded and the percentage that were privately traded.
   b. The percentage of bonds that were investment grade and the percentage that were high-yield.
   c. The percentage of bonds that had fixed coupon rates and the percentage that had floating rates.
   d. Do any patterns emerge over time?
   e. Repeat the calculations using the information for convertible bond issues (typically in Table 2).

SOLUTIONS TO
CONCEPT
checks

10.1 The callable bond will sell at the *lower* price. Investors will not be willing to pay as much if they know that the firm retains a valuable option to reclaim the bond for the call price if interest rates fall.

10.2 At a semiannual interest rate of 3%, the bond is worth $40 × Annuity factor(3%, 60) + $1,000 × PV factor(3%, 60) = $1,276.76, which results in a capital gain of $276.76. This exceeds the capital loss of $189.29 (=$1,000 − $810.71) when the semiannual interest rate increased to 5%.

10.3 Yield to maturity exceeds current yield, which exceeds coupon rate. Take as an example the 8% coupon bond with a yield to maturity of 10% per year (5% per half-year). Its price is $810.71, and therefore its current yield is 80/810.71 = 0.0987, or 9.87%, which is higher than the coupon rate but lower than the yield to maturity.

10.4 The current price of the bond can be derived from the yield to maturity. Using your calculator, set $n = 40$ (semiannual periods); PMT = $45 per period; FV = $1,000; $i = 4\%$ per semiannual period. Calculate present value as $1,098.96. Now we can calculate yield to call. The time to call is five years, or 10 semiannual periods. The price at which the bond will be called is $1,050. To find yield to call, we set $n = 10$ (semiannual periods); PMT = $45 per period; FV = $1,050; PV = $1,098.96. Calculate the semiannual yield to call as 3.72%, or 7.44% bond equivalent yield.

10.5 Price = $70 × Annuity factor(8%, 1) + $1,000 × PV factor(8%, 1) = $990.74

$$\text{Rate of return to investor} = \frac{\$70 + (\$990.74 - \$982.17)}{\$982.17} = .080 = 8\%$$

10.6 By year-end, remaining maturity is 29 years. If the yield to maturity were still 8%, the bond would still sell at par and the holding-period return would be 8%. At a higher yield, price and return will be lower. Suppose the yield to maturity is 8.5%. With annual payments of $80 and a face value of $1,000, the price of the bond is $946.70 ($n = 29$; $i = 8.5\%$; PMT = $80; FV = $1,000). The bond initially sold at $1,000 when issued at the start of the year. The holding-period return is

$$\text{HPR} = \frac{80 + (946.70 - 1,000)}{1,000} = .0267 = 2.67\%$$

which is less than the initial yield to maturity of 8%.

10.7 At the lower yield, the bond price will be $631.67 [$n = 29$, $i = 7\%$, FV = $1,000, PMT = $40]. Therefore, total after-tax income is:

Coupon	$40 × (1 − 0.38) = $24.80
Imputed interest	($553.66 − $549.69) × (1 − 0.38) = 2.46
Capital gains	($631.67 − $553.66) × (1 − 0.20) = 62.41
Total income after taxes:	$89.67

Rate of return = 89.67/549.69 = .163 = 16.3%

10.8 The yield to maturity on two-year bonds is 8.5%. The forward rate for the third year is $f_3 = 8\% + 1\% = 9\%$. We obtain the yield to maturity on three-year zeros from

$$(1 + y_3)^3 = (1 + y_2)^2(1 + f_3) = 1.085^2 \times 1.09 = 1.2832$$

Therefore, $y_3 = .0867 = 8.67\%$. We note that the yield on one-year bonds is 8%, on two-year bonds is 8.5%, and on three-year bonds is 8.67%. The yield curve is upward-sloping due solely to the liquidity premium.

Chapter

11

Managing Bond Portfolios

Learning Objectives

LO 11-1 Analyze the features of a bond that affect the sensitivity of its price to interest rates.

LO 11-2 Compute the duration of bonds, and use duration to measure interest rate sensitivity.

LO 11-3 Show how convexity affects the response of bond prices to changes in interest rates.

LO 11-4 Formulate fixed-income immunization strategies for various investment horizons.

LO 11-5 Analyze the choices to be made in an actively managed bond portfolio.

I n this chapter, we turn to various strategies that bond managers can pursue, making a distinction between passive and active strategies. A *passive investment strategy* takes market prices of securities as set fairly. Rather than attempting to beat the market by exploiting superior information or insight, passive managers act to maintain an appropriate risk-return balance given market opportunities. One special case of passive management is an immunization strategy that attempts to insulate the portfolio from interest rate risk.

An *active investment strategy* attempts to achieve returns that are more than commensurate with the risk borne. In the context of bond portfolios, this style of management can take two forms. Active managers use interest rate forecasts to predict movements in the entire bond market, or they employ some form of intra-market analysis to identify particular sectors of the market (or particular securities) that are relatively mispriced.

Because interest rate risk is crucial to formulating both active and passive strategies, we begin our discussion with an analysis of the sensitivity of bond prices to interest rate fluctuations. This sensitivity is measured by the duration of the bond, and we devote considerable attention to what determines bond duration. We discuss several passive investment strategies, and show how duration-matching techniques can be used to immunize the holding-period return of a portfolio from interest rate risk. After examining the broad range of applications of the duration measure, we consider refinements in the way that interest rate sensitivity is measured, focusing on the concept of bond convexity. Duration is important in formulating active investment strategies as well, and we next explore several of these

11.1 INTEREST RATE RISK

You know already that there is an inverse relationship between bond prices and yields and that interest rates can fluctuate substantially. As interest rates rise and fall, bondholders experience capital losses and gains. These gains or losses make fixed-income investments risky, even if the coupon and principal payments are guaranteed, as in the case of Treasury obligations.

Why do bond prices respond to interest rate fluctuations? In a competitive market, all securities must offer investors fair expected rates of return. If a bond is issued with an 8% coupon when competitive yields are 8%, then it will sell at par value. If the market rate rises to 9%, however, who would purchase an 8% coupon bond at par value? The bond price must fall until its expected return increases to the competitive level of 9%. Conversely, if the market rate falls to 7%, the 8% coupon on the bond is attractive compared to yields on alternative investments. Investors eager for that return will respond by bidding up the bond price until the total rate of return for investors who purchase at that higher price is no better than the market rate.

Interest Rate Sensitivity

The sensitivity of bond prices to changes in market interest rates is obviously of great concern to investors. To gain some insight into the determinants of interest rate risk, turn to Figure 11.1, which presents the percentage changes in price corresponding to changes in yield to maturity for four bonds that differ according to coupon rate, initial yield to maturity, and time to maturity. All four bonds illustrate that bond prices decrease when yields rise and that the price curve is convex, meaning that decreases in yields have bigger impacts on price than increases in yields of equal magnitude. We summarize these observations in the following two propositions:

1. *Bond prices and yields are inversely related: As yields increase, bond prices fall; as yields fall, bond prices rise.*
2. *An increase in a bond's yield to maturity results in a smaller price change than a decrease in yield of equal magnitude.*

Now compare the interest rate sensitivity of bonds A and B, which are identical except for maturity. Figure 11.1 shows that bond B, which has a longer maturity than bond A, exhibits greater sensitivity to interest rate changes. This illustrates another general property:

3. *Prices of long-term bonds tend to be more sensitive to interest rate changes than prices of short-term bonds.*

This is not surprising. If rates increase, for example, the bond is less valuable as its cash flows are discounted at a now-higher rate. The impact of the higher discount rate will be greater as that rate is applied to more-distant cash flows.

Notice that while bond B has six times the maturity of bond A, it has less than six times the interest rate sensitivity. Although interest rate sensitivity seems to increase with maturity, it does so less than proportionally as bond maturity increases. Therefore, our fourth property is that:

4. *The sensitivity of bond prices to changes in yields increases at a decreasing rate as maturity increases. In other words, interest rate risk is less than proportional to bond maturity.*

335

FIGURE   11.1   Change in bond price as a function of change in yield to maturity

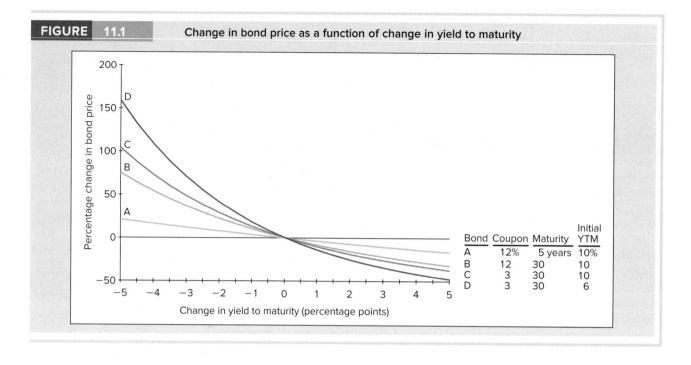

Bonds B and C, which are alike in all respects except for coupon rate, illustrate another point. The lower-coupon bond exhibits greater sensitivity to changes in interest rates. This turns out to be a general property of bond prices:

5. *Interest rate risk is inversely related to the bond's coupon rate. Prices of low-coupon bonds are more sensitive to changes in interest rates than prices of high-coupon bonds.*

Finally, bonds C and D are identical except for the yield to maturity at which the bonds currently sell. Yet bond C, with a higher yield to maturity, is less sensitive to changes in yields. This illustrates our final property:

6. *The sensitivity of a bond's price to a change in its yield is inversely related to the yield to maturity at which the bond currently is selling.*

The first five of these general properties were described by Malkiel (1962) and are sometimes known as Malkiel's bond pricing relationships. The last property was demonstrated by Homer and Leibowitz (1972).

These six propositions confirm that maturity is a major determinant of interest rate risk. However, they also show that maturity alone is not sufficient to measure interest rate sensitivity. For example, bonds B and C in Figure 11.1 have the same maturity, but the higher coupon bond has less price sensitivity to interest rate changes. Obviously, we need to know more than a bond's maturity to quantify its interest rate risk.

To see why bond characteristics such as coupon rate or yield to maturity affect interest rate sensitivity, let's start with a simple numerical example.

Table 11.1 gives bond prices for 8% annual coupon bonds at different yields to maturity and times to maturity. (For simplicity, we assume coupons are paid once a year rather than semiannually.) The shortest term bond falls in value by less than 1% when the interest rate increases from 8% to 9%. The 10-year bond falls by 6.4% and the 20-year bond by more than 9%.

Now look at a similar computation using a zero-coupon bond rather than the 8% coupon bond. The results are shown in Table 11.2.

For maturities beyond one year, the price of the zero-coupon bond falls by a greater proportional amount than the price of the 8% coupon bond. The observation that long-term bonds are

TABLE 11.1 Prices of 8% annual coupon bonds			
Bond's Yield to Maturity	**_T_ = 1 Year**	**_T_ = 10 Years**	**_T_ = 20 Years**
8%	1,000.00	1,000.00	1,000.00
9%	990.83	935.82	908.71
Percent change in price*	−0.92%	−6.42%	−9.13%

*Equals value of bond at a 9% yield to maturity minus value of bond at (the original) 8% yield, divided by the value at 8% yield.

TABLE 11.2 Prices of zero-coupon bonds			
Bond's Yield to Maturity	**_T_ = 1 Year**	**_T_ = 10 Years**	**_T_ = 20 Years**
8%	925.93	463.19	214.55
9%	917.43	422.41	178.43
Percent change in price*	−0.92%	−8.80%	−16.84%

*Equals value of bond at a 9% yield to maturity minus value of bond at (the original) 8% yield, divided by the value at 8% yield.

more sensitive to interest rate movements than short-term bonds suggests that in some sense a zero-coupon bond must represent a longer-term investment than an equal-time-to-maturity coupon bond.

In fact, this insight about the effective maturity of a bond is a useful one that we can make mathematically precise. To start, note that the times to maturity of the two bonds in this example are not perfect measures of the long- or short-term nature of the bonds. The 8% bond makes many coupon payments, most of which come years before the bond's maturity date. Each payment may be considered to have its own "maturity." In this sense, it is often useful to view a coupon bond as a "portfolio" of coupon payments. The *effective* maturity of the bond would then be measured as some sort of average of the maturities of *all* the cash flows. The zero-coupon bond, by contrast, makes only one payment at maturity. Its time to maturity is well defined.

A high-coupon rate bond has a higher fraction of its value tied to coupons rather than payment of par value, and so the portfolio is more heavily weighted toward the earlier, short-maturity payments, which give it lower "effective maturity." This explains Malkiel's fifth rule, that price sensitivity falls with coupon rate.

Similar logic explains our sixth rule, that price sensitivity falls with yield to maturity. A higher yield reduces the present value of all of the bond's payments, but more so for more distant payments. Therefore, at a higher yield, a higher proportion of the bond's value is due to its earlier payments, which have lower effective maturity. The overall sensitivity of the bond price to changes in yields is thus lower.

Duration

To deal with the concept of the "maturity" of a bond that makes many payments, we need a measure of the average maturity of the bond's promised cash flows. We would also like to use such an effective maturity measure as a guide to the sensitivity of a bond to interest rate changes because price sensitivity tends to increase with time to maturity.

Frederick Macaulay (1938) called the effective maturity concept the *duration* of the bond. **Macaulay's duration** equals the weighted average of the times to each coupon or principal payment made by the bond. The weight applied to each time to payment clearly should be related to the "importance" of that payment to the value of the bond. In fact, the weight for each payment time is the proportion of the total value of the bond accounted for by that payment, the present value of the payment divided by the bond price.

Macaulay's duration

A measure of the effective maturity of a bond, defined as the weighted average of the times until each payment, with weights proportional to the present value of the payment.

We define the weight, w_t, associated with the cash flow made at time t (denoted CF_t) as

$$w_t = \frac{CF_t/(1 + y)^t}{\text{Bond price}}$$

where y is the bond's yield to maturity. The numerator on the right-hand side of this equation is the present value of the cash flow occurring at time t, while the denominator is the present value of all the bond's payments. These weights sum to 1 because the sum of the cash flows discounted at the yield to maturity equals the bond price.

Using these values to calculate the weighted average of the times until the receipt of each of the bond's payments, we obtain Macaulay's formula for duration, denoted D.

$$D = \sum_{t=1}^{T} t \times w_t \qquad (11.1)$$

If we write out each term in the summation sign, we can express duration as:

$$D = w_1 \quad + \quad 2w_2 \quad + \quad 3w_3 \quad + \quad 4w_4 \quad + \cdots + Tw_T$$

time until weight of time until weight of
2nd cash flow 2nd CF 4th CF 4th CF

An example of how to apply Equation 11.1 appears in Spreadsheet 11.1, where we derive the durations of an 8% coupon and zero-coupon bond, each with three years to maturity. We assume that the yield to maturity on each bond is 10%. The present value of each payment is discounted at 10% for the number of years shown in column B. The weight associated with each payment time (column E) equals the present value of the payment (column D) divided by the bond price (the sum of the present values in column D).

The numbers in column F are the products of time to payment and payment weight. Each of these products corresponds to one of the terms in Equation 11.1. According to that equation, we can calculate the duration of each bond by adding the numbers in column F.

The duration of the zero-coupon bond is exactly equal to its time to maturity, three years. This makes sense for, with only one payment, the average time until payment must be the bond's maturity. The three-year coupon bond, in contrast, has a shorter duration of 2.7774 years.

While the top panel of the spreadsheet in Spreadsheet 11.1 presents numbers for our particular example, the bottom panel presents the formulas we actually entered in each cell. The inputs in the spreadsheet—specifying the cash flows the bond will pay—are given in columns B and C. In column D we calculate the present value of each cash flow using a discount rate of 10%, in column E we calculate the weights for Equation 11.1, and in column F we compute the product of time until payment and payment weight. Each of these terms corresponds to one of the terms in Equation 11.1. The sum of these terms, reported in cells F9 and F14, is therefore the duration of each bond. Using the spreadsheet, you can easily answer several "what if" questions such as the one in Concept Check 11.1.

CONCEPT check 11.1

Suppose the interest rate decreases to 9%. What will happen to the price and duration of each bond in Spreadsheet 11.1?

Duration is a key concept in bond portfolio management for at least three reasons. First, it is a simple summary measure of the effective average maturity of the portfolio. Second, it turns out to be an essential tool in immunizing portfolios from interest rate risk. We will explore this application in the next section. Third, duration is a measure of the interest rate sensitivity of a bond portfolio, which we explore here.

SPREADSHEET 11.1

Calculation of the duration of two bonds using Excel spreadsheet

	A	B	C	D	E	F
1	Interest rate:	10%				
2						
3		Time until		Payment		Column (B)
4		Payment		Discounted		×
5		(Years)	Payment	at 10%	Weight*	Column (E)
6	A. 8% coupon bond	1	80	72.727	0.0765	0.0765
7		2	80	66.116	0.0696	0.1392
8		3	1080	811.420	0.8539	2.5617
9	Sum:			950.263	1.0000	2.7774
10						
11	B. Zero-coupon bond	1	0	0.000	0.0000	0.0000
12		2	0	0.000	0.0000	0.0000
13		3	1000	751.315	1.0000	3.0000
14	Sum:			751.315	1.0000	3.0000
15						
16	*Weight = Present value of each payment (column D) divided by bond price					

	A	B	C	D	E	F
1	Interest rate:	0.1				
2						
3		Time until		Payment		Column (B)
4		Payment		Discounted		×
5		(Years)	Payment	at 10%	Weight	Column (E)
6	A. 8% coupon bond	1	80	=C6/(1+$B$1)^B6	=D6/D$9	=E6*B6
7		2	80	=C7/(1+$B$1)^B7	=D7/D$9	=E7*B7
8		3	1080	=C8/(1+$B$1)^B8	=D8/D$9	=E8*B8
9	Sum:			=SUM(D6:D8)	=D9/D$9	=SUM(F6:F8)
10						
11	B. Zero-coupon	1	0	=C11/(1+$B$1)^B11	=D11/D$14	=E11*B11
12		2	0	=C12/(1+$B$1)^B12	=D12/D$14	=E12*B12
13		3	1000	=C13/(1+$B$1)^B13	=D13/D$14	=E13*B13
14	Sum:			=SUM(D11:D13)	=D14/D$14	=SUM(F11:F13)

Spreadsheets are available in Connect

We have already seen that price sensitivity to interest rate movements generally increases with maturity. Duration enables us to quantify this relationship. It turns out that when interest rates change, the percentage change in a bond's price is proportional to its duration. Specifically, the proportional change in a bond's price can be related to the change in its yield to maturity, y, according to the rule

$$\frac{\Delta P}{P} = -D \times \left[\frac{\Delta(1+y)}{1+y}\right] \tag{11.2}$$

The proportional price change equals the proportional change in (1 plus the bond's yield) times the bond's duration. Therefore, bond price volatility is proportional to the bond's duration, and duration becomes a natural measure of interest rate exposure.[1] This relationship is key to interest rate risk management.

Practitioners commonly use Equation 11.2 in a slightly different form. They define **modified duration** as $D^* = D/(1+y)$ and rewrite Equation 11.2 as

$$\frac{\Delta P}{P} = -D^*\Delta y \tag{11.3}$$

modified duration

Macaulay's duration divided by 1 + yield to maturity. Measures interest rate sensitivity of bond.

The percentage change in bond price is just the product of modified duration and the change in the bond's yield to maturity. Because the percentage change in the bond price is proportional to modified duration, modified duration is a natural measure of the bond's exposure to interest rate volatility.

[1]Actually, as we will see later, Equation 11.3 is only approximately valid for large changes in the bond's yield. The approximation becomes exact as one considers smaller, or localized, changes in yields.

A bond with maturity of 30 years has a coupon rate of 8% (paid annually) and a yield to maturity of 9%. Its price is $897.26, and its duration is 11.37 years. What will happen to the bond price if the bond's yield to maturity increases to 9.1%?

Equation 11.3 tells us that an increase of .1% in the bond's yield to maturity ($\Delta y = .001$ in decimal terms) will result in a price change of

$$\Delta P = -(D^* \Delta y) \times P$$

$$= -\frac{11.37}{1.09} \times .001 \times \$897.26 = -\$9.36$$

To confirm the relationship between duration and the sensitivity of bond price to interest rate changes, let's compare the price sensitivity of the three-year coupon bond in Spreadsheet 11.1, which has a duration of 2.7774 years, to the sensitivity of a zero-coupon bond with maturity and duration of 2.7774 years. Both should have equal interest rate exposure if duration is a useful measure of price sensitivity.

The three-year bond sells for $950.263 at the initial interest rate of 10%. If the bond's yield increases by 1 basis point (1/100 of a percent) to 10.01%, its price will fall to $950.0231, a percentage decline of .0252%. The zero-coupon bond has a maturity of 2.7774 years. At the initial interest rate of 10%, it sells at a price of $1,000/1.10$^{2.7774}$ = $767.425. When the interest rate increases, its price falls to $1,000/1.1001$^{2.7774}$ = $767.2313, for an identical .0252% capital loss. We conclude that equal-duration assets are equally sensitive to interest rate movements.

Incidentally, this example confirms the validity of Equation 11.2. The equation predicts that the proportional price change of the two bonds should have been $-2.7774 \times .0001/1.10 = .000252$, or .0252%, just as we found from direct computation.

a. In Concept Check 11.1, you calculated the price and duration of a three-year maturity, 8% coupon bond for an interest rate of 9%. Now suppose the interest rate increases to 9.05%. What is the new value of the bond, and what is the percentage change in the bond's price?

b. Calculate the percentage change in the bond's price predicted by the duration formula in Equation 11.2 or 11.3. Compare this value to your answer for (a).

The equations for the durations of coupon bonds are tedious, and spreadsheets like Spreadsheet 11.1 are cumbersome to modify for different maturities and coupon rates. Fortunately, spreadsheet programs such as Excel come with built-in functions for duration. Moreover, these functions easily accommodate bonds that are between coupon payment dates. Spreadsheet 11.2 illustrates how to use Excel to compute duration. The spreadsheets use many of the same conventions as the bond pricing spreadsheets described in Chapter 10.

We can use the spreadsheet to reconfirm the duration of the 8% coupon bond examined in Panel A of Spreadsheet 11.1. The settlement date (i.e., today's date) and maturity date are entered in cells B2 and B3 of Spreadsheet 11.2 using Excel's date function, DATE(year, month, day). For this three-year maturity bond, we don't have a specific settlement date. We arbitrarily set the settlement date to January 1, 2000, and use a maturity date precisely three years later. The coupon rate and yield to maturity are entered as decimals in cells B4 and B5, and the payment periods per year are entered in cell B6. Macaulay and modified duration appear in cells B9 and B10. Cell B9 shows that the duration of the bond is indeed 2.7774 years. The modified duration of the bond is 2.5249, which equals 2.7774/1.10.

Consider a 9% coupon, 8-year maturity bond with annual payments, selling at a yield to maturity of 10%. Use Spreadsheet 11.2 to confirm that the bond's duration is 5.97 years. What would its duration be if the bond paid its coupon semiannually? Why intuitively does duration fall?

SPREADSHEET 11.2

Using Excel functions to compute duration

	A	B	C
1	Inputs		Formula In column B
2	Settlement date	1/1/2000	=DATE(2000,1,1)
3	Maturity date	1/1/2003	=DATE(2003,1,1)
4	Coupon rate	0.08	0.08
5	Yield to maturity	0.10	0.10
6	Coupons per year	1	1
7			
8	Outputs		
9	Macaulay duration	2.7774	=DURATION(B2,B3,B4,B5,B6)
10	Modified duration	2.5249	=MDURATION(B2,B3,B4,B5,B6)

Spreadsheets are
available in Connect

What Determines Duration?

Malkiel's bond price relations, which we laid out in the previous section, characterize the determinants of interest rate sensitivity. Duration allows us to quantify that sensitivity. For example, if we wish to speculate on interest rates, duration tells us how strong a bet we are making. Conversely, if we wish to remain "neutral" on rates, and simply match the interest rate sensitivity of a chosen bond market index, duration allows us to measure that sensitivity and mimic it in our own portfolio. For these reasons, it is crucial to understand the determinants of duration and convenient to have formulas to calculate the duration of some commonly encountered securities. Therefore, in this section, we present several "rules" that summarize most of its important properties. These rules are also illustrated in Figure 11.2, which contains plots of durations of bonds of various coupon rates, yields to maturity, and times to maturity.

We have already established:

Rule 1: The duration of a zero-coupon bond equals its time to maturity.

We also have seen that the three-year coupon bond has a lower duration than the three-year zero because coupons early in the bond's life reduce the bond's weighted-average time until payments. This illustrates another general property:

Rule 2: With time to maturity and yield to maturity held constant, a bond's duration and interest rate sensitivity are higher when the coupon rate is lower.

This property corresponds to Malkiel's fifth bond pricing relationship and is attributable to the impact of early coupons on the average maturity of a bond's payments. The lower these coupons, the less weight these early payments have on the weighted-average maturity of all the bond's payments. In other words, a lower fraction of the total value of the bond is tied up in the (earlier) coupon payments whose values are relatively insensitive to yields rather than the (later and more yield-sensitive) repayment of par value. Compare the plots in Figure 11.2 of the durations of the 3% coupon and 15% coupon bonds, each with identical yields of 15%. The plot of the duration of the 15% coupon bond lies below the corresponding plot for the 3% coupon bond.

Rule 3: With the coupon rate held constant, a bond's duration and interest rate sensitivity generally increase with time to maturity. Duration always increases with maturity for bonds selling at par or at a premium to par.

This property of duration corresponds to Malkiel's third relationship and is fairly intuitive. What is surprising is that duration need not always increase with time to maturity. For some deep discount bonds, such as the 3% coupon bond selling to yield 15% in Figure 11.2, duration may eventually fall with increases in maturity. For virtually all traded bonds, however, it is safe to assume that duration increases with maturity.

Notice in Figure 11.2 that for the zero-coupon bond, maturity and duration are equal. For all the coupon bonds, however, duration increases by less than a year for each year's increase

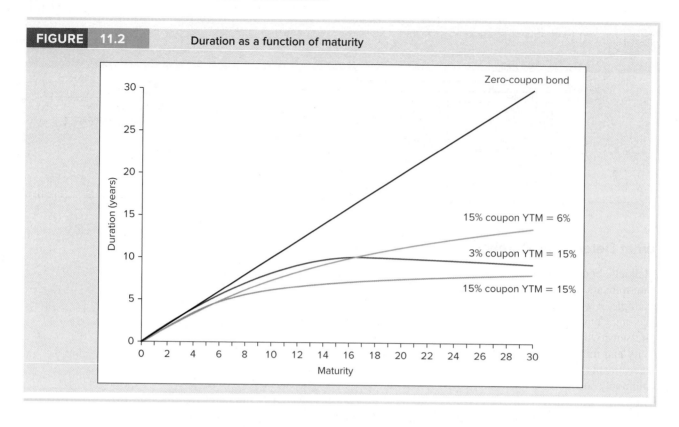

FIGURE   **11.2**   Duration as a function of maturity

in maturity. The slope of the duration graph is less than 1, and duration is always less than maturity for positive-coupon bonds.

While long-maturity bonds generally will be high-duration bonds, duration is a better measure of the long-term nature of the bond because it also accounts for coupon payments. Maturity is an adequate measure only when the bond pays no coupons; then maturity and duration are equal.

Notice also in Figure 11.2 that the two 15% coupon bonds have different durations when they sell at different yields to maturity. The lower-yield bond has longer duration. This makes sense, because at lower yields the more distant payments have relatively greater present values and thereby account for a greater share of the bond's total value. Thus, in the weighted-average calculation of duration, the distant payments receive greater weights, which results in a higher duration measure. This establishes

Rule 4: With other factors held constant, the duration and interest rate sensitivity of a coupon bond are higher when the bond's yield to maturity is lower.

As we noted above, the intuition for this rule is that while a higher yield reduces the present value of all of the bond's payments, it reduces the value of more distant payments by a greater proportional amount. Therefore, at higher yields a higher fraction of the total value of the bond lies in its earlier payments, thereby reducing effective maturity. Rule 4, which is the sixth bond pricing relationship noted above, applies to coupon bonds. For zeros, duration equals time to maturity, regardless of the yield to maturity.

Finally, we present an algebraic rule for the duration of a perpetuity. This rule is derived from and is consistent with the formula for duration given in Equation 11.1, but it is far easier to use for infinitely lived bonds.

Rule 5: The duration of a level perpetuity is

$$\text{Duration of perpetuity} = \frac{1 + y}{y} \tag{11.4}$$

TABLE 11.3 Duration of annual coupon bonds (initial yield to maturity = 6%)

| Maturity (years) | Coupon Rate | | | |
	2%	4%	6%	8%
1	1.000	1.000	1.000	1.000
5	4.786	4.611	4.465	4.342
10	8.961	8.281	7.802	7.445
20	15.170	13.216	12.158	11.495
Infinite (perpetuity)	17.667	17.667	17.667	17.667

For example, at a 15% yield, the duration of a perpetuity that pays $100 once a year forever is 1.15/.15 = 7.67 years, while at a 6% yield it is 1.06/.06 = 17.67 years.

Equation 11.4 makes it obvious that maturity and duration can differ substantially. The maturity of the perpetuity is infinite, while the duration of the instrument at a 15% yield is only 7.67 years. The present value-weighted cash flows early on in the life of the perpetuity dominate the computation of duration. Notice from Figure 11.2 that as their maturities become ever longer, the durations of the two coupon bonds with yields of 15% both converge to the duration of the perpetuity with the same yield, 7.67 years.

Durations can vary widely among traded bonds. Table 11.3 presents durations for several bonds, all paying annual coupons and yielding 6% per year. Duration decreases as coupon rates increase and increases with time to maturity. According to Table 11.3 and Equation 11.2, if the interest rate were to increase from 6% to 6.1%, the 6% coupon, 20-year bond would fall in value by about 1.15% (= −12.158 × .1%/1.06) while the 8% coupon, five-year bond would fall by only .41% (= −4.342 × .1%/1.06). Notice also from Table 11.3 that duration is independent of coupon rate only for perpetuities.

Show that the duration of a perpetuity increases as the interest rate decreases, in accordance with Rule 4.	CONCEPT check **11.4**

11.2 PASSIVE BOND MANAGEMENT

Passive managers take bond prices as fairly set and seek to control only the risk of their fixed-income portfolios. Generally, there are two ways of viewing this risk. Some institutions, such as banks, are concerned with protecting the portfolio's current net worth or net market value against interest rate fluctuations. Risk-based capital guidelines for commercial banks and thrift institutions require the setting aside of additional capital as a buffer against potential losses in market value, for example, due to interest rate fluctuations. The amount of capital required is directly related to the losses that may be incurred. Other investors, such as pension funds, may have an investment goal to be reached after a given number of years. These investors are more concerned with protecting the future values of their portfolios.

What is common to all investors, however, is interest rate risk. The net worth of the firm and its ability to meet future obligations fluctuate with interest rates. **Immunization** and dedication techniques refer to strategies that investors use to shield their net worth from interest rate risk.

immunization

A strategy to shield net worth from interest rate movements.

Immunization

Many banks and thrift institutions have a natural mismatch between the maturities of assets and liabilities. For example, bank liabilities are primarily the deposits owed to customers; these liabilities are short term in nature and consequently of low duration. Assets largely comprise commercial and consumer loans or mortgages. These assets are of longer duration,

On the MARKET FRONT

PENSION FUNDS LOSE GROUND DESPITE BROAD MARKET GAINS

With the S&P 500 providing a 16% rate of return, 2012 was a good year for the stock market, and this performance helped boost the balance sheets of U.S. pension funds. Yet despite the increase in the value of their assets, the total estimated pension deficit of 400 large U.S. companies *rose* by nearly $80 billion, and many of these firms entered 2013 needing to shore up their pension funds with billions of dollars of additional cash. Ford Motor Company alone predicted that it would contribute $5 billion to its fund.*

How did this happen? Blame the decline in interest rates during the year that were in large part the force behind the stock market gains. As rates fell, the present value of pension obligations to retirees rose even faster than the value of the assets backing those promises. It turns out that the value of pension liabilities is more sensitive to interest rate changes than is the value of the typical assets held in those funds. So even though falling rates tend to pump up asset returns, they pump up liabilities even more so. In other words, the duration of fund investments tends to be shorter than the duration of its obligations. This duration mismatch makes funds vulnerable to interest rate declines.

Why don't funds better match asset and liability durations? One reason is that fund managers are often evaluated based on their performance relative to standard bond market indexes. Those indexes tend to have far shorter durations than pension fund liabilities. So to some extent, managers may be keeping their eyes on the wrong ball, one with the wrong interest rate sensitivity.

*These estimates appear in Mike Ramsey and Vipal Monga, "Low Rates Force Companies to Pour Cash into Pensions," *The Wall Street Journal,* February 3, 2013.

and their values are correspondingly more sensitive than deposits to interest rate fluctuations. When interest rates increase unexpectedly, banks can suffer serious decreases in net worth—their assets fall in value by more than their liabilities.

Similarly, a pension fund may have a mismatch between the interest rate sensitivity of the assets held in the fund and the present value of its liabilities—the promise to make payments to retirees. The nearby box illustrates the dangers that pension funds face when they neglect the interest rate exposure of *both* assets and liabilities. It points out that when interest rates change, the present value of the fund's liabilities change. For example, in some recent years pension funds lost ground despite the fact that they enjoyed excellent investment returns. As interest rates fell, the value of their liabilities grew even faster than the value of their assets. The conclusion: Funds should match the interest rate exposure of assets and liabilities so that the value of assets will track the value of liabilities whether rates rise or fall. In other words, the financial manager might want to *immunize* the fund against interest rate volatility.

Pension funds are not alone in this concern. Any institution with a future fixed obligation might consider immunization a reasonable risk management policy. Insurance companies, for example, also pursue immunization strategies. In fact, the notion of immunization was introduced by F. M. Redington (1952), an actuary for a life insurance company. The idea is that duration-matched assets and liabilities let the asset portfolio meet the firm's obligations despite interest rate movements.

Consider, for example, an insurance company that issues a guaranteed investment contract, or GIC, for $10,000. (GICs are essentially zero-coupon bonds issued by the insurance company to its customers. They are popular products for individuals' retirement-savings accounts.) If the GIC has a five-year maturity and a guaranteed interest rate of 8%, the insurance company promises to pay $10,000 \times (1.08)^5 = \$14,693.28$ in five years.

Suppose that the insurance company chooses to fund its obligation with $10,000 of 8% *annual* coupon bonds, selling at par value, with six years to maturity. As long as the market interest rate stays at 8%, the company has fully funded the obligation, as the present value of the obligation exactly equals the value of the bonds.

Table 11.4, Panel A, shows that if interest rates remain at 8%, the accumulated funds from the bond will grow to exactly the $14,693.28 obligation. Over the five-year period, the year-end coupon income of $800 is reinvested at the prevailing 8% market interest rate. At the end of the period, the bonds can be sold for $10,000; they still will sell at par value because the coupon rate still equals the market interest rate. Total income after five years from reinvested coupons and the sale of the bond is precisely $14,693.28.

TABLE 11.4 Terminal value of a bond portfolio after five years (all proceeds reinvested)

Payment Number	Years Remaining until Obligation	Accumulated Value of Invested Payment	
A. Rates remain at 8%			
1	4	$800 \times (1.08)^4 =$	1,088.39
2	3	$800 \times (1.08)^3 =$	1,007.77
3	2	$800 \times (1.08)^2 =$	933.12
4	1	$800 \times (1.08)^1 =$	864.00
5	0	$800 \times (1.08)^0 =$	800.00
Sale of bond	0	$10,800/1.08 =$	10,000.00
			14,693.28
B. Rates fall to 7%			
1	4	$800 \times (1.07)^4 =$	1,048.64
2	3	$800 \times (1.07)^3 =$	980.03
3	2	$800 \times (1.07)^2 =$	915.92
4	1	$800 \times (1.07)^1 =$	856.00
5	0	$800 \times (1.07)^0 =$	800.00
Sale of bond	0	$10,800/1.07 =$	10,093.46
			14,694.05
C. Rates increase to 9%			
1	4	$800 \times (1.09)^4 =$	1,129.27
2	3	$800 \times (1.09)^3 =$	1,036.02
3	2	$800 \times (1.09)^2 =$	950.48
4	1	$800 \times (1.09)^1 =$	872.00
5	0	$800 \times (1.09)^0 =$	800.00
Sale of bond	0	$10,800/1.09 =$	9,908.26
			14,696.02

Note: The sale price of the bond portfolio equals the portfolio's final payment ($10,800) divided by $1 + r$, because the time to maturity of the bonds will be one year at the time of sale.

If interest rates change, however, two offsetting influences will affect the ability of the fund to grow to the targeted value of $14,693.28. If interest rates rise, the fund will suffer a capital loss, impairing its ability to satisfy the obligation. The bonds will be worth less in five years than if interest rates had remained at 8%. However, at a higher interest rate, reinvested coupons will grow at a faster rate, offsetting the capital loss. In other words, fixed-income investors face two offsetting types of interest rate risk: *price risk* and *reinvestment rate risk*. Increases in interest rates cause capital losses but at the same time increase the rate at which reinvested income will grow. If the portfolio duration is chosen appropriately, these two effects will cancel out exactly. When the portfolio duration is set equal to the investor's horizon date, the accumulated value of the investment fund at the horizon date will be unaffected by interest rate fluctuations. *For a horizon equal to the portfolio's duration, price risk and reinvestment risk are precisely offsetting.* The obligation is immunized.

In our example, the duration of the six-year maturity bonds used to fund the GIC is five years. You can confirm this using either Spreadsheet 11.1 or 11.2. The duration of the (zero-coupon) GIC is also five years. Because the fully funded plan has equal duration for its assets and liabilities, the insurance company should be immunized against interest rate fluctuations. To confirm this, let's check that the bond can generate enough income to pay off the obligation in five years regardless of interest rate movements.

FIGURE 11.3

Growth of invested funds

Note: The solid curve represents the growth of portfolio value at the original interest rate. If interest rates increase at time t^*, the portfolio value falls but increases thereafter at the faster rate represented by the broken curve. At time D (duration) the curves cross.

In Table 11.4, Panels B and C illustrate two possible interest rate scenarios: Rates either fall to 7% or increase to 9%. In both cases, the annual coupon payments are reinvested at the new interest rate, which is assumed to change before the first coupon payment, and the bond is sold in year 5 to help satisfy the obligation of the GIC.

Panel B shows that if interest rates fall to 7%, the total funds will accumulate to $14,694.05, providing a small surplus of $.77. If rates increase to 9% as in Panel C, the fund accumulates to $14,696.02, providing a small surplus of $2.74.

Several points are worth highlighting. First, duration matching balances the difference between the accumulated value of the coupon payments (reinvestment rate risk) and the sale value of the bond (price risk). That is, when interest rates fall, the coupons grow less than in the base case, but the higher value of the bond offsets this. When interest rates rise, the value of the bond falls, but the coupons more than make up for this loss because they are reinvested at the higher rate. Figure 11.3 illustrates this case. The solid curve traces the accumulated value of the bonds if interest rates remain at 8%. The dashed curve shows that value if interest rates happen to increase. The initial impact is a capital loss, but this loss eventually is offset by the now-faster growth rate of reinvested funds. At the five-year horizon date, equal to the bond's duration, the two effects just cancel, leaving the company able to satisfy its obligation with the accumulated proceeds from the bond.

We can also analyze immunization in terms of present as opposed to future values. Table 11.5, Panel A, shows the initial balance sheet for the insurance company's GIC. Both

TABLE 11.5 Market value balance sheets

A. Interest rate = 8%				
Assets			**Liabilities**	
Bonds	$10,000.00		Obligation	$10,000.00
B. Interest rate = 7%				
Assets			**Liabilities**	
Bonds	$10,476.65		Obligation	$10,476.11
C. Interest rate = 9%				
Assets			**Liabilities**	
Bonds	$ 9,551.41		Obligation	$ 9,549.62

Notes: Value of bonds = 800 × Annuity factor(r, 6) + 10,000 × PV factor(r, 6).

$$\text{Value of obligation} = \frac{14,693.28}{(1 + r)^5} = 14,693.28 \times \text{PV factor}(r, 5).$$

assets and the obligation have market values of $10,000, so the plan is just fully funded. Panels B and C in the table show that whether the interest rate increases or decreases, the value of the bonds funding the GIC and the present value of the company's obligation change by virtually identical amounts. Regardless of the interest rate change, the plan remains fully funded, with the surplus in Panels B and C just about zero. The duration-matching strategy has ensured that both assets and liabilities react equally to interest rate fluctuations.

Figure 11.4 is a graph of the present values of the bond and the single-payment obligation as a function of the interest rate. At the current rate of 8%, the values are equal, and the obligation is fully funded by the bond. Moreover, the two present value curves are tangent at $y = 8\%$. As interest rates change, the change in value of both the asset and the obligation are equal, so the obligation remains fully funded. For greater changes in the interest rate, however, the present value curves diverge. This reflects the fact that the fund actually shows a small surplus at market interest rates other than 8%.

Why is there *any* surplus in the fund? After all, we claimed that a duration-matched asset and liability mix would make the investor indifferent to interest rate shifts. Actually, such a claim is valid for only *small* changes in the interest rate, because as bond yields change, so too does duration. (Recall Rule 4 for duration.) In fact, while the duration of the bond in this example is equal to five years at a yield to maturity of 8%, the duration rises to 5.02 years when the bond yield falls to 7% and drops to 4.97 years at $y = 9\%$. That is, the bond and the obligation were not duration-matched *across* the interest rate shift, so the position was not fully immunized.

This example demonstrates the need for **rebalancing** immunized portfolios. As interest rates and asset durations continually change, managers must adjust the portfolio to realign its duration with the duration of the obligation. Moreover, even if interest rates do not change, asset durations *will* change solely because of the passage of time. Recall from Figure 11.2 that duration generally decreases less rapidly than maturity as time passes, so even if an obligation is immunized at the outset, the durations of the asset and liability will fall at different rates. Without portfolio rebalancing, durations will become unmatched and the goals of immunization will not be realized. Therefore, immunization is a passive strategy only in the sense that it does not involve attempts to identify undervalued securities. Immunization managers still actively update and monitor their positions.

rebalancing

Realigning the proportions of assets in a portfolio as needed.

An insurance company must make a payment of $19,487 in seven years. The market interest rate is 10%, so the present value of the obligation is $10,000. The company's portfolio manager wishes to fund the obligation using three-year zero-coupon bonds and perpetuities paying annual coupons. (We focus on zeros and perpetuities to keep the algebra simple.) How can the manager immunize the obligation?

Immunization requires that the duration of the portfolio of assets equal the duration of the liability. We can proceed in four steps:

Step 1. Calculate the duration of the liability. In this case, the liability duration is simple to compute. It is a single-payment obligation with duration of seven years.

Step 2. Calculate the duration of the asset portfolio. The portfolio duration is the weighted average of duration of each component asset, with weights proportional to the funds placed in each asset. The duration of the zero-coupon bond is simply its maturity, three years. The duration of the perpetuity is $1.10/.10 = 11$ years. Therefore, if the fraction of the portfolio invested in the zero is called w, and the fraction invested in the perpetuity is $(1 - w)$, the portfolio duration will be

$$\text{Asset duration} = w \times 3 \text{ years} + (1 - w) \times 11 \text{ years}$$

Step 3. Find the asset mix that sets the duration of assets equal to the seven-year duration of liabilities. This requires us to solve for w in the following equation

$$w \times 3 \text{ years} + (1 - w) \times 11 \text{ years} = 7 \text{ years}$$

(continued)

EXAMPLE 11.2

Constructing an Immunized Portfolio

FIGURE 11.4

Immunization. The coupon bond fully funds the obligation at an interest rate of 8%. Moreover, the present value curves are tangent at 8%, so the obligation will remain fully funded even if rates change by a small amount.

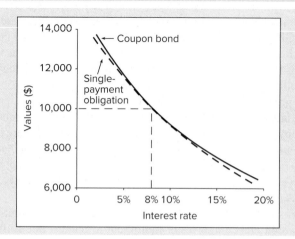

EXAMPLE 11.2

Constructing an Immunized Portfolio (concluded)

This implies that $w = 1/2$. The manager should invest half the portfolio in the zero and half in the perpetuity. This will result in an asset duration of seven years.

Step 4. Fully fund the obligation. Because the obligation has a present value of $10,000, and the fund will be invested equally in the zero and the perpetuity, the manager must purchase $5,000 of the zero-coupon bond and $5,000 of the perpetuity. Note that the face value of the zero will be $5,000 $\times$ 1.10^3 = $6,655.

Even if a position is immunized, however, the portfolio manager still cannot rest. This is because of the need for rebalancing in response to changes in interest rates. Moreover, even if rates do not change, the passage of time also will affect duration and require rebalancing. Let us continue Example 11.2 and see how the portfolio manager can maintain an immunized position.

EXAMPLE 11.3

Rebalancing

Suppose that one year has passed, and the interest rate remains at 10%. The portfolio manager of Example 11.2 needs to reexamine her position. Is the position still fully funded? Is it still immunized? If not, what actions are required?

First, examine funding. The present value of the obligation will have grown to $11,000, as it is one year closer to maturity. The manager's funds also have grown to $11,000: The zero-coupon bonds have increased in value from $5,000 to $5,500 with the passage of time, while the perpetuity has paid its annual $500 coupons and remains worth $5,000. Therefore, the obligation is still fully funded.

The portfolio weights must be changed, however. The zero-coupon bond now will have a duration of two years, while the perpetuity duration remains at 11 years. The obligation is now due in six years. The weights must now satisfy the equation

$$w \times 2 + (1 - w) \times 11 = 6$$

which implies that $w = 5/9$. To rebalance the portfolio and maintain the duration match, the manager now must invest a total of $11,000 $\times$ 5/9 = $6,111.11 in the zero-coupon bond. This requires that the entire $500 coupon payment be invested in the zero, with an additional $111.11 of the perpetuity sold and invested in the zero-coupon bond.

Of course, rebalancing the portfolio entails transaction costs as assets are bought or sold, so continuous rebalancing is not feasible. In practice, managers strike a compromise between the desire for perfect immunization, which requires continual rebalancing, and the need to control trading costs, which dictates less frequent rebalancing.

Immunization

The Excel immunization model allows you to analyze any number of time-period or holding-period immunization examples. The model is built using the Excel-supplied formulas for bond duration, which allow the investigation of any maturity bond without building a table of cash flows. In these calculations, the coupon period is assumed to be annual.

Spreadsheets are
available in Connect

	A	B	C	D	E	F	G	H
1			Holding Period Immunization					
2								
3	YTM	0.0800	Mar Price	1000.00				
4	Coupon rate	0.0800						
5	Maturity	6			Duration	4.993		
6	Par value	1000.00						
7	Holding period	5						
8	Duration	4.9927						
9								
10								
11	If rates increase by 200 basis points				If rates increase by 100 basis points			
12	Rate	0.1000			Rate	0.0900		
13	FV of CPS	488.41			FV of CPS	478.78		
14	Sales price	981.82			Sales price	990.83		
15	Total	1470.23			Total	1469.60		
16	IRR	0.0801			IRR	0.0800		
17								
18								
19								
20	If rates decrease by 200 basis points				If rates decrease by 100 basis points			
21	Rate	0.0600			Rate	0.0700		
22	FV of CPS	450.97			FV of CPS	460.06		
23	Sales price	1018.87			Sales price	1009.35		
24	Total	1469.84			Total	1469.40		
25	IRR	0.0801			IRR	0.0800		

Excel Questions

1. When rates increase by 100 basis points, what is the change in the future sales price of the bond? The value of reinvested coupons?

2. What if rates increase by 200 basis points?

3. What is the relation between price risk and reinvestment rate risk as we consider larger changes in bond yields?

Look again at Example 11.3. What would have been the immunizing weights in the second year if the interest rate had fallen to 8%?

CONCEPT **11.5**
check

Cash Flow Matching and Dedication

The problems associated with immunization seem to have a simple solution. Why not simply buy a zero-coupon bond with face value equal to the projected cash outlay? This is **cash flow matching,** which automatically immunizes a portfolio from interest rate risk because the cash flow from the bond and the obligation exactly offset each other.

Cash flow matching on a multiperiod basis is referred to as a **dedication strategy.** In this case, the manager selects either zero-coupon or coupon bonds with total cash flows that match a series of obligations. The advantage of dedication is that it is a once-and-for-all approach to eliminating interest rate risk. Once the cash flows are matched, there is no need for rebalancing. The dedicated portfolio provides the cash necessary to pay the firm's liabilities regardless of the eventual path of interest rates.

Cash flow matching is not widely pursued, however, probably because of the constraints it imposes on bond selection. Immunization/dedication strategies are appealing to firms that do not wish to bet on general movements in interest rates, yet these firms may want to immunize

cash flow matching

Matching cash flows from a fixed-income portfolio with those of an obligation.

dedication strategy

Refers to multiperiod cash flow matching.

using bonds they believe are undervalued. Cash flow matching places enough constraints on bond selection that it can make it impossible to pursue a dedication strategy using only "underpriced" bonds. Firms looking for underpriced bonds exchange exact and easy dedication for the possibility of achieving superior returns from their bond portfolios.

Sometimes, cash flow matching is not even possible. To cash flow match for a pension fund that is obligated to pay out a perpetual flow of income to current and future retirees, the pension fund would need to purchase fixed-income securities with maturities ranging up to hundreds of years. Such securities do not exist, making exact dedication infeasible. Immunization is easy, however. If the interest rate is 8%, for example, the duration of the pension fund obligation is 1.08/.08 = 13.5 years (see Rule 5 on page 342). Therefore, the fund can immunize its obligation by purchasing zero-coupon bonds with maturity of 13.5 years and a market value equal to that of the pension liabilities.

CONCEPT check	**11.6**	*a.* Suppose that this pension fund is obligated to pay out $800,000 per year in perpetuity. What should be the maturity and face value of the zero-coupon bond it purchases to immunize its obligation? *b.* Now suppose the interest rate immediately increases to 8.1%. How should the fund rebalance to remain immunized against further interest rate shocks? Ignore transaction costs.

CONCEPT check	**11.7**	How would an increase in trading costs affect the attractiveness of dedication versus immunization?

11.3 CONVEXITY

Duration clearly is a key tool in bond portfolio management. Yet, the duration rule for the impact of interest rates on bond prices is only an approximation. Equation 11.3, which we repeat here, states that the percentage change in the value of a bond approximately equals the product of modified duration times the change in the bond's yield:

$$\frac{\Delta P}{P} = -D^* \Delta y$$

This equation asserts that the percentage price change is directly proportional to the change in the bond's yield. If this were *exactly* so, however, a graph of the percentage change in bond price as a function of the change in its yield would plot as a straight line, with slope equal to $-D^*$. Yet we know from Figure 11.1, and more generally from Malkiel's five bond pricing relationships (specifically Relationship 2), that the relationship between bond prices and yields is *not* linear. The duration rule is a good approximation for small changes in bond yield, but it is less accurate for larger changes.

Figure 11.5 illustrates this point. Like Figure 11.1, this figure presents the percentage change in bond price in response to a change in the bond's yield to maturity. The curved line is the percentage price change for a 30-year maturity, 8% coupon bond, selling at an initial yield to maturity of 8%. The straight line is the percentage price change predicted by the duration rule: The modified duration of the bond at its initial yield is 11.26 years, so the straight line is a plot of $-D^* \Delta y = -11.26 \times \Delta y$. Notice that the two plots are tangent at the initial yield. Thus, for small changes in the bond's yield to maturity, the duration rule is quite accurate. However, for larger changes in yield, there is progressively more "daylight" between the two plots, demonstrating that the duration rule becomes progressively less accurate.

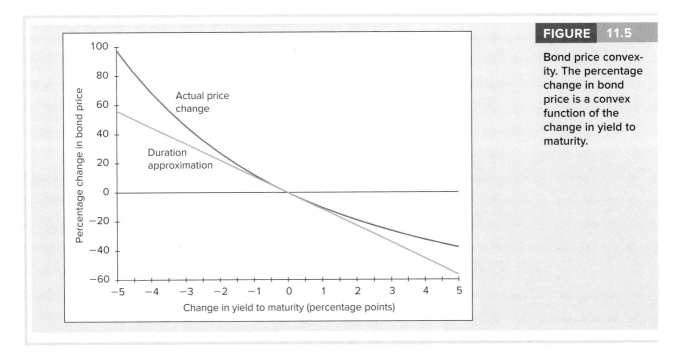

FIGURE 11.5

Bond price convexity. The percentage change in bond price is a convex function of the change in yield to maturity.

Notice from Figure 11.5 that the duration approximation (the straight line) always understates the value of the bond; it underestimates the increase in bond price when the yield falls, and it overestimates the decline in price when the yield rises. This is due to the curvature of the true price-yield relationship. Curves with shapes such as that of the price-yield relationship are said to be convex, and the curvature of the price-yield curve is called the **convexity** of the bond.

We can quantify convexity as the rate of change of the slope of the price-yield curve, expressed as a fraction of the bond price.[2] As a practical rule, you can view bonds with higher convexity as exhibiting higher curvature in the price-yield relationship. The convexity of noncallable bonds, such as that in Figure 11.5, is positive: The slope increases (i.e., becomes less negative) at higher yields.

Convexity allows us to improve the duration approximation for bond price changes. Accounting for convexity, Equation 11.3 can be modified as follows:[3]

$$\frac{\Delta P}{P} = -D^* \Delta y + \tfrac{1}{2} \times \text{Convexity} \times (\Delta y)^2 \qquad \text{(11.5)}$$

convexity

The curvature of the price-yield relationship of a bond.

---

[2]If you have taken a calculus class, you will recognize that Equation 11.3 for modified duration can be written as $dP/P = -D^*dy$. Thus, $-D^* = 1/P \times dP/dy$ is the slope of the price-yield curve expressed as a fraction of the bond price. Similarly, the convexity of a bond equals the second derivative (the rate of change of the slope) of the price-yield curve divided by bond price: Convexity $= 1/P \times d^2P/dy^2$. The formula for the convexity of a bond with a maturity of n years making annual coupon payments is

$$\text{Convexity} = \frac{1}{P \times (1 + y)^2} \sum_{t=1}^{n} \left[\frac{\text{CF}_t}{(1 + y)^t} (t^2 + t) \right]$$

where CF_t is the cash flow paid to the bondholder at date t; CF_t represents either a coupon payment before maturity or final coupon plus par value at the maturity date.

[3]To use the convexity rule, you must express interest rates as decimals rather than percentages.

The first term on the right-hand side is the same as the duration rule, Equation 11.3. The second term is the modification for convexity. Notice that for a bond with positive convexity, the second term is positive, regardless of whether the yield rises or falls. This insight corresponds to the fact noted just above that the duration rule always underestimates the new value of a bond following a change in its yield. The more accurate Equation 11.5, which accounts for convexity, always predicts a higher bond price than Equation 11.3. Of course, if the change in yield is small, the convexity term, which is multiplied by $(\Delta y)^2$ in Equation 11.5, will be extremely small and will add little to the approximation. In this case, the linear approximation given by the duration rule will be sufficiently accurate. Thus, convexity is more important as a practical matter when potential interest rate changes are large.

Convexity is the reason that the immunization examples we considered above resulted in small errors. For example, if you turn back to Table 11.5 and Figure 11.4, you will see that the single-payment obligation that was funded with a coupon bond of the same duration was well immunized for small changes in yields. However, for larger yield changes, the two pricing curves diverged a bit, implying that such changes in yields would result in small surpluses. This is due to the greater convexity of the coupon bond.

EXAMPLE 11.4

Convexity

The bond in Figure 11.5 has a 30-year maturity, an 8% coupon, and sells at an initial yield to maturity of 8%. Because the coupon rate equals yield to maturity, the bond sells at par value, or $1,000. The modified duration of the bond at its initial yield is 11.26 years, and its convexity is 212.4, which can be calculated using the formula in footnote 2. (You can find a spreadsheet to calculate the convexity of a 30-year bond in Connect. See also the nearby Excel Application.) If the bond's yield increases from 8% to 10%, the bond price will fall to $811.46, a decline of 18.85%. The duration rule, Equation 11.3, would predict a price decline of

$$\frac{\Delta P}{P} = -D^*\Delta y = -11.26 \times .02 = -.2252 = -22.52\%$$

which is considerably more than the bond price actually falls. The duration-with-convexity rule, Equation 11.5, is far more accurate:

$$\frac{\Delta P}{P} = -D^*\Delta y + \tfrac{1}{2} \times \text{Convexity} \times (\Delta y)^2$$
$$= -11.26 \times .02 + \tfrac{1}{2} \times 212.4 \times (.02)^2 = -.1827 = -18.27\%$$

which is far closer to the exact change in bond price. (Notice that when we use Equation 11.5, we must express interest rates as decimals rather than percentages. The change in rates from 8% to 10% is represented as $\Delta y = .02$.)

If the change in yield were smaller, say, .1%, convexity would matter less. The price of the bond actually would fall to $988.85, a decline of 1.115%. Without accounting for convexity, we would predict a price decline of

$$\frac{\Delta P}{P} = -D^*\Delta y = -11.26 \times .001 = -.01126 = -1.126\%$$

Accounting for convexity, we get almost the precisely correct answer:

$$\frac{\Delta P}{P} = -11.26 \times .001 + \tfrac{1}{2} \times 212.4 \times (.001)^2 = -.01115 = -1.115\%$$

Nevertheless, the duration rule is quite accurate in this case, even without accounting for convexity.

Why Do Investors Like Convexity?

Convexity is generally considered a desirable trait. Bonds with greater curvature gain more in price when yields fall than they lose when yields rise. For example, in Figure 11.6 bonds A and B have the same duration at the initial yield. The plots of their proportional price changes as a function of interest rate changes are tangent, meaning that their sensitivities to changes in yields at that point are equal. However, bond A is more convex than bond B. It enjoys greater price increases and smaller price decreases when interest rates fluctuate by larger amounts.

Convexity

The Convexity spreadsheet allows you to calculate bond convexity. You can specify yield to maturity and coupon and allow for short maturities by setting later cash flows equal to zero and setting the last cash flow equal to principal plus final coupon payment.

Spreadsheets are available in Connect

	A	B	C	D	E	F	G	H
1								
2								
3								
4			Time (t)	Cash flow	PV(CF)	t + t^2	(t + t^2) × PV(CF)	
5								
6	Coupon	3	1	3	2.871	2	5.742	
7	YTM	0.045	2	3	2.747	6	16.483	
8	Maturity	10	3	3	2.629	12	31.547	
9	Price	$88.13	4	3	2.516	20	50.314	
10			5	3	2.407	30	72.221	
11			6	3	2.304	42	96.755	
12			7	3	2.204	56	123.451	
13			8	3	2.110	72	151.888	
14			9	3	2.019	90	181.684	
15			10	103	66.325	110	7295.701	
16								
17			Sum:		88.13092273		8025.785	
18								
19				Convexity:			83.392425	

Excel Questions

1. Calculate the convexity of a "bullet" fixed-income portfolio, that is, a portfolio with a single cash flow. Suppose a single $1,000 cash flow is paid in year 5.

2. Now calculate the convexity of a "ladder" fixed-income portfolio, that is, a portfolio with equal cash flows over time. Suppose the security makes $100 cash flows in each of years 1–9, so that its duration is close to the bullet in Question 1.

3. Do ladders or bullets have greater convexity?

If interest rates are volatile, this is an attractive asymmetry that increases the expected return on the bond because bond A will benefit more from rate decreases and suffer less from rate increases. Of course, if convexity is desirable, it will not be available for free: Investors will have to pay more and accept lower yields on bonds with greater convexity.

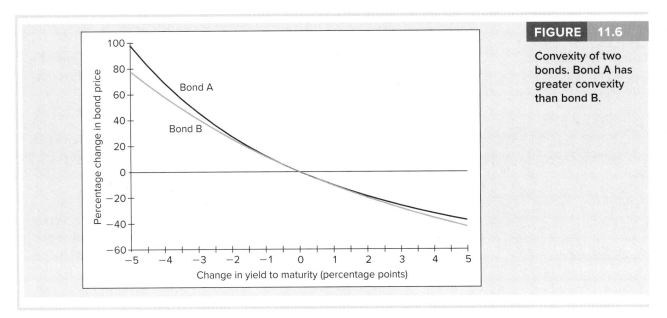

FIGURE 11.6

Convexity of two bonds. Bond A has greater convexity than bond B.

11.4   ACTIVE BOND MANAGEMENT

Sources of Potential Profit

Broadly speaking, there are two sources of potential value in active bond management. The first is interest rate forecasting, that is, anticipating movements across the entire spectrum of the fixed-income market. If interest rate declines are forecast, managers will increase portfolio duration; if increases seem likely, they will shorten duration. The second source of potential profit is identification of relative mispricing within the fixed-income market. An analyst might believe, for example, that the default premium on one bond is unnecessarily large and the bond is underpriced.

These techniques will generate abnormal returns only if the analyst's information or insight is superior to that of the market. You can't profit from knowledge that rates are about to fall if everyone else in the market is on to this. In that case, the anticipated lower future rates will be built into bond prices in the sense that long-duration bonds already sell at higher prices, reflecting the anticipated fall in future short rates. If you do not have information before the market does, you will be too late to act—prices will have already responded to the news. You know this from our discussion of market efficiency.

For now we simply repeat that valuable information is differential information. And it is worth noting that interest rate forecasters have a notoriously poor track record.

Homer and Leibowitz (1972) have developed a popular taxonomy of active bond portfolio strategies. They characterize portfolio rebalancing activities as one of four types of *bond swaps*. In the first two swaps, the investor typically believes the yield relationship between bonds or sectors is only temporarily out of alignment. Until the aberration is eliminated, gains can be realized on the underpriced bond during a period of realignment called the *workout period*.

substitution swap

Exchange of one bond for a bond with similar attributes but more attractively priced.

1. The **substitution swap** is an exchange of one bond for a nearly identical substitute. The substituted bonds should be of essentially equal coupon, maturity, quality, call features, sinking fund provisions, and so on. A substitution swap would be motivated by a belief that the market has temporarily mispriced the two bonds, with a discrepancy representing a profit opportunity.

   An example of a substitution swap would be a sale of a 20-year maturity, 6% coupon Toyota bond that is priced to provide a yield to maturity of 6.05% coupled with a purchase of a 6% coupon Honda bond with the same time to maturity that yields 6.15%. If the bonds have about the same credit risk, there is no apparent reason for the Honda bonds to provide a higher yield. Therefore, the higher yield actually available in the market makes the Honda bond seem relatively attractive. Of course, the equality of credit risk is an important condition. If the Honda bond is in fact riskier, then its higher promised yield does not represent a bargain.

intermarket spread swap

Switching from one segment of the bond market to another.

2. The **intermarket spread swap** is an exchange of two bonds from different sectors of the bond market. It is pursued when an investor believes the yield spread between two sectors of the bond market is temporarily out of line.

   For example, if the yield spread between 10-year Treasury bonds and 10-year Baa-rated corporate bonds is now 3%, and the historical spread has been only 2%, an investor might consider selling holdings of Treasury bonds and replacing them with corporates. If the yield spread eventually narrows, the Baa-rated corporate bonds will outperform the Treasury bonds.

   Of course, the investor must consider carefully whether there is a good reason that the yield spread seems out of alignment. For example, the default premium on corporate bonds might have increased because the market is expecting a severe recession. In this case, the wider spread would not represent attractive pricing of corporates relative to Treasuries but would simply be an adjustment for a perceived increase in credit risk.

rate anticipation swap

A switch made in response to forecasts of interest rate changes.

3. The **rate anticipation swap** is an exchange of bonds with different maturities. It is pegged to interest rate forecasting. Investors who believe rates will fall will swap into bonds of longer duration. For example, the investor might sell a five-year maturity

Treasury bond, replacing it with a 25-year maturity Treasury bond. The new bond has the same lack of credit risk as the old one, but it has longer duration.

4. The **pure yield pickup swap** is an exchange of a shorter-duration bond for a longer-duration bond. This swap is pursued not in response to perceived mispricing but as a means of increasing return by holding higher-yielding, longer-maturity bonds. The investor is willing to bear the interest rate risk this strategy entails.

   A yield pickup swap can be illustrated using the Treasury bond listings in Figure 10.1 in the previous chapter. You can see from that table that longer-term T-bonds offered higher yields to maturity than shorter ones. The investor who swaps the shorter-term bond for the longer one will earn a higher rate of return as long as the yield curve does not shift upward during the holding period. Of course, if it does, the longer-duration bond will suffer a greater capital loss.

   We can add a fifth swap, called a **tax swap,** to this list. This refers to a swap to exploit some tax advantage. For example, an investor may swap from one bond that has decreased in price to another similar bond if realization of capital losses is advantageous for tax purposes.

pure yield pickup swap

Moving to higher yield bonds, usually with longer maturities.

tax swap

Swapping two similar bonds to receive a tax benefit.

Horizon Analysis

One form of interest rate forecasting, which we encountered in the last chapter, is called **horizon analysis.** The analyst selects a particular investment period and predicts bond yields at the end of that period. Given the predicted yield to maturity at the end of the investment period, the bond price can be calculated. The coupon income earned over the period is then added to the predicted capital gain or loss to obtain a forecast of the total return on the bond over the holding period.

horizon analysis

Forecast of bond returns based largely on a prediction of the yield curve at the end of the investment horizon.

A 20-year maturity bond with a 10% coupon rate (paid annually) currently sells at a yield to maturity of 9%. A portfolio manager with a two-year horizon needs to forecast the total return on the bond over the coming two years. In two years, the bond will have an 18-year maturity. The analyst forecasts that two years from now 18-year bonds will sell at yields to maturity of 8% and that coupon payments can be reinvested in short-term securities over the coming two years at a rate of 7%.

To calculate the two-year return on the bond, the analyst would perform the following calculations:

1. Current price = $100 × Annuity factor(9%, 20 years) = $1,000 × PV factor(9%, 20 years)

   = $1,091.29

2. Forecast price = $100 × Annuity factor(8%, 18 years) + $1,000 × PV factor(8%, 18 years)

   = $1,187.44

3. The future value of reinvested coupons will be ($100 × 1.07) + $100 = $207

4. The two-year return is $\dfrac{\$207 + (\$1,187.44 - \$1,091.29)}{\$1,091.29}$ = .278, or 27.8%

The annualized rate of return over the two-year period would then be $1.278^{1/2} - 1 = .13$, or 13%.

EXAMPLE 11.5

Horizon Analysis

What will be the rate of return in Example 11.5 if the manager forecasts that in two years the yield to maturity on 18-year maturity bonds will be 10% and that the reinvestment rate for coupons will be 8%?

CONCEPT check 11.8

An Example of a Fixed-Income Investment Strategy

To demonstrate a reasonable, active fixed-income portfolio strategy, we discuss here the policies of Sanford Bernstein & Co., as explained in a speech by its manager of fixed-income investments, Francis Trainer. The company believes big bets on general marketwide interest movements are unwise. Instead, it concentrates on exploiting numerous instances of perceived *relative* minor pricing misalignments *within* the fixed-income sector. The firm takes as a risk benchmark the Barclays Aggregate Bond Index, which includes the vast majority of publicly traded bonds with maturities greater than one year. Any deviation from this passive or neutral position must be justified by active analysis. Bernstein considers a neutral portfolio duration to be equal to that of the index.

The firm is willing to make only limited bets on interest rate movements. As Francis Trainer puts it in his speech:

> If we set duration of our portfolios at a level equal to the index and never allow them to vary, this would imply that we are perpetually neutral on the direction of interest rates. However, we believe the utilization of these forecasts will add value and, therefore, we incorporate our economic fore-cast into the bond management process by altering the durations of our portfolios.

> However, to prevent fixed-income performance from being dominated by the accuracy of just a single aspect of our research effort, we limit the degree to which we are willing to alter our interest rate exposure. Under the vast majority of circumstances, we will not permit the duration of our portfolios to differ from that of the [Barclays] Index by more than one year.[4]

The company expends most of its effort in exploiting numerous but minor inefficiencies in bond prices that result from lack of attention by its competitors. Its analysts follow about 1,000 securities, attempting to "identify specific securities that are attractive or unattractive as well as identify trends in the richness or cheapness of industries and sectors." These two activities would be characterized as substitution swaps and intermarket spread swaps in the Homer–Leibowitz scheme.

Sanford Bernstein & Co. realizes that market opportunities will arise, if at all, only in sectors of the bond market that present the least competition from other analysts. For this reason, it tends to focus on relatively more complicated bond issues in the belief that extensive research efforts give the firm a comparative advantage in that sector. Finally, the company does not take unnecessary risks. If there do not appear to be enough seemingly attractive bonds, funds are placed in Treasury securities as a "neutral" parking space until new opportunities are identified.

To summarize the key features of this sort of strategy, we make the following observations:

1. A firm such as Bernstein has a respect for market prices. It believes that only minor mispricing usually can be detected. It works toward meaningful abnormal returns by combining numerous *small* profit opportunities, not by hoping for the success of one big bet.

2. To have value, information cannot already be reflected in market prices. A large research staff must focus on market niches that appear to be neglected by others.

3. Interest rate movements are extremely hard to predict, and attempts to time the market can wipe out all the profits of intramarket analysis.

---

[4] Sanford Bernstein & Co. brochure, September 1985.

SUMMARY

- Even default-free bonds such as Treasury issues are subject to interest rate risk. Longer-term bonds generally are more sensitive to interest rate shifts than short-term bonds. A measure of the average life of a bond is Macaulay's duration, defined as the weighted average of the times until each payment made by the security, with weights proportional to the present value of the payment.

- Modified duration is a direct measure of the sensitivity of a bond's price to a change in its yield. The proportional change in a bond's price approximately equals the negative of modified duration times the change in the bond's yield.

- Immunization strategies are characteristic of passive bond portfolio management. Such strategies attempt to render the individual or firm immune from movements in interest rates. This may take the form of immunizing net worth or, instead, immunizing the future accumulated value of a bond portfolio.

- Immunization of a fully funded plan is accomplished by matching the durations of assets and liabilities. To maintain an immunized position as time passes and interest rates change, the portfolio must be periodically rebalanced.

- Convexity refers to the curvature of a bond's price-yield relationship. Accounting for convexity can substantially improve on the accuracy of the duration approximation for the response of bond prices to changes in yields.
- A more direct form of immunization is dedication or cash flow matching. If a portfolio is perfectly matched in cash flow with projected liabilities, rebalancing will be unnecessary.
- Active bond management can be decomposed into interest rate forecasting techniques and intermarket spread analysis. One popular taxonomy classifies active strategies as substitution swaps, intermarket spread swaps, rate anticipation swaps, and pure yield pickup swaps.

KEY TERMS

cash flow matching, 349	intermarket spread swap, 354	rate anticipation swap, 354
convexity, 351		rebalancing, 347
dedication strategy, 349	Macaulay's duration, 337	substitution swap, 354
horizon analysis, 355	modified duration, 339	tax swap, 355
immunization, 343	pure yield pickup swap, 355	

KEY EQUATIONS

Macaulay's duration: $D = \sum_{t=1}^{T} t \times w_t$

Modified duration and bond price risk: $\dfrac{\Delta P}{P} = -D \times \left[\dfrac{\Delta(1+y)}{1+y} \right] = -D^* \times \Delta y$

Duration of perpetuity $= \dfrac{1+y}{y}$

Bond price risk including convexity: $\dfrac{\Delta P}{P} = -D^* \Delta y + \frac{1}{2} \times \text{Convexity} \times (\Delta y)^2$

PROBLEM SETS

 Select problems are available in McGraw-Hill's *Connect*. Please see the Supplements section of the book's frontmatter for more information.

1. How can a perpetuity, which has an infinite maturity, have a duration as short as 10 or 20 years? *(LO 11-1)*

2. You predict that interest rates are about to fall. Which bond will give you the highest capital gain? *(LO 11-1)*
   a. Low coupon, long maturity
   b. High coupon, short maturity
   c. High coupon, long maturity
   d. Zero coupon, long maturity

3. The historical yield spread between AAA bonds and Treasury bonds widened dramatically during the financial crisis. *(LO 11-4)*
   a. If you believed the spread would soon return to more typical historical levels, what should you have done?
   b. This would be an example of what sort of bond swap?

4. A bond currently sells for $1,050, which gives it a yield to maturity of 6%. Suppose that if the yield increases by 25 basis points, the price of the bond falls to $1,025. What is the duration of this bond? *(LO 11-2)*

5. Macaulay's duration is less than modified duration except for: *(LO 11-2)*
   a. Zero-coupon bonds.
   b. Premium bonds.
   c. Bonds selling at par value.
   d. None of the above.

6. Is the decrease in a bond's price corresponding to an increase in its yield to maturity more or less than the price increase resulting from a decrease in yield of equal magnitude? *(LO 11-3)*

7. Short-term interest rates are more volatile than long-term rates. Despite this, the rates of return of long-term bonds are more volatile than returns on short-term securities. How can these two empirical observations be reconciled? *(LO 11-1)*

8. Find the duration of a 6% coupon bond making *annual* coupon payments if it has three years until maturity and a yield to maturity of 6%. What is the duration if the yield to maturity is 10%? *(LO 11-2)*

9. A nine-year bond has a yield of 10% and a duration of 7.194 years. If the bond's yield changes by 50 basis points, what is the percentage change in the bond's price? *(LO 11-2)*

10. A pension plan is obligated to make disbursements of $1 million, $2 million, and $1 million at the end of each of the next three years, respectively. Find the duration of the plan's obligations if the interest rate is 10% annually. *(LO 11-2)*

11. If the plan in the previous problem wants to fully fund and immunize its position, how much of its portfolio should it allocate to one-year zero-coupon bonds and perpetuities, respectively, if these are the only two assets funding the plan? *(LO 11-4)*

12. You own a fixed-income asset with a duration of five years. If the level of interest rates, which is currently 8%, goes down by 10 basis points, how much do you expect the price of the asset to go up (in percentage terms)? *(LO 11-2)*

13. Rank the interest rate sensitivity of the following pairs of bonds. *(LO 11-1)*
    a. Bond A is a 6% coupon, 20-year maturity bond selling at par value.

    Bond B is a 6% coupon, 20-year maturity bond selling below par value.
    b. Bond A is a 20-year, noncallable coupon bond with a coupon rate of 6%, selling at par.

    Bond B is a 20-year, callable bond with a coupon rate of 7%, also selling at par.

14. Long-term Treasury bonds currently are selling at yields to maturity of nearly 6%. You expect interest rates to fall. The rest of the market thinks that they will remain unchanged over the coming year. In each question, choose the bond that will provide the higher capital gain if you are correct. Briefly explain your answer. *(LO 11-2)*
    a. (1) A Baa-rated bond with coupon rate 6% and time to maturity 20 years.
       (2) An Aaa-rated bond with coupon rate 6% and time to maturity 20 years.
    b. (1) An A-rated bond with coupon rate 4% and maturity 20 years, callable at 105.
       (2) An A-rated bond with coupon rate 6% and maturity 20 years, callable at 105.
    c. (1) A 4% coupon noncallable T-bond with maturity 20 years and YTM = 6%.
       (2) A 7% coupon noncallable T-bond with maturity 20 years and YTM = 6%.

15. You will be paying $10,000 a year in tuition expenses at the end of the next two years. Bonds currently yield 8%. *(LO 11-2)*
    a. What is the present value and duration of your obligation?
    b. What maturity zero-coupon bond would immunize your obligation?
    c. Suppose you buy a zero-coupon bond with value and duration equal to your obligation. Now suppose that rates immediately increase to 9%. What happens to your net position, that is, to the difference between the value of the bond and that of your tuition obligation?
    d. What if rates fall to 7%?

16. Pension funds pay lifetime annuities to recipients. If a firm remains in business indefinitely, the pension obligation will resemble a perpetuity. Suppose, therefore, that you are managing a pension fund with obligations to make perpetual payments of $2 million per year to beneficiaries. The yield to maturity on all bonds is 16%. *(LO 11-4)*
    a. If the duration of 5-year maturity bonds with coupon rates of 12% (paid annually) is 4 years and the duration of 20-year maturity bonds with coupon rates of 6% (paid annually) is 8 years, how much of each of these coupon bonds (in market value) will you want to hold to both fully fund and immunize your obligation?
    b. What will be the *par value* of your holdings in the 20-year coupon bond?

17. Frank Meyers, CFA, is a fixed-income portfolio manager for a large pension fund. A member of the Investment Committee, Fred Spice, is very interested in learning about the management of fixed-income portfolios. Spice has approached Meyers with several questions. Specifically, Spice would like to know how fixed-income managers position portfolios to capitalize on their expectations of future interest rates.

    Meyers decides to illustrate fixed-income trading strategies to Spice using a fixed-rate bond and note. Both bonds have semiannual coupon periods. Unless otherwise stated, all interest rate (yield curve) changes are parallel. The characteristics of these securities are shown in the following table. He also considers a nine-year floating-rate bond (floater) that pays a floating rate semiannually and is currently yielding 5%.

Characteristics of Fixed-Rate Bond and Fixed-Rate Note		
	Fixed-Rate Bond	**Fixed-Rate Note**
Price	107.18	100.00
Yield to maturity	5.00%	5.00%
Period to maturity	18	8
Modified duration	6.9848	3.5851

    Spice asks Meyers about how a fixed-income manager would position his portfolio to capitalize on expectations of increasing interest rates. Which of the following would be the most appropriate strategy? *(LO 11-5)*
    a. Shorten his portfolio duration.
    b. Buy fixed-rate bonds.
    c. Lengthen his portfolio duration.

18. Spice asks Meyers (see previous problem) to quantify price changes from changes in interest rates. To illustrate, Meyers computes the value change for the fixed-rate note in the table. Specifically, he assumes an increase in the level of interest rate of 100 basis points. Using the information in the table, what is the predicted change in the price of the fixed-rate note? *(LO 11-2)*

19. You are managing a portfolio of $1 million. Your target duration is 10 years, and you can choose from two bonds: a zero-coupon bond with maturity five years, and a perpetuity, each currently yielding 5%. *(LO 11-4)*
    a. How much of each bond will you hold in your portfolio?
    b. How will these fractions change *next year* if target duration is now nine years?

20. Find the duration of a bond with settlement date May 27, 2016, and maturity date November 15, 2025. The coupon rate of the bond is 7%, and the bond pays coupons semiannually. The bond is selling at a yield to maturity of 8%. You can use Spreadsheet 11.2, available in Connect; link to Chapter 11 material. *(LO 11-2)*

21. What is the duration of the bond in the previous problem if coupons are paid annually? Explain why the duration changes in the direction it does. *(LO 11-2)*

22. You manage a pension fund that will provide retired workers with lifetime annuities. You determine that the payouts of the fund are essentially going to resemble level perpetuities of $1 million per year. The interest rate is 10%. You plan to fully fund the obligation using five-year and 20-year maturity zero-coupon bonds. *(LO 11-2)*
    a. How much *market value* of each of the zeros will be necessary to fund the plan if you desire an immunized position?
    b. What must be the *face value* of the two zeros to fund the plan?

23. Find the convexity of a seven-year maturity, 6% coupon bond selling at a yield to maturity of 8%. The bond pays its coupons annually. (*Hint:* You can use the spreadsheet from this chapter's Excel Application on Convexity, setting cash flows after year 7 equal to zero. The spreadsheet is available in Connect; link to Chapter 11 material.) *(LO 11-3)*

24. *a.* Use a spreadsheet to calculate the durations of the two bonds in Spreadsheet 11.1 if the interest rate increases to 12%. Why does the duration of the coupon bond fall while that of the zero remains unchanged? (*Hint:* Examine what happens to the weights computed in column E.)

  b. Use the same spreadsheet to calculate the duration of the coupon bond if the coupon were 12% instead of 8%. Explain why the duration is lower. (Again, start by looking at column E.) *(LO 11-2)*

25. *a.* Footnote 2 in the chapter presents the formula for the convexity of a bond. Build a spreadsheet to calculate the convexity of the 8% coupon bond in Spreadsheet 11.1 at the initial yield to maturity of 10%.

  b. What is the convexity of the zero-coupon bond? *(LO 11-3)*

26. A 30-year maturity bond making annual coupon payments with a coupon rate of 12% has duration of 11.54 years and convexity of 192.4. The bond currently sells at a yield to maturity of 8%. *(LO 11-3)*

  a. Use a financial calculator or spreadsheet to find the price of the bond if its yield to maturity falls to 7%.

  b. What price would be predicted by the duration rule?

  c. What price would be predicted by the duration-with-convexity rule?

  d. What is the percent error for each rule? What do you conclude about the accuracy of the two rules?

  e. Repeat your analysis if the bond's yield to maturity increases to 9%. Are your conclusions about the accuracy of the two rules consistent with parts (*a*)–(*d*)?

27. Currently, the term structure is as follows: One-year bonds yield 7%, two-year bonds yield 8%, three-year bonds and greater maturity bonds all yield 9%. You are choosing between one-, two-, and three-year maturity bonds all paying *annual* coupons of 8%, once a year. Which bond should you buy if you strongly believe that at year-end the yield curve will be flat at 9%? *(LO 11-5)*

28. A 30-year maturity bond has a 7% coupon rate, paid annually. It sells today for $867.42. A 20-year maturity bond has a 6.5% coupon rate, also paid annually. It sells today for $879.50. A bond market analyst forecasts that in five years, 25-year maturity bonds will sell at yields to maturity of 8% and that 15-year maturity bonds will sell at yields of 7.5%. Because the yield curve is upward-sloping, the analyst believes that coupons will be invested in short-term securities at a rate of 6%.

  a. Calculate the expected rate of return of the 30-year bond over the five-year period.

  b. What is the expected return of the 20-year bond? *(LO 11-5)*

Challenge

29. A 12.75-year maturity zero-coupon bond selling at a yield to maturity of 8% (effective annual yield) has convexity of 150.3 and modified duration of 11.81 years. A 30-year maturity 6% coupon bond making annual coupon payments also selling at a yield to maturity of 8% has nearly identical modified duration—11.79 years—but considerably higher convexity of 231.2. *(LO 11-3)*

  a. Suppose the yield to maturity on both bonds increases to 9%.

   i. What will be the actual percentage capital loss on each bond?

   ii. What percentage capital loss would be predicted by the duration-with-convexity rule?

  b. Repeat part (*a*), but this time assume the yield to maturity decreases to 7%.

  c. Compare the performance of the two bonds in the two scenarios, one involving an increase in rates, the other a decrease. Based on their comparative investment performance, explain the attraction of convexity.

  d. In view of your answer to (*c*), do you think it would be possible for two bonds with equal duration, but different convexity, to be priced initially at the same yield to maturity if the yields on both bonds always increased or decreased by equal amounts, as in this example? *Hint:* Would anyone be willing to buy the bond with lower convexity under these circumstances?

CFA PROBLEMS

1. Rank the following bonds in order of descending duration.   *(LO 11-2)*

Bond	Coupon	Time to Maturity	Yield to Maturity
A	15%	20 years	10%
B	15	15	10
C	0	20	10
D	8	20	10
E	15	15	15

2. Philip Morris has issued bonds that pay annually with the following characteristics:
   (LO 11-2)

Coupon	Yield to Maturity	Maturity	Macaulay Duration
8%	8%	15 years	10 years

   a. Calculate modified duration using the information above.
   b. Explain why modified duration is a better measure than maturity when calculating the bond's sensitivity to changes in interest rates.
   c. Identify the direction of change in modified duration if:
      i. The coupon of the bond were 4%, not 8%.
      ii. The maturity of the bond were 7 years, not 15 years.

3. As part of your analysis of debt issued by Monticello Corporation, you are asked to evaluate two specific bond issues, shown in the table below.   *(LO 11-2)*

MONTICELLO CORPORATION BOND INFORMATION

	Bond A (callable)	Bond B (noncallable)
Maturity	2022	2022
Coupon	11.50%	7.25%
Current price	125.75	100.00
Yield to maturity	7.70%	7.25%
Modified duration to maturity	6.20	6.80
Call date	2016	—
Call price	105	—
Yield to call	5.10%	—
Modified duration to call	3.10	—

   a. Using the duration and yield information in the table, compare the price and yield behavior of the two bonds under each of the following two scenarios:
      i. Strong economic recovery with rising inflation expectations.
      ii. Economic recession with reduced inflation expectations.
   b. Using the information in the table, calculate the projected price change for bond B if the yield-to-maturity for this bond falls by 75 basis points.
   c. Describe the shortcoming of analyzing bond A strictly to call or to maturity.

4. One common goal among fixed-income portfolio managers is to earn high incremental returns on corporate bonds versus government bonds of comparable durations. The approach of some corporate-bond portfolio managers is to find and purchase those corporate bonds having the largest initial spreads over comparable-duration government

bonds. John Ames, HFS's fixed-income manager, believes that a more rigorous approach is required if incremental returns are to be maximized.

The following table presents data relating to one set of corporate/government spread relationships (in basis points, bp) present in the market at a given date: *(LO 11-5)*

CURRENT AND EXPECTED SPREADS AND DURATIONS
OF HIGH-GRADE CORPORATE BONDS (ONE-YEAR HORIZON)

Bond Rating	Initial Spread over Governments	Expected Horizon Spread	Initial Duration	Expected Duration One Year from Now
Aaa	31 bp	31 bp	4 years	3.1 years
Aa	40	50	4	3.1

- a. Recommend purchase of *either* Aaa *or* Aa bonds for a one-year investment horizon given a goal of maximizing incremental returns.
- b. Ames chooses not to rely solely on initial spread relationships. His analytical framework considers a full range of other key variables likely to impact realized incremental returns, including call provisions and potential changes in interest rates. Describe other variables that Ames should include in his analysis, and explain how each of these could cause realized incremental returns to differ from those indicated by initial spread relationships.

5. Noah Kramer, a fixed-income portfolio manager based in the country of Sevista, is considering the purchase of a Sevista government bond. Kramer decides to evaluate two strategies for implementing his investment in Sevista bonds. Table 11.6 gives the details of the two strategies, and Table 11.7 contains the assumptions that apply to both strategies.

Before choosing one of the two bond investment strategies, Kramer wants to analyze how the market value of the bonds will change if an instantaneous interest rate shift occurs immediately after his investment. The details of the interest rate shift are shown in Table 11.8. Calculate, for the instantaneous interest rate shift shown in Table 11.8, the percent change in the market value of the bonds that will occur under each strategy. *(LO 11-2)*

6. a. Janet Meer is a fixed-income portfolio manager. Noting that the current shape of the yield curve is flat, she considers the purchase of a newly issued, option-free corporate bond priced at par; the bond is described in Table 11.9. Calculate the duration of the bond.

TABLE 11.6 Investment strategies (amounts are market value invested)

Strategy	5-Year Maturity (Modified Duration = 4.83 Years)	15-Year Maturity (Modified Duration = 14.35 Years)	25-Year Maturity (Modified Duration = 23.81 Years)
I	$5 million	0	$5 million
II	0	$10 million	0

TABLE 11.7 Investment strategy assumptions

Market Value of Bonds	$10 Million
Bond maturities	5 and 25 years or 15 years
Bond coupon rates	0.00%
Target modified duration	15 years

TABLE 11.8 Instantaneous interest rate shift immediately after investment

Maturity	Interest Rate Change
5 year	Down 75 basis points
15	Up 25 bp
25	Up 50 bp

TABLE 11.9 7% option-free bond, maturity = 10 years

	Change in Yields	
	Up 10 Basis Points	**Down 10 Basis Points**
Price	99.29	100.71
Convexity	35.00	

TABLE 11.10 7.25% option-free bond, maturity = 12 years

Original issue price	Par value, to yield 7.25%
Modified duration (at original price)	7.90
Convexity measure	41.55
Convexity adjustment (yield change of 200 basis points)	1.66

b. Meer is also considering the purchase of a second newly issued, option-free corporate bond, which is described in Table 11.10. She wants to evaluate this second bond's price sensitivity to an instantaneous, downward parallel shift in the yield curve of 200 basis points. Estimate the total percentage price change for the bond if the yield curve experiences an instantaneous, downward parallel shift of 200 basis points.   *(LO 11-2)*

7. Sandra Kapple presents Maria VanHusen with a description, given in the following exhibit, of the bond portfolio held by the Star Hospital Pension Plan. All securities in the bond portfolio are noncallable U.S. Treasury securities.   *(LO 11-2)*

STAR HOSPITAL PENSION PLAN BOND PORTFOLIO

Par Value (U.S. $)	Treasury Security	Market Value (U.S. $)	Current Price	Up 100 Basis Points	Down 100 Basis Points	Effective Duration
$48,000,000	2.375% due 2015	$48,667,680	$101.391	99.245	103.595	2.15
50,000,000	4.75% due 2040	50,000,000	100.000	86.372	116.887	
98,000,000	Total bond portfolio	98,667,680	—	—	—	—

a. Calculate the effective duration of each of the following:
   i. The 4.75% Treasury security due 2040
   ii. The total bond portfolio

b. VanHusen remarks to Kapple, "If you changed the maturity structure of the bond portfolio to result in a portfolio duration of 5.25, the price sensitivity of that portfolio would be identical to the price sensitivity of a single, noncallable Treasury security that has a duration of 5.25." In what circumstance would VanHusen's remark be correct?

8. The ability to *immunize* a bond portfolio is very desirable for bond portfolio managers in some instances. *(LO 11-4)*

     a. Discuss the components of interest rate risk—that is, assuming a change in interest rates over time, explain the two risks faced by the holder of a bond.

     b. Define *immunization* and discuss why a bond manager would immunize his or her portfolio.

     c. Explain why a duration-matching strategy is a superior technique to a maturity-matching strategy for the minimization of interest rate risk.

9. You are the manager for the bond portfolio of a pension fund. The policies of the fund allow for the use of active strategies in managing the bond portfolio.

     It appears that the economic cycle is beginning to mature, inflation is expected to accelerate, and, in an effort to contain the economic expansion, central bank policy is moving toward constraint. For each of the situations below, state which one of the two bonds you would prefer. Briefly justify your answer in each case. *(LO 11-5)*

     a. Government of Canada (Canadian pay), 4% due in 2019, and priced at 101.25 to yield 3.50% to maturity;

         or

         Government of Canada (Canadian pay), 4% due in 2029, and priced at 95.75 to yield 4.19% to maturity.

     b. Texas Power and Light Co., 5½% due in 2022, rated AAA, and priced at 85 to yield 8.1% to maturity;

         or

         Arizona Public Service Co., 5.45% due in 2022, rated A−, and priced at 80 to yield 9.1% to maturity.

     c. Commonwealth Edison, 2¾% due in 2021, rated Baa, and priced at 81 to yield 7.2% to maturity;

         or

         Commonwealth Edison, 9⅜% due in 2021, rated Baa, and priced at 114 to yield 7.2% to maturity.

     d. Shell Oil Co., 6¾% sinking fund debentures due in 2029, rated AAA (sinking fund begins in 2018 at par), and priced at 89 to yield 7.1% to maturity;

         or

         Warner-Lambert, 6⅞% sinking fund debentures due in 2026, rated AAA (sinking fund begins in 2019 at par), and priced at 95 to yield 7% to maturity.

     e. Bank of Montreal (Canadian pay), 4% certificates of deposit due in 2017, rated AAA, and priced at 100 to yield 4% to maturity;

         or

         Bank of Montreal (Canadian pay), floating-rate notes due in 2021, rated AAA. Coupon currently set at 3.7% and priced at 100 (coupon adjusted semiannually to .5% above the three-month Government of Canada Treasury bill rate).

10. *a.* Which set of conditions will result in a bond with the greatest price volatility? *(LO 11-1)*

     (1) A high coupon and a short maturity.

     (2) A high coupon and a long maturity.

     (3) A low coupon and a short maturity.

     (4) A low coupon and a long maturity.

     b. An investor who expects declining interest rates would be likely to purchase a bond that has a _____ coupon and a _____ term to maturity. *(LO 11-1)*

     (1) Low, long

     (2) High, short

     (3) High, long

     (4) Zero, long

c. With a zero-coupon bond: *(LO 11-1)*
   (1) Duration equals the weighted-average term to maturity.
   (2) Term to maturity equals duration.
   (3) Weighted-average term to maturity equals the term to maturity.
   (4) All of the above.

d. As compared with bonds selling at par, deep discount bonds will have: *(LO 11-1)*
   (1) Greater reinvestment risk.
   (2) Greater price volatility.
   (3) Less call protection.
   (4) None of the above.

11. A member of a firm's investment committee is very interested in learning about the management of fixed-income portfolios. He would like to know how fixed-income managers position portfolios to capitalize on their expectations concerning three factors that influence interest rates. Assuming that no investment policy limitations apply, formulate and describe a fixed-income portfolio management strategy for each of the following interest rate factors that could be used to exploit a portfolio manager's expectations about that factor. (*Note:* Three strategies are required, one for each of the listed factors.) *(LO 11-5)*
   a. Changes in the level of interest rates.
   b. Changes in yield spreads across/between sectors.
   c. Changes in yield spreads as to a particular instrument.

12. The following bond swaps could have been made in recent years as investors attempted to increase the total return on their portfolio.

   From the information presented below, identify possible reason(s) that investors may have made each swap. *(LO 11-5)*

Action		Call	Price	YTM (%)
a. Sell	Baa1 Electric Pwr. 1st mtg. 6⅜% due 2020	108.24	95.00	7.71
Buy	Baa1 Electric Pwr. 1st mtg. 2⅜% due 2021	105.20	79.00	7.39
b. Sell	Aaa Phone Co. notes 5½% due 2021	101.50	90.00	7.02
Buy	U.S. Treasury notes 6½% due 2021	NC	97.15	6.78
c. Sell	Aa1 Apex Bank zero coupon due 2023	NC	45.00	7.51
Buy	Aa1 Apex Bank float rate notes due 2036	103.90	90.00	—
d. Sell	A1 Commonwealth Oil & Gas 1st mtg. 6% due 2026	105.75	72.00	8.09
Buy	U.S. Treasury bond 5½% due 2032	NC	80.60	7.40
e. Sell	A1 Z mart convertible deb. 3% due 2026	103.90	62.00	6.92
Buy	A2 Lucky Ducks deb. 7¾% due 2032	109.86	75.00	10.43

WEB *master*

1. Use data from **finance.yahoo.com** to answer the following questions. Enter the stock symbol "S" to locate information for Sprint Corp. Find the company's most recent annual balance sheet in the *Financials* section.
   a. Examine the company's assets and liabilities. What proportion of total assets are current assets? What proportion of total liabilities are current liabilities? Does it seem that there is a good match between the duration of the assets and the duration of the liabilities?
   b. Look at the *Annual Statement of Cash Flows* for Sprint, which is also found in the *Financials* section. Check the *Financing Activities* section to see if the company has issued new debt or reduced its debt outstanding. How much interest did the firm pay during the period?
   c. Repeat the exercise with several other companies of your choice. Try to pick companies in different industries. Do you notice any patterns that might be due to the industrial environments in which the firms operate?

2. Many bond calculators are offered on the web. For example, you can find one at Investo-
   pedia (**www.investopedia.com/calculator/mduration.aspx**). Given a bond's parameters,
   you can find duration with the click of a button.
   a. Select a bond from *The Wall Street Journal* online. (Go to **www.wsj.com**, click on *Market
      Data* under the *Markets* tab, then *Rates,* and then *Corporate Gainers* and *Decliners* under
      the *Rates* tab.).
   b. Enter the bond's characteristics into the duration calculator.
   c. Confirm the bond's duration using Excel's DURATION or MDURATION functions.
      (In general, you should always pay attention to whether calculators and spreadsheets
      are providing duration or modified duration.)
   d. Based on the bond's current price, by what percent would the price change if the yield
      were to change by .5%?
   e. Repeat the calculations by entering assumed prices of 90, 100, and 110; then answer
      the following questions:
      i. What is the duration of the bond at the each of the prices?
      ii. Is the bond price more or less sensitive to interest rates at higher prices or at
          lower ones?

SOLUTIONS TO
CONCEPT
checks

11.1 Interest rate: 0.09

		(B) Time until Payment (years)	(C) Payment	(D) Payment Discounted at 9%	(E) Weight	Column (B) times Column (E)
A. 8% coupon bond		1	80	73.394	0.0753	0.0753
		2	80	67.334	0.0691	0.1382
		3	1,080	833.958	0.8556	2.5668
	Sum:			974.687	1.0000	2.7803
B. Zero-coupon bond		1	0	0.000	0.0000	0.0000
		2	0	0.000	0.0000	0.0000
		3	1,000	772.183	1.0000	3.0000
	Sum:			772.183	1.0000	3.0000

The duration of the 8% coupon bond rises to 2.7803 years. Price increases to
$974.687. The duration of the zero-coupon bond is unchanged at 3 years, although its
price also increases when the interest rate falls.

11.2 *a.* If the interest rate increases from 9% to 9.05%, the bond price falls from $974.687
      to $973.445. The percentage change in price is $-.127\%$.
      b. The duration formula would predict a price change of

$$-\frac{2.7802}{1.09} \times .0005 = -.00127 = -.127\%$$

which is the same answer that we obtained from direct computation in part (*a*).

11.3 Use Excel to confirm that DURATION(DATE(2000,1,1), DATE(2008,1,1), .09, .10, 1)
      = 5.97 years. If you change the last argument of the duration function from 1 to 2 (to
      allow for semiannual coupons), you will find that DURATION(DATE(2000,1,1),
      DATE (2008,1,1), .09, .10, 2) = 5.80 years. Duration is lower when coupons are paid
      semiannually rather than annually because, on average, payments come earlier. Instead
      of waiting until year-end to receive the annual coupon, investors receive half the coupon
      midway through the year.

11.4 The duration of a level perpetuity is $(1 + y)/y$ or $1 + 1/y$, which clearly falls as y increases. Tabulating duration as a function of y we get:

y	D
0.01 (i.e., 1%)	101 years
0.02	51
0.05	21
0.10	11
0.20	6
0.25	5
0.40	3.5

11.5 The perpetuity's duration now would be $1.08/.08 = 13.5$. We need to solve the following equation for w

$$w \times 2 + (1 - w) \times 13.5 = 6$$

Therefore, $w = .6522$.

11.6 *a.* The present value of the fund's obligation is $\$800,000/.08 = \$10$ million. The duration is 13.5 years. Therefore, the fund should invest $10 million in zeros with a 13.5-year maturity. The face value of the zeros will be $\$10,000,000 \times 1.08^{13.5} = \$28,263,159$.

b. When the interest rate increases to 8.1%, the present value of the fund's obligation drops to $800,000/.081 = \$9,876,543$. The value of the zero-coupon bond falls by roughly the same amount, to $\$28,263,159/1.081^{13.5} = \$9,875,835$. The duration of the perpetual obligation falls to $1.081/.081 = 13.346$ years. The fund should sell the zero it currently holds and purchase $9,876,543 in zero-coupon bonds with maturity of 13.346 years.

11.7 Dedication would be more attractive. Cash flow matching eliminates the need for rebalancing and thus saves transaction costs.

11.8 Current price = $1,091.29

Forecast price = $100 × Annuity factor (10%,18 years) + $1,000 × PV factor(10%,18 years) = $1,000

The future value of reinvested coupons will be ($100 × 1.08) + $100 = $208

The two-year return is $\dfrac{\$208 + (\$1,000 - \$1,091.29)}{\$1,091.29} = .107$, or 10.7%

The annualized rate of return over the two-year period would then be $(1.107)^{1/2} - 1 = .052$, or 5.2%.

Security Analysis

PART 4

Chapters in This Part

12 Macroeconomic and Industry Analysis

13 Equity Valuation

14 Financial Statement Analysis

Tell your friends or relatives that you are studying investments and they will ask you, "What stocks should I buy?" This is the question at the heart of security analysis. How do analysts choose the stocks and other securities to hold in their portfolios?

Security analysis requires a wide mix of skills. You need to be a decent economist with a good grasp of both macroeconomics and microeconomics, the former to help you form forecasts of the general direction of the market and the latter to help you assess the relative position of particular industries or firms. You need a good sense of demographic and social trends to help identify industries with bright prospects. You need to be a quick study of the ins and outs of particular industries to choose the firms that will succeed within each industry. You need a good accounting background to analyze the financial statements that firms provide to the public. You also need to have mastered corporate finance because security analysis at its core is the ability to value a firm. In short, a good security analyst will be a generalist, with a grasp of the widest range of financial issues. This is where there is the biggest premium on "putting it all together."

The chapters in Part Four are an introduction to security analysis. We will provide you with a "top-down" approach to the subject, starting with an overview of international, macroeconomic, and industry issues, and only then progressing to the analysis of particular firms. These topics form the core of fundamental analysis. After reading these chapters, you will have a good sense of the various techniques used to analyze stocks and the stock market.

Macroeconomic and Industry Analysis

Learning Objectives

LO 12-1 Predict the effect of exchange rates as well as monetary, fiscal, and supply-side policies on business conditions.

LO 12-2 Use leading, coincident, and lagging economic indicators to describe and predict the economy's path through the business cycle.

LO 12-3 Predict which industries will be more or less sensitive to business-cycle fluctuations.

LO 12-4 Analyze the effect of industry life cycles and competitive structure on earnings prospects.

fundamental analysis

The analysis of determinants of firm value, such as prospects for earnings and dividends.

The intrinsic value of a stock depends on the dividends and earnings that can be expected from the firm. This is the heart of **fundamental analysis,** that is, the analysis of determinants of value such as earnings prospects. Ultimately, the business success of the firm determines the dividends it can pay to shareholders and the price it will command in the stock market. Because the prospects of the firm are tied to those of the broader economy, however, valuation analyses must consider the business environment in which the firm operates. For some firms, macroeconomic and industry circumstances might have a greater influence on profits than the firm's relative performance within its industry. In other words, investors need to keep the big economic picture in mind.

Therefore, in analyzing a firm's prospects it often makes sense to start with the broad economic environment, examining the state of the aggregate economy and even the international economy. From there, one considers the implications of the outside environment on the industry in which the firm operates. Finally, the firm's position within the industry is examined.

This chapter examines the broad-based aspects of fundamental analysis—macroeconomic and industry analysis. The following two chapters cover firm-specific analysis. We begin with a discussion of international factors relevant to firm performance and move on to an overview of the significance of the key variables usually used to summarize the state of the economy. We then discuss government macroeconomic policy and the determination of interest rates. We conclude the analysis of the macroeconomic environment with a discussion of business cycles. Next, we move to industry analysis, treating issues concerning the sensitivity of the firm to the business cycle, the typical life cycle of an industry, and strategic issues that affect industry performance.

12.1 THE GLOBAL ECONOMY

A top-down analysis of a firm's prospects must start with the global economy. The international economy might affect a firm's export prospects, the price competition it faces from foreign competitors, or the profits it makes on investments abroad. Table 12.1 shows the importance of the global or broad regional macroeconomy to firms' prospects. For example, stock markets throughout Europe enjoyed large gains in 2013 as the worst fears concerning the eurozone crisis abated following the restructuring of Greece's debt. In contrast, other broad regions such as Asia exhibited poor returns as previously high growth rates showed signs of slowing.

Despite the importance of regional macroeconomic conditions, there can be considerable variation in economic performance across countries, even within regions. In Europe, for example, the German economy was forecast to expand at a rate of 1.7% while the Greek economy was expected to shrink, with a forecasted growth rate of −.3%.

Perhaps surprisingly, the best stock market returns did not align with the best macroeconomic expectations. This reflects the impact of near market efficiency, where stock returns are driven by performance relative to previous expectations. For example, Greece showed the best stock market performance in Table 12.1 but had the lowest forecasted economic growth rate. While a negative growth rate is distressing, this was still better than previously expected, and Greece's emergence from the effective default on its debt was a good omen for its future growth. Asia was forecast to have much healthier growth, and the so-called BRIC countries (Brazil, Russia, India, and China), often grouped together because of their rapid recent development, were by and large expected to continue that performance.

These data illustrate that the national economic environment can be a crucial determinant of industry performance. It is far harder for businesses to succeed in a contracting economy than in an expanding one. This observation highlights the role of a big-picture macroeconomic analysis as a fundamental part of the investment process.

In addition, political uncertainty can pose considerable economic risks. The sovereign debt crisis offers a compelling illustration of the interplay between politics and economics. In the last decade, the prospects of a bailout for Greece, as well as support for struggling but much larger economies such as Spain, have been in large part political issues but with enormous consequences for the world economy. Similarly, the ongoing debate in the United States over looming budget deficits and how to address them is in large part a pitched political battle, but one with huge economic consequences. At this level of analysis, it is clear that politics and economics are intimately entwined.

Other political issues that are less sensational but still extremely important to economic growth and investment returns include issues of protectionism and trade policy, the free flow of capital, and the status of a nation's workforce.

One obvious factor that affects the international competitiveness of a country's industries is the exchange rate between that country's currency and other currencies. The **exchange rate** is the rate at which domestic currency can be converted into foreign currency. For example, in late 2014, it took about 115 Japanese yen to purchase one U.S. dollar. We would say that the exchange rate is ¥115 per dollar or, equivalently, $.0088 per yen.

As exchange rates fluctuate, the dollar value of goods priced in foreign currency similarly fluctuates. For example, in 1980, the dollar–yen exchange rate was about $.0045 per yen. Because the exchange rate in 2014 was $.0088 per yen, a U.S. citizen would have needed almost twice as many dollars in 2014 to buy a product selling for ¥10,000 as would have been

exchange rate

The rate at which domestic currency can be converted into foreign currency.

TABLE 12.1   Economic performance

	Stock Market Return, 2013 (%)		Forecasted Growth in GDP, 2013 (%)
	In Local Currency	In U.S. Dollars	
Brazil	−17.0	−28.7	2.2
Britain	14.0	15.5	2.6
Canada	9.5	1.0	2.3
China	−10.0	−7.3	7.3
France	17.0	20.7	0.8
Germany	24.8	28.7	1.7
Greece	40.9	45.4	−0.3
Hong Kong	1.5	1.5	3.8
India	6.7	6.0	6.0
Italy	19.4	23.2	0.3
Japan	55.1	27.9	1.5
Mexico	−5.0	−5.6	3.4
Russia	−1.2	−8.9	2.8
Singapore	−0.5	−4.4	3.9
South Korea	−1.9	−1.4	3.5
Spain	27.0	31.0	0.5
Thailand	−9.6	−16.4	3.8
U.S.	28.8	28.8	2.7

Source: *The Economist*, January 4, 2014.

required in 1980. If the Japanese producer were to maintain a fixed yen price for its product, the price expressed in U.S. dollars would nearly double. This would make Japanese products more expensive to U.S. consumers, however, and result in lost sales. Obviously, appreciation of the yen creates a problem for Japanese producers such as automakers that must compete with U.S. producers.

Figure 12.1 shows the change in the purchasing power of the U.S. dollar relative to the purchasing power of several major currencies in the last decade. The ratio of purchasing powers is called the "real" or inflation-adjusted exchange rate. The change in the real exchange rate measures how much more or less expensive foreign goods have become to U.S. citizens,

FIGURE   12.1

Change in real exchange rate: U.S. dollar versus major currencies, 2003–2013

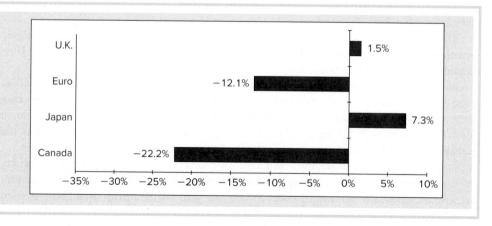

accounting for both exchange rate fluctuations and inflation differentials across countries. A positive value in Figure 12.1 means that the dollar has gained purchasing power relative to another currency; a negative number indicates a depreciating dollar. Therefore, the figure shows that goods priced in terms of euros or Canadian dollars became considerably more expensive to U.S. consumers in the last 10 years but that goods priced in British pounds or Japanese yen became somewhat cheaper. Conversely, goods priced in U.S. dollars became more expensive to Japanese consumers but more affordable to Canadian consumers.

12.2   THE DOMESTIC MACROECONOMY

The macroeconomy is the environment in which all firms operate. The importance of the macroeconomy in determining investment performance is illustrated in Figure 12.2, which compares the level of the S&P 500 stock price index to estimates of earnings per share of the S&P 500 companies. The graph shows that stock prices tend to rise along with earnings. While the exact ratio of stock price to earnings per share varies with factors such as interest rates, risk, inflation rates, and other variables, the graph does illustrate that, as a general rule, the ratio has tended to be in the range of 12 to 25. Given "normal" price-to-earnings ratios, we would expect the S&P 500 Index to fall within these boundaries. While the earnings-multiplier rule clearly is not perfect—note the dramatic increase in the P/E multiple during the dot-com boom of the late 1990s—it also seems clear that the level of the broad market and aggregate earnings do trend together.[1] Thus, the first step in forecasting the performance of the broad market is to assess the status of the economy as a whole.

The ability to forecast the macroeconomy can translate into spectacular investment performance. But it is not enough to forecast the macroeconomy well. One must forecast it *better* than one's competitors to earn abnormal profits. In this section, we will review some of the key economic statistics used to describe the state of the macroeconomy.

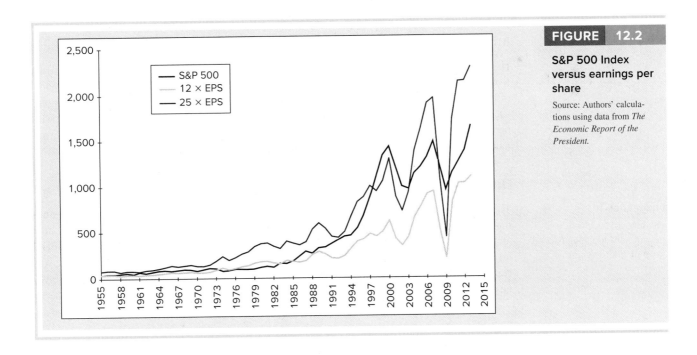

FIGURE 12.2

S&P 500 Index versus earnings per share

Source: Authors' calculations using data from *The Economic Report of the President.*

---

[1]Figure 12.2 shows that 2009 was another year in which the P/E multiple was much higher than even 25 times earnings. This reflects the fact that earnings in that year, at the height of the deep recession, were dramatically below trend projections. Market prices reflect earnings prospects well into the future, and therefore, they fell by less than earnings in that particular year. As we will see in the next chapter, P/E ratios should be interpreted relative to future earnings: Stock prices are forward-looking measures of firm value.

Gross Domestic Product

gross domestic product (GDP)

The market value of goods and services produced over a period of time.

Gross domestic product (GDP), is the measure of the economy's total production of goods and services. Rapidly growing GDP indicates an expanding economy with ample opportunity for a firm to increase sales. Another popular measure of the economy's output is *industrial production.* This statistic provides a measure of economic activity more narrowly focused on the manufacturing side of the economy.

Employment

unemployment rate

The ratio of the number of people classified as unemployed to the total labor force.

The **unemployment rate** is the percentage of the total labor force (i.e., those who are either working or actively seeking employment) yet to find work. The unemployment rate measures the extent to which the economy is operating at full capacity. The unemployment rate is a statistic related to workers only, but further insight into the strength of the economy can be gleaned from the employment rate of other factors of production. For example, analysts also look at the factory *capacity utilization rate,* which is the ratio of actual output from factories to potential output.

Inflation

inflation

The rate at which the general level of prices for goods and services is rising.

Inflation is the rate at which the general level of prices is rising. High rates of inflation often are associated with "overheated" economies, that is, economies where the demand for goods and services is outstripping productive capacity, which leads to upward pressure on prices. Most governments walk a fine line in their economic policies. They hope to stimulate their economies enough to maintain nearly full employment but not so much as to bring on inflationary pressures. The perceived trade-off between inflation and unemployment is at the heart of many macroeconomic policy disputes. There is considerable room for disagreement as to the relative costs of these policies as well as the economy's relative vulnerability to these pressures at any particular time.

Interest Rates

High interest rates reduce the present value of future cash flows, thereby reducing the attractiveness of investment opportunities. For this reason, real interest rates are key determinants of business investment expenditures. Demand for housing and high-priced consumer durables such as automobiles, which are commonly financed, also is highly sensitive to interest rates because interest rates affect interest payments. In Section 12.3 we will examine the determinants of real interest rates.

Budget Deficit

budget deficit

The amount by which government spending exceeds government revenues.

The **budget deficit** of the federal government is the difference between government spending and revenues. Any budgetary shortfall must be offset by government borrowing. Large amounts of government borrowing can force up interest rates by increasing the total demand for credit in the economy. Economists generally believe excessive government borrowing will "crowd out" private borrowing and investing by forcing up interest rates and choking off business investment.

Sentiment

Consumers' and producers' optimism or pessimism concerning the economy are important determinants of economic performance. If consumers have confidence in their future income levels, for example, they will be more willing to spend on big-ticket items. Similarly, businesses will increase production and inventory levels if they anticipate higher demand for their products. In this way, beliefs influence how much consumption and investment will be pursued and affect the aggregate demand for goods and services.

12.3 INTEREST RATES

The level of interest rates is perhaps the most important macroeconomic factor to consider in one's investment analysis. Forecasts of interest rates directly affect the forecast of returns in the fixed-income market. If your expectation is that rates will increase by more than the consensus view, you will want to shy away from longer term fixed-income securities. Similarly, increases in interest rates tend to be bad news for the stock market. Unanticipated increases in rates generally are associated with stock market declines. Thus, a superior technique to forecast rates would be of immense value to an investor attempting to determine the best asset allocation for his or her portfolio.

Unfortunately, forecasting interest rates is one of the most notoriously difficult parts of applied macroeconomics. Nonetheless, we do have a good understanding of the fundamental factors that determine the level of interest rates:

1. The supply of funds from savers, primarily households.
2. The demand for funds from businesses to be used to finance physical investments in plant, equipment, and inventories.
3. The government's net supply and/or demand for funds as modified by actions of the Federal Reserve Bank.
4. The expected rate of inflation.

Although there are many different interest rates economywide (as many as there are types of securities), these rates tend to move together, so economists frequently talk as though there were a single representative rate. We can use this abstraction to gain some insights into determining the real rate of interest if we consider the supply and demand curves for funds.

Figure 12.3 shows a downward-sloping demand curve and an upward-sloping supply curve. On the horizontal axis, we measure the quantity of funds, and on the vertical axis, we measure the real rate of interest.

The supply curve slopes up from left to right because the higher the real interest rate, the greater the supply of household savings. The assumption is that at higher real interest rates, households will choose to postpone some current consumption and set aside or invest more of their disposable income for future use.

The demand curve slopes down from left to right because the lower the real interest rate, the more businesses will want to invest in physical capital. Assuming that businesses rank

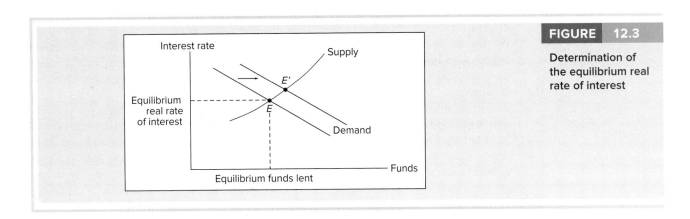

FIGURE **12.3**

Determination of the equilibrium real rate of interest

projects by the expected real return on invested capital, firms will undertake more projects the lower the real interest rate on the funds needed to finance those projects.

Equilibrium is at the point of intersection of the supply and demand curves, point E in Figure 12.3.

The government and the central bank (the Federal Reserve) can shift these supply and demand curves either to the right or to the left through fiscal and monetary policies. For example, consider an increase in the government's budget deficit. This increases the government's borrowing demand and shifts the demand curve to the right, which causes the equilibrium real interest rate to rise to point E'. That is, a forecast that indicates higher than previously expected government borrowing increases expectations of future interest rates. The Fed can offset such a rise through an increase in the money supply, which will increase the supply of loanable funds, and shift the supply curve to the right.

Thus, while the fundamental determinants of the real interest rate are the propensity of households to save and the expected productivity (or we could say profitability) of firms' investment in physical capital, the real rate can be affected as well by government fiscal and monetary policies.

The supply and demand framework illustrated in Figure 12.3 is a reasonable first approximation to the determination of the real interest rate. To obtain the *nominal* interest rate, one needs to add the expected inflation rate to the equilibrium real rate. As we discussed in Section 5.4, the inflation premium is necessary for investors to maintain a given real rate of return on their investments.

While monetary policy can clearly affect nominal interest rates, there is considerable controversy concerning its ability to affect real rates. There is widespread agreement that, in the long run, the ultimate impact of an increase in the money supply is an increase in prices with no permanent impact on real economic activity. A rapid rate of growth in the money supply, therefore, ultimately would result in a correspondingly high inflation rate and nominal interest rate, but it would have no sustained impact on the real interest rate. However, in the shorter run, changes in the money supply may well have an effect on the real interest rate.

12.4   DEMAND AND SUPPLY SHOCKS

demand shock

An event that affects the demand for goods and services in the economy.

supply shock

An event that influences production capacity and costs in the economy.

A useful way to organize your analysis of the factors that might influence the macroeconomy is to classify any impact as a supply or demand shock. A **demand shock** is an event that affects the demand for goods and services in the economy. Examples of positive demand shocks are reductions in tax rates, increases in the money supply, increases in government spending, or increases in foreign export demand. A **supply shock** is an event that influences production capacity and costs. Examples of supply shocks are changes in the price of imported oil; freezes, floods, or droughts that might destroy large quantities of agricultural crops; changes in the educational level of an economy's workforce; or changes in the wage rates at which the labor force is willing to work.

Demand shocks usually are characterized by aggregate output moving in the same direction as interest rates and inflation. For example, a big increase in government spending will tend to stimulate the economy and increase GDP. It also might increase interest rates by increasing the demand for borrowed funds by the government as well as by businesses that might desire to borrow to finance new ventures. Finally, it could increase the inflation rate if the demand for goods and services is raised to a level at or beyond the total productive capacity of the economy.

Supply shocks usually are characterized by aggregate output moving in the opposite direction of inflation and interest rates. For example, a big increase in the price of imported oil will be inflationary because costs of production will rise, which eventually will lead to increases in prices of finished goods. The increase in inflation rates over the near term can lead to higher nominal interest rates. Against this background, aggregate output will be falling. With raw materials more expensive, the productive capacity of the economy is reduced, as is the ability of individuals to purchase goods at now-higher prices. GDP, therefore, tends to fall.

How can we relate this framework to investment analysis? You want to identify the industries that will be most helped or hurt in any macroeconomic scenario you envision. For example, if you forecast a tightening of the money supply, you might want to avoid industries such as automobile producers that might be hurt by the likely increase in interest rates. We caution you again that these forecasts are no easy task. Macroeconomic predictions are notoriously unreliable. And again, you must be aware that in all likelihood your forecast will be made using only publicly available information. Any investment advantage you have will be a result only of better analysis—not better information.

12.5 FEDERAL GOVERNMENT POLICY

As the previous section would suggest, the government has two broad classes of macroeconomic tools—those that affect the demand for goods and services and those that affect their supply. For much of postwar history, demand-side policy has been of primary interest. The focus has been on government spending, tax levels, and monetary policy. Since the 1980s, however, increasing attention has also been focused on supply-side economics. Broadly interpreted, supply-side concerns have to do with enhancing the productive capacity of the economy, rather than increasing the demand for the goods and services the economy can produce. In practice, supply-side economists have focused on the appropriateness of the incentives to work, innovate, and take risks that result from our system of taxation. However, issues such as national policies on education, infrastructure (such as communication and transportation systems), and research and development also are properly regarded as part of supply-side macroeconomic policy.

Fiscal Policy

Fiscal policy refers to the government's spending and tax actions and is part of "demand-side management." Fiscal policy is probably the most direct way either to stimulate or to slow the economy. Decreases in government spending directly deflate the demand for goods and services. Similarly, increases in tax rates immediately siphon income from consumers and result in fairly rapid decreases in consumption.

fiscal policy
The use of government spending and taxing for the specific purpose of stabilizing the economy.

Ironically, although fiscal policy has the most immediate impact on the economy, the formulation and implementation of such policy is usually painfully slow and involved. This is because fiscal policy requires enormous amounts of compromise between the executive and legislative branches. Tax and spending policy must be initiated and voted on by Congress, which requires considerable political negotiations, and any legislation passed must be signed by the president, requiring more negotiation. Thus, while the impact of fiscal policy is relatively immediate, its formulation is so cumbersome that fiscal policy cannot in practice be used to fine-tune the economy.

Moreover, much of government spending, such as that for Medicare or Social Security, is nondiscretionary, meaning that it is determined by formula rather than policy and cannot be changed in response to economic conditions. This places even more rigidity into the formulation of fiscal policy.

A common way to summarize the net impact of government fiscal policy is to look at the government's budget deficit or surplus, which is simply the difference between revenues and expenditures. A large deficit means the government is spending considerably more than it is taking in by way of taxes. The net effect is to increase the demand for goods (via spending) by more than it reduces the demand for goods (via taxes), therefore, stimulating the economy.

Monetary Policy

Monetary policy refers to the manipulation of the money supply to affect the macroeconomy and is the other main leg of demand-side policy. Monetary policy works largely through its impact on interest rates. Increases in the money supply lower short-term interest rates,

monetary policy
Actions taken by the Board of Governors of the Federal Reserve System to influence the money supply or interest rates.

ultimately encouraging investment and consumption demand. Over longer periods, however, most economists believe a higher money supply leads only to a higher price level and does not have a permanent effect on economic activity. Thus, the monetary authorities face a difficult balancing act. Expansionary monetary policy probably will lower interest rates and thereby stimulate investment and some consumption demand in the short run, but these circumstances ultimately will lead only to higher prices. The stimulation/inflation trade-off is implicit in all debate over proper monetary policy.

Fiscal policy is cumbersome to implement but has a fairly direct impact on the economy, while monetary policy is easily formulated and implemented but has a less immediate impact. Monetary policy is determined by the Board of Governors of the Federal Reserve System. Board members are appointed by the president for 14-year terms and are reasonably insulated from political pressure. The board is small enough and often sufficiently dominated by its chairperson that policy can be formulated and modulated relatively easily.

Implementation of monetary policy also is quite direct. The most widely used tool is the open market operation, in which the Fed buys or sells Treasury bonds for its own account. When the Fed buys securities, it simply writes a check, thereby increasing the money supply. (Unlike us, the Fed can pay for the securities without drawing down funds at a bank account.) Conversely, when the Fed sells a security, the money paid for it leaves the money supply. Open market operations occur daily, allowing the Fed to fine-tune its monetary policy.

Other tools at the Fed's disposal are the *discount rate,* which is the interest rate it charges banks on short-term loans, and the *reserve requirement,* which is the fraction of deposits that banks must hold as cash on hand or as deposits with the Fed. Reductions in the discount rate signal a more expansionary monetary policy. Lowering reserve requirements allows banks to make more loans with each dollar of deposits and stimulates the economy by increasing the effective money supply.

While the discount rate is under the direct control of the Fed, it is changed relatively infrequently. The *federal funds rate* is by far the better guide to Federal Reserve policy. The federal funds rate is the interest rate at which banks make short-term, usually overnight, loans to each other. These loans occur because some banks need to borrow funds to meet reserve requirements, while other banks have excess funds. Unlike the discount rate, the fed funds rate is a market rate, meaning that it is determined by supply and demand rather than being set administratively. Nevertheless, the Federal Reserve Board targets the fed funds rate, expanding or contracting the money supply through open market operations as it nudges the fed funds to its targeted value. This is the benchmark short-term U.S. interest rate, and as such it has considerable influence over other interest rates in the U.S. and the rest of the world.

Monetary policy affects the economy in a more roundabout way than fiscal policy. While fiscal policy directly stimulates or dampens the economy, monetary policy works largely through its impact on interest rates. Increases in the money supply lower interest rates, which stimulates investment demand. As the quantity of money in the economy increases, investors will find that their portfolios of assets include too much money. They will rebalance their portfolios by buying securities such as bonds, forcing bond prices up and interest rates down. In the longer run, individuals may increase their holdings of stocks as well and ultimately buy real assets, which stimulates consumption demand directly. The ultimate effect of monetary policy on investment and consumption demand, however, is less immediate than that of fiscal policy.

CONCEPT check	**12.2**	Suppose the government wants to stimulate the economy without increasing interest rates. What combination of fiscal and monetary policy might accomplish this goal?

Supply-Side Policies

Fiscal policy and monetary policy are demand-oriented tools that affect the economy by stimulating the total demand for goods and services. The implicit belief is that the economy will not by itself arrive at a full-employment equilibrium and that macroeconomic policy can push the economy toward this goal. In contrast, supply-side policies treat the issue of the productive capacity of the economy. The goal is to create an environment in which workers and owners of capital have the maximum incentive and ability to produce and develop goods.

Supply-side economists also pay considerable attention to tax policy. While demand-siders look at the effect of taxes on consumption demand, supply-siders focus on incentives and marginal tax rates. They argue that lowering tax rates will elicit more investment and improve incentives to work, thereby enhancing economic growth. Some go so far as to claim that reductions in tax rates can lead to increases in tax revenues because the lower tax rates will cause the economy and the revenue tax base to grow by more than the tax rate is reduced.

CONCEPT **12.3**
check

Large tax cuts in 2001 were followed by relatively rapid growth in GDP. How would demand-side and supply-side economists differ in their interpretations of this phenomenon?

12.6   BUSINESS CYCLES

We've looked at the tools the government uses to fine-tune the economy, attempting to maintain low unemployment and low inflation. Despite these efforts, economies repeatedly seem to pass through good and bad times. One determinant of the broad asset allocation decision of many analysts is a forecast of whether the macroeconomy is improving or deteriorating. A forecast that differs from the market consensus can have a major impact on investment strategy.

The Business Cycle

The economy recurrently experiences periods of expansion and contraction, although the length and depth of these cycles can be irregular. These recurring patterns of recession and recovery are called **business cycles.** Figure 12.4 presents graphs of several measures of production and output. The production series all show clear variation around a generally rising trend. The bottom graph of capacity utilization also evidences a clear cyclical (although irregular) pattern.

business cycles

Recurring cycles of recession and recovery.

The transition points across cycles are called peaks and troughs, identified by the boundaries of the shaded areas of the graph. A **peak** is the transition from the end of an expansion to the start of a contraction. A **trough** occurs at the bottom of a recession just as the economy enters a recovery. The shaded areas in Figure 12.4 all represent periods of recession.

peak

The transition from the end of an expansion to the start of a contraction.

As the economy passes through different stages of the business cycle, the relative profitability of different industry groups might be expected to vary. For example, at a trough, just as the economy begins to recover from a recession, one would expect that **cyclical industries,** those with above-average sensitivity to the state of the economy, would tend to outperform other industries. Examples of cyclical industries are producers of durable goods, such as automobiles or washing machines. Because purchases of these goods can be deferred during a recession, sales are particularly sensitive to macroeconomic conditions. Other cyclical industries are producers of capital goods, that is, goods used by other firms to produce their own products. When demand is slack, few companies will be expanding and purchasing capital goods. Therefore, the capital goods industry bears the brunt of a slowdown but does well in an expansion.

trough

The transition point between recession and recovery.

cyclical industries

Industries with above-average sensitivity to the state of the economy.

In contrast to cyclical firms, **defensive industries** have little sensitivity to the business cycle. These are industries that produce goods for which sales and profits are least sensitive to the state of the economy. Defensive industries include food producers and processors, pharmaceutical firms, and public utilities. These industries will outperform others when the economy enters a recession.

defensive industries

Industries with below-average sensitivity to the state of the economy.

The cyclical/defensive classification corresponds well to the notion of systematic or market risk introduced in our discussion of portfolio theory. When perceptions about the health of the economy become more optimistic, for example, the prices of most stocks will increase as

Cyclical indicators

Source: The Conference Board, *Business Cycle Indicators,* December 2008.

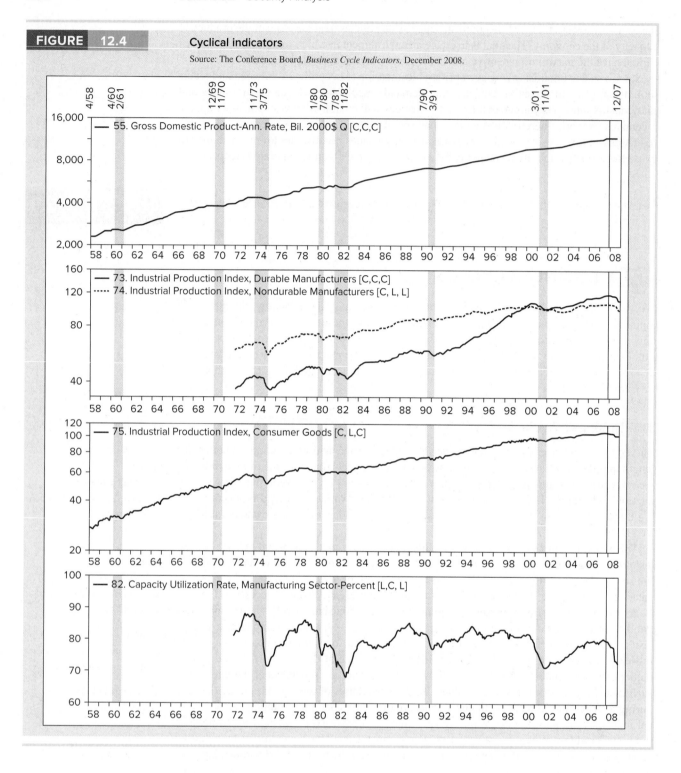

forecasts of profitability rise. Because the cyclical firms are most sensitive to such developments, their stock prices will rise the most. Thus, firms in cyclical industries will tend to have high-beta stocks. In general, then, stocks of cyclical firms will show the best results when economic news is positive, but they will also show the worst results when that news is bad. Conversely, defensive firms will have low betas and performance that is comparatively unaffected by overall market conditions.

If your assessments of the state of the business cycle were reliably more accurate than those of other investors, choosing between cyclical and defensive industries would be easy.

You would choose cyclical industries when you were relatively more optimistic about the economy, and you would choose defensive firms when you were relatively more pessimistic. As we know from our discussion of efficient markets, however, attractive investment choices will rarely be obvious. It is usually not apparent that a recession or expansion has started or ended until several months after the fact. With hindsight, the transitions from expansion to recession and back might seem obvious, but it is often quite difficult to say whether the economy is heating up or slowing down at any moment.

Economic Indicators

Given the cyclical nature of the business cycle, it is not surprising that to some extent the cycle can be predicted. The Conference Board publishes a set of cyclical indicators to help forecast, measure, and interpret short-term fluctuations in economic activity. **Leading economic indicators** are those economic series that tend to rise or fall in advance of the rest of the economy. Coincident and lagging indicators, as their names suggest, move in tandem with or somewhat after the broad economy.

leading economic indicators

Economic series that tend to rise or fall in advance of the rest of the economy.

Ten series are grouped into a widely followed composite index of leading economic indicators. Similarly, four coincident and seven lagging indicators form separate indexes. The composition of these indexes appears in Table 12.2.

Figure 12.5 graphs these three series. The dates at the top of the charts correspond to the turning points between expansions and contractions. While the index of leading indicators consistently turns before the rest of the economy, the lead time is somewhat erratic. Moreover, the lead time for peaks is consistently longer than that for troughs.

TABLE 12.2 Indexes of economic indicators

A. Leading indicators
1. Average weekly hours of production workers (manufacturing)
2. Initial claims for unemployment insurance
3. Manufacturers' new orders (consumer goods and materials industries)
4. Institute for Supply Management Index of New Orders
5. New orders for nondefense capital goods
6. New private housing units authorized by local building permits
7. Yield curve: spread between 10-year T-bond yield and federal funds rate
8. Stock prices, 500 common stocks
9. Leading credit index
10. Index of consumer expectations for business conditions

B. Coincident indicators
1. Employees on nonagricultural payrolls
2. Personal income less transfer payments
3. Industrial production
4. Manufacturing and trade sales

C. Lagging indicators
1. Average duration of unemployment
2. Ratio of trade inventories to sales
3. Change in index of labor cost per unit of output
4. Average prime rate charged by banks
5. Commercial and industrial loans outstanding
6. Ratio of consumer installment credit outstanding to personal income
7. Change in consumer price index for services

Source: The Conference Board, *Business Cycle Indicators,* October 2014.

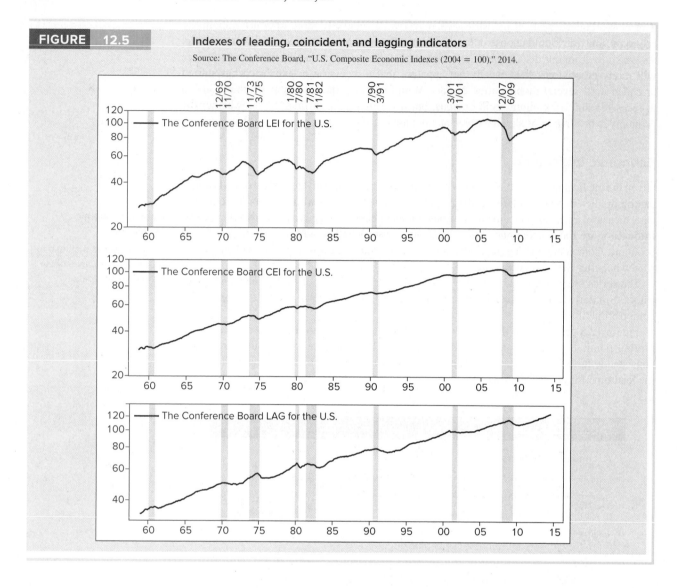

FIGURE 12.5   Indexes of leading, coincident, and lagging indicators

Source: The Conference Board, "U.S. Composite Economic Indexes (2004 = 100)," 2014.

The stock market price index is a leading indicator. This is as it should be, as stock prices are forward-looking predictors of future profitability. Unfortunately, this makes the series of leading indicators much less useful for investment policy—by the time the series predicts an upturn, the market has already made its move. While the business cycle may be somewhat predictable, the stock market may not be. This is just one more manifestation of the efficient market hypothesis.

Other leading indicators focus directly on decisions made today that will affect production in the near future. For example, manufacturers' new orders for goods, contracts and orders for plant and equipment, and housing starts all signal a coming expansion in the economy.

A wide range of economic indicators are released to the public on a regular "economic calendar." Table 12.3 lists the public announcement dates and sources for about 20 statistics of interest. These announcements are reported in the financial press, for example, *The Wall Street Journal,* as they are released. They also are available at many sites on the web, for example, at Yahoo!'s site. Figure 12.6 is a brief excerpt from a recent Economic Calendar page at Yahoo!. The page gives a list of the announcements released during the week of November 12, 2014. Notice that recent forecasts of each variable are provided along with the actual value of each statistic. This is useful because, in an efficient market, security prices will already reflect

TABLE 12.3   Economic calendar

Statistic	Release Date*	Source	Website (www.)
Auto and truck sales	2nd of month	Commerce Department	commerce.gov
Business inventories	15th of month	Commerce Department	commerce.gov
Construction spending	1st business day of month	Commerce Department	commerce.gov
Consumer confidence	Last Tuesday of month	Conference Board	conference-board.org
Consumer credit	5th business day of month	Federal Reserve Board	federalreserve.gov
Consumer price index (CPI)	13th of month	Bureau of Labor Statistics	bls.gov
Durable goods orders	26th of month	Commerce Department	commerce.gov
Employment cost index	End of first month of quarter	Bureau of Labor Statistics	bls.gov
Employment record (unemployment, average workweek, nonfarm payrolls)	1st Friday of month	Bureau of Labor Statistics	bls.gov
Existing home sales	25th of month	National Association of Realtors	realtor.org
Factory orders	1st business day of month	Commerce Department	commerce.gov
Gross domestic product	3rd–4th week of month	Commerce Department	commerce.gov
Housing starts	16th of month	Commerce Department	commerce.gov
Industrial production	15th of month	Federal Reserve Board	federalreserve.gov
Initial claims for jobless benefits	Thursdays	Department of Labor	dol.gov
International trade balance	20th of month	Commerce Department	commerce.gov
Index of leading economic indicators	Beginning of month	Conference Board	conference-board.org
Money supply	Thursdays	Federal Reserve Board	federalreserve.gov
New home sales	Last business day of month	Commerce Department	commerce.gov
Producer price index	11th of month	Bureau of Labor Statistics	bls.gov
Productivity and costs	2nd month in quarter (approx. 7th day of month)	Bureau of Labor Statistics	bls.gov
Retail sales	13th of month	Commerce Department	commerce.gov
Survey of purchasing managers	1st business day of month	Institute for Supply Management	ism.ws

*Many of these release dates are approximate.

Economic calendar at Yahoo! Finance for the week of November 12, 2014   **FIGURE** 12.6

Source: Yahoo! Finance, Earnings Calendar, **biz.yahoo.com**.

Last Week   Next Week

Date	Time (ET)	Statistic	For	Actual	Briefing Forecast	Market Expects	Prior
Nov 12	10:00 A.M.	Wholesale Inventories	Sep	0.3%	−0.1%	0.2%	0.6%
Nov 13	8:30 A.M.	Initial Claims	11/08	290K	285K	280K	278K
Nov 13	8:30 A.M.	Continuing Claims	11/01	2392K	2350K	2353K	2356K
Nov 13	10:00 A.M.	JOLTS - Job Openings	Sep	4.735M	NA	NA	4.853M
Nov 13	10:30 A.M.	Natural Gas Inventories	11/08	–	NA	NA	91 bef
Nov 13	11:00 A.M.	Crude Inventories	11/08	−1.735M	NA	NA	0.460M
Nov 13	2:00 A.M.	Treasury Budget	Oct	–	−$122.0B	−$122.0B	−$90.6B

TABLE 12.4	Useful economic indicators
CEO polls **http://businessroundtable.org**	The business roundtable surveys CEOs about planned spending, a good measure of their optimism about the economy.
Temp jobs: Search for "Temporary Help Services" at **www.bls.gov**	A useful leading indicator. Businesses often hire temporary workers as the economy first picks up, until it is clear that an upturn is going to be sustained. This series is available at the Bureau of Labor Statistics website.
Walmart sales **http://stock.walmart.com/financial-reporting/comparable-store-sales/**	Walmart sales are a good indicator of the retail sector. It publishes its same-store sales weekly.
Commercial and industrial loans **www.federalreserve.gov**	These loans are used by small and medium-sized firms. Information is published weekly by the Federal Reserve.
Semiconductors **www.semi.org/MarketInfo/Book-to-Bill**	The book-to-bill ratio (i.e., new sales versus actual shipments) indicates whether demand in the technology sector is increasing (ratio > 1) or falling. This ratio is published by Semiconductor Equipment and Materials International.
Commercial structures **www.bea.gov**	Investment in structures is an indicator of businesses' forecasts of demand for their products in the near future. This is one of the series compiled by the Bureau of Economic Analysis as part of its GDP series.

market expectations. The *new* information in the announcement will determine the market response.

Other Indicators

You can find lots of important information about the state of the economy from sources other than the official components of the economic calendar or the components of business-cycle indicators. Table 12.4, which is derived from some suggestions in *Inc.* magazine, contains a few.[2]

12.7   INDUSTRY ANALYSIS

Industry analysis is important for the same reason that macroeconomic analysis is: Just as it is difficult for an industry to perform well when the macroeconomy is ailing, it is unusual for a firm in a troubled industry to perform well. Similarly, just as we have seen that economic performance can vary widely across countries, performance also can vary widely across industries. Figure 12.7 illustrates the dispersion of industry performance. It shows return on equity for several major industry groups in 2013. ROE ranged from 4.2% for electric utilities to 37% for major airlines.

Given this wide variation in profitability, it is not surprising that industry groups exhibit considerable dispersion in their stock market performance. Figure 12.8 presents the 2013 stock market performance of the same industries included in Figure 12.7. The spread in performance across industries is remarkable, ranging from a 7.1% gain in computer systems to an 89.25% return for major airlines. The fact that in this year, each industry showed a positive return is testament to the influence of broad systematic or market factors on the performance of individual industries and firms.

The range of performance demonstrated by these industries was very much available to virtually all investors in 2014. Industry-focused exchange-traded funds such as iShares (see Chapter 4) trade like stocks and thus allow even small investors to take a position in each

[2]Gene Sperling and illustrations by Thomas Fuchs, "The Insider's Guide to Economic Forecasting," *Inc.*, August 2003, p. 96.

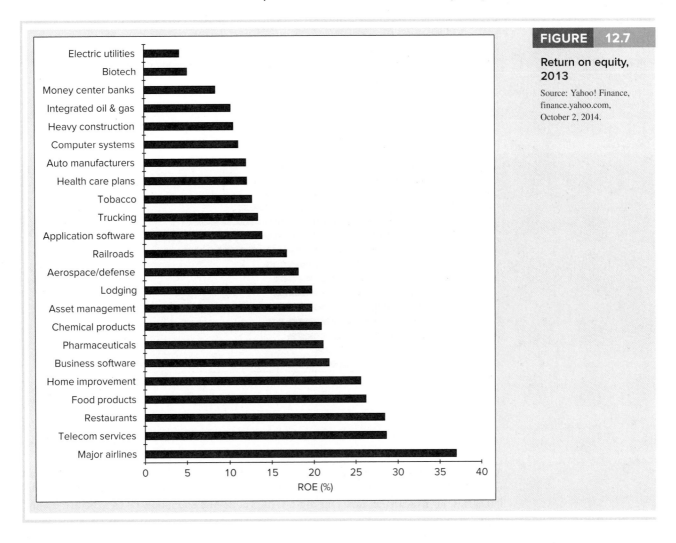

FIGURE 12.7

Return on equity, 2013

Source: Yahoo! Finance, finance.yahoo.com, October 2, 2014.

traded industry. Alternatively, one can invest in mutual funds with an industry focus. For example, Fidelity offers more than 40 sector funds, each with a particular industry focus.

Defining an Industry

While we know what we mean by an industry, it can be difficult in practice to decide where to draw the line between one industry and another. Consider, for example, one of the industries depicted in Figure 12.7, application software firms. Even within this industry, there is substantial variation by focus and product line. Their differences may result in considerable dispersion in financial performance. Figure 12.9 shows 2012 ROE for a sample of the firms included in this industry, and performance did indeed wary widely: from −6.9% for Nuance to 26.2% for Microsoft.

A useful way to define industry groups in practice is given by the North American Industry Classification System, or **NAICS, codes.**[3] These are codes assigned to group firms for statistical analysis. The first two digits of the NAICS codes denote very broad industry classifications. For example, Table 12.5 shows that the codes for all construction firms start with 23. The next digits define the industry grouping more narrowly. For example, codes starting with 236 denote *building* construction, 2361 denotes *residential* construction, and 236115

NAICS codes

Classification of firms into industry groups using numerical codes to identify industries.

[3]These codes are used for firms operating inside the NAFTA (North American Free Trade Agreement) region, which includes the U.S., Mexico, and Canada. NAICS codes replaced the Standard Industry Classification, or SIC, codes previously used in the U.S.

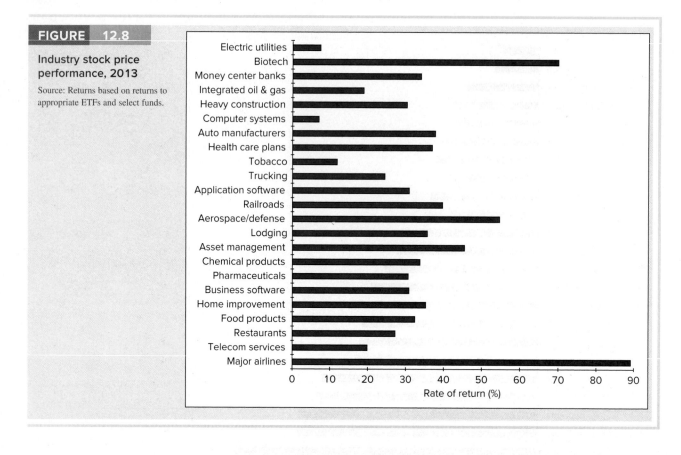

FIGURE 12.8

Industry stock price
performance, 2013

Source: Returns based on returns to
appropriate ETFs and select funds.

denotes *single-family* construction. The first five digits of NAICS codes are common across all NAFTA countries. The sixth digit is country specific and allows for a finer partition of industries. Firms with the same four-digit NAICS codes are commonly taken to be in the same industry.

Industry classifications are never perfect. For example, both Kohl's and Neiman Marcus might be classified as department stores. Yet the former is a high-volume "value" store, while the latter is a high-margin elite retailer. Are they really in the same industry? Still, these classifications are a tremendous aid in conducting industry analysis because they provide a means of focusing on very broadly or fairly narrowly defined groups of firms.

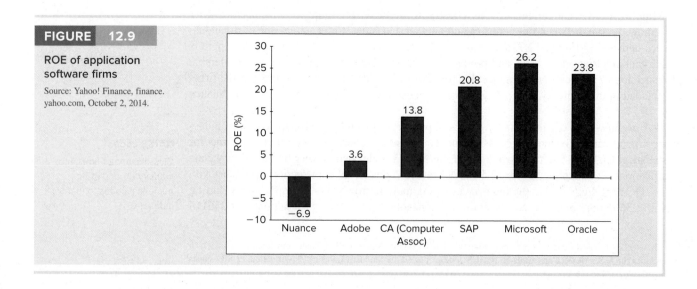

FIGURE 12.9

ROE of application
software firms

Source: Yahoo! Finance, finance.
yahoo.com, October 2, 2014.

TABLE 12.5	Examples of NAICS industry codes
NAICS Code	**NAICS Title**
23	Construction
236	Construction of Buildings
2361	Residential Building Construction
23611	Residential Building Construction
236115	New Single-Family Housing Construction
236116	New Multifamily Housing Construction
236118	Residential Remodelers
2362	Nonresidential Building Construction
23621	Industrial Building Construction
23622	Commercial and Institutional Building Construction

Several other industry classifications are provided by other analysts; for example, Standard & Poor's reports on the performance of about 100 industry groups. S&P computes stock price indexes for each group, which is useful in assessing past investment performance. The *Value Line Investment Survey* reports on the conditions and prospects of about 1,700 firms, grouped into about 90 industries. Value Line's analysts prepare forecasts of the performance of industry groups as well as of each firm.

Sensitivity to the Business Cycle

Once the analyst forecasts the state of the macroeconomy, it is necessary to determine the implication of that forecast for specific industries. Not all industries are equally sensitive to the business cycle. For example, Figure 12.10 plots changes in retail sales (year over year) in two industries: jewelry and grocery stores. Clearly, sales of jewelry, which is a luxury good, fluctuate more widely than those of grocery stores. Jewelry sales jumped in 1999 at the height of the dot-com boom but fell steeply in the recessions of 2001 and 2008-2009. In contrast,

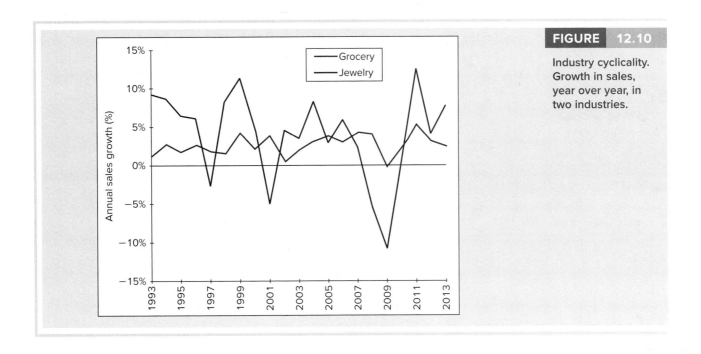

FIGURE 12.10

Industry cyclicality. Growth in sales, year over year, in two industries.

sales growth in the grocery industry is relatively stable, with no years in which sales meaningfully decline. These patterns reflect the fact that jewelry is a discretionary good, whereas most grocery products are staples for which demand will not fall significantly even in hard times.

Three factors will determine the sensitivity of a firm's earnings to the business cycle. First is the sensitivity of sales. Necessities will show little sensitivity to business conditions. Examples of industries in this group are food, drugs, and medical services. Other industries with low sensitivity are those for which income is not a crucial determinant of demand. Tobacco products are examples of this type of industry. Another industry in this group is movies, because consumers tend to substitute movies for more expensive sources of entertainment when income levels are low. In contrast, firms in industries such as machine tools, steel, autos, and transportation are highly sensitive to the state of the economy.

The second factor determining business-cycle sensitivity is operating leverage, which refers to the division between fixed and variable costs. (Fixed costs are those the firm incurs regardless of its production levels. Variable costs are those that rise or fall as the firm produces more or less product.) Firms with greater amounts of variable as opposed to fixed costs will be less sensitive to business conditions. This is because, in economic downturns, these firms can reduce costs as output falls in response to falling sales. Profits for firms with high fixed costs will swing more widely with sales because costs do not move to offset revenue variability. Firms with high fixed costs are said to have high operating leverage, as small swings in business conditions can have large impacts on profitability.

The third factor influencing business-cycle sensitivity is financial leverage, which is the use of borrowing. Interest payments on debt must be paid regardless of sales. They are fixed costs that also increase the sensitivity of profits to business conditions. We will have more to say about financial leverage in Chapter 14.

Investors should not always prefer industries with lower sensitivity to the business cycle. Firms in sensitive industries will have high-beta stocks and are riskier. But while they swing lower in downturns, they also swing higher in upturns. As always, the issue you need to address is whether the expected return on the investment is fair compensation for the risks borne.

Sector Rotation

sector rotation

An investment strategy that entails shifting the portfolio into industry sectors that are expected to outperform others based on macroeconomic forecasts.

One way that many analysts think about the relationship between industry analysis and the business cycle is the notion of **sector rotation.** The idea is to shift the portfolio more heavily into industry or sector groups that are expected to outperform based on one's assessment of the state of the business cycle.

Figure 12.11 is a stylized depiction of the business cycle. Near the peak of the business cycle, the economy might be overheated with high inflation and interest rates and price

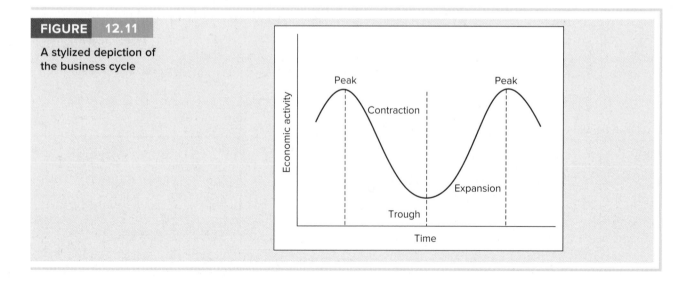

pressures on basic commodities. This might be a good time to invest in firms engaged in natural resource extraction and processing such as minerals or petroleum.

Following a peak, when the economy enters a contraction or recession, one would expect defensive industries that are less sensitive to economic conditions, for example, pharmaceuticals, food, and other necessities, to be the best performers. At the height of the contraction, financial firms will be hurt by shrinking loan volume and higher default rates. Toward the end of the recession, however, contractions induce lower inflation and interest rates, which favor financial firms.

At the trough of a recession, the economy is poised for recovery and subsequent expansion. Firms might thus be spending on purchases of new equipment to meet anticipated increases in demand. This, then, would be a good time to invest in capital goods industries, such as equipment, transportation, or construction.

Finally, in an expansion, the economy is growing rapidly. Cyclical industries such as consumer durables and luxury items will be most profitable in this stage of the cycle. Banks might also do well in expansions because loan volume will be high and default exposure low when the economy is growing rapidly.

Figure 12.12 illustrates sector rotation. When investors are relatively pessimistic about the economy, they will shift into noncyclical industries such as consumer staples or health care. When anticipating an expansion, they will prefer more cyclical industries such as materials and technology.

Let us emphasize again that sector rotation, like any other form of market timing, will be successful only if one anticipates the next stage of the business cycle better than other investors. The business cycle depicted in Figure 12.11 is highly stylized. In real life, it is never as clear how long each phase of the cycle will last, nor how extreme it will be. These forecasts are where analysts need to earn their keep.

CONCEPT check 12.4

In which phase of the business cycle would you expect the following industries to enjoy their best performance?

(a) Newspapers   (b) Machine tools   (c) Beverages   (d) Timber

---

Industry Life Cycles

Examine the biotechnology industry and you will find many firms with high rates of investment, high rates of return on investment, and very low dividends as a percentage of profits. Do the same for the electric utility industry and you will find lower rates of return, lower investment rates, and higher dividend payout rates. Why should this be?

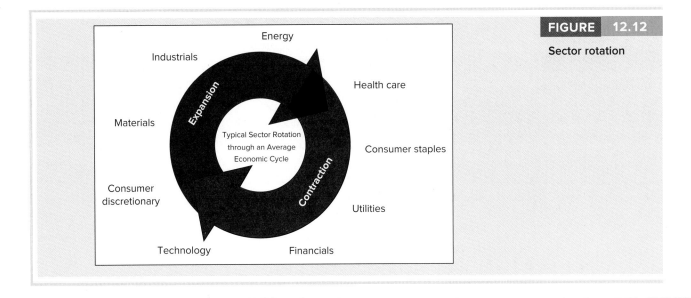

FIGURE 12.12

Sector rotation

Typical Sector Rotation through an Average Economic Cycle

The biotech industry is still new. Recently available technologies have created opportunities for the highly profitable investment of resources. New products are protected by patents, and profit margins are high. With such lucrative investment opportunities, firms find it advantageous to put all profits back into the firm. The companies grow rapidly on average.

Eventually, however, growth must slow. The high profit rates will induce new firms to enter the industry. Increasing competition will hold down prices and profit margins. New technologies become proven and more predictable, risk levels fall, and entry becomes even easier. As internal investment opportunities become less attractive, a lower fraction of profits is reinvested in the firm. Cash dividends increase.

Ultimately, in a mature industry, we observe "cash cows," firms with stable dividends and cash flows and little risk. Their growth rates might be similar to that of the overall economy. Industries in early stages of their life cycles offer high-risk/high-potential-return investments. Mature industries offer lower-risk, lower-return combinations.

industry life cycle

Stages through which firms typically pass as they mature.

This analysis suggests that a typical **industry life cycle** might be described by four stages: a start-up stage characterized by extremely rapid growth; a consolidation stage characterized by growth that is less rapid but still faster than that of the general economy; a maturity stage characterized by growth no faster than the general economy; and a stage of relative decline, in which the industry grows less rapidly than the rest of the economy or actually shrinks. This industry life cycle is illustrated in Figure 12.13. Let us turn to an elaboration of each of these stages.

START-UP STAGE   The early stages of an industry are often characterized by a new technology or product, such as desktop personal computers in the 1980s, cell phones in the 1990s, or the large-screen smartphones being introduced today. At this stage, it is difficult to predict which firms will emerge as industry leaders. Some firms will turn out to be wildly successful, and others will fail altogether. Therefore, there is considerable risk in selecting one particular firm within the industry. For example, in the smartphone industry, there is still a battle among competing technologies, such as Google's Android phones versus Apple's iPhone, and it is still difficult to predict ultimate market shares.

At the industry level, however, it is clear that sales and earnings will grow at an extremely rapid rate when the new product has not yet saturated its market. For example, in 2000 very few households had smartphones. The potential market for the product therefore was huge. In contrast to this situation, consider the market for a mature product such as refrigerators. Almost all households in the U.S. already have refrigerators, so the market for this good is primarily composed of households replacing old ones. Obviously, the growth rate in this market in the next decade will be far lower than for smartphones.

CONSOLIDATION STAGE   After a product becomes established, industry leaders begin to emerge. The survivors from the start-up stage are more stable, and market share is easier

FIGURE   12.13

The industry life cycle

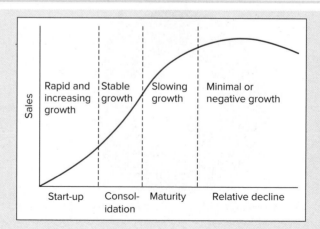

to predict. Therefore, the performance of the surviving firms will more closely track the performance of the overall industry. The industry still grows faster than the rest of the economy as the product penetrates the marketplace and becomes more commonly used.

MATURITY STAGE   At this point, the product has reached its potential for use by consumers. Further growth might merely track growth in the general economy. The product has become far more standardized, and producers are forced to compete to a greater extent on the basis of price. This leads to narrower profit margins and further pressure on profits. Firms at this stage sometimes are characterized as "cash cows," firms with reasonably stable cash flow but offering little opportunity for profitable expansion. The cash flow is best "milked from" rather than reinvested in the company.

We pointed to desktop personal computers as a start-up industry in the 1980s. By the mid-1990s it was a mature industry, with high market penetration, considerable price competition, low profit margins, and slowing sales. By the 1990s, desktops were progressively giving way to laptops, which were in their own start-up stage. Within a dozen years, laptops had in turn entered a maturity stage, with standardization, considerable market penetration, and dramatic price competition.

RELATIVE DECLINE   In this stage, the industry might grow at less than the rate of the overall economy, or it might even shrink. This could be due to obsolescence of the product, competition from new products, or competition from new low-cost suppliers; consider, for example, the steady displacement of desktops by laptops.

At which stage in the life cycle are investments in an industry most attractive? Conventional wisdom is that investors should seek firms in high-growth industries. This recipe for success is simplistic, however. If the security prices already reflect the likelihood for high growth, then it is too late to make money from that knowledge. Moreover, high growth and fat profits encourage competition from other producers. The exploitation of profit opportunities brings about new sources of supply that eventually reduce prices, profits, investment returns, and, finally, growth. This is the dynamic behind the progression from one stage of the industry life cycle to another. The famous portfolio manager Peter Lynch makes this point in *One Up on Wall Street*. He says:

> Many people prefer to invest in a high-growth industry, where there's a lot of sound and fury. Not me. I prefer to invest in a low-growth industry. . . . In a low-growth industry, especially one that's boring and upsets people [such as funeral homes or the oil-drum retrieval business], there's no problem with competition. You don't have to protect your flanks from potential rivals . . . and this gives [the individual firm] the leeway to continue to grow. [page 131]

In fact, Lynch uses an industry classification system in a very similar spirit to the life-cycle approach we have described. He places firms in the following six groups:

1. *Slow growers.* Large and aging companies that will grow only slightly faster than the broad economy. These firms have matured from their earlier fast-growth phase. They usually have steady cash flow and pay a generous dividend, indicating that the firm is generating more cash than can be profitably reinvested in the firm.

2. *Stalwarts.* Large, well-known firms like Coca-Cola or Colgate-Palmolive. They grow faster than the slow growers but are not in the very rapid growth start-up stage. They also tend to be in noncyclical industries that are relatively unaffected by recessions.

3. *Fast growers.* Small and aggressive new firms with annual growth rates in the neighborhood of 20% to 25%. Company growth can be due to broad industry growth or to an increase in market share in a more mature industry.

4. *Cyclicals.* These are firms with sales and profits that regularly expand and contract along with the business cycle. Examples are auto companies, steel companies, or the construction industry.

5. *Turnarounds.* These are firms that are in bankruptcy or soon might be. If they can recover from what might appear to be imminent disaster, they can offer tremendous

investment returns. A good example of this type of firm would be Chrysler in 1982, when it required a government guarantee on its debt to avoid bankruptcy. The stock price rose 15-fold in the next five years.

6. *Asset plays.* These are firms that have valuable assets not currently reflected in the stock price. For example, a company may own or be located on valuable real estate that is worth as much or more than the company's business enterprises. Sometimes the hidden asset can be tax-loss carryforwards. Other times the assets may be intangible. For example, a cable company might have a valuable list of cable subscribers. These assets do not immediately generate cash flow and so may be more easily overlooked by other analysts attempting to value the firm.

Industry Structure and Performance

The maturation of an industry involves regular changes in the firm's competitive environment. As a final topic, we examine the relationship between industry structure, competitive strategy, and profitability. Michael Porter (1980, 1985) has highlighted these five determinants of competition: threat of entry from new competitors, rivalry between existing competitors, price pressure from substitute products, the bargaining power of buyers, and the bargaining power of suppliers.

THREAT OF ENTRY   New entrants to an industry put pressure on price and profits. Even if a firm has not yet entered an industry, the potential for it to do so places pressure on prices because high prices and profit margins will encourage entry by new competitors. Therefore, barriers to entry can be a key determinant of industry profitability. Barriers can take many forms. For example, existing firms may already have secure distribution channels for their products based on long-standing relationships with customers or suppliers that would be costly for a new entrant to duplicate. Brand loyalty also makes it difficult for new entrants to penetrate a market and gives firms more pricing discretion. Proprietary knowledge or patent protection also may give firms advantages in serving a market. Finally, an existing firm's experience in a market may give it cost advantages due to the learning that takes place over time.

RIVALRY BETWEEN EXISTING COMPETITORS   When there are several competitors in an industry, there will generally be more price competition and lower profit margins as competitors seek to expand their share of the market. Slow industry growth contributes to this competition because expansion must come at the expense of a rival's market share. High fixed costs also create pressure to reduce prices for the reason that fixed costs put greater pressure on firms to operate near full capacity. Industries producing relatively homogeneous goods also are subject to considerable price pressure because firms cannot compete on the basis of product differentiation.

PRESSURE FROM SUBSTITUTE PRODUCTS   Substitute products mean that the industry faces competition from firms in related industries. For example, sugar producers compete with corn syrup producers. Wool producers compete with synthetic fiber producers. The availability of substitutes limits the prices that can be charged to customers.

BARGAINING POWER OF BUYERS   If a buyer purchases a large fraction of an industry's output, it will have considerable bargaining power and can demand price concessions. For example, auto producers can put pressure on suppliers of auto parts. This reduces the profitability of the auto parts industry.

BARGAINING POWER OF SUPPLIERS   If a supplier of a key input has monopolistic control over the product, it can demand higher prices for the good and squeeze profits out of the industry. One special case of this issue pertains to organized labor as a supplier of a key input to the production process. Labor unions engage in collective bargaining to increase the wages paid to workers. When the labor market is highly unionized, a significant share of the potential profits in the industry can be captured by the workforce.

The key factor determining the bargaining power of suppliers is the availability of substitute products. If substitutes are available, the supplier has little clout and cannot extract higher prices.

SUMMARY

- Macroeconomic policy aims to maintain the economy near full employment without aggravating inflationary pressures. The proper trade-off between these two goals is a source of ongoing debate.
- The traditional tools of macro policy are government spending and tax collection, which constitute fiscal policy, and manipulation of the money supply via monetary policy. Expansionary fiscal policy can stimulate the economy and increase GDP but tends to increase interest rates. Expansionary monetary policy works by lowering interest rates.
- The business cycle is the economy's recurring pattern of expansions and recessions. Leading economic indicators can be used to anticipate the evolution of the business cycle because their values tend to change before those of other key economic variables.
- Industries differ in their sensitivity to the business cycle. More sensitive industries tend to be those producing high-priced durable goods for which the consumer has considerable discretion as to the timing of purchase. Examples are automobiles or consumer durables. Other sensitive industries are those that produce capital equipment for other firms. Operating leverage and financial leverage increase sensitivity to the business cycle.

KEY TERMS

budget deficit, 374	fundamental analysis, 370	monetary policy, 377
business cycles, 379	gross domestic product	NAICS codes, 385
cyclical industries, 379	(GDP), 374	peak, 379
defensive industries, 379	industry life cycle, 390	sector rotation, 388
demand shock, 376	inflation, 374	supply shock, 376
exchange rate, 371	leading economic	trough, 379
fiscal policy, 377	indicators, 381	unemployment rate, 374

PROBLEM SETS

 Select problems are available in McGraw-Hill's *Connect*. Please see the Supplements section of the book's frontmatter for more information.

1. What are the differences between bottom-up and top-down approaches to security valuation? What are the advantages of a top-down approach? *(LO 12-1)*
2. Why does it make intuitive sense that the slope of the yield curve is considered a leading economic indicator? *(LO 12-2)*
3. Which one of the following firms would be described as having below-average sensitivity to the state of the economy? *(LO 12-3)*
   a. An asset play firm
   b. A cyclical firm
   c. A defensive firm
   d. A stalwart firm
4. The price of oil fell dramatically in 2015. What sort of macroeconomic shock would this be considered? *(LO 12-1)*
5. How do each of the following affect the sensitivity of profits to the business cycle? *(LO 12-3)*
   a. Financial leverage
   b. Operating leverage

6. The present value of a firm's projected cash flows are $15 million. The break-up value of the firm if you were to sell the major assets and divisions separately would be $20 million. This is an example of what Peter Lynch would call a(n):   *(LO 12-4)*
   a. Stalwart
   b. Slow-growth firm
   c. Turnaround
   d. Asset play

7. Define each of the following in the context of a business cycle.   *(LO 12-2)*
   a. Peak
   b. Contraction
   c. Trough
   d. Expansion

8. Which of the following is consistent with a steeply upwardly sloping yield curve?   *(LO 12-2)*
   a. Monetary policy is expansive and fiscal policy is expansive.
   b. Monetary policy is expansive while fiscal policy is restrictive.
   c. Monetary policy is restrictive and fiscal policy is restrictive.

9. Which of the following is *not* a governmental structural policy that supply-side economists believe would promote long-term growth in an economy?   *(LO 12-1)*
   a. A redistributive tax system.
   b. A promotion of competition.
   c. Minimal government interference in the economy.

10. What is typically true of corporate dividend payout rates in the early stages of an industry life cycle? Why does this make sense?   *(LO 12-4)*

11. If the nominal interest rate is 5% and the inflation rate is 3%, what is the real interest rate?   *(LO 12-1)*

12. ATech has fixed costs of $7 million and profits of $4 million. Its competitor, ZTech, is roughly the same size and this year earned the same profits, $4 million. But it operates with fixed costs of $5 million and lower variable costs.   *(LO 12-3)*
    a. Which firm has higher operating leverage?
    b. Which firm will likely have higher profits if the economy strengthens?

13. Choose an industry and identify the factors that will determine its performance in the next three years. What is your forecast for performance in that time period?   *(LO 12-3)*

14. What monetary and fiscal policies might be prescribed for an economy in a deep recession?   *(LO 12-1)*

15. If you believe the U.S. dollar is about to depreciate more dramatically than do other investors, what will be your stance on investments in U.S. auto producers?   *(LO 12-1)*

16. Unlike other investors, you believe the Fed is going to dramatically loosen monetary policy. What would be your recommendations about investments in the following industries?   *(LO 12-1)*
    a. Gold mining
    b. Construction

17. Consider two firms producing smartphones. One uses a highly automated robotics process, while the other uses human workers on an assembly line and pays overtime when there is heavy production demand.   *(LO 12-3)*
    a. Which firm will have higher profits in a recession?
    b. In a boom?
    c. Which firm's stock will have a higher beta?

18. According to supply-side economists, what will be the long-run impact on prices of a reduction in income tax rates?   *(LO 12-1)*

19. Here are four industries and four forecasts for the macroeconomy. Choose the industry that you would expect to perform best in each scenario.   *(LO 12-3)*

    Industries: housing construction, health care, gold mining, steel production.

Economic Forecasts:

Deep recession: falling inflation, falling interest rates, falling GDP.

Superheated economy: rapidly rising GDP, increasing inflation and interest rates.

Healthy expansion: rising GDP, mild inflation, low unemployment.

Stagflation: falling GDP, high inflation.

20. For each pair of firms, choose the one that you think would be more sensitive to the business cycle. *(LO 12-3)*
    a. General Autos or General Pharmaceuticals
    b. Friendly Airlines or Happy Cinemas

21. In which stage of the industry life cycle would you place the following industries? (*Warning:* There is considerable room for disagreement concerning the "correct" answers to this question.) *(LO 12-4)*
    a. Oil well equipment
    b. Computer hardware
    c. Computer software
    d. Genetic engineering
    e. Railroads

22. Why do you think the index of consumer expectations is a useful leading indicator of the macroeconomy? (See Table 12.2.) *(LO 12-2)*

23. Why do you think the change in the index of labor cost per unit of output is a useful lagging indicator of the macroeconomy? (See Table 12.2.) *(LO 12-2)*

24. You have $5,000 to invest for the next year and are considering three alternatives:
    a. A money market fund with an average maturity of 30 days offering a current annualized yield of 3%.
    b. A one-year savings deposit at a bank offering an interest rate of 4.5%.
    c. A 20-year U.S. Treasury bond offering a yield to maturity of 6% per year.

    What role does your forecast of future interest rates play in your decision? *(LO 12-1)*

25. General Weedkillers dominates the chemical weed control market with its patented product Weed-ex. The patent is about to expire, however. What are your forecasts for changes in the industry? Specifically, what will happen to industry prices, sales, the profit prospects of General Weedkillers, and the profit prospects of its competitors? What stage of the industry life cycle do you think is relevant for the analysis of this market? *(LO 12-4)*

Use the following case in answering Problems 26–28: Institutional Advisors for All Inc. (IAAI) is a consulting firm that primarily advises all types of institutions such as foundations, endowments, pension plans, and insurance companies. IAAI also provides advice to a select group of individual investors with large portfolios. One of the claims the firm makes in its advertising is that IAAI devotes considerable resources to forecasting and determining long-term trends; then it uses commonly accepted investment models to determine how these trends should affect the performance of various investments. The members of the research department of IAAI recently reached some conclusions concerning some important macroeconomic trends. For instance, they have seen an upward trend in job creation and consumer confidence and predict that this should continue for the next few years. Other domestic leading indicators that the research department at IAAI wishes to consider are industrial production, average weekly hours in manufacturing, S&P 500 stock prices, M2 money supply, and the index of consumer expectations.

In light of the predictions for job creation and consumer confidence, the investment advisers at IAAI want to make recommendations for their clients. They use established theories that relate job creation and consumer confidence to inflation and interest rates and then incorporate the forecast movements in inflation and interest rates into established models for explaining asset prices. Their primary concern is to forecast how the trends in job creation and consumer confidence should affect bond prices and how those trends should affect stock prices.

The members of the research department at IAAI also note that stocks have been trending up in the past year, and this information is factored into the forecasts of the overall economy that they deliver. The researchers consider an upward-trending stock market a positive economic indicator in itself; however, they disagree as to the reason this should be the case.

KAPLAN

SCHWESER

26. The researchers at IAAI have forecast positive trends for both job creation and consumer confidence. Which, if either, of these trends should have a positive effect on stock prices? *(LO 12-1)*

27. Stock prices are useful as a leading indicator. To explain this phenomenon, which of the following is *most* accurate? Stock prices: *(LO 12-2)*
    a. Predict future interest rates and reflect the trends in other indicators.
    b. Do not predict future interest rates, nor are they correlated with other leading indicators; the usefulness of stock prices as a leading indicator is a mystery.
    c. Reflect the trends in other leading indicators only and do not have predictive power of their own.

28. Which of the domestic series that the IAAI research department listed for use as leading indicators is *least* appropriate? *(LO 12-2)*
    a. Industrial production
    b. Manufacturing average weekly hours
    c. M2 money supply

Use the following case in answering Problems 29–32: Mary Smith, a Level II CFA candidate, was recently hired for an analyst position at the Bank of Ireland. Her first assignment is to examine the competitive strategies employed by various French wineries.

Smith's report identifies four wineries that are the major players in the French wine industry. Key characteristics of each are cited in Table 12.6. In the body of Smith's report, she includes a discussion of the competitive structure of the French wine industry. She notes that over the past five years, the French wine industry has not responded to changing consumer tastes. Profit margins have declined steadily, and the number of firms representing the industry has decreased from 10 to 4. It appears that participants in the French wine industry must consolidate to survive.

Smith's report notes that French consumers have strong bargaining power over the industry. She supports this conclusion with five key points, which she labels "Bargaining Power of Buyers":

- Many consumers are drinking more beer than wine with meals and at social occasions.
- Increasing sales over the Internet have allowed consumers to better research the wines, read opinions from other customers, and identify which producers have the best prices.
- The French wine industry is consolidating and consists of only four wineries today compared to 10 wineries five years ago.
- More than 65% of the business for the French wine industry consists of purchases from restaurants. Restaurants typically make purchases in bulk, buying four to five cases of wine at a time.
- Land where the soil is fertile enough to grow grapes necessary for the wine production process is scarce in France.

After completing the first draft of her report, Smith takes it to her boss, Ron VanDriesen, to review. VanDriesen tells her that he is a wine connoisseur himself and often makes purchases from the South Winery. Smith tells VanDriesen, "In my report I have classified the South Winery as a stuck-in-the-middle firm. It tries to be a cost leader by selling its wine at a price

TABLE 12.6   Characteristics of four major French wineries

	South Winery	North Winery	East Winery	West Winery
Founding date	1750	1903	1812	1947
Generic competitive strategy	?	Cost leadership	Cost leadership	Cost leadership
Major customer market (more than 80% concentration)	France	France	England	U.S.
Production site	France	France	France	France

that is slightly below the other firms, but it also tries to differentiate itself from its competitors by producing wine in bottles with curved necks, which increases its cost structure. The end result is that the South Winery's profit margin gets squeezed from both sides." VanDriesen replies, "I have met members of the management team from the South Winery at a couple of the wine conventions I have attended. I believe that the South Winery could succeed at following both a cost leadership and a differentiation strategy if its operations were separated into distinct operating units, with each unit pursuing a different competitive strategy." Smith makes a note to do more research on generic competitive strategies to verify VanDriesen's assertions before publishing the final draft of her report.

29. If the French home currency were to greatly appreciate in value compared to the English currency, what is the likely impact on the competitive position of the East Winery? *(LO 12-1)*
    a. Make the firm less competitive in the English market.
    b. No impact because the major market for East Winery is England, not France.
    c. Make the firm more competitive in the English market.

30. Which of Smith's points effectively support the conclusion that consumers have strong bargaining power over the industry? *(LO 12-4)*

31. Smith notes in her report that the West Winery might differentiate its wine product on attributes that buyers perceive to be important. Which of the following attributes would be the *most likely* area of focus for the West Winery to create a differentiated product? *(LO 12-4)*
    a. The method of delivery for the product
    b. The price of the product
    c. A focus on customers aged 30 to 45

32. Smith knows that a firm's generic strategy should be the centerpiece of a firm's strategic plan. On the basis of a compilation of research and documents, Smith makes three observations about the North Winery and its strategic planning process:
    i. North Winery's price and cost forecasts account for future changes in the structure of the French wine industry.
    ii. North Winery places each of its business units into one of three categories: build, hold, or harvest.
    iii. North Winery uses market share as the key measure of its competitive position.

    Which of these observation(s) *least* support the conclusion that the North Winery's strategic planning process is guided and informed by its generic competitive strategy? *(LO 12-4)*

Challenge

33. OceanGate sells external hard drives for $200 each. Its total fixed costs are $30 million, and its variable costs per unit are $140. The corporate tax rate is 30%. If the economy is strong, the firm will sell 2 million drives, but if there is a recession, it will sell only half as many. *(LO 12-3)*
    a. What will be the percentage decline in sales if the economy enters a recession?
    b. What will be the percentage decline in profits if the economy enters a recession?
    c. Comparing your answers to (a) and (b), how would you measure the operating leverage of this firm?

CFA Problems

1. As a securities analyst you have been asked to review a valuation of a closely held business, Wigwam Autoparts Heaven, Inc. (WAH), prepared by the Red Rocks Group (RRG). You are to give an opinion on the valuation and to support your opinion by analyzing each part of the valuation. WAH's sole business is automotive parts retailing. The RRG valuation includes a section called "Analysis of the Retail Auto Parts Industry," based completely on the data in Table 12.7 and the following additional information:
   - WAH and its principal competitors each operated more than 150 stores at year-end 2013.
   - The average number of stores operated per company engaged in the retail auto parts industry is 5.3.

TABLE 12.7   Selected retail auto parts industry data

	2013	2012	2011	2010	2009	2008	2007	2006	2005	2004
Population 18–29 years old (percentage change)	−1.8%	−2.0%	−2.1%	−1.4%	−0.8%	−0.9%	−1.1%	−0.9%	−0.7%	−0.3%
Number of households with income more than $40,000 (percentage change)	6.0%	4.0%	8.0%	4.5%	2.7%	3.1%	1.6%	3.6%	4.2%	2.2%
Number of households with income less than $40,000 (percentage change)	3.0%	−1.0%	4.9%	2.3%	−1.4%	2.5%	1.4%	−1.3%	0.6%	0.1%
Number of cars 5–15 years old (percentage change)	0.9%	−1.3%	−6.0%	1.9%	3.3%	2.4%	−2.3%	−2.2%	−8.0%	1.6%
Automotive aftermarket industry retail sales (percentage change)	5.7%	1.9%	3.1%	3.7%	4.3%	2.6%	1.3%	0.2%	3.7%	2.4%
Consumer expenditures on automotive parts and accessories (percentage change)	2.4%	1.8%	2.1%	6.5%	3.6%	9.2%	1.3%	6.2%	6.7%	6.5%
Sales growth of retail auto parts companies with 100 or more stores	17.0%	16.0%	16.5%	14.0%	15.5%	16.8%	12.0%	15.7%	19.0%	16.0%
Market share of retail auto parts companies with 100 or more stores	19.0%	18.5%	18.3%	18.1%	17.0%	17.2%	17.0%	16.9%	15.0%	14.0%
Average operating margin of retail auto parts companies with 100 or more stores	12.0%	11.8%	11.2%	11.5%	10.6%	10.6%	10.0%	10.4%	9.8%	9.0%
Average operating margin of all retail auto parts companies	5.5%	5.7%	5.6%	5.8%	6.0%	6.5%	7.0%	7.2%	7.1%	7.2%

- The major customer base for auto parts sold in retail stores consists of young owners of old vehicles. These owners do their own automotive maintenance out of economic necessity. *(LO 12-1)*
  a. One of RRG's conclusions is that the retail auto parts industry as a whole is in the maturity stage of the industry life cycle. Discuss three relevant items of data from Table 12.7 that support this conclusion.
  b. Another RRG conclusion is that WAH and its principal competitors are in the consolidation stage of their life cycle. Cite three items from Table 12.7 that suggest this conclusion. How can WAH be in a consolidation stage while its industry is in a maturity stage?
2. Universal Auto is a large multinational corporation headquartered in the United States. For segment reporting purposes, the company is engaged in two businesses: production of motor vehicles and information processing services.

   The motor vehicle business is by far the larger of Universal's two segments. It consists mainly of domestic United States passenger car production, but it also includes small truck manufacturing operations in the United States and passenger car production in other countries. This segment of Universal has had weak operating results for the past several years, including a large loss in 2015. Although the company does not reveal the operating results of its domestic passenger car segments, that part of Universal's business is generally believed to be primarily responsible for the weak performance of its motor vehicle segment.

Idata, the information processing services segment of Universal, was started by Universal about 15 years ago. This business has shown strong, steady growth that has been entirely internal: No acquisitions have been made.

An excerpt from a research report on Universal prepared by Paul Adams, a CFA candidate, states: "Based on our assumption that Universal will be able to increase prices significantly on U.S. passenger cars in 2016, we project a multibillion-dollar profit improvement . . ." *(LO 12-4)*

a. Discuss the concept of an industrial life cycle by describing each of its four phases.

b. Identify where each of Universal's two primary businesses—passenger cars and information processing—is in such a cycle.

c. Discuss how product pricing should differ between Universal's two businesses, based on the location of each in the industrial life cycle.

3. Adams's research report (see the previous problem) continued as follows: "With a business expansion already under way, the expected profit surge should lead to a much higher price for Universal Auto stock. We strongly recommend purchase." *(LO 12-3)*

a. Discuss the business-cycle approach to investment timing. (Your answer should describe actions to be taken on both stocks and bonds at different points over a typical business cycle.)

b. Assuming Adams's assertion is correct (that a business expansion is already under way), evaluate the timeliness of his recommendation to purchase Universal Auto, a cyclical stock, based on the business-cycle approach to investment timing.

4. Janet Ludlow is preparing a report on U.S.-based manufacturers in the electric toothbrush industry and has gathered the information shown in Tables 12.8 and 12.9. Ludlow's report concludes that the electric toothbrush industry is in the maturity (i.e., late) phase of its industry life cycle. *(LO 12-4)*

a. Select and justify three factors from Table 12.8 that support Ludlow's conclusion.

b. Select and justify three factors from Table 12.9 that refute Ludlow's conclusion.

5. The following questions have appeared on CFA examinations. *(LO 12-1)*

a. Which one of the following statements *best* expresses the central idea of counter-cyclical fiscal policy?

TABLE 12.8   Ratios for electric toothbrush industry index and broad stock market index

Year	2008	2009	2010	2011	2012	2013
Return on equity						
Electric toothbrush industry index	12.5%	12.0%	15.4%	19.6%	21.6%	21.6%
Market index	10.2	12.4	14.6	19.9	20.4	21.2
Average P/E						
Electric toothbrush industry index	28.5 ×	23.2 ×	19.6 ×	18.7 ×	18.5 ×	16.2 ×
Market index	10.2	12.4	14.6	19.9	18.1	19.1
Dividend payout ratio						
Electric toothbrush industry index	8.8%	8.0%	12.1%	12.1%	14.3%	17.1%
Market index	39.2	40.1	38.6	43.7	41.8	39.1
Average dividend yield						
Electric toothbrush industry index	0.3%	0.3%	0.6%	0.7%	0.8%	1.0%
Market index	3.8	3.2	2.6	2.2	2.3	2.1

TABLE 12.9   Characteristics of the electric toothbrush manufacturing industry

- **Industry sales growth**—Industry sales have grown at 15%–20% per year in recent years and are expected to grow at 10%–15% per year over the next three years.
- **Non-U.S. markets**—Some U.S. manufacturers are attempting to enter fast-growing non-U.S. markets, which remain largely unexploited.
- **Mail order sales**—Some manufacturers have created a new niche in the industry by selling electric toothbrushes directly to customers through mail order. Sales for this industry segment are growing at 40% per year.
- **U.S. market penetration**—The current penetration rate in the United States is 60% of households and will be difficult to increase.
- **Price competition**—Manufacturers compete fiercely on the basis of price, and price wars within the industry are common.
- **Niche markets**—Some manufacturers are able to develop new, unexploited niche markets in the United States based on company reputation, quality, and service.
- **Industry consolidation**—Several manufacturers have recently merged, and it is expected that consolidation in the industry will increase.
- **New entrants**—New manufacturers continue to enter the market.

(1) Planned government deficits are appropriate during economic booms, and planned surpluses are appropriate during economic recessions.
(2) The balanced-budget approach is the proper criterion for determining annual budget policy.
(3) Actual deficits should equal actual surpluses during a period of deflation.
(4) Government deficits are planned during economic recessions, and surpluses are utilized to restrain inflationary booms.

b. Which *one* of the following propositions would a strong proponent of supply-side economics be *most* likely to stress?
(1) Higher marginal tax rates will lead to a reduction in the size of the budget deficit and lower interest rates because they expand government revenues.
(2) Higher marginal tax rates promote economic inefficiency and thereby retard aggregate output because they encourage investors to undertake low-productivity projects with substantial tax-shelter benefits.
(3) Income redistribution payments will exert little impact on real aggregate supply because they do not consume resources directly.
(4) A tax reduction will increase the disposable income of households. Thus, the primary impact of a tax reduction on aggregate supply will stem from the influence of the tax change on the size of the budget deficit or surplus.

WEB *master*

1. Use data from **finance.yahoo.com** to answer the following questions.
   a. Go to the *Investing* tab and click on *Industries.* Find the price/book ratios for Medical Instruments & Supplies and for Electric Utilities. Do the differences make sense in light of their different stages in the industry life cycle?
   b. Now look at each industry's price–earnings ratio and dividend yield. Again, do the differences make sense in light of their different stages in the industry life cycle?
2. This exercise will give you a chance to examine data on some of the leading economic indicators.
   a. Download the data for new privately owned housing units authorized by building permits from **www.census.gov/construction/bps**. Choose the seasonally adjusted data for the United States in an Excel format. Graph the "Total" series.
   b. Download the last five years of data for manufacturers' new orders of nondefense capital goods from the St. Louis Federal Reserve site at **research.stlouisfed.org/fred2/series/NEWORDER**. Graph the data.

c. Locate data for the average weekly hours of production workers in manufacturing, available at **www.bls.gov/lpc/lpcover.htm#Data**. Select the historical time series link, and then choose the *Index* data. Choose *Manufacturing* as the sector and *Average Weekly Hours* as the measure. Retrieve the report for the past five years. Create a graph of the data that shows the quarterly trend over the last five years.

d. The data series you retrieved are all leading economic indicators. Based on the tables and your graphs, what is your opinion of where the economy is heading in the near future?

12.1 The downturn in the auto industry will reduce the demand for the product in this economy. The economy will, at least in the short term, enter a recession. This would suggest that:

a. GDP will fall.

b. The unemployment rate will rise.

c. The government deficit will increase. Income tax receipts will fall, and government expenditures on social welfare programs probably will increase.

d. Interest rates should fall. The contraction in the economy will reduce the demand for credit. Moreover, the lower inflation rate will reduce nominal interest rates.

12.2 Expansionary fiscal policy coupled with expansionary monetary policy will stimulate the economy, with the loose monetary policy keeping down interest rates.

12.3 A traditional demand-side interpretation of the tax cuts is that the resulting increase in after-tax income increased consumption demand and stimulated the economy. A supply-side interpretation is that the reduction in marginal tax rates made it more attractive for businesses to invest and for individuals to work, thereby increasing economic output.

12.4 a. Newspapers will do best in an expansion when advertising volume is increasing.

b. Machine tools are a good investment at the trough of a recession, just as the economy is about to enter an expansion and firms may need to increase capacity.

c. Beverages are defensive investments, with demand that is relatively insensitive to the business cycle. Therefore, they are good investments if a recession is forecast.

d. Timber is a good investment at a peak period, when natural resource prices are high and the economy is operating at full capacity.

Learning Objectives

LO 13-1 Use financial statements and market comparables to estimate firm value.

LO 13-2 Calculate the intrinsic value of a firm using either a constant-growth or multistage dividend discount model.

LO 13-3 Assess the growth prospects of a firm, and relate growth opportunities to the P/E ratio.

LO 13-4 Value a firm using free cash flow models.

You saw in our discussion of market efficiency that finding undervalued securities is hardly easy. At the same time, there are enough chinks in the armor of the efficient market hypothesis that the search for such securities should not be dismissed out of hand. Moreover, it is the ongoing search for mispriced securities that maintains a nearly efficient market. Even minor mispricing would allow a stock market analyst to earn his salary.

This chapter describes the ways stock market analysts try to uncover mispriced securities. The models presented are those used by *fundamental analysts,* those analysts who use information concerning the current and prospective profitability of a company to assess its fair market value. Fundamental analysts are different from *technical analysts,* who largely use trend analysis to uncover trading opportunities.

We start with a discussion of alternative measures of the value of a company. From there, we progress to quantitative tools called *dividend discount models* that security analysts commonly use to measure the value of a firm as an ongoing concern. Next, we turn to price–earnings, or P/E, ratios, explaining why they are of such interest to analysts but also highlighting some of their shortcomings. We explain how P/E ratios are tied to dividend valuation models and, more generally, to the growth prospects of the firm.

We close the chapter with a discussion and extended example of free cash flow models used by analysts to value firms based on forecasts of the cash flows that will be generated from the firm's business endeavors. We apply the several valuation tools covered in the chapter to a real firm and find that there is some disparity in their conclusions—a conundrum that will confront any security analyst—and consider reasons for these discrepancies.

13.1   VALUATION BY COMPARABLES

The purpose of fundamental analysis is to identify stocks that are mispriced relative to some measure of "true" value that can be derived from observable financial data. Of course, true value can only be estimated. In practice, stock analysts use models to estimate the fundamental value of a corporation's stock from observable market data and from the financial statements of the firm and its competitors. These valuation models differ in the specific data they use and in the level of their theoretical sophistication. But, at their heart, most of them use the notion of valuation by comparables: They look at the relationship between price and various determinants of value for similar firms and then extrapolate that relationship to the firm in question.

The Securities and Exchange Commission provides information on U.S. companies at its EDGAR website, **www.sec.gov/edgar.shtml.** The SEC requires all public companies (except foreign companies and companies with less than $10 million in assets and 500 shareholders) to file registration statements, periodic reports, and other forms electronically through EDGAR. Many websites such as **finance.yahoo.com, money.msn.com,** and **finance.google.com** also provide analysis and data derived from the EDGAR reports.

Table 13.1 shows some financial highlights for Microsoft as well as some comparable data for other firms in the software applications industry. The price per share of Microsoft's common stock is $45.95, and the total market value or capitalization of those shares (called *market cap* for short) is $378.6 billion. Under the heading "Valuation," Table 13.1 shows the ratio of Microsoft's stock price to five benchmarks. Its share price is 18.0 times its (per share) earnings in the most recent 12 months, 4.2 times its recent book value, 4.2 times its sales, and 11.7 times its cash flow. The last valuation ratio, PEG, is the P/E ratio divided by the growth rate of earnings. We would expect more rapidly growing firms to sell at higher multiples of *current* earnings (more on this to come), so PEG normalizes the P/E ratio by the growth rate.

These valuation ratios are commonly used to assess the valuation of one firm compared to others in the same industry, and we will consider all of them. The column to the right gives, where available, comparable ratios for other firms in the software applications industry. For example, an analyst might note that Microsoft's price/earnings ratio is a bit below the industry average. Microsoft's ratio of market value to **book value,** the net worth of the company

book value

The net worth of common equity according to a firm's balance sheet.

TABLE 13.1	Financial highlights for Microsoft	
Price per share	$45.95	
Common shares outstanding (billion)	8.24	
Market capitalization ($ billion)	378.64	
Latest 12 months		
Sales ($ billion)	91.5	
EBITDA ($ billion)	33.26	
Net income ($ billion)	21.37	
Earnings per share	$2.55	
Valuation	**Microsoft**	**Industry Avg**
Price/Earnings	18.0	19.4
Price/Book	4.2	7.0
Price/Sales	4.2	
Price/Cash flow	11.7	
PEG	2.6	
Profitability		
ROE (%)	24.9	21.8
ROA (%)	11.4	
Operating profit margin (%)	31.2	
Net profit margin (%)	23.4	20.5

Source: Compiled from data available at **finance.yahoo.com**, October 27, 2014.

as reported on the balance sheet, is also below industry norms, 4.2 versus 7.0. These ratios might indicate that its stock is underpriced. However, Microsoft is a more mature firm than many in the industry, and perhaps this discrepancy reflects a lower expected future growth rate. Clearly, rigorous valuation models will be necessary to sort through these sometimes conflicting signals of value.

Limitations of Book Value

Shareholders in a firm are sometimes called "residual claimants," which means that the value of their stake is what is left over when the liabilities of the firm are subtracted from its assets. Shareholders' equity is this net worth. However, the values of both assets and liabilities recognized in financial statements are based on historical—not current—values. For example, the book value of an asset equals the *original* cost of acquisition less some adjustment for depreciation, even if the market price of that asset has changed over time. Moreover, depreciation allowances are used to allocate the original cost of the asset over several years but do not reflect loss of actual value.

Whereas book values are based on original cost, market values measure *current* values of assets and liabilities. The market value of the shareholders' equity investment equals the difference between the current values of all assets and liabilities. We've emphasized that current values generally will not match historical ones. Equally or even more important, many assets such as the value of a good brand name or specialized expertise developed over many years may not even be included on the financial statements but certainly influence market price. Market prices reflect the value of the firm as a going concern.

Can book value represent a "floor" for the stock's price, below which level the market price can never fall? Although Microsoft's book value per share is considerably less than its market price, other evidence disproves this notion. While it is not common, there are always some firms selling at a market price below book value. In late 2014, for example, such troubled firms included Barclays, Citigroup, Mitsubishi, and Bank of America.

liquidation value

Net amount that can be realized by selling the assets of a firm and paying off the debt.

A better measure of a floor for the stock price is the firm's **liquidation value** per share. This represents the amount of money that could be realized by breaking up the firm, selling its assets, repaying its debt, and distributing the remainder to the shareholders. If the market price of equity drops below the liquidation value of the firm, the firm becomes attractive as a takeover target. A corporate raider would find it profitable to buy enough shares to gain control and then actually liquidate because the liquidation value exceeds the value of the business as a going concern.

replacement cost

Cost to replace a firm's assets.

Another measure of firm value is the **replacement cost** of assets less liabilities. Some analysts believe the market value of the firm cannot get too far above its replacement cost for long because, if it did, competitors would enter the market. The resulting competitive pressure would drive down the market value of all firms until they fell to replacement cost.

Tobin's q

Ratio of market value of the firm to replacement cost.

This idea is popular among economists, and the ratio of market price to replacement cost is known as **Tobin's q,** after the Nobel Prize–winning economist James Tobin. In the long run, according to this view, the ratio of market price to replacement cost will tend toward 1, but the evidence is that this ratio can differ significantly from 1 for very long periods of time.

Although focusing on the balance sheet can give some useful information about a firm's liquidation value or its replacement cost, the analyst usually must turn to expected future cash flows for a better estimate of the firm's value as a going concern. We therefore turn to the quantitative models that analysts use to value common stock based on forecasts of future earnings and dividends.

13.2   INTRINSIC VALUE VERSUS MARKET PRICE

The most popular model for assessing the value of a firm as a going concern starts from the observation that the return on a stock investment comprises cash dividends and capital gains or losses. We begin by assuming a one-year holding period and supposing that ABC stock has an expected dividend per share, $E(D_1)$, of \$4; that the current price of a share, P_0, is \$48; and that the expected price at the end of a year, $E(P_1)$, is \$52. For now, don't worry about how you derive your forecast of next year's price. At this point we ask only whether the stock seems attractively priced *today* given your forecast of *next year's* price.

The expected holding-period return is $E(D_1)$ plus the expected price appreciation, $E(P_1) - P_0$, all divided by the current price P_0.

$$\text{Expected HPR} = E(r) = \frac{E(D_1) + [E(P_1) - P_0]}{P_0}$$

$$= \frac{4 + (52 - 48)}{48} = .167 = 16.7\%$$

Note that $E(\ )$ denotes an expected future value. Thus, $E(P_1)$ represents the expectation today of the stock price one year from now. $E(r)$ is referred to as the stock's expected holding-period return. It is the sum of the expected dividend yield, $E(D_1)/P_0$, and the expected rate of price appreciation, the capital gains yield, $[E(P_1) - P_0]/P_0$.

But what is the required rate of return for ABC stock? The capital asset pricing model (CAPM) asserts that when stock market prices are at equilibrium levels, the rate of return that investors can expect to earn on a security is $r_f + \beta[E(r_M) - r_f]$. Thus, the CAPM may be viewed as providing an estimate of the rate of return an investor can reasonably expect to earn on a security given its risk as measured by beta. This is the return that investors will require of any other investment with equivalent risk. We will denote this required rate of return as k. If a stock is priced "correctly," it will offer investors a "fair" return, that is, its *expected* return will equal its *required* return. Of course, the goal of a security analyst is to find stocks that are mispriced. For example, an underpriced stock will provide an expected return greater than the required return.

Suppose that $r_f = 6\%$, $E(r_M) - r_f = 5\%$, and the beta of ABC is 1.2. Then the value of k is

$$k = 6\% + 1.2 \times 5\% = 12\%$$

The rate of return the investor expects exceeds the required rate based on ABC's risk by a margin of 4.7%. Naturally, the investor will want to include more of ABC stock in the portfolio than a passive strategy would dictate.

Another way to see this is to compare the intrinsic value of a share of stock to its market price. The **intrinsic value,** denoted V_0, of a share of stock is defined as the present value of all cash payments to the investor in the stock, including dividends as well as the proceeds from the ultimate sale of the stock, discounted at the appropriate risk-adjusted interest rate, k. Whenever the intrinsic value, or the investor's own estimate of what the stock is really worth, exceeds the market price, the stock is considered undervalued and a good investment. For ABC, using a one-year investment horizon and a forecast that the stock can be sold at the end of the year at price $P_1 = \$52$, the intrinsic value is

intrinsic value
The present value of a firm's expected future net cash flows discounted by the required rate of return.

$$V_0 = \frac{E(D_1) + E(P_1)}{1 + k} = \frac{\$4 + \$52}{1.12} = \$50$$

Equivalently, at a price of \$50, the investor would derive a 12% rate of return—just equal to the required rate of return—on an investment in the stock. However, at the current price of \$48, the stock is underpriced compared to intrinsic value. At this price, it provides better than a fair rate of return relative to its risk. Using the terminology of the CAPM, it is a positive-alpha stock, and investors will want to buy more of it than they would following a passive strategy.

In contrast, if the intrinsic value turns out to be lower than the current market price, investors should buy less of it than under the passive strategy. It might even pay to go short on ABC stock, as we discussed in Chapter 3.

In market equilibrium, the current market price will reflect the intrinsic value estimates of all market participants. This means the individual investor whose V_0 estimate differs from the market price, P_0, in effect must disagree with some or all of the market-consensus estimates of $E(D_1)$, $E(P_1)$, or k. A common term for the market-consensus value of the required rate of return, k, is the **market capitalization rate,** which we use often throughout this chapter.

market capitalization rate
The market-consensus estimate of the appropriate discount rate for a firm's cash flows.

You expect the price of IBX stock to be $59.77 per share a year from now. Its current market price is $50, and you expect it to pay a dividend one year from now of $2.15 per share.

    a. What are the stock's expected dividend yield, rate of price appreciation, and expected holding-period return?

    b. If the stock has a beta of 1.15, the risk-free rate is 6% per year, and the expected rate of return on the market portfolio is 14% per year, what is the required rate of return on IBX stock?

    c. What is the intrinsic value of IBX stock, and how does it compare to the current market price?

13.3 DIVIDEND DISCOUNT MODELS

Consider an investor who buys a share of Steady State Electronics stock, planning to hold it for one year. The intrinsic value of the share is the present value of the dividend to be received at the end of the first year, D_1, and the expected sales price, P_1. We will henceforth use the simpler notation P_1 instead of $E(P_1)$ to avoid clutter. Keep in mind, though, that future prices and dividends are unknown, and we are dealing with expected values, not certain values. We've already established that

$$V_0 = \frac{D_1 + P_1}{1 + k} \tag{13.1}$$

While this year's dividend is fairly predictable given a company's history, you might ask how we can estimate P_1, the year-end price. According to Equation 13.1, V_1 (the year-end value) will be

$$V_1 = \frac{D_2 + P_2}{1 + k}$$

If we assume the stock will be selling for its intrinsic value next year, then $V_1 = P_1$, and we can substitute this value for P_1 into Equation 13.1 to find

$$V_0 = \frac{D_1}{1 + k} + \frac{D_2 + P_2}{(1 + k)^2}$$

This equation may be interpreted as the present value of dividends plus sales price for a two-year holding period. Of course, now we need to come up with a forecast of P_2. Continuing in the same way, we can replace P_2 by $(D_3 + P_3)/(1 + k)$, which relates P_0 to the value of dividends plus the expected sales price for a three-year holding period.

More generally, for a holding period of H years, we can write the stock value as the present value of dividends over the H years plus the ultimate sales price, P_H.

$$V_0 = \frac{D_1}{1 + k} + \frac{D_2}{(1 + k)^2} + \cdots + \frac{D_H + P_H}{(1 + k)^H} \tag{13.2}$$

Note the similarity between this formula and the bond valuation formula developed in Chapter 10. Each relates price to the present value of a stream of payments (coupons in the case of bonds, dividends in the case of stocks) and a final payment (the face value of the bond or the sales price of the stock). The key differences in the case of stocks are the uncertainty of dividends, the lack of a fixed maturity date, and the unknown sales price at the horizon date. Indeed, one can continue to substitute for price indefinitely to conclude

$$V_0 = \frac{D_1}{1 + k} + \frac{D_2}{(1 + k)^2} + \frac{D_3}{(1 + k)^3} + \cdots \tag{13.3}$$

dividend discount model (DDM)

A formula for the intrinsic value of a firm equal to the present value of all expected future dividends.

Equation 13.3 states the stock price should equal the present value of all expected future dividends into perpetuity. This formula is called the **dividend discount model (DDM)** of stock prices.

It is tempting, but incorrect, to conclude from Equation 13.3 that the DDM focuses exclusively on dividends and ignores capital gains as a motive for investing in stock. Indeed, we assume explicitly in Equation 13.1 that capital gains (as reflected in the expected sales price, P_1) are part of the stock's value. At the same time, the price at which you can sell a stock in the future depends on dividend forecasts at that time.

The reason only dividends appear in Equation 13.3 is not that investors ignore capital gains. It is instead that those capital gains will reflect dividend forecasts at the time the stock is sold. That is why in Equation 13.2 we can write the stock price as the present value of dividends plus sales price for *any* horizon date. P_H is the present value at time H of all dividends expected to be paid after the horizon date. That value is then discounted back to today, time 0. The DDM asserts that stock prices are determined ultimately by the cash flows accruing to stockholders, and those are dividends.

The Constant-Growth DDM

Equation 13.3 as it stands is still not very useful in valuing a stock because it requires dividend forecasts for every year into the indefinite future. To make the DDM practical, we need to introduce some simplifying assumptions. A useful and common first pass at the problem is to assume that dividends are trending upward at a stable growth rate that we will call g. For example, if $g = .05$ and the most recently paid dividend was $D_0 = 3.81$, expected future dividends are

$$D_1 = D_0(1 + g) = 3.81 \times 1.05 = 4.00$$
$$D_2 = D_0(1 + g)^2 = 3.81 \times (1.05)^2 = 4.20$$
$$D_3 = D_0(1 + g)^3 = 3.81 \times (1.05)^3 = 4.41 \text{ etc.}$$

Using these dividend forecasts in Equation 13.3, we solve for intrinsic value as

$$V_0 = \frac{D_0(1 + g)}{1 + k} + \frac{D_0(1 + g)^2}{(1 + k)^2} + \frac{D_0(1 + g)^3}{(1 + k)^3} + \cdots$$

This equation can be simplified to

$$V_0 = \frac{D_0(1 + g)}{k - g} = \frac{D_1}{k - g} \qquad (13.4)$$

Note in Equation 13.4 that we divide D_1 (not D_0) by $k - g$ to calculate intrinsic value. If the market capitalization rate for Steady State is 12%, we can use Equation 13.4 to show that the intrinsic value of a share of Steady State stock is

$$\frac{\$4.00}{.12 - .05} = \$57.14$$

Equation 13.4 is called the **constant-growth DDM** or the Gordon model, after Myron J. Gordon, who popularized the model. It should remind you of the formula for the present value of a perpetuity. If dividends were expected not to grow, then the dividend stream would be a simple perpetuity, and the valuation formula for such a nongrowth stock would be $P_0 = D_1/k$.[1] Equation 13.4 is a generalization of the perpetuity formula to cover the case of a *growing* perpetuity. As g increases, the stock price also rises.

constant-growth DDM

A form of the dividend discount model that assumes dividends will grow at a constant rate.

Preferred stock that pays a fixed dividend can be valued using the constant-growth dividend discount model. The constant growth rate of dividends is simply zero. For example, to value a preferred stock paying a fixed dividend of $2 per share when the discount rate is 8%, we compute

$$V_0 = \frac{\$2}{.08 - 0} = \$25$$

EXAMPLE 13.1

Preferred Stock and the DDM

---

[1]Recall from introductory finance that the present value of a $1-per-year perpetuity is $1/k$. For example, if $k = 10\%$, the value of the perpetuity is $1/.10 = 10$. Notice that if $g = 0$ in Equation 13.4, the constant-growth DDM formula is the same as the perpetuity formula.

EXAMPLE 13.2

The Constant-Growth DDM

High Flyer Industries has just paid its annual dividend of $3 per share. The dividend is expected to grow at a constant rate of 8% indefinitely. The beta of High Flyer stock is 1, the risk-free rate is 6%, and the market risk premium is 8%. What is the intrinsic value of the stock? What would be your estimate of intrinsic value if you believed that the stock was riskier, with a beta of 1.25?

Because a $3 dividend has just been paid and the growth rate of dividends is 8%, the forecast for the year-end dividend is $3 × 1.08 = $3.24. The market capitalization rate (using the CAPM) is 6% + 1.0 × 8% = 14%. Therefore, the value of the stock is

$$V_0 = \frac{D_1}{k - g} = \frac{\$3.24}{.14 - .08} = \$54$$

If the stock is perceived to be riskier, its value must be lower. At the higher beta, the market capitalization rate is 6% + 1.25 × 8% = 16%, and the stock is worth only

$$\frac{\$3.24}{.16 - .08} = \$40.50$$

The constant-growth DDM is valid only when g is less than k. If dividends were expected to grow forever at a rate faster than k, the value of the stock would be infinite. If an analyst derives an estimate of g that is greater than k, that growth rate must be unsustainable in the long run. The appropriate valuation model to use in this case is a multistage DDM such as those discussed below.

The constant-growth DDM is so widely used by stock market analysts that it is worth exploring some of its implications and limitations. The constant growth rate DDM implies that a stock's value will be greater:

1. The larger its expected dividend per share.
2. The lower the market capitalization rate, k.
3. The higher the expected growth rate of dividends.

Another implication of the constant-growth model is that the stock price is expected to grow at the same rate as dividends. To see this, suppose Steady State stock is selling at its intrinsic value of $57.14, so that $V_0 = P_0$. Then

$$P_0 = \frac{D_1}{k - g}$$

Note that price is proportional to dividends. Therefore, next year, when the dividends paid to Steady State stockholders are expected to be higher by $g = 5\%$, price also should increase by 5%. To confirm this, we can write

$$D_2 = \$4(1.05) = \$4.20$$

$$P_1 = D_2/(k - g) = \$4.20/(.12 - .05) = \$60.00$$

which is 5% higher than the current price of $57.14. To generalize

$$P_1 = \frac{D_2}{k - g} = \frac{D_1(1 + g)}{k - g} = \frac{D_1}{k - g}(1 + g) = P_0(1 + g)$$

Therefore, the DDM implies that, in the case of constant expected growth of dividends, the expected rate of price appreciation in any year will equal that constant growth rate, g. For a stock whose market price equals its intrinsic value ($V_0 = P_0$), the expected holding-period return will be

$$E(r) = \text{Dividend yield} + \text{Capital gains yield}$$

$$= \frac{D_1}{P_0} + \frac{P_1 - P_0}{P_0} = \frac{D_1}{P_0} + g \tag{13.5}$$

This formula offers a means to infer the market capitalization rate of a stock, for if the stock is selling at its intrinsic value, then $E(r) = k$, implying that $k = D_1/P_0 + g$. By observing the dividend yield, D_1/P_0, and estimating the growth rate of dividends, we can compute k. This equation is known also as the *discounted cash flow (DCF) formula*.

   This is an approach often used in rate hearings for regulated public utilities. The regulatory agency responsible for approving utility pricing decisions is mandated to allow the firms to charge just enough to cover costs plus a "fair" profit, that is, one that allows a competitive return on the investment the firm has made in its productive capacity. In turn, that return is taken to be the expected return investors require on the stock of the firm. The $D_1/P_0 + g$ formula provides a means to infer that required return.

EXAMPLE 13.3

The Constant-Growth Model

Suppose that Steady State Electronics wins a major contract for its revolutionary computer chip. The very profitable contract will enable it to increase the growth rate of dividends from 5% to 6% without reducing the current dividend from the projected value of $4 per share. What will happen to the stock price? What will happen to future expected rates of return on the stock?

   The stock price ought to increase in response to the good news about the contract, and indeed it does. The stock price jumps from its original value of $57.14 to a postannouncement price of

$$\frac{D_1}{k - g} = \frac{\$4}{.12 - .06} = \$66.67$$

Investors who are holding the stock when the good news about the contract is announced will receive a substantial windfall.

   On the other hand, at the new price the expected rate of return on the stock is 12%, just as it was before the new contract was announced.

$$E(r) = \frac{D_1}{P_0} + g = \frac{\$4}{\$66.67} + .06 = .12, \text{ or } 12\%$$

This result makes sense, of course. Once the news about the contract is reflected in the stock price, the expected rate of return will be consistent with the risk of the stock. Because the risk of the stock has not changed, neither should the expected rate of return.

CONCEPT check 13.2

a. IBX's stock dividend at the end of this year is expected to be $2.15, and it is expected to grow at 11.2% per year forever. If the required rate of return on IBX stock is 15.2% per year, what is its intrinsic value?

b. If IBX's current market price is equal to this intrinsic value, what is next year's expected price?

c. If an investor were to buy IBX stock now and sell it after receiving the $2.15 dividend a year from now, what is the expected capital gain (i.e., price appreciation) in percentage terms? What is the dividend yield, and what would be the holding-period return?

Stock Prices and Investment Opportunities

Consider two companies, Cash Cow, Inc., and Growth Prospects, each with expected earnings in the coming year of $5 per share. Both companies could in principle pay out all of these earnings as dividends, maintaining a perpetual dividend flow of $5 per share. If the market capitalization rate were $k = 12.5\%$, both companies would then be valued at $D_1/k = \$5/.125 = \$40$ per share. Neither firm would grow in value, because with all earnings paid out as dividends, and no earnings reinvested in the firm, both companies' capital stock and earnings capacity would remain unchanged over time; earnings[2] and dividends would not grow.

---

[2]Actually, we are referring here to earnings net of the funds necessary to maintain the productivity of the firm's capital, that is, earnings net of "economic depreciation." In other words, the earnings figure should be interpreted as the maximum amount of money the firm could pay out each year in perpetuity without depleting its productive capacity. For this reason, the net earnings number may be quite different from the accounting earnings figure that the firm reports in its financial statements. We will explore this further in the next chapter.

FIGURE **13.1**

Dividend growth for two
earnings reinvestment
policies

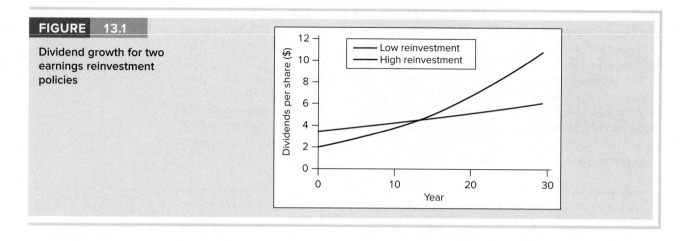

FIGURE **13.1**

Dividend growth for two
earnings reinvestment
policies

dividend payout ratio

Percentage of earnings paid
out as dividends.

**plowback ratio or earnings
retention ratio**

The proportion of the firm's
earnings that is reinvested in
the business (and not paid out
as dividends).

Now suppose one of the firms, Growth Prospects, engages in projects that generate a return on investment of 15%, which is greater than the required rate of return, $k = 12.5\%$. It would be foolish for such a company to pay out all of its earnings as dividends. If Growth Prospects retains or plows back some of its earnings into its highly profitable projects, it can earn a 15% rate of return for its shareholders, whereas if it pays out all earnings as dividends, it forgoes the projects, leaving shareholders to invest the dividends in other opportunities at a fair market rate of only 12.5%. Suppose, therefore, Growth Prospects chooses a lower **dividend payout ratio** (the fraction of earnings paid out as dividends), reducing payout from 100% to 40% and maintaining a **plowback ratio** (the fraction of earnings reinvested in the firm) of 60%. The plowback ratio also is referred to as the **earnings retention ratio.**

The dividend of the company, therefore, will be only $2 (40% of $5 earnings) instead of $5. Will the share price fall? No, it will rise! Although dividends initially fall under the earnings reinvestment policy, subsequent growth in the assets of the firm because of reinvested profits will generate growth in future dividends, which will be reflected in today's share price.

Figure 13.1 illustrates the dividend streams generated by Growth Prospects under two dividend policies. A low reinvestment rate plan allows the firm to pay higher initial dividends but results in a lower dividend growth rate. Eventually, a high reinvestment rate plan will provide higher dividends. If the dividend growth generated by the reinvested earnings is high enough, the stock will be worth more under the high reinvestment strategy.

How much growth will be generated? Suppose Growth Prospects starts with plant and equipment of $100 million and is all-equity-financed. With a return on investment or equity (ROE) of 15%, total earnings are ROE × $100 million = .15 × $100 million = $15 million. There are 3 million shares of stock outstanding, so earnings per share are $5, as posited above. If 60% of the $15 million in this year's earnings is reinvested, then the value of the firm's capital stock will increase by .60 × $15 million = $9 million, or by 9%. The percentage increase in the capital stock is the rate at which income was generated (ROE) times the plowback ratio (the fraction of earnings reinvested in more capital), which we will denote as b.

Now endowed with 9% more capital, the company earns 9% more income and pays out 9% higher dividends. The growth rate of the dividends, therefore, is[3]

$$g = \text{ROE} \times b = 15\% \times .60 = 9\%$$

---

[3]We can derive this relationship more generally by noting that with a fixed ROE, earnings (which equal ROE × Book value) will grow at the same rate as the book value of the firm. Abstracting from net new capital raised by the firm, the growth rate of book value equals reinvested earnings/book value. Therefore,

$$g = \frac{\text{Reinvested earnings}}{\text{Book value}} = \frac{\text{Reinvested earnings}}{\text{Total earnings}} \times \frac{\text{Total earnings}}{\text{Book value}} = b \times \text{ROE}$$

If the stock price equals its intrinsic value, and this growth rate can be sustained (i.e., if the ROE and payout ratios are consistent with the long-run capabilities of the firm), then the stock should sell at

$$P_0 = \frac{D_1}{k-g} = \frac{\$2}{.125 - .09} = \$57.14$$

When Growth Prospects pursued a no-growth policy and paid out all earnings as dividends, the stock price was only $40. Therefore, you can think of $40 as the value per share of the assets the company already has in place.

When Growth Prospects decided to reduce current dividends and reinvest some of its earnings in new investments, its stock price increased. The increase in the stock price reflects the fact that planned investments provide an expected rate of return greater than the required rate. In other words, the investment opportunities have positive net present value. The value of the firm rises by the NPV of these investment opportunities. This net present value is also called the **present value of growth opportunities (PVGO).**

present value of growth opportunities (PVGO)

Net present value of a firm's future investments.

Therefore, we can think of the value of the firm as the sum of the value of assets already in place, or the no-growth value of the firm, plus the net present value of the future investments the firm will make, which is the PVGO. For Growth Prospects, PVGO = $17.14 per share:

$$\text{Price} = \text{No-growth value per share} + \text{PVGO}$$
$$P_0 = \frac{E_1}{k} + \text{PVGO}$$
$$\$57.14 = \$40 + \$17.14 \qquad\qquad \textbf{(13.6)}$$

We know that, in reality, dividend cuts almost always are accompanied by steep drops in stock prices. Does this contradict our analysis? Not necessarily: Dividend cuts are usually taken as bad news about the future prospects of the firm, and it is the *new information* about the firm—not the reduced dividend yield per se—that is responsible for the stock price decline.

For example, when J.P. Morgan cut its quarterly dividend from 38 cents to 5 cents a share in 2009, its stock price actually increased by about 5%: The company was able to convince investors that the cut would conserve cash and prepare the firm to weather a severe recession. When investors were convinced that the dividend cut made sense, the stock price actually increased. Similarly, when BP announced in the wake of the massive 2010 Gulf oil spill that it would suspend dividends for the rest of the year, its stock price did not budge. The cut already had been widely anticipated, so it was not new information. These examples show that stock price declines in response to dividend cuts are really a response to the information conveyed by the cut.

It is important to recognize that growth per se is not what investors desire. Growth enhances company value only if it is achieved by investment in projects with attractive profit opportunities (i.e., with ROE > k). To see why, let's now consider Growth Prospects' unfortunate sister company, Cash Cow. Cash Cow's ROE is only 12.5%, just equal to the required rate of return, k. Therefore, the NPV of its investment opportunities is zero. We've seen that following a zero-growth strategy with b = 0 and g = 0, the value of Cash Cow will be $E_1/k = \$5/.125 = \$40$ per share. Now suppose Cash Cow chooses a plowback ratio of b = .60, the same as Growth Prospects' plowback. Then g would be

$$g = \text{ROE} \times b = .125 \times .60 = .075$$

but the stock price is still $40:

$$P_0 = \frac{D_1}{k-g} = \frac{\$2}{.125 - .075} = \$40$$

which is no different from the no-growth strategy.

In the case of Cash Cow, the dividend reduction that frees funds for reinvestment in the firm generates only enough growth to maintain the stock price at the current level. This is as it should be: If the firm's projects yield only what investors can earn on their own, then NPV is zero, and shareholders cannot be made better off by a high reinvestment rate policy. This demonstrates that "growth" is not the same as growth opportunities. To justify reinvestment, the firm must engage in projects with better prospective returns than those shareholders can find elsewhere. Notice also that the PVGO of Cash Cow is zero: PVGO = $P_0 - E_1/k = 40 - 40 = 0$. With ROE = $k,$ there is no advantage to plowing funds back into the firm; this shows up as PVGO of zero. In fact, this is why firms with considerable cash flow, but limited investment prospects, are called "cash cows." The cash these firms generate is best taken out of or "milked from" the firm.

EXAMPLE 13.4

Growth Opportunities

Takeover Target is run by entrenched management that insists on reinvesting 60% of its earnings in projects that provide an ROE of 10%, despite the fact that the firm's capitalization rate is $k = 15\%$. The firm's year-end dividend will be $2 per share, paid out of earnings of $5 per share. At what price will the stock sell? What is the present value of growth opportunities? Why would such a firm be a takeover target for another firm?

Given current management's investment policy, the dividend growth rate will be

$$g = \text{ROE} \times b = 10\% \times .6 = 6\%$$

and the stock price should be

$$P_0 = \frac{\$2}{.15 - .06} = \$22.22$$

The present value of growth opportunities is

$$\text{PVGO} = \text{Price per share} - \text{No-growth value per share}$$
$$= \$22.22 - E_1/k = \$22.22 - \$5/.15 = -\$11.11$$

PVGO is *negative*. This is because the net present value of the firm's projects is negative: The rate of return on those assets is less than the opportunity cost of capital.

Such a firm would be subject to takeover, because another firm could buy the firm for the market price of $22.22 per share and increase the value of the firm by changing its investment policy. For example, if the new management simply paid out all earnings as dividends, the value of the firm would increase to its no-growth value, $E_1/k = \$5/.15 = \$33.33$.

CONCEPT check 13.3

a. Calculate the price of a firm with a plowback ratio of .60 if its ROE is 20%. Current earnings, E_1, will be $5 per share, and $k = 12.5\%$.
b. What if ROE is 10%, which is less than the market capitalization rate? Compare the firm's price in this instance to that of a firm with the same ROE and E_1 but a plowback ratio of $b = 0$.

Life Cycles and Multistage Growth Models

As useful as the constant-growth DDM formula is, you need to remember that it is based on a simplifying assumption, namely, that the dividend growth rate will be constant forever. In fact, firms typically pass through life cycles with very different dividend profiles in different phases. In early years, there are ample opportunities for profitable reinvestment in the company. Payout ratios are low, and growth is correspondingly rapid. In later years, the firm matures, production capacity is sufficient to meet market demand, competitors enter the market, and attractive opportunities for reinvestment may become harder to find. In this mature phase, the firm may choose to increase the dividend payout ratio, rather than retain earnings. The dividend level increases, but thereafter it grows at a slower rate because the company has fewer growth opportunities.

Table 13.2 illustrates this profile. It gives Value Line's forecasts of return on capital, dividend payout ratio, and projected three-year growth rate in earnings per share of a sample of the firms included in the computer software and services industry versus those of East Coast

TABLE 13.2 Financial ratios in two industries

	Ticker	Return on Capital	Payout Ratio	Growth Rate 2016–2018
Computer software				
Adobe Systems	ADBE	13.0%	0.0%	44.2%
Cognizant	CTSH	18.5	0.0	22.2
Compuware	CPWR	12.5	72.0	20.5
Intuit	INTU	31.0	21.0	2.9
Microsoft	MSFT	23.5	45.0	13.3
Oracle	ORCL	21.0	17.0	10.5
Red Hat	RHT	14.5	0.0	10.5
PTC	PTC	17.0	0.0	9.6
SAP	SAP	16.0	33.0	10.2
Median		17.0%	17.0%	10.5%
Electric utilities (east coast)				
Dominion Resources	D	7.5%	71.0%	3.1%
Consolidated Edison	ED	5.5	64.0	2.5
Duke Energy	DUK	5.0	64.0	3.8
Northeast Utilities	NU	6.0	58.0	7.1
First Energy	FE	5.0	53.0	1.7
Public Service Enterprise	PEG	7.0	54.0	4.2
South Carolina E&G	SCG	6.0	54.0	4.3
Southern Company	SO	6.5	72.0	3.9
Tampa Electric	TE	6.5	71.0	10.5
United Illuminating	UIL	6.0	55.0	3.2
Median		6.0%	61.0%	3.8%

electric utilities. (We compare return on capital rather than return on equity because the latter is affected by leverage, which tends to be far greater in the electric utility industry than in the software industry. Return on capital measures operating income per dollar of total long-term financing, regardless of whether the source of the capital supplied is debt or equity. We will return to this issue in the next chapter.)

By and large, software firms have attractive investment opportunities. The median return on capital of these firms is forecast to be 17.0%, and the firms have responded with quite high plowback ratios. Several of these firms pay no dividends at all. The high returns on capital and high plowback ratios result in rapid growth. The median growth rate of earnings per share in this group is projected at 10.5%.

In contrast, the electric utilities are more representative of mature firms. Their median return on capital is lower, 6%; dividend payout is higher, 61%; and average growth rate is lower, 3.8%. We conclude that the higher payouts of the electric utilities reflect their more limited opportunities to reinvest earnings at attractive rates of return.

To value companies with temporarily high growth, analysts use a multistage version of the dividend discount model. Dividends in the early high-growth period are forecast and their combined present value is calculated. Then, once the firm is projected to settle down to a steady growth phase, the constant-growth DDM is applied to value the remaining stream of dividends.

We can illustrate this with a real-life example using a **two-stage DDM**. Figure 13.2 is a *Value Line Investment Survey* report on General Electric. Some of GE's relevant information of the end of 2014 is highlighted.

two-stage DDM

Dividend discount model in which dividend growth is assumed to level off only at some future date.

Value Line Investment Survey report on General Electric

Source: From *Value Line Investment Survey*, October 17, 2014.

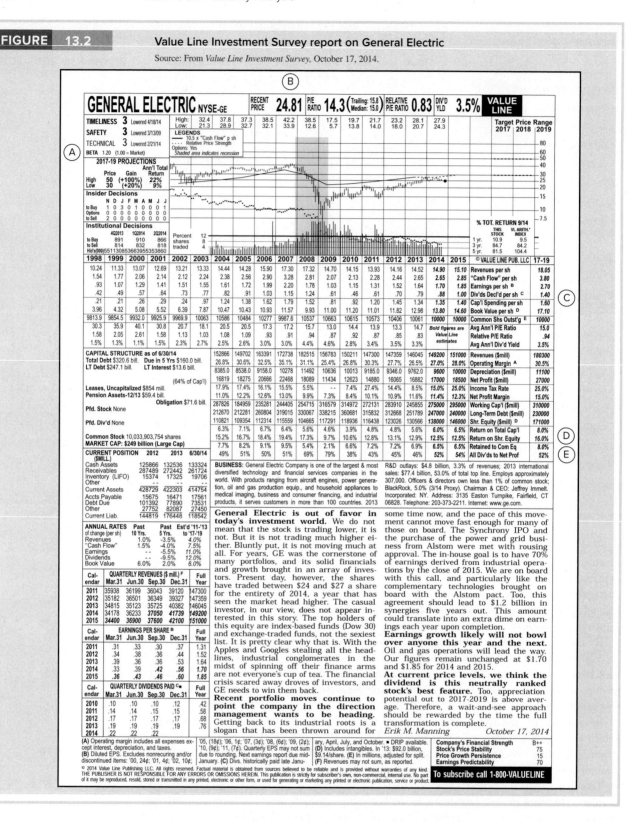

GE's beta appears at the circled A, its recent stock price at the B, the per-share dividend payments at the C, the ROE (referred to as "return on shareholder equity") at the D, and the dividend payout ratio (referred to as "all dividends to net profits") at the E. The rows ending at C, D, and E are historical time series. The boldfaced italicized entries under 2015 are estimates for that year. Similarly, the entries in the far right column (labeled 17–19) are forecasts for some time between 2017 and 2019, which we will take to be 2018.

Value Line provides explicit dividend forecasts over the relative short term, with dividends rising from $1.00 in 2015 to $1.40 in 2018. We can obtain dividend inputs for this initial period by using the explicit forecasts for 2015–2018 and linear interpolation for the years between:

2015	$1.00
2016	$1.13
2017	$1.26
2018	$1.40

Now let us assume the dividend growth rate will be steady beyond 2018. What is a reasonable guess for that steady-state growth rate? Value Line forecasts a dividend payout ratio of .52 and an ROE of 16%, implying long-term growth will be

$$g = \text{ROE} \times b = 16\% \times (1 - .52) = 7.68\%$$

Our estimate of GE's intrinsic value using an investment horizon of 2018 is therefore obtained from Equation 13.2, which we restate here:

$$V_{2014} = \frac{D_{2015}}{(1 + k)} + \frac{D_{2016}}{(1 + k)^2} + \frac{D_{2017}}{(1 + k)^3} + \frac{D_{2018} + P_{2018}}{(1 + k)^4}$$

$$= \frac{1.00}{(1 + k)} + \frac{1.13}{(1 + k)^2} + \frac{1.26}{(1 + k)^3} + \frac{1.40 + P_{2018}}{(1 + k)^4}$$

Here, P_{2018} represents the forecast price at which we can sell our shares of GE at the end of 2018, when dividends enter their constant-growth phase. That price, according to the constant-growth DDM, should be

$$P_{2018} = \frac{D_{2019}}{k - g} = \frac{D_{2018}(1 + g)}{k - g} = \frac{1.40 \times 1.0768}{k - .0768}$$

The only variable remaining to be determined to calculate intrinsic value is the market capitalization rate, k.

One way to obtain k is from the CAPM. Observe from the Value Line data that GE's beta is 1.20. The risk-free rate on long-term T-bonds in late 2014 was about 3%.[4] Suppose that the market risk premium were forecast at 8%, roughly in line with its historical average. This would imply that the forecast for the market return was

Risk-free rate + Market risk premium = 3% + 8% = 11%

Therefore, we can solve for the market capitalization rate as

$$k = r_f + \beta[E(r_M) - r_f]$$

$$= 3\% + 1.20(11\% - 3\%) = 12.6\%$$

Our forecast for the stock price in 2018 is thus

$$P_{2018} = \frac{\$1.40 \times 1.0768}{.126 - .0768} = \$30.64$$

---

[4]When valuing long-term assets such as stocks, it is common to treat the long-term Treasury bond, rather than short-term T-bills, as the risk-free asset.

and today's estimate of intrinsic value is

$$V_{2014} = \frac{1.00}{1.126} + \frac{1.13}{(1.126)^2} + \frac{1.26}{(1.126)^3} + \frac{1.40 + 30.64}{(1.126)^4} = \$22.59$$

We know from the Value Line report that GE's actual price was $24.81 (at the circled B). Our intrinsic value analysis indicates GE was overpriced by about 10%. Should we reduce our holdings or even sell the stock short?

Perhaps. But before betting the farm, stop to consider how much confidence you should place in this estimate. We've had to guess at dividends in the near future, the ultimate growth rate of those dividends, and the appropriate discount rate. Moreover, we've assumed GE will follow a relatively simple two-stage growth process. In practice, the growth of dividends can follow more complicated patterns. Even small errors in these approximations could upset a conclusion.

For example, we saw in Chapter 7 that betas are typically estimated with considerable imprecision. Suppose that GE's beta is actually 1.1 rather than 1.2. Then its risk premium will be smaller, and its market capitalization rate will be 11.8%. At this lower capitalization rate, the intrinsic value of the firm based on the two-stage model increases to $27.02, which is *more* than its recent stock price. Our conclusion regarding mispricing is reversed.

The exercise highlights the importance of assessing the sensitivity of your analysis to changes in underlying assumptions when you attempt to value stocks. Your estimates of stock values are no better than your assumptions. Sensitivity analysis will highlight the inputs that need to be most carefully examined. For example, we just found that even small changes in the estimated risk premium of the stock can result in big changes in intrinsic value. Similarly, small changes in the assumed growth rate change intrinsic value substantially. On the other hand, reasonable changes in the dividends forecast between 2015 and 2018 have a small impact on intrinsic value.

CONCEPT check   13.4

Confirm that the intrinsic value of GE using the same data as in our example, but assuming its beta is 1.1, is $27.02. (*Hint:* First calculate the discount rate and stock price in 2018. Then calculate the present value of all interim dividends plus the present value of the 2018 sales price.)

Multistage Growth Models

The two-stage growth model that we just considered for GE is a good start toward realism, but clearly we could do even better if our valuation model allowed for more flexible patterns of growth. Multistage growth models allow dividends per share to grow at several different rates as the firm matures. Many analysts use three-stage growth models. They may allow for year-by-year forecasts of dividends for the short term, a final period of sustainable growth, and a transition period in between, during which dividend growth rates taper off from the initial rate to the ultimate sustainable rate. These models are conceptually no harder to work with than a two-stage model, but they require many more calculations and can be tedious to do by hand. It is easy, however, to build an Excel spreadsheet for such a model.

Spreadsheet 13.1 is an example of such a model. Column B contains the inputs we have used so far for GE. Column E contains dividend forecasts. In cells E2 through E5 we present the Value Line estimates for the next four years. Dividend growth in this period is about 11.87% annually. Rather than assume a sudden transition to constant dividend growth starting in 2018, we assume instead that the dividend growth rate in 2018 will be 11.87% and that it will decline linearly through 2029 (see column F), finally reaching the constant terminal growth rate of 7.68% in 2029. Each dividend in the transition period is the previous year's dividend times that year's growth rate. Terminal value once the firm enters a constant-growth stage (cell G17) is computed from the constant-growth DDM. Finally, investor cash flow in each period (column H) equals dividends in each year plus the terminal value in 2030. The present value of these cash flows is computed in cell H19 as $26.52, about 17% more than the value we found in the two-stage model. We obtain a greater intrinsic value in this case because we assume that dividend growth, which at the current rate of 11.87% is quite rapid, only gradually declines to its steady-state value.

SPREADSHEET 13.1

A three-stage growth model for GE

	A	B	C	D	E	F	G	H	I
1	Inputs			Year	Dividend	Div growth	Term value	Investor CF	
2	beta	1.2		2015	1.00			1.00	
3	mkt_prem	0.08		2016	1.13			1.13	
4	rf	0.03		2017	1.27			1.27	
5	k_equity	0.1260		2018	1.40			1.40	
6	plowback	0.48		2019	1.57	0.1187		1.57	
7	roe	0.16		2020	1.75	0.1145		1.75	
8	term_gwth	0.077		2021	1.94	0.1103		1.94	
9				2022	2.14	0.1061		2.14	
10				2023	2.36	0.1019		2.36	
11				2024	2.59	0.0977		2.59	
12	Value Line			2025	2.84	0.0936		2.84	
13	forecasts of			2026	3.09	0.0894		3.09	
14	annual dividends			2027	3.35	0.0852		3.35	
15				2028	3.62	0.0810		3.62	
16				2029	3.90	0.0768		3.90	
17	Transitional period			2030	4.20	0.0768	91.96	91.96	
18	with slowing dividend								
19	growth							26.52	= PV of CF
20		Beginning of constant			E17*(1+F17)/(B5−F17)				
21		growth period						NPV(B5,H2:H17)	

Spreadsheets are available in Connect

13.4 PRICE–EARNINGS RATIOS

The Price–Earnings Ratio and Growth Opportunities

Much of the real-world discussion of stock market valuation concentrates on the firm's **price–earnings multiple,** the ratio of price per share to earnings per share, commonly called the P/E ratio. In fact, one common approach to valuing a firm is to use an earnings multiplier. The value of the stock is obtained by multiplying projected earnings per share by a forecast of the P/E ratio. This procedure seems simple, but its apparent simplicity is deceptive. First, forecasting earnings is challenging. As we saw in the previous chapter, earnings will depend on international, macroeconomic, and industry as well as firm-specific factors, many of which are highly unpredictable. Second, forecasting the P/E multiple is even more difficult. P/E ratios vary across industries and over time. Nevertheless, our discussion of stock valuation provides some insight into the factors that ought to determine a firm's P/E ratio.

price–earnings multiple

The ratio of a stock's price to its earnings per share.

Recall our discussion of growth opportunities, in which we compared two firms, Growth Prospects and Cash Cow, each of which had earnings per share of $5. Growth Prospects reinvested 60% of its earnings in prospects with an ROE of 15%, while Cash Cow paid out all of its earnings as dividends. Cash Cow had a price of $40, giving it a P/E multiple of $40/5 = 8$, while Growth Prospects sold for $57.14, giving it a multiple of $57.14/5 = 11.4$. This observation suggests the P/E ratio might serve as a useful indicator of expectations of growth opportunities. We can see this explicitly by rearranging Equation 13.6 to

$$\frac{P_0}{E_1} = \frac{1}{k}\left[1 + \frac{PVGO}{E_1/k}\right] \tag{13.7}$$

When PVGO = 0, Equation 13.7 shows that $P_0 = E_1/k$. The stock is valued like a nongrowing perpetuity of EPS_1. The P/E ratio is just $1/k$. However, as PVGO becomes an increasingly dominant contributor to price, the P/E ratio can rise dramatically.

The ratio of PVGO to E/k has a straightforward interpretation. It is the ratio of the component of firm value reflecting growth opportunities to the component of value reflecting assets already in place (i.e., the no-growth value of the firm, E/k). When future growth opportunities dominate the estimate of total value, the firm will command a high price relative to current earnings. Thus, a high P/E multiple appears to indicate that a firm is endowed with ample growth opportunities.

EXAMPLE 13.5

P/E Ratios and Growth Opportunities

Return again to Takeover Target, the firm we first encountered in Example 13.4. Earnings are $5 per share and the capitalization rate is 15%, implying that the no-growth value of the firm is $E_1/k = \$5/.15 = \$33.33$. The stock price actually is $22.22, implying that the present value of growth opportunities equals $-\$11.11$. This implies that the P/E ratio should be

$$\frac{P_0}{E_1} = \frac{1}{k}\left[1 + \frac{PVGO}{E/k}\right] = \frac{1}{.15}\left[1 + \frac{-\$11.11}{\$33.33}\right] = 4.44$$

In fact, the stock price is $22.22 and earnings are $5 per share, so the P/E ratio is $22.22/$5 = 4.44.

Let's see if P/E multiples do vary with growth prospects. Between 1996 and 2013, for example, FedEx's P/E ratio averaged about 17.5 while Consolidated Edison's average P/E was only 13.8. These numbers do not necessarily imply that FedEx was overpriced compared to Con Ed. If investors believed FedEx would grow faster, its higher price per dollar would be justified. That is, investors might well pay a higher price per dollar of *current earnings* if they expect that earnings stream to grow more rapidly. In fact FedEx's growth rate has been consistent with its higher P/E multiple. In this period, its earnings per share grew by a factor of 3.64, while Con Ed's earnings grew by only 34%. Figure 13.4 (on page 423) shows the EPS history of the two companies.

We conclude that the P/E ratio reflects the market's optimism concerning a firm's growth prospects. Analysts must decide whether they are more or less optimistic than the belief implied by the market multiple. If they are more optimistic, they will recommend buying the stock.

There is a way to make these insights more precise. Look again at the constant-growth DDM formula, $P_0 = D_1/(k - g)$. Now recall that dividends equal the earnings that are *not* reinvested in the firm: $D_1 = E_1(1 - b)$. Recall also that $g = \text{ROE} \times b$. Hence, substituting for D_1 and g, we find that

$$P_0 = \frac{E_1(1 - b)}{k - (\text{ROE} \times b)}$$

implying that the P/E ratio for a firm growing at a long-run sustainable pace is

$$\frac{P_0}{E_1} = \frac{1 - b}{k - (\text{ROE} \times b)} \qquad (13.8)$$

It is easy to verify that the P/E ratio increases with ROE. This makes sense, because high ROE projects give the firm good opportunities for growth.[5] We also can verify that the P/E ratio increases for higher plowback, b, as long as ROE exceeds k. This too makes sense. When a firm has good investment opportunities, the market will reward it with a higher P/E multiple if it exploits those opportunities more aggressively by plowing back more earnings into those opportunities.

Remember, however, that growth is not desirable for its own sake. Examine Table 13.3, where we use Equation 13.8 to compute both growth rates and P/E ratios for different combinations of ROE and b. While growth always increases with the plowback ratio (move across the rows in Panel A of Table 13.3), the P/E ratio does not (move across the rows in Panel B). In the top row of Table 13.3, Panel B, the P/E falls as the plowback rate increases. In the middle row, it is unaffected by plowback. In the third row, it increases.

This pattern has a simple interpretation. When the expected ROE is less than the required return, k, investors prefer that the firm pay out earnings as dividends rather than reinvest earnings in the firm at an inadequate rate of return. That is, for ROE lower than k, the value of the firm falls as plowback increases. Conversely, when ROE exceeds k, the firm offers superior investment opportunities, so the value of the firm is enhanced as those opportunities are more fully exploited by increasing the plowback ratio.

---

[5]Note that Equation 13.8 is a simple rearrangement of the DDM formula, with $\text{ROE} \times b = g$. Because that formula requires that $g < k$, Equation 13.8 is valid only when $\text{ROE} \times b < k$.

TABLE 13.3	Effect of ROE and plowback on growth and the P/E ratio			
	Plowback Ratio (b)			
	0	**0.25**	**0.50**	**0.75**
A. Growth rate, g				
ROE				
10%	0%	2.5%	5.0%	7.5%
12	0	3.0	6.0	9.0
14	0	3.5	7.0	10.5
B. P/E ratio				
ROE				
10%	8.33	7.89	7.14	5.56
12	8.33	8.33	8.33	8.33
14	8.33	8.82	10.00	16.67

Note: Assumption: $k = 12\%$ per year.

Finally, where ROE just equals k, the firm offers "break-even" investment opportunities with a fair rate of return. In this case, investors are indifferent between reinvestment of earnings in the firm or elsewhere at the market capitalization rate, because the rate of return in either case is 12%. Therefore, the stock price is unaffected by the plowback ratio.

We conclude that the higher the plowback ratio, the higher the growth rate, but a higher plowback ratio does not necessarily mean a higher P/E ratio. Higher plowback increases P/E only if investments undertaken by the firm offer an expected rate of return higher than the market capitalization rate. Otherwise, increasing plowback hurts investors because more money is sunk into prospects with inadequate rates of return.

Notwithstanding these fine points, P/E ratios commonly are taken as proxies for the expected growth in dividends or earnings. In fact, a common Wall Street rule of thumb is that the growth rate ought to be roughly equal to the P/E ratio. In other words, the ratio of P/E to g, often called the **PEG ratio,** should be about 1. Peter Lynch, the famous portfolio manager, puts it this way in his book *One Up on Wall Street:*

> The P/E ratio of any company that's fairly priced will equal its growth rate. I'm talking here about growth rate of earnings. . . . If the P/E ratio of Coca-Cola is 15, you'd expect the company to be growing at about 15% per year, etc. But if the P/E ratio is less than the growth rate, you may have found yourself a bargain.

PEG ratio

Ratio of P/E multiple to earnings growth rate.

Let's try his rule of thumb.

EXAMPLE 13.6

P/E Ratio versus Growth Rate

Assume:

$$r_f = 8\% \text{ (about the value when Peter Lynch was writing)}$$
$$r_M - r_f = 8\% \text{ (about the historical average market risk premium)}$$
$$b = .4 \text{ (a typical value for the plowback ratio in the U.S.)}$$

Therefore, $r_M = r_f +$ Market risk premium $= 8\% + 8\% = 16\%$, and $k = 16\%$ for an average ($\beta = 1$) company. If we also accept as reasonable that ROE = 16% (the same value as the expected return on the stock) we conclude that

$$g = \text{ROE} \times b = 16\% \times .4 = 6.4\%$$

and

$$\text{P/E} = \frac{1 - .4}{.16 - .064} = 6.26$$

(continued)

EXAMPLE 13.6

*P/E Ratio versus
Growth Rate*

(concluded)

Thus, the P/E ratio and g are about equal using these assumptions, consistent with the rule of thumb.

However, this rule of thumb, like almost all others, will not work in all circumstances. For example, the yield on long-term Treasury bonds today is more like 3%, so a comparable forecast of r_M today would be

$$r_f + \text{Market risk premium} = 3\% + 8\% = 11\%$$

If we continue to focus on a firm with $\beta = 1$, and ROE still is about the same as k, then

$$g = 11\% \times .4 = 4.4\%$$

while

$$P/E = \frac{1 - .4}{.11 - .044} = 9.1$$

The P/E ratio and g now diverge, and the PEG ratio is now 9.1/4.4 = 2.1. Nevertheless, lower-than-average PEG ratios are still widely seen as signaling potential underpricing.

Whatever its shortcomings, the PEG ratio is widely followed. The PEG ratio for the S&P over the last 20 years typically has fluctuated within the range between 1 and 1.5.

CONCEPT
check   **13.5**

ABC stock has an expected ROE of 12% per year, expected earnings per share of $2, and expected dividends of $1.50 per share. Its market capitalization rate is 10% per year.
   a. What are its expected growth rate, its price, and its P/E ratio?
   b. If the plowback rate were .4, what would be the firm's expected dividend per share, growth rate, price, P/E, and PEG ratio?

The importance of growth opportunities is most evident in the valuation of start-up firms, for example, in the Internet boom of the late 1990s. Many companies that had yet to turn a profit were valued by the market at billions of dollars. The value of these companies was *exclusively* growth opportunities. For example, the online auction firm eBay had 1998 profits of $2.4 million, far less than the $45 million profit earned by the traditional auctioneer Sotheby's; yet eBay's market value was more than 10 times greater: $22 billion versus $1.9 billion. As it turns out, the market was quite right to value eBay so much more aggressively than Sotheby's. Its net income in 2013 was $2.86 billion, about 22 times that of Sotheby's.

Of course, when company valuation is determined primarily by growth opportunities, those values can be very sensitive to reassessments of such prospects. When the market became more skeptical of the business prospects of most Internet retailers at the close of the 1990s, that is, as it revised the estimates of growth opportunities downward, their stock prices plummeted.

As perceptions of future prospects wax and wane, share price can swing wildly. Growth prospects are intrinsically difficult to tie down; ultimately, however, those prospects drive the value of the most dynamic firms in the economy.

The nearby box contains a simple valuation analysis. Facebook's 2012 IPO was among the most highly anticipated in decades, and there was widespread speculation about the price at which it would eventually trade in the stock market. There was considerable disparity among analysts about what the stock would be worth. The points of contention in their analysis turned on two key questions. First, what was a reasonable projection for the growth rate of Facebook's profits? Second, what multiple of earnings was appropriate to translate an earnings forecast into a price forecast? These are precisely the questions addressed by our stock valuation models.

FACEBOOK'S IPO

As Facebook's IPO drew near, valuation estimates by professional analysts were surprisingly disparate, ranging from as little as $50 billion to as much as $125 billion.

Disputes over fair value turned on a few key questions: Just how fast would the company be able to grow? How much profit would it be able to derive from advertising? And what earnings multiple would the market be willing to pay for that profit stream?

Everyone believed that Facebook had many years of rapid growth before it, but even so, its growth rate had already begun to slow compared to its early years. While revenue grew 88% in 2011 and net income grew 65%, that increase was nevertheless considerably below the 154% increase in revenue from 2009 to 2010.

Francis Gaskins, president of IPOdesktop.com, which analyzes IPOs for investors, estimated Facebook's value at no more than $50 billion.[6] Even that value, at the low end of the range of most analysts, seemed generous in some respects: It would have been 50 times Facebook's 2011 profits of $1 billion, and a P/E multiple of 50 was more than triple the market's average price-to-earnings ratio at the time.

However, many higher estimates were also offered. For example, Martin Pyykkonen, an analyst at Wedge Partners, believed the value could top $100 billion. If Facebook traded at 15 to 18 times next year's EBITDA (expected earnings before interest, taxes, and certain noncash charges), it would result in a stock valuation of around $89 billion. But Pyykkonen argued that if Facebook could generate faster growth in ad spending, it could justify a multiple as high as 20 times earnings, implying a $110 billion valuation. By comparison, more mature companies such as Microsoft or Google traded at 7 to 10 times EBITDA. Gaskins, of IPOdesktop, was unconvinced, pointing out that at a $100 billion valuation, Facebook would be worth about half as much as Google, even though Google's sales and profits were 10 times that of Facebook.

In the end, based on its IPO price, the market valued Facebook at about $90 billion.

[6]The valuation estimates cited in this box appeared in Randall Smith, "Facebook's $100 Billion Question," *The Wall Street Journal,* February 3, 2012.

P/E Ratios and Stock Risk

One important implication of any stock valuation model is that (holding all else equal) riskier stocks will have lower P/E multiples. We can see this in the context of the constant-growth model by examining the formula for the P/E ratio (Equation 13.8):

$$\frac{P}{E} = \frac{1 - b}{k - g}$$

Riskier firms will have higher required rates of return (i.e., higher values of k). Therefore, their P/E multiples will be lower. This is true even outside the context of the constant-growth model. For *any* expected earnings and dividend stream, the present value of those cash flows will be lower when the stream is perceived to be riskier. Hence the stock price and the ratio of price to earnings will be lower.

Of course, many small, risky, start-up companies have very high P/E multiples. This does not contradict our claim that P/E multiples should fall with risk: Instead, it is evidence of the market's expectations of high growth rates for those companies. This is why we said that high-risk firms will have lower P/E ratios *holding all else equal.* Given a growth projection, the P/E multiple will be lower when risk is perceived to be higher.

Pitfalls in P/E Analysis

No description of P/E analysis is complete without mentioning some of its pitfalls. First, consider that the denominator in the P/E ratio is accounting earnings, which are influenced by somewhat arbitrary accounting rules such as the use of historical cost in depreciation and inventory valuation. In times of high inflation, historic cost depreciation and inventory costs will tend to underrepresent true economic values because the replacement cost of both goods and capital equipment will rise with the general level of prices. As Figure 13.3 demonstrates, P/E ratios generally have been inversely related to the inflation rate. In part, this reflects the market's assessment that earnings in high inflation periods are of "lower quality," artificially distorted by inflation, and warranting lower P/E ratios.

FIGURE   13.3

P/E ratio of the S&P 500
Index and inflation

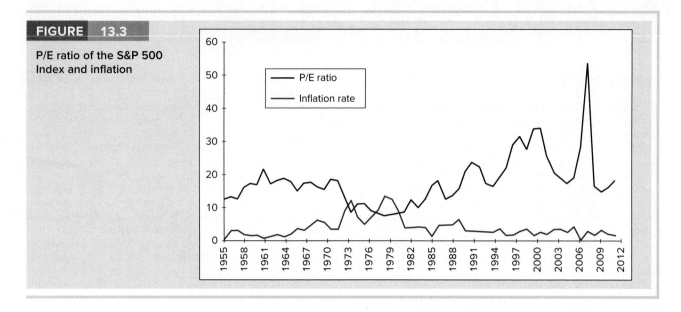

FIGURE   13.3

P/E ratio of the S&P 500
Index and inflation

earnings management

The practice of using flexibility
in accounting rules to manipulate the apparent profitability
of the firm.

Earnings management is the practice of using flexibility in accounting rules to manipulate the apparent profitability of the firm. We will have much to say on this topic in the next
chapter on interpreting financial statements. A version of earnings management that became
common in recent years was the reporting of "pro forma earnings" measures. These measures are sometimes called *operating earnings,* a term with no precise generally accepted
definition.

Pro forma earnings are calculated ignoring certain expenses, for example, restructuring
charges, stock-option expenses, or write-downs of assets from continuing operations. Firms
argue that ignoring these expenses gives a clearer picture of the underlying profitability of
the firm.

But when there is too much leeway for choosing what to exclude it becomes hard for
investors or analysts to interpret the numbers or to compare them across firms. The lack of
standards gives firms considerable leeway to manage earnings.

Even GAAP allows firms considerable discretion to manage earnings. For example, in the
late 1990s, Kellogg took restructuring charges, which are supposed to be one-time events, nine
quarters in a row. Were these really one-time events, or were they more appropriately treated
as ordinary expenses? Given the available leeway in reporting earnings, the justified P/E multiple becomes difficult to gauge.

Another confounding factor in the use of P/E ratios is related to the business cycle. We
were careful in deriving the DDM to define earnings as being net of *economic* depreciation,
that is, the maximum flow of income that the firm could pay out without depleting its productive capacity. Yet reported earnings, as we note above, are computed in accordance with generally accepted accounting principles and need not correspond to economic earnings. Beyond
this, however, notions of a normal or justified P/E ratio, as in Equation 13.7 or 13.8, assume
implicitly that earnings rise at a constant rate, or, put another way, on a smooth trend line. In
contrast, reported earnings can fluctuate dramatically around a trend line over the course of
the business cycle.

Another way to make this point is to note that the "normal" P/E ratio predicted by
Equation 13.8 is the ratio of today's price to the trend value of future earnings, E_1. The P/E
ratio reported in the financial pages of the newspaper, by contrast, is the ratio of price to the
most recent *past* accounting earnings. Current accounting earnings can differ considerably
from future economic earnings. Because ownership of stock conveys the right to future as well
as current earnings, the ratio of price to most recent earnings can vary substantially over the
business cycle, as accounting earnings and the trend value of economic earnings diverge by
greater and lesser amounts.

As an example, Figure 13.4 graphs the earnings per share of FedEx and Consolidated Edison since 1996. Note that FedEx's EPS fluctuates around its trend line more than Con Ed's. Because the market values the entire stream of future dividends generated by the company, when earnings are temporarily depressed, the P/E ratio should tend to be high—that is, the denominator of the ratio responds more sensitively to the business cycle than the numerator. This pattern is borne out well.

Figure 13.5 graphs the P/E ratios of the two firms. FedEx has greater earnings volatility and more variability in its P/E ratio. Its clearly higher average growth rate shows up in its generally higher P/E ratio. The only year in which Con Ed's ratio exceeded FedEx's was 2012, a year when FedEx's earnings rose at a far faster rate than its underlying trend. The market seems to have recognized that this earnings performance was not likely to be sustainable, and FedEx's price did not respond dramatically to this fluctuation in earnings. Consequently, its P/E ratio declined.

This example shows why analysts must be careful in using P/E ratios. There is no way to say a P/E ratio is overly high or low without referring to the company's long-run growth prospects, as well as to current earnings per share relative to the long-run trend line.

Nevertheless, Figures 13.4 and 13.5 demonstrate a clear relationship between P/E ratios and growth. Despite short-run fluctuations, FedEx's EPS clearly trended upward over the period. Its compound rate of growth in the 1996–2013 period was 7.9%. Con Edison's earnings grew far less rapidly, with a compound growth rate of 1.7%. FedEx's growth prospects are reflected in its consistently higher P/E multiple.

This analysis suggests that P/E ratios should vary across industries and, in fact, they do. Figure 13.6 shows recent P/E ratios for a sample of industries. Notice that the industries with the two highest multiples—security and application software—have attractive investment

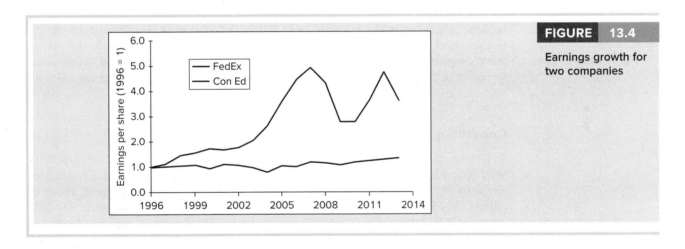

FIGURE 13.4

Earnings growth for two companies

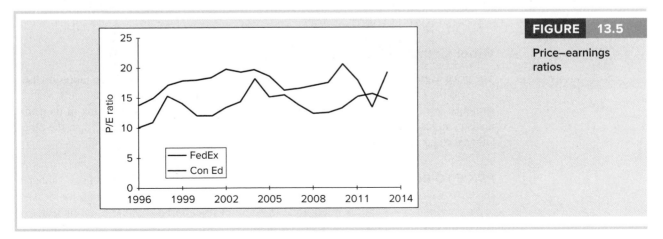

FIGURE 13.5

Price–earnings ratios

FIGURE   13.6

P/E ratios

Source: Yahoo! Finance, finance.
yahoo.com, November 14, 2014.

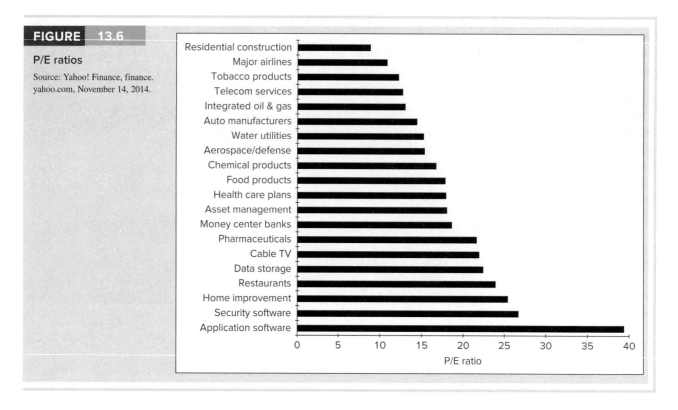

opportunities, whereas the industries with the lowest multiples—residential construction, airlines, or tobacco products—are in more mature or less profitable industries with limited growth opportunities. The relationship between P/E and growth is not perfect, which is not surprising in light of the pitfalls discussed in this section, but as a general rule, the P/E multiple does appear to track growth opportunities.

Combining P/E Analysis and the DDM

Some analysts use P/E ratios in conjunction with earnings forecasts to estimate the price of stock at an investor's horizon date. The GE analysis in Figure 13.2 shows that Value Line forecast a P/E ratio for 2018 of 15. EPS for 2018 was forecast at $2.70, implying a price in 2018 of 15 × $2.70 = $40.50. Given an estimate of $40.50 for the 2018 sales price, we would compute GE's intrinsic value as

$$V_{2014} = \frac{1.00}{(1.126)} + \frac{1.13}{(1.126)^2} + \frac{1.26}{(1.126)^3} + \frac{1.40 + 40.50}{(1.126)^4} = \$28.73$$

Other Comparative Valuation Ratios

The price–earnings ratio is an example of a comparative valuation ratio. Such ratios are used to assess the valuation of one firm versus another based on a fundamental indicator such as earnings. For example, an analyst might compare the P/E ratios of two firms in the same industry to test whether the market is valuing one firm "more aggressively" than the other. Other such comparative ratios are commonly used.

PRICE-TO-BOOK RATIO   This is the ratio of price per share divided by book value per share. As we noted earlier in this chapter, some analysts view book value as a useful measure of fundamental value and therefore treat the ratio of price to book value as an indicator of how aggressively the market values the firm.

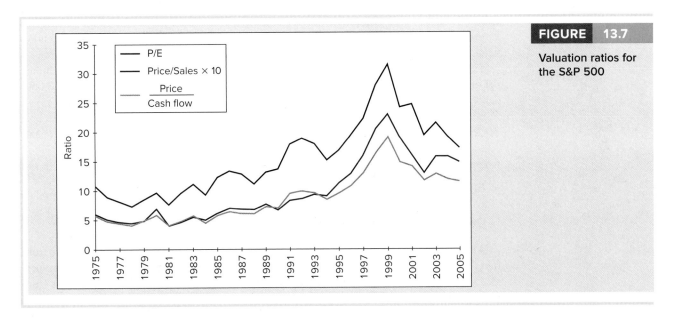

FIGURE   13.7

Valuation ratios for
the S&P 500

PRICE-TO-CASH-FLOW RATIO   Earnings as reported on the income statement can be affected by the company's choice of accounting practices and thus are commonly viewed as subject to some imprecision and even manipulation. In contrast, cash flow—which tracks cash actually flowing into or out of the firm—is less affected by accounting decisions. As a result, some analysts prefer to use the ratio of price to cash flow per share rather than price to earnings per share. Some analysts use operating cash flow when calculating this ratio; others prefer free cash flow, that is, operating cash flow net of new investment.

PRICE-TO-SALES RATIO   Many start-up firms have no earnings. As a result, the P/E ratio for these firms is meaningless. The price-to-sales ratio (the ratio of stock price to the annual sales per share) is sometimes taken as a valuation benchmark for these firms. Of course, price-to-sales ratios can vary markedly across industries because profit margins vary widely.

BE CREATIVE   Sometimes a standard valuation ratio will simply not be available, and you will have to devise your own. In the 1990s, some analysts valued retail Internet firms based on the number of hits their websites received. In retrospect, they valued these firms using too generous "price-to-hits" ratios. Nevertheless, in a new investment environment, these analysts used the information available to them to devise the best valuation tools they could.

Figure 13.7 presents the behavior of these valuation measures for the S&P 500. While the levels of these ratios differ considerably, for the most part they track each other fairly closely, with upturns and downturns at the same times.

13.5   FREE CASH FLOW VALUATION APPROACHES

An alternative approach to the dividend discount model values the firm using free cash flow, that is, cash flow available to the firm or the equityholders net of capital expenditures. This approach is particularly useful for firms that pay no dividends, for which the dividend discount model would be difficult to implement. But free cash flow models are valid for any firm, and can provide useful insights about firm value beyond the DDM.

One approach is to discount the *free cash flow* for the *firm* (FCFF) at the weighted-average cost of capital to obtain the value of the firm and then subtract the then-existing value of debt to find the value of equity. Another is to focus from the start on the free cash flow to *equityholders* (FCFE), discounting those directly at the cost of equity to obtain the market value of equity.

The free cash flow to the firm is the after-tax cash flow generated by the firm's operations, net of investments in capital and net working capital. It includes cash flows available to both debt- and equityholders.[7] It equals:

$$\text{FCFF} = \text{EBIT}(1 - t_c) + \text{Depreciation} - \text{Capital expenditures} - \text{Increase in NWC} \quad \textbf{(13.9)}$$

where

$$\text{EBIT} = \text{Earnings before interest and taxes}$$
$$t_c = \text{The corporate tax rate}$$
$$\text{NWC} = \text{Net working capital}$$

Alternatively, we can focus on cash flow available to equityholders. This will differ from free cash flow to the firm by after-tax interest expenditures, as well as by cash flow associated with net issuance or repurchase of debt (i.e., principal repayments minus proceeds from issuance of new debt).

$$\text{FCFE} = \text{FCFF} - \text{Interest expense} \times (1 - t_c) + \text{Increases in net debt} \quad \textbf{(13.10)}$$

A free cash flow to the firm valuation model discounts year-by-year cash flows plus some estimate of terminal value, P_T. In Equation 13.11, we use the constant-growth model to estimate terminal value. The appropriate discount rate is the weighted-average cost of capital.

$$\text{Firm value} = \sum_{t=1}^{T} \frac{\text{FCFF}_t}{(1 + \text{WACC})^t} + \frac{P_T}{(1 + \text{WACC})^T} \quad \textbf{(13.11)}$$

where

$$P_T = \frac{\text{FCFF}_{T+1}}{\text{WACC} - g}$$

To find equity value, we subtract the existing market value of debt from the derived value of the firm.

Alternatively, we can discount free cash flows to *equity* (FCFE) at the cost of *equity,* k_E,

$$\text{Intrinsic value of equity} = \sum_{t=1}^{T} \frac{\text{FCFE}_t}{(1 + k_E)^t} + \frac{P_T}{(1 + k_E)^T} \quad \textbf{(13.12)}$$

where

$$P_T = \frac{\text{FCFE}_{T+1}}{k_E - g}$$

As in the dividend discount model, free cash flow models use a terminal value to avoid adding the present values of an infinite sum of cash flows. That terminal value may simply be the present value of a constant-growth perpetuity (as in the formulas above), or it may be based on a multiple of EBIT, book value, earnings, or free cash flow. As a general rule, estimates of intrinsic value depend critically on terminal value.

Spreadsheet 13.2 presents a free cash flow valuation of GE using the data supplied by Value Line in Figure 13.2. We start with the free cash flow to the firm approach given in Equation 13.9. Panel A of the spreadsheet lays out values supplied by Value Line. (Entries for middle years are interpolated from beginning and final values.) Panel B calculates free cash flow. The sum of after-tax profits in row 11 plus after-tax interest payments in row 12

---

[7]This is firm cash flow assuming all-equity financing. Any tax advantage to debt financing is recognized by using an after-tax cost of debt in the computation of weighted-average cost of capital. This issue is discussed in any introductory corporate finance text.

SPREADSHEET 13.2

Free cash flow valuation of General Electric

	A	B	C	D	E	F	G	H	I	J	K	L	M
1			2014	2015	2016	2017	2018						
2	A. Input data												
3	P/E		14.60	14.70	14.80	14.90	15.00						
4	Cap spending/shr		1.35	1.40	1.47	1.53	1.60						
5	LT debt		247,000	240,000	236,667	233,333	230,000						
6	Shares		10,000	10,000	10,000	10,000	10,000						
7	EPS		1.70	1.85	2.13	2.42	2.70						
8	Working capital		275,000	295,000	300,000	305,000	310,000						
9													
10	B. Cash flow calculations												
11	Profits (after tax)		17,000	18,500	21,333	24,167	27,000						
12	Interest (after tax)		5,619	5,460	5,384	5,308	5,233			=(1-tax_rate) × r_debt × LT Debt			
13	Chg working cap			20,000	5,000	5,000	5,000						
14	Depreciation		9,600	10,000	10,367	10,733	11,100						
15	Cap spending			14,000	14,667	15,333	16,000						
16								Terminal value					
17	FCFF			−40	17,418	19,875	22,333	606,782					
18	FCFE			−12,500	8,700	11,233	13,767	393,788		assumes fixed debt ratio after 2018			
19													
20	C. Discount rate calculations												
21	Current beta	1.2								from Value Line			
22	Unlevered beta	0.729								current beta /[1+(1-tax)*debt/equity)]			
23	Terminal growth	0.04											
24	Tax_rate	0.35											
25	r_debt	0.035								YTM in 2014 on Moody's A1 rated LT debt			
26	Risk-free rate	0.03											
27	Market risk prem	0.08											
28	MV equity		248,200				405,000			Row 3 × Row 11			
29	Debt/Value		0.50	0.46	0.43	0.40	0.36			linear trend from initial to final value			
30	Levered beta		1.200	1.140	1.087	1.040	0.998			unlevered beta × [1+(1-tax)*debt/equity]			
31	k_equity		0.126	0.121	0.117	0.113	0.110	0.110		from CAPM and levered beta			
32	WACC		0.075	0.075	0.076	0.077	0.078	0.078		(1-t)*r_debt*D/V+k_equity*(1-D/V)			
33	PV factor for FCFF		1.000	0.930	0.864	0.802	0.744	0.744		Discount each year at WACC			
34	PV factor for FCFE		1.000	0.892	0.799	0.717	0.646	0.646		Discount each year at k_equity			
35													
36	D. Present values									Intrinsic val	Equity val	Intrin/share	
37	PV(FCFF)			−37	15,046	15,937	16,607	451,228		498,781	251,781	25.18	
38	PV(FCFE)			−11,149	6,947	8,058	8,898	254,536		267,291	267,291	26.73	

* 2014 P/E ratio is from Yahoo! Finance. Final input is from Value Line, and intermediate values are interpolated.

[that is, interest expense $\times (1 - t_c)$] equals EBIT$(1 - t_c)$. In row 13 we subtract the change in net working capital, in row 14 we add back depreciation, and in row 15 we subtract capital expenditures. The result in row 17 is the free cash flow to the firm, FCFF, for each year between 2015 and 2018.

To find the present value of these cash flows, we will discount at WACC, which is calculated in panel C. WACC is the weighted average of the after-tax cost of debt and the cost of equity in each year. When computing WACC, we must account for the change in leverage forecast by Value Line. To compute the cost of equity, we will use the CAPM as in our earlier (dividend discount model) valuation exercise but account for the fact that equity beta will decline each year as the firm reduces leverage.[8]

A reasonable approximation to GE's cost of debt, which was rated Aa3 by Moody's in 2014, is the yield to maturity on comparably rated long-term debt, approximately 3.5% (cell B25). GE's debt-to-value ratio (assuming its debt is selling near par value) is computed

---

[8] Call β_L the firm's equity beta at the initial level of leverage as provided by Value Line. Equity betas reflect both business risk and financial risk. When a firm changes its capital structure (debt/equity mix), it changes financial risk, and therefore equity beta changes. How should we recognize the change in financial risk? As you may remember from an introductory corporate finance class, you must first unleverage beta. This leaves us a beta that reflects only business risk. We use the following formula to find unleveraged beta, β_U, (where D/E is the firm's current debt-equity ratio):

$$\beta_U = \frac{\beta_L}{1 + (D/E)(1 - t_c)}$$

Then, we re-leverage beta in any particular year using the forecast capital structure (which reintroduces the financial risk associated with that year's capital structure):

$$\beta_L = \beta_U[1 + (D/E)(1 - t_c)]$$

in row 29. In 2014, the ratio was .50. Based on Value Line forecasts, it will fall to .36 by 2018. We interpolate the debt-to-value ratio for the intermediate years. WACC is computed in row 32. WACC increases slightly over time as the debt-to-value ratio steadily declines between 2015 and 2018. The present value factor for cash flows accruing in each year is the previous year's factor divided by (1 + WACC) for that year. The present value of each cash flow (row 37) is the free cash flow times the cumulative discount factor.

The terminal value of the firm (cell H17) is computed from the constant-growth model as $FCFF_{2018} \times (1 + g)/(WACC_{2018} - g)$, where g (cell B23) is the assumed value for the steady growth rate.[9] We assume in the spreadsheet that $g = .04$.[10] Terminal value is also discounted back to 2014 (cell H37), and the intrinsic value of the firm is thus found as the sum of discounted free cash flows between 2015 and 2018 plus the discounted terminal value. Finally, the value of debt in 2014 is subtracted from firm value to arrive at the intrinsic value of equity in 2014 (cell K37), and value per share is calculated in cell L37 as equity value divided by number of shares in 2014.

The free cash flow to equity approach yields a similar intrinsic value for the stock. FCFE (row 18) is obtained from FCFF by subtracting after-tax interest expense and net debt repurchases. The cash flows are then discounted at the equity rate. Like WACC, the cost of equity changes each period as leverage changes. The present value factor for equity cash flows is presented in row 34. Equity value is reported in cell J38, which is put on a per-share basis in cell L38.

Spreadsheet 13.2 is available in Connect.

Comparing the Valuation Models

In principle, the free cash flow approach is fully consistent with the dividend discount model and should provide the same estimate of intrinsic value if one can extrapolate to a period in which the firm begins to pay dividends growing at a constant rate. This was demonstrated in two famous papers by Modigliani and Miller (1958, 1961). However, in practice, you will find that values from these models may differ, sometimes substantially. This is due to the fact that in practice, analysts are always forced to make simplifying assumptions. For example, how long will it take the firm to enter a constant-growth stage? How should depreciation best be treated? What is the best estimate of ROE? Answers to questions like these can have a big impact on value, and it is not always easy to maintain consistent assumptions across the models.

We have now valued GE using several approaches, with estimates of intrinsic value as follows:

Model	Intrinsic Value
Two-stage dividend discount model	$22.59
DDM with earnings multiple terminal value	28.73
Three-stage DDM	26.52
Free cash flow to the firm	25.18
Free cash flow to equity	26.73
Market price in 2014	24.81

[9]Over the 2014–2018 period, Value Line predicts that GE will retire a small fraction of its outstanding debt. The implied debt repurchases are a use of cash and reduce the cash flow available to equity. Such repurchases cannot be sustained indefinitely, however, for debt outstanding would eventually be run down to zero. Therefore, in our estimate of terminal value, we compute the final cash flow assuming that by 2018 GE will begin *issuing* enough debt to maintain its debt-to-value ratio unchanged. This approach is consistent with the assumption of constant growth and constant discount rates after 2018. To maintain consistency with the assumption that debt will grow at the same rate as the rest of the firm, in the numerator in cell H18, we subtract the actual growth of debt in the most recent year and add back the change in debt that would have taken place if debt had grown at the long-run growth rate.

[10]In the long run a firm can't grow forever at a rate higher than the aggregate economy. So by the time we assert that growth is in a stable stage, it seems reasonable that the growth rate should not be significantly greater than that of the overall economy (although it can be less if the firm is in a declining industry).

What should we make of these differences? The two-stage dividend discount model is the most conservative of the estimates, probably because it assumes that the dividend growth rate will fall immediately to its terminal value after only three years. In contrast, the three-stage DDM allows growth to taper off over a longer period, and the estimate of intrinsic value from this model is much closer to those from both free cash flow models. The DDM with a terminal value provided by the earnings multiple results in the highest estimate of intrinsic value. With the exception of the two-stage DDM, all of these models produce intrinsic values greater than GE's market price. Perhaps the assumed terminal growth rate used in our valuation exercise is unrealistically high, or perhaps the stock is indeed under-priced compared to intrinsic value.

On balance, however, this valuation exercise suggests that finding bargains is not as easy as it seems. While these models are easy to apply, establishing proper inputs is more of a challenge. This should not be surprising. In even a moderately efficient market, finding profit opportunities will be more involved than analyzing Value Line data for a few hours. The models are extremely useful to analysts, however. They provide ballpark estimates of intrinsic value. More than that, they force rigorous thought about underlying assumptions and highlight the variables with the greatest impact on value and the greatest payoff to further analysis.

The Problem with DCF Models

Our estimates of GE's intrinsic value are all based on discounted cash flow (DCF) models, in which we calculate the present value of forecast cash flows and a terminal sales price at some future date. It is clear from our calculations that most of the action in these models is in the terminal value and that this value can be highly sensitive to even small changes in some input values (see, for example, Concept Check 13.4). Therefore, you must recognize that DCF valuation estimates are almost always going to be imprecise. Growth opportunities and future growth rates are especially hard to pin down.

For this reason, many value investors employ a hierarchy of valuation. They view the most reliable components of value as the items on the balance sheet that allow for a reasonable esti-mate of market price. Real estate, plant, and equipment would fall in this category.

A somewhat less reliable component of value is the economic profit on assets already in place. For example, a company such as Intel earns a far higher ROE on its investments in chip-making facilities than its cost of capital. The present value of these "economic profits," or economic value added,[11] is a major component of Intel's market value. This component of value is less certain than its balance sheet assets, however, because there is always a concern that new competitors will enter the market, force down prices and profit margins, and reduce the return on Intel's investments. Thus, one needs to carefully assess the barriers to entry that protect Intel's pricing and profit margins. We reviewed some of these barriers in the last chapter, where we discussed the role of industry analysis, market structure, and competitive position (see Section 12.7).

Finally, the least reliable components of value are growth opportunities, the purported ability of firms like Intel to invest in positive-NPV ventures that contribute to high market valuations today. Value investors don't deny that such opportunities exist, but they are skepti-cal that precise values can be attached to them and, therefore, tend to be less willing to make investment decisions that turn on the value of those opportunities.

13.6   THE AGGREGATE STOCK MARKET

The most popular approach to valuing the overall stock market is the earnings multiplier approach applied at the aggregate level. The first step is to forecast corporate profits for the coming period. Then we derive an estimate of the earnings multiplier, the aggregate P/E ratio,

---

[11]We discuss economic value added in greater detail in the next chapter.

FIGURE 13.8

Earnings yield of S&P 500 versus 10-year Treasury-bond yield

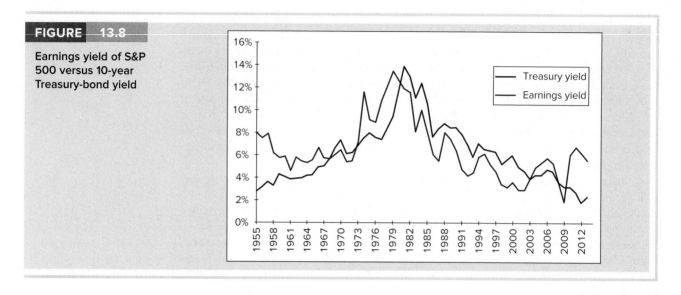

based on a forecast of long-term interest rates. The product of the two forecasts is the estimate of the end-of-period level of the market.

The forecast of the P/E ratio of the market is sometimes derived from a graph similar to that in Figure 13.8, which plots the *earnings yield* (earnings per share divided by price per share, the reciprocal of the P/E ratio) of the S&P 500 and the yield to maturity on 10-year Treasury bonds. The two series clearly move in tandem over time and suggest that one might use this relationship and the current yield on 10-year Treasury bonds to forecast the earnings yield on the S&P 500. Given that earnings yield, a forecast of earnings could be used to predict the level of the S&P in some future period. Let's consider a simple example of this procedure.

EXAMPLE 13.7

Forecasting the Aggregate Stock Market

In late 2014, the S&P 500 was at 2,040. The forecast for 12-month forward earnings per share for the S&P 500 portfolio was about $134. The 10-year Treasury-bond yield at this time was about 2.3%, but the yield curve was relatively steep, so a plausible forecast for its value next year would be higher, perhaps 2.8%. As a first approach, we might posit that the spread between the earnings yield and the Treasury yield, which was around 3.2% in 2014, will remain at that level by the end of the year. Given the assumed Treasury yield, this would imply an earnings yield for the S&P of 6% and a P/E ratio of 1/.06 = 16.67. Our forecast for the level of the S&P Index would then be 16.67 × 134 = 2,233, which would imply a one-year capital gain on the index of 193/2,040 = 9.5%.

Of course, there is uncertainty regarding all three inputs into this analysis: the actual earnings on the S&P 500 stocks, the level of Treasury yields at year-end, and the spread between the Treasury yield and the earnings yield. One would wish to perform sensitivity or scenario analysis to examine the impact of changes in all of these variables. To illustrate, consider Table 13.4, which shows a simple scenario analysis treating possible effects of variation in the Treasury-bond yield. The scenario analysis shows that the forecast level of the stock market varies inversely and with dramatic sensitivity to interest rate changes.

Some analysts use an aggregate version of the dividend discount model rather than an earnings multiplier approach. All of these models, however, rely heavily on forecasts of such macroeconomic variables as GDP, interest rates, and the rate of inflation, which are difficult to predict accurately.

TABLE 13.4 S&P 500 index forecasts under various scenarios

	Pessimistic Scenario	Most Likely Scenario	Optimistic Scenario
Treasury bond yield	3.3%	2.8%	2.3%
Earnings yield	6.5%	6.0%	5.5%
Resulting P/E ratio	15.4	16.7	18.2
EPS forecast	134	134	134
Forecast for S&P 500	2,062	2,233	2,436

Note: The forecast for the earnings yield on the S&P 500 equals the Treasury-bond yield plus 3.2%. The P/E ratio is the reciprocal of the forecast earnings yield.

Because stock prices reflect expectations of future dividends, which are tied to the economic fortunes of firms, it is not surprising that the performance of a broad-based stock index like the S&P 500 is taken as a leading economic indicator, that is, a predictor of the performance of the aggregate economy. Stock prices are viewed as embodying consensus forecasts of economic activity and are assumed to move up or down in anticipation of movements in the economy. The government's index of leading economic indicators, which is taken to predict the progress of the business cycle, is made up in part of recent stock market performance. However, the predictive value of the market is far from perfect. A well-known joke, often attributed to Paul Samuelson, is that the market has forecast eight of the last five recessions.

SUMMARY

- One approach to firm valuation is to focus on the firm's book value, either as it appears on the balance sheet or adjusted to reflect the current replacement cost of assets or the liquidation value. Another approach is to focus on the present value of expected future dividends.

- The dividend discount model holds that the price of a share of stock should equal the present value of all future dividends per share, discounted at an interest rate commensurate with the risk of the stock.

- The constant-growth version of the DDM asserts that if dividends are expected to grow at a constant rate forever, then the intrinsic value of the stock is determined by the formula

$$V_0 = \frac{D_1}{k - g}$$

- This version of the DDM is simplistic in its assumption of a constant value of g. There are more sophisticated multistage versions of the model for more complex environments. When the constant-growth assumption is reasonably satisfied, however, the formula can be inverted to infer the market capitalization rate for the stock:

$$k = \frac{D_1}{P_0} + g$$

- Stock market analysts devote considerable attention to a company's price–earnings ratio. The P/E ratio is a useful measure of the market's assessment of the firm's growth opportunities. Firms with no growth opportunities should have a P/E ratio that is just the reciprocal of the capitalization rate, k. As growth opportunities become a progressively more important component of the total value of the firm, the P/E ratio will increase.

- Many analysts form their estimates of a stock's value by multiplying their forecast of next year's EPS by a predicted P/E multiple. Some analysts mix the P/E approach with the dividend discount model. They use an earnings multiplier to forecast the terminal value of shares at a future date and add the present value of that terminal value with the present value of all interim dividend payments.

- The free cash flow approach is the one used most in corporate finance. The analyst first estimates the value of the firm as the present value of expected future free cash flows to the entire firm and then subtracts the value of all claims other than equity. Alternatively, the free cash flows to equity can be discounted at a discount rate appropriate to the risk of the stock.

- The models presented in this chapter can be used to explain or to forecast the behavior of the aggregate stock market. The key macroeconomic variables that determine the level of stock prices in the aggregate are interest rates and corporate profits.

KEY TERMS

book value, 403	liquidation value, 404	price–earnings
constant-growth DDM, 407	market capitalization	multiple, 417
dividend discount model	rate, 405	replacement cost, 404
(DDM), 406	PEG ratio, 419	Tobin's q, 404
dividend payout ratio, 410	plowback ratio, 410	two-stage DDM, 413
earnings management, 422	present value of growth	
earnings retention ratio, 410	opportunities	
intrinsic value, 405	(PVGO), 411	

KEY FORMULAS

Intrinsic value: $V_0 = \dfrac{D_1}{1+k} + \dfrac{D_2}{(1+k)^2} + \cdots + \dfrac{D_H + P_H}{(1+k)^H}$

Constant-growth DDM: $V_0 = \dfrac{D_1}{k-g}$

Growth opportunities: $\text{Price} = \dfrac{E_1}{k} + \text{PVGO}$

Determinant of P/E ratio: $\dfrac{P_0}{E_1} = \dfrac{1}{k}\left(1 + \dfrac{\text{PVGO}}{E_1/k}\right)$

Free cash flow to the firm:

$$\text{FCFF} = \text{EBIT}(1 - t_c) + \text{Depreciation} - \text{Capital expenditures} - \text{Increases in NWC}$$

Free cash flow to equity:

$$\text{FCFE} = \text{FCFF} - \text{Interest expense} \times (1 - t_c) + \text{Increase in net debt}$$

PROBLEM SETS

Select problems are available in McGraw-Hill's *Connect*. Please see the Supplements section of the book's frontmatter for more information.

1. In what circumstances would you choose to use a dividend discount model rather than a free cash flow model to value a firm? *(LO 13-4)*

2. In what circumstances is it most important to use multistage dividend discount models rather than constant-growth models? *(LO 13-2)*

3. If a security is underpriced (i.e., intrinsic value > price), then what is the relationship between its market capitalization rate and its expected rate of return? *(LO 13-2)*

4. Deployment Specialists pays a current (annual) dividend of $1 and is expected to grow at 20% for two years and then at 4% thereafter. If the required return for Deployment Specialists is 8.5%, what is the intrinsic value of Deployment Specialists stock? *(LO 13-2)*

5. Jand, Inc., currently pays a dividend of $1.22, which is expected to grow indefinitely at 5%. If the current value of Jand's shares based on the constant-growth dividend discount model is $32.03, what is the required rate of return? *(LO 13-2)*

6. A firm pays a current dividend of $1, which is expected to grow at a rate of 5% indefinitely. If the current value of the firm's shares is $35, what is the required return applicable to the investment based on the constant-growth dividend discount model (DDM)? *(LO 13-2)*

7. Tri-coat Paints has a current market value of $41 per share with earnings of $3.64. What is the present value of its growth opportunities (PVGO) if the required return is 9%? *(LO 13-2)*

8. A firm has current assets that could be sold for their book value of $10 million. The book value of its fixed assets is $60 million, but they could be sold for $90 million today. The firm has total debt with a book value of $40 million, but interest rate declines have caused the market value of the debt to increase to $50 million. What is this firm's market-to-book ratio? *(LO 13-1)*

9. The market capitalization rate for Admiral Motors Company is 8%. Its expected ROE is 10% and its expected EPS is $5. If the firm's plowback ratio is 60%, what will be its P/E ratio? *(LO 13-2)*

10. Miltmar Corporation will pay a year-end dividend of $4, and dividends thereafter are expected to grow at the constant rate of 4% per year. The risk-free rate is 4%, and the expected return on the market portfolio is 12%. The stock has a beta of .75. What is the intrinsic value of the stock? *(LO 13-2)*

11. Sisters Corp expects to earn $6 per share next year. The firm's ROE is 15% and its plowback ratio is 60%. If the firm's market capitalization rate is 10%, what is the present value of its growth opportunities? *(LO 13-3)*

12. Eagle Products' EBIT is $300, its tax rate is 35%, depreciation is $20, capital expenditures are $60, and the planned increase in net working capital is $30. What is the free cash flow to the firm? *(LO 13-4)*

13. FinCorp's free cash flow to the firm is reported as $205 million. The firm's interest expense is $22 million. Assume the tax rate is 35% and the net debt of the firm increases by $3 million. What is the market value of equity if the FCFE is projected to grow at 3% indefinitely and the cost of equity is 12%? *(LO 13-4)*

14. A common stock pays an annual dividend per share of $2.10. The risk-free rate is 7% and the risk premium for this stock is 4%. If the annual dividend is expected to remain at $2.10, what is the value of the stock? *(LO 13-2)*

15. The risk-free rate of return is 5%, the required rate of return on the market is 10%, and High-Flyer stock has a beta coefficient of 1.5. If the dividend per share expected during the coming year, D_1, is $2.50 and $g = 4\%$, at what price should a share sell? *(LO 13-2)*

16. Explain why the following statements are true/false/uncertain. *(LO 13-3)*
    a. With all else held constant, a firm will have a higher P/E if its beta is higher.
    b. P/E will tend to be higher when ROE is higher (assuming plowback is positive).
    c. P/E will tend to be higher when the plowback rate is higher.

17. *a.* Computer stocks currently provide an expected rate of return of 16%. MBI, a large computer company, will pay a year-end dividend of $2 per share. If the stock is selling at $50 per share, what must be the market's expectation of the growth rate of MBI dividends?

   b. If dividend growth forecasts for MBI are revised downward to 5% per year, what will happen to the price of MBI stock?

   c. What (qualitatively) will happen to the company's price–earnings ratio?   *(LO 13-3)*

18. Even Better Products has come out with a new and improved product. As a result, the firm projects an ROE of 20%, and it will maintain a plowback ratio of .30. Its earnings this year will be $2 per share. Investors expect a 12% rate of return on the stock.   *(LO 13-3)*

   a. At what price and P/E ratio would you expect the firm to sell?

   b. What is the present value of growth opportunities?

   c. What would be the P/E ratio and the present value of growth opportunities if the firm planned to reinvest only 20% of its earnings?

19. *a.* MF Corp. has an ROE of 16% and a plowback ratio of 50%. If the coming year's earnings are expected to be $2 per share, at what price will the stock sell? The market capitalization rate is 12%.

   b. What price do you expect MF shares to sell for in three years?   *(LO 13-2)*

20. The market consensus is that Analog Electronic Corporation has an ROE = 9% and a beta of 1.25. It plans to maintain indefinitely its traditional plowback ratio of 2/3. This year's earnings were $3 per share. The annual dividend was just paid. The consensus estimate of the coming year's market return is 14%, and T-bills currently offer a 6% return.   *(LO 13-3)*

   a. Find the price at which Analog stock should sell.

   b. Calculate the P/E ratio.

   c. Calculate the present value of growth opportunities.

   d. Suppose your research convinces you Analog will announce momentarily that it will immediately reduce its plowback ratio to 1/3. Find the intrinsic value of the stock.

   e. The market is still unaware of this decision. Explain why V_0 no longer equals P_0 and why V_0 is greater or less than P_0.

21. The FI Corporation's dividends per share are expected to grow indefinitely by 5% per year.   *(LO 13-3)*

   a. If this year's year-end dividend is $8 and the market capitalization rate is 10% per year, what must the current stock price be according to the dividend discount model?

   b. If the expected earnings per share are $12, what is the implied value of the ROE on future investment opportunities?

   c. How much is the market paying per share for growth opportunities (that is, for an ROE on future investments that exceeds the market capitalization rate)?

22. The stock of Nogro Corporation is currently selling for $10 per share. Earnings per share in the coming year are expected to be $2. The company has a policy of paying out 50% of its earnings each year in dividends. The rest is retained and invested in projects that earn a 20% rate of return per year. This situation is expected to continue indefinitely.   *(LO 13-3)*

   a. Assuming the current market price of the stock reflects its intrinsic value as computed using the constant-growth DDM, what rate of return do Nogro's investors require?

   b. By how much does its value exceed what it would be if all earnings were paid as dividends and nothing were reinvested?

   c. If Nogro were to cut its dividend payout ratio to 25%, what would happen to its stock price?

   d. What if Nogro eliminated the dividend?

23. The risk-free rate of return is 8%, the expected rate of return on the market portfolio is 15%, and the stock of Xyrong Corporation has a beta coefficient of 1.2. Xyrong pays out

40% of its earnings in dividends, and the latest earnings announced were $10 per share. Dividends were just paid and are expected to be paid annually. You expect that Xyrong will earn an ROE of 20% per year on all reinvested earnings forever. *(LO 13-2)*

a. What is the intrinsic value of a share of Xyrong stock?

b. If the market price of a share is currently $100, and you expect the market price to be equal to the intrinsic value one year from now, what is your expected one-year holding-period return on Xyrong stock?

24. The MoMi Corporation's cash flow from operations before interest and taxes was $2 million in the year just ended, and it expects that this will grow by 5% per year forever. To make this happen, the firm will have to invest an amount equal to 20% of pretax cash flow each year. The tax rate is 35%. Depreciation was $200,000 in the year just ended and is expected to grow at the same rate as the operating cash flow. The appropriate market capitalization rate for the unleveraged cash flow is 12% per year, and the firm currently has debt of $4 million outstanding. Use the free cash flow approach to value the firm's equity. *(LO 13-4)*

25. Recalculate the intrinsic value of GE using the three-stage growth model of Spreadsheet 13.1 (available in Connect; link to Chapter 13 material). Treat each of the following scenarios independently. *(LO 13-2)*

a. ROE in the constant-growth period will be 15%.

b. GE's actual beta is 1.10.

c. The market risk premium is 8.5%.

Templates and spreadsheets are available in Connect

26. Recalculate the intrinsic value of GE's shares using the free cash flow model of Spreadsheet 13.2 (available in Connect; link to Chapter 13 material). Treat each scenario independently. *(LO 13-4)*

a. GE's P/E ratio starting in 2018 (cell G3) will be 15.5.

b. GE's current stock market beta (cell B21) is 1.10.

c. The market risk premium (cell B27) is 8.5%.

Templates and spreadsheets are available in Connect

Challenge

27. Chiptech, Inc., is an established computer chip firm with several profitable existing products as well as some promising new products in development. The company earned $1 per share last year and just paid out a dividend of $.50 per share. Investors believe the company plans to maintain its dividend payout ratio at 50%. ROE equals 20%. Everyone in the market expects this situation to persist indefinitely. *(LO 13-2)*

a. What is the market price of Chiptech stock? The required return for the computer chip industry is 15%, and the company has just gone ex-dividend (i.e., the next dividend will be paid a year from now, at $t = 1$).

b. Suppose you discover that Chiptech's competitor has developed a new chip that will eliminate Chiptech's current technological advantage in this market. This new product, which will be ready to come to the market in two years, will force Chiptech to reduce the prices of its chips to remain competitive. This will decrease ROE to 15%, and, because of falling demand for its product, Chiptech will decrease the plowback ratio to .40. The plowback ratio will be decreased at the end of the second year, at $t = 2$: The annual year-end dividend for the second year (paid at $t = 2$) will be 60% of that year's earnings. What is your estimate of Chiptech's intrinsic value per share? (*Hint:* Carefully prepare a table of Chiptech's earnings and dividends for each of the next three years. Pay close attention to the change in the payout ratio in $t = 2$.)

c. No one else in the market perceives the threat to Chiptech's market. In fact, you are confident that no one else will become aware of the change in Chiptech's competitive status until the competitor firm publicly announces its discovery near the end of year 2. What will be the rate of return on Chiptech stock in the coming year (i.e., between $t = 0$ and $t = 1$)?

d. What will be the rate of return in the second year (between $t = 1$ and $t = 2$)?

e. What will be the rate of return in the third year (between $t = 2$ and $t = 3$)? (*Hint:* Pay attention to when the *market* catches on to the new situation. A table of dividends and market prices over time might help.)

CFA Problems

1. At Litchfield Chemical Corp. (LCC), a director of the company said that the use of dividend discount models by investors is "proof" that the higher the dividend, the higher the stock price. *(LO 13-2)*

   a. Using a constant-growth dividend discount model as a basis of reference, evaluate the director's statement.

   b. Explain how an increase in dividend payout would affect each of the following (holding all other factors constant):

      i. Sustainable growth rate.

      ii. Growth in book value.

2. Phoebe Black's investment club wants to buy the stock of either NewSoft, Inc. or Capital Corp. In this connection, Black prepared the following table. You have been asked to help her interpret the data, based on your forecast for a healthy economy and a strong stock market over the next 12 months. *(LO 13-2)*

	NewSoft, Inc.	Capital Corp.	S&P 500 Index
Current price	$30	$32	
Industry	Computer software	Capital goods	
P/E ratio (current)	25	14	16
P/E ratio (5-year average)	27	16	16
Price/book ratio (current)	10	3	3
Price/book ratio (5-year average)	12	4	2
Beta	1.5	1.1	1.0
Dividend yield	0.3%	2.7%	2.8%

   a. Newsoft's shares have higher price–earnings (P/E) and price–book value (P/B) ratios than those of Capital Corp. (The price–book ratio is the ratio of market value to book value.) Briefly discuss why the disparity in ratios may not indicate that NewSoft's shares are overvalued relative to the shares of Capital Corp. Answer the question in terms of the two ratios, and assume that there have been no extraordinary events affecting either company.

   b. Using a constant-growth dividend discount model, Black estimated the value of New-Soft to be $28 per share and the value of Capital Corp. to be $34 per share. Briefly discuss weaknesses of this dividend discount model, and explain why this model may be less suitable for valuing NewSoft than for valuing Capital Corp.

   c. Recommend and justify a more appropriate dividend discount model for valuing New-Soft's common stock.

3. Peninsular Research is initiating coverage of a mature manufacturing industry. John Jones, CFA, head of the research department, gathered the following fundamental industry and market data to help in his analysis: *(LO 13-3)*

Forecast industry earnings retention rate	40%
Forecast industry return on equity	25%
Industry beta	1.2
Government bond yield	6%
Equity risk premium	5%

a. Compute the price-to-earnings (P_0/E_1) ratio for the industry based on this fundamental data.

b. Jones wants to analyze how fundamental P/E ratios might differ among countries. He gathered the following economic and market data:

Fundamental Factors	Country A	Country B
Forecast growth in real GDP	5%	2%
Government bond yield	10%	6%
Equity risk premium	5%	4%

Determine whether each of these fundamental factors would cause P/E ratios to be generally higher for Country A or higher for Country B.

4. Janet Ludlow's firm requires all its analysts to use a two-stage DDM and the CAPM to value stocks. Using these measures, Ludlow has valued QuickBrush Company at $63 per share. She now must value SmileWhite Corporation. *(LO 13-2)*

   a. Calculate the required rate of return for SmileWhite using the information in the following table:

	December 2013	
	QuickBrush	SmileWhite
Beta	1.35	1.15
Market price	$45.00	$30.00
Intrinsic value	$63.00	?

Note: Risk-free rate = 4.50%; expected market return = 14.50%.

   b. Ludlow estimates the following EPS and dividend growth rates for SmileWhite:

First three years:	12% per year
Years thereafter:	9% per year

   Estimate the intrinsic value of SmileWhite using the table above and the two-stage DDM. Dividends per share in 2013 were $1.72.

   c. Recommend QuickBrush or SmileWhite stock for purchase by comparing each company's intrinsic value with its current market price.

   d. Describe *one* strength of the two-stage DDM in comparison with the constant-growth DDM. Describe *one* weakness inherent in all DDMs.

5. Rio National Corp. is a U.S.-based company and the largest competitor in its industry. Tables 13.5–13.8 present financial statements and related information for the company. Table 13.9 presents relevant industry and market data.

   The portfolio manager of a large mutual fund comments to one of the fund's analysts, Katrina Shaar: "We have been considering the purchase of Rio National Corp. equity shares, so I would like you to analyze the value of the company. To begin, based on Rio National's past performance, you can assume that the company will grow at the same rate as the industry." *(LO 13-2)*

   a. Calculate the value of a share of Rio National equity on December 31, 2015, using the constant-growth model and the capital asset pricing model.

   b. Calculate the sustainable growth rate of Rio National on December 31, 2015. Use 2015 beginning-of-year balance sheet values.

TABLE 13.5   Rio National Corp. summary year-end balance sheets (U.S. $ millions)

	2015	2014
Cash	$ 13.00	$ 5.87
Accounts receivable	30.00	27.00
Inventory	209.06	189.06
Current assets	$252.06	$221.93
Gross fixed assets	474.47	409.47
Accumulated depreciation	(154.17)	(90.00)
Net fixed assets	$320.30	$319.47
Total assets	$572.36	$541.40
Accounts payable	$ 25.05	$ 26.05
Notes payable	0.00	0.00
Current portion of long-term debt	0.00	0.00
Current liabilities	$ 25.05	$ 26.05
Long-term debt	240.00	245.00
Total liabilities	$265.05	$271.05
Common stock	160.00	150.00
Retained earnings	147.31	120.35
Total shareholders' equity	$307.31	$270.35
Total liabilities and shareholders' equity	$572.36	$541.40

TABLE 13.6   Rio National Corp. summary income statement for the year ended December 31, 2015 (U.S. $ millions)

Revenue	$300.80
Total operating expenses	(173.74)
Operating profit	$127.06
Gain on sale	4.00
Earnings before interest, taxes, depreciation & amortization (EBITDA)	$131.06
Depreciation and amortization	(71.17)
Earnings before interest & taxes (EBIT)	$59.89
Interest	(16.80)
Income tax expense	(12.93)
Net income	$ 30.16

TABLE 13.7   Rio National Corp. supplemental notes for 2015

Note 1: Rio National had $75 million in capital expenditures during the year.

Note 2: A piece of equipment that was originally purchased for $10 million was sold for $7 million at year-end, when it had a net book value of $3 million. Equipment sales are unusual for Rio National.

Note 3: The decrease in long-term debt represents an unscheduled principal repayment; there was no new borrowing during the year.

Note 4: On 1 January 2015, the company received cash from issuing 400,000 shares of common equity at a price of $25 per share.

Note 5: A new appraisal during the year increased the estimated market value of land held for investment by $2 million, which was not recognized in 2015 income.

TABLE 13.8	Rio National Corp. common equity data for 2015
Dividends paid (U.S. $ millions)	$3.20
Weighted-average shares outstanding during 2015	16,000,000
Dividend per share	$0.20
Earnings per share	$1.89
Beta	1.80

Note: The dividend payout ratio is expected to be constant.

TABLE 13.9	Industry and market data, December 31, 2015
Risk-free rate of return	4.00%
Expected rate of return on market index	9.00%
Median industry price–earnings (P/E) ratio	19.90
Expected industry earnings growth rate	12.00%

6. While valuing the equity of Rio National Corp. (from the previous problem), Katrina Shaar is considering the use of either free cash flow to the firm (FCFF) or free cash flow to equity (FCFE) in her valuation process. *(LO 13-4)*
   a. State two adjustments that Shaar should make to FCFF to obtain free cash flow to equity.
   b. Shaar decides to calculate Rio National's FCFE for the year 2015, starting with net income. Determine for each of the five supplemental notes given in Table 13.7 whether an adjustment should be made to net income to calculate Rio National's free cash flow to equity for the year 2015, and the dollar amount of any adjustment.
   c. Calculate Rio National's free cash flow to equity for the year 2015.

7. Shaar (from the previous problem) has revised slightly her estimated earnings growth rate for Rio National and, using normalized (underlying trend) EPS, which is adjusted for temporary impacts on earnings, now wants to compare the current value of Rio National's equity to that of the industry, on a growth-adjusted basis. Selected information about Rio National and the industry is given in Table 13.10.

   Compared to the industry, is Rio National's equity overvalued or undervalued on a P/E-to-growth (PEG) basis, using normalized (underlying) earnings per share? Assume that the risk of Rio National is similar to the risk of the industry. *(LO 13-3)*

8. Helen Morgan, CFA, has been asked to use the dividend discount model to determine the value of Sundanci, Inc. Morgan anticipates that Sundanci's earnings and dividends will grow at 32% for two years and 13% thereafter.

TABLE 13.10	Rio National Corp. vs. industry
Rio National	
Estimated earnings growth rate	11.00%
Current share price	$25.00
Normalized (underlying trend) EPS for 2015	$ 1.71
Weighted-average shares outstanding during 2015	16,000,000
Industry	
Estimated earnings growth rate	12.00%
Median price–earnings (P/E) ratio	19.90

TABLE 13.11 Sundanci actual 2015 and forecast 2016 financial statements for fiscal years ending May 31 ($ million, except per-share data)

Income Statement	2015	2016
Revenue	$ 474	$ 598
Depreciation	20	23
Other operating costs	368	460
Income before taxes	$ 86	$ 115
Taxes	26	35
Net income	$ 60	$ 80
Dividends	18	24
Earnings per share	$0.714	$0.952
Dividend per share	$0.214	$0.286
Common shares outstanding (millions)	84.0	84.0

Balance Sheet	2015	2016
Current assets	$ 201	$ 326
Net property, plant, and equipment	474	489
Total assets	$ 675	$ 815
Current liabilities	$ 57	$ 141
Long-term debt	0	0
Total liabilities	$ 57	$ 141
Shareholders' equity	618	674
Total liabilities and equity	$ 675	$ 815
Capital expenditures	34	38

TABLE 13.12 Selected financial information

Required rate of return on equity	14%
Growth rate of industry	13%
Industry P/E ratio	26

Calculate the current value of a share of Sundanci stock by using a two-stage dividend discount model and the data from Tables 13.11 and 13.12. *(LO 13-2)*

9. To continue with Sundanci, Abbey Naylor, CFA, has been directed to determine the value of Sundanci's stock using the free cash flow to equity (FCFE) model. Naylor believes that Sundanci's FCFE will grow at 27% for two years and 13% thereafter. Capital expenditures, depreciation, and working capital are all expected to increase proportionately with FCFE. *(LO 13-4)*

a. Calculate the amount of FCFE per share for the year 2016 using the data from Table 13.11.

b. Calculate the current value of a share of Sundanci stock based on the two-stage FCFE model.

c. i. Describe one limitation of the two-stage DDM model that is addressed by using the two-stage FCFE model.

ii. Describe one limitation of the two-stage DDM model that is *not* addressed by using the two-stage FCFE model.

10. Christie Johnson, CFA, has been assigned to analyze Sundanci using the constant-dividend-growth price–earnings (P/E) ratio model. Johnson assumes that Sundanci's earnings and dividends will grow at a constant rate of 13%.   *(LO 13-2)*

    a. Calculate the P/E ratio based on information in Tables 13.11 and 13.12 and on Johnson's assumptions for Sundanci.

    b. Identify, within the context of the constant-dividend-growth model, how each of the following factors would affect the P/E ratio.

       • Risk (beta) of Sundanci.

       • Estimated growth rate of earnings and dividends.

       • Market risk premium.

WEB *master*

1. Choose 10 firms that interest you and download their financial statements from **finance.yahoo.com**.

    a. For each firm, find the return on equity (ROE), the number of shares outstanding, the dividends per share, and the net income. Record them in a spreadsheet.

    b. Calculate the total amount of dividends paid (dividends per share × number of shares outstanding), the dividend payout ratio (total dividends paid/net income), and the plowback ratio (1 − dividend payout ratio).

    c. Compute the sustainable growth rate, $g = b \times ROE$, where b equals the plowback ratio.

    d. Compare the growth rates (g) with the P/E ratios of the firms by plotting the P/Es against the growth rates in a scatter diagram. Is there a relationship between the two?

    e. Using data from financial statements, find or calculate the ratios of price-to-book, price-to-sales, and price-to-cash flow from operations for each firm in your sample. Use a line chart to plot these three ratios on the same set of axes. What relationships do you see among the three series?

    f. For each firm, compare the three-year growth rate of earnings per share with the growth rate you calculated above. Is the actual rate of earnings growth correlated with the sustainable growth rate you calculated?

2. Now calculate the intrinsic value of three of the firms you selected in the previous question. Make reasonable judgments about the market risk premium and the risk-free rate, or find estimates from the Internet.

    a. What is the required return on each firm based on the CAPM? You can get the beta of each firm from its *Key Statistics* page.

    b. Try using a two-stage growth model, making reasonable assumptions about how future growth rates will differ from current growth rates. Compare the intrinsic values derived from the two-stage model to the intrinsic values you find assuming a constant-growth rate. Which estimate seems more reasonable for each firm?

3. Now choose one of your firms and look up other firms in the same industry. Perform a "Valuation by Comparables" analysis by looking at the price/earnings, price/book value, price/sales, and price/operating cash flow ratios of the firms relative to each other and to the industry average. Which of the firms seem to be overvalued? Which seem to be undervalued? Can you think of reasons for any apparent mispricings?

4. The actual expected return on a stock based on estimates of future dividends and future price can be compared to the "required" or equilibrium return given its risk. If the expected return is greater than the required return, the stock may be an attractive investment.

    a. First calculate the expected holding-period return (HPR) on Target Corporation's stock based on its current price, its expected price, and its expected dividend.

       i. Get information for Target (enter TGT under quote search). From the *Analyst Opinion* page, find the range for estimated target price for the next fiscal year.

       ii. Collect information about today's price and the dividend rate. What is the company's expected dividend in dollars for the next fiscal year?

       iii. Use these inputs to calculate the range of Target's HPR for the next year.

b. Calculate the required return based on the capital asset pricing model (CAPM).

   i. Use a risk-free rate from Yahoo's *Market Data* page.

   ii. Use the beta coefficient shown in the *Key Statistics* page.

   iii. Calculate the historical return on a broad-based market index of your choice. You may use any time period that you deem appropriate. Your goal is to derive an estimate of the expected return on the market index for the coming year.

   iv. Use the data you've collected as inputs for the CAPM to find the required rate of return for Target Corporation.

c. Compare the expected HPR you calculated in part (*a*) to the required CAPM return you calculated in part (*b*). What is your best judgment about the stock's current status—do you think it is selling at an appropriate price?

13.1 *a.* Dividend yield = \$2.15/\$50 = 4.3%

    Capital gains yield = (59.77 − 50)/50 = 19.54%

    Total return = 4.3% + 19.54% = 23.84%

  b. $k = 6\% + 1.15(14\% − 6\%) = 15.2\%$

  c. $V_0 = (\$2.15 + \$59.77)/1.152 = \$53.75$, which exceeds the market price. This would indicate a "buy" opportunity.

13.2 *a.* $D_1/(k − g) = \$2.15/(.152 − .112) = \$53.75$

  b. $P_1 = P_0(1 + g) = \$53.75(1.112) = \$59.77$

  c. The expected capital gain equals \$59.77 − \$53.75 = \$6.02, for a percentage gain of 11.2%. The dividend yield is $D_1/P_0 = 2.15/53.75 = 4\%$, for a holding-period return of 4% + 11.2% = 15.2%.

13.3 *a.* $g = \text{ROE} \times b = .20 \times .60 = .12$

    $P_0 = 2/(.125 − .12) = 400$

  b. When the firm invests in projects with ROE less than *k,* its stock price falls. If $b = .60$, then $g = 10\% \times .60 = 6\%$ and $P_0 = \$2/(.125 − .06) = \$30.77$. In contrast, if $b = 0$, then $P_0 = \$5/.125 = \$40$.

13.4 Because $\beta = 1.1, k = 3\% + 1.1 \times 8\% = 11.8\%.$

$$V_{2014} = \frac{1.00}{1.118} + \frac{1.13}{(1.118)^2} + \frac{1.26}{(1.118)^3} + \frac{1.40 + P_{2018}}{(1.118)^4}$$

To estimate P_{2018} in this equation, use the constant-growth dividend discount model.

$$P_{2018} = \frac{1.40 \times (1 + g)}{k − g} = \frac{1.40 \times 1.0768}{.118 − .0768} = \$36.59$$

Therefore, $V_{2014} = \$27.02.$

13.5 *a.* ROE = 12%

    $b = \$.50/\$2.00 = .25$

    $g = \text{ROE} \times b = 12\% \times .25 = 3\%$

    $P_0 = D_1/(k − g) = \$1.50/(.10 − .03) = \$21.43$

    $P_0/E_1 = 21.43/\$2 = 10.71$

  b. If $b = .4$, then $.4 \times \$2 = \$.80$ would be reinvested and the remainder of earnings, or \$1.20, would be paid as dividends.

    $g = 12\% \times .4 = 4.8\%$

    $P_0 = D_1/(k − g) = \$1.20/(.10 − .048) = \$23.08$

    $P_0/E_1 = \$23.08/\$2.00 = 11.54$

    PEG = 11.54/4.8 = 2.4

Financial Statement Analysis

14

Learning Objectives

LO 14-1 Interpret a firm's income statement, balance sheet, and statement of cash flows, and calculate standard measures of a firm's operating efficiency, leverage, and liquidity.

LO 14-2 Calculate and interpret performance measures such as economic value added and rates of return on assets, capital, and equity.

LO 14-3 Use ratio decomposition analysis to show how profitability depends on efficient use of assets, profit margin, and leverage.

LO 14-4 Identify possible sources of biases in conventional accounting data.

In the previous chapter, we explored equity valuation techniques. These techniques take as inputs the firm's dividends and earnings prospects. While the valuation analyst is interested in economic earnings streams, only financial accounting data are readily available. What can we learn from a company's accounting data that can help us estimate the intrinsic value of its common stock?

In this chapter, we show how investors can use financial data as inputs into stock valuation analysis. We start by reviewing the basic sources of such data: the income statement, the balance sheet, and the statement of cash flows. We note the difference between economic and accounting earnings. While economic earnings are more important for issues of valuation, they can at best be estimated, so, in practice, analysts always begin their evaluation of the firm using accounting data. We next show how analysts use financial ratios to explore the sources of a firm's profitability and evaluate the "quality" of its earnings in a systematic fashion. We also examine the impact of debt policy on various financial ratios.

Finally, we conclude with a discussion of the challenges you will encounter when using financial statement analysis as a tool in uncovering mispriced securities. Some of these issues arise from differences in firms' accounting procedures. Others are due to inflation-induced distortions in accounting numbers.

14.1   THE MAJOR FINANCIAL STATEMENTS

The Income Statement

income statement

A financial statement showing a firm's revenues and expenses during a specified period.

The **income statement** is a summary of the profitability of the firm over a period of time, such as a year. It presents revenues generated during the operating period, the expenses incurred during that same period, and the company's net earnings or profits, which are simply the difference between revenues and expenses.

It is useful to distinguish among four broad classes of expenses: cost of goods sold, which is the direct cost attributable to producing the product sold by the firm; general and administrative expenses, which correspond to overhead expenses, salaries, advertising, and other costs of operating the firm that are not directly attributable to production; interest expense on the firm's debt; and taxes on earnings owed to federal and local governments.

Table 14.1 presents an income statement for Home Depot (HD). At the top are the company's revenues. Next come operating expenses, the costs incurred in the course of generating these revenues, including a depreciation allowance. The difference between operating revenues and operating costs is called *operating income.* Income (or expenses) from other, primarily nonrecurring, sources is then added to obtain earnings before interest and taxes (EBIT), which is what the firm would have earned if not for obligations to its creditors and the tax authorities. EBIT is a measure of the profitability of the firm's operations abstracting from any interest burden attributable to debt financing. The income statement then goes on to subtract net interest expense from EBIT to arrive at taxable income. Finally, the income tax due the government is subtracted to arrive at net income, the "bottom line" of the income statement.

Analysts also commonly prepare a *common-size income statement,* in which all items on the income statement are expressed as a fraction of total revenue. This makes it easier to compare firms of different sizes. The right-hand column of Table 14.1 is HD's common-size income statement.

economic earnings

The real flow of cash that a firm could pay out without impairing its productive capacity.

In the previous chapter, we saw that stock valuation models require a measure of **economic earnings**—the sustainable cash flow that can be paid out to stockholders without impairing

---

TABLE 14.1   Home Depot's Income Statement

	$ Million	Percent of Revenue
Operating revenues		
Net sales	$78,812	100.0%
Operating expenses		
Cost of goods sold	$46,133	58.5%
Selling, general, and admininstrative expenses	14,970	19.0
Other	1,627	2.1
Depreciation	1,757	2.2
Total operating expenses	$64,487	81.8%
Earnings before interest and income taxes	$14,325	18.2
Interest expense	711	0.9
Taxable income	$13,614	17.3%
Taxes	3,082	3.9
Net income	$10,532	13.4%
Allocation of net income		
Dividends	2,243	2.8
Addition to retained earnings	8,289	10.5

Note: Sums subject to rounding error.
Source: Home Depot Annual Report, year ending January 2014.

the productive capacity of the firm. In contrast, **accounting earnings** are affected by several conventions regarding the valuation of assets such as inventories (e.g., LIFO versus FIFO treatment) and by the way some expenditures such as capital investments are recognized over time (as depreciation expenses). We will discuss problems with some of these accounting conventions in greater detail later in the chapter. In addition to these accounting issues, as the firm makes its way through the business cycle, its earnings will rise above or fall below the trend line that might more accurately reflect sustainable economic earnings. This introduces an added complication in interpreting net income figures. One might wonder how closely accounting earnings approximate economic earnings and, correspondingly, how useful accounting data might be to investors attempting to value the firm.

In fact, the net income figure on the firm's income statement does convey considerable information concerning a firm's products. We see this in the fact that stock prices tend to increase when firms announce earnings greater than market analysts or investors had anticipated.

accounting earnings

Earnings of a firm as reported on its income statement.

The Balance Sheet

While the income statement provides a measure of profitability over a period of time, the **balance sheet** provides a "snapshot" of the financial condition of the firm at a particular time. The balance sheet is a list of the firm's assets and liabilities at that moment. The difference in assets and liabilities is the net worth of the firm, also called *stockholders' equity* or, equivalently, *shareholders' equity*. Like income statements, balance sheets are reasonably standardized in presentation. Table 14.2 is HD's balance sheet.

balance sheet

An accounting statement of a firm's financial position at a particular time.

The first section of the balance sheet gives a listing of the assets of the firm. Current assets are presented first. These are cash and other items such as accounts receivable or inventories that will be converted into cash within one year. Next comes a listing of long-term or "fixed" assets. *Tangible fixed assets* are items such as buildings, equipment, or vehicles. HD also has several intangible assets such as a respected brand name and expertise. But accountants generally are reluctant to include these assets on the balance sheet, as they are so hard to value. However, when one firm purchases another for a premium over its book value, that difference is called *goodwill* and is listed on the balance sheet as an *intangible fixed asset*. HD lists goodwill at $1,289 million.[1]

The liability and shareholders' equity section is arranged similarly. Listed first are short-term or "current" liabilities, such as accounts payable, accrued taxes, and debts that are due within one year. Long-term debt and other liabilities due in more than a year follow. The difference between total assets and total liabilities is shareholders' equity. This is the net worth or book value of the firm. Shareholders' equity is divided into par value of stock, capital surplus (additional paid-in capital), and retained earnings, although this division is usually unimportant. Briefly, par value plus capital surplus represents the proceeds realized from the sale of stock to the public, while retained earnings represent the buildup of equity from profits plowed back into the firm. Even if the firm issues no new equity, book value will typically increase each year due to reinvested earnings.

The entries in the left columns of the balance sheet in Table 14.2 present the dollar value of each asset. To make it easier to compare firms of different sizes, analysts often present each item on the balance sheet as a percentage of total assets. This is called a *common-size balance sheet* and is presented in the right columns.

The Statement of Cash Flows

The income statement and balance sheets are based on accrual methods of accounting, which means revenues and expenses are recognized at the time of a sale even if no cash has yet been

[1]Firms are required to test their goodwill assets for "impairment" each year. If it becomes apparent that the value of the acquired firm is less than its purchase price, that amount must be charged off as an expense. For example, in 2012 Hewlett-Packard wrote off $8.8 billion on its earlier purchase of the software company Autonomy Corp. amid charges that Autonomy had overstated its profitability prior to the purchase. AOL Time Warner set a record when it recognized an impairment of $99 billion in 2002 following the January 2001 merger of Time Warner with AOL.

TABLE 14.2   Home Depot's Balance Sheet

Assets	$ Million	Percent of Total Assets	Liabilities and Shareholders' Equity	$ Million	Percent of Total Assets
Current assets			Current liabilities		
Cash and marketable securities	$ 1,929	4.8%	Debt due for repayment	$ 33	0.1%
Receivables	1,398	3.5	Accounts payable	9,379	23.1
Inventories	11,057	27.3	Other current liabilities	1,337	3.3
Other current assets	895	2.2	Total current liabilities	$10,749	26.5%
Total current assets	$15,279	37.7%	Long-term debt	14,691	36.3
Fixed assets			Other long-term liabilities	2,042	5.0
Tangible fixed assets			Deferred long-term liability charges	514	0
Property, plant, and equipment	$23,348	57.6	Total liabilities	$27,996	69.1%
Other long-term assets	602	1.5	Shareholders' equity		
Total tangible fixed assets	$23,950	59.1%	Common stock and other paid-in capital	−$10,658	−26.3
Intangible fixed assets			Retained earnings	23,180	57.2
Goodwill	1,289	3.2	Total shareholders' equity	$12,522	30.9%
Total fixed assets	$25,239	62.3%	Total liabilities and shareholders' equity	$40,518	100.0%
Total assets	$40,518	100.0%			

Note: Column sums subject to rounding error.

Source: Home Depot Annual Report, year ending January 2014.

statement of cash flows

A financial statement showing a firm's cash receipts and cash payments during a specified period.

exchanged. In contrast, the **statement of cash flows** recognizes only transactions in which cash changes hands. For example, if goods are sold now, with payment due in 60 days, the income statement will treat the revenue as generated when the sale occurs, and the balance sheet will be immediately augmented by accounts receivable, but the statement of cash flows will not recognize the transaction until the bill is paid and the cash is in hand.

Table 14.3 is the statement of cash flows for HD. The first entry listed under "Cash provided by operations" is net income. The following entries modify that figure for components of income that have been recognized but for which cash has not yet changed hands. For example, HD's accounts receivable increased by $15 million. This portion of its income was claimed on the income statement, but the cash had not yet been collected. Increases in accounts receivable are in effect an investment in working capital and, therefore, reduce the cash flows realized from operations. Similarly, increases in accounts payable mean expenses have been recognized, but cash has not yet left the firm. Any payment delay increases the company's net cash flows in this period.

Another major difference between the income statement and the statement of cash flows involves depreciation, which accounts for a substantial addition in the adjustment section of the statement of cash flows in Table 14.3. The income statement attempts to "smooth" large capital expenditures over time. The depreciation expense on the income statement does this by recognizing capital expenditures over a period of many years rather than at the specific time of purchase. In contrast, the statement of cash flows recognizes the cash implication of a capital expenditure when it occurs. Therefore, it adds back the depreciation "expense" that was used to compute net income; instead, it acknowledges a capital expenditure when it is paid. It does so by reporting cash flows separately for operations, investing, and financing activities.

TABLE 14.3 Home Depot's Statement of Cash Flows	
	$ Million
Cash provided by operations	
Net income	$5,385
Adjustments to net income	
Depreciation	1,757
Changes in working capital	
Decrease (increase) in receivables	(15)
Decrease (increase) in inventories	(455)
Increase (decrease) in other current liabilities	812
Changes due to other operating activities	144
Total adjustments	$2,243
Cash provided by operations	7,628
Cash flows from investments	
Gross investment in tangible fixed assets	($1,389)
Investments in other assets	(118)
Cash provided by (used for) investments	($1,507)
Cash provided by (used for) financing activities	
Additions to (reductions in) long-term debt	$3,933
Net issues (repurchases of) shares	(8,305)
Dividends	(2,243)
Other	(37)
Cash provided by (used for) financing activities	($6,652)
Net increase in cash	($531)

Source: Home Depot Annual Report, year ending January 2014.

This way, any large cash flows, such as those for big investments, can be recognized without affecting the measure of cash flow provided by operations.

The second section of the statement of cash flows is the accounting of cash flows from investing activities. For example, HD used $1,389 million of cash investing in tangible fixed assets. These entries are investments in the assets necessary for the firm to maintain or enhance its productive capacity.

Finally, the last section of the statement lists the cash flows realized from financing activities. Issuance of securities contributes positive cash flows, while redemption of outstanding securities uses cash. For example, HD expended $8,305 million to repurchase shares of its stock, which was a use of cash. Its dividend payments, $2,243 million, also used cash. In total, HD's financing activities absorbed $6,652 million of cash.

To summarize, HD's operations generated a cash flow of $7,628 million. The company laid out $1,507 million to pay for new investments, and financing activities used another $6,652 million. HD's cash holdings therefore changed by $7,628 − $1,507 − $6,652 = −$531 million. This is reported on the last line of Table 14.3.

The statement of cash flows provides important evidence on the well-being of a firm. If a company cannot pay its dividends and maintain the productivity of its capital stock out of cash flow from operations, for example, and it must resort to borrowing to meet these demands, this is a serious warning that the firm cannot maintain payout at its current level in the long run.

The statement of cash flows will reveal this developing problem when it shows that cash flow from operations is inadequate and that borrowing is being used to maintain dividend payments at unsustainable levels.

14.2   MEASURING FIRM PERFORMANCE

In Chapter 1, we pointed out that a natural goal of the firm is to maximize value but that various agency problems, or conflicts of interest, may impede that goal. How can we measure how well the firm is actually performing? Financial analysts have come up with a mind-numbing list of financial ratios that measure many aspects of firm performance. Before getting lost in the trees, therefore, let's first pause to consider what sorts of ratios may be related to the ultimate objective of added value.

Two broad activities are the responsibility of a firm's financial managers: investment decisions and financing decisions. Investment, or capital budgeting, decisions pertain to the firm's *use* of capital: the business activities in which it is engaged. Here, the questions we will wish to answer pertain to the profitability of those projects. How should profitability be measured? How does the acceptable level of profitability depend on risk and the opportunity cost of the funds used to pay for the firm's many projects? In contrast, financial decisions pertain to the firm's *sources* of capital. Is there a sufficient supply of financing to meet projected needs for growth? Does the financing plan rely too heavily on borrowed funds? Is there sufficient liquidity to deal with unexpected cash needs?

These questions suggest that we organize the ratios we choose to examine along the lines given in Figure 14.1. The figure shows that when evaluating the firm's investment activities, we will ask two questions: How efficiently does the firm deploy its assets, and how profitable are its sales? In turn, aspects of both efficiency and profitability can be measured with several ratios: Efficiency is typically assessed using several turnover ratios, while the profitability of sales is commonly measured with various profit margins. Similarly, when evaluating financing decisions, we look at both leverage and liquidity, and we will see that aspects of each of these two concepts also can be measured with an array of statistics.

The next section shows how to calculate and interpret some of these key financial ratios and shows how many of them are related.

14.3   PROFITABILITY MEASURES

Big firms naturally earn greater profits than smaller ones. Therefore, most profitability measures focus on earnings per dollar employed. The most common measures are return on assets, return on capital, and return on equity.

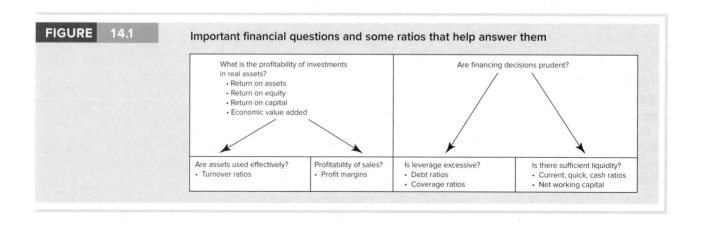

FIGURE 14.1   Important financial questions and some ratios that help answer them

Return on Assets

Return on assets (ROA) equals EBIT as a fraction of the firm's total assets.[2]

$$\text{ROA} = \frac{\text{EBIT}}{\text{Total assets}}$$

The numerator of this ratio may be viewed as total operating income of the firm. Therefore, ROA tells us the income earned per dollar deployed in the firm.

Return on Capital

Return on capital (ROC) expresses EBIT as a fraction of long-term capital, shareholders' equity plus long-term debt. It tells us the income earned per dollar of long-term capital invested in the firm.

$$\text{ROC} = \frac{\text{EBIT}}{\text{Long-term capital}}$$

Return on Equity

Whereas ROA and ROC measure profitability relative to funds raised by both debt and equity financing, **return on equity (ROE)** focuses only on the profitability of equity investments. It equals net income realized by shareholders per dollar they have invested in the firm.

$$\text{ROE} = \frac{\text{Net income}}{\text{Shareholders' equity}}$$

We noted in Chapter 13 that return on equity (ROE) is one of the two basic factors in determining a firm's growth rate of earnings. Sometimes it is reasonable to assume that future ROE will approximate its past value, but a high ROE in the past does not necessarily imply a firm's future ROE will be high. It can be dangerous to accept historical values as indicators of future values. Data from the recent past may provide information regarding future performance, but your focus should be on the future. Expectations of *future* dividends and earnings determine the intrinsic value of the company's stock.

Not surprisingly, ROA and ROE are linked, but as we will see next, the relationship between them is affected by the firm's financial policies.

Financial Leverage and ROE

ROE is affected by the firm's debt–equity mix as well as the interest rate on its debt. An example will show why. Suppose Nodett is all-equity-financed and has total assets of $100 million. Assume it pays corporate taxes at the rate of 40% of taxable earnings.

Table 14.4 shows Nodett's sales, earnings before interest and taxes, and net profits under three scenarios representing phases of the business cycle. It also shows two of the most commonly used profitability measures: operating ROA, which equals EBIT/total assets, and ROE, which equals net profits/equity.

Somdett is an otherwise identical firm to Nodett, but it has financed $40 million of its $100 million of assets with debt bearing an interest rate of 8%. It pays annual interest expenses of $3.2 million. Table 14.5 shows how Somdett's ROE differs from Nodett's.

Annual sales, EBIT, and therefore ROA for both firms are the same in each of the three scenarios; that is, business risk for the two companies is identical. But their financial risk differs: Although Nodett and Somdett have the same ROA in each scenario, Somdett's ROE exceeds that of Nodett in normal and good years and is lower in bad years.

[2]ROA sometimes is computed using EBIT $\times$ (1 − Tax rate) in the numerator. Sometimes it is computed using after-tax operating income, that is: Net income + Interest $\times$ (1 − Tax rate). Sometimes, it even is calculated using just net income in the numerator, although this definition ignores altogether the income the firm has generated for debt investors. Unfortunately, definitions of many key financial ratios are not fully standardized.

TABLE 14.4   Nodett's profitability over the business cycle

Scenario	Sales ($ million)	EBIT ($ million)	ROA (% per year)	Net Profit ($ million)	ROE (% per year)
Bad year	$ 80	$ 5	5%	$3	3%
Normal year	100	10	10	6	6
Good year	120	15	15	9	9

TABLE 14.5   Impact of financial leverage on ROE

		Nodett		Somdett	
Scenario	EBIT ($ million)	Net Profit ($ million)	ROE (%)	Net Profit* ($ million)	ROE† (%)
Bad year	$ 5	$3	3%	$1.08	1.8%
Normal year	10	6	6	4.08	6.8
Good year	15	9	9	7.08	11.8

*Somdett's after-tax profits equal .6(EBIT − $3.2 million).

†Somdett's equity is only $60 million.

We can summarize the exact relationship among ROE, ROA, and leverage in the following equation:[3]

$$ROE = (1 - \text{Tax rate}) \left[ROA + (ROA - \text{Interest rate}) \frac{\text{Debt}}{\text{Equity}} \right] \qquad \textbf{(14.1)}$$

The relationship has the following implications. If there is no debt or if the firm's ROA equals the interest rate on its debt, then ROE will simply equal (1 − tax rate) times ROA. If ROA exceeds the interest rate, then ROE will exceed (1 − tax rate) times ROA by an amount that will be greater, the higher the debt/equity ratio.

This result makes sense: If ROA exceeds the borrowing rate, the firm earns more on its money than it pays out to creditors. The surplus earnings are available to the firm's owners, the equityholders, which raises ROE. If, on the other hand, ROA is less than the interest rate paid on debt, then ROE will decline by an amount that depends on the debt/equity ratio.

EXAMPLE 14.1

Leverage and ROE

To illustrate the application of Equation 14.1, we can use the numerical example in Table 14.5. In a normal year, Nodett has an ROE of 6%, which is (1 − tax rate), or .6, times its ROA of 10%. However, Somdett, which borrows at an interest rate of 8% and maintains a debt/equity ratio of ⅔, has an ROE of 6.8%. The calculation using Equation 14.1 is

$$ROE = .6[10\% + (10\% - 8\%)⅔]$$
$$= .6(10\% + ⁴/₃\%) = 6.8\%$$

The important point is that increased debt will make a positive contribution to a firm's ROE only if the firm's ROA exceeds the interest rate on the debt.

[3]The derivation of Equation 14.1 is as follows:

$$ROE = \frac{\text{Net profit}}{\text{Equity}} = \frac{\text{EBIT} - \text{Interest} - \text{Taxes}}{\text{Equity}} = \frac{(1 - \text{Tax rate})(\text{EBIT} - \text{Interest})}{\text{Equity}}$$

$$= (1 - \text{Tax rate}) \frac{(ROA \times \text{Assets} - \text{Interest rate} \times \text{Debt})}{\text{Equity}}$$

$$= (1 - \text{Tax rate}) \left[ROA \times \frac{(\text{Equity} + \text{Debt})}{\text{Equity}} - \text{Interest rate} \times \frac{\text{Debt}}{\text{Equity}} \right]$$

$$= (1 - \text{Tax rate}) \left[ROA + (ROA - \text{Interest rate}) \frac{\text{Debt}}{\text{Equity}} \right]$$

Table 14.5 shows that financial leverage increases the risk of the equityholder returns. ROE on Somdett is worse than that of Nodett in bad years, but it is better in good years. The presence of debt makes Somdett's ROE more sensitive to the business cycle than Nodett's. Even though the two companies have equal business risk (reflected in their identical EBIT in all three scenarios), Somdett's stockholders carry greater financial risk than Nodett's because all of the firm's business risk is absorbed by a smaller base of equity investors.

Even if financial leverage increases the expected ROE of Somdett relative to Nodett (as it seems to in Table 14.5), this does not imply that Somdett's share price will be higher. Financial leverage increases the risk of the firm's equity as surely as it raises the expected ROE, and the higher discount rate will offset the higher expected earnings.

> Mordett is a company with the same assets as Nodett and Somdett but a debt/equity ratio of 1 and an interest rate of 9%. What would its net profit and ROE be in a bad year, a normal year, and a good year?

CONCEPT check 14.1

Economic Value Added

While it is common to use profitability measures such as ROA, ROC, or ROE to evaluate performance, profitability is really not enough. A firm should be viewed as successful only if the return on its projects is better than the rate investors could expect to earn for themselves (on a risk-adjusted basis) in the capital market. Plowing back funds into the firm increases share value only if the firm earns a higher rate of return on the reinvested funds than the opportunity cost of capital, that is, the market capitalization rate. To account for this opportunity cost, we might measure the success of the firm using the *difference* between the return on assets, ROA, and the opportunity cost of capital. **Economic value added** (EVA) is the spread between ROA and the cost of capital multiplied by the capital invested in the firm. It therefore measures the dollar value of the firm's return in excess of its opportunity cost. Another term for EVA (the term coined by Stern Stewart, a consulting firm that has promoted the concept) is **residual income.**

economic value added or residual income

A measure of the dollar value of a firm's return in excess of its opportunity cost.

> In 2013, Walmart had a weighted-average cost of capital of 4.29% (based on its cost of debt, its capital structure, its equity beta, and estimates derived from the CAPM for the cost of equity). Walmart's return on assets was 8.21%, fully 3.92% greater than the opportunity cost of capital on its investments in plant, equipment, and know-how. In other words, each dollar invested by Walmart earned about 3.9 cents more than the return that investors could have anticipated by investing in equivalent-risk stocks. Walmart earned this superior rate of return on a capital base of $135.45 billion. Its economic value added, that is, its return in excess of opportunity cost, was therefore $(.0821 - .0429) \times \$135.45 = \$5.31$ billion.

EXAMPLE 14.2

Economic Value Added

Table 14.6 shows EVA for a small sample of firms.[4] The EVA leader in this sample was Microsoft. But you should notice that EVA is affected by firm size. For example, the difference between AT&T's ROA and its cost of capital was $6.56\% - 4.03\% = 2.53\%$, which was less than the 3.20% spread for Intel. Yet we see that AT&T actually had the higher EVA because its margin was applied to a much larger capital base. At the other extreme, Honda earned less than its opportunity cost on a very large capital base, which resulted in a large negative EVA.

Notice that even the EVA "losers" in Table 14.6 had positive profits. For example, by conventional standards, Honda was solidly profitable with an ROA of 3.05%. But its cost of capital was higher, 7.52%. By this standard, Honda did not cover its opportunity cost of capital, and its EVA was negative. EVA treats the opportunity cost of capital as a real cost that, like other costs, should be deducted from revenues to arrive at a more meaningful "bottom line." A firm that is earning profits but is not covering its opportunity cost might be able to

---

[4]Actual EVA estimates reported by Stern Stewart differ from the values in Table 14.6 because of adjustments to the accounting data involving issues such as treatment of research and development expenses, taxes, advertising expenses, and depreciation. The estimates in Table 14.6 are designed to show the logic behind EVA but must be taken as imprecise.

TABLE 14.6 Economic value added, 2014

	Ticker	EVA ($ billion)	Capital ($ billion)	ROA (%)	Cost of Capital (%)
Microsoft	MSFT	$5.43	$113.60	11.43%	6.65%
Walmart	WMT	5.31	135.45	8.21	4.29
AT&T	T	4.28	169.00	6.56	4.03
Intel	INTC	2.24	69.88	10.21	7.01
Home Depot	HD	1.79	28.24	14.27	7.93
GlaxoSmithKline	GSK	0.80	38.04	8.39	6.30
Hewlett-Packard	HPQ	−1.08	48.25	5.27	7.52
Honda	HMC	−2.55	109.85	3.05	5.37

Source: Authors' calculations using data from **finance.yahoo.com.**

redeploy its capital to better uses. Therefore, a growing number of firms now calculate EVA and tie managers' compensation to it.[5]

14.4 RATIO ANALYSIS

Decomposition of ROE

To understand the factors affecting a firm's ROE, including its trend over time and its performance relative to competitors, analysts often "decompose" ROE into the product of a series of ratios. Each component ratio is in itself meaningful, and the process serves to focus the analyst's attention on the separate factors influencing performance. This kind of decomposition of ROE is often called the **DuPont system.**

One useful decomposition of ROE is

$$\text{ROE} = \frac{\text{Net profit}}{\text{Equity}} = \underbrace{\frac{\text{Net profit}}{\text{Pretax profit}}}_{(1)} \times \underbrace{\frac{\text{Pretax profit}}{\text{EBIT}}}_{(2)} \times \underbrace{\frac{\text{EBIT}}{\text{Sales}}}_{(3)} \times \underbrace{\frac{\text{Sales}}{\text{Assets}}}_{(4)} \times \underbrace{\frac{\text{Assets}}{\text{Equity}}}_{(5)} \qquad \textbf{(14.2)}$$

Table 14.7 shows all these ratios for Nodett and Somdett under the three different economic scenarios. Let us first focus on factors 3 and 4. Notice that their product gives us the firm's ROA = EBIT/Assets.

Factor 3 is known as the firm's operating **profit margin,** or **return on sales,** which equals operating profit per dollar of sales. In an average year, Nodett's margin is .10, or 10%; in a bad year, it is .0625, or 6.25%; and in a good year, it is .125, or 12.5%.

Factor 4, the ratio of sales to total assets, is known as **total asset turnover (ATO).** It indicates the efficiency of the firm's use of assets in the sense that it measures the annual sales generated by each dollar of assets. In a normal year, Nodett's ATO is 1 per year, meaning that sales of $1 per year were generated per dollar of assets. In a bad year, this ratio declines to .8 per year, and in a good year, it rises to 1.2 per year.

Comparing Nodett and Somdett, we see that factors 3 and 4 do not depend on a firm's financial leverage. The firms' ratios are equal to each other in all three scenarios. Similarly, factor 1, the ratio of net income after taxes to pretax profit, is the same for both firms. We call this the tax-burden ratio. Its value reflects both the government's tax code and the policies pursued by the firm in trying to minimize its tax burden. In our example, it does not change over the business cycle, remaining a constant .6.

DuPont system

Decomposition of profitability measures into component ratios.

profit margin or return on sales

The ratio of operating profits per dollar of sales (EBIT divided by sales).

total asset turnover (ATO)

The annual sales generated by each dollar of assets (sales/assets).

[5]Because it accounts for the opportunity cost of capital, EVA is a better measure of profitability than income, and this explains why firms might prefer it when evaluating their managers' performance. Nevertheless, as a measure of performance, even EVA can be distorted by factors beyond management's control.

TABLE 14.7	Ratio decomposition analysis for Nodett and Somdett

		(1)	(2)	(3)	(4)	(5)	(6)
	ROE	Net Profit Pretax Profit	Pretax Profit EBIT	EBIT Sales (Margin)	Sales Assets (Turnover)	Assets Equity	Compound Leverage Factor (2) × (5)
Bad year							
Nodett	0.030	0.6	1.000	0.0625	0.800	1.000	1.000
Somdett	0.018	0.6	0.360	0.0625	0.800	1.667	0.600
Normal year							
Nodett	0.060	0.6	1.000	0.100	1.000	1.000	1.000
Somdett	0.068	0.6	0.680	0.100	1.000	1.667	1.134
Good year							
Nodett	0.090	0.6	1.000	0.125	1.200	1.000	1.000
Somdett	0.118	0.6	0.787	0.125	1.200	1.667	1.311

While factors 1, 3, and 4 are not affected by a firm's capital structure, factors 2 and 5 are. Factor 2 is the ratio of pretax profits to EBIT. The firm's pretax profits will be greatest when there are no interest payments to be made to debtholders. In fact, another way to express this ratio is

$$\frac{\text{Pretax profits}}{\text{EBIT}} = \frac{\text{EBIT} - \text{Interest expense}}{\text{EBIT}}$$

We will call this factor the *interest-burden (IB) ratio*. It takes on its highest possible value, 1, for Nodett, which has no financial leverage. The higher the degree of financial leverage, the lower the IB ratio. Nodett's IB ratio does not vary over the business cycle. It is fixed at 1, reflecting the total absence of interest payments. For Somdett, however, because interest expense is fixed in a dollar amount while EBIT varies, the IB ratio varies from a low of .36 in a bad year to a high of .787 in a good year.

A closely related statistic to the interest-burden ratio is the **interest coverage ratio,** or **times interest earned.** The ratio is defined as

$$\text{Interest coverage} = \frac{\text{EBIT}}{\text{Interest expense}}$$

A high coverage ratio indicates that the likelihood of bankruptcy is low because annual earnings are significantly greater than annual interest obligations. It is widely used by both lenders and borrowers in determining the firm's debt capacity and is a major determinant of the firm's bond rating.

Factor 5, the ratio of assets to equity, is a measure of the firm's degree of financial leverage. It is called the **leverage ratio** and is equal to 1 plus the debt/equity ratio.[6] In our numerical example in Table 14.7, Nodett has a leverage ratio of 1, while Somdett's is 1.667.

From our discussion of Equation 14.1, we know that financial leverage helps boost ROE only if ROA is greater than the interest rate on the firm's debt. How is this fact reflected in the ratios of Table 14.7?

The answer is that the full impact of leverage in this framework equals the product of the IB and leverage ratios (that is, factors 2 and 5, in Table 14.7). This product is called the

interest coverage ratio or times interest earned

A financial leverage measure arrived at by dividing earnings before interest and taxes by interest expense.

leverage ratio

Measure of debt to total capitalization of a firm.

[6] $\dfrac{\text{Assets}}{\text{Equity}} = \dfrac{\text{Equity} + \text{Debt}}{\text{Equity}} = 1 + \dfrac{\text{Debt}}{\text{Equity}}$

compound leverage factor, and it is shown in Column 6. Nodett's compound leverage factor equals 1 in all three scenarios. But Somdett's is greater than 1 in normal years (1.134) and in good years (1.311), indicating the positive contribution of financial leverage to ROE. It is less than 1 in bad years, reflecting the fact that when ROA falls below the interest rate, ROE falls with increased use of debt.

We can summarize all of these relationships as follows:

$$ROE = Tax\ burden \times Interest\ burden \times Margin \times Turnover \times Leverage$$

Because

$$ROA = Margin \times Turnover \tag{14.3}$$

and

$$Compound\ leverage\ factor = Interest\ burden \times Leverage$$

we can decompose ROE equivalently as follows:

$$ROE = Tax\ burden \times ROA \times Compound\ leverage\ factor$$

Equation 14.3 shows that ROA is the *product* of margin and turnover. High values of one of these ratios are often accompanied by low values of the other. For example, Walmart has low profit margins but high turnover, while Tiffany has high margins but low turnover. Firms would love to have high values for both margin and turnover, but this generally will not be possible: Retailers with high markups will sacrifice sales volume, and, conversely, those with low turnover need high margins just to remain viable. Therefore, comparing these ratios in isolation usually is meaningful only in evaluating firms following similar strategies in the same industry. Cross-industry comparison can be misleading.

Figure 14.2 shows evidence of the turnover-profit margin trade-off. Industries with high turnover such as groceries or retail apparel tend to have low profit margins, while industries with high margins such as utilities tend to have low turnover. The two curved lines in the figure trace out turnover-margin combinations that result in an ROA of either 3% or 6%. You can see that most industries lie inside this range, so ROA across industries demonstrates far less variation than either turnover or margin taken in isolation.

EXAMPLE 14.3

Margin vs. Turnover

Consider two firms with the same ROA of 10% per year. The first is a discount chain and the second is a gas and electric utility.

As Table 14.8 shows, the discount chain has a "low" profit margin of 2% and achieves a 10% ROA by "turning over" its assets five times per year. The capital-intensive utility, on the other hand, has a "low" asset turnover ratio (ATO) of only .5 times per year and achieves its 10% ROA through its higher, 20%, profit margin. The point here is that a "low" margin or ATO ratio need not indicate a troubled firm. Each ratio must be interpreted in light of industry norms.

CONCEPT check 14.2

Do a ratio decomposition analysis for the Mordett corporation of Concept Check 14.1, preparing a table similar to Table 14.7.

Turnover and Asset Utilization

It is often helpful in understanding a firm's ratio of sales to assets to compute comparable efficiency-of-utilization, or turnover, ratios for subcategories of assets. For example, fixed-asset turnover would be

$$\frac{Sales}{Fixed\ assets}$$

This ratio measures sales per dollar of the firm's money tied up in fixed assets.

Median ROA, profit margin, and asset turnover for 23 industries, 1990–2004

Source: "Figure D: ROAs of Sample Firms (1977-1986)" from Thomas I. Selling and Clyde P. Stickney, "The Effects of Business Environments and Strategy on a Firm's Rate of Return on Assets." Copyright 1989, CFA Institute. Reproduced and republished from *Financial Analysts Journal,* January–February 1989, pp. 43–52, with permission from the CFA Institute. All rights reserved. Updates courtesy of Professors James Wahlen, Stephen Baginski, and Mark Bradshaw.

FIGURE 14.2

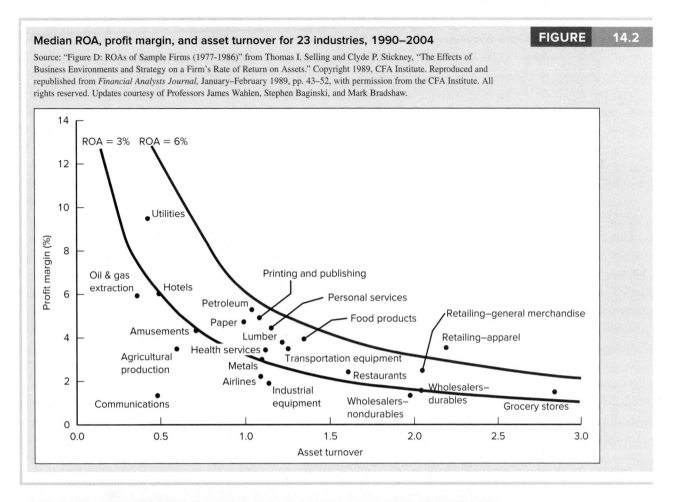

	Margin	×	ATO	=	ROA
TABLE 14.8 Differences between profit margin and asset turnover across industries					
Supermarket chain	2%		5.0		10%
Utility	20%		0.5		10%

To illustrate how you can compute this and other ratios from a firm's financial statements, consider Growth Industries, Inc. (GI). GI's income statement and opening and closing balance sheets for the years 2015–2017 appear in Table 14.9.

GI's total asset turnover in 2017 was .303, which was below the industry average of .4. To understand better why GI underperformed, we compute asset utilization ratios separately for fixed assets, inventories, and accounts receivable.

GI's sales in 2017 were $144 million. Its only fixed assets were plant and equipment, which were $216 million at the beginning of the year and $259.2 million at year's end. Average fixed assets for the year were, therefore, $237.6 million [($216 million + $259.2 million)/2]. GI's fixed-asset turnover for 2017 was $144 million per year/$237.6 million = .606 per year. In other words, for every dollar of fixed assets, there was $.606 in sales during 2017.

Comparable figures for the fixed-asset turnover ratio for 2015 and 2016 and the 2017 industry average are:

2015	2016	2017	2017 Industry Average
0.606	0.606	0.606	0.700

TABLE 14.9   Growth Industries financial statements ($ thousand)

	2014	2015	2016	2017
Income statements				
Sales revenue		$100,000	$120,000	$144,000
Cost of goods sold (including depreciation)		$ 55,000	$ 66,000	$ 79,200
Depreciation		15,000	18,000	21,600
Selling and administrative expenses		15,000	18,000	21,600
Operating income		$ 30,000	$ 36,000	$ 43,200
Interest expense		10,500	19,095	34,391
Taxable income		$ 19,500	$ 16,905	$ 8,809
Income tax (40% rate)		7,800	6,762	3,524
Net income		$ 11,700	$ 10,143	$ 5,285
Balance sheets (end of year)				
Cash and marketable securities	$ 50,000	$ 60,000	$ 72,000	$ 86,400
Accounts receivable	25,000	30,000	36,000	43,200
Inventories	75,000	90,000	108,000	129,600
Net plant and equipment	150,000	180,000	216,000	259,200
Total assets	$300,000	$360,000	$432,000	$518,400
Accounts payable	$ 30,000	$ 36,000	$ 43,200	$ 51,840
Short-term debt	45,000	87,300	141,957	214,432
Long-term debt (8% bonds maturing in 2025)	75,000	75,000	75,000	75,000
Total liabilities	$150,000	$198,300	$260,157	$341,272
Shareholders' equity (1 million shares outstanding)	$150,000	$161,700	$171,843	$177,128
Other data				
Market price per common share at year-end		$ 93.60	$ 61.00	$ 21.00

GI's fixed-asset turnover has been stable over time and below the industry average.

Notice that when a financial ratio includes one item from the income statement, which covers a period of time, and another from the balance sheet, which is a "snapshot" at a particular time, common practice is to take the average of the beginning and end-of-year balance sheet figures. Thus, in computing the fixed-asset turnover ratio, you divide sales (from the income statement) by average fixed assets (from the balance sheet).

inventory turnover ratio

Cost of goods sold divided by average inventory.

Another widely followed turnover ratio is the **inventory turnover ratio,** which is the ratio of cost of goods sold per dollar of inventory. We use the cost of goods sold (instead of sales revenue) in the numerator to maintain consistency with inventory, which is valued at cost. This ratio measures the speed with which inventory is turned over.

In 2015, GI's cost of goods sold (less depreciation) was $40 million, and its average inventory was $82.5 million [($75 million + $90 million)/2]. Its inventory turnover was .485 per year ($40 million/$82.5 million). In 2016 and 2017, inventory turnover remained the same and continued below the industry average of .5 per year. In other words, GI was burdened with a higher level of inventories per dollar of sales than its competitors. This higher investment in working capital in turn resulted in a higher level of assets per dollar of sales or profits and a lower ROA than its competitors.

days sales in receivables or average collection period

Accounts receivable per dollar of daily sales.

Another aspect of efficiency surrounds management of accounts receivable, which is often measured by **days sales in receivables,** that is, the average level of accounts receivable expressed as a multiple of daily sales. It is computed as average accounts receivable/ sales × 365 and may be interpreted as the number of days' worth of sales tied up in accounts receivable. You can also think of it as the average lag between the date of sale and the date payment is received, and it is therefore also called the **average collection period.**

For GI in 2017, this number was 100.4 days:

$$\frac{(\$36 \text{ million} + \$43.2 \text{ million})/2}{\$144 \text{ million}} \times 365 = 100.4 \text{ days}$$

The industry average was 60 days. This statistic tells us that GI's average receivables per dollar of sales exceeds that of its competitors. Again, this implies a higher required investment in working capital and ultimately a lower ROA.

In summary, use of these ratios lets us see that GI's poor total asset turnover relative to the industry is in part caused by lower-than-average fixed-asset turnover and inventory turnover and higher-than-average days receivables. This suggests GI may be having problems with excess plant capacity along with poor inventory and receivables management practices.

Liquidity Ratios

Leverage is one measure of the safety of a firm's debt. Debt ratios compare the firm's indebtedness to broad measures of its assets, and coverage ratios compare various measures of earning power against the cash flow needed to satisfy debt obligations. But leverage is not the only determinant of financial prudence. You also want to know that a firm can lay its hands on cash either to pay its scheduled obligations or to meet unforeseen obligations. **Liquidity** is the ability to convert assets into cash at short notice. Liquidity is commonly measured using the current ratio, quick ratio, and cash ratio.

liquidity
The ability to convert assets into cash at short notice.

1. **Current ratio:** current assets/current liabilities. This ratio measures the ability of the firm to pay off its current liabilities by liquidating its current assets (that is, turning them into cash). It indicates the firm's ability to avoid insolvency in the short run. GI's current ratio in 2015, for example, was $(60 + 30 + 90)/(36 + 87.3) = 1.46$. In other years, it was:

current ratio
Current assets/current liabilities.

2015	2016	2017	2017 Industry Average
1.46	1.17	0.97	2.0

This represents an unfavorable time trend and poor standing relative to the industry. This troublesome pattern is not surprising given the working capital burden resulting from GI's subpar performance with respect to receivables and inventory management.

2. **Quick ratio:** (cash + marketable securities + receivables)/current liabilities. This ratio is also called the **acid test ratio.** It has the same denominator as the current ratio, but its numerator includes only cash, cash equivalents such as marketable securities, and receivables. The quick ratio is a better measure of liquidity than the current ratio for firms whose inventory is not readily convertible into cash. GI's quick ratio shows the same disturbing trends as its current ratio:

quick ratio or acid test ratio
A measure of liquidity similar to the current ratio except for exclusion of inventories.

2015	2016	2017	2017 Industry Average
0.73	0.58	0.49	1.0

3. **Cash ratio.** A company's receivables are less liquid than its holdings of cash and marketable securities. Therefore, in addition to the quick ratio, analysts also compute a firm's cash ratio, defined as

cash ratio
Another liquidity measure. Ratio of cash and marketable securities to current liabilities.

$$\text{Cash ratio} = \frac{\text{Cash} + \text{Marketable securities}}{\text{Current liabilities}}$$

GI's cash ratios are:

2015	2016	2017	2017 Industry Average
0.487	0.389	0.324	0.70

GI's liquidity ratios have fallen dramatically over this three-year period, and by 2017, they are far below the industry average. The decline in the liquidity ratios combined with the decline in coverage ratio (you can confirm that times interest earned also has fallen over this period) suggest that its credit rating has been declining as well and, no doubt, GI is considered a relatively poor credit risk in 2017.

Market Price Ratios

market-to-book-value ratio

Market price of a share divided by book value per share.

The **market-to-book-value ratio** (P/B) equals the market price of a share of the firm's common stock divided by its *book value,* that is, shareholders' equity per share. Some analysts consider the stock of a firm with a low market-to-book value to be a "safer" investment, seeing the book value as a "floor" supporting the market price. These analysts presumably view book value as the level below which market price will not fall because the firm always has the option to liquidate, or sell, its assets for their book values. However, this view is questionable. In fact, some firms do sometimes sell for less than book value. For example, in late 2014, shares in both Bank of America and Citigroup sold for around 80% of book value per share. Nevertheless, a low market-to-book-value ratio is seen by some as providing a "margin of safety," and some analysts will screen out or reject high P/B firms in their stock selection process.

A better interpretation of the price-to-book ratio is as a measure of growth opportunities. Recall from the previous chapter that we may view the two components of firm value as assets in place and growth opportunities. As the next example illustrates, firms with greater growth opportunities will tend to exhibit higher multiples of market price to book value.

EXAMPLE 14.4

Price-to-Book and Growth Options

Consider two firms, both of which have book value per share of $10, a market capitalization rate of 15%, and a plowback ratio of .60.

Bright Prospects has an ROE of 20%, which is well in excess of the market capitalization rate; this ROE implies that the firm is endowed with ample growth opportunities. With ROE = .20, Bright Prospects will earn .20 × 10 = $2 per share this year. With its plowback ratio of .60, it pays out a dividend of $D_1 = (1 - .6) \times \$2 = \$.80$, has a growth rate of $g = b \times ROE = .60 \times .20 = .12$, and a stock price of $D_1/(k - g) = \$.80/(.15 - .12) = \$26.67$. Its P/B ratio is 26.67/10 = 2.667.

In contrast, Past Glory has an ROE of only 15%, just equal to the market capitalization rate. It therefore will earn .15 × 10 = $1.50 per share this year and will pay a dividend of $D_1 = .4 \times \$1.50 = \$.60$. Its growth rate is $g = b \times ROE = .60 \times .15 = .09$, and its stock price is $D_1/(k - g) = \$.60/(.15 - .09) = \$10$. Its P/B ratio is $10/$10 = 1. Not surprisingly, a firm that earns just the required rate of return on its investments will sell for book value, and no more.

We conclude that the price-to-book-value ratio is determined in large part by growth prospects.

---

price–earnings ratio (P/E)

The ratio of a stock's price to its earnings per share. Also referred to as the P/E multiple.

Another measure used to place firms along a growth versus value spectrum is the **price–earnings ratio (P/E).** In fact, we saw in the last chapter that the ratio of the present value of growth options to the value of assets in place largely determines the P/E multiple. While low P/E stocks allow you to pay less per dollar of *current* earnings, the high P/E stock may still be a better bargain if its earnings are expected to grow quickly enough.[7]

Many analysts nevertheless believe that low P/E stocks are more attractive than high P/E stocks. And in fact, low P/E stocks have generally been positive-alpha investments using the

---

[7]Remember, though, P/E ratios reported in the financial pages are based on *past* earnings, while price is determined by the firm's prospects of *future* earnings. Therefore, reported P/E ratios may reflect variation in current earnings around a trend line.

CAPM as a return benchmark. But an efficient market adherent would discount this track record, arguing that such a simplistic rule could not really generate abnormal returns and that the CAPM may not be a good benchmark for returns in this case.

In any event, the important points to remember are that ownership of the stock conveys the right to future as well as current earnings and, therefore, that a high P/E ratio may best be interpreted as a signal that the market views the firm as enjoying attractive growth opportunities.

Before leaving the P/B and P/E ratios, it is worth pointing out an important relationship between them.

$$\text{ROE} = \frac{\text{Earnings}}{\text{Book value}} = \frac{\text{Market price}}{\text{Book value}} \div \frac{\text{Market price}}{\text{Earnings}} \qquad \textbf{(14.4)}$$

$$= \text{P/B ratio} \div \text{P/E ratio}$$

Rearranging terms, we find that a firm's P/E ratio equals its price-to-book ratio divided by ROE:

$$\frac{P}{E} = \frac{\text{P/B}}{\text{ROE}}$$

Wall Street often distinguishes between "good firms" and "good investments." A good firm may be highly profitable, with a correspondingly high ROE. But if its stock price is bid up to a level commensurate with this ROE, its P/B ratio will also be high, and the stock price may be a relatively large multiple of earnings, thus reducing its attractiveness as an investment. The high ROE of the *firm* does not by itself imply that the *stock* is a good investment. Conversely, troubled firms with low ROEs can be good investments if their prices are low enough.

Table 14.10 summarizes the ratios reviewed in this section.

What were GI's ROE, P/E, and P/B ratios in the year 2017? How do they compare to these industry average ratios: ROE = 8.64%, P/E = 8, and P/B = .69? How does GI's earnings yield in 2017 compare to the industry average?

CONCEPT check **14.3**

Choosing a Benchmark

We have discussed how to calculate the principal financial ratios. To evaluate the performance of a given firm, however, you need a benchmark to which you can compare its ratios. One obvious benchmark is the ratio for the same company in earlier years. For example, Figure 14.3 shows Home Depot's return on assets, profit margin, and asset turnover ratio for the last few years. You can see there that most of the variation in HD's return on assets has been driven by the variation in its profit margin. In contrast, its turnover ratio was almost constant between 2001 and 2005.

It is also helpful to compare financial ratios to those of other firms in the same industry. Financial ratios for industries are published by the U.S. Department of Commerce (see Table 14.11), Dun & Bradstreet, the Risk Management Association (RMA), and others, and many ratios are available on the web, for example, on the Yahoo! Finance site.

Table 14.11 presents ratios for a sample of major industry groups to give you a feel for some of the differences across industries. Some ratios such as asset turnover or total debt ratio tend to be relatively stable. For example, asset turnover in drug development and production companies will be consistently lower than in the motor vehicle or clothing industries. However, other ratios, for example, return on assets or equity, are more sensitive to current business conditions. A value in one year cannot be assumed to reflect fundamental differences.

TABLE 14.10 Summary of key financial ratios	
Leverage ratios:	
Interest burden	$\dfrac{\text{EBIT} - \text{Interest expense}}{\text{EBIT}}$
Interest coverage (Times interest earned)	$\dfrac{\text{EBIT}}{\text{Interest expense}}$
Leverage	$\dfrac{\text{Assets}}{\text{Equity}} = 1 + \dfrac{\text{Debt}}{\text{Equity}}$
Compound leverage factor	Interest burden × Leverage
Asset utilization:	
Total asset turnover	$\dfrac{\text{Sales}}{\text{Average total assets}}$
Fixed-asset turnover	$\dfrac{\text{Sales}}{\text{Average fixed assets}}$
Inventory turnover	$\dfrac{\text{Cost of goods sold}}{\text{Average inventories}}$
Days sales in receivables	$\dfrac{\text{Average accounts receivables}}{\text{Annual sales}} \times 365$
Liquidity:	
Current ratio	$\dfrac{\text{Current assets}}{\text{Current liabilities}}$
Quick ratio	$\dfrac{\text{Cash} + \text{Marketable securities} + \text{Receivables}}{\text{Current liabilities}}$
Cash ratio	$\dfrac{\text{Cash} + \text{Marketable securities}}{\text{Current liabilities}}$
Profitability ratios:	
Return on assets	$\dfrac{\text{EBIT}}{\text{Average total assets}}$
Return on equity	$\dfrac{\text{Net income}}{\text{Average stockholders' equity}}$
Return on sales (Profit margin)	$\dfrac{\text{EBIT}}{\text{Sales}}$
Market price ratios:	
Market-to-book	$\dfrac{\text{Price per share}}{\text{Book value per share}}$
Price–earnings ratio	$\dfrac{\text{Price per share}}{\text{Earnings per share}}$
Earnings yield	$\dfrac{\text{Earnings per share}}{\text{Price per share}}$

14.5 AN ILLUSTRATION OF FINANCIAL STATEMENT ANALYSIS

In her 2017 annual report to the shareholders of Growth Industries, Inc., the president wrote: "2017 was another successful year for Growth Industries. As in 2016, sales, assets, and operating income all continued to grow at a rate of 20%."

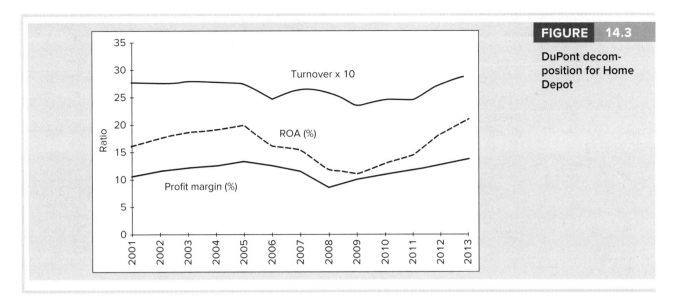

FIGURE 14.3

DuPont decomposition for Home Depot

TABLE 14.11   Financial Ratios for Major Industry Groups

	LT Debt Assets	Interest Coverage	Current Ratio	Quick Ratio	Asset Turnover	Profit Margin (%)	Return on Assets (%)	Return on Equity (%)	Payout Ratio
All manufacturing	0.22	5.42	1.38	0.94	0.78	8.48	6.63	19.87	0.33
Food products	0.27	4.71	1.61	1.00	0.98	6.33	6.18	12.81	0.34
Clothing	0.47	6.45	2.46	1.36	1.02	8.73	8.87	21.50	0.33
Printing/publishing	0.32	4.19	1.32	1.25	0.45	17.74	7.99	24.83	0.21
Chemicals	0.28	3.72	1.20	0.89	0.44	12.39	5.51	20.07	0.35
Drugs	0.28	4.00	1.22	0.95	0.34	17.50	6.01	21.69	0.41
Machinery	0.19	6.64	1.43	0.93	0.74	9.79	7.28	21.86	0.25
Electrical	0.13	5.76	1.11	0.69	0.48	9.16	4.39	14.13	0.48
Motor vehicles	0.15	5.26	1.17	0.89	1.19	4.43	5.29	15.08	0.33
Computer and electronic	0.18	5.69	1.55	1.30	0.44	11.71	5.18	20.37	0.22

Source: U.S. Department of *Commerce, Quarterly Financial Report for Manufacturing, Mining and Trade Corporations,* second quarter 2014. Available at **http://www2.census.gov/econ/qfr/current/qfr_pub.pdf.**

Is she right?

We can evaluate her statement by conducting a full-scale ratio analysis of Growth Industries. Our purpose is to assess GI's performance in the recent past, to evaluate its future prospects, and to determine whether its market price reflects its intrinsic value.

Table 14.12 shows some key financial ratios we can compute from GI's financial statements. The president is certainly right about the growth in sales, assets, and operating income. Inspection of GI's key financial ratios, however, contradicts her first sentence: 2017 was not another successful year for GI—it appears to have been another miserable one.

ROE has been declining steadily from 7.51% in 2015 to 3.03% in 2017. A comparison of GI's 2017 ROE to the 2017 industry average of 8.64% makes the deteriorating time trend especially alarming. The low and falling market-to-book-value ratio and the falling

		(1)	(2)	(3)	(4)	(5)	(6)	(7)		
		Net Profit ――――― Pretax Profit	**Pretax** **Profit** ――――― EBIT	**EBIT** ――――― Sales (Margin)	**Sales** ――――― Assets (Turnover)	**Assets** ――――― Equity	**Compound** **Leverage** **Factor** (2) × (5)	**ROA** (3) × (4)		
Year	**ROE**								**P/E**	**P/B**
2015	7.51%	0.6	0.650	30%	0.303	2.117	1.376	9.09%	8	0.58
2016	6.08	0.6	0.470	30	0.303	2.375	1.116	9.09	6	0.35
2017	3.03	0.6	0.204	30	0.303	2.723	0.556	9.09	4	0.12
Industry average	8.64	0.6	0.800	30	0.400	1.500	1.200	12.00	8	0.69

TABLE 14.12   Key financial ratios of Growth Industries, Inc.

price–earnings ratio indicate that investors are less and less optimistic about the firm's future profitability.

The fact that ROA has not been declining, however, tells us that the source of the declining time trend in GI's ROE must be due to financial leverage. And, in fact, as GI's leverage ratio climbed from 2.117 in 2015 to 2.723 in 2017, its interest-burden ratio worsened from .650 to .204—with the net result that the compound leverage factor fell from 1.376 to .556.

The rapid increase in short-term debt from year to year and the concurrent increase in interest expense make it clear that, to finance its 20% growth rate in sales, GI has incurred sizable amounts of short-term debt at high interest rates. The firm is paying rates of interest greater than the ROA it is earning on the investment financed with the new borrowing. As the firm has expanded, its situation has become ever more precarious.

In 2017, for example, the average interest rate on short-term debt was 20% versus an ROA of 9.09%. (You can calculate the interest rate on GI's short-term debt using the data in Table 14.9 as follows: The balance sheet shows us that the coupon rate on its long-term debt was 8% and its par value was $75 million. Therefore the interest paid on the long-term debt was .08 × $75 million = $6 million. Total interest paid in 2016 was $34,391,000, so the interest paid on the short-term debt must have been $34,391,000 − $6,000,000 = $28,391,000. This is 20% of GI's short-term debt at the start of the year.)

GI's problems become clear when we examine its statement of cash flows in Table 14.13. The statement is derived from the income statement and balance sheet data in Table 14.9. GI's cash flow from operations is falling steadily, from $12,700,000 in 2015 to $6,725,000 in 2017. The firm's investment in plant and equipment, by contrast, has increased greatly. Net plant and equipment (i.e., net of depreciation) rose from $150,000,000 in 2014 to $259,200,000 in 2017. This near doubling of capital assets makes the decrease in cash flow from operations all the more troubling.

The source of the difficulty is GI's enormous amount of short-term borrowing. In a sense, the company is being run as a pyramid scheme. It borrows more and more each year to maintain its 20% growth rate in assets and income. However, the new assets are not generating enough cash flow to support the extra interest burden of the debt, as the falling cash flow from operations indicates. Eventually, when the firm loses its ability to borrow further, its growth will be at an end.

At this point, GI stock might be an attractive investment. Its market price is only 12% of its book value, and with a P/E ratio of 4, its earnings yield is 25% per year. GI is a likely candidate for a takeover by another firm that might replace GI's management and build shareholder value through a radical change in policy.

TABLE 14.13	Growth Industries statement of cash flows ($ thousand)		
	2015	**2016**	**2017**
Cash flow from operating activities			
Net income	$ 11,700	$ 10,143	$ 5,285
Depreciation	15,000	18,000	21,600
Decrease (increase) in accounts receivable	(5,000)	(6,000)	(7,200)
Decrease (increase) in inventories	(15,000)	(18,000)	(21,600)
Increase in accounts payable	6,000	7,200	8,640
Cash provided by operations	$ 12,700	$ 11,343	$ 6,725
Cash flow from investing activities			
Investment in plant and equipment*	$(45,000)	$(54,000)	$(64,800)
Cash flow from financing activities			
Dividends paid†	$ 0	$ 0	$ 0
Short-term debt issued	42,300	54,657	72,475
Change in cash and marketable securities‡	$ 10,000	$ 12,000	$ 14,400

*Gross investment equals increase in net plant and equipment plus depreciation.

†We can conclude that no dividends are paid because stockholders' equity increases each year by the full amount of net income, implying a plowback ratio of 1.

‡Equals cash flow from operations plus cash flow from investment activities plus cash flow from financing activities. Note that this equals the yearly change in cash and marketable securities on the balance sheet.

CONCEPT check 14.4

You have the following information for IBX Corporation for the years 2015 and 2018 (all figures are in $ millions):

	2018	2015
Net income	$ 253.7	$ 239.0
Pretax income	411.9	375.6
EBIT	517.6	403.1
Average assets	4,857.9	3,459.7
Sales	6,679.3	4,537.0
Shareholders' equity	2,233.3	2,347.3

What is the trend in IBX's ROE, and how can you account for it in terms of tax burden, margin, turnover, and financial leverage?

14.6 COMPARABILITY PROBLEMS

Financial statement analysis gives us a good amount of ammunition for evaluating a company's performance and future prospects. But comparing financial results of different companies is not so simple. There is more than one acceptable way to represent various items of revenue and expense according to generally accepted accounting principles (GAAP). This means two firms may have exactly the same economic income yet very different accounting incomes.

Furthermore, interpreting a single firm's performance over time is complicated when inflation distorts the dollar measuring rod. Comparability problems are especially acute in this case because the impact of inflation on reported results often depends on the particular method the firm adopts to account for inventories and depreciation. The security analyst must adjust the earnings and the financial ratio figures to a uniform standard before attempting to compare financial results across firms and over time.

Comparability problems can arise out of the flexibility of GAAP guidelines in accounting for inventories and depreciation and in adjusting for the effects of inflation. Other important potential sources of noncomparability include the capitalization of leases and other expenses, the treatment of pension costs, and allowances for reserves.

Inventory Valuation

There are two commonly used ways to value inventories: **LIFO** (last-in, first-out) and **FIFO** (first-in, first-out). We can explain the difference using a numerical example.

Suppose Generic Products, Inc. (GPI), has a constant inventory of 1 million units of generic goods. The inventory turns over once per year, meaning the ratio of cost of goods sold to inventory is 1.

The LIFO system calls for valuing the million units used up during the year at the current cost of production, so that the last goods produced are considered the first ones to be sold. They are valued at today's cost. The FIFO system assumes that the units used up or sold are the ones that were added to inventory first, and goods sold should be valued at original cost.

If the price of generic goods were constant, at the level of $1, say, the book value of inventory and the cost of goods sold would be the same, $1 million under both systems. But suppose the price of generic goods rises by 10 cents per unit during the year as a result of inflation.

LIFO accounting would result in a cost of goods sold of $1.1 million, while the end-of-year balance sheet value of the 1 million units in inventory remains $1 million. The balance sheet value of inventories is given as the cost of the goods still in inventory. Under LIFO, the last goods produced are assumed to be sold at the current cost of $1.10; the goods remaining are the previously produced goods, at a cost of only $1. You can see that, although LIFO accounting accurately measures the cost of goods sold today, it understates the current value of the remaining inventory in an inflationary environment.

In contrast, under FIFO accounting, the cost of goods sold would be $1 million, and the end-of-year balance sheet value of the inventory is $1.1 million. The result is that the LIFO firm has both a lower reported profit and a lower balance sheet value of inventories than the FIFO firm.

LIFO is preferred over FIFO in computing economics earnings (that is, real sustainable cash flow), because it uses up-to-date prices to evaluate the cost of goods sold. However, LIFO accounting induces balance sheet distortions when it values investment in inventories at original cost. This practice results in an upward bias in ROE because the investment base on which return is earned is undervalued.

Depreciation

Another source of problems is the measurement of depreciation, which is a key factor in computing true earnings. The accounting and economic measures of depreciation can differ markedly. According to the *economic* definition, depreciation is the amount of a firm's operating cash flow that must be reinvested in the firm to sustain its real cash flow at the current level.

The *accounting* measurement is quite different. Accounting depreciation is the amount of the original acquisition cost of an asset that is allocated to each accounting period over an arbitrarily specified life of the asset. This is the figure reported in financial statements.

Assume, for example, that a firm buys machines with a useful economic life of 20 years at $100,000 apiece. In its financial statements, however, the firm can depreciate the machines over 10 years using the straight-line method, for $10,000 per year in depreciation. Thus, after

10 years, a machine will be fully depreciated on the books, even though it remains a productive asset that will not need replacement for another 10 years.

In computing accounting earnings, this firm will overestimate depreciation in the first 10 years of the machine's economic life and underestimate it in the last 10 years. This will cause reported earnings to be understated compared with economic earnings in the first 10 years and overstated in the last 10 years.

Depreciation comparability problems add one more wrinkle. A firm can use different depreciation methods for tax purposes than for other reporting purposes. Most firms use accelerated depreciation methods for tax purposes and straight-line depreciation in published financial statements. There also are differences across firms in their estimates of the depreciable life of plant, equipment, and other depreciable assets.

Another complication arises from inflation. Because conventional depreciation is based on historical costs rather than on the current replacement cost of assets, measured depreciation in periods of inflation is understated relative to replacement cost, and *real* economic income (sustainable cash flow) is correspondingly overstated.

For example, suppose Generic Products, Inc., has a machine with a three-year useful life that originally cost $3 million. Annual straight-line depreciation is $1 million, regardless of what happens to the replacement cost of the machine. Suppose inflation in the first year turns out to be 10%. Then the true annual depreciation expense is $1.1 million in current terms, while conventionally measured depreciation remains fixed at $1 million per year. Accounting income therefore overstates *real* economic income.

Inflation and Interest Expense

While inflation can cause distortions in the measurement of a firm's inventory and depreciation costs, it has perhaps an even greater effect on the calculation of *real* interest expense. Nominal interest rates include an inflation premium that compensates the lender for inflation-induced erosion in the real value of principal. From the perspective of both lender and borrower, therefore, part of what is conventionally measured as interest expense should be treated more properly as repayment of principal.

> **EXAMPLE 14.5**
>
> *Inflation and Real Income*
>
> Suppose Generic Products has debt outstanding with a face value of $10 million at an interest rate of 10% per year. Interest expense as conventionally measured is $1 million per year. However, suppose inflation during the year is 6%, so that the real interest rate is approximately 4%. Then $.6 million of what appears as interest expense on the income statement is really an inflation premium, or compensation for the anticipated reduction in the real value of the $10 million principal; only $.4 million is *real* interest expense. The $.6 million reduction in the purchasing power of the outstanding principal may be thought of as repayment of principal, rather than as an interest expense. Real income of the firm is, therefore, understated by $.6 million.

Mismeasurement of real interest means that inflation results in an underestimate of real income. The effects of inflation on the reported values of inventories and depreciation that we have discussed work in the opposite direction.

> **CONCEPT check 14.5**
>
> In a period of rapid inflation, companies ABC and XYZ have the same *reported* earnings. ABC uses LIFO inventory accounting, has relatively fewer depreciable assets, and has more debt than XYZ. XYZ uses FIFO inventory accounting. Which company has the higher *real* income and why?

Fair Value Accounting

Many major assets and liabilities are not traded in financial markets and do not have easily observable values. For example, we cannot simply look up the values of employee stock options, health care benefits for retired employees, or buildings and other real estate. While the true financial status of a firm may depend critically on these values, which can swing widely over time, common practice has been to simply value them at historic cost. Proponents of **fair value accounting,** also known as **mark-to-market accounting,** argue that financial statements would give a truer picture of the firm if they better reflected the current market values of all assets and liabilities.

The Financial Accounting Standards Board's Statement No. 157 on fair value accounting places assets in one of three "buckets." Level 1 assets are traded in active markets and therefore should be valued at their market price. Level 2 assets are not actively traded, but their values still may be estimated using observable market data on similar assets. These assets can be "marked to a matrix" of comparable securities. Level 3 assets are hardest to value. Here, it is difficult even to identify other assets that are similar enough to serve as benchmarks for their market values; one has to resort to pricing models to estimate their intrinsic values. Rather than mark to market, these values are often called "mark to model," although they are also disparagingly known as mark-to-make-believe, as the estimates are so prone to manipulation by creative use of model inputs. Since 2012, firms have been required to disclose more about the methods and assumptions used in their valuation models and to describe the sensitivity of their valuation estimates to changes in methodology.

Critics of fair value accounting argue that it relies too heavily on estimates. Such estimates potentially introduce considerable noise in firms' accounts and can induce great profit volatility as fluctuations in asset valuations are recognized. Even worse, subjective valuations may offer management a tempting tool to manipulate earnings or the apparent financial condition of the firm at opportune times. As just one example, Bergstresser, Desai, and Rauh (2006) find that firms make more aggressive assumptions about returns on defined benefit pension plans (which lowers the computed present value of pension obligations) during periods in which executives are actively exercising their stock options.

A contentious debate over the application of fair value accounting to troubled financial institutions erupted in 2008 when even values of financial securities such as subprime mortgage pools and derivative contracts backed by these pools came into question as trading in these instruments dried up. Without well-functioning markets, estimating (much less observing) market values was, at best, a precarious exercise.

Many observers feel that mark-to-market accounting exacerbated the financial meltdown by forcing banks to excessively write down asset values; others, that a failure to mark would have been tantamount to willfully ignoring reality and abdicating the responsibility to redress problems at nearly or already insolvent banks. The nearby box discusses the debate.

Quality of Earnings and Accounting Practices

Many firms make accounting choices that present their financial statements in the best possible light. The different choices that firms can make give rise to the comparability problems we have discussed. As a result, earnings statements for different companies may be more or less rosy presentations of true "economic earnings"—sustainable cash flow that can be paid to shareholders without impairing the firm's productive capacity. Analysts commonly evaluate the **quality of earnings** reported by a firm. This concept refers to the realism and conservatism of the earnings number, in other words, the extent to which we might expect the reported level of earnings to be sustained.

Examples of the accounting choices that influence quality of earnings are:

- *Allowance for bad debt.* Most firms sell goods using trade credit and must make an allowance for bad debt. An unrealistically low allowance reduces the quality of reported earnings. Look for a rising average collection period on accounts receivable as evidence of potential problems with future collections.

- *Nonrecurring items.* Some items that affect earnings should not be expected to recur regularly. These include asset sales, effects of accounting changes, effects of exchange rate movements, or unusual investment income. For example, in years with large equity returns, some firms enjoy large capital gains on securities held. These contribute to that

fair value or mark-to-market accounting

Use of current market values rather than historic cost in the firm's financial statements.

quality of earnings

The realism and sustainability of reported earnings.

On the MARKET FRONT

MARK-TO-MARKET ACCOUNTING: CURE OR DISEASE?

As banks and other institutions holding mortgage-backed securities revalued their portfolios throughout 2008, their net worth fell along with the value of those securities. The losses on these securities were painful enough but, in addition, they led to knock-on effects that only increased the banks' woes. For example, banks are required to maintain adequate levels of capital relative to assets. If capital reserves decline, a bank may be forced to shrink until its remaining capital is once again adequate compared to its asset base. But such shrinkage may require the bank to cut back on its lending, which restricts its customers' access to credit. It may also have to sell some of its assets; and if many banks attempt to shrink their portfolios at once, waves of forced sales may put further pressure on prices, resulting in additional write-downs and reductions to capital in a self-feeding cycle. Critics of mark-to-market accounting therefore conclude that it acted to exacerbate the problems of an already reeling economy.

Advocates, however, contend that the critics confuse the message with the messenger. Mark-to-market accounting makes transparent losses that have already been incurred, but it does not cause those losses. But the critics retort that when markets are faltering, market prices may be unreliable. If trading activity has largely broken down, and assets can be sold only at fire-sale prices, then those prices may no longer be indicative of fundamental value. Markets cannot be efficient if they are not even functioning. In the turmoil surrounding the defaulted mortgages

weighing down bank portfolios, one of the early proposals of then–Treasury Secretary Henry Paulson was for the government to buy bad assets at "hold to maturity" prices based on estimates of intrinsic value in a normally functioning market. In the same spirit, in April 2009, FASB granted financial firms more leeway to put off write-downs on assets deemed to be only "temporarily impaired."

Waiving write-down requirements may best be viewed as thinly veiled regulatory forbearance. Regulators know that losses have been incurred and that capital has been impaired. But by allowing firms to carry assets on their books at model rather than market prices, the unpleasant implications of that fact for capital adequacy may be politely ignored for a time. Even so, if the goal is to avoid forced sales in a distressed market, transparency may nevertheless be the best policy. Better to acknowledge losses and explicitly modify capital regulations to help institutions recover their footing in a difficult economy than to deal with losses by ignoring them. After all, why bother preparing financial statements if they are allowed to obscure the true condition of the firm?

Before abandoning fair value accounting, it would be prudent to consider the alternative. Traditional historic-cost accounting, which would allow firms to carry assets on the books at their original purchase price, has even less to recommend it. It would leave investors without an accurate sense of the condition of shaky institutions and, by the same token, lessen the pressure on those firms to get their houses in order. Dealing with losses must surely first require acknowledging them.

---

year's earnings but should not be expected to repeat regularly. They would be considered a "low-quality" component of earnings. Similarly, gains in corporate pension plans can generate large, but one-time, contributions to reported earnings.

- *Earnings smoothing.* In 2003, Freddie Mac was the subject of an accounting scandal, with the disclosure that it had improperly reclassified mortgages held in its portfolio in an attempt to *reduce* its current earnings. Why would it take such actions? Because later, if earnings turned down, Freddie could "release" earnings by reversing these transactions and thereby create the appearance of steady earnings growth. Similarly, in the four quarters ending in October 2012, the four largest U.S. banks released $18.2 billion in reserves, which accounted for nearly one-quarter of their pretax income.[8] Such "earnings" are clearly not sustainable over the long-term and therefore must be considered low quality.

- *Revenue recognition.* Under GAAP accounting, a firm is allowed to recognize a sale before it is paid. This is why firms have accounts receivable. But sometimes it can be hard to know when to recognize sales. For example, suppose a computer firm signs a contract to provide products and services over a five-year period. Should the revenue be booked immediately or spread out over five years? A more extreme version of this problem is called "channel stuffing," in which firms "sell" large quantities of goods to customers but give them the right to later either refuse delivery or return the product. The revenue from the "sale" is booked now, but the likely returns are not recognized until they occur (in a future accounting period). Hewlett-Packard argued in 2012 that it was led to overpay for its acquisition of Autonomy Corp. when Autonomy artificially enhanced its financial performance using channel stuffing. For example, Autonomy

[8]Michael Rapoport, "Bank Profit Spigot to Draw Scrutiny," *The Wall Street Journal,* October 11, 2012.

apparently sold software valued at more than £4 billion to Tikit Group; it booked the entire deal as revenue, but would not be paid for the software until Tikit actually sold software to its clients.[9] Thus, several years' worth of only tentative future sales was recognized in 2010.

If you see accounts receivable increasing far faster than sales, or becoming a larger percentage of total assets, beware of these practices. Given the latitude firms have in how they recognize revenue, many analysts choose instead to concentrate on cash flow, which is far harder for a company to manipulate.

- *Off-balance-sheet assets and liabilities.* Suppose that one firm guarantees the outstanding debt of another firm, perhaps a firm in which it has an ownership stake. That obligation ought to be disclosed as a *contingent liability* because it may require payments down the road. But these obligations may not be reported as part of the firm's outstanding debt. Similarly, leasing may be used to manage off-balance-sheet assets and liabilities. Airlines, for example, may show no aircraft on their balance sheets but have long-term leases that are virtually equivalent to debt-financed ownership. However, if the leases are treated as operating rather than capital leases, they may appear only as footnotes to the financial statements.

International Accounting Conventions

The examples cited above illustrate some of the problems that analysts can encounter when attempting to interpret financial data. Even greater problems arise in the interpretation of the financial statements of foreign firms. This is because these firms do not follow GAAP guidelines. Accounting practices in various countries differ to greater or lesser extents from U.S. standards. Here are some of the major issues that you should be aware of when using the financial statements of foreign firms.

RESERVING PRACTICES   Many countries allow firms considerably more discretion in setting aside reserves for future contingencies than is typical in the United States. Because additions to reserves result in a charge against income, reported earnings are far more subject to managerial discretion than in the United States.

DEPRECIATION   In the United States, firms typically maintain separate sets of accounts for tax and reporting purposes. For example, accelerated depreciation is used for tax purposes, while straight-line depreciation is used for reporting purposes. In contrast, most other countries do not allow dual sets of accounts, and most firms in foreign countries use accelerated depreciation to minimize taxes despite the fact that it results in lower reported earnings. This makes reported earnings of foreign firms lower than they would be if the firms were allowed to follow the U.S. practice.

INTANGIBLES   Treatment of intangibles can vary widely. Are they amortized or expensed? If amortized, over what period? Such issues can have a large impact on reported profits.

The effect of different country practices can be substantial. Figure 14.4, compares average P/E ratios for several countries as reported and restated on a common basis. While P/E multiples have changed considerably since this study was published, these results illustrate how different accounting rules can have a big impact on these ratios.

Some of the differences between U.S. and European accounting standards arise from different philosophies regarding regulating accounting practice. GAAP accounting in the U.S. is "rules-based," with detailed, explicit, and lengthy rules governing almost any circumstance that can be anticipated. In contrast, the **international financial reporting standards** (IFRS) used in the European Union are "principles-based," setting out general approaches for the

international financial reporting standards

A principles-based set of accounting rules adopted by about 100 countries around the world, including the European Union.

---

[9]Ben Worthen, Paul Sonne, and Justin Scheck, "Long Before H-P Deal, Autonomy's Red Flags," *The Wall Street Journal,* November 26, 2012.

FIGURE 14.4

Adjusted versus reported price–earnings ratios

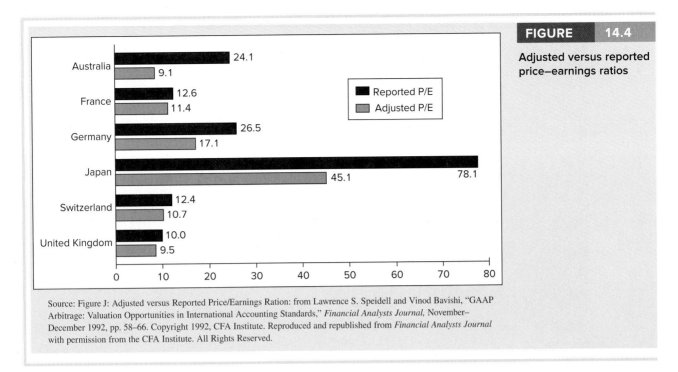

	Reported P/E	Adjusted P/E
Australia	24.1	9.1
France	12.6	11.4
Germany	26.5	17.1
Japan	78.1	45.1
Switzerland	12.4	10.7
United Kingdom	10.0	9.5

Source: Figure J: Adjusted versus Reported Price/Earnings Ration: from Lawrence S. Speidell and Vinod Bavishi, "GAAP Arbitrage: Valuation Opportunities in International Accounting Standards," *Financial Analysts Journal*, November–December 1992, pp. 58–66. Copyright 1992, CFA Institute. Reproduced and republished from *Financial Analysts Journal* with permission from the CFA Institute. All Rights Reserved.

preparation of financial statements. While EU rules are more flexible, firms must be prepared to demonstrate that their accounting choices are consistent with IFRS principles.

IFRS seem on their way to becoming global standards, even outside the European Union. By 2008, more than 100 countries had adopted them, and they are making inroads even in the United States. In 2007, the SEC began allowing foreign firms to issue securities in the U.S. if their financial statements are prepared using IFRS. In 2008, the SEC went even further when it proposed allowing large U.S. multinational firms to report earnings using IFRS rather than GAAP. The SEC has reiterated support for globally accepted accounting standards so as to make cross-border financial statements more consistent, comparable, and informative. But while differences between U.S. GAAP and IFRS have narrowed, some significant differences remain.

14.7 VALUE INVESTING: THE GRAHAM TECHNIQUE

No presentation of fundamental security analysis would be complete without a discussion of the ideas of Benjamin Graham, the greatest of the investment "gurus." Until the evolution of modern portfolio theory in the latter half of the twentieth century, Graham was the single most important thinker, writer, and teacher in the field of investment analysis. His influence on investment professionals remains very strong.

Graham's magnum opus is *Security Analysis*, written with Columbia Professor David Dodd in 1934. Its message is similar to the ideas presented in this chapter. Graham believed careful analysis of a firm's financial statements could turn up bargain stocks. Over the years, he developed many different rules for determining the most important financial ratios and the critical values for judging a stock to be undervalued. Through many editions, his book has had a profound influence on investment professionals. It has been so influential and successful, in fact, that widespread adoption of Graham's techniques has led to elimination of the very bargains they are designed to identify.

In a 1976 seminar Graham said[10]

I am no longer an advocate of elaborate techniques of security analysis in order to find superior value opportunities. This was a rewarding activity, say, forty years ago, when our textbook

---

[10]Graham's full interview is reproduced in *Financial Analysts Journal* Vol. 32, No. 5 (September/October, 1976), pp. 20–23.

"Graham and Dodd" was first published; but the situation has changed a good deal since then. In the old days any well-trained security analyst could do a good professional job of selecting under-valued issues through detailed studies; but in the light of the enormous amount of research now being carried on, I doubt whether in most cases such extensive efforts will generate sufficiently superior selections to justify their cost. To that very limited extent I'm on the side of the "efficient market" school of thought now generally accepted by the professors.

Nonetheless, in that same seminar, Graham suggested a simplified approach to identifying bargain stocks:

My first, more limited, technique confines itself to the purchase of common stocks at less than their working-capital value, or net current-asset value, giving no weight to the plant and other fixed assets, and deducting all liabilities in full from the current assets. We used this approach extensively in managing investment funds, and over a thirty-odd-year period we must have earned an average of some 20% per year from this source. For awhile, however, after the mid-1950s, this brand of buying opportunity became very scarce because of the pervasive bull market. But it has returned in quantity since the 1973–1974 decline. In January 1976 we counted over 100 such issues in the Standard & Poor's *Stock Guide*—about 10% of the total. I consider it a foolproof method of systematic investment—once again, not on the basis of individual results but in terms of the expectable group outcome.

SUMMARY

- The primary focus of the security analyst should be the firm's real economic earnings rather than its reported earnings. Accounting earnings as reported in financial statements can be a biased estimate of real economic earnings, although empirical studies confirm that reported earnings convey considerable information concerning a firm's prospects.
- A firm's ROE is a key determinant of the growth rate of its earnings. ROE is affected profoundly by the firm's degree of financial leverage. An increase in a firm's debt/equity ratio will raise its ROE and hence its growth rate only if the interest rate on the debt is less than the firm's return on assets.
- It is often helpful to the analyst to decompose a firm's ROE ratio into the product of several accounting ratios and to analyze their separate behavior over time and across companies within an industry. A useful breakdown is

$$\text{ROE} = \frac{\text{Net profits}}{\text{Pretax profits}} \times \frac{\text{Pretax profits}}{\text{EBIT}} \times \frac{\text{EBIT}}{\text{Sales}} \times \frac{\text{Sales}}{\text{Assets}} \times \frac{\text{Assets}}{\text{Equity}}$$

- Other accounting ratios that have a bearing on a firm's profitability and/or risk are fixed-asset turnover, inventory turnover, days sales in receivables, and the current, quick, and interest coverage ratios.
- Two ratios that make use of the market price of the firm's common stock in addition to its financial statements are the ratios of market-to-book value and price to earnings. Analysts sometimes take low values for these ratios as a margin of safety or a sign that the stock is a bargain.
- A major problem in the use of data obtained from a firm's financial statements is comparability. Firms have a great deal of latitude in how they choose to compute various items of revenue and expense. It is, therefore, necessary for the security analyst to adjust accounting earnings and financial ratios to a uniform standard before attempting to compare financial results across firms.
- Comparability problems can be acute in a period of inflation. Inflation can create distortions in accounting for inventories, depreciation, and interest expense.
- Fair value or mark-to-market accounting requires that most assets be valued at current market value rather than historical cost. This policy has proved to be controversial because in many instances it is difficult to ascertain true market value, and critics contend that it makes financial statements unduly volatile. Advocates argue that financial statements should reflect the best estimate of current asset values.

- International financial reporting standards have become progressively accepted throughout the world, including the United States. They differ from traditional U.S. GAAP procedures in that they are principles-based rather than rules-based.

KEY TERMS

accounting earnings, 445	FIFO, 464	price–earnings ratio (P/E), 458
acid test ratio, 457	income statement, 444	profit margin, 452
average collection	interest coverage ratio, 453	quality of earnings, 466
period, 456	international financial	quick ratio, 457
balance sheet, 445	reporting standards, 468	residual income, 451
cash ratio, 457	inventory turnover ratio, 456	return on assets (ROA), 449
current ratio, 457	leverage ratio, 453	return on capital (ROC), 449
days sales in	LIFO, 464	return on equity (ROE), 449
receivables, 456	liquidity, 457	return on sales, 452
DuPont system, 452	mark-to-market	statement of cash flows, 446
economic earnings, 444	accounting, 466	times interest earned, 453
economic value added, 451	market-to-book-value	total asset turnover
fair value accounting, 466	ratio, 458	(ATO), 452

KEY FORMULAS

ROE and leverage: $\text{ROE} = (1 - \text{Tax rate})\left(\text{ROA} + (\text{ROA} - \text{Interest rate})\dfrac{\text{Debt}}{\text{Equity}}\right)$

DuPont formula: $\text{ROE} = \dfrac{\text{Net profit}}{\text{Pretax profit}} \times \dfrac{\text{Pretax profit}}{\text{EBIT}} \times \dfrac{\text{EBIT}}{\text{Sales}} \times \dfrac{\text{Sales}}{\text{Assets}} \times \dfrac{\text{Assets}}{\text{Equity}}$

Another DuPont formula: $\text{ROA} = \text{Margin} \times \text{Turnover}$

PROBLEM SETS

 Select problems are available in McGraw-Hill's *Connect*. Please see the Supplements section of the book's frontmatter for more information.

1. Use the following financial statements of Heifer Sports Inc. in Table 14.14 to find Heifer's: *(LO 14-1)*
   a. Inventory turnover ratio in 2015.
   b. Debt/equity ratio in 2015.
   c. Cash flow from operating activities in 2015.
   d. Average collection period.
   e. Asset turnover ratio.
   f. Interest coverage ratio.
   g. Operating profit margin.
   h. Return on equity.
   i. P/E ratio.
   j. Compound leverage ratio.
   k. Net cash provided by operating activities.

2. Use the following cash flow data for Rocket Transport to find Rocket's: *(LO 14-1)*
   a. Net cash provided by or used in investing activities.
   b. Net cash provided by or used in financing activities.
   c. Net increase or decrease in cash for the year.

Cash dividend	$ 80,000
Purchase of bus	$ 33,000
Interest paid on debt	$ 25,000

(table continued on next page)

Sales of old equipment	$ 72,000
Repurchase of stock	$ 55,000
Cash payments to suppliers	$ 95,000
Cash collections from customers	$300,000

3. The Crusty Pie Co., which specializes in apple turnovers, has a return on sales higher than the industry average, yet its ROA is the same as the industry average. How can you explain this? *(LO 14-3)*

4. The ABC Corporation has a profit margin on sales below the industry average, yet its ROA is above the industry average. What does this imply about its asset turnover? *(LO 14-3)*

5. A company's current ratio is 2. If the company uses cash to retire notes payable due within one year, would this transaction increase or decrease the current ratio? What about the asset turnover ratio? *(LO 14-1)*

TABLE 14.14   Heifer Sports financial statements

Income statement	2015	
Sales	$5,500,000	
Cost of goods sold	2,850,000	
Depreciation	280,000	
Selling & administrative expenses	1,500,000	
EBIT	$ 870,000	
Interest expense	130,000	
Taxable income	$ 740,000	
Taxes	330,000	
Net income	$ 410,000	
Balance sheet, year-end	**2015**	**2014**
Assets		
Cash	$ 50,000	$ 40,000
Accounts receivable	660,000	690,000
Inventory	490,000	480,000
Total current assets	$1,200,000	$1,210,000
Fixed assets	3,100,000	2,800,000
Total assets	$4,300,000	$4,010,000
Liabilities and shareholders' equity		
Accounts payable	$ 340,000	$ 450,000
Short-term debt	480,000	550,000
Total current liabilities	$ 820,000	$1,000,000
Long-term bonds	2,520,000	2,200,000
Total liabilities	$3,340,000	$3,200,000
Common stock	$ 310,000	$ 310,000
Retained earnings	650,000	500,000
Total shareholders' equity	$ 960,000	810,000
Total liabilities and shareholders' equity	$4,300,000	$4,010,000

6. Cash flow from investing activities *excludes:* **(LO 14-1)**
   a. Cash paid for acquisitions.
   b. Cash received from the sale of fixed assets.
   c. Inventory increases due to a new (internally developed) product line.
   d. All of the above.

7. Cash flow from operating activities *includes:* **(LO 14-1)**
   a. Inventory increases resulting from acquisitions.
   b. Inventory changes due to changing exchange rates.
   c. Interest paid to bondholders.
   d. Dividends paid to stockholders.

8. Recently, Galaxy Corporation lowered its allowance for doubtful accounts by reducing bad debt expense from 2% of sales to 1% of sales. Ignoring taxes, what are the immediate effects on (*a*), operating income and (*b*) operating cash flow? **(LO 14-1)**

Use the following case in answering Problems 9–11: Hatfield Industries is a large manufacturing conglomerate based in the United States with annual sales in excess of $300 million. Hatfield is currently under investigation by the Securities and Exchange Commission (SEC) for accounting irregularities and possible legal violations in the presentation of the company's financial statements. A due-diligence team from the SEC has been sent to Hatfield's corporate headquarters in Philadelphia for a complete audit in order to further assess the situation.

Several unique circumstances at Hatfield are discovered by the SEC due-diligence team during the course of the investigation:

- Management has been involved in ongoing negotiations with the local labor union, of which approximately 40% of its full-time labor force are members. Labor officials are seeking increased wages and pension benefits, which Hatfield's management states is not possible at this time due to decreased profitability and a tight cash flow situation. Labor officials have accused Hatfield's management of manipulating the company's financial statements to justify not granting any concessions during the course of negotiations.
- All new equipment obtained over the past several years has been established on Hatfield's books as operating leases, although past acquisitions of similar equipment were nearly always classified as capital leases. Financial statements of industry peers indicate that capital leases for this type of equipment are the norm. The SEC wants Hatfield's management to provide justification for this apparent deviation from "normal" accounting practices.
- Inventory on Hatfield's books has been steadily increasing for the past few years in comparison to sales growth. Management credits improved operating efficiencies in its production methods that have contributed to boosts in overall production. The SEC is seeking evidence that Hatfield somehow may have manipulated its inventory accounts.

The SEC due-diligence team is not necessarily searching for evidence of fraud but of possible manipulation of accounting standards for the purpose of misleading shareholders and other interested parties. Initial review of Hatfield's financial statements indicates that, at a minimum, certain practices have resulted in low-quality earnings.

9. Labor officials believe that the management of Hatfield is attempting to understate its net income to avoid making any concessions in the labor negotiations. Which of the following actions by management will *most likely* result in low-quality earnings? **(LO 14-4)**
   a. Lengthening the life of a depreciable asset to lower the depreciation expense.
   b. Lowering the discount rate used in the valuation of the company's pension obligations.
   c. The recognition of revenue at the time of delivery rather than when payment is received.

10. Hatfield has begun recording all new equipment leases on its books as operating leases, a change from its consistent past use of capital leases, in which the present value of lease

payments is classified as a debt obligation. What is the *most likely* motivation behind Hatfield's change in accounting methodology? Hatfield is attempting to: *(LO 14-4)*

a. Improve its leverage ratios and reduce its perceived leverage.

b. Reduce its cost of goods sold and increase its profitability.

c. Increase its operating margins relative to industry peers.

11. The SEC due-diligence team is searching for the reason behind Hatfield's inventory build-up relative to its sales growth. One way to identify a deliberate manipulation of financial results by Hatfield is to search for: *(LO 14-4)*

a. A decline in inventory turnover.

b. Receivables that are growing faster than sales.

c. A delay in the recognition of expenses.

12. Use the DuPont system and the following data to find return on equity.   *(LO 14-3)*

- Leverage ratio   2.2
- Total asset turnover   2.0
- Net profit margin   5.5%
- Dividend payout ratio   31.8%

13. A firm has an ROE of 3%, a debt/equity ratio of .5, a tax rate of 35%, and pays an interest rate of 6% on its debt. What is its operating ROA?   *(LO 14-2)*

14. A firm has a tax burden ratio of .75, a leverage ratio of 1.25, an interest burden of .6, and a return on sales of 10%. The firm generates $2.40 in sales per dollar of assets. What is the firm's ROE?   *(LO 14-3)*

15. An analyst gathers the following information about Meyer, Inc.:

- Meyer has 1,000 shares of 8% cumulative preferred stock outstanding, with a par value of $100 and liquidation value of $110.
- Meyer has 20,000 shares of common stock outstanding, with a par value of $20.
- Meyer had retained earnings at the beginning of the year of $5,000,000.
- Net income for the year was $70,000.
- This year, for the first time in its history, Meyer paid no dividends on preferred or common stock.

What is the book value per share of Meyer's common stock?   *(LO 14-1)*

16. Here are data on two firms: *(LO 14-2)*

	Equity ($ million)	Debt ($ million)	ROC (%)	Cost of capital (%)
Acme	100	50	17	9
Apex	450	150	15	10

a. Which firm has the higher economic value added?

b. Which has higher economic value added per dollar of invested capital?

CFA Problems

1. Jones Group has been generating stable after-tax return on equity (ROE) despite declining operating income. Explain how it might be able to maintain its stable after-tax ROE.   *(LO 14-3)*

2. Which of the following *best* explains a ratio of "net sales to average net fixed assets" that *exceeds* the industry average?   *(LO 14-3)*

a. The firm added to its plant and equipment in the past few years.

b. The firm makes less efficient use of its assets than other firms.

c. The firm has a lot of old plant and equipment.

d. The firm uses straight-line depreciation.

3. The information in the following table comes from the 2014 financial statements of QuickBrush Company and SmileWhite Corporation:

Notes to the 2014 Financial Statements		
	QuickBrush	**SmileWhite**
Goodwill	The company amortizes goodwill over 20 years.	The company amortizes goodwill over 5 years.
Property, plant, and equipment	The company uses a straight-line depreciation method over the economic lives of the assets, which range from 5 to 20 years for buildings.	The company uses an accelerated depreciation method over the economic lives of the assets, which range from 5 to 20 years for buildings.
Accounts receivable	The company uses a bad-debt allowance of 2% of accounts receivable.	The company uses a bad-debt allowance of 5% of accounts receivable.

Determine which company has the higher quality of earnings by discussing *each* of the *three* notes.   *(LO 14-4)*

4. The financial statements for Chicago Refrigerator Inc. (see Tables 14.15 and 14.16) are to be used to compute the ratios *a* through *h* for 2016.   *(LO 14-2)*
   a. Quick ratio.
   b. Return on assets.
   c. Return on common shareholders' equity.
   d. Earnings per share of common stock.
   e. Profit margin.
   f. Times interest earned.
   g. Inventory turnover.
   h. Leverage ratio.

5. Janet Ludlow is a recently hired analyst. After describing the electric toothbrush industry, her first report focuses on two companies, QuickBrush Company and SmileWhite Corporation, and concludes:

   QuickBrush is a more profitable company than SmileWhite, as indicated by the 40% sales growth and substantially higher margins it has produced over the last few years. SmileWhite's sales and earnings are growing at a 10% rate and produce much lower margins. We do not think SmileWhite is capable of growing faster than its recent growth rate of 10% whereas QuickBrush can sustain a 30% long-term growth rate.   *(LO 14-3)*
   a. Criticize Ludlow's analysis and conclusion that QuickBrush is more profitable, as defined by return on equity (ROE), than SmileWhite and that it has a higher sustainable growth rate. Use only the information provided in Tables 14.17 and 14.18. Support your criticism by calculating and analyzing:
      • The five components that determine ROE.
      • The two ratios that determine sustainable growth: ROE and plowback.
   b. Explain how QuickBrush has produced an average annual earnings per share (EPS) growth rate of 40% over the last two years with an ROE that has been declining. Use only the information provided in Table 14.17.

6. Scott Kelly is reviewing MasterToy's financial statements to estimate its sustainable growth rate. Using the information presented in Table 14.19:   *(LO 14-3)*
   a. Identify and calculate the components of the DuPont formula.
   b. Calculate the ROE for 2016 using the components of the DuPont formula.
   c. Calculate the sustainable growth rate for 2016 from the firm's ROE and plowback ratios.

7. The DuPont formula defines the net return on shareholders' equity as a function of the following components: *(LO 14-3)*
   • Operating margin

TABLE 14.15   Chicago Refrigerator Inc. balance sheet, as of December 31 ($ thousand)

	2015	2016
Assets		
Current assets		
Cash	$ 683	$ 325
Accounts receivable	1,490	3,599
Inventories	1,415	2,423
Prepaid expenses	15	13
Total current assets	$3,603	$6,360
Property, plant, equipment, net	1,066	1,541
Other	123	157
Total assets	$4,792	$8,058
Liabilities		
Current liabilities		
Notes payable to bank	$ —	$ 875
Current portion of long-term debt	38	115
Accounts payable	485	933
Estimated income tax	588	472
Accrued expenses	576	586
Customer advance payment	34	963
Total current liabilities	$1,721	$3,945
Long-term debt	122	179
Other liabilities	81	131
Total liabilities	$1,924	$4,255
Shareholders' equity		
Common stock, $1 par value 1,000,000 shares authorized; 550,000 and 829,000 outstanding, respectively	$ 550	$ 829
Preferred stock, Series A 10%; $25.00 par value; 25,000 authorized; 20,000 and 18,000 outstanding, respectively	500	450
Additional paid-in capital	450	575
Retained earnings	1,368	1,949
Total shareholders' equity	$2,868	$3,803
Total liabilities and shareholders' equity	$4,792	$8,058

TABLE 14.16   Chicago Refrigerator Inc. income statement, years ending December 31 ($ thousand)

	2015	2016
Net sales	$7,570	$12,065
Other income, net	261	345
Total revenues	$7,831	$12,410
Cost of goods sold	$4,850	$ 8,048
General administrative and marketing expenses	1,531	2,025
Interest expense	22	78
Total costs and expenses	$6,403	$10,151
Net income before tax	$1,428	$ 2,259
Income tax	628	994
Net income	$ 800	$ 1,265

TABLE 14.17 Quickbrush Company financial statements: Yearly data ($000 except per-share data)

Income statement	December 2014	December 2015	December 2016
Revenue	$3,480	$5,400	$7,760
Cost of goods sold	2,700	4,270	6,050
Selling, general, and admin. expense	500	690	1,000
Depreciation and amortization	30	40	50
Operating income (EBIT)	$ 250	$ 400	$ 660
Interest expense	0	0	0
Income before taxes	$ 250	$ 400	$ 660
Income taxes	60	110	215
Income after taxes	$ 190	$ 290	$ 445
Diluted EPS	$ 0.60	$ 0.84	$ 1.18
Average shares outstanding (000)	317	346	376

Financial statistics	December 2014	December 2015	December 2016	3-Year Average
COGS as % of sales	77.59%	79.07%	77.96%	78.24%
General & admin. as % of sales	14.37	12.78	12.89	13.16
Operating margin (%)	7.18	7.41	8.51	
Pretax income/EBIT (%)	100.00	100.00	100.00	
Tax rate (%)	24.00	27.50	32.58	

Balance sheet	December 2014	December 2015	December 2016
Cash and cash equivalents	$ 460	$ 50	$ 480
Accounts receivable	540	720	950
Inventories	300	430	590
Net property, plant, and equipment	760	1,830	3,450
Total assets	$2,060	$3,030	$5,470
Current liabilities	$ 860	$1,110	$1,750
Total liabilities	$ 860	$1,110	$1,750
Stockholders' equity	1,200	1,920	3,720
Total liabilities and equity	$2,060	$3,030	$5,470
Market price per share	$21.00	$30.00	$45.00
Book value per share	$ 3.79	$ 5.55	$ 9.89
Annual dividend per share	$ 0.00	$ 0.00	$ 0.00

- Asset turnover
- Interest burden
- Financial leverage
- Income tax rate

Using *only* the data in Table 14.20:
   a. Calculate each of the five components listed above for 2013 and 2016, and calculate the return on equity (ROE) for 2013 and 2016, using all of the five components.
   b. Briefly discuss the impact of the changes in asset turnover and financial leverage on the change in ROE from 2013 to 2016.

TABLE 14.18 Smilewhite Corporation financial statements: Yearly data ($000 except per share data)

Income statement	December 2014	December 2015	December 2016
Revenue	$104,000	$110,400	$119,200
Cost of goods sold	72,800	75,100	79,300
Selling, general, and admin. expense	20,300	22,800	23,900
Depreciation and amortization	4,200	5,600	8,300
Operating income (EBIT)	$ 6,700	$ 6,900	$ 7,700
Interest expense	600	350	350
Income before taxes	$ 6,100	$ 6,550	$ 7,350
Income taxes	2,100	2,200	2,500
Income after taxes	$ 4,000	$ 4,350	$ 4,850
Diluted EPS	$ 2.16	$ 2.35	$ 2.62
Average shares outstanding (000)	1,850	1,850	1,850

Financial statistics	December 2014	December 2015	December 2016	3-Year Average
COGS as % of sales	70.00%	68.00%	66.53%	68.10%
General & admin. as % of sales	19.52	20.64	20.05	20.08
Operating margin (%)	6.44	6.25	6.46	
Pretax income/EBIT (%)	91.04	94.93	95.45	
Tax rate (%)	34.43	33.59	34.01	

Balance sheet	December 2014	December 2015	December 2016
Cash and cash equivalents	$ 7,900	$ 3,300	$ 1,700
Accounts receivable	7,500	8,000	9,000
Inventories	6,300	6,300	5,900
Net property, plant, and equipment	12,000	14,500	17,000
Total assets	$ 33,700	$ 32,100	$ 33,600
Current liabilities	$ 6,200	$ 7,800	$ 6,600
Long-term debt	9,000	4,300	4,300
Total liabilities	$ 15,200	$ 12,100	$ 10,900
Stockholders' equity	18,500	20,000	22,700
Total liabilities and equity	$ 33,700	$ 32,100	$ 33,600
Market price per share	$ 23.00	$ 26.00	$ 30.00
Book value per share	$ 10.00	$ 10.81	$ 12.27
Annual dividend per share	$ 1.42	$ 1.53	$ 1.72

TABLE 14.19   Mastertoy, Inc.: Actual 2015 and estimated 2016 financial statements for fiscal year ending December 31 ($ million, except per-share data)

	2015	2016
Income statement		
Revenue	$4,750	$5,140
Cost of goods sold	2,400	2,540
Selling, general, and administrative	1,400	1,550
Depreciation	180	210
Goodwill amortization	10	10
Operating income	$ 760	$ 830
Interest expense	20	25
Income before taxes	$ 740	$ 805
Income taxes	265	295
Net income	$ 475	$ 510
Earnings per share	$ 1.79	$ 1.96
Average shares outstanding (millions)	265	260
Balance sheet		
Cash	$ 400	$ 400
Accounts receivable	680	700
Inventories	570	600
Net property, plant, and equipment	800	870
Intangibles	500	530
Total assets	$2,950	$3,100
Current liabilities	$ 550	$ 600
Long-term debt	300	300
Total liabilities	$ 850	$ 900
Stockholders' equity	2,100	2,200
Total liabilities and equity	$2,950	$3,100
Book value per share	$ 7.92	$ 8.46
Annual dividend per share	0.55	0.60

TABLE 14.20   Income statements and balance sheets

	2013	2016
Income statement data		
Revenues	$542	$979
Operating income	$ 38	$ 76
Depreciation and amortization	3	9
Interest expense	3	0
Pretax income	$ 32	$ 67
Income taxes	13	37
Net income after tax	$ 19	$ 30
Balance sheet data		
Fixed assets	$ 41	$ 70
Total assets	245	291
Working capital	123	157
Total debt	16	0
Total shareholders' equity	159	220

1. Go to **finance.yahoo.com** to find information about Vulcan Materials Company (VMC), Southwest Airlines (LUV), Honda Motor Company (HMC), Nordstrom, Inc. (JWN), and Abbott Laboratories (ABT). Download the most recent income statement and balance sheet for each company.
   a. Calculate the operating profit margin (operating profit/sales) and the asset turnover (sales/assets) for each firm.
   b. Calculate the return on assets directly (ROA = Operating profit/Total assets), and then confirm it by calculating ROA = Operating margin × Asset turnover.
   c. In what industries do these firms operate? Do the ratios make sense when you consider the industry types?
   d. For the firms that have relatively low ROAs, does the source of the problem seem to be the operating profit margin, the asset turnover, or both?
   e. Calculate the return on equity (ROE = Net income/Equity) for each firm. For the two firms with the lowest ROEs, perform a DuPont analysis to isolate the source(s) of the problem.

2. From Yahoo's Industry Center (**biz.yahoo.com/ie/**) select *Complete Industry List* and then the Toys & Games industry. Pick two companies from the list and do the following for each firm:
   a. Retrieve the latest annual balance sheet for each company. Calculate the common-size percentages for the balance sheet in the new column.
   b. Compare the firms' investments in accounts receivable, inventory, and net plant, property, and equipment. Which firm has more invested in these items on a percentage basis?
   c. Compare the firms' investments in current liabilities and long-term liabilities. Does one firm have a significantly higher burden in either of these areas?
   d. Analyze the firms' capital structures by examining the debt ratios and the percentages of preferred and common equity. How much do the firms' capital structures differ from each other?

3. Select a company of interest to you and link to its annual cash flow statement under the company's *Financials* tab. Answer the following questions about the firm's cash flow activities.
   a. Did the firm have positive or negative cash flow from operations?
   b. Did the firm invest in or sell off long-term investments?
   c. What were the major sources of financing for the firm?
   d. What was the net change in cash?
   e. Did exchange rates have any effect on the firm's cash flows?

   Now answer these questions:
   f. How liquid is the firm?
   g. How well is the firm using its assets?
   h. How effectively is the firm using leverage?
   i. Is the firm profitable?

14.1 A debt/equity ratio of 1 implies that Mordett will have $50 million of debt and $50 million of equity. Interest expense will be .09 × $50 million, or $4.5 million per year. Mordett's net profits and ROE over the business cycle will therefore be:

		Nodett		Mordett	
Scenario	EBIT	Net Profits	ROE	Net Profits*	ROE[†]
Bad year	$5M	$3M	3%	$0.3M	0.6%
Normal year	10	6	6	3.3	6.6
Good year	15	9	9	6.3	12.6%

*Mordett's after-tax profits are given by: 0.6(EBIT 2 $4.5 million).

[†]Mordett's equity is only $50 million.

14.2 Ratio decomposition analysis for Mordett Corporation:

		(1)	(2)	(3)	(4)	(5)	(6)
Year	ROE	Net Profit / Pretax Profit	Pretax Profit / EBIT	EBIT / Sales (Margin)	Sales / Assets (Turnover)	Assets / Equity	Compound Leverage Factor (2) × (5)
a. Bad year							
Nodett	0.030	0.6	1.000	0.0625	0.800	1.000	1.000
Somdett	0.018	0.6	0.360	0.0625	0.800	1.667	0.600
Mordett	0.006	0.6	0.100	0.0625	0.800	2.000	0.200
b. Normal year							
Nodett	0.060	0.6	1.000	0.100	1.000	1.000	1.000
Somdett	0.068	0.6	0.680	0.100	1.000	1.667	1.134
Mordett	0.066	0.6	0.550	0.100	1.000	2.000	1.100
c. Good year							
Nodett	0.090	0.6	1.000	0.125	1.200	1.000	1.000
Somdett	0.118	0.6	0.787	0.125	1.200	1.667	1.311
Mordett	0.126	0.6	0.700	0.125	1.200	2.000	1.400

14.3 GI's ROE in 2017 was 3.03%, computed as follows:

$$\text{ROE} = \frac{\$5,285}{.5(\$171,843 + \$177,128)} = .0303, \text{ or } 3.03\%$$

Its P/E ratio was $21/$5.285 = 4, and its P/B ratio was $21/$177 = .12. Its earnings yield was 25% compared with an industry average of 12.5%.

Note that in our calculations the P/E does not equal (P/B)/ROE because (following common practice) we have computed ROE with *average* shareholders' equity in the denominator and P/B with *end*-of-year shareholders' equity in the denominator.

14.4 IBX ratio analysis:

ROE increased despite a decline in operating margin and a decline in the tax burden ratio because of increased leverage and turnover. Note that ROA declined from 11.65% in 2015 to 10.65% in 2018.

		(1)	(2)	(3)	(4)	(5)	(6)	(7)
Year	ROE	Net Profit / Pretax Profit	Pretax Profit / EBIT	EBIT / Sales (Margin)	Sales / Assets (Turnover)	Assets / Equity	Compound Leverage Factor (2) × (5)	ROA (3) × (4)
2018	11.4%	0.616	0.796	7.75%	1.375	2.175	1.731	10.65%
2015	10.2	0.636	0.932	8.88	1.311	1.474	1.374	11.65

14.5 LIFO accounting results in lower reported earnings than does FIFO. Fewer assets to depreciate result in lower reported earnings because there is less bias associated with the use of historic cost. More debt results in lower reported earnings because the inflation premium in the interest rate is treated as part of interest.

Derivative Markets

Chapters in This Part

15 Options Markets

16 Option Valuation

17 Futures Markets
   and Risk
   Management

Horror stories about large losses incurred by high-flying traders in derivatives markets such as those for futures and options periodically become a staple of the evening news. Indeed, there were some amazing losses to report in the last decade: several totaling hundreds of millions of dollars, and a few amounting to more than a billion dollars. Among the most notorious of these were the loss of $7.2 billion in equity futures contracts by Société Générale in January 2008 and the loss of more than $100 billion on positions in credit derivatives by American International Group that resulted in a massive government bailout in September 2008. In the wake of these debacles, some venerable institutions have gone under, notable among them Barings Bank, which once helped the U.S. finance the Louisiana Purchase and the British Empire finance the Napoleonic Wars.

These stories, while important, fascinating, and even occasionally scandalous, often miss the point. Derivatives, when misused, can indeed provide a quick path to insolvency. Used properly, however, they are potent tools for risk management and control. In fact, you will discover in these chapters that one firm was sued for *failing* to use derivatives to hedge price risk. One article in *The Wall Street Journal* on hedging applications using derivatives was entitled "Index Options Touted as Providing Peace of Mind." Hardly material for bankruptcy court or the *National Enquirer*.

Derivatives provide a means to control risk that is qualitatively different from the techniques traditionally considered in portfolio theory. In contrast to the mean-variance analysis we discussed in Parts Two and Three, derivatives allow investors to change the *shape* of the probability distribution of investment returns. An entirely new approach to risk management follows from this insight.

The following chapters will explore how derivatives can be used as parts of a well-designed portfolio strategy. We will examine some popular portfolio strategies utilizing these securities and take a look at how derivatives are valued.

Learning Objectives

LO 15-1 Calculate the profit to various option positions as a function of ultimate security prices.

LO 15-2 Formulate option strategies to modify portfolio risk-return attributes.

LO 15-3 Identify embedded options in various securities and determine how option characteristics affect the prices of those securities.

Derivative securities, or simply *derivatives*, play a large and increasingly important role in financial markets. These are securities whose prices are determined by, or "derive from," the prices of other securities.

Options and futures contracts are both derivative securities. Their payoffs depend on the value of other securities. Swap contracts, which we will discuss in Chapter 17, also are derivatives. Because the value of derivatives depends on the value of other securities, they can be powerful tools for both hedging and speculation. We will investigate these applications in the next three chapters, beginning in this chapter with options.

Trading of standardized options on a national exchange started in 1973 when the Chicago Board Options Exchange (CBOE) began listing call options. These contracts were almost immediately a great success,

crowding out the previously existing over-the-counter options market.

Options contracts now are traded on several exchanges. They are written on common stock, stock indexes, foreign exchange, agricultural commodities, precious metals, and interest rates. In addition, the over-the-counter market also has enjoyed a tremendous resurgence in recent years as its trading in custom-tailored options has exploded. Popular and potent for modifying portfolio characteristics, options have become essential tools that every portfolio manager must understand.

This chapter is an introduction to options markets. It explains how puts and calls work and examines their investment characteristics. Popular option strategies are considered next. Finally, we will examine a range of securities with embedded options such as callable or convertible bonds.

15.1 THE OPTION CONTRACT

A **call option** gives its holder the right to purchase an asset for a specified price, called the **exercise** or **strike price,** on or before some specified expiration date. For example, an October call option on Facebook stock with exercise price $80 entitles its owner to purchase Facebook stock for a price of $80 at any time up to and including the expiration date in October. The holder of the call is not required to exercise the option. She will choose to exercise only if the market value of the asset exceeds the exercise price. In this case, the option holder may "call away" the asset for the exercise price. Otherwise, the option may be left unexercised. If it is not exercised before the expiration date of the contract, a call option simply expires and becomes valueless. Therefore, if the stock price is greater than the exercise price on the expiration date, the value of the call option will equal the difference between the stock price and the exercise price; but if the stock price is less than the exercise price at expiration, the call will be worthless. The *net profit* on the call is the value of the option minus the price originally paid to purchase it.

The purchase price of the option is called the **premium.** It represents the compensation the purchaser of the call must pay for the ability to exercise the option only when exercise is desirable. Sellers of call options, who are said to *write* calls, receive premium income now as payment against the possibility they will be required at some later date to deliver the asset in return for an exercise price less than the market value of the asset. If the option is left to expire worthless, the call writer clears a profit equal to the premium income derived from the initial sale of the option. But if the call is exercised, the profit to the option writer is the premium income *minus* the difference between the value of the stock that must be delivered and the exercise price that is paid for those shares. If that difference is larger than the initial premium, the writer will incur a loss.

call option
The right to buy an asset at a specified exercise price on or before a specified expiration date.

exercise or strike price
Price set for calling (buying) an asset or putting (selling) an asset.

premium
Purchase price of an option.

Profits and Losses on a Call Option

Consider the November 2014 expiration call option on a share of Facebook with an exercise price of $80 selling on October 16, 2014, for $2.64. The exact expiration date for this option is November 21. Until then, the call holder may exercise the option to buy shares of Facebook for $80. On October 16, Facebook sells for only $75.95. Because the stock price is less than $80, it clearly does not make sense at the moment to exercise the option. Indeed, if Facebook remains below $80 by the expiration date, the call will be left to expire worthless. On the other hand, if the stock is selling above $80 at expiration, the call holder will find it optimal to exercise. For example, if the shares sell for $82 on November 21, the option will be exercised, as it will give its holder the right to pay $80 for a stock worth $82. The value of each option on the expiration date would then be

$$\text{Value at expiration} = \text{Stock price} - \text{Exercise price} = \$82 - \$80 = \$2$$

Despite the $2 payoff at expiration, the call holder still realizes a loss of $.64 on the investment because the initial purchase price was $2.64:

$$\text{Profit} = \text{Final value} - \text{Original investment} = \$2.00 - \$2.64 = -\$.64$$

Nevertheless, exercise of the call is optimal at expiration if the stock price exceeds the exercise price because the exercise proceeds will offset at least part of the purchase price. The call buyer will clear a profit if Facebook is selling above $82.64 at the expiration date. At that stock price, the proceeds from exercise will just cover the original cost of the call.

A **put option** gives its holder the right to *sell* an asset for a specified exercise or strike price on or before some expiration date. An October put on Facebook with an exercise price of $80 entitles its owner to sell shares to the put writer at a price of $80 at any time before expiration in October, even if the market price of the stock is less than $80. While profits on call options increase when the asset price rises, profits on put options increase when the asset price falls. A put will be exercised only if the exercise price is greater than the price of the underlying asset, that is, only if its holder can deliver for the exercise price an asset with market value less than that amount. (One doesn't need to own shares of Facebook to exercise the put option.

put option
The right to sell an asset at a specified exercise price on or before a specified expiration date.

Upon exercise of the put, the investor's broker purchases the necessary shares at the market price and immediately delivers or "puts them" to an option writer for the exercise price. The owner of the put profits by the difference between the exercise price and market price.)

EXAMPLE 15.2

*Profits and Losses
on a Put Option*

Now consider the November 2014 expiration put option on Facebook with an exercise price of $80, selling on October 16 for $6.74. It entitled its owner to *sell* a share of Facebook for $80 at any time until November 21. If the holder of the put buys a share of Facebook and immediately exercises the right to sell it at $80, net proceeds will be $80 − $75.95 = $4.05. Obviously, an investor who pays $6.74 for the put has no intention of exercising it immediately. If, on the other hand, Facebook is selling for $72 at expiration, the put will turn out to be a profitable investment. Its value at expiration will be

$$\text{Value at expiration} = \text{Exercise price} - \text{Stock price} = \$80 - \$72 = \$8$$

and the investor's profit will be $8 − $6.74 = $1.26. This is a holding period return of $1.26/$6.74 = .187 or 18.7%–over only 36 days! Obviously, put option sellers on October 16 (who are on the other side of the transaction) did not consider this outcome very likely.

---

in the money

An option where exercise would generate a positive cash flow.

out of the money

An option which, if exercised, would produce a negative cash flow. Out-of-the-money options are therefore never exercised.

at the money

An option where the exercise price equals the asset price.

An option is described as **in the money** when its exercise would produce a positive cash flow. Therefore, a call option is in the money when the asset price exceeds the exercise price, and a put option is in the money when the asset price is less than the exercise price. Conversely, a call is **out of the money** when the exercise price exceeds the asset value; no one would exercise the right to purchase for the exercise price an asset worth less than that amount. A put option is out of the money when the exercise price is less than the asset price. Options are **at the money** when the exercise price and asset price are equal.

Options Trading

Some options trade on over-the-counter (OTC) markets. The OTC market offers the advantage that the terms of the option contract—the exercise price, expiration date, and number of shares committed—can be tailored to the needs of the traders. The costs of establishing an OTC option contract, however, are relatively high. Today, most option trading occurs on organized exchanges.

Options contracts traded on exchanges are standardized by allowable expiration dates and exercise prices for each listed option. Each stock option contract provides for the right to buy or sell 100 shares of stock (except when stock splits occur after the contract is listed and the contract is adjusted for the terms of the split).

Standardization of the terms of listed option contracts means all market participants trade in a limited and uniform set of securities. This increases the depth of trading in any particular option, which lowers trading costs and results in a more competitive market. Exchanges, therefore, offer two important benefits: ease of trading, which flows from a central marketplace where buyers and sellers or their representatives congregate, and a liquid secondary market where buyers and sellers of options can transact quickly and cheaply.

Most options trading in the U.S. initially took place on the Chicago Board Options Exchange. However, by 2003 the International Securities Exchange, an electronic exchange based in New York, had displaced the CBOE as the largest options market. Options trading in Europe is uniformly transacted in electronic exchanges.

Figure 15.1 is a small sample of listed stock option quotations for Facebook on October 15, 2014. The last recorded price on the New York Stock Exchange for the company's stock was $75.95 per share.[1] Figure 15.1 includes options with exercise prices of $75 and $80. These values also are called the *strike prices*.

---

[1]Occasionally, this price may not match the closing price listed for the stock on the stock market page. This is because some NYSE stocks also trade on exchanges that close after the NYSE, and the stock pages may reflect the more recent closing price. The options exchanges, however, close with the NYSE, so the closing NYSE stock price is appropriate for comparison with the closing option price.

FIGURE   15.1

Facebook (FB)	Underlying stock price = $75.95		
Expiration	Strike	Call	Put
Oct-14	75	3.95	3.01
Oct-14	80	1.65	5.72
Nov-14	75	4.85	3.97
Nov-14	80	2.64	6.74

FIGURE   15.1

Options on Facebook, October 16, 2014

Source: *The Wall Street Journal Online*, October 16, 2014.

These exercise or strike prices bracket the stock price.[2] If the stock price moves outside the range of exercise prices of the existing set of options, new options with appropriate exercise prices may be offered. Therefore, at any time, both in-the-money and out-of-the-money options will be listed, as in this example.

Figure 15.1 shows both call and put options listed for each exercise price and expiration date. When we compare the prices of call options with the same expiration date but different exercise prices, we see that the value of the call is lower when the exercise price is higher. This makes sense, for the right to purchase a share is not as valuable when the purchase price is higher. Thus, the October expiration call option with strike price $75 sells for $3.95, while the $80 exercise price October call sells for only $1.65. Conversely, put options are worth *more* when the exercise price is higher: You would rather have the right to sell shares for $80 than for $75, and this is reflected in the prices of the puts. The October expiration put option with strike price $80 sells for $5.72, while the $75 exercise price October put sells for only $3.01.

Not infrequently, you will find some options that go an entire day without trading. Because trading is infrequent, it is not unusual to find option prices that appear out of line with other prices. You might see, for example, two calls with different exercise prices that seem to sell for the same price. This discrepancy arises because the last trades for these options may have occurred at different times during the day. At any moment, the call with the lower exercise price must be worth more, and the put less, than an otherwise-identical call or put with a higher exercise price.

Expirations of most exchange-traded options tend to be fairly short, ranging up to only several months. For larger firms and several stock indexes, however, longer-term options are traded with expirations ranging up to three years. These options are called LEAPS (for Long-term Equity AnticiPation Securities).

CONCEPT check   15.1

a. What will be the proceeds and net profits to an investor who purchases the October 2014 expiration Facebook calls with exercise price $80 if the stock price at option expiration is $78? What if the stock price at expiration is $84?

b. Now answer part (*a*) for an investor who purchases the October expiration put option with exercise price $80.

American and European Options

An **American option** allows its holder to exercise the right to purchase (if a call) or sell (if a put) the underlying asset on or *before* the expiration date. **European options** allow for exercise of the option only on the expiration date. American-style options, because they allow more leeway than their European-style counterparts, generally will be more valuable. Most traded options in the U.S. are American style. Foreign currency options and some stock-index options are notable exceptions to this rule, however.

American option

Can be exercised on or before its expiration.

European option

Can be exercised only at expiration.

---

[2]If a stock splits, the terms of the option—such as the exercise price—are adjusted to offset the impact of the split.

The Option Clearing Corporation

The Option Clearing Corporation (OCC), the clearinghouse for options trading, is jointly owned by the exchanges on which stock options are traded. The OCC places itself between options traders, becoming the effective buyer of the option from the writer and the effective writer of the option to the buyer. All individuals, therefore, deal only with the OCC, which effectively guarantees contract performance.

When an option holder exercises an option, the OCC arranges for a member firm with clients who have written that option to make good on the option obligation. The member firm selects from among its clients who have written that option to fulfill the contract. The selected client must deliver 100 shares of stock at a price equal to the exercise price for each call option contract written or must purchase 100 shares at the exercise price for each put option contract written.

Because the OCC guarantees contract performance, it requires option writers to post margin to guarantee that they can fulfill their contract obligations. The margin required is determined in part by the amount by which the option is in the money, because that value is an indicator of the potential obligation of the option writer upon exercise of the option. When the required margin exceeds the posted margin, the writer will receive a margin call. The *holder* of the option need not post margin because the holder will exercise the option only if it is profitable to do so. After purchasing the option, no further money is at risk.

Margin requirements also depend on whether the underlying asset is held in portfolio. For example, a call option writer owning the stock against which the option is written can satisfy the margin requirement simply by allowing a broker to hold that stock in the brokerage account. The stock is then guaranteed to be available for delivery should the call option be exercised. If the underlying security is not owned, however, the margin requirement is determined by the value of the underlying security as well as by the amount by which the option is in or out of the money. Out-of-the-money options require less margin from the writer, for expected payouts are lower.

Other Listed Options

Options on assets other than stocks also are widely traded. These include options on market indexes and industry indexes, on foreign currency, and even on the futures prices of agricultural products, gold, silver, fixed-income securities, and stock indexes. We will discuss these in turn.

INDEX OPTIONS   An index option is a call or put based on a stock market index such as the S&P 500. Index options are traded on several broad-based indexes as well as on several industry-specific indexes. We discussed many of these indexes in Chapter 2.

The construction of the indexes can vary across contracts or exchanges. For example, the S&P 100 Index is a value-weighted average of the 100 stocks in the Standard & Poor's 100 stock group. The weights are proportional to the market value of outstanding equity for each stock. The Dow Jones Industrial Average, by contrast, is a price-weighted average of 30 stocks.

Options contracts on many foreign stock indexes also trade. For example, options on the Nikkei Stock Index of Japanese stocks trade on the Singapore as well as the Chicago Mercantile Exchange. Options on European indexes such as the Financial Times Share Exchange (FTSE 100) trade on the NYSE-Euronext exchange. The Chicago Board Options Exchange also lists options on industry indexes such as the oil or high-tech industries.

In contrast to stock options, index options do not require that the call writer actually "deliver the index" upon exercise or that the put writer "purchase the index." Instead, a cash settlement procedure is used. The payoff that would accrue upon exercise of the option is calculated, and the option writer simply pays that amount to the option holder. The payoff is equal to the difference between the exercise price of the option and the value of the index. For example, if the S&P index is at 1,880 when a call option on the index with exercise price 1,870 is exercised, the holder of the call receives a cash payment equal to the difference, $1,880 - 1,870$, times the contract multiplier of $100, or $1,000 per contract.

Options on the major indexes, that is, the S&P 100 contract, often called the OEX after its ticker symbol, the S&P 500 Index (the SPX), and the Dow Jones Industrials (the DJX), are by far the most actively traded contracts on the CBOE. Together, these contracts dominate CBOE volume.

FUTURES OPTIONS   Futures options give their holders the right to buy or sell a specified futures contract, using as a futures price the exercise price of the option. Although the delivery process is slightly complicated, the terms of futures options contracts are designed in effect to allow the option to be written on the futures price itself. The option holder receives upon exercise net proceeds equal to the difference between the current futures price on the specified asset and the exercise price of the option. Thus, if the futures price is, say, $37, and the call has an exercise price of $35, the holder who exercises the call option on the futures gets a payoff of $2.

FOREIGN CURRENCY OPTIONS   A currency option offers the right to buy or sell a specified quantity of foreign currency for a specified number of U.S. dollars. Contracts are quoted in cents or fractions of a cent per unit of foreign currency.

There is an important difference between currency options and currency *futures* options. The former provide payoffs that depend on the difference between the exercise price and the exchange rate at expiration. The latter are foreign exchange futures options that provide payoffs that depend on the difference between the exercise price and the exchange rate *futures price* at expiration. Because exchange rates and exchange rate futures prices generally are not equal, the options and futures options contracts will have different values, even with identical expiration dates and exercise prices. Trading volume in currency futures options dominates by far trading in currency options.

INTEREST RATE OPTIONS   Options also are traded on Treasury notes and bonds, Treasury bills, and government bonds of other major economies such as the U.K. or Japan. Options on several interest rates also trade. Among them are contracts on Treasury bond, Treasury note, federal funds, LIBOR, Eurodollar, and British and euro-denominated yields.

15.2 VALUES OF OPTIONS AT EXPIRATION

Call Options

Recall that a call option gives the right to purchase a security at the exercise price. If you hold a call on FinCorp stock with an exercise price of $80, and FinCorp is now selling at $90, you can exercise your option to purchase the stock at $80 and simultaneously sell the shares at the market price of $90, clearing $10 per share. Yet if the shares sell below $80, you can sit on the option and do nothing, realizing no further gain or loss. The value of the call option at expiration equals

$$\text{Payoff to call holder at expiration} = \begin{cases} S_T - X & \text{if } S_T > X \\ 0 & \text{if } S_T \le X \end{cases}$$

where S_T is the value of the stock at the expiration date and X is the exercise price. This formula emphasizes the option property because the payoff cannot be negative. The option is exercised only if S_T exceeds X. If S_T is less than X, the option expires with zero value. The loss to the option holder in this case equals the price originally paid. More generally, the *profit* to the option holder is the option payoff minus the original purchase price.

The value at expiration of the call with exercise price $80 is given by the following schedule:

Stock price	$60	$70	$80	$90	$100
Option value	0	0	0	10	20

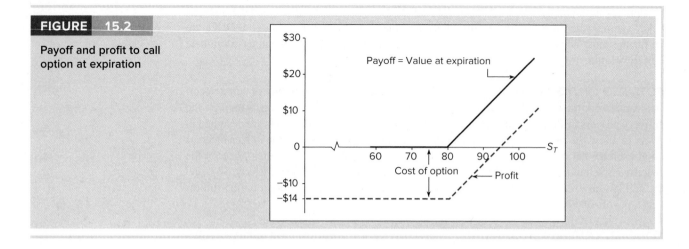

FIGURE   15.2

Payoff and profit to call
option at expiration

For stock prices at or below $80, the option expires worthless. Above $80, the option is worth the excess of the stock price over $80. The option's value increases by one dollar for each dollar increase in the stock price. This relationship is depicted in Figure 15.2.

The solid line in Figure 15.2 is the value of the call at expiration. The net *profit* to the holder of the call equals the gross payoff less the initial investment in the call. Suppose the call cost $14. Then the profit to the call holder would be as given in the dashed (bottom) line of Figure 15.2. At option expiration, the investor has suffered a loss of $14 if the stock price is less than or equal to $80.

Profits do not become positive until the stock price at expiration exceeds $94. At that price the payoff to the call, $S_T - X = \$94 - \$80 = \$14$, equals the cost paid to acquire it. Hence, the call holder shows a profit only if the stock price is higher.

Conversely, the writer of the call incurs losses if the stock price is high. In that scenario, the writer will be obligated to deliver a stock worth S_T for only X dollars.

$$\text{Payoff to call writer} = \begin{cases} -(S_T - X) & \text{if } S_T > X \\ 0 & \text{if } S_T \le X \end{cases}$$

The call writer, who is exposed to losses if the stock price increases, is willing to bear this risk in return for the option premium.

Figure 15.3 shows the payoff and profit diagrams for the call writer. These are the mirror images of the corresponding diagrams for call holders. The break-even point for the option writer also is $94. The (negative) payoff at that point just offsets the premium originally received when the option was written.

Put Options

A put option conveys the right to sell an asset at the exercise price. In this case, the holder will not exercise unless the asset price is *less* than the exercise price. For example, if FinCorp shares were to fall to $70, a put option with exercise price $80 could be exercised to give a $10 payoff. The holder would purchase a share for $70 and simultaneously deliver it to the put option writer for the exercise price of $80.

The value of a put option at expiration is

$$\text{Payoff to put holder} = \begin{cases} 0 & \text{if } S_T \ge X \\ X - S_T & \text{if } S_T < X \end{cases}$$

The solid line in Figure 15.4 illustrates the payoff at expiration to the holder of a put option on FinCorp stock with an exercise price of $80. If the stock price at option expiration is above $80, the put has no value, as the right to sell the shares at $80 would not be exercised. Below

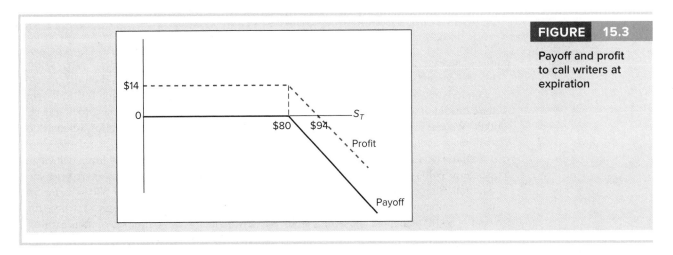

FIGURE 15.3

Payoff and profit to call writers at expiration

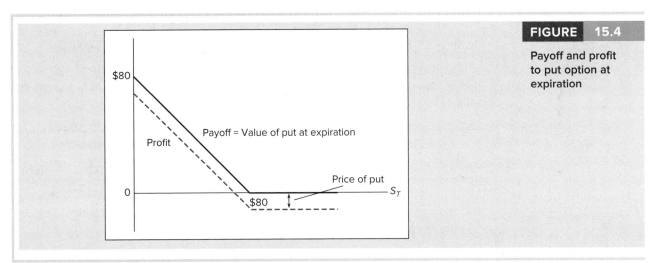

FIGURE 15.4

Payoff and profit to put option at expiration

a price of $80, the put value at expiration increases by $1 for each dollar the stock price falls. The dashed line in Figure 15.4 is a graph of the put option owner's profit at expiration, net of the initial cost of the put.

Writing puts *naked* (i.e., writing a put without an offsetting short position in the stock for hedging purposes) exposes the writer to losses if the market falls. Writing naked, deep out-of-the-money puts was once considered an attractive way to generate income, as it was believed that as long as the market did not fall sharply before the option expiration, the option premium could be collected without the put holder ever exercising the option against the writer. Because only sharp drops in the market could result in losses to the writer of the put, the strategy was not viewed as overly risky. However, in the wake of the market crash of October 1987, such put writers suffered huge losses. Participants now perceive much greater risk to this strategy.

Consider these four option strategies: (i) buy a call; (ii) write a call; (iii) buy a put; (iv) write a put.

a. For each strategy, plot both the payoff and profit diagrams as a function of the final stock price.

b. Why might one characterize both buying calls and writing puts as "bullish" strategies? What is the difference between them?

c. Why might one characterize both buying puts and writing calls as "bearish" strategies? What is the difference between them?

CONCEPT check 15.2

Options versus Stock Investments

Purchasing call options is a bullish strategy; that is, the calls provide profits when stock prices increase. Purchasing puts, in contrast, is a bearish strategy. Symmetrically, writing calls is bearish, while writing puts is bullish. Because option values depend on the price of the underlying stock, the purchase of options may be viewed as a substitute for direct purchase or sale of a stock. Why might an option strategy be preferable to direct stock transactions? We can begin to answer this question by comparing the values of option versus stock positions in FinCorp.

Suppose you believe the stock will increase in value from its current level, which we assume is $90. You know your analysis could be incorrect, however, and the share price also could fall. Suppose a six-month maturity call option with exercise price of $90 sells for $10 and the semiannual interest rate is 2%. Consider the following three strategies for investing a sum of $9,000. Suppose the firm will not pay any dividends until after the options expire.

Strategy A: Invest entirely in stock. Buy 100 shares, each selling for $90.

Strategy B: Invest entirely in at-the-money call options. Buy 900 calls, each selling for $10. (This would require 9 contracts, each for 100 shares.)

Strategy C: Purchase 100 call options for $1,000. Invest the remaining $8,000 in six-month T-bills, to earn 2% interest.

Let us trace the possible values of these three portfolios when the options expire in six months as a function of the stock price at that time.

Portfolio	Stock Price					
	$85	**$90**	**$95**	**$100**	**$105**	**$110**
A: 100 shares stock	$8,500	$9,000	$9,500	$10,000	$10,500	$11,000
B: 900 call options	0	0	4,500	9,000	13,500	18,000
C: 100 calls plus $8,000 in T-bills	8,160	8,160	8,660	9,160	9,660	10,160

Portfolio A will be worth 100 times the share price. Portfolio B is worthless unless the shares sell for more than the exercise price of the call. Once that point is reached, the portfolio is worth 900 times the excess of the stock price over the exercise price. Finally, portfolio C is worth $8,160 from the investment in T-bills ($8,000 × 1.02 = $8,160) plus any profits from the 100 call options. Remember that each of these portfolios involves the same $9,000 initial investment. The rates of return on these three portfolios are as follows:

Portfolio	Stock Price					
	$85	**$90**	**$95**	**$100**	**$105**	**$110**
A: 100 shares stock	−5.56%	0.0%	5.56%	11.11%	16.67%	22.22%
B: 900 call options	−100.0	−100.0	−50.00	0.0	50.0	100.0
C: 100 calls plus $8,000 in T-bills	−9.33	−9.33	−3.78	1.78	7.33	12.89

These rates of return are graphed in Figure 15.5.

Comparing the returns of portfolios B and C to those of the simple investment in stock represented by portfolio A, we see that options offer two interesting features. First, an option offers leverage. Compare the returns of portfolios B and A. When the stock fares poorly, ending anywhere below $90, the value of portfolio B falls precipitously to zero—a rate of return of negative 100%. Conversely, modest increases in the rate of return on the stock result in

An Excel model based on the FinCorp example discussed in the text is shown below. The model allows you to use any variety of options, stock, and lending or borrowing with a set investment amount and demonstrates the investment flexibility of options.

Z

Spreadsheets are
available in Connect

	A	B	C	D	E	F	G	H
1	Current stock price	90						
2	Exercise price	90						
3	Interest rate	0.02						
4	Investment budget	9000						
5	Call price	10						
6								
7			Dollar value of portfolio as a function of FinCorp price					
8	**Portfolio**		**$85**	**$90**	**$95**	**$100**	**$105**	**$110**
9	Portfolio A: All stock		$8,500	$9,000	$9,500	$10,000	$10,500	$11,000
10	Portfolio B: All call options		0	0	4,500	9,000	13,500	18,000
11	Portfolio C: Call plus bills		8,160	8,160	8,660	9,160	9,660	10,160
12								
13								
14			Rate of return as a function of FinCorp price					
15	**Portfolio**		**$85**	**$90**	**$95**	**$100**	**$105**	**$110**
16	Portfolio A: All stock		−5.6%	0.00%	5.6%	11.1%	16.7%	22.2%
17	Portfolio B: All call options		−100.0%	−100.0%	−50.0%	0.0%	50.0%	100.0%
18	Portfolio C: Call plus bills		−9.33%	−9.33%	−3.78%	1.78%	7.33%	12.89%

Excel Questions

1. Plot the rate of return to the call-plus-bills strategy using a diagram like that in Figure 15.5 but now assuming the investor uses an in-the-money call option with a strike price of $80. Assume the calls sell for $15. The higher cost for these calls compared to the at-the-money calls will result in less money being placed in T-bills because the investment budget is still $9,000.

2. Compare the plots of rate of return for the strategies using at-the-money calls (as in Figure 15.5) and your solution to Question 1. Which strategy is riskier?

disproportionate increases in the option rate of return. For example, a 4.8% increase in the stock price from $105 to $110 would increase the rate of return on the call from 50% to 100%. In this sense, calls are a levered investment on the stock. Their values respond more than proportionately to changes in the stock value.

Figure 15.5 vividly illustrates this point. For stock prices above $90, the slope of the all-option portfolio is far steeper than that of the all-stock portfolio, reflecting its greater proportional sensitivity to the value of the underlying security. The leverage factor is the reason that investors (illegally) exploiting inside information commonly choose options as their investment vehicle.

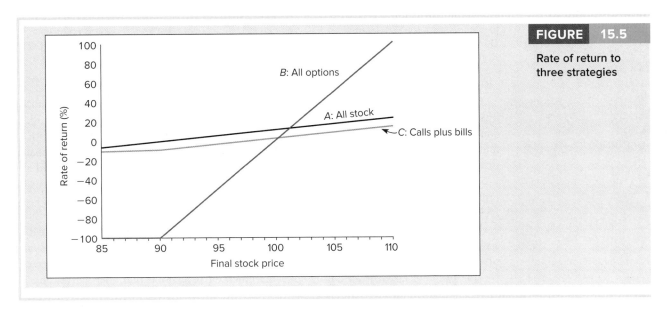

FIGURE 15.5

Rate of return to
three strategies

The potential insurance value of options is the second interesting feature, as portfolio *C* shows. The T-bill-plus-option portfolio cannot be worth less than $8,160 after six months, as the option can always be left to expire worthless. The worst possible rate of return on portfolio *C* is −9.33%, compared to a (theoretically) worst possible rate of return on the stock of −100% if the company were to go bankrupt. Of course, this insurance comes at a price: When the share price increases, portfolio *C* does not perform as well as portfolio *A,* the all-stock portfolio. For stock prices above $90, portfolio *C* underperforms portfolio *A* by about 9.33 percentage points.

This simple example makes an important point. While options can be used by speculators as effectively leveraged stock positions, as in portfolio *B,* they also can be used by investors who desire to tailor their risk exposures in creative ways, as in portfolio *C.* For example, the call-plus-T-bills strategy of portfolio *C* provides a rate of return profile quite unlike that of the stock alone. The absolute limitation on downside risk is a novel and attractive feature of this strategy. In the next section we will discuss several option strategies that provide other novel risk profiles that might be attractive to hedgers and other investors.

Option Strategies

An unlimited variety of payoff patterns can be achieved by combining puts and calls with various exercise prices. Below we explain the motivation and structure of some of the more popular ones.

PROTECTIVE PUT   Imagine you would like to invest in a stock but you are unwilling to bear potential losses beyond some given level. Investing in the stock alone seems risky to you because in principle you could lose all the money you invest. You might consider instead investing in stock and purchasing a put option on the stock.

Table 15.1 shows the total value of your portfolio at option expiration. Whatever happens to the stock price, you are guaranteed a payoff equal to the put option's exercise price because the put gives you the right to sell the share for the exercise price even if the stock price is below that value.

protective put

An asset combined with a put option that guarantees minimum proceeds equal to the put's exercise price.

Figure 15.6 illustrates the payoff and profit to this **protective put** strategy. The solid line in Figure 15.6C is the total payoff. The dashed line is displaced downward by the cost of establishing the position, $S_0 + P$. Notice that potential losses are limited.

EXAMPLE 15.3

Protective Put

Suppose the strike price is $X = \$90$ and the stock is selling for $87 at option expiration. Then the value of your total portfolio is $90: The stock is worth $87 and the value of the expiring put option is

$$X - S_T = \$90 - \$87 = \$3$$

Another way to look at it is that you are holding the stock and a put contract giving you the right to sell the stock for $90. Even if $S < \$90$, you can still sell the stock for $90 by exercising the put. On the other hand, if the stock price is above $90, say, $94, then the right to sell a share at $90 is worthless. You allow the put to expire unexercised, ending up with a share of stock worth $S_T = \$94$.

It is instructive to compare the profit on the protective put strategy with that of the stock investment. For simplicity, consider an at-the-money protective put, so that $X = S_0$. Figure 15.7 compares the profits for the two strategies. The profit on the stock is zero if the stock price remains unchanged, and $S_T = S_0$. It rises or falls by $1 for every dollar swing in the ultimate stock price. The profit on the protective put is negative and equal to the cost of the put if S_T is below S_0. The profit on the protective put increases one for one with increases in the stock price once the stock price exceeds *X*.

Figure 15.7 makes it clear that the protective put offers some insurance against stock price declines in that it limits losses. As we shall see in the next chapter, protective put strategies are the conceptual basis for the portfolio insurance industry. The cost of the protection is that, when the stock price increases, your profit is reduced by the cost of the put, which turned out to be unneeded.

risk management

Strategies to limit the risk of a portfolio.

This example also shows that despite the common perception that "derivatives mean risk," derivative securities can be used effectively for **risk management.** In fact, such risk

TABLE 15.1	Payoff to protective put strategy	
	$S_T \leq X$	$S_T > X$
Stock	S_T	S_T
Put	$X - S_T$	0
Total	X	S_T

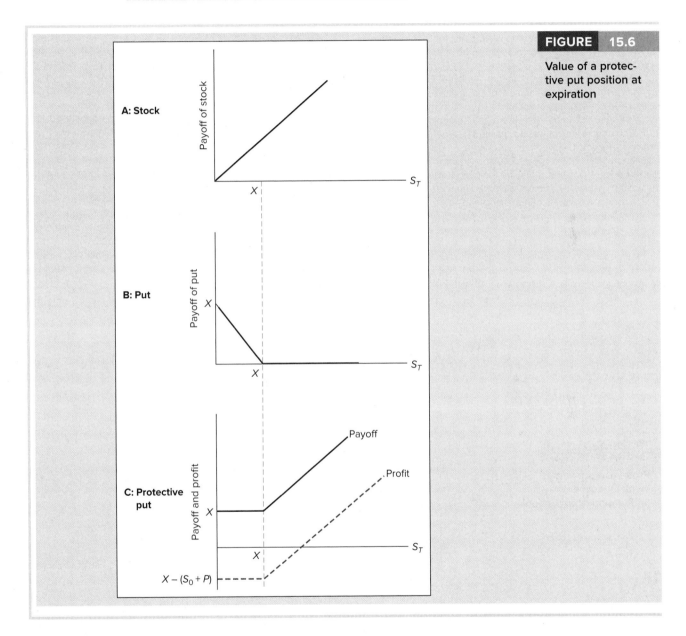

FIGURE   15.6

Value of a protective put position at expiration

A: Stock

B: Put

C: Protective put

management is becoming accepted as part of the fiduciary responsibility of financial managers. Indeed, in a highly cited court case, *Brane* v. *Roth,* a company's board of directors was successfully sued for failing to use derivatives to hedge the price risk of grain held in storage. Such hedging might have been accomplished using protective puts. Some observers believe that this case will ultimately lead to a broad legal obligation for firms to use derivatives and other techniques to manage risk.

The claim that derivatives are best viewed as risk management tools may seem surprising in light of the credit crisis of the last few years. The crisis was immediately precipitated when

DERIVATIVES, SPECULATION, AND RISK MANAGEMENT

Warren Buffett has famously described derivatives as financial weapons of mass destruction. And derivatives are widely vilified for setting off the financial crisis and the great recession that began in 2008. They are viewed as tools that enabled speculators to sink themselves and bring the economy down with them.

However, Robert Shiller, winner of the Nobel Prize in economics, has a very different outlook. While derivatives clearly can be used to speculate, they also can be used to manage risk and to lay it off onto the trader with the greatest capacity to deal with it. He compares derivatives to insurance. When you buy a fire insurance policy, for example, you pay a premium and receive a payment if a certain event occurs, in this case, if your house burns down. In isolation, it may be tempting to view the policy as gambling, specifically as a bet on a fire. But it is far more instructive to view the policy as part of a portfolio—it pays off only when some of your other assets are "losing value." Far from being a risk-increasing gamble, it is a risk-reducing hedge against losses from a fire.

Analogously, credit default swaps are also insurance tools. They pay off when other assets (corporate bonds or mortgages, for example) are similarly losing value. They therefore can be used to reduce risk on a portfolio of bonds in which you already may be invested. Admittedly, as was often the case in the crisis, they also can used to bet on bond performance. But fundamentally, they don't create risk; they simply shift it from the insured to the insurer. Shiller points out that banning the insurance product will not eliminate the underlying risk.

Shiller argues that derivatives can be used in many other ways to manage, or insure against, a wide variety of risks. At their heart, derivatives are just financial products whose payoffs depend on the prices of other assets. For example, he has advocated for the development of derivative products tied to indexes of regional home prices. Homeowners might use these products to insure against falling housing prices. By taking an appropriate position in these products, you could ensure that if housing values in your region declined, the housing price derivative contract would offset your loss. Mortgage lenders also could use these products to hedge against losses from an increase in housing foreclosures set off by declining prices.

While derivatives may have been misused leading up to the crisis, this does not refute the fact that they are potent tools that can be used to reduce risk. Shiller reminds us that these tools, like other tools, can be used badly and they can be used well. But banning innovation and foregoing their potential benefits may be the last thing we want to do as we contemplate a world filled with ever greater risks.

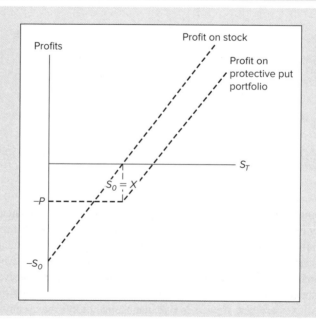

FIGURE 15.7

Protective put versus stock investment (at-the-money put option)

Straddles and Spreads

Using spreadsheets to analyze combinations of options is very helpful. Once the basic models are built, it is easy to extend the analysis to different bundles of options. The Excel model "Spreads and Straddles" shown below can be used to evaluate the profitability of different strategies.

Spreadsheets are available in Connect

	A	B	C	D	E	F	G	H	I	J	K	L
1					Spreads and Straddles							
2												
3	Stock Prices											
4	Beginning Market Price	116.5										
5	Ending Market Price	130					X 110 Straddle			X 120 Straddle		
6							Ending	Profit		Ending	Profit	
7	Buying Options:						Stock Price	-15.40		Stock Price	-24.00	
8	Call Options Strike	Price	Payoff	Profit	Return %		50	24.60		50	36.00	
9	110	22.80	20.00	-2.80	-12.28%		60	14.60		60	26.00	
10	120	16.80	10.00	-6.80	-40.48%		70	4.60		70	16.00	
11	130	13.60	0.00	-13.60	-100.00%		80	-5.40		80	6.00	
12	140	10.30	0.00	-10.30	-100.00%		90	-15.40		90	-4.00	
13							100	-25.40		100	-14.00	
14	Put Options Strike	Price	Payoff	Profit	Return %		110	-35.40		110	-24.00	
15	110	12.60	0.00	-12.60	-100.00%		120	-25.40		120	-34.00	
16	120	17.20	0.00	-17.20	-100.00%		130	-15.40		130	-24.00	
17	130	23.60	0.00	-23.60	-100.00%		140	-5.40		140	-14.00	
18	140	30.50	10.00	-20.50	-67.21%		150	4.60		150	-4.00	
19							160	14.60		160	6.00	
20	Straddle	Price	Payoff	Profit	Return %		170	24.60		170	16.00	
21	110	35.40	20.00	-15.40	-43.50%		180	34.60		180	26.00	
22	120	34.00	10.00	-24.00	-70.59%		190	44.60		190	36.00	
23	130	37.20	0.00	-37.20	-100.00%		200	54.60		200	46.00	
24	140	40.80	10.00	-30.80	-75.49%		210	64.60		210	56.00	
25												

Excel Question

1. Use the data in this spreadsheet to plot the profit on a bullish spread (see Figure 15.10) with $X_1 = 120$ and $X_2 = 130$.

the highly risky positions that many financial institutions had established in credit derivatives blew up in 2007–2008, resulting in large losses and government bailouts. Still, the same characteristics that make derivatives potent tools to increase risk also make them highly effective in managing risk, at least when used properly. Derivatives have aptly been compared to power tools: very useful in skilled hands but also very dangerous when not handled with care. The nearby box makes the case for derivatives as central to risk management.

COVERED CALLS A **covered call** position is the purchase of a share of stock with the simultaneous sale of a call option on that stock. The written option is "covered" because the potential obligation to deliver the stock can be satisfied using the stock held in the portfolio. Writing an option without an offsetting stock position is called by contrast *naked option writing*. The payoff to a covered call, presented in Table 15.2, equals the stock value minus the payoff of the call. The call payoff is subtracted because the covered call position involves issuing a call to another investor who can choose to exercise it to profit at your expense.

The solid line in Figure 15.8C illustrates the payoff pattern. You see that the total position is worth S_T when the stock price at time T is below X and rises to a maximum of X when S_T exceeds X. In essence, the sale of the call option means the call writer has sold the claim to any stock value above X in return for the initial premium (the call price). Therefore, at expiration, the position is worth at most X. The dashed line of Figure 15.8C is the net profit to the covered call.

Writing covered call options has been a popular investment strategy among institutional investors. Consider the managers of a fund invested largely in stocks. They might find it appealing to write calls on some or all of the stock in order to boost income by the premiums collected. Although they thereby forfeit potential capital gains should the stock price rise above the exercise price, if they view X as the price at which they plan to sell the stock anyway, then the call may be viewed as enforcing a kind of "sell discipline." The written call guarantees the stock sale will occur as planned.

covered call

Writing a call on an asset together with buying the asset.

TABLE 15.2 Payoff to a covered call

	$S_T \leq X$	$S_T > X$
Payoff of stock	S_T	S_T
− Payoff of call	−0	$-(S_T - X)$
Total	S_T	X

FIGURE 15.8

Value of a covered call position at expiration

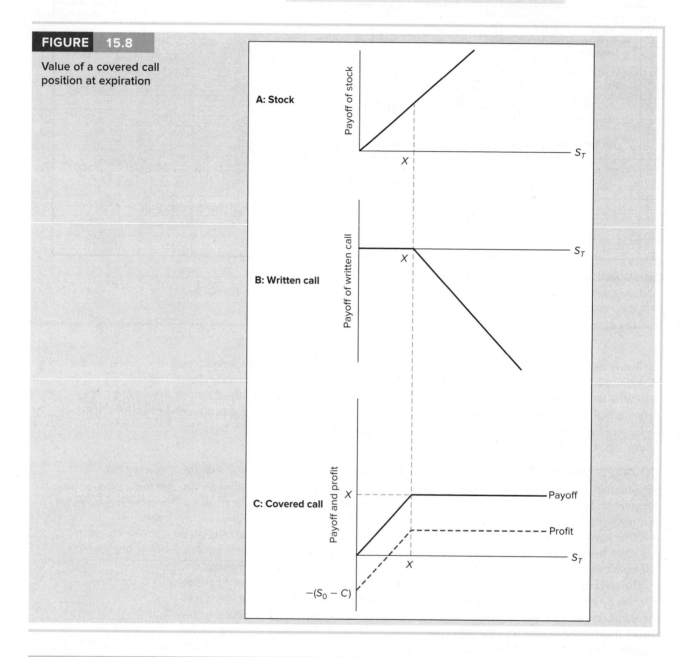

A: Stock

B: Written call

C: Covered call

EXAMPLE 15.4

Covered Call

Assume a pension fund holds 1,000 shares of GXX stock, with a current price of $130 per share. Suppose the portfolio manager intends to sell all 1,000 shares if the share price hits $140, and a call expiring in 90 days with an exercise price of $140 currently sells for $5. By writing 10 GXX call contracts (100 shares each) the fund can pick up $5,000 in extra income. The fund would lose its share of profits from any movement of GXX stock above $140 per share, but given that it would have sold its shares at $140, it would not have realized those profits anyway.

STRADDLE A long **straddle** is established by buying both a call and a put on a stock, each with the same exercise price, X, and the same expiration date, T. Straddles are useful strategies for investors who believe a stock will move a lot in price but are uncertain about the direction of the move. For example, suppose you believe an important court case that will make or break a company is about to be settled, and the market is not yet aware of the situation. The stock will either double in value if the case is settled favorably or will drop by half if the settlement goes against the company. The straddle position will do well regardless of the outcome because its value is highest when the stock price makes extreme upward or downward moves from X.

The worst-case scenario for a straddle is no movement in the stock price. If S_T equals X, both the call and the put expire worthless, and the investor's outlay for the purchase of both options is lost. Straddle positions basically are bets on volatility. An investor who establishes a straddle must view the stock as more volatile than the market does. Conversely, investors who *write* straddles—selling both a call and a put—must believe the market is less volatile. They accept the option premiums now, hoping the stock price will not change much before option expiration.

The payoff to a straddle is presented in Table 15.3. The solid line of Figure 15.9C illustrates this payoff. Notice that the portfolio payoff is always positive, except at the one point where the portfolio has zero value, $S_T = X$. You might wonder why all investors don't pursue such a no-lose strategy. To see why, remember that the straddle requires that both the put and the call be purchased. The value of the portfolio at expiration, while never negative, still must exceed the initial cash outlay for a straddle investor to clear a profit.

The dashed line of Figure 15.9C is the profit to the straddle. The profit line lies below the payoff line by the cost of purchasing the straddle, $P + C$. It is clear from the diagram that the straddle position generates a loss unless the stock price deviates substantially from X. The stock price must depart from X by the total amount expended to purchase the call *and* the put in order for the purchaser of the straddle to clear a profit.

Strips and *straps* are variations of straddles. A strip is two puts and one call on a security with the same exercise price and expiration date. A strap is two calls and one put.

straddle

A combination of a call and a put, each with the same exercise price and expiration date.

Graph the profit and payoff diagrams for strips and straps.

CONCEPT c h e c k **15.3**

SPREADS A **spread** is a combination of two or more call options (or two or more puts) on the same stock with differing exercise prices or times to expiration. Some options are bought, while others are sold, or written. A *money spread* involves the purchase of one option and the simultaneous sale of another with a different exercise price. A *time spread* refers to the sale and purchase of options with differing expiration dates.

Consider a money spread in which one call option is bought at an exercise price X_1, while another call with identical expiration date, but higher exercise price, X_2, is written. The payoff to this position will be the difference in the value of the call held and the value of the call written, as in Table 15.4.

There are now three instead of two outcomes to distinguish: the lowest-price region, where S_T is below both exercise prices; a middle region, where S_T is between the two exercise prices; and a high-price region, where S_T exceeds both exercise prices. Figure 15.10 illustrates the payoff and profit to this strategy, which is called a *bullish spread* because the payoff either increases or is unaffected by stock price increases.

One motivation for a bullish spread might be that the investor thinks one option is overpriced relative to another. For example, an investor who believes an $X = \$50$ call is cheap compared to an $X = \$55$ call might establish the spread, even without a strong desire to take a bullish position in the stock.

spread

A combination of two or more call options or put options on the same asset with differing exercise prices or times to expiration.

TABLE 15.3 Payoff to a straddle		
	$S_T \leq X$	$S_T > X$
Payoff of call	0	$S_T - X$
+Payoff of put	$+(X - S_T)$	$+0$
Total	$X - S_T$	$S_T - X$

FIGURE   15.9

Payoff and profit to a
straddle at expiration

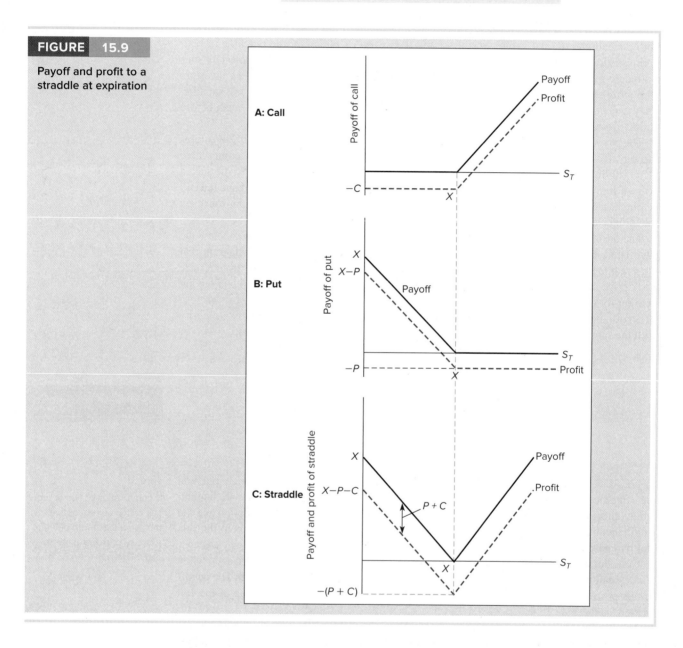

COLLARS   A **collar** is an options strategy that brackets the value of a portfolio between two
bounds. Suppose that an investor currently is holding a large position in Eagle Corp., which
is currently selling at $70 per share. A lower bound of $60 can be placed on the value of the
portfolio by buying a protective put with exercise price $60. This protection, however, requires
that the investor pay the put premium. To raise the money to pay for the put, the investor might
write a call option, say, with exercise price $80. The call might sell for roughly the same price
as the put, meaning that the net outlay for the two options positions is approximately zero.

collar

An options strategy that
brackets the value of a portfolio between two bounds.

TABLE 15.4 Payoff to a bullish spread

	$S_T \leq X_1$	$X_1 < S_T \leq X_2$	$S_T > X_2$
Payoff of first call, exercise price = X_1	0	$S_T - X_1$	$S_T - X_1$
−Payoff of second call, exercise price = X_2	−0	−0	$-(S_T - X_2)$
Total	0	$S_T - X_1$	$X_2 - X_1$

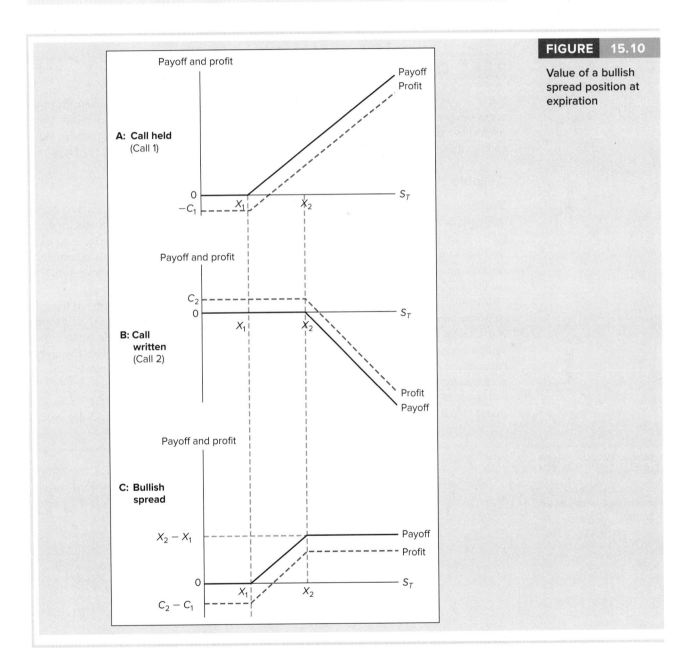

FIGURE 15.10

Value of a bullish spread position at expiration

Writing the call limits the portfolio's upside potential. Even if the stock price moves above $80, the investor will do no better than $80, because at a higher price the stock will be called away. Thus, the investor obtains the downside protection represented by the exercise price of the put by selling her claim to any upside potential beyond the exercise price of the call.

CONCEPT check **15.4**	Graph the payoff diagram for the collar described in Example 15.5.

15.3 OPTIONLIKE SECURITIES

Suppose you never intend to trade an option directly. Why do you need to appreciate the properties of options in formulating an investment plan? Many financial instruments and agreements have features that convey implicit or explicit options to one or more parties. To value and use these securities correctly, you must understand their embedded option attributes.

Callable Bonds

You know from Chapter 10 that many corporate bonds are issued with call provisions entitling the issuer to buy bonds back from bondholders at some time in the future at a specified call price. A call provision conveys a call option to the issuer, where the exercise price is equal to the price at which the bond can be repurchased. A callable bond arrangement is essentially a sale of a *straight bond* (a bond with no option features such as callability or convertibility) to the investor and the concurrent sale of a call option by the investor to the bond-issuing firm.

Investors must receive some compensation for offering this implicit call option. If the callable bond were issued with the same coupon rate as a straight bond, we would expect it to sell at a discount to the straight bond equal to the value of the call. To sell callable bonds at par, firms must issue them with coupon rates higher than the coupons on straight debt. The higher coupons are the investor's compensation for the call option retained by the issuer. Coupon rates usually are selected so that the newly issued bond will sell at par value.

Figure 15.11 illustrates this optionlike property. The horizontal axis is the value of a straight bond with otherwise identical terms as the callable bond. The dashed 45-degree line

FIGURE 15.11	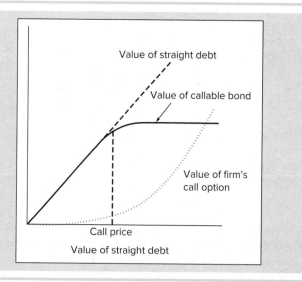
Values of callable bond compared with straight bond	

represents the value of straight debt. The solid line is the value of the callable bond, and the dotted line is the value of the call option retained by the firm. A callable bond's potential for capital gains is limited by the firm's option to repurchase at the call price.

How is a callable bond similar to a covered call strategy on a straight bond?	CONCEPT check	15.5

The option inherent in callable bonds actually is more complex than an ordinary call option because usually it may be exercised only after some initial period of call protection. The price at which the bond is callable may change over time also. Unlike exchange-listed options, these features are defined in the initial bond covenants and will depend on the needs of the issuing firm and its perception of the market's tastes.

Suppose the period of call protection is extended. How will this affect the coupon rate the company needs to offer to enable it to sell the bonds at par value?	CONCEPT check	15.6

Convertible Securities

Convertible bonds and convertible preferred stock convey options to the holder of the security rather than to the issuing firm. A convertible security typically gives its holder the right to exchange each bond or share of preferred stock for a fixed number of shares of common stock, regardless of the market prices of the securities at the time.

Should a convertible bond issued at par value have a higher or lower coupon rate than a nonconvertible bond issued at par?	CONCEPT check	15.7

For example, a bond with a conversion ratio of 10 allows its holder to convert one bond of par value $1,000 into 10 shares of common stock. Alternatively, we say the conversion price in this case is $100: To receive 10 shares of stock, the investor sacrifices bonds with face value $1,000 or $100 of face value per share. If the present value of the bond's scheduled payments is less than 10 times the value of one share of stock, it may pay to convert; that is, the conversion option is in the money. A bond worth $950 with a conversion ratio of 10 could be converted profitably if the stock were selling above $95, as the value of the 10 shares received for each bond surrendered would exceed $950. Most convertible bonds are issued "deep out of the money." That is, the issuer sets the conversion ratio so that conversion will not be profitable unless there is a substantial increase in stock prices and/or decrease in bond prices from the time of issue.

A bond's conversion value equals the value it would have if you converted it into stock immediately. Clearly, a bond must sell for at least its conversion value. If it did not, you could purchase the bond, convert it immediately, and clear a riskless profit. This condition could never persist, for all investors would pursue such a strategy and quickly bid up the price of the bond.

The straight bond value or "bond floor" is the value the bond would have if it were not convertible into stock. The bond must sell for more than its straight bond value because a convertible bond has more value; it is in fact a straight bond plus a valuable call option. Therefore, the convertible bond has two lower bounds on its market price: the conversion value and the straight bond value.

Figure 15.12 illustrates the optionlike properties of the convertible bond. Figure 15.12A shows the value of the straight debt as a function of the stock price of the issuing firm. For healthy firms, the straight debt value is almost independent of the value of the stock because default risk is small. However, if the firm is close to bankruptcy (stock prices are low), default risk increases, and the straight bond value falls. The vertical intercept in the figure shows the value of the bond when the stock price equals zero. You can interpret this as the value

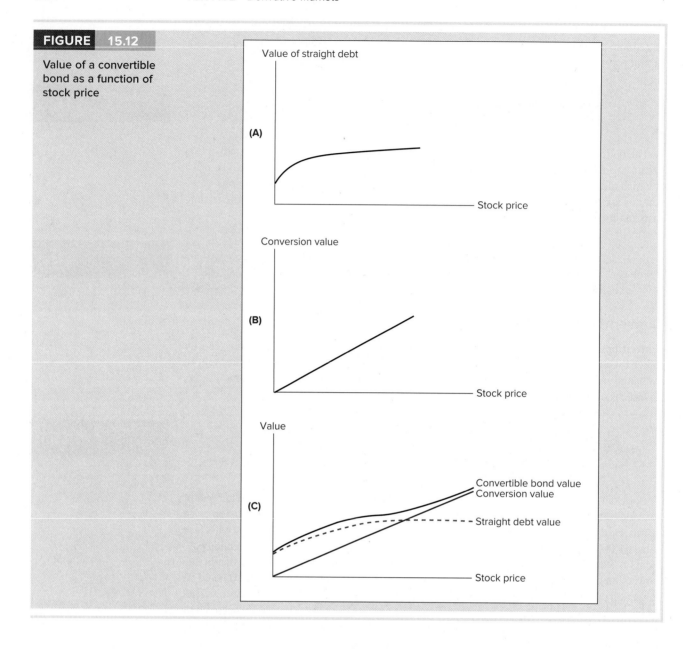

FIGURE 15.12

Value of a convertible
bond as a function of
stock price

the bondholders would receive if the firm were to enter bankruptcy and the shares become worthless. Panel B shows the conversion value of the bond. Panel C compares the value of the convertible bond to these two lower bounds.

When stock prices are low, the straight bond value is the effective lower bound, and the conversion option is nearly irrelevant. The convertible will trade like straight debt. When stock prices are high, the bond's price is determined by its conversion value. With conversion all but guaranteed, the bond is essentially equity in disguise. We can illustrate with two examples, as shown in the following table.

Bond A has a conversion value of only $600. Its value as straight debt, in contrast, is $967. This is the present value of the coupon and principal payments at a market rate for straight debt of 8.5%. The bond's price is $972, so the premium over straight bond value is only $5, reflecting the low probability of conversion. Its reported yield to maturity based on scheduled coupon payments and the market price of $972 is 8.42%, close to that of straight debt.

The conversion option on bond B is in the money. Conversion value is $1,250, and the bond's price, $1,255, reflects its value as equity (plus $5 for the protection the bond offers

	Bond A	**Bond B**
Annual coupon	$80	$80
Maturity date	10 years	10 years
Quality rating	Baa	Baa
Conversion ratio	20	25
Stock price	$30	$50
Conversion value	$600	$1,250
Market yield on 10-year Baa-rated bonds	8.5%	8.5%
Value as straight debt	$967	$967
Actual bond price	$972	$1,255
Reported yield to maturity	8.42%	4.76%

against stock price declines). The bond's reported yield is 4.76%, far below the comparable yield on straight debt. The big yield sacrifice is attributable to the far greater value of the conversion option.

In theory, we could value convertible bonds by treating them as straight debt plus call options. In practice, however, this approach is often impractical for several reasons:

1. The conversion price frequently increases over time, which means the exercise price for the option changes.
2. Stocks may pay several dividends over the life of the bond, further complicating the option value analysis.
3. Most convertibles also are callable at the discretion of the firm. In essence, both the investor and the issuer hold options on each other. If the issuer exercises its call option to repurchase the bond, the bondholders typically have a month during which they still can convert. When issuers use a call option, knowing that bondholders will choose to convert, the issuer is said to have *forced a conversion*. These conditions together mean the actual maturity of the bond is indeterminate.

Warrants

Warrants are essentially call options issued by a firm. One important difference between calls and warrants is that exercise of a warrant requires the firm to issue a new share of stock to satisfy its obligation—the total number of shares outstanding increases. Exercise of a call option requires only that the writer of the call deliver an already-issued share of stock to discharge the obligation. In this case, the number of shares outstanding remains fixed. Also unlike call options, warrants result in a cash flow to the firm when the warrant holder pays the exercise price. These differences mean warrant values will differ somewhat from the values of call options with identical terms.

warrant

An option issued by the firm to purchase shares of the firm's stock.

Like convertible debt, warrant terms may be tailored to meet the needs of the firm. Also like convertible debt, warrants generally are protected against stock splits and dividends in that the exercise price and the number of warrants held are adjusted to offset the effects of the split.

Warrants often are issued in conjunction with another security. Bonds, for example, may be packaged together with a warrant "sweetener," frequently a warrant that may be sold separately. This is called a *detachable warrant*.

Issues of warrants and convertible securities create the potential for an increase in outstanding shares of stock if exercise occurs. Exercise obviously would affect financial statistics that are computed on a per-share basis, so annual reports must provide earnings per share figures under the assumption that all convertible securities and warrants are exercised. These figures are called *fully diluted earnings per share*.[3]

---

[3]We should note that the exercise of a convertible bond need not reduce earnings per share (EPS). Diluted EPS will be less than undiluted EPS only if interest saved (per share) on the converted bonds is less than the prior EPS.

Collateralized Loans

Many loan arrangements require that the borrower put up collateral to guarantee the loan will be paid back. In the event of default, the lender takes possession of the collateral. A *nonrecourse loan* gives the lender no recourse beyond the right to the collateral. That is, the lender may not sue the borrower for further payment if the collateral turns out not to be valuable enough to repay the loan.[4]

This arrangement gives an implicit call option to the borrower. Assume the borrower is obligated to pay back L dollars at the maturity of the loan. The collateral will be worth S_T dollars at maturity. (Its value today is S_0.) The borrower has the option to wait until loan maturity and repay the loan only if the collateral is worth more than the L dollars necessary to satisfy the loan. If the collateral is worth less than L, the borrower can default on the loan, discharging the obligation by forfeiting the collateral, which is worth only S_T.

Another way of describing such a loan is to view the borrower as turning over collateral to the lender but retaining the right to reclaim it by paying off the loan. The transfer of the collateral with the right to reclaim it is equivalent to a payment of S_0 dollars less a simultaneous recovery of a sum that resembles a call option with exercise price L. In effect, the borrower turns over collateral but keeps an option to "repurchase" it for L dollars at the maturity of the loan if L turns out to be less than S_T. This is a call option.

A third way to look at a collaterized loan is to assume the borrower will repay the L dollars with certainty but also retain the option to sell the collateral to the lender for L dollars, even if S_T is less than L. In this case, the sale of the collateral would generate the cash necessary to satisfy the loan. The ability to "sell" the collateral for a price of L dollars represents a put option, which guarantees the borrower can raise enough money to satisfy the loan simply by turning over the collateral.

Figure 15.13 illustrates these interpretations. Figure 15.13A is the value of the payment to be received by the lender, which equals the minimum of S_T or L. Panel B shows that this amount can be expressed as S_T minus the payoff of the call implicitly written by the lender and held by the borrower. Panel C shows it also can be viewed as a receipt of L dollars minus the proceeds of a put option.

Leveraged Equity and Risky Debt

Investors holding stock in incorporated firms are protected by limited liability, which means that if the firm cannot pay its debts, the firm's creditors may attach only the firm's assets and may not sue the corporation's equityholders for further payment. In effect, any time the corporation borrows money, the maximum possible collateral for the loan is the total of the firm's assets. If the firm declares bankruptcy, we can interpret this as an admission that the assets of the firm are insufficient to satisfy the claims against it. The corporation may discharge its obligations by transferring ownership of the firm's assets to the creditors.

Just as is true for nonrecourse collateralized loans, the required payment to the creditors represents the exercise price of the implicit option, while the value of the firm is the underlying asset. The equityholders have a put option to transfer their ownership claims on the firm to the creditors in return for the face value of the firm's debt.

Alternatively, we may view the equityholders as retaining a call option. They have, in effect, already transferred their ownership claim to the firm to the creditors but have retained the right to reacquire the ownership claim by paying off the loan. Hence, the equityholders have the option to "buy back" the firm for a specified price, or they have a call option.

[4]In reality, of course, defaulting on a loan is not so simple. Losses of reputation are involved as well as considerations of ethical behavior. This is a description of a pure nonrecourse loan where both parties agree from the outset that only the collateral backs the loan and that default is not to be taken as a sign of bad faith if the collateral is insufficient to repay the loan.

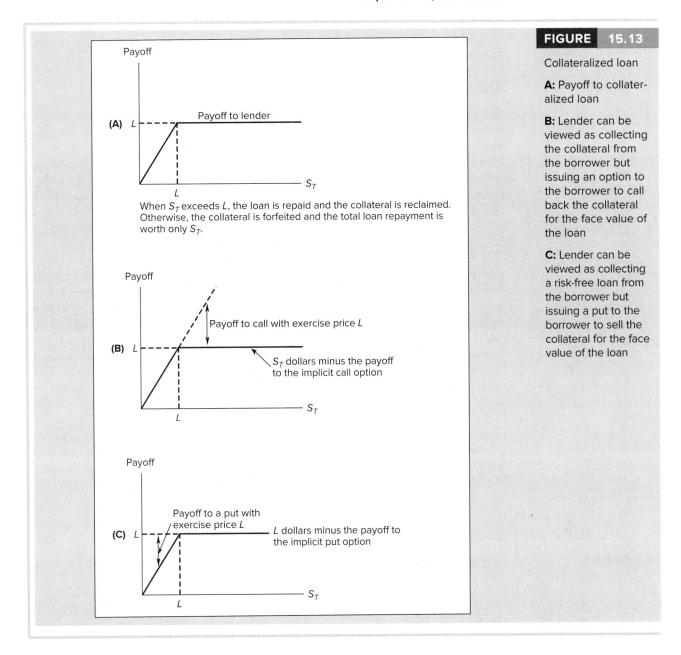

FIGURE 15.13

Collateralized loan

A: Payoff to collateralized loan

B: Lender can be viewed as collecting the collateral from the borrower but issuing an option to the borrower to call back the collateral for the face value of the loan

C: Lender can be viewed as collecting a risk-free loan from the borrower but issuing a put to the borrower to sell the collateral for the face value of the loan

The significance of this observation is that analysts can value corporate bonds using option-pricing techniques. The default premium required of risky debt in principle can be estimated using option valuation models. We will consider some of these models in the next chapter.

15.4 EXOTIC OPTIONS

Investors clearly value the portfolio strategies made possible by trading options; this is reflected in the heavy trading volume in these markets and their tremendous success. Success breeds imitation, and in recent years we have witnessed tremendous innovation in the range of option instruments available to investors. Part of this innovation has occurred in the market for customized options, which now trade in active over-the-counter markets. Many of these options have terms that would have been highly unusual even a few years ago; they therefore are called *exotic options.* In this section, we will survey a few of the more interesting variants of these new instruments.

Asian Options

You already have been introduced to American and European options. *Asian options* are options with payoffs that depend on the average (rather than final) price of the underlying asset during at least some portion of the life of the option. For example, an Asian call option may have a payoff equal to the average stock price over the last three months minus the exercise price, if that difference is positive, or zero otherwise. These options may be of interest to firms that wish to hedge a profit stream that depends on the average price of a commodity over some period of time.

Currency-Translated Options

Currency-translated options have either asset or exercise prices denominated in a foreign currency. A good example of such an option is the *quanto,* which allows an investor to fix in advance the exchange rate at which an investment in a foreign currency can be converted back into dollars. The right to translate a fixed amount of foreign currency into dollars at a given exchange rate is a simple foreign exchange option. Quantos are more interesting, however, because the amount of currency that will be translated into dollars depends on the investment performance of the foreign security. Therefore, a quanto in effect provides a *random number* of options.

Digital Options

Digital options, also called *binary* or "bet" options, have fixed payoffs that depend on whether a condition is satisfied by the price of the underlying asset. For example, a binary call option might pay off a fixed amount of $100 if the stock price at expiration exceeds the exercise price. The Chicago Board Options Exchange lists binary options on the S&P 500, but, to date, trading volume has been limited.

SUMMARY

- A call option is the right to buy an asset at an agreed-upon exercise price. A put option is the right to sell an asset at a given exercise price.
- American-style options allow exercise on or before the exercise date. European-style options allow exercise only on the expiration date. Most traded options are American in nature.
- Options are traded on stocks, stock indexes, foreign currencies, fixed-income securities, and several futures contracts.
- Options can be used either to lever up an investor's exposure to an asset price or to provide insurance against volatility of asset prices. Popular option strategies include covered calls, protective puts, straddles, and spreads.
- Many commonly traded securities embody option characteristics. Examples of these securities are callable bonds, convertible bonds, and warrants. Other arrangements, such as collateralized loans and limited-liability borrowing, can be analyzed as conveying implicit options to one or more parties.

KEY TERMS

American option, 487	exercise price, 485	risk management, 494
at the money, 486	in the money, 486	spread, 499
call option, 485	out of the money, 486	straddle, 499
collar, 500	premium, 485	strike price, 485
covered call, 497	protective put, 494	warrant, 505
European option, 487	put option, 485	

Payoff to call option $= \begin{cases} S - X & \text{if } S > X \\ 0 & \text{if } S \leq X \end{cases}$

Payoff to put option $= \begin{cases} 0 & \text{if } S_T > X \\ X - S_T & \text{if } S_T \leq X \end{cases}$

---

connect Select problems are available in McGraw-Hill's *Connect*. Please see the Supplements section of the book's frontmatter for more information.

1. We said that options can be used either to scale up or reduce overall portfolio risk. What are some examples of risk-increasing and risk-reducing options strategies? Explain each.   *(LO 15-2)*

2. Why do you think the most actively traded options tend to be the ones that are near the money?   *(LO 15-1)*

3. The following price quotations are for exchange-listed options on Primo Corporation common stock.

Company	Strike	Expiration	Call	Put
Primo 61.12	55	Feb	7.25	0.48

With transaction costs ignored, how much would a buyer have to pay for one call option contract?   *(LO 15-1)*

4. Turn back to Figure 15.1, which lists the prices of various Facebook options. Use the data in the figure to calculate the payoff and the profits for investments in each of the following November 2014 expiration options, assuming that the stock price on the expiration date is $78.   *(LO 15-1)*
   a. Call option, $X = 75$
   b. Put option, $X = 75$
   c. Call option, $X = 80$
   d. Put option, $X = 80$

5. You purchase one Facebook October $80 put contract for a premium of $5.72. What is your maximum possible profit? (See Figure 15.1.)   *(LO 15-1)*

6. An investor buys a call at a price of $4.50 with an exercise price of $40. At what stock price will the investor break even on the purchase of the call?   *(LO 15-1)*

7. You establish a straddle on Walmart using September call and put options with a strike price of $80. The call premium is $7.00 and the put premium is $8.50.   *(LO 15-2)*
   a. What is the most you can lose on this position?
   b. What will be your profit or loss if Walmart is selling for $88 in September?
   c. At what stock prices will you break even on the straddle?

8. The following diagram shows the value of a put option at expiration:

Ignoring transaction costs, which of the following statements about the value of the put option at expiration is *true?* **(LO 15-1)**

a. The expiration value of the short position in the put is $4 if the stock price is $76.

b. The expiration value of the long position in the put is −$4 if the stock price is $76.

c. The long put has a positive expiration value when the stock price is below $80.

d. The value of the short position in the put is zero for stock prices equaling or exceeding $76.

9. You are a portfolio manager who uses options positions to customize the risk profile of your clients. In each case, what strategy is best given your client's objective? **(LO 15-2)**

a. • Performance to date: Up 16%.
   • Client objective: Earn at least 15%.
   • Your scenario: Good chance of large stock price gains or large losses between now and end of year.
     i. Long straddle
     ii. Long bullish spread
     iii. Short straddle

b. • Performance to date: Up 16%.
   • Client objective: Earn at least 15%.
   • Your scenario: Good chance of large stock price losses between now and end of year.
     i. Long put options
     ii. Short call options
     iii. Long call options

10. An investor purchases a stock for $38 and a put for $.50 with a strike price of $35. The investor sells a call for $.50 with a strike price of $40. **(LO 15-1)**

a. What is the maximum profit and loss for this position?

b. Draw the profit and loss diagram for this strategy as a function of the stock price at expiration.

11. Imagine that you are holding 5,000 shares of stock, currently selling at $40 per share. You are ready to sell the shares but would prefer to put off the sale until next year due to tax reasons. If you continue to hold the shares until January, however, you face the risk that the stock will drop in value before year-end. You decide to use a collar to limit downside risk without laying out a good deal of additional funds. January call options with a strike price of $45 are selling at $2, and January puts with a strike price of $35 are selling at $3. What will be the value of your portfolio in January (net of the proceeds from the options) if the stock price ends up at (a) $30? (b) $40? (c) $50? (d) Compare these proceeds to what you would realize if you simply continued to hold the shares. **(LO 15-2)**

12. Suppose you think Apple stock is going to appreciate substantially in value in the next year. Say the stock's current price, S_0, is $100, and the call option expiring in one year has an exercise price, X, of $100 and is selling at a price, C, of $10. With $10,000 to invest, you are considering three alternatives:

a. Invest all $10,000 in the stock, buying 100 shares.

b. Invest all $10,000 in 1,000 options (10 contracts).

c. Buy 100 options (one contract) for $1,000 and invest the remaining $9,000 in a money market fund paying 4% interest annually.

What is your rate of return for each alternative for four stock prices one year from now? Summarize your results in the table and diagram below. **(LO 15-1)**

Rate of return on investment

	Price of Stock 1 Year from Now			
	$80	$100	$110	$120
a. All stocks (100 shares)				
b. All options (1,000 shares)				
c. Bills + 100 options				

13. The common stock of the P.U.T.T. Corporation has been trading in a narrow price range for the past month, and you are convinced it is going to break far out of that range in the next three months. You do not know whether it will go up or down, however. The current price of the stock is $100 per share, the price of a three-month call option with an exercise price of $100 is $10, and a put with the same expiration date and exercise price costs $7.   *(LO 15-2)*
    a. What would be a simple options strategy to exploit your conviction about the stock price's future movements?
    b. How far would the price have to move in either direction for you to make a profit on your initial investment?

14. The common stock of the C.A.L.L. Corporation has been trading in a narrow range around $50 per share for months, and you believe it is going to stay in that range for the next three months. The price of a three-month put option with an exercise price of $50 is $4, and a call with the same expiration date and exercise price sells for $7.   *(LO 15-2)*
    a. What would be a simple options strategy using a put and a call to exploit your conviction about the stock price's future movement?
    b. What is the most money you can make on this position?
    c. How far can the stock price move in either direction before you lose money?
    d. How can you create a position involving a put, a call, and riskless lending that would have the same payoff structure as the stock at expiration? The stock will pay no dividends in the next three months.
    e. What is the net cost of establishing that position now?

15. Joseph Jones, a manager at Computer Science, Inc. (CSI), received 10,000 shares of company stock as part of his compensation package. The stock currently sells at $40 a share. Joseph would like to defer selling the stock until the next tax year. In January, however, he will need to sell all his holdings to provide for a down payment on his new house. Joseph is worried about the price risk involved in keeping his shares. At current prices, he would receive $40,000 for the stock. If the value of his stock holdings falls below $35,000, his ability to come up with the necessary down payment would be jeopardized. On the other hand, if the stock value rises to $45,000, he would be able to maintain a small cash reserve even after making the down payment. Joseph considers three investment strategies:
    a. Strategy A is to write January call options on the CSI shares with strike price $45. These calls are currently selling for $3 each.
    b. Strategy B is to buy January put options on CSI with strike price $35. These options also sell for $3 each.
    c. Strategy C is to establish a zero-cost collar by writing the January calls and buying the January puts.

    Evaluate each of these strategies with respect to Joseph's investment goals. What are the advantages and disadvantages of each? Which would you recommend?   *(LO 15-2)*

16. a. A butterfly spread is the purchase of one call at exercise price X_1, the sale of two calls at exercise price X_2, and the purchase of one call at exercise price X_3. X_1 is less than X_2, and X_2 is less than X_3 by equal amounts, and all calls have the same expiration date. Graph the payoff diagram to this strategy.
    b. A vertical combination is the purchase of a call with exercise price X_2 and a put with exercise price X_1, with X_2 greater than X_1. Graph the payoff to this strategy.   *(LO 15-2)*

17. A bearish spread is the purchase of a call with exercise price X_2 and the sale of a call with exercise price X_1, with X_2 greater than X_1. Graph the payoff to this strategy and compare it to Figure 15.10.   *(LO 15-2)*

18. You are attempting to formulate an investment strategy. On the one hand, you think there is great upward potential in the stock market and would like to participate in the upward move if it materializes. However, you are not able to afford substantial stock market losses and so cannot run the risk of a stock market collapse, which you recognize is also possible. Your investment adviser suggests a protective put position: Buy shares in a market-index stock fund *and* put options on those shares with three-months until expiration and exercise price of $1,560. The stock index is currently at $1,800. However, your uncle suggests you instead buy a three-month call option on the index fund with exercise price $1,680 and buy three-month T-bills with face value $1,680.   *(LO 15-2)*

    a. On the same graph, draw the *payoffs* to each of these strategies as a function of the stock fund value in three months. (*Hint:* Think of the options as being on one "share" of the stock index fund, with the current price of each share of the index equal to $1,800.)

    b. Which portfolio must require a greater initial outlay to establish? (*Hint:* Does either portfolio provide a final payoff that is always at least as great as the payoff of the other portfolio?)

    c. Suppose the market prices of the securities are as follows:

Stock fund	$1,800
T-bill (face value $1,680)	1,620
Call (exercise price $1,680)	240
Put (exercise price $1,560)	12

    Make a table of profits realized for each portfolio for the following values of the stock price in three months: $S_T = $0, $1,400, $1,600, $1,800, and $1,920. Graph the profits to each portfolio as a function of S_T on a single graph.

    d. Which strategy is riskier? Which should have a higher beta?

19. Use the spreadsheet from the Excel Application boxes on spreads and straddles (available in Connect; link to Chapter 15 material) to answer these questions.   *(LO 15-1)*

    a. Plot the payoff and profit diagrams to a straddle position with an exercise (strike) price of $130. Assume the options are priced as they are in the Excel Application.

    b. Plot the payoff and profit diagrams to a spread position with exercise (strike) prices of $120 and $130. Assume the options are priced as they are in the Excel Application.

20. In what ways is owning a corporate bond similar to writing a put option? A call option?   *(LO 15-3)*

21. An executive compensation scheme might provide a manager a bonus of $1,000 for every dollar by which the company's stock price exceeds some cutoff level. In what way is this arrangement equivalent to issuing the manager call options on the firm's stock?   *(LO 15-3)*

22. Consider the following options portfolio: You write a November 2014 expiration call option on Facebook with exercise price $80. You also write a November expiration Facebook put option with exercise price $75.   *(LO 15-2)*

    a. Graph the payoff of this portfolio at option expiration as a function of the stock price at that time.

    b. What will be the profit/loss on this position if Facebook is selling at $77 on the option expiration date? What if it is selling at $83? Use option prices from Figure 15.1 to answer this question.

   c. At what two stock prices will you just break even on your investment?

   d. What kind of "bet" is this investor making; that is, what must this investor believe about the stock price in order to justify this position?

23. Consider the following portfolio. You *write* a put option with exercise price $90 and *buy* a put with the same expiration date with exercise price $95.   *(LO 15-2)*

   a. Plot the value of the portfolio at the expiration date of the options.

   b. Now, plot the profit of the portfolio. *Hint:* Which option must cost more?

24. A put option with strike price $60 trading on the Acme options exchange sells for $2. To your amazement, a put on the firm with the same expiration selling on the Apex options exchange but with strike price $62 also sells for $2. If you plan to hold the options position until expiration, devise a zero-net-investment arbitrage strategy to exploit the pricing anomaly. Draw the profit diagram at expiration for your position.   *(LO 15-1)*

25. You buy a share of stock, write a one-year call option with $X = \$10$, and buy a one-year put option with $X = \$10$. Your net outlay to establish the entire portfolio is $9.50. What is the payoff of your portfolio? What must be the risk-free interest rate? The stock pays no dividends.   *(LO 15-1)*

Challenge

26. Joe Finance has just purchased a stock-index fund, currently selling at $1,800 per share. To protect against losses, Joe plans to purchase an at-the-money European put option on the fund for $90, with exercise price $1,800, and three-month time to expiration. Sally Calm, Joe's financial adviser, points out that Joe is spending a lot of money on the put. She notes that three-month puts with strike prices of $1,750 cost only $70, and suggests that Joe use the cheaper put.   *(LO 15-2)*

   a. Analyze Joe's and Sally's strategies by drawing the *profit* diagrams for the stock-plus-put positions for various values of the stock fund in three months.

   b. When does Sally's strategy do better? When does it do worse?

   c. Which strategy entails greater systematic risk?

27. You write a call option with $X = \$50$ and buy a call with $X = \$60$. The options are on the same stock and have the same expiration date. One of the calls sells for $3; the other sells for $9.   *(LO 15-2)*

   a. Draw the *payoff* graph for this strategy at the option expiration date.

   b. Draw the *profit* graph for this strategy.

   c. What is the break-even point for this strategy?

   d. Is the investor bullish or bearish on the stock?

28. Devise a portfolio using only call options and shares of stock with the following value (payoff) at the option expiration date. If the stock price is currently $53, what kind of bet is the investor making?   *(LO 15-2)*

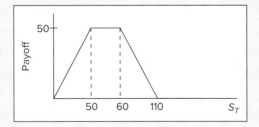

29. Some agricultural price support systems have guaranteed farmers a minimum price for their output.   *(LO 15-3)*

   a. Describe the program provisions as an option.

   b. What is the asset?

   c. What is the exercise price?

CFA Problems

1. Which one of the following statements about the value of a call option at expiration is *false?* **(LO 15-1)**

   a. A short position in a call option will result in a loss if the stock price exceeds the exercise price.

   b. The value of a long position equals zero or the stock price minus the exercise price, whichever is higher.

   c. The value of a long position equals zero or the exercise price minus the stock price, whichever is higher.

   d. A short position in a call option has a zero value for all stock prices equal to or less than the exercise price.

2. Donna Donie, CFA, has a client who believes the common stock price of TRT Materials (currently $58 per share) could move substantially in either direction in reaction to an expected court decision involving the company. The client currently owns no TRT shares, but asks Donie for advice about implementing a strangle strategy to capitalize on the possible stock price movement. A strangle is a portfolio of a put and a call with different exercise prices but the same expiration date. Donie gathers the following TRT option price data: **(LO 15-2)**

Characteristic	Call Option	Put Option
Price	$5	$4
Strike price	$60	$55
Time to expiration	90 days from now	90 days from now

   a. Recommend whether Donie should choose a long strangle strategy or a short strangle strategy to achieve the client's objective.

   b. Calculate, at expiration for the appropriate strangle strategy in part (*a*), the:

   i. Maximum possible loss per share.

   ii. Maximum possible gain per share.

   iii. Break-even stock price(s).

3. A member of an investment committee interested in learning more about fixed-income investment procedures recalls that a fixed-income manager recently stated that derivative instruments could be used to control portfolio duration, saying, "A futures-like position can be created in a portfolio by using put and call options on Treasury bonds." **(LO 15-3)**

   a. Identify the options market exposure or exposures that create a "futures-like position" similar to being long Treasury-bond futures. Explain why the position you created is similar to being long Treasury-bond futures.

   b. Explain in which direction and why the exposure(s) you identified in part (*a*) would affect portfolio duration.

   c. Assume that a pension plan's investment policy requires the fixed-income manager to hold portfolio duration within a narrow range. Identify and briefly explain circumstances or transactions in which the use of Treasury-bond futures would be helpful in managing a fixed-income portfolio when duration is constrained.

4. Suresh Singh, CFA, is analyzing a convertible bond. The characteristics of the bond and the underlying common stock are given in the nearby table.

   Compute the bond's: **(LO 15-3)**

   a. Conversion value.

   b. Market conversion price.

Convertible Bond Characteristics	
Par value	$1,000
Annual coupon rate (annual pay)	6.5%
Conversion ratio	22
Market price	105% of par value
Straight value	99% of par value
Underlying Stock Characteristics	
Current market price	$40 per share
Annual cash dividend	$1.20 per share

5. Rich McDonald, CFA, is evaluating his investment alternatives in Ytel Incorporated by analyzing a Ytel convertible bond and Ytel common equity. Characteristics of the two securities are given in the following exhibit: *(LO 15-3)*

Characteristics	Convertible Bond	Common Equity
Par value	$1,000	—
Coupon (annual payment)	4%	—
Current market price	$980	$35 per share
Straight bond value	$925	—
Conversion ratio	25	—
Conversion option	At any time	—
Dividend	—	$0
Expected market price in 1 year	$1,125	$45 per share

a. Calculate, based on the exhibit, the
   i. Current market conversion price for the Ytel convertible bond.
   ii. Expected one-year rate of return for the Ytel convertible bond.
   iii. Expected one-year rate of return for the Ytel common equity.

One year has passed and Ytel's common equity price has increased to $51 per share. Also, over the year, the yield to maturity on Ytel's nonconvertible bonds of the same maturity increased, while credit spreads remained unchanged.
b. Name the two components of the convertible bond's value. Indicate whether the value of each component should decrease, stay the same, or increase in response to the:
   i. Increase in Ytel's common equity price.
   ii. Increase in bond yield.

---

1. Use data from **finance.yahoo.com** to answer the following questions. In the *Get Quotes* box, enter stock symbol "GE" for General Electric. Go to the S&P Stock Reports section for GE.
   a. Locate the 52-week range for GE.
   b. At what price did GE last trade?
   c. Click on the link to *Options* on the left side of the Yahoo! Finance screen. Choose an expiration date three months in the future, and then choose *one* of the call options listed by selecting an exercise (strike) price. What is the last price (premium) shown for the call option?

WEB *master*

d. Is the call option in the money?

e. Draw a graph that shows the payoff and the profit to the holder of this call option over a range of prices, including the prices you found in the 52-week range of the S&P Stock Report.

f. Repeat the steps for a put option on GE with the same expiration date and the same strike price.

2. Go to **www.nasdaq.com** and select Facebook (FB) in the quote section. Once you have the information quote, request the information on *Option Chain*. Use options with about 1-month time to expiration that are as close as possible to at-the-money.

a. What are the prices for these puts and calls?

b. What would be the cost of a straddle using these options?

c. At expiration, what would be the break-even stock prices for the straddle?

d. What would be the percentage increase or decrease in the stock price required to break even?

e. What are the prices for the put and call with a later expiration date?

f. What would be the cost of a straddle using the later expiration date? At expiration, what would be the break-even stock prices for the straddle?

g. What would be the percentage increase or decrease in the stock price required to break even?

15.1 *a.* Proceeds = $S_T - X = S_T - \$80$ if this value is positive; otherwise, the call expires worthless. Profit = Proceeds − Price of call option = Proceeds − $1.65.

	$S_T = \$78$	$S_T = \$84$
Proceeds	$0	$4
Profits	−1.65	2.35

b. Proceeds = $X - S_T = \$80 - S_T$ if this value is positive; otherwise, the put expires worthless. Profit = Proceeds − Price of put option = Proceeds − $5.72.

	$S_T = \$78$	$S_T = \$84$
Proceeds	$2	$0
Profits	−3.72	−5.72

15.2 *a.*

b. The payoffs and profits to both buying calls and writing puts generally are higher when the stock price is higher. In this sense, both positions are bullish. Both involve potentially taking delivery of the stock. However, the call holder will *choose* to take delivery when the stock price is high, while the put writer *is obligated* to take delivery when the stock price is low.

c. The payoffs and profits to both writing calls and buying puts generally are higher when the stock price is lower. In this sense, both positions are bearish. Both involve potentially making delivery of the stock. However, the put holder will *choose* to make delivery when the stock price is low, while the call writer *is obligated* to make delivery when the stock price is high.

15.3

Payoff to a Strip

	$S_T \leq X$	$S_T > X$
2 Puts	$2(X - S_T)$	0
1 Call	0	$S_T - X$

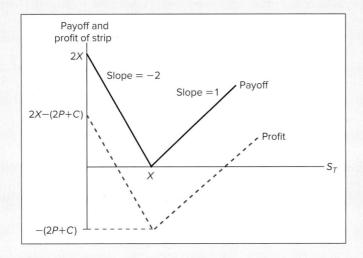

Payoff to a Strap

	$S_T \leq X$	$S_T > X$
1 Put	$X - S_T$	0
2 Calls	0	$2(S_T - X)$

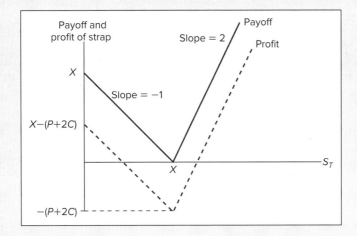

15.4 The payoff table on a per-share basis is as follows:

	$S_T < 60$	$60 < S_T < 80$	$S_T > 80$
Buy put ($X = 60$)	$60 - S_T$	0	0
Share	S_T	S_T	S_T
Write call ($X = 80$)	0	0	$-(S_T - 80)$
Total	60	S_T	80

The graph of the payoff follows. If you multiply the per-share values by 2,000, you will see that the collar provides a minimum payoff of $120,000 (representing a maximum loss of $20,000) and a maximum payoff of $160,000 (which is the cost of the house).

15.5 The covered call strategy would consist of a straight bond with a call written on the bond. The payoff value of the covered call position at option expiration as a function of the value of the straight bond is given in the following figure, and is virtually identical to the value of the callable bond in Figure 15.11.

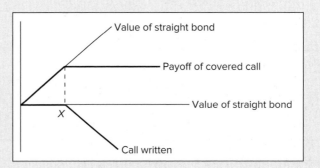

15.6 The call option is less valuable as call protection is expanded. Therefore, the coupon rate need not be as high.

15.7 Lower. Investors will accept a lower coupon rate in return for the conversion option.

Option Valuation

Learning Objectives

LO 16-1 Identify the features of an option that affect its market value.

LO 16-2 Compute an option value in two-scenario and binomial models of the economy.

LO 16-3 Compute the Black-Scholes value and implied volatility of an option.

LO 16-4 Compute the proper relationship between call and put prices.

LO 16-5 Compute the hedge ratio of an option, and use that ratio to manage risk.

In the previous chapter, we examined option markets and strategies. We ended by noting that many securities contain embedded options that affect both their values and their risk-return characteristics. In this chapter, we turn our attention to option valuation issues. Understanding most of these models requires considerable mathematical and statistical background. Still, many of their ideas and insights can be demonstrated in simple examples, and we will concentrate on these.

We start with a discussion of the factors that ought to affect option prices. After this qualitative discussion, we present a simple "two-state" quantitative option valuation model and show how we can generalize it into a useful and accurate pricing tool. Next, we move on to one particular option valuation formula, the famous Black-Scholes model. Option-pricing models allow us to "back out" market estimates of stock price volatility, and we will examine these estimates of implied volatility.

Next we turn to some of the more important applications of option-pricing theory in risk management. Finally, we take a brief look at some of the empirical evidence on option pricing and the implications of that evidence concerning the limitations of the Black-Scholes model.

16.1   OPTION VALUATION: INTRODUCTION

Intrinsic and Time Values

Consider a call option that is out of the money at the moment, with the stock price below the exercise price. This does not mean the option is valueless. Even though immediate exercise would be unprofitable, the call retains a positive value because there is always a chance the stock price will increase sufficiently by the expiration date to allow for profitable exercise. If not, the worst that can happen is that the option will expire with zero value.

The value $S_0 - X$ is sometimes called the **intrinsic value** of an in-the-money call option because it gives the payoff that could be obtained by immediate exercise. Intrinsic value is set equal to zero for out-of-the-money or at-the-money options. The difference between the actual call price and the intrinsic value is commonly called the **time value** of the option.

Time value is an unfortunate choice of terminology because it may confuse the option's time value with the time value of money. Time value in the options context simply refers to the difference between the option's price and the value the option would have if it were expiring immediately. It is the part of the option's value that may be attributed to the fact that it still has positive time to expiration.

Most of an option's time value typically is a type of "volatility value." As long as the option holder can choose not to exercise, the payoff cannot be worse than zero. Even if a call option is out of the money now, it still will sell for a positive price because it offers the potential for a profit if the stock price increases, while imposing no risk of additional loss should the stock price fall. The volatility value lies in the right *not* to exercise the option if that action would be unprofitable. The option to exercise, as opposed to the obligation to exercise, provides insurance against poor stock price performance.

As the stock price increases substantially, it becomes more likely that the call option will be exercised by expiration. In this case, with exercise all but assured, the volatility value becomes minimal. As the stock price gets ever larger, the option value approaches the "adjusted" intrinsic value—the stock price minus the present value of the exercise price, $S_0 - \text{PV}(X)$.

Why should this be? If you *know* the option will be exercised and the stock purchased for X dollars, it is as though you own the stock already. The stock certificate might as well be sitting in your safe-deposit box now, as it will be there in only a few months. You just haven't paid for it yet. The present value of your obligation is the present value of X, so the present value of the net payoff of the call option is $S_0 - \text{PV}(X)$.[1]

Figure 16.1 illustrates the call option valuation function. The value curve shows that when the stock price is low, the option is nearly worthless because there is almost no chance that it will be exercised. When the stock price is very high, the option value approaches adjusted intrinsic value. In the midrange case, where the option is approximately at the money, the option curve diverges from the straight lines corresponding to adjusted intrinsic value. This is because, while exercise today would have a negligible (or negative) payoff, the volatility value of the option is quite high in this region.

The call option always increases in value with the stock price. The slope is greatest, however, when the option is deep in the money. In this case, exercise is all but assured, and the option increases in price one-for-one with the stock price.

Determinants of Option Values

We can identify at least six factors that should affect the value of a call option: the stock price, the exercise price, the volatility of the stock price, the time to expiration, the interest rate, and the dividend rate of the stock. The call option should increase in value with the stock price and decrease in value with the exercise price because the payoff to a call, if exercised, equals $S_T - X$. The magnitude of the expected payoff from the call increases with the difference $S_0 - X$.

---

[1]This discussion presumes the stock pays no dividends until after option expiration. If the stock does pay dividends before expiration, then there *is* a reason you would care about getting the stock now rather than at expiration—getting it now entitles you to the interim dividend payments. In this case, the adjusted intrinsic value must subtract the value of the dividends the stock will pay out before the call is exercised. Adjusted intrinsic value would more generally be defined as $S_0 - \text{PV}(X) - \text{PV}(D)$, where D represents dividends to be paid before option expiration.

intrinsic value

Stock price minus exercise price, or the cash flow that could be attained by immediate exercise of an in-the-money call option.

time value

Difference between an option's price and its intrinsic value.

FIGURE   16.1

Call option value
before expiration

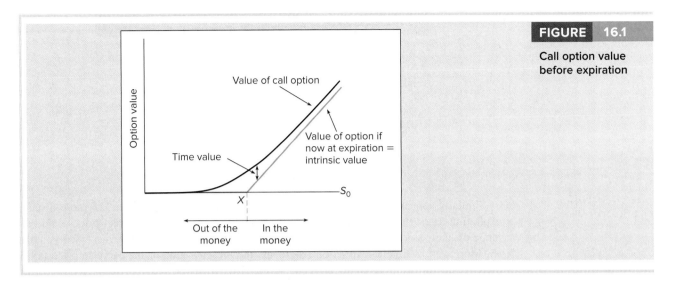

Call option value also increases with the volatility of the underlying stock price. To see why, consider circumstances where possible stock prices at expiration may range from $10 to $50 compared to a situation where they range only from $20 to $40. In both cases, the expected, or average, stock price will be $30. Suppose the exercise price on a call option is also $30. What are the option payoffs?

High-Volatility Scenario

Stock price	$10	$20	$30	$40	$50
Option payoff	0	0	0	10	20

Low-Volatility Scenario

Stock price	$20	$25	$30	$35	$40
Option payoff	0	0	0	5	10

If each outcome is equally likely, with probability .2, the expected payoff to the option under high-volatility conditions will be $6, but under the low-volatility conditions, the expected payoff to the call option is half as much, only $3.

Despite the fact that the average stock price in each scenario is $30, the average option payoff is greater in the high-volatility scenario. The source of this extra value is the limited loss an option holder can suffer, or the volatility value of the call. No matter how far below $30 the stock price drops, the option holder will get zero. Obviously, extremely poor stock price performance is no worse for the call option holder than moderately poor performance.

In the case of good stock performance, however, the call option will expire in the money, and it will be more profitable the higher the stock price. Thus, extremely good stock outcomes can improve the option payoff without limit, but extremely poor outcomes cannot worsen the payoff below zero. This asymmetry means volatility in the underlying stock price increases the expected payoff to the option, thereby enhancing its value.[2]

Should a put option increase in value with the volatility of the stock?

CONCEPT
check   **16.1**

[2]You should be careful interpreting the relationship between volatility and option value. Neither the focus of this analysis on total (as opposed to systematic) volatility nor the conclusion that options buyers seem to like volatility contradicts modern portfolio theory. In conventional discounted cash flow analysis, we find the discount rate appropriate for a *given* distribution of future cash flows. Greater risk implies a higher discount rate and lower present value. Here, however, the cash flow from the *option* depends on the volatility of the *stock*. The option value increases not because traders like risk but because the expected cash flow to the option holder increases along with the volatility of the underlying asset.

TABLE 16.1	Determinants of call option values
If This Variable Increases	**The Value of a Call Option**
Stock price, S	Increases
Exercise price, X	Decreases
Volatility, σ	Increases
Time to expiration, T	Increases
Interest rate, r_f	Increases
Dividend payouts	Decreases

Similarly, longer time to expiration increases the value of a call option. For more distant expiration dates, there is more time for unpredictable future events to affect prices, and the range of likely stock prices increases. This has an effect similar to that of increased volatility. Moreover, as time to expiration lengthens, the present value of the exercise price falls, thereby benefiting the call option holder and increasing the option value. As a corollary to this issue, call option values are higher when interest rates rise (holding the stock price constant), because higher interest rates also reduce the present value of the exercise price.

Finally, the dividend payout policy of the firm affects option values. A high dividend payout policy puts a drag on the rate of growth of the stock price. For any expected total rate of return on the stock, a higher dividend yield must imply a lower expected rate of capital gain. This drag on stock appreciation decreases the potential payoff from the call option, thereby lowering the call value. Table 16.1 summarizes these relationships.

CONCEPT
check   16.2

Prepare a table like Table 16.1 for the determinants of put option values. How should put values respond to increases in S, X, T, σ, r_f, and dividend payout?

16.2 BINOMIAL OPTION PRICING

Two-State Option Pricing

A complete understanding of commonly used option valuation formulas is difficult without a substantial mathematics background. Nevertheless, we can develop valuable insight into option valuation by considering a simple special case. Assume a stock price can take only two possible values at option expiration: The stock will either increase to a given higher price or decrease to a given lower price. Although this may seem an extreme simplification, it allows us to begin understanding more complicated and realistic models. Moreover, we can extend this approach to describe far more reasonable specifications of stock price behavior. In fact, several major financial firms employ variants of this simple model to value options and securities with optionlike features.

Suppose the stock now sells at $100, and the price will either increase by a factor of $u = 1.2$ to $120 ($u$ stands for "up") or fall by a factor of $d = .9$ to $90 ($d$ stands for "down") by year-end. A call option on the stock might specify an exercise price of $110 and a time to expiration of one year. The interest rate is 10%. At year-end, the payoff to the holder of the call option will be either zero, if the stock falls, or $10, if the stock price goes to $120.

These possibilities are illustrated by the following "value trees":

Stock price   Call option value

Compare this payoff to that of a portfolio consisting of one share of the stock and borrowing of $81.82 at the interest rate of 10%. The payoff of this portfolio also depends on the stock price at year-end.

	$ 90	$ 120
Value of stock at year-end	$ 90	$ 120
−Repayment of loan with interest	−90	−90
Total	$ 0	$ 30

We know the cash outlay to establish the portfolio is $18.18: $100 for the stock less the $81.82 proceeds from borrowing. Therefore, the portfolio's value tree is

The payoff of this portfolio is exactly three times that of the call option for either value of the stock price. In other words, three call options will exactly replicate the payoff to the portfolio; it follows that three call options should have the same price as this "replicating portfolio." Therefore,

$$3C = \$18.18$$

or each call should sell at $C = \$6.06$. Thus, given the stock price, exercise price, interest rate, and volatility of the stock price (as represented by the spread between the up or down movements), we can derive the fair value for the call option.

This valuation approach relies heavily on the notion of *replication*. With only two possible end-of-year values of the stock, the payoffs to the levered stock portfolio replicate the payoffs to three call options and so need to command the same market price. This notion of replication is behind most option-pricing formulas. For more complex price distributions for stocks, the replication technique is correspondingly more complex, but the principles remain the same.

One way to view the role of replication is to note that, using the numbers assumed for this example, a portfolio made up of one share of stock and three call options written is perfectly hedged. Its year-end value is independent of the ultimate stock price:

	$90	$120
Stock value	$90	$120
−Obligations from 3 calls written	−0	−30
Net payoff	$90	$ 90

The investor has formed a riskless portfolio with a payout of $90. Its value must be the present value of $90, or $90/1.10 = $81.82. The value of the portfolio, which equals $100 from the stock held long minus $3C$ from the three calls written, should equal $81.82. Hence, $100 − 3C = \$81.82$, or $C = \$6.06$.

The ability to create a perfect hedge is the key to this argument. The hedge locks in the end-of-year payout, which therefore can be discounted using the *risk-free* interest rate. To find the value of the option in terms of the value of the stock, we do not need to know the option's or the stock's beta or expected rate of return. When a perfect hedge can be established, the final stock price does not affect the investor's payoff, so the stock's risk and return parameters have no bearing.

The hedge ratio of this example is one share of stock to three calls, or one-third. This ratio has an easy interpretation in this context: It is the ratio of the range of the values of the option to those of the stock across the two possible outcomes. The stock, which originally sells for $S_0 = \$100$, will be worth either $d \times \$100 = \$90$ or $u \times \$100 = \$120$, for a range of $30. If the stock price increases, the call will be worth $C_u = \$10$, whereas if the stock price decreases, the call will be worth $C_d = 0$, for a range of $10. The ratio of ranges, $10/$30, is one-third, which is the hedge ratio we have established.

The hedge ratio equals the ratio of ranges because the option and stock are perfectly correlated in this two-state example. Because they are perfectly correlated, a perfect hedge requires that they be held in a fraction determined only by relative volatility.

We can generalize the hedge ratio for other two-state option problems as

$$H = \frac{C_u - C_d}{uS_0 - dS_0}$$

where C_u or C_d refers to the call option's value when the stock goes up or down, respectively, and uS_0 and dS_0 are the stock prices in the two states. The hedge ratio, H, is the ratio of the swings in the possible end-of-period values of the option and the stock. If the investor writes one option and holds H shares of stock, the value of the portfolio will be unaffected by the stock price. In this case, option pricing is easy: Simply set the value of the hedged portfolio equal to the present value of the known payoff.

Using our example, the option-pricing technique would proceed as follows:

1. Given the possible end-of-year stock prices, $uS_0 = \$120$ and $dS_0 = \$90$, and the exercise price of $110, calculate that $C_u = \$10$ and $C_d = \$0$. The stock price range is $30, while the option price range is $10.
2. Find that the hedge ratio is $10/$30 = ⅓.
3. Find that a portfolio made up of ⅓ share with one written option would have an end-of-year value of $30 with certainty.
4. Show that the present value of $30 with a one-year interest rate of 10% is $27.27.
5. Set the value of the hedged position equal to the present value of the certain payoff:

$$⅓ S_0 - C_0 = \$27.27$$
$$\$33.33 - C_0 = \$27.27$$

6. Solve for the call's value, $C_0 = \$6.06$.

What if the option were overpriced, perhaps selling for $6.50? Then you can make arbitrage profits. Here is how:

	Initial Cash Flow	Cash Flow in 1 Year for Each Possible Stock Price	
		$S_1 = \$90$	$S_1 = \$120$
1. Write 3 options	$ 19.50	$ 0	$−30
2. Purchase 1 share	−100	90	120
3. Borrow $80.50 at 10% interest; repay in 1 year	80.50	−88.55	−88.55
Total	$ 0	$ 1.45	$ 1.45

Although the net initial investment is zero, the payoff in one year is positive and riskless. If the option were underpriced, one would simply reverse this arbitrage strategy: Buy the option, and sell the stock short to eliminate price risk. Note, by the way, that the present value of the profit to the above arbitrage strategy equals three times the amount by which the option is overpriced. The present value of the risk-free profit of $1.45 at a 10% interest rate is $1.32. With three options written in the strategy above, this translates to a profit of $.44 per option, exactly the amount by which the option was overpriced: $6.50 versus the "fair value" of $6.06.

Suppose the call option had been underpriced, selling at $5.50. Formulate the arbitrage strategy to exploit the mispricing, and show that it provides a riskless cash flow in one year of $.6167 per option purchased. Compare the present value of this cash flow to the option mispricing.

Generalizing the Two-State Approach

Although the two-state stock price model seems simplistic, we can generalize it to incorporate more realistic assumptions. To start, suppose we were to break up the year into two six-month segments and then assert that over each half-year segment the stock price could take on two values. In this example, we will say it can increase 10% (i.e., $u = 1.10$) or decrease 5% (i.e., $d = .95$). A stock initially selling at $100 could follow the following possible paths over the course of the year:

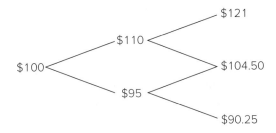

The midrange value of $104.50 can be attained by two paths: an increase of 10% followed by a decrease of 5%, or a decrease of 5% followed by an increase of 10%.

There are now three possible end-of-year values for the stock and three for the option:

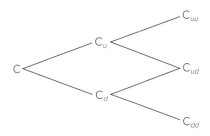

Using methods similar to those we followed above, we could value C_u from knowledge of C_{uu} and C_{ud}, then value C_d from knowledge of C_{du} and C_{dd}, and finally value C from knowledge of C_u and C_d. And there is no reason to stop at six-month intervals. We could next break the year into 4 three-month units, or 12 one-month units, or 365 one-day units, each of which would be posited to have a two-state process. Although the calculations become quite numerous and correspondingly tedious, they are easy to program into a computer, and such computer programs are used widely by participants in the options market.

Suppose that the risk-free interest rate is 5% per six-month period and we wish to value a call option with exercise price $110 on the stock described in the two-period price tree just above. We start by finding the value of C_u. From this point, the call can rise to an expiration-date value of $C_{uu} = \$11$ (because at this point the stock price is $u \times u \times S_0 = \$121$) or fall to a final value of $C_{ud} = 0$ (because at this point the stock price is $u \times d \times S_0 = \$104.50$, which is less than the $110 exercise price). Therefore, the hedge ratio at this point is

$$H = \frac{C_{uu} - C_{ud}}{uuS_0 - udS_0} = \frac{\$11 - 0}{\$121 - \$104.5} = \frac{2}{3}$$

(continued)

Thus, the following portfolio will be worth $209 at option expiration regardless of the ultimate stock price:

	$udS_0 = \$104.50$	$uuS_0 = \$121$
Buy 2 shares at price $uS_0 = \$110$	$209	$242
Write 3 calls at price C_u	0	−33
Total	$209	$209

The portfolio must have a current market value equal to the present value of $209:

$$2 \times \$110 - 3C_u = \$209/1.05 = \$199.047$$

Solve to find that $C_u = \$6.984$.

Next we find the value of C_d. It is easy to see that this value must be zero. If we reach this point (corresponding to a stock price of $95), the stock price at option expiration will be either $104.50 or $90.25; in both cases, the option will expire out of the money. (More formally, we could note that with $C_{ud} = C_{dd} = 0$, the hedge ratio is zero, and a portfolio of *zero* shares will replicate the payoff of the call!)

Finally, we solve for C by using the values of C_u and C_d. The following Concept Check leads you through the calculations that show the option value to be $4.434.

Show that the initial value of the call option in Example 16.1 is $4.434.
a. Confirm that the spread in option values is $C_u - C_d = \$6.984$.
b. Confirm that the spread in stock values is $uS_0 - dS_0 = \$15$.
c. Confirm that the hedge ratio is .4656 shares purchased for each call written.
d. Demonstrate that the value in one period of a portfolio comprising .4656 shares and one call written is riskless.
e. Calculate the present value of this payoff.
f. Solve for the option value.

Making the Valuation Model Practical

As we break the year into progressively finer subintervals, the range of possible year-end stock prices expands. For example, when we increase the number of subperiods to three, the number of possible stock prices increases to four, as demonstrated in the following stock price tree:

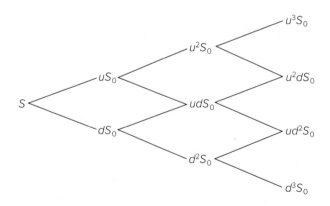

Thus, by allowing for an ever-greater number of subperiods, we can overcome one of the apparent limitations of the valuation model: that the number of possible end-of-period stock prices is small.

Notice that extreme outcomes such as u^3S_0 or d^3S_0 will be relatively rare, as they require either three consecutive increases or decreases in the three subintervals. More moderate, or midrange, results such as u^2dS_0 can be arrived at by more than one path; any combination of two price increases and one decrease will result in stock price u^2dS_0. There are three of these paths: *uud, udu, duu.* In contrast, only one path, *uuu,* results in a stock price of u^3S_0. Thus, midrange values are more likely. As we make the model more realistic and break up the option maturity into more and more subperiods, the probability distribution for the final stock price begins to resemble the familiar bell-shaped curve, with highly unlikely extreme outcomes and far more likely midrange outcomes. The exact probability of each outcome is given by the binomial probability distribution, and this multiperiod approach to option pricing is called the **binomial model.**

But we still need to answer an important practical question. Before the binomial model can be used to value actual options, we need a way to choose reasonable values for u and d. The spread between up and down movements in the price of the stock reflects the volatility of its rate of return, so the choice for u and d should depend on that volatility. Call σ your estimate of the standard deviation of the stock's continuously compounded annualized rate of return and Δt the length of each subperiod. To make the standard deviation of the stock in the binomial model match your estimate of σ, it turns out that you can set $u = \exp(\sigma\sqrt{\Delta t})$ and $d = \exp(-\sigma\sqrt{\Delta t})$.[3] You can see that the proportional difference between u and d increases with annualized volatility as well as the duration of the subperiod. This makes sense, as both higher σ and longer holding periods make future stock prices more uncertain. The following example illustrates how to use this calibration.

binomial model

An option valuation model predicated on the assumption that stock prices can move to only two values over any short time period.

EXAMPLE 16.2

Calibrating u and d to Stock Volatility

Suppose you are using a three-period model to value a one-year option on a stock with volatility (i.e., annualized standard deviation) of $\sigma = .30$. With a time to expiration of $T = 1$ year, and three subperiods, you would calculate $\Delta t = T/n = 1/3$, $u = \exp(\sigma\sqrt{\Delta t}) = \exp(.30\sqrt{1/3}) = 1.189$ and $d = \exp(-\sigma\sqrt{\Delta t}) = \exp(-.30\sqrt{1/3}) = .841$. Given the probability of an up movement, you could then work out the probability of any final stock price. For example, suppose the probability that the stock price increases is .554 and the probability that it decreases is .446.[4] Then the probability of stock prices at the end of the year would be as follows:

Event	Possible Paths	Probability	Final Stock Price
3 down movements	*ddd*	$0.446^3 = 0.089$	$59.48 = 100 \times 0.841^3$
2 down and 1 up	*ddu, dud, udd*	$3 \times 0.446^2 \times 0.554 = 0.330$	$84.10 = 100 \times 1.189 \times 0.841^2$
1 down and 2 up	*uud, udu, duu*	$3 \times 0.446 \times 0.554^2 = 0.411$	$118.89 = 100 \times 1.189^2 \times 0.841$
3 up movements	*uuu*	$0.554^3 = 0.170$	$168.09 = 100 \times 1.189^3$

We plot this probability distribution in Figure 16.2, Panel A. Notice that the two middle end-of-period stock prices are, in fact, more likely than either extreme.

---

[3]Notice that $d = 1/u$. This is the most common, but not the only, way to calibrate the model to empirical volatility. For alternative methods, see Robert L. McDonald, *Derivatives Markets,* 3rd ed. (Boston: Pearson/Addison-Wesley, 2013), chap. 11, sec. 11.3.

[4]Using this probability, the continuously compounded expected rate of return on the stock is .10. In general, the formula relating the probability of an upward movement with the annual expected rate of return, r, is $p = \dfrac{\exp(r\Delta t) - d}{u - d}$.

Probability distributions
for final stock price:
possible outcomes and
associated probabili-
ties. In each panel, the
stock's expected annual-
ized, continuously com-
pounded rate of return
is 10% and its standard
deviation is 30%.

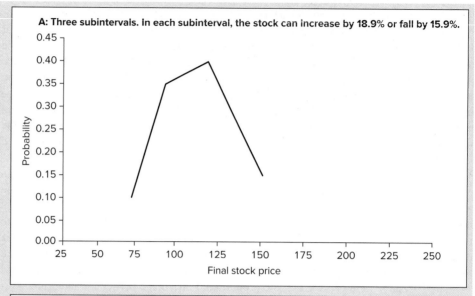

A: Three subintervals. In each subinterval, the stock can increase by 18.9% or fall by 15.9%.

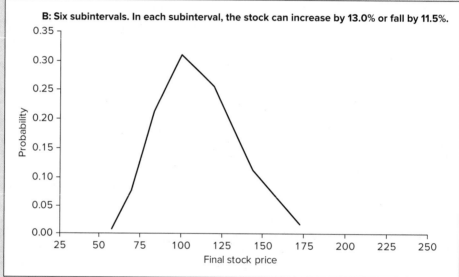

B: Six subintervals. In each subinterval, the stock can increase by 13.0% or fall by 11.5%.

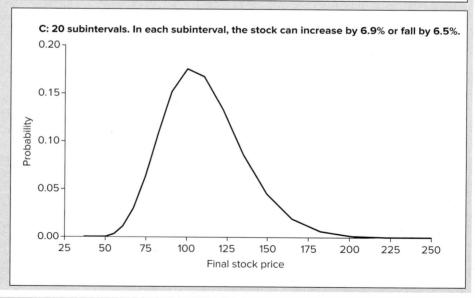

C: 20 subintervals. In each subinterval, the stock can increase by 6.9% or fall by 6.5%.

Now we can extend Example 16.2 by breaking up the option maturity into ever-shorter subintervals. As we do, the stock price distribution becomes increasingly plausible, as we demonstrate in Example 16.3.

> In Example 16.2, we broke up the year into three subperiods. Let's also look at the cases of 6 and 20 subperiods.
>
> | Subperiods, n | $\Delta t = T/n$ | $u = \exp(\sigma\sqrt{\Delta t})$ | $d = \exp(-\sigma\sqrt{\Delta t})$ |
> |---|---|---|---|
> | 3 | 0.333 | $\exp(0.173) = 1.189$ | $\exp(-0.173) = 0.841$ |
> | 6 | 0.167 | $\exp(0.123) = 1.130$ | $\exp(-0.095) = 0.885$ |
> | 20 | 0.015 | $\exp(0.067) = 1.069$ | $\exp(-0.067) = 0.935$ |
>
> We plot the resulting probability distributions in Panels B and C of Figure 16.2.[5]
>   Notice that the right tail of the distribution in Panel C is noticeably longer than the left tail. In fact, as the number of intervals increases, the distribution progressively approaches the skewed log-normal (rather than the symmetric normal) distribution. Even if the stock price were to decline in *each* subinterval, it can never drop below zero. But there is no corresponding upper bound on its potential performance. This asymmetry gives rise to the skewness of the distribution.

EXAMPLE 16.3

Increasing the Number of Subperiods

Eventually, as we divide the option maturity into an ever-greater number of subintervals, each node of the event tree corresponds to a smaller and smaller time interval. The possible stock price movement within each time interval is correspondingly small. As those many intervals pass, the end-of-period stock price more and more closely resembles a lognormal distribution.[6] Thus, the apparent oversimplification of the two-state model can be overcome by progressively subdividing any period into many subperiods.

At any node, one still can set up a portfolio that is perfectly hedged over the next time interval. Then, at the end of that interval, on reaching the next node, a new hedge ratio can be computed and the portfolio composition revised to remain hedged over the coming small interval. By continuously revising the hedge position, the portfolio remains hedged and earns a riskless rate of return over each interval. This is called *dynamic hedging,* the continued updating of the hedge ratio as time passes. As the dynamic hedge becomes ever finer, the resulting option valuation procedure becomes more precise. The nearby box offers further refinements on the use of the binomial model.

> In the table in Example 16.3, u and d both get closer to 1 (u is smaller and d is larger) as the time interval Δt shrinks. Why does this make sense? Does the fact that u and d are each closer to 1 mean that the total volatility of the stock over the remaining life of the option is lower?

CONCEPT check   16.5

16.3   BLACK-SCHOLES OPTION VALUATION

While the binomial model we have described is extremely flexible, it requires a computer to be useful in actual trading. An option-pricing *formula* would be far easier to use than the tedious algorithm involved in the binomial model. It turns out that such a formula can be

[5]We adjust the probabilities of up versus down movements using the formula in footnote 4 to make the distributions in Figure 16.2 comparable. In each panel, p is chosen so that the stock's expected annualized, continuously compounded rate of return is 10%.

[6]Actually, more complex considerations enter here. The limit of this process is lognormal only if we assume also that stock prices move continuously, by which we mean that over small time intervals only small price movements can occur. This rules out rare events such as sudden, extreme price moves in response to dramatic information (like a takeover attempt). For a treatment of this type of "jump process," see John C. Cox and Stephen A. Ross, "The Valuation of Options for Alternative Stochastic Processes," *Journal of Financial Economics* 3 (January–March 1976), pp. 145–166; or Robert C. Merton, "Option Pricing When Underlying Stock Returns Are Discontinuous," *Journal of Financial Economics* 3 (January–March 1976), pp. 125–144.

A RISK-NEUTRAL SHORTCUT

We pointed out earlier in the chapter that the binomial-model valuation approach is arbitrage-based. We can value the option by replicating it with shares of stock plus borrowing. The ability to replicate the option means that its price relative to the stock and the interest rate must be based only on the technology of replication, and *not* on risk preferences. It cannot depend on risk aversion or the capital asset pricing model or any other model of equilibrium risk-return relationships.

This insight—that the pricing model must be independent of risk aversion—leads to a very useful shortcut to valuing options. Imagine a *risk-neutral economy,* that is, an economy in which all investors are risk-neutral. This hypothetical economy must value options the same as our real one, because risk aversion cannot affect the valuation formula.

In a risk-neutral economy, investors would not demand risk premiums and would therefore value all assets by discounting expected payoffs at the risk-free rate of interest. Therefore, a security such as a call option would be valued by discounting its expected cash flow at the risk-free rate: $C = \dfrac{"E"(CF)}{1 + r_f}$. We put the expectation operator in quotation marks to signify that this is not the true expectation but the expectation that would prevail in the hypothetical risk-neutral economy. To be consistent, we must calculate this expected cash flow using the expected rate of return the stock *would* have in the risk-neutral economy, *not* using its actual expected rate of return. But if we can successfully maintain consistency, the value derived for the hypothetical economy should match the one in our own.

How do we compute the expected cash flow from the option in the risk-neutral economy? Because there are no risk premiums, the stock's expected rate of return must equal the risk-free rate. Call p the probability that the stock price increases. Then p must be chosen to equate the expected rate of increase of the stock price to the risk-free rate (we ignore dividends here):

$$"E"(S_1) = p(uS) + (1 - p)dS = (1 + r_f)S$$

This implies that $p = \dfrac{1 + r_f - d}{u - d}$. We call p a *risk-neutral probability* to distinguish it from the true or "objective" probability. To illustrate, in our two-state example at the beginning of Section 16.2, we had $u = 1.2$, $d = .9$, and $r_f = .10$. Given these values,

$$p = \frac{1 + .10 - .9}{1.2 - .9} = \frac{2}{3}.$$

Now let's see what happens if we use the discounted cash flow formula to value the option in the risk-neutral economy. We continue to use the two-state example from Section 16.2. We find the present value of the option payoff using the risk-neutral probability and discount at the risk-free interest rate:

$$C = \frac{"E"(CF)}{1 + r_f} = \frac{p\,C_u + (1 - p)\,C_d}{1 + r_f} = \frac{\frac{2}{3} \times 10 + \frac{1}{3} \times 0}{1.10} = 6.06$$

This answer exactly matches the value we found using our no-arbitrage approach!

We repeat: This is not truly an expected discounted value.

- The *numerator* is not the true expected cash flow from the option because we use the risk-neutral probability, p, rather than the true probability.
- The *denominator* is not the proper discount rate for option cash flows because we do not account for the risk.
- In a sense these two "errors" cancel out. But this is not just luck: We are *assured* to get the correct result because the no-arbitrage approach implies that risk preferences cannot affect the option value. Therefore, the value computed for the risk-neutral economy *must* equal the value that we obtain in our economy.

When we move to the more realistic multiperiod model, the calculations are more cumbersome but the idea is the same. Footnote 4 shows how to relate p to any expected rate of return and volatility estimate. Simply set the expected rate of return on the stock equal to the risk-free rate, use the resulting probability to work out the expected payoff from the option, discount at the risk-free rate, and you will find the option value. These calculations are actually fairly easy to program in Excel.

---

derived if one is willing to make just two more assumptions: that both the risk-free interest rate and stock price volatility are constant over the life of the option. In this case, as the time to expiration is divided into ever more subperiods, the distribution of the stock price at expiration progressively approaches the lognormal distribution, as suggested by Figure 16.2. When the stock price distribution is actually lognormal, we can derive an exact option-pricing formula.

The Black-Scholes Formula

Black-Scholes pricing formula

A formula to value an option that uses the stock price, the risk-free interest rate, the time to expiration, and the standard deviation of the stock return.

Financial economists searched for years for a workable option-pricing model before Black and Scholes (1973) and Merton (1973) derived a formula for the value of a call option. Now widely used by options market participants, the **Black-Scholes pricing formula** for a European-style call option is

$$C_0 = S_0 e^{-\delta T} N(d_1) - X e^{-rT} N(d_2) \tag{16.1}$$

where

$$d_1 = \frac{\ln(S_0/X) + (r - \delta + \sigma^2/2)T}{\sigma\sqrt{T}}$$

$$d_2 = d_1 - \sigma\sqrt{T}$$

and where

C_0 = Current call option value.

S_0 = Current stock price.

$N(d)$ = The probability that a random draw from a standard normal distribution will be less than d. This equals the area under the normal curve up to d, as in the shaded area of Figure 16.3. In Excel, this function is called NORMSDIST( ) or NORM.S.DIST( ).

X = Exercise price.

e = The base of the natural log function, approximately 2.71828. In Excel, e^x can be evaluated using the function EXP(x).

δ = Annual dividend yield of underlying stock. (We assume for simplicity that the stock pays a continuous income flow, rather than discrete periodic payments, such as quarterly dividends.)

r = Risk-free interest rate, expressed as a decimal (the annualized continuously compounded rate[7] on a safe asset with the same maturity as the expiration date of the option, which is to be distinguished from r_f, the discrete period interest rate).

T = Time remaining until expiration of option (in years).

ln = Natural logarithm function. In Excel, ln(x) can be calculated using the built-in function LN(x).

σ = Standard deviation of the annualized continuously compounded rate of return of the stock, expressed as a decimal, not a percent.

Notice a surprising feature of Equation 16.1: The option value does not depend on the expected rate of return on the stock. In a sense, this information is already built into the formula with inclusion of the stock price, which itself depends on the stock's risk and return characteristics. This version of the Black-Scholes formula is predicated on the assumption that the underlying asset has a constant dividend (or income) yield.

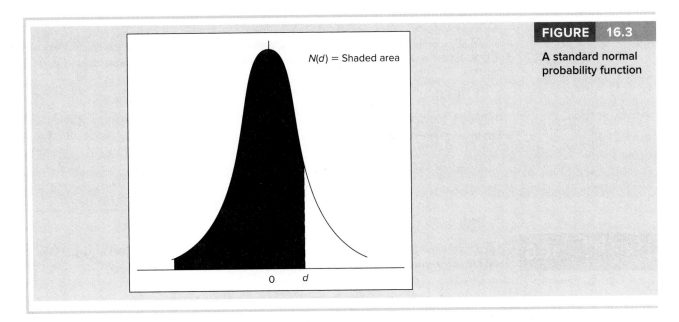

FIGURE   16.3

A standard normal probability function

$N(d)$ = Shaded area

0   d

---

[7]See Chapter 5, Section 5.1, for a review of continuous compounding.

Although you may find the Black-Scholes formula intimidating, we can explain it at a somewhat intuitive level. Consider a nondividend-paying stock, for which $\delta = 0$. Then $S_0 e^{-\delta T} = S_0$.

The trick is to view the $N(d)$ terms (loosely) as risk-adjusted probabilities that the call option will expire in the money. First, look at Equation 16.1 assuming both $N(d)$ terms are close to 1, that is, when there is a very high probability that the option will be exercised. Then the call option value is equal to $S_0 - Xe^{-rT}$, which is what we called earlier the adjusted intrinsic value, $S_0 - PV(X)$. This makes sense; if exercise is certain, we have a claim on a stock with current value S_0 and an obligation with present value $PV(X)$, or with continuous compounding, Xe^{-rT}.

Now look at Equation 16.1 assuming the $N(d)$ terms are close to zero, meaning the option almost certainly will not be exercised. Then the equation confirms that the call is worth nothing. For middle-range values of $N(d)$ between 0 and 1, Equation 16.1 tells us that the call value can be viewed as the present value of the call's potential payoff adjusting for the probability of in-the-money expiration.

How do the $N(d)$ terms serve as risk-adjusted probabilities? This question quickly leads us into advanced statistics. Notice, however, that d_1 and d_2 both increase as the stock price increases. Therefore, $N(d_1)$ and $N(d_2)$ also increase with higher stock prices. This is the property we would desire of our "probabilities." For higher stock prices relative to exercise prices, future exercise is more likely.

EXAMPLE 16.4

Black-Scholes Call Option Valuation

You can use the Black-Scholes formula fairly easily. Suppose you want to value a call option under the following circumstances:

Stock price	$S_0 = 100$
Exercise price	$X = 95$
Interest rate	$r = .10$
Dividend yield	$\delta = 0$
Time to expiration	$T = .25$ (one-quarter year)
Standard deviation	$\sigma = .50$

First calculate

$$d_1 = \frac{\ln(100/95) + (.10 - 0 + .5^2/2).25}{.5\sqrt{0.25}} = .43$$

$$d_2 = .43 - .5\sqrt{.25} = .18$$

Next find $N(d_1)$ and $N(d_2)$. The normal distribution function is tabulated and may be found in many statistics textbooks. A table of $N(d)$ is provided as Table 16.2. The normal distribution function $N(d)$ is also provided in any spreadsheet program. In Microsoft Excel, for example, the function name is NORMSDIST or NORM.S.DIST. Using either Excel or Table 16.2 (using interpolation for .43), we find that

$$N(.43) = .6664$$

$$N(.18) = .5714$$

Finally, remember that with $\delta = 0$, $S_0 e^{-\delta T} = S_0$. Thus, the value of the call option is

$$C = 100 \times .6664 - 95e^{-.10 \times .25} \times .5714$$

$$= 66.64 - 52.94 = \$13.70$$

CONCEPT check 16.6

Calculate the call option value if the standard deviation on the stock is .6 instead of .5. Confirm that the option is worth more using this higher volatility.

What if the option price in Example 16.4 were $15 rather than $13.70? Is the option mispriced? Maybe, but before betting your career on that, you may want to reconsider the valuation

TABLE 16.2   Cumulative normal distribution

d	N(d)	d	N(d)	d	N(d)	d	N(d)	d	N(d)	d	N(d)
−3.00	0.0013	−1.58	0.0571	−0.76	0.2236	0.06	0.5239	0.88	0.8106	1.70	0.9545
−2.95	0.0016	−1.56	0.0594	−0.74	0.2297	0.08	0.5319	0.90	0.8159	1.72	0.9573
−2.90	0.0019	−1.54	0.0618	−0.72	0.2358	0.10	0.5398	0.92	0.8212	1.74	0.9591
−2.85	0.0022	−1.52	0.0643	−0.70	0.2420	0.12	0.5478	0.94	0.8264	1.76	0.9608
−2.80	0.0026	−1.50	0.0668	−0.68	0.2483	0.14	0.5557	0.96	0.8315	1.78	0.9625
−2.75	0.0030	−1.48	0.0694	−0.66	0.2546	0.16	0.5636	0.98	0.8365	1.80	0.9641
−2.70	0.0035	−1.46	0.0721	−0.64	0.2611	0.18	0.5714	1.00	0.8414	1.82	0.9656
−2.65	0.0040	−1.44	0.0749	−0.62	0.2676	0.20	0.5793	1.02	0.8461	1.84	0.9671
−2.60	0.0047	−1.42	0.0778	−0.60	0.2743	0.22	0.5871	1.04	0.8508	1.86	0.9686
−2.55	0.0054	−1.40	0.0808	−0.58	0.2810	0.24	0.5948	1.06	0.8554	1.88	0.9699
−2.50	0.0062	−1.38	0.0838	−0.56	0.2877	0.26	0.6026	1.08	0.8599	1.90	0.9713
−2.45	0.0071	−1.36	0.0869	−0.54	0.2946	0.28	0.6103	1.10	0.8643	1.92	0.9726
−2.40	0.0082	−1.34	0.0901	−0.52	0.3015	0.30	0.6179	1.12	0.8686	1.94	0.9738
−2.35	0.0094	−1.32	0.0934	−0.50	0.3085	0.32	0.6255	1.14	0.8729	1.96	0.9750
−2.30	0.0107	−1.30	0.0968	−0.48	0.3156	0.34	0.6331	1.16	0.8770	1.98	0.9761
−2.25	0.0122	−1.28	0.1003	−0.46	0.3228	0.36	0.6406	1.18	0.8810	2.00	0.9772
−2.20	0.0139	−1.26	0.1038	−0.44	0.3300	0.38	0.6480	1.20	0.8849	2.05	0.9798
−2.15	0.0158	−1.24	0.1075	−0.42	0.3373	0.40	0.6554	1.22	0.8888	2.10	0.9821
−2.10	0.0179	−1.22	0.1112	−0.40	0.3446	0.42	0.6628	1.24	0.8925	2.15	0.9842
−2.05	0.0202	−1.20	0.1151	−0.38	0.3520	0.44	0.6700	1.26	0.8962	2.20	0.9861
−2.00	0.0228	−1.18	0.1190	−0.36	0.3594	0.46	0.6773	1.28	0.8997	2.25	0.9878
−1.98	0.0239	−1.16	0.1230	−0.34	0.3669	0.48	0.6844	1.30	0.9032	2.30	0.9893
−1.96	0.0250	−1.14	0.1271	−0.32	0.3745	0.50	0.6915	1.32	0.9066	2.35	0.9906
−1.94	0.0262	−1.12	0.1314	−0.30	0.3821	0.52	0.6985	1.34	0.9099	2.40	0.9918
−1.92	0.0274	−1.10	0.1357	−0.28	0.3897	0.54	0.7054	1.36	0.9131	2.45	0.9929
−1.90	0.0287	−1.08	0.1401	−0.26	0.3974	0.56	0.7123	1.38	0.9162	2.50	0.9938
−1.88	0.0301	−1.06	0.1446	−0.24	0.4052	0.58	0.7191	1.40	0.9192	2.55	0.9946
−1.86	0.0314	−1.04	0.1492	−0.22	0.4129	0.60	0.7258	1.42	0.9222	2.60	0.9953
−1.84	0.0329	−1.02	0.1539	−0.20	0.4207	0.62	0.7324	1.44	0.9251	2.65	0.9960
−1.82	0.0344	−1.00	0.1587	−0.18	0.4286	0.64	0.7389	1.46	0.9279	2.70	0.9965
−1.80	0.0359	−0.98	0.1635	−0.16	0.4365	0.66	0.7454	1.48	0.9306	2.75	0.9970
−1.78	0.0375	−0.96	0.1685	−0.14	0.4443	0.68	0.7518	1.50	0.9332	2.80	0.9974
−1.76	0.0392	−0.94	0.1736	−0.12	0.4523	0.70	0.7580	1.52	0.9357	2.85	0.9978
−1.74	0.0409	−0.92	0.1788	−0.10	0.4602	0.72	0.7642	1.54	0.9382	2.90	0.9981
−1.72	0.0427	−0.90	0.1841	−0.08	0.4681	0.74	0.7704	1.56	0.9406	2.95	0.9984
−1.70	0.0446	−0.88	0.1894	−0.06	0.4761	0.76	0.7764	1.58	0.9429	3.00	0.9986
−1.68	0.0465	−0.86	0.1949	−0.04	0.4841	0.78	0.7823	1.60	0.9452	3.05	0.9989
−1.66	0.0485	−0.84	0.2005	−0.02	0.4920	0.80	0.7882	1.62	0.9474		
−1.64	0.0505	−0.82	0.2061	0.00	0.5000	0.82	0.7939	1.64	0.9495		
−1.62	0.0526	−0.80	0.2119	0.02	0.5080	0.84	0.7996	1.66	0.9515		
−1.60	0.0548	−0.78	0.2177	0.04	0.5160	0.86	0.8051	1.68	0.9535		

analysis. First, like all models, the Black-Scholes formula is based on some simplifying abstractions that make the formula only approximately valid.

Some of the important assumptions underlying the formula are the following:

1. The stock will pay a constant, continuous dividend yield until the option expiration date.
2. Both the interest rate, r, and variance rate, σ^2, of the stock are constant (or in slightly more general versions of the formula, both are *known* functions of time—any changes are perfectly predictable).
3. Stock prices are continuous, meaning that sudden extreme jumps, such as those in the aftermath of an announcement of a takeover attempt, are ruled out.

Variants of the Black-Scholes formula have been developed to deal with many of these limitations.

Second, even within the context of the Black-Scholes model, you must be sure of the accuracy of the parameters used in the formula. Four of these—S_0, X, T, and r—are straightforward. The stock price, exercise price, and time to expiration are readily determined. The interest rate used is the money market rate for a maturity equal to that of the option, and the dividend yield is usually reasonably stable, at least over short horizons.

The last input, though, the standard deviation of the stock return, is not directly observable. It must be estimated from historical data, from scenario analysis, or from the prices of other options, as we will describe momentarily. Because the standard deviation must be estimated, it is always possible that discrepancies between an option price and its Black-Scholes value are simply artifacts of error in the estimation of the stock's volatility.

In fact, market participants often give the option valuation problem a different twist. Rather than calculating a Black-Scholes option value for a given stock standard deviation, they ask instead: What standard deviation would be necessary for the option price that I actually observe to be consistent with the Black-Scholes formula? This is called the **implied volatility** of the option, the volatility level for the stock that the option price implies. Investors can then judge whether they think the actual stock standard deviation exceeds the implied volatility. If it does, the option is considered a good buy; if actual volatility seems greater than the implied volatility, the option's fair price would exceed the observed price.

Another variation is to compare two options on the same stock with equal expiration dates but different exercise prices. The option with the higher implied volatility would be considered relatively expensive because a higher standard deviation is required to justify its price. The analyst might consider buying the option with the lower implied volatility and writing the option with the higher implied volatility.

The Black-Scholes call option valuation formula, as well as the implied volatility, is easily calculated using an Excel spreadsheet, as in Spreadsheet 16.1. The model inputs are provided in column B, and the outputs are given in column E. The formulas for d_1 and d_2 are provided in the spreadsheet, and the Excel formula NORMSDIST(d_1) is used to calculate $N(d_1)$. Cell E6 contains the Black-Scholes call option formula.

To compute an implied volatility, we can use the Goal Seek command from the What-If Analysis menu (which may be found under the Data tab) in Excel. (See Figure 16.4 for an

implied volatility

The standard deviation of stock returns that is consistent with an option's market value.

SPREADSHEET 16.1

Spreadsheet to calculate Black-Scholes call-option values

Spreadsheets are available in Connect

	A	B	C	D	E	F	G	H	I	J
1	INPUTS			OUTPUTS			FORMULA FOR OUTPUT IN COLUMN E			
2	Standard deviation (annual)	0.2783		d1	0.0029		(LN(B5/B6)+(B4−B7+.5*B2^2)*B3)/(B2*SQRT(B3))			
3	Expiration (in years)	0.5		d2	−0.1939		E2−B2*SQRT(B3)			
4	Risk-free rate (annual)	0.06		N(d1)	0.5012		NORMSDIST(E2)			
5	Stock price	100		N(d2)	0.4231		NORMSDIST(E3)			
6	Exercise price	105		B/S call value	7.0000		B5*EXP(−B7*B3)*E4−B6*EXP(−B4*B3)*E5			
7	Dividend yield (annual)	0		B/S put value	8.8967		B6*EXP(−B4*B3)*(1−E5)−B5*EXP(−B7*B3)*(1−E4)			

FIGURE   16.4

Using Goal Seek to find implied volatility

FIGURE   16.4

	A	B	C	D	E	F	G	H	I	J	K
1	INPUTS			OUTPUTS			FORMULA FOR OUTPUT IN COLUMN E				
2	Standard deviation (annual)	0.2783		d1	0.0029		(LN(B5/B6)+(B4−B7+.5*B2^2)*B3)/(B2*SQRT(B3))				
3	Expiration (in years)	0.5		d2	−0.1939		E2−B2*SQRT(B3)				
4	Risk-free rate (annual)	0.06		N(d1)	0.5012		NORMSDIST(E2)				
5	Stock price	100		N(d2)	0.4231		NORMSDIST(E3)				
6	Exercise price	105		B/S call value	7.0000		B5*EXP(−B7*B3)*E4−B6*EXP(−B4*B3)*E5				
7	Dividend yield (annual)	0		B/S put value	8.8968		B6*EXP(−B4*B3)*(1−E5)−B5*EXP(−B7*B3)*(1−E4)				
8											
9											
10											
11											
12											
13											
14											
15											
16											
17											

Goal Seek

Set cell: $E$6

To value: 7

By changing cell: $B$2

OK   Cancel

illustration.) Goal Seek asks us to change the value of one cell to make the value of another cell (called the *target cell*) equal to a specific value. For example, if we observe a call option selling for $7 with other inputs as given in the spreadsheet, we can use Goal Seek to change the value in cell B2 (the standard deviation of the stock) to set the option value in cell E6 equal to $7. The target cell, E6, is the call price, and the spreadsheet manipulates cell B2. When you click *OK,* the spreadsheet finds that a standard deviation equal to .2783 is consistent with a call price of $7; therefore, 27.83% would be the call's implied volatility if it were selling at $7.

CONCEPT
check   16.7

Consider the call option in Example 16.4. If it sells for $15 rather than the value of $13.70 found in the example, is its implied volatility more or less than .5? Use Spreadsheet 16.1 (available in Connect) to find its implied volatility at this price.

The Chicago Board Options Exchange regularly computes the implied volatility of major stock indexes. Figure 16.5 is a graph of the implied (30-day) volatility of the S&P 500. During periods of turmoil, implied volatility can spike quickly. Notice the peaks in January 1991 (Gulf War), in August 1998 (collapse of Long-Term Capital Management), on September 11, 2001, in 2002 (buildup to invasion of Iraq), and, most dramatically, during the credit crisis of 2008. Because implied volatility correlates with crisis, it is sometimes called an "investor fear gauge."

A futures contract on the 30-day implied volatility of the S&P 500 has traded on the CBOE Futures Exchange since 2004. The payoff of the contract depends on market implied volatility at the expiration of the contract. The ticker symbol of the contract is VIX.

Figure 16.5 also reveals an awkward empirical fact. While the Black-Scholes formula is derived assuming that stock volatility is constant, the time series of implied volatilities consistent with that formula is in fact far from constant. This contradiction reminds us that the Black-Scholes model (like all models) is a simplification that does not capture all aspects of real markets. In this particular context, extensions of the pricing model that allow stock volatility to evolve randomly over time would be desirable, and, in fact, many extensions of the model along these lines have been developed.[8]

---

[8]Influential articles on this topic are Hull and White (1987), Wiggins (1987), and Heston (1993). For a more recent review, see Ghysels, Harvey, and Renault (1996).

FIGURE 16.5

Implied volatility of the S&P 500 (VIX index), expressed as an annualized standard deviation

Source: Chicago Board Options Exchange.

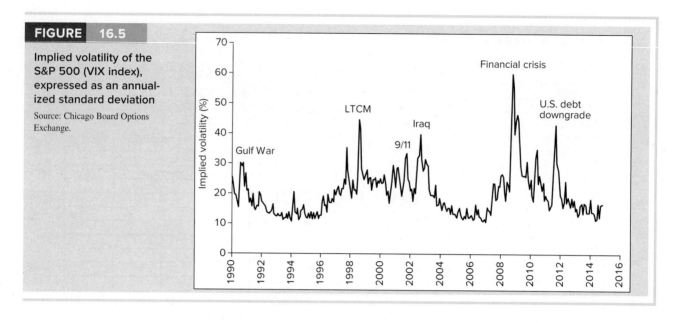

The fact that volatility changes unpredictably means that it can be difficult to choose the proper volatility input to use in any option-pricing model. A considerable amount of recent research has been devoted to techniques to predict changes in volatility. These techniques, which are known as *ARCH* and *stochastic volatility models,* posit that changes in volatility are partially predictable and that by analyzing recent levels and trends in volatility, one can improve predictions of future volatility.[9]

The Put-Call Parity Relationship

So far, we have focused on the pricing of call options. In many important cases, put prices can be derived simply from the prices of calls. This is because prices of European put and call options are linked together in an equation known as the put-call parity relationship. Therefore, once you know the value of a call, finding the value of the put is easy.

To derive the parity relationship, suppose you buy a call option and write a put option, each with the same exercise price, X, and the same expiration date, T. At expiration, the payoff on your investment will equal the payoff to the call minus the payoff that must be made on the put. The payoff for each option will depend on whether the ultimate stock price, S_T, exceeds the exercise price at contract expiration.

	$S_T \leq X$	$S_T > X$
Payoff of call held	0	$S_T - X$
− Payoff of put written	$-(X - S_T)$	0
Total	$S_T - X$	$S_T - X$

Figure 16.6 illustrates this payoff pattern. Compare the payoff to that of a portfolio made up of the stock plus a borrowing position, where the money to be paid back will grow, with interest, to X dollars at the maturity of the loan. Such a position is a *levered* equity position in which $PV(X) = Xe^{-rT}$ dollars is borrowed today (so that X will be repaid at maturity), and S_0 dollars is invested in the stock. The total payoff of the levered equity position is $S_T - X$, the same as that of the option strategy. Thus, the long call–short put position replicates the levered equity position. Again, we see that option trading provides leverage.

[9]For an introduction to these models, see Alexander (2001).

FIGURE 16.6

The payoff pattern
of a long call–short
put position

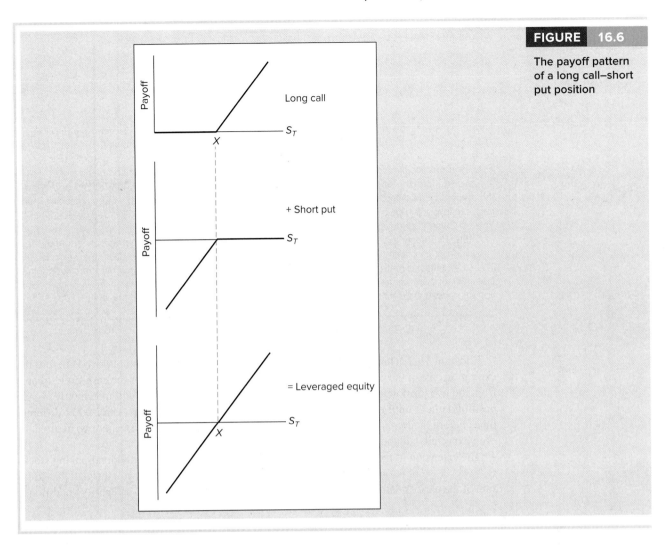

Because the option portfolio has a payoff identical to that of the levered equity position, the costs of establishing them must be equal. The net cash outlay necessary to establish the option position is $C - P$: The call is purchased for C, while the written put generates income of P. Likewise, the levered equity position requires a net cash outlay of $S_0 - Xe^{-rT}$, the cost of the stock less the proceeds from borrowing. Equating these costs, we conclude

$$C - P = S_0 - Xe^{-rT} \qquad \textbf{(16.2)}$$

Equation 16.2 is called the **put-call parity relationship** because it represents the proper relationship between put and call prices. If the parity relationship is ever violated, an arbitrage opportunity arises.

put-call parity relationship

An equation representing the proper relationship between put and call prices.

EXAMPLE 16.5

Put-Call Parity

Suppose you observe the following data for a certain stock.

Stock price	$110
Call price (six-month maturity, $X = \$105$)	14
Put price (six-month maturity, $X = \$105$)	5
Risk-free interest rate	5% continuously compounded rate

(continued)

EXAMPLE 16.5

Put-Call Parity
(concluded)

We use these data in the put-call parity relationship to see if parity is violated.

$$C - P \overset{?}{=} S_0 - Xe^{-rT}$$
$$14 - 5 \overset{?}{=} 110 - 105e^{-.05 \times .5}$$
$$9 \overset{?}{=} 7.59$$

This result, a violation of parity (9 does not equal 7.59) indicates mispricing and leads to an arbitrage opportunity. You can buy the relatively cheap portfolio (the stock plus borrowing position represented on the right-hand side of Equation 16.2) and sell the relatively expensive portfolio (the long call–short put position corresponding to the left-hand side, that is, write a call and buy a put).

Let's examine the payoff to this strategy. In six months, the stock will be worth S_T. You borrowed the present value of the exercise price, $105, and must pay back the loan with interest, resulting in a cash outflow of $105. The written call will result in a cash outflow of $S_T - \$105$ if S_T exceeds $105. The purchased put pays off $105 - S_T$ if the stock price is below $105.

Table 16.3 summarizes the outcome. The immediate cash inflow is $1.41, precisely equal to the mispricing of the option. In six months, the various positions provide exactly offsetting cash flows: The $1.41 inflow is realized risklessly without any offsetting outflows. This is an arbitrage opportunity that investors will pursue on a large scale until buying and selling pressure restores the parity condition expressed in Equation 16.2.

Equation 16.2 actually applies only to options on stocks that pay no dividends before the expiration date of the option. It also applies only to European options, as the cash flow streams from the two portfolios represented by the two sides of Equation 16.2 will match only if each position is held until expiration. If a call and a put may be optimally exercised at different times before their common expiration date, then the equality of payoffs cannot be assured, or even expected, and the portfolios will have different values.

The extension of the parity condition for European call options on dividend-paying stocks is, however, straightforward. Problem 32 at the end of the chapter leads you through the extension of the parity relationship. The more general formulation of the put-call parity condition is

$$P = C - S_0 + PV(X) + PV(\text{dividends}) \tag{16.3}$$

where PV(dividends) is the present value of the dividends that will be paid by the stock during the life of the option. If the stock does not pay dividends, Equation 16.3 becomes identical to Equation 16.2.

Notice that this generalization would apply as well to European options on assets other than stocks. Instead of using dividend income in Equation 16.3, we would let any income paid out by the underlying asset play the role of the stock dividends. For example, European put and call options on bonds would satisfy the same parity relationship, except that the bond's coupon income would replace the stock's dividend payments in the parity formula.

TABLE 16.3 Arbitrage strategy

Position	Immediate Cash Flow	Cash Flow in Six Months	
		$S_T < 105$	$S_T \geq 105$
Buy stock	−110	S_T	S_T
Borrow $Xe^{-rT} = \$102.41$	+102.41	−105	−105
Sell call	+14	0	$-(S_T - 105)$
Buy put	−5	$105 - S_T$	0
Total	1.41	0	0

Sheffield Hallam University
Adsetts Library (4)

Borrowed Items 03/02/2020 13:42
XXXXX3974

Item Title	Due Date
˄ Essentials of investments	10/02/2020
Investment and portfolio management : a practical introduction	09/02/2020
Asset management : equities demystified	10/02/2020
The Financial Times guide to wealth management : how to plan, invest and protect your financial assets	10/02/2020
The new wealth management : the financial advisor's guide to managing and investing client assets	10/02/2020

˄ Indicates items borrowed today

Adsetts Library
Email: library@shu.ac.uk
Items normally renewed automatically
unless requested by another borrower

Let's see how well parity works using the data in Figure 15.1 (from the previous chapter) on the Facebook options. The November expiration call with exercise price $80 and time to expiration of 36 days cost $2.64, while the corresponding put option cost $6.74. Facebook was selling for $75.95, and the annualized short-term interest rate on this date was 0.1%. Facebook was not expected to pay a dividend prior to option expiration. According to parity, we should find that

$$P = C + PV(X) - S_0 + PV(\text{dividends})$$
$$6.74 = 2.64 + \frac{80}{(1.001)^{36/365}} - 75.95 + 0$$
$$6.74 = 2.64 + 79.99 - 75.95 + 0$$
$$6.74 = 6.68$$

So parity is violated by about $.06 per share. Is this a big enough difference to exploit? Almost certainly not. You have to weigh the potential profit against the trading costs of the call, put, and stock. More important, given the fact that options may trade relatively infrequently, this deviation from parity might not be "real" but may instead be attributable to "stale" (i.e., out-of-date) price quotes at which you cannot actually trade.

Put Option Valuation

As we saw in Equation 16.3, we can use the put-call parity relationship to value put options once we know the call option value. Sometimes, however, it is easier to work with a put option valuation formula directly. The Black-Scholes formula for the value of a European put option is[10]

$$P = Xe^{-rT}[1 - N(d_2)] - S_0e^{-\delta T}[1 - N(d_1)] \qquad \textbf{(16.4)}$$

EXAMPLE 16.6

Black-Scholes Put Option Valuation

Using data from the Black-Scholes call option in Example 16.4, we find that a European put option on that stock with identical exercise price and time to expiration is worth

$$\$95e^{-.10 \times .25}(1 - .5714) - \$100(1 - .6664) = \$6.35$$

Notice that this value is consistent with put-call parity:

$$P = C + PV(X) - S_0 + PV(\text{Div}) = 13.70 + 95e^{-.10 \times .25} - 100 + 0 = 6.35$$

As we noted traders can do, we might then compare this formula value to the actual put price as one step in formulating a trading strategy.

Equation 16.4 is valid for European puts. Most listed put options are American-style, however, and offer the opportunity of early exercise. Because an American option allows its owner to exercise at any time before the expiration date, it must be worth at least as much as the corresponding European option. However, while Equation 16.4 describes only the lower bound on the true value of the American put, in many applications the approximation is very accurate.

16.4 USING THE BLACK-SCHOLES FORMULA

Hedge Ratios and the Black-Scholes Formula

In the last chapter, we considered two investments in FinCorp stock: 100 shares or 900 call options. We saw that the call option position was more sensitive to swings in the stock price

---

[10]This formula is consistent with the put-call parity relationship and in fact can be derived from it. If you want to try, remember to take present values using continuous compounding, and use the fact that when a stock pays a continuous flow of income in the form of a constant dividend yield, δ, the present value of that dividend flow is $S_0(1 - e^{-\delta T})$. (Notice that $e^{-\delta T}$ approximately equals $1 - \delta T$, so the value of the dividend flow is approximately $\delta T S_0$.)

than the all-stock position. To analyze the overall exposure to a stock price more precisely, however, it is necessary to quantify these relative sensitivities. We can summarize the overall exposure of portfolios of options with various exercise prices and times to expiration using the hedge ratio. An option's **hedge ratio** is the change in the option price for a $1 increase in the stock price. A call option, therefore, has a positive hedge ratio, and a put option has a negative hedge ratio. The hedge ratio is commonly called the option's **delta.**

If you were to graph the option value as a function of the stock value, as we have done for a call option in Figure 16.7, the hedge ratio is simply the slope of the value function evaluated at the current stock price. For example, suppose the slope of the curve at $S_0 = \$120$ equals .60. As the stock increases in value by $1, the option increases by approximately $.60, as the figure shows.

For every call option written, .60 shares of stock would be needed to hedge the investor's portfolio. If one writes 10 options and holds six shares of stock, according to the hedge ratio of .6, a $1 increase in stock price will result in a gain of $6 on the stock holdings, while the loss on the 10 options written will be $10 \times \$.60$, an equivalent $6. The stock price movement leaves total wealth unaltered, which is what a hedged position is intended to do. The investor holding both the stock and options in proportions dictated by their relative price movements hedges the portfolio.

Black-Scholes hedge ratios are particularly easy to compute. The hedge ratio for a call is $N(d_1)$, while the hedge ratio for a put is $N(d_1) - 1$. We defined $N(d_1)$ as part of the Black-Scholes formula in Equation 16.1. Recall that $N(d)$ stands for the area under the standard normal curve up to d. Therefore, the call option hedge ratio must be positive and less than 1.0, while the put option hedge ratio is negative and of smaller absolute value than 1.0.

Figure 16.7 verifies the insight that the slope of the call option valuation function is less than 1, approaching 1 only as the stock price becomes extremely large. This tells us that option values change less than one-for-one with changes in stock prices. Why should this be? Suppose an option is so far in the money that you are absolutely certain it will be exercised. In that case, every $1 increase in the stock price would increase the option value by $1. But if there is a reasonable chance the call option will expire out of the money, even after a moderate stock price gain, a $1 increase in the stock price will not necessarily increase the ultimate payoff to the call; therefore, the call price will not respond by a full $1.

The fact that hedge ratios are less than 1 does not contradict our earlier observation that options offer leverage and are sensitive to stock price movements. Although *dollar* movements in option prices are less than dollar movements in the stock price, the *rate of return* volatility of options remains greater than stock return volatility because options sell at lower prices. In our example, with the stock selling at $120, and a hedge ratio of .6, an option with exercise price $120 may sell for $5. If the stock price increases to $121, the call price would

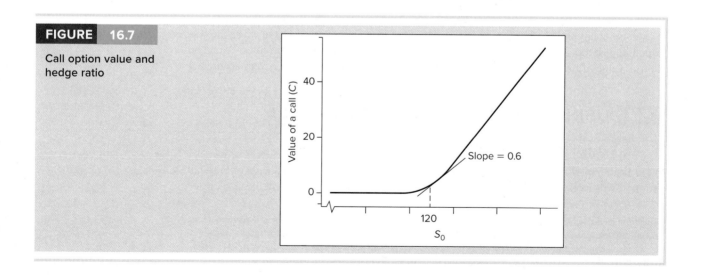

FIGURE 16.7

Call option value and hedge ratio

be expected to increase by only \$.60, to \$5.60. The percentage increase in the option value is \$.60/\$5 = 12%, however, while the percentage stock price increase is only \$1/\$120 = .83%. The ratio of the percent changes is 12%/.83% = 14.4. For every 1% increase in the stock price, the option price increases by 14.4%. This ratio, the percent change in option price per percent change in stock price, is called the **option elasticity.**

The hedge ratio is an essential tool in portfolio management and control. An example will show why.

option elasticity

The percentage increase in an option's value given a 1% increase in the value of the underlying security.

EXAMPLE 16.7

Portfolio Hedge Ratios

Consider two portfolios, one holding 750 FinCorp calls and 200 shares of FinCorp and the other holding 800 shares of FinCorp. Which portfolio has greater dollar exposure to FinCorp price movements? You can answer this question easily using the hedge ratio.

Each option changes in value by H dollars for each dollar change in stock price, where H stands for the hedge ratio. Thus, if H equals .6, the 750 options are equivalent to 450 shares (= .6 × 750) in terms of the response of their market value to FinCorp stock price movements. The first portfolio has less dollar sensitivity to stock price change because the 450 share-equivalents of the options plus the 200 shares actually held are less than the 800 shares held in the second portfolio.

This is not to say, however, that the first portfolio is less sensitive to the stock's rate of return. As we noted in discussing option elasticities, the first portfolio may be of lower total value than the second, so despite its lower sensitivity in terms of total market value, it might have greater rate-of-return sensitivity. Because a call option has a lower market value than the stock, its price changes more than proportionally with stock price changes, even though its hedge ratio is less than 1.

What is the elasticity of a put option currently selling for \$4 with exercise price \$120 and hedge ratio −.4 if the stock price is currently \$122?

CONCEPT check 16.8

Portfolio Insurance

In Chapter 15, we showed that protective put strategies offer a sort of insurance policy on an asset. The protective put has proven to be extremely popular with investors. Even if the asset price falls, the put conveys the right to sell the asset for the exercise price, which is a way to lock in a minimum portfolio value. With an at-the-money put ($X = S_0$), the maximum loss that can be realized is the cost of the put. The asset can be sold for X, which equals its original price, so even if the asset price falls, the investor's net loss over the period is just the cost of the put. If the asset value increases, however, upside potential is unlimited. Figure 16.8 graphs the profit or loss on a protective put position as a function of the change in the value of the underlying asset.

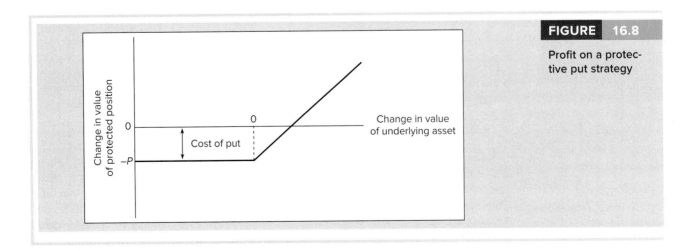

FIGURE 16.8

Profit on a protective put strategy

portfolio insurance

Portfolio strategies that limit investment losses while maintaining upside potential.

While the protective put is a simple and convenient way to achieve **portfolio insurance,** that is, to limit the worst-case portfolio rate of return, there are practical difficulties in trying to insure a portfolio of stocks. First, unless the investor's portfolio corresponds to a standard market index for which puts are traded, a put option on the portfolio will not be available for purchase. And if index puts are used to protect a nonindexed portfolio, tracking error can result. For example, if the portfolio falls in value while the market index rises, the put will fail to provide the intended protection. Moreover, the maturities of traded options may not match the investor's horizon. Therefore, rather than using option strategies, investors may use trading strategies that mimic the payoff to a protective put option.

Here is the general idea. Even if a put option on the desired portfolio with the desired expiration date does not exist, a theoretical option-pricing model (such as the Black-Scholes model) can be used to determine how that option's price *would* respond to the portfolio's value if the option did trade. For example, if stock prices were to fall, the put option would increase in value. The option model could quantify this relationship. The net exposure of the (hypothetical) protective put portfolio to swings in stock prices is the sum of the exposures of the two components of the portfolio: the stock and the put. The net exposure of the portfolio equals the equity exposure less the (offsetting) put option exposure.

We can create "synthetic" protective put positions by holding a quantity of stocks with the same net exposure to market swings as the hypothetical protective put position. The key to this strategy is the option delta, or hedge ratio, that is, the change in the price of the protective put option per change in the value of the underlying stock portfolio.

EXAMPLE 16.8

Synthetic Protective Puts

Suppose a portfolio is currently valued at $100 million. An at-the-money put option on the portfolio might have a hedge ratio or delta of −.6, meaning the option's value swings $.60 for every dollar change in portfolio value, but in an opposite direction. Suppose the stock portfolio falls in value by 2%. The profit on a hypothetical protective put position (if the put existed) would be as follows (in millions of dollars):

Loss on stocks:	2% of $100 = $2.00
+Gain on put:	.6 × $2.00 = 1.20
Net loss	$0.80

We create the synthetic option position by selling a proportion of shares equal to the put option's delta (i.e., selling 60% of the shares) and placing the proceeds in risk-free T-bills. The rationale is that the hypothetical put option would have offset 60% of any change in the stock portfolio's value, so one must reduce portfolio risk directly by selling 60% of the equity and putting the proceeds into a risk-free asset. Total return on a synthetic protective put position with $60 million in risk-free investments such as T-bills and $40 million in equity is:

Loss on stocks:	2% of $40 = $.80
+Loss on bills:	0
Net loss	$.80

The synthetic and actual protective put positions have equal returns. We conclude that if you sell a proportion of shares equal to the put option's delta and place the proceeds in cash equivalents, your exposure to the stock market will equal that of the desired protective put position.

---

dynamic hedging

Constant updating of hedge positions as market conditions change.

The challenge with synthetic positions is that deltas constantly change. Figure 16.9 shows that as the stock price falls, the absolute value of the appropriate hedge ratio increases. Therefore, market declines require extra hedging, that is, additional conversion of equity into cash. This constant updating of the hedge ratio is called **dynamic hedging,** as discussed in Section 16.2. Another term for such hedging is delta hedging, because the option delta is used to determine the number of shares that need to be bought or sold.

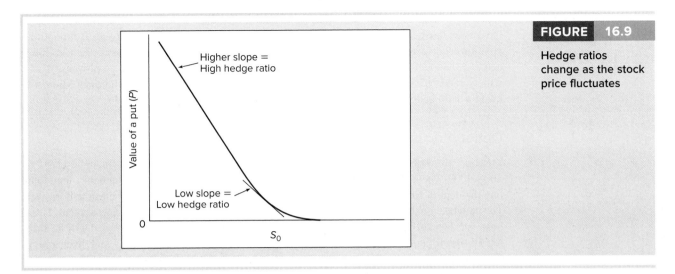

FIGURE 16.9

Hedge ratios change as the stock price fluctuates

Dynamic hedging is one reason portfolio insurance has been said to contribute to market volatility. Market declines trigger additional sales of stock as portfolio insurers strive to increase their hedging. These additional sales are seen as reinforcing or exaggerating market downturns.

In practice, portfolio insurers do not actually buy or sell stocks directly when they update their hedge positions. Instead, they minimize trading costs by buying or selling stock-index futures as a substitute for sale of the stocks themselves. As you will see in the next chapter, stock prices and index future prices usually are very tightly linked by cross-market arbitrageurs so that futures transactions can be used as reliable proxies for stock transactions. Instead of selling equities based on the put option's delta, insurers will sell an equivalent number of futures contracts.[11]

Several portfolio insurers suffered great setbacks during the market "crash" of October 19, 1987, when the Dow Jones Industrial Average fell more than 20%. A description of what happened then should help you appreciate the complexities of applying a seemingly straightforward hedging concept.

1. Market volatility at the crash was much greater than ever encountered before. Put option deltas computed from historical experience were too low; insurers underhedged, held too much equity, and suffered excessive losses.

2. Prices moved so fast that insurers could not keep up with the necessary rebalancing. They were "chasing deltas" that kept getting away from them. The futures market saw a "gap" opening, where the opening price was nearly 10% below the previous day's close. Prices dropped before insurers could update their hedge ratios.

3. Execution problems were severe. First, current market prices were unavailable, with trade execution and the price quotation system hours behind, which made computation of correct hedge ratios impossible. Moreover, trading in stocks and stock futures ceased during some periods. The continuous rebalancing capability that is essential for a viable insurance program vanished during the precipitous market collapse.

4. Futures prices traded at steep discounts to their proper levels compared to reported stock prices, thereby making the sale of futures (as a proxy for equity sales) to increase hedging seem expensive. While you will see in the next chapter that stock-index futures prices commonly exceed the value of the stock index, on October 19, futures sold far below the stock-index level. When some insurers gambled that the futures price would recover to its expected premium over the stock index and chose to defer sales, they remained underhedged. As the market fell farther, their portfolios experienced substantial losses.

---

[11]Notice, however, that the use of index futures reintroduces the problem of tracking error between the portfolio and the market index.

While most observers believe that the portfolio insurance industry will never recover from the market crash, dynamic hedges are still widely used to hedge potential losses from options positions. For example, when Microsoft ended its employee stock option program in 2003, and J. P. Morgan purchased many already-issued options from Microsoft employees, it was widely expected that Morgan would protect its options position by selling shares in Microsoft using a delta hedging strategy.

Option Pricing and the Crisis of 2008–2009

Merton[12] shows how option-pricing models can provide insight into the financial crisis of 2008-2009. The key to understanding his argument is to recognize that when banks lend to or buy the debt of firms with limited liability, they implicitly write a put option to the borrower. To see why, consider the payoff to the lender when the loan comes due for repayment. If the borrower has sufficient assets to pay off the loan, it will do so, and the lender will be fully repaid. But if the borrower has insufficient assets, it can declare bankruptcy and discharge its obligations by transferring ownership of the firm to its creditors. The borrower's ability to satisfy a loan by transferring ownership is equivalent to the right to "sell" itself to the creditor for the face value of the loan. This arrangement is therefore just like a put option on the firm with exercise price equal to the stipulated loan repayment.

Figure 16.10 shows the payoff to the lender at loan maturity (time T) as a function of the value of the borrowing firm, V_T, when the loan, with face value L, comes due. If $V_T \geq L$, the lender is paid off in full. But if $V_T < L$, the lender gets the firm, which is worth less than the promised payment L.

We can write the payoff in a way that emphasizes the implicit put option:

$$\text{Payoff} = \begin{cases} L \\ V_T \end{cases} = L - \begin{cases} 0 & \text{if } V_T \geq L \\ L - V_T & \text{if } V_T < L \end{cases} \quad \textbf{(16.5)}$$

Equation 16.5 shows that the payoff on the loan equals L (when the firm has sufficient assets to pay off the debt) *minus* the payoff of a put option on the value of the firm (V_T) with an exercise price of L. Therefore, we may view risky lending as a combination of safe lending, with a guaranteed payoff of L, with a short position in a put option on the borrower.

When firms sell credit default swaps (see Chapter 10), the implicit put option is even clearer. Here, the CDS seller agrees to make up any losses due to the insolvency of a bond issuer. If the bond issuer goes bankrupt, leaving assets of only V_T for the creditors, the CDS seller is obligated to make up the difference, $L - V_T$. This is in essence a pure put option.

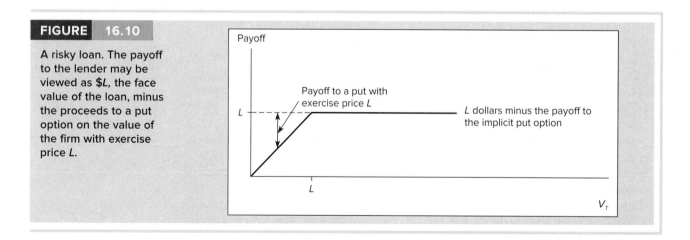

FIGURE 16.10

A risky loan. The payoff to the lender may be viewed as \$$L$, the face value of the loan, minus the proceeds to a put option on the value of the firm with exercise price L.

[12]This material is based on a lecture given by Robert Merton at MIT in March 2009. You can find the lecture online at **http://video.mit.edu/watch/observations-on-the-science-of-finance-in-the-practice-of-finance-9449/**

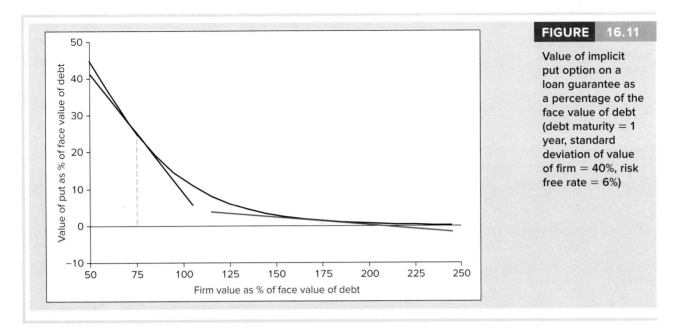

FIGURE   16.11

Value of implicit put option on a loan guarantee as a percentage of the face value of debt (debt maturity = 1 year, standard deviation of value of firm = 40%, risk free rate = 6%)

Now think about the exposure of these implicit put writers to changes in the financial health of the underlying firm. The value of a put option on V_T appears in Figure 16.11. When the firm is financially strong (i.e., V is far greater than L), the slope of the curve is nearly zero, implying that there is little exposure of the implicit put writer (either the lender or the CDS writer) to the value of the borrowing firm. For example, when firm value is 1.75 times the value of the debt, the lighter line drawn tangent to the put value curve has a slope of only $-.040$. But if there is a big shock to the economy, and firm value falls, not only does the value of the implicit put rise, but its slope is now steeper, implying that exposure to further shocks is now greater. When firm value is only 75% of the value of the loan, the slope of the line tangent to the put value valuation curve is far steeper, $-.644$. You can see how as you get closer to the edge of the cliff, it gets easier and easier to slide right off.

We often hear people say that a shock to asset values of the magnitude of the financial crisis was a 10-sigma event, by which they mean that such an event was so extreme that it would be 10 standard deviations away from an expected outcome, making it virtually inconceivable. But this analysis shows that standard deviation may be a moving target, increasing dramatically as the firm weakens. As the economy falters and put options go further into the money, their sensitivity to further shocks increases, increasing the risk that even worse losses may be around the corner. The built-in instability of risk exposures makes a scenario like the crisis more plausible and should give us pause when we discount an extreme scenario as "almost impossible."

16.5   EMPIRICAL EVIDENCE

There have been an enormous number of empirical tests of the Black-Scholes option-pricing model. For the most part, the results of the studies have been positive in that the Black-Scholes model generates option values close to the actual prices at which options trade. At the same time, some regular empirical failures of the model have been noted.

The biggest problem concerns volatility. If the model were accurate, the implied volatility of all options on a particular stock with the same expiration date would be equal—after all, the underlying asset and expiration date are the same for each option, so the volatility inferred from each also ought to be the same. But, in fact, when one actually plots implied volatility as a function of exercise price, the typical results appear as in Figure 16.12, which treats S&P 500 Index options as the underlying asset. Implied volatility steadily falls as the exercise price rises. Clearly, the Black-Scholes model is missing something.

Source: Mark Rubinstein,
"Implied Binomial Trees,"
Journal of Finance 49 (July 1994),
pp. 771–818, Figure 2.

FIGURE   16.12

Implied volatility as a
function of exercise
price

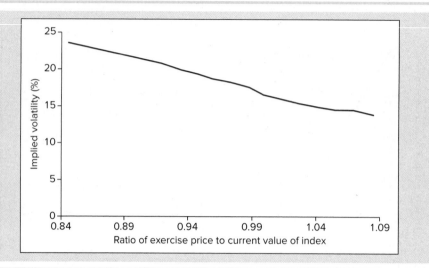

Rubinstein (1994) argues that the problem with the model has to do with fears of a market crash like that of October 1987. The idea is that deep out-of-the-money puts would be nearly worthless if stock prices evolve smoothly because the probability of the stock falling by a large amount (and the put option thereby moving into the money) in a short time would be very small. But a possibility of a sudden large downward jump that could move the puts into the money, as in a market crash, would impart greater value to these options. Thus, the market might price these options as though there is a bigger chance of a large drop in the stock price than would be suggested by the Black-Scholes assumptions. The result of the higher option price is a greater implied volatility derived from the Black-Scholes model.

Interestingly, Rubinstein points out that prior to the 1987 market crash, plots of implied volatility like the one in Figure 16.12 were relatively flat, consistent with the notion that the market was then less attuned to fears of a crash. However, postcrash plots have been consistently downward-sloping, exhibiting a shape often called the *option smirk*. When we use option-pricing models that allow for more general stock price distributions, including large downward jumps and random changes in volatility, they generate downward-sloping implied volatility curves similar to the one observed in Figure 16.12.[13]

SUMMARY

- Option values may be viewed as the sum of intrinsic value plus time or "volatility" value. The volatility value is the right to choose not to exercise if the stock price moves against the holder. Thus, option holders cannot lose more than the cost of the option regardless of stock price performance.

- Call options are more valuable when the exercise price is lower, when the stock price is higher, when the interest rate is higher, when the time to expiration is greater, when the stock's volatility is greater, and when dividends are lower.

- Options may be priced relative to the underlying stock price using a simple two-period, two-state pricing model. As the number of periods increases, the model can approximate more realistic stock price distributions. The Black-Scholes formula may be seen as a limiting case of the binomial option model, as the holding period is divided into progressively smaller subperiods.

- The put-call parity theorem relates the prices of put and call options. If the relationship is violated, arbitrage opportunities will result. Specifically, the relationship that must be satisfied is

$$P = C - S_0 + PV(X) + PV(\text{dividends})$$

[13]For an extensive discussion of these more general models, see R. L. McDonald, *Derivatives Markets,* 3rd ed. (Boston: Pearson Education, Addison-Wesley, 2013).

where X is the exercise price of both the call and the put options and $PV(X)$ is the present value of the claim to X dollars to be paid at the expiration date of the options.

- The implied volatility of an option is the standard deviation of stock returns consistent with an option's market price. It can be backed out of an option-pricing model by finding the stock volatility that makes the option's value equal to its observed price.

- The hedge ratio (or option delta) is the number of shares of stock required to hedge the price risk involved in writing one option. Hedge ratios are near zero for deep out-of-the-money call options and approach 1 for deep in-the-money calls.

- Although option deltas are less than 1, call options have elasticities greater than 1. The rate of return on a call (as opposed to the dollar return) responds more than one-for-one with stock price movements.

- Portfolio insurance can be obtained by purchasing a protective put option on an equity position. When the appropriate put is not traded, portfolio insurance entails a dynamic hedge strategy where a fraction of the equity portfolio equal to the desired put option's delta is sold, with proceeds placed in risk-free securities.

- Empirically, implied volatilities derived from the Black-Scholes formula tend to be lower on options with higher exercise prices. This may be evidence that the option prices reflect the possibility of a sudden dramatic decline in stock prices. Such "crashes" are inconsistent with the Black-Scholes assumptions.

KEY TERMS

binomial model, 527
Black-Scholes pricing
   formula, 530
delta, 540
dynamic hedging, 542

hedge ratio, 540
implied volatility, 534
intrinsic value, 520
option elasticity, 541
portfolio insurance, 542

put-call parity
   relationship, 537
time value, 520

KEY FORMULAS

Binomial model: $u = \exp(\sigma\sqrt{\Delta t});$ $d = \exp(-\sigma\sqrt{\Delta t});$ $p = \dfrac{\exp(r\Delta t) - d}{u - d}$

Put-call parity: $P = C + PV(X) - S_0 + PV(\text{Dividends})$

Black-Scholes formula: $C_0 = S_0 e^{-\delta T} N(d_1) - Xe^{-rT} N(d_2)$

$$d_1 = \frac{ln(S_0/X) + (r - \delta + \sigma^2/2)T}{\sigma\sqrt{T}}$$

$$d_2 = d_1 - \sigma\sqrt{T}$$

Delta (or hedge ratio): $H = \dfrac{\text{Change in option value}}{\text{Change in stock value}}$

PROBLEM SETS

Select problems are available in McGraw-Hill's *Connect*. Please see the Supplements section of the book's frontmatter for more information.

1. A call option with a strike price of $50 on a stock selling at $55 costs $6.50. What are the call option's intrinsic and time values? *(LO 16-1)*

2. A put option on a stock with a current price of $33 has an exercise price of $35. The price of the corresponding call option is $2.25. According to put-call parity, if the effective annual risk-free rate of interest is 4% and there are three months until expiration, what should be the price of the put? *(LO 16-4)*

3. A call option on Jupiter Motors stock with an exercise price of $75 and one-year expiration is selling at $3. A put option on Jupiter stock with an exercise price of $75 and one-year expiration is selling at $2.50. If the risk-free rate is 8% and Jupiter pays no dividends, what should the stock price be?   *(LO 16-4)*

4. We showed in the text that the value of a call option increases with the volatility of the stock. Is this also true of put option values? Use the put-call parity relationship as well as a numerical example to prove your answer.   *(LO 16-4)*

5. In each of the following questions, you are asked to compare two options with parameters as given. The risk-free interest rate for *all* cases should be assumed to be 6%. Assume the stocks on which these options are written pay no dividends.   *(LO 16-1)*

    a.

Put	T	X	σ	Price of Option
A	0.5	50	0.20	10
B	0.5	50	0.25	10

    Which put option is written on the stock with the lower price?
    (1) A
    (2) B
    (3) Not enough information

    b.

Put	T	X	σ	Price of Option
A	0.5	50	0.2	10
B	0.5	50	0.2	12

    Which put option must be written on the stock with the lower price?
    (1) A
    (2) B
    (3) Not enough information

    c.

Call	S	X	σ	Price of Option
A	50	50	0.20	12
B	55	50	0.20	10

    Which call option must have the lower time to expiration?
    (1) A
    (2) B
    (3) Not enough information

    d.

Call	T	X	S	Price of Option
A	0.5	50	55	10
B	0.5	50	55	12

    Which call option is written on the stock with higher volatility?
    (1) A
    (2) B
    (3) Not enough information

e.

Call	*T*	*X*	*S*	Price of Option
A	0.5	50	55	10
B	0.5	55	55	7

Which call option is written on the stock with higher volatility?

(1) A

(2) B

(3) Not enough information

6. Reconsider the determination of the hedge ratio in the two-state model (Section 16.2), where we showed that one-third share of stock would hedge one option. What would be the hedge ratio for each of the following exercise prices: (*a*) \$120; (*b*) \$110; (*c*) \$100; (*d*) \$90? What do you conclude about the hedge ratio as the option becomes progressively more in the money? *(LO 16-5)*

7. Show that Black-Scholes call option hedge ratios increase as the stock price increases. Consider a one-year option with exercise price \$50 on a stock with annual standard deviation 20%. The T-bill rate is 3% per year. Find $N(d_1)$ for stock prices (*a*) \$45, (*b*) \$50, and (*c*) \$55. *(LO 16-3)*

8. We will derive a two-state put option value in this problem. Data: $S_0 = 100$; $X = 110$; $1 + r = 1.10$. The two possibilities for S_T are 130 and 80. *(LO 16-2)*

   a. Show that the range of S is 50 while that of P is 30 across the two states. What is the hedge ratio of the put?

   b. Form a portfolio of three shares of stock and five puts. What is the (nonrandom) payoff to this portfolio?

   c. What is the present value of the portfolio?

   d. Given that the stock currently is selling at 100, show that the value of the put must be 10.91.

9. Calculate the value of a *call* option on the stock in the previous problem with an exercise price of 110. Verify that the put-call parity relationship is satisfied by your answers to both Problems 8 and 9. (Do not use continuous compounding to calculate the present value of X in this example, because the interest rate is quoted as an effective per-period rate.) *(LO 16-2)*

Use the following case in answering Problems 10–15.

Mark Washington, CFA, is an analyst with BIC. One year ago, BIC analysts predicted that the U.S. equity market would most likely experience a slight downturn and suggested delta-hedging the BIC portfolio. As predicted, the U.S. equity markets did indeed experience a downturn of approximately 4% over a 12-month period. However, portfolio performance for BIC was disappointing, lagging its peer group by nearly 10%. Washington has been told to review the options strategy to determine why the hedged portfolio did not perform as expected.

10. Which of the following *best* explains a delta-neutral portfolio? A delta-neutral portfolio is hedged against: *(LO 16-5)*

    a. Small price changes in the underlying asset.

    b. Small price decreases in the underlying asset.

    c. All price changes in the underlying asset.

11. After discussing the concept of a delta-neutral portfolio, Washington determines that he needs to further explain the concept of delta. Washington draws the value of an option as a function of the underlying stock price. Draw such a diagram, and indicate how delta is interpreted. Delta is the: *(LO 16-5)*

    a. Slope in the option price diagram.

    b. Curvature of the option price graph.

    c. Level in the option price diagram.

12. Washington considers a put option that has a delta of $-.65$. If the price of the underlying asset decreases by $6, then what is the best estimate of the change in option price? *(LO 16-5)*

13. BIC owns 51,750 shares of Smith & Oates. The shares are currently priced at $69. A call option on Smith & Oates with a strike price of $70 is selling at $3.50 and has a delta of .69. What is the number of call options necessary to create a delta-neutral hedge?   *(LO 16-5)*

14. Return to the previous problem. Will the number of call options written for a delta-neutral hedge increase or decrease if the stock price falls?   *(LO 16-5)*

15. Which of the following statements regarding the goal of a delta-neutral portfolio is *most* accurate? One example of a delta-neutral portfolio is to combine a: *(LO 16-5)*
    a. Long position in a stock with a short position in call options so that the value of the portfolio does not change with changes in the value of the stock.
    b. Long position in a stock with a short position in a call option so that the value of the portfolio changes with changes in the value of the stock.
    c. Long position in a stock with a long position in call options so that the value of the portfolio does not change with changes in the value of the stock.

Templates and spreadsheets are available in Connect

16. Use the Black-Scholes formula to find the value of a call option on the following stock:

    Time to expiration = 6 months

    Standard deviation = 50% per year

    Exercise price = $50

    Stock price = $50

    Interest rate = 3%

    Dividend = 0

    (LO 16-3)

Templates and spreadsheets are available in Connect

17. Find the Black-Scholes value of a put option on the stock in the previous problem with the same exercise price and expiration as the call option.   *(LO 16-3)*

18. Recalculate the value of the option in Problem 16, successively substituting one of the changes below while keeping the other parameters as in Problem 16:
    a. Time to expiration = 3 months
    b. Standard deviation = 25% per year
    c. Exercise price   = $55
    d. Stock price   = $55
    e. Interest rate   = 5%

    Consider each scenario independently. Confirm that the option value changes in accordance with the prediction of Table 16.1.   *(LO 16-3)*

Templates and spreadsheets are available in Connect

19. What would be the Excel formula in Spreadsheet 16.1 for the Black-Scholes value of a straddle position?   *(LO 16-3)*

20. Would you expect a $1 increase in a call option's exercise price to lead to a decrease in the option's value of more or less than $1?   *(LO 16-1)*

21. All else being equal, is a put option on a high-beta stock worth more than one on a low-beta stock? The firms have identical firm-specific risk.   *(LO 16-1)*

22. All else being equal, is a call option on a stock with a lot of firm-specific risk worth more than one on a stock with little firm-specific risk? The betas of the stocks are equal.   *(LO 16-1)*

23. All else being equal, will a call option with a high exercise price have a higher or lower hedge ratio than one with a low exercise price?   *(LO 16-5)*

24. Should the rate of return of a call option on a long-term Treasury bond be more or less sensitive to changes in interest rates than the rate of return of the underlying bond?   *(LO 16-1)*

25. If the stock price falls and the call price rises, then what has happened to the call option's implied volatility?   *(LO 16-1)*

26. If the time to expiration falls and the put price rises, then what has happened to the put option's implied volatility?   *(LO 16-1)*

27. According to the Black-Scholes formula, what will be the hedge ratio (delta) of a call option as the stock price becomes infinitely large? Explain briefly.   *(LO 16-5)*

28. According to the Black-Scholes formula, what will be the hedge ratio (delta) of a put option for a very small exercise price?   *(LO 16-5)*

29. The hedge ratio (delta) of an at-the-money call option on IBM is .4. The hedge ratio of an at-the-money put option is −.6. What is the hedge ratio of an at-the-money straddle position on IBM?   *(LO 16-5)*

30. Consider a six-month expiration European call option with exercise price $105. The underlying stock sells for $100 a share and pays no dividends. The risk-free rate is 5%. What is the implied volatility of the option if the option currently sells for $8? Use Spreadsheet 16.1 (available in Connect; link to Chapter 16 material) to answer this question.   *(LO 16-3)*

    ☒
    Templates and spreadsheets are available in Connect

    a. Go to the *Data* tab of the spreadsheet and select *Goal Seek* from the What-If menu. The dialog box will ask you for three pieces of information. In that dialog box, you should *set cell* E6 *to value* 8 *by changing cell* B2. In other words, you ask the spreadsheet to find the value of standard deviation (which appears in cell B2) that forces the value of the option (in cell E6) equal to $8. Then click *OK,* and you should find that the call is now worth $8, and the entry for standard deviation has been changed to a level consistent with this value. This is the call's implied standard deviation at a price of $8.

    b. What happens to implied volatility if the option is selling at $9? Why?

    c. What happens to implied volatility if the option price is unchanged at $8 but the time until option expiration is lower, say, only four months? Why?

    d. What happens to implied volatility if the option price is unchanged at $8 but the exercise price is lower, say, only $100? Why?

    e. What happens to implied volatility if the option price is unchanged at $8 but the stock price is lower, say, only $98? Why?

31. These three put options all are written on the same stock. One has a delta of −.9, one a delta of −.5, and one a delta of −.1. Assign deltas to the three puts by filling in the table below.   *(LO 16-5)*

Put	X	Delta
A	10	
B	20	
C	30	

32. In this problem, we derive the put-call parity relationship for European options on stocks that pay dividends before option expiration. For simplicity, assume that the stock makes one dividend payment of $D per share at the expiration date of the option.   *(LO 16-4)*

    a. What is the value of the stock-plus-put position on the expiration date of the option?

    b. Now consider a portfolio consisting of a call option and a zero-coupon bond with the same expiration date as the option and with face value $(X + D)$. What is the value of this portfolio on the option expiration date? You should find that its value equals that of the stock-plus-put portfolio, regardless of the stock price.

    c. What is the cost of establishing the two portfolios in parts (a) and (b)? Equate the cost of these portfolios, and you will derive the put-call parity relationship, Equation 16.3.

33. A collar is established by buying a share of stock for $50, buying a six-month put option with exercise price $45, and writing a six-month call option with exercise price $55. Based on the volatility of the stock, you calculate that for an exercise price of $45 and maturity of six months, $N(d_1) = .60$, whereas for the exercise price of $55, $N(d_1) = .35$.   *(LO 16-5)*

    a. What will be the gain or loss on the collar if the stock price increases by $1?

    b. What happens to the delta of the portfolio if the stock price becomes very large?

    c. Very small?

34. You are *very* bullish (optimistic) on stock EFG, much more so than the rest of the market. In each question, choose the portfolio strategy that will give you the biggest dollar profit if your bullish forecast turns out to be correct. Explain your answer. *(LO 16-5)*
    a. *Choice A:* $100,000 invested in calls with $X = 50$.
       Choice B: $100,000 invested in EFG stock.
    b. *Choice A:* 10 call options contracts (for 100 shares each), with $X = 50$.
       Choice B: 1,000 shares of EFG stock.

35. You are attempting to value a call option with an exercise price of $100 and one year to expiration. The underlying stock pays no dividends, its current price is $100, and you believe it has a 50% chance of increasing to $120 and a 50% chance of decreasing to $80. The risk-free rate of interest is 10%. Calculate the call option's value using the two-state stock price model. *(LO 16-2)*

36. Consider an increase in the volatility of the stock in the previous problem. Suppose that if the stock increases in price, it will increase to $130, and that if it falls, it will fall to $70. Show that the value of the call option is higher than the value derived using the original assumptions. *(LO 16-2)*

37. a. Return to Example 16.1. Use the binomial model to value a one-year European put option with exercise price $110 on the stock in that example.
    b. Show that your solution for the put price satisfies put-call parity. *(LO 16-2)*

Challenge

38. Imagine you are a provider of portfolio insurance. You are establishing a four-year program. The portfolio you manage is currently worth $100 million, and you promise to provide a minimum return of 0%. The equity portfolio has a standard deviation of 25% per year, and T-bills pay 5% per year. Assume for simplicity that the portfolio pays no dividends (or that all dividends are reinvested). *(LO 16-5)*
    a. What fraction of the portfolio should be placed in bills? What fraction in equity?
    b. What should the manager do if the stock portfolio falls by 3% on the first day of trading?

39. You would like to be holding a protective put position on the stock of XYZ Co. to lock in a guaranteed minimum value of $100 at year-end. XYZ currently sells for $100. Over the next year, the stock price will either increase by 10% or decrease by 10%. The T-bill rate is 5%. Unfortunately, no put options are traded on XYZ Co. *(LO 16-5)*
    a. Suppose the desired put option were traded. How much would it cost to purchase?
    b. What would have been the cost of the protective put portfolio?
    c. What portfolio position in stock and T-bills will ensure you a payoff equal to the payoff that would be provided by a protective put with $X = \$100$? Show that the payoff to this portfolio and the cost of establishing the portfolio match those of the desired protective put.

40. Suppose you are attempting to value a one-year maturity option on a stock with volatility (i.e., annualized standard deviation) of $\sigma = .40$. What would be the appropriate values for u and d if your binomial model is set up using the following? *(LO 16-2)*
    a. 1 period of one year
    b. 4 subperiods, each 3 months
    c. 12 subperiods, each 1 month

41. You build a binomial model with one period and assert that over the course of a year the stock price will either rise by a factor of 1.5 or fall by a factor of ⅔. What is your implicit assumption about the volatility of the stock's rate of return over the next year? *(LO 16-2)*

42. Use the put-call parity relationship to demonstrate that an at-the-money call option on a nondividend-paying stock must cost more than an at-the-money put option. Show that the prices of the put and call will be equal if $S = (1 + r)^T$. *(LO 16-4)*

43. Return to Problem 35. Value the call option using the risk-neutral shortcut described in the box. Confirm that your answer matches the value you get using the two-state approach. *(LO 16-2)*

44. *a.* Return to Problem 37. What will be the payoff to the put, P_u, if the stock goes up?
    b. What will be the payoff, P_d, if the stock price falls?
    c. Value the put option using the risk-neutral shortcut described in the box. Confirm that your answer matches the value you get using the two-state approach. *(LO 16-2)*

CFA Problems

1. Ken Webster manages a $400 million equity portfolio benchmarked to the S&P 500 Index. Webster believes the market is overvalued when measured by several traditional fundamental/economic indicators. He is therefore concerned about potential losses but recognizes that the S&P 500 Index could nevertheless move above its current 1,766 level. Webster is considering the following *option collar* strategy:
   - Protection for the portfolio can be attained by purchasing S&P 500 Index puts with a strike price of 1,760 (just out of the money).
   - The put can be partially financed by selling an equal number of call options with strike price 1,800 (further out-of-the-money) for every put purchased.
   - Because the combined delta of the call and put positions (see the following table) is greater than −1, (that is, −.44 −.30 = −.74), the options will not lose more than the underlying portfolio will gain if the market advances.

   The information in the following table describes the two options used to create the collar. *(LO 16-5)*

Characteristics	1,800 Call	1,760 Put
Option price	$27.20	$32.20
Option implied volatility	20%	22%
Option's delta	0.30	−0.44

Notes:
Ignore transaction costs.
S&P 500 historical 30-day volatility = 21%.
Time to option expiration = 30 days.

   a. Describe the potential returns of the combined portfolio (the underlying portfolio plus the option collar) if after 30 days the S&P 500 Index has:
       i. Risen approximately 5% to 1,854.
       ii. Remained at 1,766 (no change).
       iii. Declined by approximately 5% to 1,682.
       (No calculations are necessary.)
   b. Discuss the effect on the hedge ratio (delta) of *each* option as the S&P 500 approaches the level of *each* of the potential outcomes listed in part (*a*).
   c. Evaluate the pricing of each of the following in relation to the volatility data provided:
       i. The put
       ii. The call

2. Michael Weber, CFA, is analyzing several aspects of option valuation, including the determinants of the value of an option, the characteristics of various models used to value options, and the potential for divergence of calculated option values from observed market prices. *(LO 16-1)*
   a. What is the expected effect on the value of a call option on common stock if (i) the volatility of the underlying stock price decreases; (ii) the time to expiration of the option increases.
   b. Using the Black-Scholes option-pricing model, Weber calculates the price of a three-month call option and notices the option's calculated value is different from its market price. With respect to Weber's use of the Black-Scholes option-pricing model,

(i) discuss why the calculated value of an out-of-the-money European option may differ from its market price; (ii) discuss why the calculated value of an American option may differ from its market price.

3. A stock index is currently trading at 50. Paul Tripp, CFA, wants to value two-year index options using the binomial model. In any year, the stock will either increase in value by 20% or fall in value by 20%. The annual risk-free interest rate is 6%. No dividends are paid on any of the underlying securities in the index.   *(LO 16-2)*
   a. Construct a two-period binomial tree for the value of the stock index.
   b. Calculate the value of a European call option on the index with an exercise price of 60.
   c. Calculate the value of a European put option on the index with an exercise price of 60.
   d. Confirm that your solutions for the values of the call and the put satisfy put-call parity.

1. Use information from **finance.yahoo.com** to answer the following questions.
   a. What is Coke's current price?
   b. Now enter the ticker "KO" (for Coca-Cola) and find the *Analyst Opinion* tab. What is the mean 12-month target price for Coke? Based on this forecast, would at-the-money calls or puts have the higher expected profit?
   c. What is the spread between the high and low target stock prices, expressed as a percentage of Coke's current stock price? How (qualitatively) should the spread be related to the price at which Coke options trade?
   d. Calculate the implied volatility of the call option closest to the money with time to expiration of about three months. You can use Spreadsheet 16.1 (available in Connect) to calculate implied volatility using the Goal Seek command.
   e. Now repeat the exercise for Pepsi (ticker: PEP). What would you expect to be the relationship between the high versus low target price spread and the implied volatility of the two companies? Are your expectations consistent with actual option prices?
   f. Suppose you believe that the volatility of KO is going to increase from currently anticipated levels. Would its call options be overpriced or underpriced? What about its put options?
   g. Could you take positions in both puts and calls on KO in such a manner as to speculate on your volatility beliefs without taking a stance on whether the stock price is going to increase or decrease? Would you buy or write each type of option?
   h. How would your relative positions in puts and calls be related to the delta of each option?

2. Calculating implied volatility can be difficult if you don't have a spreadsheet handy. Fortunately, many tools are available on the web to perform the calculation; for example, **www.numa.com** contains option calculators that also compute implied volatility.

   Using daily price data, calculate the annualized standard deviation of the daily percentage change in a stock price. For the same stock, use these websites to find the implied volatility. Option price data can be retrieved from **www.cboe.com**.

   Recalculate the standard deviation using three months, six months, and nine months of daily data. Which of the calculations most closely approximates implied volatility? What time frame does the market seem to use for assessing stock price volatility?

SOLUTIONS TO
CONCEPT
check

16.1 Yes. Consider the same scenarios as for the call.

Stock price	$10	$20	$30	$40	$50
Put payoff	20	10	0	0	0
Stock price	20	25	30	35	40
Put payoff	10	5	0	0	0

The low volatility scenario yields a lower expected payoff.

16.2

If This Variable Increases . . .	The Value of a Put Option
S	Decreases
X	Increases
σ	Increases
T	Increases/Uncertain*
r_f	Decreases
Dividend payouts	Increases

*For American puts, increase in time to expiration *must* increase value. One can always choose to exercise early if this is optimal; the longer expiration date simply expands the range of alternatives open to the option holder, thereby making the option more valuable. For a European put, where early exercise is not allowed, longer time to expiration can have an indeterminate effect. Longer maturity increases volatility value because the final stock price is more uncertain, but it reduces the present value of the exercise price that will be received if the put is exercised. The net effect on put value is ambiguous.

16.3 Because the option now is underpriced, we want to reverse our previous strategy.

	Initial Cash Flow	Cash Flow in 1 Year for Each Possible Stock Price	
		$S = \$90$	$S = \$120$
Buy 3 options	−$16.50	$ 0	$ 30
Short-sell 1 share; repay in 1 year	100	−90	−120
Lend $83.50 at 10% interest rate	−83.50	91.85	91.85
Total	$ 0	$ 1.85	$ 1.85

The riskless cash flow in one year per option is $1.85/3 = $.6167, and the present value is $.6167/1.10 = $.56, precisely the amount by which the option is underpriced.

16.4 *a.* $C_u - C_d = \$6.984 - 0 = \$6.984$

   b. $uS_0 - dS_0 = \$110 - \$95 = \$15$

   c. $6.984/15 = .4656$

   d.

Action Today (time 0)	Value in Next Period as Function of Stock Price	
	$dS_0 = \$95$	$uS_0 = \$110$
Buy .4656 shares at price $S_0 = \$100$	$44.232	$51.216
Write 1 call at price C_0	0	−6.984
Total	$44.232	$44.232

The portfolio must have a market value equal to the present value of $44.232.

   e. $\$44.232/1.05 = \$42.126$

   f. $.4656 \times \$100 - C_0 = \$42.126$

   $C_0 = \$46.56 - \$42.126 = \$4.434$

16.5 When Δt shrinks, there should be lower possible dispersion in the stock price by the end of the subperiod because each shorter subperiod offers less time in which new information can move stock prices. However, as the time interval shrinks, there will be a correspondingly greater number of these subperiods until option expiration. Thus, *total* volatility over the remaining life of the option will be unaffected. In fact, take another look at Figure 16.2. There, despite the fact that u and d each get closer to 1 as the number of subintervals increases and the length of each subinterval falls, the total volatility of the stock return until option expiration is unaffected.

16.6 Because $\sigma = .6$, $\sigma^2 = .36$.

$$d_1 = \frac{\ln(100/95) + (.10 + .36/2).25}{.6\sqrt{.25}} = .4043$$

$$d_2 = d_1 - .6\sqrt{.25} = .1043$$

Using Table 16.2 and interpolation, or a spreadsheet function,

$$N(d_1) = .6570$$

$$N(d_2) = .5415$$

$$C = 100 \times .6570 - 95e^{-.10 \times .25} \times .5415 = 15.53$$

16.7 Implied volatility exceeds .5. Given a standard deviation of .5, the option value is $13.70. A higher volatility is needed to justify the actual $15 price. Using Spreadsheet 16.1 and Goal Seek, we find the implied volatility is .5714, or 57.14%.

16.8 A $1 increase in stock price is a percentage increase of $1/122 = .82\%$. The put option will *fall* by $(.4 \times \$1) = \$.40$, a percentage decrease of $\$.40/\$4 = 10\%$. Elasticity is $-10/.82 = -12.2$.

Futures Markets and Risk Management

Learning Objectives

LO 17-1 Calculate the profit on futures positions as a function of current and eventual futures prices.

LO 17-2 Formulate futures market strategies for hedging or speculative purposes.

LO 17-3 Compute the futures price appropriate to a given price on the underlying asset.

LO 17-4 Design arbitrage strategies to exploit futures market mispricing.

LO 17-5 Determine how swaps can be used to mitigate interest rate risk.

utures and forward contracts are like options in that they specify the purchase or sale of some underlying security at some future date. The key difference is that the holder of an option to buy is not compelled to buy and will not do so if the trade is unprofitable. A futures or forward contract, however, carries the obligation to go through with the agreed-upon transaction.

A forward contract is not an investment in the strict sense that funds are paid for an asset. It is only a commitment today to transact in the future. Forward arrangements are part of our study of investments, however, because they offer a powerful means to hedge other investments and generally modify portfolio characteristics.

Forward markets for future delivery of various commodities go back at least to ancient Greece. Organized *futures markets,* though, are a relatively modern development, dating only to the 19th century. Futures markets replace informal forward contracts with highly standardized, exchange-traded securities.

While futures markets have their roots in agricultural products and commodities, the markets today are dominated by trading in financial futures such as those on stock indexes, interest rate–dependent securities such as government bonds, and foreign exchange. The markets themselves also have changed, with trading today largely taking place in electronic markets.

This chapter describes the workings of futures markets and the mechanics of trading in these markets. We show how futures contracts are useful investment vehicles for both hedgers and speculators and how

17.1 THE FUTURES CONTRACT

To see how futures and forwards work and how they might be useful, consider the portfolio diversification problem facing a farmer growing a single crop, let us say wheat. The entire planting season's revenue depends critically on the highly volatile crop price. The farmer can't easily diversify his position because virtually his entire wealth is tied up in the crop.

The miller who must purchase wheat for processing faces a risk management problem that is the mirror image of the farmer's. He is subject to profit uncertainty because of the unpredictable cost of the wheat.

forward contract

An arrangement calling for future delivery of an asset at an agreed-upon price.

Both parties can hedge their risk by entering into a **forward contract** calling for the farmer to deliver the wheat when harvested at a price agreed upon now, regardless of the market price at harvest time. No money need change hands at this time. A forward contract is simply a deferred-delivery sale of some asset with the sales price agreed upon now. All that is required is that each party be willing to lock in the ultimate delivery price. The forward contract protects each from future price fluctuations.

Futures markets formalize and standardize forward contracting. Buyers and sellers do not have to rely on a chance matching of their interests; they can trade in a centralized market. The futures exchange also standardizes the types of contracts that may be traded: It establishes contract size, the acceptable grade of commodity, contract delivery dates, and so forth. While standardization eliminates much of the flexibility available in informal forward contracting, it has the offsetting advantage of liquidity because many traders will concentrate on the same small set of contracts. Futures contracts also differ from forward contracts in that they call for a daily settling up of any gains or losses on the contract. By contrast, no money changes hands in forward contracts until the delivery date.

In a centralized market, buyers and sellers can trade through brokers without searching for trading partners. The standardization of contracts and the depth of trading in each contract allows futures positions to be liquidated easily rather than personally renegotiated with the other party to the contract. Because the exchange guarantees the performance of each party, costly credit checks on other traders are not necessary. Instead, each trader simply posts a good-faith deposit, called the *margin,* to guarantee contract performance.

The Basics of Futures Contracts

futures price

The agreed-upon price to be paid on a futures contract at maturity.

The futures contract calls for delivery of a commodity at a specified delivery or maturity date, for an agreed-upon price, called the **futures price,** to be paid at contract maturity. The contract specifies precise requirements for the commodity. For agricultural commodities, the exchange sets allowable grades (e.g., No. 2 hard winter wheat or No. 1 soft red wheat). The place or means of delivery of the commodity is specified as well. Delivery of agricultural commodities is made by transfer of warehouse receipts issued by approved warehouses. For financial futures, delivery may be made by wire transfer; for index futures, delivery may be accomplished by a cash settlement procedure such as those used for index options. (Although the futures contract technically calls for delivery of an asset, delivery rarely occurs. Instead, parties to the contract much more commonly close out their positions before contract maturity, taking gains or losses in cash. We will show you how this is done later in the chapter.)

Because the futures exchange specifies all the terms of the contract, the traders need bargain only over the futures price. The trader taking the **long position** commits to purchasing the commodity on the delivery date. The trader who takes the **short position** commits to delivering the commodity at contract maturity. The trader in the long position is said to "buy" a contract; the short-side trader "sells" a contract. The words *buy* and *sell* are figurative only, because a contract is not really bought or sold like a stock or bond; it is entered into by mutual agreement. At the time the contract is entered into, no money changes hands.

long position

The futures trader who commits to purchasing the asset.

short position

The futures trader who commits to delivering the asset.

Figure 17.1 shows prices for a sample of futures contracts as they appear in *The Wall Street Journal*. The boldface heading lists in each case the commodity, the exchange where the futures contract is traded in parentheses, the contract size, and the pricing unit. For example, the first contract listed under "Agriculture Futures" is for corn, traded on the Chicago Board of Trade (CBT). Each contract calls for delivery of 5,000 bushels, and prices in the entry are quoted in cents per bushel.

The next several rows detail price data for contracts expiring on various dates. The December maturity corn contract, for example, opened during the day at a futures price of 374.75 cents per bushel. The highest futures price during the day was 381, the lowest was 371.50, and the settlement price (a representative trading price during the last few minutes of trading) was 374.00. The settlement price fell by 1.25 cents from the previous trading day. Finally, open interest, or the number of outstanding contracts, was 629,009. Similar information is given for each maturity date.

The trader holding the long position, that is, the person who will purchase the good, profits from price increases. Suppose that when the contract matures, the price of corn turns out to be 379 cents per bushel. The long position trader who entered the contract at the futures price of 374 cents on October 30 (the date of *The Wall Street Journal* listing) earns a profit of 5 cents per bushel: The eventual price is 5 cents higher than the originally agreed-upon futures price. As each contract calls for delivery of 5,000 bushels, the profit to the long position equals $5,000 \times \$.05 = \$250$ per contract. Conversely, the short position loses 5 cents per bushel. The short position's loss equals the long position's gain.

To summarize, at maturity

$$\text{Profit to long} = \text{Spot price at maturity} - \text{Original futures price}$$
$$\text{Profit to short} = \text{Original futures price} - \text{Spot price at maturity}$$

where the spot price is the actual market price of the commodity at the time of the delivery.

The futures contract, therefore, is a *zero sum game,* with losses and gains to all positions netting out to zero. Every long position is offset by a short position. The aggregate profits to futures trading, summing over all investors, also must be zero, as is the net exposure to changes in the commodity price.

Figure 17.2, Panel A, is a plot of the profits realized by an investor who enters the long side of a futures contract as a function of the price of the asset on the maturity date. Notice that profit is zero when the ultimate spot price, P_T, equals the initial futures price, F_0. Profit per unit of the underlying asset rises or falls one-for-one with changes in the final spot price. Unlike the payoff of a call option, the payoff of the long futures position can be negative: This will be the case if the spot price falls below the original futures price. Unlike the holder of a call, who has an *option* to buy, the long futures position trader cannot simply walk away from the contract. Also unlike options, in the case of futures there is no need to distinguish gross payoffs from net profits. This is because the futures contract is not purchased; it is simply a contract that is agreed to by two parties. The futures price adjusts to make the present value of either side of the contract equal to zero.

The distinction between futures and options is highlighted by comparing Panel A of Figure 17.2 to the payoff and profit diagrams for an investor in a call option with exercise price, *X*, chosen equal to the futures price F_0 (see Panel C). The futures investor is exposed to considerable losses if the asset price falls. In contrast, the investor in the call cannot lose more than the cost of the option.

Futures listings for October 30, 2014

Source: From *The Wall Street Journal*, October 31, 2014.

Futures Prices

Metal & Petroleum Futures

	Open	High	hi lo	Low	Settle	Chg	Open Interest
Copper-High (CMX)-25,000 lbs.; $ per lb.							
Nov	3.0910	3.0910		3.0500	3.0720	−0.0395	2,111
Dec	3.0820	3.0875		3.0360	3.0625	−0.0420	103,395
Gold (CMX)-100 troy oz.; $ per troy oz.							
Nov	1213.70	1214.70		1195.80	1198.10	−26.20	274
Dec	1211.20	1216.50		1195.50	1198.60	−26.30	275,404
Feb'15	1212.70	1217.30		1196.60	1199.50	−26.40	55,851
April	1217.70	1217.70		1197.20	1200.10	−26.30	25,700
June	1214.70	1215.80		1197.90	1200.70	−26.30	17,581
Dec	1216.30	1217.60		1199.60	1202.90	−26.10	14,360
miNY Gold (CMX)-50 troy oz.; $ per troy oz.							
Dec	1212.50	1214.00		1195.75	1198.50	−26.50	838
Feb'15	1214.00	1215.00		1197.75	1199.50	−26.50	28
June	1206.00	1216.00		1201.75	1200.75	−26.25	10
Dec	1203.00	1203.00	▼	1203.00	1203.00	−26.00	n.a.
Palladium (NYM)-50 troy oz.; $ per troy oz.							
Nov	772.50	772.50		772.45	780.35	−20.00	5
Dec	795.35	795.40		775.30	780.70	−20.00	30,097
March'15	792.00	792.00		778.40	781.50	−20.00	2,769
June	784.35	784.35		784.35	781.45	−20.00	31
Platinum (NYM)-50 troy oz.; $ per troy oz.							
Nov	1243.50	1243.50		1243.50	1246.90	−23.10	2
Jan'15	1260.80	1262.20		1240.00	1245.90	−23.30	56,872
Silver (CMX)-5,000 troy oz.; $ per troy oz.							
Nov	16.350	16.350	▼	16.340	16.391	−0.833	519
Dec	17.095	17.205	▼	16.330	16.420	−0.844	118,765
miNY Silver (CMX)-2500 troy oz.; $ per troy oz.							
Dec	17.075	17.200	▼	16.325	16.425	−0.837	200
Jan'15	16.475	16.475	▼	16.475	16.438	−0.850	8
March	16.700	16.700	▼	16.400	16.475	−0.850	20
Crude Oil, Light Sweet (NYM)-1,000 bbls.; $ per bbl.							
Dec	81.93	82.09		80.72	81.12	−1.08	324,039
Jan'15	81.78	81.82		80.49	80.90	−1.06	178,360
March	81.32	81.43		80.25	80.64	−1.04	118,247
June	81.09	81.21		80.16	80.51	−0.88	135,563
Dec	80.75	80.84		80.08	80.41	−0.68	151,244
Dec'16	80.55	80.68		80.05	80.50	−0.42	70,259
Heating Oil No. 2 (NYM)-42,000 gal.; $ per gal.							
Nov	2.5315	2.5335		2.5005	2.5128	−.0222	12,481
Dec	2.5184	2.5220		2.4907	2.5050	−.0185	113,490
Gasoline-NY RBOB (NYM)-42,000 gal.; $ per gal.							
Nov	2.2211	2.2243		2.1853	2.1958	−.0249	11,016
Dec	2.1800	2.1848		2.1486	2.1610	−.0206	125,328
Natural Gas (NYM)-10,000 MMBtu.; $ per MMBtu.							
Dec	3.793	3.873		3.768	3.827	.039	165,409
Jan'15	3.883	3.948		3.848	3.906	.035	188,329
Feb	3.869	3.940		3.842	3.900	.034	61,548
March	3.813	3.867		3.776	3.831	.032	97,465
April	3.614	3.666		3.590	3.642	.028	78,384
May	3.588	3.651		3.577	3.623	.028	48,581

Agriculture Futures

	Open	High	hi lo	Low	Settle	Chg	Open Interest
Corn (CBT)-5,000 bu.; cents per bu.							
Dec	374.75	381.00		371.50	374.00	−1.25	629,009
March'15	388.00	394.25		384.25	387.00	−1.50	306,156
Ethanol (CBT)-29,000 gal.; $ per gal.							
Nov	1.808	1.844		1.804	1.837	−.00	113
Dec	1.750	1.755		1.725	1.744	−.01	2,304
Oats (CBT)-5,000 bu.; cents per bu.							
Dec	350.50	353.00		338.00	338.50	−12.00	6,862
March'15	340.00	343.50		330.50	331.25	−10.25	2,589
Soybeans (CBT)-5,000 bu.; cents per bu.							
Nov	1042.50	1053.75		1023.50	1024.25	−18.75	49,653
Jan'15	1048.50	1059.25		1029.00	1029.75	−19.25	304,088
Soybean Meal (CBT)-100 tons; $ per ton.							
Dec	400.50	408.50		379.00	380.00	−17.20	124,448
Jan'15	375.20	384.00		360.00	361.10	−13.50	77,586
Soybean Oil (CBT)-60,000 lbs.; cents per lb.							
Dec	34.26	34.59		33.80	34.31	.13	157,989
Jan'15	34.45	34.80		34.03	34.54	.13	97,883
Rough Rice (CBT)-2,000 cwt.; $ per cwt.							
Nov	1204.50	1215.50		1183.00	1191.00	−22.00	927
Jan'15	1229.50	1242.50		1214.00	1221.00	−16.50	6,649
Wheat (CBT)-5,000 bu.; cents per bu.							
Dec	538.25	545.50		532.50	536.00	−2.25	219,598
March'15	553.75	558.00		544.75	549.00	−2.00	106,615
Wheat (KC)-5,000 bu.; cents per bu.							
Dec	606.00	611.75		599.50	602.00	−4.50	79,515
March'15	611.00	616.25		604.50	607.25	−4.00	39,277
Wheat (MPLS)-5,000 bu.; cents per bu.							
Dec	581.50	586.50	▲	575.75	577.75	−4.75	27,284
March'15	592.50	596.75	▲	587.00	588.75	−3.75	19,971
Cattle-Feeder (CME)-50,000 lbs.; cents per lb.							
Oct	239.400	239.850		239.400	239.750	.900	3,351
Jan'15	228.000	229.375		226.950	228.475	.525	17,885
Cattle-Live (CME)-40,000 lbs.; cents per lb.							
Oct	169.400	171.350	▲	169.100	170.500	1.500	991
Dec	166.925	168.000		166.100	167.325	.575	141,548
Hogs-Lean (CME)-40,000 lbs.; cents per lb.							
Dec	89.200	89.550		86.150	87.200	−1.400	92,857
Feb'15	88.600	88.750		86.100	86.950	−1.100	58,234
Lumber (CME)-110,000 bd.ft., $ per 1,000 bd.ft.							
Nov	322.80	324.80		321.00	323.60	2.00	716
Jan'15	322.30	325.00		320.00	322.60	1.70	2,924
Milk (CME)-200,000 lbs.; cents per lb.							
Nov	21.30	21.39		21.23	21.25	−.12	4,508
Dec	19.21	19.39		19.21	19.28	−.08	3,920
Cocoa (ICE-US)-10 metric tons; $ per ton.							
Dec	2,925	2,953		2,917	2,946	9	64,841
March'15	2,908	2,943		2,906	2,939	14	66,139

	Open	High	hi lo	Low	Settle	Chg	Open Interest
Coffee (ICE-US)-37,500 lbs.; cents per lb.							
Dec	189.95	190.95		186.25	187.60	−2.00	68,232
March'15	193.80	195.25		190.65	192.00	−1.95	59,546
Sugar-World (ICE-US)-112,000 lbs.; cents per lb.							
March	16.34	16.37		16.15	16.30	...	473,691
May	16.60	16.64		16.45	16.59	−.01	106,207
Sugar-Domestic (ICE-US)-112,000 lbs.; cents per lb.							
Jan	24.75	24.75		24.75	24.70	−.16	1,427
March	25.25	25.25		25.25	25.00	−.01	1,459
Cotton (ICE-US)-50,000 lbs.; cents per lb.							
Dec	65.34	66.05		64.33	64.50	−.85	96,533
March'15	63.20	63.80		62.77	63.02	−.20	73,723
Orange Juice (ICE-US)-15,000 lbs.; cents per lb.							
Nov	135.50	136.45		133.95	134.45	−1.20	1,606
Jan'15	139.20	139.80		137.95	139.05	.15	9,999

Interest Rate Futures

	Open	High	hi lo	Low	Settle	Chg	Open Interest
Treasury Bonds (CBT)-$100,000; pts 32nds of 100%							
Dec	141−150	142−040		141−080	141−180	6.0	849,866
June'15	150−200	151−000		150−100	140−200	10.0	254
Treasury Notes (CBT)-$100,000; pts 32nds of 100%							
Dec	126−175	126−245		126−100	126−200	5.5	2,714,061
March'15	125−275	126−010		125−195	125−285	6.0	15,635
5 Yr. Treasury Notes (CBT)-$100,000; pts 32nds of 100%							
Dec	119−167	119−207		119−115	119−190	4.7	1,877,372
March'15	118−240	118−240		118−195	118−267	5.0	14,027
2 Yr. Treasury Notes (CBT)-$200,000; pts 32nds of 100%							
Dec	109−260	109−270		109−245	109−260	.2	1,353,724
March'15	109−140	109−150		109−132	109−142	.5	3,920
30 Day Federal Funds (CBT)-$5,000,000; 100-daily avg.							
Oct	99.910	99.913		99.910	99.913	...	33,626
April'15	99.885	99.890		99.885	99.885	...	62,890
10 Yr. Del. Int. Rate Swaps (CBT)-$100,000; pts 32nds of 100%							
Dec	104.531	104.875		104.531	104.656	.172	52,366
1 Month Libor (CME)-$3,000,000; pts of 100%							
Nov	...	...		...	99.8450	−.0050	851
Eurodollar (CME)-$1,000,000; pts of 100%							
Nov	99.7650	99.7675		99.7650	99.7650	−.0050	39,278
March'15	99.7400	99.7500		99.7300	99.7400	...	1,311,638
June	99.6050	99.6300		99.5950	99.6150	.0100	1,137,595
Dec	99.1650	99.2000		99.1450	99.1850	.0250	1,320,450

Currency Futures

	Open	High	hi lo	Low	Settle	Chg	Open Interest
Japanese Yen (CME)-¥12,500,000; $ per 100¥							
Dec	.9191	.9197		.9137	.9149	−.0047	183,867
June'16	...	...		...	.9268	−.0045	7,000
Canadian Dollar (CME)-CAD 100,000; $ per CAD							
Dec	.8929	.8946		.8899	.8924	.0002	86,303
March'15	.8909	.8924		.8880	.8903	.0002	8,189
British Pound (CME)-£62,500; $ per £							
Dec	1.6008	1.6032		1.5944	1.5997	−.0016	138,889
March'15	1.5997	1.6018		1.5935	1.5984	−.0016	1,206
Swiss Franc (CME)-CHF 125,000; $ per CHF							
Dec	1.0481	1.0484		1.0407	1.0463	−.0026	57,361
March'15	1.0460	1.0486		1.0420	1.0474	−.0026	345
Australian Dollar (CME)-AUD 100,000; $ per AUD							
Dec	.8765	.8813	▲	.8728	.8803	.0033	103,907
March'15	.8680	.8755		.8672	.8746	.0028	501
Mexican Peso (CME)-MXN 500,000; $ per MXN							
Nov	...	...	▲	...	.07431	.00022	
Dec	.07386	.07432		.07373	.07418	.00022	121,711
Euro (CME)-€125,000; $ per €							
Dec	1.2639	1.2643		1.2548	1.2616	−.0033	437,202
March'15	1.2643	1.2643		1.2550	1.2624	−.0032	6,589
Euro/Japanese Yen (ICE-US)-€125,000; ¥ per €							
Dec	137.61	137.61		137.08	137.89	.34	358
Euro/British Pound (ICE-US)-€125,000; £ per €							
Dec	.7899	.7899		.7899	.7887	−.0013	983
Euro/Swiss Franc (ICE-US)-€125,000; CHF per €							
Dec	...	...	▲	...	1.2058	−.0001	1,106

Index Futures

	Open	High	hi lo	Low	Settle	Chg	Open Interest
DJ Industrial Average (corn)-$10 x index							
Dec	16932	17145		16832	17114	190	11,263
Mini DJ Industrial Average (CBT)-$5 x index							
Dec	16912	17152		16831	17114	190	115,609
March'15	16790	17066	▲	16790	17042	194	222
S&P 500 Index (CME)-$250 x index							
Dec	1970.90	1993.50		1959.30	1988.60	16.40	148,145
March'15	1963.90	1985.40		1960.40	1980.80	16.40	6,840
Mini S&P 500 (CME)-$50 x index							
Dec	1971.75	1994.25		1959.25	1988.50	16.25	2,854,076
March'15	1963.00	1986.25		1951.50	1980.75	16.25	28,128
Mini S&P Midcap 400 (CME)-$100 x index							
Dec	1392.10	1401.90		1381.80	1399.30	6.60	105,977
Nasdaq 100 (CME)-$100 x index							
Dec	4064.25	4104.00		4043.50	4089.50	17.25	10,117
Mini Nasdaq 100 (CME)-$20 x index							
Dec	4072.3	4102.5		4043.0	4089.5	17.3	327,531
March'15	4070.5	4096.3		4039.0	4082.5	17.8	393
Mini Russell 2000 (ICE-US)-$100 x index							
Dec	1139.80	1158.30		1131.60	1153.80	12.10	377,986
March'15	1125.80	1154.10		1125.80	1149.30	12.10	13,013
Mini Russell 1000 (ICE-US)-$100 x index							
Dec	1092.00	1108.20		1092.00	1105.50	8.00	8,576
U.S. Dollar Index (ICE-US)-$1,000 x index							
Dec	86.10	86.59		86.08	86.23	.20	76,417
March'15	86.30	86.70		86.28	86.40	.20	3,275

FIGURE 17.2

Profits to buyers and sellers of futures and options contracts

A: Long futures position (buyer), **B:** Short futures position (seller), **C:** Buy call option

A: Long futures profit = $P_T - F_0$

B: Short futures profit = $F_0 - P_T$

C: Buy a call option

Figure 17.2, Panel B, is a plot of the profits realized by an investor who enters the short side of a futures contract. It is the mirror image of the profit diagram for the long position.

> **CONCEPT check 17.1**
>
> a. Compare the profit diagram in Figure 17.2, Panel B, to the payoff diagram for a long position in a put option. Assume the exercise price of the option equals the initial futures price.
>
> b. Compare the profit diagram in Figure 17.2, Panel B, to the payoff diagram for an investor who writes a call option.

Existing Contracts

Futures and forward contracts are traded on a wide variety of goods in four broad categories: agricultural commodities, metals and minerals (including energy commodities), foreign currencies, and financial futures (fixed-income securities and stock market indexes). In addition to indexes on broad stock indexes, one can now trade so-called **single stock futures** on individual stocks and narrowly based indexes. OneChicago has operated an entirely electronic market in single stock futures since 2002. The exchange maintains futures markets in actively traded stocks with the most liquidity as well as in some popular ETFs such as those on the S&P 500 (ticker SPY), the NASDAQ 100 (ticker QQQ), or the Dow Jones Industrial Average (DIA). However, trading volume in single stock futures has to date been disappointing.

single stock futures
A futures contract on the shares of an individual company.

Innovation in financial futures has been rapid and is ongoing. Table 17.1 offers a sample of contracts trading in 2014. Contracts now trade on items that would not have been considered possible only a few years ago. For example, there are now electricity as well as weather futures and options contracts. Weather derivatives (which trade on the Chicago Mercantile Exchange) have payoffs that depend on average weather conditions, for example, the number of degree-days by which the temperature in a region exceeds or falls short of 65 degrees Fahrenheit. The potential use of these derivatives in managing the risk surrounding electricity or oil and natural gas use should be evident.

While Table 17.1 includes many contracts, the large and ever-growing array of markets makes this list necessarily incomplete. The nearby box discusses some comparatively fanciful futures markets in which payoffs may be tied to the winner of presidential elections, the box office receipts of a particular movie, or anything else in which participants are willing to take positions.

Outside the futures markets, a well-developed network of banks and brokers has established a forward market in foreign exchange. This forward market is not a formal exchange in

PREDICTION MARKETS

If you find S&P 500 or T-bond contracts a bit dry, perhaps you'd be interested in futures contracts with payoffs that depend on the winner of the next presidential election, or the severity of the next influenza season, or the host city of the 2024 Olympics. You can now find "futures markets" in these events and many others.

For example, both Iowa Electronic Markets (www.biz.uiowa .edu/iem) and the *Politics* page of Betfair (www.betfair.com) maintain presidential futures markets. In July 2011, you could have purchased a contract that would pay off $1 in November 2012 if the Republican candidate won the presidential race but nothing if he lost. The contract price (expressed as a percentage of face value) therefore may be viewed as the probability of a Republican victory, at least according to the consensus view of market participants at the time. If you believed in July that the probability of a Republican victory was 55%, you would have been prepared to pay up to $.55 for the contract. Alternatively, if you had wished to bet against the Republicans, you could have *sold* the contract. Similarly, you could bet on (or against) a Democrat victory using the Democrat contract. (When there are only two relevant parties, betting on one is equivalent to betting against the other, but in other elections, such as primaries where there are several viable candidates, selling one candidate's contract is not the same as buying another's.)

The accompanying figure shows the price of each contract from July 2011 through Election Day 2012. The price clearly tracks each candidate's perceived prospects. You can see Obama's price rise dramatically in the days shortly before the election as it became ever clearer that he would win.

Interpreting prediction market prices as probabilities actually requires a caveat. Because the contract payoff is risky, the price of the contract may reflect a risk premium. Therefore, to be precise, these probabilities are actually risk-neutral probabilities. In practice, however, it seems unlikely that the risk premium associated with these contracts is substantial.

Prediction markets for the 2012 presidential election. Contract on each party pays $1 if the party wins the election. Price is in cents.

Source: Iowa Electronic Markets, downloaded January 25, 2013.

the sense that the exchange specifies the terms of the traded contract. Instead, participants in a forward contract may negotiate for delivery of any quantity of goods at any time, whereas, in the formal futures markets, contract size and delivery dates are set by the exchange. In forward arrangements, banks and brokers simply negotiate contracts for clients (or themselves) as needed. This market is huge: More than $5 trillion of currency trades each day.

TABLE 17.1	Sample of futures contracts			
Foreign Currencies	**Agricultural**	**Metals and Energy**	**Interest Rate Futures**	**Equity Indexes**
British pound	Corn	Copper	Eurodollars	Dow Jones Industrials
Canadian dollar	Oats	Aluminum	Euroyen	S&P Midcap 400
Japanese yen	Soybeans	Gold	Euro-denominated	NASDAQ 100
Euro	Soybean meal	Platinum	bond	NYSE Index
Swiss franc	Soybean oil	Palladium	Euroswiss	Russell 2000 Index
Australian dollar	Wheat	Silver	Sterling	Nikkei 225 (Japanese)
Mexican peso	Barley	Crude oil	British gov't bond	FTSE Index (British)
Brazilian real	Flaxseed	Heating oil	German gov't bond	CAC Index (French)
New Zealand dollar	Canola	Gas oil	Italian gov't bond	DAX Index (German)
	Rye	Natural gas	Canadian gov't bond	All ordinary (Australian)
	Cattle	Gasoline	Treasury bonds	Toronto 35 (Canadian)
	Milk	Propane	Treasury notes	Titans 30 (Italian)
	Hogs	Commodity index	Treasury bills	Dow Jones Euro STOXX 50
	Pork bellies	Electricity	LIBOR	Industry indexes, e.g.,
	Cocoa	Weather	EURIBOR	banking
	Coffee		Municipal bond index	natural resources
	Cotton		Federal funds rate	chemical
	Orange juice		Bankers' acceptance	health care
	Sugar		S&P 500 Index	technology
	Lumber		Interest rate swaps	retail
	Rice			utilities
				telecom

17.2 TRADING MECHANICS

The Clearinghouse and Open Interest

Until about 15 years ago, most futures trades in the United States occurred among floor traders in the "trading pit" for each contract. Today, however, trading is overwhelmingly conducted through electronic networks, particularly for financial futures.

The impetus for this shift originated in Europe, where electronic trading is the norm. Eurex, which is jointly owned by the Deutsche Börse and Swiss exchange, is among the world's largest derivatives exchanges. It operates a fully electronic trading and clearing platform and, in 2004, received clearance from regulators to list contracts in the U.S. In response, the Chicago Board of Trade adopted an electronic platform provided by Eurex's European rival Euronext.liffe,[1] and the CBOT's Treasury contracts are now traded electronically. The Chicago Mercantile Exchange maintains another electronic trading system called Globex. These electronic exchanges enable trading around the clock. The CBOT and CME merged in 2007 into one combined company, named the CME Group, with all electronic trading from both exchanges moving onto Globex.

---

[1]Euronext.liffe is the international derivatives market of Euronext. It resulted from Euronext's purchase of LIFFE (the London International Financial Futures and Options Exchange) and a merger with the Lisbon exchange in 2002. Euronext was itself the result of a 2000 merger of the exchanges of Amsterdam, Brussels, and Paris.

clearinghouse

Established by exchanges to facilitate trading. The clearing-house may interpose itself as an intermediary between two traders.

Once a trade is agreed to, the **clearinghouse** enters the picture. Rather than having the long and short traders hold contracts with each other, the clearinghouse becomes the seller of the contract for the long position and the buyer of the contract for the short position. The clearing-house is obligated to deliver the commodity to the long position and to pay for delivery from the short; consequently, the clearinghouse's position nets to zero. This arrangement makes the clearinghouse the trading partner of each trader, both long and short. The clearinghouse, bound to perform on its side of each contract, is the only party that can be hurt by the failure of any trader to observe the obligations of the futures contract. This arrangement is necessary because a futures contract calls for future performance, which cannot be as easily guaranteed as an immediate stock transaction.

Figure 17.3 illustrates the role of the clearinghouse. Panel A shows what would happen in the absence of the clearinghouse. The trader in the long position would be obligated to pay the futures price to the short position, and the trader in the short position would be obligated to deliver the commodity. Panel B shows how the clearinghouse becomes an intermediary, acting as the trading partner for each side of the contract. The clearinghouse's position is neutral, as it takes a long and a short position for each transaction.

The clearinghouse makes it possible for traders to liquidate positions easily. If you are currently long in a contract and want to undo your position, you simply instruct your broker to enter the short side of a contract to close out your position. This is called a *reversing trade*. The exchange nets out your long and short positions, reducing your net position to zero. Your zero net position with the clearinghouse eliminates the need to fulfill at maturity either the original long or reversing short position.

The *open interest* on the contract is the number of contracts outstanding. (Long and short positions are not counted separately, meaning that open interest can be defined as either the number of long or short contracts outstanding.) The clearinghouse's position nets out to zero, and so it is not counted in the computation of open interest. When contracts begin trading, open interest is zero. As time passes, open interest increases as progressively more contracts are entered.

There are many apocryphal stories about futures traders who wake up to discover a small mountain of wheat or corn on their front lawn. But the truth is that futures contracts rarely result in actual delivery of the underlying asset. Traders establish long or short positions in contracts that will benefit from a rise or fall in the futures price and almost always close out those positions before the contract expires. The fraction of contracts that result in actual delivery is estimated to range from less than 1% to 3%, depending on the commodity and activity

FIGURE   17.3   **Trading with and without a clearinghouse**

in the contract. In the unusual case of actual deliveries of commodities, they occur via regular channels of supply, usually via warehouse receipts.

You can see the typical pattern of open interest in Figure 17.1. In the gold contract, for example, the November delivery contracts are close to maturity and open interest is small; most contracts have been reversed already. The next few maturities have significantly greater open interest. Finally, the most distant maturity contracts have less open interest, as they have been available only recently and few participants have yet traded. For other contracts such as crude oil futures, for which the nearest maturity is still more than a month away, open interest is highest in the nearest contract.

Marking to Market and the Margin Account

The total profit or loss realized by the long trader who buys a contract at time 0 and closes, or reverses, it at time t is just the change in the futures price over the period, $F_t - F_0$. Symmetrically, the short trader earns $F_0 - F_t$.

The process by which profits or losses accrue to traders is called **marking to market.** At initial execution of a trade, each trader establishes a margin account. The margin is a security account consisting of cash or near-cash securities, such as Treasury bills, that ensures the trader will be able to satisfy the obligations of the futures contract. Because both parties to the futures contract are exposed to losses, both must post margin. To illustrate, return to the December corn contract listed in Figure 17.1. If the initial required margin on corn, for example, is 10%, the trader must post $1,870 per contract for the margin account. This is 10% of the value of the contract ($3.74 per bushel × 5,000 bushels per contract).

marking to market

The daily settlement of obligations on futures positions.

Because the initial margin may be satisfied by posting interest-earning securities, the requirement does not impose a significant opportunity cost of funds on the trader. The initial margin is usually set between 5% and 15% of the total value of the contract. Contracts written on assets with more volatile prices require higher margins.

On any day that futures contracts trade, futures prices may rise or fall. Instead of waiting until the maturity date for traders to realize all gains and losses, the clearinghouse requires all positions to recognize profits as they accrue daily. If the futures price of corn rises from 374 to 376 cents per bushel, for example, the clearinghouse credits the margin account of the long position for 5,000 bushels times 2 cents per bushel, or $100 per contract. Conversely, for the short position, the clearinghouse takes this amount from the margin account for each contract held. Therefore, as futures prices change, proceeds accrue to the trader's account immediately.

Marking to market is the major way in which futures and forward contracts differ, besides contract standardization. Futures follow this pay- (or receive-) as-you-go method. Forward contracts are simply held until maturity, and no funds are transferred until that date, although the contracts may be traded.

What must be the net inflow or outlay from marking to market for the clearinghouse?	**CONCEPT** check	**17.2**

If a trader accrues sustained losses from daily marking to market, the margin account may fall below a critical value called the **maintenance margin.** If the value of the account falls below this value, the trader receives a *margin call,* requiring that the margin account be replenished or the position be reduced to a size commensurate with the remaining funds. Margins and margin calls safeguard the position of the clearinghouse. Positions are closed out before the margin account is exhausted—the trader's losses are covered, and the clearinghouse is not put at risk.

maintenance margin

An established value below which a trader's margin may not fall. Reaching the maintenance margin triggers a margin call.

EXAMPLE 17.1

Suppose the maintenance margin is 5% while the initial margin was 10% of the value of the corn, or $1,870. Then a margin call will go out when the original margin account has fallen about in half, or by $935. Each 1-cent decline in the corn price results in a $50 loss to the long position. Therefore, the futures price need fall only by 19 cents to trigger a margin call.

Maintenance Margin

On the contract maturity date, the futures price will equal the spot price of the commodity. As a maturing contract calls for immediate delivery, the futures price on that day must equal the spot price—the cost of the commodity from the two competing sources is equalized in a competitive market.[2] You may obtain delivery of the commodity either by purchasing it directly in the spot market or by entering the long side of a maturing futures contract.

A commodity available from two sources (the spot and futures markets) must be priced identically, or else investors will rush to purchase it from the cheap source in order to sell it in the high-priced market. Such arbitrage activity could not persist without prices adjusting to eliminate the arbitrage opportunity. Therefore, the futures price and the spot price must converge at maturity. This is called the **convergence property.**

convergence property

The convergence of futures prices and spot prices at the maturity of the futures contract.

For an investor who establishes a long position in a contract now (time 0) and holds that position until maturity (time T), the sum of all daily settlements will equal $F_T - F_0$, where F_T stands for the futures price at contract maturity. Because of convergence, however, the futures price at maturity, F_T, equals the spot price, P_T, so total futures profits also may be expressed as $P_T - F_0$. Thus, we see that profits on a futures contract held to maturity perfectly track changes in the value of the underlying asset.

EXAMPLE 17.2

Marking to Market and Futures Contract Profits

Assume the current futures price for silver for delivery five days from today is $16.10 per ounce. Suppose that over the next five days, the futures price evolves as follows:

Day	Futures Price
0 (today)	$16.10
1	16.20
2	16.25
3	16.18
4	16.18
5 (delivery)	16.21

The daily mark-to-market settlements for each contract held by the long positions will be as follows:

Day	Profit (loss) per Ounce	× 5,000 Ounces/Contract = Daily Proceeds
1	$16.20 − $16.10 = $0.10	$500
2	16.25 − 16.20 = 0.05	250
3	16.18 − 16.25 = −0.07	−350
4	16.18 − 16.18 = 0	0
5	16.21 − 16.18 = 0.03	150
		Sum = $550

The profit on day 1 is the increase in the futures price from the previous day, or ($16.20 − $16.10) per ounce. Because each silver contract on the Commodity Exchange calls for purchase and delivery of 5,000 ounces, the profit per contract is 5,000 times $.10, or $500. On day 3, when the futures price falls, the long position's margin account will be debited by $350. By day 5, the sum of all daily proceeds is $550. This is exactly equal to 5,000 times the difference between the final futures price of $16.21 and the original futures price of $16.10. Because the final futures price equals the spot price on that date, the sum of all the daily proceeds (per ounce of silver held long) equals $P_T - F_0$.

---

[2]Small differences between the spot and futures prices at maturity may persist because of transportation costs, but this is a minor factor.

Cash versus Actual Delivery

Most futures markets call for delivery of an actual commodity, such as a particular grade of wheat or a specified amount of foreign currency, if the contract is not reversed before maturity. For agricultural commodities, where quality of the delivered good may vary, the exchange sets quality standards as part of the futures contract. In some cases, contracts may be settled with higher- or lower-grade commodities. In these cases, a premium or discount is applied to the delivered commodity to adjust for the quality differences.

Some futures contracts call for **cash settlement.** An example is a stock-index futures contract where the underlying asset is an index such as the Standard & Poor's 500 Index. Delivery of every stock in the index clearly would be impractical. Hence, the contract calls for "delivery" of a cash amount equal to the value that the index attains on the maturity date of the contract. The sum of all the daily settlements from marking to market results in the long position realizing total profits or losses of $S_T - F_0$, where S_T is the value of the stock index on the maturity date T, and F_0 is the original futures price. Cash settlement closely mimics actual delivery, except the cash value of the asset rather than the asset itself is delivered.

More concretely, the S&P 500 Index contract calls for delivery of $250 times the value of the index. At maturity, the index might list at 1,800, a market value–weighted index of the prices of all 500 stocks in the index. The cash settlement contract would then call for delivery of $250 × 1,800, or $450,000 cash in return for $250 times the futures price. This yields exactly the same profit as would result from directly purchasing 250 units of the index for $450,000 and then delivering it for $250 times the original futures price.

cash settlement
The cash value of the underlying asset (rather than the asset itself) is delivered to satisfy the contract.

Regulations

Futures markets are regulated by the federal Commodity Futures Trading Commission (CFTC). The CFTC sets capital requirements for member firms of the futures exchanges, authorizes trading in new contracts, and oversees maintenance of daily trading records.

The futures exchange may set limits on the amount by which futures prices may change from one day to the next. For example, if the price limit on silver contracts is $1, and silver futures close today at $16.10 per ounce, trades in silver tomorrow may vary only between $15.10 and $17.10 per ounce. The exchange may increase or reduce these price limits in response to perceived changes in the price volatility of the contract. Price limits often are eliminated as contracts approach maturity, usually in the last month of trading.

Price limits traditionally are viewed as a means to limit violent price fluctuations. This reasoning seems dubious. Suppose an international monetary crisis overnight drives up the spot price of silver to $25. No one would sell silver futures at prices for future delivery as low as $16.10. Instead, the futures price would rise each day by the $1 limit, although the quoted price would represent only an unfilled bid order—no contracts would trade at the low quoted price. After several days of limit moves of $1 per day, the futures price would finally reach its equilibrium level, and trading would occur again. This process means no one could unload a position until the price reached its equilibrium level. This example shows that price limits offer no real protection against fluctuations in equilibrium prices.

Taxation

Because of the mark-to-market procedure, investors do not have control over the tax year in which they realize gains or losses. Instead, price changes are realized gradually, with each daily settlement. Therefore, taxes are paid at year-end on cumulated profits or losses regardless of whether the position has been closed out. As a general rule, 60% of futures gains or losses are treated as long term and 40% as short term.

17.3   FUTURES MARKET STRATEGIES

Hedging and Speculation

Hedging and speculating are two polar uses of futures markets. A speculator uses a futures contract to profit from movements in futures prices; a hedger, to protect against price movements.

If speculators believe prices will increase, they will take a long position for expected profits. Conversely, they exploit expected price declines by taking a short position.

EXAMPLE 17.3

Speculating with Oil Futures

Suppose you believe that crude oil prices are going to increase. You might purchase crude oil futures. Each contract calls for delivery of 1,000 barrels of oil, so for every dollar increase in the price of crude, the long position gains $1,000 and the short position loses that amount.

Conversely, suppose you think that prices are heading lower and therefore sell a contract. If crude oil prices fall, then your short position gains $1,000 for every dollar that prices decline.

If the futures price for delivery in March is $89.48 and crude oil is selling for $91.48 at the contract maturity date, the long side will profit by $2,000 per contract purchased. The short side will lose an identical amount on each contract sold. On the other hand, if oil has fallen to $87.48, the long side will lose, and the short side will gain, $2,000 per contract.

Why would a speculator buy a futures contract? Why not buy the underlying asset directly? One reason lies in transaction costs, which are far smaller in futures markets.

Another reason is the leverage futures trading provides. Recall that futures contracts require traders to post margin considerably less than the value of the asset underlying the contract. Therefore, they allow speculators to achieve much greater leverage than is available from direct trading in a commodity.

EXAMPLE 17.4

Futures and Leverage

Suppose the initial margin requirement for the oil contract is 10%. At a current futures price of $89.48, and contract size of 1,000 barrels, this would require margin of $.10 \times 89.48 \times 1,000 = \$8,948$. A $2 jump in oil prices represents an increase of 2.235%, and results in a $2,000 gain on the contract for the long position. This is a percentage gain of 22.35% in the $8,948 posted as margin, precisely 10 times the percentage increase in the oil price. The 10-to-1 ratio of percentage changes reflects the leverage inherent in the futures position because the contract was established with an initial margin of one-tenth the value of the underlying asset.

Hedgers, by contrast, use futures to insulate themselves against price movements. A firm planning to sell oil, for example, might anticipate a period of market volatility and wish to protect its revenue against price fluctuations. To hedge the total revenue derived from the sale, the firm enters a short position in oil futures. As the following example illustrates, this locks in its total proceeds (i.e., revenue from the sale of the oil plus proceeds from its futures position).

EXAMPLE 17.5

Hedging with Oil Futures

Consider an oil distributor planning to sell 100,000 barrels of oil in March that wishes to hedge against a possible decline in oil prices. Because each contract calls for delivery of 1,000 barrels, it would sell 100 contracts. Any decrease in prices would then generate a profit on the contracts that would offset the lower sales revenue from the oil.

To illustrate, suppose that the only three possible prices for oil in March are $87.48, $89.48, and $91.48 per barrel. The revenue from the oil sale will be 100,000 times the price per barrel. The profit on each contract sold will be 1,000 times any decline in the futures price. At maturity, the convergence property ensures that the final futures price will equal the spot price of oil. Therefore, the profit on the 100 contracts sold will equal $100,000 \times (F_0 - P_T)$, where P_T is the oil price on the delivery date and F_0 is the original futures price, $89.48.

(continued)

Now consider the firm's overall position. The total revenue in March can be computed as follows:

EXAMPLE 17.5

Hedging with Oil Futures

(concluded)

	Oil Price in March, P_T		
	$87.48	**$89.48**	**$91.48**
Revenue from oil sale: $100{,}000 \times P_T$	$8,748,000	$8,948,000	$9,148,000
+ Profit on futures: $100{,}000 \times (F_0 - P_T)$	200,000	0	−200,000
Total Proceeds	$8,948,000	$8,948,000	$8,948,000

The revenue from the oil sale plus the proceeds from the contracts equals the current futures price, $89.48 per barrel. The variation in the price of the oil is precisely offset by the profits or losses on the futures position. For example, if oil falls to $87.48 a barrel, the short futures position generates $200,000 profit, just enough to bring total revenues to $8,948,000. The total is the same as if one were to arrange today to sell the oil in March at the futures price.

Figure 17.4 illustrates the nature of the hedge in Example 17.5. The upward-sloping line is the revenue from the sale of oil. The downward-sloping line is the profit on the futures contract. The horizontal line is the sum of sales revenue plus futures profits. This line is flat, as the hedged position is independent of oil prices.

To generalize Example 17.5, note that oil will sell for P_T per barrel at the maturity of the contract. The profit per barrel on the futures will be $F_0 - P_T$. Therefore, total revenue is $P_T + (F_0 - P_T) = F_0$, which is independent of the eventual oil price.

The oil distributor in this example engaged in a *short hedge,* taking a short futures position to offset risk in the sales price of a particular asset. A *long hedge* is the analogous hedge for someone who wishes to eliminate the risk of an uncertain purchase price. For example, a petrochemical firm planning to purchase oil may be afraid that prices might rise by the time

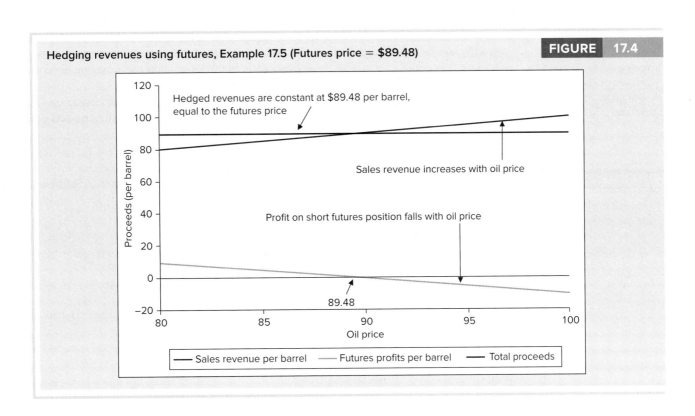

FIGURE 17.4

Hedging revenues using futures, Example 17.5 (Futures price = $89.48)

of the purchase. As the following Concept Check illustrates, the firm might *buy* oil futures to lock in the net purchase price at the time of the transaction.

CONCEPT check 17.3

Suppose as in Example 17.5 that oil will be selling in March for $87.48, $89.48, or $91.48 per barrel. Consider a firm that plans to buy 100,000 barrels of oil in March. Show that if the firm buys 100 oil contracts, its net expenditures will be hedged and equal to $8,948,000.

Exact futures hedging may be impossible for some goods because the necessary futures contract is not traded. For example, a portfolio manager might want to hedge the value of a diversified, actively managed portfolio for a period of time. However, futures contracts are listed only on indexed portfolios. Nevertheless, because returns on the manager's diversified portfolio will have a high correlation with returns on broad-based indexed portfolios, an effective hedge may be established by selling index futures contracts. Hedging a position using futures on another asset is called *cross-hedging*.

CONCEPT check 17.4

What are the sources of risk to an investor who uses stock-index futures to hedge an actively managed stock portfolio? How might you estimate the magnitude of that risk?

Basis Risk and Hedging

basis

The difference between the futures price and the spot price.

The **basis** is the difference between the futures price and the spot price.[3] As we have noted, on the maturity date of a contract, the basis must be zero: The convergence property implies that $F_T - P_T = 0$. Before maturity, however, the futures price for later delivery may differ substantially from the current spot price.

For example, in Example 17.5, we discussed the case of a short hedger who manages risk by entering a short position to deliver oil in the future. If the asset and futures contract are held until maturity, the hedger bears no risk. Risk is eliminated because the futures price and spot price at contract maturity must be equal: Gains and losses on the futures and the underlying asset will exactly cancel. If the contract and asset are to be liquidated early, before contract maturity, however, the hedger bears **basis risk,** because the futures price and spot price need not move in perfect lockstep until the delivery date. In this case, gains and losses on the contract and the asset may not exactly offset each other.

basis risk

Risk attributable to uncertain movements in the spread between a futures price and a spot price.

Some speculators try to profit from movements in the basis. Rather than betting on the direction of the futures or spot prices per se, they bet on the changes in the difference between the two. A long spot–short futures position will profit when the basis narrows.

EXAMPLE 17.6

Speculating on the Basis

Consider an investor holding 100 ounces of gold, who is short one gold futures contract. Suppose that gold today sells for $1,191 an ounce, and the futures price for June delivery is $1,196 an ounce. Therefore, the basis is currently $5. Tomorrow, the spot price might increase to $1,194, while the futures price increases to $1,198.50, so the basis narrows to $4.50. The investor's gains and losses are as follows:

Gain on holdings of gold (per ounce): $1,194 − $1,191 = $3.00
Loss on gold futures position (per ounce): $1,198.50 − $1,196 = $2.50

The investor gains $3 per ounce on the gold holdings but loses $2.50 an ounce on the short futures position. The net gain is the decrease in the basis, or $.50 an ounce.

---

[3]Usage of the word *basis* is somewhat loose. It sometimes is used to refer to the futures-spot difference, $F - P$, and other times it is used to refer to the spot-futures difference, $P - F$. We will consistently call the basis $F - P$.

A related strategy is a **spread** position, where the investor takes a long position in a futures contract of one maturity and a short position in a contract on the same commodity but with a different maturity. Profits accrue if the difference in futures prices between the two contracts changes in the hoped-for direction, that is, if the futures price on the contract held long increases by more (or decreases by less) than the futures price on the contract held short. Like basis strategies, spread positions aim to exploit movements in relative price structures rather than to profit from movements in the general level of prices.

spread (futures)

Taking a long position in a futures contract of one maturity and a short position in a contract of a different maturity, both on the same commodity.

Consider an investor who holds a September maturity contract long and a June contract short. If the September futures price increases by 5 cents while the June futures price increases by 4 cents, the net gain will be 5 cents − 4 cents, or 1 cent.

EXAMPLE 17.7

Speculating on the Spread

17.4   FUTURES PRICES

Spot-Futures Parity

There are at least two ways to obtain an asset at some date in the future. One way is to purchase it now and store it until the targeted date. The other way is to take a long futures position that calls for purchase of the asset on the date in question. As each strategy leads to an equivalent result, namely, the ultimate acquisition of the asset, you would expect the market-determined cost of pursuing these strategies to be equal. There should be a predictable relationship between the current price of the asset, including the costs of holding and storing it, and the futures price.

To make the discussion more concrete, consider a futures contract on gold. This is a particularly simple case: Explicit storage costs for gold are minimal, gold provides no income flow for its owners (in contrast to stocks or bonds that make dividend or coupon payments), and gold is not subject to the seasonal price patterns that characterize most agricultural commodities. Instead, in market equilibrium, the price of gold will be at a level such that the expected rate of capital gains will equal the fair expected rate of return given gold's investment risk. Two strategies that will ensure possession of the gold at some future date T are:

> *Strategy A:* Buy the gold now, paying the current or "spot" price, S_0, and hold it until time T, when its spot price will be S_T.
>
> *Strategy B:* Initiate a long futures position, and invest enough money now to pay the futures price when the contract matures.

Strategy B will require an immediate investment of the *present value* of the futures price in a riskless security such as Treasury bills, that is, an investment of $F_0/(1 + r_f)^T$ dollars, where r_f is the interest rate on T-bills. Examine the cash flow streams of the following two strategies.[4]

	Action	Initial Cash Flow	Cash Flow at Time T
Strategy A:	Buy gold	$-S_0$	S_T
Strategy B:	Enter long position	0	$S_T - F_0$
	Invest $F_0/(1 + r_f)^T$ in bills	$-F_0/(1 + r_f)^T$	F_0
	Total for strategy B	$-F_0/(1 + r_f)^T$	S_T

The initial cash flow of strategy A is negative, reflecting the cash outflow necessary to purchase the gold at the current spot price, S_0. At time T, the gold will be worth S_T.

---

[4]We ignore the margin requirement on the futures contract and treat the cash flow involved in establishing the futures position as zero for the two reasons mentioned above: First, the margin is small relative to the amount of gold controlled by one contract; and second, and more important, the margin requirement may be satisfied with interest-bearing securities. For example, the investor merely needs to transfer Treasury bills already owned into the brokerage account. There is no time-value-of-money cost.

Strategy B involves an initial investment equal to the present value of the futures price that will be paid at the maturity of the futures contract. By time T, the investment will grow to F_0. In addition, the profits to the long position at time T will be $S_T - F_0$. The sum of the two components of strategy B will be S_T dollars, exactly enough to purchase the gold at time T regardless of its price at that time.

Each strategy results in an identical value of S_T dollars at T. Therefore, the cost, or initial cash outflow, required by these strategies also must be equal; it follows that

$$F_0/(1 + r_f)^T = S_0$$

or

$$F_0 = S_0(1 + r_f)^T \tag{17.1}$$

This gives us a relationship between the current price and the futures price of the gold. The interest rate in this case may be viewed as the "cost of carrying" the gold from the present to time T. The cost in this case represents the time-value-of-money opportunity cost—instead of investing in the gold, you could have invested risklessly in Treasury bills to earn interest income.

EXAMPLE 17.8

Futures Pricing

Suppose that gold currently sells for $1,200 an ounce. If the risk-free interest rate is .1% per month, a six-month maturity futures contract should have a futures price of

$$F_0 = S_0(1 + r_f)^T = \$1,200(1.001)^6 = \$1,207.22$$

If the contract has a 12-month maturity, the futures price should be

$$F_0 = \$1,200(1.001)^{12} = \$1,214.48$$

If Equation 17.1 does not hold, investors can earn arbitrage profits. For example, suppose the six-month maturity futures price in Example 17.8 were $1,210 rather than the "appropriate" value of $1,207.22 that we just derived. An investor could realize arbitrage profits by pursuing a strategy involving a long position in strategy A (buy the gold) and a short position in strategy B (sell the futures contract and borrow enough to pay for the gold purchase).

Action	Initial Cash Flow	Cash Flow at Time T (6 months)
Borrow $1,200, repay with interest at time T	+$1,200	$-\$1,200(1.001)^6 = \$1,207.22$
Buy gold for $1,200	−1,200	S_T
Enter short futures position ($F_0 = \$1,210$)	0	$1,210 - S_T$
Total	$ 0	$2.78

The net initial investment of this strategy is zero. Moreover, its cash flow at time T is positive and riskless: The total payoff at time T will be $2.78 regardless of the price of gold. The profit is precisely equal to the mispricing of the futures contract, $1,210 rather than $1,207.22. Risk has been eliminated because profits and losses on the futures and gold positions exactly offset each other. The portfolio is perfectly hedged.

Such a strategy produces an arbitrage profit—a riskless profit requiring no initial net investment. If such an opportunity existed, all market participants would rush to take advantage of it. The results? The price of gold would be bid up, and/or the futures price offered down, until Equation 17.1 is satisfied. A similar analysis applies to the possibility that F_0 is less than $1,207.22. In this case, you simply reverse the above strategy to earn riskless profits.

Spot-Futures Parity

The Spot-Futures Parity spreadsheet allows you to calculate futures prices corresponding to a spot price for different maturities, interest rates, and income yields. You can use the spreadsheet to see how prices of more distant contracts will fluctuate with spot prices and the cost of carry.

You can learn more about this spreadsheet by using the version available in Connect.

Spreadsheets are available in Connect

	A	B	C	D	E
1					
2	**Spot-Futures Parity and Time Spreads**				
3					
4	Spot price	100			
5	Income yield (%)	2		Futures prices versus maturity	
6	Interest rate (%)	4.5			
7	Today's date	5/14/15		Spot price	100.00
8	Maturity date 1	11/17/15		Futures 1	101.26
9	Maturity date 2	1/2/16		Futures 2	101.58
10	Maturity date 3	6/7/16		Futures 3	102.66
11					
12	Time to maturity 1	0.51			
13	Time to maturity 2	0.63			
14	Time to maturity 3	1.06			

Excel Questions

1. Experiment with different values for both income yield and interest rate. What happens to the size of the time spread (the difference in futures prices for the long- versus short-maturity contracts) if the interest rate increases by 2%?

2. What happens to the time spread if the income yield increases by 2%?

3. What happens to the spread if the income yield equals the interest rate?

We conclude, therefore, that in a well-functioning market in which arbitrage opportunities are competed away, $F_0 = S_0(1 + r_f)^T$.

CONCEPT check 17.5

Return to the arbitrage strategy just laid out. What would be the three steps of the strategy if F_0 were too low, say, $1,206? Work out the cash flows of the strategy now and at time T in a table like the one above. Confirm that your profits equal the mispricing of the contract.

The arbitrage strategy can be represented more generally as follows:

Action	Initial Cash Flow	Cash Flow at Time T
1. Borrow S_0	$+S_0$	$-S_0(1 + r_f)^T$
2. Buy gold for S_0	$-S_0$	S_T
3. Enter short futures position	0	$F_0 - S_T$
Total	0	$F_0 - S_0(1 + r_f)^T$

The initial cash flow is zero by construction: The money necessary to purchase the gold in step 2 is borrowed in step 1, and the futures position in step 3, which is used to hedge the value of the gold, does not require an initial outlay. Moreover, the total cash flow at time T is riskless because it involves only terms that are already known when the contract is entered. This situation could not persist, as all investors would try to cash in on the arbitrage opportunity. Ultimately prices would change until the time T cash flow was reduced to zero, at which point F_0 would equal $S_0(1 + r_f)^T$. This result is called the **spot-futures parity theorem** or **cost-of-carry relationship;** it gives the normal or theoretically correct relationship between spot and futures prices.

spot-futures parity theorem or cost-of-carry relationship

Describes the theoretically correct relationship between spot and futures prices. Violation of the parity relationship gives rise to arbitrage opportunities.

We can easily extend the parity theorem to the case where the underlying asset provides a flow of income to its owner. For example, consider a futures contract on a stock index such as the S&P 500. In this case, the underlying asset (i.e., the stock portfolio indexed to the S&P 500 index) pays a dividend yield to the investor. If we denote the dividend yield as d, then the net cost of carry is only $r_f - d$; the forgone interest earnings on the wealth tied up in the stock are offset by the flow of dividends from the stock. The net opportunity cost of holding the stock is the forgone interest less the dividends received. Therefore, in the dividend-paying case, the spot-futures parity relationship is[5]

$$F_0 = S_0(1 + r_f - d)^T \qquad \textbf{(17.2)}$$

where d is the dividend yield on the stock. Problem 10 at the end of the chapter leads you through a derivation of this result.

Notice that when the dividend yield is less than the risk-free rate, Equation 17.2 implies that futures prices will exceed spot prices and by greater amounts for longer times to contract maturity. But when $d > r_f$, as is the case today, the income yield on the stock actually exceeds the forgone (risk-free) interest that could be earned on the money invested; in this event, the futures price will be less than the current stock price, again by greater amounts for longer maturities. You can confirm that this is so by examining any of the stock-index futures listings in Figure 17.1.

Although dividends of individual securities may fluctuate unpredictably, the annualized dividend yield of a broad-based index such as the S&P 500 is fairly stable, recently in the neighborhood of a bit more than 2% per year. The yield is seasonal, however, with regular peaks and troughs, so the dividend yield for the relevant months must be the one used. Figure 17.5 illustrates the yield pattern for the S&P 500. Some months, such as January or April, have consistently low yields, while others, such as May, have consistently high ones.

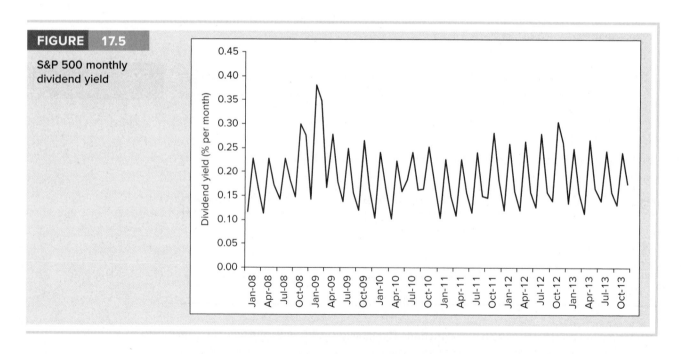

FIGURE 17.5

S&P 500 monthly dividend yield

---

[5]This relationship is only approximate in that it assumes the dividend is paid just before the maturity of the contract.

The arbitrage strategy just described should convince you that these parity relationships are more than just theoretical results. Any violations of the parity relationship give rise to arbitrage opportunities that can provide large profits to traders. We will see shortly that index arbitrage in the stock market is a tool used to exploit violations of the parity relationship for stock-index futures contracts.

Suppose that the risk-free interest rate is .1% per month, the dividend yield on the stock index is .2% per month, and the stock index is currently 1,800. The net cost of carry is therefore negative, .1% − .2% = −.1% per month. Given this, a three-month contract should have a futures price of $1,800(1 − .001)^3 = 1,794.61$, while a six-month contract should have a futures price of $1,800(1 − .001)^6 = 1,789.23$. If the index rises to 1,810, both futures prices will rise commensurately: The three-month futures price will rise to $1,810(1 − .001)^3 = 1,804.58$, while the six-month futures price will rise to $1,810(1 − .001)^6 = 1,799.17$.

EXAMPLE 17.9

Stock-Index Futures Pricing

Spreads

Just as we can predict the relationship between spot and futures prices, there are similar ways to determine the proper relationships among futures prices for contracts of different maturity dates. Equation 17.2 shows that the futures price is in part determined by time to maturity. If $r_f < d$, as was true of S&P 500 stock-index futures in 2014, then the futures price will be lower on longer-maturity contracts. You can easily verify this by examining Figure 17.1, which includes *Wall Street Journal* listings of several stock-index futures contracts. For futures on assets like gold, which pay no "dividend yield," we can set $d = 0$ and conclude that F must increase as time to maturity increases.

Equation 17.2 shows that futures prices should all move together. It is not surprising that futures prices for different maturity dates move in unison, for all are linked to the same spot price through the parity relationship. Figure 17.6 plots futures prices on gold for three maturity dates. It is apparent that the prices move in virtual lockstep and that the more distant delivery dates command higher futures prices, as Equation 17.2 predicts should be the case for gold, for which $d = 0$.

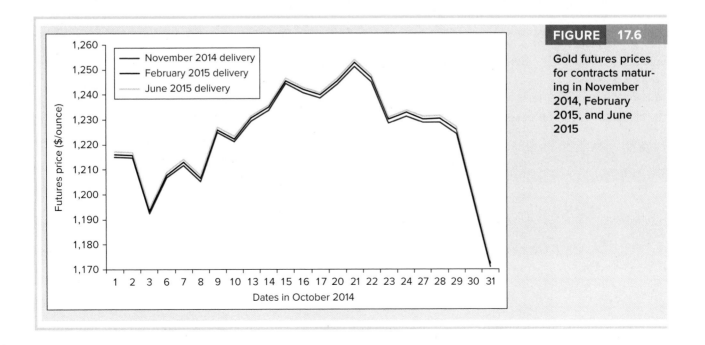

FIGURE   17.6

Gold futures prices for contracts maturing in November 2014, February 2015, and June 2015

17.5 FINANCIAL FUTURES

Although futures markets have their origins in agricultural commodities, today's market is dominated by contracts on financial assets. We review the most important of these contracts in this section: stock-index contracts, foreign exchange contracts, and interest rate contracts.

Stock-Index Futures

Futures trade actively on stock market indexes such as the Standard & Poor's 500. In contrast to most futures contracts, which call for delivery of a specified asset, these contracts are settled by a cash amount equal to the value of the stock index in question on the contract maturity date times a multiplier that scales the size of the contract. This cash settlement duplicates the profits that would arise with actual delivery.

There are several stock-index futures contracts currently traded. Table 17.2 lists some contracts on major indexes, showing under "Contract Size" the multiplier used to calculate contract settlements. An S&P 500 contract with an initial futures price of 1,200 and a final index value of 1,210, for example, would result in a profit for the long side of $250 \times (1,210 - 1,200) = \$2,500$. The S&P contract by far dominates the market in stock-index futures.[6]

The broad-based U.S. stock market indexes are all highly correlated. Table 17.3 presents a correlation matrix for five U.S. indexes. Notice that the correlations among the Dow Jones Industrial Average, the New York Stock Exchange Index, and the S&P 500 are all well above .97. The NASDAQ Composite Index, which is dominated by technology firms, and the Russell 2000 Index of smaller-capitalization firms have smaller correlations with the large-cap indexes and with each other, but even these are all above .85.

TABLE 17.2   Sample of stock-index futures

Contract	Underlying Market Index	Contract Size	Exchange
S&P 500	Standard & Poor's 500 Index, a value-weighted arithmetic average of 500 stocks	$250 times the S&P 500 Index	Chicago Mercantile Exchange
Dow Jones Industrials (DJIA)	Price-weighted arithmetic average of 30 blue-chip stocks	$10 times the Dow Jones Industrial Average	Chicago Board of Trade
NASDAQ 100	Value-weighted arithmetic average of 100 of the largest over-the-counter stocks	$100 times the OTC index	Chicago Mercantile Exchange
Russell 2000	Index of 2,000 smaller firms	$500 times the index	Intercontinental Exchange, ICE
Nikkei 225	Nikkei 225 stock average	$5 times the Nikkei Index	Chicago Mercantile Exchange
FTSE 100	Financial Times–Stock Exchange Index of 100 U.K. firms	£10 times the FTSE Index	London International Financial Futures Exchange (Euronext)
CAC 40	Index of 40 of the largest French firms	10 euros times the index	Euronext Paris
DAX 30	Index of 30 of the largest German firms	25 euros times the index	Eurex
Hang Seng	Value-weighted index of largest firms in Hong Kong	50 Hong Kong dollars times the index	Hong Kong Exchange

---

[6]We should point out that while the multipliers on these contracts may make the resulting positions too large for many small investors, there are effectively equivalent futures contracts with smaller multipliers, *Minis*. Mini contracts trade in several stock indexes as well as foreign currencies.

TABLE 17.3 Correlations among major U.S. stock market indexes, 2006–2011					
	DJIA	**NYSE**	**NASDAQ**	**S&P 500**	**Russell 2000**
DJIA	1.000				
NYSE	0.977	1.000			
NASDAQ	0.861	0.859	1.000		
S&P 500	0.977	0.978	0.918	1.000	
Russell 2000	0.863	0.890	0.921	0.931	1.000

Source: Authors' calculations.

Creating Synthetic Stock Positions

One reason stock-index futures are so popular is that they can substitute for holdings in the underlying stocks themselves. Index futures let investors participate in broad market movements without actually buying or selling large numbers of stocks.

Because of this, we say futures represent "synthetic" holdings of the market position. Instead of holding the market directly, the investor takes a long futures position in the index. Such a strategy is attractive because the transaction costs involved in establishing and liquidating futures positions are much lower than what would be required to take actual spot positions. Investors who wish to buy and sell market positions frequently find it much cheaper and easier to play the futures market. Market timers who speculate on broad market moves rather than individual securities are large players in stock-index futures for this reason.

One way to market time is to shift between Treasury bills and broad-based stock market holdings. Timers attempt to shift from bills into the market before market upturns and to shift back into bills to avoid market downturns, thereby profiting from broad market movements. Market timing of this sort, however, can result in huge trading costs with the frequent purchase and sale of many stocks. An attractive alternative is to invest in Treasury bills and hold varying amounts of market-index futures contracts.

The strategy works like this: When timers are bullish, they will establish many long futures positions that they can liquidate quickly and cheaply when expectations turn bearish. Rather than shifting back and forth between T-bills and stocks, traders buy and hold T-bills and adjust only the futures position. (Recall strategies A and B of the preceding section where we showed that a T-bill plus futures position resulted in a payoff equal to the stock price.) This strategy minimizes transaction costs. An advantage of this technique for timing is that investors can implicitly buy or sell the market index in its entirety, whereas market timing in the spot market would require the simultaneous purchase or sale of all the stocks in the index. This is technically difficult to coordinate and can lead to slippage in the execution of a timing strategy.

Index Arbitrage

Whenever the actual futures price differs from its parity value, there is an opportunity for profit. This is why the parity relationships are so important. **Index arbitrage** is an investment strategy that exploits divergences between the actual futures price on a stock market index and its theoretically correct parity value.

In principle, index arbitrage is simple. If the futures price is too high, short the futures contract and buy the stocks in the index. If it is too low, go long in futures and short the stocks. You can perfectly hedge your position and should earn arbitrage profits equal to the mispricing of the contract.

In practice, however, index arbitrage can be difficult to implement. The problem lies in buying the stocks in the index. Selling or purchasing shares in all 500 stocks in the S&P 500 is difficult for two reasons. The first is transaction costs, which may outweigh any profits to be

index arbitrage

Strategy that exploits divergences between actual futures prices and their theoretically correct parity values to make a riskless profit.

made from the arbitrage. Second, index arbitrage calls for the purchase or sale of shares of 500 different firms simultaneously—and any lags in the execution of such a strategy can destroy the effectiveness of a plan to exploit short-lived price discrepancies.

Arbitrageurs need to trade an entire portfolio of stocks quickly and simultaneously if they hope to exploit temporary disparities between the futures price and its corresponding stock index. For this they need a coordinated trading program; hence the term **program trading,** which refers to coordinated purchases or sales of entire portfolios of stocks. Such strategies can be executed using electronic trading, which enables traders to send coordinated buy or sell programs to the floor of the stock exchange over computer lines. (See Chapter 3 for a discussion of electronic trading.)

Foreign Exchange Futures

Exchange rates between currencies vary continually and often substantially. This variability can be a source of concern for anyone involved in international business. A U.S. exporter who sells goods in England, for example, will be paid in British pounds, and the dollar value of those pounds depends on the exchange rate at the time payment is made. Until that date, the U.S. exporter is exposed to foreign exchange rate risk. This risk can be hedged through currency futures or forward markets. For example, if you know you will receive £100,000 in 60 days, you can sell those pounds forward today in the forward market and lock in an exchange rate equal to today's forward price.

The forward market in foreign exchange is relatively informal. It is simply a network of banks and brokers that allows customers to enter forward contracts to trade currency in the future at a currently agreed-upon rate of exchange. The bank market in currencies is among the largest in the world, and most large traders with sufficient creditworthiness execute their trades here rather than in futures markets. Contracts in these markets are not standardized in a formal market setting. Instead, each is negotiated separately. Moreover, there is no marking to market as would occur in futures markets. Forward contracts call for execution only at the maturity date.

For currency futures, however, there are formal markets established by the Chicago Mercantile Exchange (International Monetary Market), the London International Financial Futures Exchange, and other exchanges. Here, contracts are standardized by size, and daily marking to market is observed. Moreover, there are standard clearing arrangements that allow traders to enter or reverse positions easily.

Figure 17.7 reproduces a *Wall Street Journal* listing of foreign exchange spot and forward rates. The listing gives the number of U.S. dollars required to purchase a unit of foreign currency and then the amount of foreign currency needed to purchase $1.

The forward quotations in Figure 17.7 always apply to rolling delivery in 30, 90, or 180 days. Thus, tomorrow's forward listings will apply to a maturity date one day later than today's listing. In contrast, foreign exchange futures contracts mature only on four specified dates in any year, in March, June, September, and December.

Interest Rate Futures

The major U.S. interest rate contracts currently traded are on Eurodollars, Treasury bills, Treasury notes, and Treasury bonds. The range of these securities provides an opportunity to hedge against interest rate risk in a wide spectrum of maturities from very short (T-bills) to long term (T-bonds). In addition, futures contracts tied to interest rates in Europe, Japan, the United Kingdom, and several other countries actively trade. Figure 17.1 shows listings of some of these contracts.

The Treasury contracts call for delivery of a Treasury bond, bill, or note. Should interest rates rise, the market value of the security at delivery will be less than the original futures price, and the deliverer will profit. Hence, the short position in the interest rate futures contract gains when interest rates rise and bond prices fall.

FIGURE 17.7

Spot and forward prices in foreign exchange

Source: From *The Wall Street Journal,* October 30, 2014.

Currencies

U.S.-dollar foreign-exchange rates in late New York trading

Country/currency	Wed in US$	Wed per US$	US$vs, YTD chg (%)	Country/currency	Wed in US$	Wed per US$	US$vs, YTD chg (%)
Americas				**Europe**			
Argentina peso	.1176	8.5010	**30.4**	**Czech Rep.** koruna	.04551	21.973	**10.5**
Brazil real	.4064	2.4605	**4.2**	**Denmark** krone	.1697	5.8931	**8.6**
Canada dollar	.8942	1.1183	**5.3**	**Euro area** euro	1.2632	.7917	**8.8**
Chile peso	.001729	578.36	**10.0**	**Hungary** forint	.004082	245.00	**13.3**
Colombia peso	.0004887	2046.45	**6.0**	**Norway** krone	.1491	6.7047	**10.4**
Ecuador US dollar	1	1	**unch**	**Poland** zloty	.2991	3.3436	**10.6**
Mexico peso	.0741	13.4973	**3.5**	**Russia** ruble	.02316	43.172	**31.1**
Peru new sol	.3430	2.916	**4.0**	**Sweden** krona	.1358	7.3657	**14.4**
Uruguay peso	.04115	24.2985	**14.7**	**Switzerland** franc	1.0472	.9549	**6.9**
Venezuela b. fuerte	.157480	6.3500	**unch**	1-mos forward	1.0474	.9547	**6.5**
				3-mos forward	1.0482	.9540	**6.5**
Asia-Pacific				6-mos forward	1.0493	.9530	**6.5**
Australian dollar	.8797	1.1367	**1.3**	**Turkey** lira	.4518	2.2134	**3.0**
1-mos forward	.8779	1.1391	**1.3**	**UK pound**	1.6013	.6245	**3.4**
3-mos forward	.8739	1.1443	**1.4**	1-mos forward	1.6009	.6247	**3.3**
6-mos forward	.8683	1.1516	**1.4**	3-mos forward	1.6001	.6250	**3.3**
China yuan	.1635	6.1145	**1.0**	6-mos forward	1.5987	.6255	**3.3**
Hong Kong dollar	.1290	7.7547	**unch**				
India rupee	.01627	61.480	**−0.6**	**Middle East/Africa**			
Indonesia rupiah	.0000826	12102	**−0.5**	**Bahrain** dinar	2.6526	.3770	**unch**
Japan yen	.009183	108.90	**3.4**	**Egypt** pound	.1398	7.1540	**2.9**
1-mos forward	.009184	108.88	**3.3**	**Israel** shekel	.2656	3.7652	**8.5**
3-mos forward	.009192	108.79	**3.2**	**Jordan** dinar	1.4127	.7079	**unch**
6-mos forward	.009200	108.69	**3.2**	**Kuwait** dinar	3.4504	.2898	**2.6**
Malaysia ringgit	.3054	3.2741	**−0.3**	**Lebanon** pound	.0006610	1512.95	**0.5**
New Zealand dollar	.7802	1.2817	**5.4**	**Saudi Arabia** riyal	.2665	3.7518	**unch**
Pakistan rupee	.00970	103.040	**−2.2**	**South Africa** rand	.0913	10.9470	**4.4**
Philippines peso	.0224	44.728	**0.8**	**UAE** dirham	.2723	3.6730	**unch**
Singapore dollar	.7825	1.2779	**1.2**				
South Korea won	.0009518	1050.69	**−0.5**		Close	Net Chg	%ChgYTD%Chg
Taiwan dollar	.03292	30.374	**1.5**				
Thailand baht	.03076	32.506	**−0.6**	**WSJ Dollar Index**	77.94	0.54 0.70	**5.59**
Vietnam dong	.00004701	21274	**0.7**	Sources: ICAP plc., WSJ Market Data Group			

Similarly, Treasury-bond futures can be useful hedging vehicles for bond dealers or underwriters. Consider, for example, these problems:

1. A fixed-income manager holds a bond portfolio on which considerable capital gains have been earned. She foresees an increase in interest rates but is reluctant to sell her portfolio and replace it with a lower-duration mix of bonds because such rebalancing would result in large trading costs as well as realization of capital gains for tax purposes. Still, she would like to hedge her exposure to interest rate increases.

2. A corporation plans to issue bonds to the public, but it cannot issue the bonds for another three months because of the lags inherent in SEC registration. It would like to hedge the uncertainty surrounding the yield at which it eventually will be able to sell the bonds.

3. A pension fund will receive a large cash inflow next month that it plans to invest in long-term bonds. It is concerned that interest rates may fall by the time it can make the investment and would like to lock in the yield currently available on long-term issues.

In each of these cases, the investment manager wishes to hedge interest rate changes. To illustrate the procedures that might be followed, we will focus on the first example and suppose that the portfolio manager has a $10 million bond portfolio with a modified duration of

9 years.[7] If, as feared, market interest rates increase and the bond portfolio's yield also rises, say by 10 basis points (.10%), the fund will suffer a capital loss. Recall from Chapter 11 that the capital loss in percentage terms will be the product of modified duration, D^*, and the change in the portfolio yield. Therefore, the loss will be

$$D^* \times \Delta y = 9 \times .10\% = .9\%$$

price value of a basis point (PVBP)

The change in the value of an asset due to a 1-basis-point change in its yield to maturity.

or $90,000. This establishes that the sensitivity of the value of the unprotected portfolio to changes in market yields is $9,000 per 1-basis-point change in the yield. Market practitioners call this ratio the **price value of a basis point (PVBP).** The PVBP represents the sensitivity of the dollar value of the portfolio to changes in interest rates. Here, we've shown that

$$\text{PVBP} = \frac{\text{Change in portfolio value}}{\text{Predicted change in yield}} = \frac{\$90,000}{10 \text{ basis points}} = \$9,000 \text{ per basis point}$$

One way to hedge this risk is to take an offsetting position in an interest rate futures contract, for example, the Treasury-bond contract. The bond nominally calls for delivery of $100,000 par value T-bonds with 6% coupons and 20-year maturity. In practice, the contract delivery terms are fairly complicated because many bonds with different coupon rates and maturities may be substituted to settle the contract. However, we will assume that the bond to be delivered on the contract already is known and has a modified duration of 10 years. Finally, suppose that the futures price currently is $90 per $100 par value. Because the contract requires delivery of $100,000 par value of bonds, the contract multiplier is $1,000.

Given these data, we can calculate the PVBP for the futures contract. If the yield on the delivery bond increases by 10 basis points, the bond value will fall by $D^* \times .1\% = 10 \times .1\% = 1\%$. The futures price also will decline 1%, from 90 to 89.10.[8] Because the contract multiplier is $1,000, the gain on each short contract will be $1,000 \times .90 = \$900$. Therefore, the PVBP for one futures contract is $900/10-basis-point change, or $90 for a change in yield of 1 basis point.

Now we can easily calculate the hedge ratio as follows:

$$H = \frac{\text{PVBP of portfolio}}{\text{PVBP of hedge vehicle}} = \frac{\$90,000}{\$90 \text{ per contract}} = 100 \text{ contracts}$$

Therefore, 100 T-bond futures contracts will serve to offset the portfolio's exposure to interest rate fluctuations.

CONCEPT check   17.6

Suppose the bond portfolio is twice as large, $20 million, but that its modified duration is only 4.5 years. Show that the proper hedge position in T-bond futures is the same as the value just calculated, 100 contracts.

---

cross-hedging

Hedging a position in one asset by establishing an offsetting position in a related, but different, asset.

Although the hedge ratio is easy to compute, the hedging problem in practice is more difficult. For example, we assumed in our example that the yields on the T-bond contract and the bond portfolio would move perfectly in unison. Although interest rates on various fixed-income instruments do tend to vary in tandem, there is considerable slippage across sectors of the fixed-income market.

This problem highlights the fact that most hedging activity is in fact **cross-hedging,** meaning that the hedge vehicle is a different asset from the one to be hedged. To the extent that there is slippage between prices or yields of the two assets, the hedge will not be perfect. Nevertheless, even cross-hedges can eliminate a large fraction of the total risk of the unprotected portfolio.

---

[7]Recall that modified duration, D^*, is related to duration, D, by the formula $D^* = D/(1 + y)$, where y is the bond's yield to maturity. If the bond pays coupons semiannually, then y should be measured as a semiannual yield. For simplicity, we will assume annual coupon payments and treat y as the effective annual yield to maturity.

[8]This assumes the futures price will be exactly proportional to the bond price, which ought to be nearly true.

17.6 SWAPS

Swaps are multiperiod extensions of forward contracts. For example, rather than agreeing to exchange British pounds for U.S. dollars at an agreed-upon forward price at one single date, a **foreign exchange swap** would call for an exchange of currencies on several future dates. For example, the parties might exchange $1.6 million for £1 million in each of the next five years. Similarly, **interest rate swaps** call for the exchange of a series of cash flows proportional to a given interest rate for a corresponding series of cash flows proportional to a floating interest rate.[9] For example, one party might exchange a variable cash flow equal to $1 million times a short-term interest rate for $1 million times a fixed interest rate of 6% for each of the next seven years.

The swap market is a huge component of the derivatives market, with over $650 trillion in interest rate and exchange rate swap agreements outstanding. We will illustrate how these contracts work using a simple interest rate swap as an example.

foreign exchange swap

An agreement to exchange a sequence of payments denominated in one currency for payments in another currency at an exchange rate agreed to today.

interest rate swaps

Contracts between two parties to trade cash flows corresponding to different interest rates.

EXAMPLE 17.10

Interest Rate Swap

Consider the manager of a large portfolio that currently includes $100 million par value of long-term bonds paying an average coupon rate of 7%. The manager believes that interest rates are about to rise. As a result, he would like to sell the bonds and replace them with either short-term or floating-rate issues. However, it would be exceedingly expensive in terms of transaction costs to replace the portfolio every time the forecast for interest rates is updated. A cheaper and more flexible way to modify the portfolio is for the manager to "swap" the $7 million a year in interest income the portfolio currently generates for an amount of money that is tied to the short-term interest rate. That way, if rates do rise, so will the portfolio's interest income.

A swap dealer might advertise its willingness to exchange, or "swap," a cash flow based on the six-month LIBOR rate for one based on a fixed rate of 7%. (The LIBOR, or London InterBank Offered Rate, is the interest rate at which banks borrow from each other in the Eurodollar market. It is the most commonly used short-term interest rate in the swap market.) The portfolio manager would then enter into a swap agreement with the dealer to *pay* 7% on **notional principal** of $100 million and *receive* payment of the LIBOR rate on that amount of notional principal.[10] In other words, the manager swaps a payment of .07 × $100 million for a payment of LIBOR × $100 million. The manager's *net* cash flow from the swap agreement is therefore (LIBOR − .07) × $100 million. Note that the swap arrangement does not mean that a loan has been made. The participants have agreed only to exchange a fixed cash flow for a variable one.

Now consider the net cash flow to the manager's portfolio in three interest rate scenarios:

notional principal

Principal amount used to calculate swap payments.

	LIBOR Rate		
	6.5%	**7.0%**	**7.5%**
Interest income from bond portfolio (= 7% of $100 million bond portfolio)	$7,000,000	$7,000,000	$7,000,000
Cash flow from swap [= (LIBOR − 7%) × notional principal of $100 million]	(500,000)	0	500,000
Total (= LIBOR × $100 million)	$6,500,000	$7,000,000	$7,500,000

Notice that the total income on the overall position—bonds plus swap agreement—is now equal to the LIBOR rate in each scenario times $100 million. The manager has, in effect, converted a fixed-rate bond portfolio into a synthetic floating-rate portfolio.

---

[9]Interest rate swaps have nothing to do with the Homer-Leibowitz bond swap taxonomy described in Chapter 11.

[10]The participants to the swap do not loan each other money. They agree only to exchange a fixed cash flow for a variable cash flow that depends on the short-term interest rate. This is why the principal is described as *notional*. The notional principal is simply a way to describe the size of the swap agreement. In this example, the parties to the swap exchange a 7% fixed rate for the LIBOR rate; the difference between LIBOR and 7% is multiplied by notional principal to determine the cash flow exchanged by the parties.

Swaps and Balance Sheet Restructuring

Example 17.10 illustrates why interest rate swaps have tremendous appeal to fixed-income managers. These contracts provide a means to quickly, cheaply, and anonymously restructure the balance sheet. Suppose a corporation that has issued fixed-rate debt believes that interest rates are likely to fall; it might prefer to have issued floating-rate debt. In principle, it could issue floating-rate debt and use the proceeds to buy back the outstanding fixed-rate debt. It is faster and easier to convert the outstanding fixed-rate debt into synthetic floating-rate debt by entering a swap to receive a fixed interest rate (offsetting its fixed-rate coupon obligation) and pay a floating rate.

Conversely, a bank that pays current market interest rates to its depositors, and thus is exposed to increases in rates, might wish to convert some of its financing to a fixed-rate basis. It would enter a swap to receive a floating rate and pay a fixed rate on some amount of notional principal. This swap position, added to its floating-rate deposit liability, would result in a net liability of a fixed stream of cash. The bank might then be able to invest in long-term fixed-rate loans without encountering interest rate risk.

As a final example, consider a fixed-income portfolio manager. Swaps enable the manager to switch back and forth between a fixed- or floating-rate profile quickly and cheaply as the forecast for the interest rate changes. A manager who holds a fixed-rate portfolio can transform it into a synthetic floating-rate portfolio by entering a pay fixed–receive floating swap and can later transform it back by entering the opposite side of a similar swap.

The Swap Dealer

What about the swap dealer? Why is the dealer, which is typically a financial intermediary such as a bank, willing to take on the opposite side of the swaps desired by these participants in these hypothetical swaps?

Consider a dealer who takes on one side of a swap, let's say paying LIBOR and receiving a fixed rate. The dealer will search for another trader in the swap market who wishes to receive a fixed rate and pay LIBOR. For example, company A may have issued a 7% coupon fixed-rate bond that it wishes to convert into synthetic floating-rate debt, while company B may have issued a floating-rate bond tied to LIBOR that it wishes to convert into synthetic fixed-rate debt. The dealer will enter a swap with company A in which it pays a fixed rate and receives LIBOR and will enter another swap with company B in which it pays LIBOR and receives a fixed rate. When the two swaps are combined, the dealer's position is effectively neutral on interest rates, paying LIBOR on one swap and receiving it on another. Similarly, the dealer pays a fixed rate on one swap and receives it on another. The dealer becomes little more than an intermediary, funneling payments from one party to the other.[11] The dealer finds this activity profitable because it will charge a bid–asked spread on the transaction.

This rearrangement is illustrated in Figure 17.8. Company A has issued 7% fixed-rate debt (the leftmost arrow in the figure) but enters a swap to pay the dealer LIBOR and receive a 6.95% fixed rate. Therefore, the company's net payment is 7% + (LIBOR − 6.95%) = LIBOR + .05%. It has thus transformed its fixed-rate debt into synthetic floating-rate debt. Conversely, company B has issued floating-rate debt paying LIBOR (the rightmost arrow) but enters a swap to pay a 7.05% fixed rate in return for LIBOR. Therefore, its net payment is LIBOR + (7.05% − LIBOR) = 7.05%. It has thus transformed its floating-rate debt into synthetic fixed-rate debt. The bid–asked spread, the source of the dealer's profit, in the example illustrated in Figure 17.8 is .10% of notional principal each year.

CONCEPT check 17.7 A pension fund holds a portfolio of money market securities that the manager believes are paying excellent yields compared to other comparable-risk short-term securities. However, the manager believes that interest rates are about to fall. What type of swap will allow the fund to continue to hold its portfolio of short-term securities while at the same time benefiting from a decline in rates?

[11]Actually, things are a bit more complicated. The dealer is more than just an intermediary because it bears the credit risk that one or the other of the parties to the swap might default on the obligation. Referring to Figure 17.8, if firm A defaults on its obligation, for example, the swap dealer still must maintain its commitment to firm B. In this sense, the dealer does more than simply pass through cash flows to the other swap participants.

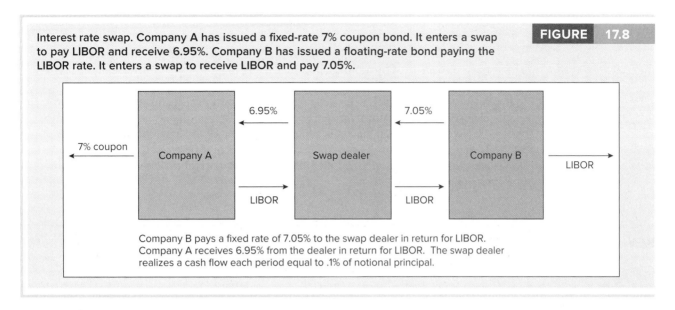

Interest rate swap. Company A has issued a fixed-rate 7% coupon bond. It enters a swap to pay LIBOR and receive 6.95%. Company B has issued a floating-rate bond paying the LIBOR rate. It enters a swap to receive LIBOR and pay 7.05%.

FIGURE 17.8

Company B pays a fixed rate of 7.05% to the swap dealer in return for LIBOR. Company A receives 6.95% from the dealer in return for LIBOR. The swap dealer realizes a cash flow each period equal to .1% of notional principal.

SUMMARY

- Forward contracts are arrangements that call for the future delivery of an asset at a currently agreed-upon price. The long trader is obligated to purchase the good, and the short trader is obligated to deliver it. If the price at the maturity of the contract exceeds the forward price, the long side benefits by virtue of acquiring the good at the contract price.

- A futures contract is similar to a forward contract, differing most importantly in the aspects of standardization and marking to market, which is the process by which gains and losses on futures contract positions are settled daily. In contrast, forward contracts call for no cash transfers until contract maturity.

- Futures contracts are traded on organized exchanges that standardize the size of the contract, the grade of the deliverable asset, the delivery date, and the delivery location. Traders negotiate only the contract price. This standardization creates increased liquidity in the marketplace and means buyers and sellers can easily find many traders for a desired purchase or sale.

- The clearinghouse steps in between each pair of traders, acting as the short position for each long and as the long position for each short, so traders need not be concerned about the performance of the trader on the opposite side of the contract. Traders are required to post margins to guarantee their own performance on the contracts.

- The long position's gain or loss on a contract held between time 0 and t is $F_t - F_0$. Because $F_T = P_T$ at maturity, the long's profit if the contract is held until maturity is $P_T - F_0$, where P_T is the spot price at time T and F_0 is the original futures price. The gain or loss to the short position is $F_0 - P_T$.

- Futures contracts may be used for hedging or speculating. Speculators use the contracts to take a stand on the ultimate price of an asset. Short hedgers take short positions in contracts to offset any gains or losses on the value of an asset already held in inventory. Long hedgers take long positions in futures contracts to offset gains or losses in the purchase price of a good.

- The spot-futures parity relationship states that the equilibrium futures price on an asset providing no service or payments (such as dividends) is $F_0 = P_0(1 + r_f)^T$. If the futures price deviates from this value, then market participants can earn arbitrage profits.

- If the asset provides services or payments with yield d, the parity relationship becomes $F_0 = P_0(1 + r_f - d)^T$. This model is also called the cost-of-carry model, because it states that the futures price must exceed the spot price by the net cost of carrying the asset until maturity date T.

- Futures contracts calling for cash settlement are traded on various stock-market indexes. The contracts may be mixed with Treasury bills to construct artificial equity positions, which makes them potentially valuable tools for market timers. Market-index contracts also are used by arbitrageurs who attempt to profit from violations of the parity relationship.
- Interest rate futures allow for hedging against interest rate fluctuations in several different markets. The most actively traded contract is for Treasury bonds.
- The interest rate swap market is a major component of the fixed-income market. In these arrangements, parties trade the cash flows of different securities without actually exchanging any securities directly. This is a useful tool to manage the interest rate exposure of a portfolio.

KEY TERMS			
	basis, 570	forward contract, 558	price value of a basis point,
	basis risk, 570	futures price, 558	(PVBP) 580
	cash settlement, 567	index arbitrage, 577	program trading, 578
	clearinghouse, 564	interest rate swaps, 581	short position, 559
	convergence property, 566	long position, 559	single stock futures, 561
	cost-of-carry	maintenance margin, 565	spot-futures parity
	relationship, 574	marking to market, 565	theorem, 574
	cross-hedging, 580	notional principal, 581	spread, 571
	foreign exchange swap, 581		

KEY FORMULAS   Spot futures parity: $F_0 = (1 + r_f - d)^T$

PROBLEM SETS   Select problems are available in McGraw-Hill's *Connect*. Please see the Supplements section of the book's frontmatter for more information.

1. On January 1, you sold one March maturity S&P 500 Index futures contract at a futures price of 1,800. If the futures price is 1,850 on February 1, what is your profit? The contract multiplier is $250.   *(LO 17-1)*

2. The current level of the S&P 500 is 1,800. The dividend yield on the S&P 500 is 2%. The risk-free interest rate is 1%. What should a futures contract with a one-year maturity be selling for?   *(LO 17-3)*

3. A one-year gold futures contract is selling for $1,141. Spot gold prices are $1,200 and the one-year risk-free rate is 2%.   *(LO 17-4)*
   a. According to spot-futures parity, what should be the futures price?
   b. What risk-free strategy can investors use to take advantage of the futures mispricing, and what will be the profits on the strategy?

4. You purchase a Treasury-bond futures contract with an initial margin requirement of 15% and a futures price of $115,098. The contract is traded on a $100,000 underlying par value bond. If the futures price falls to $108,000, what will be the percentage loss on your position?   *(LO 17-1)*

5. a. Turn to Figure 17.1 and locate the contract on the Standard & Poor's 500 Index. If the margin requirement is 10% of the futures price times the multiplier of $250, how much must you deposit with your broker to trade the December contract?
   b. If the December futures price were to increase to 2,000, what percentage return would you earn on your net investment if you entered the long side of the contract at the price shown in the figure?

    c. If the December futures price falls by 1%, what is the percentage gain or loss on your net investment? *(LO 17-1)*

6. Why might individuals purchase futures contracts rather than the underlying asset? *(LO 17-2)*

7. What is the difference in cash flow between short-selling an asset and entering a short futures position? *(LO 17-1)*

8. Suppose the value of the S&P 500 Stock Index is currently $1,800. *(LO 17-3)*
   - *a.* If the one-year T-bill rate is 3% and the expected dividend yield on the S&P 500 is 2%, what should the one-year maturity futures price be?
   - *b.* What if the T-bill rate is less than the dividend yield, for example, 1%?

9. It is now January. The current interest rate is 3%. The June futures price for gold is $1,246.30, while the December futures price is $1,251. Is there an arbitrage opportunity here? If so, how would you exploit it? *(LO 17-4)*

10. Consider a stock that will pay a dividend of D dollars in one year, which is when a futures contract matures. Consider the following strategy: Buy the stock, short a futures contract on the stock, and borrow S_0 dollars, where S_0 is the current price of the stock. *(LO 17-3)*
   - *a.* What are the cash flows now and in one year? (*Hint:* Remember the dividend the stock will pay.)
   - *b.* Show that the equilibrium futures price must be $F_0 = S_0(1 + r) - D$ to avoid arbitrage.
   - *c.* Call the dividend yield $d = D/S_0$, and conclude that $F_0 = S_0(1 + r - d)$.

11. *a.* A single stock futures contract on a nondividend-paying stock with current price $150 has a maturity of one year. If the T-bill rate is 3%, what should the futures price be?
   - *b.* What should the futures price be if the maturity of the contract is three years?
   - *c.* What if the interest rate is 5% and the maturity of the contract is three years? *(LO 17-3)*

12. The Excel Applications box in the chapter (available in Connect; link to Chapter 17 material) shows how to use the spot-futures parity relationship to find a "term structure of futures prices," that is, futures prices for various maturity dates. *(LO 17-3)*
   - *a.* Suppose that today is January 1, 2015. Assume the interest rate is 1% per year and a stock index currently at 1,800 pays a dividend yield of 2%. Find the futures price for contract maturity dates of February 14, 2015, May 21, 2015, and November 18, 2015.
   - *b.* What happens to the term structure of futures prices if the dividend yield is lower than the risk-free rate? For example, what if the interest rate is 3%?

Templates and spreadsheets are available in Connect

13. One Chicago has just introduced a new single stock futures contract on the stock of Brandex, a company that currently pays no dividends. Each contract calls for delivery of 1,000 shares of stock in one year. The T-bill rate is 6% per year. *(LO 17-3)*
   - *a.* If Brandex stock now sells at $120 per share, what should the futures price be?
   - *b.* If the Brandex stock price drops by 3%, what will be the change in the futures price and the change in the investor's margin account?
   - *c.* If the margin on the contract is $12,000, what is the percentage return on the investor's position?

14. The multiplier for a futures contract on the stock-market index is $250. The maturity of the contract is one year, the current level of the index is 2,000, and the risk-free interest rate is .5% per month. The dividend yield on the index is .2% per month. Suppose that after one month, the stock index is at 2,010. *(LO 17-1)*
   - *a.* Find the cash flow from the mark-to-market proceeds on the contract. Assume that the parity condition always holds exactly.
   - *b.* Find the one-month holding-period return if the initial margin on the contract is $10,000.

15. Suppose the S&P 500 Index portfolio pays a dividend yield of 2% annually. The index currently is 1,800. The T-bill rate is 3%, and the S&P futures price for delivery in one year is $1,833. Construct an arbitrage strategy to exploit the mispricing and show that your profits one year hence will equal the mispricing in the futures market.   *(LO 17-4)*

16. *a.* How should the parity condition (Equation 17.2) for stocks be modified for futures contracts on Treasury bonds? What should play the role of the dividend yield in that equation?
    b. In an environment with an upward-sloping yield curve, should T-bond futures prices on more distant contracts be higher or lower than those on near-term contracts?
    c. Confirm your intuition by examining Figure 17.1.   *(LO 17-3)*

17. Desert Trading Company has issued $100 million worth of long-term bonds at par at a fixed rate of 7%. The firm then enters into an interest rate swap where it pays LIBOR and receives a fixed 6% on notional principal of $100 million. What is the firm's effective interest rate on its borrowing?   *(LO 17-5)*

18. What type of interest rate swap would be appropriate for a speculator who believes interest rates soon will fall?   *(LO 17-5)*

19. The margin requirement on the S&P 500 futures contract is 10%, and the stock index is currently 1,800. Each contract has a multiplier of $250.   *(LO 17-1)*
    a. How much margin must be put up for each contract sold?
    b. If the futures price falls by 1% to 1,782, what will happen to the margin account of an investor who holds one contract?
    c. What will be the investor's percentage return based on the amount put up as margin?

20. The multiplier for a futures contract on a certain stock market index is $250. The maturity of the contract is one year, the current level of the index is 1,000, and the risk-free interest rate is .2% per *month*. The dividend yield on the index is .1% per month. Suppose that *after one month,* the stock index is at 1,020.   *(LO 17-1)*
    a. Find the cash flow from the mark-to-market proceeds on the contract. Assume that the parity condition always holds exactly.
    b. Find the holding-period return if the initial margin on the contract is $10,000.

21. You are a corporate treasurer who will purchase $1 million of bonds for the sinking fund in three months. You believe rates soon will fall and would like to repurchase the company's sinking fund bonds, which currently are selling below par, in advance of requirements. Unfortunately, you must obtain approval from the board of directors for such a purchase, and this can take up to two months.   *(LO 17-2)*
    a. What action can you take in the futures market to hedge any adverse movements in bond yields and prices until you actually can buy the bonds?
    b. Will you be long or short? Why?

22. A manager is holding a $1 million bond portfolio with a modified duration of eight years. She would like to hedge the risk of the portfolio by short-selling Treasury bonds. The modified duration of T-bonds is 10 years. How many dollars' worth of T-bonds should she sell to minimize the risk of her position?   *(LO 17-2)*

23. A corporation plans to issue $10 million of 10-year bonds in three months. At current yields the bonds would have modified duration of eight years. The T-note futures contract is selling at $F_0 = 100$ and has modified duration of six years. How can the firm use this futures contract to hedge the risk surrounding the yield at which it will be able to sell its bonds? Both the bond and the contract are at par value.   *(LO 17-2)*

Challenge

24. The S&P 500 Index is currently at 1,800. You manage a $9 million indexed equity portfolio. The S&P 500 futures contract has a multiplier of $250.   *(LO 17-2)*
    a. If you are temporarily bearish on the stock market, how many contracts should you sell to fully eliminate your exposure over the next six months?

    b. If T-bills pay 2% per six months and the semiannual dividend yield is 1%, what is the parity value of the futures price?

    c. Show that if the contract is fairly priced, the total risk-free proceeds on the hedged strategy in part (*a*) provide a return equal to the T-bill rate.

25. *a.* How would your hedging strategy in the previous problem change if, instead of holding an indexed portfolio, you hold a portfolio of only one stock with a beta of .6?

    b. How many contracts would you now choose to sell? Would your hedged position be riskless?

    c. What would be the beta of the hedged position? *(LO 17-2)*

26. A corporation has issued a $10 million issue of floating-rate bonds on which it pays an interest rate 1% over the LIBOR rate. The bonds are selling at par value. The firm is worried that rates are about to rise, and it would like to lock in a fixed interest rate on its borrowings. The firm sees that dealers in the swap market are offering swaps of LIBOR for 7%. *(LO 17-5)*

    a. What swap arrangement will convert the firm's borrowings to a synthetic fixed-rate loan?

    b. What interest rate will it pay on that synthetic fixed-rate loan?

27. The one-year futures price on a particular stock-index portfolio is 1,825, the stock index currently is 1,800, the one-year risk-free interest rate is 3%, and the year-end dividend that will be paid on a $1,800 investment in the index portfolio is $25. *(LO 17-4)*

    a. By how much is the contract mispriced?

    b. Formulate a zero-net-investment arbitrage portfolio, and show that you can lock in riskless profits equal to the futures mispricing.

    c. Now assume (as is true for small investors) that if you short-sell the stocks in the market index, the proceeds of the short sale are kept with the broker and you do not receive any interest income on the funds. Is there still an arbitrage opportunity (assuming you don't already own the shares in the index)? Explain.

    d. Given the short-sale rules, what is the no-arbitrage *band* for the stock-futures price relationship? That is, given a stock index of 1,800, how high and how low can the futures price be without giving rise to arbitrage opportunities?

CFA Problems

1. The open interest on a futures contract at any given time is the total number of outstanding: *(LO 17-1)*

    a. Contracts.

    b. Unhedged positions.

    c. Clearinghouse positions.

    d. Long and short positions.

2. In futures trading, the minimum level to which an equity position may fall before requiring additional margin is *most accurately* termed the: *(LO 17-1)*

    a. Initial margin.

    b. Variation margin.

    c. Cash flow margin.

    d. Maintenance margin.

3. A silver futures contract requires the seller to deliver 5,000 Troy ounces of silver. Jerry Harris sells one July silver futures contract at a price of $28 per ounce, posting a $6,000 initial margin. If the required maintenance margin is $2,500, what is the *first* price per ounce at which Harris would receive a maintenance margin call? *(LO 17-1)*

4. In each of the following cases, discuss how you, as a portfolio manager, could use financial futures to protect a portfolio. *(LO 17-2)*

    a. You own a large position in a relatively illiquid bond that you want to sell.

    b. You have a large gain on one of your long Treasuries and want to sell it, but you would like to defer the gain until the next accounting period, which begins in four weeks.

    c. You will receive a large contribution next month that you hope to invest in long-term corporate bonds on a yield basis as favorable as is now available.

5. Futures contracts and options contracts can be used to modify risk. Identify the fundamental distinction between a futures contract and an option contract, and briefly explain the difference in the manner that futures and options modify portfolio risk.   *(LO 17-2)*

6. Joan Tam, CFA, believes she has identified an arbitrage opportunity for a commodity as indicated by the information given in the following exhibit: *(LO 17-4)*

Commodity Price and Interest Rate Information	
Spot price for commodity	$120
Futures price for commodity expiring in one year	$125
Interest rate for one year	8%

    a. Describe the transactions necessary to take advantage of this specific arbitrage opportunity.

    b. Calculate the arbitrage profit.

7. Several Investment Committee members have asked about interest rate swap agreements and how they are used in the management of domestic fixed-income portfolios.   *(LO 17-5)*

    a. Define an interest rate swap, and briefly describe the obligation of each party involved.

    b. Cite and explain two examples of how interest rate swaps could be used by a fixed-income portfolio manager to control risk or improve return.

8. Janice Delsing, a U.S.-based portfolio manager, manages an $800 million portfolio ($600 million in stocks and $200 million in bonds). In reaction to anticipated short-term market events, Delsing wishes to adjust the allocation to 50% stocks and 50% bonds through the use of futures. Her position will be held only until "the time is right to restore the original asset allocation." Delsing determines a financial futures-based asset allocation strategy is appropriate. The stock futures index multiplier is $250, and the denomination of the bond futures contract is $100,000. Other information relevant to a futures-based strategy is given in the following exhibit: *(LO 17-2)*

Information for Futures-Based Strategy	
Bond portfolio modified duration	5 years
Bond portfolio yield to maturity	7%
Price value of basis point (PVBP) of bond futures	$97.85
Stock-index futures price	1378
Stock portfolio beta	1.0

    a. Describe the financial futures-based strategy needed, and explain how the strategy allows Delsing to implement her allocation adjustment. No calculations are necessary.

    b. Compute the number of each of the following needed to implement Delsing's asset allocation strategy:

      i. Bond futures contracts.

      ii. Stock-index futures contracts.

9. Maria VanHusen, CFA, suggests that forward contracts on fixed-income securities can be used to protect the value of the Star Hospital Pension Plan's bond portfolio against the possibility of rising interest rates. VanHusen prepares the following example to illustrate how such protection would work:

    • A 10-year bond with a face value of $1,000 is issued today at par value. The bond pays an annual coupon.

- An investor intends to buy this bond today and sell it in six months.
- The six-month risk-free interest rate today is 5% (annualized).
- A six-month forward contract on this bond is available, with a forward price of $1,024.70.
- In six months, the price of the bond, including accrued interest, is forecast to fall to $978.40 as a result of a rise in interest rates.   *(LO 17-2)*

a. Should the investor buy or sell the forward contract to protect the value of the bond against rising interest rates during the holding period?

b. Calculate the value of the forward contract for the investor at the maturity of the forward contract if VanHusen's bond price forecast turns out to be accurate.

c. Calculate the change in value of the combined portfolio (the underlying bond and the appropriate forward contract position) six months after contract initiation.

WEB *master*

1. Suppose that you want to create a spread position using S&P 500 futures contracts. Go to **www.cmegroup.com** and listed under Equity Index Products, select *S&P 500*. Click on *Contract Specifications* at the top of the product listing. Review the contract's specifications. Click on the *Contract Months* link to see the contracts that are available for trading. Note the code for one contract that expires in approximately three months and the code for another that expires in approximately nine months.

2. Assume that you bought the three-month contract and sold the nine-month contract about two months ago. *The Wall Street Journal Online* provides a comprehensive list of current and historical prices (under the *Market Data* tab). Specifically, navigate to the *Commodities & Futures* tab and then the *Index* tab. Choose the S&P 500 Comp Index, and click on the *Chart* icon. From here you can move your mouse over any day and retrieve the closing price on that day. Choose a trading date that occurred two months ago and note the price. Find the closing prices for the two contracts that you selected.

3. Return to the CME listings and find the closing prices of the two contracts on today's date. Assume that you close your positions in both contracts.

4. Using the beginning and ending prices for the futures contracts that you bought and sold, calculate the return you earned on the spread position during the two-month period, before commissions.

SOLUTIONS TO CONCEPT *checks*

17.1 *a.* The payoff on the put looks like that on the short futures contract when the asset price falls below X or F_0, but when the asset price rises above F_0, the futures payoff turns negative whereas the value of the put cannot fall below zero. The put (which must be purchased) gives you upside potential if the asset price falls but limits downside risk, whereas the futures gives you both upside and downside exposure.

b. The payoff on the written call looks like that on the short futures contract when the asset price rises above F_0, but when the asset price falls, the futures payoff is positive, whereas the payoff on the written call is never positive. The written call gives you downside exposure, but your upside potential is limited to the premium you received for the option.

17.2 The clearinghouse has a zero net position in all contracts. Its long and short positions are offsetting, so that net cash flow from marking to market must be zero.

17.3

	Oil Price in March, P_T		
	$87.48	**$89.48**	**$91.48**
Cash flow to purchase oil: $-100,000 \times P_T$	$-\$8,748,000$	$-\$8,948,000$	$-\$9,148,000$
+ Profit on long futures: $100,000 \times (P_T - F_0)$	$-200,000$	0	$+200,000$
Total cash flow	$-\$8,948,000$	$-\$8,948,000$	$-\$8,948,000$

17.4 The risk would be that the index and the portfolio do not move perfectly together. Thus, risk involving the spread between the futures price and the portfolio value could persist even if the index futures price were set perfectly relative to index itself. You can measure this risk using the index model introduced in Chapter 7. If you regress the return of the active portfolio on the return of the index portfolio, the regression R-square will equal the proportion of the variance of the active portfolio's return that could have been hedged using the index futures contract. You can also measure the risk of the imperfectly hedged position using the standard error of the regression, which tells you the standard deviation of the residuals in the index model. Because these are the components of the risky returns that are independent of the market index, this standard deviation measures the variability of the portion of the active portfolio's return that *cannot* be hedged using the index futures contract.

17.5 The future price, $1,206 is $1.22 below the parity value of $1,207.22. The cash flow to the following strategy is riskless and equal to this mispricing.

Action	Initial Cash Flow	Time-T Cash Flow
Lend $1,200	$-\$1,200$	$\$1,200(1.001)^6 = \$1,207.22$
Sell gold short	$+1,200$	$-S_T$
Long futures	0	$S_T - \$1,206$
Total	$\$0$	$\$1.22$ risklessly

17.6 The price value of a basis point is still $9,000, as a 1-basis-point change in the interest rate reduces the value of the $20 million portfolio by $.01\% \times 4.5 = .045\%$. Therefore, the number of futures needed to hedge the interest rate risk is the same as for a portfolio half the size with double the modified duration.

17.7 The manager would like to hold on to the money market securities because of their attractive relative pricing compared to other short-term assets. However, there is an expectation that rates will fall. The manager can hold this *particular* portfolio of short-term assets and still benefit from the drop in interest rates by entering a swap to pay a short-term interest rate and receive a fixed interest rate. The resulting synthetic fixed-rate portfolio will increase in value if rates do fall.

Active Investment Management

PART 6

Chapters in This Part

18 Portfolio Performance Evaluation

19 Globalization and International Investing

20 Hedge Funds

21 Taxes, Inflation, and Investment Strategy

22 Investors and the Investment Process

Passive investment, or indexing, is the preferred strategy for investors who believe markets are essentially efficient. While administration of passive portfolios requires efficient organization and trading structure, there is no need for security analysis or portfolio strategy. In contrast, active managers believe that markets are not efficient and that bargains can be found in security markets by application of asset valuation and portfolio theory.

Earlier in the text we asked how to effectively exploit security mispricing—how to balance superior expected returns with the increased risk from reduced diversification. In a market economy, we look to incentives: How will portfolio managers behave when evaluated using standard performance measures? They will choose portfolios that are expected to provide them with the best evaluation. Superior results, in turn, will lead to increased assets under management and higher profits. Accordingly, Chapter 18 discusses performance evaluation and techniques to achieve superior performance.

Investing across borders is conceptually a simple extension of efficient diversification. This pursuit confronts the effects of political risk and uncertain exchange rates on future performance, however. These issues, unique to international investing, are addressed in Chapter 19.

Chapter 20 covers hedge funds, probably the most active of active managers. It also focuses on some of the special problems encountered in evaluation of hedge fund performance.

Investments originate with a savings plan that diverts funds from consumption to investment. Taxes and inflation complicate the relationship between how much you save and what you will be able to achieve with your accumulating investment fund. Chapter 21 introduces a framework to formulate an effective household savings/investment plan.

Professional management of active investment begins with a contractual relationship between a client and a portfolio manager. The economic needs of clients must be articulated and their objectives translated into an operational financial plan. For this purpose, the CFA Institute has laid out a broad framework for active investment management. Chapter 22 familiarizes you with this framework.

Portfolio Performance Evaluation

Learning Objectives

LO 18-1 Compute risk-adjusted rates of return, and use them to evaluate investment performance.

LO 18-2 Determine which risk-adjusted performance measure is appropriate in a variety of investment contexts.

LO 18-3 Apply style analysis to assess portfolio strategy.

LO 18-4 Decompose portfolio returns into components attributable to asset allocation choices versus security selection choices.

LO 18-5 Assess the presence and value of market-timing ability.

In previous chapters, we derived predictions for expected return as a function of risk. In this chapter, we ask how we can evaluate the actual performance of a portfolio accounting for risk. Adjusting returns for risk presents a host of issues because the proper measure of risk may not be obvious and risk levels may change along with portfolio composition.

We begin with conventional approaches to risk adjustment. These use the risk measures developed earlier to rank investment results. We show the problems with these approaches when you try to apply them in a real and complex world. Finally, we examine evaluation procedures used in the field. We show how overall investment results are decomposed and attributed to asset allocation and security selection decisions of the portfolio manager.

We finally turn to two specific forms of active management: market timing based solely on macroeconomic factors, and security selection based on microeconomic forecasting.

18.1 RISK-ADJUSTED RETURNS

Investment Clients, Service Providers, and Objectives of Performance Evaluation

Individual households as well as institutional money managers must decide whether to use passive or active management. **Passive management** involves (1) capital allocation between **cash** (almost-risk-free vehicles such as money market funds) and a designated risky portfolio constructed from one or more index funds or ETFs. Passive investors will change their allocations only infrequently in response to significant changes in circumstances or estimates of risk derived, for example, from VIX (the volatility indexes, discussed in Chapter 16) or other sources.

Alternatively, households and institutional endowments may choose **active management,** in which case they usually become clients of professional portfolio managers.[1] The dividing line between passive and active management is the forecasting of future rates of return on asset classes and/or individual assets. Competition among the vast number of investors means that security prices generally reflect publicly available information. Thus, successful forecasting of future prices and rates of return requires *differential* private information. Accordingly, active managers forecast returns in conjunction with risk to construct optimal portfolios. A few professionals restrict their activity to *market timing* (switching between risky portfolios and cash), some concentrate on asset allocation only, and most engage in both asset allocation and security selection.[2]

Both clients and professionals are interested in performance evaluation. Clients need to know whether their chosen professionals produce adequate net-of-fee returns. Professionals need to shore up their methodology and maintain qualified staff with adequate compensation to compete in the market for these services. Lapses in performance can cost them dearly as evidence shows that funds under management flow quickly from underachievers to superperformers.

Performance evaluation of a portfolio is difficult because of the great volatility of asset returns. A portfolio's average return over an evaluation period is inadequate to measure performance. To begin with, the average return realized over any particular period may not represent the *expected* return. Surely, luck (good *or* bad) should not be allowed to dominate the evaluation process. Even when the average return does approximate expected return, it still would be invalid as a measure of performance because it ignores risk—we expect higher-risk investments to outperform lower-risk ones in average to boom markets and to underperform in bear markets. Hence, we must estimate portfolio risk to determine the adequacy of the average return. Because volatility generates statistical errors in estimates of both expected return and risk, we must remain skeptical of the evaluation process.

Comparison Groups

The simplest and most popular way to adjust returns for portfolio risk is to compare rates of return with those of other investment funds with similar risk characteristics. For example, high-yield bond portfolios are grouped into one "universe," growth stock equity funds are grouped into another universe, and so on. Then the average returns of each fund within the universe are ordered, and each portfolio manager receives a percentile ranking depending on relative performance within the **comparison universe,** the collection of funds to which performance is compared. For example, the manager with the ninth-best performance in a universe of 100 funds would be the 90th percentile manager: Her performance was better than 90% of all competing funds over the evaluation period.

These relative rankings usually are displayed in a chart like Figure 18.1. The chart summarizes performance rankings over four periods: one quarter, one year, three years, and five

---

passive management

Holding a well-diversified portfolio without attempting to search for mispriced securities.

cash

Shorthand for virtually risk-free money market securities.

active management

Attempts to achieve returns higher than commensurate with risk by forecasting broad markets and/or by identifying mispriced securities.

comparison universe

The set of portfolio managers with similar investment styles that is used to assess relative performance.

---

[1]Households and institutional endowments that conduct active management in-house become their own clients.
[2]Many professional managers are prohibited from extensive market timing by a prospectus or contract that limits the range of weights in cash instruments.

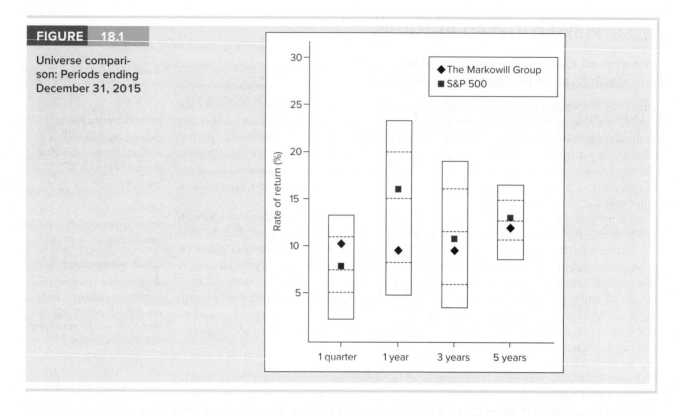

FIGURE 18.1

Universe comparison: Periods ending December 31, 2015

years. The top and bottom lines of each box are drawn at the rate of return of the 95th and 5th percentile managers. The three dotted lines correspond to the rates of return of the 75th, 50th (median), and 25th percentile managers. The diamond is drawn at the average return of a particular fund, the Markowill Group, and the square is drawn at the average return of a benchmark index such as the S&P 500. This format provides an easy-to-read representation of the performance of the fund relative to the comparison universe.

This comparison with other managers of similar investment groups is a useful first step in evaluating performance. Even so, such rankings can be misleading. Consider that within a particular universe some managers may concentrate on particular subgroups, so that portfolio characteristics are not truly comparable. For example, within the equity universe, one manager may concentrate on high-beta stocks. Similarly, within fixed-income universes, interest rate risk can vary across managers. These considerations suggest that we need more precise risk adjustment.

Basic Performance-Evaluation Statistics

Basic performance evaluation relies on the index model discussed in Sections 6.5 and 7.2 and on the CAPM of Section 7.1. The single-index model equation applied to a portfolio P is

$$R_{Pt} = \beta_P R_{Mt} + \alpha_P + e_{Pt} \qquad \text{(18.1)}$$

where $R_{Pt} = r_{Pt} - r_{ft}$ is portfolio P's excess return over cash equivalents during period t, r_{ft} is the return on cash, and R_{Mt} is the excess return on the market index. β_P is the portfolio's sensitivity to the market index, hence its measure of systematic risk, and $\beta_P R_{Mt}$ is the component of return that is driven by the market. The extra-market or nonsystematic component, $\alpha_P + e_{Pt}$, includes the portfolio alpha plus zero-mean noise, e, called the *residual*, which is uncorrelated with R_M. Thus, the expected excess return of the portfolio for some evaluation period is

$$E(R_P) = \beta_P E(R_M) + \alpha_P \qquad \text{(18.2)}$$

We measure *expected* returns over the period (unfortunately, with sampling error) using the *sample average* return.

The CAPM hypothesis is that the market portfolio is mean-variance efficient. The index model uses an index portfolio, *M*, to proxy for the theoretical market portfolio, and hence it is the benchmark passive strategy against which competing portfolios are measured. The CAPM hypothesis is that the alpha of all securities and competing portfolios is zero. A professional who claims to outperform the index must produce a positive alpha; the validity of the CAPM doesn't preclude some professionals from doing so, as long as the totality of investments that exhibit positive alpha is not large relative to aggregate wealth in the economy.

What about portfolio risk? As noted above, beta measures *systematic* risk given that the variance of the market-driven return component is

$$\text{Var}(\beta_P R_{Mt}) = \beta_P^2 \, \sigma_M^2 \tag{18.3}$$

and the term σ_M^2 is the same for all portfolios. The extra-market component of return contributes the quantity $\text{Var}(e_P)$ to portfolio variance. The standard deviation of the residual return *e*, which we will denote here as σ_e, is called *residual risk* or *residual SD*. The variance of the return on *P* is thus the sum of the systematic and residual variances (since the systematic and residual components of return are uncorrelated):

$$\sigma_P^2 = \beta_P^2 \sigma_M^2 + \sigma_e^2 \tag{18.4}$$

We may now prepare the statistics that are used for performance evaluation of a portfolio *P* from a sample of observations over an interval of *T* periods (usually months). The procedure includes the following steps:

1. Obtain the time series of R_{Pt} for portfolio *P*, and R_{Mt} for the benchmark *M*.
2. Compute the arithmetic averages of the series $\bar{R}_P$, $\bar{R}_M$. These are taken as estimates of the expected returns of portfolios *P* and *M* for the evaluation period.
3. Compute the standard deviations of returns for portfolios *P* and *M*, σ_P and σ_M. These serve as estimates of the total risk of *P* and *M*.
4. Run a regression of R_{Pt} on R_{Mt} to obtain estimates of *P*'s beta, alpha, residual SD, and correlation with the benchmark. Check the significance statistics to see that the sample is reasonable. In particular, if the beta coefficient estimate is not significant, the sample may be insufficient for the performance-evaluation statistics discussed below.
5. Recall from Equation 18.2 that the regression intercept is *P*'s alpha, $\alpha_P = \bar{R}_P - \beta_P \bar{R}_M$.
6. Recall from Equation 18.4 that the standard error, or residual standard deviation, of the regression is $\sigma_e = \text{SQRT}(\sigma_P^2 - \beta_P^2 \sigma_M^2)$.

Table 18.1 presents performance-evaluation statistics for two professionally managed portfolios, *P* and *Q*, the benchmark, *M*, and cash. Notice that *P* is aggressive with a beta of 1.25. *Q* might be a hedge fund, not completely market-neutral (which would entail a beta of zero), but still with a defensive beta of .5. Thus, most of the volatility of *Q* is due to its residual SD.

Performance Evaluation of Entire-Wealth Portfolios Using the Sharpe Ratio and M-Square

Consider the Do Well Foundation, a small charity, whose board has decided to invest its endowment in one of the three portfolios of Table 18.1. In this case, the total risk of the chosen portfolio will also be the endowment's risk. Accordingly, the familiar **Sharpe ratio,**

$$S = \frac{\bar{R}}{\sigma} \tag{18.5}$$

Sharpe ratio

Reward-to-volatility ratio; ratio of portfolio excess return to standard deviation.

which measures risk by total volatility (SD), must determine the choice. Table 18.1 shows that the Sharpe ratio of portfolio *P* (.398) is highest; hence *P* would be the charity's choice. Notice that *P*'s average return is sufficiently large to compensate for the fact that it is the highest SD portfolio; conversely, although *Q* is the least volatile, its Sharpe ratio is the lowest.

The Sharpe ratio has a clear interpretation, namely, the incremental return an investor may expect for every increase of 1% of standard deviation. It is the slope of the capital allocation

TABLE 18.1 Performance of two managed portfolios, P and Q, the benchmark portfolio, M, and cash equivalents				
	Portfolio P	**Portfolio Q**	**Benchmark**	**Cash**
Average return	13.6	9.5	10.4	4
Average excess return (%)	9.60	5.50	6.37	0
Standard deviation (%)	24.1	18.0	18.5	0
Beta (pure number)	1.25	0.50	1.0	0
Alpha (%)	1.6	2.3	0	0
Residual SD (%)	6.79	15.44	0	0
Correlation with benchmark	0.96	0.51	1	0
Sharpe ratio	0.398	0.306	0.344	0
M-square (%)	1.00	−0.72	0	0
Treynor measure	7.68	11.00	6	0
Information ratio	0.24	0.15	0	0

line supported by that portfolio. But should investors consider the difference in Sharpe ratios between portfolio P and the benchmark portfolio M (.398 − .344 = .054) large? That is harder to interpret and leads us to a variant on the Sharpe ratio.

Imagine a portfolio with the same standard deviation as the benchmark, σ_M. Then the difference between the Sharpe ratios of the portfolio and the benchmark would be the difference in their risk premiums divided by that common standard deviation. Put differently, ranking portfolios with a common volatility by Sharpe ratio will be equivalent to ranking them very simply by risk premium—estimated from the sample excess returns, as in Equation 18.5. This makes comparison of portfolios with equal standard deviation easy to interpret.

Can we transform P to an equivalent portfolio with the same standard deviation as the benchmark, σ_M, without affecting its Sharpe ratio? Yes, we can: Recall that the slope of P's CAL is the Sharpe ratio of *all* portfolios on that line. Therefore, we just choose the portfolio on CAL_P that has standard deviation σ_M. All portfolios on CAL_P are mixtures of portfolio P with risk-free borrowing or lending. When we invest a weight w in P and $1 − w$ in the risk-free asset, we just slide up (when $w > 1$) or down (when $w < 1$) the CAL. Call P^* the portfolio created by mixing P with the risk-free asset in just the right proportion to make the standard deviation match that of the benchmark. In other words, portfolio P^* is portfolio P with just the right amount of leverage to make the standard deviation match that of the benchmark.

We form P^* by choosing $w = \sigma_M/\sigma_P$ because this makes the SD of P^* equal to $w\sigma_P = \sigma_M$. The risk premium of portfolio P^* therefore can be written in terms of the Sharpe ratio of P:

$$\bar{R}_{P*} = w\bar{R}_P = \frac{\sigma_M}{\sigma_P}\bar{R}_P = \sigma_M S_P$$

Similarly, the risk premium of the benchmark can be written in terms of its Sharpe ratio:

$$\bar{R}_M = \sigma_M \frac{\bar{R}_M}{\sigma_M} = \sigma_M S_M$$

M-square (M^2)

Return difference between a managed portfolio leveraged to match the volatility of a passive index and the return on that index.

The difference between the risk premium of P^*, the leverage-adjusted version of P, and the benchmark is known as **M-square** (after Leah and Franco Modigliani)[3] and is written M^2.

$$M^2 = \bar{R}_{P*} - \bar{R}_M = \sigma_M(S_P - S_M) \qquad \text{(18.6)}$$

---

[3]The M-square measure was developed independently by Graham and Harvey (1997) and by Modigliani and Modigliani (1997).

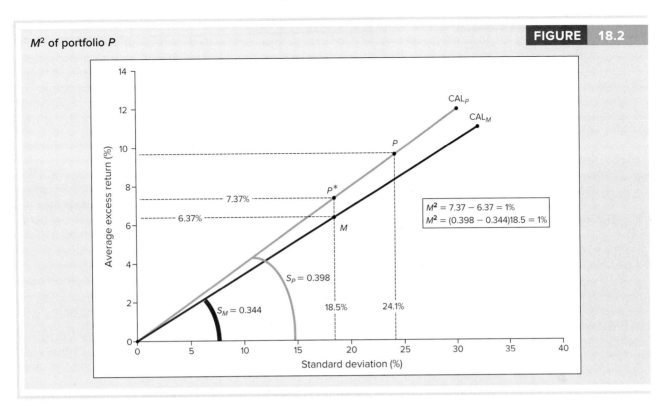

FIGURE 18.2

M^2 of portfolio P

M-square is the rate-of-return differential between P^* and M, a legitimate and easy-to-interpret performance measure because the portfolios are volatility-matched. Equation 18.6 shows us that it also is a simple transformation of the difference between their Sharpe ratios. Table 18.1 and Figure 18.2 show this vividly.

Suppose that instead of investing all its funds in P, the endowment had invested only $\sigma_M/\sigma_P = 18.5/24.1 = .7676$ or 76.76% of its funds, with the remainder placed in risk-free assets. The average excess return on this P^* would have been $.7676 \times 9.6\% = 7.37\%$. Thus, M-square of P is $7.37\% - 6.37\% = 1\%$. We also could find this measure directly from the difference in Sharpe ratios: $18.5\% \times (.398 - .344) = 1\%$. (For practice, verify that the M-square of portfolio Q is -0.72%.)

Performance Evaluation of Fund of Funds Using the Treynor Measure

We have used the Sharpe ratio, or its variant M-square, to choose between an actively managed portfolio competing with a passive benchmark as the sole risky position for an endowment. But some funds are so large that they engage *several* managers to run risky component portfolios. For example, CalPERS (the California Public Employee Retirement System) is a huge pension fund with an investment portfolio of about $300 billion in 2015. Like many large plans, it uses a **fund of funds** approach, allocating the endowment among a number of professional managers (funds) based in part on performance. This requires a different performance measure.

To see why, suppose CalPERS considers two managers, and it so happens that both establish portfolios with average returns, beta, and residual standard deviation equal to those of portfolio Q in Table 18.1. If Q were considered as the *sole* investment portfolio, the endowment fund would reject it because it has a negative M-square of $-.72\%$. But if the residuals of the two Q-like portfolios are uncorrelated, the residual SD of an equally weighted portfolio of the two would be only $\sqrt{2 \times (\frac{1}{2} \times 15.44)^2} = 10.92\%$. In turn, the total portfolio SD would be $\sqrt{(\beta\sigma_M)^2 + \text{Var}(e)} = \sqrt{(.5 \times 18.5)^2 + 10.92^2} = 14.31\%$. With the same average return as Q,

fund of funds

Mutual funds or hedge funds that invest in other funds.

the Sharpe ratio of the combined portfolio is 5.5/14.31 = .384, and its M-square is *positive:* 18.5(.384 − .344) = .74%. The improvement is due to the benefits of diversification that arise when we combine the two funds into an equally weighted portfolio. With residual risk lessened due to diversification, the trade-off of excess return to total volatility is enhanced.

This exercise suggests that for a fund of funds, where residual risk can be largely diversified away, we should compare average excess return to nondiversifiable or *systematic,* rather than total, risk. Because beta measures systematic risk, Treynor (1965) proposed the following measure, since named after him:

$$T = \frac{\bar{R}}{\beta} \tag{18.7}$$

Treynor measure

Ratio of portfolio excess return to beta.

As Table 18.1 demonstrates, the **Treynor measure** can differ from Sharpe's, suggesting that the proper performance measure depends on the role of the risky position in the investor's overall portfolio.

Performance Evaluation of a Portfolio Added to the Benchmark Using the Information Ratio

Now we consider yet another scenario, one in which an endowment considers adding a position in an actively managed portfolio to an already existing passive portfolio. The Central State University endowment has so far been a passive investor. Presented with a positive alpha achieved by the managers of *P* and *Q,* the board decides to add a position in just one of the portfolios. Which should it choose? To answer, we must choose the portfolio which, when combined with the benchmark, generates the higher Sharpe ratio. In Section 6.5 we saw that the key to this problem is the **information ratio.**

information ratio

Ratio of alpha to the standard deviation of diversifiable risk.

We can calculate the Sharpe ratio of the optimized portfolio from the Sharpe ratio of the benchmark *M,* and the information ratio of the added portfolio using Equation 6.17, which we repeat here:

$$S_O = \text{SQRT} \left[S_M^2 + \left(\frac{\alpha_P}{\sigma_e} \right)^2 \right] \tag{18.8}$$

where $\frac{\alpha_P}{\sigma_e}$ is the information ratio of portfolio *P.* Table 18.1 indicates that the information ratio of *P,* .24, is higher than that of *Q,* .15. Equation 18.8 tells us that the Sharpe ratio of the optimized portfolio using *P* will be .42, but only .38 using *Q*—still better than the benchmark's .34. Once again, we see that the role of the evaluated portfolio in the investor's complete portfolio determines the choice of performance measure. A different measure can lead to different judgment of superiority. The following table summarizes our conclusions:

Performance Measure	Definition	Application
Sharpe	$\dfrac{\text{Excess return}}{\text{Standard deviation}}$	When choosing among portfolios competing for the overall risky portfolio
Treynor	$\dfrac{\text{Excess return}}{\text{Beta}}$	When ranking many portfolios that will be mixed to form the overall risky portfolio
Information ratio	$\dfrac{\text{Alpha}}{\text{Residual standard deviation}}$	When evaluating a portfolio to be mixed with the benchmark portfolio

The Relation of Alpha to Performance Measures

Jensen measure

The alpha of an investment.

Alpha, also known as the **Jensen measure** after Michael Jensen, who first proposed it, appears everywhere in performance evaluation; why then, did we not present it as a performance measure? To answer, we must see its relation in the three performance measures.

When short sales are allowed, a negative alpha is as good as, or even better than, a positive one when constructing the optimal portfolio. A negative, or short, position in a negative-alpha stock will turn the alpha positive. If the stock's beta is positive, a negative position in it will also reduce systematic and therefore overall risk. Thus, a negative-alpha, positive-beta stock serves double duty in optimizing a portfolio.[4] However, if short sales are prohibited, a negative-alpha stock is worse than a zero-alpha one because it must be ignored.

The foregoing notwithstanding, when it comes to performance evaluation, we judge *ex post* (after the fact) portfolio returns. We cannot directly observe the manager's *ex ante* (before the fact) expectations. We know that the manager must have judged the alpha positive ex ante. But either forecasting errors or just bad luck could have driven a perceived positive-alpha portfolio into negative-alpha territory. Nevertheless, in performance evaluation, a negative realized alpha is taken to indicate below-average performance, if sometimes unfairly.

The relation of the Jensen measure to the Sharpe and Treynor measures can be gleaned from Equation 18.2. Substituting the right-hand side of the equation for the average excess return and employing some manipulation, we find that the Sharpe measure is

$$S_P = \frac{\bar{R}_P}{\sigma_P} = \frac{\beta_P \bar{R}_M}{\sigma_P} + \frac{\alpha_P}{\sigma_P}; \beta_P = \rho \frac{\sigma_P}{\sigma_M}$$

$$S_P = S_M \rho + \frac{\alpha_P}{\sigma_P} \tag{18.9}$$

$$S_P - S_M = S_M(\rho - 1) + \frac{\alpha_P}{\sigma_P}$$

where ρ is the correlation between the excess return of P and the benchmark. First, observe that alpha alone does not determine which portfolio has a larger Sharpe ratio. The standard deviation of P and its correlation with the benchmark are also important. Thus, positive alpha is *not* a sufficient condition for a managed portfolio to offer a higher Sharpe measure than the passive benchmark.

While it is not sufficient, a positive alpha is *necessary* to obtain a higher Sharpe ratio than the benchmark's S_M, because $S_M(\rho - 1)$ is negative. Superior performance in this context is a stiff challenge because, to achieve a positive alpha, it is necessary to construct a portfolio that is different from the benchmark. But this, in turn, will increase residual risk (which lowers the correlation coefficient) and offset the improvement in alpha. Notice that portfolio Q has a larger alpha, 2.3%, than P, 1.6%. Moreover, its ratio of alpha to standard deviation (2.3/18 = .128) is far greater than P's (1.6/24.1 = .066). Despite all this, Q's Sharpe ratio is smaller because its correlation coefficient with M is low (.51) compared with P's (.96).

The Treynor measure, which measures performance of a portfolio within a fund of funds, also is related to the portfolio alpha via Equation 18.2 as follows:

$$T_P = \frac{\bar{R}_P}{\beta_P} = \frac{\beta_P \bar{R}_M + \alpha_P}{\beta_P} = \bar{R}_M + \frac{\alpha_P}{\beta_P}$$

$$\beta_M = 1 \quad T_M = \bar{R}_M \tag{18.10}$$

$$T_P - T_M = \frac{\alpha_P}{\beta_P}$$

$\bar{R}_M$ is common to all portfolios; therefore, the relative rank of T_P is determined by the ratio $\frac{\alpha_P}{\beta_P}$. Thus, here too, a positive alpha is necessary but not sufficient to rank alternative active portfolios; we also need to know beta.

Finally, to complete the list, a positive alpha is needed to increase the Sharpe ratio of any portfolio to which the measured one is added. At the stage of constructing a portfolio, negative-alpha securities are useful because one can take a short position in them. But in performance evaluation we are asking whether the realized return on a manager's portfolio suggests we should

[4]Because a negative-beta stock is a rarity, negative alpha is generally better than a positive one when short sales are allowed.

employ the manager in the future to construct a piece of our overall portfolio. We are willing to do so only if the manager's forecasts have translated to realized returns with a positive alpha.

However, here, too, alpha alone cannot rank portfolios, given that a portfolio with lower alpha but also lower residual risk still can be judged of better overall performance (Sharpe ratio). We can be sure, though, that a negative alpha indicates inferior performance by all performance measures.

CONCEPT check 18.1

Consider the following data for a particular year when returns were high:

	Portfolio *P*	Market *M*
Average return	35%	28%
Beta	1.2	1.0
Standard deviation	42%	30%

Calculate alpha and the three performance measures for portfolio *P* and the market. The T-bill rate during the period was 6%. By which measures did portfolio *P* outperform the market?

Performance Evaluation with a Multi-Index Model

The Fama-French (FF) three-factor model discussed in Section 7.4 has almost completely replaced the single-index model in academic performance evaluation, and has been gaining "market share" in the investment services industry.[5] Evidence in favor of augmenting the market index with the size (SMB) and value (HML) portfolios is compelling. How should this affect performance evaluation?

Expanding Equation 18.1 to include the size and value factors, we have,[6]

$$R_{Pt} = \beta_P R_{Mt} + \beta_{SMB} r_{SMBt} + \beta_{HML} r_{HMLt} + \alpha_P + e_{Pt}$$
$$\bar{R}_{Pt} = \beta_P \bar{R}_{Mt} + \beta_{SMB} \bar{r}_{SMBt} + \beta_{HML} \bar{r}_{HMLt} + \alpha_P \qquad \text{(18.11)}$$

Equation 18.11 states that expected return is determined by betas on three factors, not just by beta relative to the market index. Notice that the index portfolio, *M,* has zero alpha; if you regress R_M on the three right-hand-side portfolios, it will be completely explained by the first factor, R_M, and so it will have an intercept of zero. The same applies to SMB and HML, and thus any portfolio formed from one or more index portfolios will have zero alpha.

In a three-factor security market as described by Equation 18.11, the market index is no longer the single efficient portfolio. Instead, we can use as our benchmark (default) portfolio the combination of factor portfolios that maximizes the Sharpe ratio. Once this benchmark is identified, the Treynor-Black method can be deployed: First identify the optimal active portfolio based on alpha values from security analysis; then mix the active portfolio with the said benchmark to find the optimal risky portfolio. This implies that the information ratio from the multifactor equation is the appropriate performance measure for an active portfolio to be added to the multifactor benchmark.

Failure to recognize the multi-index equation (when valid) in favor of a misspecified single-index equation can lead one to overestimate performance. Apparent alpha values that reflect the impact of omitted factors will be mistaken for superior performance.

Recent research by Cremers, Petajisto, and Zitzewitz (2013) shows that indexes such as the S&P 500 and Russell 2000 demonstrate significant nonzero alphas when evaluated using the

---

[5]The three FF factors (market, SMB, and HML) sometimes are augmented by a momentum portfolio (long in recent losers and short in recent gainers) and/or by a liquidity portfolio (long in liquid and short in illiquid stocks).

[6]Notice that while we use uppercase *R* (which denotes an excess return relative to the risk-free rate) for the market index, we use lowercase *r* for the SMB and HML factors because these portfolios already are excess returns, for example, small-stock returns over large-stock returns.

Performance Measures

The Excel model "Performance Measures" calculates all of the performance measures discussed in this chapter. The model available on our website is built to allow you to compare eight different portfolios and to rank them on all measures discussed in this chapter.

Spreadsheets are available in Connect

	A	B	C	D	E	F	G	H	I	J	K
1					Performance Measurement						
2											
3											
4											
5		Average	Standard	Beta	Unsystematic	Sharpe	Treynor	Jensen	M^2	T^2	Appraisal
6	Fund	Return	Deviation	Coefficient	Risk	Ratio	Measure	Alpha	Measure	Measure	Ratio
7	Alpha	0.2800	0.2700	1.7000	0.0500	0.8148	0.1294	-0.0180	-0.0015	-0.0106	-0.3600
8	Omega	0.3100	0.2600	1.6200	0.0600	0.9615	0.1543	0.0232	0.0235	0.0143	0.3867
9	Omicron	0.2200	0.2100	0.8500	0.0200	0.7619	0.1882	0.0410	-0.0105	0.0482	2.0500
10	Millennium	0.4000	0.3300	2.5000	0.2700	1.0303	0.1360	-0.0100	0.0352	-0.0040	-0.0370
11	Big Value	0.1500	0.1300	0.9000	0.0300	0.6923	0.1000	-0.0360	-0.0223	-0.0400	-1.2000
12	Momentum Watcher	0.2900	0.2400	1.4000	0.1600	0.9583	0.1643	0.0340	0.0229	-0.0243	0.2125
13	Big Potential	0.1500	0.1100	0.5500	0.0150	0.8182	0.1636	0.0130	-0.0009	0.0236	0.8667
14	S&P Index Return	0.2000	0.1700	1.0000	0.0000	0.8235	0.1400	0.0000	0.0000	0.0000	0.0000
15	T-Bill Return	0.06		0							
16											
17	Ranking by Sharpe										
18		Return	S.D.	Beta	Unsy. Risk	Sharpe	Treynor	Jensen	M^2	T^2	Appraisal
19	Millennium	0.4000	0.3300	2.5000	0.2700	1.0303	0.1360	-0.0100	0.0352	-0.0040	-0.0370
20	Omega	0.3000	0.2600	1.6200	0.0600	0.9615	0.1543	0.0232	0.0235	0.0143	0.3867
21	Momentum Watcher	0.2900	0.2400	1.4000	0.1600	0.9583	0.1643	0.0340	0.0229	0.0243	0.2125
22	S&P Index Return	0.2000	0.1700	1.0000	0.0000	0.8235	0.1400	0.0000	0.0000	0.0000	0.0000
23	Big Potential	0.1500	0.1100	0.5500	0.0150	0.8182	0.1636	0.0130	-0.0009	0.0236	0.8667
24	Alpha	0.2800	0.2700	1.7000	0.0500	0.8148	0.1294	-0.0180	-0.0015	-0.0106	-0.3600
25	Omicron	0.2200	0.2100	0.8500	0.0200	0.7619	0.1882	0.0410	-0.0105	0.0482	2.0500
26	Big Value	0.1500	0.1300	0.9000	0.0300	0.6923	0.1000	-0.0360	-0.0223	-0.0400	-1.2000
27											
28	Ranking by Treynor										
29		Return	S.D.	Beta	Unsy. Risk	Sharpe	Treynor	Jensen	M^2	T^2	Appraisal
30	Omicron	0.2200	0.2100	0.8500	0.0200	0.7619	0.1882	0.0140	-0.0105	0.0482	2.0500
31	Momentum Watcher	0.2900	0.2400	1.4000	0.1600	0.9583	0.1643	0.0340	0.0229	0.0243	0.2125
32	Big Potential	0.1500	0.1100	0.5500	0.0150	0.8182	0.1636	0.0130	-0.0009	0.0236	0.8667
33	Omega	0.3100	0.2600	1.6200	0.0600	0.9615	0.1543	0.0232	0.0235	0.0143	0.3867
34	S&P Index Return	0.2000	0.1700	1.0000	0.0000	0.8235	0.1400	0.0000	0.0000	0.0000	0.0000
35	Millennium	0.4000	0.3300	2.5000	0.2700	1.0303	0.1360	-0.0100	0.0352	-0.0040	-0.0370
36	Alpha	0.2800	0.2700	1.7000	0.0500	0.8148	0.1294	-0.0180	-0.0015	-0.0106	-0.3600

Excel Questions

1. Examine the performance measures of the funds included in the spreadsheet. Rank the funds by the five performance measures. Are the rankings across funds consistent? What explains these results?

2. Which fund would you choose if you were considering investing the entire risky portion of your portfolio? What if you were considering adding a small position in one of these funds to a portfolio invested in the market index?

FF model even when a momentum factor is added. The problem in finding adequate passive benchmarks tells us that performance evaluation is really (after more than 40 years) still in its infancy and our inferences should elicit some healthy skepticism.

18.2 STYLE ANALYSIS

Style analysis was introduced by Nobel Laureate William Sharpe (1992). The popularity of the concept was aided by a widely cited study (Brinson et al., 1991) concluding that 91.5% of the variation in returns of 82 mutual funds could be explained by the funds' asset allocation to bills, bonds, and stocks. While later studies have argued with the exact interpretation of Brinson's results, there is widespread agreement that asset allocation is responsible for a high proportion of the variation across funds in investment performance.

Sharpe considered 12 asset class (style) portfolios. His idea was to regress fund returns on indexes representing a range of asset classes. The regression coefficient on each index would then measure the implicit allocation to that "style." Because funds are barred from short positions, the regression coefficients are constrained to be either zero or positive and to sum to 100%, so as to represent a complete asset allocation. The R-square of the regression would then measure the percentage of return variability due to style choice rather than security selection. Finally, in this regression there is no intercept, and residuals are not constrained to sum to zero. The residuals measure the *total return from security selection* of the fund portfolio. They therefore track the success of security selection over time.

To illustrate the approach, consider Sharpe's study of the monthly returns on Fidelity's Magellan Fund over the period January 1985 through December 1989, shown in Table 18.2. While there are 12 asset classes, each one represented by a stock index, the regression coefficients are positive for only four of them. We can conclude that the fund returns are well explained by only four style portfolios. Moreover, these four style portfolios alone explain 97.3% of the variance of returns.

The proportion of return variability *not* explained by asset allocation can be attributed to security selection within asset classes. For Magellan, this was $100 - 97.3 = 2.7\%$. To evaluate the average contribution of stock selection to fund performance we track the residuals from the regression, displayed in Figure 18.3. The figure plots the cumulative effect of these residuals; the steady upward trend confirms Magellan's success at stock selection in this period. Notice that the plot in Figure 18.3 is far smoother than the plot in Figure 18.4, which shows Magellan's performance compared to a standard benchmark, the S&P 500. This reflects the fact that the regression-weighted index portfolio tracks Magellan's overall style much better than the S&P 500. The performance spread is much noisier using the S&P as the benchmark.

Of course, Magellan's consistently positive residual returns (reflected in the steadily increasing plot of cumulative return difference) is hardly common. Figure 18.5 shows the frequency distribution of average residuals across 636 mutual funds. The distribution has the familiar bell shape with a slightly negative mean of −.074% per month.

Style analysis has become very popular in the investment management industry and has spawned quite a few variations on Sharpe's methodology. Many portfolio managers utilize websites that help investors identify their style and stock selection performance.

TABLE 18.2 Sharpe's style portfolios for the Magellan fund	
	Regression Coefficient*
Bills	0
Intermediate bonds	0
Long-term bonds	0
Corporate bonds	0
Mortgages	0
Value stocks	0
Growth stocks	47
Medium-cap stocks	31
Small stocks	18
Foreign stocks	0
European stocks	4
Japanese stocks	0
Total	100
R-squared	97.3%

*Regressions are constrained to have nonnegative coefficients and to have coefficients that sum to 100%.

Source: William F. Sharpe, "Asset Allocation: Management Style and Performance Evaluation," *Journal of Portfolio Management,* Winter 1992, pp. 7–19.

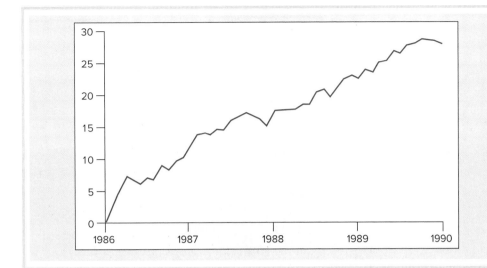

FIGURE 18.3

Fidelity Magellan Fund cumulative return difference: Fund versus style benchmark

Source: William F. Sharpe, "Asset Allocation: Management Style and Performance Evaluation," *Journal of Portfolio Management*, Winter 1992, pp. 7–19. Figure 17, p. 18.

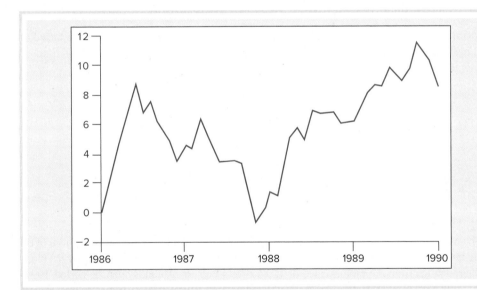

FIGURE 18.4

Fidelity Magellan Fund cumulative return difference: Fund versus S&P 500

Source: William F. Sharpe, "Asset Allocation: Management Style and Performance Evaluation," *Journal of Portfolio Management*, Winter 1992, pp. 7–19. Figure 16, p. 17.

18.3 MORNINGSTAR'S RISK-ADJUSTED RATING

The commercial success of Morningstar, Inc., the premier source of information on mutual funds, has made its *Risk Adjusted Rating* (RAR) among the most widely used performance measures. The Morningstar five-star rating is coveted by the managers of the thousands of funds covered by the service.

Morningstar calculates a number of RAR performance measures that are similar, although not identical, to the standard mean-variance measures (see Chapter 4 for a more detailed discussion). The most distinct measure, the Morningstar Star Rating, is based on comparison of each fund to a peer group. The peer group for each fund is selected on the basis of the fund's investment universe (e.g., international, growth versus value, fixed-income) as well as portfolio characteristics such as average price-to-book value, price–earnings ratio, and market capitalization.

FIGURE 18.5

Average tracking error, 636 mutual funds, 1985–1989

Source: William F. Sharpe, "Asset Allocation: Management Style and Performance Evaluation," *Journal of Portfolio Management,* Winter 1992, pp. 7–19. Figure 18, p. 18.

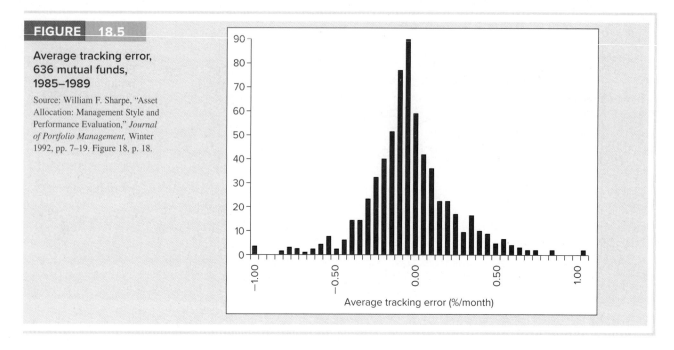

Morningstar computes fund returns (adjusted for loads) as well as a risk measure based on fund performance in its worst years. The risk-adjusted performance is ranked across funds in a style group, and stars are awarded based on the following table:

Percentile	Stars
0–10	1
10–32.5	2
32.5–67.5	3
67.5–90	4
90–100	5

The Morningstar RAR method produces results that are similar but not identical to those of the mean/variance-based Sharpe ratios. Figure 18.6 demonstrates the fit between ranking by RAR and by Sharpe ratios from the performance of 1,286 diversified equity funds over the period 1994–1996. Sharpe notes that this period is characterized by high returns that contribute to a good fit.

FIGURE 18.6

Rankings based on Morningstar's category RARs and excess return Sharpe ratios

Source: William F. Sharpe (1997), "Morningstar Performance Measures," **www.stanford.edu/~wfsharpe/art/stars/stars0.htm**.

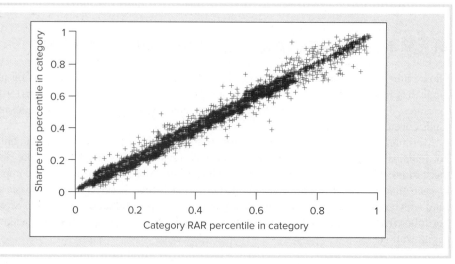

18.4 RISK ADJUSTMENTS WITH CHANGING PORTFOLIO COMPOSITION

One potential problem with risk-adjustment techniques is that they all assume that portfolio risk, whether measured by standard deviation or beta, is constant over the relevant time period. This isn't necessarily so. If a manager attempts to increase portfolio beta when she thinks the market is about to go up and to decrease beta when she's pessimistic, both the standard deviation and the beta of the portfolio will change over time. This can wreak havoc with our performance measures, as illustrated by the following example.

EXAMPLE 18.1

Risk Measurement with Changing Portfolio Composition

Suppose the Sharpe measure of the passive strategy (investing in a market-index fund) is .4. A portfolio manager is in search of a better, active strategy. Over an initial period of, say, four quarters, she executes a low-risk or defensive strategy with an annualized mean excess return of 1.5% and a standard deviation of 3.4%. This makes for a Sharpe measure of .44, which beats the passive strategy.

Over the next period of another four quarters, this manager finds that a high-risk strategy is optimal, with an annual mean excess return of 8.75% and standard deviation of 20%. Here again the Sharpe measure is .44. Over the two years, our manager maintains a better-than-passive Sharpe measure.

Figure 18.7 shows a pattern of (annualized) quarterly returns that is consistent with our description of the manager's strategy over two years. In the first four quarters, the excess returns are −3%, 5%, 1%, and 3%, consistent with the predicted mean and SD. In the next four quarters, the excess returns are −9%, 27%, 25%, and −8%, also consistent with predictions for the higher-volatility period. Thus, *each* year exhibits a Sharpe measure of .44.

But if we treat the eight-quarter sequence as a single measurement period instead of two independent periods, the portfolio's mean and standard deviation over the full period are 5.125% and 13.8% respectively, resulting in a Sharpe measure of only .37, apparently inferior to the passive strategy!

What went wrong in Example 18.1? Sharpe's ratio does not recognize the shift in the mean from the first four quarters to the next as a result of a strategy change. Instead, the difference in mean returns in the two years adds to the *appearance* of volatility in portfolio returns. The change in mean returns across time periods contributed to the variability of returns over the same period. Unfortunately, an outside observer cannot tell that policy changes within the

FIGURE 18.7

Portfolio returns. In the first four quarters, the firm follows a low-risk, low-return policy. In the next four quarters, it shifts to a high-risk, high-return policy.

sample period are the source of some of the return variability. Therefore, the active strategy with shifting means appears riskier than it really is, which biases the estimate of the Sharpe measure downward.

When assessing the performance of actively managed portfolios, it is important to keep track of portfolio composition and changes in portfolio mean return and risk. We will see another example of this problem when we turn to market timing.

Another warning: When we address the performance of mutual funds selected *because* they have been successful, we need to be highly cautious in evaluating their track records. In particular, we need to recognize that even if all managers were equally skilled, a few "winners" would emerge by sheer chance each period. With thousands of funds in operation, the best-performing funds will have been wildly successful, even if these results reflect luck rather than skill. The nearby box addresses this issue. Another manifestation of selection bias arises when we limit a sample of funds to those for which returns are available over an entire sample period. This practice implies that we exclude from consideration all funds that were closed down over the sample period. The ensuing bias is called **survivorship bias.** It turns out that when even a small number of funds have failed, the upward bias in the performance of surviving funds can be substantial. Most mutual fund databases now include failed funds so that samples can be protected from survivorship bias.

survivorship bias

Upward bias in average fund performance due to the failure to account for failed funds over the sample period.

Performance Manipulation

Imagine a manager whose performance is measured over two-year return periods, as in Example 18.1, for which the Sharpe ratio in each year is .44. Now we are at the end of the first year, when the manager's portfolio has returned the aforementioned four annualized quarterly rates of -3%, 5%, 1%, and 3%, providing the assumed Sharpe ratio of .44.

At this point the manager identifies the high-risk but better-than-passive strategy of the example; but he recognizes that following this strategy, he can expect a losing Sharpe ratio of .37. But what if the portfolio is "de-levered" by shifting $5/6$ of its value into bills. With this shift to safety (and zero excess return), the four second-year returns would be -1.5%, 4.5%, 4.17%, and -1.33%. Because the Sharpe ratio is invariant to shifts between the risky portfolio and risk-free asset, the second-year Sharpe ratio is still .44. Despite this, the eight-quarter Sharpe ratio is now evaluated at .47.[8] So far, little damage has been wrought. But given that the prospectuses of many funds promise general investment strategies (for example, investing in equity), they may not allow significant investments in bills. In that event, managers may reduce risk by moving into low-beta stocks. This distorts their security selection decisions, and investors end up with less-than-optimal portfolios due to the attempted manipulation of the Sharpe ratio.

This type of manipulation is only one in a menu that includes investments in derivatives. These strategies also can be used to manipulate the other performance measures discussed earlier in the chapter. A manipulation-free performance measure exists, but since it hasn't yet penetrated the industry, we leave it for future consideration.

18.5 PERFORMANCE ATTRIBUTION PROCEDURES

Rather than focus on risk-adjusted returns, practitioners often want simply to ascertain which decisions resulted in superior or inferior performance. Superior investment performance depends on an ability to be in the "right" securities at the right time. Timing and selection ability may be considered broadly, such as being in equities as opposed to fixed-income securities when the stock market is performing well. Or it may be defined at a more detailed level, such as choosing the relatively better-performing stocks within a particular industry.

[8]The two-year Sharpe ratio can be higher than that of each of the two individual years in part because of the bias correction to the SD (having to do with degrees of freedom). Instead of multiplying each annual estimate of SD by 4/3, we multiply the two-year estimate by "only" 8/7.

On the MARKET FRONT

THE MAGELLAN FUND AND MARKET EFFICIENCY: ASSESSING THE PERFORMANCE OF MONEY MANAGERS

Fidelity's Magellan Fund outperformed the S&P 500 in eleven of the thirteen years ending in 1989, when its manager, Peter Lynch, retired. Is such performance consistent with the efficient market hypothesis? Casual statistical analysis would suggest not.

If outperforming the market were like flipping a fair coin, as would be the case if all securities were fairly priced, then the odds of an arbitrarily selected manager producing eleven out of thirteen winning years would be only about 0.95%, or 1 in 105. The Magellan Fund, however, is not a randomly selected fund. Instead, it is the fund that emerged after a thirteen-year "contest" as a clear winner. Given that we have chosen to focus on the winner of a money management contest, should we be surprised to find performance far above the mean? Clearly not.

Once we select a fund precisely because it has outperformed all other funds, the proper benchmark for predicted performance is no longer a standard index such as the S&P 500. The benchmark must be the expected performance of the best-performing fund out of a sample of randomly selected funds.

Consider as an analogy a coin flipping contest. If fifty contestants were to flip a coin thirteen times, and the winner were to flip eleven heads out of thirteen, we would not consider that evidence that the winner's coin was biased. Instead, we would recognize that with fifty contestants, the probability is greater than 40% that the individual who emerges as the winner would in fact flip heads eleven or more times. (In contrast, a coin chosen at random that resulted in eleven out of thirteen heads would be highly suspect!)

How then ought we evaluate the performance of those managers who show up in the financial press as (recently) superior performers. We know that after the fact some managers will have been lucky. When is the performance of a manager so good that even after accounting for selection bias—the selection of the ex post winner—we still cannot account for such performance by chance?

SELECTION BIAS AND PERFORMANCE BENCHMARKS

Consider this experiment. Allow fifty money managers to flip a coin thirteen times, and record the maximum number of heads realized by any of the contestants. (If markets are efficient, the coin will have the same probability of turning up heads as that of a money manager beating the market.) Now repeat the contest, and again record the winning number of heads. Repeat this experiment 10,000 times. When we are done, we can compute the frequency distribution of the winning number of heads over the 10,000 trials.

The table (column 1) presents the results of such an experiment simulated on a computer. The table shows that in 9.2% of the

PROBABILITY DISTRIBUTION OF NUMBER OF SUCCESSFUL YEARS OUT OF THIRTEEN FOR THE BEST-PERFORMING MONEY MANAGER

Winning Years	Managers in Contest			
	50	100	250	500
8	0.1%	0	0	0
9	9.2	0.9	0	0
10	47.4	31.9	5.7	0.2
11	34.8	51.3	59.7	42.3
12	7.7	14.6	31.8	51.5
13	0.8	1.2	2.8	5.9
Mean winning years of best performer	10.43	10.83	11.32	11.63

contests, the winning number of heads was nine; in 47.4% of the trials ten heads would be enough to emerge as the best manager. Interestingly, in 43.3% of the trials, the winning number of heads was eleven or better out of thirteen.

Viewed in this context, the performance of Magellan is still impressive but somewhat less surprising. The simulation shows that out of a sample of 50 managers, chance alone would provide a 43.3% probability that *someone* would beat the market at least eleven out of thirteen years. Averaging over all 10,000 trials, the mean number of winning years necessary to emerge as most reliable manager over the thirteen-year contest was 10.43.

Therefore, once we recognize that Magellan is not a fund chosen at random, but a fund that came to our attention precisely because it turned out to perform so well, the frequency with which it beat the market is no longer high enough to be considered a violation of market efficiency. Indeed, using the conventional 5% confidence level, we could not reject the hypothesis that the consistency of its performance was due to chance.

The other columns in the table present the frequency distributions of the winning number of successful coin flips (analogously, the number of years in which the best-performing manager beats an efficient market) for other possible sample sizes. Not surprisingly, as the pool of managers increases, the predicted best performance steadily gets better. By providing as a benchmark the probability distribution of the best performance, rather than the average performance, the table tells us how many grains of salt to add to reports of the latest investment guru.

SOURCE: Alan J. Marcus, "The Magellan Fund and Market Efficiency." *The Journal of Portfolio Management,* Fall 1990, pp. 85–86.

Portfolio managers constantly make both broad-brush asset market allocation decisions as well as more detailed sector and security allocation decisions within markets. Performance attribution studies attempt to decompose overall performance into discrete components that may be identified with a particular level of the portfolio selection process.

Attribution analysis starts from the broadest asset allocation choices and progressively focuses on ever-finer details of portfolio choice. The difference between a managed portfolio's performance and that of a benchmark portfolio may be expressed as the sum of the contributions to performance of a series of decisions made at the various levels of the construction process. For example, one common attribution system decomposes performance into three components: (1) broad asset market allocation choices *across* equity, fixed-income, and money markets; (2) industry (sector) choice *within* each market; and (3) security choice within each sector.

To illustrate this method, consider the attribution results for a hypothetical portfolio. The portfolio invests in stocks, bonds, and money market securities. The portfolio return over the period is 5.34%. An attribution analysis appears in Tables 18.3 through 18.6.

The first step is to establish a benchmark level of performance against which performance ought to be compared. This benchmark is called the **bogey.** It is the portfolio designed to fit the fund prospectus in the absence of any active choice, in other words, the fund's passive or default portfolio. A fund's prospectus likely dictates a "normal" range for investment weights, say 50%–70% in equities, 20%–40% in bonds, and 0%–10% in bills. We will use the middle of these ranges to form the bogey, with a neutral asset allocation of 60% in equities, 30% in bonds, and 10% in bills, as shown in Table 18.3.

The prospectus also likely specifies benchmarks for each asset class. For instance, the S&P 500 often serves as the benchmark for equity investments, and the Barclays Capital U.S. Aggregate Bond Index may be used for fixed income. Table 18.3 shows the returns on these benchmarks for the relevant period. The neutral asset allocation, along with the returns on the benchmark indexes, generates the bogey return shown in Table 18.3, 3.97%. The table also records the actual portfolio return, 5.34%. The difference between actual and bogey returns, 1.37%, is the excess return of the managed portfolio. We next try to measure the relative contributions of asset allocation versus security selection decisions to this advantageous performance.

bogey

The benchmark portfolio an investment manager is compared to for performance evaluation.

Asset Allocation Decisions

The managed portfolio is actually invested in the equity, fixed-income, and money markets with weights of 70%, 7%, and 23%, respectively. The portfolio's performance could be due to the departure of this weighting scheme from the benchmark 60/30/10 weights and/or to superior or inferior results *within* each of the three broad markets.

TABLE 18.3	Performance of the managed portfolio		
Bogey Performance and Excess Return			
Component		Benchmark Weight	Return of Index during Month (%)
Equity (S&P 500)		0.60	5.81
Bonds (U.S. Aggregate Index)		0.30	1.45
Cash (money market)		0.10	0.48
Bogey = (0.60 × 5.81) + (0.30 × 1.45) + (0.10 × 0.48) = 3.97%			
Return of managed portfolio			5.34%
−Return of bogey portfolio			3.97
Excess return of managed portfolio			1.37%

To isolate the effect of the manager's asset allocation choice, we measure the performance of a hypothetical portfolio that would have been invested in the *indexes* for each market with the actual weights of 70/7/23. This return measures the effect of the shift away from the benchmark 60/30/10 weights without allowing for any effects attributable to active management of the securities selected within each market.

Superior performance relative to the bogey is achieved by overweighting investments in markets that outperform the bogey and by underweighting poorly performing markets. The contribution of asset allocation to superior performance equals the sum over all markets of the excess weight in each market times the return of the index for each market.

Table 18.4, Panel A demonstrates that asset allocation contributed 31 basis points to the portfolio's excess return of 137 basis points. The major contribution of asset allocation to superior performance in this period comes from the heavy weighting of the equity market when the equity market has an excellent return of 5.81%.

Sector and Security Selection Decisions

If .31% of the excess performance can be attributed to advantageous asset allocation across markets, the remaining 1.06% then must be attributable to sector selection and security selection within each market. Table 18.4, Panel B details the contribution of the managed portfolio's sector and security selection to total performance.

Panel B shows that the equity component of the managed portfolio has a return of 7.28% versus a return of 5.81% for the S&P 500. The fixed-income return is 1.89% versus 1.45% for the Aggregate Bond Index. The superior performance in both equity and fixed-income markets weighted by the portfolio proportions invested in each market sums to the 1.06% contribution to performance attributable to sector and security selection.

Table 18.5 documents the sources of the equity market performance by each sector within the market. The first three columns detail the allocation of funds within the equity market compared to their representation in the S&P 500. Column (4) shows the rate of return of each sector, and column (5) equals the product of the difference in the sector weight and the sector's performance.

TABLE 18.4 | Performance attribution

A. Contribution of Asset Allocation to Performance

Market	(1) Actual Weight in Market	(2) Benchmark Weight in Market	(3) Excess Weight	(4) Index Return (%)	(5) = (3) × (4) Contribution to Performance (%)
Equity	0.70	0.60	0.10	5.81	0.5810
Fixed-income	0.07	0.30	−0.23	1.45	−0.3335
Cash	0.23	0.10	0.13	0.48	0.0624
Contribution of asset allocation					0.3099

B. Contribution of Selection to Total Performance

Market	(1) Portfolio Performance (%)	(2) Index Performance (%)	(3) Excess Performance (%)	(4) Portfolio Weight	(5) = (3) × (4) Contribution (%)
Equity	7.28	5.81	1.47	0.70	1.03
Fixed-income	1.89	1.45	0.44	0.07	0.03
Contribution of selection within markets					1.06

TABLE 18.5	Sector allocation within the equity market				
	(1)	**(2)**	**(3)**	**(4)**	**(5) = (3) × (4)**
	Beginning-of-Month Weights				
Sector	**Portfolio**	**S&P 500**	**Difference in Weights**	**Sector Return (%)**	**Contribution of Sector Allocation (%)**
Basic materials	0.0196	0.083	−0.0634	6.9	−0.437
Business services	0.0784	0.041	0.0374	7.0	0.262
Capital goods	0.0187	0.078	−0.0593	4.1	−0.243
Consumer cyclical	0.0847	0.125	−0.0403	8.8	−0.355
Consumer noncyclical	0.4037	0.204	0.1997	10.0	1.997
Credit sensitive	0.2401	0.218	0.0221	5.0	0.111
Energy	0.1353	0.142	−0.0067	2.6	−0.017
Technology	0.0195	0.109	−0.0895	0.3	−0.027
Total	1.0000	1.000	0.0000		1.290

Note that good performance derives from overweighting well-performing sectors such as consumer noncyclicals, as well as underweighting poorly performing sectors such as technology. The excess return of the equity component of the portfolio attributable to sector allocation alone is 1.29%. As the equity component of the portfolio outperformed the S&P 500 by 1.47%, we conclude that the effect of security selection within sectors must have contributed an additional 1.47 − 1.29, or .18%, to the performance of the equity component of the portfolio.

A similar sector analysis can be applied to the fixed-income portion of the portfolio, but we do not show those results here.

Summing Up Component Contributions

In this attribution period, all facets of the portfolio selection process were successful. Table 18.6 details the contribution of each aspect of performance. Asset allocation across

TABLE 18.6	Portfolio attribution: summary	
		Contribution (basis points)
1. Asset allocation		31.0
2. Selection		
a. Equity excess return		
i. Sector allocation	129	
ii. Security selection	18	
	147 × 0.70 (portfolio weight) =	102.9
b. Fixed-income excess return	44 × 0.07 (portfolio weight) =	3.1
Total excess return of portfolio		137.0

Performance Attribution

The Excel model "Performance Attribution" that is available on our website is built on the example that appears in Section 18.5. The model allows you to specify different allocations and to analyze the contribution sectors and weightings for different performances.

Spreadsheets are available in Connect

	A	B	C	D	E	F
1			Chapter 18			
2			Performance Attribution			
3	Solution to Question				Contribution	
4	Bogey Portflio		Weight	Return on	to Portfolio	
5	Component	Index	Benchmark	Index	Return	
6	Equity	S&P500	0.6	5.8100%	3.4860%	
7	Bonds	Aggregate Index	0.3	1.4500%	0.4350%	
8	Cash	Money Market	0.1	0.4800%	0.0480%	
9						
10	Return on Bogey				3.9690%	
11						
12				Contribution		
13	Managed Portfolio	Portfolio	Actual	to Portfolio		
14	Component	Weight	Return	Return		
15	Equity	0.75	6.5000%	4.8750%		
16	Bonds	0.12	1.2500%	0.1500%		
17	Cash	0.13	0.4800%	0.0624%		
18						
19	Return on Managed			5.0874%		
20						
21	Express Return			1.1184%		
22						
23						
24			Contribution of Asset Allocation			
25		Actual Weight	Benchmark	Excess	Market	Performance
26	Market	in Portfolio	Weight	Weight	Return	Contribution
27	Equity	0.75	0.6	0.15	5.8100%	0.8715%
28	Fixed Income	0.12	0.3	-0.18	1.4500%	-0.2610%
29	Cash	0.13	0.1	0.03	0.4800%	0.0144%
30	Contribution of					
31	Asset Allocation					0.6249%

Excel Questions

1. What would happen to the contribution of asset allocation to overall performance if the actual weights had been 70/17/13 in the three markets rather than 75/12/13? Explain your result.

2. Show what would happen to the contribution of security selection to performance if the actual return on the equity portfolio had been 7.5% instead of 6.5% and the return on the S&P 500 had been 6.81% instead of 5.81%. Explain your result.

the major security markets contributes 31 basis points. Sector and security allocation within those markets contributes 106 basis points, for total excess portfolio performance of 137 basis points.

The sector and security allocation of 106 basis points can be partitioned further. Sector allocation within the equity market results in excess performance of 129 basis points, and security selection within sectors contributes 18 basis points. (The total equity excess performance of 147 basis points is multiplied by the 70% weight in equity to obtain the contribution to portfolio performance.) Similar partitioning could be done for the fixed-income sector.

CONCEPT check 18.2

a. Suppose the benchmark weights had been set at 70% equity, 25% fixed-income, and 5% cash equivalents. What then would be the contributions of the manager's asset allocation choices?

b. Suppose the S&P 500 return had been 5%. Recompute the contribution of the manager's security selection choices.

18.6 MARKET TIMING

market timing

A strategy that moves funds between the risky portfolio and cash, based on forecasts of relative performance.

Pure **market timing** involves switching funds between the risky portfolio and cash in response to forecasts of relative performance. To evaluate the potential of a pure market-timing strategy, consider the fortunes of three families of investors who had $1 to invest on December 1, 1926. Their heirs counted their blessings 82 years later, in 2008. The investment history of the families included the Great Depression, a major bear market in 2008 (when the S&P 500 lost 39%), and seven other recessions in between. The families differed wildly in their investment strategy:

1. Family A invested solely in a money market or cash equivalents.
2. Family B invested solely in stocks (the S&P 500 portfolio), reinvesting all dividends.
3. Family C switched, *every month,* 100% of its funds between stocks and cash, based on its forecast of which sector would do better next month.

While the strategies of families A and B are straightforward, that of family C is worth pondering. Try asking friends: "What would it take to be a perfect market timer?" Many would venture that to accomplish perfect timing, the timer would need to be able to forecast the rate of return on stocks at the start of every month. But actually, you wouldn't need the precise rate of return: "All" the perfect timer would have to know is whether stocks will outperform cash! You might think that such elementary knowledge wouldn't be worth all that much. But examine Table 18.7, computed from the actual return history on cash and stocks.

The first panel of Table 18.7 provides the punch line: After 82 years, $1 returned $20 to the cash fund of family A, and most of those nominal profits were undone by inflation over the period. Despite the Great Depression and recessions of varying severity, the stock fund of family B outdid the cash fund by a factor of more than 80, ending up with $1,626. But the gains to the perfect-timing family C would have been otherworldly indeed (as was the family's power of prediction); the timing fund starting with $1 would have ended with $36.7 *billion.*

CONCEPT check 18.3

Use annual rates of return from Connect to replicate Table 18.7 for the 1926–2008 period for a market timer who could perfectly forecast only once a year, rather than every month. Why is the performance of the annual timer not as good as that of the monthly timer?

TABLE 18.7 Performance of cash, stocks, and perfect-timing strategies

I. Family fund as of the end of 2008

	Family/Strategy		
	A. Cash	**B. Stocks**	**C. Perfect Timing**
Final proceeds	$20	$1,626	$36,699,302,473

II. Annualized monthly rate-of-return statistics (%)

	A. Cash	B. Stocks	C. Perfect Timing
Geometric average	3.71	9.44	34.54
Arithmetic average	3.71	11.48	35.44
Minimum monthly rate*	−0.03	−28.73	−0.03
Maximum monthly rate†	1.52	41.65	41.65
Average excess return	0.00	7.77	31.73
Standard deviation	3.54	19.38	12.44

*Occurred in September 1931.

†Occurred in April 1933.

Both extreme values occurred during the Great Depression.

These results have some lessons for us. The first has to do with the power of compounding. This effect is particularly important as ever more funds under management represent pension savings. The horizons of pension investments may not be as long as 82 years, but they are measured in decades, making compounding an important factor.

The second is a huge difference between the end value of the all-safe asset strategy ($20) and of the all-equity strategy ($1,626). Why would anyone invest in safe assets? By now you know the reason: risk. The annual standard deviation of the equity strategy was 19.38%. The high standard deviation of the return on the equity portfolio is commensurate with its significantly higher average return. The higher average excess return reflects the long-term risk premium.

Is the return premium on the perfect-timing strategy also a risk premium? It can't be: Because the perfect timer never does worse than either bills or the market, the extra return cannot be compensation for the possibility of poor returns; instead it is attributable to superior analysis. The value of superior information is reflected in the tremendous ending value of the portfolio. This value does not reflect compensation for risk.

Consider how you might choose between two hypothetical strategies. Strategy 1 offers a sure rate of return of 5%; strategy 2 offers an uncertain return that is given by 5% *plus* a random number that is equally likely to be either 0% or 5%. The results for each strategy are:

	Strategy 1 (%)	Strategy 2 (%)
Expected return	5	7.5
Standard deviation	0	2.5
Highest return	5	10.0
Lowest return	5	5.0

Clearly, strategy 2 dominates strategy 1, as its rate of return is *at least* equal to that of strategy 1 and sometimes greater. No matter how risk averse you are, you will always prefer strategy 2 to strategy 1, even though strategy 2 has a significant standard deviation. Compared to strategy 1, strategy 2 provides only good surprises, so the standard deviation in this case cannot be a measure of risk.

You can look at these strategies as analogous to the case of the perfect timer compared with either an all-equity or all-cash strategy. In every period, the perfect timer obtains at least as good a return, in some cases better. Therefore, the timer's standard deviation is a misleading measure of risk when you compare perfect timing to an all-equity or all-cash strategy.

Valuing Market Timing as an Option

Merton (1981) shows that perfect market timing can be viewed as a call option on the market index in this sense: Investing 100% in T-bills plus holding a call option on the equity portfolio will yield returns identical to those of the portfolio of the perfect timer who invests 100% in either the safe asset or the equity portfolio, whichever will yield the higher return. The perfect timer's return is shown in Figure 18.8. The rate of return is bounded from below by the risk-free rate, r_f.

To see how timing ability can be treated as an option, suppose the market index currently is at S_0 and a call option on the index has exercise price of $X = S_0(1 + r_f)$. If the market outperforms bills over the coming period, S_T will exceed X; it will be less than X otherwise. Now look at the payoff to a portfolio consisting of this option plus S_0 dollars invested in bills.

	Payoff to Portfolio	
Outcome:	$S_T \leq X$	$S_T > X$
Bills	$S_0(1 + r_f)$	$S_0(1 + r_f)$
Call option	0	$S_T - X$
Total	$S_0(1 + r_f)$	S_T

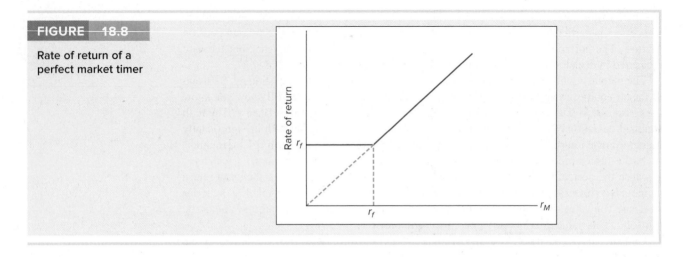

FIGURE 18.8

Rate of return of a
perfect market timer

The portfolio returns the risk-free rate when the market return is less than the risk-free rate and pays the market return when the market beats bills. This represents perfect market timing. Consequently, the value of perfect-timing ability must equal the value of the call option.

Valuation of the call option embedded in market timing is relatively straightforward using the Black-Scholes formula. Set $S_0 = \$1$ (to find the value of the call per dollar invested in the market), use an exercise price of $X = (1 + r_f)$ (for example, the current risk-free rate is about .12%), and a volatility of $\sigma = 18\%$ (about the historical annual standard deviation of the S&P 500). For a once-a-month timer, $T = \frac{1}{12}$. According to the Black-Scholes formula, the call option conveyed by market-timing ability is worth 2.1% of assets, and this is the monthly fee one could presumably charge for such services. Annualized, that fee is about 28%, similar to the excess return of the market timer in Table 18.7. Less frequent timing would be worth less (see Concept Check 18.3). If one could time the market only on an annual basis, then $T = 1$ and the value of perfect timing would be about 7.2% per year.

The Value of Imperfect Forecasting

But managers are not perfect forecasters. While managers who are right most of the time presumably do very well, "right most of the time" does not mean merely the *percentage* of the time a manager is right. A Tucson, Arizona, weather forecaster who *always* predicts "no rain" may be right 90% of the time, but this "stopped clock" strategy does not require any forecasting ability.

Neither is the overall proportion of correct forecasts an appropriate measure of market forecasting ability. If the market is up two days out of three, and a forecaster always predicts a market advance, the two-thirds success rate is not a measure of forecasting ability. We need to examine the proportion of bull markets ($r_M > r_f$) correctly forecast *as well as* the proportion of bear markets ($r_M < r_f$) correctly forecast.

If we call P_1 the proportion of correct forecasts of bull markets and P_2 the proportion for bear markets, then $P_1 + P_2 - 1$ is the correct measure of timing ability. For example, a forecaster who always guesses correctly will have $P_1 = P_2 = 1$ and will show ability of 1 (100%). An analyst who always bets on a bear market will mispredict all bull markets ($P_1 = 0$), will correctly "predict" all bear markets ($P_2 = 1$), and will end up with timing ability of $P_1 + P_2 - 1 = 0$. If C denotes the (call option) value of a perfect market timer, then $(P_1 + P_2 - 1)C$ measures the value of imperfect forecasting ability.

The incredible potential payoff to accurate timing versus the relative scarcity of billionaires suggests that market timing is far from a trivial exercise and that very imperfect timing is the most that we can hope for.

Measurement of Market-Timing Performance

In its pure form, market timing involves shifting funds between a market-index portfolio and cash equivalents, such as T-bills or a money market fund, depending on whether the market as a whole is expected to outperform cash. In practice, most managers do not shift fully between cash and the market. How might we measure partial shifts into the market when it is expected to perform well?

To simplify, suppose the investor holds only the market-index portfolio and T-bills. If the weight on the market were constant, say, .6, then the portfolio beta would also be constant, and the portfolio characteristic line would plot as a straight line with a slope .6, as in Figure 18.9, Panel A. If, however, the investor could correctly time the market and shift funds into it in periods when the market does well, the characteristic line would plot as in Figure 18.9, Panel B. The idea is that if the timer can predict bull and bear markets, more will be shifted into the market when the market is about to go up. The portfolio beta and the slope of the characteristic line will be higher when r_M is higher, resulting in the curved line that appears in Figure 18.9, Panel B.

Treynor and Mazuy (1966) tested to see whether portfolio betas did in fact increase prior to market advances, but they found little evidence of timing ability. A similar test was implemented by Henriksson (1984). Overall, 62% of the funds in his study had negative point estimates of timing ability.

In sum, empirical tests to date show little evidence of market-timing ability. Perhaps this should be expected; given the tremendous values to be reaped by a successful market timer, it would be surprising to uncover clear-cut evidence of such skills in nearly efficient markets.

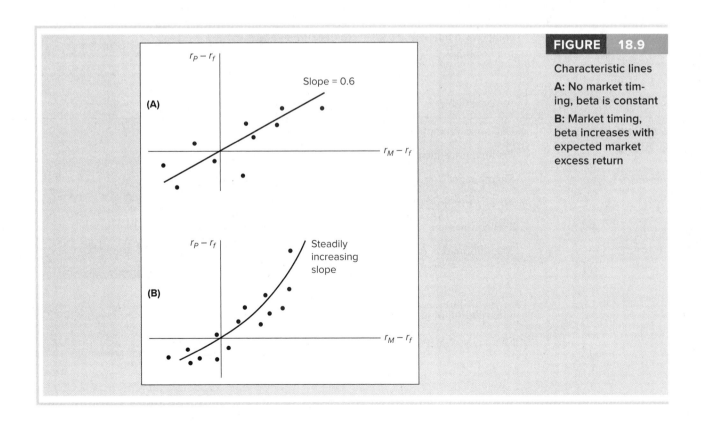

FIGURE   18.9

Characteristic lines
A: No market timing, beta is constant
B: Market timing, beta increases with expected market excess return

SUMMARY

- The appropriate performance measure depends on the investment context. The Sharpe measure is most appropriate when the portfolio represents the entire investment fund. The Treynor measure is appropriate when the portfolio is to be mixed with several other assets, allowing for diversification of firm-specific risk outside each portfolio. The information ratio may be used when evaluating a portfolio to be mixed with the passive index portfolio.
- The shifting mean and variance of actively managed portfolios make it harder to assess performance. A typical example is the attempt of portfolio managers to time the market, resulting in ever-changing portfolio betas and standard deviations.
- Common attribution procedures partition performance improvements to asset allocation, sector selection, and security selection. Performance is assessed by calculating departures of portfolio composition from a benchmark or neutral portfolio.
- Active management has two components: market timing (or, more generally, asset allocation) and security analysis.
- The value of perfect market-timing ability is enormous. The rate of return to a perfect market timer will be uncertain, but the risk cannot be measured by standard deviation, because perfect timing dominates a passive strategy, providing only "good" surprises.
- Perfect-timing ability is equivalent to having a call option on the market portfolio. The value of that option can be determined using valuation techniques such as the Black-Scholes formula.
- The value of *imperfect* market timing depends on the sum of the probabilities of the true outcome conditional on the forecast: $P_1 + P_2 - 1$. Because the value of perfect timing equals that of the implicit call option C, imperfect timing can be valued by: $(P_1 + P_2 - 1)C$.

KEY TERMS

active management, 593
bogey, 608
cash, 593
comparison universe, 593
fund of funds, 597

information ratio, 598
Jensen measure, 598
M-square (M^2), 596
market timing, 612
passive management, 593

Sharpe ratio, 595
survivorship bias, 606
Treynor measure, 598

KEY FORMULAS

Decomposition of the variance of a portfolio, P: $\sigma_P^2 = \beta_P^2 \sigma_M^2 + \sigma_e^2$

Performance measures:

Sharpe ratio: $S = \dfrac{\bar{R}}{\sigma}$

M^2 of portfolio P relative to its Sharpe ratio: $M^2 = \bar{R}_{P*} - \bar{R}_M = \sigma_M(S_P - S_M)$

Treynor measure: $T = \dfrac{\bar{R}}{\beta}$

The information ratio of an incremental portfolio and the overall Sharpe ratio:

$$S_O = \text{SQRT}\left[S_M^2 + \left(\frac{\alpha_P}{\sigma_e}\right)^2 \right]$$

The relation of alpha to other performance measures:

Sharpe ratio: $S_P = \dfrac{\bar{R}_P}{\sigma_P} = \dfrac{\beta_P R_M}{\sigma_P} + \dfrac{\alpha_P}{\sigma_P};$ $\beta_P = \rho\dfrac{\sigma_P}{\sigma_M}$

$$S_P = S_M\rho + \frac{\alpha_P}{\sigma_P}$$

$$S_P - S_M = S_M(\rho - 1) + \frac{\alpha_P}{\sigma_P}$$

Treynor measure:

$$T_P = \frac{\bar{R}_P}{\beta_P} = \frac{\beta_P\bar{R}_M + \alpha_P}{\beta_P} = \bar{R}_M + \frac{\alpha_P}{\beta_P}$$

$$\beta_M = 1 \qquad T_M = R_M$$

$$T_P - T_M = \frac{\alpha_P}{\beta_P}$$

Performance evaluation using the Fama-French 3-factor model:

$$R_{Pt} = \beta_P R_{Mt} + \beta_{SMB} r_{SMBt} + \beta_{HML} r_{HMLt} + \alpha_P + e_{Pt}$$

and

$$\bar{R}_{Pt} = \beta_P \bar{R}_{Mt} + \beta_{SMB} \bar{r}_{SMBt} + \beta_{HML} \bar{r}_{HMLt} + \alpha_P$$

Select problems are available in McGraw-Hill's *Connect*. Please see the Supplements section of the book's frontmatter for more information.

PROBLEM SETS

1. The finance committee of an endowment has decided to shift part of its investment in an index fund to one of two professionally managed portfolios. Upon examination of past performance, a committee member proposes to choose the portfolio that achieved a greater alpha value. *(LO 18-1)*
   a. Do you agree? Why or why not?
   b. Could a positive alpha be associated with inferior performance? Explain.

2. The board of a large pension fund noticed that the alpha value of the portfolio of one of its contract managers has recently increased. Should the fund increase the allocation to this portfolio? *(LO 18-1)*

3. Could portfolio *A* show a higher Sharpe ratio than that of *B* and at the same time a lower M^2 measure? Explain. *(LO 18-2)*

4. Two portfolio managers use different procedures to estimate alpha. One uses a single-index model regression, the other the Fama-French model. Other things equal, would you prefer the portfolio with the larger alpha based on the index model or the FF model? *(LO 18-2)*

5. Based on current dividend yields and expected capital gains, the expected rates of return on portfolios *A* and *B* are 11% and 14%, respectively. The beta of *A* is .8, while that of *B* is 1.5. The T-bill rate is currently 6%, while the expected rate of return of the S&P 500 index is 12%. The standard deviation of portfolio *A* is 10% annually, while that of *B* is 31%, and that of the index is 20%. *(LO 18-2)*
   a. If you currently hold a market-index portfolio, would you choose to add either of these portfolios to your holdings? Explain.
   b. If instead you could invest *only* in bills and *one* of these portfolios, which would you choose?

6. Evaluate the timing and selection abilities of the four managers whose performances are plotted in the following four scatter diagrams. *(LO 18-5)*

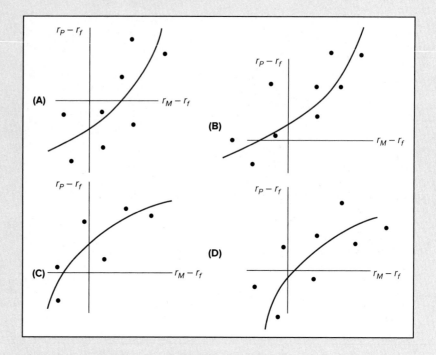

7. Consider the following information regarding the performance of a money manager in a recent month. The table presents the actual return of each sector of the manager's portfolio in column (1), the fraction of the portfolio allocated to each sector in column (2), the benchmark or neutral sector allocations in column (3), and the returns of sector indexes in column (4).   *(LO 18-4)*

	(1) Actual Return	(2) Actual Weight	(3) Benchmark Weight	(4) Index Return
Equity	2.0%	0.70	0.60	2.5% (S&P 500)
Bonds	1.0	0.20	0.30	1.2 (Aggregate Bond Index)
Cash	0.5	0.10	0.10	0.5

a. What was the manager's return in the month? What was her over- or underperformance?
b. What was the contribution of security selection to relative performance?
c. What was the contribution of asset allocation to relative performance? Confirm that the sum of selection and allocation contributions equals her total "excess" return relative to the bogey.

8. Conventional wisdom says one should measure a manager's investment performance over an entire market cycle. What arguments support this contention? What arguments contradict it?   *(LO 18-1)*

9. Does the use of universes of managers with similar investment styles to evaluate relative investment performance overcome the statistical problems associated with instability of beta or total variability?   *(LO 18-3)*

10. During a particular year, the T-bill rate was 6%, the market return was 14%, and a portfolio manager with beta of .5 realized a return of 10%. Evaluate the manager based on the portfolio alpha.   *(LO 18-1)*

11. Bill Smith is evaluating the performance of four large-cap equity portfolios: funds A, B, C, and D. As part of his analysis, Smith computed the Sharpe ratio and the Treynor measure for all four funds. Based on his finding, the ranks assigned to the four funds are as follows:

Fund	Treynor Measure Rank	Sharpe Ratio Rank
A	1	4
B	2	3
C	3	2
D	4	1

The difference in rankings for funds *A* and *D* is most likely due to: *(LO 18-2)*
a. A lack of diversification in fund *A* as compared to fund *D*.
b. Different benchmarks used to evaluate each fund's performance.
c. A difference in risk premiums.

Use the following information to answer Problems 12–16.

Primo Management Co. is looking at how best to evaluate the performance of its managers. Primo has been hearing more and more about benchmark portfolios and is interested in trying this approach. As such, the company hired Sally Jones, CFA, as a consultant to educate the managers on the best methods for constructing a benchmark portfolio, how best to choose a benchmark, whether the style of the fund under management matters, and what they should do with their global funds in terms of benchmarking.

For the sake of discussion, Jones put together some comparative two-year performance numbers that relate to Primo's current domestic funds under management and a potential benchmark.

| Style Category | Weight | | Return | |
	Primo	Benchmark	Primo	Benchmark
Large-cap growth	0.60	0.50	17%	16%
Mid-cap growth	0.15	0.40	24	26
Small-cap growth	0.25	0.10	20	18

As part of her analysis, Jones also takes a look at one of Primo's global funds. In this particular portfolio, Primo is invested 75% in Dutch stocks and 25% in British stocks. The benchmark invested 50% in each—Dutch and British stocks. On average, the British stocks outperformed the Dutch stocks. The euro appreciated 6% versus the U.S. dollar over the holding period, while the pound depreciated 2% versus the dollar. In terms of the local return, Primo outperformed the benchmark with the Dutch investments but underperformed the index with respect to the British stocks.

12. What is the within-sector selection effect for each individual sector? *(LO 18-4)*

13. Calculate the amount by which the Primo portfolio out- (or under-) performed the market over the period, as well as the contribution to performance of the pure sector allocation and security selection decisions. *(LO 18-4)*

14. If Primo decides to use return-based style analysis, will the R^2 of the regression equation of a passively managed fund be higher or lower than that of an actively managed fund? *(LO 18-3)*

15. Which of the following statements about Primo's global fund is most correct? Primo appears to have a positive currency allocation effect as well as: *(LO 18-4)*
a. A negative market allocation effect and a positive security allocation effect.
b. A negative market allocation effect and a negative security allocation effect.
c. A positive market allocation effect and a negative security allocation effect.

16. Kelli Blakely is a portfolio manager for the Miranda Fund (Miranda), a core large-cap equity fund. The market proxy and benchmark for performance measurement purposes is the S&P 500. Although the Miranda portfolio generally mirrors the asset class and

sector weightings of the S&P, Blakely is allowed a significant amount of leeway in managing the fund. Her portfolio holds only stocks found in the S&P 500 and cash.

Blakely was able to produce exceptional returns last year (as outlined in the table below) through her market-timing and security selection skills. At the outset of the year, she became extremely concerned that the combination of a weak economy and geopolitical uncertainties would negatively impact the market. Taking a bold step, she changed her market allocation. For the entire year her asset class exposures averaged 50% in stocks and 50% in cash. The S&P's allocation between stocks and cash during the period was a constant 97% and 3%, respectively. The risk-free rate of return was 2%.   *(LO 18-1)*

One-Year Trailing Returns		
	Miranda Fund	**S&P 500**
Return	10.2%	−22.5%
Standard deviation	37.0%	44.0%
Beta	1.10	1.00

    a. What are the Sharpe ratios for the Miranda Fund and the S&P 500?
    b. What are the M^2 measures for Miranda and the S&P 500?
    c. What is the Treynor measure for the Miranda Fund and the S&P 500?
    d. What is the Jensen measure for the Miranda Fund?

17. Log in to Connect and link to the material for Chapter 18, where you will find five years of monthly returns for two mutual funds, Vanguard's U.S. Growth Fund and U.S. Value Fund, as well as corresponding returns for the S&P 500 and the Treasury-bill rate.   *(LO 18-2)*

    a. Set up a spreadsheet to calculate each fund's excess rate of return over T-bills in each month.
    b. Calculate the standard deviation of each fund over the five-year period.
    c. What was the beta of each fund over the five-year period? (You may wish to review the spreadsheets from Chapters 5 and 6 on the Index model.)
    d. What were the Sharpe, Jensen, and Treynor measures for each fund?

Challenge

18. Historical data suggest the standard deviation of an all-equity strategy is about 5.5% per month. Suppose the risk-free rate is now 1% per month and market volatility is at its historical level. What would be a fair monthly fee to a perfect market timer, according to the Black-Scholes formula?   *(LO 18-5)*

19. A fund manager scrutinizing the record of two market timers comes up with this information: *(LO 18-5)*

Number of months that $r_M > r_f$	135
Correctly predicted by timer A	78
Correctly predicted by timer B	86
Number of months that $r_M < r_f$	92
Correctly predicted by timer A	57
Correctly predicted by timer B	50

    a. What are the conditional probabilities, P_1 and P_2, and the total ability parameters for timers A and B?
    b. Using the data given in this problem, and the historical data in the previous problem, what is a fair monthly fee for the two timers?

CFA Problems

1. A plan sponsor with a portfolio manager who invests in small-capitalization, high-growth stocks should have the plan sponsor's performance measured against which *one* of the following? *(LO 18-3)*
   a. S&P 500 Index.
   b. Wilshire 5000 Index.
   c. Dow Jones Industrial Average.
   d. Russell 2000 Index.

2. The chairman provides you with the following data, covering one year, concerning the portfolios of two of the fund's equity managers (manager A and manager B). Although the portfolios consist primarily of common stocks, cash reserves are included in the calculation of both portfolio betas and performance. By way of perspective, selected data for the financial markets are included in the following table. *(LO 18-1)*

	Total Return	Beta
Manager A	24.0%	1.0
Manager B	30.0	1.5
S&P 500	21.0	
Aggregate Bond Index	31.0	
91-day Treasury bills	12.0	

   a. Calculate and compare the alpha of the two managers relative to each other and to the S&P 500.
   b. Explain *two* reasons the conclusions drawn from this calculation may be misleading.

3. Carl Karl, a portfolio manager for the Alpine Trust Company, has been responsible since 2015 for the City of Alpine's Employee Retirement Plan, a municipal pension fund. Alpine is a growing community, and city services and employee payrolls have expanded in each of the past 10 years. Contributions to the plan in fiscal 2020 exceeded benefit payments by a three-to-one ratio.

   The plan's board of trustees directed Karl five years ago to invest for total return over the long term. However, as trustees of this highly visible public fund, they cautioned him that volatile or erratic results could cause them embarrassment. They also noted a state statute that mandated that not more than 25% of the plan's assets (at cost) be invested in common stocks.

   At the annual meeting of the trustees in November 2020, Karl presented the following portfolio and performance report to the board.

ALPINE EMPLOYEE RETIREMENT PLAN

Asset Mix as of 9/30/20	At Cost (millions)		At Market (millions)	
Fixed-income assets:				
Short-term securities	$ 4.5	11.0%	$ 4.5	11.4%
Long-term bonds and mortgages	26.5	64.7	23.5	59.5
Common stocks	10.0	24.3	11.5	29.1
	$41.0	100.0%	$39.5	100.0%

INVESTMENT PERFORMANCE

	Annual Rates of Return for Periods Ending 9/30/20	
	5 Years	1 Year
Total Alpine Fund:		
Time-weighted	8.2%	5.2%
Dollar-weighted (Internal)	7.7%	4.8%
Assumed actuarial return	6.0%	6.0%
U.S. Treasury bills	7.5%	11.3%
Large sample of pension funds (average 60% equities, 40% fixed income)	10.1%	14.3%
Common stocks—Alpine Fund	13.3%	14.3%
Average portfolio beta coefficient	0.90	0.89
Standard & Poor's 500 Stock Index	13.8%	21.1%
Fixed-income securities—Alpine Fund	6.7%	1.0%
Salomon Brothers' Bond Index	4.0%	−11.4%

Karl was proud of his performance and was chagrined when a trustee made the following critical observations:

a. "Our one-year results were terrible, and it's what you've done for us lately that counts most."

b. "Our total fund performance was clearly inferior compared to the large sample of other pension funds for the last five years. What else could this reflect except poor management judgment?"

c. "Our common stock performance was especially poor for the five-year period."

d. "Why bother to compare your returns to the return from Treasury bills and the actuarial assumption rate? What your competition could have earned for us or how we would have fared if invested in a passive index (which doesn't charge a fee) are the only relevant measures of performance."

e. "Who cares about time-weighted return? If it can't pay pensions, what good is it!" Appraise the merits of each of these statements and give counterarguments that Karl can use. *(LO 18-2)*

4. A portfolio manager summarizes the input from the macro and micro forecasts in the following table: *(LO 18-2)*

MICRO FORECASTS

Asset	Expected Return (%)	Beta	Residual Standard Deviation (%)
Stock A	20	1.3	58
Stock B	18	1.8	71
Stock C	17	0.7	60
Stock D	12	1.0	55

MACRO FORECASTS

Asset	Expected Return (%)	Standard Deviation (%)
T-bills	8	0
Passive equity portfolio	16	23

a. Calculate expected excess returns, alpha values, and residual variances for these stocks.

b. Construct the optimal risky portfolio.

c. What is Sharpe's measure for the optimal portfolio and how much of it is contributed by the active portfolio? What is the M^2?

Morningstar has an extensive ranking system for mutual funds, including a screening program that allows you to select funds based on a number of factors. Open the Morningstar website at **www.morningstar.com** and click on the *Funds* link. Select the *Mutual Fund Quickrank* link. Use the Quickrank screener to find a list of the Large Stock funds with the highest one-year returns. Repeat the process to find the funds with the highest three-year returns. How many funds appear on both lists?

Select three of the funds that appear on both lists. For each fund, click on the ticker symbol to get its Morningstar report and look in the Ratings & Risk section.

1. What is the fund's standard deviation?
2. What is the fund's Sharpe ratio?
3. What is the standard index? What is the best-fit index?
4. What are the beta and alpha coefficients using both the standard index and the best-fit index? How do these compare to the fund's parameters?

Look at the Management section of the report. Was the same manager in place for the entire 10-year period?

18.1 Sharpe: $(\bar{r} - \bar{r}_f)/\sigma$

$S_P = (35 - 6)/42 = .69$

$S_M = (28 - 6)/30 = .733$

Jensen (or alpha): $\bar{r} - [\bar{r}_f + \beta(\bar{r}_M - \bar{r}_f)]$

$\alpha_P = 35 - [6 + 1.2(28 - 6)] = 2.6\%$

$\alpha_M = 0$

Treynor: $(\bar{r} - \bar{r}_f)/\beta$

$T_P = (35 - 6)/1.2 = 24.2$

$T_M = (28 - 6)/1.0 = 22$

18.2 Performance attribution

First compute the new bogey performance as

$$(.70 \times 5.81) + (.25 \times 1.45) + (.05 \times .48) = 4.45\%$$

a. Contribution of asset allocation to performance:

Market	(1) Actual Weight in Market	(2) Benchmark Weight in Market	(3) Excess Weight	(4) Index Return (%)	(5) = (3) × (4) Contribution to Performance (%)
Equity	0.70	0.70	0.00	5.81	0.000
Fixed-income	0.07	0.25	−0.18	1.45	−0.261
Cash	0.23	0.05	0.18	0.48	0.086
Contribution of asset allocation					−0.175

b. Contribution of selection to total performance:

Market	(1) Portfolio Performance (%)	(2) Index Performance (%)	(3) Excess Performance (%)	(4) Portfolio Weight	(5) = (3) × (4) Contribution (%)
Equity	7.28	5.00	2.28	0.70	1.60
Fixed-income	1.89	1.45	0.44	0.07	0.03
Contribution of selection within markets					1.63

18.3 Import the series of annual returns on T-bills and large stocks (S&P 500).

    a. Compute the return to the perfect timer. You can use the Excel function = max (stock return, bill return) to select the greater of the two returns each year.

    b. Use Excel functions to estimate average and SD.

    c. Generate the wealth-index series. Set the wealth index at the end of 1925 to 1. Because the rates of return are expressed in percentages, the index value at the end of 1926 = 1 + rate(1926)/100. For the following years, index = previous index × (1 + this year's return/100).

    d. The wealth index for 2008 is the terminal value of the fund per \$1 invested at the beginning of 1926.

    e. The geometric average equals: Terminal value^(1/82) − 1. Notice that this calculation results in a return expressed as a decimal, not percent.

    f. The performance of the annual timer is not as good as the monthly timer. The annual timer may switch funds between the market and T-bills only once per year. He cannot advantageously move funds between the market and bills across months *within* each year. Someone who can time perfectly will always be better off when allowed to make more frequent allocation choices.

18.4 The timer will guess bear or bull markets randomly. One-half of all bull markets will be preceded by a correct forecast, and, similarly, one-half of all bear markets will be preceded by a correct forecast. Hence, $P_1 + P_2 - 1 = \frac{1}{2} + \frac{1}{2} - 1 = 0$.

Globalization and International Investing

Learning Objectives

LO 19-1 Understand the special issues that affect the efficacy of international diversification.

LO 19-2 Formulate hedge strategies to offset the currency risk involved in international investments.

LO 19-3 Implement international investment strategies.

LO 19-4 Decompose investment returns into contributing factors such as country, currency, and stock selection.

The S&P 500 market index is widely used in practice as "the" risky market portfolio. This may be justified on the grounds that an S&P 500 Index fund or ETF is the simplest acceptable passive portfolio of U.S. equities, and thus can be viewed as an appropriate benchmark. But the S&P index does not cover all U.S. equity, and even the broadest U.S. equities index makes up less than 40% of world equity market value. In this chapter, we look beyond domestic markets to survey issues of extended diversification.

In one sense, international investing may be viewed as no more than a straightforward generalization of our earlier treatment of portfolio selection with a larger menu of assets from which to construct a portfolio. One faces similar issues of diversification, security analysis, security selection, and asset allocation. On the other hand, international investments pose some problems not encountered in domestic markets: exchange rate risk, restrictions on capital flows across national boundaries, political risk, country-specific regulations, and differing accounting practices.

We begin by looking at market capitalizations of stock exchanges around the world and their relation to home-country GDP. Next, we examine exchange rate risk and how such risk can be mitigated by using foreign exchange futures and forward contracts. We also introduce political and country-specific risk that must be considered in the overall risk assessment of international investments.

We then examine the efficacy of investing globally in the context of equilibrium in international capital markets with and without hedging foreign exchange risk. Finally, we show how performance attribution procedures can be adapted to an international setting.

19.1 GLOBAL MARKETS FOR EQUITIES

You can easily invest today in capital markets of nearly 100 countries and obtain up-to-date data about your investments in each of them. More than 50 nations have stock markets with aggregate market capitalization above $1 billion. The data and discussion in this chapter are based on these countries.

The investments industry commonly distinguishes between "developed" and "emerging" markets. A typical emerging economy still is undergoing industrialization, is growing faster than developed economies, and its capital markets usually entail greater risk. We will use the criteria employed by the Financial Times Share Exchange (FTSE),[1] which emphasize capital market conditions, to classify markets as emerging or developed.

Developed Countries

To appreciate the myopia of an exclusive investment focus on U.S. stocks and bonds, consider the data in Table 19.1. Our list includes 32 "developed" countries, accounting for 85% of world equity capitalization in 2011 and 68% of the world gross domestic product in 2010.

The first two columns of Table 19.1 show market capitalization in 2000 and 2011. The first line shows capitalization for all world exchanges, showing total capitalization of corporate equity in 2011 as $38.2 trillion, of which U.S. stock exchanges made up $13.9 trillion, or 36.4%. The year-to-year changes in the figures in these columns demonstrate the volatility of these markets.

The next three columns of Table 19.1 compare country equity capitalization as a percentage of the world's in 2000 and 2011, as well as the growth in capitalization over those 12 years. The two crises of the first dozen years of the 21st century, the bursting of the tech bubble in 2000–2001, and the financial crisis of 2008–2009 hit the developed countries hardest. Average growth of developed-country equity markets over these years was an anemic 1.7%, compared with a world average of 2.79% and 16.3% for emerging markets.

The last three columns of Table 19.1 show GDP, per capita GDP, and the equity capitalization as a percentage of GDP in 2010. Although per capita GDP in developed countries is not as variable across countries as total GDP, which is determined in part by total population, market capitalization as a percentage of GDP is quite variable. This suggests widespread differences in economic structure even across developed countries.

Emerging Markets

For a passive strategy, one could argue that a portfolio of equities of just the six countries with the largest capitalization would make up 64% (in 2011) of the world portfolio and may be sufficiently diversified. However, this argument will not hold for active portfolios that seek to tilt investments toward promising assets. Active portfolios will naturally include many stocks or indexes of emerging markets.

Table 19.2 makes the point. Surely, active portfolio managers must prudently scour stocks in markets such as China with an annual growth rate so far in the 21st century in excess of 33% (⅓ per year!). Table 19.2 shows data from the 20 largest emerging markets. But managers also would not want to have missed other markets that exhibited marked, if not quite so dramatic, growth over the same years.

These 20 emerging markets make up 24% of the world GDP and, together with the developed markets in Table 19.1, make up 92% of the world GDP. Per capita GDP in these emerging markets was quite variable, ranging from $1,019 (Pakistan) to $41,122 (Singapore). Market capitalization as a percent of GDP of the BRIC countries (Brazil, Russia, India, China) is still below 70% (only 11% in China!), suggesting that these emerging markets can enjoy significant growth over the coming years, even without spectacular growth in GDP.

The growth of capitalization in emerging markets over this period was much more volatile than growth in developed countries, implying that both risk and rewards in this segment of the globe may be substantial.

---

[1]FTSE Index Co., the sponsor of the British FTSE stock market index, uses 14 specific criteria to divide countries into "developed" and "emerging" categories. Our list of developed countries includes all 25 countries that appear on FTSE's list.

TABLE 19.1 Market capitalization of stock exchanges in developed countries

| | Market Capitalization | | | | Annual Growth (%) | GDP | GDP per Capita | Market Capitalization as % of GDP |
| | Billions of U.S. Dollars | | Percent of World | | | | | |
	2000	2011	2000	2011	2000–2011	2010	2010	2010
World	**27,473**	**38,200**	**100%**	**100%**	**2.8**	**63,124**	**9,228**	**68**
U.S.	12,900	13,917	47.0	36.4	0.6	14,587	47,199	98
Japan	3,140	3,289	11.4	8.6	0.4	5,459	42,831	69
U.K.	2,566	2,794	9.3	7.3	0.7	2,249	36,144	133
Canada	615	1,581	2.2	4.1	8.2	1,577	46,236	114
France	1,278	1,455	4.7	3.8	1.1	2,560	39,460	70
Hong Kong	564	1,369	2.1	3.6	7.7	225	31,758	701
Germany	1,061	1,177	3.9	3.1	0.9	3,281	40,152	43
Switzerland	783	1,062	2.9	2.8	2.6	528	67,464	224
Australia	349	1,039	1.3	2.7	9.5	925	42,131	132
Korea	123	763	0.4	2.0	16.4	1,015	20,757	86
Spain	331	546	1.2	1.4	4.2	1,407	30,542	44
Italy	716	460	2.6	1.2	−3.6	2,051	33,917	28
Sweden	274	440	1.0	1.2	4.0	459	48,936	118
Netherlands	680	376	2.5	1.0	−4.8	779	46,915	60
Mexico	112	372	0.4	1.0	10.5	1,035	9,123	39
Norway	52	238	0.2	0.6	13.5	413	84,538	61
Chile	44	229	0.2	0.6	14.7	213	12,431	136
Belgium	159	216	0.6	0.6	2.6	469	43,144	54
Denmark	99	176	0.4	0.5	4.9	310	55,891	67
Turkey	50	164	0.2	0.4	10.4	734	10,094	34
Finland	280	139	1.0	0.4	−5.7	239	44,512	86
Israel	46	119	0.2	0.3	8.3	217	28,504	80
Poland	27	112	0.1	0.3	12.5	469	12,293	34
Austria	28	85	0.1	0.2	9.8	379	45,209	33
Ireland	82	65	0.3	0.2	−1.9	211	47,170	30
Portugal	64	59	0.2	0.2	−0.6	229	21,505	35
Czech Rep.	12	39	0.0	0.1	10.4	192	18,245	23
New Zealand	20	35	0.1	0.1	5.0	136	31,067	35
Luxemburg	28	34	0.1	0.1	1.7	53	105,438	79
Greece	72	29	0.3	0.1	−7.1	301	26,600	21
Hungary	12	19	0.0	0.0	4.1	129	12,852	22
Slovenia	2	6	0.0	0.0	11.2	47	22,851	18

Source: Market capitalization: Datastream, **online.thomsonreuters.com/datastream;** GDP and GDP per capita: The World Bank, **data.worldbank.org.**

TABLE 19.2 Market capitalization of stock exchanges in emerging markets

	Market Capitalization								
	Billions of U.S. Dollars		Percent of World		Growth (%)	GDP	GDP per Capita	Market Capitalization as % of GDP
	2000	2011	2000	2011	2000–2011	2010	2010	2010
Brazil	180	1,056	0.7	2.8	15.9	2,088	10,710	66
India	107	868	0.4	2.3	19.0	1,727	1,475	69
Russia	19	694	0.1	1.8	34.9	1,480	10,440	58
China	13	499	0.0	1.3	35.2	5,927	4,428	11
Taiwan	177	455	0.6	1.2	8.2	430	18,300	134
Singapore	136	428	0.5	1.1	10.1	209	41,122	241
South Africa	104	405	0.4	1.1	12.0	364	7,275	134
Malaysia	83	330	0.3	0.9	12.1	238	8,373	135
Indonesia	21	301	0.1	0.8	24.8	707	2,946	41
Thailand	23	219	0.1	0.6	20.7	319	4,608	70
Colombia	4	191	0.0	0.5	37.3	288	6,225	70
Philippines	20	141	0.1	0.4	17.6	200	2,140	67
Peru	5	77	0.0	0.2	25.9	157	5,401	64
Argentina	24	36	0.1	0.1	3.6	369	9,124	15
Pakistan	5	26	0.0	0.1	15.2	177	1,019	17
Sri Lanka	1	14	0.0	0.0	27.5	50	2,375	31
Romania	0	14	0.0	0.0	36.9	162	7,538	9
Venezuela	6	6	0.0	0.0	-0.2	392	13,590	3
Cyprus	9	3	0.0	0.0	-9.7	23	28,779	28
Bulgaria	0	2	0.0	0.0	29.6	48	6,325	4

Source: Market capitalization: Datastream, **online.thomsonreuters.com/datastream**; GDP and GDP per capita: The World Bank, **data.worldbank.org.**

Market Capitalization and GDP

A contemporary view of economic development (rigorously stated in de Soto, 2000) holds that an important requirement for economic advancement is a developed code of business laws, institutions, and regulations that allows citizens to legally own, capitalize, and trade capital assets. As a corollary, we expect that development of equity markets will serve as a catalyst for enrichment of the population, that is, that countries with larger relative capitalization of equities will tend to be richer. For rich countries, with already-large equity markets, this relationship will be weaker.

Figure 19.1 depicts the relationship[2] between per capita GDP and market capitalization (where both variables have been transformed to log10 scale). Figure 19.1, Panel A,

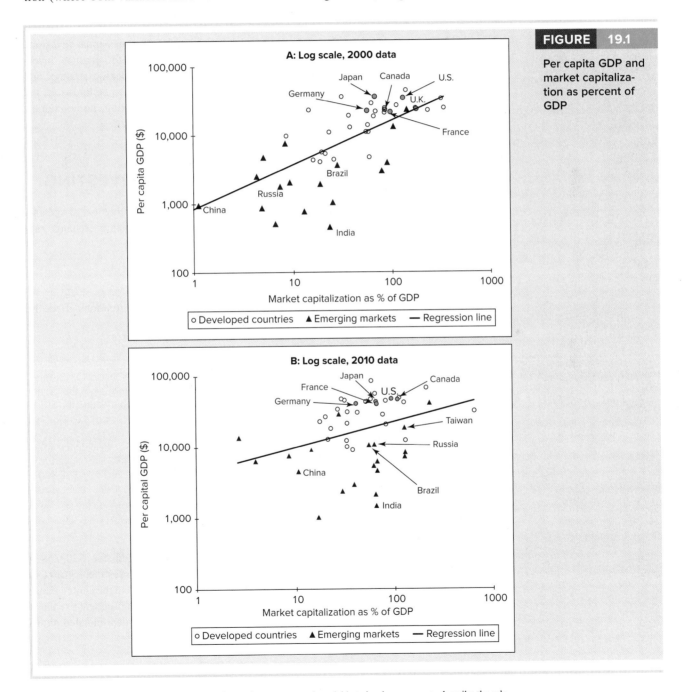

FIGURE 19.1

Per capita GDP and market capitalization as percent of GDP

[2] This simple single-variable regression is put forward not as a causal model but simply as a way to describe the relation between per capita GDP and the size of markets.

shows a scatter diagram and regression line for 2000, while the situation in 2011 is shown in Figure 19.1, Panel B. While developed markets are mostly above the line and emerging markets mostly below it, the latter dramatically moved up in relative market capitalization over these years. This move was sufficient to greatly moderate the slope of the line. One can also easily see the upward shift of the whole world on the vertical axis that measures per capita GDP.

The regression slope coefficient measures the average percent change in per capita income when market capitalization increases by 1%. In 2000, this value was .64, but it fell to .35 in 2011. The scatter around the regression line has also visibly grown, as reflected in an R-square of .52 in 2000 but only .10 in 2011.

Home-Country Bias

One would expect that most investors, particularly institutional and professional investors, would be aware of the opportunities offered by international investing. Yet in practice, investors grossly overweight home-country stocks compared to a neutral indexing strategy and underweight, or even completely ignore, foreign equities. This has come to be known as the *home-country bias.* Despite a continuous increase in cross-border investing, home-country bias still pervades investor portfolios. We return to this issue in Section 19.3.

19.2 RISK FACTORS IN INTERNATIONAL INVESTING

Opportunities in international investments do not come free of risk or of the cost of specialized analysis. The risk factors that are unique to international investments are exchange rate risk and country-specific risk, discussed in the next two sections.

Exchange Rate Risk

It is best to begin with a simple example showing how exchange rate fluctuations affect the returns of investments denominated in foreign currencies.

EXAMPLE 19.1

Exchange Rate Risk

Consider an investment in risk-free British government bills paying 10% annual interest in British pounds. While these U.K. bills would be the risk-free asset to a British investor, this is not the case for a U.S. investor. Suppose, for example, the current exchange rate is $2 per pound, and the U.S. investor starts with $20,000. That amount can be exchanged for £10,000 and invested at a riskless 10% rate in the United Kingdom to provide £11,000 in one year.

What happens if the dollar–pound exchange rate varies over the year? Say that during the year, the pound depreciates relative to the dollar, so that by year-end only $1.80 is required to purchase £1. The £11,000 can be exchanged at the year-end exchange rate for only $19,800 (= £11,000 × $1.80/£), resulting in a loss of $200 relative to the initial $20,000 investment. Despite the positive 10% pound-denominated return, the dollar-denominated return is negative 1%.

We can generalize from Example 19.1. The $20,000 is exchanged for $20,000/$E_0$ pounds, where E_0 denotes the original exchange rate ($2/£). The U.K. investment grows to $(20,000/E_0) \times [1 + r_f(\text{UK})]$ British pounds, where $r_f(\text{UK})$ is the risk-free rate in the United Kingdom. The pound proceeds ultimately are converted back to dollars at the subsequent exchange rate E_1, for total dollar proceeds of $20,000(E_1/E_0)[1 + r_f(\text{UK})]$. The dollar-denominated return on the investment in British bills, therefore, is

$$1 + r(\text{US}) = [1 + r_f(\text{UK})]E_1/E_0 \qquad \textbf{(19.1)}$$

We see in Equation 19.1 that the dollar-denominated return for a U.S. investor equals the pound-denominated return times the exchange rate "return." For a U.S. investor, the investment

Stock market returns in U.S. dollars and local currencies for 2014

Source: *The Economist*, January 3, 2015.

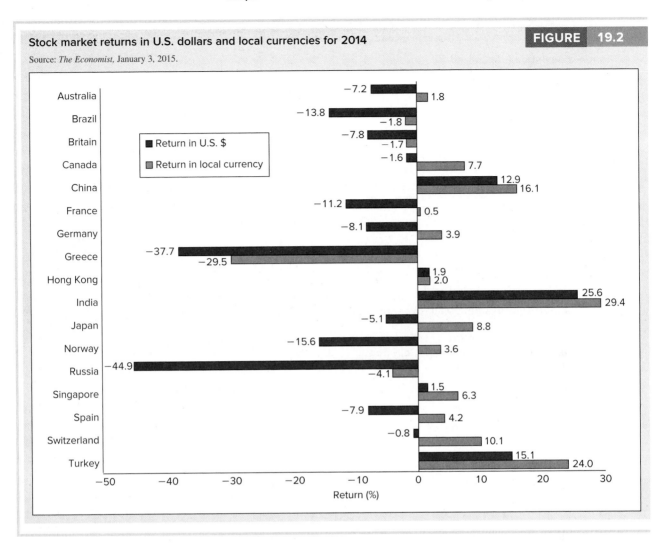

FIGURE   19.2

in British bills is a combination of a safe investment in the United Kingdom and a risky investment in the performance of the pound relative to the dollar. Here, the pound fared poorly, falling from a value of $2 to only $1.80. The loss on the pound more than offsets the earnings on the British bill.

Figure 19.2 illustrates this point. It presents rates of returns on stock market indexes in several countries for 2014. Returns are shown in local currencies as well as in dollars, adjusted for exchange rate movements. It's clear that exchange rate fluctuations over this period had large effects on dollar-denominated returns in several countries.

CONCEPT check 19.1

Using the data in Example 19.1, calculate the rate of return in dollars to a U.S. investor holding the British bill if the year-end exchange rate is (*a*) $E_1 = \$2/£$; (*b*) $E_1 = \$2.20/£$.

Pure **exchange rate risk** is the risk borne by investments in foreign safe assets. The investor in U.K. bills of Example 19.1 bears only the risk of the U.K./U.S. exchange rate. We can assess the magnitude of exchange rate risk by examination of historical rates of change in various exchange rates and their correlations.

Table 19.3, Panel A, shows historical exchange rate risk measured by the standard deviation of monthly percent changes in the exchange rates of major currencies against the U.S. dollar over the period 2001–2011. The data show that currency risk is quite high. The annualized standard

exchange rate risk

The uncertainty in asset returns due to movements in the exchange rates between the U.S. dollar and foreign currency.

TABLE 19.3 Rates of change in major currencies against the U.S. dollar, 2002–2011 (annualized monthly rate)

A. Standard deviation (annualized %)

	Euro (€)	U.K. (£)	Switzerland (SF)	Japan (¥)	Australia (A$)	Canada (C$)
	11.04	9.32	11.94	9.13	13.87	10.04

B. Correlation matrix

	Euro (€)	U.K. (£)	Switzerland (SF)	Japan (¥)	Australia (A$)	Canada (C$)
U.K. (£)	0.63	1				
Switzerland (SF)	0.83	0.51	1			
Japan (¥)	0.27	0.08	0.42	1		
Australia (A$)	0.75	0.60	0.61	0.05	1	
Canada (C$)	0.51	0.49	0.37	20.02	0.72	1

C. Average annual returns from rolling over one-month LIBOR rates (%)

Country	Currency	Return in Local Currency	Expected Gain from Currency	Actual Gain from Currency	Actual Return in U.S. Dollars	Surprise Component of Return	SD of Annual Return
U.S.	$	2.18			2.18		
Euro	€	2.38	−0.20	4.38	6.77	4.58	11.04
U.K.	£	3.51	−1.32	1.09	4.60	2.41	9.32
SF	SF	0.90	1.28	6.46	7.36	5.17	11.94
Japan	¥	0.24	1.94	5.75	5.99	3.81	9.13
Australia	A$	5.25	−3.07	7.94	13.19	11.01	13.87
Canada	C$	2.50	−0.31	5.01	7.51	5.32	10.04

Source: Exchange rates: Datastream, **online.thomsonreuters.com/datastream**; LIBOR rates: **www.economagic.com**.

deviation of the percent changes in the exchange rate ranged from 9.13% (Japanese yen) to 13.87% (Australian dollar). The standard deviation of returns on U.S. large stocks for the same period was 16%. Hence, exchange rate volatility was roughly 70% that of the volatility on stocks. Clearly, an active investor who believes that a foreign stock is underpriced but has no information about any mispricing of its currency should consider hedging the currency risk exposure when tilting the portfolio toward the stock. Exchange rate risk of the major currencies seems to have increased in this century. For example, a study by Solnik (1999) for the period 1971–1998 found lower standard deviations, ranging from 4.8% (Canadian dollar) to 12% (Japanese yen).

In the context of international portfolios, exchange rate risk may be mostly diversifiable. This is evident from the low correlation coefficients in Table 19.3, Panel B. (There are notable exceptions in the table, though, and this observation will be reinforced when we compare the risk of hedged and unhedged country portfolios in a later section.) Thus, passive investors with well-diversified international portfolios need not be overly concerned with hedging exposure to foreign currencies.

The effect of exchange rate fluctuations also shows up in Panel C, which presents the returns on money market investments in different countries. While these investments are virtually risk-free in local currency, they are risky in dollar terms because of exchange rate risk. International investment flows by currency speculators should roughly equalize the expected dollar returns in various currencies, adjusted for risk. Moreover, exchange rate risk is largely diversifiable, as Panel B shows, and hence we would expect similar dollar returns from cash investments in major currencies.

We can illustrate exchange rate risk using a yen-denominated investment during this period. The low yen-denominated LIBOR rate, .24%, compared to the U.S.-dollar LIBOR rate, 2.18%, suggests that investors expected the yen to appreciate against the dollar by around 1.94%, the interest rate differential across the two countries. But those expectations were not realized; in fact, the yen actually appreciated against the dollar at an annual rate of 5.75%, leading to an annual dollar-denominated return on a yen investment of 5.99% (the .24% yen interest rate together with the realized exchange rate appreciation of 5.75%). However, such deviations between prior expectations and actual returns of this magnitude are not shocking. The "surprise" return in a yen LIBOR investment (converted into dollars) was the difference between the actual return in dollars, 5.99%, and the dollar-denominated LIBOR rate of 2.18%, amounting to 3.81%. This surprise is actually considerably less than the yen standard deviation of 9.13%. In fact, none of the six surprises exceeded the standard deviation, which is actually the surprising event here.

Investors can hedge exchange rate risk using a forward or futures contract in foreign exchange. Recall that such contracts entail delivery or acceptance of one currency for another at a stipulated exchange rate. To illustrate, recall Example 19.1. In this case, to hedge her exposure to the British pound, the U.S. investor would agree to deliver pounds for dollars at a fixed exchange rate, thereby eliminating the future risk involved with conversion of the pound investment back into dollars.

EXAMPLE 19.2

Hedging Exchange Rate Risk

If the futures exchange rate in Example 19.1 had been $F_0 = \$1.93/£$ when the investment was made, the U.S. investor could have ensured a riskless dollar-denominated return by locking in the year-end exchange rate at $\$1.93/£$. In this case, the riskless U.S. return would have been 6.15%:

$$[1 + r_f(\text{UK})]F_0/E_0$$

$$= (1.10)1.93/2.00$$

$$= 1.0615$$

Here are the steps to lock in the dollar-denominated returns. The futures contract entered in the second step exactly offsets the exchange rate risk incurred in step 1.

Initial Transaction	End-of-Year Proceeds in Dollars
Exchange $20,000 for £10,000 and invest at 10% in the United Kingdom.	£11,000 × E_1
Enter a contract to deliver £11,000 for dollars at the (forward) exchange rate $1.93/£.	£11,000(1.93 − E_1)
Total	£11,000 × $1.93/£ = $21,230

You may have noticed that the futures hedge in Example 19.2 is the same type of hedging strategy at the heart of the spot-futures parity relationship discussed in Chapter 17. In both instances, futures markets are used to eliminate the risk of holding another asset. The U.S. investor can lock in a riskless dollar-denominated return either by investing in the United Kingdom and hedging exchange rate risk or by investing in riskless U.S. assets. Because the returns on two riskless strategies must provide equal returns, we conclude that

$$[1 + r_f(\text{UK})]F_0/E_0 = 1 + r_f(\text{US})$$

or

$$\frac{F_0}{E_0} = \frac{1 + r_f(\text{US})}{1 + r_f(\text{UK})} \qquad (19.2)$$

This relationship is called the **interest rate parity relationship** or **covered interest arbitrage relationship**.

interest rate parity relationship or covered interest arbitrage relationship

The spot-futures exchange rate relationship that precludes arbitrage opportunities.

Consider the intuition behind this result. If $r_f(US)$ is greater than $r_f(UK)$, money invested in the United States will grow at a faster rate than money invested in the United Kingdom. If this is so, why wouldn't all investors decide to invest their money in the United States? One important reason is that the dollar may be depreciating relative to the pound. Although dollar investments in the United States grow faster than pound investments in the United Kingdom, each dollar is worth progressively fewer pounds as time passes. Such an effect will exactly offset the advantage of the higher U.S. interest rate.

To complete the argument, we need only determine how a depreciating dollar will be reflected in Equation 19.2. If the dollar is depreciating, meaning that progressively more dollars are required to purchase each pound, then the forward exchange rate, F_0 (which equals the dollars required to purchase 1 pound for delivery in the future), must exceed E_0, the current exchange rate.

That is exactly what Equation 19.2 tells us: When $r_f(US)$ exceeds $r_f(UK)$, F_0 must exceed E_0. The depreciation of the dollar embodied in the ratio of F_0 to E_0 exactly compensates for the difference in interest rates available in the two countries. Of course, the argument also works in reverse: If $r_f(US)$ is less than $r_f(UK)$, then F_0 will be less than E_0.

EXAMPLE 19.3

Covered Interest Arbitrage

What if the interest rate parity relationship were violated? Suppose $r_f(US)$ is 6.15% but the futures price is $1.90/£ instead of $1.93/£. You could adopt the following strategy to reap arbitrage profits. In this example, let E_1 denote the exchange rate that will prevail in one year. E_1 is, of course, a random variable from the perspective of today's investors.

Action	Initial Cash Flow (in $)	Cash Flow in One Year (in $)
1. Borrow 1 British pound in London. Repay in one year.	$ 2	$-E_1(1.10)$
2. Convert the pound to $2 and lend in the United States.	−2	2(1.0615)
3. Enter a contract to purchase 1.10 pounds at a (futures) price of $F_0 = \$1.90/£$	0	$1.10(E_1 - 1.90)$
Total	$ 0	$.033

In step 1, you borrow 1 pound in the United Kingdom (worth $2 at the current exchange rate) and, after one year, repay the pound borrowed with interest. Because the loan is made in the United Kingdom at the U.K. interest rate, you would repay 1.10 pounds, which would be worth $E_1(1.10)$ dollars. The U.S. loan in step 2 is made at the U.S. interest rate of 6.15%. The futures position in step 3 results in receipt of 1.10 pounds, for which you would first pay F_0 (i.e., 1.90) dollars each and then convert into dollars at exchange rate E_1.

The exchange rate risk here is exactly offset between the pound obligation in step 1 and the futures position in step 3. The profit from the strategy is, therefore, riskless and requires no net investment. This is an arbitrage opportunity.

CONCEPT check 19.2

What are the arbitrage strategy and associated profits if the initial future price is $F_0 = \$1.95$/pound?

Ample empirical evidence bears out this theoretical relationship. For example, on May 10, 2015, the one-year dollar-dominated LIBOR rate was .736%, while the Euro LIBOR rate was .173%. The spot exchange rate was $1.115/€. Substituting these values into Equation 19.2, we find that interest rate parity implies that the forward exchange rate for delivery in one year should have been $1.115 \times 1.00736/1.00173 = 1.121/€$. The actual forward rate was $1.124/€, which was so close to the parity value that transaction costs would have prevented arbitrageurs from profiting from the discrepancy.

DIRECT VERSUS INDIRECT QUOTES The exchange rate in Example 19.1 is expressed as dollars per pound. This is an example of what is termed a *direct* exchange rate quote. The euro–dollar exchange rate is also typically expressed as a direct quote. In contrast, exchange rates for other currencies such as the Japanese yen or Swiss franc are typically expressed as *indirect* quotes, that is, as units of foreign currency per dollar, for example, 120 yen per dollar. For currencies expressed as indirect quotes, depreciation of the dollar would result in a *decrease* in the quoted exchange rate ($1 buys fewer yen); in contrast, dollar depreciation versus the pound would show up as a *higher* exchange rate (more dollars are required to buy £1). When the exchange rate is quoted as foreign currency per dollar, the domestic and foreign exchange rates in Equation 19.2 must be switched: In this case the equation becomes

$$F_0(\text{foreign currency/\$}) = \frac{1 + r_f(\text{foreign})}{1 + r_f(\text{U.S.})} \times E_0(\text{foreign currency/\$})$$

For example, if the interest rate in the U.S. is higher than in Japan, the dollar will sell in the forward market at a lower price than in the spot market.

Imperfect Exchange Rate Risk Hedging

Unfortunately, perfect exchange rate hedging usually is not so easy. In Example 19.2, we knew exactly how many pounds to sell in the forward or futures market because the pound-denominated proceeds in the United Kingdom were riskless. If the U.K. investment had not been in bills, but instead had been in risky U.K. equity, we would not know the ultimate value in pounds of our U.K. investment and therefore would also not know how many pounds to sell forward. That is, the hedging opportunity offered by foreign exchange forward contracts would be imperfect.

To summarize, the generalization of Equation 19.1 is that

$$1 + r(\text{US}) = [1 + r(\text{foreign})]E_1/E_0 \tag{19.3}$$

where $r(\text{foreign})$ is the possibly risky return earned in the currency of the foreign investment. You can set up a perfect hedge only in the special case that $r(\text{foreign})$ is itself a known number. In that case, you know you must sell in the forward or futures market an amount of foreign currency equal to $[1 + r(\text{foreign})]$ for each unit of that currency you purchase today.

How many pounds would the investor in Example 19.2 need to sell forward to hedge exchange rate risk if (*a*) *r*(UK) = 20%, and (*b*) *r*(UK) = 30%?	CONCEPT check **19.3**

Political Risk

In principle, security analysis at the macroeconomic, industry, and firm-specific level is similar in all countries. Such analysis aims to provide estimates of expected returns and risk of individual assets and portfolios. However, to achieve the same quality of information about assets in a foreign country is by nature more difficult and hence more expensive. Moreover, the risk of coming by false or misleading information is greater.

Consider two investors: an American wishing to invest in Indonesian stocks and an Indonesian wishing to invest in U.S. stocks. While each would have to consider macroeconomic analysis of the foreign country, the task would be much more difficult for the American investor. The reason is not that investment in Indonesia is necessarily riskier than investment in the U.S. You can easily find many U.S. stocks that are, in the final analysis, riskier than a number of Indonesian stocks. The difference lies in the fact that U.S. financial markets are more transparent than those of Indonesia.

In the past, when international investing was novel, the added risk was referred to as **political risk** and its assessment was an art. As cross-border investment has increased and more resources have been utilized, the quality of related analysis has improved. A leading organization in the

political risk

Possibility of expropriation of assets, changes in tax policy, restrictions on the exchange of foreign currency for domestic currency, or other changes in the business climate of a country.

field is the PRS (Political Risk Services) Group, and the presentation here follows the PRS methodology.[3]

PRS's country risk analysis results in a country composite risk rating on a scale of 0 (most risky) to 100 (least risky). Countries are then ranked by the composite risk measure and divided into five categories: very low risk (100–80), low risk (79.9–70), moderate risk (69.9–60), high risk (59.9–50), and very high risk (less than 50). To illustrate, Table 19.4 shows the placement of countries in the January 2011 issue of the PRS *International Country Risk Guide.* It is not surprising to find Norway at the top of the very-low-risk list, and small emerging markets at the bottom, with Somalia (ranked 140) closing the list. What may be surprising is the fairly mediocre ranking of the U.S. (ranked 32), comparable to Bahrain (29), both in the low-risk category.

The composite risk rating is a weighted average of three measures: political risk, financial risk, and economic risk. Political risk is measured on a scale of 100–0, while financial and economic risk are measured on a scale of 50–0. The three measures are added and divided by 2 to obtain the composite rating. The variables used by PRS to determine the composite risk rating from the three measures are shown in Table 19.5.

Table 19.6 shows the three risk measures for seven of the countries in Table 19.4, in order of the January 2011 ranking of the composite risk ratings. The table shows that by political risk, the United States ranked third among these seven countries. But in the financial risk measure, the U.S. ranked sixth among the seven. The surprisingly poor performance

TABLE 19.4	Composite risk ratings for January 2011 versus February 2010			
Rank in January 2011	Country	Composite Risk Rating January 2011	Composite Risk Rating February 2012	January 2011 versus February 2010	Rank in February 2010
	Very low risk				
1	Norway	**90.5**	90.00	0.50	1
11	Germany	**83.5**	83.50	0.00	5
13	Canada	**82.8**	82.75	0.00	6
16	Qatar	**82.0**	81.25	0.75	11
19	Japan	**81.0**	80.00	1.00	17
	Low risk				
31	United Kingdom	**77.3**	73.75	3.50	39
32	United States	**77.0**	77.25	−0.25	26
39	China, Peoples' Rep.	**75.0**	76.25	−1.25	30
44	Brazil	**74.5**	72.75	1.75	46
68	Spain	**70.0**	71.00	−1.00	58
	Moderate risk				
78	Indonesia	**68.5**	67.25	1.25	81
86	India	**67.3**	70.50	−3.25	62
104	Egypt	**64.5**	66.50	−2.00	84
111	Turkey	**63.3**	63.50	−0.25	100
	High risk				
124	Venezuela	**59.5**	53.75	5.75	133
127	Iraq	**58.5**	59.25	−0.75	119
129	Pakistan	**57.3**	57.00	0.25	125
	Very high risk				
138	Haiti	**48.5**	49.75	−1.25	137
140	Somalia	**41.5**	36.75	4.75	140

Source: *International Country Risk Guide,* January 2011, Table 1, The PRS Group, Inc.

[3]You can find more information on the website **www.prsgroup.com**. We are grateful to the PRS Group for supplying us data and guidance.

TABLE 19.5 Variables used in PRS's political risk score

Political Risk Variables	Financial Risk Variables	Economic Risk Variables
Government stability	Foreign debt (% of GDP)	GDP per capita
Socioeconomic conditions	Foreign debt service (% of GDP)	Real annual GDP growth
Investment profile	Current account (% of exports)	Annual inflation rate
Internal conflicts	Net liquidity in months of imports	Budget balance (% of GDP)
External conflicts	Exchange rate stability	Current account balance (% GDP)
Corruption		
Military in politics		
Religious tensions		
Law and order		
Ethnic tensions		
Democratic accountability		
Bureaucracy quality		

TABLE 19.6 Current risk ratings and composite risk forcasts

Country	Composite Ratings		Current Ratings		
	February 2010	January 2011	Political Risk January 2011	Financial Risk January 2011	Economic Risk January 2011
Norway	90.00	**90.50**	88.5	46.5	46.0
Canada	82.75	**82.75**	86.5	40.0	39.0
Japan	80.00	**81.00**	78.5	44.0	39.5
United States	77.25	**77.00**	81.5	37.0	35.5
China, Peoples' Rep.	76.25	**75.00**	62.5	48.0	39.5
India	70.50	**67.25**	58.5	43.5	32.5
Turkey	63.50	**63.25**	57.0	34.5	35.0

Source: *International Country Risk Guide,* January 2011, Table 2B, The PRS Group, Inc.

of the U.S. in this dimension was probably due to its exceedingly large government and balance-of-trade deficits, which put considerable pressure on its exchange rate. Exchange rate stability, foreign trade imbalance, and foreign indebtedness all enter PRS's computation of financial risk.

Country risk is captured in greater depth by scenario analysis for the composite measure and each of its components. Table 19.7 (Panels A and B) shows one- and five-year worst-case and best-case scenarios for the composite ratings and for the political risk measure. Risk stability is based on the difference in the rating between the best- and worst-case scenarios and is quite large in most cases. The worst-case scenario can move a country to a higher risk category. For example, Table 19.7, Panel B, shows that in the worst-case five-year scenario, China and Turkey were particularly vulnerable to deterioration in the political environment.

Finally, Table 19.8 shows ratings of political risk by each of its 12 components. Corruption (variable F) in Japan is rated better than in the U.S. In democratic accountability (variable K), China ranked worst, and the United States, Canada, and India best, while China ranked best in government stability (variable A).

Each monthly issue of the *International Country Risk Guide* of the PRS Group includes great detail and runs some 250 pages. Other organizations compete in supplying such evaluations. The result is that today's investor can become well equipped to properly assess the risk involved in international investing.

TABLE 19.7	Composite and political risk forecasts

A. Composite risk forecasts

Country	Current Rating January 2011	One Year Ahead			Five Years Ahead		
		Worst Case	Best Case	Risk Stability	Worst Case	Best Case	Risk Stability
Norway	**90.5**	88.3	93.3	5.0	83.3	92.8	9.5
Canada	**82.8**	78.3	84.3	6.0	75.3	86.5	11.3
Japan	**81.0**	77.0	84.3	7.3	72.5	87.5	15.0
United States	**77.0**	73.3	80.3	7.0	69.5	83.0	13.5
China, Peoples' Rep.	**75.0**	70.8	79.0	8.3	61.3	82.0	20.8
India	**67.3**	64.0	72.3	8.3	57.5	77.0	19.5
Turkey	**63.3**	57.8	67.5	9.8	53.8	71.5	17.8

B. Political risk forecasts

Country	Current Rating January 2011	One Year Ahead			Five Years Ahead		
		Worst Case	Best Case	Risk Stability	Worst Case	Best Case	Risk Stability
Norway	**88.5**	88.0	92.0	4.0	86.0	89.5	3.5
Canada	**86.5**	83.0	88.5	5.5	81.5	89.5	8.0
Japan	**78.5**	75.5	84.0	8.5	72.0	88.0	16.0
United States	**81.5**	77.5	85.5	8.0	76.0	87.0	11.0
China, Peoples' Rep.	**62.5**	58.5	68.5	10.0	55.0	73.0	18.0
India	**58.5**	55.0	64.0	9.0	53.5	71.0	17.5
Turkey	**57.0**	52.5	63.5	11.0	51.5	69.0	17.5

Source: **A:** *International Country Risk Guide,* January 2011, Table 2C; **B:** *International Country Risk Guide,* January 2011, Table 3C. The PRS Group, Inc.

TABLE 19.8	Political risk points by component, January 2011

This table lists the total points for each of the following political risk components out of the maximum points indicated. The final columns in the table show the overall political risk rating (the sum of the points awarded to each component) and the change from 2010.

A	Government stability	12		G	Military in politics	6
B	Socioeconomic conditions	12		H	Religious tensions	6
C	Investment profile	12		I	Law and order	6
D	Internal conflict	12		J	Ethnic tensions	6
E	External conflict	12		K	Democratic accountability	6
F	Corruption	6		L	Bureaucracy quality	4

Country	A	B	C	D	E	F	G	H	I	J	K	L	Risk Rating January 2011	Change from December 2010
Canada	8.5	9.0	11.5	11.0	11.0	5.0	6.0	6.0	5.5	3.5	5.5	4.0	86.5	0.5
China, Peoples' Rep.	9.0	8.0	6.5	9.0	9.0	2.0	3.0	5.0	4.0	3.5	1.5	2.0	62.5	0.0
India	6.0	4.5	8.5	6.0	9.5	2.0	4.0	2.5	4.0	2.5	6.0	3.0	58.5	−1.5
Japan	5.0	8.5	11.5	10.0	9.0	4.5	5.0	5.5	5.0	5.5	5.0	4.0	78.5	−0.5
Norway	7.5	10.5	11.5	11.0	11.0	5.0	6.0	5.5	6.0	4.5	6.0	4.0	88.5	0.0
Turkey	8.5	5.5	7.5	7.5	7.5	2.5	2.0	4.0	3.5	2.0	4.5	2.0	57.0	0.0
United States	8.0	8.5	12.0	10.0	9.5	4.0	4.0	5.5	5.0	5.0	6.0	4.0	81.5	0.5

Source: *International Country Risk Guide,* January 2011, Table 3B, The PRS Group, Inc.

19.3 INTERNATIONAL INVESTING: RISK, RETURN, AND BENEFITS FROM DIVERSIFICATION

U.S. investors have several avenues through which they can invest internationally. The most obvious method, which is available in practice primarily to larger institutional investors, is to purchase securities directly in the capital markets of other countries. However, even small investors now can take advantage of several investment vehicles with an international focus.

Shares of several foreign firms are traded in U.S. markets in the form of American Depositary Receipts (ADRs). A U.S. financial institution such as a bank will purchase shares of a foreign firm in that firm's country and then issue claims to those shares in the United States. Each ADR is then a claim on a given number of the shares of stock held by the bank. In this way, the stock of foreign companies can be traded on U.S. stock exchanges. Trading foreign stocks with ADRs is therefore as easy as trading U.S. stocks.

There is also a wide array of mutual funds and exchange-traded funds with an international focus. Single-country funds invest in the shares of only one country. In addition to single-country funds, there are several open-end mutual and exchange-traded funds with an international focus. For example, Fidelity offers funds with investments concentrated overseas, generally in Europe, in the Pacific Basin, and in developing economies in its emerging opportunities fund. Vanguard, consistent with its indexing philosophy, offers separate index funds for Europe, the Pacific Basin, and emerging markets. The nearby box discusses a wide range of single-country exchange-traded index funds.

U.S. investors also can trade derivative securities based on prices in foreign security markets. For example, they can trade options and futures on the Nikkei stock index of 225 stocks on the Tokyo stock exchange, or on FTSE indexes of U.K. and European stocks.

Risk and Return: Summary Statistics

Illustrations for most of our discussions in the remaining part of this chapter derive from a database of country market-index returns. We use 10 years of monthly returns over 2002–2011 for 48 non-U.S. country market indexes as well as the U.S. S&P 500. This decade stretches from the beginning of the recovery from the bursting of the tech bubble in 2001, through the low–interest rate boom period that followed and the ensuing financial crisis of 2008, and, finally, to the beginning of the slow recovery from that crisis.

Analysis of risky assets typically focuses on *excess* returns over the risk-free rate. This alone adds a perplexing aspect to international investing because the appropriate risk-free rate varies around the globe. Rates of return on identical indexes (as well as individual assets) will generate different excess returns when safe bonds are denominated in different currencies. Although our perspective here is U.S.-based, our methodology would serve investors in any country, yet the numbers may differ when applied to risk-free rates denominated in other currencies.

The tumultuous period we analyze resulted in unexpected low average excess returns, primarily in developed markets, while most emerging markets continued unabated growth. This fact alone conveys an important lesson. It provides an extreme example of the general observation that realized returns are very noisy reflections of investor expectations and cannot provide accurate forecasts of future returns. Past returns do, however, provide an indication of risk, at least for the near future. While the near-efficient market hypothesis applies *to expected returns* (specifically, future returns cannot be forecast from past returns), it does *not* apply to forecasting risk. Thus, our exercise will allow us to demonstrate the distinction between what you can and cannot learn from historical returns that evidently departed from prior expectations.

While active-strategy managers engage in individual-market asset allocation and security selection, we will restrict our international diversification to country market-index portfolios, keeping us on the side of an enhanced passive strategy. Nevertheless, our analysis illustrates the essential features of extended active management as well.

LOW-COST FOREIGN INDEX FUNDS CALLED WEBS ELIMINATE SOME OF THE GUESSWORK AND COSTS OF INVESTING ABROAD

With foreign markets generally stronger this year, a new way to invest abroad has appeared at a good time. WEBS, an acronym for World Equity Benchmark Shares, represents an investment in a portfolio of publicly traded foreign stocks in a selected country. Each WEBS Index Series seeks to generate investment results that generally correspond to the price and yield performance of a specific Morgan Stanley Capital International (MSCI) index.

You sell these shares rather than redeeming them, but there the similarity to closed-end country funds ends. WEBS are equity securities, not mutual funds. WEBS shares trade continuously during regular trading hours, just like any other publicly traded U.S. stock. In contrast, mutual fund shares do not trade in the secondary market, and are normally bought and sold from the issuing mutual fund at prices determined only at the end of the day. The new funds create and redeem shares in large blocks as needed, thus preventing the big premiums or discounts to net asset value typical of closed-end country funds. As index portfolios, WEBS are passively managed, so their expenses run much lower than for current open- or closed-end country funds.

WEBS shares offer U.S. investors portfolio exposure to country-specific equity markets, in a single, listed security you can easily buy, sell, or short on the Amex. Unlike American Depositary Receipts (ADRs) that give you an investment in just one company, WEBS shares enable you to gain exposure to a broad portfolio of a desired foreign country's stocks. You gain broad exposure in the country or countries of your choice without the complications usually associated with buying, owning, or monitoring direct investments in foreign countries. You also have the conveniences of trading on a major U.S. exchange and dealing in U.S. dollars.

Some investors may prefer the active management, diversity, and flexibility of open-end international equity index funds as a way to limit currency and political risks of investing in foreign markets. As conventional open-end funds, however, the international funds are sometimes forced by net redemptions to sell stocks at inopportune times, which can be a particular problem in foreign markets with highly volatile stocks.

You pay brokerage commissions on the purchase and sale of WEBS, but because their portfolios are passively managed, their management and administrative fees are relatively low and they eliminate most of the transaction charges typical of managed funds.

FOREIGN INDEX BASKETS

WEBS	Ticker Symbol	WEBS	Ticker Symbol
Australia	EWA	Malaysia	EWM
Austria	EWO	Mexico	EWW
Belgium	EWK	Netherlands	EWN
Canada	EWC	Singapore	EWS
France	EWQ	Spain	EWP
Germany	EWG	Sweden	EWD
Hong Kong	EWH	Switzerland	EWL
Italy	EWI	U.K.	EWU
Japan	EWJ		

SOURCES: Modified from *The Outlook*, May 22, 1996, published by Standard and Poor's; and Amex website, **www.amex.com**, February 2000.

We begin with an investigation of the characteristics of individual markets and then proceed to analyze the benefits of diversification, using portfolios constructed from these individual markets. The market capitalization of individual-country indexes can be found in Tables 19.1 and 19.2, and the aggregated results for the portfolios are shown in Table 19.9A. This table also displays the performance of two types of portfolios: portfolios aggregated from country indexes and regional-index portfolios. The performances of individual-country-index portfolios are shown in Table 19.9B.

For the aggregated country-index portfolios, we examine a strategy that constructs value-weighted portfolios of developed and emerging markets based on market capitalizations at the beginning of 2002. These portfolios are rebalanced after five years, in 2007, based on capitalizations at the end of 2006, and held for another five years. (Dividends are reinvested throughout the 10-year experiment.) Such a strategy is feasible to a large degree because many (although, admittedly, not all) country-index portfolios are investable as index funds or ETFs. Because not all country indexes are investable, this hypothetical strategy perhaps generates a bit more efficient diversification than is actually possible. On the other hand, if actually held, these value-weighted portfolios would automatically be rebalanced to value weights continually. In contrast, we rebalance only once after five years, which slightly attenuates diversification benefits. On balance, then, we expect these hypothesized portfolios to perform about as well as a feasible country-based, passive international strategy.

TABLE 19.9A Market value and performance of country portfolio combinations compared with regional-index portfolios

Country–Index Portfolios	Market Value ($ billion)			Performance 2002–2011 ($-denom. returns, %)		
	2001	2006	2011	Average	SD	Sharpe Ratio
U.S.	11,850	15,520	13,917	0.21	4.63	0.0444
Developed Ex U.S	10,756	22,065	18,487	0.48	5.48	0.0869
Emerging	1,230	5,319	5,765	1.35	6.86	0.1971
Developed + EM	11,987	27,384	24,251	0.61	5.63	0.1077
U.S. + Developed	22,606	37,585	32,403	0.34	4.99	0.0680
U.S. + EM	13,080	20,839	19,681	0.36	4.94	0.0736
World	23,836	42,904	38,168	0.50	5.32	0.0948
Regional-Index Portfolios						
MSCI EAFE (Europe + Australia + Far East) = Developed				0.42	5.41	0.0771
MSCI emerging markets				1.21	7.00	0.1734
MSCI World excluding U.S.				0.46	5.41	0.0841
World				0.31	4.90	0.0637

Source: Datastream.

TABLE 19.9B Performance of individual-country-index portfolios, monthly excess returns in U.S. dollars over 2002–2011

Individual-Country-Index Portfolios	Average	SD	Sharpe Ratio	Regression against U.S.				
				Corr. w/U.S.	Beta	Alpha	Residual SD	Info Ratio
Developed								
U.S.	0.21	4.63	0.0444	1	1	0	0	0
Australia	1.17	6.75	0.1728	0.82	1.20	0.92	3.84	0.24
Austria	0.78	8.87	0.0876	0.74	1.42	0.49	6.00	0.08
Belgium	0.32	7.47	0.0434	0.79	1.28	0.06	4.56	0.01
Canada	0.99	6.33	0.1557	0.80	1.10	0.76	3.77	0.20
Denmark	0.97	6.48	0.1496	0.78	1.10	0.74	4.04	0.18
Finland	0.09	8.93	0.0101	0.77	1.49	−0.22	5.72	−0.04
France	0.37	6.76	0.0548	0.88	1.29	0.11	3.19	0.03
Germany	0.58	7.80	0.0743	0.89	1.49	0.27	3.64	0.08
Greece	−0.51	10.10	−0.0506	0.66	1.43	−0.81	7.65	−0.11
Hong Kong	0.74	6.33	0.1175	0.69	0.94	0.55	4.61	0.12
Ireland	−0.37	7.69	−0.0477	0.79	1.31	−0.64	4.73	−0.13
Israel	0.56	6.19	0.0904	0.64	0.86	0.38	4.76	0.08
Italy	0.21	7.18	0.0291	0.82	1.27	−0.05	4.11	−0.01
Japan	0.23	4.95	0.0463	0.56	0.60	0.11	4.11	0.03
Netherlands	0.41	6.95	0.0589	0.88	1.32	0.14	3.32	0.04
New Zealand	0.97	6.22	0.1554	0.67	0.90	0.78	4.64	0.17
Norway	1.35	8.98	0.1507	0.78	1.51	1.04	5.68	0.18
Portugal	0.35	6.74	0.0524	0.73	1.06	0.13	4.63	0.03
Singapore	0.99	6.71	0.1475	0.75	1.09	0.77	4.43	0.17
Spain	0.76	7.53	0.1009	0.79	1.29	0.49	4.62	0.11
Sweden	0.94	8.01	0.1177	0.86	1.49	0.64	4.11	0.16
Switzerland	0.60	5.04	0.1194	0.79	0.86	0.42	3.10	0.14
U.K.	0.38	5.29	0.0725	0.87	1.00	0.18	2.60	0.07

(continued)

TABLE 19.9B   *(Concluded)*

Individual-Country-Index Portfolios	Average	SD	Sharpe Ratio	Regression against U.S.				
				Corr. w/U.S.	Beta	Alpha	Residual SD	Info Ratio
Emerging								
Argentina	1.32	11.05	0.1191	0.44	0.44	1.05	1.10	0.96
Brazil	2.10	10.86	0.1931	0.71	0.71	1.66	1.76	0.94
Chile	1.46	6.69	0.2179	0.63	0.63	0.91	1.27	0.72
China	1.37	8.13	0.1683	0.62	0.62	1.10	1.14	0.96
Colombia	2.95	8.76	0.3367	0.53	0.53	1.00	2.74	0.36
Czech Republic	2.06	7.93	0.2593	0.62	0.62	1.06	1.84	0.58
Egypt	2.17	10.29	0.2111	0.40	0.40	0.89	1.99	0.45
Hungary	1.25	10.78	0.1155	0.70	0.70	1.64	0.91	1.80
India	1.53	9.13	0.1676	0.62	0.62	1.21	1.28	0.95
Indonesia	2.77	10.01	0.2766	0.54	0.54	1.17	2.53	0.46
Jordan	0.59	6.32	0.0932	0.28	0.28	0.38	0.51	0.75
Malaysia	1.07	5.27	0.2033	0.59	0.59	0.67	0.93	0.71
Mexico	1.28	7.09	0.1809	0.83	0.83	1.27	1.02	1.24
Morocco	1.18	6.01	0.1970	0.31	0.31	0.41	1.10	0.37
Pakistan	1.87	10.09	0.1849	0.14	0.14	0.31	1.80	0.17
Peru	2.53	9.54	0.2655	0.52	0.52	1.08	2.31	0.47
Philippines	1.27	7.37	0.1725	0.48	0.48	0.77	1.11	0.69
Poland	1.19	10.24	0.1162	0.75	0.75	1.65	0.85	1.94
Russia	1.50	10.30	0.1457	0.61	0.61	1.35	1.22	1.10
South Africa	1.61	7.93	0.2031	0.68	0.68	1.16	1.37	0.84
Korea	1.34	8.76	0.1526	0.75	0.75	1.41	1.05	1.35
Sri Lanka	1.82	10.92	0.1663	0.19	0.19	0.45	1.72	0.26
Taiwan	0.52	7.44	0.0697	0.70	0.70	1.12	0.29	3.86
Thailand	1.92	8.34	0.2298	0.57	0.57	1.03	1.70	0.61
Turkey	1.66	13.14	0.1267	0.59	0.59	1.67	1.32	1.27

Source: Datastream, **online.thomsonreuters.com/datastream.**

These portfolios are contrasted with completely feasible international diversification by investing in regional-index funds, which are also shown in Table 19.9A. This comparison is based on standard performance statistics, namely, average and standard deviation of excess returns (denominated in U.S. dollars), as well as beta and alpha estimated against a U.S.-only portfolio. We will assess these performance statistics after we first take a broad-brush look at the return behavior of developed versus emerging market indexes.

Are Investments in Emerging Markets Riskier?

In Figure 19.3, developed countries and emerging markets are separately ordered from lowest to highest standard deviation. The standard deviations of investments in emerging markets are charted with those in developed countries. The graphs clearly show that, considered as total portfolios, emerging markets are generally riskier than developed countries because risk is measured by total volatility of returns. Still, you can find emerging markets that appear safer than some developed countries. However, if one considers adding a foreign country index to an indexed U.S. portfolio, the relevant risk measure is the country's beta against the U.S.[4]

Figure 19.4 ranks and charts the betas of country returns (in U.S. dollars) against the U.S. index. It shows that betas of six developed and eight emerging markets were estimated to be below 1. Notice, however, that this is only about one-third of all 48 foreign markets. Thus, we can foresee the conclusion: A well-diversified international portfolio may well be riskier than the U.S. alone, which has consistently exhibited the lowest standard deviation of all countries.

[4]A sufficient condition to reduce the standard deviation of a portfolio by adding an asset is that the beta of the asset on the portfolio be less than 1.

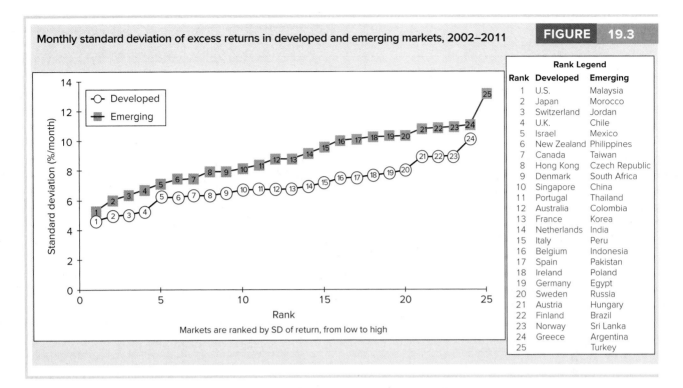

Monthly standard deviation of excess returns in developed and emerging markets, 2002–2011

FIGURE 19.3

Rank Legend		
Rank	**Developed**	**Emerging**
1	U.S.	Malaysia
2	Japan	Morocco
3	Switzerland	Jordan
4	U.K.	Chile
5	Israel	Mexico
6	New Zealand	Philippines
7	Canada	Taiwan
8	Hong Kong	Czech Republic
9	Denmark	South Africa
10	Singapore	China
11	Portugal	Thailand
12	Australia	Colombia
13	France	Korea
14	Netherlands	India
15	Italy	Peru
16	Belgium	Indonesia
17	Spain	Pakistan
18	Ireland	Poland
19	Germany	Egypt
20	Sweden	Russia
21	Austria	Hungary
22	Finland	Brazil
23	Norway	Sri Lanka
24	Greece	Argentina
25		Turkey

This is not to say, however, that an international portfolio with higher variance would be inferior. In fact, when a risk-free asset is available, minimum-variance portfolios are never efficient (they are dominated by the maximum Sharpe ratio, or tangency, portfolio on the efficient frontier). But, then, the international portfolio must show a sufficiently larger average return to provide a larger Sharpe ratio.

Comparison between developed and emerging markets' betas in Figure 19.4 shows that, in contrast to the picture painted by standard deviation, emerging markets are not meaningfully riskier to U.S. investors than developed markets. This is the most important lesson from this exercise.

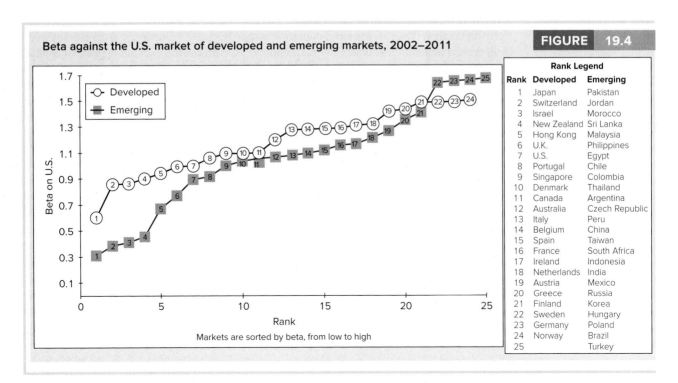

Beta against the U.S. market of developed and emerging markets, 2002–2011

FIGURE 19.4

Rank Legend		
Rank	**Developed**	**Emerging**
1	Japan	Pakistan
2	Switzerland	Jordan
3	Israel	Morocco
4	New Zealand	Sri Lanka
5	Hong Kong	Malaysia
6	U.K.	Philippines
7	U.S.	Egypt
8	Portugal	Chile
9	Singapore	Colombia
10	Denmark	Thailand
11	Canada	Argentina
12	Australia	Czech Republic
13	Italy	Peru
14	Belgium	China
15	Spain	Taiwan
16	France	South Africa
17	Ireland	Indonesia
18	Netherlands	India
19	Austria	Mexico
20	Greece	Russia
21	Finland	Korea
22	Sweden	Hungary
23	Germany	Poland
24	Norway	Brazil
25		Turkey

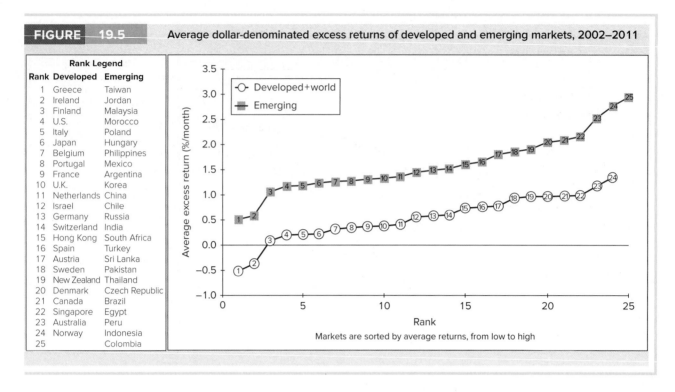

FIGURE 19.5   Average dollar-denominated excess returns of developed and emerging markets, 2002–2011

Rank Legend

Rank	Developed	Emerging
1	Greece	Taiwan
2	Ireland	Jordan
3	Finland	Malaysia
4	U.S.	Morocco
5	Italy	Poland
6	Japan	Hungary
7	Belgium	Philippines
8	Portugal	Mexico
9	France	Argentina
10	U.K.	Korea
11	Netherlands	China
12	Israel	Chile
13	Germany	Russia
14	Switzerland	India
15	Hong Kong	South Africa
16	Spain	Turkey
17	Austria	Sri Lanka
18	Sweden	Pakistan
19	New Zealand	Thailand
20	Denmark	Czech Republic
21	Canada	Brazil
22	Singapore	Egypt
23	Australia	Peru
24	Norway	Indonesia
25		Colombia

Are Average Returns Higher in Emerging Markets?

Figure 19.5 repeats the previous exercise for average excess returns. The graph shows that emerging markets generally provided higher average returns than developed markets over the period 2002–2011. The fact that only 2 (developed) of the 49 markets averaged a lower rate than the risk-free alternative is quite unusual given the volatility of these markets. However, this result is partially due to the weak U.S. dollar over these years. When returns are hedged, that is, returns are measured in local currencies, returns in eight countries, all developed, average below U.S. T-bills over the 10-year period. Beyond that, we see that countries with relatively low betas (e.g., Pakistan) earned higher returns than countries with relatively high betas, even the highest-beta country, Turkey. Further, average returns in emerging markets were generally higher than those in developed countries despite the fact that emerging market betas were not higher, implying that emerging markets provided better diversification opportunities than developed markets in this period.

We shouldn't be too surprised by these results. Remember again that the SD of an average estimated over 120 months (without serial correlation, which is very low) is given by SD(10-year average) = SD(1-month return)/$\sqrt{120}$. Thus, the SD of the 10-year average monthly return for Pakistan would be about .92%, and that of Turkey about 1.20%. An outcome of one SD in opposite directions for these two portfolios would span a distance of about 2.12%, while the difference in average returns is only .21%. The conclusion is one we've noted before: We cannot read too much into realized averages even over periods as long as 10 years.

Instinct calls for estimating alpha or information ratios for individual markets, to see whether they are distributed around zero. Recall from our discussion of performance evaluation in Chapter 18 that, without positive alpha, we cannot conclude that an asset has shown superior performance on any measure. The information ratio measures the potential increase in the Sharpe ratio if the country index were to be added in an optimal proportion to the U.S index.

Figure 19.6 verifies that information ratios in emerging markets were, on the whole, clearly better than those in developed markets. This is a result of inferior performance of the eight markets most affected by the financial crisis, all developed countries, and four stellar emerging market performers. The performance of the other 36 markets cannot be distinguished in terms of emerging versus developed. Here again, given the high volatilities, finding four outperformers and eight underperformers in a group of 48 countries is not surprising or significant.

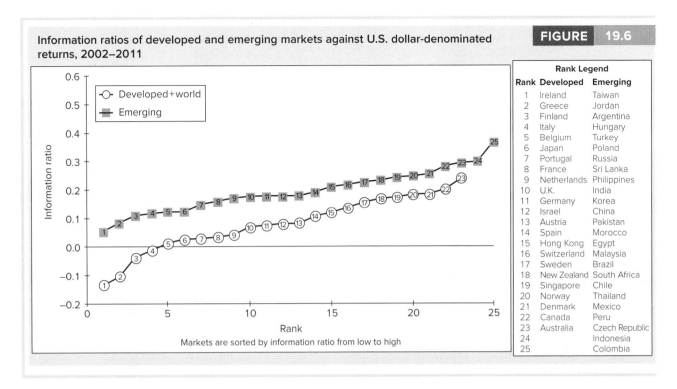

Information ratios of developed and emerging markets against U.S. dollar-denominated returns, 2002–2011

FIGURE 19.6

	Rank Legend	
Rank	Developed	Emerging
1	Ireland	Taiwan
2	Greece	Jordan
3	Finland	Argentina
4	Italy	Hungary
5	Belgium	Turkey
6	Japan	Poland
7	Portugal	Russia
8	France	Sri Lanka
9	Netherlands	Philippines
10	U.K.	India
11	Germany	Korea
12	Israel	China
13	Austria	Pakistan
14	Spain	Morocco
15	Hong Kong	Egypt
16	Switzerland	Malaysia
17	Sweden	Brazil
18	New Zealand	South Africa
19	Singapore	Chile
20	Norway	Thailand
21	Denmark	Mexico
22	Canada	Peru
23	Australia	Czech Republic
24		Indonesia
25		Colombia

Is Exchange Rate Risk Important in International Portfolios?

Table 19.3 revealed that changes in exchange rates vary widely across country pairs. In Figures 19.7 to 19.10 we compare results for SD, beta coefficients, average excess return, and information ratios for both developed and emerging markets using dollar and local-currency returns. Figures 19.7 and 19.8 look at the issue of risk. Both measures show that returns in local currency are convincingly less risky than dollar-denominated returns. The difference (at least over the recent 10 years) is greater when comparing beta. Remember, however, that this result applies only to adding one country to the U.S. portfolio; relative contributions to risk could change if one were to consider broader diversification.

Standard deviation of excess returns in dollar-denominated and local currencies, 2002–2011

FIGURE 19.7

	Rank Legend		
Rank	Country	Rank	Country
1	U.S.	27	Czech Republic
2	Japan	28	South Africa
3	Switzerland	29	Sweden
4	Malaysia	30	China
5	U.K.	31	Thailand
6	Morocco	32	Colombia
7	Israel	33	Korea
8	New Zealand	34	Austria
9	Jordan	35	Finland
10	Canada	36	Norway
11	Hong Kong	37	India
12	Denmark	38	Peru
13	Chile	39	Indonesia
14	Singapore	40	Pakistan
15	Portugal	41	Greece
16	Australia	42	Poland
17	France	43	Egypt
18	Netherlands	44	Russia
19	Mexico	45	Hungary
20	Italy	46	Brazil
21	Philippines	47	Sri Lanka
22	Taiwan	48	Argentina
23	Belgium	49	Turkey
24	Spain		
25	Ireland		
26	Germany		

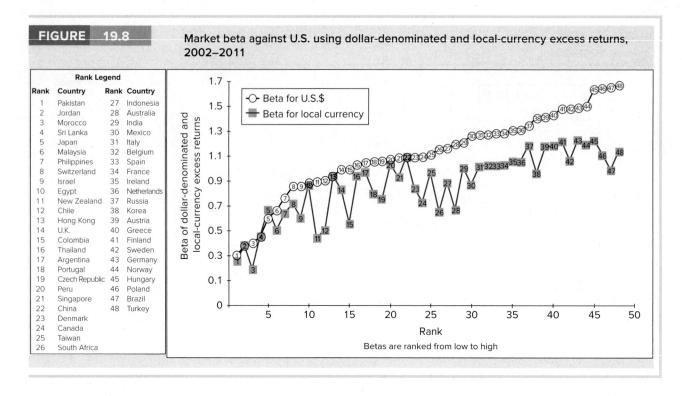

FIGURE 19.8 Market beta against U.S. using dollar-denominated and local-currency excess returns, 2002–2011

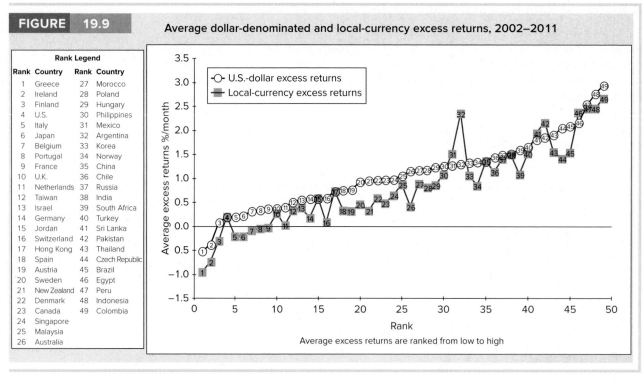

FIGURE 19.9 Average dollar-denominated and local-currency excess returns, 2002–2011

Hedging currency risk when investing internationally is often undertaken to reduce overall portfolio risk. However, the decision of whether to hedge foreign currencies in an internationally diversified portfolio can also be made as part of active management. If a portfolio manager believes the U.S. dollar is, say, overvalued against a given currency, then hedging the exposure to that currency would, if correct, enhance the portfolio return in U.S dollars. The potential gain from this decision depends on the weight of that currency in the overall portfolio. Such a decision applied to investments in only one country would have a small effect on

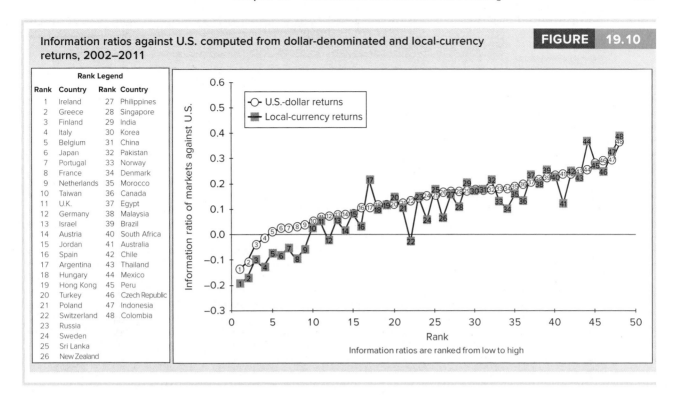

Information ratios against U.S. computed from dollar-denominated and local-currency returns, 2002–2011

FIGURE 19.10

Rank Legend

Rank	Country	Rank	Country
1	Ireland	27	Philippines
2	Greece	28	Singapore
3	Finland	29	India
4	Italy	30	Korea
5	Belgium	31	China
6	Japan	32	Pakistan
7	Portugal	33	Norway
8	France	34	Denmark
9	Netherlands	35	Morocco
10	Taiwan	36	Canada
11	U.K.	37	Egypt
12	Germany	38	Malaysia
13	Israel	39	Brazil
14	Austria	40	South Africa
15	Jordan	41	Australia
16	Spain	42	Chile
17	Argentina	43	Thailand
18	Hungary	44	Mexico
19	Hong Kong	45	Peru
20	Turkey	46	Czech Republic
21	Poland	47	Indonesia
22	Switzerland	48	Colombia
23	Russia		
24	Sweden		
25	Sri Lanka		
26	New Zealand		

overall risk. But what if the manager estimates that the dollar is generally overvalued against most or all currencies? In this case, hedging the entire exposure would constitute a bet with significant effect on total risk. At the same time, if the decision is correct, such a large position can provide handsome gains.

Figures 19.9 and 19.10 show that dollar-denominated average excess returns and information ratios are a bit better than those denominated in local currencies. Given that the risk-adjusted returns are no better in local currency than in dollars, we must conclude that the superior performance of emerging market portfolios is due to surprises about their economic performance and not solely due to the decline in the U.S. dollar.

Benefits from International Diversification

Table 19.10 tells the story of international diversification. First, notice the strong trend of increasing correlation. Of the 16 countries, only four show stable correlation from the late 1960s through 2011. The rest show significant increases. In the most recent decade, the correlation of the portfolio of tradeable world country portfolios excluding the U.S. with that of the U.S. is .90. Hence, the benefits of diversification can be expected to emanate from countries with relatively lower correlations (admittedly, among themselves, as well as with the U.S.). Table 19.9B shows that such low correlations are found mostly in the emerging markets.

To assess the value of international diversification, we return to Table 19.9A, where we first viewed portfolio standard deviation. We find that whether we diversify from U.S.-only investments either to the entire world or to emerging markets only, the standard deviation of the portfolio increases. This results from higher standard deviations of foreign markets that are not offset by the relatively low correlations of emerging markets.

Nevertheless, the objective of diversification is *not* merely risk reduction. Rather, it is to increase the Sharpe ratio. Here we see that, in any configuration, the Sharpe ratio of internationally diversified portfolios is higher than that of the U.S. alone. Even without any notion about emerging versus developed markets, holding the world portfolio results in a significantly higher Sharpe ratio. Using the more revealing M^2 measure (see Chapter 18), the advantage of the world countries portfolio amounts to 284 basis points annually. Even the less diversified world ETF portfolio earned an annual risk-adjusted premium of 107 basis points.

TABLE 19.10 Correlation of foreign investments with U.S. returns over time (dollar-denominated excess returns)		
	2002–2011	**1967–2001**
World	0.97	0.95
World (excluding U.S.)	0.90	NA
Germany	0.89	0.75
Netherlands	0.88	0.71
France	0.88	0.70
United Kingdom	0.87	0.83
Sweden	0.86	0.73
Australia	0.82	0.71
Italy	0.82	0.55
Canada	0.80	0.82
Spain	0.79	0.65
Switzerland	0.79	0.65
Belgium	0.79	0.46
Denmark	0.78	0.67
Norway	0.78	0.63
Austria	0.74	0.46
Hong Kong	0.69	0.67
Japan	0.56	0.58

NA = not available.

Source: Datastream **online.thomsonreuters.com/datastream;** 1970–1989: Campbell R. Harvey, "The World Price of Covariance Risk," *Journal of Finance* 46 (March 1991), issue 1, pp. 111–158.

Thus, the data clearly indicate that despite increasing correlations, even a passive strategy of holding a world ETF is still superior to the U.S.-only portfolio. Figure 19.11 shows diversification benefits based on 1995 correlations and diversification into randomly selected stocks from around the world compared with a one-stock portfolio.

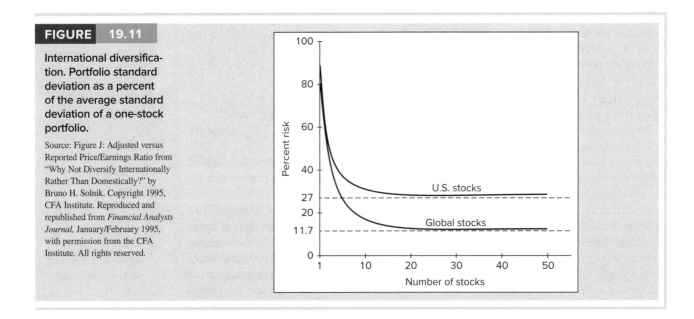

FIGURE 19.11

International diversification. Portfolio standard deviation as a percent of the average standard deviation of a one-stock portfolio.

Source: Figure J: Adjusted versus Reported Price/Earnings Ratio from "Why Not Diversify Internationally Rather Than Domestically?" by Bruno H. Solnik. Copyright 1995, CFA Institute. Reproduced and republished from *Financial Analysts Journal,* January/February 1995, with permission from the CFA Institute. All rights reserved.

DANCING IN STEP

Individual stock markets are increasingly being driven by global rather than local factors. But why do national markets not have minds of their own? They did have once.

Traditionally, one way that investors sought to reduce risk was by diversifying overseas: when American shares slumped, the loss there would be offset by a gain in, say, European shares. That, at any rate, was the theory. In recent years, however, stock markets seem to have moved more closely in step with one another. The correlation between changes in American and European share prices has risen from 0.4 in the mid-1990s to 0.8 last year.

The health of a market's home economy may matter less than it used to for a number of reasons. First, the scrapping of controls on capital (combined with more efficient trading systems) has increased cross-border trading of shares, creating something closer to a global equity market. Second, it has become increasingly common for big companies to be listed on more than one market. Third, as a result of the wave of cross-border mergers and

acquisitions, overseas profits account for a bigger slice of many companies' overall profits—high-tech firms are especially global in their reach. And finally, the Internet has made it easier for investors to get information on foreign firms. So firms in the same industry, but in different economies, are valued on a similar basis.

By breaking down movements in share prices into global effects, country-specific effects, and firm-specific effects, a new study by economists at the IMF tries to find out what percentage of a stock's performance is due to global rather than country factors. The model distinguishes between two kinds of global factors: the global business cycle and global-industry effects, which similarly influence firms in the same sector but in different countries.

The study finds that there has indeed been a big increase in the importance of global factors—of both kinds—in explaining movements in share prices since the mid-1990s.

Misleading Representation of Diversification Benefits

The baseline technique for constructing efficient portfolios is the efficient frontier. A useful efficient frontier is constructed from *expected* returns and an estimate of the covariance matrix of returns. This frontier, combined with cash assets, generates the capital allocation line—the set of efficient complete portfolios, as elaborated in Chapters 6 and 7. The benefit from this efficient diversification is reflected in the curvature of the efficient frontier. Other things equal, the lower the covariance across stocks, the greater the curvature of the efficient frontier and the greater the risk reduction for any desired *expected* return. So far, so good. But suppose we replace *expected* returns with *realized* average returns from a particular sample period to construct an efficient frontier; what is the proper use of this graph?

The ex-post efficient frontier (derived from realized returns) describes the portfolio choices of only one investor—the clairvoyant who actually expected the precise averages of realized returns on all assets and estimated a covariance matrix that materialized, precisely, in the actual realizations of the sample period returns on all assets. Obviously, we are talking about a slim to empty set of investors. For all other, less-than-clairvoyant investors such a frontier may have value only for purposes of performance evaluation.

In the world of volatile stocks, some stocks are bound to realize large, *unexpected* average returns. This will be reflected in ex-post efficient frontiers of enormous "potential." They will, however, suggest exaggerated diversification benefits. Such (elusive) potential was enumerated in Chapter 18 on performance evaluation. It has no use as a tool to discuss the potential for future investments for real-life investors.

Realistic Benefits from International Diversification

While recent realized returns can be highly misleading estimates of expected future returns, they are more useful for measuring prospective risk. There are two compelling reasons for this. First, market efficiency (or even near efficiency) implies that stock price movements will be impossible to predict with any accuracy, but no such implication applies to risk measures. Second, it is a statistical fact that errors in estimates of standard deviation and correlation from realized data are of a lower order of magnitude than estimates of expected returns. For these reasons, using risk estimates from realized returns does not exaggerate as much the potential benefits from diversification.

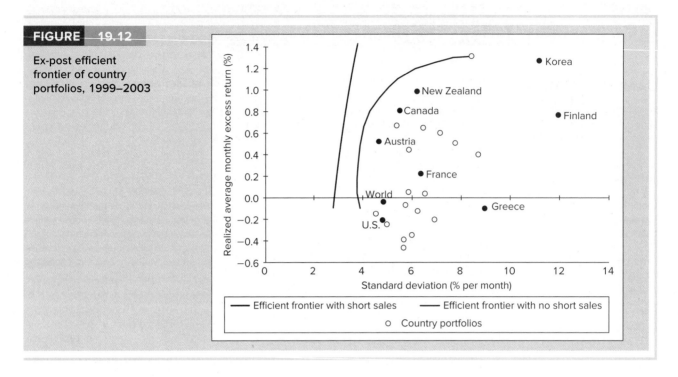

FIGURE 19.12

Ex-post efficient frontier of country portfolios, 1999–2003

Figure 19.12 shows the efficient frontier using realized average monthly returns on the stock indexes of the 25 developed countries, with and without short sales. Even when the (ex-post) efficient frontier is constrained to preclude short sales, it greatly exaggerates the realistic benefits from diversification. Unfortunately, such misleading efficient frontiers are presented in many articles and texts on the benefits of diversification.

A more reasonable description of diversification is achievable only when we input reasonable equilibrium expected returns. In the absence of superior information, such expected returns are best based on appropriate risk measures of the assets. The capital asset pricing model (CAPM) suggests using the beta of the stock against the world portfolio. To generate expected excess returns (over the risk-free rate) for all assets, we specify the expected excess return on the world portfolio. We obtain the expected excess return on each asset by multiplying the beta of the asset by the world portfolio expected excess return. This procedure presupposes that the world portfolio will lie on the efficient frontier, at the point of tangency with the world capital market line.

We perform this procedure with risk measures estimated from actual returns and further impose the likely applicable constraint on short sales. We use the betas to compute the expected return on individual markets, assuming the expected excess return on the world portfolio is either .3% or .6% per month. These excess returns are in the range of averages realized over the period 1999–2003 and in line with the average return over the previous 50 years. Varying this estimate would not qualitatively affect the results shown in Figure 19.13 (Panels A and B). The figures reveal quite modest benefits for U.S. investors from international diversification using only developed markets. Incorporating emerging markets would slightly increase these benefits.

Are Benefits from International Diversification Preserved in Bear Markets?

Some studies (e.g., Longin and Solnik, 1995, or Jacquier and Marcus, 2001) suggest that correlation in country portfolio returns increases during periods of turbulence in capital markets. If so, benefits from diversification would be lost exactly when they are needed the most. For example, a study by Roll (1988) of the crash of October 1987 shows that all 23 country indexes studied declined over the crash period of October 12–26. This correlation is reflected in the highly synchronized movements of regional indexes depicted in Figure 19.14A.

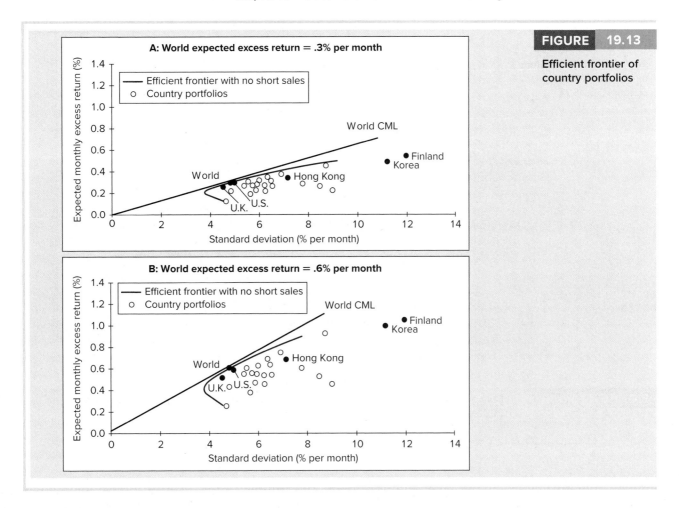

FIGURE   19.13

Efficient frontier of
country portfolios

Roll found that the beta of a country index on the world index (estimated prior to the crash) was the best predictor of that index's response to the October crash of the U.S. stock market. This suggests a common factor underlying the movement of stocks around the world. This model predicts that a macroeconomic shock would affect all countries and that diversification can mitigate only country-specific events.

The 2008 crash of stock markets around the world allows us to test Roll's prediction. The data in Figure 19.14B include average monthly rates of return for both the 10-year period 1999–2008 and the crisis period corresponding to the last four months of 2008, as well as the beta on the U.S. market and monthly standard deviation for several portfolios. The graph shows that both beta against the U.S. and the country-index standard deviation explain the difference between crisis period returns and overall period averages. Market behavior during the 1987 crisis, that is, larger correlations in extreme bad times, repeated itself in the crisis of 2008, vindicating Roll's prediction.

Active Management and International Diversification

As we mentioned at the outset, the great potential of adding foreign stocks and bonds to the investable universe is obvious. The likelihood of identifying a diversified set of mispriced securities directly increases with the number of analyzed securities.

The hierarchy of active management entails two levels. At the ground level, security selection and asset allocation (plus currency hedging as deemed optimal) within each market would lead to a country portfolio superior to the passive index. At the next level, an international portfolio would optimize allocation across country portfolios. Take a second look at Table 19.9B, and observe the large ex-post values of alpha and information ratios. Analysis leading to even very noisy forecasts of these values would result in a portfolio of greatly superior performance.

FIGURE   19.14A

Regional indexes around the crash, October 14–October 26, 1987

Source: From Richard Roll, "The International Crash of October 1987," *Financial Analysts Journal,* September–October 1988.

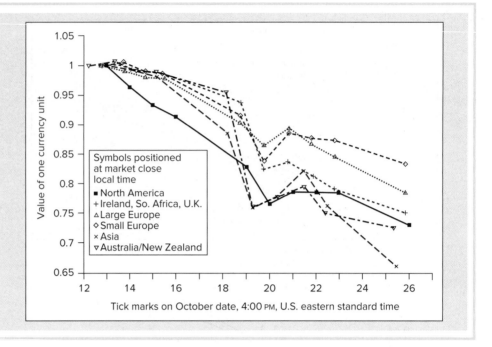

Symbols positioned at market close local time
- North America
- + Ireland, So. Africa, U.K.
- △ Large Europe
- ◇ Small Europe
- × Asia
- ▽ Australia/New Zealand

Tick marks on October date, 4:00 PM, U.S. eastern standard time

FIGURE   19.14B   Beta and SD of portfolios against deviation of monthly return over September–December 2008 from average over 1999–2008

Source: Authors' calculations.

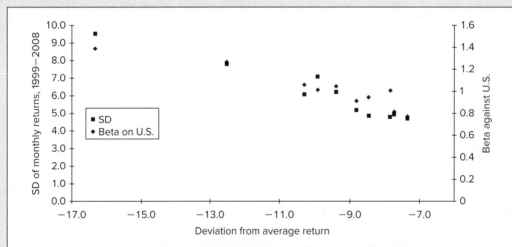

■ SD
◆ Beta on U.S.

Market	Average Monthly Return 1999–2008	2008: Sept.–Dec.	Deviation from Average	Beta on U.S.	SD
USA	−0.47	−8.31	−7.84	1	4.81
World largest six (non-U.S.) markets	−0.16	−7.51	−7.35	0.77	4.71
EU developed markets	−0.05	−10.34	−10.29	1.06	6.08
Other Europe developed markets	0.14	−7.59	−7.73	0.82	4.95
Australia + Far East	0.10	−9.29	−9.38	1.04	6.21
Emerging Far East + South Africa	0.20	−9.70	−9.90	1.01	7.10
Emerging Latin America	0.80	−11.72	−12.52	1.27	7.83
Emerging markets in Europe	0.90	−15.43	−16.32	1.38	9.54
World minus U.S. (48 countries by cap)	0.01	−8.79	−8.81	0.91	5.19
World portfolio (by country cap)	−0.15	−8.60	−8.45	0.94	4.88

19.4 INTERNATIONAL INVESTING AND PERFORMANCE ATTRIBUTION

The benefits from international diversification may be modest for passive investors, but for active managers international investing offers greater opportunities. International investing calls for specialization in additional fields of analysis: currency, country and worldwide industry, as well as a greater universe for stock selection.

Constructing a Benchmark Portfolio of Foreign Assets

Active international investing, as well as passive, requires a benchmark portfolio (called the bogey). One widely used index of non-U.S. stocks is the **European, Australian, Far East (EAFE) index** computed by Morgan Stanley. Additional indexes of world equity performance are published by Capital International Indices, Credit Suisse First Boston, and Goldman Sachs. Portfolios designed to mirror or even replicate the country, currency, and company representation of these indexes would be the obvious generalization of the purely domestic passive equity strategy.

An issue that sometimes arises in the international context is the appropriateness of market-capitalization weighting schemes in the construction of international indexes. Capitalization weighting is far and away the most common approach. However, some argue that it might not be the best weighting scheme in an international context. This is in part because different countries have differing proportions of their corporate sector organized as publicly traded firms.

Table 19.11 shows 1998 and 2011 data for market-capitalization weights versus GDP weights for countries in the EAFE index. These data reveal substantial disparities between the relative sizes of market capitalization and GDP. Because market capitalization is a stock figure (the value of equity at one point in time), while GDP is a flow figure (production of goods and services during the entire year), we expect capitalization to be more volatile and the relative shares to be more variable over time. Some discrepancies are persistent, however. For example, Hong Kong's share of capitalization in 2011 is about eight times its share of GDP, while Germany's share of capitalization is much less than its share of GDP. These disparities indicate that a greater proportion of economic activity is conducted by publicly traded firms in Hong Kong than in Germany.

Some argue that it would be more appropriate to weight international indexes by GDP rather than market capitalization. The justification for this view is that an internationally diversified portfolio should purchase shares in proportion to the broad asset base of each country, and GDP might be a better measure of the importance of a country in the international economy than the value of its outstanding stocks. Others have even suggested weights proportional to the import share of various countries. The argument is that investors who wish to hedge the price of imported goods might choose to hold securities in foreign firms in proportion to the goods imported from those countries.

Performance Attribution

We can measure the contribution of each of the following components of active management in a manner similar to the performance attribution techniques introduced in Chapter 18.

1. **Currency selection** measures the contribution to total portfolio performance attributable to exchange rate fluctuations relative to the investor's benchmark currency, which we will take to be the U.S. dollar. We might use a benchmark such as the EAFE index to compare a portfolio's currency selection for a particular period to a passive benchmark. EAFE currency selection would be computed as the weighted average of the currency appreciation of the currencies represented in the EAFE portfolio using as weights the fraction of the EAFE portfolio invested in each currency.

European, Australian, Far East (EAFE) index

A widely used index of non-U.S. stocks computed by Morgan Stanley.

currency selection

Asset allocation in which the investor chooses among investments denominated in different currencies.

TABLE 19.11 Weighting schemes for EAFE countries

Country	2011		1998	
	% of EAFE Market Capitalization	% of EAFE GDP	% of EAFE Market Capitalization	% of EAFE GDP
Japan	21.1%	23.7%	26.8%	29.1%
United Kingdom	17.9	9.8	22.4	10.5
France	9.3	11.1	7.2	10.7
Germany	7.5	14.2	8.9	15.8
Switzerland	6.8	2.3	6.0	1.9
Italy	2.9	8.9	3.9	8.8
Netherlands	2.4	3.4	5.9	2.9
Hong Kong	8.8	1.0	4.0	1.2
Australia	6.7	4.0	2.9	2.7
Spain	3.5	6.1	2.7	4.3
Sweden	2.8	2.0	2.4	1.8
Finland	0.9	1.0	0.7	1.0
Belgium	1.4	2.0	1.4	1.8
Singapore	2.7	0.9	1.1	0.6
Denmark	1.1	1.3	0.9	1.3
Norway	1.5	1.8	0.6	1.1
Ireland	0.4	0.9	0.5	0.6
Greece	0.2	1.3	0.3	0.9
Portugal	0.4	1.0	0.6	0.8
Austria	0.5	1.6	0.4	1.6
New Zealand	0.2	0.6	0.4	0.4

Source: Datastream, **online.thomsonreuters.com/datastream.**

country selection

Asset allocation in which the investor chooses among investments in different countries.

2. **Country selection** measures the contribution to performance attributable to investing in the better-performing stock markets of the world. It can be measured as the weighted average of the equity-*index* returns of each country using as weights the share of the manager's portfolio in each country. We use index returns to abstract from the effect of security selection within countries. To measure a manager's contribution relative to a passive strategy, we might compare country selection to the weighted average across countries of equity-index returns using as weights the share of the EAFE portfolio in each country.

stock selection

Choice of specific stocks within a country's equity market.

3. **Stock selection** ability may, as in Chapter 18, be measured as the weighted average of equity returns *in excess of the equity index* in each country. Here, we would use local-currency returns and use as weights the investments in each country.

cash/bond selection

Choice between money market and longer-term bonds.

4. **Cash/bond selection** may be measured as the excess return derived from weighting bonds and bills differently from some benchmark weights.

Table 19.12 gives an example of how to measure the contribution of the decisions an international portfolio manager might make.

CONCEPT check 19.4

Using the data in Table 19.12, compute the manager's country and currency selection if portfolio weights had been 40% in Europe, 20% in Australia, and 40% in the Far East.

This Excel model provides an efficient frontier analysis similar to that in Chapter 6. In Chapter 6 the frontier was based on individual securities, whereas this model examines the returns on international exchange-traded funds. Using the model with this return data enables us to analyze the benefits of international diversification.

Spreadsheets are available in Connect

	A	B	C	D	E	F	G	H	I
58				Bordered Covariance Matrix for Target Return Portfolio					
59			EWD	EWH	EWI	EWJ	EWL	EWP	EWW	SP 500
60	Weights		0.00	0.00	0.08	0.38	0.02	0.00	0.00	0.52
61		0.0000	0.00	0.00	0.00	0.00	0.00	0.00	0.00	0.00
62		0.0000	0.00	0.00	0.00	0.00	0.00	0.00	0.00	0.00
63		0.0826	0.00	0.00	4.63	3.21	0.55	0.00	0.00	7.69
64		0.3805	0.00	0.00	3.21	98.41	1.82	0.00	0.00	53.79
65		0.0171	0.00	0.00	0.55	1.82	0.14	0.00	0.00	2.09
66		0.0000	0.00	0.00	0.00	0.00	0.00	0.00	0.00	0.00
67		0.0000	0.00	0.00	0.00	0.00	0.00	0.00	0.00	0.00
68		0.5198	0.00	0.00	7.69	53.79	2.09	0.00	0.00	79.90

Excel Questions

1. Find three points on the efficient frontier corresponding to three different expected returns. What are the portfolio standard deviations corresponding to each expected return?

2. Now assume that the correlation between the S&P 500 and the other country indexes is cut in half. Find the new standard deviations corresponding to each of the three expected returns. Are they higher or lower? Why?

TABLE 19.12 Example of performance attribution: international

	EAFE Weight	Return on Equity Index	Currency Appreciation $E_1 / E_0 - 1$	Manager's Weight	Manager's Return
Europe	0.30	10%	10%	0.35	8%
Australia	0.10	5	−10	0.10	7
Far East	0.60	15	30	0.55	18

Overall performance (dollar return = return on index + currency appreciation)

EAFE: $0.30(10 + 10) + 0.10(5 - 10) + 0.60(15 + 30) = 32.5\%$
Manager: $0.35(8 + 10) + 0.10(7 - 10) + 0.55(18 + 30) = 32.4\%$
Loss of 0.10% relative to EAFE

Currency selection

EAFE: $(0.30 \times 10\%) + (0.10 \times (-10\%)) + (0.60 \times 30\%) = 20\%$ appreciation
Manager: $(0.35 \times 10\%) + (0.10 \times (-10\%)) + (0.55 \times 30\%) = 19\%$ appreciation
Loss of 1% relative to EAFE

Country selection

EAFE: $(0.30 \times 10\%) + (0.10 \times 5\%) + (0.60 \times 15\%) = 12.5\%$
Manager: $(0.35 \times 10\%) + (0.10 \times 5\%) + (0.55 \times 15\%) = 12.25\%$
Loss of 0.25% relative to EAFE

Stock selection

$(8\% - 10\%) \times 0.35 + (7\% - 5\%) \times 0.10 + (18\% - 15\%) \times 0.55 = 1.15\%$

Contribution of 1.15% relative to EAFE

Sum of attributions (equal to overall performance)

Currency (-1%) + country ($-.25\%$) + selection (1.15%) = -0.10%

SUMMARY

- U.S. assets are only a part of the world portfolio. International capital markets offer important opportunities for portfolio diversification with enhanced risk-return characteristics.
- Exchange rate risk imparts an extra source of uncertainty to investments denominated in foreign currencies. Much of that risk can be hedged in foreign exchange futures or forward markets, but a perfect hedge is not feasible unless the foreign currency rate of return is known.
- Several world market indexes can form a basis for passive international investing. Active international management can be partitioned into currency selection, country selection, stock selection, and cash/bond selection.

KEY TERMS

cash/bond selection, 654	currency selection, 653	interest rate parity
country selection, 654	European, Australian, Far	relationship, 633
covered interest arbitrage	East (EAFE) index, 653	political risk, 635
relationship, 633	exchange rate risk, 631	stock selection, 654

KEY FORMULAS

Interest rate parity (covered interest arbitrage) for direct ($/foreign currency) exchange rates:

$$F_0 = E_0 \frac{1 + r_f(\text{US})}{1 + r_f(\text{foreign})}$$

Interest rate parity for indirect (foreign currency/$) exchange rates:

$$F_0 = E_0 \frac{1 + r_f(\text{foreign})}{1 + r_f(\text{US})}$$

PROBLEM SETS

Select problems are available in McGraw-Hill's *Connect*. Please see the Supplements section of the book's frontmatter for more information.

For Questions 1–4, answer true or false. Explain your answer.

1. Due to currency risk, dollar-denominated returns of international portfolios will have a higher standard deviation than local-currency-denominated returns.   *(LO 19-1)*

2. The principle of diversification assures us that diversifying a U.S. portfolio internationally will reduce standard deviation.   *(LO 19-1)*

3. For a passive investor, the minimum-variance portfolio of country indexes is optimal.   *(LO 19-3)*

4. A currency-hedged foreign-stock portfolio return is the weighted average of the foreign stock returns *in local currency.*   *(LO 19-1)*

5. Suppose a U.S. investor wishes to invest in a British firm currently selling for £40 per share. The investor has $10,000 to invest, and the current exchange rate is $2/£. *(LO 19-2)*
   a. How many shares can the investor purchase?
   b. Fill in the table below for rates of return after one year in each of the nine scenarios (three possible prices per share in pounds times three possible exchange rates).

Price per Share (£)	Pound-Denominated Return (%)	Dollar-Denominated Return for Year-End Exchange Rate		
		$1.80/£	$2/£	$2.20/£
£35				
£40				
£45				

   c. When is the dollar-denominated return equal to the pound-denominated return?

6. If each of the nine outcomes in Problem 5 is equally likely, find the standard deviation of both the pound- and dollar-denominated rates of return. *(LO 19-2)*

7. Now suppose the investor in Problem 5 also sells forward £5,000 at a forward exchange rate of $2.10/£. *(LO 19-2)*
   a. Recalculate the dollar-denominated returns for each scenario.
   b. What happens to the standard deviation of the dollar-denominated return? Compare it to both its old value and the standard deviation of the pound-denominated return.

8. Calculate the contribution to total performance from currency, country, and stock selection for the manager in the following table. All exchange rates are expressed as units of foreign currency that can be purchased with one U.S. dollar. *(LO 19-4)*

	EAFE Weight	Return on Equity Index	E_1 / E_0	Manager's Weight	Manager's Return
Europe	0.30	20%	0.9	0.35	18%
Australia	0.10	15	1.0	0.15	20
Far East	0.60	25	1.1	0.50	20

9. If the current exchange rate is $1.75/£, the one-year forward exchange rate is $1.85/£, and the interest rate on British government bills is 8% per year, what risk-free dollar-denominated return can be locked in by investing in the British bills? *(LO 19-2)*

10. If you were to invest $10,000 in the British bills of Problem 5, how would you lock in the dollar-denominated return? *(LO 19-2)*

11. Suppose that the spot price of the euro is currently $1.30. The one-year futures price is $1.35. Is the U.S. interest rate higher than the euro rate? *(LO 19-2)*

12. *a.* Suppose the spot price of the British pound is currently $1.50. If the risk-free interest rate on one-year government bonds is 4% in the United States and 3% in the United Kingdom, what must the forward price of the pound be for delivery one year from now?
   b. How could an investor make risk-free arbitrage profits if the forward price were higher than the price you gave in answer to (*a*)? Give a numerical example. *(LO 19-2)*

13. Consider the following information: *(LO 19-2)*

$$r_{US} = 5\%$$
$$r_{UK} = 7\%$$
$$E_0 = \$2 \text{ per pound}$$
$$F_0 = \$1.97/£ \text{ (one-year delivery)}$$

where the interest rates are annual yields on U.S. or U.K. bills. Given this information:
   a. Where would you lend?
   b. Where would you borrow?
   c. How could you arbitrage?

Challenge

14. Suppose you forecast the information ratios of the seven international portfolios (as shown in Table 19.9B). Construct the optimal portfolio of the U.S. index with the seven portfolios and assess its performance. *(LO 19-3)*

CFA Problems

1. Renée Michaels, CFA, plans to invest $1 million in U.S. government cash equivalents for the next 90 days. Michaels's client has authorized her to use non-U.S. government cash equivalents, but only if the currency risk is hedged to U.S. dollars by using forward currency contracts. *(LO 19-2)*

    a. Calculate the U.S.-dollar value of the hedged investment at the end of 90 days for each of the two cash equivalents in the table below. Show all calculations.

    b. Briefly explain the theory that best accounts for your results.

    c. Based upon this theory, estimate the implied interest rate for a 90-day U.S. government cash equivalent.

Interest Rates 90-Day Cash Equivalents	
Japanese government	7.6%
Swiss government	8.6

Exchange Rates: Currency Units per U.S. Dollar		
	Spot	90-Day Forward
Japanese yen	133.05	133.47
Swiss franc	1.5260	1.5348

2. John Irish, CFA, is an independent investment adviser who is assisting Alfred Darwin, the head of the Investment Committee of General Technology Corporation, to establish a new pension fund. Darwin asks Irish about international equities and whether the Investment Committee should consider them as an additional asset for the pension fund. *(LO 19-3)*

    a. Explain the rationale for including international equities in General's equity portfolio. Identify and describe three relevant considerations in formulating your answer.

    b. List three possible arguments against international equity investment, and briefly discuss the significance of each.

    c. To illustrate several aspects of the performance of international securities over time, Irish shows Darwin the accompanying graph of investment results experienced by a U.S. pension fund in the recent past. Compare the performance of the U.S.-dollar and non-U.S.-dollar equity and fixed-income asset categories, and explain the significance of the result of the account performance index relative to the results of the four individual asset class indexes.

3. You are a U.S. investor considering purchase of one of the following securities. Assume that the currency risk of the Canadian government bond will be hedged, and the six-month discount on Canadian-dollar forward contracts is −.75% versus the U.S. dollar.

Bond	Maturity	Coupon	Price
U.S. government	6 months	6.50%	100.00
Canadian government	6 months	7.50%	100.00

Calculate the expected price change required in the Canadian government bond that would result in the two bonds having equal total returns in U.S. dollars over a six-month horizon. Assume that the yield on the U.S. bond is expected to remain unchanged. *(LO 19-2)*

4. After much research on the developing economy and capital markets of the country of Otunia, your firm, GAC, has decided to include an investment in the Otunia stock market in its Emerging Markets Commingled Fund. However, GAC has not yet decided whether to invest actively or by indexing. Your opinion on the active versus indexing decision has been solicited. The following is a summary of the research findings:

Otunia's economy is fairly well diversified across agricultural and natural resources, manufacturing (both consumer and durable goods), and a growing finance sector. Transaction costs in securities markets are relatively large in Otunia because of high commissions and government "stamp taxes" on securities trades. Accounting standards and disclosure regulations are quite detailed, resulting in wide public availability of reliable information about companies' financial performance.

Capital flows into and out of Otunia, and foreign ownership of Otunia securities is strictly regulated by an agency of the national government. The settlement procedures under these ownership rules often cause long delays in settling trades made by nonresidents. Senior finance officials in the government are working to deregulate capital flows and foreign ownership, but GAC's political consultant believes that isolationist sentiment may prevent much real progress in the short run. *(LO 19-3)*

a. Briefly discuss aspects of the Otunia environment that favor investing actively, and aspects that favor indexing.
b. Recommend whether GAC should invest in Otunia actively or by indexing. Justify your recommendation based on the factors identified in part (a).

WEB *master*

A common misconception is that investors can earn excess returns by investing in foreign bonds with higher interest rates than are available in the U.S. Interest rate parity implies that any such interest rate differentials will be offset by premiums or discounts in the forward or futures market for foreign currency.

Interest rates on government bonds in the U.S., U.K., Japan, Germany, Brazil, and Australia can be found at **www.bloomberg.com.** (Look for the link to *Markets,* and then *Rates + Bonds.*) Spot exchange rates on international currencies can be found at **www.bloomberg.com.** (Look for the link to *Markets,* and then *Currencies.*) Forward exchange rates on currency futures contracts can be found at **www.cmegroup.com.** (Look for the link to *Trading* and then *FX.*)

1. Select one of these countries and record the yield on a short-term government security from the Bloomberg website. Also make note of the U.S. Treasury yield on an instrument with the same maturity.

2. Record the spot exchange rate from the Bloomberg site and the futures contract exchange rate from the CME website for the date closest to the maturity of the investment you chose in the previous step.

3. Calculate the rate of return available on the foreign government security, converting the foreign currency transactions into dollars at the current and forward exchange rates.

4. How well does interest rate parity seem to hold? Are there bargains to be found in other currencies? What factors might account for interest rate parity violation?

19.1 $1 + r(US) = [(1 + r_f(UK))] \times (E_1/E_0)$
   a. $1 + r(US) = 1.1 \times 1.0 = 1.10$. Therefore, $r(US) = 10\%$.
   b. $1 + r(US) = 1.1 \times 1.1 = 1.21$. Therefore, $r(US) = 21\%$.

19.2   According to interest rate parity, F_0 should be $1.93. As the futures price is too high, we should reverse the arbitrage strategy just considered.

Action	Cash Flow Now ($)	Cash Flow in One Year ($)
Borrow $2 in the United States.	$ 2	$-\$2(1.0615)$
Convert the borrowed dollars to pounds, and lend in the United Kingdom at a 10% interest rate.	−2	$1.10E_1$
Enter a contract to sell 1.10 pounds at a futures price of $1.95/£.	0	$1.10(1.95 - E_1)$
Total	$ 0	$0.022

19.3   You must sell forward the number of pounds you will end up with at the end of the year. This value cannot be known with certainty, however, unless the rate of return of the pound-denominated investment is known.
   a. $10,000 \times 1.20 = 12,000$ pounds
   b. $10,000 \times 1.30 = 13,000$ pounds

19.4   *Country selection:*

$$(.40 \times 10\%) + (.20 \times 5\%) + (.40 \times 15\%) = 11\%$$

This is a loss of 1.5% (11% versus 12.5%) relative to the EAFE passive benchmark.
Currency selection:

$$(.40 \times 10\%) + [.20 \times (-10\%)] + (.40 \times 30\%) = 14\%$$

This is a loss of 6% (14% versus 20%) relative to the EAFE benchmark.

Hedge Funds

Learning Objectives

LO 20-1 Identify directional versus nondirectional or market-neutral investment strategies.

LO 20-2 Formulate "pure plays" on seemingly misaligned security prices, and identify the risks that are hedged in these strategies as well as the risks that remain.

LO 20-3 Cite the various difficulties entailed in evaluating hedge fund investment performance.

LO 20-4 Interpret incentive fees charged by hedge funds as implicit options and value them using option-pricing methods.

While mutual funds are still the dominant form of investing in securities markets for most individuals, hedge funds enjoyed far greater growth rates in the last two decades. Assets under hedge fund management increased from around $200 billion in 1997 to about $2.3 trillion in 2014. Like mutual funds, hedge funds allow private investors to pool assets to be invested by a fund manager. Unlike mutual funds, however, they are commonly organized as private partnerships and thus not subject to many SEC regulations. They typically are open only to wealthy or institutional investors.

Hedge funds touch on virtually every issue discussed in the earlier chapters of the text, including liquidity, security analysis, market efficiency, portfolio analysis, hedging, and option pricing. For example, these funds often bet on relative mispricing of specific securities but hedge broad market exposure. This sort of pure "alpha-seeking" behavior requires a procedure for optimally mixing a hedge fund position with a more traditional portfolio. Other funds engage in aggressive market timing; their risk profiles can shift rapidly and substantially, raising difficult questions for performance evaluation. Many hedge funds take extensive derivatives positions. Even those funds that do not trade derivatives charge incentive fees that resemble the payoff to a call option; an option-pricing background therefore is necessary to interpret both hedge fund strategies and costs. In short, hedge funds raise the full range of issues that one might confront in active portfolio management.

We begin with a survey of various hedge fund orientations. We devote considerable

20.1 HEDGE FUNDS VERSUS MUTUAL FUNDS

hedge fund

A private investment pool, open to wealthy or institutional investors, that is largely exempt from SEC regulation and therefore can pursue more speculative policies than mutual funds.

Like mutual funds, the basic idea behind **hedge funds** is investment pooling. Investors buy shares in these funds, which then invest the pooled assets on their behalf. The net asset value of each share represents the value of the investor's stake in the portfolio. In this regard, hedge funds operate much like mutual funds. However, there are important differences between the two.

TRANSPARENCY Mutual funds are subject to the Securities Act of 1933 and the Investment Company Act of 1940 (designed to protect unsophisticated investors), which require transparency and predictability of strategy. They periodically must provide the public with information on portfolio composition. In contrast, hedge funds usually are set up as limited liability partnerships and provide minimal information about portfolio composition and strategy to their investors only.

INVESTORS Hedge funds traditionally have no more than 100 "sophisticated" investors, in practice usually defined by minimum net worth and income requirements. They do not advertise to the general public, although the recent trend is to market as well to ever-smaller and less sophisticated investors. Minimum investments are usually between $250,000 and $1 million.

INVESTMENT STRATEGIES Mutual funds lay out their general investment approach (e.g., large, value stock orientation versus small-cap growth orientation) in their prospectus. They face pressure to avoid *style drift* (departures from their stated investment orientation), especially given the importance of retirement funds such as 401(k) plans to the industry and the demand of such plans for predictable strategies. Most mutual funds promise to limit their use of short-selling and leverage, and their use of derivatives is highly restricted. Some so-called 130/30 funds, serving primarily institutional clients, have prospectuses that explicitly allow for more active short-selling and derivatives positions, but even these have less flexibility than hedge funds.[1] In contrast, hedge funds may effectively partake in any investment strategy and may act opportunistically as conditions evolve. For this reason, it would be a mistake to view hedge funds as anything remotely like a uniform asset class. Hedge funds by design are empowered to invest in a wide range of investments, with various funds focusing on derivatives, distressed firms, currency speculation, convertible bonds, emerging markets, merger arbitrage, and so on. Other funds may jump from one asset class to another as perceived investment opportunities shift.

lock-up period

Period in which investors cannot redeem investments in the hedge fund.

LIQUIDITY Hedge funds often impose **lock-up periods,** that is, periods as long as several years in which investments cannot be withdrawn. Many also employ redemption notices requiring investors to provide notice weeks or months in advance of their desire to redeem funds. These restrictions limit the liquidity of investors but in turn enable the funds to invest in illiquid assets where returns may be higher, without worrying about meeting unanticipated demands for redemptions.

---

[1]These are funds that may sell short up to 30% of the value of their portfolios, using the proceeds of the sale to increase their positions in invested assets. So for every $100 in net assets, the fund could sell short $30, investing the proceeds to increase its long positions to $130. This gives rise to the 130/30 moniker.

COMPENSATION STRUCTURE Hedge funds also differ from mutual funds in their fee structure. Whereas mutual funds assess management fees equal to a fixed percentage of assets, for example, between .5% and 1.5% annually for typical equity funds, hedge funds charge a management fee, usually between 1% and 2% of assets, *plus* a substantial *incentive fee* equal to a fraction of any investment profits beyond some benchmark. The incentive fee is often 20%. The threshold return to earn the incentive fee is often a money market rate such as LIBOR. Indeed, some observers only half-jokingly characterize hedge funds as "a compensation scheme masquerading as an asset class."

20.2 HEDGE FUND STRATEGIES

Table 20.1 presents a list of most of the common investment themes found in the hedge fund industry. The list contains a wide diversity of styles and suggests how hard it can be to speak generically about hedge funds as a group. We can, however, divide hedge fund strategies into two general categories: directional and nondirectional.

Directional and Nondirectional Strategies

Directional strategies are easy to understand. They are simply bets that one sector or another will outperform other sectors of the market.

In contrast, **nondirectional strategies** are usually designed to exploit temporary misalignments in security valuations. For example, if the yield on corporate bonds seems abnormally high compared to that on Treasury bonds, the hedge fund would buy corporates and short-sell Treasury securities. Notice that the fund is *not* betting on broad movements in the entire bond market: It buys one type of bond and sells another. By taking a long corporate–short Treasury

directional strategy

Speculation that one market sector will outperform other sectors.

nondirectional strategy

A position designed to exploit temporary misalignments in relative pricing; typically involves a long position in one security hedged with a short position in a related security.

TABLE 20.1 Hedge fund styles*	
Convertible arbitrage	Hedged investing in convertible securities, typically long convertible bonds and short stock.
Dedicated short bias	Net short position, usually in equities, as opposed to pure short exposure.
Emerging markets	Goal is to exploit market inefficiencies in emerging markets. Typically long-only because short-selling is not feasible in many of these markets.
Equity market neutral	Commonly uses long-short hedges. Typically controls for industry, sector, size, and other exposures, and establishes market-neutral positions designed to exploit some market inefficiency. Commonly involves leverage.
Event driven	Attempts to profit from situations such as mergers, acquisitions, restructuring, bankruptcy, or reorganization.
Fixed-income arbitrage	Attempts to profit from price anomalies in related interest rate securities. Includes interest rate swap arbitrage, U.S. versus non-U.S. government bond arbitrage, yield-curve arbitrage, and mortgage-backed arbitrage.
Global macro	Involves long and short positions in capital or derivative markets across the world. Portfolio positions reflect views on broad market conditions and major economic trends.
Long-short equity hedge	Equity-oriented positions on either side of the market (i.e., long or short), depending on outlook. *Not* meant to be market neutral. May establish a concentrated focus regionally (e.g., U.S. or Europe) or on a specific sector (e.g., tech or health care stocks). Derivatives may be used to hedge positions.
Managed futures	Uses financial, currency, or commodity futures. May make use of technical trading rules or a less structured judgmental approach.
Multistrategy	Opportunistic choice of strategy depending on outlook.
Fund of funds	Fund allocates its cash to several other hedge funds to be managed.

*CS/TASS (Credit Suisse/Tremont Advisors Shareholder Services) maintains one of the most comprehensive databases on hedge fund performance. It categorizes hedge funds into these 11 different investment styles.

position, the fund hedges its interest rate exposure while making a bet on the *relative* valuation across the two sectors. The idea is that when yield spreads converge back to their "normal" relationship, the fund will profit from the realignment regardless of the general trend in the level of interest rates. In this respect, it strives to be **market neutral,** or hedged with respect to the direction of interest rates, which gives rise to the term *hedge fund.*

market neutral

A strategy designed to exploit relative mispricing within a market, but which is hedged to avoid taking a stance on the direction of the broad market.

Nondirectional strategies are sometimes further divided into *convergence* or *relative value* positions. The difference between convergence and relative value is a time horizon at which one can say with confidence that any mispricing ought to be resolved. An example of a convergence strategy would entail mispricing of a futures contract that must be corrected by the time the contract matures. In contrast, the corporate versus Treasury spread we just discussed would be a relative value strategy, because there is no obvious horizon during which the yield spread would "correct" from unusual levels.

EXAMPLE 20.1

Market-Neutral Positions

We can illustrate a market-neutral position with a strategy used extensively by several hedge funds, which observed that newly issued or "on-the-run" 30-year Treasury bonds regularly sell at higher prices (lower yields) than 29½-year bonds with almost identical duration. The yield spread presumably is a premium due to the greater liquidity of the on-the-run bonds. Hedge funds, which have relatively low liquidity needs, therefore buy the 29½-year bond and sell the 30-year bond. This is a hedged, or market-neutral, position that will generate a profit when the yields on the two bonds converge, as typically happens when the 30-year bonds age, are no longer the most liquid on-the-run bond, and are no longer priced at a premium.

Notice that this strategy should generate profits regardless of the general direction of interest rates. The long-short position will return a profit as long as the 30-year bonds underperform the 29½-year bonds, as they should when the liquidity premium dissipates. Because the pricing discrepancies between these two securities almost necessarily *must* disappear at a given date, this strategy is an example of convergence arbitrage. While the convergence date in this application is not quite as definite as the maturity of a futures contract, one can be sure that the currently on-the-run T-bonds will lose that status by the time the Treasury next issues 30-year bonds.

Long-short positions such as in Example 20.1 are characteristic of hedged strategies. They are designed to *isolate* a bet on some mispricing without taking on market exposure. Profits are made regardless of broad market movements once prices "converge" or return to their "proper" levels. Hence, use of short positions and derivatives is part and parcel of the industry.

A more complex long-short strategy is *convertible bond arbitrage.* Noting that a convertible bond may be viewed as a straight bond plus a call option on the underlying stock, the market-neutral strategy in this case involves a position in the bond offset by an opposite position in the stock. For example, if the convertible is viewed as underpriced, the fund will buy it and offset its resultant exposure to declines in the stock price by shorting the stock.

pure plays

Bets on particular mispricing across two or more securities, with extraneous sources of risk such as general market exposure hedged away.

Although these market-neutral positions are hedged, they are *not* risk-free arbitrage strategies. Rather they should be viewed as **pure plays,** that is, bets on *particular* (perceived) mispricing between two sectors or securities, with extraneous sources of risk such as general market exposure hedged away. Moreover, because the funds often operate with considerable leverage, returns can be quite volatile.

CONCEPT check 20.1

Classify each of the following strategies as directional or nondirectional.

a. The fund buys shares in the India Investment Fund, a closed-end fund that is selling at a discount to net asset value, and sells the MSCI India Index Swap.

b. The fund buys shares in Petrie Stores and sells Toys "R" Us, which is a major component of Petrie's balance sheet.

c. The fund buys shares in Generic Pharmaceuticals, betting that it will be acquired at a premium by Pfizer.

Statistical Arbitrage

Statistical arbitrage is a version of a market-neutral strategy, but one that merits its own discussion. It differs from pure arbitrage in that it does not exploit risk-free positions based on unambiguous mispricing (such as index arbitrage). Instead, it uses quantitative and often automated trading systems that seek out many temporary and modest misalignments in prices among securities. By taking relatively small positions in many of these opportunities, the law of averages would make the probability of profiting from the collection of apparently positive-value bets very high, ideally almost a "statistical certainty." Of course, this strategy presumes that the fund's modeling techniques can actually identify reliable, if small, market inefficiencies. The law of averages will work for the fund only if the expected return is positive!

Statistical arbitrage often involves trading in hundreds of securities a day with holding periods that can be measured in minutes or less. Such rapid and heavy trading requires extensive use of quantitative tools such as automated trading and mathematical algorithms to identify profit opportunities and efficient diversification across positions. These strategies try to profit from the smallest of perceived mispricing opportunities and require the fastest trading technology and the lowest possible trading costs. They would not be possible without the algorithmic trading tools discussed in Chapter 3.

A particular form of statistical arbitrage is **pairs trading,** in which stocks are paired up based on an analysis of either fundamental similarities or market exposures (betas). The general approach is to pair up similar companies whose returns are highly correlated but where one company seems to be priced more aggressively than the other.[2] Market-neutral positions can be formed by buying the relatively cheap firm and selling the expensive one. Many such pairs comprise the hedge fund's overall portfolio. Each pair may have an uncertain outcome, but with many such matched pairs, the presumption is that the large number of long-short bets will provide a very high probability of a positive abnormal return. More general versions of pairs trading allow for positions in clusters of stocks that may be relatively mispriced.

Statistical arbitrage is commonly associated with **data mining,** which refers to sorting through huge amounts of historical data to uncover systematic patterns in returns that can be exploited by traders. The risk of data mining, and statistical arbitrage in general, is that historical relationships may break down when fundamental economic conditions change or, indeed, that the apparent patterns in the data may be due to pure chance. Enough analysis applied to enough data is sure to produce apparent patterns that do not reflect real relationships that can be counted on to persist in the future.

statistical arbitrage

Use of quantitative systems to uncover many perceived misalignments in relative pricing and ensure profit by diversifying across these small bets.

pairs trading

Stocks are paired up based on underlying similarities, and long-short positions are established to exploit any relative mispricing between each pair.

data mining

Sorting through large amounts of historical data to uncover systematic patterns that can be exploited.

20.3 PORTABLE ALPHA

An important implication of the market-neutral pure play is the notion of **portable alpha.** Suppose that you wish to speculate on a stock that you think is underpriced, but you think that the market is about to fall. Even if you are right about the stock being *relatively* underpriced, it still might decline in response to declines in the broad market. You would like to separate the stock-specific bet from the implicit asset allocation bet on market performance that arises because the stock's beta is positive. The solution is to buy the stock and eliminate the resultant market exposure by selling enough index futures to drive beta to zero. This long stock–short futures strategy gives you a pure play or, equivalently, a *market-neutral* position on the stock.

More generally, you might wish to separate asset allocation from security selection. The idea is to invest wherever you can "find alpha." You would then hedge the systematic risk of that investment to isolate its alpha from the asset market where it was found. Finally, you establish exposure to desired market sectors by using passive products such as indexed mutual

portable alpha or alpha transfer

A strategy in which you invest in positive alpha positions, then hedge the systematic risk of that investment, and, finally, establish market exposure where you want it using passive indexes.

---

[2]Rules for deciding relative "aggressiveness" of pricing may vary. In one approach, a computer scans for stocks whose prices historically have tracked very closely but have recently diverged. If the differential in cumulative return typically dissipates, the fund will buy the recently underperforming stock and sell the outperforming one. In other variants, pricing aggressiveness may be determined by evaluating the stocks based on the ratio of price to some measure of intrinsic value.

funds, ETFs, or index futures. In other words, you have created portable alpha that can be mixed with an exposure to whatever sector of the market you choose. This procedure is also called **alpha transfer,** because you transfer alpha from the sector where you find it to the asset class in which you ultimately establish exposure. Finding alpha requires skill. By contrast, beta, or market exposure, is a "commodity" that can be supplied cheaply through index funds or ETFs and does not provide value added.

An Example of a Pure Play

Suppose you manage a $2.5 million portfolio. You believe that the alpha of the portfolio is positive, $\alpha > 0$, but also that the market is about to fall, that is, that $r_M < 0$. You would therefore try to establish a pure play on the perceived mispricing.

The return on the portfolio over the next month may be described by Equation 20.1, which states that the portfolio return will equal its "fair" CAPM return (the first two terms on the right-hand side), plus firm-specific risk reflected in the "residual," e, plus an alpha that reflects perceived mispricing:

$$r_{\text{portfolio}} = r_f + \beta(r_M - r_f) + e + \alpha \qquad \text{(20.1)}$$

To be concrete, suppose that $\beta = 1.20$, $\alpha = .02$, $r_f = .01$, the current value of the S&P 500 Index is $S_0 = 2,000$, and, for simplicity, the portfolio pays no dividends. You want to capture the positive alpha of 2% per month, but you don't want the positive beta that the stock entails because you are worried about a market decline. So you choose to hedge your exposure by selling S&P 500 futures contracts.

Because the S&P contracts have a multiplier of $250, and the portfolio has a beta of 1.20, your stock position can be hedged for one month by selling six futures contracts:[3]

$$\text{Hedge ratio} = \frac{\$2,500,000}{2,000 \times \$250} \times 1.20 = 6 \text{ contracts}$$

The dollar value of your portfolio after one month will be

$$\$2,500,000 \times (1 + r_{\text{portfolio}}) = \$2,500,000 \, [1 + .01 + 1.20 \, (r_M - .01) + .02 + e]$$
$$= \$2,545,000 + \$3,000,000 \times r_M + \$2,500,000 \times e$$

The dollar proceeds from your futures position will be:

$6 \times \$250 \times (F_0 - F_1)$	Mark-to-market on 6 contracts sold
$= \$1,500 \times [S_0 \, (1.01) - S_1]$	Substitute for futures price, F_0, from parity relationship
$= \$1,500 \times S_0 \, [1.01 - (1 + r_M)]$	Because $S_1 = S_0(1 + r_M)$ when no dividends are paid
$= \$1,500 \times [S_0 \, (.01 - r_M)]$	Simplify
$= \$30,000 - \$3,000,000 \times r_M$	Because $S_0 = 2,000$

The total value of the stock plus futures position at month's end will be the sum of the portfolio value plus the futures proceeds, which equals

$$\text{Hedged proceeds} = \$2,575,000 + \$2,500,000 \times e \qquad \text{(20.2)}$$

Notice that the dollar exposure to the market from your futures position precisely offsets your exposure from the stock portfolio. In other words, you have reduced beta to zero. Your investment is $2.5 million, so your total monthly rate of return is 3% plus the remaining non-systematic risk (the second term of Equation 20.2). The fair or equilibrium expected rate of return on such a zero-beta position is the risk-free rate, 1%, so you have preserved your alpha of 2%, while eliminating the market exposure of the stock portfolio.

[3]We simplify here by assuming that the maturity of the futures contract precisely equals the hedging horizon, in this case, one month. If the contract maturity were longer, one would have to slightly reduce the hedge ratio in a process called "tailing the hedge."

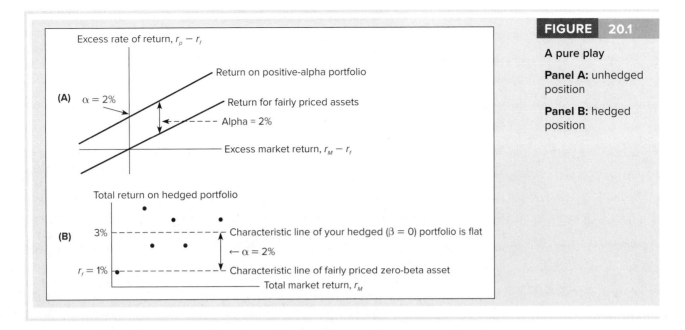

FIGURE 20.1

A pure play

Panel A: unhedged position

Panel B: hedged position

This is an idealized example of a pure play. In particular, it simplifies by assuming a known and fixed portfolio beta, but it illustrates that the goal is to speculate on the stock while hedging out the undesired market exposure. Once this is accomplished, you can establish any desired exposure to other sources of systematic risk by buying indexes or entering index futures contracts in those markets. Thus, you have made alpha portable.

Figure 20.1 is a graphical analysis of this pure play. Panel A shows the excess returns to betting on a positive-alpha stock portfolio "naked," that is, unhedged. Your *expected* return is better than an equilibrium return given your risk, but because of your market exposure you still can lose if the market declines. Panel B shows the characteristic line for the position with systematic risk hedged out. There is no market exposure.

A warning: Even market-neutral positions are still bets, and they can go wrong. This is not true arbitrage because your profits still depend on whether your analysis (your perceived alpha) is correct. Moreover, you can be done in by simple bad luck, that is, your analysis may be correct but a bad realization of idiosyncratic risk (negative values of e in Equation 20.1 or 20.2) can still result in losses.

What would be the dollar value and rate of return on the market-neutral position if the value of the residual turns out to be −4%? If the market return in that month is 5%, where would the plot of the strategy return lie in each panel of Figure 20.1?

An apparently market-neutral bet misfired badly in 1998. While the 30- versus 29½-year maturity T-bond strategy (see Example 20.1) worked well over several years, it blew up when Russia defaulted on its debt, triggering massive investment demand for the safest, most liquid assets that drove up the price of the 30-year Treasury relative to its 29½-year counterpart. The big losses that ensued illustrate that even the safest bet—one based on convergence arbitrage—carries risks. Although the T-bond spread had to converge eventually, and in fact it did several weeks later, Long Term Capital Management (LTCM) and other hedge funds suffered large losses on their positions when the spread widened temporarily. The ultimate convergence came too late for LTCM, which was also facing massive losses on its other positions and had to be bailed out.[4]

---

[4]This timing problem is a common one for active managers. We saw other examples of this issue when we discussed limits to arbitrage in Chapter 9. More generally, when security analysts think they have found a mispriced stock, they usually acknowledge that it is hard to know how long it will take for price to converge to intrinsic value.

Even market-neutral bets can result in considerable volatility because most hedge funds use considerable leverage. Most incidents of relative mispricing are fairly minor, and the hedged nature of long-short strategies makes overall volatility low. The hedge funds respond by scaling up their bets. This amplifies gains when their bets work out, but also amplifies losses. In the end, the volatility of the funds is not small.

20.4   STYLE ANALYSIS FOR HEDGE FUNDS

While the classic hedge fund strategy may have focused on market-neutral opportunities, as the market has evolved, the freedom to use derivatives contracts and short positions means that hedge funds can in effect follow any investment strategy. While many hedge funds pursue market-neutral strategies, a quick glance at the range of investment styles in Table 20.1 should convince you that many, if not most, funds pursue directional strategies. In these cases, the fund makes an outright bet, for example, on currency movements, the outcome of a takeover attempt, or the performance of an investment sector. These funds are most certainly not hedged, despite their name.

In Chapter 18, we introduced you to style analysis, which uses regression analysis to measure the exposure of a portfolio to various factors or asset classes. The analysis thus measures the implicit asset class exposure of a portfolio. The betas on a series of factors measure the fund's exposure to each source of systematic risk. A market-neutral fund will have no sensitivity to an index for that market. In contrast, directional funds will exhibit significant betas, often called *loadings* in this context, on whatever factors the fund tends to bet on. Observers attempting to measure investment style can use these factor loadings to impute exposures to a range of variables.

We present a simple style analysis for the hedge fund indexes in Table 20.2. The four systematic factors we consider are

- *Interest rates*—the return on long-term U.S. Treasury bonds.
- *Equity markets*—the return on the S&P 500.
- *Credit conditions*—the difference in the return on Baa-rated bonds over Treasury bonds.
- *Foreign exchange*—the percentage change in the value of the U.S. dollar against a basket of foreign currencies.

The excess returns on hedge fund index i in month t may be statistically described by

$$R_{it} = \alpha_i + \beta_{i1} \text{Factor1}_t + \cdots + \beta_{i4} \text{Factor4}_t + e_{it} \tag{20.3}$$

The betas (equivalently, factor loadings) measure the sensitivity to each factor. As usual, the residual, e_{it}, measures "nonsystematic" risk that is uncorrelated with the set of explanatory factors, and the intercept, α_i, measures average performance of fund i net of the impact of these systematic factors.

Table 20.2 presents factor exposure estimates for 13 hedge fund indexes. The results confirm that most funds are in fact directional with very clear exposures to one or more of the four factors. Moreover, the estimated factor betas seem reasonable in terms of the funds' stated style. For example:

- The equity market–neutral funds have uniformly low and statistically insignificant factor betas, as one would expect of a market-neutral posture.
- Dedicated short bias funds exhibit substantial negative betas on the S&P index.
- Distressed-firm funds have significant exposure to credit conditions (more positive credit spreads in this table indicate better economic conditions) as well as to the S&P 500. This exposure arises because restructuring activities often depend on access to borrowing, and successful restructuring depends on the state of the economy.
- Global macro funds show negative exposure to a stronger U.S. dollar, which would make the dollar value of foreign investments less valuable.

We conclude that, by and large, most hedge funds are making very explicit directional bets on a wide array of economic factors.

TABLE 20.2   Style analysis for a sample of hedge fund indexes

Funds Group*	Alpha	S&P 500	Long T-bond	Credit Conditions	U.S. Dollar
All funds	0.0052	0.2718	0.0189	0.1755	−0.1897
	3.3487	5.0113	0.3064	2.0462	−2.1270
Market neutral	0.0014	0.1677	−0.0163	0.3308	−0.5097
	0.1990	0.6917	−0.0589	0.8631	−1.2790
Short bias	0.0058	−0.9723	0.1310	0.3890	−0.2630
	1.3381	−6.3684	0.7527	1.6113	−1.0476
Event driven	0.0071	0.2335	0.0000	0.2056	−0.1165
	5.1155	4.7858	−0.0002	2.6642	0.1520
Risk arbitrage	0.0034	0.1498	0.0130	−0.0006	−0.2130
	3.0678	3.8620	0.0442	−0.0097	−3.3394
Distressed	0.0068	0.2080	0.0032	0.2521	−0.1156
	5.7697	4.9985	0.0679	3.8318	−1.6901
Emerging markets	0.0082	0.3750	0.2624	0.4551	−0.2169
	2.8867	3.7452	2.2995	2.8748	−1.3173
Fixed-income arb	0.0018	0.1719	0.2284	0.5703	−0.1714
	1.0149	2.8139	3.2806	5.9032	−1.7063
Convertible arb	0.0005	0.2477	0.2109	0.5021	−0.0972
	0.2197	3.1066	2.3214	3.9825	−0.7414
Global macro	0.0079	0.0746	0.0593	0.1492	−0.2539
	3.5217	0.9437	0.6587	1.1938	−1.9533
Long-short equity	0.0053	0.4442	−0.0070	0.0672	−0.1471
	2.5693	6.1425	−0.0850	0.5874	−1.2372
Managed futures	0.0041	0.2565	−0.2991	−0.5223	−0.2703
	0.8853	1.5944	−1.6310	−2.0528	−1.0217
Multistrategy	0.0075	0.2566	−0.0048	0.1781	−0.1172
	4.2180	4.1284	−0.0684	1.8116	−1.1471

*Fund definitions given in Table 20.1.

Note: Top line of each entry is the estimate of the factor beta. Lower line is the *t*-statistic for that estimate.

Source: Authors' calculations. Hedge fund returns are on indexes computed by Credit Suisse/Tremont Index, LLC.

Analyze the betas of the fixed-income arbitrage index in Table 20.2. Based on these results, are these funds typically market neutral? If not, do their factor exposures make sense in terms of the markets in which they operate?

CONCEPT check 20.3

20.5   PERFORMANCE MEASUREMENT FOR HEDGE FUNDS

Table 20.3 shows basic performance data for a collection of hedge fund indexes computed from the standard index model with the S&P 500 used as the market benchmark. The model is estimated using monthly returns over the five-year period ending in October 2014. We report for

TABLE 20.3	Index-model regressions for hedge fund indexes*			
	Beta	**Serial Correlation**	**Alpha**	**Sharpe Ratio**
Hedge fund composite index	0.288	0.099	0.18%	0.327
Convertible arbitrage	0.154	0.259	0.32%	0.346
Short bias	−0.926	−0.050	0.04%	−0.361
Emerging markets	0.426	0.015	−0.09%	0.168
Equity market neutral	0.272	−0.102	−0.11%	0.086
Event driven: Composite	0.372	0.277	0.11%	0.268
Event driven: Distressed	0.283	0.310	0.33%	0.393
Event driven: Multi-strategy	0.432	0.258	−0.02%	0.213
Event driven: Risk arbitrage	0.164	0.036	0.03%	0.110
Fixed income arbitrage	0.053	0.196	0.63%	0.902
Global macro	0.095	−0.182	0.47%	0.394
Long/short equity	0.510	0.059	−0.09%	0.227
Managed futures	0.206	−0.128	−0.01%	0.040
Multi-strategy	0.224	0.156	0.40%	0.532
S&P 500	1.000	−0.126	0.00%	0.337
Average across hedge funds	0.182	0.086	0.16%	0.260

*Estimation period: November 2009–October 2014.

Source: Authors' calculations using data downloaded from Credit Suisse, *Hedge Fund Indexes,* hedgeindex.com, November 2014.

each index the beta relative to the S&P 500, the serial correlation of returns, the Sharpe ratio, and the alpha. Betas tend to be considerably less than 1; not surprisingly, the beta of the short bias index is large and negative. The beta of the equity market-neutral index is .272, quite low for an asset class invested exclusively in the equity market. Most of the alpha estimates are positive, and the average alpha is substantial, .16% per month. What might be the source of such performance?

One possibility, of course, is the obvious one: these results may reflect a high degree of skill among hedge fund managers. Another possibility is that funds maintain some exposure to omitted risk factors that convey a positive risk premium. One likely candidate for such a factor would be liquidity, and we will see shortly that liquidity and liquidity risk are associated with average returns. Moreover, several other factors make hedge fund performance difficult to evaluate, and these also are worth considering.

Liquidity and Hedge Fund Performance

One explanation for apparently attractive hedge fund performance is liquidity. Recall that one of the more important extensions of the CAPM is a version that allows for the possibility of a return premium for investors willing to hold less liquid assets. Hedge funds tend to hold more illiquid assets than other institutional investors such as mutual funds. They can do so because of restrictions such as the lock-up provisions that commit investors to keep their investment in the fund for some period of time. Therefore, it is important to control for liquidity when evaluating performance. If it is ignored, what may be no more than compensation for illiquidity may appear to be true alpha, that is, risk-adjusted abnormal returns.

Aragon (2007) demonstrates that hedge funds with lock-up restrictions do tend to hold less liquid portfolios. Moreover, once he controlled for lock-ups or other share restrictions (such as redemption notice periods), the apparently positive average alpha of those funds turned insignificant. Aragon's work suggests that the typical "alpha" exhibited by hedge funds may be better interpreted as an equilibrium liquidity premium rather than a sign of stock-picking ability, in other words as a "fair" reward for providing liquidity to other investors.

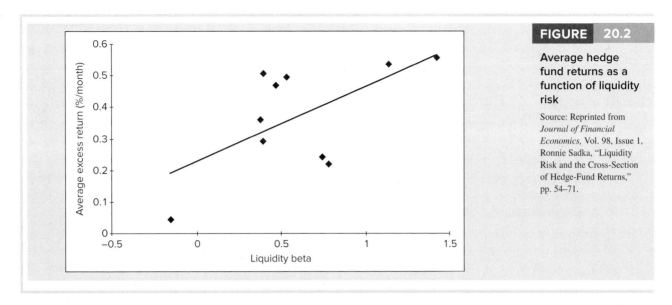

FIGURE 20.2

Average hedge fund returns as a function of liquidity risk

Source: Reprinted from *Journal of Financial Economics,* Vol. 98, Issue 1, Ronnie Sadka, "Liquidity Risk and the Cross-Section of Hedge-Fund Returns," pp. 54–71.

Whereas Aragon focuses on the average level of liquidity, Sadka (2009) addresses the liquidity *risk* of hedge funds. He shows that exposure to unexpected declines in market liquidity is an important determinant of hedge fund returns, and that the spread in average returns across the funds with the highest and lowest liquidity exposure may be as much as 6% annually. Hedge fund performance may therefore reflect significant compensation for liquidity risk. Figure 20.2, constructed from data reported in his study, is a scatter diagram relating average return for the hedge funds in each style group of Table 20.2 to the liquidity-risk beta for that group.[5] Average return clearly rises with exposure to changes in market liquidity.

One symptom of illiquid assets is serial correlation in returns. Positive serial correlation means that positive returns are more likely to be followed by positive than by negative returns. Such a pattern is often taken as an indicator of less liquid markets for the following reason: When accurate and timely prices are not available because an asset is not actively traded, the hedge fund must estimate its value to calculate net asset value and rates of return. But such procedures are at best imperfect and, as demonstrated by Getmansky, Lo, and Makarov (2004), tend to result in serial correlation in prices as firms either smooth out their value estimates or only gradually mark prices to true market values. Positive serial correlation is therefore often interpreted as evidence of liquidity problems; in nearly efficient markets with frictionless trading, we would expect serial correlation or other predictable patterns in prices to be minimal.[6]

Hasanhodzic and Lo (2007) find that hedge fund returns in fact exhibit significant serial correlation. This symptom of smoothed prices has two important implications. First, it lends further support to the hypothesis that hedge funds are holding less liquid assets and that their apparent alphas may in fact be liquidity premiums. Second, it implies that their performance measures are upward-biased, because any smoothing in the estimates of portfolio value will reduce total volatility (thereby increasing the Sharpe ratio) as well as covariances and therefore betas with systematic factors (thereby increasing risk-adjusted alphas).

In fact, Figure 20.3 shows that both the alphas and the Sharpe ratios of the hedge fund indexes in Table 20.3 increase with the serial correlation of returns. These results are consistent with the fund-specific results of Hasanhodzic and Lo and suggest that price smoothing may account for some part of the apparently superior hedge fund performance.

---

[5]Just as the market beta of a stock measures sensitivity of returns to changes in overall market performance as reflected in the return on a broad market index, the liquidity beta measures sensitivity to changes in market liquidity. Because liquidity risk is nondiversifiable, stocks with greater liquidity betas should compensate investors with higher expected rates of return.

[6]Of course, in any particular sample period, the point estimate of serial correlation may be positive or negative. With long data series, we find that serial correlations generally are in fact small.

Hedge funds with higher serial correlation in returns, an indicator of illiquid portfolio holdings, exhibit both higher alphas (Panel A) and higher Sharpe ratios (Panel B).

Source: Prepared using data in Table 20.3.

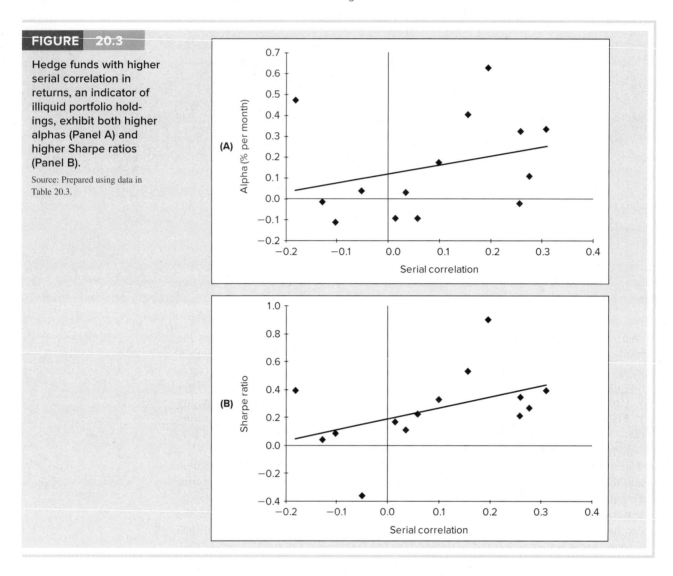

Performance can be even more difficult to interpret if a hedge fund takes advantage of illiquid markets to manipulate returns by purposely misvaluing illiquid assets. In this regard, it is worth noting that, on average, hedge funds report average returns in December that are substantially greater than their average returns in other months (Agarwal, Daniel, and Naik, 2011). The pattern is stronger for lower-liquidity funds and for funds that are near or beyond the threshold return at which performance incentive fees kick in. It appears that funds use their discretion in valuing assets to move returns to December when that will enhance their annual incentive fees. It also appears that some hedge funds attempt to manipulate their measured performance by buying additional shares in stocks they already own in an effort to push up their prices (Ben-David, Franzoni, Landier, and Moussawi, 2013). The buying takes place just before market close at the end of the month when hedge fund performance is reported. Moreover, the effort is concentrated in less liquid stocks where the price impact would be expected to be greater. If, as these papers suggest, funds take advantage of illiquid markets to manage returns, then accurate performance measurement becomes almost impossible.

Hedge Fund Performance and Survivorship Bias

We already know that survivorship bias (when only successful funds remain in a database) can affect the estimated performance of a sample of mutual funds. The same problems, as well as related ones, apply to hedge funds. **Backfill bias** arises because hedge funds report

backfill bias

Bias in the average returns of a sample of funds induced by including past returns on funds that entered the sample only if they happened to be successful.

returns to database publishers only if they choose to. Funds started with seed capital will open to the public and therefore enter standard databases only if their past performance is deemed sufficiently successful to attract clients. Therefore, the prior performance of funds that are eventually included in the sample may not be representative of typical performance. **Survivorship bias** arises when unsuccessful funds that cease operation stop reporting returns and leave a database, leaving behind only the successful funds. Malkiel and Saha (2005) find that attrition rates for hedge funds are far higher than for mutual funds—in fact, commonly more than double the attrition rate of mutual funds—making this an important issue to address. Estimates of survivorship bias in various studies are typically substantial, in the range of 2%–4%.[7]

survivorship bias

Bias in the average returns of a sample of funds induced by excluding past returns on funds that left the sample because they happened to be unsuccessful.

Hedge Fund Performance and Changing Factor Loadings

In Chapter 18, we pointed out that an important assumption underlying conventional performance evaluation is that the portfolio manager maintains a reasonably stable risk profile over time. But hedge funds are designed to be opportunistic and have considerable flexibility to change that profile. This too can make performance evaluation tricky. If risk is not constant, then estimated alphas will be biased if we use a standard, linear index model. And if the risk profile changes systematically with the expected return on the market, performance evaluation is even more difficult.

To see why, look at Figure 20.4, which illustrates the characteristic line of a perfect market timer (see Chapter 18, Section 18.6) who engages in no security selection but moves funds from T-bills into the market portfolio only when the market will outperform bills. The characteristic line is nonlinear, with a slope of 0 when the market underperforms T-bills, and a slope of 1 when it outperforms. But a naïve attempt to estimate a regression equation from this pattern would result in a fitted line with a slope between 0 and 1 and a positive alpha. Neither statistic accurately describes the fund.

As we noted in Chapter 18, and as is evident from Figure 20.4, an ability to conduct perfect market timing is much like obtaining a call option on the underlying portfolio without having to pay for it. Similar nonlinearities would arise if the fund actually buys or writes options. Figure 20.5, Panel A, illustrates the case of a fund that holds a stock portfolio and writes put options on it, and Panel B illustrates the case of a fund that holds a stock portfolio and writes call options. In both cases, the characteristic line is steeper when portfolio returns are poor—in other words, the fund has greater sensitivity to the market when it is falling than when it is rising. This is the opposite profile that would arise from timing ability, which is much like acquiring rather than writing options, and therefore would give the fund greater sensitivity to market advances.[8]

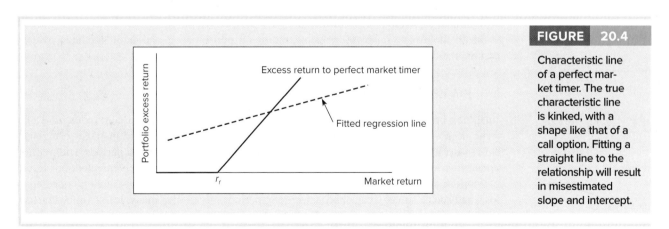

FIGURE 20.4

Characteristic line of a perfect market timer. The true characteristic line is kinked, with a shape like that of a call option. Fitting a straight line to the relationship will result in misestimated slope and intercept.

[7]For example, Malkiel and Saha (2005) estimate the bias at 4.4%, Amin and Kat (2003) find a bias of about 2%, and Fung and Hsieh (2000) find a bias of about 3.6%.

[8]But the fund that writes options would at least receive fair compensation for the unattractive shape of its characteristic line in the form of the premium received when it writes the options.

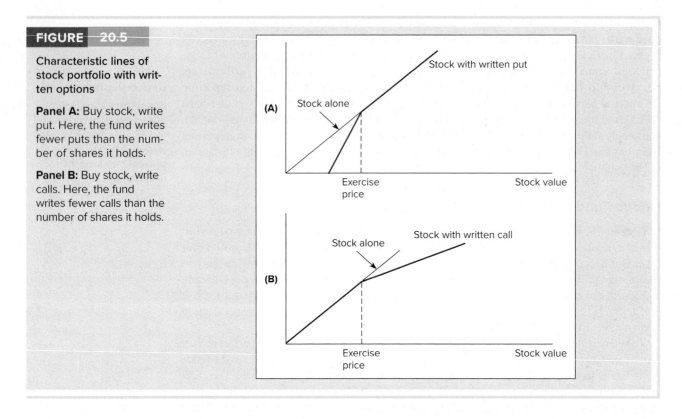

FIGURE 20.5

Characteristic lines of stock portfolio with written options

Panel A: Buy stock, write put. Here, the fund writes fewer puts than the number of shares it holds.

Panel B: Buy stock, write calls. Here, the fund writes fewer calls than the number of shares it holds.

Figure 20.6 presents evidence on these sorts of nonlinearities. A nonlinear regression line is fitted to the scatter diagram of returns on hedge fund indexes plotted against returns on the S&P 500. The fitted lines in Panels A and B, for hedge funds concentrating on fixed-income arbitrage or distressed firms, show higher down-market betas (higher slopes) than up-market betas. This is precisely what investors presumably do *not* want: higher market sensitivity when the market is weak. This is evidence that these funds may be *writing* options, either explicitly or implicitly through dynamic trading strategies (see Chapter 16, Section 16.4, for a discussion of such dynamic strategies).

Not all funds show this pattern, however. Panel C, for global macro funds that bet on differences in performance across countries or currencies, shows the opposite pattern, with betas increasing along with the return on the S&P 500. The attractive asymmetry is characteristic of a position that is long in S&P call options, benefiting from good market performance, but with limited exposure to downturns.

In all three panels, however, using traditional performance evaluation methods, which assume fixed market exposures, is hazardous.

Tail Events and Hedge Fund Performance

Imagine a hedge fund whose entire investment strategy is to hold an S&P 500 Index fund and write deep out-of-the-money put options on the index. Clearly the fund manager brings no skill to his job. But if you knew only his investment results over limited periods, and not his underlying strategy, you might be fooled into thinking that he is extremely talented. For if the put options are written sufficiently out-of-the-money, they will only rarely end up imposing a loss, and such a strategy can appear over long periods—even over many years—to be consistently profitable. In most periods, the strategy brings in a modest premium from the written puts and therefore outperforms the S&P 500, yielding the impression of consistently superior performance. Every so often, however, such as in the market crash of October 1987, the strategy may lose multiples of its entire gain over the last decade. But if you are lucky enough to avoid these rare but extreme *tail events* (so named because they fall in the far-left tail of the probability distribution), the strategy might appear to be gilded.

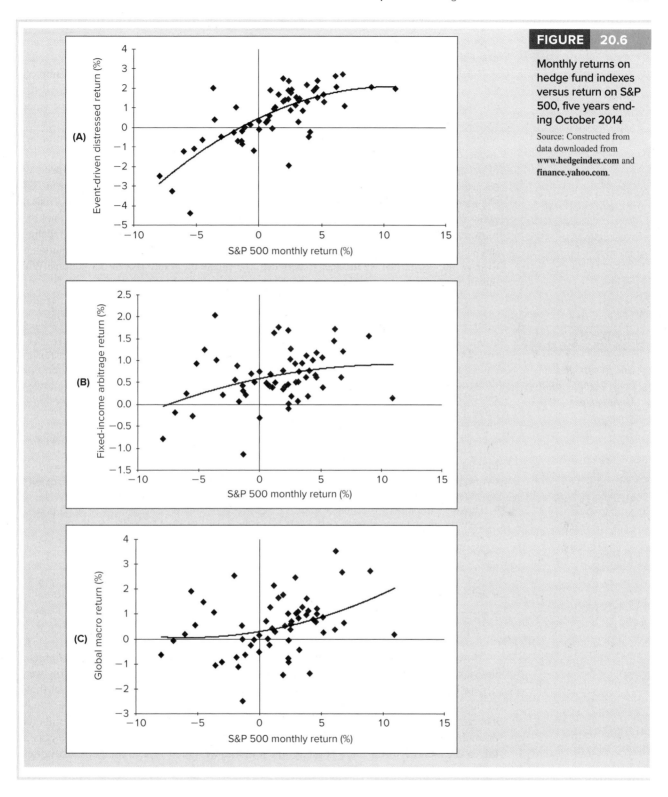

FIGURE   20.6

Monthly returns on hedge fund indexes versus return on S&P 500, five years ending October 2014

Source: Constructed from data downloaded from **www.hedgeindex.com** and **finance.yahoo.com**.

The evidence in Figure 20.6 indicating that hedge funds are at least implicitly option writers should make us nervous about taking their measured performance at face value. The problem in interpreting strategies with exposure to extreme tail events (such as short options positions) is that these events by definition occur very infrequently, so it can take *decades* of results to fully appreciate their true risk and reward attributes. Nassim Taleb (2004, 2007) who is a hedge fund operator himself, makes the case that many hedge funds are analogous to our hypothetical manager, racking up fame and fortune through strategies that make money *most* of the time, but expose investors to rare but extreme losses.

Taleb uses the metaphor of the black swan to discuss the importance of highly improbable, but highly impactful, events. Until the discovery of Australia, Europeans believed that all swans were white: They had never encountered swans that were not. In their experience, the black swan was outside the realm of reasonable possibility, in statistical jargon, an extreme outlier relative to their sample of observations. Taleb argues that the world is filled with black swans, deeply important developments that simply could not have been predicted from the range of accumulated experience to date. While we can't predict which black swans to expect, we nevertheless know that some black swan may be making an appearance at any moment. The October 1987 crash, when the market fell by more than 20% in one day, or the financial crisis of 2008–2009 might be viewed as black swans—events that had never taken place before, ones that most market observers would have dismissed as impossible and certainly not worth modeling, but with high impact. These sorts of events seemingly come out of the blue, and they caution us to show humility when we use past experience to evaluate the future risk of our actions. With this in mind, consider again the example of Long Term Capital Management.

EXAMPLE 20.3 *Tail Events and Long Term Capital Management*	In the late 1990s, Long Term Capital Management was widely viewed as the most successful hedge fund in history. It had consistently provided double-digit returns to its investors, and it had earned hundreds of millions of dollars in incentive fees for its managers. The firm used sophisticated computer models to estimate correlations across assets and believed that its capital was almost 10 times the annual standard deviation of its portfolio returns, presumably enough to withstand any "possible" shock to capital (at least, assuming normal distributions!). But in the summer of 1998, things went badly. On August 17, 1998, Russia defaulted on its sovereign debt and threw capital markets into chaos. LTCM's *one-day* loss on August 21 was $550 million (approximately nine times its estimated *monthly* standard deviation). Total losses in August were about $1.3 billion, despite the fact that LTCM believed that most of its positions were market-neutral relative value trades. Losses accrued on virtually all of its positions, flying in the face of the presumed diversification of the overall portfolio. How did this happen? The answer lies in the massive flight to quality and, even more so, to liquidity that was set off by the Russian default. LTCM was typically a seller of liquidity (holding less liquid assets, selling more liquid assets with lower yields, and earning the yield spread) and suffered huge losses. This was a different type of shock from those that appeared in its historical sample/modeling period. In the liquidity crisis that engulfed asset markets, the unexpected commonality of liquidity risk across asset classes previously believed to be uncorrelated became obvious. Losses that seemed statistically impossible on past experience had in fact come to pass; LTCM fell victim to a black swan.

However, Figure 20.6 shows that hedge funds as a group did not exhibit noticeably greater tail risk than other stock investments during the financial crisis. While equity returns were generally dismal in that period, typical hedge fund returns were far less negative that those of the S&P 500. This, of course, is consistent with the generally low betas of these funds. The noteworthy observation from the scatter diagrams of Figure 20.6 is that no points fall dramatically below the trend lines. While hedge funds suffered along with other assets in the crisis, their performance was pretty much in line with their typical market sensitivities, no better but no worse.

20.6   FEE STRUCTURE IN HEDGE FUNDS

incentive fee

A fee charged by hedge funds equal to a share of any investment returns beyond a stipulated benchmark performance.

The typical hedge fund fee structure is a management fee of 1% to 2% of assets plus an **incentive fee** equal to 20% of investment profits beyond a stipulated benchmark performance, annually. Incentive fees are effectively call options on the portfolio with a strike price equal to current portfolio value times 1 + benchmark return. The manager gets the fee if the portfolio

FIGURE   20.7

Incentive fees as a call option. The current value of the portfolio is denoted S_0 and its year-end value is S_T. The incentive fee is equivalent to .20 call options on the portfolio with exercise price $S_0(1 + r_f)$.

value rises sufficiently, but loses nothing if it falls. Figure 20.7 illustrates the incentive fee for a fund with a 20% incentive fee and a hurdle rate equal to the money market rate, r_f. The current value of the portfolio is denoted S_0 and the year-end value is S_T. The incentive fee is equivalent to .20 call options on the portfolio with exercise price $S_0(1 + r_f)$.

Suppose the standard deviation of a hedge fund's annual rate of return is 30% and the incentive fee is 20% of any investment return over the risk-free money market rate. If the portfolio currently has a net asset value of $100 per share, and the effective annual risk-free rate is 5% (or 4.88% expressed as a continuously compounded rate), then the implicit exercise price on the incentive fee is $105. The Black-Scholes value of a call option with $S_0 = 100$, $X = 105$, $\sigma = .30$, $r = .0488$, $T = 1$ year is $11.92, just a shade below 12% of net asset value. Because the incentive fee is worth 20% of the call option, its value is just about 2.4% of net asset value. Together with a typical management fee of 2% of net asset value, the investor in the fund pays fees with a total value of 4.4%.

EXAMPLE 20.4

Black-Scholes Valuation of Incentive Fees

The major complication to this description of the typical compensation structure is the **high water mark.** If a fund experiences losses, it may not be able to charge an incentive fee unless and until it recovers to its previous higher value. With large losses, this may be difficult. High water marks therefore give managers an incentive to shut down funds that have performed poorly, and likely are a cause of the high attrition rate for funds noted above.

A notable fraction of the hedge fund universe is invested in **funds of funds,** which are hedge funds that invest in one or more other hedge funds. Funds of funds are also called *feeder funds,* because they feed assets from the original investor to the ultimate hedge fund. They market themselves as providing investors the capability to diversify across funds and also as providing the due diligence involved in screening funds for investment worthiness. In principle, this can be a valuable service because many hedge funds are opaque and feeder funds may have greater insight than typical outsiders.

However, when Bernard Madoff was arrested in December 2008 after admitting to a $60 billion Ponzi scheme, it emerged that many large feeder funds were among his biggest clients and that their "due diligence" may have been, to put it mildly, lacking. At the head of the list was Fairfield Greenwich Advisors, with exposure reported at $7.5 billion, but several other feeder funds and asset management firms around the world were also on the hook for amounts greater than $1 billion. In the end, it appears that some funds had in effect become little more than marketing agents for Madoff. The nearby box presents further discussion of the Madoff affair.

Optionality can have a big impact on expected fees in funds of funds. This is because the fund of funds pays an incentive fee to each underlying fund that outperforms its benchmark, even if the aggregate performance of the fund of funds is poor. In this case, diversification can hurt you (Brown, Goetzmann, and Liang, 2004)!

high water mark

The previous value of a portfolio that must be reattained before a hedge fund can charge incentive fees.

funds of funds

Hedge funds that invest in several other hedge funds.

On the MARKET FRONT

THE BERNARD MADOFF SCANDAL

Bernard Madoff seemed like one of the great success stories in the annals of finance. His asset management firm, Bernard L. Madoff Investment Securities, reported to its clients that their investments of around $20 billion had grown to about $65 billion in 2008. But that December, Madoff reportedly confessed to his two sons that he had for years been operating a Ponzi scheme. A Ponzi scheme is an investment fraud in which a manager collects funds from clients, claims to invest those funds on their behalf, reports extremely favorable investment returns, but in fact uses the funds for his own purposes. (The schemes are named after Charles Ponzi, whose success with this scheme in the early 1900s made him notorious throughout the United States.) Early investors who ask to redeem their investments are paid back with the funds coming in from new investors rather than with true earnings. The scheme can continue as long as new investors provide enough funds to cover the redemption requests of the earlier ones—and these inflows are attracted both by the superior returns "earned" by early investors and their apparent ability to redeem funds as requested.

As a highly respected member of the Wall Street establishment, Madoff was in a perfect position to perpetrate such a fraud. He was a pioneer in electronic trading and had served as chairman of the NASDAQ stock market. Aside from its trading operations, Bernard L. Madoff Investment Securities LLC also acted as a money manager, and it claimed to achieve highly consistent annual returns, between 10% and 12% in good markets as well as bad. Its strategy was supposedly based on option hedging strategies, but Madoff was never precise about his approach. Still, his stature on Wall Street and the prestige of his client list seemed to testify to his legitimacy. Moreover, he played hard-to-get with new investors, and it appeared that one needed connections to join the fund, which

only increased its appeal. The scheme seems to have operated for decades, but in the 2008 stock market downturn several large clients requested redemptions totaling around $7 billion. With less than $1 billion of assets left in the firm, the scheme collapsed.

Not everyone was fooled, and, in retrospect, several red flags should have aroused suspicion. For example, some institutional investors shied away from the fund, objecting to its unusual opacity. Given the magnitude of the assets supposedly under management, the option hedging trades purportedly at the heart of Madoff's investment strategy should have dominated options market trading volume, yet there was no evidence of their execution. Moreover, Madoff's auditor, a small firm with only three employees (including only one active accountant!), seemed grossly inadequate to audit such a large and complex operation. In addition, Madoff's fee structure was highly unusual. Rather than acting as a hedge fund that would charge a percentage of assets plus incentive fees, he claimed to profit instead through trading commissions on the account—if true, this would have been a colossal price break to clients. Finally, rather than placing assets under management with a custodial bank as most funds do, Madoff claimed to keep the funds in house, which meant that no one could independently verify their existence. In 2000, the SEC received a letter from an industry professional named Harry Markopolos concluding that "Madoff Securities is the world's largest Ponzi scheme," but Madoff continued to operate unimpeded.

Even today, several questions remain. How much help did Madoff receive from others? Exactly how much money was lost? Most of the "lost" funds represented fictitious profits that had never actually been earned, but some money was returned to early investors. How much was skimmed off to support Madoff's lifestyle? And perhaps most important, why didn't the red flags and early warnings prompt a more aggressive response from regulators?

EXAMPLE 20.5

Incentive Fees in Funds of Funds

Suppose a fund of funds is established with $1 million invested in each of three hedge funds. For simplicity, we will ignore the asset-value-based portion of fees (the management fee) and focus only on the incentive fee. Suppose that the hurdle rate for the incentive fee is a zero return, so each fund charges an incentive fee of 20% of total return (if positive). The following table shows the performance of each underlying fund over a year, the gross rate of return, and the return realized by the fund of funds net of the incentive fee. Funds 1 and 2 have positive returns, and therefore earn an incentive fee, but Fund 3 has terrible performance, so its incentive fee is zero.

	Fund 1	Fund 2	Fund 3	Fund of Funds
Start of year (millions)	$1.00	$1.00	$1.00	$3.00
End of year (millions)	$1.20	$1.40	$0.25	$2.85
Gross rate of return	20%	40%	−75%	−5%
Incentive fee (millions)	$0.04	$0.08	$0.00	$0.12
End of year, net of fee	$1.16	$1.32	$ .25	$2.73
Net rate of return	16%	32%	−75%	−9%

Even though the return on the aggregate portfolio of the fund of funds is *negative* 5%, it still pays incentive fees of $.12 for every $3 invested because incentive fees are paid on the first two well-performing funds. The incentive fees amount to 4% of net asset value. As demonstrated in the last column, this reduces the rate of return earned by investors in the fund of funds from −5% to −9%.

The idea behind funds of funds is to spread risk across several different funds. However, investors need to be aware that these funds of funds may operate with considerable leverage, on top of the leverage of the primary funds in which they invest, which can make returns highly volatile. Moreover, if the various hedge funds in which these funds of funds invest have similar investment styles, the diversification benefits of spreading investments across several funds may be illusory—but the extra layer of steep management fees paid to the manager of the fund of funds certainly is not.[9]

[9]One small silver lining: While funds of funds pay incentive fees to each of the underlying funds, the incentive fees they charge their own investors tend to be lower, typically around 10% rather than 20%.

SUMMARY

- Like mutual funds, hedge funds pool the assets of several clients and manage the pooled assets on their behalf. However, hedge funds differ from mutual funds with respect to disclosure, investor base, flexibility and predictability of investment orientation, regulation, and fee structure.
- Directional funds take a stance on the performance of broad market sectors. Nondirectional funds establish market-neutral positions on relative mispricing. However, even these hedged positions still present idiosyncratic risk.
- Statistical arbitrage is the use of quantitative systems to uncover many perceived misalignments in relative pricing and ensure profits by averaging over all of these small bets. It often uses data-mining methods to uncover past patterns that form the basis for the established investment positions.
- Portable alpha is a strategy in which one invests in positive-alpha positions, then hedges the systematic risk of that investment, and, finally, establishes market exposure where desired by using passive indexes or futures contracts.
- Performance evaluation of hedge funds is complicated by survivorship bias, by the potential instability of risk attributes, by the existence of liquidity premiums, and by unreliable market valuations of infrequently traded assets. Performance evaluation is particularly difficult when the fund engages in option positions. Tail events make it hard to assess the true performance of positions involving options without extremely long histories of returns.
- Hedge funds typically charge investors both a management fee and an incentive fee equal to a percentage of profits beyond some threshold value. The incentive fee is akin to a call option on the portfolio. Funds of hedge funds pay the incentive fee to each underlying fund that beats its hurdle rate, even if the overall performance of the portfolio is poor.

KEY TERMS

alpha transfer, 665
backfill bias, 672
data mining, 665
directional strategy, 663
funds of funds, 677
hedge fund, 662

high water mark, 677
incentive fee, 676
lock-up period, 662
market neutral, 664
nondirectional strategy, 663
pairs trading, 665

portable alpha, 665
pure plays, 664
statistical arbitrage, 665
survivorship bias, 673

PROBLEM SETS

 Select problems are available in McGraw-Hill's *Connect.* Please see the Supplements section of the book's frontmatter for more information.

1. Would a market-neutral hedge fund be a good candidate for an investor's entire retirement portfolio? If not, would there be a role for the hedge fund in the overall portfolio of such an investor? *(LO 20-1)*
2. A fund manages a $2.4 billion equity portfolio with a beta of .6. If the S&P contract multiplier is $250 and the index is currently at 1,600, how many contracts should the fund sell to make its overall position market neutral? *(LO 20-2)*

3. A hedge fund charges an incentive fee of 20% of any investment returns above the T-bill rate, which currently is 2%. In the first year, the fund suffers a loss of 8%. What rate of return must it earn in the second year to be eligible for an incentive fee?   *(LO 20-4)*

4. Which of the following is *most* accurate in describing the problems of survivorship bias and backfill bias in the performance evaluation of hedge funds?   *(LO 20-3)*

   a. Survivorship bias and backfill bias both result in upwardly biased hedge fund index returns.

   b. Survivorship bias and backfill bias both result in downwardly biased hedge fund index returns.

   c. Survivorship bias results in upwardly biased hedge fund index returns, but backfill bias results in downwardly biased hedge fund index returns.

5. Which of the following would be the *most* appropriate benchmark to use for hedge fund evaluation?   *(LO 20-3)*

   a. A multifactor model.

   b. The S&P 500.

   c. The risk-free rate.

6. With respect to hedge fund investing, the net return to an investor in a fund of funds would be lower than that earned from an individual hedge fund because of: *(LO 20-4)*

   a. Both the extra layer of fees and the higher liquidity offered.

   b. No reason; funds of funds earn returns that are equal to those of individual hedge funds.

   c. The extra layer of fees only.

7. Which of the following hedge fund types is *most likely* to have a return that is closest to risk free?   *(LO 20-1)*

   a. A market-neutral hedge fund.

   b. An event-driven hedge fund.

   c. A long-short hedge fund.

8. How might the incentive fee of a hedge fund affect the manager's proclivity to take on high-risk assets in the portfolio?   *(LO 20-4)*

9. Why is it harder to assess the performance of a hedge fund portfolio manager than that of a typical mutual fund manager?   *(LO 20-3)*

10. Is statistical arbitrage true arbitrage? Explain.   *(LO 20-2)*

11. A hedge fund with $1 billion of assets charges a management fee of 2% and an incentive fee of 20% of returns over a money market rate, which currently is 5%. Calculate total fees, both in dollars and as a percent of assets under management, for portfolio returns of: *(LO 20-4)*

    a. −5%

    b. 0

    c. 5%

    d. 10%

12. A hedge fund with net asset value of $62 per share currently has a high water mark of $66. Is the value of its incentive fee more or less than it would be if the high water mark were $67?   *(LO 20-4)*

13. Reconsider the hedge fund in the previous problem. Suppose it is January 1, the standard deviation of the fund's annual returns is 50%, and the risk-free rate is 4%. The fund has an incentive fee of 20%, but its current high water mark is $66, and net asset value is $62.   *(LO 20-4)*

    a. What is the value of the annual incentive fee according to the Black-Scholes formula?

    b. What would the annual incentive fee be worth if the fund had no high water mark and it earned its incentive fee on its total return?

c. What would the annual incentive fee be worth if the fund had no high water mark and it earned its incentive fee on its return in excess of the risk-free rate? (Treat the risk-free rate as a continuously compounded value to maintain consistency with the Black-Scholes formula.)

d. Recalculate the incentive fee value for part (*b*) now assuming that an increase in fund leverage increases volatility to 60%.

14. Log in to Connect, link to Chapter 20, and find there a spreadsheet containing monthly values of the S&P 500 Index. Suppose that in each month you had written an out-of-the-money put option on one unit of the index with an exercise price 5% lower than the current value of the index. *(LO 20-3)*

Templates and spreadsheets are available in Connect

a. What would have been the average value of your gross monthly payouts on the puts over the 10-year period October 1977–September 1987? The standard deviation?

b. Now extend your sample by one month to include October 1987, and recalculate the average payout and standard deviation of the put-writing strategy.

c. What do you conclude about tail risk in naked put writing?

15. Suppose a hedge fund follows the following strategy: Each month it holds $100 million of an S&P 500 Index fund and writes out-of-the-money put options on $100 million of the index with exercise price 5% lower than the current value of the index. Suppose the premium it receives for writing each put is $.25 million, roughly in line with the actual value of the puts. *(LO 20-3)*

Templates and spreadsheets are available in Connect

a. Calculate the Sharpe ratio the fund would have realized in the period October 1982–September 1987. Compare its Sharpe ratio to that of the S&P 500. Use the data from the previous problem (available in Connect), and assume the monthly risk-free interest rate over this period was .7%.

b. Now calculate the Sharpe ratio the fund would have realized if we extend the sample period by one month to include October 1987.

c. What do you conclude about performance evaluation and tail risk for funds pursuing optionlike strategies?

16. The following is part of the computer output from a regression of monthly returns on Waterworks stock against the S&P 500 Index. A hedge fund manager believes that Waterworks is underpriced, with an alpha of 2% over the coming month. *(LO 20-2)*

Beta	R-square	Standard Deviation of Residuals
0.75	0.65	0.06 (i.e., 6% monthly)

a. If he holds a $6 million portfolio of Waterworks stock and wishes to hedge market exposure for the next month using one-month maturity S&P 500 futures contracts, how many contracts should he enter? Should he buy or sell contracts? The S&P 500 currently is at 2,000 and the contract multiplier is $250.

b. What is the standard deviation of the monthly return of the hedged portfolio?

c. Assuming that monthly returns are approximately normally distributed, what is the probability that this market-neutral strategy will lose money over the next month? Assume the risk-free rate is .5% per month.

Challenge

17. Return to the previous problem. *(LO 20-2)*

a. Suppose you hold an equally weighted portfolio of 100 stocks with the same alpha, beta, and residual standard deviation as Waterworks. Assume the residual returns (the *e* terms in Equations 20.1 and 20.2) on each of these stocks are independent of each other. What is the residual standard deviation of the portfolio?

b. Recalculate the probability of a loss on a market-neutral strategy involving equally weighted, market-hedged positions in the 100 stocks over the next month.

18. Return to Problem 16. Now suppose that the manager misestimates the beta of Water-works stock, believing it to be .50 instead of .75. The standard deviation of the monthly market rate of return is 5%.   *(LO 20-2)*

   a. What is the standard deviation of the (now improperly) hedged portfolio?

   b. What is the probability of incurring a loss over the next month if the monthly market return has an expected value of 1% and a standard deviation of 5%? Compare your answer to the probability you found in Problem 16.

   c. What would be the probability of a loss using the data in Problem 17 if the manager similarly misestimated beta as .50 instead of .75? Compare your answer to the probability you found in part (*b*).

   d. Why does the misestimation of beta matter so much more for the 100-stock portfolio than it does for the 1-stock portfolio?

19. Here are data on three hedge funds. Each fund charges its investors an incentive fee of 20% of total returns. Suppose initially that a fund of funds (FF) manager buys equal amounts of each of these funds and also charges its investors a 20% incentive fee. For simplicity, assume also that management fees other than incentive fees are zero for all funds.   *(LO 20-4)*

	Hedge Fund 1	Hedge Fund 2	Hedge Fund 3
Start of year value (millions)	$100	$100	$100
Gross portfolio rate of return	20%	10%	30%

   a. Compute the rate of return after incentive fees to an investor in the fund of funds.

   b. Suppose that instead of buying shares in each of the three hedge funds, a stand-alone (SA) hedge fund purchases the same *portfolio* as the three underlying funds. The total value and composition of the SA fund is therefore identical to the one that would result from aggregating the three hedge funds. Consider an investor in the SA fund. After paying 20% incentive fees, what would be the value of the investor's portfolio at the end of the year?

   c. Confirm that the investor's rate of return in SA is higher than in FF by an amount equal to the extra layer of fees charged by the fund of funds.

   d. Now suppose that the return on the portfolio held by hedge fund 3 were −30% rather than +30%. Recalculate your answers to parts (*a*) and (*b*).

   e. Will either FF or SA charge an incentive fee in the scenario in part (*d*)? Why then does the investor in FF still do worse than the investor in SA?

WEB *master*

Log on to **www.hedgeindex.com,** a site run by Credit Suisse/Tremont, which maintains the TASS Hedge Funds Database of the performance of more than 2,000 hedge funds and produces indexes of investment performance for several hedge fund classes. Click the *HFRI Indexes* tab, and then look for the link to *All Hedge Indexes.* Click the *Download Historical Performance* link (free registration is required for access to this part of the website). Select *Credit Suisse Broad Hedge Fund Indexes,* and you will obtain historical rates of return on each of the hedge fund subclasses (e.g., market neutral, event driven, dedicated short bias, and so on).

1. Download the most recent five years of monthly returns for each subclass and download returns on the S&P 500 for the same period from **finance.yahoo.com.**

2. Calculate the beta of the equity market–neutral and dedicated short bias funds. Do the results seem reasonable in terms of the orientation of these funds?

3. Look at the year-by-year performance of indexes for several hedge fund classes. How does the variability of performance results in different years compare to that of the S&P 500?

20.1 *a.* Nondirectional. The shares in the fund and the short position in the index swap constitute a hedged position. The hedge fund is betting that the discount on the closed-end fund will shrink and that it will profit regardless of the general movements in the Indian market.

   b. Nondirectional. The value of both positions is driven by the value of Toys "R" Us. The hedge fund is betting that the market is undervaluing Petri relative to Toys "R" Us and that as the *relative* values of the two positions come back into alignment, it will profit regardless of the movements in the underlying shares.

   c. Directional. This is an outright bet on the price that Generic Pharmaceuticals will eventually command at the conclusion of the predicted takeover attempt.

20.2 The expected rate of return on the position (in the absence of any knowledge about idiosyncratic risk reflected in the residual) is 3%. If the residual turns out to be −4%, then the position will lose 1% of its value over the month or $25,000 and fall to $2,475,000. (Alternatively, in Equation 20.2, set $e = -.04$ and verify that the hedged proceeds are $2,475,000.) The excess return on the market in this month over T-bills would be 5% − 1% = 4%, while the excess return on the hedged strategy would be −1% −1% = −2%, so the strategy would plot in Panel A as the point (4%, −2%). In Panel B, which plots *total* returns on the market and the hedge position, the strategy would plot as the point (5%, −1%).

20.3 Fixed-income arbitrage portfolios show positive exposure to the long bond and to the credit spread. This pattern suggests that these are *not* hedged arbitrage portfolios but in fact are directional portfolios.

Taxes, Inflation, and Investment Strategy

Learning Objectives

LO 21-1 Analyze and design lifetime savings plans.

LO 21-2 Account for inflation in formulating savings and investment plans.

LO 21-3 Account for taxes in formulating savings and investment plans.

LO 21-4 Understand tax shelters.

LO 21-5 Show how adverse selection and moral hazard affect markets such as those for insurance or annuity products.

A good deal of investment management in practice revolves around the individual's lifetime savings and investment plan. We all confront many real-world complications such as taxes and tax shelters, Social Security, insurance, and inflation. In this chapter, we introduce the *principles* of managing personal savings in a complex environment in which taxes and inflation interact, rather than provide a detailed analysis of the (ever-changing) tax code.

Retirement, purchase of a home, and financing the education of children are the major objectives of saving in most households. Inflation and taxes make the task of gearing investment to accomplish these objectives complex. The long-term nature of savings intertwines the power of compounding with inflation and tax effects. Only experienced investors integrate these issues into their investment strategies. Appropriate investment strategy also must address adequate insurance coverage for contingencies such as death, disability, and property damage.

We start with the long-term goal of formulating a retirement plan. We investigate the effect of inflation on the savings plan and examine how tax shelters may be integrated into it. The analysis may be adapted to the tax code of other countries. Next we incorporate Social Security and show how to generalize the savings plan to meet other objectives such as owning a home and financing children's education. Finally, we discuss uncertainty about longevity and other contingencies. Understanding the spreadsheets we develop along the way will enable you to devise savings/investment plans for yourself and others and adapt them to a changing environment.

21.1 SAVING FOR THE LONG RUN

Our objective in this chapter is to quantify the essentials of savings/investment plans and adapt them to the presence of both inflation and taxes. In the next chapter we describe the framework that the CFA Institute has established to help financial advisers communicate with and involve client households in structuring their savings/investment plans.[1] As a first step, we set up a spreadsheet for a simple retirement plan, ignoring saving for other objectives.

Before we dive in, a brief word on what we mean by saving. Economists think of saving as a way to smooth out the lifetime consumption stream; you save when you have high earnings in order to support consumption in low-income years. In a "global" sense, the concept implies that you save for retirement so that consumption during the retirement years will not be too low relative to consumption during the saving years. In a "local" sense, smoothing consumption implies that you might finance a large purchase such as a car, rather than buy it for cash. Clearly, local consumption smoothing is of second-order importance; that is, how you purchase durable goods has little effect on the overall savings plan, except, perhaps, for very large expenditures such as buying a home or sending children to college. We begin therefore with a savings plan that ignores even large expenditures and later discuss how to integrate these needs.

A Hypothetical Household

Imagine you are now 30 years old and have already completed your formal education, accumulated some work experience, and settled down to plan the rest of your economic life. Your plan is to retire at age 65 with a remaining life expectancy of an additional 25 years. Later on, we will further assume that you have two small children and plan to finance their college education.

For starters, we assume you desire to obtain a (level) annuity for your 25-year retirement period; we postpone discussion of planning for the uncertain time of death. (You may well live to over 100; what then?) Suppose your gross income this year was $50,000, and you expect annual income to increase at a rate of 7% per year. In this section, we assume that you ignore the impact of inflation and taxes. You intend to steadily save 15% of income and invest in safe government bonds that will yield 6% over the entire period. Proceeds from your investments will be automatically reinvested at the same 6% until retirement. Upon retirement, your funds in the retirement account will be used to purchase a 25-year annuity (using the same 6% interest rate) to finance a steady consumption annuity. Let's examine the consequences of this framework.

The Retirement Annuity

We can easily obtain your **retirement annuity** from Spreadsheet 21.1, where we have hidden some age lines. All of the spreadsheets in the chapter are available in Connect.

Let's see how this spreadsheet was constructed. To view the formulas of all cells in an Excel spreadsheet, click on the "Formulas" tab on the command ribbon and choose "Show Formulas." The formula view of Spreadsheet 21.1 is shown in the lower panel (numbers are user inputs).

Inputs in row 2 include the number of retirement years (cell A2 = 25); the income growth rate (cell B2 = .07); nominal portfolio rate of return (cell D2 = .06); age (column A); and income at age 30 (B4 = 50,000). Column B computes income in future years using the growth rate in cell B2; column C computes annual savings by applying the savings rate (cell C2) to income; and column E computes consumption as the difference between income and savings: column B − column C. Cumulative savings appear in column D. To obtain the value in D6, for example, multiply cell D5 by 1 plus the assumed rate of return in cell D2 (the ROR) and

retirement annuity

Stream of level cash flows available for consumption during one's retirement years.

---

[1] Even if you do not read Chapter 22 carefully, you may want to skim through it to get an idea of how financial planners articulate a saver's objectives, constraints, and investment policy.

SPREADSHEET 21.1

The savings plan

Spreadsheets are
available in Connect

	A	B	C	D	E
1	Retirement Years	Income Growth	Savings Rate	ROR	
2	**25**	**0.07**	**0.15**	**0.06**	
3	Age	Income	Savings	Cumulative Savings	Consumption
4	30	50,000	7,500	7,500	42,500
5	31	53,500	8,025	15,975	45,475
9	35	70,128	10,519	61,658	59,608
19	45	137,952	20,693	308,859	117,259
29	55	271,372	40,706	943,477	230,666
39	65	533,829	80,074	2,457,518	453,755
40	Total	**7,445,673**	**1,116,851**	Retirement Annuity	**192,244**

	A	B	C	D	E
1	Retirement Years	Income Growth	Savings Rate	ROR	
2	**25**	**0.07**	**0.15**	**0.06**	
3	Age	Income	Savings	Cumulative Savings	Consumption
4	30	50000	=B4*$C$2	=C4	=B4-C4
5	31	=B4*(1+$B$2)	=B5*$C$2	=D4*(1+$D$2)+C5	=B5-C5
39	65	=B38*(1+$B$2)	=B39*$C$2	=D38*(1+$D$2)+C39	=B39-C39
40	Total	=SUM(B4:B39)	=SUM(C4:C39)	Retirement Annuity	=PMT($D$2,$A$2,-$D$39,0,0)

then add current savings from column C. Finally, C40 shows the sum of dollars saved over the lifetime, and E40 converts cumulative savings (including interest) at age 65 to a 25-year annuity using the financial function PMT from Excel's function menu: PMT(rate, nper, PV, FV).

We observe that your retirement fund will accumulate approximately $2.5 million (cell D39) by age 65. This hefty sum shows the power of compounding because your contributions to the savings account were only $1.1 million (C40). This fund will yield an annuity of $192,244 per year (E40) for your 25-year retirement, which seems quite attractive, except that the standard of living you'll have to get accustomed to in your retirement years is much lower than your consumption at age 65 (E39). In fact, if you unhide the hidden lines, you'll see that upon retirement, you'll have to make do with what you used to consume at age 51. This may not worry you much because, with your children having flown the coop and the mortgage paid up, you may be able to maintain the luxury to which you recently became accustomed. But your projected well-being is deceptive: Get ready to account for inflation and taxes.

CONCEPT check 21.1

If you project an ROR of only 5%, what savings rate would you need to provide the same retirement annuity?

21.2   ACCOUNTING FOR INFLATION

Inflation puts a damper on your plans in two ways: First, it erodes the purchasing power of the cumulative dollars you have so far saved. Second, the *real* dollars you earn on your portfolio each year depend on the *real* interest rate, which is approximately equal to the nominal rate minus inflation. Because an appropriate savings plan must generate a decent *real* annuity, we must recast the entire plan in real dollars. We will assume your income still is forecast to grow at a 7% rate, but now you recognize that part of income growth is due to inflation, which is running at 3% per year.

A Real Savings Plan

To convert nominal dollars to real dollars we need to calculate the price level in future years relative to today's prices. The "deflator" (or relative price level) for a given year is that year's price level divided by today's. It equals the dollars required at that future date to provide the same purchasing power as $1 today (at age 30). For an inflation rate of $i = 3\%$, the deflator for age 35 is $(1 + i)^5$, or in Excel notation, $(1 + i)^\wedge 5 = 1.03^\wedge 5 = 1.16$. By age 65, the deflator is 2.81. Thus, even with a moderate rate of inflation, nominal dollars will lose a lot of purchasing power over long horizons. We also can compute the *real* rate of return (rROR) from the nominal ROR of 6%: rROR = (ROR − i)/(1 + i) = 3/1.03 = 2.91%.

Spreadsheet 21.2, with the formula view below it, is the reworked Spreadsheet 21.1 adjusted for inflation. In addition to the rate of inflation (cell C2) and the real rate of return (F2), the major addition to this sheet is the price level deflator (column C). Instead of nominal consumption, we present **real consumption** (column F), calculated by dividing nominal consumption (column B − column D) by the price deflator, column C.

real consumption

Nominal consumption divided by the price deflator.

The numbers have changed considerably. Gone is the luxurious retirement we anticipated earlier. At age 65 and beyond, with a real annuity of $49,668 (cell F40), you will have to revert to a standard of living equal to that you attained at age 34; this is less than a third of your real consumption in your last working year, at age 65. The reason is that the retirement fund of $2.5 million (E39) is worth only $873,631 in today's purchasing power (E39/C39). Such is the effect of inflation. If you wish to do better than that, you must save more.

In our initial plan (Spreadsheet 21.1), we envisioned consuming a level, nominal annuity for the retirement years. This is an inappropriate goal once we account for inflation because it would imply a declining standard of living starting at age 65. Its purchasing power at age 65 in terms of current dollars would be $68,320 (i.e., $192,244/1.03^{35}$), and at age 90 only $32,630. (Check this!)

It is tempting to contemplate solving the problem of an inadequate retirement annuity by increasing the assumed rate of return on investments. However, this can be accomplished only by putting your savings at risk. Much of this text elaborates on how to do so efficiently; yet it also emphasizes that while taking on risk will give you an *expectation* for a better retirement, it implies as well a nonzero probability of doing a lot worse. At the age of 30, you should be able to tolerate some risk to the retirement annuity for the simple reason that if things go wrong, you can change course, increase your savings rate, and work harder. As you get older, this option progressively fades, and increasing risk becomes less of a viable option. If you do choose to increase risk, you can set a "safety-first target" (i.e., a minimum acceptable goal) for the retirement annuity and continuously monitor your risky portfolio. If the portfolio does poorly and approaches the safety-first target, you progressively shift into risk-free bonds—you may recognize this strategy as a version of dynamic hedging.

The difficulty with this strategy is twofold: First, it requires monitoring, which is time-consuming and may be nerve-racking as well. Second, when decision time comes, it may

SPREADSHEET 21.2

A real retirement plan

	A	B	C	D	E	F
1	Retirement Years	Income Growth	Rate of Inflation	Savings Rate	ROR	rROR
2	25	0.07	0.03	0.15	0.06	0.0291
3	Age	Income	Deflator	Saving	Cumulative Savings	rConsumption
4	30	50,000	1.00	7,500	7,500	42,500
5	31	53,500	1.03	8,025	15,975	44,150
9	35	70,128	1.16	10,519	61,658	51,419
19	45	137,952	1.56	20,693	308,859	75,264
29	55	271,372	2.09	40,706	943,477	110,167
39	65	533,829	2.81	80,074	2,457,518	161,257
40	Total	7,445,673		1,116,851	Real Annuity	49,668

Spreadsheets are available in Connect

	A	B	C	D	E	F
1	Retirement Years	Income Growth	Rate of Inflation	Savings Rate	ROR	rROR
2	25	0.07	0.03	0.15	0.06	=(E2-C2)/(1+C2)
3	Age	Income	Deflator	Savings	Cumulative Savings	rConsumption
4	30	50000	1	=B4*$D$2	=D4	=(B4-D4)/C4
5	31	=B4*(1+$B$2)	=C4*(1+$C$2)	=B5*$D$2	=E4*(1+$E$2)+D5	=(B5-D5)/C5
39	65	=B38*(1+$B$2)	=C38*(1+$C$2)	=B39*$D$2	=E38*(1+$E$2)+D39	=(B39-D39)/C39
40	Total	=SUM(B4:B39)		=SUM(D4:D39)	Real Annuity	=PMT($F$2,$A$2,-$E$39/$C$39,0,0)

be psychologically hard to withdraw. By shifting out of the risky portfolio if and when your portfolio is hammered, you give up any hope of recovery. This is hard to do, and many investors fail the test. For these investors, therefore, the right approach is to stick with a safe, lower ROR and make the effort to balance standard of living before and after retirement. Avoiding sleepless nights is ample reward.

Therefore, the only variable under your control in this spreadsheet is the rate of saving. To improve retirement lifestyle relative to the preretirement years, without jeopardizing its safety, you will have to reduce consumption during the saving years—there is no free lunch.

CONCEPT check	21.2	If you project a rate of inflation of 4%, what nominal ROR on investments would you need to maintain the same real retirement annuity as in Spreadsheet 21.2?

An Alternative Savings Plan

In Spreadsheet 21.2, we saved a constant fraction of income. But since real income grows over time (nominal income is expected to grow at 7% while inflation is only 3%), we might consider deferring our savings toward future years when real income is higher. By applying a higher savings rate to future (higher) real income, we are able to reduce the current savings rate. In Spreadsheet 21.3, we use a base savings rate of 10% (lower than the savings rate in the previous spreadsheet), but we increase it by 3% per year. Saving in each year therefore equals a fixed savings rate times annual income (column B), times the exponential growth factor 1.03^t. By saving a larger fraction of income in later years, when real income is larger, you create a smoother profile of real consumption.

Spreadsheet 21.3 shows that with an *initial* savings rate of 10%, compared with the unchanging 15% rate in the previous spreadsheet, you can achieve a retirement annuity of $59,918, larger than the $49,668 annuity in the previous plan.

Notice that real consumption in the early years is greater than with the previous plan. What you have done is to postpone some saving until your income is higher. At first blush, this plan is preferable: It allows for a more comfortable consumption of 90% of income at the outset and a consistent increase in standard of living during your earning years, all without significantly affecting the retirement annuity. But this program has one serious downside: By postponing the bulk of your savings to a later age, you come to depend on your health,

---

	A	B	C	D	E	F
1	Retirement Years	Income Growth	Rate of Inflation	Savings Rate	ROR	rROR
2	25	0.07	0.03	0.1	0.06	0.0291
3	Age	Income	Deflator	Savings	Cumulative Savings	rConsumption
4	30	50,000	1.00	5,000	5,000	45,000
5	31	53,500	1.03	5,511	10,811	46,592
9	35	70,128	1.16	8,130	44,351	53,480
19	45	137,952	1.56	21,492	260,927	74,751
29	55	271,372	2.09	56,819	947,114	102,471
39	65	533,829	2.81	150,212	2,964,669	136,331
40	Total	7,445,673		1,572,466	Real Annuity	59,918

	A	B	C	D	E	F
1	Retirement Years	Income Growth	Rate of Inflation	Savings Rate	ROR	rROR
2	25	0.07	0.03	0.1	0.06	=(E2-C2)/(1+C2)
3	Age	Income	Deflator	Savings	Cumulative Savings	rConsumption
4	30	50000	1	=B4*C4*$D$2	=D4	=(B4-D4)/C4
5	31	=B4*(1+$B$2)	=C4*(1+$C$2)	=B5*C5*$D$2	=E4*(1+$E$2)+D5	=(B5-D5)/C5
39	65	=B38*(1+$B$2)	=C38*(1+$C$2)	=B39*C39*$D$2	=E38*(1+$E$2)+D39	=(B39-D39)/C39
40	Total	=SUM(B4:B39)		=SUM(D4:D39)	Real Annuity	=PMT($F$2,$A$2,-$E$39/$C$39,0,0)

longevity, and, more ominously *(and without possibility of insurance),* on a successful future career. Put differently, this plan achieves comfort by increasing risk, making this choice a matter of risk tolerance.

Suppose you like the plan of tilting saving toward later years, but worry about the increased risk of postponing the bulk of your saving to later years. Is there anything you can do to mitigate the risk?	**CONCEPT** check **21.3**

21.3 ACCOUNTING FOR TAXES

To initiate a discussion of taxes, let's assume that you are subject to a **flat tax** rate of 25% on taxable income less one exemption of $15,000. This is similar to several proposals for a simplified U.S. tax code that have been floated from time to time. An important feature of this (and the existing) tax code is that the tax rate is levied on nominal income and applies as well to investment income. (The tax on investment income is sometimes characterized as double taxation—you pay taxes when you earn income and then you pay taxes again when your savings earn interest.) Some relief from the effect of taxing nominal dollars both in this proposal and the current U.S. code is provided by raising the exemption, annually, by the rate of inflation. To adapt our spreadsheet to this simple tax code, we must add columns for taxes and after-tax income. The tax-adjusted plan is shown in Spreadsheet 21.4. It adapts the savings plan of Spreadsheet 21.2, that is, saving 15% of nominal income.

The top panel of the sheet deals with the earning years. Column D adjusts the exemption (D2) by the price level (column C). Column E applies the tax rate (cell E2) to taxable income (column B − column D). The savings rate (F2) is applied to after-tax income (column B − column E), allowing us to calculate cumulative savings (column G) and real consumption (column H). The formula view shows the detailed construction.

flat tax

A tax code that taxes all income above some exemption at a fixed rate.

SPREADSHEET 21.4

Saving with a simple tax code

	A	B	C	D	E	F	G	H
1	Retirement Years	Income Growth	Rate of Inflation	Exemption Now	Tax Rate	Savings Rate	ROR	rROR
2	25	0.07	0.03	15000	0.25	0.15	0.06	0.0291
3	Age	Income	Deflator	Exemption	Taxes	Savings	Cumulative Savings	rConsumption
4	30	50,000	1.00	15,000	8,750	6,188	6,188	35,063
5	31	53,500	1.03	15,450	9,605	6,584	13,143	36,224
9	35	70,128	1.16	17,389	13,775	8,453	50,188	41,319
19	45	137,952	1.56	23,370	31,892	15,909	245,334	57,864
29	55	271,372	2.09	31,407	69,943	30,214	733,467	81,773
39	65	533,829	2.81	42,208	148,611	57,783	1,874,346	116,365
40	Total				1,884,163	834,226	Real Annuity=	37,882
41	RETIREMENT							
42	Age	Nom Withdraw	Deflator	Exemption	Taxes		Funds Left	rConsumption
43	66	109,792	2.90	43,474	17,247		1,877,014	31,931
47	70	123,572	3.26	48,931	15,743		1,853,382	33,056
52	75	143,254	3.78	56,724	12,200		1,721,015	34,656
57	80	166,071	4.38	65,759	6,047		1,422,954	36,503
62	85	192,521	5.08	76,232	0		883,895	37,882
67	90	223,185	5.89	88,374	0		0	37,882
68	Total	4,002,944			203,199			

	A	B	C	D	E	F	G	H
1	Retirement Years	Income Growth	Rate of Inflation	Exemption Now	Tax Rate	Savings Rate	ROR	rROR
2	25	0.07	0.03	15000	0.25	0.15	0.06	=(G2-C2)/(1+C2)
3	Age	Income	Deflator	Exemption	Taxes	Savings	Cumulative Savings	rConsumption
4	30	50000	1	=$D$2*C4	=(B4-D4)*$E$2	=(B4-E4)*$F$2	=F4	=(B4-E4-F4)/C4
5	31	=B4*(1+$B$2)	=C4*(1+$C$2)	=$D$2*C5	=(B5-D5+G4*$G$2)*$E$2	=(B5-E5)*$F$2	=G4*(1+$G$2)+F5	=(B5-E5-F5)/C5
39	65	=B38*(1+$B$2)	=C38*(1+$C$2)	=$D$2*C39	=(B39-D39+G38*$G$2)*$E$2	=(B39-E39)*$F$2	=G38*(1+$G$2)+F39	=(B39-E39-F39)/C39
40	Total				=SUM(E4:E39)	=SUM(F4:F39)	Real Annuity	=PMT($H$2,$A$2,-$G$39/$C$39,0,0)
41	RETIREMENT							
42	Age	Nom Withdraw	Deflator	Exemption	Taxes		Funds Left	rConsumption
43	66	=$H$40*C43	=C39*(1+$C$2)	=$D$2*C43	=MAX(0,(G39*$G$2-D43)*$E$2)		=G39*(1+$G$2)-B43	=(B43-E43)/C43
44	67	=$H$40*C44	=C43*(1+$C$2)	=$D$2*C44	=MAX(0,(G43*$G$2-D44)*$E$2)		=G43*(1+$G$2)-B44	=(B44-E44)/C44
67	90	=$H$40*C67	=C66*(1+$C$2)	=$D$2*C67	=MAX(0,(G66*$G$2-D67)*$E$2)		=G66*(1+$G$2)-B67	=(B67-E67)/C67
68	Total	=SUM(B43:B67)			=SUM(E43:E67)			

𝕏

Spreadsheets are available in Connect

As you might have expected, real consumption is lower in the presence of taxes, as are savings and the retirement fund. The retirement fund provides for a real, before-tax annuity of only $37,882, compared with $49,668 absent taxes in Spreadsheet 21.2.

The bottom panel of the sheet shows the further reduction in real consumption due to taxes paid during the retirement years. While you do not pay taxes on the cumulative savings in the retirement plan (you did that already as the savings accrued interest), you do pay taxes on interest earned by the fund while you are drawing it down. These taxes are quite significant and further deplete the fund and its net-of-tax earning power. For this reason, your consumption annuity is lower in the early years when your fund has not yet been depleted and taxable interest income is higher.

In the end, despite a handsome income that grows at a real rate of almost 4%, an aggressive savings rate of 15%, a modest rate of inflation, and a realistic tax, you will be able to achieve only a modest (but at least low-risk) real retirement income. This is a reality with which most people must struggle. Whether to sacrifice more of today's standard of living through an increased rate of saving, or take some risk in the form of saving a real annuity and/or invest in a risky portfolio with a higher expected return, is a question of preference and risk tolerance.

One often hears complaints about the double taxation resulting from taxing income earned on savings from dollars on which taxes were already paid. It is interesting to see what effective tax rate is imposed on your lifetime earnings by double taxation. To do so, we use Spreadsheet 21.4 to set up your lifetime earnings, exemptions, and taxes:

Income		
(1) Lifetime labor income		$7,445,673
Total exemptions during working years	949,139	
(2) Lifetime taxable labor income		6,496,534
Taxes		
During labor years	$1,884,163	
During retirement	203,199	
(3) Lifetime taxes		$2,087,362
Lifetime average tax rate = (3)/(1)		28%
Lifetime tax rate on taxable income = (3)/(2)		32%

Thus, double taxation is equivalent to raising the tax rate on taxable income to 32%. It creates a lifetime *average* tax rate (28%) that is higher than the prescribed *marginal* rate of 25%.

CONCEPT check 21.4   Would a 1% increase in the exemption compensate you for a 1% increase in the tax rate?

21.4   THE ECONOMICS OF TAX SHELTERS

tax shelters

Means by which to postpone payment of tax liabilities for as long as possible.

Tax shelters range from the simple to the mind-bogglingly complex, yet they all have one common objective: to postpone payment of tax liabilities for as long as possible. We know already that this isn't a minor issue. Postponement implies a smaller present value of tax payment, and a tax paid with a long delay can have present value near zero. However, the advantage of delay also depends on how tax rates are projected to change over time. If the tax rate on retirement income is higher than during earning years, the value of a tax deferral may be questionable; on the other hand, if the tax rate will decline, deferral is even more preferable.

A Benchmark Tax Shelter

Postponing tax payments is the only attainable objective because, whenever you have taxable income, a tax liability is created that can (almost) never be erased.[2] For this reason, a benchmark tax shelter *postpones* all taxes on savings and the income on those savings. We will assume that taxes on your entire savings account will be paid during retirement, as you draw down the retirement fund. This sort of shelter is actually equivalent to the tax treatment of Individual Retirement Accounts (IRAs) which we discuss later, so we will describe this structure as having an "IRA style."

To examine the impact of an IRA-style structure (assuming you could shelter all your savings) in a situation comparable to the nonsheltered flat-tax case, we maintain the same consumption level as in Spreadsheet 21.4 (flat tax with no shelter) but now input the new, sheltered savings plan in Spreadsheet 21.5. This focuses the entire effect of the tax shelter onto retirement consumption.

In this sheet, we input desired real consumption (column H, copied from Spreadsheet 21.4). Taxes (column E) are then calculated by applying the tax rate (E2) to nominal consumption less the exemption (H × C − D). Thus, savings are the residual from nominal income (B) minus taxes (E), minus nominal consumption (H × C). The retirement panel shows that you pay taxes on all withdrawals—all funds in the retirement account are subject to tax.

The results are interesting. Total lifetime taxes paid with the IRA tax shelter amount to $2.5 million, a lot more than $2.1 million without the shelter. The reason is that the tax shelter allows for larger savings that increase lifetime income to $3.7 million compared with only $1.9 million without the shelter. Because in this comparison, income and consumption

---

SPREADSHEET 21.5

Saving with a flat tax and an IRA-style tax shelter

	A	B	C	D	E	F	G	H
1	Retirement Years	Income Growth	Rate of Inflation	Exemption Now	Tax Rate	Savings Rate	ROR	rROR
2	25	0.07	0.03	15000	0.25	0.15	0.06	0.0291
3	Age	Income	Deflator	Exemption	Taxes	Savings	Cumulative Savings	rConsumption
4	30	50,000	1.00	15,000	5,016	9,922	9,922	35,063
5	31	53,500	1.03	15,450	5,465	10,724	21,242	36,224
9	35	70,128	1.16	17,389	7,628	14,600	83,620	41,319
19	45	137,952	1.56	23,370	16,695	31,106	438,234	57,864
29	55	271,372	2.09	31,407	34,952	65,205	1,393,559	81,773
39	65	533,829	2.81	42,208	71,307	135,087	3,762,956	116,365
40	Total				944,536	1,773,854	Real Annuity	76,052
41	**RETIREMENT**							
42	Age	Nom Withdraw	Deflator	Exemption	Taxes		Funds Left	rConsumption
43	66	220,420	2.90	43,474	44,236		3,768,313	60,789
47	70	248,085	3.26	48,931	49,789		3,720,867	60,789
52	75	287,598	3.78	56,724	57,719		3,455,127	60,789
57	80	333,405	4.38	65,759	66,912		2,856,737	60,789
62	85	386,508	5.08	76,232	77,569		1,774,517	60,789
67	90	448,068	5.89	88,374	89,924		0	60,789
68	Total	8,036,350			1,612,828			

	A	B	C	D	E	F	G	H
1	Retirement Years	Income Growth	Rate of Inflation	Exemption Now	Tax Rate	Savings Rate	ROR	rROR
2	25	0.07	0.03	15000	0.25	0.15	0.06	=(G2-C2)/(1+C2)
3	Age	Income	Deflator	Exemption	Taxes	Savings	Cumulative Savings	rConsumption
4	30	50000	1	=$D$2*C4	=(H4*C4-D4)*$E$2	=B4-E4-H4*C4	=F4	35062.5
5	31	=B4*(1+$B$2)	=C4*(1+$C$2)	=$D$2*C5	=(H5*C5-D5)*$E$2	=B5-E5-H5*C5	=G4*(1+$G$2)+F5	36223.7712378641
39	65	=B38*(1+$B$2)	=C38*(1+$C$2)	=$D$2*C39	=(H39*C39-D39)*$E$2	=B39-E39-H39*C39	=G38*(1+$G$2)+F39	116364.980523664
40	Total				=SUM(E4:E39)	=SUM(F4:F39)	Real Annuity	=PMT($H$2,$A$2,-$G$39/$C$39,0,0)
41	**RETIREMENT**							
42	Age	Nom Withdraw	Deflator	Exemption	Taxes		Funds Left	rConsumption
43	66	=$H$40*C43	=C39*(1+$C$2)	=$D$2*C43	=MAX(0,(B43-D43)*$E$2)		=G39*(1+$G$2)-B43	=(B43-E43)/C43
44	67	=$H$40*C44	=C43*(1+$C$2)	=$D$2*C44	=MAX(0,(B44-D44)*$E$2)		=G43*(1+$G$2)-B44	=(B44-E44)/C44
67	90	=$H$40*C67	=C66*(1+$C$2)	=$D$2*C67	=MAX(0,(B67-D67)*$E$2)		=G66*(1+$G$2)-B67	=(B67-E67)/C67
68	Total	=SUM(B43:B67)			=SUM(E43:E67)			

Spreadsheets are available in Connect

---

[2]Bankruptcy or death can erase some tax liabilities, though. We will avoid dealing with these unhappy outcomes.

during the earnings years are as before, the entire net gain from the shelter is pushed to the retirement years. Thus, the real annuity (pretax) during retirement increases from $37,882 to $76,052.

CONCEPT check **21.5**	With the IRA-style tax shelter, all your taxes are due during retirement. Is the trade-off between exemption and tax rate different from the circumstance where you have no shelter?

The Effect of the Progressive Nature of the Tax Code

Because of the exemption, the flat tax is somewhat progressive: Taxes as a fraction of income increase along with income. For very high incomes, the marginal tax rate (25%) is only slightly higher than the average rate. With income of $50,000 at the outset, the average tax rate is 17.5% (.25 × 35,000/50,000), and it grows steadily over time. In general, with a flat tax, the ratio of the average to marginal rate equals the ratio of taxable to gross income. This ratio becomes .89 at age 45, at which point the average tax rate is above 22%. The current U.S. tax code, with multiple income brackets, is much more progressive than our assumed structure.

progressive tax

Taxes are an increasing fraction of income.

In Spreadsheet 21.6 we work with a more **progressive tax** structure that is closer to the U.S. federal tax code augmented with an average state tax. Our hypothetical tax schedule is described in Table 21.1.

We have seen that taxes on income during the earning period have a greater effect because of the time value of money; early tax payments (during earning years) have a larger effect than later payments during retirement years. In a progressive tax environment, this effect is magnified if your retirement income (withdrawal from the retirement fund) is lower than income during the earning years. This has been the case in all the alternatives that we have analyzed so far.

Spreadsheet 21.6, which continues to maintain the same income and consumption during the earning years, differs from Spreadsheet 21.4 only in that column E replaces the flat tax with the schedule of Table 21.1. Surprisingly, the effect on consumption in both earning and retirement years is small. This is due to two offsetting effects. The higher tax rate applied to the high incomes of the later earning years increases the tax bite. At the same time, the lower income and corresponding lower tax bracket during both early earning and retirement years dampen that effect. The bottom line is that a roughly typical life cycle of earnings mitigates the difference between flat and progressive tax schedules. This is an important

SPREADSHEET 21.6

Saving with a progressive tax

𝕏

Spreadsheets are available in Connect

	A	B	C	D	E	F	G	H
1	Retirement Years	Income Growth	Rate of Inflation	Exemption Now	Tax rates in	Savings Rate	ROR	rROR
2	25	0.07	0.03	10000	Table 21.1	0.15	0.06	0.0291
3	Age	Income	Deflator	Exemption	Taxes	Savings	Cumulative Savings	rConsumption
4	30	50,000	1.00	10,000	8,000	6,300	6,300	35,700
5	31	53,500	1.03	10,300	8,716	6,718	13,396	36,958
9	35	70,128	1.16	11,593	12,489	8,646	51,310	42,262
19	45	137,952	1.56	15,580	32,866	15,763	248,018	57,333
29	55	271,372	2.09	20,938	76,587	29,218	731,514	79,076
39	65	533,829	2.81	28,139	186,335	52,124	1,833,644	104,970
40	Total			Total	632,759	2,116,533	799,371	Real Annuity	37,059
41	RETIREMENT							
42	Age	Nom Withdraw	Deflator	Exemption	Taxes		Fund Left	rConsumption
43	66	107,408	2.90	28,983	16,207		1,836,254	31,467
47	70	120,889	3.26	32,620	15,371		1,813,134	32,347
52	75	140,143	3.78	37,816	13,083		1,683,643	33,599
57	80	162,464	4.38	43,839	8,831		1,392,054	35,045
62	85	188,341	5.08	50,821	1,757		864,701	36,714
67	90	218,338	5.89	58,916	0		0	37,059
68	Total	3,916,018			227,675			

TABLE 21.1   Income tax schedule used for the progressive tax

Taxable Income* Over	But Not Over	The Tax Is	of the Amount Over
$ 0	$ 50,000	$ 0 + 20%	$ 0
50,000	150,000	10,000 + 30%	50,000
150,000	. . .	40,000 + 40%	150,000

*Current exemption with this code is assumed to be $10,000; that is, taxable income = income − 10,000. The exemption and tax brackets are continuously adjusted for inflation.

point in favor of a flat tax that is simpler and reduces the incentive to devote resources to avoiding taxation.

Spreadsheet 21.7 augments the progressive tax code with our benchmark (IRA-style) tax shelter that allows you to pay taxes on consumption (minus an exemption) and accumulate a tax liability to be paid during your retirement years. The construction of this spreadsheet is identical to Spreadsheet 21.5, with the only difference being the tax structure built into column E. We copied the real preretirement consumption stream from Spreadsheet 21.6 to focus the effect of the tax shelter on the standard of living during the retirement years. Spreadsheet 21.7 shows that the lower tax bracket during the retirement years allows you to pay lower taxes over the life of the plan and significantly increases retirement consumption. The use of the IRA-style tax shelter increases the retirement annuity by an average of $32,000 a year, a better improvement than we obtained from the shelter with the flat tax.

The effectiveness of the shelter also has a sort of hedge quality. If you become fortunate and strike it rich, the tax shelter will be less effective because your tax bracket will be higher at retirement. However, mediocre or worse outcomes will result in low marginal rates upon retirement, making the shelter more effective and the tax bite lower.

Are you indifferent between an increase in the low-income-bracket tax rate versus an equal increase in the high-bracket tax rates?

CONCEPT check   21.6

SPREADSHEET 21.7

The benchmark (IRA) tax shelter with a progressive tax code

	A	B	C	D	E	F	G	H
1	Retirement Years	Income Growth	Rate of Inflation	Exemption Now	Tax rates in	Savings Rate	ROR	rROR
2	25	0.07	0.03	10000	Table 21.1	0.15	0.06	0.0291
3	Age	Income	Deflator	Exemption	Taxes	Savings	Cumulative Savings	rConsumption
4	30	50,000	1.00	10,000	5,140	9,160	9,160	35,700
5	31	53,500	1.03	10,300	5,553	9,880	19,590	36,958
9	35	70,128	1.16	11,593	7,480	13,654	77,112	42,262
19	45	137,952	1.56	15,580	14,749	33,880	434,916	57,333
29	55	271,372	2.09	20,938	32,920	72,885	1,455,451	79,076
39	65	533,829	2.81	28,139	66,100	172,359	4,125,524	104,970
40	Total			632,759	879,430	2,036,474	Real Annuity	83,380
41	RETIREMENT							
42	Age	Nom Withdraw	Deflator	Exemption	Taxes		Funds Left	rConsumption
43	66	241,658	2.90	28,983	49,311		4,131,398	66,366
47	70	271,988	3.26	32,620	55,500		4,079,381	66,366
52	75	315,309	3.78	37,816	64,340		3,788,036	66,366
57	80	365,529	4.38	43,839	74,588		3,131,989	66,366
62	85	423,749	5.08	50,821	86,467		1,945,496	66,366
67	90	491,241	5.89	58,916	100,239		0	66,366
68	Total	8,810,670	Total		1,797,848			

Spreadsheets are available in Connect

21.5 A MENU OF TAX SHELTERS

Defined Benefit Plans

The Employee Retirement Income Security Act (ERISA) of 1974 sets out rules that govern the management of one of two types of employee pension funds: a "defined benefit" retirement plan, or a "defined contribution" retirement plan, to be discussed later.

defined benefit plan

A pension fund that promises a specified level of income to vested retired employees.

An employer that offers a **defined benefit plan** must dedicate and manage a stand-alone fund that promises to pay vested retired employees (those who have served the required number of years to qualify for pension payouts) a specified (or "defined") amount of income for their lifetimes. Corporations are responsible for investing sufficient funds in qualified capital and money market assets so that the projected cash flows from these investments will be sufficient to satisfy the payouts owed to vested employees. Thus, the corporation bears the risk that arises when the pension fund is invested in risky capital assets.

The government plays a dual role in this pension coverage: First, it exempts from taxes contributions to defined benefit funds as well as earnings on pension fund assets. Second, the government has established the Pension Benefit Guarantee Corporation (PBGC) to guarantee at least a portion of the pension benefits promised to vested employees if the sponsoring firm defaults and has underfunded the pension plan. As you might guess from this arrangement, corporations may renege on their promises of benefits when filing for bankruptcy. Thus, the risk borne by corporations funding defined benefit plans is limited, while employees bear the potentially catastrophic risk of bankruptcy, mitigated by PBGC benefits that are often far smaller than promised defined benefits. This arrangement may encourage sponsoring corporations to opt for higher expected return but riskier investment strategies in the pension fund, as they are able to off-load a good portion of investment risk onto their employees and the government; the ensuing conflict of interest leads many economists to argue for the elimination of defined benefit plans in favor of defined contribution ones. Indeed, the market seems to be coming around to this judgment; the popularity of defined benefit plans, once the vast majority of pension funds, has waned to less than 25% of all pension plans.

Defined benefit plans vary in their particulars, but in general they amount to an annuity that replaces a certain percentage of employee income upon retirement. When the benefit is indexed to inflation, as is sometimes the case, it is a real annuity. Employees expecting a defined benefit annuity (that is taxable) can easily incorporate it into their retirement planning as in Spreadsheets 21.1 to 21.7, with the caveat that they are not risk-free. When a company files for bankruptcy, the PBGC's guarantee is usually quite a bit smaller than that promised by defined benefit plans.

Employee Defined Contribution Plans

Defined contribution plans are better known as 401k (private-sector) plans or 403b (not-for-profit) plans from the relevant paragraphs of the ERISA legislation that enabled them (the two are essentially identical and we will refer to all of them as 401k plans).

401 k plans

Defined contribution pension plans wherein the employer matches the employee's contribution up to a set percentage.

In a **401k plan,** the employer sets up an account for each employee with an administrator, usually a management company such as Fidelity or Vanguard. The employee contributes a fraction of wages, and the employer likewise contributes a fraction of wages to the account. Like wages, this type of compensation is tax deductible to the firm. It is a tax-efficient form of employee compensation because the contributed funds (and investment earnings) are shielded from individual taxes until later in life. To limit the cost to the government in terms of lost tax revenue, annual contributions by employees are limited (in 2015) to $18,000 until the age of 50 and to $24,000 for those aged 50 and over. Combined annual contributions by employer and employee are limited to the minimum of either 100% of wages or $53,000.

An immediate implication of the employer match is that 401k employees should contribute, at a minimum, the amount that maximizes the employer's matching contributions, even if this calls for borrowing to pay for consumption needs.

Individual Retirement Accounts

Individual Retirement Accounts (IRAs) were set up by Congress in 1984 to further increase the incentives to save for retirement. The limited scope of these accounts is an important feature. Currently, annual contributions are limited (in 2015) to $5,500. Workers 50 years of age and older can increase annual contributions by up to another $1,000. IRAs are somewhat illiquid (as are most shelters), in that there is a 10% penalty on withdrawals prior to age 59½. However, allowances for early withdrawal with no penalty for qualified reasons such as (one-time) purchase of a home or higher education expenses substantially mitigate the problem.

As far as retirees are concerned, 401k plans and IRAs are in most respects identical; employees can use both, combining the benefits from each. Hence, from this point on, we refer to them both simply as retirement "accounts" or retirement "plans."

The IRS allows you to choose two very different schedules of tax shelters for your retirement accounts: one is called *traditional* (introduced first) and the other, *Roth* (after the congressman who proposed it). The choice between them is not trivial.

TRADITIONAL RETIREMENT PLANS Contributions to **traditional retirement accounts** are tax deductible, as are the earnings in the account until retirement. In principle, if you were able to contribute all your savings to a traditional account, your savings plan would be identical to our benchmark tax shelter (Spreadsheets 21.5 and 21.7), with the effectiveness of tax mitigation depending on your marginal tax rate upon retirement.

traditional retirement account

Contributions to the account and investment earnings are tax sheltered until retirement.

ROTH RETIREMENT PLANS A **Roth account** is a variation on the traditional tax shelter, with both a drawback and an advantage. Contributions to Roth plans are *not* tax deductible. However, earnings on the accumulating funds in the Roth account are tax-free, and unlike a traditional plan, no taxes are paid upon withdrawals of savings during retirement. The trade-off is not easy to evaluate. To gain insight and illustrate how to analyze the trade-off, we contrast Roth with traditional plans under the currently more realistic, progressive tax code.

Roth account

Contributions are not tax sheltered, but investment earnings are tax free.

Roth Accounts with the Progressive Tax Code

As we have noted, a traditional plan is identical to the benchmark tax shelter set up under two alternative tax codes in Spreadsheets 21.5 and 21.7. We saw that, as a general rule, the effectiveness of a tax shelter depends on the progressivity of the tax code: Lower tax rates during retirement favor the postponement of tax obligations until one's retirement years. However, with a Roth plan, you pay no taxes at all on withdrawals during the retirement phase. In this case, therefore, the effectiveness of the shelter does not depend on the tax rates during the retirement years. The question for any investor is whether this advantage is sufficient to compensate for the nondeductibility of contributions, which is the primary advantage of the traditional plan.

To evaluate the trade-off, Spreadsheet 21.8 modifies Spreadsheet 21.7 (progressive tax) to conform to the features of a Roth plan; that is, we eliminate deductibility of contributions and taxes during the retirement phase. We keep consumption during the earning years the same as they were in the benchmark (traditional) tax shelter to compare the standard of living in retirement afforded by a Roth tax shelter.

Table 21.2 demonstrates the difference between the two types of shelters. In both cases, lifetime income and real consumption during the earning years, as well as the progressive tax scheme, are identical. The only difference is which plan you choose, traditional or Roth. Hence the first line of Table 21.2, lifetime labor income, is fixed at $7.4 million. But the shelter works differently in each case. The traditional plan shelters more income during the earning years, resulting in total taxes of only $879,430, compared with $1.75 million under the Roth plan. In the retirement years, however, the Roth plan entails no taxes, while the traditional plan results in taxes of just under $1.8 million. Lifetime taxes are $2.7 million using the traditional account compared with only $1.75 million for the Roth plan. Despite this, the larger accumulation in the traditional IRA account results in a larger retirement fund ($4.1 million compared with $2.4 million) and a larger real after-tax retirement annuity of $66,366.

Spreadsheets are
available in Connect

	A	B	C	D	E	F	G	H
3	Retirement Years	Income Growth	Rate of Inflation	Exemption Now	Tax Rates in	Savings Rate	ROR	rROR
4	25	0.07	0.03	10000	Table 21.1	0.15	0.06	0.0291
5	Age	Income	Deflator	Exemption	Taxes	Savings	Cumulative Savings	rConsumption
6	30	50,000	1.00	10,000	8,000	6,300	6,300	35,700
7	31	53,500	1.03	10,300	8,640	6,793	13,471	36,958
11	35	70,128	1.16	11,593	11,764	9,370	52,995	42,262
21	45	137,952	1.56	15,580	28,922	19,707	278,528	57,333
31	55	271,372	2.09	20,938	64,661	41,143	883,393	79,076
41	65	533,829	2.81	28,139	145,999	92,460	2,432,049	104,970
42	Total	7,445,673		632,759	1,752,425	1,163,478	**Real Annuity**	49,153
43	**RETIREMENT**							
44	Age	Nom Withdraw	Deflator	Exemption	Taxes		Funds Left	rConsumption
45	66	142,460	2.90	28,983	0		2,435,512	49,153
49	70	160,340	3.26	32,620	0		2,404,847	49,153
54	75	185,879	3.78	37,816	0		2,233,096	49,153
59	80	215,484	4.38	43,839	0		1,846,348	49,153
64	85	249,805	5.08	50,821	0		1,146,895	49,153
69	90	289,593	5.89	58,916	0		0	49,153
70	Total	5,194,003			0			

TABLE 21.2 Traditional vs. Roth plan tax shelters under a progressive tax code		
	Traditional Plan	**Roth Plan**
Lifetime labor income	**$7,445,673**	**$7,445,673**
Taxes ($):		
Earning years	$ 879,430	$ 1,752,425
Retirement years	1,797,848	0
Total paid over lifetime	**$2,677,278**	**$1,752,425**
Lifetime average tax rate (%)	35.96%	23.54%
Retirement annuity:		
Before-tax	$ 83,380	$ 49,153
After-tax	66,366	49,153

The bottom line is that the traditional plan is more effective for the middle-income family we examine here.

The explanation of why the traditional plan is better for a middle-income family also indicates when the Roth plan may be preferred. If earnings are sharply back-loaded, that is, most of your earnings are close to retirement, then tax-free accumulation of investment income is less important, and the Roth plan may dominate. This can happen if you start with fewer years to retirement and your income grows faster. Without changing the number of years to retirement, you would need to change nominal income growth in both spreadsheets from 7% to an extreme 40% for the Roth plan to dominate. (Another advantage of Roth plans has to do with IRA contribution limits: Limits on Roth contributions apply to after-tax rather than to pretax dollars, allowing more funds to be funneled into your retirement account than are allowed in the traditional plans.)

Notice in Table 21.2 that the lifetime average tax rate for saving with a traditional plan is 35.96%. This is a result of a large accumulation of earnings on savings that are taxed on retirement and shows the importance of early accumulation. Despite the higher lifetime taxes, this tax shelter ends up with larger after-tax real consumption during retirement. The lifetime average tax rate is not a good measure of the effect of taxes on lifetime consumption, because it does not fully account for the timing of tax collections. In the circumstances we postulated (a long period with middle-class earnings levels), the tax savings with Roth trumps the traditional plan.

Suppose all taxpayers were like you, and the IRS wished to raise a fixed tax revenue. Is the traditional or Roth plan the better choice?

CONCEPT check **21.7**

Risky Investments and Capital Gains as Tax Shelters

So far we have limited our examples to assume safe investments that yield a sure 6%. This number, coupled with the inflation assumption (3%), determined the results of various savings rules given the appropriate tax configuration. Clearly, the 6% return and 3% inflation assumptions are not hard numbers, and you must consider the implications of other possible scenarios over the life of the savings plan. The spreadsheets we developed make scenario analysis quite easy. Once you set up a spreadsheet with a contemplated savings plan, you simply vary the inputs for ROR (the nominal rate of return) and inflation and record the implications for each scenario. The probabilities of possible deviations from the expected numbers and your risk tolerance will dictate which savings plan provides you with sufficient security of obtaining your goals. This sensitivity analysis will be even more important when you consider risky investments.

The tax shelters we described allow you to invest in a broad array of securities and mutual funds, and you can invest your nonsheltered savings in any asset. Which portfolio to choose is a matter of risk versus return. That said, taxes lend importance to the otherwise largely irrelevant aspect of cash dividends and interest income versus capital gains.

According to current U.S. tax law, there are three applicable capital gains rates for most investments: 0% for lower to moderate income investors, 15% once your marginal tax bracket on ordinary income reaches 25%, and 20% if you are in the highest marginal tax bracket.[3] More important, you pay the applicable rate only when you sell the security. Thus, investing in nondividend-paying securities is an implicit partial tax shelter with no restrictions on contributions or withdrawals. Because this investment is not tax deductible, it is similar to a Roth plan, but somewhat inferior in that you do pay a tax on withdrawal, however low. Still, such investments can be more effective than traditional plans, as we discussed earlier. Because annual contributions to all plans are quite limited, investment in a low- or no-dividend portfolio may be the efficient shelter for many investors who wish to exceed the contribution limit. Another advantage of such portfolios is that you can sell securities that have lost value to realize capital losses and thereby reduce your tax bill in any given year. This virtue of risky securities is called the *tax-timing option*. Managing a portfolio with efficient utilization of the tax-timing option requires expert attention, however, and may not be appropriate for many savers.

The average dividend yield on the S&P 500 stocks is on the order of 2%, and other indexes (such as NASDAQ) bear an even lower yield. This means that you can easily construct a well-diversified portfolio with a very low dividend yield. Such a portfolio allows you to utilize the tax advantage of capital gains versus dividends. Spreadsheet 21.9 adapts Spreadsheet 21.6 (progressive tax with no shelter) to a no-dividend portfolio of stocks, maintaining the same preretirement consumption stream, holding the ROR at 6%, and assuming 15% capital gains tax. Real retirement consumption, averaging $45,105, is almost identical to that supported by a Roth plan (Spreadsheet 21.8).[4]

Sheltered versus Unsheltered Savings

Suppose your desired level of savings is double the amount you are able to shelter. At the same time you wish to invest equal amounts in stocks and bonds. Where should you keep the stocks and where the bonds? You will be surprised by how many investors make the costly mistake of

---

[3]High income investors also face an additional potential tax surcharge on their investment earnings.

[4]In Spreadsheet 21.9 we did not take full advantage of the tax code. You can defer capital gains longer by specifying the particular shares you sell so that you sell first new shares with little capital gains and old shares last.

SPREADSHEET 21.9

Saving with no-dividend stocks under a progressive tax

Spreadsheets are
available in Connect

	A	B	C	D	E	F	G	H
3	Retirement Years	Income Growth	Rate of Inflation	Exemption Now	Tax rates in	Savings Rate	ROR	rROR
4	**25**	**0.07**	**0.03**	**10000**	**Table 21.1**	**0.15**	**0.06**	**0.0291**
5	Age	Income	Deflator	Exemption	Taxes	Savings	Cumulative Savings	rConsumption
6	30	50,000	1.00	10,000	8,000	6,300	6,300	35,700
7	31	53,500	1.03	10,300	8,640	6,793	13,471	36,958
11	35	70,128	1.16	11,593	11,764	9,370	52,995	42,262
21	45	137,952	1.56	15,580	28,922	19,707	278,528	57,333
31	55	271,372	2.09	20,938	64,661	41,143	883,393	79,076
41	65	533,829	2.81	28,139	145,999	92,460	2,432,049	104,970
42	Total				1,752,425	1,163,478	**Real Annuity**	**49,153**
43	**RETIREMENT**				Tax Rate	Capital Gains		0.15
44	Age	Nom Withdraw	Deflator	Cum Cap Gains	on Exemption	Taxes	Funds Left	rConsumption
45	66	142,460	2.90	1,340,186	28,983	6,799	2,435,512	46,808
49	70	160,340	3.26	1,561,124	32,620	10,178	2,404,847	46,033
54	75	185,879	3.78	1,660,844	37,816	14,598	2,233,096	45,293
59	80	215,484	4.38	1,503,386	43,839	19,338	1,846,348	44,742
64	85	249,805	5.08	995,489	50,821	24,535	1,146,895	44,326
69	90	289,593	5.89	1,500	58,916	30,626	0	43,955
70	Total				1,056,691	445,850		

holding the stocks in a tax-protected account and the bonds in an unsheltered account. Most of the return from bonds is in the form of taxable interest payments, while stocks already provide some tax shelter.

Recall that tax shelters enhance the retirement annuity with two elements: (1) tax deferral on contributions and (2) tax deferral on income earned on savings. The effectiveness of each element depends on the tax rate on withdrawals. Of the two types of tax shelters we analyzed, traditional plans contain both elements, while Roth plans provide only the second, but with the advantage that the tax rate on withdrawals is zero. Therefore, we need to analyze the stock–bond shelter question separately for each type of retirement plan. Table 21.3 shows the hierarchy of this analysis when a Roth plan is used. The difference is apparent by comparing the taxes in each column. With stocks inside and bonds outside the shelter you pay taxes early and at the ordinary income rate. When you remove stocks from and move bonds into the shelter, you pay taxes later at the lower capital gains rate.

When you use a traditional plan, contributions are tax deferred regardless of whether you purchase stocks or bonds, so we need to compare only taxes on income from savings and withdrawal. Table 21.4 shows the trade-off for a traditional plan.

The advantage ends up being the same as with the Roth plan. By removing stocks from and moving bonds into the shelter, you gain the deferral on the bond interest during the savings phase. During the retirement phase you gain the difference between the ordinary income and the capital gains rate on the gains from the stocks.

TABLE 21.3 Investing Roth plan contributions in stocks and bonds

Phase	Asset	Stocks Inside; Bonds Outside	Stocks Outside; Bonds Inside
Savings	Bonds	Taxed upon accrual	No taxes
	Stocks	No taxes	Taxes deferred
Withdrawal*	Bonds	No taxes	No taxes
	Stocks	No taxes	Taxed at capital gains rate

*Because the retirement annuity is similar in both plans, taxes on this annuity are ignored.

		Stocks Inside;	Stocks Outside;
Phase	**Asset**	**Bonds Outside**	**Bonds Inside**
Savings	Bonds	Taxed on accrual	Taxes deferred
	Stocks	Tax deferred	Taxes deferred
Withdrawal*	Bonds	No taxes	Taxed at marginal rate
	Stocks	Taxed at marginal rate	Taxed at capital gains rate

TABLE 21.4 Investing stocks and bonds in traditional plans

*Because the retirement annuity is similar in both plans, taxes on this annuity are ignored.

Does the rationale of sheltering bonds rather than stocks apply to preferred stocks?

CONCEPT check **21.8**

21.6 SOCIAL SECURITY

Social Security (SS) is a cross between a pension and an insurance plan. It is quite regressive in that employees pay a proportional (currently 7.65%) tax on gross wages with no exemption but with an income cap ($118,500 in 2015). Employers match employees' contributions and pay SS directly.[5]

On the other hand, SS is progressive in the way it allocates benefits; low-income individuals receive a relatively larger replacement of preretirement income upon retirement. Of the SS tax of 7.65%, 6.2% goes toward retirement benefits and 1.45% toward retirement health care services provided by Medicare. Thus, combining your payments with your employer's, the real retirement annuity is financed by $2 \times 6.2 = 12.4\%$ of your income (up to the aforementioned cap); we do not examine the Medicare component of SS.

SS payments are made throughout one's entire working life, but only the highest 35 years of contributions count for the determination of benefits. Benefits are in the form of a lifetime real annuity based on a retirement age of 67, although you can retire earlier (as of age 62) or later (up to age 70) and draw a smaller or larger annuity, respectively.[6]

One reason SS is projected to face fiscal difficulties in future years is the increased longevity of the population. Over the next 35 years, longevity is expected to increase by almost two years, increasing steady-state expenditures by more than 10%. To keep a level population (ignoring immigration) requires an average of 2.1 children per female, yet the current average of 2.0 is expected to decline further.[7] The projected large deficits in future Social Security budgets require reform of the program. Increasing the retirement age to account for increased longevity does not constitute a reduction in the present value of expected benefits to plan participants and therefore seems a reasonable solution to deficits arising from this factor. Eliminating the deficit resulting from declining birth rates is more difficult. It is projected that doing so by increasing the SS tax may require an increase in the combined SS tax of as much as 10% within your working years. Such a simple solution is considered politically difficult. Another possiblity is changes in benefits, also politically difficult.

Social Security

Federally mandated pension plan established to provide minimum retirement benefits to all workers.

---

[5]Without the SS tax, it is reasonable to assume that the amount contributed by employers would be added to your pretax income; hence your actual contribution is really 15.3%. For this reason, self-employed individuals are required to contribute 15.3% to SS.

[6]Retirement age for individuals born before 1960 is 66. For a complete listing of retirement ages, go to **www .socialsecurity.gov**.

[7]Fertility rates in Europe, Japan, and (until recently) China are even lower, exacerbating the problems of their Social Security systems.

Part of your retirement expenditures will be paid for with your Social Security benefits. Part will come from your retirement savings. Compare the risks surrounding the income stream that will be generated from each of these sources.

21.7   LARGE PURCHASES

Sending a child to a private college can cost a family in excess of $50,000 a year, in current dollars, for four years. Even a state college can cost in excess of $30,000 a year. Many families will send two or more children to college within a few years, creating a need to finance large expenditures within a few years. Other large expenditures such as a second home (we deal with the primary residence in the next section) or an expensive vehicle present similar problems on a smaller scale.

The question is whether planned, large outflows during the working years require a major innovation in our planning tools. The answer is no. All you need to do is add a column to your spreadsheet for extra-consumption expenditures that come out of savings. As long as cumulative savings do not turn negative as the outflows take place, the only effect to consider is the reduction in the retirement annuity that results from these expenditures. To respond to a lower-than-desired retirement annuity you have four options: (1) Increase the savings rate, (2) live with a smaller retirement annuity, (3) do away with or reduce the magnitude of the expenditure item, or (4) increase expected ROR by taking on more risk. Recall though, that in Section 21.2, we suggested option 4 isn't viable for many investors.

The situation is a little more complicated when the extra-consumption expenditures create negative cumulative savings in the retirement plan. In principle, one can simply borrow to finance these expenditures with debt (as is common for large purchases such as automobiles). Again, the primary variable of interest is the retirement annuity. The problem, however, is that if you arrive at a negative savings level quite late in your savings plan, you will be betting the farm on the success of the plan in later years. Pushing risk into later years, other things equal, is more dangerous because you will have little time to recover from any setback.

An illuminating example requires adding only one column to Spreadsheet 21.2, as shown in Spreadsheet 21.10. Column G adds the extra-consumption expenditures. We use as input (cell G2) a hypothetical $40,000 cost of one college year per child. We assume your first child will be college-bound when you are 48 years old and the second when you are 50. The expenditures in column G are inflated by the price level in column C and subtracted from cumulative savings in column E.

The real retirement annuity prior to this extra-consumption expenditure was $49,688, but "after-children" only $22,048, less than half. The expenditure of $320,000 in today's dollars

SPREADSHEET 21.10

Financing children's education

Spreadsheets are available in Connect

	A	B	C	D	E	F	G
1	Retirement Years	Income Growth	Rate of Inflation	Savings Rate	ROR	rROR	Extra-Cons
2	25	0.07	0.03	0.15	0.06	0.0291	40,000
3	Age	Income	Deflator	Savings	Cumulative Savings	rConsumption	Expenditures
4	30	50,000	1.00	7,500	7,500	42,500	0
5	31	53,500	1.03	8,025	15,975	44,150	0
9	35	70,128	1.16	10,519	61,658	51,419	0
19	45	137,952	1.56	20,693	308,859	75,264	0
22	48	168,997	1.70	25,349	375,099	84,378	68,097
23	49	180,826	1.75	27,124	354,588	87,654	70,140
24	50	193,484	1.81	29,023	260,397	91,058	144,489
25	51	207,028	1.86	31,054	158,252	94,595	148,824
26	52	221,520	1.92	33,228	124,331	98,268	76,644
27	53	237,026	1.97	35,554	88,401	102,084	78,943
28	54	253,618	2.03	38,043	131,748	106,049	0
29	55	271,372	2.09	40,706	180,359	110,167	0
39	65	533,829	2.81	80,074	1,090,888	161,257	0
40	Total			1,116,851	Real Annuity	22,048	

lowers your lifetime real consumption by $25 \times (\$49{,}688 - \$22{,}048) = \$690{,}514$ because of the loss of interest on the funds that would have been saved. If you change the input in G2 to $25,000 (a reasonable cost estimate for many public colleges), the retirement annuity falls to $32,405, a loss of "only" 35% in the standard of living.

A more recent tax shelter comes in the form of a "529 plan" that allows for tax-exempt saving for higher education (see, for example, **www.saveforcollege.com**). These plans are similar to Roth plans in that they are funded with after-tax dollars, but investment earnings are not taxed. Deployment of such plans can further reduce the impact of children's education on lifetime consumption.

What, if anything, should you do about the risk of a rapid increase in college tuition?

CONCEPT check **21.10**

21.8 HOME OWNERSHIP: THE RENT-VERSUS-BUY DECISION

Many people dream of owning a home and for good reason. In addition to the natural desire for roots that goes with owning your home, this investment is an important hedge for most families. Dwelling is the largest long-term consumption item, and fluctuations in the cost of dwelling are responsible for the largest consumption risk they face. Dwelling costs, in turn, are subject to general price inflation, as well as to significant fluctuations specific to geographic location.

The common belief is that the mortgage tax break (interest is tax deductible) is the major financial advantage of investing in rather than renting a home. In competitive markets, though, rents will reflect the mortgage interest tax deduction that applies to rental residence as well. Moreover, homes are illiquid assets, and transaction costs in buying/selling a house are high. Therefore, purchasing a home that isn't expected to be a long-term residence for the owner may well be a speculative investment with inferior expected returns. Speculative investments in real estate ought to be made in a portfolio context through instruments such as Real Estate Investment Trusts (REITs).

With all this in mind, it is evident that investment in a home enters the savings plan in two ways. First, during the working years the cash down payment and mortgage payments should be treated just like any other large, extra-consumption expenditure as discussed earlier. Second, home ownership affects your retirement plan because if you own your home free and clear by the time you retire, you will need a smaller annuity to get by; moreover, the value of the house is part of retirement (and bequest) wealth.

Should you have any preference for fixed- versus variable-rate mortgages?

CONCEPT check **21.11**

21.9 UNCERTAIN LONGEVITY AND OTHER CONTINGENCIES

Perhaps the most daunting uncertainty in our life is the time it will end. This uncertainty has economic implications. Old age is hard enough without worrying about expenses. Yet the amount of money you may need is at least linear in longevity, if not exponential. Not knowing how much you will need, plus a healthy degree of risk aversion, requires saving a lot more than necessary just to insure against the fortune of longevity.

One solution to this problem is to invest in a life annuity to supplement Social Security benefits, your base life annuity. When you own a **life annuity** that pays until you die, the provider bears the risk of the time of death. To survive, the provider must be sure to earn a

life annuity
An annuity that matures when you die.

rate of return commensurate with the risk. Except for wars and natural disasters, however, an individual's time of death is a unique, nonsystematic risk.[8] It would appear, then, that the cost of a life annuity should be a simple calculation of interest rates applied to life expectancy from mortality tables. Unfortunately, adverse selection comes in the way.

adverse selection

The tendency for any proposed deal to attract the type of party who would make the deal a losing proposition to the offering party.

Adverse selection is the tendency for any proposed contract (deal) to attract the type of party who would make the contract a losing proposition to the offering party. A good example of adverse selection arises in health care. Suppose that Blue Cross offers health coverage where you choose your doctor and Blue Cross pays 80% of the costs. Another HMO covers 100% of the cost but charges a fixed fee per treatment. If HMOs were to price the services on the basis of a survey of the average health care needs in the population at large, they would be in for an unpleasant surprise. People who need frequent and more expensive care would prefer the fixed-fee HMO plan over the cost-sharing Blue Cross plan. The adverse selection in this case is that higher-need individuals will choose the plan that provides more complete coverage. The individuals that the HMO most wants *not* to insure are most likely to sign up for coverage. Hence, to stay in business HMOs must expect their patients to have greater than average needs, and price the policy on this basis.

Providers of life annuities can expect a good dose of adverse selection as well, as people with the longest life expectancies will be their most enthusiastic customers. Therefore, it is advantageous to acquire these annuities at a younger age, before either individuals or insurers learn much about their particular life expectancies. The Social Security trust does not face adverse selection because virtually the entire population is forced into the purchase.

Unfortunately we also must consider untimely death or disability of a member of the household. These require an appropriate amount of life and disability insurance, particularly in the early stage of the life cycle. The appropriate coverage should be thought of in the context of a retirement annuity. Coverage should replace at least the most essential part of the retirement annuity.

Finally, there is the need to hedge labor income. Because you cannot insure wages, the least you can do is maintain a portfolio that is uncorrelated with your labor income. As Lehman Brothers and other recent bankruptcies have demonstrated, too many are unaware of the perils of having their pension income tied to their career, employment, and compensation. Investing a significant fraction of your portfolio in the industry you work in, not to mention the company you work for, is akin to a "Texas hedge": betting on the horse you own.

CONCEPT check 21.12   Insurance companies offer life insurance on your children. Does it make economic sense to buy such insurance?

21.10 MATRIMONY, BEQUEST, AND INTERGENERATIONAL TRANSFERS

In the context of a retirement plan, we think of risk in terms of safety first. The imperative to avoid disastrous outcomes makes mean-variance analysis inadequate. We touched on this issue in the context of (1) raising the ROR by tilting toward riskier investments, (2) avoiding savings plans that rely too heavily on savings in later years, and (3) acquiring life insurance and life annuities.

moral hazard

The phenomenon whereby a party to a contract has an incentive to change behavior in a way that makes the contract less attractive to the other party.

One sort of insurance the market cannot supply is wage insurance. If we could obtain wage insurance, a savings plan would be a lot easier to formulate. **Moral hazard** is the reason for this void in the marketplace. Moral hazard is the phenomenon whereby a party to a contract (deal) has an incentive to change behavior in a way that makes the deal less attractive to the other party.[9] A person who buys wage insurance would then have an incentive to consume leisure at the expense of work effort. Moral hazard is also why insuring items for more than their market or intrinsic value is prohibited. If your warehouse were insured for lots more than its value, you might have less incentive to prevent fires, an obvious moral hazard.

[8]For this reason, life insurance policies typically exclude coverage of wars, epidemics, and famine.
[9]Moral hazard and adverse selection can reinforce each other. Restaurants that offer an all-you-can-eat meal attract big eaters (adverse selection) and induce "normal" eaters to overeat (moral hazard).

In contrast, marriage provides a form of co-insurance that extends also to the issue of longevity. A married couple has a greater probability that at least one will survive to an older age, giving greater incentive to save for a longer life. Put differently, saving for a longer life has a smaller probability of going to waste.

Bequest is another motive for saving. There is something special about bequest that differentiates it from other "expense" items. When you save for members of the next generation (or beyond), you double the planning horizon, and by considering later generations as well, you can make it effectively infinite. This has implications for the composition of the savings portfolio. For example, the conventional wisdom that, as you grow older, you should gradually shift out of stocks and into bonds is not as true when bequest is an important factor in the savings plan.[10]

Having discussed marriage co-insurance and bequest, we cannot fail to mention that despite the virtues of saving for the longest term, many individuals overshoot the mark. When a person saves for old age and passes on before taking full advantage of the nest egg, the estate is called an "involuntary, intergenerational transfer." Data show that such transfers are widespread. Kotlikoff and Summers (1981) estimate that about 75% of wealth left behind is actually involuntary transfer. This suggests that people make too little use of the market for life annuities. Hopefully you will not be one of them, both because you will live to a healthy old age and because you'll have a ball spending your never-expiring annuity.

[10]Those who wish to reduce retirement risk as they grow older can use target date retirement funds (TDRFs). Asset allocation in this sort of fund is linked to your planned retirement date. As time passes and you approach retirement, the fund gradually shifts your asset allocation from risky to risk-free investments, usually ending risk-free upon your retirement date.

SUMMARY

- The major objective of a savings plan is to provide for adequate retirement income.
- Even moderate inflation will affect the purchasing power of the retirement annuity. Therefore, the plan must be cast in terms of real consumption and retirement income.
- From a standpoint of smoothing consumption, it is advantageous to save a fixed or rising fraction of real income. However, postponement of savings to later years increases the risk of the retirement fund.
- The traditional-style tax shelter defers taxes on both contributions and investment earnings.
- The progressive tax code sharpens the importance of taxes during the retirement years. High tax rates during retirement reduce the effectiveness of the tax shelter.
- A Roth-style tax shelter does not shield contributions but eliminates taxes during retirement. Savers who anticipate high retirement income (and taxes) must examine whether this shelter is more beneficial than a traditional account.
- 401k plans are similar to traditional Individual Retirement Accounts but allow matched contributions by employers. This benefit should not be forgone.
- Capital gains can be postponed and later taxed at a lower rate. Therefore, investment in low-dividend stocks is a natural tax shelter. Investments in interest-bearing securities should be sheltered first.
- Social Security benefits are an important component of retirement income.
- Savings plans should be augmented for large expenditures such as children's education.
- Home ownership can be viewed in part as a hedge against increases in rental cost.
- Uncertain longevity and other contingencies can be managed using life annuities and appropriate insurance coverage.

KEY TERMS

adverse selection, 702
defined benefit plan, 694
flat tax, 689
401k plans, 694
life annuity, 701
moral hazard, 702
progressive tax, 692
real consumption, 687
retirement annuity, 685
Roth account, 695
Social Security, 699
tax shelters, 690
traditional retirement
account, 695

PROBLEM SETS

Select problems are available in McGraw-Hill's *Connect*. Please see the Supplements section of the book's frontmatter for more information.

X

Templates and spreadsheets are available in Connect

1. A ship owner is attempting to insure an old vessel for twice its current market value. Is this an adverse selection or moral hazard issue? *(LO 21-5)*

2. The same ship owner advertises a tariff whereby the freight charged per pound for all cargo will be the same. What kind of good can the ship owner expect to attract? *(LO 21-5)*

3. What type of investors would be interested in a target date retirement fund? Why? *(LO 21-1)*

4. What is the insurance aspect of the Social Security annuity? *(LO 21-1)*

5. Why does a progressive tax code produce a retirement annuity for a middle-class household that is similar to that which would follow from a flat tax? *(LO 21-3)*

6. With no taxes or inflation (Spreadsheet 21.1), what would be your retirement annuity if you increase the savings rate by 1%? *(LO 21-1)*

7. With a 3% inflation rate (Spreadsheet 21.2), by how much would your retirement annuity grow if you increase the savings rate by 1%? Is the benefit greater in the face of inflation? *(LO 21-2)*

8. What savings rate from real income (Spreadsheet 21.3) will produce the same retirement annuity as a 15% savings rate from nominal income? *(LO 21-2)*

9. Under the flat tax (Spreadsheet 21.4), will a 1% increase in ROR offset a 1% increase in the tax rate? *(LO 21-3)*

10. With a traditional tax shelter (Spreadsheet 21.5), compare the effect on real consumption during retirement of a 1% increase in the rate of inflation to a 1% increase in the tax rate. *(LO 21-4)*

11. With a progressive tax (Spreadsheet 21.6), compare the effects of an increase of 1% in the lowest tax bracket to an increase of 1% in the highest tax bracket. *(LO 21-4)*

12. Verify that the traditional tax shelter with a progressive tax (Spreadsheet 21.7) acts as a hedge. Compare the effect of a decline of 2% in the ROR to an increase of 2% in ROR. *(LO 21-4)*

13. What is the trade-off between ROR and the rate of inflation with a Roth plan under a progressive tax (Spreadsheet 21.8)? *(LO 21-3)*

14. Suppose you could defer capital gains tax to the last year of your retirement (Spreadsheet 21.9). Would it be worthwhile given the progressivity of the tax code? *(LO 21-3)*

15. Project your Social Security benefits with the parameters of Section 21.6. *(LO 21-1)*

16. Using Spreadsheet 21.10, assess the present value of a 1% increase in college tuition as a fraction of the present value of labor income. *(LO 21-4)*

17. Give another example of adverse selection. *(LO 21-5)*

18. In addition to expected longevity, what traits might affect an individual's demand for a life annuity? *(LO 21-5)*

19. Give another example of a moral hazard problem. *(LO 21-5)*

WEB *master*

Visit the AARP's Financial Planning and Retirement website at **www.aarp.org.** Locate *Work and Retirement Tools* and then the *Retirement Planner*. The calculator allows you to enter information about your retirement plans, your current level of assets, expected benefits from other sources, and your spouse's financial data and needs. Use the AARP Retirement Planning Calculator to enter your specific data and assumptions.

1. On the Results page, do you have a projected excess of funds or a shortfall of funds at the end of the retirement period? Can you meet your goals by following your current financial path?

2. Look at the list of parameters toward the bottom of the page. Which one would be the easiest for you to change to make your goals attainable? Some people might choose to work longer, some to spend less in retirement, and so on. Choose the combination of factors that would work best for you, and then recalculate to see the new results. Can you come up with a plan that has a combination of factors that offer you an acceptable level of comfort?

21.1 When ROR falls by 1% to 5%, the retirement annuity falls from $192,244 to $149,855 (i.e., by 22.45%). To restore this annuity, the savings rate must rise by 4.24 percentage points to 19.24%. With this savings rate, the entire loss of 1% in ROR falls on consumption during the earning years.

21.2 Intuition suggests you need to keep the real rate (2.91%) constant, that is, increase the nominal rate to 7% (confirm this). However, this will not be sufficient because the nominal income growth of 7% (column B) has a lower real growth when inflation is higher. Result: You must increase the real ROR to compensate for a lower growth in real income, ending with a nominal rate of 7.67%.

21.3 There are two components to the risk of relying on future labor income: disability/death and career failure/unemployment. You can insure the first component but not the second.

21.4 With before-tax income held constant, your after-tax income will remain unchanged if your average tax rate, and hence total tax liability, is unchanged:

$$\text{Total tax} = (\text{Income} - \text{Exemption}) \times \text{Tax rate, or } T = (I - E) \times t$$

A 1% increase in the tax rate will increase T by $.01(I - E)$. A 1% increase in the exemption will decrease T by $.01 \times E \times t$. Realistically, $I - E$ will be greater than $E \times t$ and hence you will be worse off with the increase in exemption and tax rate.

21.5 The qualitative result is the same. However, with no shelter you are worse off early and hence also lose the earning power of the additional tax bills.

21.6 No, an increase in the low-bracket tax rate applies to your entire taxable income, while an increase in the high-bracket tax rate applies only to a fraction of your taxable income.

21.7 Using the same inputs as in Spreadsheet 21.8, the Roth plan will generate less taxes yet still result in a smaller real retirement annuity. The reason is the timing of the taxes. The timing issue does not affect the stream of tax revenues to the IRS because at any point in time, taxpayers are distributed over all ages. In this case, the IRS can replace all Roth plans with traditional ones and lower the tax rates. The IRS will collect similar revenue each year, and retirees will enjoy higher real retirement annuities.

21.8 No, in terms of cash income, preferred stocks are more similar to bonds.

21.9 Your projected retirement fund is risky because of uncertainty about future labor income and future real returns on savings. The projected Social Security real annuity is risky because of political uncertainty about future benefits. It's hard to judge which risk is greater.

21.10 You need an investment that pays more when tuition is higher. Several states now offer "tuition futures" contracts that allow you to lock in the price of future tuition expenditures.

21.11 A fixed-rate mortgage is the lower-risk, higher-expected-cost option. Homeowners with greater risk tolerance might opt for a variable-rate mortgage which is expected to average a lower rate over the life of the mortgage.

21.12 In the old days, children were more than a bundle of joy; they also provided a hedge for old-age income. Under such circumstance, insuring children would make economic sense. These days, children may well be a financial net expenditure, ruling out insurance on economic grounds. Other nonfinancial considerations are a matter of individual preference.

Chapter

22

Investors and the Investment Process

Learning Objectives

LO 22-1 Specify investment objectives of individual and institutional investors.

LO 22-2 Identify constraints on individual and institutional investors.

LO 22-3 Develop investment policy statements consistent with a client's objectives and constraints.

Translating the aspirations and circumstances of diverse households into appropriate investment decisions is a daunting task. A novice financial consultant often asks: "How do you engage members of a household in financial planning when they do not know what standard deviation is, never studied Economics 101, and have little, if any, quantitative background?" Finance advisers spend most of their time in the trenches doing just that.

The task is equally difficult for institutions, most of which have many stakeholders and often are regulated by various authorities. The investment process is not easily reduced to a simple or mechanical algorithm.

While many principles of investments are quite general and apply to virtually all investors, some issues are peculiar to the specific investor. Tax bracket, age, risk tolerance, wealth, job prospects, and uncertainties make each investor's circumstances somewhat unique. In this chapter we focus on the process by which investors systematically review their particular objectives, constraints, and circumstances. Along the way, we survey some of the major classes of institutional investors and examine the special issues they must confront.

There is no unique "correct" investment process, but some approaches are better than others. It can be helpful to take one high-quality approach as a useful case study. For this reason, we examine the systematic approach suggested by the CFA Institute. The CFA Institute is one of the most important professional organizations for finance practitioners. It confers the Chartered Financial Analyst designation on those who meet its requirements, which include both work experience and a set of three exams. There are currently around 125,000 CFA charterholders employed in about 150 countries. (The nearby box describes how to become a CFA charterholder.) Dozens of countries have adopted the CFA Institute's Global Investment Performance Standards. The CFA curriculum thus influences the training of the highest-level and most respected investment managers around the world. Throughout its history, the CFA Institute has maintained rigorous standards, and its curriculum has evolved over the years to keep up with developments in both financial theory and practice.

The CFA Institute has created a framework to help professionals develop and explain financial policy to individual and institutional clients. This chapter presents the CFA Institute's approach. As you read about it, concentrate on the methodology underlying its design of the investment process.

The basic framework divides the investment process into four stages: specifying objectives, specifying constraints, formulating policy, and monitoring and updating the portfolio. We start with a description of major types of investors, both individual and institutional, as well as their special objectives. We turn next to the constraints or circumstances peculiar to each investor class and consider some of the investment policies that each can choose.

22.1 THE INVESTMENT MANAGEMENT PROCESS

The CFA Institute divides the process of investment management into elements that constitute a dynamic feedback loop: planning, execution, and feedback. Figure 22.1 and Table 22.1 describe the steps in that process. *Planning* is focused largely on establishing the inputs necessary for decision making. These include data about the client as well as the capital market, leading to broad policy guidelines (strategic asset allocation). *Execution* fleshes out the details of optimal asset allocation and security selection. Finally, *feedback* is the process of adapting to changes in expectations and objectives as well as to changes in portfolio composition that result from changes in market prices.

CFA Institute investment management process

FIGURE 22.1

TABLE 22.1 Components of the investment management process

I. Planning
    A. Identifying and specifying the investor's objectives and constraints
    B. Creating the *investment policy statement* [See Table 22.2]
    C. Forming capital market expectations
    D. Creating the strategic asset allocation (Target minimum and maximum class weights)

II. Execution: Portfolio construction and revision
    A. Asset allocation (including tactical) and portfolio optimization (combining assets to meet risk and return objectives)
    B. Security selection
    C. Implementation and execution

III. Feedback
    A. Monitoring (investor, economic, and market input factors)
    B. Rebalancing
    C. Performance evaluation

Source: John L. Maginn, Donald L. Tuttle, Dennis W. McLeavey, and Jerald E. Pinto, "The Portfolio Management Process and the Investment Policy Statement," in *Managing Investment Portfolios: A Dynamic Process,* 3rd ed. (CFA Institute, 2007) and correspondence with Tom Robinson, head of educational content.

TABLE 22.2 Components of the investment policy statement (IPS)

1. Brief client description
2. Purpose of establishing policies and guidelines
3. Duties and investment responsibilities of parties involved
4. Statement of investment goals, objectives, and constraints
5. Schedule for review of investment performance and the IPS
6. Performance measures and benchmarks
7. Any considerations in developing strategic asset allocation
8. Investment strategies and investment styles
9. Guidelines for rebalancing

TABLE 22.3 Determination of portfolio policies

Objectives	Constraints
Return requirements	Liquidity
Risk tolerance	Horizon
	Regulations
	Taxes
	Unique needs, such as:
	Ethical concerns
	Specific hedging needs
	Age
	Wealth

The result of this analysis can be summarized in an *investment policy statement* (IPS) addressing the topics specified in Table 22.2. In the next sections we elaborate on the steps leading to an IPS. We start with the planning phase, the top panel of Table 22.1.

Table 22.1 indicates that the management planning process starts off by analyzing one's investment clients—in particular, by considering the objectives and constraints that govern their decisions. Portfolio objectives center on the risk-return trade-off between the expected return the investors need (return requirements in the first column of Table 22.3) and how much risk they are willing to assume (risk tolerance). Investment managers must know the

HOW TO BECOME A CHARTERED FINANCIAL ANALYST

The CFA Institute is a nonprofit international organization with a mission of serving investors by educating investment professionals and setting high standards for ethical practice. The Institute also has established a *Code of Ethics and Standards of Professional Conduct* that lays out guidelines of practice for investment professionals.

The CFA Institute was established in January 1990 through the combination of the previously existing Financial Analysts Federation and the Institute of Chartered Financial Analysts. The CFA Institute administers the program through which an investment professional can be designated as a Chartered Financial Analyst (CFA). This designation has become a progressively more important requirement for a career in institutional money management. About 125,000 investment professionals were members of the CFA Institute in 2015, and the Institute was affiliated with 144 professional societies in 69 countries.

To become a CFA, you must pass a series of three annual examinations that demonstrate knowledge of:

- Valuation principles for fixed-income, equity, and derivative securities.
- Financial statement analysis and corporate finance.
- Industry and company analysis.
- Microeconomic and macroeconomic theory.
- Quantitative methods.
- Principles of portfolio construction and management.
- Capital market theory.
- Financial markets and instruments.
- The CFA Institute Code of Ethics and Standards of Professional Conduct.

Beyond these exams, the candidate must have four years of work experience in money management and must join the CFA Institute and apply for membership in a local CFA member society.

For more information, you can visit the CFA Institute website at **www.cfainstitute.org.**

---

level of risk that can be tolerated in the pursuit of higher expected return. Investors also must deal with various constraints on their portfolio choice that derive from considerations such as liquidity needs, regulations, or tax concerns. The second column of Table 22.3 lists the more important constraints.

In the next sections, we explore some of these objectives and constraints.

22.2 INVESTOR OBJECTIVES

Individual Investors

The basic factors affecting an individual investor's objectives usually arise from that investor's stage in the life cycle. The first significant investment decision for most individuals concerns education, which is an investment in "human capital." The major asset most people have during their early working years is the earning power derived from their skills. For these people, the financial risk due to illness or injury is far greater than that associated with the rate of return on their portfolios of financial assets. At this point in the life cycle, the most important financial decisions concern insurance against the possibility of disability or death.

As one ages and accumulates savings to provide for consumption during retirement, the composition of wealth shifts from human capital toward financial capital. At this point, portfolio choices become progressively more important. In middle age, most investors will be willing to take on a meaningful amount of portfolio risk to increase their expected rates of return. As retirement draws near, however, risk tolerance seems to diminish.

Questionnaire results confirm that attitudes shift away from risk tolerance and toward risk aversion as investors near retirement age. (See the questionnaire in the nearby box.) With age, individuals lose the potential to recover from a disastrous investment performance. When they are young, investors can respond to a loss by working harder and saving more of their income. But as retirement approaches, investors realize there will be less time to recover, hence the shift to safe assets.

The task of life-cycle financial planning is formidable for most people. It is not surprising that a whole industry has sprung up to provide personal financial advice.

TIME FOR INVESTING'S FOUR-LETTER WORD

What four-letter word should pop into mind when the stock market takes a harrowing nose dive?

No, not those. R-I-S-K.

Risk is the potential for realizing low returns or even losing money, possibly preventing you from meeting important objectives, like sending your kids to the college of their choice or having the retirement lifestyle you crave.

Assessing your risk tolerance, however, can be tricky. You must consider not only how much risk you can *afford* to take but also how much risk you can *stand* to take. Determining how much risk you can stand—your temperamental tolerance for risk—is more difficult. It isn't quantifiable.

To that end, many financial advisers, brokerage firms, and mutual fund companies have created risk quizzes to help people determine whether they are conservative, moderate, or aggressive investors. Some firms that offer such quizzes include Merrill Lynch; T. Rowe Price Associates Inc., Baltimore; Zurich Group Inc.'s Scudder Kemper Investments Inc., New York; and Vanguard Group in Malvern, Pa.

Typically, risk questionnaires include 7 to 10 questions about a person's investing experience, financial security, and tendency to make risky or conservative choices.

The benefit of the questionnaires is that they are an objective resource people can use to get at least a rough idea of their risk tolerance. "It's impossible for someone to assess their risk tolerance alone," says Mr. Bernstein. "I may say I don't like risk, yet will take more risk than the average person."

Many experts warn, however, that the questionnaires should be used simply as a first step to assessing risk tolerance. The second step, many experts agree, is to ask yourself some difficult questions, such as: How much can you stand to lose over the long term?

"Most people can stand to lose a heck of a lot temporarily," says Mr. Schatsky. The real acid test, he says, is how much of your portfolio's value you can stand to lose over months or years.

As it turns out, most people rank as middle-of-the-road risk-takers, say several advisers. "Only about 10% to 15% of my clients are aggressive," says Mr. Roge.

WHAT'S YOUR RISK TOLERANCE?

Circle the letter that corresponds to your answer.

1. Just 60 days after you put money into an investment, its price falls 20%. Assuming none of the fundamentals have changed, what would you do?

   a. Sell to avoid further worry and try something else.
   b. Do nothing and wait for the investment to come back.
   c. Buy more. It was a good investment before; now it's a cheap investment, too.

2. Now look at the previous question another way. Your investment fell 20%, but it's part of a portfolio being used to meet investment goals with three different time horizons.

2A. What would you do if the goal were five years away?

   a. Sell
   b. Do nothing
   c. Buy more

2B. What would you do if the goal were 15 years away?

   a. Sell
   b. Do nothing
   c. Buy more

Professional Investors

Professional investors provide investment management services for a fee. Some are employed directly by wealthy individual investors. Most professional investors, however, either pool the funds of many individual investors and manage them or serve institutional investors.

personal trust

An interest in an asset held by a trustee for the benefit of another person.

PERSONAL TRUSTS   A **personal trust** is established when an individual confers legal title to property to another person or institution, which then manages that property for one or more beneficiaries. The holder of the title is called the *trustee*. The trustee is usually a bank, a lawyer, or an investment professional. Investment of a trust is subject to state trust laws and *prudent investor rules* that limit the types of allowable trust investment.

The objectives of personal trusts normally are more limited in scope than those of the individual investor. Because of their fiduciary responsibility, personal trust managers typically are expected to invest with more risk aversion than individual investors. Certain asset classes, such as options and futures contracts, for example, and some strategies, such as short-selling or buying on margin, are ruled out. Short sales and margin purchases were discussed in Chapter 3.

mutual fund

A firm pooling and managing funds of investors.

MUTUAL FUNDS   **Mutual funds** are firms that manage pools of individual investor money. They invest in accordance with their objectives and issue shares that entitle investors to a pro rata portion of the income generated by the funds.

2C. What would you do if the goal were 30 years away?

a. Sell
b. Do nothing
c. Buy more

3. The price of your retirement investment jumps 25% a month after you buy it. Again, the fundamentals haven't changed. After you finish gloating, what do you do?

a. Sell it and lock in your gains
b. Stay put and hope for more gain
c. Buy more: It could go higher

4. You're investing for retirement, which is 15 years away. Which would you rather do?

a. Invest in a money-market fund or guaranteed investment contract, giving up the possibility of major gains, but virtually assuring the safety of your principal
b. Invest in a 50-50 mix of bond funds and stock funds, in hopes of getting some growth, but also giving yourself some protection in the form of steady income
c. Invest in aggressive growth mutual funds whose value will probably fluctuate significantly during the year, but have the potential for impressive gains over five or 10 years

5. You just won a big prize! But which one? It's up to you.

a. $2,000 in cash
b. A 50% chance to win $5,000
c. A 20% chance to win $15,000

6. A good investment opportunity just came along. But you have to borrow money to get in. Would you take out a loan?

a. Definitely not
b. Perhaps
c. Yes

7. Your company is selling stock to its employees. In three years, management plans to take the company public. Until then, you won't be able to sell your shares and you will get no dividends. But your investment could multiply as much as 10 times when the company goes public. How much money would you invest?

a. None
b. Two months' salary
c. Four months' salary

SCORING YOUR RISK TOLERANCE

To score the quiz, add up the number of answers you gave in each category a–c; then multiply as shown to find your score:

(a) answers _____ × 1 = _____ points
(b) answers _____ × 2 = _____ points
(c) answers _____ × 3 = _____ points

YOUR SCORE_____points

If you scored . . . You may be a:

9–14 points   Conservative investor
15–21 points   Moderate investor
22–27 points   Aggressive investor

The return requirement and risk tolerance across mutual funds are highly variable because funds segment the investor market. Various funds appeal to distinct investor groups and will adopt a return requirement and risk tolerance that fit a particular market niche. For example, "income" funds cater to the conservative investor, while "high-growth" funds seek out the more risk-tolerant ones. Tax-free bond funds segment the market by tax bracket.

A mutual fund's objectives are spelled out in its prospectus. We discussed mutual funds in detail in Chapter 4.

PENSION FUNDS   There are two basic types of pension plans: *defined contribution* and *defined benefit*. Defined contribution plans are in effect savings accounts established by the firm for its employees. The employer contributes funds to the plan, but the employee bears all the risk of the fund's investment performance. These plans are called defined contribution because the firm's only obligation is to make the stipulated contributions to the employee's retirement account. The employee is responsible for directing the management of the assets, usually by selecting among several investment funds in which the assets can be placed. Investment earnings in these retirement plans are not taxed until the funds are withdrawn, usually after retirement. These plans are discussed in Chapter 21.

In defined benefit plans, by contrast, the employer has an obligation to provide a specified annual retirement benefit. That benefit is defined by a formula that typically takes into account years of service and the level of salary or wages. For example, the employer may pay the retired employee a yearly amount equal to 2% of the employee's final annual salary for each year of service. A 30-year employee would then receive an annual benefit equal to 60% of his or her final salary. The payments are an obligation of the employer, and the assets in the pension fund provide collateral for the promised benefits. If the investment performance of the assets is poor, the firm is obligated to make up the shortfall by contributing additional assets to the fund. Therefore, in contrast to defined contribution plans, the risk surrounding investment performance in defined benefit plans is borne by the firm.

The pension fund sponsor, the corporation that sets up the fund, appoints a pension fund manager. While its presumed constituency is the group of retirees covered by the fund, the sponsor's management still exerts influence over the fund manager. Between these two entities, asset allocation is hatched. At this point, the pension actuary retained by the fund must sign off on the expected rate of return assumed for the asset portfolio. This is used as the discount rate to compute the present value of fund obligations, which determines whether the pension liabilities are adequately funded or additional funds need to be endowed by the sponsor to meet these liabilities. For example, if the actuary assumes a rate of return of 10%, then the firm must contribute $385.54 now to fund $1,000 of pension liabilities that will arise in 10 years, because $385.54 \times 1.10^{10} = \$1,000$.

If a pension fund's *actual* rate of return exceeds the actuarial *assumed* rate, the firm's shareholders reap the gain, because the excess return can be used to reduce future contributions. If the plan's actual rate of return falls short of the assumed rate, however, the firm will have to increase future contributions. Because the sponsoring firm's shareholders bear the risk in a defined benefit pension plan, the objective of the plan will be consistent with the objective of the firm's shareholders. Thus, a conflict of interest is created: Although the fund in principle should be run for the benefit of the retirees, because the pension plan manager and actuary are retained and compensated by the sponsor, the interests of shareholders may, in practice, be treated as paramount.

Life Insurance Companies

Life insurance companies generally invest to hedge their liabilities, which are defined by the policies they write. The company can reduce risk by investing in assets that will return more in the event the insurance policy coverage becomes more expensive.

For example, if the company writes a policy that pays a death benefit linked to the consumer price index, then the company is subject to inflation risk. It might search for assets expected to return more when the rate of inflation rises, thus hedging the price-index linkage of the policy.

There are as many objectives as there are distinct types of insurance policies. Until the 1970s, only two types of life insurance policies were available for individuals: whole-life and term.

A *whole-life insurance policy* combines a death benefit with a kind of savings plan that provides for a gradual buildup of cash value that the policyholder can withdraw later in life, usually at age 65. *Term insurance,* on the other hand, provides death benefits only, with no buildup of cash value.

The interest rate embedded in the schedule of cash value accumulation promised under the whole-life policy is a fixed rate. One way life insurance companies try to hedge this liability is by investing in long-term bonds. Often the insured individual has the right to borrow at a prespecified fixed interest rate against the cash value of the policy.

During the high-interest-rate years of the 1970s and early 1980s, many older whole-life policies allowed policyholders to borrow at rates as low as 4% or 5% per year; some holders borrowed heavily against the cash value to invest in assets paying double-digit yields. Other actual and potential policyholders abandoned whole-life policies and took out term insurance, which accounted for more than half the volume of new sales of individual life policies.

In response to these developments, the insurance industry came up with two new policy types: variable life and universal life. A *variable life policy* entitles the insured to a fixed death benefit plus a cash value that can be invested in the policyholder's choice of mutual funds. A *universal life policy* allows policyholders to increase or reduce either the insurance premium (the annual fee paid on the policy) or the death benefit (the cash amount paid to beneficiaries in the event of death) according to their changing needs. Furthermore, the interest rate on the cash value component changes with market interest rates. The great advantage of variable and universal life insurance policies is that earnings on the cash value are not taxed until the money is withdrawn.

Non-Life-Insurance Companies

Non-life-insurance companies such as property and casualty insurers have investable funds primarily because they pay claims *after* they collect policy premiums. Typically, they are conservative in their attitude toward risk.

A common thread in the objectives of pension plans and insurance companies is the need to hedge predictable long-term liabilities. Investment strategies typically call for hedging these liabilities with bonds of various maturities.

Banks

Most bank investments are loans to businesses and consumers, and most of their liabilities are accounts of depositors. As investors, banks try to match the risk of assets to liabilities while earning a profitable spread between the lending and borrowing rates.

Most liabilities of banks and thrift institutions are checking accounts, time or savings deposits, and certificates of deposit (CDs). Checking account funds may be withdrawn at any time, so they are of the shortest maturity. Time or savings deposits are of various maturities. Some time deposits may extend as long as seven years, but, on average, they are of fairly short maturity. CDs are bonds of various maturities that the bank issues to investors. While the range of maturities is from 90 days to 10 years, the average is about one year.

In the past, a large part of the loan portfolio of savings and loan (S&L) institutions was in home mortgages, with typical maturities of 15 to 30 years. Today, the bulk of thrifts' portfolios are business loans. The maturities of these loans typically are less than those of mortgages but still generally exceed the maturities of sources of financing. Thus, profits are exposed to interest rate risk. When rates rise, thrifts have to pay higher rates to depositors, while the income from their longer-term investments is relatively fixed.

Banks earn profit from the interest rate spread between loans extended (the bank's assets) and deposits and CDs (the bank's liabilities), as well as from fees for services. Managing bank assets calls for balancing the loan portfolio with the portfolio of deposits and CDs. A bank can increase the interest rate spread by lending to riskier borrowers and by increasing the proportion of longer-term loans. However, both of these policies increase risk. Because bank capital regulations now are risk-based, so higher-risk strategies will elicit higher capital requirements as well as the possibility of greater regulatory interference in the bank's affairs.

As we noted in Chapter 2, most long-term fixed-rate mortgages today are securitized into pass-through certificates and held as securities in the portfolios of mutual funds, pension funds, and other institutional investors. Mortgage originators typically sell a portion of the mortgages they originate to pass-through agencies like Fannie Mae or Freddie Mac rather than holding them in a portfolio. They earn their profits on mortgage origination and servicing fees. The trend away from maintaining portfolio holdings of long-term mortgages also has reduced interest rate risk.

Endowment Funds

Endowment funds are held by organizations chartered to use their money for specific non-profit purposes. They are financed by gifts from one or more sponsors and are typically managed by educational, cultural, and charitable organizations or by independent foundations established solely to carry out the fund's specific purposes. Generally, the investment objectives of an endowment fund are to produce a steady flow of income subject to only a moderate degree of risk. Trustees of an endowment fund, however, can specify other objectives as circumstances dictate.

endowment funds
Portfolios operated for the benefit of a nonprofit entity.

TABLE 22.4   Matrix of objectives

Type of Investor	Return Requirement	Risk Tolerance
Individual and personal trusts	Life cycle (education, children, retirement)	Life cycle (younger are more risk tolerant)
Mutual funds	Variable	Variable
Pension funds	Assumed actuarial rate	Depends on proximity of payouts
Endowment funds	Determined by current income needs and need for asset growth to maintain real value	Generally conservative
Life insurance companies	Should exceed new money rate by sufficient margin to meet expenses and profit objectives; also actuarial rates important	Conservative
Non-life-insurance companies	No minimum	Conservative
Banks	Interest spread	Variable

CONCEPT check   22.1   Describe several distinguishing characteristics of endowment funds that differentiate them from pension funds.

Table 22.4 summarizes the objectives governing these classes of investors.

22.3   INVESTOR CONSTRAINTS

Even with identical attitudes toward risk, different households and institutions might choose different investment portfolios because of their differing circumstances. These circumstances include tax status, requirements for liquidity or a flow of income from the portfolio, or various regulatory restrictions. These circumstances impose *constraints* on investor choice. Together, objectives and constraints determine investment policy.

As noted, constraints usually have to do with investor circumstances. For example, if a family has children about to enter college, there will be a high demand for liquidity because cash will be needed to pay tuition bills. Other times, however, constraints are imposed externally. For example, banks and trusts are subject to legal limitations on the types of assets they may hold in their portfolios. Finally, some constraints are self-imposed. For example, *social investing* means that investors will not hold shares of firms involved in ethically objectionable activities. Some criteria that have been used to judge firms as ineligible for a portfolio are involvement in countries with human rights abuses, production of tobacco or alcohol, and participation in polluting activities.

Five common types of constraints are described below.

Liquidity

liquidity

The speed and ease with which an asset can be converted to cash.

Liquidity is the speed and ease with which an asset can be sold and still fetch a fair price, or the price discount necessary to achieve an immediate sale. It is a relationship between the time dimension (how long it will take to sell) and the price dimension (the discount from fair market price) of an investment asset.

When an actual concrete measure of liquidity is necessary, one thinks of the discount when an immediate sale is unavoidable.[1] Cash and money market instruments such as Treasury bills

---

[1]In many cases, it is impossible to know the liquidity of an asset with certainty until it is put up for sale. In more active markets, however, the liquidity of the traded assets can be observed from the bid–ask spread, that is, the difference between the "bid" quote (the lower price available when someone wishes to sell an asset) and the "ask" quote (the higher price a buyer would have to pay to acquire the asset).

and commercial paper, where the bid–ask spread is a small fraction of 1%, are the most liquid assets, and real estate is among the least liquid. Office buildings and manufacturing structures in extreme cases can suffer a 50% liquidity discount.

Both individual and institutional investors must consider how likely they are to require cash at short notice. From this likelihood, they establish the minimum level of liquid assets they need in the investment portfolio.

Investment Horizon

This is the *planned* liquidation date of the investment. Examples of an individual's **investment horizon** could be the time to fund a college education or the retirement date for a wage earner. For a university or hospital endowment, an investment horizon could relate to the time to fund a major construction project. Horizon dates must be considered when investors choose between assets of various maturities. For example, the maturity date of a bond might make it a more attractive investment if it coincides with a date on which cash is needed. This idea is analogous to the matching principle from corporate finance: Strive to match financing maturity to the economic life of the financed asset.

investment horizon
The planned liquidation date.

Regulations

Only professional and institutional investors are constrained by regulations. First and foremost is the **prudent investor rule.** That is, professional investors who manage other people's money have a fiduciary responsibility to restrict investment to assets that would have been approved by a prudent investor. The law is purposefully nonspecific. Every professional investor must stand ready to defend an investment policy in a court of law, and interpretation may differ according to the standards of the times.

prudent investor rule
The fiduciary responsibility of a professional investor.

Also, specific regulations apply to various institutional investors. For instance, U.S. mutual funds may not hold more than 5% of the shares of any publicly traded corporation.

Sometimes, "self-imposed" regulations also affect the investment choice. We have noted several times, for example, that mutual funds describe their investment policies in a prospectus. These policy guidelines amount to constraints on the ability to choose portfolios freely.

Tax Considerations

Tax consequences are central to investment decisions. The performance of any investment strategy should be measured by its rate of return *after* taxes. For household and institutional investors who face significant tax rates, tax sheltering and deferral of tax obligations may be pivotal in their investment strategy.

Unique Needs

Virtually every investor faces special circumstances. Imagine husband-and-wife aeronautical engineers holding high-paying jobs in the same aerospace corporation. The entire human capital of that household is tied to a single player in a rather cyclical industry. This couple would need to hedge the risk of a deterioration in the economic well-being of the aerospace industry.

Similar issues would confront an executive on Wall Street who owns an apartment near work. Because the value of the home in that part of Manhattan probably depends on the vitality of the securities industry, the individual is doubly exposed to the vagaries of the stock market. Because both job and home already depend on the fortunes of Wall Street, the purchase of a typical diversified stock portfolio would actually increase the exposure to the stock market.

These examples illustrate that the job, or more generally, human capital, is often an individual's biggest "asset," and the unique risk profile that results from employment can play a big role in determining a suitable investment portfolio.

TABLE 22.5	Matrix of constraints			
Type of Investor	**Liquidity**	**Horizon**	**Regulatory**	**Taxes**
Individuals and personal trusts	Variable	Life cycle	Prudent investor laws (for trusts)	Variable
Mutual funds	Low	Short	Little	None
Pension funds	Young, low; mature, high	Long	ERISA	None
Endowment funds	Little	Long	Little	None
Life insurance companies	Low	Long	Complex	Yes
Non-life-insurance companies	High	Short	Little	Yes
Banks	Low	Short	Changing	Yes

Other unique needs of individuals often center around their stage in the life cycle, as previously discussed. Retirement, housing, and children's education constitute three major demands for funds, and investment policy will depend in part on the proximity of these expenditures.

Institutional investors also face unique needs. For example, pension funds will differ in their investment policy, depending on the average age of plan participants. Another example of a unique need for an institutional investor would be a university whose trustees allow the administration to use only cash income from the endowment fund. This constraint would translate into a preference for high-dividend-paying assets.

Table 22.5 presents a matrix of constraints for various investors. As you would expect, liquidity and tax constraints for individuals are variable because of wealth and age differentials.

A particular constraint for mutual funds arises from investor response to the fund's performance. When a mutual fund earns an unsatisfactory rate of return, investors often redeem their shares—they withdraw money from the fund. The mutual fund then contracts. The reverse happens when a mutual fund earns an unusually high return: It can become popular with investors overnight, and its asset base will grow dramatically.

Pension funds are heavily regulated by the Employee Retirement Income Security Act of 1974 (ERISA). This law revolutionized savings for retirement in the United States and remains a major piece of social legislation. Thus, for pension funds, regulatory constraints are relatively important. Also, mature pension funds are required to pay out more than young funds and hence need more liquidity.

Endowment funds, on the other hand, usually do not need to liquidate assets, or even use dividend income, to finance payouts. Contributions are expected to exceed payouts and increase the real value of the endowment fund, so liquidity is not an overriding concern.

Life insurance companies are subject to complex regulation. The corporate tax rate, which today is 35% for large firms, also applies to insurance company investment income, so taxes are an important concern.

Property and casualty insurance, like term life insurance, is written on a short-term basis. Most policies must be renewed annually, which means property and casualty insurance companies are subject to short-term horizon constraints.

The short horizon constraint for banks comes from the interest rate risk component of the interest rate spread (i.e., the risk of interest rate increases that banks face when financing long-term assets with short-term liabilities).

CONCEPT check 22.2

a. Think about the financial circumstances of your closest relative in your parents' generation (for example, your parents' household if you are fortunate enough to have them around). Write down the objectives and constraints for their investment decisions.

b. Now consider the financial situation of your closest friend or relative who is in his or her 30s. Write down the objectives and constraints that would fit his or her investment decision.

c. How much of the difference between the two statements is due to the age of the investors?

On the MARKET FRONT

22.4 INVESTMENT POLICIES

Once objectives and constraints are determined, an investment policy that suits the investor can be formulated. That policy must reflect an appropriate risk-return profile as well as needs for liquidity, income generation, and tax positioning. Institutional investors such as pension plans and endowments often must issue formal statements of their investment policy. These policy statements should be based on, and often make explicit, the objectives and constraints of the investment fund.

The investment policy statement serves as a strategic guide to the planning and implementation of an investment program.[2] When implemented successfully, the IPS anticipates issues related to governance of the investment program, planning for appropriate asset allocation, implementing an investment program with internal and/or external managers, monitoring the results, risk management, and appropriate reporting. The IPS also establishes accountability for the various entities that may work on behalf of an investor. Perhaps, most importantly, the IPS serves as a policy guide that can offer an objective course of action to be followed during periods of disruption when emotional or instinctive responses might otherwise motivate less prudent actions.

The nearby box suggests desirable components of an investment policy statement for use with individual and/or high-net-worth investors. Not every component will be appropriate for every investor or every situation, and there may be other components that are desirable for inclusion reflecting unique investor circumstances.

The following is an example of a portion of a policy statement for a defined benefit pension plan.

The Plan should emphasize production of adequate levels of real return as its primary return objective, giving special attention to the inflation-related aspects of the plan. To the extent consistent with appropriate control of portfolio risk, investment action should seek to maintain or increase the surplus of plan assets relative to benefit liabilities over time. Five-year periods, updated annually, shall be employed in planning for investment decision making; the plan's actuary shall update the benefit liabilities breakdown by country every three years.

The orientation of investment planning shall be long term in nature. In addition, minimal liquidity reserves shall be maintained so long as annual company funding contributions and investment income exceed annual benefit payments to retirees and the operating expenses of the plan. The plan's actuary shall update plan cash flow projections annually. Plan administration shall ensure compliance with all laws and regulations related to maintenance of the plan's tax-exempt status and with all requirements of the Employee Retirement Income Security Act (ERISA).

---

[2]This material is adapted from documents of the CFA Institute that were made available to the authors in draft form. They may differ from the final published documents.

The most important portfolio decision an investor makes is the proportion of the total investment fund allocated to risky as opposed to safe assets. This choice is the most fundamental means of controlling investment risk.

It follows that the first decision an investor must make is the asset allocation decision. Asset allocation refers to the allocation of the portfolio across major asset categories such as:

1. Money market assets (cash equivalents).
2. Fixed-income securities (primarily bonds).
3. Stocks.
4. Non-U.S. stocks and bonds.
5. Real estate.
6. Precious metals and other commodities.

Only after the broad asset classes to be held in the portfolio are determined can one sensibly choose the specific securities to purchase.

Investors who have relatively high degrees of risk tolerance will choose asset allocations more concentrated in higher-risk investment classes, such as equity, to obtain higher expected rates of return. More conservative investors will choose asset allocations with a greater weight in bonds and cash equivalents.

Asset allocation also will depend on expectations for capital market performance in the coming period. (Look back at Figure 22.1 and Table 22.1, and you will see that the CFA Institute classifies this part of the planning process as the formation of "capital market expectations.") Given the risk-return positioning of the investor and the set of expectations, an optimal asset mix may be formed (see step II, Execution, in Table 22.1).

Top-Down Policies for Institutional Investors

Individual investors need not concern themselves with organizational efficiency. But professional investors with large amounts to invest must structure asset allocation activities to decentralize some of the decision making.

A common feature of large organizations is the investment committee and the asset universe. The investment committee includes top management officers, senior portfolio managers, and senior security analysts. The committee determines investment policies and verifies that portfolio managers and security analysts are operating within the bounds of specified policies. A major responsibility of the investment committee is to translate the objectives and constraints of the company into an **asset universe,** an approved list of assets for each of the company's portfolios.

asset universe

Approved list of assets in which a portfolio manager may invest.

Thus, the investment committee has responsibility for broad asset allocation. While the investment manager might have some leeway to tilt the portfolio toward or away from one or another asset class, the investment committee establishes the benchmark allocation that largely determines the risk characteristics of the portfolio. The task of choosing specific securities from the approved universe is more fully delegated to the investment manager.

Figure 22.2 illustrates the stages of the portfolio choice process for Palatial Investments, a hypothetical firm that invests internationally. The first two stages are asset allocation choices. The broadest choice is in the weighting of the portfolio between U.S. and Japanese securities. Palatial has chosen a weight of 75% in the United States and 25% in Japan. The allocation of the portfolio across asset classes may now be determined. For example, 15% of the U.S. portfolio is invested in cash equivalents, 40% in fixed income, and 45% in equity. The asset-class weights are, in general, a policy decision of the investment committee, although the investment manager might have some authority to alter the asset allocation to limited degrees based on her expectations concerning the investment performance of various asset classes. Finally, security selection within each country is determined by the portfolio manager from the approved universe. For example, 45% of funds held in the U.S. equity market will be placed in IBM, 35% in GE, and 20% in ExxonMobil. (We show only three securities in the figure because of space limitations. Obviously a $1 billion fund will hold securities of many more firms.)

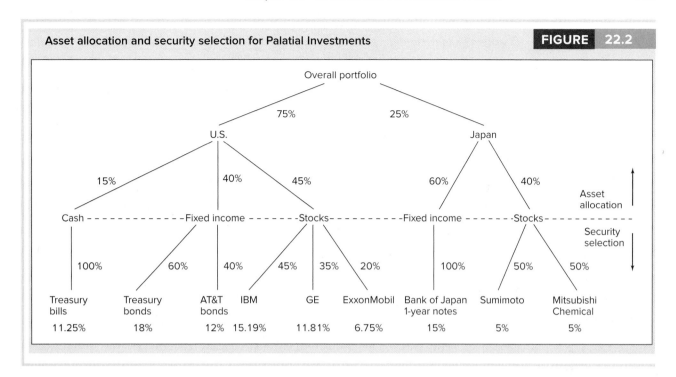

Asset allocation and security selection for Palatial Investments

FIGURE 22.2

These ever-finer decisions determine the proportion of each individual security in the overall portfolio. As an example, consider the determination of the proportion of Palatial's portfolio invested in ExxonMobil, 6.75%. This fraction results from the following decisions: First, the United States receives a weight of 75% of the overall portfolio, and equities comprise 45% of the U.S. component of the portfolio. These are asset allocation choices. ExxonMobil comprises 20% of the U.S. equity component of the portfolio. This is a security selection choice. Therefore, ExxonMobil's weight in the overall portfolio is .75 × .45 × .20 = .0675, or 6.75%. If the entire portfolio is $1 billion, $67,500,000 will be invested in ExxonMobil. If ExxonMobil is selling for $90 a share, 750,000 shares must be purchased. The bottom line in Figure 22.2 shows the percentage of the overall portfolio held in each asset.

This example illustrates a top-down approach that is consistent with the needs of large organizations. The top managers set the overall policy of the portfolio by specifying asset allocation guidelines. Lower-level portfolio managers fill in the details with their security selection decisions.

Active versus Passive Policies

One choice that must be confronted by all investors, individual as well as institutional, is the degree to which the portfolio will be actively versus passively managed. Recall that passive management is based on the belief that security prices usually are close to "fair" levels. Instead of spending time and other resources attempting to "beat the market," that is, to find mispriced securities with unusually attractive risk-return characteristics, the investor simply assumes that she will be fairly compensated for the risk she is willing to take on and selects a portfolio consistent with her risk tolerance.[3]

Passive management styles can be applied to both the security selection and the asset allocation decisions. With regard to asset allocation, passive management simply means that the manager does not depart from his or her "normal" asset-class weightings in response to changing expectations about the performance of different markets. Those "normal" weights are based on the investor's risk and return objectives, as discussed earlier. For example, an asset allocation for a 45-year-old investor of 65% equity, 20% bonds, and 15% cash

[3]We discussed arguments for passive management in previous chapters.

equivalents would be considered fairly conventional. A purely passive manager would not depart from these weights in response to forecasts of market performances. The weighting scheme would be adjusted only in response to changes in risk tolerance as age and wealth change over time.

Next consider passive security selection. Imagine that you must choose a portfolio of stocks without access to any special information about security values. This would be the case if you believed that anything you know about a stock is already known by the rest of the investors in the market and therefore is already reflected in the stock price. If you cannot predict which stocks will be winners, you should broadly diversify your portfolio to avoid putting all your eggs in one basket. A natural course of action for such an investor would be to choose a portfolio with "a little bit of everything."

This reasoning leads one to look for a portfolio that is invested across the entire security market. We saw in Chapter 4 that some mutual fund operators have established index funds that follow just such a strategy. These funds hold each stock or bond in proportion to its representation in a particular index, such as the Standard & Poor's 500 stock price index or the Barclays Capital Aggregate Bond Index. Holding an indexed portfolio represents purely passive security selection in that the investor's return simply duplicates the return of the overall market without making a bet on one or another stock or sector of the market.

In contrast to passive strategies, active management assumes an ability to outguess other investors and to identify either securities or asset classes that will shine in the near future. Active security selection for institutional investors typically requires two layers: security analysis and portfolio choice. Security analysts specialize in particular industries and companies and prepare assessments of their particular market niches. The portfolio managers then sift through the reports of many analysts. They use forecasts of market conditions to make asset allocation decisions and use the security analysts' recommendations to choose the particular securities to include within each asset class.

The choice between active and passive strategies need not be all-or-nothing. One can pursue both active security selection and passive asset allocation, for example. In this case, the manager would maintain fixed asset allocation targets but would actively choose the securities within each asset class. Or one could pursue active asset allocation and passive security selection. In this case, the manager might actively shift the allocation between equity and bond components of the portfolio but hold indexed portfolios within each sector. Another mixed approach is called a *passive core* strategy. In this case, the manager indexes *part* of the portfolio, the passive core, and actively manages the rest of the portfolio.

Is active or passive management the better approach? It might seem at first blush that active managers have the edge because active management is necessary to achieve outstanding performance. But remember that active managers start out with some disadvantages as well. They incur significant costs when preparing their analyses of markets and securities and incur heavier trading costs from the more rapid turnover of their portfolios. If they don't uncover information or insights currently unavailable to other investors (not a trivial task in a nearly efficient market), then all of this costly activity will be wasted, and they will underperform a passive strategy. In fact, low-cost passive strategies have performed surprisingly well in the last few decades, as we saw in Chapters 4 and 8.

CONCEPT check 22.3

Classify the following statements according to where each fits in the objective-constraints-policies framework.

a. Invest 5% in bonds and 95% in stocks.
b. Do not invest more than 10% of the budget in any one security.
c. Shoot for an average rate of return of 11%.
d. Make sure there is $95,000 in cash in the account on December 31, 2030.
e. If the market is bearish, reduce the investment in stocks to 80%.
f. As of next year, we will be in a higher tax bracket.
g. Our new president believes pension plans should take no risk whatsoever with the pension fund.
h. Our acquisition plan will require large sums of cash to be available at any time.

22.5 MONITORING AND REVISING INVESTMENT PORTFOLIOS

Choosing the investment portfolio requires the investor to set objectives, acknowledge constraints, determine asset-class proportions, and perform security analysis. Is the process ever finished and behind us? By the time we have completed all of these steps, many of the inputs we have used will be out of date. Moreover, our circumstances as well as our objectives change over time. Therefore, the investment process requires that we continually monitor and update our portfolios. This is the task of rebalancing, part of the feedback process described earlier in Table 22.1 and Figure 22.1.

Moreover, even when circumstances do not change, our portfolios necessarily will. Suppose you currently hold 1,000 shares of ExxonMobil, selling at $90 a share, and 1,000 shares of Microsoft, selling at $50. If the price of ExxonMobil falls to $80 a share, while that of Microsoft rises to $60, the fractions of your portfolio allocated to each security change without your taking any direct action. The value of your investment in ExxonMobil is now lower, and the value of the Microsoft investment is higher. Unless you are happy with this reallocation of investment proportions, you will need to take some action to restore the portfolio weights to desired levels.

Asset allocation also will change over time, as the investment performance of different asset classes diverges. If the stock market outperforms the bond market, the proportion of your portfolio invested in stocks will increase while the proportion invested in bonds will decrease. If you are uncomfortable with this shift in the asset mix, you must rebalance the portfolio by selling some of the stocks and purchasing bonds.

Therefore, investing is a *dynamic process,* meaning that you must continually update and reevaluate your decisions over time.

- The CFA Institute has developed a systematic framework for the translation of investor goals to investment strategy. Its three main parts are objectives, constraints, and policy. Investor objectives include the return requirement and risk tolerance, reflecting the overriding concern of investment with the risk-return trade-off. Investor constraints include liquidity requirements, investment horizon, regulatory concerns, tax obligations, and the unique needs of various investors. Investment policies specify the portfolio manager's asset allocation and security selection decisions.
- Major institutional investors include pension funds, mutual funds, life insurance companies, non-life-insurance companies, banks, and endowment funds. For individual investors, life-cycle concerns are the most important factor in setting objectives, constraints, and policies.
- Major asset classes include cash (money market assets), fixed-income securities (bonds), stocks, real estate, precious metals, and collectibles. Asset allocation refers to the decision made as to the investment proportion to be allocated to each asset class. An active asset allocation strategy calls for the production of frequent market forecasts and the adjustment of asset allocation according to these forecasts.
- Active security selection requires security analysis and portfolio choice. Analysis of individual securities is required to choose securities that will make up a coherent portfolio and outperform a passive benchmark.
- Perhaps the most important feature of the investment process is that it is dynamic. Portfolios must be continually monitored and updated. The frequency and timing of various decisions are in themselves important decisions. Successful investment management requires management of these dynamic aspects.

SUMMARY

KEY TERMS

asset universe, 718	liquidity, 714	personal trust, 710
endowment funds, 713	mutual fund, 710	prudent investor rule, 715
investment horizon, 715		

PROBLEM SETS

Select problems are available in McGraw-Hill's *Connect.* Please see the Supplements section of the book's frontmatter for more information.

1. You are being interviewed for a job as a portfolio manager at an investment counseling partnership. As part of the interview, you are asked to demonstrate your ability to develop investment portfolio policy statements for the clients listed below:

   a. A pension fund that is described as a mature defined benefit plan, with the workforce having an average age of 54, no unfunded pension liabilities, and wage cost increases forecast at 5% annually.

   b. A university endowment fund that is described as conservative, with investment returns being utilized along with gifts and donations received to meet current expenses, the spending rate is 5% per year, and inflation in costs is expected at 3% annually.

   c. A life insurance company that is described as specializing in annuities; policy premium rates are based on a minimum annual accumulation rate of 7% in the first year of the policy and a 4% minimum annual accumulation rate in the next five years.

   List and discuss separately for *each* client described above the objectives and constraints that will determine the portfolio policy you would recommend for that client.   *(LO 22-3)*

CFA Problems

1. You are P. J. Walter, CFA, a managing partner of a prestigious investment counseling firm that specializes in individual rather than institutional accounts. The firm has developed a national reputation for its ability to blend modern portfolio theory and traditional portfolio methods. You have written a number of articles on portfolio management. You are an authority on the subject of establishing investment policies and programs for individual clients, tailored to their particular circumstances and needs.

   Dr. and Mrs. A. J. Mason have been referred to your firm and to you in particular. At your first meeting on June 2, 2015, Dr. Mason explained that he is an electrical engineer and long-time professor at the Essex Institute. He is also an inventor, and, after 30 years of teaching, the rights to one of his patented inventions, the "inverse thermothrocle valve," have just been acquired by a new electronics company, ACS, Inc.

   In anticipation of the potential value of his invention, Dr. Mason had followed his accountant's advice and established a private corporation, wholly owned by the Masons, to hold the title to the inverse thermothrocle valve patent. It was this corporation that ACS acquired from the Masons for $1 million in cash, payable at the closing on June 7, 2015. In addition, ACS has agreed to pay royalties to Dr. Mason or his heirs based on its sales of systems that utilize the inverse thermothrocle valve.

   Because ACS has no operating record, it is difficult for either the company or Dr. Mason to forecast future sales and royalties. While all parties are optimistic about prospects for success, they are also mindful of the risks associated with any new firm, especially those exposed to the technological obsolescence of the electronics industry. The management of ACS has indicated to Dr. Mason that he might expect royalties of as much as $100,000 in the first year of production and maximum royalties of as much as $500,000 annually thereafter.

   During your counseling meeting, Mrs. Mason expressed concern for the proper investment of the $1,000,000 initial payment. She pointed out that Dr. Mason has invested all of their savings in his inventions. Thus, they will have only their Social Security retirement benefits and a small pension from the Essex Institute to provide for their retirement. Dr. Mason will be 65 in 2019. His salary from the Essex Institute is $55,000 per year. Additionally, he expects to continue earning $10,000 to $25,000 annually from consulting and speaking engagements.

The Masons have two daughters and a son, all of whom are married and have families of their own. Dr. and Mrs. Mason are interested in helping with the education of their grandchildren and have provided in their wills for their estate to be divided among their children and grandchildren.

In the event that the royalty payments from ACS meet the projections cited above, Mrs. Mason is interested in providing a scholarship fund in the name of Dr. Mason for the benefit of enterprising young engineers attending the Essex Institute. The scholarship fund ranks third behind the provision for the Masons' retirement and for the education of their grandchildren.

In your discussions with Dr. and Mrs. Mason, you have stressed the importance of identifying investment objectives and constraints and having an appropriate investment policy. Identify and describe an appropriate set of investment objectives and investment constraints for Dr. and Mrs. Mason, and prepare a comprehensive investment policy statement based on these investment objectives and constraints. *(LO 22-1, 22-2)*

2. Your client says, "With the unrealized gains in my portfolio, I have almost saved enough money for my daughter to go to college in eight years, but educational costs keep going up." Based on this statement alone, which one of the following appears to be least important to your client's investment policy? *(LO 22-2)*
   a. Time horizon
   b. Purchasing power risk
   c. Liquidity
   d. Taxes

3. The aspect least likely to be included in the portfolio management process is: *(LO 22-3)*
   a. Identifying an investor's objectives, constraints, and preferences.
   b. Organizing the management process itself.
   c. Implementing strategies regarding the choice of assets to be used.
   d. Monitoring market conditions, relative values, and investor circumstances.

4. A clearly written investment policy statement is critical for: *(LO 22-3)*
   a. Mutual funds.
   b. Individuals.
   c. Pension funds.
   d. All investors.

5. The investment policy statement of an institution must be concerned with all of the following *except:* *(LO 22-3)*
   a. Its obligations to its clients.
   b. The level of the market.
   c. Legal regulations.
   d. Taxation.

6. Under the provisions of a typical corporate defined benefit pension plan, the employer is responsible for: *(LO 22-2)*
   a. Paying benefits to retired employees.
   b. Investing in conservative fixed-income assets.
   c. Counseling employees in the selection of asset classes.
   d. Maintaining an actuarially determined, fully funded pension plan.

7. Which of the following statements reflects the importance of the asset allocation decision to the investment process? The asset allocation decision: *(LO 22-3)*
   a. Helps the investor decide on realistic investment goals.
   b. Identifies the specific securities to include in a portfolio.
   c. Determines most of the portfolio's returns and volatility over time.
   d. Creates a standard by which to establish an appropriate investment time horizon.

8. You are a portfolio manager and senior executive vice president of Advisory Securities Selection, Inc. Your firm has been invited to meet with the trustees of the Wood Museum Endowment Funds. Wood Museum is a privately endowed charitable institution that is

dependent on the investment return from a $25 million endowment fund to balance the budget. The treasurer of the museum has recently completed the budget that indicates a need for cash flow of $3 million in 2016, $3.2 million in 2017, and $3.5 million in 2018 from the endowment fund to balance the budget in those years. Currently, the entire endowment portfolio is invested in Treasury bills and money market funds because the trustees fear a financial crisis. The trustees do not anticipate any further capital contributions to the fund.

The trustees are all successful businesspeople, and they have been critical of the fund's previous investment advisers because they did not follow a logical decision-making process. In fact, several previous managers have been dismissed because of their inability to communicate with the trustees and their preoccupation with the fund's relative performance rather than the cash flow needs.

Advisory Securities Selection, Inc., has been contacted by the trustees because of its reputation for understanding and relating to the client's needs. The trustees have asked you, as a prospective portfolio manager for the Wood Museum Endowment Fund, to prepare a written report in response to the following questions. Your report will be circulated to the trustees before the initial interview on June 15, 2016.

Explain in detail how each of the following relates to the determination of either investor objectives or investor constraints that can be used to determine the portfolio policies for this three-year period for the Wood Museum Endowment Fund.
(LO 22-1, 22-2)

a. Liquidity requirements.
b. Return requirements.
c. Risk tolerance.
d. Time horizon.
e. Tax considerations.
f. Regulatory and legal considerations.
g. Unique needs and circumstances.

9. Mrs. Mary Atkins, age 66, has been your firm's client for five years, since the death of her husband, Dr. Charles Atkins. Dr. Atkins had built a successful newspaper business that he sold two years before his death to Merit Enterprises, a publishing and broadcasting conglomerate, in exchange for Merit common stock. The Atkinses have no children, and their wills provide that upon their deaths the remaining assets shall be used to create a fund for the benefit of Good Samaritan Hospital, to be called the Atkins Endowment Fund.

Good Samaritan is a 180-bed, not-for-profit hospital with an annual operating budget of $12.5 million. In the past, the hospital's operating revenues have often been sufficient to meet operating expenses and occasionally even generate a small surplus. In recent years, however, rising costs and declining occupancy rates have caused Good Samaritan to run a deficit. The operating deficit has averaged $300,000 to $400,000 annually over the last several years. Existing endowment assets (that is, excluding the Atkins's estate) of $7.5 million currently generate approximately $375,000 of annual income, up from less than $200,000 five years ago. This increased income has been the result of somewhat higher interest rates, as well as a shift in asset mix toward more bonds. To offset operating deficits, the Good Samaritan Board of Governors has determined that the endowment's current income should be increased to approximately 6% of total assets (up from 5% currently). The hospital has not received any significant additions to its endowment assets in the past five years.

Identify and describe an appropriate set of investment objectives and constraints for the Atkins Endowment Fund to be created after Mrs. Atkins's death. *(LO 22-1, 22-2)*

10. Several discussion meetings have provided the following information about one of your firm's new advisory clients, a charitable endowment fund recently created by means of a one-time $10 million gift:

Objectives

Return requirement. Planning is based on a minimum total return of 8% per year, including an initial current income component of $500,000 (5% on beginning capital). Realizing this current income target is the endowment fund's primary return goal. (See "unique needs" below.)

Constraints

Time horizon. Perpetuity, except for requirement to make an $8,500,000 cash distribution on June 30, 2017. (See "unique needs.")

Liquidity needs. None of a day-to-day nature until 2017. Income is distributed annually after year-end. (See "unique needs.")

Tax considerations. None; this endowment fund is exempt from taxes.

Legal and regulatory considerations. Minimal, but the prudent investor rule applies to all investment actions.

Unique needs, circumstances, and preferences. The endowment fund must pay out to another tax-exempt entity the sum of $8,500,000 in cash on June 30, 2017. The assets remaining after this distribution will be retained by the fund in perpetuity. The endowment fund has adopted a "spending rule" requiring a first-year current income payout of $500,000; thereafter, the annual payout is to rise by 3% in real terms. Until 2017, annual income in excess of that required by the spending rule is to be reinvested. After 2017, the spending rate will be reset at 5% of the then-existing capital.

With this information and information found in this chapter, do the following:

(LO 22-3)

a. Formulate an appropriate investment policy statement for the endowment fund.

b. Identify and briefly explain three major ways in which your firm's initial asset allocation decisions for the endowment fund will be affected by the circumstances of the account.

11. You have been named as investment adviser to a foundation established by Dr. Walter Jones with an original contribution consisting entirely of the common stock of Jomedco, Inc. Founded by Dr. Jones, Jomedco manufactures and markets medical devices invented by the doctor and collects royalties on other patented innovations.

All of the shares that made up the initial contribution to the foundation were sold at a public offering of Jomedco common stock, and the $5 million proceeds will be delivered to the foundation within the next week. At the same time, Mrs. Jones will receive $5 million in proceeds from the sale of her stock in Jomedco.

Dr. Jones's purpose in establishing the Jones Foundation was to "offset the effect of inflation on medical school tuition for the maximum number of worthy students."

You are preparing for a meeting with the foundation trustees to discuss investment policy and asset allocation. *(LO 22-1, 22-2, 22-3)*

a. Define and give examples that show the differences between an investment objective, an investment constraint, and investment policy.

b. Identify and describe an appropriate set of investment objectives and investment constraints for the Jones Foundation.

c. Based on the investment objectives and investment constraints identified in part *(b)*, prepare a comprehensive investment policy statement for the Jones Foundation to be recommended for adoption by the trustees.

The proper asset allocation for an investor planning for retirement changes dramatically over time. Investors who do *not* frequently update their asset allocation could be caught in a tragic investment scenario that significantly delays retirement. This is exactly what occurred in 2008, when many investors planning for retirement realized they had not reallocated their portfolios away from stocks and into fixed-income securities over the years, as they should have.

WEB *master*

Go to **money.cnn.com** and under the *Personal Finance* tab, select *Calculators*. Then choose the Asset Allocation calculator in the *Investing* category. Calculate an asset allocation for the following two scenarios:

A. Need the money: 20 + years

How much risk: As much as possible

How flexible: If I miss my goal . . . OK

During market sell-offs: See an opportunity to buy

B. Need the money: 3–5 years

How much risk: Not much at all

How flexible: I can't afford to miss my target

During market sell-offs: Do nothing

1. What is the ratio of stock to bonds in each scenario? Notice the dramatic shift from risky assets to safe assets. How would this change have impacted an investor during the stock market crash of 2008?

2. Explain the impact on an investor planning to retire in 3–5 years if the investor had maintained asset allocation A and not asset allocation B during the 2008 stock market crash.

3. How frequently do you think investors should examine their asset allocation? What else should investors review on a periodic basis in addition to asset allocation?

SOLUTIONS TO
CONCEPT
checks

22.1 A convenient and effective way to organize the answer to this question is to cast it in the context of the investment policy statement framework.

Risk: Endowment funds have no "safety nets" such as pension funds enjoy in the event of difficulty, either in the form of corporate assets to fall back on or a call on public assistance, such as from the Pension Benefit Guaranty Corporation. Moreover, endowment fund cash flows may be highly erratic due to the uncertain timing of income from gifts and/or bequests, while pension fund cash flows tend to be very predictable and steady. These differences suggest the typical endowment fund will adopt a more conservative risk-bearing posture than will the typical pension fund, both to asset-class exposures and to the type of security content of such exposures.

Return: Because investment-related spending usually is limited to "income yield," endowment funds often focus their return goals on the matter of current spendable income; pension funds, on the other hand, tend to adopt total return approaches, at least until a plan matures. Although inflation protection should be of great importance to both types of funds, endowment funds appear to be less concerned with real return production than are pension funds, perhaps because of their common emphasis on "income now" in setting return goals.

Time horizon: Theoretically, an endowment fund is a perpetuity, while a pension fund may well have a finite life span. Therefore, an endowment fund should operate with a very long-term view of investment. However, such funds in practice tend to adopt shorter horizons than are typical of pension funds (just as they typically assume less risk). Their tendency to emphasize income production in the near term is the probable reason for this common occurrence.

Liquidity: Endowment funds, particularly those that use gifts and bequests to supplement their investment income, often have fairly large liquidity reserves— both to protect against fluctuations in their cash flows and to reflect their generally conservative outlooks—while, except for very mature plans, pension funds tend to require minimum liquidity reserves. Endowment funds also frequently maintain substantial liquid holdings to provide for known future cash payout requirements, such as for new buildings.

Taxes: Here, although differing in detail, the situations of the two forms of institutions are very much the same. In the United States, tax considerations are normally of minimal importance in both cases.

Regulatory/legal: Endowment fund investment is carried out under state governance, while pension fund investment, in the United States, is carried out under federal law, specifically under ERISA. The difference is significant. Endowment funds operate under the prudent investor rule, whereby each investment must be judged on its own merits apart from any other portfolio holdings, while pension plans operate under a broader context for investment—each security being judged in terms of the portfolio as a whole—and an ERISA-mandated diversification requirement that often leads to wider asset-class exposures.

Unique circumstances: Endowment funds often are faced with unique situations that sometimes affect pension fund management, including the scrutiny of such special-interest groups as trustees, alumni, faculty, student organizations, local community pressure groups, etc., each with separate and often incompatible constraints and goals that may need to be accommodated in policy setting and/or in investment content. Similarly, endowment funds may be subjected to severe "social pressures" that, as in the case of tobacco firm divestment, can have an important investment impact by restricting the available universe of investment securities, mandating participation or nonparticipation in certain industries, sectors, or countries, or otherwise changing investment action from what it would otherwise have been. In pension fund investment, ERISA mandates that no other interests be put ahead of the interests of the beneficiaries in determining investment actions.

22.2 Identify the elements that are life-cycle driven in the two schemes of objectives and constraints.

22.3 *a.* Policy, asset allocation.
   b. Constraint, regulation.
   c. Objective, return requirement.
   d. Constraint, horizon.
   e. Policy, market timing.
   f. Constraint, taxes.
   g. Objectives, risk tolerance.
   h. Constraint, liquidity.

Appendix A

References

Affleck-Graves, John, and Richard R. Mendenhall. "The Relation between the Value Line Enigma and Post-Earnings-Announcement Drift." *Journal of Financial Economics* 31 (February 1992), pp. 75–96.

Agarwal, Vikas; Naveen D. Daniel; and Narayan Y. Naik. "Why Is Santa So Kind to Hedge Funds? The December Return Puzzle!" March 29, 2007, **http://ssrn.com/abstract=891169.**

Alexander, C. *Market Models.* Chichester, England: Wiley, 2001.

Alexander, Sidney. "Price Movements in Speculative Markets: Trends or Random Walks, No. 2." In *The Random Character of Stock Market Prices,* ed. Paul Cootner. Cambridge, MA: MIT Press, 1964.

Amihud, Yakov, and Haim Mendelson. "Asset Pricing and the Bid-Ask Spread." *Journal of Financial Economics* 17 (December 1986), pp. 223–50.

———. "Liquidity, Asset Prices, and Financial Policy." *Financial Analysts Journal* 47 (November–December 1991), pp. 56–66.

Amin, G., and H. Kat. "Stocks, Bonds and Hedge Funds: Not a Free Lunch!" *Journal of Portfolio Management* 29 (Summer 2003), pp. 113–20.

Aragon, George O. "Share Restrictions and Asset Pricing: Evidence from the Hedge Fund Industry." *Journal of Financial Economics* 83 (2007), pp. 33–58.

Arbel, Avner. "Generic Stocks: An Old Product in a New Package." *Journal of Portfolio Management,* Summer 1985, pp. 4–13.

Arbel, Avner, and Paul J. Strebel. "Pay Attention to Neglected Firms." *Journal of Portfolio Management,* Winter 1983, pp. 37–42.

Arnott, Robert. "Orthodoxy Overwrought." *Institutional Investor,* December 18, 2006.

Asness, Cliff. "The Value of Fundamental Indexing." *Institutional Investor,* October 16, 2006, pp. 94–99.

Ben-David, Itzhak; Francesco Franzoni; Augustin Landier; and Rabih Moussawi. "Do Hedge Funds Manipulate Stock Prices?" *Journal of Finance* 68 (December 2013), pp. 2383–2434.

Ball, R., and P. Brown. "An Empirical Evaluation of Accounting Income Numbers." *Journal of Accounting Research* 9 (1968), pp. 159–78.

Banz, Rolf. "The Relationship between Return and Market Value of Common Stocks." *Journal of Financial Economics* 9 (March 1981), pp. 3–18.

Barber, B.; R. Lehavy; M. McNichols; and B. Trueman. "Can Investors Profit from the Prophets? Security Analysts Recommendations and Stock Returns." *Journal of Finance* 56 (April 2001), pp. 531–63.

Barber, Brad, and Terrance Odean. "Trading Is Hazardous to Your Wealth: The Common Stock Investment Performance of Individual Investors." *Journal of Finance* 55 (2000), pp. 773–806.

———. "Boys Will Be Boys: Gender, Overconfidence, and Common Stock Investment." *Quarterly Journal of Economics* 16 (2001), pp. 262–92.

Barberis, Nicholas, and Richard Thaler. "A Survey of Behavioral Finance." In *The Handbook of the Economics of Finance,* ed. G. M. Constantinides, M. Harris, and R. Stulz. Amsterdam: Elsevier, 2003.

Basu, Sanjoy. "The Investment Performance of Common Stocks in Relation to Their Price-Earnings Ratios: A Test of the Efficient Market Hypothesis." *Journal of Finance* 32 (June 1977), pp. 663–82.

———. "The Relationship between Earnings Yield, Market Value, and Return for NYSE Common Stocks: Further Evidence." *Journal of Financial Economics* 12 (June 1983), pp. 129–56.

Battalio, R. H., and R. Mendenhall. "Earnings Expectation, Investor Trade Size, and Anomalous Returns around Earnings Announcements." *Journal of Financial Economics* 77 (2005), pp. 289–319.

Benveniste, Lawrence, and William Wilhelm. "Initial Public Offerings: Going by the Book." *Journal of Applied Corporate Finance* 10 (March 1997), pp. 98–108.

Bergstresser, D.; M. Desai; and J. Rauh. "Earnings Manipulation, Pension Assumptions, and Managerial Investment Decisions." *Quarterly Journal of Economics* 121 (2006), pp. 157–95.

Berk, J. B., and R. C. Green. "Mutual Fund Flows and Performance in Rational Markets." *Journal of Political Economy* 112 (2004), pp. 1269–95.

Bernard, Victor L., and Jacob K. Thomas. "Post-Earnings-Announcement Drift: Delayed Price Response or Risk Premium?" *Journal of Accounting Research* 27 (1989), pp. 1–36.

Bernard, V., and J. Thomas. "Evidence That Stock Prices Do Not Fully Reflect the Implications of Current Earnings for Future Earnings." *Journal of Accounting and Economics* 13 (1990), pp. 305–40.

Bernhard, Arnold. *Value Line Methods of Evaluating Common Stocks.* New York: Arnold Bernhard, 1979.

Black, Fischer. "Yes, Virginia, There Is Hope: Tests of the Value Line Ranking System." Graduate School of Business, University of Chicago, 1971.

Black, Fischer; Michael C. Jensen; and Myron Scholes. "The Capital Asset Pricing Model: Some Empirical Tests." In *Studies in the Theory of Capital Markets,* ed. Michael C. Jensen. New York: Praeger, 1972.

Black, Fischer, and Myron Scholes. "The Pricing of Options and Corporate Liabilities." *Journal of Political Economy* 81 (May–June 1973), pp. 637–59.

"From Black-Scholes to Black Holes: New Frontiers in Options." London: *Risk* Magazine, 1992.

Blake, Christopher; Edwin J. Elton; and Martin J. Gruber. "The Performance of Bond Mutual Funds." *Journal of Business* 66 (July 1993), pp. 371–404.

Blume, Marshall E., and Robert F. Stambaugh. "Biases in Computed Returns: An Application to the Size Effect." *Journal of Finance Economics,* 1983, pp. 387–404.

Bogle, John C. "Investing in the 1990s: Remembrance of Things Past, and Things Yet to Come." *Journal of Portfolio Management,* Spring 1991, pp. 5–14.

———. *Bogle on Mutual Funds.* Burr Ridge, IL: Irwin, 1994.

Bollen, Nicolas P. B., and Jeffrey A. Busse. "Short-Term Persistence in Mutual Fund Performance." *Review of Financial Studies* 19 (2004), pp. 569–97.

Brav, Alon; Christopher Geczy; and Paul A. Gompers. "Is the Abnormal Return Following Equity Issuances Anomalous?" *Journal of Financial Economics* 56 (2000), pp. 209–49.

Brennan, Michael. "Taxes, Market Valuation and Corporate Financial Policy." *National Tax Journal,* 1970.

Brinson, G.; C. R. Hood; and G. Beebower. "Determinants of Portfolio Performance." *Financial Analysts Journal,* July–August 1986.

Brinson, Gary; Brian Singer; and Gilbert Beebower. "Determinants of Portfolio Performance." *Financial Analysts Journal,* May–June 1991.

Brock, William; Josef Lakonishok; and Blake LeBaron. "Simple Technical Trading Rules and the Stochastic Properties of Stock Returns." *Journal of Finance* 47 (December 1992), pp. 1731–64.

Brown, David, and Robert H. Jennings. "On Technical Analysis." *Review of Financial Studies* 2 (1989), pp. 527–52.

Brown, Lawrence D., and Michael Rozeff. "The Superiority of Analysts' Forecasts as Measures of Expectations: Evidence from Earnings." *Journal of Finance,* March 1978.

Brown, S. J.; W. N. Goetzmann; and B. Liang. "Fees on Fees in Funds of Funds." *Journal of Investment Management* 2 (2004), pp. 39–56.

Busse, J. A., and T. C. Green. "Market Efficiency in Real Time." *Journal of Financial Economics* 65 (2002), pp. 415–37.

Campbell, John Y., and Robert Shiller. "Stock Prices, Earnings and Expected Dividends." *Journal of Finance* 43 (July 1988), pp. 661–76.

Carhart, Mark. "On Persistence in Mutual Fund Performance." *Journal of Finance* 52 (1997), pp. 57–82.

Chen, Nai-fu; Richard Roll; and Stephen Ross. "Economic Forces and the Stock Market." *Journal of Business* 59 (1986), pp. 383–403.

Chen, Y.; W. E. Ferson; and H. Peters. "Measuring the Timing Ability and Performance of Bond Mutual Funds." *Journal of Financial Economics* 98 (2010), pp. 72–89.

Chopra, Navin; Josef Lakonishok; and Jay R. Ritter. "Measuring Abnormal Performance: Do Stocks Overreact?" *Journal of Financial Economics* 31 (1992), pp. 235–68.

Chordia, Tarun; Avanidhar Subrahmanyam; and Qing Tong. "Trends in the Cross-Section of Expected Stock Return." 2012, available at SSRN, **http://ssrn .com/abstract=2029057** or **http://dx.doi .org/10.2139/ssrn.2029057.**

Clarke, Roger, and Mark P. Kritzman. *Currency Management: Concepts and Practices.* Charlottesville: Research Foundation of the Institute of Chartered Financial Analysts, 1996.

Clayman, Michelle. "In Search of Excellence: The Investor's Viewpoint." *Financial Analysts Journal,* May–June 1987.

Connolly, Robert. "An Examination of the Robustness of the Weekend Effect." *Journal of Financial and Quantitative Analysis* 24 (June 1989), pp. 133–69.

Conrad, Jennifer, and Gautam Kaul. "Time-Variation in Expected Returns." *Journal of Business* 61 (October 1988), pp. 409–25.

Copeland, Thomas E., and David Mayers. "The Value Line Enigma (1965–1978): A Case Study of Performance Evaluation Issues." *Journal of Financial Economics,* November 1982.

Coval, Joshua D., and Tyler Shumway. "Do Behavioral Biases Affect Prices?" *Journal of Finance* 60 (February 2005), pp. 1–34.

Cremers, Martijn; Antti Petajisto; and Eric Zitzewitz. "Should Benchmark Indices Have Alpha? Revisiting Performance Evaluation." *Critical Finance Review* 2 (2013), pp. 1–48.

Davis, James L.; Eugene F. Fama; and Kenneth R. French. "Characteristics, Covariances, and Average Returns, 1929 to 1997." *Journal of Finance* 55 (2000), pp. 389–406.

De Bondt, W.F.M., and R. H. Thaler. "Does the Stock Market Overreact?" *Journal of Finance* 40 (1985), pp. 793–805.

———. "Further Evidence on Investor Overreaction and Stock Market Seasonality." *Journal of Finance* 42 (1987), pp. 557–81.

———. "Do Security Analysts Overreact?" *American Economic Review* 80 (1990), pp. 52–57.

———. "Financial Decision Making in Markets and Firms." In *Handbooks in Operations Research and Management Science, Vol. 9: Finance,* ed. R. A. Jarrow, V. Maksimovic, and W. T. Ziemba. Amsterdam: Elsevier, 1995.

Del Guercio, Diane, and Jonathan Reuter. "Mutual Fund Performance and the Incentive to Generate Alpha." *Journal of Finance* 69 (2014), pp. 1673–1704.

DeLong, J. Bradford; Andrei Schleifer; Lawrence Summers; and Robert Waldmann. "Noise Trader Risk in Financial Markets." *Journal of Political Economy* 98 (August 1990), pp. 704–38.

DeMarzo, Peter M.; Ron Kaniel; and Ilan Kremer. "Diversification as a Public Good: Community Effects in Portfolio Choice." *Journal of Finance* 59 (August 2004), pp. 1677–1716.

de Soto, Hernando. *The Mystery of Capital: Why Capitalism Triumphs in the West and Fails Everywhere Else.* New York: Basic Books, 2000.

Dimson, E.; P. R. Marsh; and M. Staunton. *Millennium Book II: 101 Years of Investment Returns.* London: ABN-Amro and London Business School, 2001.

Douglas, George W. "Risk in Equity Markets: An Empirical Appraisal of Market Efficiency." *Yale Economic Essays* IX (Spring 1969).

Dunn, Patricia, and Rolf D. Theisen. "How Consistently Do Active Managers Win?" *Journal of Portfolio Management* 9 (Summer 1983), pp. 47–53.

Errunza, Vihang, and Etienne Losq. "International Asset Pricing under Mild Segmentation: Theory and Test." *Journal of Finance* 40 (March 1985), pp. 105–24.

Fama, Eugene. "The Behavior of Stock Market Prices." *Journal of Business* 38 (January 1965), pp. 34–105.

———. "Market Efficiencies, Long-Term Returns, and Behavioral Finance." *Journal of Financial Economics* 49 (September 1998), pp. 283–306.

Fama, Eugene, and Marshall Blume. "Filter Rules and Stock Market Trading Profits." *Journal of Business* 39 (Supplement, January 1966), pp. 226–41.

Fama, Eugene F., and Kenneth R. French. "Permanent and Temporary Components of Stock Prices." *Journal of Political Economy* 96 (1988), pp. 246–73.

———. "Dividend Yields and Expected Stock Returns." *Journal of Financial Economics* 22 (October 1988), pp. 3–25.

———. "Business Conditions and Expected Returns on Stocks and Bonds." *Journal of Financial Economics* 25 (November 1989), pp. 3–22.

———. "The Cross Section of Expected Stock Returns." *Journal of Finance* 47 (June 1992), pp. 427–65.

———. "Common Risk Factors in the Returns on Stocks and Bonds." *Journal of Financial Economics* 33 (1993), pp. 3–56.

———. "Multifactor Explanations of Asset Pricing Anomalies." *Journal of Finance* 51 (1996), pp. 55–84.

———. "The Equity Premium." *Journal of Finance* 57 (April 2002), pp. 637–60.

———. "Luck versus Skill in the Cross-Section of Mutual Fund Returns." *Journal of Finance* 65 (2010), pp. 1915–47.

Fama, Eugene, and James MacBeth. "Risk, Return and Equilibrium: Empirical Tests." *Journal of Political Economy* 81 (March 1973).

Fisher, Irving. *The Theory of Interest: As Determined by Impatience to Spend Income and Opportunity to Invest It.* New York: Augustus M. Kelley, 1965, originally published in 1930.

Flannery, Mark J., and Christopher M. James. "The Effect of Interest Rate Changes on the Common Stock Returns of Financial Institutions." *Journal of Finance* 39 (September 1984), pp. 1141–54.

Foster, George; Chris Olsen; and Terry Shevlin. "Earnings Releases, Anomalies, and the Behavior of Security Returns." *The Accounting Review* 59 (October 1984).

French, Kenneth. "Stock Returns and the Weekend Effect." *Journal of Financial Economics* 8 (March 1980), pp. 55–69.

Froot, K. A., and E. M. Dabora. "How Are Stock Prices Affected by the Location of Trade?" *Journal of Financial Economics* 53 (1999), pp. 189–216.

Fung, William, and David Hsieh. "Empirical Characteristics of Dynamic Trading Strategies: The Case of Hedge Funds." *Review of Financial Studies* 10 (1997), pp. 275–302.

———. "Performance Characteristics of Hedge Funds and CTA Funds: Natural versus Spurious Biases." *Journal of Financial and Quantitative Analysis* 35 (2000), pp. 291–307.

Gervais, S., and T. Odean. "Learning to Be Overconfident." *Review of Financial Studies* 14 (2001), pp. 1–27.

Geske, Robert, and Richard Roll. "On Valuing American Call Options with the Black-Scholes European Formula." *Journal of Finance* 39 (June 1984), pp. 443–56.

Getmansky, Mila; Andrew W. Lo; and Igor Makarov. "An Econometric Model of Serial Correlation and Illiquidity in Hedge Fund Returns." *Journal of Financial Economics* 74 (2004), pp. 529–609.

Ghysels, E.; A. Harvey; and E. Renault. "Stochastic Volatility." In *Statistical Methods in Finance,* eds. C. Rao and G. Maddala. Amsterdam: Elsevier Science, North-Holland Series in Statistics and Probability, 1996.

Gibbons, Michael, and Patrick Hess. "Day of the Week Effects and Asset Returns." *Journal of Business* 54 (October 1981), pp. 579–98.

Givoly, Dan, and Dan Palmon. "Insider Trading and Exploitation of Inside Information: Some Empirical Evidence." *Journal of Business* 58 (1985), pp. 69–87.

Goetzmann, William N., and Roger G. Ibbotson. "Do Winners Repeat?" *Journal of Portfolio Management,* Winter 1994, pp. 9–18.

Graham, J. R., and C. R. Harvey. "Grading the Performance of Market Timing Newsletters." *Financial Analysts Journal* 53 (November–December 1997), pp. 54–66.

———. "Expectations of Equity Risk Premia, Volatility and Asymmetry from a Corporate Finance Perspective." 2001, available at SSRN, **http://ssrn.com/abstract=292623**.

Grieves, Robin, and Alan J. Marcus. "Riding the Yield Curve: Reprise." *Journal of Portfolio Management,* Winter 1992.

Grinblatt, Mark, and Bing Han. "Prospect Theory, Mental Accounting, and Momentum." *Journal of Financial Economics* 78 (November 2005), pp. 311–39.

Grinblatt, Mark, and Sheridan Titman. "Mutual Fund Performance: An Analysis of Quarterly Portfolio Holdings." *Journal of Business* 62 (1989), pp. 393–416.

Grossman, Sanford J., and Joseph E. Stiglitz. "On the Impossibility of Informationally Efficient Markets." *American Economic Review* 70 (June 1980), pp. 393–408.

Hasanhodzic, Jasmina, and Andrew W. Lo. "Can Hedge Fund Returns Be Replicated? The Linear Case." *Journal of Investment Management* 5 (2007), pp. 5–45.

Haugen, Robert A. *The New Finance: The Case against Efficient Markets.* Englewood Cliffs, NJ: Prentice Hall, 1995.

Henriksson, Roy D. "Market Timing and Mutual Fund Performance: An Empirical Investigation." *Journal of Business* 57 (January 1984).

Heston, S. L. "A Closed-Form Solution for Options with Stochastic Volatility with Applications to Bonds and Currency Options." *Review of Financial Studies* 6 (1993), pp. 327–43.

Hirshleifer, David. "Investor Psychology and Asset Pricing." *Journal of Finance* 56 (August 2001), pp. 1533–97.

Homer, Sidney, and Martin L. Leibowitz. *Inside the Yield Book: New Tools for Bond Market Strategy.* Englewood Cliffs, NJ: Prentice Hall, 1972.

Hull, J. C., and A. White. "The Pricing of Options on Assets with Stochastic Volatilities." *Journal of Finance* 42 (1987), pp. 281–300.

Ibbotson, Roger G. "Price Performance of Common Stock New Issues." *Journal of Financial Economics* 2 (September 1975).

Ibbotson, Roger; Richard C. Carr; and Anthony W. Robinson. "International Equity and Bond Returns." *Financial Analysts Journal,* July–August 1982.

Ibbotson, R. G., and L. B. Siegel. "The World Market Wealth Portfolio." *Journal of Portfolio Management,* Winter 1983.

Ibbotson, R. G.; L. B. Siegel; and K. Love. "World Wealth: Market Values and Returns." *Journal of Portfolio Management,* Fall 1985.

Jacquier, Eric, and Alan Marcus. "Asset Allocation Models and Market Volatility." *Financial Analysts Journal* 57 (March–April 2001), pp. 16–30.

Jaffe, Jeffrey F. "Special Information and Insider Trading." *Journal of Business* 47 (July 1974), pp. 410–28.

———. "Gold and Gold Stocks as Investments for Institutional Portfolios." *Financial Analysts Journal* 45 (March–April 1989), pp. 53–59.

Jagannathan, R.; E. R. McGrattan; and A. Scherbina. "The Declining U.S. Equity Premium." *Federal Reserve Bank of Minneapolis Quarterly Review* 24 (Fall 2000), pp. 3–19.

Jagannathan, Ravi, and Zhenyu Wang. "The Conditional CAPM and the Cross-Section of Expected Returns." *Staff Report 208,* Federal Reserve Bank of Minneapolis, 1996.

Jegadeesh, Narasimhan. "Evidence of Predictable Behavior of Security Returns." *Journal of Finance* 45 (September 1990), pp. 881–98.

Jegadeesh, N.; J. Kim; S. D. Krische; and C. M. Lee. "Analyzing the Analysts: When Do Recommendations Add Value?" *Journal of Finance* 59 (June 2004), pp. 1083–1124.

Jegadeesh, Narasimhan, and Sheridan Titman. "Returns to Buying Winners and Selling Losers: Implications for Stock Market Efficiency." *Journal of Finance* 48 (March 1993), pp. 65–91.

Jensen, Michael C. "The Performance of Mutual Funds in the Period 1945–1964." *Journal of Finance,* May 1968.

———. "Risk, the Pricing of Capital Assets, and the Evaluation of Investment Portfolios." *Journal of Business* 42 (April 1969), pp. 167–247.

Kahneman, D., and A. Tversky. "Subjective Probability: A Judgment of Representativeness." *Cognitive Psychology* 3 (1972), pp. 430–54.

———. "On the Psychology of Prediction." *Psychology Review* 80 (1973), pp. 237–51.

Keim, Donald B. "Size Related Anomalies and Stock Return Seasonality: Further Empirical Evidence." *Journal of Financial Economics* 12 (June 1983), pp. 13–32.

Keim, Donald B., and Robert F. Stambaugh. "Predicting Returns in the Stock and Bond Markets." *Journal of Financial Economics* 17 (1986), pp. 357–90.

Kendall, Maurice. "The Analysis of Economic Time Series, Part I: Prices." *Journal of the Royal Statistical Society* 96 (1953), pp. 11–25.

Kopcke, Richard W., and Geoffrey R. H. Woglom. "Regulation Q and Savings Bank Solvency—The Connecticut Experience." In *The Regulation of Financial Institutions,* Federal Reserve Bank of Boston Conference Series, No. 21, 1979.

Kosowski, R.; A. Timmermann; R. Wermers; and H. White. "Can Mutual Fund 'Stars' Really Pick Stocks? New Evidence from a Bootstrap Analysis." *Journal of Finance* 61 (December 2006), pp. 2551–95.

Kothari, S. P.; Jay Shanken; and Richard G. Sloan. "Another Look at the Cross-Section of Expected Stock Returns." *Journal of Finance* 50 (March 1995), pp. 185–224.

Kotlikoff, Laurence J., and Avia Spivack. "The Family as an Incomplete Annuities Market." *Journal of Political Economy* 89, no. 2 (April 1981), pp. 372–91.

Kotlikoff, Laurence J., and Lawrence H. Summers. "The Role of Intergenerational Transfers in Aggregate Capital Accumulation." *Journal of Political Economy* 89, no. 4 (August 1981), pp. 706–32.

Lakonishok, Josef; Andrei Shleifer; and Robert W. Vishny. "Contrarian Investment, Extrapolation, and Risk." *Journal of Finance* 50 (1995), pp. 1541–78.

Lamont, O. A., and R. H. Thaler. "Can the Market Add and Subtract? Mispricing in Tech Carve-Outs." *Journal of Political Economy* 111 (2003), pp. 227–68.

La Porta, Raphael. "Expectations and the Cross-Section of Stock Returns." *Journal of Finance* 51 (December 1996), pp. 1715–42.

Latane, H. A., and C. P. Jones. "Standardized Unexpected Earnings—1971–1977." *Journal of Finance,* June 1979.

Lease, R.; W. Lewellen; and G. Schlarbaum. "Market Segmentation: Evidence on the Individual Investor." *Financial Analysts Journal* 32 (1976), pp. 53–60.

Lee, C. M.; A. Shleifer; and R. H. Thaler. "Investor Sentiment and the Closed-End Fund Puzzle." *Journal of Finance* 46 (March 1991), pp. 75–109.

Lehmann, Bruce. "Fads, Martingales and Market Efficiency." *Quarterly Journal of Economics* 105 (February 1990), pp. 1–28.

Levy, Robert A. "The Predictive Significance of Five-Point Chart Patterns." *Journal of Business* 44 (July 1971), pp. 316–23.

Liebowitz, Martin L., and Alfred Weinberger. "Contingent Immunization—Part I: Risk Control Procedure." *Financial Analysts Journal* 38 (November–December 1982).

Lo, Andrew W., and Craig MacKinlay. "Stock Market Prices Do Not Follow Random Walks: Evidence from a Simple Specification Test." *Review of Financial Studies* 1 (Spring 1988), pp. 41–66.

Loeb, T. F. "Trading Cost: The Critical Link between Investment Information and Results." *Financial Analysts Journal,* May–June 1983.

Longin, F., and B. Solnik. "Is the Correlation in International Equity Returns Constant: 1960–1990?" *Journal of International Money and Finance* 14 (1995), pp. 3–26.

Lynch, Peter, with John Rothchild. *One Up on Wall Street.* New York: Penguin Books, 1989.

Macaulay, Frederick. *Some Theoretical Problems Suggested by the Movements of Interest Rates, Bond Yields, and Stock Prices in the United States since 1856.* New York: National Bureau of Economic Research, 1938.

Malkiel, Burton G. "Expectations, Bond Prices, and the Term Structure of Interest Rates." *Quarterly Journal of Economics* 76 (May 1962), pp. 197–218.

———. "Returns from Investing in Equity Mutual Funds: 1971–1991." *Journal of Finance* 50 (June 1995), pp. 549–72.

Malkiel, Burton G., and Atanu Saha. "Hedge Funds: Risk and Return." *Financial Analysts Journal* 61 (2005), pp. 80–88.

Malmendier, U., and G. Tate. "Who Makes Acquisitions? CEO Overconfidence and the Market's Reaction." *Journal of Financial Economics* 89 (July 2008) pp. 20–43.

Marcus, Alan J. "The Magellan Fund and Market Efficiency." *Journal of Portfolio Management* 17 (Fall 1990), pp. 85–88.

Mayers, David. "Nonmarketable Assets and Capital Market Equilibrium under Uncertainty." In *Studies in the Theory of Capital Markets,* ed. M. C. Jensen. New York: Praeger, 1972.

McDonald, Robert L. *Derivative Markets,* 2nd ed. Boston: Addison-Wesley, 2005.

McLean, R. David, and Jeffrey E. Pontiff. "Does Academic Research Destroy Stock Return Predictability," *Journal of Finance,* forthcoming (2015).

Merton, Robert C. "Theory of Rational Option Pricing." *Bell Journal of Economics and Management Science* 4 (Spring 1973), pp. 141–83.

———. "On Market Timing and Investment Performance: An Equilibrium Theory of Value for Market Forecasts." *Journal of Business* 54 (July 1981).

———. "A Simple Model of Capital Market Equilibrium with Incomplete Information." *Journal of Finance* 42 (1987), pp. 483–510.

Miller, Merton H., and Myron Scholes. "Rate of Return in Relation to Risk: A Reexamination of Some Recent Findings." In *Studies in the Theory of Capital Markets,* ed. Michael C. Jensen. New York: Praeger, 1972.

Modigliani, Franco, and M. Miller. "The Cost of Capital, Corporation Finance, and the Theory of Investment." *American Economic Review,* June 1958.

———. "Dividend Policy, Growth, and the Valuation of Shares." *Journal of Business,* October 1961.

Modigliani, Franco, and Leah Modigliani. "Risk-Adjusted Performance." *Journal of Portfolio Management,* Winter 1997, pp. 45–54.

Morrell, John A. "Introduction to International Equity Diversification." In *International Investing for U.S. Pension Funds,* Institute for Fiduciary Education, London/Venice, May 6–13, 1989.

Niederhoffer, Victor, and Patrick Regan. "Earnings Changes, Analysts' Forecasts, and Stock Prices." *Financial Analysts Journal,* May–June 1972.

Norby, W. C. "Applications of Inflation-Adjusted Accounting Data." *Financial Analysts Journal,* March–April 1983.

Odean, T. "Are Investors Reluctant to Realize Their Losses?" *Journal of Finance* 53 (1998), pp. 1775–98.

Patel, J. M., and M. A. Wolfson. "The Intraday Speed of Adjustment of Stock Prices to Earnings and Dividend Announcements." *Journal of Financial Economics* 13 (June 1984), pp. 223–52.

Perold, André. "Fundamentally Flawed Indexing." HBS mimeo, January 2007.

Perry, Kevin, and Robert A. Taggart. "The Growing Role of Junk Bonds in Corporate Finance." *Continental Bank Journal of Applied Corporate Finance* 1 (Spring 1988).

Pontiff, Jeffrey. "Closed-End Fund Premia and Returns Implications for Financial Market Equilibrium." *Journal of Financial Economics* 37 (1995), pp. 341–70.

———. "Costly Arbitrage: Evidence from Closed-End Funds." *Quarterly Journal of Economics* 111 (November 1996), pp. 1135–51.

Porter, Michael E. *Competitive Strategy: Techniques for Analyzing Industries and Competitors.* New York: Free Press, 1980.

———. *Competitive Advantage: Creating and Sustaining Superior Performance.* New York: Free Press, 1985.

Poterba, James M., and Lawrence Summers. "Mean Reversion in Stock Market Prices: Evidence and Implications." *Journal of Financial Economics* 22 (1988), pp. 27–59.

Rau, P. R.; O. Dimitrov; and M. Cooper. "A Rose.com by Any Other Name." *Journal of Finance* 56 (2001), pp. 2371–88.

Ready, Mark J. "Profits from Technical Trading Rules." *Financial Management* 31 (Autumn 2002), pp. 43–62.

Redington, F. M. "Review of the Principle of Life-Office Valuations." *Journal of the Institute of Actuaries* 78 (1952), pp. 286–340.

Reinganum, Marc R. "The Anomalous Stock Market Behavior of Small Firms in January: Empirical Tests for Tax-Loss Effects." *Journal of Financial Economics* 12 (June 1983), pp. 89–104.

———. "The Anatomy of a Stock Market Winner." *Financial Analysts Journal,* March–April 1988, pp. 272–84.

Rendleman, Richard J., Jr.; Charles P. Jones; and Henry A. Latané. "Empirical Anomalies Based on Unexpected Earnings and the Importance of Risk Adjustments." *Journal of Financial Economics* 10 (November 1982), pp. 269–87.

Ritter, Jay R. "The Buying and Selling Behavior of Individual Investors at the Turn of the Year." *Journal of Finance* 43 (July 1988), pp. 701–17.

Roberts, Harry. "Stock Market 'Patterns' and Financial Analysis: Methodological Suggestions." *Journal of Finance* 14 (March 1959), pp. 11–25.

Roll, Richard. "A Critique of the Capital Asset Theory Tests: Part I: On Past and Potential Testability of the Theory." *Journal of Financial Economics* 4 (1977).

———. "The International Crash of October 1987." *Financial Analysts Journal,* September–October 1988.

Ross, Stephen A. "Return, Risk and Arbitrage." In *Risk and Return in Finance,* ed. I. Friend and J. Bicksler. Cambridge, MA: Ballinger, 1976.

———. "Neoclassical Finance, Alternative Finance and the Closed End Fund Puzzle." *European Financial Management* 8 (2002), pp. 129–37, **ssrn.com/abstract=313444.**

Rubinstein, Mark. "Implied Binomial Trees." *Journal of Finance* 49 (July 1994), pp. 771–818.

Sadka, Ronnie. "Liquidity Risk and the Cross-Section of Hedge-Fund Returns." *Journal of Financial Economics* 98 (October 2010), pp. 54–71.

Samuelson, Paul. "The Judgment of Economic Science on Rational Portfolio Management." *Journal of Portfolio Management* 16 (Fall 1989), pp. 4–12.

Schleifer, Andrei. *Inefficient Markets.* New York: Oxford University Press, 2000.

Schleifer, Andrei, and Robert Vishny. "Equilibrium Short Horizons of Investors and Firms." *American Economic Review* 80 (May 1990), pp. 148–53.

———. "The Limits of Arbitrage." *Journal of Finance* 52 (March 1997), pp. 35–55.

Seyhun, H. Nejat. "Insiders' Profits, Costs of Trading and Market Efficiency." *Journal of Financial Economics* 16 (1986), pp. 189–212.

Sharpe, William F. "A Simplified Model for Portfolio Analysis." *Management Science* IX (January 1963), pp. 277–93.

———. "Mutual Fund Performance." *Journal of Business* 39 (January 1966).

———. "Asset Allocation: Management Style and Performance Evaluation." *Journal of Portfolio Management,* Winter 1992, pp. 7–19.

Shefrin, Hersh. *Beyond Greed and Fear.* Boston: Harvard Business School Press, 2002.

Shefrin, Hersh, and Meir Statman. "The Disposition to Sell Winners Too Early and Ride Losers Too Long: Theory and Evidence." *Journal of Finance* 40 (July 1985), pp. 777–90.

Shiller, Robert. "Do Stock Prices Move Too Much to Be Justified by Subsequent Changes in Dividends?" *American Economic Review* 71 (June 1981).

Solnik, B. *International Investing,* 4th ed. Reading, MA: Addison-Wesley, 1999.

Solnik, Bruno, and A. De Freitas. "International Factors of Stock Price Behavior." CESA Working Paper, February 1986 (cited in Bruno Solnik, *International Investments.* Reading, MA: Addison-Wesley, 1988).

Speidell, Lawrence S., and Vinod Bavishi. "GAAP Arbitrage: Valuation Opportunities in International Accounting Standards." *Financial Analysts Journal,* November–December 1992, pp. 58–66.

Statman, Meir. "Behavioral Finance." *Contemporary Finance Digest* 1 (Winter 1997), pp. 5–22.

Statman, Meir. "What Is Behavioral Finance?" *Handbook of Finance,* vol. II, chap. 9 (2008), pp. 79–84.

Statman, Meir; Kenneth L. Fisher; and Deniz Anginer. "Affect in a Behavioral Asset-Pricing Model." *Financial Analysts Journal* 64 (2008), pp. 20–29.

Stickel, Scott E. "The Effect of Value Line Investment Survey Rank Changes on Common Stock Prices." *Journal of Financial Economics* 14 (1986), pp. 121–44.

Taleb, Nassim N. *Fooled by Randomness: The Hidden Role of Chance in Life and in the Markets.* New York: TEXERE (Thomson), 2004.

———. *The Black Swan: The Impact of the Highly Improbable.* New York: Random House, 2007.

Thaler, Richard H. *The Winner's Curse.* Princeton, NJ: Princeton University Press, 1992.

———. *Advances in Behavioral Finance.* New York: Russell Sage Foundation, 1993.

Tobin, James. "Liquidity Preference as Behavior toward Risk." *Review of Economic Studies* XXVI (February 1958), pp. 65–86.

Treynor, Jack L. "How to Rate Management Investment Funds." *Harvard Business Review* 43 (January–February 1965).

Treynor, Jack, and Fischer Black. "How to Use Security Analysis to Improve Portfolio Selection." *Journal of Business* 46 (January 1973).

Treynor, Jack L., and Kay Mazuy. "Can Mutual Funds Outguess the Market?" *Harvard Business Review* 43 (July–August 1966).

Trippi, Robert R., and Duane Desieno. "Trading Equity Index Futures with Neural Networks." *Journal of Portfolio Management* 19 (Fall 1992).

Trippi, Robert R.; Duane Desieno; and Efraim Turban, eds. *Neural Networks in Finance and Investing.* Chicago: Probus, 1993.

Wallace, A. "Is Beta Dead?" *Institutional Investor* 14 (July 1980), pp. 22–30.

Wermers, R. R. "Mutual Fund Performance: An Empirical Decomposition into Stock-Picking Talent, Style, Transaction Costs, and Expenses." *Journal of Finance* 55 (2000), pp. 1655–1703.

Whaley, Robert E. "Valuation of American Call Options on Dividend-Paying Stocks: Empirical Tests." *Journal of Financial Economics* 10 (1982), pp. 29–58.

Wiggins, J. B. "Option Values under Stochastic Volatilities." *Journal of Financial Economics* 19 (1987), pp. 351–72.

Womack, K. L. "Do Brokerage Analysts' Recommendations Have Investment Value?" *Journal of Finance* 51 (March 1996), pp. 137–67.

Appendix B

References to CFA Questions

Each end-of-chapter CFA question is reprinted with permission from the CFA Institute, Charlottesville, Virginia.[1] Following is a list of the CFA questions in the end-of-chapter material and the exams/study guides from which they were taken and updated.

Chapter 2

CFA 1. 1986 Level II CFA
Study Guide, © 1986.

Chapter 3

CFA 1–2. 1986 Level I CFA Study
Guide, © 1986.

Chapter 5

CFA 1–3. 1998 Level I CFA Study
Guide, © 1998.

CFA 4–6. 1991 Level I CFA Study
Guide, © 1991.

CFA 7–11. 1993 Level I CFA Study
Guide, © 1993.

Chapter 6

CFA 1. 1998 Level I CFA Study
Guide, © 1998.

CFA 2. 2001 Level III CFA
Study Guide, © 2001.

CFA 3. 2001 Level II CFA
Study Guide, © 2001.

CFA 4–6. 1982 Level III CFA
Study Guide, © 1982.

CFA 7. 2000 Level II CFA
Study Guide, © 2000.

Chapter 7

CFA 1. 1998 Level I CFA Study
Guide, © 1998.

CFA 2. 2000 Level II CFA
Study Guide, © 2000.

[1]The CFA Institute does not endorse, promote, review, or warrant the accuracy of the product or services offered by McGraw-Hill Education.

CFA 3. 2002 Level II CFA
Study Guide, © 2002.

CFA 4. 2001 Level II CFA
Study Guide, © 2001.

CFA 5–14. Various CFA exams.

Chapter 8

CFA 1–5. 1993 Level I CFA Study
Guide, © 1993.

CFA 6. 1998 Level I CFA Study
Guide, © 1998.

CFA 7. 1981 Level I CFA Study
Guide, © 1981.

CFA 8. 1989 Level III CFA
Study Guide, © 1989.

CFA 9. 1996 Level III CFA
Study Guide, © 1996.

CFA 10. 1996 Level III CFA
Study Guide, © 1996.

CFA 11. 1996 Level III CFA
Study Guide, © 1996.

Chapter 9

CFA 1. 2000 Level III CFA
Study Guide, © 2000.

CFA 2. 2001 Level III CFA
Study Guide, © 2001.

CFA 3. 2004 Level III CFA
Study Guide, © 2004.

CFA 4. 2003 Level III CFA
Study Guide, © 2003.

CFA 5. 2002 Level III CFA
Study Guide, © 2002.

Chapter 10

CFA 1. From various CFA
exams.

CFA 2. 1999 Level II CFA
Study Guide, © 1999.

CFA 3. 1992 Level II CFA
Study Guide, © 1992.

CFA 4. 1993 Level I CFA Study
Guide, © 1993.

CFA 5. 1994 Level I CFA Study
Guide, © 1994.

Chapter 11

CFA 1. 1985 Level I CFA Study
Guide, © 1985.

CFA 2. 1985 Level I CFA Study
Guide, © 1985.

CFA 3. 1992 Level II CFA
Study Guide, © 1992.

CFA 4. 1983 Level III CFA
Study Guide, © 1983.

CFA 5. 2001 Level II CFA
Study Guide, © 2001.

CFA 6. 2003 Level II CFA
Study Guide, © 2003.

CFA 7. 2004 Level II CFA
Study Guide, © 2004.

CFA 8–9. 1983 Level III CFA
Study Guide, © 1983.

CFA 10. From various CFA
exams.

CFA 11–12. 1983 Level III CFA Study
Guide, © 1983.

Chapter 12

CFA 1. 1995 Level II CFA
Study Guide, © 1995.

CFA 2. 1993 Level II CFA
Study Guide, © 1993.

CFA 3. 1993 Level II CFA
Study Guide, © 1993.

CFA 4. 1998 Level II CFA
Study Guide, © 1998.

CFA 5. From various CFA
exams.

Chapter 13

CFA 1. 1995 Level II CFA
Study Guide, © 1995.

CFA 2. 1987 Level I CFA Study
Guide, © 1987.

CFA 3. 2001 Level II CFA Study Guide, © 2001.

CFA 4. 1994 Level II CFA Study Guide, © 1994.

CFA 5. 2003 Level I CFA Study Guide, © 2003.

CFA 6. 2003 Level I CFA Study Guide, © 2003.

CFA 7. 2003 Level II CFA Study Guide, © 2003.

CFA 8. 2001 Level II CFA Study Guide, © 2001.

CFA 9. 2001 Level II CFA Study Guide, © 2001.

CFA 10. 2001 Level II CFA Study Guide, © 2001.

Chapter 14

CFA 1. 2002 Level II CFA Study Guide, © 2002.

CFA 2. 1988 Level I CFA Study Guide, © 1988.

CFA 3. 1998 Level II CFA Study Guide, © 1998.

CFA 4. 1987 Level I CFA Study Guide, © 1987.

CFA 5. 1998 Level II CFA Study Guide, © 1998.

CFA 6. 1999 Level II CFA Study Guide, © 1999.

CFA 7. 1998 Level II CFA Study Guide, © 1998.

Chapter 15

CFA 1. 1984 Level III CFA Study Guide, © 1984.

CFA 2. 2000 Level II CFA Study Guide, © 2000.

CFA 3. 1984 Level III CFA Study Guide, © 1984.

CFA 4. 2001 Level II CFA Study Guide, © 2001.

CFA 5. 2002 Level II CFA Study Guide, © 2002.

Chapter 16

CFA 1. 2000 Level I CFA Study Guide, © 2000.

CFA 2. 2000 Level I CFA Study Guide, © 2000.

CFA 3. 2000 Level II CFA Study Guide, © 2000.

Chapter 17

CFA 1–3. 1998 Level I CFA Study Guide, © 1998.

CFA 4. 1982 Level III CFA Study Guide, © 1982.

CFA 5. 1986 Level III CFA Study Guide, © 1986.

CFA 6. 2000 Level II CFA Study Guide, © 2000.

CFA 7. 1993 Level I CFA Study Guide, © 1993.

CFA 8. 2000 Level III Study Guide, © 2000.

CFA 9. 2004 Level II CFA Study Guide, © 2004.

Chapter 18

CFA 1. From various CFA exams.

CFA 2. 1981 Level I Study Guide, © 1981.

CFA 3. 1981 Level I Study Guide, © 1981.

CFA 4. 2000 Level I Study Guide, © 2000.

Chapter 19

CFA 1. 1986 Level III Study Guide, © 1986.

CFA 2. 1986 Level III Study Guide, © 1986.

CFA 3. 1991 Level II Study Guide, © 1991.

CFA 4. 1998 Level II Study Guide, © 1998.

Chapter 22

CFA 1. 1984 Level II CFA Study Guide, © 1984.

CFA 2. 1988 Level I CFA Study Guide, © 1988.

CFA 3. 1988 Level I CFA Study Guide, © 1988.

CFA 4. From various CFA exams.

CFA 5. From various CFA exams.

CFA 6. 1981 Level II CFA Study Guide, © 1981.

CFA 7. 1985 Level III CFA Study Guide, © 1985.

CFA 8. 1988 Level I CFA Study Guide, © 1988.

CFA 9. 1982 Level III CFA Study Guide, © 1982.

CFA 10–11. From various CFA exams.

Index

Entries in **bold** indicate a definition on that page. Page numbers with *f* indicate material found in figures; *n*, notes; and *t*, tables.

A

Accenture, 67
Accounting
  fair value, 465–467
  GAAP, 464, 467, 468–469
  IFRS, 468–469
Accounting earnings, 445
Accrued interest, 292–293, 301
Acid test ratio, 457
Active investment strategy, 334
Active management, 11, 591; *see also* Hedge funds; International investing; Investors; Personal finance; Portfolio performance evaluation
  bonds, 334, 354–356
  ETFs, 96
  expenses, 139
  international investing and, 626, 628t, 651, 653
  as investment policy decision, 719–720
  mutual funds and, 99
  overconfidence and, 266
  overview, 591
  passive management versus, 239–240
  rates of return, 100f
Active portfolio, 166, **175**–176, 177t, 195
Adjustable rate mortgages (ARMs), 18
Adjusted R-square, 205
Adobe Systems, 274–275, 385, 413t
ADRs (American Depositary Receipts), 40, 639
Adverse selection, 702
Affect, in behavioral finance, 268
Agarwal, Vikas, 672
Agency problems, 7–8, 19, 38
AIG (American International Group), 20, 21, 319, 483
Alexander, C., 536n
Algorithmic trading, 65, **66,** 67
Alibaba, 57
Allen, F., 272n7

Allowance for bad debt, 466
Alpha, 169, 199; *see also* Capital asset pricing model
  in CAPM, 193
  hedge funds, 671–672
  mutual fund benchmarks and, 253–255
  portable, 665–668
  in portfolio performance evaluation, 598–600
Alpha transfer, 665–666
American Depositary Receipts (ADRs), 40, 639
American International Group (AIG), 20, 21, 319, 483
American options, 487, 539
American Stock Exchange (Amex), 65, 68, 640
Ameritrade, 69
Amihud, Yakov, 209, 246
Analysis; *see also* Financial statement analysis; Fundamental analysis; Industry analysis; Macroeconomic analysis; Ratio analysis; Technical analysis
  horizon, 307, 355
  mean-variance, 125, 200
  scenario, 116–117, 121–122
  security, 10, 174–176, 177t, 369, 376–377
  style, 601–603
Analysts, mutual fund, 252–256
Analysts, stock market, 250, 252
Angel, James J., 60n, 64n
Angel investors, 15
Anginer, Deniz, 268, 732
Annual percentage rate (APR), 113–114
Annual percentage yield (APY), 114
Annuity factor, 297–298
Anomalies, 245
  interpretation of, 249–251
  semistrong tests and, 244–249
AOL Time Warner, 445n
Apple Inc., 46–47, 55, 56, 67, 216t, 390

APR (annual percentage rate), 113–114
APY (annual percentage yield), 114
Aragon, George O., 670–671
Arbel, Avner, 245
Arbitrage, 214
  convertible bond, 664
  covered interest, 633–634
  futures contracts and, 572–575
  index, 577–578
  limits to, 269–272
  options and, 524, 530, 537–538
  statistical, 665
Arbitrage portfolio, 215–218
Arbitrage pricing theory (APT), 214
  CAPM and, 218
  introduction, 192–193
  multifactor generalization of, 218–220
  well-diversified portfolios and, 215–218
Archipelago ECN, 68
Archipelago Exchange, 63, 65
ARCH models, 208, 536
Arithmetic average, 111–112, 131
ARMs (adjustable rate mortgages), 18
Arthur Andersen, 9
Asian options, 508
Ask price, 27, 59
Asset allocation, 9, 133
  active versus passive policies, 719–720
  asset classes and, 26
  of complete portfolio, 161–162
  by institutional investors, 718–719
  international diversification, 651
  investment performance and, 601, 608–611
  investment policy statements and, 718
  mutual fund benchmarks and, 253
  portable alpha and, 665
  rebalancing and, 721
  risky assets or portfolios and, 133–137

Asset allocation—*Cont.*
  target date retirement funds, 703n
  with two risky assets
    covariance and correlation,
      150–153
    historical data usage, 153–154
    mean-variance criterion,
      157–159
    risk-return trade-off, 155–157
    rules, 154–155
Asset allocation funds, 89
Asset-backed bonds, 295
Asset-backed commercial paper, 28
Asset-backed securities, 37–38
Asset beta, 206n
Asset classes and financial
    instruments
  bond market, 32–38
  derivative markets, 46–48
  equity securities, 38–40
  indexes, 40–46
  money market, 27–32
Asset location, 697–699
Asset plays, 392
Assets
  financial, 3–6, 12, 13t, 709
  human capital as, 709, 715
  real, 3–5
Asset universe, 718
Asset utilization ratios, 454–457, 460t
Atlantic Richfield, 278
ATO (total asset turnover), 452
AT&T, 452t, 452
At the money, 486
Auction markets, 59
Auditors, 9
Autonomy Corp., 445n, 467–468
Average collection period, 456–457

B

Back-end load, 91–92
Backfill bias, 672–673
Baginski, Stephen, 455n
Balanced funds, 89
Balance sheet, 445
  financial assets on, 3, 12,
    13t, 446t
  restructuring with swaps, 582
Ball, R., 247
Bank-discount method, 27–28
Bankers' acceptances, 29
Bank of America, 14, 21, 68,
  404, 458
Banks, as professional investors,
  713, 716
Banz, Rolf, 245, 246f
Barber, B., 252, 266

Barberis, Nicholas, 265n
Barclays, 30, 45, 127, 404
Barclays Aggregate Bond Index,
  356, 609
Barclays Capital U.S. Aggregate
  Bond Index, 239, 608, 720
Barclay's Global Investors, 95
Barings Bank, 483
Barron's, 279
Basel accord, 122
Basis, 570
Basis risk, 570
Basu, Sanjoy, 245
BATS exchange, 60, 62, 64, 65
Battalio, R. H., 247n
Bavishi, Vinod, 469f
Bear markets, 650–651
Bear Stearns, 14, 76, 289
Behavioral finance, 265; *see also*
  Technical analysis
  arbitrage limits, 269–272
  biases, 267–269
  bubbles and, 272–273
  critique of, 265, 273–274
  information processing, 266–267
  introduction, 264–265
  law of one price, 270–272
Benchmarks
  bond market, 239, 356, 608,
    609, 720
  choosing, 459
  international markets, 95, 96t,
    640, 653
  mutual funds, 253–255
  in portfolio evaluation, 608
  S&P 500, 176, 200–201, 253,
    594, 608, 625, 720
Ben-David, Itzhak, 672
Bequests, 703
Bergstresser, D., 466
Berk, J. B., 255
Berkshire Hathaway, 216t, 256
Bernard, V., 247n
Bernard L. Madoff Investment
  Securities, 678
Bernstein, Mr., 710
Beta, 169; *see also* Capital asset
  pricing model
  anomalies and, 245–247, 250
  equity beta versus asset beta, 206n
  expected return relationship, 197–198
  portfolio performance evaluation
    and, 598–600, 605
  predicting, 208
  real-world evidence, 208–209
  in single-index model, 170–171
Beta coefficient, 194

Biases
  behavioral, 267–269
  home-country, 630
  information processing, 266–267
  selection, 241–242
  survivorship, 672–673
Bid-ask spread, 27, 58, **59**–63, 69,
  714–715
Bid price, 27, **59**
Binary options, 508
Binomial model, 527
Binomial option pricing
  practical applications, 526–529
  two-state, 522–525
  two-state generalization, 525–526
Black, Fischer, 175, 209, 530
BlackRock, 95, 96t
Black-Scholes option valuation
  empirical evidence, 545–546
  financial crisis of 2008-2009 and,
    544–545
  hedge ratios and, 539–541
  incentive fees, 677
  introduction, 529–536
  market timing and, 614
  portfolio insurance, 541–544
  put-call parity relationship, 536–539
  put option valuation, 539
Black-Scholes pricing formula,
  530–536
Black swans, 676
Blake, Christopher, 255
Blocks, 67
Blue Cross, 702
Blue sky laws, 76
B/M (book-to-market) ratio,
  211–212, 250
Bogey, 608
Bogle, John, 133
Bollen, Nicholas P. B., 255
Bond characteristics
  accrued interest, 292–293, 301
  call provisions, 36, 293–294,
    502–503
  convertibility, 36, 294, 503–505
  government agency, 33, 37f, 295
  innovative features, 295–297
  international bonds, 33, 295
  municipal bonds, 295
  preferred stock features and, 40,
    294–295
  price and yield relationship, 299,
    299f, 335–337
  tax features, 34–36
  Treasury bonds and notes, 291–293
Bond-equivalent yield, 28
Bond funds, 88, 89, 90t, 255–256

Bond indentures, 291, 314–315
Bond market
  asset-backed securities, 37–38
  benchmark indexes, 239, 356, 608, 609, 720
  components, 46f
  corporate bonds, 36
  Federal agency debt, 33, 37f, 295
  innovation in, 295–297
  international bonds, 33, 295
  introduction, 289
  mortgages and MBS, 36–37
  municipal bonds, 34–36
  Treasury notes and bonds, 32–33
Bond market indexes, 45–46
Bond maturity
  duration concept, 337–341
  duration rules, 341–343
  interest rate risk and, 335–337
Bond portfolio management
  active strategies, 334, 354–356
  convexity, 350–353
  interest rate risk
    duration concept, 337–341
    duration rules, 341–343
    interest rate sensitivity, 335–337
  introduction, 334–335
  passive strategies
    cash flow matching and dedication, 349–350
    immunization, 343–349
Bond prices and yields; *see also* Duration
  after-tax returns and, 310–311
  calculations, 298–299, 301–302
  convexity and, 350–353
  between coupon dates, 300–301
  default risk and pricing
    bond indentures, 291, 314–315
    credit default swaps, 317–319
    junk bonds, 312
    safety determinants, 312–314
    yield to maturity and, 315–317
  introduction, 289–291
  over time, 308–311
  present value, 297–300
  Treasury notes and bonds, 32–33
  Treasury STRIPS, 310
  yield-price relationship, 229, 299f, 335–337
  yield to maturity versus holding-period return, 309–310
  zero-coupon bonds, 310
Bonds, 291; *see also* Bond characteristics
  asset-backed, 295
  collateralized, 315

corporate, 35–36, 293–294, 299–300
  floating-rate, 294
  indexed, 296–297
  innovative, 295–297
  international, 33, 295
  investment grade, 312
  long-term, 335–337, 342
  mortgage, 36–37, 315
  original-issue discount, 310
  predictors of returns in, 244
  puttable, 294
  rating agencies, 19, 28, 289, 312, 313f, 314, 387, 427
  as risky debt, 507
  serial, 315
  sheltered versus unsheltered plans, 697–699
  speculative grade, 312
  straight, 502–505
  trading, 59, 64, 68
Bond swaps, 354–355
Bond yields
  realized compound return versus yield to maturity, 306–307
  yield curve and, 319–324
  yield to call, 304–306
  yield to maturity, 302–304
Book, 57
Bookbuilding, 57
Book-to-market effect, 246–247, 249–250
Book-to-market (B/M) ratio, 211–212, 250
Book value, 403–404, 458
Borsa Italiana, 68
Boston Stock Exchange, 68
Bowie, David, 295
BP, 411
Bradshaw, Mark, 455n
Brane v. Roth, 495
Brazil, 626
Breadth, 277–278, 279t
Break-even inflation, 127
Brealey, R. A., 272n7
Brennan, Michael, 197
BRIC countries, 626
Brinson, Gary, 601
British Bankers Association, 30
Brokerage firms, 61–62, 69, 252
Brokered markets, 59
Brokers' call loans, 29, 70
Brown, P., 247
Brown, S. J., 677
Bubbles, 248–249, 270, 272–273, 626
Budget deficit, 289, 374, 377, 637

Buffett, Warren, 256
Bulldog bonds, 295
Bullish spread, 500–501
Business cycles, 379–381, 387–389, 422–423
Busse, J. A., 234
Busse, Jeffrey A., 255
Buying on margin, 70–72

C

CAL (capital allocation line), 135–137, 159–161, 194–195
California Public Employee Retirement System (CalPERS), 597
Callable bonds, 36, 293, 502–503
Call options, 46, 485; *see also* Options valuation
  hedge ratio for, 540
  incentive fees as, 676–677
  introduction, 5, 46–47
  profits and losses on, 485
  put-call parity relationship, 536–539
  put/call ratio and, 280
  stock portfolio with, 673–674
  values at expiration, 489–490, 491f
Call price, 293
Campbell, John Y., 244
Capacity utilization rate, 374
Capital allocation line (CAL), 135–137, 159–161, 194–195
Capital allocation to risky assets, 133
Capital asset pricing model (CAPM), 193
  applications of, 199–200
  arbitrage pricing theory and, 214–220
  assumptions and implications, 193–194
  expected return-beta relationship, 197–198
  index models
    data collection and processing, 202–203, 204f
    estimation conclusions, 206–208
    estimation introduction, 201–202
    estimation results, 203–206
    as market portfolio proxy, 200–201
  in realized returns, 201
  realized returns and mean-beta equation, 201

Capital asset pricing model (CAPM)—*Cont.*
international investments, 650
introduction, 192–193
market portfolio and, 194–195, 196, 197–198
multifactor models and, 210–214
passive strategy and, 195–196
portfolio performance evaluation and, 594–595
portfolio risk and, 197, 245
real world evidence, 208–209
risk premiums and, 196
security market line, 198–199
Capital budgeting, 200
Capital gains, 39
Capital International Indices, 653
Capital market, 5
Capital market line (CML), 137–139, 195, 199
CAPM; *see* Capital asset pricing model
Carhart, Mark M., 101n, 253–254
Case-Shiller index, 17f
Cash, 26, **593**
Cash/bond selection, 654
Cash cows, 391
Cash equivalents, 26
Cash flow matching, 349–350
Cash flow-to-debt ratio, 314
Cash ratio, 457–458
Cash settlement, 567
Catastrophe bonds, 296
CBOE (Chicago Board Options Exchange), 484, 486, 508, 535
CBOT or CBT (Chicago Board of Trade), 47–48, 68, 292n2, 559, 563
CDOs (collateralized debt obligations), 19
CDS (credit default swap), 19–20, **317**–319, 544
Certificates of deposit (CDs), 28, 31
CFA (Chartered Financial Analyst), 706–707, 709
CFA Institute, 76, 77, 591, 685, 706–707, 709
CFTC (Commodity Futures Trading Commission), 75, 567
Channel stuffing, 467–468
Chartered Financial Analyst (CFA), 706–707, 709
Chartists, 237
Chase Manhattan, 14
Chen, Y., 256
Chicago Board of Trade (CBOT or CBT), 47–48, 68, 292n2, 559, 563

Chicago Board Options Exchange (CBOE), 484, 486, 508, 535
Chicago Mercantile Exchange (CME), 68, 488, 561, 563, 578
China, 626
Chopra, Navin, 244, 267
Chordia, Tarun, 63n, 251
Chrysler, 392
Churchill, Winston, 6
Circuit breakers, 67
Citigroup, 14, 45, 68, 404, 458
Class A, B, and C shares, 92
Clearinghouse, 564
Closed-end funds, 86–87, 271–272
CME (Chicago Mercantile Exchange), 68, 488, 561, 563, 578
CME Group, 563
CML (capital market line), 137–139, 195, 199
CNBC network programs, 234
Coca-Cola, 391, 419
Cognizant, 413t
Coincident economic indicators, 381–384
Coin toss analogies, 242, 267, 607
Colgate-Palmolive, 391
Collars, 500–502
Collateral, 315
Collateralized debt obligations (CDOs), 19
Collateralized loans, 506, 507f
Collateral trust bond, 315
College expenses, 700–701
Co-location, 66–67
Commercial banking, 14
Commercial paper (CP), 21, 28–29
Commingled funds, 87
Commodity Futures Trading Commission (CFTC), 75, 567
Common-size balance sheet, 445
Common-size income statement, 444
Common stocks, 38–39
Company stock, 149
Comparison universe, 593–594
Competition, 10–11, 235–236, 392–393
Complete portfolio, 133, 134–136, 161–162
Compounding
annual costs effect on, 139
annual percentage rates and, 113–114
geometric average and, 112
historical returns and, 127–128
market timing and, 613
retirement plans and, 685–686

Compuware, 413t
Conference Board, 381
Confidence index, 279
Conforming mortgages, 18, 37
Congestion area, 277
Conrad, Jennifer, 243
Conservatism bias, 266
Consolidated Edison, 413t, 418, 423
Consolidation stage, 390–391
Constant-growth DDM, 272, 273, 407–409, 416, 421
Constantinides, G. M., 265n
Constraints, investor, 714–716
Consumption timing, 6–7
Contingent liabilities, 468
Continuous compounding, 115, 120, 127
Contrarian investment strategy, 244, 280
Convergence, 664
Convergence property, 566
Conversion premium, 294
Conversion ratio, 294
Convertible bond arbitrage, 664
Convertible bonds, 36, 294, 503–505
Convertible preferred stock, 40, 503–505
Convexity, 299, 350–353, **351**
Cooper, M., 273
Corporate bonds, 35–36, 293–294, 299–300
Corporate ethics, 8–9
Corporate governance, 8–9
Corrections, market, 274–279
Correlation and covariance, 150–153
Correlation coefficient, 152, 155, 157–159, 171–172
Cost-of-carry relationship, 574
Costs
active management, 139
annual fee compounding, 139
college, 700–701
hedge funds, 139, 663, 676–679
implementation, 270
mutual funds, 91–93
passive strategy, 138–139
replacement, 404
securities trading, 69
Counterparty risk, 319
Country-index portfolios; *see* International investing
Country risk, 637
Country selection, 654
Coupon payments, 32, 291, 300–301
Coupon rate, 291, 298n6

Coval, Joshua D., 268
Covariance and correlation, 150–153
Coverage ratios, 312
Covered calls, 497–498
Covered interest arbitrage relationship, 633–634
Covering the short position, 72
Cox, John C., 529n6
CP (commercial paper), 21, 28–29
Craigslist, 58
Crashes and bubbles
  2000–2001 technology bubble, 6, 15, 241, 272–273, 626, 639
  historical returns and, 612
  May 2010 flash crash, 66, 67, 98
  October 1987
    hedge fund effects, 674–676
    international market effects, 650–651, 652f
    option market effects, 491, 543, 546
    risk premiums and, 31t, 32
Credit default swap (CDS), 19–20, 317–319, 544
Credit ratings, 19
Credit risk; *see* Default risk
Credit spreads, 317
Credit Suisse, 14
Credit Suisse First Boston, 653
Cremers, Martijn, 600
"A Critique of Capital Asset Pricing Tests" (Roll), 209
Cross-hedging, 570, 580
CRSP indexes of U.S. equities, 239, 240
Cumulative preferred stock, 40
Currency futures, 578, 579f
Currency risk, 631–632, 646–647
Currency selection, 653
Currency-translated options, 508
Current ratio, 313, 457
Current yield, 304
Cyclical industries, 379–381, 391
Cyclical stocks, 169

D

Dabora, E. M., 270n4
Dana Computer Corporation, 148, 170–171, 175–176, 177t
Daniel, Naveen D., 672
Dark pools, 66, 67
Das, S., 253n12
Data mining, 251, 665
David Bowie bonds, 295
DAX index, 45
Days sales in receivables, 456–457

DCF (discounted cash flow) formula, 409, 429
Dealer markets, 58–59, 61–62
Debentures, 36, 315
De Bondt, W. F. M., 244, 266, 268
Debt (fixed-income) securities, 5; *see also* Bond characteristics; Bond portfolio management; Bond prices and yields; Bonds
  as balance sheet liabilities, 3
  corporate bonds, 35–36, 293–294, 299–300
  introduction, 289–291
  preferred stocks, 40, 294–295
Debt-to-equity ratio, 313
Dedication strategy, 349–350
Default premium, 317
Default risk
  bond pricing and
    bond indentures, 291, 314–315
    junk bonds, 312
    safety determinants, 312–314
    yield to maturity and, 315–317
  corporate bonds and, 36
  credit default swaps and, 19–20, 317–319, 544
Defensive industries, 379–381
Defensive stocks, 169, 171
Deferred callable bonds, 293
Defined benefit plans, 694, 711–712, 717
Defined contribution plans, 694, 711–712; *see also* 401(k) plans
Del Guercio, Diane, 255
DeLong, J. B., 269n
Delta, 540, 542–543
Delta Air Lines, 197
Delta hedging, 542–544
Demand curve, 375–376
Demand shock, 376–377
Depositary receipts, 40, 639
Depreciation, 446–447, 464–465, 468
Depth, 59, 60f
Derivative assets, 46–48, 639
Derivative markets, 46–48, 483; *see also* Futures markets; Options valuation
Derivative securities, 5–6, 484
Desai, M., 466
De Soto, Hernando, 629
Detachable warrants, 505
Deutsche Bank, 14
Deutsche Börse, 68, 563
Developed countries
  capitalization and GDP, 626, 627t
  emerging market comparisons
    beta, 642–643, 645–646

information ratios, 644–645, 647
  SD of excess returns, 644–647
  SD of volatility, 642–643
"Diamonds" (DIA), 95, 96t
Digital options, 508
Dimitrov, O., 273
Dimson, Elroy, 130n, 138
Direct+, 65
Direct Edge, 64
Direct exchange rate quote, 635
Directional strategies, 663–664
Directory of Mutual Funds (Investment Company Institute), 101
Direct search markets, 58
Discount, price, 86–87, 271–272
Discount bonds, 304
Discount brokers, 69
Discounted cash flow (DCF) formula, 409, 429
Discount rate, 378
Discretionary accounts, 69
Disposition effect, 274
Diversifiable risk, 148
Diversification
  asset allocation with two risky assets
    covariance and correlation, 150–153
    historical data usage, 153–154
    mean-variance criterion, 157–159
    risk-return trade-off, 155–157
    rules, 154–155
  definition, 11
  international investing
    active management and, 651
    in bear markets, 650–651
    benefits from, 647–648
    misleading representation of, 649
    realistic expectations from, 649–650
    risk and return statistics, 639–642
  long-term investment risk, 176–179
  with many risky assets, 163–168
  optimal risky portfolio with risk-free asset, 159–162
  portfolio risk and, 148–149
  single-index stock market
    index models, 168–170
    security analysis with, 174–176, 177t
    statistical and graphical representation, 170–172
    systematic and nonsystematic variances, 172–174

Dividend discount model (DDM), 406
constant-growth, 272, 273, 407–409, 416, 421
introduction, 402, 406–407
multistage growth models, 416–417
multistage growth models and life cycles, 412–416
P/E analysis combined with, 424
stock prices and investment opportunities, 409–412
two-stage, 413, 428–429
Dividend payout ratio, 410
Dividends
bond indenture limits on, 315
bond interest compared with, 293n3
capital gains strategy versus, 697
efficient frontier and, 165
preferred stock, 294–295
spot-futures parity and, 574
Dividend yield, 111, 244, 697
Dodd, David, 469–470
Dodd-Frank Wall Street Reform and Consumer Protection Act, 14, 21–22, 319
Dollar-weighted average return, 112–113
Domestic macroeconomy, 373–375
Domestic net worth, 3–4
Dominion Resources, 413t
Domino's Pizza, 295
Dot-com bubble, 6, 15, 241, 248, 272–273, 626, 639
DOT (Designated Order Turnaround), 65
Doubling option, 315
Dow Jones indexes, ETFs on, 95, 96t
Dow Jones Industrial Average
flash crash of May 6, 2010, 66, 67, 98
futures contracts on, 576–577
index options on, 488–489
October 1987 crash, 543
overview, 40–42, 43t
single stock futures contracts, 561
Drexel Burnham Lambert, 312
Dreyfus funds, 88, 92
Duke Energy, 413t
Dun & Bradstreet, 459
DuPont system, 452, 461f
Duration, 337
concept of, 334–335, 337–341
interest rate sensitivity and, 337–341

modified, 339, 580n7
of a perpetuity, 342–343
rules of, 341–343
Dynamic hedging, 529, 542–544
Dynamic process, 721

E

EAFE (European, Australian, Far East) index, 653
Eagle Corp., 500
EAR (effective annual rate), 113–114
Earnings announcements and price drift, 247–248
Earnings management, 422
Earnings per share, 373, 505
Earnings retention ratio, 410
Earnings smoothing, 467
Earnings surprises, 247
Earnings yield, 430
Eaton Vance, 96
eBay, 420
ECNs (electronic communication networks), 62–64, 65
Economic calendar, 382–383
Economic conditions; *see also* Financial crisis of 2008; Macroeconomic analysis
business cycle analysis, 232, 250
domestic, 373–375
economic indicators, 324, 381–384
global, 371–373
sentiment indicators, 278f, 279–280, 374
Economic earnings, 444–445
Economic indicators, 324, 381–384
Economic risk, 636–637
Economic value added, 451–452
EDGAR website, 403
Education savings accounts, 709
Effective annual rate (EAR), 113–114
Efficient diversification; *see* Diversification
Efficient frontier, 163–168, 649–650, 651f
Efficient market hypothesis (EMH), 233
active versus passive portfolio management, 239–240
anomalies, 244–249
anomalies interpretation, 249–251
broad market return predictors, 244
competition and, 235–236
conclusions, 256

fundamental analysis and, 238–239, 244
inside information and, 249
introduction, 11, 232
lucky event issue, 241
magnitude issue, 241
mutual fund manager performance, 252–256
portfolio management role in, 240
random walks and, 233–237
resource allocation and, 240–241
selection bias issue, 241–242
semistrong-form, 236–237, 244–249
stock market analyst performance, 250, 252–256
strong-form, 236–237, 249
technical analysis and, 237–238, 244
weak-form, 236–237, 243–244
Efficient portfolios, 163–168, 233n
Electronic communication networks (ECNs), 62–64, 65
Electronic trading, 62–64, 65
Elliott wave theory, 275
Elton, Edwin J., 255
Elton, E. J., 253n12
Emerging market funds, 89
Emerging markets
capitalization and GDP, 626, 628t
developed country comparisons
beta, 642–643, 645–646
information ratios, 644–645, 647
SD of excess returns, 644–647
SD of volatility, 642–643
Employee Retirement Income Security Act of 1974 (ERISA), 694, 716
Endowment funds, 713, 716
Engle, Robert F., 208n
Enron, 9, 76
Equally weighted indexes, 44–45
Equilibrium nominal interest rate, 115–116
Equilibrium risk premium, 196
Equipment obligation bonds, 315
Equity, 5
Equity beta, 206n
Equity carve-outs, 270–271
Equity funds, 89, 90t, 254
Equity securities; *see also* Stocks
common stocks, 38–39
depositary receipts, 40, 639
global markets for, 626–630
preferred stock, 40, 294–295
Equity trusts, 87

Equity valuation
  aggregate stock market, 429–431
  by comparables, 403–404
  dividend discount models
    constant-growth, 272, 273,
      407–409, 416, 421
    definition and overview,
      406–407
    life cycles and multistage
      growth models, 412–416
    multistage growth models,
      416–417
    stock prices and investment
      opportunities, 409–412
  free cash flow approaches,
    425–429
  intrinsic value versus market
    price, 404–406
  introduction, 402
  price-earnings ratios
    comparative ratios in
      combination with,
      424–425
    DDM combined with, 424
    growth opportunities and,
      417–421
    pitfalls in, 421–424
    stock risk and, 421
Equivalent taxable yield, 35
ERISA (Employee Retirement
  Income Security Act) of 1974,
  694, 716
Ethics, 8–9
ETNs (exchange-traded notes),
  96–97
E*Trade, 69
ETVs (exchange-traded vehicles),
  96–97
Eurex, 562
EURIBOR (European Interbank
  Offer Rate), 30
Euro, 33
Eurobonds, 33, 295
Eurodollar bonds, 33
Eurodollars, 29
Euronext, 65, 68, 563
Euronext.liffe, 563
**European, Australian, Far East
  (EAFE) index, 653**
European Interbank Offer Rate
  (EURIBOR), 30
European options, 487, 536, 539
European Union, 68, 133n16,
  468–469
Eurosterling bonds, 295
Euroyen bonds, 295
Evans, Richard, 253n14, 254n

Ex-ante, 599
Excess returns, 123, 169
  arbitrage pricing theory and, 215
  decomposition of, 169–170
  emerging market versus
    developed country
    investments, 644–645
  in index model estimates,
    201–202
  portfolio risk and, 128
Exchange rate, 371–373
Exchange rate risk, 630–635,
  645–647
Exchange-traded funds (ETFs), 95
  2010 flash crash effects on, 67
  as index fund alternative, 44,
    239–240, 561
  international investments, 639
  overview, 95–98
Exchange-traded notes (ETNs),
  96–97
Exchange-traded vehicles (ETVs),
  96–97
Ex-dividend, 293n3
Execution process, 707
Exercise price, 46
Exercise price, 485, 486–487
Exotic options, 507–508
Expectations hypothesis, 319–322,
  320
Expected holding-period return,
  405, 408
Expected return, 116–117
  alpha and, 169
  beta and, 169
  on individual securities, 197–198
  portfolio performance evaluation
    and, 593, 594
  risk and, 134–135
  risk-return tradeoff and, 10
**Expected return-beta relationship,
  197**–198, 201
Expected yield versus promised
  yield, 315–317
Expert-network providers, 235, 236
Ex-post, 599
Express Scripts Hldg & Co., 293f
Extendable bond, 294
ExxonMobil, 148, 216t,
  718–719, 721

F

Facebook, 57, 59, 60, 420–421,
  485–487, 539
Face value, 291
Factor loadings, 250, 673–674, 675f
Factor portfolios, 219

Fads hypothesis, 243–244
Fairfield Greenwich Advisors, 677
Fair value accounting,
  465–**466,** 467
"Fallen angels," 312
Fama, Eugene, 138, 209, 211–214,
  243, 244, 246, 250, 253, 273
Fama-French Three-Factor Model,
  211–214, 250, 253, 600–601
Fannie Mae
  as bond issuer, 295
  financial crisis role of, 17–18, 19,
    20, 33, 37
  securitization by, 17–18, 37, 713
Farm Credit agencies, 295
FASB (Financial Accounting
  Standards Board), 466, 467
Fast growers, 391
Fat tail risk, 122, 129–131
FCFE (free cash flow to
  equityholders), 426
FCFF (free cash flow to firm),
  425–426, 428–429
Federal agency debt, 33, 37f, 295
Federal debt, 289, 374, 377, 637
Federal Deposit Insurance
  Corporation, 28
Federal funds, 29–30
Federal funds rate, 30, 378
Federal government policy, 377–379
Federal Home Loan Bank Board, 295
Federal Home Loan Bank
  (FHLB), 33
Federal Home Loan Mortgage
  Corporation (FHLMC); see
  Freddie Mac
Federal Housing Finance
  Agency, 33
Federal National Mortgage
  Association (FNMA); see
  Fannie Mae
Federal Reserve
  economic business cycle roles, 126
  financial crisis of 2008 and, 14, 15
  interest rate influences by, 375,
    377–378
  macroeconomic analysis roles,
    375, 376, 377, 378
  margin loan rates and, 70
  monetary policy, 116
  regulatory oversight by, 14, 29
FedEx, 418, 423
Feedback process, 707
Feeder funds, 677
Ferson, W. E., 256
FHLB (Federal Home Loan Bank),
  33, 295

FHLMC (Federal Home Loan Mortgage Corporation); *see* Freddie Mac
Fidelity funds, 88, 89, 385, 639, 694
Fidelity Magellan Fund, 256, 602–603, 607
FIFA (Fédération Internationale de Football Association), 296
FIFO (first-in, first-out), 464
Financial Accounting Standards Board (FASB), 466, 467
Financial assets, 3–6
Financial crisis of 2008–2009
    antecedents of, 15–17
    banking industry and, 14, 15, 122n
    as black swan, 676
    bond market impacts by, 289, 312, 316–317
    credit default swaps and, 19–20, 318–319
    credit spreads during, 317
    derivatives role in, 495–497
    developed countries impacts by, 626, 627t
    Dodd-Frank Reform Act and, 14, 21–22, 319
    hedge fund impacts by, 289
    housing finance changes and, 17–19, 20, 33, 37
    international diversification and, 651, 652f
    market collapse, 20–21
    money market impacts by, 21, 31–32
    option pricing and, 544–545
    S&P 500 volatility, 535, 536f
    systemic risk and, 15, 20, 169
Financial futures, 576–580
Financial Industry Regulatory Authority (FINRA), 76
Financial intermediaries, 12–14
Financial leverage, 388, 449–451
Financial markets; *see also specific market, e.g.,* stock market
    competitive nature of, 10–11
    consumption timing and, 6–7
    economy and, 6–9
    efficiency of, 11
    informational role of, 6
    participants, 11–15
    primary versus secondary, 15
    risk and, 7
    summary, 27t
Financial ratios, 312–314, 413t, 459–462
Financial risk, 636–637

Financial Services Authority, 76
Financial statement analysis
    comparability problems
        depreciation, 464–465
        earnings quality and accounting practices, 466–468
        fair value accounting, 465–466
        inflation and interest expense, 465
        international accounting conventions, 468–469
        inventory valuation, 464
    illustration of, 460–463
    introduction, 443
    performance measures, 448
    profitability measures, 448–452
    ratio analysis
        benchmark choices, 459
        industry groups, 459–461
        liquidity ratios, 313, 457–458, 460t
        market price ratios, 458–459, 460t
        ROE decomposition, 452–454, 455f
        summary, 460t
        turnover and asset utilization ratios, 454–457, 460t
    value investing and, 469–470
Financial supermarkets, 91
Financial Times (FTSE) indexes, 40, 45, 239, 488, 576t, 626, 639
Financial Times Share Exchange (FTSE), 626
Financial Times Share Exchange index (FTSE 100), 488, 576t
FINRA (Financial Industry Regulatory Authority), 76
Firm commitment, 56
Firm performance measures, 448
Firms as investors, 11–12
Firm-specific risk, 148, 168, 169, 170, 171, 174, 175
Firm value, 426; *see also* Equity valuation
First Energy, 413t
First-in, first-out (FIFO), 464
Fiscal policy, 376, 377
Fisher, Irving, 115–116
Fisher, Kenneth L., 268
Fisher equation, 115–116, 125, 126
Fitch Investors Service, 19, 312
529 plans, 701
Fixed-charge coverage ratio, 312
Fixed-income capital market, 32, 46f; *see also* Bond market
Fixed-income investment strategies, 355–356

Fixed-income mutual funds, 255–256
Fixed-income (debt) securities, 5; *see also* Bond characteristics; Bond portfolio management; Bond prices and yields; Bonds
    corporate bonds, 35–36, 293–294, 299–300
    overview, 289–291
    preferred stocks, 40, 294–295
Flash crash of May 6, 2010, 66, 67, 98
Flat prices, 301
Flat tax, 689
Flexible funds, 89
Floating-rate bonds, 294
FNMA (Federal National Mortgage Association); *see* Fannie Mae
Forcing a conversion, 505
Ford Motor Company, 316–317, 344
Forecasting, aggregate stock market, 429–431
Forecasting errors, 266
Foreign bonds, 295
Foreign currency options, 489
Foreign exchange futures, 578, 579f
Foreign exchange swap, 581
Foreign stocks, 40, 45
Forward contracts, 558, 633
Forward rate, 321–322
401(k) plans, 149, **694**
403(b) plans, 694
Four-factor model, 253–255
Framing, 267
Franzoni, Francesco, 672
Freddie Mac
    as bond issuer, 295
    earnings smoothing by, 467
    financial crisis role of, 17–18, 19, 20, 33, 37
    securitization by, 17–18, 37, 713
Free cash flow to equityholders (FCFE), 426
Free cash flow to firm (FCFF), 425–426, 428–429
Free cash flow valuation, 425–429
French, Kenneth, 126f, 130n, 138, 202n4, 209, 211–214, 243, 244, 246, 247n, 250, 253
Front-end load, 91
Froot, K. A., 270n4
FTSE 100 (Financial Times Share Exchange index), 488
FTSE (Financial Times Share Exchange), 626
FTSE Index Co., 626
FTSE (Financial Times) indexes, 40, 45, 239, 488, 576t, 626, 639

Fuchs, Thomas, 384n
Full-service brokers, 69
Fully diluted earnings per share, 505
Fundamental analysis, 238–239, 244, **370,** 402; *see also* Financial statement analysis
Fundamental risk, 269–270
Funds of funds, 89, 597–598, **677**–679
Futures contracts, 47
   basics of, 47–48, 558–561
   categories, 561–563
   currency, 578, 579f
   financial, 576–580
   foreign exchange, 578, 579f, 633
   hedging with, 568–570, 633
   interest rate, 578–580
   prediction, 562
   stock-index, 543, 567, 575, 576–577
   swaps, 581–583
  Futures markets
   arbitrage opportunities, 572–575
   introduction, 557–558
   regulation of, 75, 567
   strategies, 568–571
   tax issues, 567
   trading mechanics, 563–567
Futures options, 489
Futures price, 47, 489, **558**–561, 571–575

G

GAAP (generally accepted accounting principles), 464, 467, 468–469
Gabelli, Mario, 256
Galleon Group hedge fund, 235
Gambling versus speculation, 124
GAMCO, 256
Garber, Peter, 249n
Gaskins, Francis, 421
GDP (gross domestic product), 374, 626, 627t, 628t, 629–630, 653
Gender and overconfidence, 266
General Electric (GE), 7, 39, 216t, 413–416, 426–428, 718–719
Generally accepted accounting principles (GAAP), 464, 467, 468–469
General obligation bonds, 34
Geometric average, 112, 128
Gerson Lehrman Group, 236
Gervais, S., 274
Getmansky, Mila, 671
Ghysels, E., 535n

GIC (guaranteed investment contract), 344–348
Ginnie Mae, 33, 295
Givoly, Dan, 249
Glass-Steagall Act, 14
GlaxoSmithKline, 452t
Global Crossing, 9
Global economy, 371–373
Global funds, 89
Globalization, 68–69; *see also* International investing
Globex, 563
GNMA (Government National Mortgage Association), 33, 295
Goetzmann, W. N., 677
Going public, 56
Goldgar, Anne, 249n
Goldman Sachs, 14, 15, 68, 293f, 653
Goodwill, 445
Google
   in capital asset pricing model, 195, 201–208, 211–213
   industry life cycle and, 390, 421
   as information source, 403
   optimal portfolio construction with, 174–176, 177t
Gordon, Myron J., 407
Gordon model, 407
Government National Mortgage Association (GNMA), 33, 295
Governments as investors, 11–12
Government securities, 133n16; *see also* Treasury bills; Treasury notes or bonds
Graham, Benjamin, 469–470
Graham, J. R., 138, 209n10, 596n
Graphical representation of single-index models, 170–172
Great Depression, 116, 612
Greece, 133n16, 317–318, 371
Green, R. C., 255
Green, T. C., 234
Greenspan, Alan, 272
Grinblatt, Mark, 274
Grocery stores, industry cyclicality of, 387–388
Gross domestic product (GDP), 374, 626, 627t, 628t, 629–630, 653
Grossman, Sanford J., 235
Growth firms, 211
Growth funds, 89
Growth Industries, Inc.
   financial statement, 455–458
   financial statement analysis, 460–463
Growth models, 412–417

Growth opportunities, 411–412, 417–421
Growth stocks, 103, 251
Gruber, Martin J., 255
Gruber, M. J., 253n12
Guaranteed investment contract (GIC), 344–348

H

Han, Bing, 274
Hang Seng index, 45
Harris, Lawrence E., 60n, 64n
Harris, M., 265n
Harvey, A., 535n
Harvey, Campbell R., 648n
Harvey, C. R., 138, 209n10, 596n
Hasanhodzic, Jasmina, 671
Health insurance, 702
HealthSouth, 9
Hedge funds, 88, 662
   benefits of, 139
   expert-network providers, 236
   fee structure, 139, 663, 676–679
   financial crisis effects on, 289
   introduction, 13–14, 661–662
   mutual funds versus, 662–663
   performance measurement
     factor loading changes, 673–674, 675f
     liquidity and, 670–672
     survivorship bias and, 672–673
     tail events and, 674–676
   portable alpha and, 665–668
   strategies, 663–665
   style analysis for, 663, 668–669
Hedge ratio, 540
   binomial option pricing and, 523–524, 529
   Black-Scholes formula and, 539–541
   portfolio insurance and, 543
   PVBP for futures contract, 580
Hedging
   basis risk and, 570–571
   currency risk, 646–647
   dynamic, 529, 542–544
   exchange rate risk, 633, 635
   futures market, 568–570, 633
   protective puts, 494–497, 541–542
Henriksson, Roy D., 615
Heston, S. L., 535n
Hewlett-Packard, 67, 445n, 452t, 467
High-frequency trading, 65–67, **66**
High minus low (HML) portfolios, 212–213, 250, 600

High water mark, 677
High-yield (junk) bonds, 312
Historical returns
  asset allocation and, 153–154
  calculating, 122–123
  compounding and, 127–128
  crashes and bubbles effects, 612
  interest rates and inflation and,
    125–127
  risk premium and, 131–132,
    137–138
  S&P 500 Index, 9, 16f, 137–138,
    150, 196, 201, 203t, 204t
  stocks, 9, 10, 137–138
  Treasury bills, 9–10, 15–16,
    125–127, 129f, 203t, 204t, 207
  Treasury notes or bonds, 129f,
    430
  world and U.S. stocks and bonds,
    127–132
Hlavka, M., 253n12
HML (high minus low) portfolios,
  212–213, 250, 600
Holding-period return (HPR), 111
  after-tax returns, 311
  bonds, 308
  expected, 321, 405, 408
  yield to maturity versus, 309–310
Home-country bias, 630
Home Depot, 444–447, 452t, 459,
  461f
Home ownership, 701
Homer, Sidney, 336, 354, 356,
  581n9
Homogeneous expectations, 194
Honda, 3, 354, 451t, 452
Horizon analysis, 307, 355
Households as investors, 11
Household wealth, 3–4, 12; *see also*
  Personal finance
House money effect, 267
Housing market, 17–19
Housing price bubble, 248
HPR; *see* Holding-period return
HSBC, 14
Hull, J. C., 535n
Human capital as asset, 709, 715
Hybrid funds, 90t

I

IBM, 269, 718–719
IB (interest-burden) ratio, 453
Icahn, Carl, 8
ICE (Intercontinental Exchange),
  65, 68
**IFRS (international financial
  reporting standards), 468**–469

IMF (International Monetary Fund),
  649
Immunization, 343
  GIC example, 343–348
  rebalancing, 347–349
Implementation costs, 270
Implied volatility, 534–536, 545–546
Incentive fees, 663, **676**–679
Inc. magazine, 384
Income funds, 89
Income statement, 444–445
Indentures, 291, **314**–315
Index arbitrage, 577–578
Indexed bonds, 296–297
Index funds, 44, 89–90, **239,** 640,
  720
Index futures, 543, 567, 575,
  576–577
Indexing, 137, 266, 591
Index models, 168
  CAPM and, 193, 200–201
  data collection and processing,
    202–203, 204f
  estimation conclusions, 206–208
  estimation introduction, 201–202
  estimation results, 203–206
  in realized returns, 201
  realized returns and mean-beta
    equation, 201
  security analysis with, 174–176,
    177t
  single-, 168–170
  statistical and graphical
    representation, 170–172
Index options, 488–489
India, 626
Indirect exchange rate quote, 635
Individual investors
  constraints on, 714–716
  investment policies for, 717–720
  objectives of, 709–711
  portfolio monitoring and revising,
    721
  risk tolerance of, 708–709
Individual Retirement Accounts
  (IRAs), 691, 695–696
Industrial development bonds, 34
Industrial production, 374
Industry analysis
  business cycle sensitivity,
    387–388
  definitions, 385–387
  financial ratios for, 459–461
  importance of, 384–385
  life cycles, 389–392
  ROA, profit margin, and asset
    turnove., 455f

  ROE comparisons, 384, 385f,
    386f
  sector rotation, 388–389
  stock price performance, 386f
  structure and performance,
    392–393
Industry life cycle, 389–392, **390**
INET, 68
Inflation, 374
  historical rates, 125–127
  interest expense and, 465
  P/E ratio relation to, 421–422
  real interest rate and, 114–116
  retirement savings plans and,
    686–689
  Treasury bill rates and, 125,
    126–127
Inflation-protected Treasury bonds,
  33, 127, 133, 216t, 296–297
Inflation rate, 115, 217t
Inflow, 298
Information
  competition and, 235–236
  earnings announcements,
    247–248
  in efficient markets, 233–234
  EMH versions and, 236–237
  technical or fundamental analysis
    of, 237–239, 244
Information processing, 266–267
Information ratio, 175, 598
Information sources
  EDGAR website, 403
  equity valuation, 387, 413–416
  financial ratios, 459
  mutual funds, 101–103, 603–604
Initial public offering (IPO), 56,
  57, 58f
Inside information, 78, 235–236,
  249
Inside quotes, 60
Insider trading, 78, 235–237, 249
Instinet, 63, 68
Institutional investors
  asset allocation policies of,
    718–719
  constraints on, 714–716
  objectives of, 710–714
  as players, 11–12
Insurance, health and life, 702
Insurance principle, 148
Intangible fixed assets, 445
Intangibles, 468
Intel, 5, 429, 452t, 452
Intercontinental Exchange (ICE),
  65, 68
Interest-burden (IB) ratio, 453

Interest coverage ratio, 453
Interest expense, 465
Interest rate forecasting, 354
Interest rate futures, 578–580
Interest rate options, 489
Interest rate parity relationship, 633–634
Interest rate risk
  bond maturity and, 335–337
  duration concept, 337–341
  duration rules, 341–343
  fixed-income investments and, 345
  interest rate sensitivity and, 335–337
  liquidity preference theory and, 322
Interest rates
  financial crisis of 2008 and, 15–17
  historical record, 125–127
  macroeconomic analysis and, 374, 375–376
  nominal, 115
  real, 115
  risk structure of, 317–318
Interest rate sensitivity
  concept of, 335–337
  duration and, 337–341
  pension fund risks, 344
Interest rate swap, 581–583
Intergenerational transfers, 703
Intermarket spread swap, 354
Internal rate of return (IRR), 200
Internal Revenue Service (IRS), 311
International accounting
  conventions, 468–469
International bonds, 33, 295
International Country Risk Guide
  (PRS), 636–638
International financial reporting standards (IFRS), 468–469
International funds, 89
International investing
  diversification
    active management and, 651
    in bear markets, 650–651, 652f
    benefits from, 647–648
    misleading representation of, 649
    realistic expectations from, 649–650
    risk and return statistics, 639–642
  emerging markets versus developed countries
    average returns, 644–645
    risk factors, 642–643
  equity markets, 626–630
  foreign index funds, 640

introduction, 625
performance attribution, 653–655
risk factors
  exchange rate risk, 630–635, 645–647
  political risk, 635–638
International Monetary Fund (IMF), 649
International Money Market, 578
International Securities Exchange (ISE), 68, 486
International stocks, 58
In the money, 486
Intrade, 562
Intrinsic value, 404–406, **405, 520**
Intrinsic value of equity, 426
Intuit, 413t
Inventory turnover ratio, 456
Inventory valuation, 464
Inverse ETFs, 96
Inverse floaters, 295
Investment bankers, 14–15
Investment companies, 12, 85;
  see also Hedge funds; Mutual funds
  assets under management, 97f
  commingled, 87
  managed, 86–87
  real estate investment trusts, 87–88
  regulation of, 88, 92, 95, 96, 101
  unit investment trusts, 86
Investment Company Act of 1940, 85, 662
Investment Company Institute, 101
Investment grade bonds, 312
Investment horizon, 176–179, **715**
Investment management process
  introduction, 707–709
  investor objectives of
    banks, 713
    endowment funds, 713
    individual investors, 709–711
    life insurance companies, 712–713
    non-life-insurance companies, 713
    pension funds, 711–712
    summary, 714t
  monitoring and revisions, 721
Investment opportunity set, 156–159
Investment policy statement (IPS), 708, 717–720
Investments, 2; *see also* Asset classes and financial instruments;
  Financial crisis of 2008; Investment companies; Securities markets

financial assets, 5–6
financial markets, 6–11
participants, 11–15
portfolio construction, 9–10
real versus financial assets, 3–5
Investor constraints, 714–716
Investor objectives
  banks, 713
  endowment funds, 713
  individual investors, 709–711
  life insurance companies, 712–713
  non-life-insurance companies, 713
  pension funds, 711–712
  summary, 714t
Investors; *see also* Behavioral finance; individual investors
  convexity attractiveness to, 352–353
  gender and overconfidence, 266
  introduction, 706–707
  time horizon of, 176–179
  unique needs of, 715–716
Invoice price, 292, 301
Iowa Electronic Markets, 562
IPOdesktop.com, 421
IPO (initial public offering), 56, 57, 58f
IPS (investment policy statement), 708, 717–720
IRAs (Individual Retirement Accounts), 691, 695–696
Irrational exuberance, 248n, 272
IRR (internal rate of return), 200
IRS (Internal Revenue Service), 311
ISE (International Securities Exchange), 68, 486
IShares, 67, 95–96, 384

J

Jacquier, Eric, 650
Jaffe, Jeffrey F., 78, 249
Jagannathan, R., 138
Jagannathan, Ravi, 209
JCPenney, 386
Jegadeesh, N., 243n, 252
Jegadeesh, Narasimhan, 243
Jensen, Michael C., 209, 598
Jensen measure, 598–600
Jewelry stores, industry cyclicality of, 387–388
Jiau, Winifred, 236
Johnson & Johnson, 216t
Joint tests, 245
Jones, C., 76n
Jones, C. P., 247, 248n

J. P. Morgan, 14, 411, 544
JPMorgan Chase, 14, 216t, 293f
Junk bonds, 312

K

Kahneman, D., 266, 268n
Karabell, Zachary, 496n
Kaul, Gautam, 243
Keim, Donald B., 244
Kellogg, 422
Kendall, Maurice, 232–233
Keown, Arthur, 234n
Keynes, John Maynard, 270
Kim, J., 252
Kondratieff waves, 275
Kosowski, R., 256
Kothari, S. P., 246n
Kotlikoff, Laurence J., 703
Krische, S. D., 252
Kurtosis, 122, 130–131

L

Labor income, hedging, 702
Lagging economic indicators,
    381–384
Lakonishok, Josef, 244, 250, 267
Lamont, O. A., 76n, 270n5, 271n
Landier, Augustin, 672
La Porta, Raphael, 250
Large purchases, 700–701
Last-in, first-out (LIFO), 464
Latané, H. A., 247, 248n
Latency, 65
Law of One Price, 270–272
Leading economic indicators, 324,
    381–384
LEAPS (Long-term Equity
    AnticiPation Securities), 487
Lee, C. M., 252, 271
Legg Mason Value Trust, 243
Lehavy, R., 252
Lehman Brothers, 9, 14, 15, 21, 31,
    45, 76, 88n, 240, 702
Lehmann, B., 243n
Leibowitz, Martin L., 336, 354,
    356, 581n9
Leverage, in futures market, 568
Leveraged equity, 506
Leveraged ETFs, 96
Leverage ratio, 313, **453,** 460t
Liabilities, 3
Liang, B., 677
Liar loans, 19
LIBOR (London Interbank
    Offer Rate), 15–16, **30,** 632t,
    633–634
Liew, J., 250n

Life annuity, **701**–702
Life cycle financial planning, 709, 716
Life-cycle funds, 89
Life cycles, industry, 389–392,
    412–416
Life expectancy, 701–702
Life insurance, 702
Life insurance companies, 712–713,
    716
LIFFE (London International
    Financial Futures and Options
    Exchange), 68, 563n, 578
LIFO (last-in, first-out), 464
Limit buy (sell) orders, 59–61
Limited liability, 39
Limit order book, 59–60
Lintner, J., 193
Liquidation value, 404
Liquidity, 457, 714
    concept of, 20n, 55
    depth as component of, 59
    in Fama-French model, 213n16,
        214
    hedge funds, 662, 670–672
    as investor constraint, 714–715
    as risk factor, 209
    specialist roles, 62
Liquidity effect, 246
Liquidity preference theory,
    322–323
Liquidity premium, 322–323
Liquidity ratios, 313, 457–458, 460t
Lloyds, 30
Lo, Andrew W., 243, 671
Load, 87
Loans, collateralized, 506, 507f
Lock-up periods, 662
London Interbank Offer Rate
    (LIBOR), 15–16, **30,** 632t,
    633–634
London International Financial
    Futures and Options Exchange
    (LIFFE), 68, 563n, 578
London Stock Exchange, 9
Longevity, 702–703
Long hedge, 569
Longin, F., 650
Long position, 559
Long-term bonds, 335–337, 342
Long-Term Capital Management
    (LTCM), 31t, 32, 289, 535,
    536f, 676
Long-term Equity AnticiPation
    Securities (LEAPS), 487
Long-term investment risk, 176–179
Loughran, T., 58n
Low-load funds, 91

LSE, 68
LTCM (Long-Term Capital
    Management), 31t, 32, 289,
    535, 536f, 676
Lucky event issue of EMH, 241
Lynch, Peter, 256, 391, 419

M

M^2 **(M-square), 596**–597, 647
Macaulay, Frederick, 337, 338
Macaulay's duration, 337
MacBeth, James, 209
MacKinlay, Craig, 243
Macroeconomic analysis
    business cycles, 379–381
    demand and supply shocks,
        376–377
    domestic macroeconomy,
        373–375
    economic indicators, 324, 381–384
    federal government policy and,
        377–379
    global economy, 371–373
    industry analysis
        business cycle sensitivity,
            387–388
        definitions, 385–387
        financial ratios for, 459–461
        importance of, 384–385
        life cycles, 389–392
        ROA, profit margin, and asset
            turnover, 455f
        ROE comparisons, 384, 385f, 386f
        sector rotation, 388–389
        stock price performance, 386f
        structure and performance,
            392–393
    interest rates and, 375–376
    introduction, 370–371
Madoff, Bernard, 677–678
Maginn, John L., 708n
Magnitude issue of EMH, 241
Maintenance margin, 70–71,
    565–566
Major expenditures, 700–701
Makarov, Igor, 671
Malkiel, Burton G., 99–100, 336,
    337, 341, 350, 673
Malmendier, U., 266, 731
Managed investment companies,
    86–87
Management, ownership separation
    from, 7–8
Marcus, Alan J., 607n, 650
Margin, 70
    buying securities on, 20, 29,
        70–72

futures contracts and, 558
maintenance, 70–71, 565–566
option contracts and, 488
short sales and, 72–75, 76
Margin calls, 70, 74, 565
Market capitalization
international investments, 626,
627t, 628t, 653, 654t
per capita GDP and, 629–630
valuation by comparables and,
211–212, 403
Market capitalization rate, 405
Market conversion value, 294
Market depth, 59, 60f
Market interest rate, 297–300
Market neutral, 664–665
Market orders, 59
**Market portfolio (M),
194**–198, 595
Market price, 404–406
Market price of risk, 124
Market price ratios, 458–459, 460t
Market risk, 148, 171, 172,
174, 196
Market timing, 577, 593, **612**–615,
673–674
Market-to-book-value ratio,
211–212, 250, **458;** *see also*
Book-to-market effect
Market types, 58–59
Market value-weighted indexes,
42–44
Marking to market, 565–566
Markopolos, Harry, 678
Markowill Group, 594
Markowitz, Harry, 11, 147, 163, 175
**Mark-to-market accounting,
466,** 467
Marriage and longevity, 703
Marsh, Paul, 130n, 138
Maturity stage, 391
Mayers, David, 197
Mazuy, Kay, 615
McDonald, Robert L., 527n3
McGrattan, E. R., 138
McLean, R. David, 251
McLeavey, Dennis W., 708n
McNichols, M., 252
Mean of the distribution, 116
Mean return, 116–118; *see also*
Expected return
Mean reversion, 208
Mean-variance analysis, 125, 200
Mean-variance criterion, 157–159
Medicare, 699
Medtronic, 293f
Memory bias, 266

Mendelson, Haim, 209, 246
Mendenhall, R., 247n
Mental accounting, 267
Merck, 10
Mergers and acquisitions, 65, 68, 266
Merrill Lynch, 14, 15, 21, 45, 68,
96t, 710
Merton, Robert C., 210, 214, 246,
529n6, 530, 544, 613
**M (market portfolio),
194**–198, 595
Microsoft, 8, 216t, 385, 403–404,
413t, 421, 451t, 452, 544, 721
Midday Call (CNBC), 234
Milken, Michael, 312
Miller, Bill, 243
Miller, M., 428
Minimum-variance portfolio (MIN),
159–160
Minsky, Hyman, 248
Miramax, 295
Mitsubishi, 404
Mobil Corp., 315, 316f
Model risk, 270
Modern portfolio theory, 11
Modified duration, 339, 580n7
Modigliani, Franco, 428, 596
Modigliani, Leah, 596
Momentum, 213n16, 214, 274–276
Momentum effect, 243, 249–250
Monetary policy, 376, **377**–378
Money market, 27; *see also*
Treasury bills
bankers' acceptances, 29
brokers' calls, 29, 70
CDs, 28, 31
commercial paper, 21, 28–29
Eurodollars, 29
Federal funds, 29–30
financial crisis of 2008 and, 21,
31–32
LIBOR market, 30
overview, 5
repos and reverses, 29
yields, 30–32
Money market mutual funds, 21, 31,
88, 90t, 134
Money spread, 499
Monga, Vipal, 344n
Moody's Investor Services, 19, 312,
313f, 427
Moral hazard, 702
Morgan Stanley, 14, 293f, 653
Morgan Stanley Capital
International (MSCI) index,
45, 640
Morning Call (CNBC), 234

Morningstar, Inc., 101–103, 603–604
Mortgage-backed securities, 17–19,
36–37
Mortgage bonds, 36–37, 315
Mortgage market, 17–19
Mortgage origination, 713
Mortgages, subprime, 18–20,
28–29, 37
Mortgage trusts, 87
Mossin, J., 193
Moussawi, Rabih, 672
Moving averages, 274–276
MSCI (Morgan Stanley Capital
International) index, 45, 640
MSN, 403
M-square (M^2), 596–597, 647
Multifactor models, 210
arbitrage pricing theory and
CAPM, 218–220
CAPM validity and, 214
Fama-French Three-Factor Model,
211–214, 250, 253, 254f
four-factor model, 253–255
two-factor illustration, 210–211
Multistage growth models, 412–417
Municipal bond funds, 89
Municipal bonds, 34–36
Mutual funds, 710; *see also*
Exchange-traded funds; Hedge
funds; Portfolio performance
evaluation
analyst performance, 252–256
asset allocation, 89
benchmarks for, 253–255
bond, 88, 89, 90t, 255–256
constraints on, 715
emerging market, 89
equity, 89, 90t, 254
fee structure, 91–93
global, 89
hedge funds versus, 662–663
index, 44, 89–90, 239, 640, 720
information sources for, 101–103,
603–604
international, 89, 639, 640
investment policies of, 88–90
net asset value, 85, 87, 97,
271–272
performance of, 98–101
as professional investors, 710–711
rate of return, 93–94
regional, 89
regulation of, 88, 92, 95, 96, 101,
715
sales and marketing, 90–91
sector, 89, 385
tax issues, 94–95

Mutual Fund Sourcebook
(Morningstar), 101
Mutual fund theorem, 195
Myers, S. C., 272n7

N

NAFTA (North American Free
Trade Agreement), 385n, 386
**NAICS (North American Industry
Classification System) codes,
385**–387
Naik, Narayan Y., 672
Naked options, 491, 497
Naked short-selling, 72n
Napoleon, 76
NASDAQ 100 index, 95, 96t, 561
NASDAQ Composite Index, 270,
576–577
NASDAQ OMX Group, 64, 68
NASDAQ Stock Market, 62
crashes and bubbles, 67, 272
electronic trading on, 63–64
listing on, 39
market share, 64
market value indexes, 44
mergers and acquisitions by, 68
overview, 64–65
as secondary market, 55
specialist markets on, 62
trading mechanisms, 61–63
National Association of Securities
Dealers (NASD), 44, 61, 63, 76
National Market System, 62, 63–64
Neglected-firm effect, 245–246
Neiman Marcus, 386
Net asset value (NAV), 85, 87, 97,
271–272
Net present value, 411
Newsletter schemes, 242
New York Stock Exchange (NYSE);
see NYSE
New York Stock Exchange Index,
576–577
Nikkei Average, 40
Nikkei Stock Index, 45, 488, 639
No-load funds, 91
Nominal interest rate, 115, 217t
Nominal return, 296
Nonconforming mortgages, 18
Nondirectional strategies, 663–664
Nondiversifiable risk, 148
Non-life-insurance companies, 713
Nonrecourse loans, 506
Nonrecurring items, 466–467
Nonsystematic risk, 148, 174
Normal distribution, 118–119,
121–122

Normality over time, 120
North American Free Trade
Agreement (NAFTA), 385n, 386
**North American Industry
Classification System
(NAICS) codes, 385**–387
Northeast Utilities, 413t
Notional principal, 581
NYSE (New York Stock Exchange)
as auction market, 59
bond trading on, 68
circuit breakers, 67
crashes and bubbles, 67
market share, 64
mergers and acquisitions by, 65, 68
options trading on, 486–487
overview, 65
self regulation, 76
NYSE Amex, 65
NYSE Arca, 63, 64
NYSE Bonds, 68
NYSE Euronext, 65, 68, 488
NYSE Group, 65, 68
NYSE Hybrid Market, 65
NYSE Index, 576–577

O

Obama, Barack, 562
Obligation, 48
OCC (Option Clearing
Corporation), 488
Odean, Terrance, 266, 267, 274
Off-balance-sheet assets and
liabilities, 468
Office of Credit Ratings, 22
Official Summary (SEC), 249
OID (original-issue discount) bonds,
310–311
OMX, 64, 68
OneChicago, 561
One Up on Wall Street (Lynch), 419
OPEC (Organization of Petroleum
Exporting Countries), 31–32
Open-end funds, 86, 87; *see also*
Mutual funds
Open interest, 564–565
Open market operations, 378
Operating earnings, 422
Operating expenses, 91
Operating income, 444
Operating leverage, 388
Optimal risky portfolio, 160
choosing, 165
constructing, 166–168
index models and, 174–176, 177t
market portfolio as, 194–195
with risk-free assets, 159–162

Option Clearing Corporation
(OCC), 488
Option elasticity, 541
Optionlike securities
callable bonds, 36, 293–294,
502–503
collateralized loans, 506, 507f
convertible securities, 36, 294,
503–505
leveraged equity and risky debt,
506–507
warrants, 505
Options
American, 487, 539
contracts, 46–47, 484–489
European, 487, 536, 539
exotic, 507–508
foreign currency, 489
futures, 489
futures contracts compared with,
559
interest rate, 489
markets, 484, 486–487
naked, 491, 497
stock investments versus,
492–494, 496f
trading, 486–487
Option smirk, 546
Option strategies
collars, 500–502
covered calls, 497–498
protective puts, 494–497
spreads, 499–501
stock portfolio with options,
673–674, 675f
straddles, 497, 499, 500f
T-bills plus options, 492–494,
613–615
Options valuation
binomial option pricing, 522–529
Black-Scholes formula
empirical evidence, 545–546
financial crisis effect on,
544–545
hedge ratios and, 539–541
introduction, 529–536
portfolio insurance, 541–544
put-call parity relationship,
536–539
put option valuation, 539
determinants of, 520–522
at expiration, 489–491
introduction, 519–522
volatility relationship to,
520–521, 527
Oracle, 413t
Order types, 59–61

Organization of Petroleum Exporting Countries (OPEC), 31–32
Oriental Land Co., 296
Original-issue discount (OID) bonds, 310–311
Osaka Stock Exchange, 68
Outflow, 298
Out of the money, 486
Overconfidence, 266
Over-the-counter (OTC) market, 59, **61,** 68, 75, 486
Ownership, management separation from, 7–8

P

Pairs trading, 66, **665**
Palatial Investments, 718–719
Palm, 270–271
Palmon, Dan, 249
Parmalat, 9
Par value, 291
Passive core strategy, 720
Passive investment strategy, 239–240, 334
Passive management, 11, 591
    bonds
        cash flow matching and dedication, 349–350
        immunization, 334, 343–349
        international investments, 626, 628t, 653
    as investment policy decision, 719–720
    mutual funds, 99, 100f
Passive portfolio, 174–176
Passive strategy, 137
    capital market line and, 137–139
    costs and benefits, 138–139
    efficiency of, 195–196
    index funds and, 89–90
    optimal portfolios and, 166
    overconfidence and, 266
Pass-throughs, 18
Patel, J. M., 234
Paulson, Henry, 467
Paulson, John, 289, 318
Pay-in-kind bonds, 296
Payoff of loan, 544
PBGC (Pension Benefit Guarantee Corporation), 694
Peak, 379
P/E effect, 245, 249–250, 266
PEG ratio, 403, 419–420
Penn Square Bank, 31t, 32
Pension Benefit Guarantee Corporation (PBGC), 694

Pension funds, 344, 466, 711–712, 716
Pension plans, 717
P/E ratio; see Price-earnings ratio
Perfect correlation, 172
Performance attribution, 606–611, 653–655
Performance evaluation; see Portfolio performance evaluation
Performance manipulation, 606
Perpetuity, 407
Perpetuity, duration of, 342–343
Personal finance
    bequests and, 702–703
    home ownership, 701
    inflation and, 686–689
    intergenerational transfers and, 702–703
    introduction, 684
    large purchases, 700–701
    longevity and, 701–702
    matrimony and, 702–703
    savings plans, 685–686
    Social Security, 699
    taxes and, 689–690, 692–693
    tax shelters
        asset location and, 697–699
        economics of, 690–693
        types, 694–699
Personal trusts, 710
Petajisto, Antti, 600
Peters, H., 256
Pfizer, 10, 216t
Pinkerton, John, 234n
Pinto, Jerald E., 708n
Planning process, 707–709
Plowback ratio, 410, 418–419
Point and figure charts, 276–277, 278f
Political risk, 635–638
Political Risk Services (PRS) Group, 636–638
Pontiff, Jeffrey E., 87, 251, 271
Ponzi, Charles, 678
Ponzi schemes, 677–678
Portable alpha, 665–668
Porter, Michael, 392
Portfolio insurance, 541–544, **542**–544
Portfolio management; see also Asset allocation; Bond portfolio management; Hedge funds; International investing; Investment management process; Personal finance; Portfolio performance evaluation

active versus passive, 239–240
behavioral finance and, 273–274
in efficient markets, 240
hedge ratios and, 541
index models and, 207–209
investment policy statements and, 708, 717–720
swaps and, 581–583
Portfolio performance evaluation
    attribution procedures, 606–611
    hedge funds
        factor loading changes, 673–674, 675f
        liquidity and, 670–672
        survivorship bias and, 672–673
        tail events and, 674–676
    introduction, 592
    market timing and, 612–615
    Morningstar ratings, 603–604
    risk-adjusted returns
        alpha relation to, 598–600
        comparison groups, 593–594
        with a multi-index model, 600–601
        objectives, 593
        statistics, 594–595
        using information ratios, 598
        using Jensen measure, 598–600
        using Sharpe ratio and M^2, 595–597
        using Treynor measure, 597–598
    risk adjustments with changing portfolio composition, 605–606
    style analysis, 601–603, 604n
Portfolio risk; see also Diversification
    CAPM and, 197, 245
    diversification and, 148–149
    expected return and, 134–135
    mutual fund performance and, 99
    risk aversion and, 124
    Sharpe ratio and, 125
Portfolios; see also Risky assets or portfolios
    arbitrage, 215–218
    investment process and, 9
    monitoring and revising, 721
    riskless, 523
    style, 250
    well-diversified, 215–218
Portfolio theory, 109; see also Arbitrage pricing theory; Behavioral finance; Capital asset pricing model; Diversification; Efficient market hypothesis; Risk and return; Technical analysis

Poterba, James M., 243
Preferred stock, 40, 294–295
Premium, 48, **485**
Premium, price, 86–87, 271–272
Premium bonds, 304
Present value
    of an annuity, 297
    of a bond, 297
    of a price in the future, 571
    of single payment in *T* periods,
        298
**Present value of growth
    opportunities (PVGO),
    411–412**
Presidential futures markets, 562
Price-contingent orders, 59–61
Price drift, post-earnings-
    announcement, 247–248
Price-earnings multiple, 417
Price-earnings (P/E) ratio, 458
    comparative ratios in combination
        with, 424–425
    DDM combined with, 424
    growth opportunities and,
        417–421
    by industry, 423–424
    international reporting standards,
        468, 469f
    overview, 39
    pitfalls in, 421–424
    ROE and, 418–419, 459
    stock risk and, 421
Price of risk, 124
Price risk, 345
Prices and efficient market
    hypothesis, 232–233, 237
Price-to-book ratio, 424
Price-to-cash flow ratio, 425
Price-to-sales ratio, 425
**Price value of a basis point
    (PVBP), 580**
Price-weighted averages, 41–42, 44
Primary global research, 236
Primary market, 15, 55, 58
Principles-based regulation, 78
Private equity, 15
Privately held firms, 38, 55
Private placement, 55
Probability distribution, 116–117
Procter & Gamble, 216t
Professional investors
    asset allocation policies of,
        718–719
    constraints on, 714–716
    investment objectives of, 710–714
    as players, 11–12
Profitability measures, 448–452

Profitability ratios, 313–314, 460t
Profit margin, 452
Pro forma earnings, 422
Program trading, 578
Progressive tax, 692–693, 695–696
Promised yield versus expected
    yield, 315–317
Property and casualty insurance
    companies, 713, 716
Proprietary trading, 14
Prospect theory, 268–269
Prospectus, 56, 88, 92, 95, 101
Protective puts, 494–497,
    541–542
Proxy, 38
Proxy contests, 8
PRS (Political Risk Services)
    Group, 636–638
Prudent investor rule, 710, 715
PTC, 413t
Publicly traded firms, 55–56
Public Service Enterprise, 413t
Pulp Fiction (film), 295
Purchasing power, 372–373
Pure plays, 664, 666–668
Pure yield pickup swap, 355
Put bonds, 294
**Put-call parity relationship,
    536–539, 537**
Put/call ratio, 280
Putnam Prime Money Market
    Fund, 31
Put options, 46, 485
    hedge ratio for, 540
    introduction, 46–47
    profits and losses on, 485–486
    protective puts, 494–497,
        541–542
    put-call parity relationship,
        536–539
    put/call ratio and, 280
    stock portfolio with, 673–675
    valuation of, 539
    values at expiration, 490–491
**PVBP (price value of a basis
    point), 580**
PV factor, 298
**PVGO (present value of growth
    opportunities), 411–412**
Pyykkonen, Martin, 421

Q

Quality of earnings, 466–468
Quantos, 508
"Qubes" (QQQ), 95, 96t
Quick ratio, 313, 457
Qwest Communications, 9

R

Rabobank, 30
Rajaratnam, Raj, 235
Ramsey, Mike, 344n
Random walk, 233
Rapoport, Michael, 467n
RAR (Risk Adjusted Rating),
    603–604
Rate anticipation swap, 354–355
Rating agencies, 19, 28, 289, 312,
    313f, 314, 387, 427
Ratio analysis
    benchmark choices, 459
    industry groups, 459–461
    liquidity ratios, 313, 457–458,
        460t
    market price ratios, 458–459, 460t
    ROE decomposition, 452–454,
        455f
    summary, 460t
    turnover and asset utilization
        ratios, 454–457, 460t
Ratios; *see also* Price-earnings ratio;
    Sharpe ratio
    asset utilization, 454–457, 460t
    book-to-market, 211
    cash flow-to-debt, 314
    conversion, 294
    coverage, 312
    debt-to-equity, 313
    dividend payout, 410
    financial, 312–314, 413t, 459–462
    information, 598
    interest-burden, 453
    interest coverage, 453
    inventory turnover, 456
    leverage, 313, 453, 460t
    liquidity, 313, 457–458, 460t
    market price, 458–459, 460t
    plowback or earnings retention,
        410
    price-to-book, 424
    price-to-cash flow, 425
    price-to-sales, 425
    profitability, 313–314, 460t
    put/call, 280
    turnover, 454–457
Rau, P. R., 273
Rauh, J., 466
Real assets, 3–5
Real consumption, 687
Real Estate Investment Trusts
    (REITs), 87–88, 701
Real interest rate, 115
    annual standard deviation, 217t
    historical record, 125–127

inflation and, 114–116
macroeconomic analysis and, 375–376
Realized compound return, 306
Real return, 297
Rebalancing, 45, **347**–348, 721
Recession, 150–152
Redeemable preferred stock, 40
Redeemable trust certificates, 86
Red Hat, 413t
Redington, F. M., 344
Refunding, 293
Regional funds, 89
Regression equation, 170–171
Regret avoidance, 268
Regulation
    Dodd-Frank Wall Street Regulation, 14, 21–22, 319
    of futures markets, 75, 567
    of hedge funds, 662
    insider trading and, 78, 235–237, 249
    of investment companies, 88, 92, 95, 96, 101
    as investor constraint, 715
    rules-based versus principles-based, 78
    Sarbanes-Oxley Act, 76–78
    of securities markets, 28, 55–56, 61, 63, 75–78
    self-regulation, 76
Regulation NMS, 63, 65
Reinvestment rate risk, 307, 345
REITs (Real Estate Investment Trusts), 87–88, 701
Relative decline stage, 391
Relative strength, 237, **278**
Relative value, 664
Renault, E., 535n
Rendleman, R. J., Jr., 247, 248n
Replacement cost, 404
Replication, 523, 530
Representativeness bias, 266–267
Repurchase agreements (RPs), 29
Reserve Primary Fund, 31, 88n
Reserve requirement, 378
Reserving practices, 468
Residual claims, 39
Residual income, 451–452
Residual risk, 169, 595
Residual standard deviation (SD), 174–175, 202, 595
Resistance levels, 237–238
Resource allocation, 240–241
Retirement, 685–689
Retirement annuity, 685–686

Return on assets (ROA), 449, 455f
Return on capital (ROC), 413, **449**
Return on equity (ROE), 449
    decomposition of, 452–454, 455f
    financial leverage and, 449–451
    in industry analysis, 384, 385f, 386f
    P/E ratio and, 418–419, 459
Return on sales, 452
Returns; *see also* Anomalies; Excess returns; Historical returns
    annualizing, 113–114
    broad market predictors, 244
    expected, 10, 116–117
    holding-period, 111
    mutual fund fees and, 93–94
    nominal, 296
    over long horizons, 243–244
    over multiple periods, 111–113
    over short horizons, 243
    real, 297
Reuter, Jonathan, 255
Revealed preference, 124
Revenue bonds, 34
Revenue recognition, 467–468
Revenue sharing, 91
Reversal effect, 244, 249–250
Reverse repos, 29
Reversing trades, 564
Reward-to-volatility ratio, 135
Rights, 48
Risk; *see also* Interest rate risk; Portfolio risk; Risky assets or portfolios
    allocation of, 7
    country, 637
    currency, 631–632, 646–647
    diversifiable, 148
    economic, 636–637
    exchange rate, 630–635, 645–647
    financial, 636–637
    firm-specific, 148, 168, 169
    fundamental, 269–270
    of long-term investments, 176–179
    market, 148, 172
    model, 270
    nondiversifiable, 148
    nonsystematic, 148
    political, 635–638
    price, 345
    reinvestment rate, 307, 345
    residual, 169
    retirement savings and, 686–688
    systemic, 15, 20, 148, 168, 169, 319
    unique, 148

Risk Adjusted Rating (RAR), 603–604
Risk-adjusted returns
    alpha relation to, 598–600
    comparison groups, 593–594
    with a multi-index model, 600–601
    objectives, 593
    portfolio composition changes and, 605–606
    statistics, 594–595
    using information ratios, 598
    using Jensen measure, 598–600
    using Sharpe ratio and M^2, 595–597
    using Treynor measure, 597–598
Risk and return
    asset allocation and, 133–137
    historical record
        interest rates and inflation, 125–127
        risky assets and portfolios, 127–132
    inflation and real interest rate, 114–116
    international investing statistics, 639–642
    with long-term investments, 176–179
    market timing and, 612–615
    passive strategies and, 137–139
    rates of return, 111–114
Risk and risk premiums
    deviation from normality and VaR, 121–122
    normal distribution, 118–119
    normality over time, 120
    risk aversion and, 123–125
    scenario analysis and probability distributions, 116–117
    Sharpe ratio, 125
    time series of return, 122–123
Risk aversion, 124; *see also* Risk tolerance
    capital market line and, 136–137
    risk-neutral economy and, 530
    risk premiums and, 123–125, 196
Risk-free assets, 133–134
Risk-free rate, 123, 297
Riskless portfolio, 523
Risk management, 494–497
Risk Management Association, 459
Risk-neutral economy, 530
Risk-neutral probability, 530

Risk premium, 123; *see also* Risk and risk premiums
  anomalies and, 249–250
  of complete portfolios, 134–136
  equities, 137–138
  historical returns and, 131–132, 137–138
  of market portfolio, 196
  during periods of stability, 248
  risk aversion and, 123–125
Risk-return trade-off, 10–11, 155–157
Risk structure of interest rates, 317–318
Risk tolerance; *see also* Risk aversion
  concept of, 137n
  of individual investors, 708–709
  investment policy statement and, 717–718, 719
  portfolio management benefits, 240
  of professional investors, 710–714
  questionnaire, 710–711
  retirement plans and, 689, 690
Risky assets or portfolios
  asset allocation and, 133–137
  bond, 127–132
  complete portfolio and separation property, 165–166
  efficient diversification, 163–168
  expected return and risk, 134–135
  optimal, 159–162, 165–168
  stock, 127–132
  U.S. assets, 127–132
  world assets, 127–132
Risky debt and option valuation models, 507
Rite Aid, 9
Ritter, Jay, 57, 58n, 267
Ritter, Jay R., 244
Road shows, 57
ROA (return on assets), 449, 455f
Roberts, Harry, 280, 281f
Robinson, Tom, 708n
Roge, Mr., 710
Roll, Richard, 63n, 209, 650–651, 652n
Ross, Stephen A., 214, 272, 313n, 529n6
Roth, Brane v., 495
Roth accounts, 695–696, 698
Royal Bank of Scotland, 30
Royal Dutch Petroleum, 270–271
RPs (repurchase agreements), 29
Rubinstein, Mark, 546
Rules-based regulation, 78

Russell 2000 index, 59, 60f, 96t, 576–577, 600–601
Russia, 626, 676
Rydqvist, K., 58n

S
SAC Capital Advisors, 235, 236
Sadka, Ronnie, 671
Saha, Atanu, 673
SAI (Statement of Additional Information), 101
Sales charge (load), 87
Sales sensitivity, 388
Salomon Smith Barney, 14, 45, 68
Sample-size neglect, 266–267
Samuelson, Paul, 256, 431
Samurai bonds, 33, 295
Sanford Bernstein & Co., 355–356
SAP, 413t
Sarbanes-Oxley Act, 9, 76–78
Savings and loan (S&L) institutions, 713
Savings plans, 685–686
Scenario analysis, 116–117, 121–122
Schatsky, Mr., 710
Scheck, Justin, 468n
Scherbina, A., 138
Schleifer, A., 269n
Scholes, Myron, 209, 530
Schwab, 69
SCL (security characteristic line), 170, 203
Scudder Kemper Investments, Inc., 710
Seasoned equity offering, 56
Secondary market, 15, 55
Sector funds, 89, 385
Sector rotation, 388–389
Sector selection decisions, 609–611, 663
Securities Act of 1933, 75, 662
Securities and Exchange Commission (SEC)
  credit ratings agency oversight by, 22
  financial statement standards, 469
  flash crash of 2010 report, 67
  foreign bond registration with, 295
  as information source, 403
  insider trading restrictions by, 78, 236, 249
  investment company regulation by, 88, 92, 95, 96, 101
  Madoff scandal and, 678
  securities markets regulation by, 28, 55–56, 61, 63, 75, 76, 78

Securities Exchange Act of 1934, 62, 75
Securities Investor Protection Act of 1970, 75
Securities Investor Protection Corporation (SIPC), 75
Securities markets
  electronic trading, 62–64
  globalization of, 68–69
  margin accounts, 70–72
  regulation of, 28, 55–56, 61, 63, 75–78
  securities issuance, 55–57
  short sales, 72–75
  trading, 57–62
  trading costs, 69
  trading strategies, 65–68
  U.S. markets, 64–65
Securitization, 17–18, 37, 713
Security analysis, 10, 174–176, 177t, 369; *see also* Equity valuation; Macroeconomic analysis
Security Analysis (Graham and Dodd), 469–470
Security characteristic line (SCL), 170, 203
Security Exchange Act of 1934, 236
Security market line (SML), 198–199, 210, 214
Security selection, 9
  active versus passive policies, 651, 719–720
  hedge fund investments and, 665
  introduction, 26
  as investment policy, 609–611, 718–719
Security valuation; *see* Bond prices and yields
Selection bias issue of EMH, 241–242, 607
Self-destructing price patterns, 238, 251
Self-regulation, 76
Selling, Thomas I., 455n
Selling short; *see* Short sales
Semistrong-form EMH, 236–237, 244–249
Sentiment indicators, 278f, 279–280, 374
Separate Trading of Registered Interest and Principal of Securities (STRIPS), 310
Separation property, 166
Serial bonds, 315
Serial correlation of returns, 243
Settlement date, 301
Seyhun, Nejat H., 249, 259

Shanken, Jay, 246n

Shareholders, residual status of, 404

Shareholders' equity, 445, 458

Sharpe, William F., 11, 135, 169, 192, 193, 209, 601–603, 604n

Sharpe ratio, 125, 595
capital allocation line and, 135–137
hedge funds, 671–672
historical returns and, 131
international investments and, 643, 644, 647
optimal risky portfolio, 160–161, 164–165, 166, 168, 175, 176
risk-adjusted returns and, 595–604
risk adjustments with changing portfolio composition, 605–606

Shefrin, Hersh, 267

Shelf registration, 56

Shell Transport, 270–271

Shiller, Robert, 244, 496

Shleifer, A., 271

Shleifer, Andrei, 250

Short hedge, 569

Short interest, 280

Short position, 559

Short sales, 60, **72**–75, 76, 599, 662, 664

Short-term bonds and interest rates, 335–337

Shumway, Tyler, 268

"Siamese Twin" companies, 270–271

Single-index stock market
diversification in, 172–174
index models, 168–170, 594–595
security analysis with, 174–176, 177t
statistical and graphical representation, 170–172

Single stock futures, 561

Sinking funds, 314–315

SIPC (Securities Investor Protection Corporation), 75

Skew, 122, 130–131

S&L (savings and loan) institutions, 713

Sloan, Richard G., 246n

Slow growers, 391

Small-firm effect, 245–246, 249–250, 251

Small minus big (SMB) portfolios, 212–213, 250, 600

Smith, Randall, 421n

SML (security market line), 198–199, 210, 214

Social investing, 714

Social Science Research Network, 251

Social Security, 699, 702

Société Générale, 483

Soft dollars, 94

Solnik, Bruno, 632, 648n, 650

Sonne, Paul, 468n

Sotheby's, 420

South Carolina E&G, 413t

Southern Company, 413t

South Sea Company, 248

Southwest Airlines, 195

Sovereign debt, 133n16

S&P 500 Index; *see* Standard & Poor's 500 Index

S&P 500 volatility index (VIX), 535, 536f, 593

Spatt, Chester, 60n, 64n

Specialist markets, 62

Specialists, 62, 64, 65

Speculation, 124, 568–570

Speculative grade bonds, 312

Speidell, Lawrence S., 469f

Sperling, Gene, 384n

"Spiders" (SPDRs), 95, 96t

Spot-futures parity theorem, 571–575, **574,** 633

Spot price, 559, 566

Spread (bid-ask), 58–63

Spread (futures), 571, 575

Spread (options), 499–501

Stalwarts, 391

Stambaugh, Robert F., 244

Standard deviation, 117
of complete portfolios, 134–136
expected return and, 117
normal distribution and, 118–119
normality over time, 120
residual, 202
risky assets and portfolios, 128–131
Sharpe ratio and, 125
from time series of return, 122–123
Treasury bill rate, 126
of two-risky-asset portfolios, 157–158

Standard error of the regression, 216

Standard & Poor's 100 Index, 489

Standard & Poor's 500 Index (S&P 500)
annual standard deviation of, 241
arbitrage portfolios and, 216–218
as benchmark, 176, 200–201, 253, 594, 608, 625, 720
characteristics of, 42–44
dividend yield of, 574, 697

earnings per share versus, 373

earnings yield of, 430–431

ETFs on, 96t

forecasts, 431

futures contracts on, 567, 574, 576–577

hedge fund indexes compared with, 674, 675f

historical returns, 9, 16f, 137–138, 150, 196, 201, 203t, 204t

implied volatility of, 535–536, 545–546

index funds and, 89, 239

indexing, 137

largest-capitalization stocks in, 216t

market depth, 59, 60f

as market portfolio proxy, 200–201

options on, 488–489, 508

P/E ratios and inflation rates, 421–422

portfolio performance evaluation and, 594, 600–601, 602–603

regression statistics, 216, 217t

single stock futures contracts, 561

Standard & Poor's Corporation, 19, 28, 289, 312, 313f, 314, 387

Standard & Poor's Depository Receipts (SPDRs), 95

Start-up stage, 390

Statement of Additional Information (SAI), 101

Statement of cash flows, 445–448, **446**

State Street, 96t

Statistical arbitrage, 665

Statistical representation of single-index models, 170–172

Statman, Meir, 149n, 267, 268

Staunton, Mike, 130n, 138

Stern Stewart, 451, 452n4

Stickney, Clyde P., 455n

Stiglitz, Joseph E., 235

Stochastic volatility models, 536

Stock exchanges, 65

Stockholders, residual status of, 404

Stockholders' equity, 445, 458

Stock-index futures, 543, 567, 575, 576–577

Stock market analysts, 250, 252

Stock market indexes
equally weighted, 44–45
foreign and international, 45
market-value weighted, 42–44
price-weighted, 41–42, 44

Stock market listings, 39
Stock markets; *see also* Crashes and
    bubbles
    anomalies in, 244–249
    global/international, 372t, 631
    globalization of, 68–69
    listings, 39
    price analysis of, 232
    scenario analysis, 117
    valuation of, 429–431
Stock options, 8
Stock price
    investment opportunities and,
        409–412
    performance by industry, 386f
Stocks; *see also* Equity valuation;
        International investing
    common, 38–39
    company, 149
    cyclical/defensive, 169, 171
    depositary receipts, 40, 639
    global market for, 40, 45, 58,
        626–630
    growth, 103, 251
    historical returns, 9, 10, 137–138
    leveraged equity, 506
    market portfolio and, 194
    options investments versus, 492–494,
        496f
    predictors of returns in, 244
    preferred, 40, 294–295
    in sheltered versus unsheltered
        plans, 697–699
    synthetic positions, 577
    trading, 58–62, 69, 266
    trading strategies, 65–68
    value, 103, 211, 251
Stock selection, 654
Stock splits, 41–42, 487
Stop-buy orders, 60–61, 74–75
Stop-loss orders, 60–61
Stop orders, 60–61
Straddles, 497, **499,** 500f
Straight bonds, 502–505
Straps, 499
Strebel, Paul J., 245
Strike price, 46, **485,** 486–487
Strips (option), 499
STRIPS (Separate Trading of
    Registered Interest and
    Principal of Securities), 310
Strong-form EMH, 236–237, 249
Stub value, 271
Stulz, R., 265n
Style analysis, 601–603
Style drift, 662
Style portfolios, 250

Subordinated debentures, 36
Subordination clauses, 315
Subprime mortgages, 18–20,
    28–29, 37
Subrahmanyam, Avanidhar,
    63n, 251
Substitution swap, 354
Summers, L., 269n
Summers, Lawrence, 243
Summers, Lawrence H., 703
SuperDOT, 65
Supply curve, 375–376
Supply shock, 376–377
Supply-side policies, 378–379
Support levels, 237
Survivorship bias, 606, 672–**673**
Swap dealers, 582–583
Swaps, 19–20, 317–319, 354–355,
    581–583
Synthetic ETFs, 96
Synthetic protective puts, 542
Synthetic stock positions, 577
Systematic risk, 148
    APT and CAPM generalization,
        218–220
    beta and, 595
    diversification and, 168, 169, 170,
        171, 172, 174
    Treynor measure and, 598
Systemic risk, 15, **20,** 148, 168,
    169, 319

T

Tail events, 674–676
Tail risk, 122, 129–131
Taleb, Nassim, 675–676
Tampa Electric, 413t
Tangible fixed assets, 445
Target date retirement funds
    (TDRFs), 703n
Targeted-maturity funds, 89
Tate, G, 266
Taxable bonds, 34–36
Tax anticipation notes, 34
Taxes
    capital gains, 697
    on ETFs, 98
    flat, 689
    on futures gains or losses, 567
    as investor constraint, 715
    on municipal bond interest, 34
    on mutual fund income, 94–95
    on OID bond interest, 310–311
    progressive, 692–693, 695–696
    on retirement plans, 689–690
Tax-exempt bonds, 34–36

Tax shelters, 690
    economics of, 690–693
    sheltered versus unsheltered
        savings, 697–699
    types, 694–699
Tax swap, 355
Tax-timing option, 697
TDRFs (target date retirement
    funds), 703n
Technical analysis, 237
    efficient markets and, 237–238,
        244
    introduction, 274, 402
    sentiment indicators, 279–280
    trends and corrections
        breadth, 277–278, 279t
        momentum and moving
            averages, 274–276
        point and figure charts,
            276–277
        relative strength, 278
    warning about, 280–281
TED spread, 16–17, 21, 32
Templeton, John, 256
Templeton Funds, 256
Term insurance, 712
Term repos, 29
Term structure of interest rates, 319
Thaler, R. H., 244, 270n5
Thaler, Richard, 265n
Thaler, Richard H., 266, 268, 271
Thomas, J., 247n
3Com, 270–271
Three-factor model, 211–214, 250,
    253, 600–601
Three-stage growth models,
    416–417, 428–429
Tick size, 32, 62
Tikit Group, 468
Time diversification, 176–179
Time series of return, 122–123
Times interest earned, 453
Times-interest-earned ratio, 312
Time spread, 499
Time value, 520
Time value of money, 310
Time Warner, 445n
Time-weighted average return,
    112
Timmerman, A., 256
TIPS (Treasury Inflation-Protected
    Securities), 33, 127, 133, 216t,
    296–297
Titman, Sheridan, 243
Tobin, James, 166, 404
Tobin's q, 404
Tokyo Disneyland, 296

Tokyo Stock Exchange, 68
Tong, Qing, 251
Total asset turnover (ATO), 452
Toyota, 3–4, 7, 240, 278, 354
Trading
    algorithmic, 65, 66, 67
    bonds, 59, 64, 68
    costs, 69
    futures, 563–567
    gender and overconfidence, 266
    insider, 78, 235–237, 249
    market types, 58–59
    options, 486–487
    order types, 59–61
    pairs, 66, 665
    program, 578
    proprietary, 14
    stocks, 61–62
Trading strategies, 65–68
Traditional retirement accounts, 695–696, 698–699
Trainer, Francis, 355–356
Tranches, 19
Transparency, 8
Treasury bills, 27
    annualizing returns, 114
    historical returns, 9–10, 15–16, 125–127, 129f, 203t, 204t, 207
    inflation rates and, 125, 126–127
    in options, stock, and lending strategy, 492–494, 613–615
    pricing and yields, 27–28
    as risk-free assets, 9, 30–31, 123, 133, 159–162
    as zero-coupon instruments, 310
Treasury-bond futures, 579–580
Treasury Inflation-Protected Securities (TIPS), 33, 127, 133, 216t, 296–297
Treasury notes or bonds, 32
    characteristics, 291–293
    historical returns, 129f, 430
    open market operations, 378
    price and yield, 32–33
Treasury securities, yield curves on, 320f, 323–324
Treasury strips, 310
Trends, market, 274–279
Treynor, Jack L., 175, 193, 598, 615
Treynor-Black model, 175–176, 193, 207, 600
Treynor measure, 597–598, 599
Trin statistic, 279
Triumph of the Optimists (Dimson, Marsh, and Staunton), 138

Trough, 379
T. Rowe Price Associates, Inc., 710
Trueman, B., 252
Trustees, 710
TSX index, 45
Tulip mania bubble, 248
Turnarounds, 391–392
Turnover, 94
Turnover ratio, 454–457
Tuttle, Donald L., 708n
Tversky, A., 266, 268n
12b-1 fees, 92–93
Two-factor model, 210–211
Two-risky-assets portfolios
    covariance and correlation, 150–153
    historical data usage, 153–154
    mean-variance criterion, 157–159
    risk-return trade-off, 155–157
    rules of, 154–155
Two-stage DDM, 413
Two-state option pricing, 522–529
Tyco, 76

U

UBS, 14, 30
Underwriters, 15, 56–57
Unemployment rate, 374
Uniform Securities Act, 76
Unique risk, 148
United Illuminating, 413t
U.S. bond portfolios, 127–132
U.S. Department of Commerce, 459
U.S. securities markets, 64–65
U.S. stock portfolios, 127–132
U.S. Treasury, 31
U.S. Treasury bills; *see* Treasury bills
Unit investment trusts, 86
Units, 87
Universal life policy, 712–713
Unmanaged trusts, 86
Updegrave, Walter, 149n

V

Value at risk (VaR), 119, 121–122
Value investing, 469–470
Value Line Investment Survey, 387, 413–416
Value premium, 211
Value stocks, 103, 211, 251
Vanguard 500 Index Fund, 239
Vanguard Bond Index Fund, 239
Vanguard funds, 88, 89–90, 93, 96t, 98, 99, 133, 639, 694
Vanguard Group, 710
Vanguard Total Stock Market Index Fund, 99

VaR (value at risk), 119, 121–122
Variable life policy, 712
Variance, 117
    of excess returns, 170
    normality over time, 120
    risky assets and portfolios, 130–131
    Sharpe ratio and, 125
    from time series of return, 122–123
Vassalou, M, 250n
Venture capital (VC), 15
Vishny, R., 250, 269n
VIX (S&P 500 volatility index), 535, 536f, 593
Volatility
    Black-Scholes model and, 545–546
    implied, 534–536
    October 1987 crash and, 31t, 32, 543, 546
    option value relationship to, 521n, 527
Volcker, Paul, 14
Volcker Rule, 14, 21
Voting rights, 38

W

Waddell & Reed Financial, 67
Wahlen, James, 455n
Waldmann, R., 269n
Wallace, A., 209n11
Walmart, 451
Wang, Zhenyu, 209
Warrants, 505
Weak-form EMH, 236–237, 243–244
WEBS (World Equity Benchmark Shares), 95, 96t, 640
Well-diversified portfolios, 215–218
Wells Fargo, 216t
Wells Fargo Advantage Growth Fund, 101, 102f
Wermers, R., 256
Wermers, R. R., 253
Westerfield, Randolph W., 313n
White, A., 535n
White, H., 256
Whole-life insurance policy, 712
Wiggins, J. B., 535n
Wilshire 5000 index, 44, 96t, 99, 100f, 252
Wolfson, M. A., 234
Womack, K. L., 252
Workout period, 354
World bond portfolios, 127–132
WorldCom, 9, 76

World Equity Benchmark Shares
    (WEBS), 95, 96t, 640
World stock portfolios, 127–132
Worthen, Ben, 468n

Y

Yahoo!, 8, 101, 319, 382, 383f, 403,
    459
Yan, Jinghua, 234n
Yang, Jerry, 8
Yankee bonds, 33, 295
Yield curve, 319–324
Yields
    annual percentage, 114
    bond-equivalent, 28

current, 304
dividend, 111, 244, 697
earnings, 430
expected versus promised, 315–317
municipal versus corporate debt,
    35–36
Treasury bills, 27–28
Yield to call, 304–306
Yield to maturity (YTM), 302
    default risk and, 315–317
    duration and, 338–343
    holding-period return versus,
        309–310
    interest rate sensitivity and,
        335–337

overview, 33, 302–304
realized compound return versus,
    306–307

Z

Zero-coupon bonds, 291
    duration of, 338–341
    guaranteed investment contracts,
        344–348
    interest rate sensitivity of,
        336–337
    Treasury STRIPS and, 310
Zero sum game, 559
Zitzewitz, Eric, 600
Zurich Group Inc., 710

Praise for *Mistress of Justice* and Jeffery Dea

'An intelligently written thriller.' *klist*

"This novel is a solid achievement.' *tery News*

'The best psychological thriller writ *The Times*

'If you want thrills, Deaver is you. *Guardian*

'The twists and turns from devilish Deaver will have you burning the midnight oil, then using it to set fire to the candle you'll be burning at both ends until you finish this . . . This is the perfect accompaniment on a winter's night, curled up on the sofa with a glass of your favourite tipple.' *Sun*

'No one is better at narrative misdirection. Just at the point you think "That's impossible!" Deaver demonstrates the exact opposite.' *Evening Standard*

'Jeffery Deaver is grand master of the ticking-clock thriller.' Kathy Reichs

'Deaver is a master of manipulation himself; his skillfully constructed plots are devilishly tricky to track and impossible to solve, just the way we like them.' *New York Times Book Review*

'Jeffery Deaver is a master at crafting intricate crimes that are solved through guile, tenacity and sheer creative genius. And Lincoln Rhyme is one of a kind.' Harlan Coben

Also by Jeffery Deaver

Mistress of Justice
The Lesson of Her Death
Praying for Sleep
Speaking in Tongues
The Devil's Teardrop
The Blue Nowhere
Garden of Beasts
The Bodies Left Behind
Edge
The October List

The Rune Series
Manhattan is My Beat
Death of a Blue Movie Star
Hard News

The Location Scout Series
Shallow Graves
Bloody River Blues
Hell's Kitchen

The Lincoln Rhyme Thrillers
The Bone Collector
The Coffin Dancer
The Empty Chair
The Stone Monkey
The Vanished Man
The Twelfth Card
The Cold Moon
The Broken Window
The Burning Wire
The Kill Room
The Skin Collector
The Steel Kiss

The Kathryn Dance Thrillers
The Sleeping Doll
Roadside Crosses
XO
Solitude Creek

A James Bond Novel
Carte Blanche

Short Stories
Twisted
More Twisted
Trouble in Mind

JEFFERY DEAVER

MISTRESS OF JUSTICE

HODDER

First published in Great Britain in 1992 by Hodder & Stoughton
An Hachette UK company

This Hodder paperback edition 2016

1

A CIP catalogue record for this title is available from the British Library

Paperback ISBN 978 1 473 63191 5
eBook ISBN 978 1 848 94178 6

Typeset by Palimpsest Book Production Ltd, Falkirk, Stirlingshire

Printed and bound by Clays Ltd, St Ives plc

Hodder & Stoughton policy is to use papers that are natural, renewable and
recyclable products and made from wood grown in sustainable forests.
The logging and manufacturing processes are expected to conform to
the environmental regulations of the country of origin.

Hodder & Stoughton Ltd
Carmelite House
50 Victoria Embankment
London EC4Y 0DZ

www.hodder.co.uk

About the Author

Two of my most heartfelt beliefs about writing suspense fiction are these: First, it's a craft—a skill that can be learned and refined and improved with practice. Second, we writers of suspense fiction have a duty to entertain and to—as the other moniker for the genre suggests—thrill our readers.

In rereading the first version of this book, which I wrote thirteen years ago, I realized that, while it was a perfectly acceptable dramatic, character-driven study of life on Wall Street, it didn't make my—and presumably my readers'— palms sweat.

It didn't, in other words, thrill.

I considered just letting the book stand as a curiosity among the suspense novels I've written but I felt the nag of the second belief I mentioned above—that overarching duty to readers. I know how much I enjoy the experience of reading a roller coaster of a story and I felt that the premise of this novel and the characters I'd created would lend themselves to more of a carnival ride of a book. Hence, I dismantled the book completely and rewrote nearly all of it.

I had a chance recently to write an introduction to a new edition of Mary Shelley's Frankenstein and during the course of researching her work I learned that she significantly revised the novel thirteen years after it was first published (how's that for a coincidence?). Many of the changes in the later edition of Frankenstein reflected the author's altered worldview. Not so in the case of Mistress of Justice. The current edition stands true to its view of Wall Street in the chaotic era of the 1980s—takeover fever, uncontrolled wealth, too-chic-for-words Manhattan clubs, ruthlessness in boardrooms and bedrooms . . . and the many hardworking lawyers who wished for nothing more than to help their clients and to make a living at their chosen profession.

My special thanks to editor Kate Miciak for giving me this chance and for helping this book realize its potential.

—J.D., Pacific Grove, CA, 2001

ONE

Conflicts of Interest

"Let the jury consider their verdict," the King said, for about the twentieth time that day.

"No, no," said the Queen. "Sentence first—verdict afterwards."

—Lewis Carroll, *Alice's Adventures in Wonderland*

CHAPTER ONE

The drapery man had been warned that even though it was now well after midnight, Sunday morning of the Thanksgiving holiday, there would very likely be people in the firm here, attorneys and paralegals, still working.

And so he carried the weapon at his side, pointed downward.

It was a curious thing—not a knife exactly, more of an ice pick, but longer and made of a blackened, tempered metal.

He held it with the confidence of someone who was very familiar with the device. And who had used it before.

Dressed in gray coveralls bearing the stencil of a bogus drapery cleaning service and wearing a baseball cap, the big, sandy-haired man now paused and, hearing footsteps, slipped into an empty office. Then there was silence. And he continued on, through shadows, pausing for a long moment, frozen like a fox near a ground nest of skittish birds.

He consulted the diagram of the firm, turned along one corridor and continued, gripping the handle of the weapon tightly in his hand, which was as muscular as the rest of his body.

As he neared the office he sought, he reached up and pulled a paper face mask over his mouth. This was not so that he wouldn't be recognized but because he was concerned that he might lose a fleck of spit that could be retrieved as evidence and used in a DNA match.

The office, which belonged to Mitchell Reece, was at the end of the corridor, not far from the front door of the firm. Like all the offices here, the lights were left on, which meant that the drapery man wasn't sure that it was unoccupied. But he glanced in quickly, saw that the room was empty and stepped inside.

The office was very cluttered. Books, files, charts, thousands of sheets of papers. Still, the man found the filing cabinet easily—there was only one here with two locks on it—and crouched, pulling on tight latex gloves and extracting his tool kit from his coverall pockets.

The drapery man set the weapon nearby and began to work on the locks.

Scarf, Mitchell Reece thought, drying his hands in the law firm's marble-and-oak rest room. He'd forgotten his wool scarf.

Well, he was surprised he'd managed to remember his coat and briefcase. The lanky thirty-three-year-old associate, having had only four hours' sleep, had arrived at the firm around 8 A.M. yesterday, Saturday, and had worked straight through until about an hour ago, when he'd fallen asleep at his desk.

A few moments before, something had startled him out of that sleep. He'd roused himself and decided to head home for a few hours of shut-eye the old-fashioned way—horizontally. He'd grabbed his coat and briefcase and made this brief pit stop.

But he wasn't going outside without his scarf—1010

WINS had just reported the temperature was 22 degrees and falling.

Reece stepped into the silent corridor.

Thinking about a law firm at night.

The place was shadowy but not dark, silent yet filled with a white noise of memory and power. A law firm wasn't like other places: banks or corporations or museums or concert halls; it seemed to remain alert even when its occupants were gone.

Here, down a wide wallpapered corridor, was a portrait of a man in stern sideburns, a man who left his partnership at the firm to become governor of the state of New York.

Here, in a small foyer decorated with fresh flowers, was an exquisite Fragonard oil painting, no alarm protecting it. In the hall beyond, two Keith Harings and a Chagall.

Here, in a conference room, were reams of papers containing the magic words required by the law to begin a corporate breach of contract suit for three hundred million dollars, and in a similar room down the hall sat roughly the same amount of paper, assembled in solemn blue binders, which would create a charitable trust to fund private AIDS research.

Here, in a locked safe-file room, rested the last will and testament of the world's third-richest man—whose name most people had never heard of.

Mitchell Reece put these philosophical meanderings down to sleep deprivation, told himself to mentally shut up and turned down the corridor that would lead to his office.

Footsteps approaching.

In a soldier's instant the drapery man was on his feet, the ice pick in one hand, his burglar tools in the other. He eased behind the door to Reece's office and quieted his breathing as best he could.

He'd been in this line of work for some years. He'd been hurt in fights and had inflicted a great deal of pain. He'd

killed seven men and two women. But this history didn't
dull his emotions. His heart now beat hard, his palms
sweated and he fervently hoped he didn't have to hurt anyone tonight. Even people like him vastly preferred to avoid
killing.

Which didn't mean he'd hesitate to if he were found out
here.

The steps grew closer.

█████

Mitchell Reece, walking unsteadily from exhaustion,
moved down the corridor, his feet tapping on the marble
floor, the sound occasionally muffled when he strode over
the Turkish rugs carefully positioned throughout the firm
(and carefully mounted on antiskid pads; law firms are extremely cognizant of slip-and-fall lawsuits).

In his mind was a daunting list of tasks to complete before the trial that was scheduled in two days. Reece had
graduated from Harvard Law fourth in his class, largely
thanks to lists—memorizing for his exams volumes of cases
and rules of law and statutes. He was now the firm's most
successful senior litigation associate for much the same reason. Every single aspect of the case—the civil trial of *New
Amsterdam Bank & Trust, Ltd. v. Hanover & Stiver, Inc.*—was
contained in a complicated series of lists, which Reece was
constantly reviewing and editing in his mind.

He supposed he'd been reviewing his lists when he'd
neglected to pick up his scarf.

He now approached the doorway and stepped inside.

Ah, yes, there it was, the tan cashmere given to him by a
former girlfriend. It sat just where he'd left it, next to the refrigerator in the coffee room across from his office. When
he'd arrived that morning—well, make that *yesterday* morning at this point—he'd stopped first in this canteen room to
make a pot of coffee and had dropped the scarf on the table
while getting the machine going.

He now wrapped it around his neck and stepped out

into the corridor. He continued to the front door of the firm. He hit the electric lock button and—hearing the satisfying click that he'd come to know so well, thanks to his thousands of late hours at the firm—Mitchell Reece stepped into the lobby, where he summoned the elevator.

As he waited it seemed to him that he heard a noise somewhere in the firm—nearby. A faint whine of a door hinge maybe. Followed by the *snick-snick* of two metal objects faintly colliding.

But then the elevator arrived. Reece stepped in and began once again reciting his scrolls of lists silently to himself.

"I think we may have a misunderstanding," Taylor Lockwood said.

"Not really," returned the voice, also female though much older, from the phone.

Taylor dropped into her squeaky chair and rolled against the wall of her cubicle. *Not really?* What did *that* mean? She continued, "I'm the lead paralegal on the SCB closing. That's at four today."

It was 8:30 A.M., the Tuesday after the Thanksgiving holiday, and she'd just arrived back here after a few hours' sleep at home, having spent most of the night at the firm, editing, assembling and stapling hundreds of documents for the closing this afternoon.

Ms. Strickland, on the other end of the line, said, "You've been reassigned. Something urgent."

This'd never happened that Taylor knew about. It was general knowledge—as solid as Newton's laws—that a law firm partner was incapable of handling a business closing without the presence of the paralegal who'd worked on the deal. Law is manifest in the details, and a firm's paralegals are the gurus of minutiae.

The only reason for a last-minute reassignment was if a major screwup had occurred.

But Taylor Lockwood did not screw up and a cursory

review of her ball-busting work on the case over the past weeks revealed no glitches the remedy for which would involve her summarily getting kicked off the deal.

"What're my options?" she asked the paralegal supervisor.

"Actually," the word stretching into far more syllables than it had, "there *are* no options."

Taylor spun her chair one way, then the other. A paper cut inflicted by a UCC security agreement last night had started to bleed again and she wrapped her finger in a napkin with a happy turkey printed on it, a remnant from a firm cocktail party the week before. "Why—?"

"Mitchell Reece needs your help."

Reece? Taylor reflected. So I'll be playing with the big boys. . . . Good news, but still odd. "Why me? I've never worked for him."

"Apparently your reputation has preceded you." Ms. Strickland sounded wary, as if she hadn't known that Taylor had a reputation. "He said you and only you."

"Is this long-term? I'm taking a vacation next week. I'm scheduled to go skiing."

"You can negotiate with Mr. Reece. I mentioned your schedule to him."

"What was his reaction?"

"He didn't seem overly concerned."

"Why would he be? *He's* not the one going skiing." Blood seeping through the napkin had stained the turkey's smiling face. She pitched it out.

"Be in his office in an hour."

"What sort of project?"

A pause, while Ms. Strickland perhaps selected from among her quiver of delicate words. "He wasn't specific."

"Should I call Mr. Bradshaw?"

"It's all taken care of."

"I'm sorry?" Taylor asked. "What's been taken care of?"

"Everything. You've been transferred and another paralegal—two actually—are working with Mr. Bradshaw."

"Already?"

"Be in Mr. Reece's office in one hour," Ms. Strickland reminded.

"All right."

"Oh, one more thing."

"What's that?"

"Mr. Reece said you're not supposed to mention this to anyone. He said that was very important. Not to anyone."

"Then I won't."

They hung up.

Taylor walked through the carpeted cubicles of the paralegal pen to the one window in this part of the firm. Outside, the Financial District was bathed in early-morning, overcast light. She didn't care much for the scenery today. Too much old grimy stone, like weathered, eerie mountains. In one window of a building across the way, a maintenance man was struggling to erect a Christmas tree. It seemed out of place in the huge marble lobby.

She focused on the window in front of her and realized she was looking at her own reflection.

Taylor Lockwood was not heavy but neither was she fashionably bony or angular. Earthy. That was how she thought of herself. When asked her height she would answer five-five (she was five-four and a quarter) but she had a dense black tangle of hair that added another two inches. A boyfriend once said that with her hair hanging frizzy and loose she looked like she belonged in a pre-Raphaelite painting.

On days when she was in a good mood she believed she resembled a young Mary Pickford. On not-so-good days she felt like a thirty-year-old little girl, standing pigeon-toed, impatiently waiting for the arrival of maturity, decisiveness, authority. She thought she looked her best in imperfect reflections, like storefronts painted black.

Or Wall Street law firm windows.

She turned away and walked back to her cubicle. It was now close to nine and the firm was coming awake, growing busier—catching up with her; this was usually the case; Taylor Lockwood was often one of the first employees to arrive. Other paralegals were making their way to their desks. Shouts of greetings—and warnings of impending crises—were crisscrossing the paralegal pen, war stories of subway snarls and traffic jams were exchanged. She sat down in her chair and thought about how abruptly the course of life can change, and at someone else's whim.

Mr. Reece said you're not supposed to mention this to anyone. He said that was very important. Not to anyone.

Then I won't.

Taylor glanced at her finger and went to find a Band-Aid for the paper cut.

CHAPTER TWO

■■■■■■On a warm morning in April of 1887, a balding, thirty-two-year-old sideburned lawyer named Frederick Phyle Hubbard walked into a small office on lower Broadway, slipped his silk hat and Prince Albert coat onto a hook and said wryly to his partner, "Good morning, Mr. White. Have you secured any clients yet?"

The life of a law firm began.

Both Hubbard and George C. T. White had graduated from Columbia Law School and had promptly come under the acutely probing eye of Walter Carter, Esquire, the senior partner at Carter, Hughes & Cravath. Carter hired them without pay for a year then turned them into professionals at the end of their probation by paying them the going salary of twenty dollars a month.

Six years later, the two men—as ambitious as Carter had pegged them to be—borrowed three thousand dollars from White's father, hired one law clerk and a male secretary and opened their own firm.

Though they dreamed of offices in the state-of-the-art Equitable Building at 120 Broadway they settled for less.

Rent in the old building they chose near Trinity Church was sixty-four dollars a month, which bought the partners two dark rooms. Still, their quarters had central heat (though they kept the office's two fireplaces going throughout most of January and February) and an elevator that one operated by pulling a thick rope running through the middle of the car with pieces of tapestry carpeting Hubbard's wife had cut and stitched; the felt pads provided by the building management were, Hubbard felt, inelegant, and he feared they might "impress clients adversely."

Over lunch at Delmonico's on Fifth Avenue, where Hubbard and White sunk much of their first profits feeding existing and would-be clients, they would brag about the firm's new letterpress, which used a damp cloth to make copies of firm correspondence. The firm had a typewriter but the lawyers wrote most of their correspondence in ink with steel pens. Hubbard and White both insisted that their secretary fill the firm's ink-blotting shakers with Lake Champlain black sand. The men had looked at, though rejected, a telephone—it would have cost ten dollars a month (besides, there was no one to call but court clerks and a few government officials).

In school both men had dreamed of becoming great trial lawyers and during their clerking days at Carter, Hughes they'd spent many hours in courtrooms watching famous litigators cajole, charm and terrorize juries and witnesses alike. But in their own practice economics could not be ignored and the lucrative field of corporate law became the mainstay of their young practice. They billed at fifty-two cents an hour though they added arbitrary and generous bonuses for certain assignments.

Those were the days before income tax, before the Antitrust Division of the Justice Department, before the SEC; corporations rode like Assyrians over the landscape of American free enterprise and Messrs. Hubbard and White were their warlords. As their clients became exceedingly wealthy so did they. A third senior partner, Colonel Benjamin Willis, joined the firm in 1920. He died several years later of pneumonia related to a World War One mustard gassing but he left as a legacy to the firm one railroad, two banks and several major utilities as clients. Hubbard and White also inherited the matter of what to do with his name—appending it to theirs had been the price for both the colonel and his fat clients. Nothing of the bargain was in writing but after his death the remaining partners kept their word; the firm would forever be known as a triumvirate.

By the time the mantles passed, in the late 1920s, Hubbard, White & Willis had grown to thirty-eight attorneys and had moved into its cherished Equitable Building. Banking, corporate law, securities and litigation made up the bulk of the work, which was still performed as it had been in the nineteenth century—by gentlemen, and a certain type of gentleman only. Attorneys seeking work who were in fact or by appearance Jewish, Italian or Irish were interviewed with interest and cordiality and were never offered positions.

Women were always welcome—good stenographers being hard to find.

The firm continued to grow, occasionally spinning off satellite firms or political careers (invariably Republican). Several attorneys general issued from Hubbard, White & Willis, as did an SEC commissioner, a senator, two governors and a vice president of the United States. Yet the firm, unlike many of its size and prestige on Wall Street, wasn't a major political breeding ground. It was common knowledge that politics was power without money and the partners at Hubbard, White saw no reason to forsake one reward of Wall Street practice when they could have both.

The present-day Hubbard, White & Willis had over two hundred fifty attorneys and four hundred support employees, placing it in the medium-sized category of Manhattan firms. Of the eighty-four partners, eleven were women, seven were Jewish (including four of the women), two were Asian-American and three were black (one of whom was, to the great delight of the EEOC-conscious executive committee, Latino as well).

Hubbard, White & Willis was now big business. Overhead ran $3 million a month and the partners had upped the billing rates considerably higher than the small change charged by Frederick Hubbard. An hour of a partner's time could hit $650 and in big transactions a premium (referred to by associates as a no-fuck-up bonus) of perhaps $500,000 would be added to the client's final tab.

Twenty-five-year-old associates fresh out of law school made around $100,000 a year.

The firm had moved from sooty limestone into glass and metal and now occupied four floors in a skyscraper near the World Trade Center. An interior designer had been paid a million dollars to awe clients with dramatic understatement. The theme was lavender and burgundy and sea blue, rich stone, smoky glass, brushed metal and dark oak. Spiral marble staircases connected the floors, and the library was a three-story atrium with fifty-foot windows offering a stunning view of New York Harbor. The firm's art collection was appraised at close to fifty million dollars.

Within this combination MOMA and *Interior Design* centerfold, Conference Room 16–2 was the only one large enough to hold all of the partners of the firm. This Tuesday morning, though, only two men were sitting here, at the end of a U-shaped conference table surfaced with dark red marble and edged in rosewood.

Amid an aroma of baseboard heat and brewing coffee they together read a single sheet of paper, gazing at it like next of kin identifying a body.

"Lord, I can't believe this." Donald Burdick, the man pinning the sheet to the table, had been the head of the firm's executive committee for the past eight years. At sixty-seven he was lean and had sleek gray hair trimmed short by a barber who visited Burdick's office fortnightly, the old Italian brought to the firm in the partner's Rolls Royce— "fetched," as Burdick said.

People often described the partner as dapper but this was offered only by those who didn't know him well. "Dapper" suggested weakness and a lack of grit and Donald

Burdick was a powerful man, more powerful than his remarkable resemblance to Laurence Olivier and his suede-glove manners suggested.

His was a power that could not be wholly quantified—it was an amalgam of old money and old friends in strategic places and old favors owed. One aspect of his power, however, did lend itself to calculation: the enigmatic formula of partnership interest in Hubbard, White & Willis. Which was not in fact so mysterious at all if you remembered that the votes you got to cast and the income you took home varied according to the number of clients you brought to the firm and how much they paid in fees.

Donald Burdick's salary was close to five million dollars a year. (And augmented—often doubled—by a complicated network of other "investments," to use his preferred euphemism.)

"My Lord," he muttered again, pushing the sheet toward William Winston Stanley. Sixty-five years old, Stanley was stout, ruddy, grim. You could easily picture him in Pilgrim garb, cheeks puffing out steam on a frigid New England morning as he read an indictment to a witch.

Burdick was Dartmouth and Harvard Law; Stanley had gone to Fordham Law School at night while working in the Hubbard, White mailroom. By a crafty mix of charm, bluntness and natural brilliance for business he'd fought his way up through a firm of men with addresses (Locust Valley and Westport) as foreign to him as his (Canarsie in Brooklyn) was to them. His saving grace among the society-minded partners was membership in an Episcopalian church.

Burdick asked, "How can this be accurate?"

Stanley gazed at the list. He shrugged.

"How on earth did Clayton do it?" Burdick muttered. "How did he get this many in his camp without our hearing?"

Stanley laughed in a thick rasp. "We just *have* heard."

The names contained on the list had been compiled by one of Burdick's spies—a young partner who was not particularly talented at practicing law but was a whiz kid at getting supposedly secret information out of people at the firm. The list showed how many partners were planning on voting in favor of a proposed merger between Hubbard, White & Willis and a Midtown law firm, a merger that would end the life of Hubbard, White as it then existed, as well as Burdick's control of the firm—and very likely his practice of law on Wall Street altogether.

Until now Burdick and Stanley were convinced that the pro-merger faction, led by a partner named Wendall Clayton, would not have enough votes to ram the deal through. But, if this tally was accurate, it was clear that the rebels probably would succeed.

And the memo contained other information that was just as troubling. At the partnership meeting scheduled for later this morning the pro-merger side was going to try to accelerate the final merger vote to a week from today. Originally it had been planned for next January. Burdick and Stanley had been counting on the month of December to win, or bully, straying partners back into their camp. Moving the vote forward would be disastrous.

Burdick actually felt a sudden urge to break something. His narrow, dry hand snatched up the paper. For a moment it seemed he would crumple it into a tight ball but instead he folded the paper slowly and slipped it into the inside pocket of his trim-fitting suit.

"Well, he's not *going* to do it," Burdick announced.

"What do we do to stop him?" Stanley barked.

Burdick began to speak then shook his head, rose and, stately as ever, buttoned his suit jacket. He nodded toward the complicated telephone sitting near them on the conference table, which unlike the phones in his office was not regularly swept for microphones. "Let's not talk here. Maybe a stroll in Battery Park. I don't think it's that cold out."

CHAPTER THREE

His eyes were the first thing about him she noticed.

They were alarmingly red, testifying to a lack of sleep, but they were also troubled.

"Come on into the lion's den." Mitchell Reece nodded Taylor Lockwood into his office then swung the door shut. He sat slowly in his black leather chair, the mechanism giving a soft ring.

Lion's den . . .

"I should tell you right up front," Taylor began, "I've never worked in litigation. I—"

He held up a hand to stop her. "Your experience doesn't really matter. Not for what I have in mind. Your discretion's what's important."

"I've worked on a lot of sensitive deals. I appreciate client confidentiality."

"Good. But this situation requires more than confidentiality. If we were the government I guess we'd call it top secret."

When Taylor was a little girl her favorite books were

about exploration and adventure. The two at the top of her list were the Alice stories—*Wonderland* and *Through the Looking-Glass*. She liked them because the adventures didn't take the heroine to foreign lands or back through history; they were metaphoric journeys through the bizarre side of life around us.

Taylor was now intrigued. *Lion's den. Top secret.*

She said, "Go ahead."

"Coffee?"

"Sure. Just milk, no sugar."

Reece stood up stiffly, as if he'd been sitting in one position for hours. His office was a mess. A hundred files—bulging manila folders and Redwelds stuffed with documents—filled the floor, the credenza, his desk. Stacks of legal magazines, waiting to be read, filled the spaces between the files. She smelled food and saw the remains of a take-out Chinese dinner sitting in a greasy bag beside the door.

He stepped into the canteen across the hall and she glanced out, watched him pour two cups.

Taylor studied him: the expensive but wrinkled slacks and shirt (there was a pile of new Brooks Brothers' shirts on the credenza behind him; maybe he wore one of these to court if he didn't have time to pick up his laundry). The tousled dark hair. The lean physique. She knew that the trial lawyer, with dark straight hair a touch long to go unnoticed by the more conservative partners, was in his mid-thirties. He specialized in litigation and had a reputation of his own. The firm's clients loved him because he won cases; the firm loved him because he ran up huge tabs doing so. (Taylor had heard that he'd once billed twenty-six hours in a single day; working on a flight to L.A., he'd taken advantage of the time zones.)

Young associates idolized Reece though they burned out working for him. Partners were uncomfortable supervising him; the briefs and motion papers he wrote under their names were often way beyond the older lawyers' skills at legal drafting.

Reece also was the driving force behind the firm's pro

bono program, volunteering much of his time to represent indigent clients in criminal cases.

On the personal side, Reece was *the* trophy of the firm, according to many women paralegals. He was single and probably straight (the proof wasn't conclusive—a divorce— but the ladies were willing to accept that circumstantial evidence as entirely credible). He'd had affairs with at least two women at the firm, or so the rumor went. On the other hand, they lamented, he was your standard Type A workaholic and thus a land mine in the relationship department. Which, nonetheless, didn't stop most of them from dreaming, if not flirting.

Reece returned to his office and closed the door with his foot, handed her the coffee. He sat down.

"Okay, here it is—our client's been robbed," he said.

She asked, "As in what they do to you on the subway or what they do at the IRS?"

"Burglary."

"Really?" Taylor again swallowed the yawn that had been trying to escape and rubbed her own stinging eyes.

"What do you know about banking law?" he asked.

"The fee for bounced checks is fifteen dollars."

"That's all?"

"I'm afraid so. But I'm a fast learner."

Reece said seriously, "I hope so. Here's your first lesson. One of the firm's clients is New Amsterdam Bank & Trust. You ever work for them?"

"No." She knew about the place, though; it was the firm's largest banking client and had been with Hubbard, White for nearly a hundred years. Taylor took a steno pad out of her purse and uncapped a pen.

"Don't write."

"I like to get the facts straight," she said.

"No, don't write," he said bluntly.

"Well, okay." The pad vanished.

Reece continued. "Last year the bank loaned two hundred fifty million dollars to a company in Midtown. Hanover & Stiver, Inc."

"What do they do?"

"They make things. I don't know. Widgets, baubles, bangles, bright, shiny beads." Reece shrugged then continued, "Now the first installments of the loan were due six months ago and the company missed the payments. They go back and forth, the bank and Hanover, but it's pretty clear that the company's never going to pay the money back. So, under the loan agreement, the whole amount comes due—a quarter-billion dollars."

"What'd they do with the money?"

"Good question. My feeling is it's still sitting somewhere—hell, they didn't have *time* to spend that much. But anyway, what happens at New Amsterdam—our revered client—is this: The economy melts down and the bank's reserves are shrinking. Now, the government says to all banks, Thou shalt have X amount of dollars on hand at all times. But New Amsterdam doesn't *have* X amount anymore. They need more in their reserves or the feds're going to step in. And the only way to get a big infusion of cash is to get back Hanover's loan. If they don't, the bank could go under. And that results in a couple of problems: First, Amsterdam is Donald Burdick's plum client. If the bank goes under he will not be a happy person, nor will the firm, because they pay us close to six million a year in fees. The other problem is that New Amsterdam happens to be a bank with a soul. They have the largest minority-business lending program in the country. Now, I'm not a flaming liberal, but you may have heard that one of my pet projects here—"

"The criminal pro bono program."

"Right. And I've seen firsthand that the one thing that helps improve shitty neighborhoods is to keep businesses in them. So I have a philosophical stake in the outcome of this . . . situation."

"And what exactly *is* the situation, Mitchell?"

"Earlier in the fall we filed suit against Hanover for the two hundred fifty million plus interest. Now if we can get a judgment fast we can levy against the assets of the company before the other creditors know what hit them. But if there's a delay in enforcing that judgment the company'll go into bankruptcy, the assets'll disappear and New Amsterdam might just go into receivership."

Taylor tapped the pen on her knee. She didn't mean to be projecting the impatience she felt though she knew maybe she was. "And the burglary part?"

He replied, "I'm getting to that. To loan the money the bank made Hanover sign a promissory note—you know, a negotiable instrument that says Hanover promises to pay the money back. It's like your savings bond."

Not like one of *mine,* Taylor reflected, considering what *theirs* was worth.

"Now the trial was set for yesterday. I had the case all prepared. There was no way we'd lose." Reece sighed. "Except...When you're going to sue to recover money on a note you have to produce the note in court. On Saturday the bank couriered the note to me. I put it in the safe there." He nodded at a big filing cabinet bolted to the floor. There were two heavy key locks on the front.

Shocked, Taylor said, "*That's* what was stolen? The note?"

Reece said in a low voice, "Somebody took it right out of my fucking safe. Just walked right in and walked out with it."

"You need the original? Can't you use a copy?"

"We could still win the case but not having the note'll delay the trial for months. I managed to finagle a postponement till next week but the judge won't grant any more extensions."

She nodded at the file cabinet. "But when...how was it stolen?"

"I was here until about three on Sunday morning. I went home to get some sleep and was back here by nine-thirty that morning. I almost thought of camping out." He gestured toward a sleeping bag in the corner. "I should have."

"What'd the police say?"

He laughed. "No, no. No police. Burdick'd find out that the note's missing, the client too. The newspapers..." He held her eyes. "So I guess you know why I asked you here."

"You want me to find out who took it?"

"Actually, I'd like you to find the note itself. I don't really care who did it."

She laughed. The whole idea was ridiculous. "But why me?"

"I can't do it by myself." Reece leaned back in his chair; the singing metal rang again. He looked at ease, as if she had already accepted his offer—a bit of haughtiness that irritated her some. "Whoever took it'll know I can't go to the cops and he'll be anticipating me. I need somebody else to help me. I need you."

"I just—"

"I know about your ski trip. I'm sorry. You'd have to postpone it."

Well, so much for the negotiations, Ms. Strickland....

"Mitchell, I don't know. I'm flattered you called me but I don't have a clue how to go about it."

"Well, let me just say one thing. We work with a lot of, you know, private eyes—"

"Sam Spade, sure."

"Actually, no, *not* Sam Spade at all. This's what I'm saying: The best detectives're women. They listen better than men. They're more empathic. They observe more carefully. You're smart, popular at the firm and—if we can mix our gender metaphor for a minute—the grapevine here says you've got balls."

"Does it now?" Taylor asked, frowning and feeling immensely pleased.

"And if you want another reason: I trust you."

Trust me? she wondered. He doesn't even know me. He— But then she understood. She smiled. "And you know I didn't steal it. I've got an alibi."

Reece nodded unabashedly. "Yep, you were out of town."

She'd gone to Maryland to spend the Thanksgiving holiday with her parents.

Taylor said, "I could've hired somebody."

"I think whoever was behind the theft *did* hire somebody." A nod toward the cabinet. "It's a professional break-in—the burglar picked the lock and, whatever you see in the movies, that ain't easy. But the point is that you don't have a motive, and motive is the number one reason somebody becomes a suspect in a crime. Why would *you* steal it? You have a good relationship with everybody at the firm. You don't need money. You've applied to law school—three of the best in the country. Besides, I just can't imagine Samuel Lockwood's daughter stealing a note."

She felt a troubled jolt that he'd peered so far into her life. "Well, I suspect Ted Bundy had upright parents too. It's just that this is out of my depth, Mitchell. You need a pro—one of those private eyes you've hired before."

"That wouldn't work," he said bluntly, as if it were obvious. "I need somebody with a reason to be here, who won't raise eyebrows. You'll have to poke into a lot of different places at the firm."

Like Alice on the other side of the looking glass.

Still seeing the hesitancy in her face, he added, "It could work out well for you too." He toyed with his coffee cup. She lifted an enquiring eyebrow and he continued, "I'm a trial lawyer and I lost my delicacy the first time I ever stood up in court. The fact is if that note doesn't turn up and I lose the case then I'm not going to make partner this year and that just isn't acceptable. I might even get fired. But if we *can* find it and nobody learns about the theft then it's pretty likely I'll make partner here or, if I don't want to stay at Hubbard, White, at some other firm."

"And?" she asked, still not certain where his comments were headed.

"I'll be in a position to make sure you get into whatever law school you want and get you a job when you graduate. I've got contacts everywhere—corporate firms, the government, public welfare law, environmental law firms."

As a paralegal Taylor Lockwood had learned that the engine of law ran on many fuels and that it would seize and burn without the delicate web of contacts and networks and unspoken obligations that Reece was not so subtly referring to.

But she also knew that you could always take a higher path and, with luck, sweat and smarts make your own way in this world. She said stiffly, "I appreciate that, Mitchell, but my undergrad professors're writing me all the letters of recommendation I need."

He blinked and held up a hand. "Look, I'm sorry. That was out of line. I'm used to dealing with clients who're either crooks or greedy bastards." A sour laugh. "And I'm not sure which are my pro bono criminal clients and which are the white-shoe folks we wine and dine at the Downtown Athletic Club."

She nodded, accepting his apology but glad certain ground rules were clear.

Reece looked her over for a moment, as if he suddenly saw her differently. A faint smile bloomed on his face. "I'm kind of like you."

"How do you mean?" she asked.

"I get the sense that you *never* ask for help."

She shrugged.

"I don't either. Never. But now I *need* help and it's hard for me to ask. I don't even know how to. . . . So, let me try again." A boyish laugh. "Will you help me?" he asked in a voice filled with what seemed to be uncharacteristic emotion.

Taylor looked out the window. The pale sun went behind thick clouds and the sky became as dark as its reflection in the choppy harbor. "I love views," she said. "In my apartment, you can see the Empire State Building. Provided you lean out the bathroom window."

Silence. Reece brushed his hair aside then rubbed his eyes with his knuckles. The brass clock on his desk ticked softly.

Taylor mentally asked the opinion of Alice, the young

girl in the English countryside who decided out of summer boredom to follow a talking white rabbit down its hole to a world very different from her own. Finally Taylor said to the lawyer, "All right. I frankly don't have a clue what to do but I'll help you."

Reece smiled and leaned forward suddenly then stopped fast. There's a code of chastity within law firms. Whatever liaisons occurred in hotel rooms or attorneys' beds at home, when you were within the labyrinth of the office, cheeks were not kissed and lip never met lip. Even embracing was suspect. Reece's concession to gratitude was taking Taylor's hand in both of his. She smelled a mix of expensive aftershave and sweat in his wake as he sat back.

"So, first of all," she said, "what does it look like? The note."

"Nothing fancy. One piece of eight-and-a-half-by-eleven paper." He showed her a binder containing a copy of it.

She looked over the undistinguished document then asked, "Tell me what happened and when."

"The bank messengered the note to me at five in the afternoon on Saturday—they were closed on Sunday and since the trial started at nine on Monday I needed it early to make copies for pleadings. Well, I locked it in my file cabinet as soon as it came in. I made the copies about ten or eleven that night, put it back in the cabinet, locked it. I left at three on Sunday morning. I got some sleep, came back around nine-thirty. I noticed some scratch marks on the lock and opened it up. The note was gone. I spent the rest of Sunday looking for it. I appeared in court yesterday, got the continuance for a week from today and then came back here to find somebody to help me."

"Did you see anybody at the firm that night?"

"Not after five or six. Not a soul. But I was at my desk practically the whole time."

"Well." She sat back, reflecting. "You mentioned motive. Who has a motive to steal it? You said it was negotiable. Could somebody cash it in?"

"No, nobody in the world'd take paper like that. Too big

and too easily traced. I'm sure it was just to delay the case—to give Lloyd Hanover a chance to hide his assets."

"Who knew you had it?"

"The messenger didn't know what was in the bag but it was an armed courier service so they'd know it was valuable. At the bank, as far as I know, the only one who knew I took delivery was the vice president who worked on the deal."

"Could he have been bribed by Hanover?"

Reece said, "Anything's possible, but he's a career officer. Been with the bank for twenty years. I know him personally. He and his wife live in Locust Valley and they've got plenty of money on their own. Anyway, he's the point man on the deal. If the bank doesn't collect on this note, he'll be fired."

"Who here knew you were working on the case?"

Reece laughed. He slid a memo across to her.

> *From: M. A. Reece*
> *To: Attorneys of Hubbard, White & Willis*
> *Re: Conflicts of Interest*
>
> *I am representing our client New Amsterdam Bank & Trust in a lawsuit against Hanover & Stiver, Inc. Please advise if you have ever represented Hanover & Stiver or have any other conflicts of interest involving these companies of which the firm should be aware.*

"This is the standard conflicts of interest memo. To let everybody know who we're suing. If any lawyers here have ever represented Hanover we have to drop the case or do a Chinese wall to make sure there was no appearance that we were compromising either client. . . . So, in answer to your question, *everybody* here knew what I was doing. And by checking copies of my correspondence in the file room they could figure out when I'd be receiving the note."

Taylor prodded the conflicts memo with the fork of her fingers.

"What do you know about the executives at Hanover?"

"I've had murderers in the pro bono program who're more upright than the CEO—Lloyd Hanover. He's unadulterated scum. He thinks he's some kind of smooth operator. You know the kind—late fifties, crew-cut, tanned. Has three mistresses. Wears so much gold jewelry he'd never get through a metal detector."

"That's not a crime," Taylor said.

"No, but his three SEC violations and two RICO and one IRS convictions were."

"Ah."

Taylor glanced out the window: across the street was a wall of office windows, a hundred of them. And beyond that building were others with more office windows, and still more beyond that. Taylor Lockwood was, momentarily, overwhelmed by the challenges they faced. Needles and haystacks . . . She asked, "Are you sure we're looking for something that still exists?"

"How do you mean?"

"If nobody's going to cash the note why wouldn't they just burn it?"

"Good question. I've thought about that. When I was an assistant U.S. prosecutor—and when I do my criminal defense work now—I always put myself in the mind of the perp. In this case, if the note disappears forever that implies a crime. If it's just misplaced until Hanover's hidden his assets and then it resurfaces, well, that suggests, just legal malpractice on Hubbard, White's part; nobody looks any farther for a bad guy than us. That's why I think the note's still in the firm. Maybe in the file room, maybe stuck in a magazine in a partner's office, maybe behind a copier—wherever the thief hid it.

Thief. . . . Lockwood felt her first uneasy twinge—not only at the impossibility of the task but that there was potential danger too.

In Wonderland the Queen of Hearts' favorite slogan was "Off with their heads."

She sat back. "I don't know, Mitchell. It seems hopeless. There're a million places the note could be."

"We don't have the facts yet. There's a huge amount of information at the firm about where people have been at various times and what they've been doing. Billing department, payroll, things like that. I guess the first thing I'd do is check the door key entry logs and time sheets to find out who was in the firm on Saturday."

She nodded at the lock. "But we think it was a pro, don't we? Not a lawyer or employee?"

"Still, somebody had to let him in. Either that or they lent him their key card—or one they'd stolen." Reece then took out his wallet and handed her a thousand dollars in hundreds.

She looked at the cash with a funny smile, embarrassed, curious.

"For expenses."

"Expenses." Did he mean bribes? She wasn't going to ask. Taylor held the bills awkwardly for a moment then slipped them into her purse. She noticed a sheet of paper on Reece's desk. It was legal-sized and pale green—the color of corridors in old hospitals and government buildings. She recognized it as the court calendar the managing attorney of Hubbard, White circulated throughout the firm daily. It contained a grid of thirty days beginning with today. Filling these squares were the times and locations of all court appearances scheduled for the firm's litigators. She leaned forward. In the square indicating one week from today were the words:

> New Amsterdam Bank & Trust v. Hanover & Stiver.
> Jury trial. Ten a.m. No continuance.

He looked at his watch. "Let's talk again tomorrow. But we should keep our distance when we're at the firm. If anybody asks tell them you're helping me with some year-end billing problems."

"But who'd ask? Who'd even know?"

He laughed and seemed to consider this a naive comment. "How's the Vista Hotel at nine-thirty?"

"Sure."

"If I call you at home I can leave a message, can't I?"

"I've got an answering machine."

"No, I mean, there won't be anybody else there to pick it up, right? I heard you lived alone."

She hesitated momentarily and said only, "You can leave messages there."

CHAPTER FOUR

██████████ "I have a breakfast meeting in half an hour then the partnership meeting for the rest of the morning," Wendall Clayton said into the phone. "Get me the details as soon as possible."

"I'll do what I can, Wendall," Sean Lillick, a young paralegal who worked for Clayton regularly, replied uneasily. "But it's, like, pretty confidential."

" 'Like' confidential. It is confidential or not?"

A sigh from the other end of the phone line. "You know what I mean."

The partner muttered, "You meant it *is* confidential. Well, find out who has the information and aristocratize them. I want the particulars. Which you might just have found out *before* you called. You'd know I'd want them."

"Sure, Wendall," Lillick said.

The partner dropped the phone into the cradle.

Wendall Clayton was a handsome man. Not big—under six feet—but solid from running (he didn't jog; he *ran*) and tennis and skippering the forty-two-foot *Ginny May* around Newport every other weekend from April through

September. He had a thick bundle of professorial hair and he wore European suits, slitless in the back, forgoing the burdened sacks of dark pinstripe that cloaked most of the pear-shaped men of the firm. Killer looks, the women in the firm said. Another three inches and he could have been a model. Clayton worked hard at his image, the way nobility worked hard. A duke had to be handsome. A duke enjoyed dusting his suits with pig-bristle brushes and getting a radiant glow on his burgundy-colored Bally's.

A duke took great pleasures in the small rituals of fastidiousness.

Aristocratize them....

Sometimes Clayton would write the word in the margin of a memo one of his associates had written. Then watch the girl or boy, flustered, trying to pronounce it. *Ar-is-TOC-ratize* ... he'd made up the term himself. It had to do with attitude mostly. Much of it was knowing the law, of course, and much was circumstance.

But mostly it was attitude.

Clayton practiced often and he was very good at it.

He hoped Sean Lillick would, in turn, be good at aristocratizing some underling in the steno department to get the information he wanted.

By searching through the correspondence files, time sheets and limousine and telephone logs the young paralegal had learned that Donald Burdick had recently attended several very secretive meetings and made a large number of phone calls during firm hours that had not been billed to any clients. This suggested to Clayton that Burdick was plotting something that could jeopardize the merger. That might not be the case, of course; his dealings could be related to some private business plans that Burdick or his Lucrezia Borgia of a wife, Vera, were involved in. But Clayton hadn't gotten to his present station in life by assuming that unknown maneuverings of his rivals were benign.

Hence, his sending Lillick off on the new mission to find out the details.

The Tuesday morning light filtered into his office, the

corner office, located on the firm's executive row, the seventeenth floor. The room measured twenty-seven by twenty—a
size that by rights should have gone to a partner more senior
than Clayton. When it fell vacant, however, the room was assigned to him. Even Donald Burdick never found out why.

Clayton glanced at the Tiffany nautical clock on his
desk. Nearly time. He rocked back in his chair, his throne, a
huge construction of oak and red leather he had bought in
England for two thousand pounds.

Aristocratize.

He ordered his secretary to have his car brought
around. He rose, donned his suit jacket and left the office.
The breakfast get-together he was about to attend was perhaps the most important of any meeting he'd been to in
the past year. But Clayton didn't go immediately to the
waiting car. Rather, he decided he'd been a bit harsh on
the young man and wandered down to Lillick's cubicle in
the paralegal department to personally thank the young
man and tell him a generous bonus would be forthcoming.

■■■

"You ever been here, Wendall?" the man across the bur-
nished copper table asked.

When Clayton spoke, however, it was to the captain of
the Carleton Hotel on Fifty-ninth Street, off Fifth Avenue.
"The nova, Frederick?"

"No, Mr. Clayton." The captain shook his head. "Not
today."

"Thanks. I'll have my usual."

"Very good, Mr. Clayton."

"Well, that answers my question," John Perelli said with
an explosive laugh. "How's the yogurt today, Freddie?"

"It's—"

"That's a joke," Perelli barked. "Gimme a bowl. Dry
wheat toast and a fruit cup."

"Yessir, Mr. Perelli."

Perelli was stocky and dark, with a long face. He wore a
navy pinstripe suit.

Clayton shot his cuffs, revealing eighteen-karat-Wedgwood cuff links, and said, "I feel, in answer to your question, right at home here."

Though this was not completely true. Recently Wendall Clayton had been coming to this dining room—where many of Perelli's partners breakfasted and lunched—to make inroads into Midtown. Yet this was not his natural turf, which had always been Wall Street, upper Fifth Avenue, his weekend house in Redding, Connecticut, his ten-room cabin in Newport.

Clayton had a stock portfolio worth around twenty-three million (depending on how the Gods of the Dow were feeling at any particular moment). Hanging on the oak paneling in his Upper East Side den were a Picasso, three Klees, a Mondrian, a Magritte. He drove a Jaguar and a Mercedes station wagon. Yet his wealth was of the hushed, Victorian sort: a third inherited, a third earned at the practice of law (and cautious investment of the proceeds), the rest from his wife.

But here, in Midtown, he was surrounded by a different genre of money. It was loud money. Acquired from new wellsprings. This money was from media, from advertising, from public relations, from junk bonds, from leveraged buyouts, from alligator spreads and dividend-snatching. Commission money. Sales money. Real estate money. Italian money. Jewish money. Japanese money.

Clayton's wealth was money with cobwebs and therefore it was, ironically, suspect—at least around here. In this part of town, when it came to wealth the slogan was: the more respectable, the less acceptable.

He tried not to give a damn. Yet here Clayton felt as if he were "without passport," the phrase whose acronym gave rise to the derisive term for Italians. Wendall Clayton in Midtown was an immigrant in steerage.

"So why the call, Wendall?" Perelli asked.

Clayton replied, "We need to move faster. I'm trying to accelerate the vote on the merger."

"Faster? Why?"

"The natives are restless."

Perelli barked, "What does that mean? I don't know what it means. That your people wanta go forward or that Burdick and his cronies're trying to fuck the deal?"

"A little bit of both."

"What's Donald doing? Setting up an office in D.C. and London to goose up your operating expense?"

"Something like that. I'm finding out," Clayton conceded with a nod.

The waiter set the plates on the table. Clayton hunched over the soft mounds of eggs and ate hungrily, cutting the food into small bites.

Perelli waited until the server was gone then examined Clayton carefully and said, "We want this to work. We've got labor clients we can parlay into your SEC base. We've got products liability cases that are gold mines. You've got corporate people and litigators who'd be a natural fit. Obviously we want your banking department and you want our real estate group. It's made in heaven, Wendall. What's Burdick's problem?"

"Old school. I don't know."

"The fact we've got Jewish partners? The fact we have Eye-talian partners?"

"Probably."

"But there's more to it, right?" the keen-eyed Perelli asked. "Cut the crap, Wendall. You've got an agenda that's scaring the shit out of Burdick and his boys. What?"

Okay, Clayton thought. This is it. . . . He reached into his jacket and handed Perelli a piece of paper.

Perelli read then looked up questioningly. "A hit list?"

Clayton tapped the paper dramatically. "Yep. That's who I want out within a year after the merger."

"There are—what?—twenty-five names here?" Perelli read. "Burdick, Bill Stanley, Woody Crenshaw, Lamar Fredericks, Ralph Dudley . . . Wendall, these men *are* Hubbard, White & Willis. They've been there for decades."

"They're deadwood, has-beens. This is the last piece of the deal, John. For the merger to work they have to go."

Perelli chewed some of his toast and washed it down with

coffee. "You said you wanted to accelerate the merger." He waved at the paper. "But if you're asking us to agree to *this* it'll only slow things up. I've got to run these names by the management committee. We'll have to review each one of their partnership contracts. Christ, they're all over forty-five. You know the kind of trouble they could make in court for us?"

Clayton laughed with genuine amusement. "John, with my connections you really think the EEOC would be a problem?"

"All right, maybe not. But these're still dangerous men."

"And they're the ones who're bleeding the firm dry. They have to go. If we want to the firm to succeed they have to go." He pushed aside his empty plate. "A week, John. I want the merger papers signed in a week."

"Impossible."

"Considering that you might have to move slightly more quickly," Clayton said, "we would be willing to alter our partnership share price."

"You—"

"If we ink the deal next week, Hubbard, White and Willis is willing to reduce our first-year share take by eight percent."

"Are you out of your fucking mind? You're talking millions of dollars, Wendall."

"*Thirteen* million dollars."

This meant that the Hubbard, White and Willis partners would in effect give the incoming partners a huge bonus simply for expediting the deal—and for ousting Burdick and his cronies.

Clayton continued, "We'll claim it has to be done by year end for tax reasons. That'll be our excuse."

"Just tell me: If I insisted that Burdick stay for, say, five years, would you still be willing to proceed?"

Clayton signed his name to the check. He offered no credit card.

"Let me tell you something, John. Twenty years ago Donald Burdick was asked by the President to head a special committee looking into abuses in the steel industry."

"The Justice Department was involved. I heard about that."

"Burdick was picked because he was known in both Albany and Washington. The executive committee at Hubbard, White—it was called a steering committee then—was ecstatic. Publicity for the firm, a chance for Burdick to do some serious stroking on the Hill. Afterward, a triumphant return. Well, Donald Burdick told the committee he'd accept the appointment on one condition. That when he returned he and a man of his choosing would be placed on the executive committee and three particular partners would be asked to leave the firm. Now, John, that was at a time when law firms did not fire partners. It simply was not done."

"And?"

"Three months later, a memo went around the office congratulating three partners who were unexpectedly leaving Hubbard, White and starting their own firm." Clayton pushed back from the table. "The answer to your question is this: The only way the deal works is without Burdick . . . and everyone else on that list. That's the quid pro quo. What do you say?"

"You really fucking want this, don't you?"

"Deal?" Clayton asked, sticking out his hand.

Perelli hesitated for a moment before pronouncing, "Deal," and shaking Clayton's hand but the delay was merely because he had to swallow the piece of bacon he'd snuck off Clayton's plate and wipe his fingers.

■

Who are these men and women?

What do I know about them other than the baldest facts of their wealth, their brilliance, their aspirations?

In the back of the massive sixteenth-floor conference room Donald Burdick heard the grandfather clock chime and begin its ringing climb toward 11 A.M. The partners were arriving. Most carried foolscap pads or stacks of files and their ubiquitous leather personal calendars.

Over the years I've seen men like this, women now too,

display stubbornness and brutality and brilliance and cruelty.

And generosity and sacrifice.

But those are the mere *manifestations* of their souls; what's truly in their hearts?

The partners took their places around the table in the dark conference room. Some, the less confident, the younger ones, examined the dings in the rosewood and traced the pattern of the marble with their fingers and eyes and made overly loud comments about their Thanksgivings and about football games. They wore jackets with their suits. Others, the veterans, were in shirtsleeves and had no time for chatter or the administrivia of meetings like this. They appeared inconvenienced. And why shouldn't they? Isn't the point of a law firm, after all, to practice law?

They're my partners . . . but how many are my friends?

Donald Burdick, sitting at the apogee of the table, however, understood that this was a pointless question. The real one was: How many of my friends will stab me in the back? If the tally that Bill Stanley had showed him earlier was accurate the answer to this question was one hell of a lot.

To Stanley, Burdick whispered, "Nearly fifteen'll be missing. That could swing it one way or another."

"They're dead," Stanley replied in a growl. "And we'll never find the bodies."

Wendall Clayton entered the room and took a seat in the middle of one leg of the U. He wasn't particularly far away from Burdick and not particularly close. He busied himself jotting notes and, smiling, chatting with the partner next to him.

At eleven-fifteen Burdick nodded for a partner to close the door. The lock mechanism gave a solid click. It seemed to Burdick that the pressure in the room changed and that they were sealed in, as if this were a chamber in the Great Pyramid.

Donald Burdick called the meeting to order. Minutes were read and not listened to, a brief report from the executive committee on staff overtime went ignored. Committee

reports were recited at breakneck speed, with uncharacteristically few interruptions and little debate.

"Do you want to hear about the hiring committee's
schedule?" asked a sanguine young partner, who had probably stayed up half the night to prepare it.

"I think we'll postpone that one," Burdick said evenly,
and—seeing several partners smile—realized that the royal
pronoun was an unfortunate slip.

There was silence in the room, punctuated by the popping of soda cans and papers being organized. Dozens of
pens made graffiti on legal pads. Burdick studied the agenda
for a moment and then it was time for Wendall Clayton to
make his move. He slipped his suit jacket off, opened a file
and said, "May I have the floor?"

Burdick nodded in his direction. In a rehearsed baritone
Wendall Clayton said, "I'd like to make a motion relevant to
the proposed merger of our firm with Sullivan & Perelli."

Burdick shrugged. "You have the floor."

Sipping had stopped. Doodling had stopped. Some
partners—like the aging, oblivious Ralph Dudley—were
confused because the final vote on the merger wasn't scheduled until January. They were terrified that they might have
to make a decision without someone's telling them what
to do.

"I'm moving to change the date of the ratification vote
regarding the merger to November 28, one week from
today."

Clayton's trim young protégé, Randy Simms III, whom
Burdick detested, said quickly, "Second."

There was complete silence. And Burdick was mildly
surprised that Clayton's bid caught some people off guard.
But then Burdick and his wife were rumored to have the
best intelligence sources on Wall Street and were often one
step ahead of everybody else.

One voice called, "Can we discuss it?"

"The rules of order allow for debate," Clayton said.

And debate ensued. Clayton was clearly prepared for it.
He met every objection, making a good case for the acceler-

ation—the year-end tax planning, for instance, hinting that the merger would put significant money into the pockets of all the partners and that they needed to know before December 31 how much this might be.

More voices joined in and a tide of comments and tension-breaking laughter filled the room.

Clayton managed to insert into the discussion a comment on Sullivan & Perelli's income cap on the executive committee partners. Burdick observed that this was irrelevant to the immediate motion under consideration but would not go unnoticed by the younger, poorer partners: The gist of the comment was that after the merger the senior partners could earn no more than two million a year, leaving that much more to be distributed to the rest of the partners. Hubbard, White & Willis currently had no such cap, which was the reason that five partners on the executive committee—such as Burdick and Stanley—earned 18 percent of the firm's income and junior partners often earned less than they did as salaried associates.

"What is the cap?" one partner, obviously impressed, asked.

Goddamn socialism, Burdick thought, then he interrupted the youngster to say bluntly, "We're not here now to discuss the substantive issue of the merger. It's merely a procedural matter on *when* the vote should be. And my opinion is that it's impossible to review the material in one week. We need until January."

"Well, Donald," Clayton pointed out, "you've had everything for two weeks already. And I'd imagine you, like all the rest of us, read it as soon as they messengered the binders to us from Perelli & Sullivan."

He *had* read it, of course, and so had the team of lawyers he and Vera had hired.

A new partner at the end of the table made a comment. "I don't think we can debate this too much. It's not inappropriate to talk about the substance of the merger now, I think." His dialect put him within five minutes of the Charles River.

"Yes, it is inappropriate," Burdick said shortly, silencing him. Then to Clayton: "Go ahead with your vote. It makes no sense to me but if two thirds of the partners are in favor—"

Clayton gave a very minuscule frown. "A simple majority, Donald."

Burdick shook his head. A trace of confusion now crossed *his* face. "Majority? No, Wendall, I don't think so. The issue is the merger of the firm and that requires a vote of two thirds."

Clayton said, "No, we'd be voting simply on establishing an agenda and timetable. Under the partnership rules, Donald, that requires only a simple majority."

Burdick was patient. "Yes, but it's an agenda and timetable that *pertain* to a merger."

Each of the two partners pulled out a copy of the partnership documents, like dueling knights drawing swords.

"Section fourteen, paragraph four, subparagraph d." Clayton said this as if reading from the tome though everyone knew he'd memorized it long ago.

Burdick continued reading for a few moments. "It's ambiguous. But I won't make an issue of it. We'll be here all day at this rate. And I, for one, have some work to do for clients."

The senior partner knew, of course, that Clayton was absolutely correct about the majority vote on this matter. However, it had been vitally important to make clear to everyone in the room exactly where Burdick stood on the merger—how adamantly against it he was.

"Go ahead," Burdick said to Stanley.

As the rotund partner growled off names, Burdick sat calmly, pretending to edit a letter though he was keeping a perfect tally in his head of the fors and againsts.

Distraction on his face, agony in his heart, Burdick added them up. His mood slipped from cautious to alarmed to despairing. Clayton prevailed—and by almost a two-thirds majority, the magic percentage needed to win the entire war.

The list Stanley had shown Burdick earlier was not accurate. Clayton was *stronger* than they'd thought.

Clayton looked at Burdick, studying his opponent from behind the emotionless guise of the great. His gold pen danced on a pad. "If anyone needs any information from Perelli—to make a better-informed decision next week—just let me know."

Burdick said, "Thank you, Wendall. I appreciate the time you've spent on the matter." Looking around the room—at both his supporters and his Judases—with as neutral a face as he could muster, he added, "Now, any more issues we ought to discuss?"

CHAPTER FIVE

"Dimitri." Taylor Lockwood's voice was a whisper. "Don't say 'satin touch' tonight. Please."

"Hey, come on," the man replied in a deep Greek-accented voice, "the guys in the audience, they like it."

"It's embarrassing."

"It's sexy," he replied petulantly.

"No, it's not, and all it does is get me moony looks from the lechers."

"Hey, they like to fantasize. So do I. You got the lights?"

She sighed and said, "Yeah, I got the lights."

From the amplifier his voice filled the bar: "Ladies and gentlemen, Miracles Pub is pleased to bring you the silky and oh-so-smooth satin touch of Taylor Lockwood on the keys. A warm round of applause please. And don't forget to ask your waitress about the Miracles menu of exotic drinks."

Oh-so-smooth satin touch?

Taylor clicked the switch that turned the house lights down and ignited the two overhead spots trained on her. Dimitri had made the spotlights himself—pineapple cans painted black.

Smiling at them all, even the moony lechers, she began to play Gershwin on the battered Baldwin baby grand.

It wasn't a bad gig. The temperamental owner of the club in the West Village—a lech himself—had figured that an attractive woman jazz pianist would help sell bad food, so he'd hired her for Tuesday nights, subject only to sporadic preemption by Dimitri's son-in-law's balalaika orchestra.

With her day job at the firm and this gig, Taylor had found a type of harmony in her life. Music was her pure sensual love; her paralegal job gave her the pleasures of intellect, organization, function. She sometimes felt like those men with two wives who know nothing of the other. Maybe someday she'd get nailed but so far the secret was safe.

A half hour later Taylor was doing the bridge to "Anything Goes" when the front door swung open with its familiar D to B-flat squeak. The woman who entered was in her mid-twenties, with a round, sweet, big-sister face framed by hair pulled back in a ponytail. She wore a sweater decorated with reindeer, black ski pants and, on her petite, out-turned feet, Top-Siders. She smiled nervously and waved broadly to Taylor then stopped suddenly, afraid of disrupting the show.

Taylor nodded back and finished the tune. Then she announced a break and sat down.

"Carrie, thanks for coming."

The young girl's eyes sparkled. "You are so good. I didn't know you were a musician. Where did you study? Like, Juilliard?"

Taylor sipped her Seagram's and soda. "Juilliard? Try Mrs. Cuikova's. A famous music school. Freddy Bigelow went there. And Bunny Grundel."

"I never heard of them."

"Nobody has. We were all in the same grade school. We'd go to Frau Cuikova's in Glen Cove every Tuesday and Thursday at four to be abused about arpeggios and finger position."

Several men in the audience were restless, about to make their moves, so Taylor did the lech maneuver—positioning her chair with her back to them—and turned her whole attention to Carrie.

Taylor had spent the day looking through documents on the *New Amsterdam Bank v. Hanover & Stiver* case, collecting the names of everyone who'd worked on it: partners, associates and all the paralegals, typists, messengers and other support staff. But the case had been in the works for months and the cast of characters at Hubbard, White who'd been involved totaled nearly thirty people. She needed to narrow down the suspects and to get the key entry logs and the time sheets, as Reece had suggested. But to do this, she'd found, you needed to be a registered user and to have a pass code. Carrie Mason, a friend of hers at the firm, was the paralegal who oversaw the billing and time recording system and so Taylor had asked the girl to meet her here after work.

Taylor now looked at the girl's Coach attaché case. "You've got what I asked for?"

"I feel like a, you know, spy," the girl joked, though uneasily. She opened the briefcase and pulled out stacks of computer papers.

"I wouldn't have asked if it weren't important. Are these the door key logs?"

"Yeah."

Taylor sat forward and examined the papers. On top was a copy of the computer key entry ledger for the firm's front and back doors. Like many Wall Street firms Hubbard, White had installed computer security locks that were activated with ID cards. To enter the firm you had to slide the card through a reader, which sent the information to the central computer. To leave, or to open the door for someone outside, you had only to hit a button inside the firm.

Taylor read through the information, noting who'd used their keys to get into the firm on Saturday and Sunday morning. There were fifteen people who'd entered on Saturday, two on Sunday.

"Where're the time sheet reports?"

More documents appeared on the table. It was on these

time sheets that lawyers recorded in exasperating detail exactly how they spent each minute at the firm: which clients they worked for and what tasks they'd performed, when they took personal time during office hours, when they worked on business for the firm that was unrelated to clients.

Taylor looked through papers and, cross-checking the owner of the key code with the hours billed, learned that fourteen of the fifteen who'd checked in on Saturday morning had billed no more than six hours, which meant they would have left by four or five in the afternoon—a typical pattern for those working weekends: Get the work done early then play on Saturday night.

The one lawyer who'd remained was Mitchell Reece.

Flipping to the Sunday key entries, she saw that Reece had returned, as he'd told her, later that morning, at 9:23. But there was an entry *before* that, well before it, in fact. Someone had entered the firm at 1:30 A.M. But the only lawyer for whom there were time sheet entries was Reece.

Why on earth would somebody come into the firm that late and not do any work?

Maybe to open the door for a thief who would steal a gazillion-dollar note.

She flipped through the key assignment file and found that the person who'd entered at 1:30 had been Thomas Sebastian.

"Sebastian." Taylor tried to picture him but couldn't form an image; so many of the young associates looked alike. "What do you know about him?"

Carrie rolled her eyes. "Gag me. He's a total party animal. Goes out every night, dates a different girl every week, sometimes two—if you want to call it a date. We went out once and he couldn't keep his hands to himself."

"Is he at the firm now, tonight?"

"When I left, maybe a half hour ago, he was still working. But he'll probably be going out later. Around ten or eleven. I think he goes to clubs every night."

"You know where he hangs out?"

"There's a club called The Space. . . ."

Taylor said, "Sure, I've been there." She then asked, "Did you bring copies of the time sheet summaries from the *New Amsterdam v. Hanover & Stiver* case?"

Carrie slid a thick wad of Xerox copies to Taylor, who thumbed through them. These would show how much time each person spent on the case. Those more familiar with the case, Taylor was figuring, would be more likely to have been the ones approached by Hanover to steal the note.

Of the list of thirty people who'd been involved, though, only a few had spent significant time on it: Burdick and Reece primarily.

"Man," Taylor whispered, "look at the hours Mitchell worked. Fifteen hours in one day, sixteen hours, fourteen— on a Sunday. He even billed ten hours on Thanksgiving."

"That's why I love being a corporate paralegal," Carrie said, sounding as if she devoutly meant it. "You do trial work, you can kiss personal time so long."

"Look at this." Taylor frowned, tapping the "Paralegals" column on the case roster. "Linda Davidoff."

Carrie stared silently at her frothy drink. Then she said, "I didn't go to her funeral. Were you there?"

"Yes, I was."

Many people at the firm had attended. The suicide of the pretty, shy paralegal last fall had stunned everyone in the firm—though such deaths weren't unheard of. The subject wasn't talked about much in Wall Street law circles but paralegals who worked for big firms were under a lot of pressure—not only at their jobs but at home as well: Many of them were urged by their parents or peers to get into good law schools when they in fact had no particular interest in or aptitude for the law. There were many breakdowns and more than a few suicide attempts.

"I didn't know her too good," Carrie said. "She was kind of a mystery." A faint laugh. "Like you in a way. I didn't know you were a musician. Linda was a poet. You know that?"

"I think I remember something from the eulogy," Taylor said absently, eyes scanning the time sheets. "Look, in

September Linda stopped working on the case and Sean Lillick took over for her as paralegal."

"Sean? He's a strange boy. I think he's a musician too. Or a stand-up comic, I don't know. He's skinny and wears weird clothes. Has his hair all spiked up. I like him, though. I flirted with him some but he never asked me out. You ask me, Mitchell's cuter." Carrie played with the pearls around her neck and her voice flattened to a gossipy hush. "I heard you were with him all day."

Taylor didn't glance up. "With who?" she asked casually but felt her heart gallop.

"Mitchell Reece."

She laughed. "How'd you hear that?"

"Just the rumor around the paralegal pen. Some of the girls were jealous. They're dying to work for him."

Who the hell had noticed them? she wondered. She hadn't seen a soul outside his office when she entered or left. "I just met with him for a few minutes is all."

"Mitchell's hot," the girl said.

"Is he?" Taylor replied. "I didn't take his temperature." Nodding at the papers: "Can I keep them?"

"Sure, they're copies."

"Can I get any of this information myself?"

"Not if it's in the computer. You need to be approved to go on-line and have a pass code and everything. But the raw time sheets—before they're entered—anybody can look at. They're in the file room, organized by the attorney assigned as lead on the case or deal. The other stuff... just tell one of the girls what you want and they'll get it for you. Uhm, Taylor, can you, like, tell me what's going on?"

She lowered her voice and looked gravely into the eyes of the young woman. "There was a mega mix-up on the New Amsterdam bill. I don't know what happened but the client's totally pissed. It was kind of embarrassing—with all the merger talks going on and everything. Mitchell wanted me to get to the bottom of it. On the Q.T."

"I won't say a word."

Taylor put the rest of the papers into her attaché case.

"Ms. Satin Touch?" Dimitri called from behind the bar in a singsongy voice.

"Brother." Taylor grimaced. "Gotta go pay the rent," she said and climbed back under Dimitri's homemade spotlights.

A trickle of fear ran through her as she began to play.

Who else had seen Mitchell and her together?

Taylor suddenly gave a brief laugh as she realized the title of the tune she found herself playing, selected by some subconscious hiccup.

The song was "Someone to Watch Over Me."

■■■■■

"Hey," the young man shouted over the music cascading from the club's million-decibel sound system, "I'm sorry I'm late. Are you still speaking to me?"

The blond woman glanced at the chubby man. "What?" she called.

"I can't believe I kept you waiting."

She looked over his smooth baby-fatted skin, the newscaster's perfect hair, the gray suit, wing tips, Cartier watch. He examined her right back: red angular dress, paisley black stockings, black hat and veil. Small tits, he noticed, but a lot of skin was exposed.

"What?" she shouted again. Though she'd heard his words; he knew she had.

"I got held up," he explained, hands clasped together in prayer. "I can't really go into it. It's an unpleasant story."

These were lines he used a lot in clubs like this. Cute lines, silly lines. As soon as the women realized that they'd never seen him before and that he was hitting on them in a major way, they usually rolled their eyes and said, "Fuck off."

But sometimes, just sometimes, they didn't. This one said nothing yet. She was taking her time. She watched him sending out Morse code with something in his hand, tapping it against the bar absently, while he smiled his flirts toward her.

Tap, tap, tap.

"I thought for sure you would've left. Would've served me right. Keeping a beautiful woman waiting," said this young man with a slight swell of double chin and a belly testing his Tripler's 42-inch alligator belt.

The process of scoring in a place like this was, of course, like negotiating. You had to play a role, act, be somebody else.

Tap, tap, tap.

The club was an old warehouse, sitting on a commercial street in downtown Manhattan, deserted except for the cluster of supplicants crowding around the ponytailed, baggy-jacketed doorman, who selected Those Who Might Enter with a grudging flick of a finger.

Thom Sebastian was never denied entrance.

Tap, tap, tap.

True, mostly the women roll their eyes and tell him to fuck off. But sometimes they did what she was doing now: looking down at the telegraph key—a large vial of coke—and saying, "Hi, I'm Veronica."

He reacted to the gift of her name like a shark tasting blood in the water. He moved in fast, sitting next to her, shaking her hand for a lengthy moment.

"Thom," he said.

The sound system's speakers, as tall as the six-foot-six, blue-gowned transvestite dancing in front of them, sent fluttering bass waves into their faces and chests. The smell was a pungent mix of cigarette smoke and a gassy, ozonelike scent—from the fake fog.

Tap, tap, tap.

He offered his boyish grin while she rambled on about careers—she sold something in some store somewhere but wanted to get into something else. Sebastian nodded and murmured single-word encouragements and mentally tumbled forward, caught in the soft avalanche of anticipation. He saw the evening unfold before him: They'd hit the john, duck into a stall and do a fast line or two of coke. No nookie yet, nor would he expect any. After that they'd leave and go over to Meg's, where he was a regular. Then out for pasta. After that, when it was pushing 3 A.M., he'd ask her with mock trepidation if she ever went north of Fourteenth Street.

A car-service Lincoln up to his apartment.

Your condom or mine . . .

And later, after a Val or 'lude to come down, they'd sleep. Up at eight-thirty the next morning, share the shower, take turns with the hair dryer, give her a kiss. She'd cab it home. He'd down some speed and head to Hubbard, White & Willis for another day of lawyering.

Tap, tap, tap . . .

"Hey," Thom said, interrupting her as she was saying *something,* "how about—"

But there was a disturbance. Another incarnation of Veronica appeared: a young woman walking toward them. Different clothes but the same high cheeks, pale flesh, laces, silks, a flea market's worth of costume jewelry. Floral perfume. They were interchangeable, these two women. Clones. They bussed cheeks. Behind Veronica II stood a pair of quiet, preoccupied young Japanese men dressed in black, hair greased and spiked high like porcupine quills. One wore a medal studded with rhinestones.

Sebastian suddenly detested them—not because of the impending kidnapping of his new love but for no reason he could figure out. He wanted to lean forward and ask the young man if he'd won the medal at Iwo Jima. Veronica nodded to her other half, lifted her eyebrows at Sebastian with regret and a smile that belied it and disappeared into the mist.

Tap, tap, tap.

"*Quo vadis,* Veronica?" Sebastian whispered, pronouncing the v's like w's the way his Latin professor had instructed. He turned back to the bar and noticed that somebody had taken Veronica's space. Someone who was the exact opposite of her: homey, pretty, dressed conservatively but stylishly in black. She was vaguely familiar; he must've seen her here before. The woman ordered a rum and Coke, gave a laugh to herself.

She was hardly his type but Sebastian couldn't help raise an eyebrow at the laugh. She noticed and said in response, "That woman over there? She's decided I'm her soul mate. I don't know what she wants but I don't think it's healthy."

Instinctively he glanced where the woman was nodding and studied the gold lamé dress, the stiletto heels. He said, "Well, the good news is it's not a woman."

"What?"

"Truly. But the bad news is that I'm betting what he has in mind is still pretty perverse."

"Maybe I better head for the hills," she said.

"Naw, hang out here. I'll protect you. You can cheer me up. My true love just left me."

"The true love you just met four minutes ago?" the woman asked. "*That* true love?"

"Ah, you witnessed that, did you?"

She added, "Mine just stood me up. I won't go so far as to say true love. He was a blind date."

His mind raced. Yes, she *was* familiar. . . . She now squinted at him as if she recognized him too. Where did he know her from? Here? The Harvard Club? Piping Rock?

He wondered if he'd slept with her, and, if he had, whether he'd enjoyed it. Shit, had he called her the next day?

She was saying, "I couldn't believe it. The bouncer wasn't going to let me in. It took all my political pull."

"Political?"

"A portrait of Alexander Hamilton." She slung out the words and Sebastian thought he heard something akin to mockery in her voice, as if he wasn't quick enough to catch the punch line.

"Gotcha," Sebastian said, feeling defensive.

"This drink sucks. The Coke tastes moldy."

Now he felt offended too, taking this as a criticism of the club, which was one of his homes away from home. He sipped his own drink and felt uncharacteristically out of control. Veronica was easier to handle. He wondered how to get back in the driver's seat.

"Look, I know I know you. You're?"

"Taylor Lockwood." They shook hands.

"Thom Sebastian."

"Right," she said, understanding dawning in his eyes.

With this, his mind made the connection. "Hubbard, White?"

"Corporate paralegal. Hey, you ever fraternize with us folks?"

"Only if we blow this joint. Let's go—there's nothing happening here."

The tall gold-clad transvestite had begun a striptease in front of them, while ten feet away Tina Turner and Calvin Klein paused to watch.

"There isn't?" Taylor asked.

Sebastian smiled, took her hand and led her through the crowd.

CHAPTER SIX

The drapery man was having a busy night.

He pushed a canvas cart ahead of him, filled with his props—draperies that needed to be cleaned but never would be. They were piled atop one another and the one on top was folded carefully; it hid his ice-pick weapon, resting near to hand.

This man had been in many different offices at all hours of the day and night. Insurance companies with rows of ghastly gray desks bathed in green fluorescence. CEOs' offices that were like the finest comp suites in Vegas casinos. Hotels and art galleries. Even some government office buildings. But Hubbard, White & Willis was unique.

At first he'd been impressed with the elegant place. But now, pushing the cart through quiet corridors, he felt belittled. He sensed contempt for people like him, sensed it from the walls themselves. Here, he was nothing. His neck prickled as he walked past a dark portrait of some old man from the 1800s. He wanted to pull out his pick and slash the canvas.

The drapery man's face was a map of vessels burst in

fistfights on the streets and in the various prisons he'd been incarcerated in and his muscles were dense as a bull's. He was a professional, of course, but part of him was hoping one of these scrawny prick lawyers, hunched over stacks of books in the offices he passed (no glances, no nods, no smiles—well, fuck you and your mother)... hoping one of them would walk up to him and demand to see a pass or permit so he could shank them through the lung.

But they all remained oblivious to him. An underling.

Not even worth noticing.

Glancing around to make sure no one was approaching, he stepped into the coffee room on the main floor and took a dusty container of Coffee-mate from the back of a storage shelf. In thirty seconds he'd slid out the tape recorder, removed the cassette, put in a new one and replaced the unit in the canister. He knew it was safe in this particular container because he'd observed that the prissy lawyers here insisted on real milk—half-and-half or 2 percent—and wouldn't think of drinking, or serving their clients, anything artificial. The Coffee-mate tube had been here, untouched, for months.

Making sure the corridor was empty again, the drapery man walked across the hall to Mitchell Reece's office and, listening carefully for footsteps, checked the receiver of Reece's phone.

On Saturday night, when he'd been here to steal the promissory note, he'd placed in the handset of the phone unit an Ashika Electronics omnidirectional ambient-filtering microphone and transmitter. The device was roughly the size of a Susan B. Anthony silver dollar. It was, however, considerably more popular and was used by every security, private eye or industrial espionage outfit that could afford the eight-thousand-dollar price tag. This bug broadcast a razor-clear transmission of all of Reece's conversations on the phone or with anyone else in the office to the radio receiver and tape recorder in the Coffee-mate container across the hall. One feature of the transmitter was that it contained a frequency-canceling feature, which made it virtually invisible to most commercial bug-detecting sweepers. He checked the battery and found it was still good.

When he was finished he spent another three or four minutes arranging the drapes so they looked nice. This was, after all, his purported job.

He peeled off the gloves and walked out into the halls, which greeted him once again with their silence and their real, or imagined, disdain.

"I suffer from the fallacy of the beautiful woman."

The Lincoln Town Car limo crashed through the meat-packing district in the western part of Greenwich Village, near the river. Taylor leaned sideways to hear Thom Sebastian over the crackly sound of the talk show on the driver's AM radio.

He continued, "Which is this: that because a woman is attractive she can do no wrong. You think, Christ, the way she lights a cigarette is the right way, the restaurants she picks are the right restaurants, the way she fakes an orgasm—pardon my French—is the right way so *I* must be doing something wrong. For instance, we're now on our way to Meg's. The club. You know it?"

"Absolutely no idea."

"There, my point exactly. I'm thinking: Jesus, I'm doing something wrong. Taylor is a primo woman but she doesn't know about this club. *I've* fucked up. *I've* got it wrong."

Taylor smirked. "Does this usually work?"

Sebastian paused then slouched back in the cab seat and lit a cigarette. "What?"

"That line? The one you're using on me now?"

Sebastian waited a few more seconds and must've decided there'd be no recovery from her busting him. "You'd be surprised at some of the lines I've gotten away with." He laughed. "The thing is *women* suffer from the fallacy of the man who knows what he's doing. We never do, of course." He gave her what might pass for a sincere glance and said, "I like you."

They pulled up in front of nothing. A row of ware-houses and small factories, not a streetlight in sight, only the distant aurora borealis of industrial Jersey across the Hudson River.

"Welcome to my main club."

"Here?"

"Yep. I'm here six, seven nights a week."

Sebastian led them through an unguarded, unmarked door into what looked like a Victorian bordello. The walls were covered with dark tapestry. The tables were marble and brass. Oak columns and sideboards were draped with tooling and floral chintz. Tiffanyesque lamps were every-where. The uniform for men was tuxedo or Italian suits, for the women, dark, close-fitting dresses with necklines that required pure willpower to keep nipples hidden. The rooms were chockablock with high-level celebs and politicos, the sort that regularly make *New York* magazine and Liz Smith's columns.

Sebastian whispered, "The three little piggies," and pointed out a trio of hip young novelists whom a *Times* critic had just vivisected en masse in an article called "Id as Art: The Care and Feeding of Self-Indulgence." Skinny women hovered around the threesome. Sebastian eyed the women with dismay and said, "Why are they wasting time with those dudes? Didn't they see the article?"

Taylor said dryly, "You assume they can read." And bumped into Richard Gere. He glanced at her with a polite acknowledgment, apologized and continued on.

"Oh my God." She gasped, staring at the man's broad back. "*He's* here."

"Yes," Sebastian said, bored. "And so are we."

The music wasn't as loud as at the previous club and the pace was less frantic. Sebastian waved to some people.

"What're you drinking?" he asked.

"Stick with R&C."

They sipped their drinks for a few minutes. Sebastian leaned over again and asked, "What's your biggest passion? After handsome men like me, I mean."

"Skiing, I guess." Taylor was circumspect about telling people her second career—the music—and was particularly reluctant to give a robbery suspect too much information about herself.

"Skiing? Sliding down a mountain, getting wet and cold and breaking bones, is that it?"

"Breaking bones is optional."

"I did some exercise once," Sebastian said, shaking his head. "I got over it. I'm okay now."

She laughed and studied him in the mirror. The lawyer didn't look good. His eyes were puffy and red. He blew his nose often and his posture was terrible. The coke and whatever other drugs he was doing were taking their toll. He seemed deflated as he hunched over his drink, sucking his cocktail through the thin brown straw. Suddenly he straightened, slipped his arm around her shoulders and kissed her hair. "Does anyone ever get lost in there?"

She kept the smile on her face but didn't lean into him. She said evenly, "It's true that I had date failure tonight. But I still do things the old-fashioned way. Real slow." She eased away and looked at him. "Just want the ground rules understood."

He left his arm where it was for a noncommittal ten seconds, then dropped it. "Fair enough," he said with a tone that suggested: all rights reserved.

"You go out a lot?" she asked.

"Work hard and play hard. By the time I burn out at forty-five ..." His voice faded and he was looking at her expectantly.

Tap, tap, tap.

She saw his hand swinging against the bar. A brown vial.

"You want to retire to the facilities with me? Build strong bodies twelve ways?"

"Not me. I have to keep in shape for breaking bones."

He blinked, surprised. "Yeah? You sure?"

"Never touch the stuff."

He laughed. Then put the bottle away.

Just then another man appeared from the crowd and walked up to Sebastian though his attention seemed fixed on Taylor. He resembled Sebastian some but was thinner, shorter, a few years younger. He wore a conservative gray suit but bright red sunglasses, from which a green cord hooked to the earpieces dangled down the back of his neck.

She noted Sebastian's surprise when the young man approached.

Sebastian said, "Hey, Taylor, meet my main man, Bosk. Hey, Bosk, Taylor." They shook hands.

"Will you marry me?" Bosk asked her in a slurred voice. He'd had a great deal to drink and she knew that beneath the silly Elton John sunglasses his eyes would be unfocused.

"Oh, gosh," she answered brightly, "I can't tonight."

"Story of my life." He turned back to Sebastian. "Hey, you never fucking called me back. We've gotta talk. He called and wanted to know where—"

Bosk suddenly fell silent and as Taylor reached for her drink she observed in the mirror behind the bar two very subtle gestures by Sebastian, a nod toward her and a wag of his finger, whose only possible meaning was that the topic Bosk was raising was not to be discussed in front of her.

Bosk recovered, though not very well, by saying, "What it is, I've still got some room on that New Jersey project if you're interested."

"How leveraged?"

Bosk said, "We'll need to come up with probably six five."

"No fucking way." Sebastian laughed.

"Sea Bass, come on. . . ."

"Three eight was the top, dumbo. I'm not going over three eight."

These figures might have referred to percentages or shares of stock or money, in which case, considering that the context was New York metro area business or real estate, they might be talking about hundreds of thousands or even millions of dollars.

And Alice thought Wonderland was topsy-turvy....

"Don't be such a fucking wuss," Bosk muttered drunkenly. Studying Taylor.

Sebastian grinned and grabbed Bosk, swung him into a neck lock then rapped him on the head.

Bosk broke away and shouted, laughing, "You're a fucking cow chip, you know that?" He replaced his gaudy sunglasses. "Hey, you want to come out to Long Island for dinner on Friday? My mother'll be out with her cook. Bunch of the gang. Brittany said she, like, forgives you for not calling."

An electronic pocket calendar appeared in Sebastian's pudgy hand. He studied it. "Can do, dude," he said at last. They slapped palms and Bosk vanished.

"Primo guy," Sebastian said.

"He's a lawyer?"

"Among other things. We go way back. We're doing some projects together."

Projects ... as vague a euphemism as there was.

"Like real estate?" Taylor asked.

"Yeah." But she heard a lie in his voice.

Taylor turned back to her drink. "I'd like to do some investing. But I got one problem. No money."

"Why's that a problem?" Sebastian said, frowning, genuinely perplexed. "You never use your own money. Use somebody else's. It's the only way to invest."

"Hubbard, White lets you work on your own? Don't you have to clear it with somebody?"

Sebastian laughed, a sharp exhalation of bitterness that surprised her. "We aren't on such good terms lately, Messrs. Hubbard, White and Willis and myself." He apparently decided to drop the fast-lane image. Deflated, he sighed and muttered, "They passed me over for partner." His lips tightened into a bleak smile and she got what she thought was her first real look at Thom Sebastian.

"I'm sorry." Taylor knew that this would have been a devastating blow to him. Partnership was the golden ring young associates strived for. They worked sixty or seventy hours a week for years for the chance to be asked to join the firm as one of the partners—the owners.

Taylor, on the trail of a thief, after all, sensed he might be revealing a motive to lift the promissory note—revenge—and wanted him to keep talking. She said, "Must've been tough."

"After they told me, I tried to convince myself I didn't really *want* to be partner. I mean, Christ, you can make more money at real estate or investment banking. I said, 'Fuck it. Who needs them? It's just a bunch of old men....' Well, that's what I told myself. But, damn, I wanted it bad. I've worked all my professional life to get my name on the letterhead of Hubbard, White & Willis. And this is what they do to me."

"Did they tell you why?"

His pale jaw, round with fat, trembled. "Bullshit. I mean, finances was what they said. 'Effecting economies,' if I may quote. But that wasn't the reason." He turned to her and said, "See, I don't fit the Hubbard, White mold."

"What's the mold?"

"Ha, that's the catch. They can't tell you; they just know whether you've got it or not. And that prick Clayton didn't think I had it."

"Wendall Clayton? What did he have to do with it?"

"I'm not one of his chosen few. Most of the partnership slots this year got filled with his boys and girls. Look at that asshole Randy Simms."

She had a vague memory of a young, square-jawed blond partner.

"Randy Simms III," Sebastian spat out. "The 'third,'" he mused bitterly. "But, hey, he's gotta be the end of *that* family line though. I'm sure the guy doesn't have a dick."

"But Clayton's not even on the executive committee," Taylor said.

He laughed. "What difference does *that* make? He's got ten times more power than Burdick or Stanley think. He's going to ramrod the merger through."

"The merger?" she said. "That's just a rumor. It's been going around for months."

Sebastian looked at her and detected no irony. He snorted. "Just a rumor? You think that, then you don't know Wendall Clayton. Two months from now, you won't be able to recognize our firm. . . ." His voice dwindled. "I should say, *your* firm. Ain't mine no more."

"What're you going to do?"

He was about to say something but grew cautious. She could sense he was selecting his words carefully. "Oh, I'll get a new job. Probably go in-house, become chief general counsel for a client. That's what happens to most senior associates after they cut your balls off."

Okay, Taylor told herself. Go for it.

"Then why're you working so hard?" she asked. "If I got passed over *I* sure wouldn't be working holiday weekends."

A brief hesitation. "Weekends?" he asked.

"Yeah, you were in the firm on Sunday morning, weren't you?"

He took a long sip of his drink then said, "Me? No. I was here all night. I left about three, when they were getting ready to close."

She frowned. "That's funny. I was doing some billing for . . . who was it? I don't remember. Anyway, I saw your key card number. You came in real early on Sunday." He looked at her for a long moment. His face was completely blank but she sensed that his thoughts were grinding hard and fast. Then he nodded in understanding. "Ralph Dudley," he said angrily.

"Dudley? The old partner?"

"Yeah, Grandpa. Yesterday he dropped my key off in my office. He said I left it in the library and he'd picked it up by mistake on Friday. He must've used it on Sunday."

She couldn't tell whether to believe him or not.

Agitated at this news, Sebastian fished in his pocket and found the little vial. He held it up. "You sure?" She shook her head and he looked toward the men's room. "Excusez-moi."

After he disappeared, Taylor motioned the bartender over to her and said, "You working last Saturday night?"

He normally didn't get questions like this. He polished glasses. But finally he said, "Yeah."

"Was Thom in here from one to three or so on Sunday morning?"

"I don't remember."

She slid two twenties toward him furtively. He blinked. This only happened in movies and the man seemed to be considering how his favorite actor would handle it. The bills disappeared into tight black jeans. "No. He left around one—without a girl. That *never* happens. If he's by himself usually he closes the place. He's even slept here a couple times."

When Sebastian returned he took Taylor's purse and slipped it around her—over one shoulder and under the other arm, the way paranoid tourists do. "Come on. I'm wound, I'm flying like a bird. I gotta dance. . . ."

"But—"

He pulled her onto the small floor. After fifteen minutes, her hair was down, streaming in thick, sweaty tangles. Her toes were on fire, her calves ached. Sebastian kept jerking away in time to the reggae beat, eyes closed, lost in the catharsis of the motion and music and the coke. Taylor collapsed on his shoulder. "Enough."

"I thought you were a skier."

"Exhausted." She was gasping.

His brow arched and the surprise in his eyes was genuine. "But we haven't eaten yet."

Taylor said, "It's one A.M. I've been up for nearly twenty-four hours."

"Time for penne!"

"But—"

"Come on. One plate of darling little squigglies of pasta in alfredo sauce with cilantro and basil, one teeny endive salad, one bottle of Mersault."

Taylor was weakening.

"*Belgium* endive! . . ." Then he lowered his head. "Okay."

Sebastian the negotiator was now speaking. "How's this for a deal? We have dinner and you can tell me about the Pine Breath Inn in Vermont or wherever the hell it is you ski and we'll call it a night. Or I can take you home now and you'll have to fight off my frontal assault at your door. Few women have been able to resist."

"Thom—"

"I take no prisoners."

She lowered her head on his shoulder then straightened up, smiling. "Does this place have spaghetti and meat balls with thick red sauce, à la Ragú?"

"I'll never be able to show my face there again. But if you want it I'll force the chef to make it."

She sighed, took his arm and together they made their way toward the door.

CHAPTER SEVEN

The alarm clock wailed like a smoke detector.

Taylor Lockwood opened one eye. Was this the worst headache of her life? she wondered.

She lay still for five minutes while the votes rolled in. Yes, no?

Sitting up decided the contest—a clear victory for the pain. She slammed her palm down on the alarm then scooted gingerly to the edge of the bed. She still wore her panty hose and bra; the elastic bands had cut deep purple lines into her skin and she was momentarily concerned that she'd have permanent discolorations.

Oh, man, I feel lousy. . . .

Taylor's one-bedroom apartment was small and dark. It was located in the Fifth Avenue Hotel, a dark, Gothic building distinguished only by the prestige of the street it was located on and its reputation for being the place that New York's Judge Crater was supposedly on his way to when he disappeared seventy years before—still an open case on the NYPD books.

Her parents had offered to send her whatever furniture

she wanted from their eight-bedroom house in Chevy Chase or from one of their summer homes but Taylor had wanted this apartment to be exclusively hers. It was furnished post-collegiate—Conran's, Crate & Barrel, Pottery Barn. A lot of fake stone, Formica, black and white plastic. A huge pillow sofa. Canvas chairs that, looked at straight on, seemed to be grinning. A number of interesting pieces from the Twenty-sixth Street flea market on Sixth Avenue.

The bedroom was the homiest room in the place, decorated with lace tulle, art deco lamps and old furniture—battered but loaded with personality—a hundred books, souvenirs from the trips young Taylor took to Europe with her parents.

On the wall was a large poster—one of Arthur Rackham's sepia illustrations of Lewis Carroll's *Alice's Adventures in Wonderland.*

The picture wasn't like the Disney cartoon or the original Sir John Tenniel drawings but was a masterful work by the brilliant artist. It showed an alarmed Alice lifting her hands to protect herself as the Red Queen's playing card soldiers flew into the air.

The caption read:

> At this the whole pack rose up into the air,
> and came flying down upon her.

The framed poster had been a graduation present from her roommates at Dartmouth. Taylor loved the Carroll books, and Alice memorabilia were sure bets as birthday and Christmas presents. There were many other *Wonderland* and *Through the Looking-Glass* artifacts throughout her apartment.

Taylor sent her tongue around her parched mouth; she didn't enjoy the trip. She staggered into the bathroom, where she downed two glasses of water and brushed her teeth twice. She squinted at the clock. Let's see, Sebastian had dropped her off at about four. Do the math. . . . Okay, we're talking about three and a half hours' sleep.

And, more troubling, it turned out that she'd largely wasted her time. Thom Sebastian had denied being in the firm on Saturday or Sunday and had remained tight-lipped about his dealings with Bosk though he'd continued to talk bitterly about the firm's decision to pass him over. He'd had no response when she'd casually mentioned Hanover & Stiver, Inc.

She kneaded her belly, which swelled slightly over the top of her panties, recalling that there were a hundred fifty calories in each cocktail. . . . She squeezed her temples. Her vision swam.

A blinking red light across the room coincided with the throbbing in her head. It was her answering machine, indicating a message from last night. She hit the play button, thinking it might be a call from Mitchell Reece, remembering his asking her if it was okay to call her at home.

Beep.

"Hello, counselor."

Ah, her father, she realized with a thud in her turbulent stomach.

"Just wanted to tell you: You owe me lunch. Earl Warren was chief justice when the case was decided. Call when you can. Love you."

Click.

Shit, she thought. I shouldn't've bet with him.

Taylor didn't mind losing to him, of course; half the lawyers in Washington, D.C., had lost a case or motion or argument to Samuel Lockwood at one time or another in their careers. The *Washington Post* had called him "The Unbeatable Legal Eagle" (the article was framed and displayed prominently in their living room at home). No, it was that even though she could see clearly that he was testing her, she'd weakened and agreed to the pointless bet.

It was very, very difficult to say no to Samuel Lockwood.

He called her two or three times a week but unless he had something specific to ask her he usually picked "safe" times: During the day he'd call her home, at night he'd call the firm, leaving messages—fulfilling his parental duty and making his royal presence felt in her territory but making sure he didn't waste time actually talking to her. (She noted cynically that she might reasonably have been expected to be home last night when he'd phoned—because the purpose of that call had been to gloat.)

Well, she could hardly point fingers; Taylor did the same—generally calling home when she knew he was working so she could chat with her mother untroubled by the brooding presence of her father hovering near the receiver, a presence she could sense from even three hundred miles away.

She winced as the headache pounded on her again, just for the pure fun of it, it seemed. A glance at the clock.

Okay, Alice, you got twenty minutes to get yourself up and running. Go for it.

Sitting before Mitchell Reece in the glaringly lit Vista Hotel dining room was a plate of scrambled eggs, hash browns, bacon and a bagel. Taylor was nursing a grapefruit juice and seltzer.

She'd already been stared down by her dry toast.

Reece said, "You feeling okay?"

"I was out dancing last night till four."

"All work and no play . . ."

Taylor grunted. "The good news is I've got us a suspect." The juice was reviving traces of rum lurking in her bloodstream. This resuscitation was not pleasant. "Thom Sebastian."

She explained to him about cross-referencing the computer key entries and the time sheets.

"Brilliant," he told her, lifting an eyebrow.

She nodded noncommittally and downed two more Advils.

"Sebastian?" Reece pondered. "In the corporate group, right? He's done work for New Amsterdam in the past. He might even've done some of the work on the original loan to Hanover. But what's his motive? Money?"

"Revenge. He was passed over for partner."

"Ouch." Sympathy crept into Reece's face, which revealed the fatigue-dulled skin and damp red eyes that Taylor knew matched hers. Still, his suit of textured charcoal wool was perfectly pressed and his shirt was as smooth and white as the starched napkin that lay across his lap. His dark hair was combed back, slick and smooth from either a recent shower or some lotion. He sat comfortably upright at the table and ate hungrily.

Taylor braved the toast again and managed to eat a small piece. "And he acted real odd about something. He's got a quote project going on with somebody nicknamed Bosk. Another lawyer here in town, young kid. But he wouldn't talk about it. He also claims he was in a club on Saturday but the bartender there said he wasn't. He left about one. I asked Sebastian about it and he claims Ralph Dudley took his computer door key."

"Old Man Dudley? Working on Sunday at one-thirty? No way. Past his bedtime." Reece then reconsidered. "Funny, though, I heard Dudley had money problems. He's borrowed big against his partnership equity."

Taylor said, "How'd you find that out?" The individual partners' financial situations were closely guarded secrets.

As if citing an immutable rule of physics Reece said, "*Always* know the successful partners from the losers."

"I'll check out Dudley today."

"I can't imagine he was in the firm on legitimate business. Dudley hasn't worked a weekend in his life. But I also can't see him as our thief. He's such a bumbler. And he's got that granddaughter of his he's looking after. I don't see how he'd risk going to jail and leaving her alone. She doesn't have any other family."

"That cute little girl he brought to the outing last year? She's about sixteen?"

"I heard that Dudley's son abandoned her or something.

Anyway, she's in boarding school in town and he takes care of her." He laughed. "Kids. I can't imagine them."

Taylor asked, "You don't have any?"

He grew wistful for a few seconds. "No. I thought I would once." The stoic lawyer's facade returned immediately. "But my wife wasn't so inclined. And, after all, it does take two, you know."

"When I hit thirty-eight I'm going to find a genetically acceptable man, get pregnant and send him on his way."

"You could always try marriage, of course."

"Oh, yeah, I've heard about that."

He looked at her eyes for a moment then started laughing.

She asked, "What?"

"I was thinking, we should start a group."

"What?"

"The Visine Club," he said.

"I can get by with seven hours' sleep. Less than that, no way."

Reece said, "Five's pretty much standard for me." He finished the bacon and held a forkful of eggs toward her. She smiled, fought down the nausea and shook her head. She noticed, behind the bar, a stack of wine bottles and felt her stomach twist. Reece ate some of his breakfast and asked, "Where you from?"

"Burbs of D.C. Chevy Chase in Maryland. Well, I was born on Long Island but my parents moved to Maryland when I was in middle school. My father got a job in the District."

"Oh, I read that article in the *Post* about him last month. His argument before the Supreme Court."

"Tell me about it," she grumbled. "I've heard the blow-by-blow a half-dozen times. He overnighted me a copy of his argument. For my leisure-time reading, I guess."

"So how'd you end up on Wall Street?" Reece asked.

"Very long story," she said with a tone that told him that this was not the time or place to share it.

"School?

"Dartmouth . . . music and poly sci."

"Music?"

"I play piano. Jazz mostly."

This seemed to intrigue him. He asked, "Who do you listen to?"

"Billy Taylor's my fave, I guess. But there's something about the fifties and sixties. Cal Tjader, Desmond, Brubeck."

Reece shook his head. "I'm mostly into horn. Dexter Gordon, Javon Jackson."

"No kidding," she said, surprised. Usually only jazzophiles knew these players. "I love Jabbo Smith."

He nodded at this. "Sure, sure. I'm also a big Burrell fan."

She nodded. "Guitar? I still like Wes Montgomery, I've got to admit. For a while I was into a Howard Roberts phase."

Reece said, "Too avant-garde for me."

"Oh, yeah, I hear you," she said. "A melody . . . that's what music's got to have—a tune people can hum. A movie's got to have a story, a piece of music's got to have a tune. That's my philosophy of life."

"You perform?"

"Sometimes. Right now my big push is to get a record contract. I just dropped a bundle making a demo of some of my own tunes. I rented a studio, hired union backup. The works. Sent them to about a hundred companies."

"Yeah?" He seemed excited. "Give me a copy if you think about it. You have any extra?"

She laughed. "Dozens. Even after I give them away as Christmas presents this year."

"How's the response been?"

"Next question?" she asked, sighing. "I've sent out ninety-six tapes—agents, record companies, producers. So far, I've gotten eighty-four rejections. But I did get one 'maybe.' From a big label. They're going to present it to their A&R committee."

"I'll keep my fingers crossed."

"Thanks."

"So," he asked, "how's the music jibe with the law school track?"

"Oh, I can handle them both," she said without really thinking about her response. She wondered if the comment came off as pompous.

He glanced at his watch, and Taylor felt the gesture abruptly push aside the personal turn their conversation had taken. She asked, "There is one thing I wanted to ask you about. Linda Davidoff worked on the Hanover & Stiver case, right?"

"Linda? The paralegal? Yeah, for a few months when the case got started."

"It struck me as a little curious that she quit working on the case pretty suddenly then she killed herself."

He nodded. "That's odd, yeah. I never thought about it. I didn't know her very well. She was a good paralegal. But real quiet. It doesn't seem likely she'd be involved," Reece said, "but if you asked me it if was likely somebody'd steal a note from a law firm, I'd say no way."

The waitress asked if they wanted anything else. They shook their heads. "You women, always dieting," Reece said, nodding at her uneaten toast.

Taylor smiled. Thinking: We women, always trying not to throw up in front of our bosses.

"What's up next?" he asked.

"Time to be a spy," she said.

■

Taylor sat in her cubicle at the firm and dialed a number.

She let the telephone ring. When the system shifted the call over to voice mail she hung up, left her desk and wandered down the halls. Up a flight of stairs. She turned down a corridor that led past the lunchroom then past the forms room, where copies of prototype contracts and pleadings were filed. At the end of this corridor—in the law firm's Siberia—was a single office. On the door was a nameplate: *R. Dudley.* Most of these plates in the firm were plastic; this one, though it designated the smallest partner's office in Hubbard, White, was made of polished brass.

Inside the office were crammed an Italian Renaissance desk, a tall bookcase, two shabby leather chairs, dozens of prints of nineteenth-century sailing ships and eighteenth-century foxhunting scenes. Through a small window you could see a brick wall and a tiny sliver of New York Harbor. On the desk rested a large brass ashtray, a picture of an unsmiling, pretty teenage girl, a dozen Metropolitan Opera *Playbills,* a date book and one law book—a Supreme Court *Reporter.*

Taylor Lockwood opened the *Reporter* and bent over it. Her eyes, though, camouflaged by her fallen hair, were not reading the twin columns of type but rather Ralph Dudley's scuffed leather date book, opened to the present week.

She noticed the letters *W.S.* penned into the box for late Saturday evening or early Sunday morning, just before the time Dudley—if Sebastian was right—had used the associate's key to get into the firm.

The initials *W.S.* were also, she observed, written in the 10 P.M. slot for tomorrow. Who was this person? A contact at Hanover? The professional thief? Taylor then opened the calendar to the phone number/address section. There was no one listed with those initials. She should—

"Can I help you?" a man's voice snapped.

Taylor forced herself not to jump. She kept her finger on the *Reporter* to mark her spot and looked up slowly.

A young man she didn't recognize stood in the doorway. Blond, scrubbed, chubby. And peeved.

"Ralph had this *Reporter* checked out from the library," she said, nodding at the book. "I needed to look up a case." Taking the offensive, she asked bluntly, "Who're you?"

"Me? I'm Todd Stanton. I work for Mr. Dudley." He squinted. "Who are *you?*"

"Taylor Lockwood. A paralegal." She forced indignation into her voice.

"A paralegal." His tone said, Oh, well, that doesn't really count. "Does Mr. Dudley know you're here?"

"No."

"If you need anything, you can ask me for it. Mr. Dudley doesn't like"—he sought the least disparaging term—"anyone in his office when he's not here."

"Ah," Taylor said and then turned back to the book and slowly finished reading a long paragraph.

Stanton shifted then said with irritation, "Excuse me but—"

Taylor closed the book softly. "Hey," she said, offering a concerned glance. "Don't sweat it. You're excused." And walked past him back into the deserted corridor.

CHAPTER EIGHT

"Dactyloscopy," the man said. "Repeat after me: dactyloscopy."

Taylor did.

More or less.

"Good," the man said. "Now you know the first thing about fingerprinting. It's called dactyloscopy. The second is that it is a royal pain in the butt."

She sat in the office of John Silbert Hemming. His card explained that he was a vice president in the corporate security department at Manhattan Allied Security, Inc.

The man, in his mid-thirties, had been recommended by a friend from the music world who did word processing for Allied Security to support his addiction to the saxophone.

Taylor had spent most of the day at Hubbard, White, poring over records of the *New Amsterdam Bank v. Hanover & Stiver* case, trying to find a reference to anyone who might have shown unusual interest in the promissory note or who'd requested files on the deal when there didn't seem to be a reason for them to do so.

But after nearly eight hours of mind-numbing legal babble Taylor found not a shred of evidence to suggest that Ralph
Dudley or Thom Sebastian—or anyone else—was the thief.

She'd decided to give up on the subtle approach and try
a more traditional tack, à la *Kojak* or *Rockford Files*.

Hence, the tall shamus she was now sitting across from.

When Hemming had come to meet her in the reception
area she'd blinked and looked up. He was six feet ten. His
height had led, he had explained on their way back to his
office, to his becoming a backroom security man—the company technical and forensic expert.

"You've got to be unobtrusive in private detective work.
A lot of what we do is surveillance, you know."

She said, "Tailing."

"Pardon?"

"Don't you say 'tailing'? You know, like you tail somebody?"

"Hmmm, no, we say say 'surveillance.'"

"Oh."

"If you stand out like me that's not so good. When we
recruit we have a space on our evaluation form—'Is subject
unobtrusive?' We mean 'boring.'"

His hair was tawny and unruly and Taylor's impression
of Hemming was that he was a huge little boy. He had eyes
that seemed perpetually amused and that belied a face that
was dramatically long (what else could it be, given that it sat
atop a body like his?). Despite this quirky appearance there
was something rather appealing about him.

Now, John Silbert Hemming was aiming a startlingly
long finger at her and saying, "I hope you mean that, about
wanting to know everything. Because there's a lot, and here
it comes. Let's start with: What *are* fingerprints?"

"Uh—"

"I know. You paid the money, I've got the answers. But I
like people to participate. I like interaction. Time's up. No
idea? I'd suggest you avoid *Jeopardy!* Now: Fingerprints are
the impressions left by the papillary ridges of the fingers
and thumb, primarily in perspiration. Also called friction

ridges. There are no sebaceous glands in the fingertips themselves but people sometimes leave fingerprints in human oils picked up elsewhere on the body. Yes, in answer to the first most-often-asked question, they are all different. Even more different than snowflakes, I can say safely, because for hundreds of years people have been collecting fingerprints from all over the world and comparing them, and nobody—none of *my* close friends, I'll tell you—have been doing that with snowflakes. Go ahead, ask the next-most-popular question."

"Uh, do animals have fingerprints?"

"Primates do, but who cares? We don't give apes government clearances or put them on the ten-most-wanted list. That's not the question. The question is twins."

"Twins?"

"And the answer is that twins, quadruplets, duodeceplets—they all have different fingerprints. Now, who first discovered fingerprints?"

"I have a feeling you're going to tell me?"

"Guess."

"Scotland Yard?" Taylor offered.

"Prehistoric tribes in France were aware of fingerprints and used them as cave decorations. In the sixteen and seventeen hundreds they were used as graphic designs and trademarks. The first attempt to study them seriously was in 1823—Dr. J. E. Purkinje, an anatomy professor, came up with a crude classification system. Fingerprints became sexy in the late 1800s. Sir Francis Galton, who was a preeminent scholar in the field of . . ." He cocked his eyebrows at Taylor. "Daily Double?"

"Dactyloscopy?"

"Nice try but no. In the field of heredity. He established that all fingerprints are different and they never change throughout one's life. The British government appointed Edward Richard Henry to a commission to consider using fingerprints to identify criminals. By around the turn of the century Henry had created the basic classification system they use in most countries. His system is called, coincidentally, the Henry system. New York was the first state to start fingerprinting all prisoners. Around 1902."

While she found this fascinating the urgency of the Hanover case kept prodding her. When he came up for air she asked, "If one were going to look for fingerprints, how would one do it?"

" 'One'?" he asked coyly. "You?"

"No, just . . . one."

"Well, it depends on the surface. You—excuse me, *one*—should wear cloth gloves—not latex. If the surface is light-colored one would use a carbon-based dark powder. On dark, one would use an aluminum-and-chalk mixture; it's light gray. One would dust on the powder with a very soft, long-bristle brush. Then one removes the excess—"

"How?"

"Flip a coin," the detective said.

"One blows it off."

"A lot of rookies think that. But you tend to spit and ruin the whole print. No, use a brush. Now, powders only work on smooth surfaces. If you've got to take a print from paper there are different techniques. If the print's oily maybe it'll show up in iodine vapor. The problem is that you have to expose it in an enclosed cabinet and take a picture of the print very quickly because the vapors evaporate right away. Sometimes latents come out with a nitrate solution or ninhydrin or superglue. But that's the big league, probably over your—one's—skill level.

"Now, once *one* has the print, he or"—a nod toward her—"*she* has to capture it. You lift it off the surface with special tape or else take a picture of it. Remember: Fingerprints are *evidence*. They have to get into the courtroom and in front of an expert witness."

"Now," she said, "just speaking theoretically, could someone like me take fingerprints?"

"If you practiced, sure. But could you testify that prints A and B were the same? No way. Could you even tell if they were the same or different? Not easy, mama, not at all. They squoosh out, they move, they splot. They look different when they're the same, they look identical except for some little significant difference you miss. . . . No, it isn't easy. Fingerprinting is an art."

"How 'bout a machine, or something? A computer?"

"The police use them, sure. The FBI. But not private citizens. Say, Ms. Lockwood?"

"Taylor," she prompted.

"Perhaps if you told me exactly what your problem is I could offer some specific solutions."

"It's somewhat sensitive."

"It always is. That's why companies like us exist."

"Best to keep mum for the time being."

"Understood. Just let me know if you'd like another lesson. Though I do recommend keeping in mind the experts." He grew serious and the charming banter vanished. "Should the matter become, let's say, more than *sensitive*—a lot of our people here have carry permits."

" 'Carry'?"

"They're licensed to carry weapons."

"Oh," she said in a soft voice.

"Just something to think about."

"Thanks, John." Then she said, "I do have one question."

The hand in which a basketball would look so at home rose and a finger pointed skyward. "Allow me to deduce. The inquiry is: Where you can get a Dick Tracy fingerprint kit?" Before she answered yes, he was writing an address on the back of his business card. "It's a police equipment supply house. You can buy anything but weapons and shields there."

"Shields?"

"Badges, you know. Those you can buy—*one* can buy— in Times Square arcades for about ten bucks. But you're not supposed to. Oh, not to be forward, but I did happen to write my home phone number on the back of the card. In case any questions occur to you after hours, say."

She decided she liked this guy. "This's been fascinating, John. Thank you." She stood and he escorted her toward the elevator, pointing out a glass case containing a collection of blackjacks and saps.

"Oh, and Miss Lockwood? Taylor?"

"Yes?"

"Before you leave I was just wondering: Would you like to hear the lecture I give to our new employees on the laws against breaking and entering and invading privacy?"

Taylor said, "No, I don't believe I would."

███████

She'll be moody today.

Ralph Dudley sat in his creaky office chair. The nape of his neck eased into the tall leather back and he stared at the thin slice of sky next to the brick wall outside his window. Gray sky, gray water. November.

Yes, Junie would be in one of her moods.

It was a talent, this intuition of his. Whereas Donald Burdick, to whom he constantly—obsessively—compared himself, was brilliant, Ralph Dudley was intuitive. He charmed clients, he told them jokes appropriate to their age, gender and background, he listened sympathetically to their tales of sorrow at infidelities and deaths and to their stories of joy at grandchildren's births. He told war stories of his courtroom victories with a dramatic pacing that only fiction—which they were, of course—permits. With his patented vestigial bow Dudley could charm the daylights out of the wives of clients and potential clients.

He had sense and feeling while Burdick had reason and logic.

And, sure enough, he was now right. Here came fifteen-year-old Junie, a sour look on her face, trooping sullenly into his office, ignoring the woman from the word processing pool who was handling a typing job for him.

The girl stopped in the doorway, a hip-cocked stance, unsmiling.

"Come on in, honey," Dudley said. "I'm almost finished."

She wore a jumper, white blouse and white stockings. A

large blue bow was in her hair. She gave him a formal kiss on the cheek and plopped into one of his visitor's chairs, swinging her legs over the side.

"Sit like a lady, now."

She waited a defiant thirty seconds then slipped on her Walkman headset and swiveled slowly in the chair, planting her feet on the lime-green carpet.

Dudley laughed. He picked up the handle of his dictating machine. "Look, I've got one, too—a recorder."

She looked perplexed and he realized she couldn't hear what he was saying (and would probably have thought his joke was idiotic if she'd been able to). But Dudley had learned not to be hurt by the girl's behavior and he unemotionally proceeded to dictate a memo that gave the gist of some rules of law he believed he remembered. At the end of the tape he included instructions to Todd Stanton, his associate at the firm, who would rewrite the memo and look up the law Dudley hoped existed to support his points.

Ralph Dudley knew they sometimes laughed at him, the young associates here. He never raised his voice, he never criticized, he was solicitous toward them. He supposed the young men (Dudley had never quite come to terms with the idea of women lawyers) held him in all the more contempt for this obsequiousness. There were a few loyal boys, like Todd, but on the whole no one had much time for Old Man Dudley.

"Grandpa," he'd heard that the associates called him. Partners, too, although somewhat more subtly, joined in the derision. Yet though this treatment soiled his days here—and obliterated whatever loyalty he had once felt for Hubbard, White & Willis—he was not overly troubled. His relation with the firm became just what his marriage to Emma had been: one of respectful acknowledgment. He was usually able to keep his bitterness contained.

Junie's eyes were closed, her patent-leather shoes swaying in time to the music. My God, she was growing up. Fifteen. It gave him a pang of sorrow. At times he had flashes—poses she struck, the way the light might catch her face—of her as a woman in her twenties. He knew that she, abandoned in adolescence, carried the seeds of adulthood within her more fertilely than other children.

And he often felt she was growing up far too fast for him.

He handed the dictated tape to the typist, who left.

"So," he said to the girl, "are we going to do some shopping?"

"I guess."

That question she heard perfectly, Dudley observed. "Well, let's go."

She shrugged and hopped off the chair, tugging at her dress in irritation, which meant she wanted to be wearing jeans and a T-shirt—clothes that she loved and that he hated.

They were at the elevator when a woman's voice asked, "Ralph, excuse me, you have a minute?"

He recognized the young woman from around the firm but couldn't recall a name. It stung him slightly that she had the effrontery to call him by his first name but because he was a gentlemen he did nothing other than smile and nod. "Yes, you're . . ."

"Taylor Lockwood."

"Sure, of course. This is my granddaughter, Junie. Junie, say hello to Miss Lockwood. She's a lawyer here."

"Paralegal, actually." Taylor smiled and said to the girl pleasantly, "You look like Alice."

"Huh?"

"*Alice in Wonderland.* It's one of my favorite books."

The girl shrugged and returned to the oblivion of her music.

Dudley wondered what this woman wanted. Had he given her some work? An assignment?

"I'd like to ask you something."

"What's that?"

"You went to Yale Law School, didn't you?"

"That's right, I did."

"I'm thinking of applying there."

Dudley felt a bit of alarm. He hadn't quite graduated, despite what he'd told the firm, and so couldn't exactly send a letter of recommendation for her.

But she added, "My application and letters and everything're in. I just want to know a little about the school. I'm trying to decide between there and Harvard and NYU."

Relieved, Dudley said, "Oh, I went there before you were born. I don't think anything I'd have to tell you would be much help."

"Well, somebody here said you helped them decide to go to law school, that you were very helpful. I was sort of hoping you could spare a half hour or so."

Dudley felt the pleasure he always did at even minor adulation like this. "Tonight?"

She said, "I was thinking tomorrow night maybe. After work? I could take you out to dinner."

A woman taking a man out to dinner? Dudley was nearly offended.

The paralegal added, "Unless you have plans."

He did, of course—plans he *wouldn't* miss. But that was at 10 P.M. He said, "I'm busy later in the evening. But how would seven be?" A charming smile. "I'll take you to my club."

Junie of the selective hearing said, "Like, Poppie, you told me they didn't let women in there."

Dudley said to her, "That's only as members, honey." To Taylor he said, "Come by tomorrow at six, we'll take a cab uptown. . . ." Then, calculating the taxi fare, he added, "No, actually a subway would be better. That time of day, traffic is terrible."

■

"Now he's going after the clients."

Donald Burdick knotted the silk tie carefully with his long fingers. He liked the feel of good cloth, the way it yielded yet was tough. Tonight, though, the smooth texture gave him little pleasure.

"First he rams through the accelerated vote and now I hear he's targeting the clients."

"The clients," Vera Burdick repeated, nodding. "We should've thought of that." She sat at her dressing table in the bedroom of their Park Avenue co-op, rubbing prescription retin-A cream on her neck. She wore a red and black silk dress, which revealed pale freckled skin along the unzipped V in the back. She was leaning forward studiously, watching the cream disappear.

A resolute woman, in her early sixties, she'd battled age by making tactical concessions. She gave up tanning fifteen years ago and carefully gained a little weight, refusing to join in the dieting obsession of many of her friends, who were now knobby scarecrows. She let her hair go white but she kept it shiny with Italian conditioner and wore it pulled back in the same style as her granddaughter. She'd allowed herself one face-lift and had flown to Los Angeles to have a particular Beverly Hills surgeon perform the operation.

She was now as she'd always been: attractive, reserved, stubborn, quiet. And virtually as powerful as the two men who'd influenced her life—her father and Donald Burdick, her husband of thirty-two years. Arguably she was *more* powerful in some ways than each of these men because people were always on guard with the masters of Wall Street, like Donald Burdick, but tended to get careless around women and be too chatty, to give away secrets, to reveal weaknesses.

Burdick sat on the bed. His wife offered her back and he carefully zipped up the dress and hooked the top eyelet. The partner continued, "Clayton's moving against them. It's pretty clever, I have to admit. While Bill Stanley and Lamar and I've been taking on as much debt as we can to poison the merger Wendall's been spending time with the clients, trying to convince *them* to pressure the partners at the firm to support the merger."

Vera too felt admiration for what Wendall was doing. Although a firm's clients have no official vote in firm affairs they ultimately pay the bills and accordingly can exert astonishing influence over which way the partners vote. She'd often said that if clients unionized against law firms it would be time for her husband to find a new line of work.

"How's he doing it?" she asked, curious to learn his technique.

"Probably promising big discounts in legal fees if they support the merger. Those that still don't go along with him—my clients or Bill's, the ones who won't support the merger in any case—we're afraid he's going to sabotage."

"Sabotage. Oh, my. What's the vote so far?"

"It's closer than it should be."

"You've got the long-term lease with Rothstein, right?" Vera asked. "That should slow him up some. When are you signing it?"

"Friday or the weekend," he answered glumly.

"Not till then?" She winced.

"I know," he said. "The fastest they could get the papers together. But it's okay—Clayton doesn't know anything about it. Then I've been talking to Steve Nordstrom."

"At McMillan Holdings," Vera recalled. "Your biggest client. Steve's the chief financial officer, right?"

A nod. "I'm closer to him than I am to Ed Gliddick, the CEO. I'm going to get them to lobby some of the other partners against the merger."

"And Steve'll agree?"

"I'm sure he will. Gliddick's in charge. But he listens to Steve. Wendall doesn't know about that either. I've been excruciatingly discreet. I . . ."

Burdick realized that he sounded desperate and hated the tone of his voice. Then he glanced at his wife, who was gazing at him with a savvy smile on her face. "We can do it," she said. "Clayton's not in our league, dear."

"Neither was that cobra on vacation last year. That doesn't mean he's not dangerous."

"But look what happened to it."

Hiking in Africa, Burdick had accidentally stepped on the snake in the brush. It had puffed out its hood and prepared to strike. Vera had taken its head off with a swipe of a sharp machete.

Burdick found his teeth clenched. "Wendall just doesn't understand what Wall Street law practice is. He's crude, he bullies. He has affairs."

"Irrelevant." She began on her makeup.

"Oh, I think it *is* relevant. I'm talking about the survival of the firm. Wendall doesn't have *vision*. He doesn't understand what Hubbard, White is, what it should be."

"And how do you define 'should be'?"

Touché, Burdick thought. He grinned involuntarily. "All right, what *I've* made it. Bill and Lamar and I. Wendall wants to turn the firm into a mill. Into a big merger-and-acquisition house."

"Every generation has its own specialties. That's very profitable work." She set down the blush. "I'm not justifying him, darling. I'm only saying we should stay focused. We can't make logical arguments against the nature of the legal work he wants the new firm to handle. We have to remember that the risk is that as part of the merger he's going to burn the firm to the ground and then sow the ashes with salt. *That's* why we have to stop him."

She was, as usual, right. He reached for her hand but the phone rang and he walked to the nightstand to answer it.

Burdick took the call and listened in dismay as Bill Stanley's gruff voice delivered the message. He hung up and looked at his wife, who stared at him, clearly alarmed by his drawn expression.

"He's done it again."

"Clayton?"

Burdick sighed and nodded. He walked to the window and gazed outside into the trim, windswept courtyard. "There's a problem with the St. Agnes case."

Donald Burdick's oldest and second-most-lucrative client was Manhattan's St. Agnes Hospital. It had recently been sued for malpractice and Fred LaDue, a litigation partner, was handling the trial, which was in its fourth day now.

The case was routine and it was likely that the hospital was going to win. Stanley had just reported, however, that the plaintiff's attorneys—from a tough Midtown personal injury firm—had found a new witness, a doctor whose testimony could be devastating to St. Agnes. Even though he was a surprise witness, the judge was going to let him testify tomorrow.

The judgment could be for tens of millions and a loss this big might mean that St. Agnes—which was self-insured—would fire Hubbard, White & Willis altogether. Even if the hospital didn't do so, though, the credibility of Burdick and his litigation department would be seriously eroded and the hospital might push to support the merger; John Perelli's firm was renowned for its brutal handling of personal injury defense work.

"Damn," Burdick muttered. "Damn."

Vera's eyes narrowed. "You don't think that Wendall slipped your client's files to the other side, do you?"

"It did occur to me."

Vera took a sip of scotch and set the Waterford glass down on the table. Burdick's eyes were distant, trying to process this news. His wife's, however, had coalesced into dark dots. "One thing I'd say, darling."

The wind rattled the leaded-glass windows. Burdick glanced at the sound.

She said, "With a man like Wendall, we have to hit him hard the first time. We won't have a second chance."

Burdick's eyes dropped to the Pakistani carpet on the bedroom floor. Then he picked up the phone and called the night operator at the law firm. "This is Donald Burdick," he said politely. "Please locate Mitchell Reece and have him call me at home. Tell him it's urgent."

CHAPTER NINE

Taylor Lockwood walked through the breezy evening streets of the East Village, the curbs banked with trash, and thought of a funeral she'd attended several months earlier.

She'd sat in the front pew of the church in Scarsdale, north of the city, a wood-and-stone building built, someone behind her had whispered, by contributions from tycoons like J. P. Morgan and Vanderbilt. Although Taylor had been in black, that color did not seem to be requisite at funerals any longer; any somber shade was acceptable—purple, forest green, even dusk-brown tapestry. She sat on the hard pew and watched the family members, lost in their personal rituals of grief, tears running in halting streams, hands squeezing hands, fingers rubbing obsessively against fingers. The minister had spoken of Linda Davidoff with genuine sorrow and familiarity. He knew the parents better than the daughter, that was clear, but he was eulogizing well.

Most attendees had seemed sad or bewildered but not everyone had cried; suicide makes for an ambivalent mourning.

The minister had closed the service with one of Linda's poems, one published in her college literary magazine.

As he'd read, images of Linda had returned and the tears that Taylor Lockwood had told herself not to cry appeared fast, stinging the corners of her eyes and running with maddening tickles down her cheeks, even though she hadn't known the paralegal very well.

Then the organ had played a solemn cue and the mourners had filed outside for the drive to the interment.

As she'd told Reece, nothing that she'd found suggested that Linda Davidoff had had any connection with Hanover & Stiver or the loan deal. But there was something suspicious to Taylor about the way the girl had worked such long hours on the case then stopped abruptly—and then committed suicide.

She felt she needed to follow up on this question. Alice, after all, had wandered everywhere throughout Wonderland—a place, however, in which you sure wouldn't find the disgusting six-story tenement she now stood in front of. In the foul entry foyer the intercom had been stolen and the front door was open, swinging in the breeze like a batwing door in a ghost town saloon. She started up the filthy steps.

"It may look impressive, but the bank owns most of it," Sean Lillick said.

The young paralegal was sitting on the drafty floor, shirtless and shoeless, shoving a backpack under the bed as she walked in.

Taylor Lockwood, catching her breath from the climb, was surveying what Lillick was referring to: a wall of keyboards, wires, boxes, a computer terminal, speakers, guitar, amps. Easily fifty thousand dollars' worth of musical equipment.

Lillick—thin, dark-haired, about twenty-four—was smelling socks, discarding them. He wore black jeans, a sleeveless T-shirt. His boots sat in front of him. The only clue as to his day job at Hubbard, White & Willis were two dark suits and three white shirts, in various stages of recycling, hanging on nails pounded crookedly into the wall. He studied her for a moment. "You look impressed or confused. I can't tell."

"Your place is a little more alternative than I expected." The apartment was a patchwork. Someone had nailed pieces of plywood, plastic or sheet metal over cracks and holes. Joints didn't meet, plaster was rotting, floorboards were cracked or missing. In the living room: one hanging bare bulb, one floor lamp, one daybed, one desk.

And a ton of bank-owned musical instruments and gear.

"Have a seat."

She looked helplessly about her.

"Oh. Well, try the daybed. . . . Hey, Taylor, listen to this. I just thought it up. I'm going to use it in one of my pieces: You know what a preppy is?"

"I give up."

"A yuppie with papers."

She smiled politely. He didn't seem concerned about the tepid response and wrote the line down in a notebook. "So what do you do?" she asked. "Stand-up comedy?"

"Performance art. I like to rearrange perceptions."

"Ah, musically speaking," she joked, "you're a re-arranger."

He seemed to like her observation too and mentally stored it somewhere.

Taylor walked over to a music keyboard.

Lillick said, "You're thinking organ, I know. But—"

"I'm thinking Yamaha DX-7 synthesizer with a digital sampler, MIDI and a Linn sequencer that should store about a hundred sequences in RAM. You mind?"

He laughed and waved his hand. She sat on a broken stool and clicked on the Yamaha. She ran through "Ain't Misbehavin'."

Lillick said, "This machine cannot deal with music like that. I think it's having a breakdown."

"What do you play?" she asked him.

"Postmodern, post–New Wave. What I do is integrate music and my show. I call myself a sound painter. Is that obnoxious?"

Taylor thought it was but just smiled and read through some of his lead sheets. In addition to standard musical notation they included drawings of pans and hammers, lightbulbs, bells, a pistol.

"When I started composing I was a serialist and then I moved to minimalism. Now I'm exploring nonmusical elements, like choreography and performance art. Some sound sculpture, too. I love what Philip Glass does only I'm less thematic. Laurie Anderson, that sort of thing. I believe there should be a lot of randomness in art. Don't you think?"

She shook her head, recalling what she'd told Reece that morning: How she believed music should stay close to melodies that resonated within people's hearts. She said, "You're talking to Ms. Mainstream, Sean," and shut off the system. She asked, "Got a beer?"

"Oh. Sure. Help yourself. I'll take one, too, while you're at it."

She popped them and handed him one. He asked, "You perform?"

"You wouldn't approve. Piano bars."

"They serve a valuable function."

Irritated by his too hip, and too righteous, attitude, Taylor asked, "Are you being condescending?"

"No. I mean it. I like classics too." Lillick was up, hobbling on one boot to his rows of records and CDs and tapes. "Charlie Parker. I got every Bird record ever made. Here, listen." He put on an LP, which sounded scratchy and authentic. "Man, that was the life," Lillick said. "You get up late, practice a bit, hang out, play sax till three, watch the sunrise with your buddies."

Taylor, lost in one of Bird's solos, mused, "Man died young."

"Thirty-five," Lillick said.

"World lost a lot of music."

"Maybe it wouldn't have been so, you know, deep, so righteous if he'd lived longer."

Taylor said, "Maybe just the opposite. Hooked on smack's gotta affect you."

He nodded at his record collection, which did contain a lot of mainstream jazz. "See, I'm not a snob. We need people like that. If you don't have rules and traditions there's nothing to break."

If it ain't broke, don't fix it, Taylor thought. But she wasn't here to debate the philosophy of music with him.

Lillick retrieved a fat joint and lit it up. He passed it toward Taylor. She shook her head and, examining the musical armada of equipment, asked, "What're you doing at a law firm, you're so into artsy-fartsy?"

"Steady salary, what else. The way I look at it, Hubbard, White & Willis is supporting the arts." He seemed uneasy, as if the conversation was going down paths he didn't want to tread.

He suddenly pulled out a pad of music staff paper and a pencil. "Keep talking. I work best when I'm only using half my mind."

She asked, "What I came to ask you about . . . You took over for Linda Davidoff on the Hanover & Stiver case, right?"

"Yeah."

"What do you know about her?"

Lillick looked at his cracked plaster walls for a moment and wrote a measure of music. She sensed he was performing for her—playing the distracted artist.

"Linda Davidoff?" she repeated.

After a moment he looked up. "Sorry . . . Linda? Well, we went out a few times. I thought she was more interesting than most of the prep princesses you see around the firm. She wanted to be a writer. It didn't go very far between us."

"Why'd she stop working on the Hanover case?"

Silent for a moment, Lillick thought back. "I'm not sure. I think she was sick."

"Sick? What was wrong with her?"

"I don't know. I remember she didn't look good. She was—"

"—pale," Taylor recalled.

"Yeah, exactly. I saw her filling out insurance forms a couple of times. I asked her about it but she didn't tell me anything."

"Do you know why she killed herself?" Taylor asked.

"No, but I'll tell you I wasn't wildly amazed she did. She was too sensitive, you know? She took things too much to heart. I don't what she was doing working for a law firm." Lillick erased and rewrote a line. He hummed it. "Give me a B-flat diminished."

Taylor turned on the DX-7 and hit the chord.

"Thanks." He wrote some more musical notations.

"Where'd she live?"

"I don't know—in the Village somewhere, I think. What's up? Why're you so interested in Linda?"

"Screwup with the New Amsterdam bill, going way back. They were majorly underbilled and I'm supposed to check out what happened. When you took over for her did she say anything about the case?"

Lillick shook his head.

Taylor asked, "You're still billing time on the case, aren't you?"

"Some. But Mitchell's handling most of it himself." Lillick didn't seem to have any reaction to her questions.

"Anybody she was close to?"

"Her roommate, Danny Stuart. He's an editor or something. Lives in the West Village. Over on Greenwich Street, I think." He rummaged in a stack of papers. "I've got the number somewhere." He handed it to her. "Hey, back in a flash."

He ducked into the john.

Which gave Taylor the chance she'd been waiting for. She dropped to her knees and found the backpack that Lillick had been stashing when she'd entered. It had seemed to her that he'd hidden it just a little too quickly when she walked inside.

A fast unzip revealed cash. A lot of it. Taylor had only ten seconds for a fast estimate but figured the total would probably be something on the order of thirty or forty thousand dollars. An amount equal to his yearly salary at the firm—which didn't, of course, pay in greenbacks.

And, a regular of the Downtown performing circuit herself, Taylor knew that, to quote her father, there was no way in Satan's backyard that anyone would ever make any kind of serious money playing music in bars.

Which meant that, no, Sean, the bank *didn't* own most of your equipment.

She'd come here only for information but had found another suspect.

Taylor shoved the bag back a few seconds before the young man returned. "Better roll," she said. "Thanks for the beer."

"You like goat?"

"What?"

"I'm thinking of going over to this place on Fourteenth. The goat's the best in the city. It's a totally happening place."

The thought of another night partying was more than she could handle. Besides, she had a mission back at the firm.

"Not tonight."

"Hey, this place is mondo cool. Bowie hangs out there. It's so packed you can hardly get in. And they play industrial out of one set of speakers and the Sex Pistols out of the other. I mean in the same room! Like, at a thousand decibels."

"Kills me to say no, Sean. But I'll take a pass."

Wendall Clayton liked the firm at night.

He liked the silence, the jeweled dots of boat lights in New York Harbor, liked taking a mouthful of cigar smoke and holding it against his palate, free from the critical glances his secretary and some of the more reckless younger lawyers shot his way when he lit up a Macanudo in the firm.

This after-hours atmosphere took him back to his days just after law school, when he'd spend many of his nights proofreading the hundreds of documents that make up typical business deals: loan agreements, guarantees, security agreements, cross-collateralization documents, certificates of government filings, corporate documents and board resolutions.

Proofreading . . . and carefully watching the partners he was working for.

Oh, he'd learned the law, yes, because in order to be good a lawyer must have a flawless command of the law. But to be a *great* lawyer—that requires much more. It requires mastering the arts of demeanor, tactics, leadership, extortion, anger and even flirtation.

Sabotage too.

He now looked over statements by a witness in a case that Hubbard, White was currently defending on behalf of one of Donald Burdick's prize clients, St. Agnes Hospital in Manhattan. Sean Lillick and Randy Simms, Clayton's head of the SS, had dug up the identity of a doctor who had firsthand knowledge of the hospital malpractice St. Agnes was allegedly guilty of.

Clayton had slipped the identity of this man to the plaintiff—in effect, scuttling the case against his firm's own client.

This troubled him some, of course, but as he read through the witness's statements and realized that the St. Agnes doctors had indeed committed terrible malpractice, he concluded that his sabotage was in fact loyalty to a higher authority than the client or the firm: loyalty to abstract justice herself.

He rolled these thoughts around in his complex mind for a few minutes and reached this conclusion: that he could live with St. Agnes Hospital's extremely expensive loss in the trial.

He hid these documents away and then opened another sealed envelope. Sean Lillick had dropped it off just before he'd left for the night. He read the memo the paralegal had written him.

Clayton's money was being well spent, he decided. Lillick had apparently aristocratized the right people. Or begged them or fucked them or whatever. In any case the information was as valuable as it was alarming.

Burdick was taking an extreme measure. The firm's lease for its present office space in Wall Street would be up next year. This expiration had been a plus for Clayton's merger because it meant that the firm could move to Perelli's Midtown office, which was much cheaper, without a difficult and expensive buyout of an existing lease.

The purpose of the secret talks Lillick had learned about between Burdick, Stanley and Harry Rothstein, the head of the partnership that owned the building, was to negotiate a new, extremely expensive long-term lease for the existing office space.

By entering the lease, the firm would take on a huge financial commitment that would cost millions to buy its way out of. This would make Hubbard, White a much less attractive target for a merger. The full partnership didn't need to approve the lease, only the executive committee, which Burdick's side controlled.

The lease agreement, Lillick had learned, wouldn't be signed until this weekend.

Son of a bitch, he raged. Well, he'd have to stop the deal somehow.

He put Lillick's memo away and began thinking about defensive measures. If Burdick learned what Clayton was up to, particularly with the St. Agnes case and the lease, he and his bitchy wife would strike back hard. Clayton began to worry about loose ends.

He picked up the phone and called Lillick.

The boy's cheerful voice drooped when he realized who the caller was.

"That information was . . . helpful."

This was one of Clayton's highest forms of compliments.
Helpful.

"Like . . . I mean, I'm glad."

"I'm a little concerned though, Sean. You *are* being careful, aren't you?"

The boy hesitated and Clayton wondered if there was
anything more to his uneasiness than a phone call from his
boss.

"Of course."

"I'm aware of people asking questions around the firm,
Sean. Anybody been asking you questions?"

"Uh, no."

"You are making sure you cover tracks? Being a good
Boy Scout or nature guide or something?"

"Yeah, I'm not stupid, Wendall."

"No, of course you're not. Just make sure everything's
covered up carefully, no way to trace what you and I've been
up to. You know legal defense fees can be *so* expensive.
They can eat up all one's savings in a flash."

The boy's silence told him that the threat had been received.

Clayton looked up into the doorway, where a young
woman stood at attention. "Better go, Sean. Be in early tomorrow. Snip any ends, okay?"

"Sure."

The partner hung up, his eyes on the woman. She was
one of the night stenographers from the word processing
department. Her name was Carmen and she was slim and
had a complexion like a week-old tan. She wore tight
blouses and dark skirts that would be too short for the day,
but on the evening shift the dress code was more relaxed.

"I got your call, Mr. Clayton. You need some dictation?"

Clayton looked at her legs then her breasts. "Yes, I do."

Carmen had a five-year-old son, fathered by a man who
was currently in prison. She lived with her mother in the
Bronx. She had a patch of stretch marks on her lower belly
and a tattoo of a rose on her left buttock.

"Why don't you close the door," he said. "We don't want the cleaning staff to disturb us."

She waited until he'd taken his wallet from his suit jacket pocket and opened it up before she swung the door shut and locked it.

CHAPTER TEN

It was nearly 8 P.M. but for some reason the closing of a corporate merger that had begun at 2 that afternoon ran into difficulties and was not yet completed—some delay in Japanese regulatory approvals.

The Hubbard, White & Willis lawyers and paralegals working on the case, clutching stacks of documents, scurried back and forth between the several conference rooms devoted to the closing like ants stealing bread crumbs from a picnic though with considerably more content faces than their insect counterparts—presumably because ants don't make a collective $4,000 per hour for carting around bits of soggy food. The clients, on the other hand—the *payers* of those legal fees—were nothing but frustrated.

Back from her trip to Lillick's apartment, Taylor Lockwood had learned many intimate details about the closing because she'd been dodging the lawyers and clients for the past hour. Like the clients in the delayed deal, Taylor had her own frustrations.

John Silbert Hemming had neglected to tell her that dactyloscopy powder didn't come off.

She'd just finished fingerprinting Reece's burglarized file cabinet and painstakingly transferring the sticky tape of the two dozen latents she'd found to cards. She thought back to what Hemming'd told her. Yes, he'd mentioned the different kinds of powders. He'd mentioned how to spread it around and how to brush, not blow, the excess away.

But he hadn't told her the stuff was like dry ink.

Once you—once *one*—dusted it onto the surface the damn stuff didn't wipe off. The smear just got bigger and bigger.

She wasn't concerned about the file cabinet that had contained the note. She was concerned about Mitchell Reece's coffee mug, emblazoned with "World's Greatest Lawyer," which she'd dusted to get samples of his prints to eliminate those from the ones she lifted off his cabinet.

Fingerprinting powder coated the mug like epoxy paint. She did her best to clean it then noticed she'd gotten some on her blouse. She pinched the midriff of the shirt and fluffed the poor garment to see if that would dislodge the powder. No effect. She tried to blow it away, and—as her tall private eye had warned—spit into the smear, which immediately ran the powder into the cloth. Permanently, she suspected.

Taylor sighed and pulled on her suit jacket to cover the smudge.

She hurried down to Ralph Dudley's office, where she lifted samples of his fingerprints, then on to Thom Sebastian's, where she did the same.

Finally, back in the paralegal pens, she took samples of Sean Lillick's prints from several objects in his cubicle. Then back in her own cubicle she put the fingerprint cards in an envelope and hid it under a stack of papers in the bottom drawer of her desk.

She found the phone number that Lillick had given her—Danny Stuart, Linda Davidoff's roommate—and called him. He wasn't in but she left a message asking if they could meet; there was something about Linda she wanted to ask him about.

She hung up and then happened to look down at her desktop and, with a twist in her gut, noticed the managing attorney's daily memo. In the square for Tuesday of next week were these words:

> New Amsterdam Bank & Trust v. Hanover & Stiver.
> Jury trial. Ten a.m. No continuance.

As she stared there was suddenly a huge explosion behind her.

Taylor spun around, inhaling a scream.

Her eyes met those of a young man in a white shirt. He was standing in the hall, staring back at her. He held a bottle of French champagne he'd just opened. "Hey, sorry," he said. Then smiled. "We just closed. We finally got Bank of Tokyo approval."

"I'm happy for you," she said and snagged her coat then started down the hallway as he turned his groggy attention to opening more bottles and setting them on a silver tray.

———

The drapery man watched her pull her overcoat on and step into the lobby, the door swinging shut behind her.

He patiently waited a half hour, just in case she'd forgotten anything, and when she didn't return he walked slowly down the corridor to Taylor Lockwood's cubicle, pushing the drapery cart in front of him, his hand near his ice-pick weapon.

Upstairs the firm was bustling like mid-morning—some big fucking business deal going on, dozens of lawyers and assistants ignoring him—but down here the place was dark and empty. He paused in the Lockwood woman's cubicle, checked the hallways again and dropped to his knees. In two minutes he'd fitted the transmitting microphone, like the one he planted in Mitchell Reece's phone, into hers.

The drapery man finished the job, tested the device, ran a sweep to make sure it wasn't detectable and walked to the entranceway of the paralegal cubicles.

Nearby was a conference room, in which he saw a half-dozen open bottles of champagne sitting on a silver tray. When he touched one with the back of his hand he found it was still cold. He glanced behind him, pulled on his gloves and lifted the first bottle to his mouth. He took a sip then ran his tongue around the lip of the bottle. He did the same with the others.

Then feeling the faint buzz from the dry wine—and a huge sense of satisfaction—he returned to the hallway and started pushing his cart toward the back door.

—

"Never take a job," Sean Lillick said pensively, holding the door open, "where you have to hold things in your teeth."

Carrie Mason, standing in the door of his shabby East Village walk-up, blinked. "Never what?" she asked, entering.

"That's a line from a piece I'm working on right now. I'm, like, a performance artist. This one's about careers. I call it 'W2 Blues.' Like your W2 form, the tax thing. It's spoken over music."

"Never take a job that..." Pained, she said, "I don't think I get it."

"There's nothing to get," he explained, a little irritated. "It's more of a social comment, you know, than a joke. It's about how we're defined in terms of what we do for a living. You know, like the first thing lawyers say when you meet them is what they do for a living. The point is we should be human beings first and then have a career."

She nodded. "So when you just said you were a performance artist, that was, like, being ironic?"

Now, *he* blinked. Then, even more irritated, he nodded. "Yeah, exactly. Ironic."

He examined her from the corner of his eye. The girl was hardly his type. Although on the whole Lillick preferred women to men (he'd had his share of both since he came to New York from Des Moines five years ago) the sort of women he wanted to fuck were willowy, quiet, beautiful and passed cold judgment on anyone they bothered to glance at.

Carrie Mason didn't come close to meeting his specifications. For one thing, she was fat. Well, okay, not fat, but round—round in a way that needed pleated skirts and billowy blouses to make her look good. For another, she was polite and laughed a lot, which was evidence that she would rarely pass moody judgments on anyone at all.

Lillick also suspected she blushed frequently and he couldn't see himself getting involved with anybody who blushed.

"You know," she said after a moment, "tailors hold pins and things in their teeth. Fashion designers too. And carpenters hold nails when they're building houses."

That was true. He hadn't thought of that. And her comment made him even angrier with her. "I meant more like, you know, maybe holding bits of tape or tools or something." Then he added quickly, "The point is, like, just to make people think about things."

"Well, it *does* make you think," she conceded.

Lillick took her coat. "You want a beer?"

She was studying the keyboards and computers. "Sure."

"Have a seat."

She ran her hand over the tie-dye bedspread and glanced at her fingers to make sure the coloring didn't come off.

Excuse me, your royal highness. . . .

She sat down. He opened a Pabst and handed it to her, thinking only after he did that he probably should have poured it into a glass. But to take it back and find a clean mug would now seem stupid.

"I was surprised when you called, Sean."

"Yeah?" Lillick punched on a Meredith Monk tape. "I've been meaning to. You know, you work with somebody and you think, I'm going to call her up, yadda, yadda, yadda, but you get caught up in things."

"That's sure true."

"Anyway, I was thinking of going over to this place for

goat. . . ." But he stopped speaking fast, thinking what the hell would his buddies from the East Village say if they saw him at Carlos' with a fat preppy princess?

But he didn't need to worry; Carrie wrinkled her nose at the food. "Goat?"

"Maybe," he said, "we'll find someplace else. Whatta you like?"

"Burgers and fries and salads. Usual stuff, you know. I usually hang out at the bars on Third Avenue. They're fun. You know, sing along."

"When Irish Eyes Are Smiling . . ." God in heaven save me.

"You want me to . . .," Carrie began.

"Huh?"

"Well, I was going to say: If you want me to iron your shirt I'm, like, way good at that sort of thing."

The garment was a tan shirt printed with tiny brown scenes of European landmarks. It was one of his favorites and the cloth was wrinkled as a prune.

He laughed. "You iron this poor thing, it'd curl up and die."

Carrie said, "I like ironing. It's therapeutic. Like washing dishes."

In his five years in Manhattan he'd never ironed a single piece of clothing. He *did* do the dishes. Occasionally.

Outside a man's scream cut through the night. Then another, followed by a long moan. Carrie looked up, alarmed.

Lillick laughed. "It's just a hooker. There's a guy turns tricks across the air shaft. He's a howler." He pointed to a machine. "That's a digital sampler. It's a computer that records a sound and lets you play it back through your synthesizer on any note you want."

Carrie looked at the device.

Lillick continued, "I recorded the screaming one night. It was totally the best!" He laughed. "I performed a piece from Bach's *Well-Tempered Clavier,* only instead of the harpsichord sound it's a gay hooker shouting, 'Deeper, deeper!'"

She laughed hard. Then looked out the window toward

the diminishing wails. "I don't get downtown as much as I'd like."

"Where do you live?"

"East Eighty-fourth."

"Ah."

"I know," she said, blushing, as he'd predicted. "It's not so cool. But I kinda ended up there and I've got a three-year lease."

"So, how's Mexican?" he asked. He glanced down at his shirt. It wasn't *that* fucking wrinkled. "There's a place around the corner. I call it the Hacienda del Hole. Kinda a dive but the food's good."

"Sure, whatever." Then she suggested, "Or we could just hang out here. Like, maybe order pizza, watch the tube." Carrie nodded at his dusty TV set. "I like *Cheers*," she said. "And *M*A*S*H*."

Lillick only watched TV to pick up on pop culture icons he could trash in his performance pieces. He had to admit, though, he liked *M*A*S*H*. Well, and *Lucy* reruns. And *Gilligan's Island* (though not a soul in the universe knew *that*).

"It's kinda broken. I mean, the reception's pretty shitty."

He walked over to his Yamaha keyboard and turned it on. The amps sent a moan of anticipation through the warm air. "I'll show you how the sampler works. I'll play something for you."

"Good, I'd like to hear it. Hey, got another beer?"

He went to the fridge. "Those were the last. How 'bout wine?"

"Sure."

He poured two large tumblers and handed one to her. They tapped glasses. She picked a piece of cork or lint or something out of hers and they both drank.

Then she slipped off her white plastic headband and lay back on the bed. She ran her hand over the middle part of the mattress. "What's this?"

"What?"

"This lump?"

"I don't know. A pillowcase, I think."

But Carrie was frowning. "No, it's, like, weird. You better check it out."

He stood up and sat on the bed next to her, rummaged under the covers to find the lump. It turned out to be not a pillowcase but a woman's red high-heel shoe.

"How'd that get there?" Carrie laughed, teasing.

"I used it in one of my pieces."

"Uh-huh," she said, not believing him.

It's true, goddamn it, he thought angrily. I'm not a fucking transvestite....

She looked into his eyes and, without even thinking about it, he leaned forward and kissed her. He tasted lipstick and the Binaca she'd sprayed into her mouth when he was busy pouring the wine.

Then she lifted the red shoe away, dropped it on the floor and directed his hand to her breasts.

This is weird....

Carrie reached up and turned off the skewed floor lamp. The only illumination in the room was from the display lights on the synthesizer.

Weird...

He began to kiss her hard, desperately, and she kissed him right back.

She pulled off her jeans and sweater. Lillick stared at the huge breasts defined by the netlike cloth of her bra, nipples dark circles.

He kissed her for a full minute.

Weird.

Lillick realized that he'd left the recorder on the sampler running; it would store every sound in the room for the next twenty minutes. He supposed he should shut it off but in fact he didn't really want to get up. Besides, he figured, you never knew when you could use some good sound effects.

CHAPTER ELEVEN

Taylor wasn't sure when the idea occurred to her—probably 4 or 5 A.M. as she lay in bed, listening to the sounds of the city. She was in a half-waking, half-dreaming state—in Wonderland or on the far side of the looking glass.

She'd been thinking about the evidence she'd gathered. A brief comparison of the prints on the safe with her suspects—Sebastian, Lillick and Dudley—wasn't conclusive but it was more likely than not that Sebastian had left several prints on the safe.

But was there any way to verify that he—or someone else—had been in the firm that Saturday night, other than through the time sheets and key card entry logs?

Sure, she realized, there was: The thief might've taken a cab or car service limo to the firm that late at night. And he might've just used his real name and employee number on the reimbursement or payment voucher.

And copiers too. If he'd been in the firm for some legitimate reason he might've used a copier—you had to use a special key, with your number on it, to activate the machine.

Or, she thought, excited about these leads, the thief might have logged onto one of the Lexis/Nexis computers.

Or used the phone.

Every service or function within the firm that can be charged to a client (plus a delightful 300 percent markup for overhead) is recorded in the firm computers.

She glanced at the clock: 7:40 A.M.

Brother.

Exhausted, she rolled out of bed. At least she didn't have a hangover—and she'd managed to change into boxers and a T-shirt last night, saving her skin from more stigmatas of Victoria's Secret.

Let's go, Alice. . . . This is getting curiouser and curiouser. . . .

At 9 A.M. exactly Taylor was standing in the accounting department at Hubbard, White & Willis.

"I'm doing a bill for Mitchell Reece," she told the computer operator. "Can you let me see the copier card, taxi and car service voucher ledger, phone records and Lexis/Nexis log-ons for last Saturday and Sunday?"

"It's not the end of the month." The operator snapped her gum.

"Mitchell wants to give the client an estimate."

Snap.

"An estimate of disbursements? It couldn't be more than a thousand bucks. Who'd care?"

"If you don't mind," Taylor said sweetly. "Please."

Snap. "I guess." The woman hunched over the keys and typed several lines. She frowned and typed again.

Taylor bent over the computer screen. The screen was blank.

Snap, snap . . .

"I don't know what's going on. There's no taxi vouchers. There *always* are on Saturday." Taylor knew this very well. The rule was if you had to work on Saturday the firm paid for your taxi to and from your apartment or house.

Alarmed, Taylor said, "How about the copiers?"

The fingernails tapped. The operator squinted, tapped some more and stared at the screen. "Well, this's damn funny."

"Nobody made any copies either."

"You got it."

Snap.

"Phones? Lexis/Nexis?"

The clattering of keys. "Nothing."

Taylor asked, "You think the files were erased?"

"Hold on a minute." Her fingers tapped as noisily as her popping gum.

Snap, snap . . .

The young woman looked up. "That's it. Erased. Must've had a software hiccup or something. The disbursement and incidental expense files for the past week've been deleted. Taxis, meals, copiers, even the phones. All gone."

"Has that ever happened before?"

"Nup. Never."

Snap.

████

Sean Lillick stopped by Carrie Mason's cubicle to say good morning to her.

He could tell immediately how pleased she was to see him comply with the famous morning-after rule.

They talked for a few minutes and then he said how much he wanted a cup of coffee and, as he'd expected, she was on her feet immediately and asking him, "How do you want it?"

"Black," he answered because even though he liked a lot of sugar it was cooler to say "Black."

"Sure. I'll be right back."

"You don't have to—," he started to say.

"No problem."

She trotted off down the hallway.

Which gave him the chance to put her computer room access card back into her purse.

That's what'd been so weird last night.

The fact that the sex had been initiated by *her.*

Because the whole point of calling her up was to get her over to his place, get her drunk, seduce her and when she was dozing afterward steal her access card, which would allow him to erase the telltale files of expenses—like the taxi he'd taken from the firm to the office of the plaintiff's lawyer in the St. Agnes case, or the phone calls he'd made about the new lease with Rothstein. After he'd talked to Wendall Clayton earlier Lillick had realized that he *had* been pretty careless and needed to, as the partner had said, "snip some ends."

Hence, the grand seduction last night.

Weird...

Carrie now returned with the coffee and when she handed it to him their hands met and they looked into each other's eyes for a moment. It took perhaps two seconds for the guilt to prod him into looking away and he said quickly, "Got a big project. Better run. I'll call you."

Donald Burdick believed that bringing one's first client into a law firm was the most significant milestone in the career of a Wall Street lawyer.

Unlike graduation from law school, unlike admission to the bar, unlike being made partner—all of which are significant but abstract stages in a lawyer's life—hooking a money-paying client was what distinguished, in his metaphor, the nobility from the gentry.

Many years ago Burdick—a young, newly made partner at Hubbard, White & Willis—had just finished the eighteenth hole at Meadowbrook Club on Long Island when one of the foursome turned to him and said, "Say, Donald, I hear good things about you. Legal-wise, I'm saying. You interested in doing a little work for a hospital?"

That had been on a Sunday afternoon and two days later Burdick had presented to the executive committee of the firm his first signed retainer agreement—with the huge St. Agnes Hospital complex in Manhattan.

At nine-thirty this morning Donald Burdick sat in his office with the chief executive officer of St. Agnes, a tall, middle-aged, mild-spoken veteran of hospital administration. Also present were Fred LaDue, the senior litigation partner handling the malpractice case against the hospital, and Mitchell Reece.

Three of these four appeared very unhappy, though for different reasons. Burdick, because of what he'd learned last night—that with the new witness St. Agnes would probably lose the malpractice trial, which would make the hospital throw its support to Clayton and the pro-merger crowd. The CEO, of course, because his hospital now stood to lose millions of dollars. Lawyer LaDue, because Burdick had summarily ordered that he stand down today and that a young associate Mitchell Reece, take over the cross-examination of the new witness.

Reece, on the other hand, was calm as a priest though it was clear the man hadn't had more than a few hours' sleep. He'd been preparing virtually nonstop since Burdick and LaDue had briefed him last night around 9 p.m.

"Who is this guy?" the CEO asked. "The witness?"

"That's the problem. He was working at St. Agnes when they brought the plaintiff in. He didn't treat the patient himself but he was in the room the whole time."

"One of our own people? Testifying against us?" The CEO was dumbfounded.

"Apparently he was a visiting professor from UC San Diego."

"Can't we object?"

"I did," LaDue said plaintively. "Judge overruled me. The best he did was give us a chance to depose the witness before he goes on."

Reece said, "I'll do that in a half hour. The guy goes on the stand at eleven."

"How bad do you think his testimony's going to be?" the administrator asked.

"From what the other side's lawyer said," Reece explained bluntly, "it could lose you the case."

Burdick, who realized he had been squeezing his teeth together with fierce pressure, said, "Well, Mitchell, perhaps it isn't as hopeless as you're painting it."

Reece shrugged. "I don't think it's hopeless. I never said it's hopeless. But the plaintiff's lawyers've upped their settlement offer to thirty million and they're holding firm. That means that this witness is the smoking gun."

LaDue sat and stewed. The doughy man was as pale as always though at this particular moment his waxen complexion was largely due to the fact that he'd done a very clumsy job at the trial so far.

Burdick played with a manicured thumbnail. He was furious that Clayton had probably spent thousands of dollars to track down this witness and had anonymously sent his name to the plaintiff's attorney.

"What do you have in mind, Mitchell?" LaDue asked. "How're you going to handle the cross?"

Reece looked up and started to answer but then Burdick's secretary walked into the doorway. "Mr. Reece, your secretary said you've just got an important call. You can take it in the conference room there."

"Thank you," he said to her. Then glanced at his watch. "I'll be busy for the rest of the morning, gentlemen. I'll see you in court."

CHAPTER TWELVE

If she hadn't been initiated, Taylor Lockwood would never have known she was watching a trial.

She saw a bored judge rocking back in his chair, distracted lawyers. She saw clerks walking around casually, no one really concentrating on what was going on. She saw dazed jurors and few spectators—a half dozen or so, retirees, she guessed, like the unshaven men who take trains out to Belmont or Aqueduct racetracks in the morning, just for a place to spend their slow days.

She'd found Reece in the hall at the firm earlier and wanted to update him on what she'd learned—the fingerprints and the erased files. But he was jogging from the library to his office, two huge Redweld folders under his arms. He paused briefly to tell her that he'd been called in to handle an emergency cross-examination and that he could see her at the courthouse on Centre Street later, around noon.

Taylor had decided to sit in on this portion of the trial and catch him in the hall afterward. Maybe they could have lunch.

She now looked around the courtroom in which *Marlow v. St. Agnes Hospital and Health Care Center* was being tried and located the plaintiff. Mr. Marlow sat in a wheelchair, pale and unmoving. Unshaven, his hair disheveled. His wife was nearby, with her hand resting on his arm. Taylor's father, a trial lawyer himself, had instilled enough cynicism in his daughter to make her believe that, while undoubtedly the man had suffered a serious injury, the wheelchair might just be a prop and there was no need for him to be looking as destroyed as he did here.

The door opened, and in walked a man she recognized from the firm. It took her a moment to place the name. Randy Simms—either the III or the IV. She recalled that he was a protégé of Wendall Clayton. He sat in the back row, by himself, putting away a cellular phone. He put his hands in his lap and sat perfectly still, perfectly upright.

She scanned the rest of the visitors and was surprised to find Donald Burdick himself in the gallery. He too glanced at Randy Simms, a faint frown on the old partner's face.

Finally, papers were sorted out and the judge pulled off his glasses. In a gruff voice he told the plaintiff's counsel that he could present his witness.

The lawyer rose and called to the stand a handsome, gray-haired man in his mid-fifties. He gazed pleasantly out at the jury. Under questioning from the plaintiff's counsel, he began his testimony.

Taylor Lockwood worked primarily for corporate lawyers at Hubbard, White & Willis but she knew the basics of personal injury law. This man's testimony was clearly devastating to St. Agnes.

Dr. William Morse's credentials were impeccable and, unlike many expert witnesses, who testify based only on what they've read in reports long after the accident, he was actually present at the hospital when the alleged malpractice occurred. The jury members took in his comments and looked at each other with lifted eyebrows, obviously impressed with the man's demeanor and by what he was saying.

"Let's reiterate what happened here," the plaintiff's lawyer

said. "In March of last year a doctor at St. Agnes treated a patient—Mr. Marlow there in the wheelchair, the plaintiff in
this case—who was suffering from arthritis and adrenal insufficiency with seventy milligrams of cortisone acetate in
conjunction with one hundred milligrams of indomethacin."

"That's correct," Morse said.

"Did you observe him do this?"

"I saw the injection and then looked at the chart afterward and told him immediately the mistake he'd make."

"And why was that a mistake?"

"Mr. Marlow had a preexisting ulcerous condition.
Everyone knows that such a patient should absolutely not
be treated with the drugs he was administered."

"I'd object, sir," Reece said politely. "The witness can't
speak for, quote, everyone."

Dr. Morse corrected, "The medical literature is quite
clear that such a patient should not be treated with those
particular drugs."

The plaintiff's lawyer continued, "What was this doctor's
reaction when you told him that?"

"He said that I was not on the staff, I was a visiting
physician and, in effect, I should mind my own business."

"Objection," Reece called again. "Hearsay."

The plaintiff's lawyer said, "I'll rephrase. Sir, after you
called attention to what you perceived as a dangerous condition, did anyone take any steps to correct it?"

"No."

"What happened then?"

"I told a nurse to monitor the patient carefully and that I
thought he might have serious adverse reactions. Then I
went to see the chief of staff."

"That would be Harold Simpson?"

"Yessir."

"And what was his reaction?"

"Dr. Simpson was not available. I was told he was playing golf."

"Objection. Hearsay."

"He was not available," the witness corrected.

"What happened then?"

"I returned to Mr. Marlow's ward to see how he was doing but he was unconscious, comatose. The nurse I'd left to monitor his condition was gone. We stabilized his condition. But he remained comatose."

"Would it have been possible, when you called attention to the drugs that had been improperly prescribed, to administer an antidote—"

"Objection," Reece called. "He's suggesting that we poisoned the plaintiff."

"You *did*," Dr. Morse snapped.

"Your honor?" Reece asked.

"A more neutral term, counselor," the judge said to the plaintiff's lawyer.

"Yessir. Dr. Morse, would it have been possible to administer other drugs to counteract the damaging effects of the drugs that the St. Agnes staff doctor administered?"

"Absolutely. But it would have to be done immediately."

"And what happened then?"

"That was my last day at the hospital. I returned to California the next day and as soon as I arrived I called the hospital to check on the status of the patient. I was told that he'd come out of the coma but had suffered irreparable brain damage. I left messages for the chief of staff, the head of the procedures committee and the head of the department of internal medicine. No one ever called me back."

"No further questions."

A murmur from the peanut gallery at the deadly testimony. Taylor concurred with the apparent reaction. She thought, Okay, we just lost the case.

The judge rocked back in his chair and said, "Mr. Reece, cross-examination?"

Mitchell Reece stood and—in smooth motions—buttoned his jacket, straightened his paisley tie.

"Thank you, your honor. First of all"—he turned to the jury—"I'd like to introduce myself. I'm Mitch Reece. I work for Hubbard, White & Willis, along with my friend and colleague, Fred LaDue, who I think you know. And he's been gracious enough to let me visit with you for a few hours to-day." He smiled, creating a camaraderie with six men and women bored numb from days of medical testimony.

Hunkered down behind two octogenarian trial buffs, Taylor watched him pace back and forth slowly.

Reece said, "Now, sir, you know I'm getting paid for asking you questions."

The witness blinked. "I—"

Reece laughed. "It's not a question. I'm just telling you that I'm getting paid to be here, and I assume you're getting paid to testify. But I don't think it's fair to ask you how much *you're* getting, if I'm not prepared to tell you how much *I'm* getting. And I'm not. Lawyers're overpaid anyway." Laughter filled the room. "So we'll just let it go at the fact that we're both professionals. Are we all together on that?"

"Yessir."

"Good.

The plaintiff's lawyers grew wary at this. One of the first ways cross-examining lawyers attack experts is to make them sound like mercenaries.

"Now, Doctor," Reece said, "let me ask you, how often do you testify at medical malpractice cases like this one?"

"Rarely."

"How rare would that be?"

The witness lifted his hand. "I've probably testified three or four times in my life. Only when I feel a terrible injustice has been done and—"

Reece held up his hand and, still smiling, said, "Maybe if we could just stick to answering my questions, please."

"The jury will disregard the witness's last sentence," the judge mumbled.

"So it's safe to say that you spend most of your time *practicing* medicine. Not testifying against other doctors."

"That's right."

"That's so refreshing, Doctor. I mean that. It's clear you care about your patients."

"Helping patients is the most important thing in the world to me."

"I applaud that, sir. And I welcome your appearance here—I mean that. Because these are very tricky technical matters that my friends on the jury and I have to wrestle with, and cooperative witnesses like you can make the issues clearer."

The witness laughed. "I *have* had a bit of experience."

"Let's talk about that, sir. Now, you practice internal medicine, correct?"

"That's correct."

"You're board-certified in internal medicine?"

"I am."

"And you have occasion to administer various drugs?"

"Oh, yessir."

"Would you say you have great experience administering them?"

"I would say so, sure."

"Those ways of administering them would include sublingual—that's under the tongue, right?"

"That's right."

Reece continued, "And rectally as well as administering injected medicines, like the sort that the plaintiff received."

"That's true."

"I don't want you to think I'm up to anything here, sir. You've testified that my client did something wrong in administering certain medicines and all I want to do is make it clear that your observations about what my client did are valid because of your expertise. We're all together on that?"

"All together, yessir."

"Good."

Taylor could see that the jury had brightened up. Something was happening. Reece was being *nice* to the witness. Shouldn't they be screaming at each other? The jury was confused and because of that they'd started paying attention.

She noticed something else: Though she hadn't seen him change his appearance, Reece's jacket, at some point, had become unbuttoned and in lifting his hand to straighten his hair he'd mussed it. He looked boyish. She thought of him suddenly as a young Southern lawyer—a hero in a John Grisham book.

The witness too had relaxed. He was less stiff, less cautious.

Taylor, though, thought that Reece had gone too far with the good-old-boy approach. The witness was looking good in the eyes of the jury; the credibility of his testimony was improving. By now, she reflected, her father would've cut the balls off this doctor and had him cowering on the stand.

Reece said, "Now, let me quote from the record as best I can." He squinted and recited, "'In March of last year a doctor from St. Agnes treated a patient—Mr. Marlow there in the wheelchair, the plaintiff—who has arthritis and adrenal insufficiency with seventy milligrams of cortisone acetate in conjunction with one hundred milligrams of indomethacin.'"

"That's right."

"And you testified that you wouldn't have done that."

"Correct."

"Because of his preexisting ulcerous condition."

"Yes."

"But I've looked through his charts. There's no record of his having an ulcer."

The witness said, "I don't know what happened with the charts. But he told the doctors he had an ulcer. I was there. I heard the exchange."

"He was in the emergency room," Reece said. "Generally a busy place, a lot of doctors trying to cope with all kinds of problems. I've been in them myself—cut my thumb bad last year. . . ." Reece winced and smiled at the jury. "I'm a real klutz," he told them. Then back to the doctor: "So will you agree that it's *possible* that the person Mr. Marlow told about his ulcer wasn't the person who administered the drugs?"

"That doesn't—"

Reece smiled. "Please, sir."

"It's possible. But—"

"Please. Just the question."

Taylor saw that Reece was preventing the witness from reminding the jury that it didn't matter who knew before the injection because Dr. Morse had brought it to the staff's attention just *after* the injection, when there was still time to correct it, but the staff had ignored him.

"It's possible."

Reece let this sit for a moment. "Now, Dr. Morse, there's been a lot of talk in this trial about what is and is not an accepted level of medical treatment, right?"

Morse paused before answering, as if trying to figure out where Reece was going. He looked at his own lawyer then answered, "Some, I suppose."

"I'm thinking that if, as you say, you wouldn't've treated the patient with these medications then I assume you feel that St. Agnes's treatment was below the standards of proper medical care?"

"Certainly."

Reece walked to a whiteboard in the corner of the courtroom, near the jury, and drew a thick line horizontally across it. "Doctor, let's say this is the standard-of-care line, all right?"

"Sure."

Reece drew a thin dotted line an inch below it. "Would you say that the level of care St. Agnes provided in administering those drugs was this far below the standard level of care? Just a little bit below?"

Morse looked at his lawyer and was greeted with a shrug.

"No. It wasn't just a little bit below. They almost killed the man."

"Well." Reece drew another line, farther down. "This far?"

"I don't know."

Another line. "This far below?"

Dr. Morse said in a solemn voice, "It was very far below."

Reece drew another two lines then stopped writing. He asked, "Once you get below a certain level of the standard of care . . . well, how'd you describe that?"

Another uncertain look at his lawyer then the witness answered, "I'd say . . . I'd guess I'd say it was malpractice."

"You'd characterize St. Agnes's treatment of Mr. Marlow," Reece said in a sympathetic voice, "as malpractice."

"Well, yes, I would."

A murmur of surprise from several people in the court-room. Not only was Reece befriending the witness but his cross-examination was having the effect of making the wit-ness repeat over and over again that the hospital had made a mistake. He had even gotten the witness to characterize the staff's behavior as malpractice—a legal conclusion that no defense lawyer in the world would have accepted from a plaintiff's witness. Yet it had been Reece himself who elicited this opinion.

What was going on here? Taylor glanced at Burdick and saw him sitting forward, clearly troubled.

A dozen rows behind him Clayton's representative, Randy Simms, sat immobile though with a slight smile on his face.

The judge looked at Reece, opposing counsel looked at Reece.

"I appreciate your candor, Doctor. Malpractice, mal-practice." Reece walked back to the table slowly, letting the word sink into the jury's consciousness. He stopped and then added brightly, "Oh, Doctor, if you don't mind, I just have a few matters of clarification."

"Not at all."

Reece said, "Doctor, where are you licensed to practice?"

"As I said before, California, New Jersey and New York."

"No other state?"

"No."

Reece turned to look into Morse's eyes. "How about any other *country*?"

"Country?"

"Yessir," Reece said. "I'm just curious if you've ever been licensed to practice in any other country."

A hesitation. Then a smile. "No."

"Have you ever *practiced* medicine in another country?"

"I just said I wasn't licensed."

"I caught that, sir. But what I just asked was 'practiced,' Doctor, not licensed. Have you ever *practiced* medicine anywhere outside of the United States?"

The man swallowed, a look of horror in his eyes. "I've done some volunteer work...."

"Outside of the country."

"Yes, that's right."

"And would you be so kind as to tell us which country, if that isn't too much trouble, Doctor?"

"Mexico."

"Mexico," Reece repeated. "What were you doing in Mexico?"

"I was getting a divorce. I liked the country and I decided to stay for a while—"

"This was when?"

"Eight years ago."

"And you practiced medicine in Mexico?"

Morse was looking at his fingertips. "Yes, for a while. Before I moved back to California. I set up a practice in Los Angeles. I found Los Angeles to be—"

Reece waved his hand. "I'm much more interested in Mexico than Los Angeles, Doctor. Now, why did you leave Mexico?"

Dr. Morse took a sip of water, his hands trembling. The plaintiff's lawyers looked at each other. Even the poor plaintiff seemed to have sat up higher in his wheelchair and was frowning.

"The divorce was final.... I wanted to move back to the States."

"Is that the only reason?"

The witness lost his composure for a moment as a time-lapse bloom of anger spread on his face. Finally he controlled it. "Yes."

Reece said, "Did you run into some kind of trouble down in Mexico?"

"Trouble, like the food?" He tried to laugh. It didn't work and he cleared his throat again and swallowed.

"Doctor, what is Ketaject?"

Pause. Morse rubbed his eyes. He muttered something.

"Louder, please," Reece asked, his own voice calm and utterly in control of himself, the witness, the universe.

The doctor repeated: "It's the brand name of a drug whose generic name I don't recall."

"Could it be the brand name for ketamine hydrochloride?"

The witness whispered, "Yes."

"And what does that do?"

Morse breathed deeply several times. "It is a general anesthetic." His eyes were joined to Reece's by a current full of fear and hate.

"And what is a general anesthetic, Doctor?"

"You know. Everybody knows."

"Tell us anyway, please."

"It's a solution or gas that renders a patient unconscious."

"Doctor, when you were in Mexico, did you have a patient, a Miss Adelita Corrones, a seventeen-year-old resident of Nogales?"

Hands gripped together. Silence. He wanted water but was afraid to reach for the glass.

"Doctor, shall I repeat the question?"

"I don't recall."

"Well, I'm sure she recalls you. Why don't you think back to the St. Teresa Clinic in Nogales. Think back seven years ago. And try to recall if you had such a patient. Did you?"

"It was all a setup! They set me up! The locals—the police and the judge—blackmailed me! I was innocent!"

"Doctor," Reece continued, "please just respond to my questions." His tie was loose, his face was ruddy with excitement, and even from the back of the courtroom Taylor could see his eyes shining with lust.

"On September seventeenth of that year, pursuant to a procedure for the removal of a nevus—that is, a birthmark—from Miss Corrones's leg, did you administer

Ketaject to her and then, when you perceived her to be unconscious, partially undress her, fondle her breasts and genitals and masturbate until you reached a climax?"

"Objection!" Marlow's lead lawyer was on his feet.

The judge said, "Overruled."

"No! It's a lie," the witness cried.

Reece returned to the counsel table and picked up a document. "Your honor, I move to introduce Defense Exhibit Double G: a certified copy of a complaint from the federal prosecutor's office in Nogales, Mexico."

He handed it to the judge and a copy to the plaintiff's counsel, who read it, grimaced and said in disgust, "Let it in."

"So admitted," the judge intoned and looked back to the witness.

Dr. Morse's head was in his hands. "They set the whole thing up. They blackmailed me. I paid the fine and they said they'd seal the record."

"Well, I guess it's been unsealed," Reece responded. "Now, the report goes on to say that the reason Miss Corrones was aware you were molesting her was that you not only administered the wrong dosage of Ketaject but that you injected it improperly so that most of the drug didn't even reach her bloodstream. Is this what the prosecutor's report says?"

"I—"

"True or not true? Answer the question."

"They set me—"

"Is this what the report says?"

Sobbing, the man said, "Yes, but—"

"Wouldn't you say, sir, that you can hardly state my client is guilty of malpractice because of the improper administration of drugs when you can't even knock out a teenager enough to rape her?"

"Objection."

"Withdrawn."

"They set me up," the witness said. "Just to blackmail me. They—"

Reece turned on him. "Well, then, Doctor, did you at

any time contact the law enforcement authorities in Mexico City or in the United States to report that you were being blackmailed?"

"No," he raged. "I paid them the extortion money and they said I could leave the country and they'd seal the record. I—"

"You mean," Reece said, "you paid the *fine* for your *punishment*. Like any other criminal. No further questions."

Taylor found herself sitting forward on the edge of the pew. She now saw Reece's brilliant tactic. First, he'd gotten the jury's attention. Expecting petty bickering, they'd seen Reece befriend the witness, surprising them and getting them to sit up and listen. Then he got the man to say the magic word that, by rights, Reece or LaDue or anyone on the St. Agnes legal team would try never even to allow into testimony, let alone elicit themselves: "malpractice."

And then, in a masterful stroke, he'd linked that characterization—that one magic word—to the witness's terrible behavior and completely destroyed his credibility.

Taylor saw a gleam in Reece's face, a flushing of the cheeks, fists balled up in excitement.

Reece turned. He noticed Donald Burdick in the back of the courtroom. The two men looked at each other. Neither smiled, but Burdick touched his forehead in a salute of respect.

Taylor turned and looked at Burdick then behind him. Finally Randy Simms showed some emotion. His lips were tight and his eyes bored into the back of Donald Burdick's head. He rose and stepped out of the courtroom, which was utterly silent.

Except for the sobbing of the witness.

CHAPTER THIRTEEN

███████ She stopped him in the hallway of the court.

Reece smiled when he saw her.

"How'd I do?"

"How do you think? I'd say you mopped up the floor with him."

"We'll see." Reece continued, "What most lawyers don't realize is that cross-examination isn't about being an orator. It's about having information. I called a private eye I've used out in San Diego and he dug up the dirt on the guy. Cost me—well, cost St. Agnes—fifty thousand. But it saved them a lot more than that."

"You enjoyed it, didn't you?"

"Handling the cross? Yep." He hesitated a moment, and finally spoke, though whether it was what he'd originally intended to say or not she couldn't tell. "I sometimes feel bad for them—people like that witness—when I tear apart their testimony. But in this case it was easy. He was a rapist."

"You believe he did it? What happened in Mexico?"

He considered. "I *chose* to believe he did something

wrong. It's a mind-set thing. Hard to explain but, yes, I believe it."

Taylor reflected: You could certainly argue that their client, the hospital, had done something wrong too—destroying the plaintiff's life; and she wasn't sure if the rape, if it had actually occurred, undermined the legitimacy of Morse's opinion about that.

She said nothing about any of this though and, indeed, she secretly envied Reece his fervent view of right and wrong. For her, justice wasn't quite as clear as that. It was a moving target, like the birds she'd watch her father hunt every fall. Some he hit and some he missed and there was no grand design as to which.

"Listen," she said. "I've got some leads. Have time for lunch?"

"Can't. I'm meeting one of the vice presidents from New Amsterdam. I've got to be at the Downtown Athletic Club fifteen minutes ago."

He looked around. "Let's talk later. But tell you what: Come over to my place for dinner."

"I'm playing Mata Hari tonight. What's tomorrow? Friday—how's that?"

"Make it Saturday. I'm meeting with the bank people all day tomorrow and I'm sure it'll go into dinner." He fell silent as someone walked by, a sandy-haired man in coveralls, who glanced at them quickly and then continued on. Reece's eyes followed the man uneasily as he walked away.

"Paranoid," he muttered with a smile, gave her hand a fast squeeze and then left the courthouse.

On her way back to the firm Taylor's willpower faded, her lust for a fast-food burger won and she decided she'd get something to eat.

This was how she found out that Mitchell Reece had lied to her.

Instead of going back to the office she'd headed north, to a Burger King, and as she turned the corner she saw Reece ahead of her. But he was walking *away* from the

Downtown Athletic Club, where he'd said he was going for lunch. She slowed, stung at first, then thinking, No, he probably meant another athletic club: the *New York* Athletic Club on Central Park South in Midtown.

Only, if that was so, why was he disappearing into the Lexington Avenue subway stop? The train went uptown but there were no stops anywhere near the NYAC. And why was he taking a train in the first place? The rule on Wall Street was that if you went anywhere on firm business, you always took the car service or a cab.

Taylor had had four or five serious relationships in her life and one thing about men that irked her was that their fondness for the truth fell far short of other appreciations. Honesty was her new standard for love and she didn't think that it was too much to ask.

Reece, of course, was nothing more than her employer—but still the lie hurt; she was surprised at how much.

Well, maybe his plans had changed—maybe he'd checked his messages, found the witness had canceled and was on his way to Tripler's to pick up a couple of new shirts.

But on impulse she found herself pulling a token out of her purse and hurrying down the subway stairs.

Why? she wondered.

Because she was Alice. That was the only answer. And once you slip into the rabbit hole, Taylor Lockwood had learned, you go where fate directs you.

Which happened to be Grand Central Terminal.

Taylor followed the lawyer, climbing up the stairs, skirting a small colony of homeless. She watched Reece buy a train ticket and walk toward the gates. She stopped.

Squinting though the misty afternoon light that spilled across the huge cavern of the terminal, she caught a glimpse of him standing at a vending cart in front of a gate. A crowd of passengers walked between them, obscuring him.

She jockeyed aside to get a better view. Then she laughed to herself when she saw what he'd bought.

One mystery of Mitchell Reece had been solved.

He was walking to one of the commuter trains carrying a large bouquet of flowers.

He had a girlfriend after all.

Digging another token from her purse, she descended once more into the piquant subway to return to the firm.

■

Sometimes he felt like a juggler.

Thom Sebastian was thinking of an off-Broadway magic show he'd seen some years ago.

Sebastian remembered the juggler most clearly. He hadn't used balls or Indian clubs but a hatchet, a lit blow-torch, a crystal vase, a full bottle of wine and a wineglass.

From time to time, Sebastian thought of that show, of the tension that wound your guts up as the man would add a new object and send it sailing up in an arc, a smile on his face, eyes at the apogee. Everyone waited for the metal to cut, the torch to burn, the glass to shatter. But nope, the man's no-sweat smile silently said to the audience: So far, so good.

Sebastian, sitting in his office this afternoon, feeling de-pleted, coked out, 'phetamined out, now told himself the same thing.

So far, so good.

When he had learned that Hubbard, White & Willis had chosen not to make him a partner Thom Sebastian had held a conference with himself and decided after consider-able negotiation to cut back on his working hours; he was going to relax.

But that didn't work. Clients still called. They were of-ten greedy, they were occasionally bastards, but a lot of times they were neither. And whether they were or not was irrelevant. They were still clients and they were scared and troubled and needed help that only a smart, hardworking lawyer could give them.

Sebastian found to his surprise that he was physically incapable of slowing down. He continued at a frantic pace, his hours completely absorbed by two refinancings, a leveraged buyout, a revolving credit agreement.

By his own real estate transactions, by his special project with Bosk, by his girlfriends, by arranging buys with his drug dealer, Magaly, by his family, by his pro bono clients, all in motion, all spinning, all just barely under control.

So far . . .

He desperately wanted sleep and that thought momentarily brought to mind another: The brown glass vial hidden in his briefcase. But it was no more than that—a passing image. Sebastian did not even consider slipping into the men's room to partake. He never did drugs within the walls of Hubbard, White & Willis. That would be a sin.

. . . so good.

He closed the door to his office then pulled a manila envelope out of his desk. He removed the computer printouts and began to read—all about Ms. Taylor Lockwood.

He found the information fascinating. He jotted a few notes and hid them under the blotter on the desk then fed the printouts themselves and the envelope through the shredder in his office.

Sweeping the phone from the cradle, Sebastian dialed her number from memory.

"Hello?"

"Hey, Taylor . . ."

He heard tension and anxiety in his own voice. This was bad. Take charge.

"Thom?"

"Yeah. How you doing?"

"Fine, but guilty. I'm finishing a Whopper."

With any other woman he'd have jumped on that line with both feet and flirted relentlessly. But he resisted and said casually, "Hey, you survived an evening with me. Not a lot of girls can make that claim. Oops, women. Meant to say 'women.' Have I offended you yet?"

"You're not even on the radar screen."

"I'll try harder." In fact he wasn't really in the mood to joke but he forced himself to maintain a certain level of patented Sebastian banter. "You realize that we're leaving for the airport in a half hour."

"And the 'we' would be who?"

"You and me."

"Ah. Our elopement. Your friend Bosk was first in line. You can be best lawyer."

Damn, she was fast. He'd run out of jokes. "Listen, speaking of your betrothed, I'm going out to dinner in the Hamptons tomorrow with him and a few other folks."

"I remember you mentioning that."

She had? That was interesting. Why'd she been paying attention to their offhand comments? "Hey, it's totally last-minute, I know, but any chance you'd like to come? It'll give me the chance to kill him so that I can move to the number one spot."

"Chivalrous."

He added gravely, "I have to warn you..."

"Yes?"

"It's not a stretch limo."

"That's not a deal-breaker. What's the occasion?"

"It's Take Someone to Dinner in the Hamptons Day. You *do* know about that, don't you?"

"I saw the card rack at Hallmark. I thought I'd have to celebrate by myself with popcorn and the tube."

"How 'bout it? Leave early, five-ish. We'll be back by midnight, one."

"Fair enough. Dress?"

"Business."

"Cool," she said. "I'll come by your office."

Sebastian set down the receiver and closed his eyes. He breathed deeply. He relaxed.

The motion of his imaginary juggler slowed. Unnecessary thoughts fell away. Projects that weren't immediate dissolved. The image of the Chinese-American girl he'd picked up last night and would be meeting at The Space tonight vanished. Some technical financial aspects of his project with Bosk rose then faded, as did a nasty, dark portrait of Wendall Clayton. Finally Sebastian was left with two thoughts, tossing them around slowly. One was the loan agreement he was working on, spread out on his desk before him.

The other was Taylor Lockwood.

He pulled the agreement toward him and looked at the words with a grave intensity. But ten minutes passed before he started to read them.

For Donald Burdick there was no square in New York City more beautiful than that at Lincoln Center.

The buoyant fountain, the soaring white rock architecture, the energetic Chagall . . . these all came together as a testament to the power of culture and moved him now, as they always did. It was especially stunning on fall nights like this, when the concert halls radiated their rich glow into the misty dimness of the city.

Burdick, his hands in his cashmere coat pockets, paced slowly in front of the fountain. It was chilly but waiting inside the Metropolitan Opera, where he and his wife had tickets for Stravinsky later that night, would undoubtedly require him to speak to any number of other box holders, who like him were major patrons of the arts and arrived early for dinner in the private dining room.

At the moment he didn't want to be distracted.

He glanced up and saw the Silver Cloud ease to the curb and Sergei leap out to open Vera's door. She stepped onto the pavement in her sable coat. He remembered how a few years ago, as Vera had waited for a light to change on Madison Avenue, an animal rights activist had sprayed her mink with orange paint. His wife had grabbed the young woman's arm and wrestled her to the ground, pinned her there until the police arrived.

They hugged and she took his arm as they walked to the private entrance that led to the club reserved for the most generous patrons. Burdick had once calculated that, even adjusted for the charitable deduction, each glass of champagne here cost him roughly two hundred dollars.

They let another couple go ahead of them so they could
take an elevator alone.

"St. Agnes?" Vera asked abruptly.

"Mitchell won. Well, they dropped their settlement offer
to five million. We'll pay one. That's nothing. Everybody at
the hospital's ecstatic."

"Good," she said. "And the lease? Did you sign it up?"

"Not yet. It's on for Monday now. Rothstein...I *hate*
dealing with him. And we have to keep everything hush-
hush so Wendall doesn't find out."

"Monday," she said, troubled, then his wife glanced at
her reflection in the elevator's metal panel. She turned back
to her husband. "I made some calls today. Talked to Bill
O'Brien's wife."

This was an executive of McMillan Holdings, which was
Hubbard, White's biggest client. The company was Burdick's
client alone and he took home personally about three million a year from McMillan.

"Trouble?" Burdick asked quickly.

"Apparently not. Wendall hasn't approached them about
the merger."

"Good," Burdick said. "He doesn't even know the
board's meeting in Florida this week or if he does he hasn't
made any rumblings about going down there."

Burdick had assumed that Clayton wouldn't waste the
time trying to sway McMillan since it was so firmly in the
antimerger court.

"But the board's been talking among themselves. They're
wondering if the merger'd be good or bad for them."

"Bill's wife knows that?"

Vera nodded matter-of-factly. "She's sleeping with one of
the board members: Frank Augustine."

Burdick nodded. "I wondered who he was seeing."

Vera said, "I think you have to get down to Florida and
talk to them. As soon as possible. Hold their hands, rally
them against the merger. Warn them about Clayton."

"I'll go this weekend. It'll be a good excuse to miss

Clayton's party on Sunday. Last thing in the world I want to do is spend time in that pompous ass's house."

Vera smiled. "I'll go," she said cheerfully. "One of us should be there, I think. Just to keep him a little unsettled."

And, Burdick thought as the elevator door opened, you're just the woman to do it.

CHAPTER FOURTEEN

Ms. Lockwood:

We cannot thank you enough for the opportunity to review your demo tape.

Taylor hurried to her apartment from her building's mailroom, clutching three return envelopes from three record companies. She'd called Dudley and told him that she wanted to change before seeing him for dinner at his club in Midtown and that she'd meet him there.

As she walked down the hallway she fantasized about the contents of the envelopes.

It so captivated the initial screener that he sent it to our A&R department, where it made the rounds in record (forgive the pun) time. Your masterly reinterpretations of the old standards in juxtaposition with your own works (masterpieces in fusion) make the tape itself worthy of production, but we would propose a three-record project of primarily original material.

Enclosed you will find our standard recording contract, already executed by our senior vice president, and, as an advance, a check in the amount of fifty thousand dollars. A limousine will be calling for you. . . .

Not able to wait until she got inside, she ripped the envelopes open with her teeth, all of them at once. The torn-off tops lay curled like flat yellow worms on the worn carpet behind her as she read the form rejection letters which were a far cry from the one that her imagination had just composed.

The one that said the most about the music business, she decided, began with the salutation "Dear Submitter."

Shit.

Taylor stepped out of the elevator and tossed the letters into the sand-filled ashtray next to the call button.

Inside her apartment, she saw a blinking light on her answering machine, and pushed the replay button as she stripped off her coat and kicked her shoes in an arc toward the closet.

Her machine had a number of messages:

Ralph Dudley, giving her the address of his club again.

Sebastian, confirming dinner tomorrow.

Reece, confirming dinner on Saturday.

Danny Stuart, Linda Davidoff's roommate, apologizing for not getting back to her but suggesting they meet for lunch in the Village tomorrow.

Three dinners and a lunch. Damn, how *do* spies manage to stay trim?

One more message remained. She hit play.

"Hello, counselor. Got some news. I'll be in town in a week or so and I'm going to take my little legal eagle out to dinner. Call me and we'll make plans."

Taylor instantly looked around her room to see how straightened up it was—as if the phone contained a video camera beaming the images directly to her father's law office.

She sat down slowly on the arm of the couch, Samuel Lockwood's call reviving a question Mitchell Reece had asked yesterday.

So how'd you end up in New York?

Taylor recalled perfectly sitting in front of her father two years ago, the man of medium build, jowly and pale—by rights, he should have broadcast an anemic image, but he filled the living room of their house in Chevy Chase, Maryland, with his powerful image.

She tried to gaze back at him.

But couldn't, of course.

Finally, the sound of spring lawn mowing from outside was broken by his asking, "You can simply try it, Taylor."

"I have other priorities, Dad."

"'Priorities,'" the lawyer said quickly, pouncing. "See, that very word suggests that there are several directions you'd want to go in." A smile. "In the back of your mind you're already entertaining the possibility that you'd like to be a lawyer."

"I mean—"

What *had* she meant? She was too flustered to remember.

"My talent—"

"And you *are* talented, darling. I've always recognized that. Your grades...Honey, A's in every government, politics, philosophy course you've ever taken."

And in music composition, music theory, improvisation and performance.

"Music too," he added, with perfect timing, diffusing her anger. Then he laughed, "But there's no way in Satan's backyard that anyone would ever make any kind of serious money playing music in bars."

"I don't do it for the money, Dad. You know that."

"Look, you should pursue everything. Lord knows I do."

And he had. Law, business, golf, tennis, skydiving, sailing, teaching.

"It's just that it's easier to get your law degree now. Going back after you're older...it limits your opportunities."

Reduced to a child before him, Taylor could think of no logical retorts. Well, the best legal minds in the country had engaged in forensic battle with Samuel Lockwood and lost. She said weakly, "I just feel alive when I play music, Dad. That's all there is to it."

"And what a feeling that must be," he said. "But remember that we go through stages in life. What excites us now isn't necessarily what sustains us all forever. I pitched a dozen no-hitters in college. And I never felt higher than being on the pitcher's mound. What a thrill that was! But making that my life? A pro ball player? No, I had other things to do. And I found getting up in court gave me exactly the same thrill. Even better, in fact, because I was in harmony with my nature."

"Music isn't a sport to me, Dad." She believed she was whining and hated herself for it.

"Of course not. I know it's an important part of your life." He then tactically reminded, "I was at every single one of your recitals." A pause. "I'm only saying that it would be better to excel in a profession—doesn't have to be the law, not by any means."

Oh, right ...

"And work at the music part-time. That way if the ... you call them gigs, right? If they *don't* happen, well, you'd still have something. Or you could do both. Your music could come first and law could be second."

He seemed to have forgotten that he'd absolved her from the practice of law just a moment earlier.

Continuing, Samuel Lockwood said, "There's a whole different approach to practicing nowadays. There are part-time arrangements. A lot of women have other 'priorities'— families and so on. Firms are flexible."

"I'm supporting myself playing, Dad. Not a lot of people are." Not that the eighteen thousand a year she'd made in clubs and playing weddings and a few corporate shows last year could be considered supporting herself.

"And what a feather in your cap that is," he said. Then frowned. "I've got a thought. How about a compromise? What if you got a job as a paralegal at one of the firms in Washington, one of our affiliated firms. I'll get you in. You can try out law firm life, see if you like it. I'll put aside some funds for school."

She'd said no at first but Samuel Lockwood was relentless and she'd finally given in.

"But I'll get a job on my own, Dad. I'll support myself. If I like it I'll apply to law school. But I'll play music at nights. Nothing's going to interfere with that."

"Taylor . . ." He frowned.

"It's the best I can do. And not in D.C. I'll go to New York."

He took a breath and then nodded his concession to her victory over him. "You've got backbone, counselor."

And he gave her a smile that chilled her soul—because it unwittingly revealed that this "spontaneous" thought of his had been born some time ago and nurtured over many nights as he lay in his twin bed, three feet from his wife's, trying to figure out exactly how to manipulate her.

Taylor was furious with herself for letting her guard down. He'd never intended that she work in Washington, wouldn't have presumed to link her with him by getting her a job and would never have threatened her music directly—out of fear that he'd push her away completely.

In the end, even though she'd defiantly resisted him, it turned out that Taylor had played right into his hand.

"You understand I'm doing this because I love you and care for you," he said.

No, she thought, I understand you're doing this because the thought of being unable to control the slightest aspect of your life is abhorrent to you.

She'd said, "I know, Dad."

But, as it turned out, the paralegal life was not as bad as she'd anticipated. Smart, tireless, unintimidated by the culture of Wall Street money and Manhattan society, Taylor had made a reputation for herself at the firm, quickly becoming one of the most popular paralegals, always in demand. She found that she enjoyed the work and had considerable aptitude for it.

So when a cycle came around for applying to law schools and Samuel Lockwood asked her which schools she'd decided to apply to (not *if* she intended to apply), she said what the hell and plunged forward with a yes and basked in the sunlight of her father's approval.

Taylor, lost in this complex answer to Reece's simple question, now realized that she was still frozen in place, perched on a sofa arm, her hand floating above her answering machine.

Why exactly was her father coming here? Where could they eat? Would the place she picked please him? Would he want to come see her perform? They sure couldn't eat at Miracles or one of the other clubs she played at; he'd make a fuss about the menu. Want to know what kind of oil they cooked with, send food back if it wasn't prepared just right.

The electronic woman in the answering machine told her, *"To save this message, press two. To erase this message, press three."*

She hit two and walked into the bedroom to dress for her Mata Hari date.

This is a Midtown club? she thought.

Taylor had expected that it would be more, well, spiffy. More of a power, platinum-card corporate watering hole and less of a tawdry college lounge. Well, maybe old money was allowed a little shabbiness. In any case, Taylor Lockwood looked at the fiercely bright lighting, the dusty moose head sprouting from the wall, the threadbare school banners and uncarpeted floor, and asked herself again, This is a club?

But Ralph Dudley was excited about the Knickerbocker Businessmen's Club. He was at home here and buoyant at showing off his nest to a stranger.

"Come along now," the partner said. And he ushered her into the club's dining room. He walked to what must've been his regular table and, amusing her beyond words, actually held the chair out for her and bowed after she'd sat.

"Have the steak, Miss Lockwood. They have chicken, too, but order the steak. Rare, like mine." The old partner's excitement was infectious, his eyes gleaming as if he were back in the arms of his alma mater.

They ordered. Dudley took instantly to his task as mentor and launched into a series of stories about his law school. It seemed an endless tumble of hard work, harmless collegiate pranks, chorale singers, respectable young gentlemen in suits and ties and tearfully inspiring professors.

All forty years out of date, if it wasn't complete fiction.

She nodded, smiled till she felt jowls and said "Uh-huh" or "No kidding" or "How 'bout that" every so often. She got good mileage out of "That's very helpful, just what I was wondering."

The waiter brought the steaks, charred and fatty, and although she wasn't particularly hungry, she found hers tasted very good. Dudley made sure she was looked after. He was a natural host. They ate in silence for a few minutes as Taylor took in the young men at the tables around them—recent grads, she assumed. In white shirts and striped ties and suspenders, they were just beginning the journeys that, in four decades, would take them to the destinations at which Donald Burdick and Ralph Dudley and Bill Stanley had arrived.

She looked at her watch. "You said you had some plans tonight. I don't want to interfere with them. I hope you're not working late?"

He gave her a charming smile. "Just meeting some friends."

The mysterious W.S.

Taylor took a sip of the heavy wine he'd ordered. "I'd rather work late than on weekends."

"Weekends?" He shook his head. "Never."

"Really?" she asked casually. "I was in on Saturday night. I thought I saw you. Actually I think it was early Sunday morning."

He hesitated a moment but there was nothing evasive about his demeanor when he answered. "Not I. Maybe it was Donald Burdick. Yes, that was probably it. I'm told we look alike. No, I haven't worked on a weekend since, let's see, '79 or '80. That was a case involving the seizure of foreign assets. Iranian, I think. Yes, it was. Let me tell you about it. Fascinating case."

Which it may very well have been. But Taylor wasn't

paying any attention. She was trying to decide if he'd been lying or not.

Well, looking at his frayed cuffs and overwashed shirt, she observed a motive for stealing the note: money. Dudley was a charming old man but he wasn't a player in Wall Street law and probably never had been. His savings dwindling, his partnership share decreasing as he made less and less money for the firm, he would have been an easy target when somebody from Hanover approached and asked him to let a man inside the firm—an industrial spy, they'd probably said.

Dudley finished his story and glanced at his watch.

It was nine-thirty and he was meeting W.S. in a half hour, she recalled.

He signed the bill and they wandered out of the club into the cold, damp ozone of a New York evening on the shag end of November.

Taylor hoped the cool air would wake her but it had no effect. The narcotics of red wine and heavy food numbed her mind. She groggily followed the partner down the front steps, half-wishing she partook in Thom Sebastian's magic wake-up powder.

She thanked Dudley for his insights and for dinner and said that his school had slipped into the front-runner spot.

This seemed to genuinely please him.

He said, "You all right, Taylor?"

"Fine, just a little tired."

"Tired?" Dudley said, as if he had never heard of the word. "I'll walk you to the subway." He started down the sidewalk in long, enthusiastic but gentlemanly strides.

CHAPTER FIFTEEN

"Wait."

Sean Lillick's voice was sufficiently urgent that Wendall Clayton stopped, frozen in the back entrance of the Knickerbocker Club.

"What is it?" the partner asked.

"There, didn't you see them? It was Ralph Dudley and Taylor Lockwood. They were going out the front."

Clayton frowned. It was a constant source of irritation that a has-been like Dudley belonged to the same club that he did. He resumed his aristocratic stride. "So?"

"What are they doing here?" Lillick wondered uneasily.

"Fucking?" Clayton suggested. He glanced toward the stairway, which led to the club's private bedrooms.

"No, they came out of the dining room, it looked like."

"Maybe he bought her dinner and *now* he's going to fuck her. I wonder if he can still get it up."

"I don't want them to see us," Lillick said.

"Why not?"

"I just don't."

Clayton shrugged. He looked at his watch. "Randy's late. What's going on?"

Lillick said, "I've got to leave about midnight, Wendall. If it's okay." His suit didn't fit well and he looked like a college boy out to dinner with Dad.

"Midnight?"

"It's important."

"What's up?" Clayton smiled. "Do you have a date?" He dragged the last word out teasingly.

"Just seeing some friends."

"I don't think it's 'okay.' Not tonight."

Lillick said nothing for a moment. Then: "It's pretty important. I've really got to."

Clayton examined the young man. Like most denizens of the East Village, he seemed damp and unclean. "One of your performances?"

"Yeah."

"Yeah," the partner mocked.

"Yes," Lillick corrected himself instantly though in a tone that approached rebellious.

"We've got so much to do. . . ."

"I mentioned it a week ago."

"And what a busy week it's been, don't you agree?"

"It'll just be a few hours. I'll still be at the office at six if you want."

Clayton had let him dangle enough. He said, "This once, I suppose, it's all right." He had plans of his own tonight and didn't give a rat's rosy ass what Lillick did after they were finished here.

"Thanks—"

Clayton waved him off and gave a reserved smile to Randy Simms, who now walked through the revolving door of the club.

Ignoring Lillick, as he always did, Simms said, "I saw Ralph Dudley outside. With a woman."

Piqued again by the reference to the old partner, Clayton snapped, "Appreciate the weather report, Randy."

Simms was six feet three, thin and solid. Ralph Lauren might have designed a line of Connecticut sportswear around him. A mother and her teenage daughter entered the lobby. They eyed the young lawyer with similar degrees of desire.

"How'd they get the lowdown on our witness?" Clayton was referring to the evisceration of Dr. Morse on the witness stand in the St. Agnes Hospital case.

"Reece used some private eye in San Diego."

"Fuck, that was good," Clayton said with admiration. He didn't know Reece well but he'd make sure the associate was guaranteed a partnership slot next year or the year after.

"When's our guest arriving?" Clayton asked him.

"Any minute now."

"Give me the details."

"His name's Harry Rothstein. Senior partner in the general partnership that owns the firm's building. He's got full authority to go forward or pull the plug. He and Burdick are planning to sign the new lease on Monday. Rothstein doesn't seem to have any mistresses but I found some accounts in the Caymans. Son's got two drug convictions."

"What kind?"

"Cocaine."

"I mean what kind of *convictions*?"

"Felony. One sale, one possession."

"Is he a good friend of Burdick's?"

Simms's face eased into a faint smile.

"What's that supposed to mean?" Clayton snapped again.

"How can he be a friend of Donald's?" Simms asked. "Rothstein's a Jew."

A tall, bald man walked through the door and looked around.

"That's him," Simms said.

Clayton's face broke into a huge smile as he strode forward. "Mr. Rothstein. I'm Wendall Clayton," he called. "Come join us, my friend."

━━━━━

At the corner of Madison Avenue and Forty-fourth Street Taylor and Ralph Dudley paused and shook hands.

He inclined his head toward her in a Victorian way she found quaint and said, "Which train're you taking?"

"I'll walk."

"I'll cab it, I suppose. Good luck to you. Let me know how you fare with Yale." He turned and walked away.

Taylor had thought she'd have to do a private-eye number: *Hey, follow that cab; there's a fiver in it for you.* But no: Dudley didn't flag down a taxi at all. He was on foot, going to meet the mysterious W.S., whom he had visited the night the note was stolen.

When he was a half block away, Taylor followed. They moved west through the eerie illumination of a city at night—the glossy wetness of the streets and storefront windows lit for security. Still plenty of traffic, some theaters letting out now, people leaving restaurants en route to clubs and bars. Taylor felt infused with the luminous energy of New York; she found that she'd sped up to keep pace with it and had nearly overtaken Dudley. She slowed and let him regain a long lead.

Out of the brilliant, cold, fake daylight of Times Square. Only now did Taylor feel the first lump of fear as she crossed an invisible barrier, into pimp city. The public relations firms hired by New York developers called this area Clinton; almost everyone else knew it by its historical name—the more picturesque Hell's Kitchen.

Taylor continued her pursuit even when Dudley hit Twelfth Avenue, near the river, and turned south, where the streetlights grew sparser and the neighborhoods were deserted, abandoned even by the hookers.

Then Dudley stopped so suddenly, catching Taylor in mid-thought, that she had to jump into a doorway to avoid being seen.

The concrete reeked of sour urine. Hugging the shadows,

she felt nauseous. When she looked again Dudley was gone. Taylor waited for five minutes, breathing shallow gasps of cold air, listening to the sticky rush of traffic on the West Side Highway. Then she walked toward the spot where Dudley had disappeared: the doorway of a small two-story building. There were no lights radiating from the windows; she saw they were painted over. An old sign, faded, read, *West Side Art and Photography Club.*

W.S. on his calendar. So, a place, not a person.

He'd come here on Saturday night and then—possibly—gone to the firm around the time the note had disappeared.

But was there a connection?

Or was this just his hobby? Taking pictures or attending lectures on Ansel Adams and Picasso?

She cocked her head and listened. She thought she heard something. Wait, wait. Taylor tried to block out the rush of the cars and trucks and believed she heard music, something syrupy, full of strings, like Mantovani. Standing in the doorway, her feet stinging from the unaccustomed exercise in very unsensible Joan and David heels, she leaned against the stone and watched a cluster of intrepid rats browse through a garbage pile across the street.

He goes in, she figured, he's got to come out.

Forty minutes later he did.

The door swung wide. Taylor caught an image of pink and lavender. Soft music and softer light spilled out into the street. A radio cab—owned by the company that the firm used—pulled up. Dudley vanished immediately into the car, which sped away.

The question was, what would Mitchell do?

No, that wasn't the question at all. She *knew* what he would do. The question really was, did she have the guts to do the same thing?

The grapevine says you've got balls.

Yeah, well...Taylor walked to the front door and pressed the buzzer.

A handsome black man, large and trapezoidal, opened the door. "Yes?" he asked, poised and polite.

Taylor said, "Um, I'm here. . . ." Her voice clogged.

"Yes, you are."

"I'm here because a customer—"

"A member?"

"Right, a member referred me."

The bouncer looked past her and then opened the door. Taylor stepped inside.

It was like the lobby of an exclusive hotel. Smoky pastels, brushed copper, leather furniture, a teak bar. Three Japanese men, all in dark suits, sat on a plush couch, smoking furiously. They looked at Taylor briefly—hopefully—then, when she met their gaze with chill defiance, looked away fast.

A woman in her forties, wearing a conservative navy suit and white blouse, walked silently up to her. "How may I help you?" The smile of a maitre d'.

"I had a little time free tonight. I thought I'd check the place out."

"Well," the woman said, now playing tour director, "the West Side Art and Photography Club is one of the oldest art appreciation clubs in the city. Here's some literature." She handed Taylor a glossy brochure. There were programs of music, art shows, classes.

But how could she find out who Dudley met here?

Taylor nodded. "Ralph can't say enough good things about you."

"Ralph?"

"Ralph Dudley's a friend. I was going to meet him here earlier but—"

"Oh," the woman said quickly, "you just missed him. You should've said you knew him." She took back the brochure and tossed it in a drawer. "Sorry. I didn't know he'd referred you. ID, please."

"I—"

"Driver's license or passport."

What was Alice to do?

Play by the rules of topsy-turvy, what else?

She handed the license over and crossed her arms as the woman compared face and picture then went to a computer and typed in some information.

Apparently favorable results came back and the woman returned the license. "Can't be too careful, you know. Now, our membership fee is one thousand, and the hourly fee is five hundred per model. If you want a man, he'll have to wear a condom. Oral sex is completely up to the individual model; most do, some don't. Tipping is expected. The fee includes any standard toys but if you want something special it can probably be arranged. Will that be cash or charge?"

"Uh, American Express?"

"It'll show up as art instruction on your statement. One hour?"

"One hour, sure."

The woman took the card and asked, "Do you have any special requests?"

Taylor said, "Actually, I was thinking about something a little unusual. Could I have the, uh, model that Ralph Dudley sees?"

The hostess, trained to be unflappable, didn't look up from the charge voucher but hesitated for a millisecond. "You're sure?"

Thinking she'd never been less sure about anything in her life, Taylor Lockwood gave a slight smile and said, "Positive."

"There's a premium. Double."

"No problem." Smiling, Taylor took the credit card slip and a pen.

See the steadiness of my hand as I sign for the *two thousand Jesus Christ what am I doing dollars.* . . .

The hostess disappeared into the back room. Muzak played quietly, a guitar rendition of "Pearly Shells." She returned a moment later with a key. "I've talked to her. She hasn't been with too many women but she's game to try."

"Good."

"I think you'll find her quite nice. Up the stairs, last room on the right. Liquor's free. Coke we can give you at cost."

"That's okay." Taylor walked into the cool corridor.

Topsy-turvy. . .

She knocked on the door. A voice called, "Come on in."

Taylor took a deep breath, exhaled and pushed into the room. She stopped, total shock in her eyes—an expression that perfectly matched the one on the face of the girl who stood, topless, in the center of the room.

It was the teenage girl she'd met in Dudley's office, Junie. His granddaughter.

The garter belt in the girl's hand fell to the floor with a dull clink. She said, "Oh, shit. Like, it's you."

CHAPTER SIXTEEN

"You gotta, like, close the door," Junie said, regaining some composure. "It's a rule. Johnny, he's the bouncer, comes around and gets pissed, you don't."

Taylor stepped into the room, shut the door.

Junie said darkly, "Like, Ralph isn't going to be so happy this happened, you know."

Taylor whispered, "You're his granddaughter?"

"Like, helloooo. Whatta you think? Of course not. That's only what he tells people."

The girl was heavily made up, with dark streaks of brown and blue eye shadow that made her face sleek and serpentine. She retrieved the garter and began untangling it. "What it is, he's one of my oldest customers." Then she laughed. "I mean one of the dudes I've been seeing for the longest time. But, you know, he's one of the oldest, too. Probably, like, *the* oldest."

Taylor looked at a plush armchair. "Can I sit down?"

"It's your hour. Have a drink, you want."

Taylor poured sparkling wine into a crystal champagne glass. "You want any?"

"Me?" Junie looked horrified. "I can't drink. I'm under-age, you know."

Taylor blinked.

The girl laughed. "That's, like, a fucking joke. Of *course* I drink. Only they don't let us when we're working."

Taylor said, "You mind?" as she eased her shoes off. A swell of pain went through her feet then slowly vanished.

"Mind? Usually people take off a lot more than their shoes."

"So tell me about you and Ralph."

"I guess I oughta ask why."

"He could be in trouble. I need to find out whether he is or not."

The girl shrugged, meaning: That's not a good enough answer.

"I'll pay you."

This was a better response.

"I guess I oughta see the duckets."

"The what?"

The girl held her palm out.

Taylor opened her purse. She hadn't brought much of Reece's bribe money. She wadded together about two hundred dollars, keeping twenty for herself for cab fare home.

"I get that as a tip for a blow job," Junie said. "If the son of a bitch's cheap."

Taylor handed her more money. "That's all I have."

Junie shrugged and put the money in a dresser drawer. She pulled out a T-shirt and worked it over her head. "So, Poppie—that's what I call him—he likes girls my age. He came to the house last year and we had a date. It was like to-tally bizotic but we kind of hit it off, you know?" She whis-pered, "We started meeting outside the club. They get really pissed, they find out. But we did it anyway. He brought me some totally def clothes. Nice shit, you know. From the good stores. Anyway, we did some weird things, like, he took me to this art museum, which was a real bore. But then we went to the zoo. . . . Like, I've never been there before. It was way

wild. We just kept hanging out more and more. He's lonely.
His wife died and his daughter is a total bowhead."

"Junie . . . is that really your name?"

"June. I like June."

"June, last Saturday night, was Ralph here?"

"Yeah."

"When?"

"Around ten or eleven, I guess. We had our regular appointment, you know. I'm his on Saturday night. Sorta a tradition."

"Then what?"

She fell silent. Shrugged.

"Another two hundred."

The girl said, "I thought you don't have any more
money."

"I can give you a check."

"A check?" Junie laughed.

"I promise it won't bounce."

"That was, what, five hundred, you said?"

Taylor hesitated. "You have a good memory." She wrote
the check out and handed it to her. Mitchell, you're going to
see a very weird expense account for this project.

Junie slipped the check into her purse. "Okay, but he
didn't want me to tell anybody. . . . He went to your company."

"The law firm?"

"Yeah."

"What was he doing?"

"That's the thing: He wouldn't say. I'm, like, what're you
going there for this time of night? I mean, it's midnight or
whatever. He said he had to—something about a lot of
money. But he wouldn't tell me what. And he told me never
tell anybody."

At least anybody who didn't pay her seven hundred dollars.

Taylor asked, "Has he ever mentioned a company called
Hanover & Stiver?"

"Naw, but he don't talk—I mean, he *doesn't* talk about his business too much. He's always correcting what I say. It's so mundo-boring."

Taylor stood slowly, slipped her swollen feet back into her shoes. She walked painfully to the door. She paused.

"How old are you?"

"Eighteen. And I've got a driver's license."

"I've had fake ones too, honey."

"Okay, I'm sixteen. But I tell Ralph I'm fifteen. He likes it that I'm younger."

"Do you go to school or anything?"

A laugh. "Where're you from? I made sixty-eight thousand dollars last year and have a hundred Gs in a, you know, retirement fund. Why the fuck would I want to go to school?"

Why indeed?

Taylor let herself out into the hallway, through which echoed a cacophony of voices and sounds very different from those she was used to at Hubbard, White & Willis.

At lunchtime the next day, her feet only marginally recovered from their abuse the day before, Taylor Lockwood was sitting across from a diminutive young man in a West Village diner: Danny Stuart, Linda Davidoff's former roommate.

The menu of the place, which had been Stuart's choice, was heavy on foods that had swayed in the wind when alive, and light on main courses that had walked around on two or four legs, the latter being by far Taylor's favorite.

"So," she asked, "you know Sean Lillick too?"

"Not at all really. I met him through Linda and went to some of his shows. But he's a little avante-garde for me."

"You're an editor?"

"That's mostly a hobby. Some of us put together an alternative literary magazine. I'm a computer programmer by profession."

Taylor yawned and stretched. A joint popped. The walls of the place were badly painted, swirls of dark paint didn't cover the lighter enamel underneath. The decorations were à la *Mother Jones* and Woodstock. But the space, she knew, had been a Beat club in the fifties. William Burroughs and Allen Ginsberg had hung out here—the ancient floor felt spongy under the chairs and the wooden columns were carved with the initials of hundreds of former patrons. What these walls have heard, she thought.

Danny ordered sprouts and nuts and yogurt; Taylor, a garden burger. "Bacon?"

"No bacon," the waitress replied through her pierced lips.

"Ketchup," Taylor tried.

"We don't have ketchup."

"Mustard?"

"Sesame-soy paste or eggless mayo."

"Cheese?"

"Not your kind of cheese," the waitress responded.

"Plain'll be just fine."

The woman vanished.

Stuart said, "I think I remember you from Linda's funeral."

Taylor nodded. "I didn't know many people there, except the ones from the firm."

"You a lawyer?" he asked.

"Paralegal. How did you meet her?"

"Just a fluke. You know, your typical New York story. You come to New York from a small town, look for a place to live, you need a roommate 'cause the rents are so high. The guy I was rooming with got AIDS and moved back home. I needed to split the rent and Linda'd been staying at some residence hall for women. She hated it. We roomed together for, I guess, about nine or ten months. Until she died."

"Did you know her well?"

"Pretty well. I read some of her pieces and did some editing for her. She wrote reviews for us and I was hoping eventually to publish some of her poems."

"Was she good?"

"She was young; her work was unformed. But if she'd kept at it I know she would've gone someplace."

"What was her style like? Plath?" Taylor had read some of Sylvia Plath's poetry and recalled that she too had committed suicide.

Stuart said, "Her poetry was more traditionally structured than Plath's. But her personal life? Yep, just as turbulent. The wrong men, always heartbroken. Too stoic. She needed to scream and throw things more. But she kept it all inside."

The food came and Danny Stuart dug eagerly into his huge mass of rabbit food. Taylor started working on the sandwich, which she decided should be named not the garden but the cardboard burger.

"How did it happen, the suicide?" she asked.

"She was up at her parents' summer house in Connecticut. The back deck was above this big gorge. One night, she jumped. The fall didn't kill her but she hit her head and got knocked out. She drowned in a stream."

Taylor closed her eyes and shook her head. "Did she leave a note?"

He nodded. "Well, it wasn't really a note. It was one of her poems. When you called and said you were curious about her I thought you'd like to see it. I made you a copy. It's dated the day before she died. It talks about leaving life behind her, all the cares. . . . I was going to publish it in my magazine but, you know, I haven't had the heart."

He handed her the Xerox copy. Taylor read the title: "When I Leave."

She looked at Danny and said, "I hope I can ask you something in confidence. Something that won't go any further."

"Sure."

"Do you think Linda killed herself because of something that happened at work?"

"No."

"You sound pretty certain."

"I am. I know exactly why she killed herself."

"I thought no one knew."

"Well, I did. She was pregnant."

"Pregnant?"

"I don't think anybody knew except me. She got an EPT kit? It was just a couple of weeks before she died. I saw the kit in the bathroom and asked her about it. You know, we were like girlfriends. She confided in me."

"But why would she kill herself?"

"I think the father dumped her."

"Who was the father?"

"I don't know. She was seeing somebody but never talked about him or brought him around the apartment. She was real secretive about him."

"Breaking up . . . that upset her so much she killed herself?"

Stuart considered. She thought, studying his face: poet's eyes, artist's eyes. Unlike Sean Lillick, this was the real thing. He said, "There's more to it. See, Linda had no business working at that law firm. She was too sensitive. The business world was way too much for her. She got thrown too easily. Then when her personal life came crashing down I think it pushed her over the edge."

"But you don't know if there was anything specific at the firm that upset her? Anything she might've felt guilty about?"

"Nope. She never mentioned a word about that. And she probably would have. As I said, she and I were like, well, sisters."

So, the rabbit hole of Wall Street had proved too much for poor Linda Davidoff.

Without the heart to read the girl's suicide poem, Taylor put it in her purse and continued to eat her bland lunch while she and Danny talked about life in the Village.

Her face broke into another major yawn. She laughed and Stuart joined her.

"Not getting enough sleep lately?" he wondered.

"The problem," she explained, "is that I've been living an after-hours life when I'm not an after-hours person. I'm a during-hours person."

CHAPTER SEVENTEEN

Alice was on another trip through the looking glass.

This time, in a limo.

Taylor and Thom Sebastian were speeding down the Long Island Expressway Friday after work. The driver's eyes flicked to the radar detector needle as often as they glanced at the highway.

"I'm totally psyched you came," Sebastian said with apparent sincerity. "I thought you were going to boogie in with the Big E."

"E?"

"Excuse, you know. I—"

"Get that a lot?" she filled in.

"Yeah." He grimaced. "Now let me tell you about Bosk."

"What's the story behind the name?"

"His real handle's Brad Ottington Smith. B-O-S. Bosk. I'm Sea-bastian. Sea Bass. Get it? Okay. His father and mother have been separated practically since he was born. She has a house in Boston and his father has an apartment on the Upper East Side. They kept the summer place in the

Hamptons and have it on alternate weeks. They—that's the parents they—can't talk to each other without bloodshed so they have their lawyers schedule the visits to the house."

"And we're the mother's week."

"Right."

"Sounds like it's going to be a bucket of kicks and giggles. What is she, a wicked witch?" Taylor asked.

"All I'll say is she's more powerful than his father."

"What does *he* do?"

"Dad? What he does is he's rich. He's a senior partner at Ludlum Morgan, the investment bank."

"Bosk." She laughed. "I feel like I want to give him a Milk-Bone when I call him that. What firm does he work at?"

As he'd done the other night, though, he grew reluctant to give much away about Bosk professionally.

"Little shop in Midtown." Sebastian busied himself opening a Budweiser, handed it to her. Popped another.

"The mother?"

"Ada travels, entertains, does what any fifty-five-year-old sorority sister does: manages her portfolio. It's about a hundred million." Sebastian sipped the beer and let his hand stray—accidentally on purpose—to her knee. "Ho, boy, Taylor. This's gonna be primo. Good food, good drink, good people."

She lifted his pudgy fingers off her skirt. "And good behavior."

Sebastian moaned, then sat back in silence, and they gazed out the dim windows as dusk enveloped the flat, sandy landscape.

The Ottington Smith family manse was a three-story Gothic Victorian house, white with dark blue trim, about a hundred miles east of New York on the South Shore of Long Island. Two towers rose to widow's walks, which overlooked a huge yard and three connected outbuildings. The house itself was covered with skeletons of vines and wisteria. A spiked, wrought-iron fence surrounded a labyrinth of grounds. Much of the property had been reclaimed by tangles of forsythia, which sported sparse tags of brown and yellow leaves.

"Addams Family," Taylor said.

The circular driveway was full of cars. The limo paused and they got out. "God, more German cars than in Brazil," Sebastian said.

"Porches. I love porches," Taylor said. She sat on a wooden swing and rocked back and forth. "Wish it were thirty degrees warmer."

He rang the bell. A woman in her mid-fifties came to the door. Her dry, blond hair swept sideways Jackie Kennedy–style and was sprayed firmly into place. She wore a lime-green silk dress woven with pink and black triangles that pointed feverishly in all directions. Taylor bird-spotted Chanel.

The woman's face was long and glossy, the high bones holding the skin like a taut sail. Her jewelry was large. A blue topaz on her tanned, wrinkled finger was easily fifty carats.

"Thomas." They pressed cheeks and Taylor was introduced to Ada Smith—introduced, then promptly examined: the dynamics of the eyes, the contour of skin. The mouth especially. The review was mixed and Taylor believed she understood why: Bosk's little girlfriends—age twenty-three or twenty-four—could be forgiven their youth. Taylor had broken the three-oh barrier and yet had hardly a crow's foot or defining jowl.

She hates me, Taylor thought.

Yet Ada's smile and charm didn't waver; she'd been brought up right. "Call me Ada, please. I don't know where Bradford is. The others are in the den. Bradford's the cock-tail and cigar director. I'm in charge of dinner. That will be at eight."

Then she was gone.

From the back hallway, a bellowing voice: "Sea Bass, Sea Bass!"

Sebastian ran toward him and grunted. "Bosk-meister! Yo!"

They slapped fists, reminding Taylor of bull rams smacking horns.

Their host was in chinos, Top-Siders and a green Harvard sweatshirt. His hands and face were red, his eyes watering from the cold. "We've been chopping wood for the fire."

A girl giggled at the apparent lie.

"Well," Bosk said, "carting it in. Same as chopping it. Just as much work."

Bosk leaned forward, his arm on Sebastian's shoulders. He whispered, "Jennie's here and she brought Billy-boy, you can believe it."

"No way! Is she totally fucked, or what?" Sebastian looked around uneasily. "And how 'bout Brittany?"

"Couldn't make it."

The lawyer's eyes were immeasurably relieved and Taylor remembered something from the club about unreturned phone calls.

Then Bosk's eyes danced to Taylor. "'Lo. You're...?"

"Taylor Lockwood."

"Right, you're the one who won't marry me."

"True, but you're in good company." She nodded at Sebastian. "I won't marry him either. You have a nice place here."

"Thanks. I'll show you around later. Come on inside. We've got a fire going."

After she'd washed up she joined the crowd in the den. They were mostly in their twenties. Names went past—Rob and Mindy and Gay-Gay and Trevor and Windham and MacKenzie (the latter both female), clusters of contemporary syllables more distinct than the faces of the handsome men and pretty women they identified.

Taylor smiled and waved and forgot the names instantly. They were friendly but reserved and Taylor wondered what they were thinking of her—a woman with more wop and mick in her than Brit, with a mass of kinky black hair, not a pert ponytail, and wearing a long paisley skirt and a black blouse, not a J. Crew stitch upon her body.

Suspicion... That was the message from the women.

From the men there was something very different. Something between casual flirtation and a knee-jerk invitation to hump. Taylor supposed that soon there'd be a lot of female fingers twining possessively through the belt loops of their men.

Bosk made martinis for the crowd but Taylor stuck with beer.

"Are you a lawyer?" one blonde asked.

"A paralegal."

"Oh," the woman said, blinking. "That's interesting."

"We need you folks," one handsome young man said as he tinkered nervously with his Rolex. "You save our butts every day." It seemed he wasn't being condescending; he was simply embarrassed for her and trying to salvage her pride.

"Where're you from? Boston, right? I detect Bostonian."

"Born on the North Shore."

"Oh, Locust Valley?" a pretty blond woman asked. The residence of the crème de la crème. J. P. Morgan's home.

"No, Glen Cove." A pleasant but strip-malled city. "But we moved to Maryland when I was twelve."

"Is your father or mother in the business?"

"Which business would that be?" Taylor asked innocently.

"Law, banking?" As if no other businesses existed.

"He manages a convenience store," she replied.

Sebastian, who'd already commented about her father and his renowned law practice, glanced at her with a cryptic look.

"Well, retail," one girl finally said, nodding with robust approval. "Good margins in retail lately."

"Very good," somebody else added.

And to her relief, Taylor Lockwood ceased to be a human being as far as they were concerned and their own conversation—the real and important conversation—resumed.

■■■■

Dinner was Ada's jurisdiction.

She presided with the quiet authority of someone

for whom social propriety is statutory. Somewhere, in a three-decades-old volume of Emily Post, this very layout of Waterford and Wedgwood was represented. Though the clothing was supposed to be casual, Ada's appearance in a rustling silk dress, black-velvet headband and necklace gripping a lemon-colored stone the size of a fat thumb made it clear that, whatever happened in the frat dining halls or eating clubs these youngsters were accustomed to, dinner in this particular house would be governed by a respectable modicum of formality.

Taylor tried a vain end run around the seating ("Oh, I'm sorry, was I supposed to sit there?"); Ada smilingly steered her away from Bosk's girlfriend (a potential source of information about the "project"), scolding, "Boy, girl, boy, girl..."

Lobster bisque, a pear-and-Camembert salad, tiny veal chops surrounded by a yin-yang swirl of pureed peas and carrots, a green salad. A real butler served the meal.

Between polite words with the young man on her right Taylor tried to overhear the conversation between Bosk and Sebastian but Ada's voice was too loud—she was a lock-jawed caricature of Long Island money. She touched the men's arms with her dark, bony fingers and flirted fiercely. Yet their hostess knew this game as well as she knew the proper wording for bread-and-butter notes. She had no intention of seducing these boys; the only organ at play here was her ego—though sex was a strong undercurrent of the meal and crude jokes, some of them really disgusting, flew back and forth. (The upper class, Taylor remembered, had by and large not been Puritans.)

Halfway through the profiteroles and espresso with anisette, the doorbell rang. Bosk rose and a few minutes later returned with a man of about forty-five. He was introduced as Dennis Callaghan.

Taylor disliked him at once.

She wasn't sure why. What she might in fairness have read as groomed, discerning and charming she believed was vain (spun, sprayed hair combed forward, a close-fitting suit with shot cuffs, gold bracelet), pompous (a disdaining look at the children around him) and dishonest (a broad smile he could not have felt).

He was also insulting: He ignored Taylor while he studied the bloused or sweatered breasts of every woman younger than herself at the table before turning a flattering smile on Ada with the respect due a matriarch.

Taylor then noticed that the climate at the table had changed considerably. Sebastian's expression was one of anger. He shot a dark, mystified glance at Bosk, who shrugged with a look that meant, It wasn't my fault. When she saw that, Taylor's interest immediately perked up. Perhaps Callaghan had some connection with the "project."

The visitor, whose beach house was apparently nearby, announced that he'd played hooky from Wall Street today to hold a couple of meetings out here and happened to notice the cars as he was driving back to the city. He thought he'd stop in and see Bosk and Sebastian.

The man glanced at Sebastian, and Taylor saw another finger wag, just like the other night. Callaghan nodded subtly.

And so the conversation remained social. As he sat down at the table and took a glass of wine—he'd eaten already—they talked about problems in finding groundskeepers and the advantages and risks of helicoptering into Manhattan. Sebastian remained nervous as hell and when Taylor asked Callaghan what he did for a living the young lawyer answered for the businessman, offering quickly, "Wall Street, darling. *Everybody* out here's on Wall Street. Well, you've got an artist or two from time to time—Taylor's a musician, by the way."

"Really?"

The conversation turned back to her momentarily and before she could ask anything more about Callaghan, dinner was over and Sebastian had quickly shepherded Bosk and the businessman downstairs, explaining that they were going to check out Bosk's cigar cellar.

No one else was invited but the herd of preppies didn't

take any offense. Ada nodded toward the port, sherry and liqueur and, armed with yet more alcohol, this contingent ambled into the panoramic living room for more gossip.

It was then that Taylor recalled: She hadn't told Sebastian that she was a musician.

Soon several people lit up cigarettes, Ada among them.

The smoke gave Taylor an excuse to drain her Grand Marnier and say she was going to step outside to get some air. Whether anyone thought this was rude, or suspicious, didn't matter; they all seemed relieved that the 7-Eleven heiress was leaving and they could spend some time dishing in earnest.

She took her leather jacket from the closet and walked out the front door, then strolled around the house until she spotted a four-foot-deep window well. She climbed down into it. A piece of glass was loose and she worked it free. She could not see the three men downstairs but their words, carried on the warm air, streamed up to her with the awkward-sounding hesitancies of conversations overheard but not witnessed.

"Got to be more careful," Sebastian said. "Jesus, I shit when I saw you here."

Callaghan said, "We've still got some details to work out. And you're impossible to get ahold of, Thom."

"Well, we can't just fucking waltz into each other's office and take a meeting now, can we? We've got to be careful about it, set it up ahead of time, keep everything secret."

Callaghan sighed. "I've been doing this sort of thing a lot longer than you have, Thom. We're going to get away with it. Stop worrying so much."

"I'm thinking about the phones," Bosk said. "You really think they're bugged?"

Sebastian said, "Of course they're fucking bugged. Jesus, don't be so naive.

Bosk: "Well, I can't run downstairs to make a call from a

pay phone every time I want to talk to you. Somebody sees me doing that a couple of times and what're they going to think?"

Sebastian: "Well, that's what you're going to have to do. You can pick up cell phone transmissions even easier than landlines."

Callaghan: "What we could do—I've done this before— what we could do is get an answering service. You call and leave messages. I'll call on a separate line and pick them up. We'll have a second answering service going the other way."

Clever, Taylor Lockwood thought, though being truly clever, Thom, would have meant wearing gloves when you check out the file cabinet you're about to break into so you don't leave fingerprints.

Suddenly she felt a curious thrill. What was it? The excitement of the pursuit, she supposed, getting closer to her quarry. What Reece felt in the courtroom yesterday. What her father undoubtedly felt—in court, on the golf course, with his beloved shotgun out in the fields.

When she was young her father would take her with him when he'd go hunting on Saturday mornings in the fall. She'd hated those times, wanted to be back home in bed, watching cartoons or playing on her upright piano, shopping with her mother. But Samuel Lockwood, eyes keen and hungry for a kill, had insisted she come along. He'd carried the tiny, still-warm corpses of the birds back to the car, where came the moment she dreaded: To make her understand that the dead birds couldn't hurt her, he had her touch each one with her index finger.

There, that wasn't so bad, was it? Didn't hurt. They can't bite when they're dead, Taylie, remember that.

Dennis Callaghan now said, "Look, yeah, we have to be careful but we can't let this paralyze us."

"We're fucking thieves," Sebastian said. "Am I the only one taking this seriously?"

Bosk's laugh was flinty. "Well, whatta you want, Thom? You want to get walkie-talkies and scramblers? Disguises?"

"I'm just a little paranoid, okay? There was a weird fuckup."

"What?"

"Well, last Saturday night, when I was in the firm?"

"Right," Callaghan offered.

"I made sure nobody knew I was there—on Friday I taped the back door latch down so I could get in without leaving any record I was in. But what happens is this old asshole, a partner, cops my key and uses it to get in early Sunday morning. So now I'm in the system."

Gotcha, thought Taylor Lockwood. John Silbert Hemming, her tall private eye, would be proud of her.

"Shit," Bosk said. "Why'd he do it?"

"How the fuck do I know? Alzheimer's."

Callaghan said, "Not the end of the world. They don't know what you were doing there, right?"

"I don't think so."

"Well, relax. You've covered up everything real well, Thom. . . . Oh, here. Got a present."

"Ah, nectar of the gods," Sebastian said.

"Sure," Bosk said. A long pause.

Then a sniff. Another.

The magic powder boosted Sebastian's spirits considerably. When he spoke next he said with a laugh, "I like this— fucking the firm that fucked me and getting rich in the process."

"You want a Lamborghini?" Callaghan asked.

Bosk said seriously, "I don't like the ride. Rough, you know."

Sebastian: "I live in Manhattan. What'm I gonna do, alternate-side-of-the-street parking with a two-hundred-thousand-dollar car?"

"Keep it out at your summer house, Thom, like we all do."

"I don't have a summer house. And I don't want one."

The wind was dicing her face and ears. She closed her eyes against the cold. Her legs and thighs, the last stronghold

of heat, were going numb. She touched the glass that separated her from a room that was fifty degrees warmer, where
she heard the sounds of two chubby, spoiled boys sniffing the
residue of cocaine into their nostrils.

Bosk said, "So what's with this Taylor cunt? She put out?"

"Fuck you," Sebastian said unemotionally.

"No, does she fuck *you*? That's what I'm asking."

Callaghan sniffed his white powder then said, "You've
got gonads for brains, Bosk. Is that all you think about? Sex?"

"Money, too. I think a lot about money but mostly I
think about sex. Tell me about Taylor."

"I don't want to talk about her," Sebastian said menac-
ingly.

"Does she have big tits? I couldn't tell. . . . Hey, chill, will
you, man? That's a fucking scary look. I was just curious."

There was a pause. And with an ominous tone in his
voice Sebastian said, "Well, don't get too interested in her.
You hear me?"

Taylor felt a ping of fear at that.

"I'm just—"

"You hear what I'm saying?"

"Hey, chill. . . . I hear you, Sea Bass, I hear you."

Then the conversation turned to sports and, stinging
with cold, Taylor left them to their banter. She walked inside and rejoined the crowd in front of the fireplace, observing how the conversation grew sedate when she entered the
room. She nudged herself into the center of the group and
sat on the hearth with her back to the fire until the pain
from the cold became a fierce itch and then finally died
away.

███████

Around 10 P.M. the drapery man walked through
Greenwich Village under huge trapezoids of bruise-purple
clouds, lit from the perpetual glow of the city.

He was concentrating on the buildings and finally arrived at the address he sought.

At the service entrance, which smelled of sour garbage,

he inserted his lock gun and flicked the trigger a dozen times until the teeth of the tumblers were aligned. The door opened easily. He climbed to the fourth floor and picked another set of locks—on the door of the particular apartment he sought.

Inside, he slipped his ice-pick weapon into his belt, handle up, ready to grab it if he had to, and began to search. He found a bag of needlepoint (one a Christmas scene that sure wouldn't be finished in time for the holiday), a box of Weight Watchers apple snacks, a garter belt in its original gift box, apparently never worn, cartons of musty sheet music. An elaborate, expensive-looking reel-to-reel tape recorder. Dozens of tape cassettes with the same title: *The Heat of Midnight. Songs by Taylor Lockwood.*

Inside the woman's briefcase, in addition to sheet music, he found time sheets, key entry logs and other documents from Hubbard, White & Willis. He looked through them carefully and memorized exactly what they contained.

He found and read through the woman's address book, her calendar and her phone bills. He listened to her answering machine tapes. His client had hoped that she'd have a diary but very few people kept diaries anymore and Taylor Lockwood was no exception.

The drapery man continued his search, walking slowly through the apartment, taking his time. He knew his client would grill him at length about what he'd found here and he wanted to make sure he overlooked nothing.

CHAPTER EIGHTEEN

Taylor dropped into the chair in her cubicle.

It was six-thirty, Saturday morning. The gods of the furnace had decided that not even Type A attorneys would be in the office yet and so Hubbard, White & Willis was cold as Anchorage.

She shivered both from the temperature and from exhaustion too. She and Thom Sebastian had arrived back in the city late last night. The lawyer had been subdued. She'd sensed that he was worried she'd ask about Callaghan and he wouldn't be able to come up with a credible story. But there was something else troubling him. His jokey self was gone. And once she caught him looking at her with an odd, troubled expression on his face.

She had an image of herself as a condemned prisoner and him as a prison guard, distancing himself from someone about to die.

Ridiculous, she thought. Still, she could hear his words in her head:

Well, don't get too interested in her.

What did *that* mean?

And how the hell had he known she was a musician?

She noticed a flashing light on her phone, indicating that she had a message. She picked up the receiver to check voice mail.

Reece had called again to remind her about dinner at his place that night.

There was one other message.

Beep.

"*Hey, counselor, how you doing? Saw an article about your shop in the* Law Journal. *About the merger. You've probably seen it but I'm faxing it to you. Always stay on top of firm politics. . . .*"

If you only knew, Dad, she thought.

"*We're planning Christmas dinner and we've got an RSVP from a Supreme Court justice; I'll let you guess who. I'm putting him next to you at the table. Just keep your more liberal views to yourself, counselor. I'm serious about that. Okay, I'll be in town week after next. Your mother says hi.*"

Supreme Court? Samuel Lockwood never did anything without a purpose. What did he have in mind? Was the dinner table placement intended to help her career? she wondered.

Or *his?* she appended cynically.

Taylor found the fax her father had sent about the merger of the firms, scanned it quickly. It described the vicious infighting among the partners at Hubbard, White & Willis—Burdick v. Clayton—and how, despite the animosity, the merged firms would probably succeed much better in the new business climate than if they remained separate. The picture featured Burdick and his wife.

An idea occurred to her.

She wrote on the top, "Thom, FYI." And signed her name.

Using this as an excuse, she hurried to his office, propped the article on his chair and, with a glance into the deserted corridor, proceeded to search the room like an eager rookie cop on crime scene detail.

In his desk she found: condoms, Bamboo paper, an unopened bottle of Chivas Regal, matches from the Harvard

Club, the Palace Hotel and assorted late-night clubs around town, dozens of take-out menus from downtown restaurants, chatty letters from his brother and father and mother (all neatly organized, some with margin notes), brokerage house statements, checkbooks (Jesus, where'd he get all this *money*?), some popular spy and military paperbacks, a coffee-stained copy of the *Lawyer's Code of Professional Responsibility,* assorted photographs from vacations, newspaper articles on bond issues and stock offerings, the *Pennystock News,* candy bars, crumbs and paper clips.

Nothing about the note, no information linking him, Bosk or Callaghan to Hanover & Stiver.

On Sebastian's bookshelves were hundreds of huge books, bound in navy and burgundy and deep green. They'd contain copies of all the closing documents in a business transaction that Sebastian had worked on. They would be great places to hide stolen promissory notes and other incriminating evidence. But it would take several days to look through all of them. She saw Sebastian's name embossed in gold at the bottom of each one.

It was then that she noticed the corner of a piece of paper protruding from beneath Sebastian's desk blotter. Another glance into the corridor—still no signs of life—and she pulled the paper out.

The jottings were brief and to the point.

Taylor Lockwood. 24 Fifth Avenue.

Her age, schools attended. Home address in Chevy Chase. Phone numbers at the firm and at home. The unlisted one too.

Father: Samuel Lockwood. Mother: housewife. No siblings. Applied to law school. Employed by HWW for two years. Merit raises and bonuses at top levels.

"Musician. Every Tuesday. Miracles Pub."

The son of a bitch, she whispered. Then replaced the sheet exactly where she'd found it.

She left his office and returned to the chilly corridor, hearing echoes of footsteps, hearing the click of guns being cocked and the hiss of knives being unsheathed.

And hearing over and over Thom Sebastian's words:
Well, don't get too interested in her.

In the firm's library she logged on to several of the computer databases that the firm subscribed to, including the Lexis/Nexis system, which contains copies of nearly all court decisions, statutes and regulations in the United States, as well as articles from hundreds of magazines and newspapers around the world.

She spent hours trying to find information about Dennis Callaghan, Bosk and Sebastian.

There wasn't much that was helpful. Bradford Smith had been admitted to the New York and federal bars and currently practiced at a Midtown firm, which didn't, however, seem to have any connection to Hanover & Stiver or New Amsterdam Bank.

Dennis Callaghan wasn't a lawyer but a businessman. He dabbled in dozens of different activities and had been under investigation for stock fraud and real estate scams though he'd never been indicted. He was currently connected with about twenty different companies, some of which were incorporated offshore and which, she guessed, were fronts.

But still no connection between any of them and Hanover & Stiver.

The information about Sebastian—found in alumni magazine archives and legal magazines he'd contributed articles to—wasn't incriminating either, though she found, interestingly, that the Upper East Side preppy image was fake. Sebastian had grown up outside of Chicago, his father the manager of a Kroger grocery store (hence, she realized, another reason for the funny look when he'd heard her tell the youngsters at Ada's that Dad managed a convenience store). Sebastian did have an undergrad degree from Harvard but it had taken him six years because he'd gone part-time—presumably while working to support himself.

The Yale Law School certificates she'd noticed on his

wall must have been for continuing education courses; he'd gotten his law degree from Brooklyn Law at night while working as a process server during the day—serving subpoenas in some of the toughest parts of the outer boroughs.

So, there was a different Thom Sebastian beneath the jokey party animal. One who was driven, ambitious, tough. And, Taylor knew, recalling the conversation in Ada's downstairs den, also a thief—fucking the firm that fucked him.

More associates were filing into the library now and she didn't want anybody to see what she was doing so she logged off the computer and went to the administrative floor.

There she walked into the file room Carrie Mason had told her about, a large, dingy space filled with row upon row of cabinets. It was here that the billing department kept the original time sheets that lawyers filled out daily.

Making certain the room was empty, Taylor opened the "D" drawer—where Ralph Dudley's sheets would reside—and found the most recent ones. They were little blue slips of carbon paper filled with his imperial scrawl, describing every ten-minute period during working hours. She read through and replaced them and then did the same in the "L" drawer for Lillick and the "S" for Thom Sebastian.

Taylor rose to leave but then paused.

The "R" cabinet was right next to her.

She rested her fingers on the handle and after a moment's hesitation, pulled it open and looked inside. She stared in astonishment at the booklets with Mitchell Reece's name on them. There were hundreds of them. Christ Almighty . . . nearly twice as many as for most other lawyers.

She pulled one out at random—September—and thumbed through it, looking at a typical day in the life of Mitchell Reece:

New Client relations—½ hour.
New Amsterdam Bank & Trust v. Hanover & Stiver—4½ hours (depositions).
Westron Electronic et al. v. Larson Associates—3¼ hours (motion to quash subpoena, J. Brietell).

State of New York v. Kowalski—½ hour *(conference
with DA's office; pro bono).*
State of New York v. Hammond—½ hour *(meeting
with defendant; pro bono).*
In re Summers Publishing—2½ hours *(research,
briefing Chapter 7 bankruptcy issue).*

She skimmed ahead.

*Lasky v. Allied Products...Mutual Indemnity of
New Jersey v. New Amsterdam Bank...State of
New York v. Williams.*

She totaled the hours: Sixteen were billed to clients.
That was sixteen hours of *productive* work, not commuting
time, lunch, trips to the rest rooms and the water fountain.

Sixteen hours in one day!

And every day was pretty much the same.

*Arguing motion, arguing motion, on trial, writing brief, on
trial, on trial, settlement conference, arguing motion, on trial,
pro bono meetings with criminal clients and prosecutors.*

On trial on trial on trial...

He never stopped.

A thought occurred to her and she smiled to herself.
Yes, no?

Go for it, Alice.

She opened the binder containing the most recent of his
sheets. She flipped through them until she found the day
that she'd followed him to Grand Central Station.

For the three hours he was out of the office he'd marked
the time Code 03.

Which meant personal time.

The time you spend at the dentist's office.

The time you spend at PTA conferences.

The time you spend in Westchester, with your girlfriend.

Taylor felt her skin buzzing with embarrassment as she
flipped through other lunch hours over the past several

months. In September he'd done the same—taken long lunches—only usually it was two or three times a week. Recently, in the month of November, for instance, he'd done so only once a week.

Three hours in the middle of the day for a workaholic like Reece?

Well, Taylor Lockwood understood; she'd had lovers herself.

She put the time sheets back and closed the drawer.

Outside, the air was cold but the city was ablaze with Christmas decorations and she decided to walk home. She slipped her Walkman headset on, then her earmuffs, and began to walk briskly, thinking about the evening ahead, dinner with Mitchell Reece—at least until the hiss of the cassette grew silent, Miles Davis started into "Seven Steps to Heaven" and the rest of the world was lost to Taylor Lockwood.

CHAPTER NINETEEN

██████████ Well, look at this.

Mitchell Reece could've been a professional interior designer.

Taylor would have thought he'd have no time for decor—or interest in the subject. So when he opened his door and ushered her into the huge loft, she exhaled a sharp, surprised laugh.

She was looking at a single room, probably twenty-five hundred square feet. There was a separate elevated sleeping area with a brass railing around it, containing an oak armoire and a matching dresser—and a bed, which caught her attention immediately. It was dark mahogany, with a massive headboard that would have dwarfed any smaller space. The headboard was carved in a Gothic style and the characters cut into the wood were cracked and worn. She couldn't tell exactly what they were—perhaps gargoyles and dragons.

She thought of the mythical creature in *Through the Looking-Glass*.

Beware the Jabberwock, my son!
The jaws that bite, the claws that catch!

Around the loft were plants, sculpture, antiques, tall bookshelves, tapestries. Pin spots shot focused streams of light onto small statues and paintings, many of which looked ugly enough to be very valuable. The walls were brick and plaster, painted mottled white and gray and pink. The floors were oak, stained white.

If this boy cooks, she joked to herself, I may just reconsider my baby-by-mail plan and marry him.

"You did this just to impress me, I know."

He laughed. "Let me take your coat." Reece wore baggy pants and a blousy white shirt. Sockless slippers. His hair was still damp from a shower.

Taylor had chosen noncommittal vamp. Black stockings but shoes with low, functional heels. A black Carolina Herrera dress, tight but high-necked. (Cleavage? A roommate had once bluntly assessed, *Forget boobs, Taylor: Avoid low-cut. But the rest of your bod—it's to die for. Wear short and tight. Remember that. Short and tight.*)

Taylor noted the sweep of Reece's eyes all along her body. He was subtle, but not subtle enough; she caught him in reflection in one of the mirrors near the Jabberwock bed.

Okay, Ms. Westchester, she thought to Reece's mysterious girlfriend, can *you* shoehorn into a dress like this?

She followed him across an oriental rug. The dinner table had feet, and on the side, carved faces of the sun. They were solemn.

"Your table looks unhappy."

"He gets bored. I don't have much company. He'll be happy tonight."

As Reece took the wine she'd brought she looked at him carefully and decided he wasn't very happy either. His eyes were still bloodshot and he seemed to be forcing himself to relax, to push the intruding distractions of the law firm away.

He walked into the kitchen area and put the chardonnay into a refrigerator. She looked inside; it contained nothing but wine. "You should try groceries sometime," she said. "Lettuce, oranges. You can even get chicken, I'm told, ready to cook."

"Wine cellar," Reece said, laughing. He pulled out a bottle of white, a Puligny-Montrachet. Her father's favorite Burgundy, Taylor recalled. Reece added, "The fridge's over there." He pointed to a tall Sub-Zero then took two crystal goblets in one hand and carried the wine and a ceramic cooler out into the living area.

Man, she thought, he's really slick at this.

He poured and they touched glasses. "To winning."

Taylor held his eye for a moment and repeated the toast. The wine was rich and sour-sweet, more like a food than a drink. The goblet was heavy in her hand.

They sat and he told her how he'd found the loft. It was raw space when he'd moved in and he'd had it finished himself. The project had taken nearly a year because he'd had three full-fledged trials that year and had been unable to meet with the contractors. "I slept in sawdust a lot," he explained. "But I won the cases."

"Have you ever lost a trial?" she asked.

"Of course. Everybody loses trials. I seem to win a few more than most people. But that's not magic. Or luck. Preparation is the key. And will to win."

"Preparation and Will. That could be your motto."

"Maybe I should get a crest. I wonder what it'd be in Latin."

Taylor rose and walked toward a long wooden shelf. "My mother," she said, "would call this a knickknack shelf. I used to think 'knickknack' was French for 'small, ugly ceramic poodle.'" He laughed.

She found herself looking at an army of metal soldiers.

"I collect them," Reece said. "Winston Churchill probably had the biggest collection in the world and Malcolm Forbes's wasn't too shabby either. I've only been at it for twenty years or so."

"What are they, tin?"

"Lead."

Taylor said, "One year my father got the idea that I should get soldiers, not dolls, for Christmas. I must've been eight or nine. He gave me bags and bags of these green plastic guys. He gave me a B-52 too so I nuked most of them and went back to Barbie and Pooh. You have other things, too? Like cannons and catapults?"

"Everything. Soldiers, horses, cannons, and caissons..."

She sipped the wine and was thinking: Sometimes in life this craziness falls right on top of you and you find yourself almost floating up and away from your body like a guru or psychic, looking down at yourself, and all you can say is, Shit a brick, this is *so* weird. I mean, here I am, Alice in Wonderland, in a fab loft, next to a handsome man I'm playing detective with, drinking hundred-dollar wine and talking toy soldiers.

Taylor told herself not, under any circumstances, to get drunk.

Reece played with some of the figures. "I have a British Square. I made it when I was sixteen."

"Like a park? Like Trafalgar Square?"

Reece was laughing. "Taylor, British Square? A fighting formation? You know, Gunga Din."

"Kipling," she said.

He nodded. "The ranks divided into two lines. One stood and reloaded, the other knelt and fired. The fuzzy-wuzzies were the only warriors to break through the square."

"The, uh..."

"Zulus. African tribal warriors."

"Ah. Boer War."

"That was twenty years later."

"Oh, sure," she said seriously, nodding in recognition.

"You're laughing at me, aren't you?"

She shook her head but couldn't keep a straight face and said through the grin, "Definitely."

He hit her playfully on the arm and let his hand pause on the thin cotton of her blouse for a moment.

He put on some music jazz.

"Any word about your demo tapes?"

"The responses ain't been jim-dandy."

"It only takes one record company."

She shrugged. And glanced at an antique clock. Eight-thirty. She could smell nothing simmering. Well, scratch one: He can't cook. Maybe they were going out. But—

The door buzzer sounded.

"Excuse me."

He let a young man into the loft. He nodded politely to Taylor and, from a large shopping bag, took out plates wrapped in stippled foil. Reece set the table with bone china plates, silver and a candlestick.

The portable butler said, "Would you like me to pour the wine, Mr. Reece?"

"No, thank you anyway, Robert." Reece signed the proffered slip of paper. A bill changed hands.

"Then good night, sir."

———

Dinner turned out to be blini with beluga caviar and sour cream, veal medallions with slivers of fresh truffles in a marsala sauce, braised endive and cold marinated green beans.

No fake burgers and sprouts for this boy . . .

They sat at the table and began to eat. Reece said, "Now, tell me what you've found out about the note."

Taylor organized her thoughts. "First, somebody got into the computer and erased all the disbursements, expenses and phone call logs for Saturday and Sunday."

"All of them?" He winced.

She nodded. "All last week, actually. Everything that'd link a particular person to the firm—except the door card keys and the time sheets."

"Okay." He nodded, taking this in. "Who can get into the system?"

"It's not that hard. You need an access card but it'd be

easy to steal one." More of the wonderful wine—he'd opened a second bottle. "Let me go through the suspects. First, Thom Sebastian."

He nodded. "Go ahead."

"Well, I fingerprinted your safe and found his on the top and side."

He laughed. "You did what?"

"I got a private-eye kit—deerstalker cap and decoder ring, the works. I dusted the scene of the crime and came up with twenty-five latents—that's prints, to you. Fifteen completely unrecognizable. The other ten, most were partials but seven seem to be the same person—you, I'm pretty sure. I dusted your coffee cup—I owe you a new one, by the way; the powder didn't come off too well. I threw it out."

"I wondered what happened to it."

"And three others. A couple of prints are unidentified but there are a dozen or so that're smooth smudges, as if somebody'd worn gloves. Thom's're pretty clear."

"Thom?" Reece frowned. "Son of a bitch."

She said, "I don't think he actually broke into the safe; from the position on the metal it looks like the guy who did that was the one wearing the gloves—the pro. But Sebastian may have checked it out before—or tried to open it that night and when he couldn't called in an expert. Is there any reason why he'd've been going through your files?"

"He's worked for New Amsterdam in the past though not on the Hanover & Stiver deal—not that I've *heard* about. Anyway, he'd have no business going through anybody's office without asking." He laughed and looked at her admiringly. "Fingerprints . . . That never occurred to me."

She continued, explaining to him that Sebastian had lied about how late he'd stayed at the club on Saturday night and that she'd confirmed he was in fact in the firm. She told him too about Bosk and Dennis Callaghan. How they'd talked about stealing something from the firm and how they were going to spend their money.

She asked, "You ever hear the name Callaghan in connection with the Hanover & Stiver case?"

"No." Reece shook his head. "But what about Sebastian's motive? He's risking prison just to get even with the firm?"

"Why not? The firm was his entire life. Besides, he's got a dark side to him. He was a process server in Brooklyn and Queens."

Reece nodded. "Yeah, those guys are tough."

Sebastian's implicit threat echoed in her mind again.

She said, "I think he wants revenge. But mostly I think he looks at the money Hanover'd pay him to lose the note as something the firm owes him—for not getting made partner. Think about it: He's a product of Hubbard, White— which's been training him for six or seven years to go for the throat, look only at the bottom line. He's also been checking me out."

"You?"

She nodded. "He's got a little dossier on me."

"Why?"

"Know your enemy?" She then continued, "Remember I mentioned Dudley? Well, are you ready for this?"

She told him about Junie and the West Side Art and Photography Club.

"Whoa," Reece blurted. "That little girl's a hooker? Dudley's mad. They'll put him away forever for that. Statutory rape, contributing to the delinquency."

"And it looks like he's paying a thousand bucks a week cash for her. You told me he's got money problems to start with. That's *his* motive. And as for being in the firm on Saturday I know he was there and he told Junie that some project he was working on was going to mean a lot of money. I checked his time sheets and he didn't bill any time Saturday or Sunday. So whatever he was doing at the firm then was personal. . . ."

Taylor added, "Now, we've got a third-party candidate."

"Who?"

"Sean Lillick."

"The paralegal? Hell, he's been working for me on the case—he knows all the details about the note. But what's his motive?"

"Also money. I found thousands of dollars hidden in his apartment. He didn't get it from a paralegal's salary. And he *sure* didn't make it doing that performance art crap of his."

"But he wasn't in the firm when the note was stolen, was he?"

"I'm not sure. He did come in Saturday morning, according to his key entry card. I assumed he left, because he only billed a few hours to a client. But he might've stayed all night."

Reece had a thought. "Something interesting...Lillick hangs around with Wendall Clayton a lot."

She nodded. She'd seen them together.

"But you know what's curious?" Reece mused. "Lillick's assigned to the litigation department. Not corporate. Why'd he be working for Clayton?"

"I don't know."

A frown on the lawyer's face. "Lillick'd be familiar with the St. Agnes files too. He might've fed Clayton some information that led him to that surprise witness from San Diego."

"You think *Clayton's* behind that?" she asked.

Reece shrugged. "St. Agnes is Donald's client and so's New Amsterdam Bank. All Clayton cares about is getting the merger through, and sabotaging Burdick's clients is a pretty efficient way to do it."

He stood, walked into the kitchen and returned with two glasses of cognac. He handed one to Taylor, the liqueur leaving thin, syrupy waves on the glass. "Tomorrow, Wendall's having a party at his Connecticut place. Why don't you come along. You might be able to find something."

"Oh, I couldn't go. I'm just a paralegal."

"It's a *firm* function; they just have it at his house. A party for the new associates, an annual thing. You can come with me."

"We shouldn't be seen together."

"We'll split up once we get inside. We'll get there late and just slip in." He tipped his glass to her. "Good job, counselor."

They clinked glasses but she must've winced a bit.

"What?"

" 'Counselor.' "

"You don't like that?"

"My father's pet name for me. Fingernails on the blackboard."

"Noted," he said. "I can imagine it's tough being Samuel Lockwood's child."

If you only knew, she thought, echoing the words she'd just directed to her father's phone message earlier that day.

They sipped the cognac and talked about the firm, partners, affairs, who was gay, who was on partnership track and who was not. She supplied most of the information and was surprised he knew so little about the gossipy side of the firm and its politics.

It was more astonishing to her that he knew so little about the merger. Although the lawyers and staffers of Hubbard, White spent more hours debating the merger than billing time for clients, Reece seemed oblivious to the whole thing. She mentioned the rumor that Clayton had a German lawyer inquire about accounts Burdick might have opened in Switzerland.

"Really?" Reece asked with what seemed unsophisticated surprise.

"Aren't you worried about it?" Taylor asked. "About what'll happen if Wendall wins?"

He laughed. "No. Doesn't make a bit of difference to me—as long as I can try cases, good cases, that's all I care about. Whether it's Donald in charge or Wendall or John Perelli, doesn't matter."

Together they cleared the dishes. He nodded toward the leather sofa and they walked over to it, sitting and sinking into the deep, supple piece of furniture.

There was a moment of quiet. The ticking clock. A siren far away. A distant shout.

That was when he kissed her.

And she kissed him back.

They embraced for a moment, his right hand sliding down the side of her face but coming to rest, ambiguously, at her collarbone.

His palm started downward but it stopped.

Perhaps because he sensed something coming from her—the reserve, the caution, that she in fact suddenly felt.

"Sorry," he said. "I'm impulsive and pushy. Tell me to go to hell."

"I would if I wanted to."

If you only knew . . .

He sat back and after a moment said, "There's something I wanted to say."

"Sure."

"It's nothing really. But it's been bugging me. Remember when I said I couldn't have lunch after the cross? Yesterday?"

"Right." She found her heart beating hard.

"I didn't have a meeting."

She pictured the three-hour lunch reference on the time sheet. The flowers.

"I went up to Westchester."

Taylor nodded, said nothing.

He continued. "There's something I don't talk about too much. My mother's in a home up there."

"Oh, I'm sorry, Mitchell."

He was stoic but she believed she could see pain somewhere behind his eyes. "Schizophrenia. It's pretty bad. I go to see her a couple times a week. Sometimes she remembers me." He smiled. "Yesterday she was pretty good. I took her some flowers and she went on and on about them for a long time."

"She's on medication?"

"Oh, yeah. And the nurses at the home are real good to her. The thing is, it's hard for me to talk about it. In fact, you're the only one I've told."

She felt a burst of pleasure at this confidence, even more than being singled out by Reece to help him find the promissory note. "I won't say anything. . . . If there's anything I can do—"

"Hey, how 'bout just a kiss to forgive me for not being honest."

She laughed and squeezed his arm. And leaned forward. Kissed him quickly.

Then eased her arms around his neck and kept kissing him.

Hard.

Where are we going with this? she wondered.

As she kissed and was kissed, as she touched and was touched, her mind counted her marriage proposals (two), the live-in boyfriends (three), the men she'd slept with (thirteen).

She thought of the ones she felt mere fondness for who'd claimed they were madly in love with her. And the flip side: the ones she'd lusted or pined for who hadn't cared she existed.

But maybe *this* time would be different, she thought. Maybe getting older, maybe simply getting by, *surviving* in this world had changed her, made her more discerning, given her better judgment.

Maybe she'd broken into a different place—that Wonderland where her father and Mitchell Reece resided. Where she was their equal.

But be careful, she thought. Remember Thom Sebastian's myth of the beautiful woman? Well, beware the myth of the absolute moment, a moment like this—when we sit, or lie, close together, muscles ticking, limbs at their most relaxed, bathed in the certainty of love. The absolute moment, when conversation soars, confidences are shared, coincidences between you and your lover pop up like crocuses in April.

The absolute moment—when we forget that most loves aren't forever, that most words are mere vibrations of insubstantial air, that most unions are a nest of comic and aching differences that no other animal in the world would tolerate, let alone desperately pursue.

She eased back slightly, wiped the war paint of lipstick off his cheek. He glanced down at her empty glass. He stood up and filled both of theirs again and returned, sat down, slouching back into the leather, playing with the top button of his shirt. His hair was mussed. He tried to brush it back but the thick comma stayed put.

"Know what?" he asked.

"What's that?"

"I'm glad."

"About what?" Taylor felt it then, that unwinding feeling within her. Despite the keen warning to herself a moment ago, the spring had been set loose.

Was it going to be good or bad? The time was coming soon, quick as a wet-leaf skid. Okay? Decide, good or bad? Decide fast, Alice; you've got about three minutes.

"I'm glad we haven't caught our thief yet. I like working with you." His voice was husky.

Reece held his glass up.

Come on, this is the moment. Now. You going, or staying? You've still got the power. It hasn't tipped yet. You can do it easy, diffuse the whole thing. Thank him for dinner. Stand up. That's all it would take.

One way or another, decide: In the end, is this good or bad?

She lifted her glass too and tapped but as he sipped, some of the cognac spilled onto the front of his shirt.

"Oh, hell," he muttered.

Come on, good or bad? Make it your decision. Choose. . . .

"Here, let me clean it up," she said.

Good or bad?

She thought that question to herself a dozen times in the space of five seconds or maybe two seconds or maybe just one but it never got answered; his mouth closed on hers and his hands—surprisingly large and strong for a bookish man—were covering her breasts and she felt the heat in his fingers as they then slid inside her dress, probing for fasteners.

Taylor in turn sought the smooth cloth of his shirt, gripped it hard and pulled him down on top of her.

Good or bad, good or bad...

This Saturday night, late, Donald Burdick and Bill Stanley sat beside each other in tall-backed leather chairs and looked into the valet room of their private club on Broad Street.

It was in that room that every morning one of the club employees would iron the *New York Times, International Herald Tribune* and *Wall Street Journal* for the members. This had been a perk ever since the club had been founded in the mid-1800s. At that time, of course, when New York City boasted more than a dozen papers, the valet was busy all day long. Now, however, with no evening papers of worth, the room was used at night only for its junction box, to which telephones on long wires were connected. When a call came in these phones were carried to members; cellular phones were, of course, forbidden in the club.

Burdick and Stanley watched the poised black man, in a dinner jacket, now carrying one of these phones to Burdick, who took it with a nod of thanks.

The conversation lasted only four minutes.

Burdick absorbed the information, closed his eyes and, thinking that in Roman days the messenger would have been killed had he delivered news like this, nonetheless politely thanked the caller.

He dropped the receiver into the cradle. The valet appeared instantly and removed the phone.

"What the hell was that?" Stanley asked.

"The lease," Burdick said, shaking his head.

"Oh, no," Stanley grumbled.

Burdick nodded. "He did it. Somehow Clayton deepsixed the lease."

The caller had been an underling of Rothstein's, the head of the real estate syndicate that owned the building where Hubbard, White & Willis was located. The syndicate had suddenly withdrawn from the negotiations for the expensive long-term lease and was going to let the current lease lapse.

This meant that it would now make much more financial sense to merge the firm with Perelli and move into the Midtown firm's space.

Damn . . . Burdick clenched his fist.

"*Clayton's* telling *Jews* what to do with their Manhattan real estate?" Stanley barked. There was no need to lower his voice. The only non-Protestant sect represented in the club was Papist and none of the three Catholic members was here tonight. "How the hell did he do it?"

Burdick didn't know and didn't care but, as his wife had admitted not long ago, he couldn't help but admire Clayton. He hadn't thought that the partner even *knew* about the negotiations, let alone that he could put together some bribery—or extortion—plan to sabotage the lease this quickly.

Now, with the lease gone, all Burdick had left to use as leverage was urging McMillan Holdings to take a stand against the merger.

"I'm going down to Florida tomorrow," he said.

"McMillan?" Stanley asked.

Burdick nodded. "Their board meeting. I'll do whatever I have to to make sure they let Perelli know where they stand."

"That'll help some, I guess." Then Stanley muttered something that Burdick couldn't hear.

"What was that?" the partner asked him.

"I said, 'Remember the days when all we had to do was get clients and practice law?' "

"No," Burdick replied sourly. "That must've been before my time."

CHAPTER TWENTY

The law professor and legal philosopher Karl Llewellyn wrote a book called *The Bramble Bush*. The foliage in his title was a metaphor for the study and practice of law and his meaning was that this field, in all its many incarnations, is endless. In that book he wrote that "the only cure for law is more law," by which he was suggesting that you cannot dabble at the profession. When you are overwhelmed by the case, the business deal, the jurisprudential study, when you are exhausted, when you cannot bear the thought of proceeding one more moment, you can find salvation only by pushing forward, deeper into the tangle.

The law, he was suggesting, is an infinitely complex, uncompromising mistress.

Wendall Clayton thought of Professor Llewellyn's writing now as he sat across his desk from Randy Simms, late Sunday morning at the firm.

The smarmy young lawyer had just delivered troubling news. They had managed to sabotage the long-term lease that Burdick had been trying to put into place. But some of the old-guard partners at the firm were refusing to vote in favor of the merger. Burdick's win in the St. Agnes trial had heartened them and a bit of cheerleading on Bill Stanley's part had gotten them to switch their votes back to Burdick's camp.

Which meant that there was now some doubt that Clayton would have enough votes, come Tuesday, for the merger to be approved.

"How close is it?" Clayton asked.

"Pretty evenly balanced. Right down the middle, more or less."

"Then we have to make it less 'pretty even.' "

"Yessir."

"Stay on call. I'll be right back." Clayton rose and walked down the stairs to the paralegal pen.

To his surprise he found Sean Lillick was not alone.

The pretty boy was standing with a girl, another paralegal in the firm.

Clayton didn't understand what Lillick saw in her. She seemed shy, timid, unassertive. A bit, well, rotund too.

A consolation fuck at best.

When they saw him coming they stepped apart and Clayton noticed, though he pretended not to, that they'd been fighting about something. The girl's eyes were red from crying and Lillick's otherwise pasty face was flushed.

"Sean," the partner said.

The boy nodded. "Hi, Wendall."

"And you are? . . ."

"Carrie Mason."

"Ah."

"I hope I'm not interrupting anything," Clayton said.

"No. Not at all."

Carrie said quickly, "We were just talking."

"Ah. Talking. Well, if you'll excuse us, Carrie. Sean and I have some business."

Neither of them moved. Lillick looked at the floor. Carrie cleared her throat and said, "We've got some documents to copy. For the SCI deal."

Clayton didn't say anything. He just stared from one to the other.

Lillick said to her, "Why don't you get started."

She hesitated then hefted an armful of papers and walked moodily down the hall on her solid legs.

Clayton said, "You'll be at my party tonight, won't you, Carrie? My place in Connecticut."

The girl looked back and said to the partner, "Yeah, I'll be there."

"I'm so pleased," the partner said, smiling.

When she'd vanished, Clayton said to the young man, "We've got some problems. About the vote. I need some information. Good information. And I need it fast. The vote's day after tomorrow."

It was, of course, the paralegals—and the support staff—who had the best access to information at the firm. As with the butlers and maids on *Upstairs, Downstairs,* the higher echelons of the firm babbled like schoolgirls in front of the hired help at Hubbard, White & Willis. This is why Clayton had swooped down on poor Lillick last year and began bribing him for information.

Lillick swallowed and looked down. "I think I've already done enough."

"You've been very helpful," the partner agreed smoothly.

"I don't want to help you anymore." He looked in the direction Carrie had disappeared.

Clayton nodded. There were times to push and times to placate. "I know it's been tough for you. But everything you've done has been for the good of everybody who works here." He rested his hand on the boy's shoulder. "We're very close, Sean, close to winning. And if we win, well, that'll be . . . rewarding for the whole firm, you included."

When the paralegal said nothing more Clayton said, "There've been some defections. I need any unusual phone calls that Burdick might've made. Travel plans. Anything like that. He's a desperate man and desperate men are his enemy's best friends. Know why? Because they make mistakes. You understand that?"

"Yessir."

"You're grasping it, you're committing it to memory?"

"Yes."

"Good. Find something and it'll be worth a lot of money. I mean five-figure money."

Clayton said nothing further but just leveled his eyes at the boy. After thirty seconds Lillick said slowly, "Let me look around. See if I can find something sort of helpful."

"Ah, wonderful," Clayton said. "Actually, though, it really has to be *very* helpful. I don't have any time left for subtleties."

Every color clashed.

Taylor Lockwood looked over the apparel of the crowd milling in the living room of Wendall Clayton's country home in Redding, Connecticut. She saw plaid. She saw lemon yellow with orange. She saw lime shirts with red slacks.

She saw madras!

Her mother had told her about madras: In the ancien régime of the sixties, star-burst tie-dye marked the hippies; madras flagged the nerds.

To be fair, the collision of hues was almost exclusively on the frames of the older lawyers. The younger crowd of associates were in chinos and Izod shirts or skirts and sweaters. A lot of pearls, a lot of blond hair, a lot of pretty faces.

It was Sunday, around five-thirty, and Reece and Taylor had cruise-controlled their way here along the wide parkway in a car he'd rented. They had found Clayton's place after asking directions twice and, after they'd parked, had walked into the house without knocking. They stood, unnoticed, in the entrance foyer.

"We're overdressed," she observed.

Reece pulled his tie off and stuffed it in his pocket. "How do I look?"

"Like an overdressed lawyer who lost his tie."

He said, "I'll take the first floor. You take the second."

"Okay," she said quickly. Then she hesitated.

"What's wrong?" Reece asked.

"We're kind of like burglars, aren't we?"

He recited quickly, "Burglary is entering a dwelling without permission with the intention of committing a felony." He gave her a fast smile. "We've got permission to be here. Therefore, it's not burglary."

If you say so . . .

Reece disappeared and Taylor found the bar. The bartender was doing a big business with mugs of sweet, mint-laced Southsiders. Taylor shook her head at the offered drink and got a glass of Stag's Leap Chardonnay. Before the first sip a man was right beside her, gripping her arm.

Thom Sebastian.

She shivered, hearing in her mind's ear Sebastian's comment to Bosk, his warning not to get too interested in her, the dangers it implied.

"Hey," the pudgy associate said, "you recovered okay?"

"Recovered?"

"From a night out with me."

"Nothing to report to any official governmental bodies."

"Excellent." His eyes were evasive, almost as if he had something he wanted to confess to her. After a glance around the room he asked casually, "You doing anything tomorrow night?"

What was on his mind?

"I think I've got some time free."

"Maybe dinner?"

"Sure," she said.

"Great. I'll call you." He gazed at her, expressionless, for a moment and she believed suddenly, as she looked into his cryptic eyes, that if he *was* the thief he wanted to come clean with her.

And if he confessed and produced the note? What then? she wondered.

Reece or her father . . . well, they would, of course, destroy Sebastian's life: force him into leaving the practice of law in New York. But *her* inclination would be to reward a confession with anonymity and to let him go.

But, as she watched him walk down a corridor in search of more liquor, she realized that she was getting ahead of herself.

Find the note first, then we'll consider justice. . . .

Taylor made her way through the hallway. As she did she noticed an older woman scrutinizing her carefully, with a look of almost amused curiosity. The woman reminded her of Ada Smith, Bosk's mother. Taylor tried to avoid her but once their eyes met and held, she felt the power of a silent summons and she remained where she was as the woman approached.

"You're Taylor Lockwood," the woman said.

"Yes."

"I'm Vera Burdick, Donald's wife."

"Nice to see you," Taylor said recalling the name from the newspaper article her father had just faxed to her. They shook hands. The woman must have seen the surprise in Taylor's face—surprise that the Burdick camp would be represented in enemy territory. Vera said, "Donald had business tonight. He asked me to come in his stead."

"It's a nice party," Taylor said.

"Wendall was kind enough to donate his house for the evening. He does the same for the summer associates in July. It's a sort of fresh-air outing for lawyers."

Silence filled the small space between them.

Taylor broke the stalemate with "Well, I think I'll mingle a little."

Vera Burdick nodded, as if her examination of Taylor had produced all the information she needed. "A pleasure seeing you again, dear. And good luck."

Taylor watched the partner's wife join a cluster of associates nearby. *Good luck?* As the woman's voice rose in laughter Taylor started again for the stairs. She'd gotten halfway across the hall when she heard another voice—a man's voice, soft, directed at her. "And who are you again?"

Her neck hair bristled.

Taylor turned to look into the face of Wendall Clayton.

She was, at first, surprised that he was only a couple of inches taller than she. Then she noticed that he was much more handsome up close than he seemed from a distance.

And then her mind went blank. For three or four seconds she was utterly without a conscious thought. Clayton's eyes were the reason. They were the eyes of a man who knew how to control people, a man to whom it would be excruciating to say no, even if he made his demands with silence.

A man exactly like her father.

"Pardon?" Taylor asked.

He smiled. "I asked who you were again?"

She thought: The same person I've always been, no "again" about it, hotshot. Then she got lost in his eyes once more and didn't try a snappy comeback. She said, "Taylor Lockwood."

"I'm Wendall Clayton."

She said, "Yes, I know. I'd thank you for inviting me, Wendall, but I'm afraid I crashed. Are you going to kick me out?" She found a smile somewhere and slipped it on, reminding herself to resist the urge to call him "Mr. Clayton."

"On the contrary, you're probably the only person in this crew worth talking to."

"I don't think I'd go that far."

He took her arm. She had never been touched in this way. His grip wasn't a disciplinarian's or a friend's or a lover's. In the contraction of the muscles was a consuming pressure of authority. As if he'd squeezed her soul. After a moment he lowered his hand.

Clayton said, "Would you like a tour of the house?"

"Sure.

"It's an authentic 1780s. I—"

"Taylor! You're here!" Carrie Mason trotted up to them.

"Hello, Carrie."

"Welcome." Clayton took Carrie Mason's hard-pumping hand. "Sean's not here?"

Carrie hesitated and said, "No, he had something else to do." It seemed there was a darkness in her face.

"Ah, maybe one of his performances."

"Carrie," Taylor said, "Wendall was just going to give me a tour of his house. Join us."

"Sure," the chubby girl said.

Clayton didn't appreciate that they were now a three-some but his reaction vanished as Vera Burdick walked past.

The woman stopped and extended a hand to Clayton.

He smiled and shook it graciously, clasping hers in both of his. "Vera. How good to see you again. Donald made it, I hope."

"Unfortunately not. That fund-raiser at City Hall?"

"When the mayor summons you—" Clayton said.

"The governor actually," she corrected.

"—you better go."

Taylor felt the tension between them like sparking wires. Vera Burdick clearly detested the partner, and while Clayton obviously returned the feeling, it was she who easily held his eye and the lawyer who looked defensively away as he made trivial conversation.

In this tableau Taylor recognized a truth about Clayton: While the partner knew men and how to handle them, he was only comfortable with women he could sexualize or control as his lessers.

She was nearly queasy, observing a man like this feeling threatened—a powerful man and, considering that he might have engineered the theft of the New Amsterdam note, one who was quite dangerous.

"I'll leave you to your friends," Vera said, the disdain visible like breath on a cold spring day. A glance at Taylor and Carrie. A meaningless smile.

Clayton said, "I hope Donald enjoys the fund-raiser."

███████

"Donald, you're white as snow. Damn it, man, you've got to get more fresh air. Brought your racket, I hope?"

Burdick leaned against the railing of the penthouse suite in the Fleetwood Hotel in Miami Beach and looked at the cool disk of the setting sun. "More business than pleasure today, I'm afraid, Steve."

Burdick was tired. The firm's private Canadair jet hadn't been available—some maintenance problem—and he'd had to fly down to Miami in a commercial airliner. First class, of course, but he'd still had to stand in lines and then there'd been a delay on the runway that put him an hour off schedule.

He'd arrived exhausted but had ordered the car service to bring him directly here before checking in to a room.

Steve Nordstrom, shaking martinis like an ace bartender, was the president of McMillan Holdings. He was thick and square, with gray hair trimmed so impeccably it might have been injection-molded in the company's Teterboro plant, and was wearing a purple Izod shirt and white slacks.

"Drink?"

Burdick didn't want alcohol but he knew he would take the offered glass from Nordstrom, a man of fifty, whose face was already in bloom from the damaged blood vessels.

"How's the board meeting going?" Burdick asked.

Nordstrom licked martini off his finger. He grinned happily. "We're cutting a melon this year, Donald. Three sixty-three a share."

"Ah," Burdick said approvingly.

"You read the *Journal,* you read the *Times*—everybody's cratering but us. Hey, tomorrow, we're meeting on the new industry association. You want to sit in?"

"Can't. But tell your people to watch what they say. I told you that Justice is heating up again and Antitrust is looking at price-fixing. Don't even mention dollars. No numbers at all. Remember what happened in '72."

"Always looking out for your client, Donald?" Nordstrom's question contained the silent modifiers "biggest" and "most lucrative."

They sat down at a table. The bellboy, who had been waiting patiently, brought out lobster salads in half pineapples and set them on the balcony table. The men ate the salad and raisin rolls—the lawyer struggling to down the food, which he had no appetite for—while they talked about vacations and family and house prices and the administration in Washington.

When they were finished eating, Burdick accepted another martini and pushed away from the table. "Which of our boys is down here helping you with the board meeting, Steve?"

"From Hubbard, White? Stan Johannsen is here and Thom Sebastian did most of the advance work last week. He's covering the front in New York. I understand he didn't make partner. What happened? He's a good man."

Burdick looked out over the flat scenery at a line of cars shooting flashes of glare from the expressway. After a moment he realized he had been asked a question and said, "I don't remember exactly about Thom."

He wished Bill Stanley were with him. Or Vera. He wanted allies nearby.

Nordstrom frowned. "But that's not what you're here for, is it? About the board meeting."

"No, Steve, it's not. . . ." Burdick stood and paced, hands clasped behind his back. "Hubbard, White's been doing your legal work for, let's see, thirty-five years?"

"About that. Before my time."

"Steve, I'd ask you to keep what I'm going to tell you between you and me and Ed Gliddick. For the time being, at least. No bullshit between us."

"Never has been." The businessman looked the partner over coyly. "This's about the merger, I assume?"

"Yes. And there's more to it than meets the eye." Burdick explained to him about Clayton and his planned massacre after the merger was completed.

Nordstrom said, "So you'd be out? That's crap. You've made the firm what it is. You *are* Hubbard, White."

Burdick laughed. "I hate to put it this way, Steve, but McMillan is our largest single source of revenue."

"Well, you give us good service. And we're happy to pay for it."

"So when you or Ed talk, partners at the firm listen."

"And you want me to talk against the merger."

"It'd be bad for you and bad for dozens of other clients. Wendall Clayton has no vision of what a law firm should be. He wants to turn us into some kind of assembly line. Profit's all he thinks about."

Nordstrom picked up a fat piece of lobster and sucked it clean of dressing, then chewed and swallowed it slowly. "What's the time frame?"

"Clayton ramrodded the merger vote through early. It'll be this Tuesday."

"Day after tomorrow? Fuck me," Nordstrom said. "That man is crazy." He probed for more lobster. He settled for raisins. "Ed's in a dinner meeting right now but he should be free in an hour or so. I'll have him call and we'll have after-dinner drinks. About ten or so? By the pool over there. Don't worry, Donald. We'll work *something* out."

CHAPTER TWENTY-ONE

▬▬▬ Clayton moved them quickly through his old manse like a tour guide goosed by a tight schedule.

It was a rambling house—big, though the rooms themselves were small and cockeyed. Beams were uneven, floorboards sprung. Much of the furniture was painted in drab Colonial colors. The gewgaws were of hammered tin and wicker and carved wood.

He led them upstairs. Taylor pretended to be studying portraits of horses, Shaker furniture and armoires while in fact she looked for places where he might have hidden information about Hanover & Stiver or the note. She glanced into a small room that seemed to be an office and saw a desk.

"Are you with us, Taylor?" Clayton asked and she hurried to join them. He continued the tour. "...Mark Twain's house, the house he died in, isn't far from here."

"Are you a Son of the American Revolution?" Carrie asked.

Clayton spoke with a feigned indignity that rested on real pride. "The Revolutionaries? They were *newcomers*. My family was one of the original settlers of Nieuw Nederlandt. We came over in 1628."

"Are you Dutch?"

"No. My ancestors were Huguenots."

Taylor said, "I always got those mixed up in school—the Huguenots and the Hottentots."

Clayton smiled coldly.

Ooooh, doesn't like potshots into the family tree.

"The Huguenots were French Protestants," he explained. "They were badly persecuted. In the 1620s Cardinal Richelieu ordered a siege of La Rochelle, a large Huguenot town. My family escaped and settled here. New Rochelle, New York, by the way, is named after La Rochelle."

Carrie asked, "What did your ancestors do when they got here?"

"There was considerable prejudice against the Huguenots, even here. We were barred from many businesses. My family became artisans. Silversmiths mostly. Paul Revere was one of us. But my family were always better merchants than craftsmen. . . . We moved into manufacturing and then finance though that field had largely been preempted by . . . other groups." For a moment he looked wily and Taylor suspected he was suppressing an opinion about early Jewish settlers.

"My family," he continued, "ended up in Manhattan and stayed there. Upper East Side. I was born within a five-block radius of my father's and grandfather's birthplaces."

That touched Taylor. "You don't see that much anymore. Today, everybody's spread all over the world."

"You shouldn't let that happen," Clayton said sincerely. "Your family history is all you have. You should keep your ancestry and be proud of it. This year I'm steward of the French Society. . . ."

Carrie, of the front row in law school, blinked. "Oh, I've heard of that. Sure."

Clayton said to Taylor, "After the Holland Society it's the most prestigious of the hereditary societies in New York."

The chubby paralegal was impressed but another need intruded. "Say, Mr. Clayton, where's the little girls' room?"

Oh, honey, don't fail me now. . . . Taylor wanted Carrie to keep Clayton busy, giving her a chance to take a look in the office.

But he said, "We've been having problems with the one up here. Why don't you go downstairs. We'll meet you there in a bit."

Carrie trotted off, and it was then that Taylor realized they had ended the tour at Clayton's bedroom. The room was dramatic, filled with Ralph Lauren rust and red florals, English-hunt green, brass. This was the room of a nobleman.

Beware the Jabberwock, my son. . . .

Clayton closed the door. "You're very attractive."

Taylor sighed. Doesn't go much for subtlety, does he? She said, "I should be getting downstairs."

He took her hand. To her astonishment she let him and the next thing she knew some undefinable pressure overwhelmed her. She found herself sitting on the bed next to him.

"Wendall . . ."

"Look at me."

Taylor did, feeling a growing power from the partner, a magnet tugging at her soul—and at everything around her. It seemed to Taylor that her hair actually stirred in this invisible wind.

She thought of the playing-card soldiers swirling around Alice. *Beware the . . .*

"Wendall—"

"I want to tell you one thing," he said calmly. "This has to be completely clear. Whatever happens—or doesn't happen—has no affect on your career at Hubbard, White. Is that understood?"

She pulled her arm away. "I don't even know you. I've never even spoken to you before." But she was shocked to hear that her words seemed weak, as if she were wavering.

He shrugged. "Spoken to me? I don't want to have a discussion. I want to make love to you."

There was no physical impediment to her leaving. He wasn't even standing in her way. One foot, then the other, and she could troop right out the door. Yet she didn't.

Clayton crossed his legs. He brushed the tassel of his hair off his forehead.

"I have commitments," she explained.

No, no, no... Don't say that. You're meeting his argument. It's like making excuses to your father. Tell him to fuck off. Forget who he is. Forget the case. Just say it now: Fuck off. Fuck. Off.

Say it!

"Well, Taylor, we all have commitments. That's not really the issue."

She felt her throat thicken.

Don't swallow. It's a weakness.

She swallowed. "We don't even know each other."

Clayton smiled, shaking his head. "Hey, look, I don't want to marry you. I want to make love to you. That's all. Two adults. I'm telling you that you're an attractive woman."

"I have to go."

"It's not a compliment," he continued. "It's an observation. I know how to make love to women. I'm good at it. Don't you find me attractive?"

"That's not the point—"

"So you do?" he said quickly. He stroked the bed and repeated, "I want to make love with you. Harmless and simple."

Taylor smiled. "You don't want to make love at all. You want to fuck me."

"No!" he whispered harshly. Then he smiled. "I want us to fuck *together*."

Mistake, girl. He likes dirty talk.

"Look." He waved his hand in front of his crotch like a magician. He was erect. "You did this. Not everybody does."

She found herself leaning back, first her palms on the rich bedspread, then her elbows.

"Do you know the first thing I noticed about you?" Clayton whispered, touching a renegade strand of her hair. "Your eyes. Even from across the room."

She rolled onto her side. She glanced down between his legs and said, "You're a pretty gifted man, Wendall. I would have thought that with all the excitement at the firm you'd be more distracted."

He hesitated then asked, " 'Excitement'?"

"The merger."

He didn't move for a moment. She'd thrown him off stride. He laughed seductively. "I've got a pretty big appetite."

Taylor scanned his face, which was no more than twelve inches from hers. "I read somewhere that hunters make love before the hunt," she said. "Sex is supposed to steady the hand." She shook her head. "Me, I think it's dissipating."

"Ah, dissipate me, dissipate me...." But the words fell short of their intended playfulness and he sounded like a college boy making an inappropriate joke. And suddenly the balance of this contest shifted—barely—to her.

He whispered, "Lie down, put your head on the pillow." He spoke in a mesmerizing voice and Taylor was suddenly aware of his penis pressing through layers of cloth against her leg. Clayton said, "I have some toys."

"Do you?"

"I can make you feel very, very good. Like you've never felt before."

She laughed and more power slipped to her side of the board. When the spell wasn't working, his lines began to sound silly. She asked, "Why do you hate Donald Burdick?"

"I'm not interested in talking about him. Or about the merger."

"Why not?"

"I'd rather make love to you."

"The merger is all everybody's talking about."

"Are you worried about your job? You won't have to be. I promise you that," he said.

"I haven't worried about a job for years. I'm mostly just curious why you dislike Donald Burdick so much."

She sat up. Clayton seemed befuddled. The evidence of his passion hadn't diminished but he seemed uncertain—as if he had met and overcome all types of reluctance in seducing women over the years yet had suddenly run into a new defense: a barrage of questions.

"Go on," she said. "Tell me why."

"Well," Clayton finally offered, "I don't dislike Donald personally. He's one of the most charming men I know. Socially, I admire him. He's a fine representative of old money."

"The rumor is that you want to destroy him."

Clayton considered his answer. "I hear lots of rumors at the firm. I suspect those that I hear aren't any more accurate than the ones you hear. The merger is solely business. Destroying people is far too time-consuming...."

Finally the partner's spell broke completely.

Taylor Lockwood rolled off the bed and ran her fingers through her hair. "You should go downstairs, I think. You are the host, after all."

Clayton tried one last time. "But..." His hand strayed across the bulging front of his slacks.

"You know, Wendall," Taylor said, smiling, "that's the best compliment I've had in months. Does a girl's heart good. But if you'll excuse me."

████

After leaving the bedroom Taylor walked into the upstairs bathroom (which, she noticed, seemed to be in perfect working order). There she waited until Clayton was out of sight. Then she slipped into his office.

Inside, in addition to the desk, were an armchair, a Victorian tea serving table, several floor lamps, two large armoires; there were no closets. She turned on a lamp and pushed the door partially closed.

The desk was unlocked. Its cubbyholes were filled with hundreds of slips of paper. Bank statements, canceled checks, memos, notes, personal bills, receipts. Taylor sighed at the volume of material she'd have to look through then sat in the red-leather chair and started going through the items one by one.

She'd been doing this for fifteen minutes when she heard a voice in the doorway say, "Ah, here you are. . . ."

The man speaking was Wendall Clayton.

CHAPTER TWENTY-TWO

Taylor spun around and stood up, knocking a stack of papers to the floor. The sheets spread like spilled water.

Wendall Clayton was outside the door, talking to someone else. Just out of his line of sight, she reached toward the papers then heard Clayton say, "Let's go inside here for a minute, shall we?"

Desperately she kicked the papers under the desk; they disappeared—except for the corner of one letter. She reached down for it but the door was swinging open. Taylor leapt behind the largest armoire. She pressed herself flat against the wall, her head pressing painfully into the hard, cold plaster. Another voice spoke. A man's voice, one she recognized. Ralph Dudley asked, "What is it exactly you wanted to see me about, Wendall?"

The door closed. Clayton said, "Have a seat."

"Is something wrong?"

Clayton's voice was curious. "I don't remember this light being on."

Taylor eased back harder against the wall.

Silence. What were they doing? Could they see the tips of her shoes, the corner of the paper under the desk? Was the chair she'd sat in still warm?

Clayton said, "Ralph, you're part of, I guess I'd call it, the old guard, the old-boy network at the firm."

"I go back a ways, that's true."

"You and Donald started at about the same time, didn't you?"

"Bill Stanley, too. And Lamar Fredericks."

"I see you at the DAC with Joe Wilkins and Porter quite a bit, don't I?"

"Yes, we go there often. What do you—"

"Enjoying yourself tonight, are you?"

"Quite, Wendall." The old partner's voice was filled with anxiety as Clayton asked these pleasant questions with a slightly sadistic edge.

Silence. Feet shifting.

Clayton continued. "Young people here tonight. Lots of young people. It's funny, isn't it, Ralph? When I was their age I was making . . . fifty, seventy-five dollars a week. These youngsters make ninety thousand dollars a year. Amazing."

"Wendall, is there something you want?"

"Ralph, I want you to vote in favor of the merger on Tuesday. That's what I want."

A long pause. The old man's voice was trembling when he said, "I can't, Wendall. You know that. If the merger goes through I lose my job. Donald loses his; a lot of people do."

"You'll be well provided for, Ralph. A good severance."

"I can't. I can't afford to retire."

"No, of course not. You've got expenses."

Dudley sounded very cautious now. "That's right. It costs a lot to live here."

"Manhattan . . . most expensive city on earth."

"I'm sorry, Wendall. I'll have to say no to the merger."

Silence again. Taylor imagined Dudley's thoughts racing to catch up with Clayton's. Taylor's, however, had already arrived at their sad destination.

"You don't mind blunt talk?" Clayton asked.

"Of course not. I appreciate candor and—"

"If you don't vote in favor of the merger I'll go public with your affair with a sixteen-year-old girl."

The choked laugh didn't mask the despair. "What are you talking about?"

"Ralph, I respect your intelligence; I hope you'll respect mine. The little whore, the one you dress up and parade around as your granddaughter, which makes it all the more disgusting. You—"

Taylor heard the slap of a blow, a laugh of surprise from Clayton, feet dancing in the awkward shuffle of wrestling. Finally: a sad, desperate groan from Dudley—a sound filled with pain and hate and hopelessness.

Clayton laughed again. "Really, Ralph...Are you all right? There, sit down now. Are you hurt?"

"Don't touch me," Dudley said, his voice cracking. The sounds of the older man's sobbing echoed softly in the room.

Clayton said patiently, "Let's not be emotional. There's no reason for me to tell anyone. Let's negotiate a little bit. You're the firm's charmer, aren't you? You're suave, debonaire. You're a holdout from the days when a lawyer's manners were as important as his intelligence. So, now, how's this? You and three of your cronies switch your votes in favor of the merger and I won't share your secret."

"Three others?"

"Say, Joe, Porter, pick somebody else. But—here's the good part—you bring me any *more* and I'll kick in fifty thousand each to your severance package. That should keep you in teenage pussy for another year or so."

"You're vile," Dudley spat out.

"More vile than you?" Clayton asked. "I wonder. The vote's day after tomorrow, Ralph. Why don't you think about it." Clayton's was the voice of luxurious moderation. "Just think about it. It's your decision. Come on, go downstairs, have a drink. Relax."

"If you only understood—"

Clayton's voice cut through the room like a knife. "Oh, but that's the point, Ralph. I can't understand. And no one else will either."

The door opened. Two pairs of feet receded. Both slowly. One pair in triumph, one in despair, but the sound they made was the same.

■■■■■■■

Still in the quiet den Taylor was concentrating on a single noise.

Rhythmic and soft.

She had stayed here, hiding behind the armoire, after the partners had left because Clayton had remained upstairs; she'd heard his voice from nearby.

Then after five minutes or so the sound began. What is that?

A voice chanting? Primitive music?

She couldn't place it at first. It seemed very familiar but she associated it with an entirely different place.

Rhythmic and soft.

No, couldn't be. . . .

She walked to the far wall and pressed her head against the plaster again. The sound was coming from the other side—Clayton's bedroom.

Oh, Taylor realized. *That's* the sound. Of course. Not one voice, but two.

The nature of the activity didn't surprise Taylor much, considering what she now knew about Wendall Clayton. What did surprise her, however, was that the other participant was Carrie Mason, who was contributing half of the sound effects.

"Fuck me, fuck me, fuck me. . . . I'm almost there. . . . Yeah, yeah, yeah. . . ."

Carrie may have finished quickly but it took Clayton considerably longer. Long enough, in fact, for Taylor to go through the partner's desk carefully. The sound track conveniently helped her gauge how much time she had.

She found only one thing that interested her: an invoice

for a security firm. The bill was for ongoing services, which had begun last month. The job description was "As directed by client."

She debated stealing it. What would her detective friend John Silbert Hemming do? He'd use a spy camera, she guessed. But ill-equipped Taylor Lockwood did the next best thing: She carefully copied all the information and put the invoice back.

Downstairs she noticed the crowd had dwindled considerably, as you'd expect for a Sunday night party. Only the hard-core partiers remained. Thom Sebastian, for instance, who swooped in for another sloppy bear hug. She ducked away from it. He said good-bye and reiterated his dinner invitation for tomorrow. Taylor ambled through the house, aiming toward the buffet and listening to the snatches of muted, often drunken, conversation.

He's going to do it. For sure. Next month, we're going to be Hubbard, White, Willis, Sullivan & Perelli.

You're out to lunch, dude. No way'll Burdick let it happen.

Do you realize the vote is Tuesday? Day after tomorrow.

You hear about the detective that was going through Burdick's Swiss accounts?

You hear Burdick had somebody check Clayton's law review article to see if he plagiarized?

That's bullshit.

You want to talk bullshit, this merger is bullshit. Nobody's getting any work done.

Where's Donald?

He doesn't need to be here. He sent Himmler instead.

Who?

His wife. See, Burdick would charm a man out of his balls; Vera'd just cut 'em off. You know the stories about her, don't you? Lady Macbeth . . .

Taylor noticed that Burdick's wife was no longer here.

She then surveyed the long table where there'd once sat mounds of caviar, roast beef, steak tartare and sesame chicken. All that now remained was broccoli.

Taylor Lockwood hated broccoli.

On the patio deck of the Fleetwood Hotel's penthouse on the Miami Beach strip Ed Gliddick sent a golf ball near the putting cup embedded in the roof's AstroTurf.

"Hell," he said of the miss and looked at the trim young man near him, who watched the shot without emotion. Standing ramrod-straight, he offered Gliddick no false compliments and said only, "I play tennis, not golf."

The man was Randall Simms III, Wendall Clayton's protégé. It was he who'd pirated the Hubbard, White & Willis chartered jet to beat Donald Burdick down to Florida to meet with the executives of McMillan Holdings.

While Burdick himself was cooling his heels with the second-in-command of the company, Steve Nordstrom, Simms had been meeting with Gliddick, the chairman of the board and CEO of McMillan.

McMillan was a company that did nothing but own other companies, which either manufactured obscure industrial parts or provided necessary though obscure services to other businesses or in turn owned other companies or portions of them. The vagaries of this structure and function, however, were not to suggest that Gliddick didn't know how to satisfy a market need when he saw one. McMillan was consistently in the top twenty of the most profitable companies in the world.

At sixty-five, Gliddick was stooped and paunchy amidships. His ruddy skin was wrinkled from years of sun on golf courses and tennis courts around the world. Sparse gray hair, a hook of a nose.

So he said to Simms, "Wendall didn't come down to see me. He sent you instead."

Simms said nothing.

Gliddick held up a hand. "Which means only one thing. You're the muscle, right?"

Unsmiling, Simms folded his arms and watched Gliddick miss another easy putt. "Wendall wanted a little distance between himself and what I'm going to say to you."

"This's all about that fucking merger, isn't it?"

"I'd suggest we go inside," Simms said. "Somebody could have an antenna trained on us. They really make those things, you know. They're not just in the movies."

"I know."

Gliddick walked into the room, shut the window and drew the curtains. Simms mixed whiskey sours for them both. Gliddick wondered how this man, whom he'd never met, had known that this was his drink.

The chairman sipped the sweet concoction. "You know Donald Burdick's meeting with Steve Nordstrom right now."

"We know."

We.

"So what is it that you want, I mean, Wendall wants?"

"We want you to let it be known around the firms—ours and John Perelli's—that you want the merger to go through."

"Why would we *not* want it to go through?"

Simms said bluntly, "Donald and his cronies won't be there afterward."

"Ah." Gliddick nodded. "I see."

"You might feel some loyalty to him," Simms said.

"Fuck, I do feel loyalty to him."

"Of course you do. You've been friends for years. But putting that aside for a moment, let's talk about why you *would* want the firms to merge," Simms said.

This is one slick boy—I like him, Gliddick thought, but immediately gave up the idea of trying to wrest him away from Hubbard, White to work for McMillan. Wendall Clayton was not somebody you stole employees from.

Simms continued, "We've gone over your billings, Ed. Burdick's robbing you blind. Your legal costs are totally out of control. You're paying two hundred bucks an hour for first-year associates who know shit. You're paying for limo deliveries when messengers can take public transportation. You're paying premium bonuses for routine legal work. If you help the merger along we'll pare your expenses by an easy five million a year."

"Five?"

"Five. And if the merger goes through, Perelli can take over your labor law work. Right now you've got Mavern, Simpson handling it and, frankly, they're idiots. They didn't do shit to keep the unions out of your subs' Oregon and Washington State operations. Perelli's the toughest labor lawyer in New York. He'll fuck your unions in the ass."

Gliddick shook his head. "Donald was on our board for I don't know how long. He's got friends all over the company. There're a lot of people won't take it kindly that we've sold him out."

" 'Kindly'?" Simms said the word as if it were in a foreign language. "Well, loyalty's important. But it works both ways. I'd think you'd have to *earn* loyalty. And do you think a lawyer who misses a takeover plan against his client deserves it?"

"A . . . What're you talking about?"

"There's a rumor. . . . Only a rumor but Wendall and I think it's valid."

"We're always hearing that. Hell, we beat projections every quarter last year. Everybody'd love to acquire us."

"But does everybody contact your institutional investors on the sly?"

Gliddick's glass froze halfway to his mouth. "Who?"

"GCI in Toronto."

"Weinraub, that fucking Jew prick." A glance to Simms to see if the young man was Semitic but the results of the scan came back reassuringly Aryan. "I saw him just last week in London. He gave me the great stone face."

Simms continued, "We're thinking four months till a tender offer. If you wait you'll pay a takeover firm a million or two to defend. Perelli can preempt it for a quarter of that. And he can handle it in a way that your stockholders and key employees won't get nervous and bail out. That's what he does best."

"Donald doesn't know about it?"

"Nope. We found out through Perelli.

He finished his drink. Simms poured another.

"Randy, I don't know. I can't argue with what you're saying, with the numbers. It's a moral decision. I don't like moral decisions. Maybe—"

There was a knock on the door. A young woman. Blond, about five-two, wearing a short leather miniskirt and tight white blouse, walked into the suite.

"Mr. Simms, I've got the file you asked for."

"Thank you, Jean." He took a thick manila folder. "Jean, this is Mr. Gliddick."

They shook hands. Gliddick's eyes skimmed the white silk over her breasts, the lacy bra clearly visible beneath.

"Jean's an assistant with a firm we use down here occasionally."

"Nice to meet you, Jean."

Simms tapped the folder. "There's a lot of other material in there about how the merger'd be good for your company, Ed." He looked at his watch. "Say, I've got a conference call scheduled now. I'll make it from my room so I don't bother you. Look over that stuff, think about what I'm saying."

"Sure," Gliddick said, eyes still scanning Jean's figure. She smiled broadly at the paunchy businessman.

"Say, Jean," Simms said, "you know Miami, right?

"Well, now, I've lived here all my life" came the lilting accent.

"Then maybe you could help Mr. Gliddick figure out a place where he and I could go listen to some music. Jazz or Cuban or something."

"I'd be happy to." The young woman sat on the bed and picked up an entertainment guide. Her skirt hiked up high. "If that's all right with him."

"I'd appreciate your input," Gliddick said.

Simms said, "We're off-duty now, Jean, how 'bout you fix yourself a drink. And another one for Mr. Gliddick too."

"Thanks, Randy. I believe I will."

"I'll be back in about an hour," Simms said.

"That'd be fine," Gliddick replied, setting the file on the table and watching Jean scoot pertly off the bed and walk to the bar. Somehow her shoes had come off in the process.

Moral decision...

As Simms was about to step through the door, Gliddick said, "One thing, Randy?"

The tall lawyer turned.

"Maybe you could call first—before coming back to the room?"

"Not a problem, Ed."

At 10 P.M., as Reece was accelerating south onto the highway that would take them from Clayton's Connecticut home back to the city, Taylor stretched out in the reclining seat of the rented Lincoln.

She was listening to the moan of the transmission. The flabby suspension swayed her nearly to sleep. She'd told him about Clayton's blackmailing Dudley and then about the invoice she'd found.

"'Client-directed' security services?" Reece asked. Then he nodded. "A euphemism for industrial espionage. Good job, finding that. How much was it for?"

"Two thousand a month."

"That's pretty low for stealing a note. Maybe it's for spying on people for the merger."

"Did you hear the talk at the party? My God, these are first-year associates and all they were talking about was the merger. Wendall's out on a limb. If he doesn't get it through he's lost a lot of credibility...."

Reece laughed. "Ha, if he doesn't get the merger through he's lost his *job*...." He looked over and caught her in the midst of another huge yawn. "You okay?"

"I used to sleep."

"I tried it once," Reece said, shrugging. "It wears off."

He reached over and began massaging her neck.

"Oh, that's nice...." She closed her eyes. "You ever made love in a car?"

"Never have."

"I never have either. I've never even been to a drive-in movie."

Reece said, "One time when I was in high school, I— Jesus!"

A huge jolt. Taylor's eyes snapped open and she saw a white car directly in front of them. It'd veered into their lane. Reece swerved onto the shoulder but the Lincoln slipped off the flat surface and started down a steep embankment.

"Mitchell!" Taylor screamed and threw her arms up as trees and plants raced at them at seventy miles an hour. The undercarriage scraping and groaning, metal and plastic supports popping apart. Then brush and reeds were flashing past the car's windows.

Reece called, "That car, that car! He ran us off the road! He ran us—"

He was braking, trying to grip the wheel as it spun furiously back and forth, the front tires buffeted by rocks and branches. The car slowed as it chewed through the underbrush, the buff-colored rushes and weeds whipping into the windshield.

Taylor's head slammed against the window; she was stunned. She felt nausea and fear and a huge pain in her back.

Then they were slowing as the slope flattened out. The car was still skewing but the wheels started to track, coming under control.... She heard Reece say reverently, "Son of a bitch," and saw him smile as the car started a slow skid on the slippery vegetation. Thirty miles an hour, twenty-five...

"Okay, okay...," Reece muttered to himself. He steered carefully into the skids, braking lightly, regaining control, losing and then regaining it. "Okay, come on," he whispered seductively to the huge Lincoln.

The car slowed to ten miles an hour. Taylor took his arm and whispered, "Oh, Mitchell." They smiled at each other, giddy with relief.

But as she looked at his face his smile vanished.

"God!" He shoved his foot onto the brake with all his weight. Taylor looked forward and she saw the brush disappear as they broke out of the foliage and dropped over a ridge, onto a steep incline that led down to the huge reservoir, a half mile across, its surface broken with choppy waves. The locked wheels slid without resistance along the frost and dewy leaves.

"Taylor!" he called. "We're going in, we're going in!"

With a last huge rocking jolt, the scenery and the distant gray horizon disappeared. A wave of black oily water crashed into the windshield and started coming into the car from a dozen places at once.

CHAPTER TWENTY-THREE

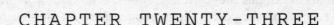At eleven that night, in Miami, the phone in Donald Burdick's hotel room rang.

The partner had been waiting for Ed Gliddick all evening and had fallen asleep, fully dressed, on the couch in his room.

"Yes, hello?" he asked groggily.

"Mr. Burdick?" a woman's voice asked.

"That's right. Who's this?"

"My name's Jean. I'm calling for Mr. Gliddick."

Jean? Burdick wondered. Who was this? Ed Gliddick had had the same secretary, Helen, for twenty years and never traveled anywhere without her.

"Yes, Jean, well, I've been waiting to see Ed all night. Is he all right?"

"Mr. Gliddick asked me to call you and apologize. He won't be able to see you, I'm afraid."

Burdick was angry and disappointed but he said, "Well, it's late anyway. We can meet for breakfast. I'll—"

"Actually, sir, I'm afraid he won't be able to see you at all this trip. He's got meetings nonstop for the next two days and then he's got to get home to Battle Creek."

Burdick closed his eyes and sighed. So, ambushed by Clayton yet again.

"I see. By any chance was there another attorney from Hubbard, White & Willis in town tonight?"

"I wouldn't know, sir."

"Okay," Burdick said wearily, realizing it would be pointless to call Steve Nordstrom—the coward wouldn't even pick up the phone. "If you could deliver a message to Ed for me."

"I'd be happy to."

" 'And you too, Brutus?' Do you have that?"

"Uhm, I do, sir. Will he know what it means?"

"I'm sure he will." Burdick dropped the phone in the cradle then picked it up once more to call his wife.

———

In front of them the huge reservoir extended in faintly lapping waves to the trees on the opposite shore. The moon reflected off the water, broken into a thousand crescents on the textured surface. It would've been quite romantic if they hadn't been wet and freezing.

Taylor Lockwood and Reece sat in the front seat of the rental Lincoln, legs crossed to keep their feet out of the six inches of water that filled the bottom of the car's interior.

After the skid to the bottom of the hill, with its dramatic conclusion—a braking splash like a Disneyland ride—the Lincoln had settled into about eighteen inches of water and stopped sinking.

The reservoir was huge but here, apparently, very shallow.

They'd laughed—edgy and a bit hysterical—but then the humor wore off quickly when they realized that while they could open the door, they'd have a thirty- or forty-foot trek through freezing water up to a deserted road, where they'd have to wait for help with no way to keep warm.

Reece called the police on his cell phone and then they curled their legs up and huddled in their coats.

The dispatcher had assured them that a squad car and rescue truck would be there in ten minutes. But that had been some time ago and, since Reece had been unable to tell them exactly where they'd run off the road, he guessed their rescue might not be imminent even now.

"Who was it?" Taylor asked.

"The thief, I assume. I didn't get a good look at him. Middle-aged guy, white, hat, collar turned up. I didn't even see what kind of car it was. Just a white streak."

"An accident?"

"No way," Reece answered. "He was steering for us."

"Who was at the party—who'd know we were there?"

Reece shrugged. "Thom Sebastian, Dudley. And most of Clayton's little goose-stepping clones, except Randy Simms." Then he fell silent for a moment, finally saying, "I'm thinking it's time to tell the police what happened. Tell them everything."

"No." She shook her head.

"I didn't think this was going to happen, Taylor. I never thought it could turn violent."

She said, "It wouldn't make sense to kill us. That'd bring the police in for sure, and he doesn't want that any more than we do. He didn't know we'd go off the road. He was just scaring us."

Reece considered.

Taylor scooted closer to him. "We're almost there. I can feel it. The trial's day after tomorrow. Let's just hold out until then." She took his head in both her hands. "Just until then?"

"I don't know."

But he was weakening. She repeated, "Just until then," though when she said the words this time, they were not spoken as a question but as a command. He opened his mouth to protest, but she shook her head and touched his lips with her finger.

He leaned close, following the motion of her finger to

her own lips. They kissed hard and their arms wound around each other.

A moment later this embrace was interrupted by several probing flashlights, their fierce halogen beams converging on the car. As Reece and Taylor leapt apart they could hear a laugh and an amused voice. "Whoa, lookit that car! Looks like it's floating. Hank, lookit! I mean, you ever seen anything like that?"

To which another voice replied, "I surely haven't. Not in a month of Sundays."

At lunch on Monday, the day before the New Amsterdam trial, Taylor Lockwood sat in Mc Sorley's Old Ale House in Manhattan and watched John Silbert Hemming down a mug of ale.

He may not've been the traditional private eye who tossed back Scotch on the job but this boy loved his beer. The tall man finished his sixth mug of dark brew and called for three more. "They're small."

True, they were, though Taylor was having trouble with her second. She'd drunk more wine than she'd intended at Clayton's and had not gotten much sleep, thanks to the dip in the reservoir—and Reece's presence in bed next to her.

She told Hemming about the Supreme Court case that required the pub to allow women in; for many years it had been a men-only establishment.

"Some achievement," Hemming muttered, looking at the carved-up bare wood tables, the wishbone collection growing a dark fur of dust and the crowds of young frat boys shouting and hooting. He glowered at a drunk, beer-spilling student stumbling toward them. The boy caught the huge man's gaze and changed direction quickly. With some true curiosity in his voice the detective asked Taylor, "Are we having a date?"

"I don't think so."

"Ah," he said and nodded. "How did the fingerprints work out?"

"Not bad. I'll send you a postcard."

"If you want I'll show you how to do plantars."

"Vegetable prints?"

"Very good but no—feet, Ms. Lockwood."

"Taylor."

"Feet."

Taylor handed him the piece of paper with the information from the invoice she'd found in Wendall Clayton's desk. "John, have you ever heard of this company?"

He read, "Triple A Security? They're not around New York. But we can assume it's a sleazy outfit."

"Why's that?"

"It's an old trick to get in the front of the phone book—to have your listing first. Name your company with a lot of A's. You want me to check it out?"

"Can you?"

"Sure." A waiter carrying fifteen mugs in one hand swooped past and dropped two more, unasked-for.

"Would somebody from a security service—say, this disreputable Triple A outfit—commit a crime?"

"Jaywalking?"

"Worse."

"Stealing apples?"

"That category. More valuable than fruit."

He sat up and towered over her for an instant then hunched forward again. "At the big security firms, like our place, absolutely not. You commit a crime, you lose your license and your surety bond's invalidated. But these small outfits"—he tapped the paper—"there's a fine line between the good guys and the bad guys. I mean, somebody's got to *plant* the bugs that my company finds, right? And planting bugs is illegal."

"Any funny stuff?"

"That's not a term of art in my profession."

"Say, hypothetically, trying to run somebody off the road."

"Run somebody off..."

Taylor whispered, "...the road."

Hemming hesitated a moment and said, "This sort of

place—Triple A Security—yeah, you could possibly find somebody there who might be willing to do that. Worse too."

Taylor finished the bitter dark ale. She opened her purse, pulled out a twenty and signaled the waiter.

"Is there a Mr. Lockwood?" Hemming asked.

"Yes, but you wouldn't really like my father."

"Well, anything in the fiancé-boyfriend category. You know, those pesky fellows that tend to get there first?"

"Not exactly."

John Silbert Hemming said, "How about dinner?"

"Can't."

"I was going to let *you* take *me* out so you could deduct it."

She laughed and said, "I've got plans for the immediate future."

"Plans are what contractors and shipbuilders use."

"Some other time?" she asked. "I mean it."

"Sure," Hemming said. Then, as she started to stand, he held up a finger, which returned her to her seat. "One thing...there's this friend I have. He wears a badge and works at a place called One Police Plaza and I was thinking maybe it's time you gave him a call. Just to have a chat."

Taylor replayed the drive through the foliage down to the reservoir last night and thought Hemming's was an excellent idea.

But she answered, "No."

CHAPTER TWENTY-FOUR

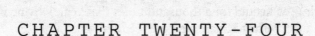They walked together through Battery Park.

Ralph Dudley's eyes were on the Statue of Liberty, rising from the harbor like a sister of the figure of blind justice. Junie walked silently beside him. He wanted to hold her hand but of course he did not. Like tourists, they were on their way to see the monument up close.

Dudley wondered how many people Junie's age knew the lines carved on the base of the statue, knew they were from a poem called "The New Colossus" by Emma Lazarus.

> *Give me your tired, your poor,*
> *Your huddled masses, yearning to breathe free,*
> *The wretched refuse of your teeming shore....*

Hardly any.

But, he also wondered, how many Wall Street lawyers knew it?

Not many of them either.

"Is it, like, cold on the boat?"

"You're saying 'like' again a lot. Remember, you were going to watch it."

"Whatever."

"I'm sure we can sit downstairs where it's warm. We'll get some hot chocolate."

"Or a beer," she muttered.

"Ha," Dudley said. "Come on over here for a minute."

He nodded to a bench and they sat down, Dudley wondering, as he had for a thousand times that year, why he was so taken with this little creature.

"Yo, so wassup?" she said. Sometimes she talked black and there was nothing he could say to get her out of this mode. He'd learned that it was best to ignore her affectations. They went away sooner or later.

"I've got some papers here. For you to sign. We couldn't do it in the firm."

She put her Walkman headsets on. He took them off her and smoothed her hair. She wrinkled her face.

"You've got to sign them."

"Like, okay."

He dug them out of his briefcase and handed them to her.

"Okay," she said, snapping her gum. "Gimme a pen."

Dudley reached into his jacket pocket and found that he'd accidentally picked up his Cross mechanical pencil. "Damn, I forgot mine."

"I, like, have one." She reached into her purse and pulled it out. But as she did a piece of paper fell to the ground. Dudley had picked it up and started to hand it back when he looked at the check.

He saw Junie's name.

He saw Taylor Lockwood's name.

His hand froze in midair between them.

Dudley looked at her with rage in his face. "What is this?"

"I—"

"What the hell have you done?"

"Poppie?" she asked, dropping her Walkman. It broke apart on the asphalt.

"How could you?" he whispered. "How could you?"

_____

The going rate to get Alice into the rabbit hole of a Manhattan apartment was a sob story.

I feel so stupid, Ralph Dudley's my uncle? And my aunt— that's his wife—passed away two years ago today and he was feeling really lousy. I wanted to make him dinner, just to cheer him up.

She held up the Food Emporium bag as evidence.

Here's fifty for your trouble. Don't say anything, okay? It's a surprise.

Taylor Lockwood had dressed in her business finest, to allay the doorman's concerns. He looked her over, pocketed the money, slipped her a spare key and turned back to a tiny television.

She knew Dudley wouldn't be here. She'd run into him in the halls and he'd told her that he was taking the afternoon off to show Junie the Statue of Liberty. The sullen girl had been in the lobby, waiting for him. Taylor shivered at the thought of the two of them together. For the girl's part, she looked from Dudley's face to Taylor's and back again. And just seemed bored.

Taylor now walked inside and found that Dudley's apartment was much smaller and more modest than she'd expected.

Although she knew about his financial problems, she'd assumed that an elderly Wall Street law firm partner like Dudley would be living at least in simple elegance, jaded though it might be. In fact, the four rooms in the prewar building didn't not have much more square footage than her own apartment. The walls were covered with cheap paint, which blotched where it was thin and peeled where the painters had bothered to apply several coats. There was no way the windows would ever open again.

She gave a cursory once-over to the living room, which was filled with old furniture, some of whose tattered, cracked arms and legs were tied together neatly with twine. She saw chipped vases, lace that had been torn and carelessly

resewn, books, afghans, walking sticks, a collection of
dented silver cigarette cases. Walls were covered with old
framed pictures of relatives, including several of Dudley as a
young man with a large, unfriendly-looking woman. He was
handsome but very thin and he stared at the camera with
solemn introspection.

In his bedroom, beside a neatly made bed, she found
what looked like a wooden torso with one of Dudley's suit
jackets hanging on the shoulders. A clothes brush rested on
a small rack on the torso's chest and on the floor in front of it
was a pair of carefully polished shoes with well-worn heels.

His fussiness made her job as burglar easy. Each of the
pigeonholes in his oak rolltop desk contained a single, well-
marked category of documents. Con Ed bills, phone bills,
letters from his daughter (the least-filled compartment),
business correspondence, warranty cards for household ap-
pliances, letters from his alumni organization, receipts. He
separated opera programs from symphony programs from
ballet programs.

Taylor finished the desk in ten minutes but could find
nothing linking Dudley to the note or to Hanover & Stiver.
Discouraged and feeling hot and filthy from the search, she
walked into the kitchen, illuminated with pallid light from the
courtyard that the room's one small window looked out on.

Taylor leaned against the sink. In front of her was
Dudley's small kitchen table, on either side of which were
two mahogany chairs. One side of the table was empty. On
the other was a faded place mat on which sat an expensive,
nicked porcelain plate, a setting of heavy silverware, a wineglass—all arranged for his solitary dinner that evening. A
starched white napkin, rolled and held by a bright red napkin ring, rested in the center of the plate. The gaudy ring was
the one item glaringly out of place. Taylor picked up the
cheap plastic, the kind sold at the bargain stores in Times
Square where tourists buy personalized souvenirs—cups,
dishes, tiny license plates.

She turned it over; the name sloppily embossed in the
plastic was *Poppie*.

A present from June, the object of his perverse desire.

Her hour was up. Book on outta here, Alice....

Nothing, she thought angrily. I didn't find a thing. Not a single hint as to where the note might be. She stuffed the grocery bag, which had been filled only with wadded-up newspapers, into the trash chute and left.

So, can we eliminate Dudley? she wondered.

No, but we can put him lower on the list than Thom Sebastian.

Well, don't get too interested in her....

She'd charm the young lawyer, interrogate him—the prick who'd been collecting information on her. She remembered his troubled expression yesterday. Maybe a confession *would* be forthcoming at dinner tonight. She still held out that hope.

Outside, she paused for a moment, rubbed her eyes.

Tomorrow, she thought in alarm, the trial was tomorrow.

Taylor stepped into the street to flag down a cab.

Thom Sebastian sat at the bar of the Blue Devil on the far edge of West Fifty-seventh, near the Hudson River.

An excellent place, he assessed, it had a mostly black audience, dressed super-sharp. He was working on a vodka gimlet, imagining his juggler and thinking, So far, so good.

But also thinking *goddamn,* I'm nervous.

He was considering what was about to happen tonight.

Was this a way-major mistake?

For a while he'd thought so. But now he wasn't so sure. Had no idea.

But it *was* going to happen; the die had been cast, he thought, phrasing the situation in a cliché that he found unworthy of a lawyer of his caliber.

He found himself coolly considering partnership at Hubbard, White & Willis and he remembered—almost with amusement—that he'd always considered achieving partnership a matter of life and death.

Death...

After Wendall Clayton had called him into his office and told him in that soft voice of his that the firm had concluded it would be unable to extend the offer of partnership to him, Sebastian had sat motionless for three or four minutes, smiling at the partner, listening to the man describe the firm's plans for Sebastian's severance.

A smile, yes, but it was really a rictus gaze, what to Clayton—had the fucking prick even noticed—must have seemed like a grin of madness: teeth bared, eyes crinkling in a psychotic squint.

"We'd like to make you a partner, Thom—you're respected here—but you understand that economies have to be effected."

Meaning simply that Sebastian was not a clone of Wendall Clayton and was, therefore, expendable.

Effecting economies... Oh, how that term—pure corporatespeak—had inflamed him like acid.

Listening to Clayton, he'd lowered his head and had seen something resting on the partner's desk: an inlaid dish of Arabic design. Sebastian's eyes had clung to the dish as if he could encapsulate the terrible reality in the cloisonné and escape, leaving his sorrow trapped behind him.

And now he thought about the problem of Taylor Lockwood.

But he tried as hard as he could to push her away, put her out of his mind, and replaced her with the image of the juggler once more.

He glanced at his watch.

Okay, let's do it. He stood up from the bar, told the bartender he'd be back in five.

So far...

███████

Without really thinking about it, the man in the Dodge reached over to the passenger seat and felt the breakdown—a Remington automatic 12-gauge shotgun.

Six shells in the extended magazine. Six more wedged into the seat, business end down.

He wasn't concentrating on the hardware, though; his eyes were on the woman walking down the street toward the fat boy, Thom Sebastian, who waved at her, smiling a weird smile. Looking all shit-his-pants.

All right, so this bitch was the one.

The man in the Dodge watched her, wondering what kind of body she had underneath the overcoat. He would've liked it if she'd been wearing high heels. He liked high heels, not those stupid black flat shoes this broad wore.

The man in the Dodge checked for blue-and-whites and pedestrians who might block the shot.

Clear street, clear shooting zone.

He eased the car forward then braked slowly to a halt twenty feet from the woman. She glanced at him with casual curiosity. Her eyes met his and, as he lifted the gun, she realized what was going down. She screamed, holding up her hands.

Nowhere for her to run...

He aimed over the bead sight and pulled the trigger. The huge recoil stunned his shoulder. He had a fast image of the woman as she took one load of buckshot in the side, a glancing hit. He fired two more toward her back but the way she fell, it seemed that only one cluster struck her and even that wasn't a square hit.

Well, if she wasn't dead yet she probably would be soon. And at the very worst she'd be out of commission for months.

People screamed and horns wailed as cars screeched to a halt, avoiding the pedestrians who dived into the street for safety.

The man in the Dodge accelerated fast to the next intersection, skidded through the red then slowed and, once out of sight of the hit, drove carefully uptown, well within the speed limit, diligently stopping at every red light he came to.

CHAPTER TWENTY-FIVE

Thom Sebastian, hands cuffed, was led into the precinct house by two uniformed cops.

Everybody stared at him—the cops, the drunk drivers, the hookers, a lawyer or two.

"Man," somebody whispered.

It was the blood, which covered Sebastian's jacket and white shirt. Nobody could figure out how somebody could be covered with this much blood and not have a dozen stab wounds.

The chubby lawyer slumped on a bench, waiting for the booking officer to get around to him, staring at his brown wing tips. A girl sat next to him, a tall black hooker with a tank top and hot pants under her fake fur coat. She looked at the blood then shook her head quickly, a shiver.

"Jesus," she whispered.

Sebastian felt a shadow over him, someone walking close. He looked up and blinked.

Taylor Lockwood said, "Are you all right? The blood..."

Sebastian nodded then closed his eyes and lowered his head again slowly. "Nosebleed," he muttered.

The desk sergeant said gruffly to her, "Who're you?"

Taylor said, "What happened?"

He looked over her black nylons, short black skirt and leather jacket. "Get outta here, lady. He's missin' his date for the night."

A bit of her father's temper popped within her. "And I'm making the trip down here to meet with my client. So I guess I'm missing mine too. Anything else you'd like to put on the record?"

The man's face reddened. "Hey, I didn't know you was a lawyer."

She had no idea what had happened. She'd shown up at the restaurant and found a crime scene investigation under way. Somebody'd been shot and Sebastian had been arrested.

She barked, "What's he been booked on?"

"Nothing yet. The arresting's on the phone to the medical examiner." He turned back to a mass of papers.

Man, that was a lot of blood.

A uniformed officer came up, a thin man, slicked-back hair, gray at the temples. He looked over Taylor and was not pleased. His would be a joint prejudice: against defense lawyers in general (who spent hours tormenting cops on the witness stand and reducing them to little piles of incompetence) and women defense lawyers in particular (who had to prove they could torment more brutally than their male counterparts).

Taylor Lockwood cocked her head and tried to look like a ballbuster. "I'm Mr. Sebastian's lawyer. What's going on?"

Suddenly a roar of a voice filled the station house. "Hey, Taylor!"

She froze. Oh, brother—why now? It was one of those moments when the gods get bored and decide to skewer you just for the fun of it. Taylor gave an inaudible sigh and turned toward the voice, now booming again, "Taylor Lockwood, right?"

A huge cop, a faceful of burst vessels, tan from a vacation in Vegas or the Bahamas, stalked across the room. He was off-duty, wearing designer jeans and a windbreaker. Early forties, thirty pounds overweight. Trim, razor-cut blond hair. A boyish face.

There was nothing to do, she decided, but go all the way. Her father's advice: If you're going to bluff, bluff like there's no tomorrow.

"Hey," she said, smiling.

"It's Tommy Blond. Don'tcha remember? Tommy Bianca, from the Pogiolli case."

"Sure, Tommy. How you doing?" She took his massive, callused hand.

The man was looking down at Sebastian. "He okay?"

"Nosebleed is all," the arresting said. "We thought he'd taken one, too. EMS looked him over, said he'll be okay, he keeps an eye on his nostrils."

Tommy Blond looked at the arresting and the desk sergeant. "Hey, treat this lady right. She's okay. She was working with the lawyer got off Joey, youse remember—Joey Pogiolli from the Sixth? Got him off last year some asshole sued him, said Joey worked him over on a bust....Hey, Taylor, you was a paralegal then. What, you go to law school?"

"Nights," Taylor said, grinning and wondering if the nervous sweat that had gathered on her forehead would start running down to her chin and carrying her makeup with it.

"That's great. My kid's applying to Brooklyn. Wants to be FBI. I told him agents don't got to have law degrees anymore but he wants to do it right. Maybe sometime he could talk to you about school? Got a card?"

"None with me. Sorry."

She glanced at Sebastian, staring at the floor.

Tommy Blond said, "Whatsa story, Frank?"

The arresting said, "We got a vic got took out outside the Blue Devil, name of Magaly Sanchez. Upscale coke dealer moving into the wrong territory. We think whoever did her wasn't sure what she looked like and was using him"—he nodded toward Sebastian—"to ID the hit. Or maybe they wanted to whack her in front of a customer. Send a message, you know. She had about ten grams on her, all packaged and ready for delivery. And Mr. Sebastian had a quarter gram. . . . That's why we brought him in."

Taylor rolled her eyes. "A quarter gram? Come on, you guys."

"Taylor, I know what you're asking. . . ." Tommy Blond said, then: "That's a lot of blood. You're sure it's just a nose-bleed?"

She remembered a buzzword. "What was your probable cause for search?"

"Probable cause?" The arresting blinked in surprise. "He was waving at a known drug dealer who got whacked right in front of him? That's not probable cause—that's for-damn-fucking-sure cause."

"Let's talk." She walked over to the bulletin board. Tommy Blond and the arresting looked at each other and then followed her. She stood with her head down and whispered harshly to the arresting, "Come on, he's never been arrested before. Sure, the guy's an asshole, but a quarter gram? You and I both know a collar like that's optional."

Taylor was making this up.

The arresting: "I don't know. . . . Everybody's pissed off about these assholes from Wall Street think they can buy and sell blow and we're not going to do anything about it."

"Let's cut a deal," Taylor continued. "Tell you what. Give him back to me and he'll give you a statement about the late Miss Sanchez and her friends—as long as it's anonymous and he never has to testify in court against anybody. And I'll make him promise to get off the stuff."

"Whatta you say?" Tommy Blond said to the uniformed officer.

"Look," Taylor pushed, "he works for the same firm got your buddy Joey off. That oughta count for something."

Joey, Taylor remembered, was the patrolman who maybe *did* get a little carried away with his nightstick on that black kid who maybe lifted a wallet but maybe didn't. And who maybe reached for that tire iron, even though,

funny thing, it was found twenty feet away from the scuffle.
Took the ER fifty-eight stitches to repair Officer Joey's hand-
iwork on the kid's face.

The arresting gave Taylor a look that's shorthand in law
enforcement. It translates to: I don't need this shit.

"Okay, get him out of here. But tell him to clean up his
act. I mean, like really. Next time they won't leave *nobody*
around. Have him down to Narcotics at the Plaza next week
and give 'em a statement." He wrote a name on a card. "Ask
for this detective here."

Taylor said, "Thanks, gentlemen."

Tommy Blond shook her hand again. "Proud of you, little lady. A lawyer. That's all right." He walked off toward the
locker room.

Taylor walked back to Sebastian, who'd been slumped
in his seat, out of earshot of the bargaining. He didn't yet
know he was free.

She knelt down next to him, looked at the blood on his
face and shirt. It was quite brilliant. She said, "Thom, I may
be able to help you out. But I've got to ask you something. I
need an honest answer. . . . Look at me."

Boy's eyes. Indignant, hurt, scared boy's eyes.

"You went through Mitchell Reece's file cabinet sometime recently. Why?"

A furrow ran through his bloody forehead as he
frowned. He sniffed. "What are you talking about?"

Taylor said brutally, "Fuck it, Thom, I can get you out of
here or I can make sure they book you. That'll be the end of
your life in New York. Now, it's your call."

He wiped tears from his cheeks. "Mitchell does trial
work for New Amsterdam. I handle a lot of their corporate
work. I probably needed some files he had."

"You've been in his safe file?"

Sebastian frowned again. "That thing he's got in his office with the locks on it? Yeah, a few months ago I got some
files out of it, some settlement agreements from a secured-
loan suit a couple of years ago. I needed them. It wasn't

locked and Reece was out of town on business. What's this all about?"

"You know New Amsterdam pretty well?"

"What's this—"

"Answer me," she snapped.

"Know them?" He wiped his face with a tissue and looked at the blood. He laughed bitterly. "I've worked for them for years! I baby-sit them! I hold their hands and walk them through the deals. While Burdick's collecting their fucking check *I'm* the grunt doing all the work for them. While Fred LaDue takes 'em out to dinner and plays tennis with them *I'm* the one who's up till three A.M. doing the documents. *I'm* their lawyer." He sighed. "Yeah, I know them pretty well."

Taylor looked into his eyes and she believed him. But she persisted. "You were in the firm on Saturday night, a week ago. You lied to me about it. You snuck in through the back door."

"How did you know that?" he asked. But his voice faded as he noticed her gaze grow cold again. "I'm sorry. Yeah, I was there. I did lie . . . but I had to. Look, when I got passed over for partner I decided to start my own firm. That's what Bosk and I're doing. Dennis Callaghan's doing the real estate for us, brokering some office space downtown. I just don't want anybody at Hubbard, White to know yet. That's why I lied."

"Prove it."

Numb, he pulled out his cell phone and placed a call. "Dennis? It's Thom. I'm putting somebody on the line. Tell her exactly what you're doing for Bosk and me."

She took the phone and said simply, "Go ahead."

Callaghan hesitated a moment then told her the same thing Sebastian had. "Okay, thanks." She disconnected and handed Sebastian back the phone.

"Why'd you get all that information about me? The stuff under your desk blotter."

Another blink. Another dip of the head. "You showed

up in my life all of a sudden. You were just *there* and I didn't know why. You were . . . interesting. I liked you. I was trying to find out about you. That's what I do—I'm a lawyer. That's how I work."

She looked over the miserable fat boy and knew he was innocent. He glanced at her once but had to look away quickly as if he were frightened by what he saw.

An odd feeling swept through her. Her face burned; she felt queasy. And she understood that for the first time in her life she'd done what her father would have done, what Mitchell Reece would have done: She'd been brutal in victory.

Power.

That was what she sensed. Sebastian, defeated in front of her, bloody and fearful as a child, was hers. The cops were hers. The sensation was exhilarating.

"Can you tell me what's going on?" he asked.

"No," she replied firmly. "I can't." She stood up. He looked uneasily at the cops.

"It's okay," she said. "You can go home."

"I can—"

"You can leave. It's all right."

Sebastian rose to his feet slowly and she took his arm to steady him. They started toward the door.

The hooker watched them leave and said cynically, "My, my, this be some justice system we got ourselves. Anybody gotta ciggie?"

Late Monday evening—the merger vote a mere fifteen hours away—Wendall Clayton sat in a conference room across across from John Perelli.

Fatigue had settled on Clayton like a wet coat. But, unlike Perelli, Clayton had not loosened his tie or rolled up the sleeves of his white, Sea Island cotton shirt. He sat the way he had been sitting for the past four hours: upright, only occasionally lowering his head to rub his bloodshot eyes or to stretch.

Beside him sat Randy Simms and another of Clayton's young partners. Perelli too had several of his lieutenants here.

Simms and the other young man were on the executive committee of Hubbard, White. Burdick had rallied hard to keep them off but Clayton had maneuvered their elections through, though Burdick had retained control. Before them were drafts of a document, the merger agreement, spread out like a patient under a surgeon's careful eyes.

Clayton glanced outside the door at a young woman, a secretary from a freelance legal services staffing firm. The woman knew every major word processing system in the United States, could take dictation and could keyboard 110 words a minute. These skills were fetching her forty-two dollars an hour though at the moment she was being paid that fee solely to sip coffee and read a battered paperback called *Surrender, My Love.*

He wondered if he'd still have the energy to fuck her in an hour or two, after the final negotiations were completed. Clayton thought it might be dicey; he was utterly exhausted.

Perelli wore half-rim glasses, low on his nose. He looked up and stared into Clayton's eyes. "I should tell you—my people aren't happy about your demand. About ousting Burdick. Even with the giveback."

"What're you saying?" Clayton asked coolly.

"He could sue. Older man, EEOC. He could make a mess."

"We're lawyers. Our job is to make messes go away."

"We'd prefer to keep him for a while. Say, a year. Phase him out."

Clayton laughed. "You don't phase people like Donald Burdick out. Either he's in charge or he's gone completely. That's his nature."

Perelli pulled off his glasses and rubbed the bridge of his nose.

The gesture explained that there'd been considerable rebellion in the ranks at Perelli's firm over Burdick. And Clayton knew that he had to act immediately.

"If you want Hubbard, White—Burdick has to go," he continued casually. He gestured in an aristocratic way toward the window, outside of which Wall Street at night glistened. "If you want Burdick, John, go find yourself another firm."

"You'd walk?"

"And not look back."

Perelli's assistants shifted uncertainly in their chairs.

A moment passed and not a cell in Wendall Clayton's face revealed the electric tension he felt.

Finally Perelli laughed. "Goddamn, you and I're going to make some serious fucking money together." He and Clayton shook hands with finality.

Perelli stood and stretched. "You going to use a special pen to sign the merger agreement, Wendall? Like the President does?"

"No, I'll just use this old thing."

He displayed a battered Parker fountain pen, one he had used for years. Not long after Clayton had started at Hubbard, White he found himself at a closing without a pen. Donald Burdick had shot him a gruff glance and slid this very pen to him. "You should always be prepared, Wendall. Keep that one as a reminder."

Wendall Clayton put the pen away and helped the other men organize the documents while he dictated instructions for the copying and assembly of the execution copies to the *Surrender, My Love* woman. After the firm approved the merger tomorrow, these papers would be brought into the large conference room for the signing of the agreement with Perelli's partners itself. Since so many people had to sign, the logistics of closing the deal were massive.

A half hour later, walking back toward his office, Clayton stopped and turned quickly, aware of someone approaching fast from down a dark corridor.

The person was making right for him.

For a moment he actually thought that Donald Burdick had lost his mind and was about to assault him.

But, no, it was Sean Lillick.

The red-eyed paralegal raged at Clayton. "You fucked her! You son of a bitch!"

"Quiet, you little shit!" Clayton whispered. John Perelli hadn't left yet.

"You fucked her!"

"Who?"

"Carrie Mason."

Clayton regarded the young man with some amusement. "And?"

"How could you do it?"

"Last time I looked, Sean, that girl was over eighteen and unattached." He lifted an eyebrow. "Was she wearing your Art Carved engagement ring? A tasteful but small solitaire? I didn't notice one."

"I don't want your fucking sarcasm, Wendall."

So, the puppy has some teeth. He'd never seen them bared before.

"Calm down, Sean. What the hell is she to you? She's a fat little inbred preppy and you're the point man of the avant-garde. Capulets and Montagues. You have nothing in common except gonads engorged by your differences."

"How could you treat her like that?"

"I treated her very well. Besides, the word 'consensual' comes to mind."

"She was drunk. She thinks you used her."

"She's an adult. What she thinks is her business. Not yours or mine." Clayton glanced back toward the conference room. He lowered his face and asked, "What? Did you think you two were going to move to Locust Valley and have babies? For God's sake, Sean. You're not crazy. Go find some girl with a crew cut, pierced labia and dirty fingernails."

"I hate you."

"No you don't, Sean. But even if you did your hatred is irrelevant. What is relevant is that you need me. Now, the merger vote's tomorrow and I don't have time for this. Learn a lesson, son: If somebody fucks your girlfriend the question isn't who did it and how can I get even—it's *why* did she want to? Think about that."

The boy fell silent.

Clayton could still see the anger and bitterness in his face. In a calmer tone he said, "It happened once. She was drunk, I was drunk. I have no intention of ever seeing her again." This was as close to a sincere apology as Wendall Clayton would ever come.

Lillick seemed to realize this. He wasn't pleased but Clayton saw that he'd pulled the rug out from underneath his rage.

"I'll tell her," Clayton joked, "what a wonderful human being you are."

"I—"

Clayton held up an finger. He said, "Tomorrow, early—in my office? We've got a big day tomorrow. We've got a thousand documents to get ready. The phalanxes will be marching through Rome."

CHAPTER TWENTY-SIX

North of Fourteenth Street, where Taylor Lockwood had risen from the hot, pungent subway on her way to Mitchell Reece's, the broad sidewalks were sparse.

After she'd put Thom Sebastian into a cab Taylor had returned to her apartment, changed and was now on her way to report to Reece that one suspect had been eliminated— but that she still had no clue where the note might be, the note that he'd need in court tomorrow morning, a little over twelve hours from now.

She zigged around patches of ice, remembering how her music teacher taught her to think of footsteps as musical beats. As she walked she'd break the spaces between the tap of the steps into half notes, quarter notes, eighths, triplets, dotted quarters and eighths, whispering the rhythms.

One two and uh three four...

A noise behind her, footsteps on the gritty concrete.

She turned quickly but saw no one.

A block farther. Now the streets were completely deserted. This area, Chelsea, near Sixth Avenue, contained some residential lofts and cavernous restaurants. But this particular street was the home of professional photographers, printers, warehouses and Korean importers. At night it was empty, a gloomy, dark, functional place, and she felt another chill of uneasiness.

One and two and three and—

Suddenly the scenery vanished as the arm went around her chest and a hand clamped over her mouth.

She screamed.

The man started to drag her into the alley.

Goddamn, no . . .

She struggled to free herself but managed only to force her attacker to fall, still clutching her fiercely around the neck. They landed on some boxes and tumbled to the slick cobblestones. The man ended up on top of her and knocked the breath from her body. Choking, gasping, she threw her hands over her face, unable to call for help.

The man rose to his knees. Taylor took this chance to twist away, smelling rotting bean sprouts and chicken bones and garlic from restaurant trash. She saw a fist rise up, about to come plunging down toward her face.

But anger detonated within her and, still breathless, she pushed hard with her legs, slamming into the man's hip and knocking him against a wall. Taylor grabbed the first thing she could find as a weapon—a piece of jagged concrete—and staggered to her feet, about to swing the sharp stone.

Her hand paused as she heard the man's sobbing. The raspy voice wheezed between the sobs. "Why, why, why? . . ."

"You!" she whispered.

Ralph Dudley wiped his face and stared at her at her in raw hatred. He didn't pay any attention to the rock in her hand. He stiffly rose, walked to an overturned trash drum and sat on it, gasping for breath. "Why did you do it?"

"Are you out of your mind?" She pitched the rock away and began brushing her coat off, rubbing at the oil and grease stains. "Look at this! Are you crazy?"

The old partner stared blankly at the ground. "I followed you from your apartment. I don't know what I wanted to do. I actually thought about killing you."

"What are you talking about?"

"You followed me. You bribed my . . . You bribed Junie to find out about me. Then I asked an associate if he'd seen you in my office and he said you had."

Taylor shrugged. "You lied to me, Ralph. You lied about being in the firm a week ago Saturday."

"So?" He smoothed his mussed hair, examined his damaged coat.

"What were you doing in the firm?"

"It's not any of your business."

"Maybe not. But maybe it is. What were you doing?"

"I love that girl."

Taylor said nothing.

"She makes me feel so alive. I hate it that she's in that business. She does too, I know she does. But she doesn't have any choice."

In her mind she saw the cheap red plastic napkin ring. *Poppie* . . .

Taylor's fear had changed into pity. The desires to flee, to slap him, to put her hand on his shoulder and comfort him were balanced.

He lifted his head; the cold light, shining down from above, hit his narrow face and made him look deranged and cadaverous. He started to speak then lowered his face into his hands. A dozen cars crashed over a pothole in the street next to them before he spoke. "Why did you do it?"

"Do what, Ralph?"

"Tell Wendall Clayton about us."

"I didn't tell Clayton anything."

"Somebody . . ." He wiped his face again. "Somebody told him."

"Oh, please . . ." Taylor laughed. "That law firm is like Machiavelli's villa. Everybody's got spies."

"But why did you go to the West Side Club? Why did you follow me?"

"There are problems at the firm. I needed to know where some people were at a certain time. I got the feeling you were lying to me so I followed you after dinner. Now, tell me what you were doing at the firm."

He shook his head.

Just as she had with the cop who'd arrested Sebastian, Taylor now lowered her head and said, "Ralph, I can put you in jail for a long time—because of that girl. And I'll do it if you don't cooperate. No bullshit. Tell me what you were doing in the firm."

The look of hatred in his face chilled her but he finally said, "Junie's father died two years ago and left her some money. But her mother and stepfather're keeping it all tied up. They're trying to get it for themselves. I've been spending every weekend and half my nights at the firm, learning trusts and estates and fiduciary law. I'm going to get the money back for her." He wiped tears. "I couldn't tell anybody at the firm because they'd find out she's not my granddaughter and then . . . they might find out the real situation. Besides, I've borrowed against my partnership draw so much the firm'd fire me if they knew I was spending my time on a project that wasn't making Hubbard, White any money."

He looked up, wretched and lost. "I'm really not a very good lawyer. I can charm people, I can entertain clients . . . but this is the only real law I've done in years."

"Prove it to me."

He said stiffly, "I don't think I owe you anything more."

Once again the same dark power she'd felt before filled Taylor Lockwood's heart and she whispered harshly, "Prove it to me or I go to the cops."

A wounded animal, Dudley hesitated. Then he glanced down, opened his briefcase. Shoved it toward her.

She knew little about trusts and estates law but it was clear that these documents—petitions to the Surrogate's Court, copies of cases and correspondence—bore out what he'd told her.

"You were in the firm early Sunday morning after Thanksgiving."

"Yes" he answered as if he were a witness under cross-examination.

"You used Thom Sebastian's key?"

"Yes. I didn't want anybody to know I was in that night. I got there about one-thirty. After I'd been to the West Side Club."

She asked, "Where *were* you in the firm?"

"Just the library and my office. The rest room. The canteen—for some coffee."

"Did you see anyone else there?"

Dudley rocked slowly back and forth on the trash can, under the rain of harsh streetlight. His breath popped out in small puffs as he worried the tear in his coat. "As a matter of fact," he answered, "I did."

The loft door was open. She paused in the hallway, seeing the trapezoid of ashen light fall into the corridor. Taylor felt a jab of panic. In a burst of frightening memory she remembered the white car driving them off the road and, though at the time she believed the thief had intended only to scare them, she thought for an instant that the man had come back and killed Mitchell. She ran to the door and pushed inside.

He was lying on the couch, wearing blue jeans and a wrinkled dress shirt. His hair was mussed and his arms lolled at his sides. His eyes stared unmoving at the ceiling.

"Mitchell?" she asked. "Are you all right?

He turned on his side slowly and looked at her. A faint smile. "Must've dozed off."

Taylor crouched next to him and took his hand. "I thought . . . you were hurt or something."

She felt the slight pressure of his hand on hers. He looked at her jacket and jeans. "What happened to you?"

Taylor laughed. "Little wrestling match."

"Are you all right?"

"You should see the other guy." Then she said, "I know who the thief is."

"What?" His eyes returned to life. "Who?"

"Wendall Clayton."

"How do you know?"

"I eliminated Thom and Dudley." She told him about Sebastian's adventure with the police and the old partner's attack on her. Then she said, "Clayton let the thief in that night."

"But he wasn't in the firm," Reece said.

"Yes he was. Dudley saw him. And Clayton's key entry didn't show up because he got to the firm on *Friday*."

Reece nodded, eyes closing at the obvious answer. "Of course. He was there all weekend, working on the merger. He didn't leave until Sunday. He stayed two nights. Must've slept on the couch. I should've thought about that."

Taylor continued. "I just went back to the firm and checked his time sheets. We would've seen that he'd ordered food in and made phone calls and photocopies but all those records were erased, remember?"

Reece's smile faded. "That doesn't mean he stole the note though."

"But Dudley told me something else. About three-thirty or four on Sunday morning he saw this man, like a janitor, walking through the firm with an envelope. Dudley thought it was odd that he was carrying something like that. He noticed he went into Clayton's office with the envelope but came out without it. Dudley didn't say anything to him—or to anyone else about him—because he was working on something unrelated to firm business.

"I talked to my private detective. He said there is a Triple A Security—the receipt I found in Wendall's desk—and he checked the grapevine. It's in Florida. He said they're a firm that has a reputation for doing labor work. Which he tells me is a euphemism for rough stuff, like stealing documents and bugging offices and even driving people off the road. That's who Dudley saw. Clayton let him into the firm and he stole the note after you went home."

Reece said, "And you think the note's in that envelope?"

"I think so. Like you said, he probably hid it in a stack

of documents in his office. I'm going to search it. Only we have to wait. He was still at his desk when I left the firm and it didn't look like he was going to leave anytime soon. I'll go back to the firm and wait till he leaves for the night."

"Taylor . . . What can I say?" He hugged her, hard, and she threw her arms around him. Their hands began coursing up and down each other's backs and suddenly it was as if all the compressed tension they'd felt over the past week had been converted into a very different kind of energy . . . and now suddenly erupted.

The room vanished into motion: his arms around her, under her legs, sweeping her up. Reece carried her to the huge dining room table and lay her upon it, books falling, papers sailing off onto the floor. He eased her down onto the tabletop, her blouse and skirt spiraling off and away, his own clothes flying in a wider trajectory. He was already hard. He pressed his mouth down on hers, their teeth met and he worked down her neck, biting. Pulling hard on her nipples, her stomach, her thighs. She tried to rise up to him but he held her captive, her butt and leg cut by the sharp corners of a law book: The pain added to the hunger.

Then he was on top of her, his full weight on her chest, as his hands curled around the small of her back and tugged her toward him. She was completely immobile, her breath forced out of her lungs by his demanding strokes.

Taylor felt a similar hunger and she dug her nails into his solid back, her teeth clenched in a salivating lust for the pain it was causing.

They moved like this for minutes, or hours—she had no idea. Finally she screamed as she shuddered, her toes curling, her head bouncing against the table. He finished a moment later and collapsed against her.

Taylor lifted her hands. Two nails were bloody. She shoved the law book out from underneath her; it fell with a resonant thud. She closed her eyes and they remained locked this way for a long time.

She dozed briefly.

When she awoke a half hour later she found that Reece

was at his desk, dressed only in a shirt, scribbling notes, reading cases. She watched his back for a moment then walked to him, kissed the top of his head.

He turned and pressed his head against her breasts.

"It's up to you now," he said. "I'm going to proceed with the case as if we can't find the note." He nodded at the papers surrounding him. "But I'll hope for the best."

██████

At three in the morning, wearing her cat burglar outfit of Levi's and a black blouse, Taylor Lockwood walked into Hubbard, White & Willis.

Her black Sportsac contained a pair of kidskin gloves, a set of screwdrivers, a pair of pliers, a hammer. The firm seemed empty but she moved through the corridors in complete quiet, pausing in darkened conference rooms, listening for voices or footsteps.

Nothing.

Finally she made it to Wendall Clayton's office and began her search.

By four-thirty, she'd covered most of it and found no sign of the note. But there were still two tall stacks of documents, on the floor beside his credenza, that she hadn't looked through yet.

She continued searching. She finished one and found nothing. She started on the second one.

Which was when jaunty footsteps sounded on the marble floor in the corridor nearby and Wendall Clayton's voice boomed to someone, "The merger vote's in six hours. I need those fucking documents now!"

CHAPTER TWENTY-SEVEN

He didn't truly live anywhere but here.

In murky, echoing rotundas of courthouses like this.

In marble corridors lit by milky sunlight filtering through fifty-year-old grimy windows, in oak hallways smelling of bitter paper from libraries and file rooms.

At counsel tables like the one at which he now sat.

Mitchell Reece studied the courtroom around him, where the opening volley in *New Amsterdam Bank & Trust, Ltd. v. Hanover & Stiver, Inc.* would be fired in a short while. He studied the vaulted ceilings, the austere jury box and a judge's bench reminiscent of a conning tower on a warship, the dusty flag, the pictures of stern nineteenth-century judges. The room was unlit at the moment. There was a scuffed, well-worn aspect to the place; it reminded him of old subway cars. Well, that was appropriate; after all, justice was just another service provided by government to its citizens, like public transportation and trash collection.

He sat for a few minutes but grew restless; he stood suddenly and began to pace.

And what, he speculated, would happen if Taylor *didn't* find the note?

He supposed he could find alternatives. But because Mitchell Reece was so very driven, because he was someone who, as Taylor had once said, had left behind reason and logic and even safety in this mad sojourn, he felt a fierce desperation to find that tiny piece of paper.

He wanted to win this one oh-so-badly.

He rose and walked to the soiled window, through which he watched men and women hurrying along Centre Street: attorneys and judges and clients. Everyone was wearing a suit but making the distinction among them was easy. Lawyers carried big litigation bags, clients carried briefcases and judges carried nothing.

He wandered to the judge's bench then to the jury gallery.

Theater.

Winning is about theater, he reflected.

The revelation had come to him early in his career—he was representing a young boy blinded in one eye when a lawn mower fired a rock out of the grass chute and into the child's face. The boy's father had used a hacksaw to cut off the safety deflector panel, believing the motor labored harder with the deflector in place and used more gas. Reece sued the manufacturer, claiming that the unit was defective because there was no warning that users should *not* cut the panel off.

It was understood by virtually everyone that—because the proximate cause of the injury was the father's removal of the device—Reece had absolutely no chance of winning. The bored judge knew this, as did the arrogant lawyer for the defendant and the complacent lawyer for the defendant's insurance company.

Seven people did *not* know the impossibility of the suit, however. One was Mitchell Reece. The others were the six members of the jury, who awarded the snotty, self-pitying little kid one point seven million bucks.

Theater.

That was the key to litigation: a dab of logic, a bit of law, a lot of personality, and considerable theater.

He glanced at the door to the courtroom, willing it to open and Taylor Lockwood to hurry inside, the note in hand.

But of course it remained closed.

After he'd heard nothing more from her after she left to go to the firm at 3 A.M. He'd gotten a few hours' sleep, shaved and showered then dressed in his finest litigation Armani. He'd gathered his documents, called the clients to have them meet him at the courthouse then limoed downtown, where he slipped into the cavernous domed cathedral of New York State Supreme Court.

Well, the matter was out of his hands, he now reflected. Either Taylor would find it and life would move in one direction, or she would not and an entirely different set of consequences would occur.

Mitchell Reece had not prayed for perhaps thirty years but today he addressed a short message to a vague deity, whom he pictured looking somewhat like blind Justice, and asked that she keep Taylor Lockwood safe and to please, please let her find the note.

You've done so much, Taylor; now do just a little more. For both of us. . . .

Taylor Lockwood stood in Wendall Clayton's private bathroom.

The time was now 9 A.M. and she'd hidden here for hours, waiting for the partner to take a break so that she could continue going through the remaining stack of papers.

But Clayton had never even stood up to stretch. In this entire time he'd remained rooted at his desk, reading, picking up the phone and calling partners and clients. The news he was receiving was apparently good for his side; it was clear to her that the merger would be approved and that both firms would sign it up later in the day.

Reece would be in court by now, probably despairing that he hadn't heard from her.

But there was nothing she could do other than wait.

Ten minutes passed. Then ten more. And finally Clayton rose.

Thank God. He was going to check on something.

She would grab the remaining stack and flee with it to her cubicle, looking through it there. Then—

Her gut jumped hard. Clayton wasn't leaving the office at all. He needed to use the rest room and was walking directly toward where Taylor Lockwood now hid, a room without a single closet or shower stall where she might hide.

"Bench conference, your honor?" Mitchell Reece asked. He was standing in front of the plaintiff's table.

The judge looked surprised and Reece could understand why. The trial had just started. The opening statements had been completed and it was rare that a bench conference—a brief informal meeting between lawyers, out of earshot of the jury—should occur at this early stage; nothing had happened so far that the two attorneys could argue about.

The judge raised his eyebrows and Hanover & Stiver's slick, gray-haired lawyer rose to his feet and walked slowly to the bench.

The courtroom was half empty but Reece was distressed to see some reporters present. He didn't know why they were here; they never covered cases of this sort.

Someone's political hand? he wondered.

At the defendant's table sat Lloyd Hanover, tanned and trim, his hair combed forward in bangs, his face an expression of blasé confidence.

The two lawyers stood at the bench. Reece said softly, "Your honor, I have a best-evidence situation. I'd like to move to introduce a copy of the promissory note in question."

Hanover's lawyer turned his head slowly to look at Reece. It was the judge, however, who was more astonished. "You don't have the note itself?"

No one in the jury box or elsewhere in the courtroom could hear this exchange but the surprise on the jurist's face was evident. Several spectators looked at each other and a reporter or two leaned forward slightly, sharks smelling blood.

The Hanover lawyer said tersely, "No way. Not acceptable. I'll fight you on this all the way, Reece."

The judge said, "Was it a negotiable instrument?"

"Yes, your honor. But there is precedent for admitting a copy at this stage, as long as the original is surrendered before execution of the judgment."

"Assuming you *get* a judgment," the Hanover lawyer countered.

"Bickering pisses me off, gentlemen." When the jury wasn't listening the judge could curse to his heart's delight.

"Sorry, sir," Hanover's lawyer murmured contritely. Then he said, "You prove to me the note's destroyed—I mean, show me ashes—and then you can put a copy into evidence. But if not, I'm moving for dismissal."

"What happened to the original?" the judge asked.

"We have it at the firm," Reece said casually. "We're having some technical failure accessing it."

"'Technical failure accessing it'?" the judge blurted. "What the fuck does that mean?"

"Our security systems aren't functioning right, as I understand it."

"Well, wouldn't that be convenient, to have the note disappear just now?" the Hanover lawyer said. "Especially since we intend to call into question certain aspects of the execution of the note."

Reece gave a bitter laugh. "Let me get this right—you're saying that you gladly took my client's money but now you're not sure they executed the loan agreement correctly so you don't have to pay it back?"

"Our thinking is that the bank tried to give itself an out because interest rates turned and they want to invest the capital elsewhere."

"Your client missed six months of interest payments,"

Reece said, raising his voice just loud enough for the jury to hear. "How exactly—"

"Was I not making myself goddamn clear? No bickering, no fucking comments on the merits of the case in a bench conference.... Now, Mr. Reece, this is very unusual. A suit on a note, especially a negotiable note, requires the original document. Under the best-evidence rule if you can't explain the note's destruction, you're precluded from entering a copy into evidence."

Reece said calmly, "I'd like to make a motion to submit other evidence of the existence of the note."

"Your honor," opposing counsel said, "I would point out that it is Mr. Reece's client that sued on the note it alleges is properly executed. It is his responsibility to present that note. A copy won't show that there's been tampering on the part of Mr. Reece's client."

Reece countered, "Your honor, it is very important that the administration of justice not get bogged down in technicalities. The note is merely *evidence* of the debt owed—and remaining unpaid, I should point out—by Hanover & Stiver. It is true that the best-evidence rule generally requires the original but there are exceptions. We're all familiar with the rules of civil procedure, I'm sure."

"But this isn't a bill of sale, Mr. Reece," the judge said. "It's a negotiable instrument worth hundreds of millions of dollars."

"With all due respect to Mr. Reece," the Hanover lawyer said, "I am reminded of a case once in which a similar claim of a missing note was made and it turned out that the document in question had been sold by the bank to a third party. I would never suggest that New Amsterdam Bank was guilty of such wrongdoing but ... we can't take that chance."

Reece walked to the counsel table and returned with some documents. He handed one copy to the lawyer and one to the judge. "Motion papers. I move to allow the introduction of secondary evidence of the note. I've briefed the issue in here. If you would like to recess for twenty-four hours to allow my opponent here to respond—"

"No more delays," the judge snapped. "This case has fucked up my calendar enough."

The other lawyer shook his head. "You lost the note, Reece, I'm ready for trial. Your honor, I move for a directed verdict in my client's favor."

The judge flipped through the lengthy brief that Reece had prepared then lifted an impressed eyebrow. "Good work, Mr. Reece. Brilliant analysis." Then he tossed the brief aside. "But it doesn't cut it. No secondary evidence will be allowed."

Reece's heart sank.

"On the other hand, I won't grant a directed verdict for Hanover. What I will do is grant a motion to dismiss *without* prejudice. That will allow Mr. Reece to bring his case in the future. However, given the nature of defendant's financial condition, I doubt they'll have much money for your client to collect, Mr. Reece. You'd better talk to your malpractice carrier. I think your client may look to you for restitution in this matter. And that's to the tune of two hundred and fifty million dollars."

The opposing counsel began the formalities: "Your honor, I move for dismissal of—"

"Mitchell!" a woman's voice called from the back of the courtroom.

The judge looked up, glaring at the intrusion. Everyone in the gallery and the jury box swiveled to watch Taylor Lockwood hurry down the aisle.

"It's customary to ask permission before shouting in my courtroom, young lady," the judge snapped sarcastically.

"Forgive me, sir. I need to speak to plaintiff's counsel for a moment."

Hanover's lawyer said, "Your honor, I—"

The judge waved him silent and nodded Taylor forward.

CHAPTER TWENTY-EIGHT

"I *am* sorry, your honor," Taylor Lockwood said.

Judges were public servants, catering to the will of the people, but as her father had reminded from a young age, you could never be too deferential to jurists or, as he put it even to grade-school Taylie, you could never kiss too much judicial ass.

She walked to Reece and handed him an envelope. Inside was the promissory note, looking as mundane and matter-of-fact as the copy he'd showed her at their first meeting.

Mitchell Reece took out the document and exhaled slowly.

"Your honor, at this time the plaintiff would like to introduce Exhibit A." He handed it to the opposing counsel, who looked at Taylor with a gaze of distilled hate. "No objection." He returned the note to Reece's unsteady hands.

Reece walked back to his favorite space, in front of the jury box. "Your honor, before continuing with my case, I first must apologize to the court and to the jury for this delay." He smiled contritely. The six men and women smiled or nodded back and forgave him; the interruption had added an element of drama to the case.

"Fine, fine, Mr. Reece, let's move this along," the judge grumbled, his chances for a fast escape to golf or tennis ruined.

"One moment, your honor." The Hanover & Stiver attorney bent toward one of his clients, probably Lloyd Hanover, Taylor guessed, to judge from his slick, tanned appearance, which matched what Reece had told her of him. After a bit of conversation the attorney stood up. "Approach the bench again? With opposing counsel?"

The judge gestured them up. The defense lawyer said, "Your honor, my clients would like to present a settlement offer to the plaintiff."

The judge lifted an eyebrow to Reece. Taylor's father had also taught his daughter that settlement was the Holy Grail of judges. Burdened by an endless workload, they infinitely preferred the parties' agreeing to work out their differences rather than slugging it out at trial. The judge might even be able to get in nine holes today.

"We'll entertain it," Reece said stiffly.

The lawyer moved closer to Reece and whispered, "Look, you can get a judgment entered for the face value of the note plus interest but there's no way there'll be enough cash left in the company to collect that much by the time you enforce it. Not to mention your legal fees' eating up a lot of the rest."

"A number," Reece said. "Just give me a number."

"I—"

The judge: "Give him a number."

"Sixty-five cents on the dollar."

Reece said, "Eighty cents on the dollar. U.S. cash, not negotiable instruments or assets or tangible property, even gold."

"We're trying to be cooperative. But we have to be realistic," Hanover's lawyer said. Then he added ominously, "The money just won't be there in a few months."

"Then we'll just have to go a-lookin'," Reece said

cheerfully. "Now, Lloyd Hanover personally guaranteed the debt. I'm ready to interrogate—excuse me, *depose*—every one of his relatives and every business associate of his for the past ten years to find out where he hid the money."

"He didn't hide—"

"We'll look into every deal he's ever been involved in, every charity he ever gave money to, his kid's college funds."

"He's completely innocent of secreting funds if that's what you're suggesting."

Reece shrugged. "Dismissal without prejudice. Eighty cents on the dollar. Cash. And we close within one week. If not, then Lloyd Hanover and everybody he's ever known won't have a minute's peace."

The lawyer held his eye for a moment and strode back to his client, who listened, gave a searing look to Reece then whispered something to the lawyer.

When the man returned he said, "Agreed."

Reece nodded and said, "We'll execute the stipulation now."

"We don't want to take the court's time. I suggest—"

"I think his honor would prefer to spend a few extra minutes now rather than risk being back here in a few weeks for a full-fledged trial. Am I right about that, your honor?"

"You are, Mr. Reece. Write out the stipulation by hand and we'll get it signed up."

The defense lawyer sighed and scurried back to give the bad news to the client.

After the paperwork was completed hands were shaken among comrades, glares delivered between opponents and the courtroom emptied.

In the courthouse rotunda, the New Amsterdam vice presidents and executives clustered together, enjoying their relief. Taylor followed Reece to a small vestibule that contained public phones, which unlike most in the city were in old-fashioned booths with closing doors. He pulled her inside one and kissed her hard. After a moment he released her and leaned back. "What on earth happened? Where were you?"

"I was almost through searching Clayton's office but he came in early to take care of some last-minute things for the merger. I hid in the bathroom."

"Jesus. What happened then?"

"About nine or so he had to use the john. But I unscrewed the lightbulbs before he got there. So he went up the hall. When he did I grabbed the last stack of paper and ran down to my cubicle with them. I found all of this in the envelope the note was in."

Reece took the sheets of paper that Taylor offered. Shaking his head, he looked at them closely. A copy of a letter to the *National Law Journal.* "Re: Careless Security Costs Firm Client." The letter blamed Burdick and the executive committee. There was also a typewritten list with the names of several other clients and cases that Clayton was going to sabotage while, presumably, shifting the blame to Burdick.

From her purse Taylor then took a small tape recorder and held up a tiny microcasette. "This was in the envelope too." She inserted the cassette into the player and hit a button. They heard Reece's voice, thick with static, talking to her about the promissory note. She shut it off.

"Son of a bitch," Reece said. "He bugged my office. That's how he knew we were after him. He's known all along. He..." Then Reece paused and looked at his watch. "Oh, no."

"What?

"The firm's voting on the merger any minute now. We've got to tell Donald about this. It'll change everything."

He grabbed the phone and dug in his pocket for some change.

■■■■

Perpetual motion does exist.

In business, in fact, where the mere laws of science

mean zip compared with the power of greed and ambition, it's one of the essential principles.

Donald Burdick sensed the undercurrent of this energy surrounding each partner as he or she entered the big conference room. Mostly they were uneasy. They lingered at the door, pretending to leave messages with the conference room secretary, pretending to wait for comrades so they might enter with human shields, or at least with allies to deflect the glare of the partners representing the other side of the merger issue from theirs.

As always, few of the younger partners would make eye contact with Burdick but this morning he felt this evasion was due not to distance in social station but to hostility on the part of his opponents and shame in the hearts of those who had betrayed him.

The Danish pastries on the Limoges china, the coffee in the sterling urn were practically untouched. Burdick, looking down, reviewed a loan document that did not need reviewing. He heard conversations about the Jets and Giants, about concerts, about vacations, about closings, about the faux pas of opposing counsel, about the Supreme Court's latest excursions to Olympus, about rumors of other law firms breaking up.

Finally, at eleven o'clock, Burdick started to call the meeting to order. He was about to ask for a quorum vote when:

"Excuse me," said Randy Simms, whom Donald Burdick couldn't help but picture as a handsome leech.

"Yes?" Burdick drew the word out threateningly.

Simms said, "We're not all present."

Eyes coursing leisurely around the table, Burdick said, "But we have a quorum."

"Well, Mr. Clayton isn't here."

"Either we have a quorum, in which case the meeting proceeds, or we do not, in which case it doesn't. Whom that quorum is made up of is not, to my memory, an issue of any concern in *Robert's Rules of Order*."

"I'm just thinking that it might be appropriate—"

But the slick young sycophant's words were interrupted by a bold knock. The door opened and Burdick's secretary walked inside with a sealed envelope. Ignoring everyone in the room, the older partner took it, slit the seal open with his gold pen and read the note. He handed it to Bill Stanley, who blinked in surprise.

Burdick said, "If you'll excuse us for a moment please. There's something that needs attending to. We'll adjourn for fifteen minutes. Bill, you come too."

■

Donald Burdick was as angry as Taylor had ever seen him. He glanced at her and she looked away from his towering fury.

They sat in Burdick's office. Bill Stanley was on the couch, a fat ankle resting on a fat knee, and read over the papers Taylor had found in Clayton's office.

Stanley muttered, "What a stupid, stupid thing to do."

But Burdick was venting at Reece. "Why the hell didn't you tell me about the note?"

Reece said, "It was a judgment call. I didn't want word to get out. I had my own way of handling it."

"You almost lost the case," Burdick spat out. "You almost got yourselves killed."

Reece withstood the anger easily. "Clayton wasn't going to hurt us. I'm sure the car incident was just to scare us. As far as losing goes, well, yes, I took that chance."

"You risked our client because you were afraid you'd lose your job."

The associate fired back, "Of course that was one reason. But it was also because if word got out it would be bad for the firm. In my assessment we had to act covertly."

"'Covertly.' You sound like a damn spy." Burdick took the papers and the tape recorder from Stanley. "He wanted the merger so badly, he'd do this?" Burdick's anger was giving way to astonishment.

Stanley considered something. "You introduced the note into evidence, right?"

Reece nodded. "Hanover's agreed to settle. We're going to close in Boston next week."

"Well, then Clayton will've heard you found it. He'll know he's in trouble."

Burdick nodded. "That's why he's not at the meeting." The old partner rubbed his eyes. "What a mess."

"Fucking scandal," Stanley growled. "Last thing we need."

"Give me some thoughts on the damage assessment," Burdick said to the rotund partner.

"Probably not terrible." He nodded at Reece and Taylor. "They didn't tell anyone." A piercing glance at Taylor. "Right? You didn't mention it to anybody?"

"No, of course not. When I found those things in Clayton's office I took them right to Mitchell at the court-house. I didn't even call—because I thought the phones might be bugged. Nobody else knows what I was doing."

Stanley nodded and continued, "The problem's going to be talking him into leaving. He knows we're afraid of publicity so we're not going to go to the police or going to sue him. Fucking clever when you think about it. He arranges to misplace a note, nearly loses our client and when we catch him red-handed he's practically got immunity from the liability."

Burdick was shaking his head. "We'll find a way to oust him. That man has to..." His voice faded as there was an urgent knock on the door.

"Come in."

The door opened fast and one of Burdick's secretaries stood there. Her face was white and her eyes were red from crying.

"What is it, Carol?"

Oh, no, Taylor thought: Just what they were afraid of had happened—word had gotten out that Clayton had stolen the note.

But the tragedy was of a somewhat different order.

The woman gasped, "Oh, Mr. Burdick... it's terrible. They just found Wendall Clayton in the garage downstairs. In his car... He's..."

"What, Carol?"

"He shot himself. He's dead."

TWO

Men of Most
Renowned Virtue

"You will observe the Rules of Battle, of course?" the White Knight remarked, putting on his helmet....

"I always do," said the Red Knight, and they began banging away at each other with such fury that Alice got behind a tree to be out of the way of the blows.

—Lewis Carroll, *Through the Looking-Glass*

CHAPTER TWENTY-NINE

███████ Only a few hours had elapsed since Clayton's suicide. But it seemed to Taylor Lockwood that days had passed—given all the conjuring that Donald Burdick had done in the wake of the tragedy.

First, he'd appeared at the merger vote meeting and delivered the news to the partners. Then, leaving the stunned men and women to make what they would of the man's death, he'd returned immediately to his office, where Reece and Taylor had been ordered to remain.

The senior partner had handled an endless stream of phone calls and meetings with his cronies. So far he'd talked to the mayor's and the governor's offices, the medical examiner's office, the police, the Justice Department, the press.

Taylor was startled to see Burdick's wife make an appearance, walking into her husband's office unannounced, without the least acknowledgment of Reece or Taylor. The woman apparently knew all about the suicide and she and her husband retired to the small conference room off his office and closed the door. Five minutes later Burdick returned alone.

He sat down, leaned back in the chair and then asked Reece and Taylor, "Do you have anything else that has to do with Wendall or the theft? Anything at all?"

Reece shook his head and looked at Taylor, who said numbly, "I didn't think this would happen."

Burdick looked at her blankly for a moment then repeated, "Anything else?"

"No," she said.

He nodded and took an envelope out of his pocket. "There was that suicide note in the car, the one the police found. Talking about pressures at work, being despondent." Burdick looked at both Reece and Taylor. He added, "But he wrote another one. It was on his desk, addressed to me."

He handed a sheet of paper to Reece, who read it and then passed it on to Taylor.

> *Donald, forgive me. I'm sending this to you privately to keep my theft of the note out of the news. It will be better for everyone.*
>
> *I want you to know that I truly believed the merger would save the firm. But I lost sight of how far I should go. All I'll offer is this from Milton: "Men of most renowned virtue have sometimes by transgressing most truly kept the law."*

Burdick took the letter back and locked it in his desk. "I'm going to try to keep this note quiet." He nodded at the drawer. "I'll talk to the police commissioner and I don't think he'll have a problem with it. This is Hubbard, White's dirty laundry and no one else's. Publicity would be bad for everyone. Bad for the firm. Bad for Clayton's widow too."

"Widow?" Taylor asked suddenly.

Burdick replied, "Yes, Wendall was married. Didn't you know?"

"No," she said. "She wasn't in Connecticut the other day.

I've never seen her at any of the firm functions. He never wore a ring."

"Well, I guess he wouldn't now, would he? Given his extracurricular activities."

His widow...

The words stung. Before his death Clayton the man had been hidden beneath Clayton the ruthless aristocrat. That he had a wife—and maybe children or living parents, siblings—was a shock.

"The newspapers'll get a watered-down story," Burdick continued. "I've called the public relations company. Bill Stanley's with them now. They're preparing a statement. If anybody asks we'll refer questions to them." He lowered his head and looked into Reece's eyes, then Taylor's. She had the same sense as when she met Reece's gaze, or Clayton's. Or her father's. They drew you in, made you forget who you were, forget your own thoughts. In Burdick's eyes she saw will and confidence, strong as bronze. Her mind went blank. He asked, "Will you back me on this? If I thought there was anything to be gained by a full disclosure I wouldn't hesitate to reveal everything. But I can't see any upside to it."

Men of most renowned virtue.

Reece said, "I won't perjure myself, Donald. But I won't volunteer anything."

"Fair enough." The partner looked at Taylor.

She nodded. "Sure. I agree."

The hairs on the back of her neck stirred.

Widow...

Taylor looked into the conference room, inside which Vera Burdick, her gray hair piled on her head in a stately bun, was on the telephone. She glanced back and caught Taylor's gaze. The woman half-rose and swung the door closed.

Burdick's phone rang and he took the call. He mouthed something about its being from someone at City Hall but Taylor was preoccupied. She was seeing in her mind's eye the real suicide note, tucked away in Burdick's desk. She vaguely heard Burdick speaking to the caller in a low, reassuring tone. She watched his long, jowly face, carefully shaved, his sparse gray hair brushed into precise alignment.

And Taylor Lockwood thought: What the hell had she been doing all along? What did she *think* would happen when she fingered the thief? Had she ever considered the consequences?

Never once.

Renowned virtue.

Burdick hung up the receiver and nodded with satisfaction. "I think we'll get away with it."

Taylor tried to figure out what he meant.

"The Medical Examiner's office is going to rule the death suicide. The AG agrees. And we can keep our other suicide note private."

Reece blurted an astonished laugh. "The ME ruled *already*?"

Burdick nodded then looked at Taylor and Reece with a vaguely ominous gaze, which she interpreted as: Don't be too curious about this.

The partner looked at his watch. He held out his hand to Reece, then to Taylor, who first wanted to wipe her palm. It was damp as a washcloth; Burdick's was completely dry.

"You two get some rest. You've been through a hellish week. If you want any personal time I'll arrange it. Won't come out of your vacation or sick leave. Are you busy now?"

Reece walked toward the door. "I've got the Hanover settlement closing in Boston next week. That's the only thing on the front burner."

"You, Ms. Lockwood?"

"No, nothing," she replied, still numb.

"Then take some time off. In fact, I'd urge you to. Might be best."

Taylor nodded and began to speak but hesitated. She

was waiting for some significant thought to arrive, some phrase that neatly summarized what had just happened.

Nothing occurred; her mind had jammed.

Get away with it?

"Oh, Mitchell," Burdick said, smiling, as if the suicide no longer occupied even a portion of his thoughts.

Reece turned.

"Congratulations on the Hanover settlement," the partner said. "I myself would have settled for seventy cents on the dollar. That's why you're a litigator and I'm not."

He rose and walked to the small conference room, where his wife awaited him. Burdick didn't open the door right away, though. He waited, Taylor noticed, until she and Reece had left the office.

███

They walked in silence to the paralegal pen.

Everyone in the corridors seemed to be staring at her. As if they knew the part she'd played in the partner's death.

Near her cubicle, in a place where the hall was empty, Reece took her by the arm. He bent down and whispered, "I know how you feel, Taylor. I know how *I* feel. But this wasn't our fault. There's no way we could've anticipated this."

She said nothing.

He continued, "Even if the police'd been involved the same thing would've happened."

"I know," she said in a soft voice. But it sounded lame, terribly lame. Because, of course, she didn't know anything of the kind.

Reece asked, "Come over for dinner tonight."

She nodded. "Okay, sure."

"How's eight?" Then he frowned. "Wait, it's Tuesday . . . you're playing piano at your club, right?"

Was it Tuesday? The thought of the leches in the audience and Dimitri's reference to her satin touch suddenly repulsed her. "Think I'll cancel for tonight."

Reece gave a wan smile. "I'll see you later." He seemed to be looking for something to add but said nothing more. He looked up and down the hallway to make sure it was empty then hugged her hard and walked away.

Taylor called Ms. Strickland and told her she was taking the rest of the day off. She couldn't get the supervisor off the line, though; all the woman wanted to do was talk about Clayton's suicide. Finally she managed to hang up. Taylor avoided Carrie Mason and Sean Lillick and a half dozen of the other paralegals and snuck out the back door of the firm.

At home she loaded dirty clothes into the basket but got only as far as the front door. She stopped and set the laundry down. She turned on her Yamaha keyboard and played music for a few hours then took a nap.

At six that night she called Reece at home.

"Look," she said. "I'm sorry, I can't come over tonight."

"Sure," he said uncertainly. Then he asked, "Are you all right?"

"Yeah. I've got the fatigues. Bad."

"I understand." But he sounded edgy. "Is this ... Come on, tell me, is what happened going to affect us?"

Oh, brother ... you can hardly *ever* get men to talk seriously. And then, at the worst possible time, you can't stop them. "No, Mitch. It's not that. I just need some R&R time."

"Whatever you want," he said. "That's fine. I'll be here. It's just ... I guess I miss you."

" 'Night."

"Sleep well. Call me tomorrow."

She took a long bath then called home. Taylor was troubled to hear her father answer.

"Jesus, Taylie, what the hell happened at your shop?"

No "counselor" now. They were regressing to her grade-school nickname.

"I just heard," her father continued. "Was that somebody you worked for, this Clayton fellow?"

"I knew him, yeah. Not too well."

"Well, take some advice: You keep a low profile, young lady."

"What?" she asked, put off by his professorial tone.

"You keep your head down. The firm's going to have some scars from a suicide. We don't want any of it to rub off on you."

How can scars rub off? Taylor thought cynically. But of course she said nothing other than: "I'm just a paralegal, Dad. Reporters from the *Times* aren't going to be writing me up."

Although, she added to herself, if they'd told the whole story by rights they *should*.

"Killed himself?" Samuel Lockwood mused. "If you can't stand the heat stay out of the kitchen."

"Maybe there was more to it than standing the heat, Dad."

"He took the coward's way out and he hurt your shop."

"Not mine," Taylor said. But her voice was soft and Samuel Lockwood didn't hear.

"You want to talk to your mother?" he asked.

"Please."

"I'll get her. Just remember what I said, Taylie."

"Sure, Dad."

Her mother, who'd clearly had a glass of wine too many, was happy to hear from her daughter and, to Taylor's relief, wasn't the least alarmist about what had happened at the firm. Taylor slipped into a very different mode with her—far less defensive and tense—and the women began chatting about soap operas and distant relatives and Taylor's Christmas trip home to Maryland.

The woman was so cheerful and comforting in fact that Taylor, on a whim, upped the length of her stay from three days to seven. Hell, Donald Burdick wants me to take some time off? Okay, I'll take some time off.

Her mother was delighted and they talked for a few minutes longer but then Taylor said she had to go; she was afraid her father would come back on the line.

She put a frozen pouch of spaghetti into a pot of water.

That and an apple were dinner. Then she lay on her couch, watching a *Cheers* rerun.

Mitchell Reece called once but she let her answering machine do the talking for her. He left a short message, saying only that he was thinking of her. The words shored her up a bit.

But still, she didn't call back.

Taylor Lockwood, curled on the old sofa, the TV yammering mindlessly in front of her, thought about when she was a teenager and her Labrador retriever would pile into bed next to her and lie against an adjacent pillow until she scooted him off. She'd then lie still, waiting for sleep, while she felt, in the warmth radiating from the empty pillow, the first glimmerings of understanding that the pain that solitude conjures within us is a false pain and has nothing to do with solitude at all.

Indeed, being alone was curative, she believed.

She thought about Reece and wondered if he was different, if he was like her father, who sought company when he was troubled—though it was not the presence of his family Samuel Lockwood had ever needed but that of business associates, politicians, fellow partners and clients.

But that's a different story, she thought wearily.

She lay back on the couch and ten hours later opened her eyes to a gray morning.

She took the next day off and spent much of the morning and early afternoon Christmas shopping. When she returned home, in the late afternoon, there was another call from Reece and a curious one from Sean Lillick. He seemed drunk and he rambled on for a few minutes about Clayton's death, an edge to his voice. He mentioned that Carrie Mason wasn't going to Clayton's memorial service with him and asked if Taylor wanted to go.

No, she thought. But didn't call him back.

Thom Sebastian too had left a message, asking her to phone back. She didn't call him either.

She rummaged through the mail she'd picked up downstairs and found, mixed in among the Christmas cards, a self-addressed envelope from a music company. Her heart sank as she felt the thick tape inside and realized what it contained. Ripping the envelope open, she upended it and let her demo tape clatter out onto the table.

This wasn't the last of the tapes she'd sent out for consideration—there were still about a half dozen out at various companies—but it was the important one, the only tape that had made it to a label's Artists and Repertoire committee.

There was no response letter; someone had simply jotted on her own cover note, "Thanks, but not for us."

She tossed it into a Macy's box with the rest of them and, finally, opened that morning's *New York Times*. She read the article she'd been avoiding all day, headlined:

WALL STREET LAWYER KILLS SELF
PRESSURE AT WHITE-SHOE FIRM
CITED IN DEATH OF PARTNER, 52

Burdick apparently had indeed gotten away with it.

His artistry was astonishing. Not a word about the Hanover & Stiver case, nothing about the theft of the promissory note. Nothing about her or Mitchell or the merger.

Burdick was quoted, calling the death a terrible tragedy and saying that the profession had lost a brilliant attorney. The reporter also quoted several members of the firm—Bill Stanley mostly (well, the PR firm)—discussing Clayton's huge workload and his moodiness. The article reported that in the past year Clayton had billed over twenty-six hundred hours, a huge number for lawyers of his seniority. There was a sidebar on stress among overworked professionals.

She sighed and threw the newspaper away then washed the ink off her hands as if it were blood.

At five-thirty the doorbell rang.

Who could it be? Neighbors? Thom Sebastian assaulting her to beg for a date?

Ralph Dudley simply assaulting her?

She opened the door.

Mitchell Reece, wearing a windbreaker, walked inside and asked her if she had a cat.

"What?" she asked, bewildered by his quick entrance.

"A cat," he repeated.

"No, why? Are you allergic? What are you doing here?"

"Or fish, or anything you have to feed regularly?"

She was so pleased to see him in a playful mood—so different from the shock in his face after Clayton's death—that she joked back, "Just occasional boyfriends. But none at the moment, as I think you know."

"Come on downstairs. I want to show you something."

"But—"

He held his finger to his lips. "Let's go." She followed him out to the street, where a limo awaited, a black Lincoln. He opened the door and pointed inside, where she saw three large bags from Paragon Sporting Goods and two sets of new Rossignol skis propped across the seats.

Taylor laughed. "Mitchell, what are you doing?"

"Time for my lesson. Don't you remember? You were going to teach me to ski."

"Where? Central Park?"

"You know of someplace called Cannon? It's in New Hampshire. I just called the weather number. Four inches of new powder. I don't know what that means but even the recorded voice sounded excited so I assume it's good."

"But when?"

"But now," he said.

"Just like that?"

"The firm's jet's on the ramp at La Guardia. And they bill us by the hour so I suggest you hustle your butt. Go pack."

"This is crazy. What about work?"

"Donald called—he or his wife found out you like to ski so he ordered us to take some time off. He's giving us the trip all-expenses-paid. He called it a Christmas bonus. I've bought everything we need, I think. The store told me what to get. Skis, poles, black stretch pants, boots, bindings, sweaters, goggles. And . . ." He held up a box.

"What's that?" Taylor asked.

"That? The most important thing of all."

She opened it. "A crash helmet?"

"That's for me." He shrugged. "Maybe you're a good teacher." He smiled. "And maybe you're not."

CHAPTER THIRTY

The helmet wasn't a bad idea. Reece had been on the bunny slope at the Cannon ski resort in New Hampshire for only fifteen minutes when he fell and jammed his thumb.

One of the resort doctors, a cheerful Indian, had taped it.

"Is it broken?" Reece had asked.

"No, is no fracture."

"Why does it hurt so much?"

"Lots of nerves in fingers," the doctor said, beaming. "Many, many nerves."

Afterward, they sat in the small lounge in the inn.

"Oh, Mitchell, I feel so bad," she said. "But you did a very respectable first run."

"My thumb doesn't feel too respectable. Is it always this cold?"

"Cannon's got the coldest, windiest runs in New England, dear," she said, pulling his head against her neck. "People have frozen to death not far from here."

"Really? Well, we wouldn't want to have too much fun now, would we?"

Reece actually didn't seem too upset about either the accident or the weather. And she soon learned why: He preferred to sit out the day with what he had smuggled with him—files from the Hanover settlement closing. Taylor too didn't mind; she was eager to get out onto the double-diamond trails and kick some ski butt, not baby-sit him on the beginner slopes or worry about him on the intermediates.

She kissed him. "Sit in the lodge and behave yourself."

As she crunched her way toward the lifts, he called, "Good luck. I assume you don't say, 'Break a leg.'"

She smiled, stomped into her skis and slid down the slight incline to the bottom of the lift.

At the top of the mountain, she eased off the chair and braked to a stop just past the lift house. She bent down and washed her goggles in snow. The White Mountains were, as she'd told him, son-of-a-bitch cold and the wind steadily scraped across her face. She pulled silk hand liners on and replaced her mittens, then poled her way into position and looked down the mountain. Her impression had always been that most runs never look as steep from the top as they do from the bottom but as she gazed down toward the lodge, over a half mile straight below her, she saw a plunge, not a slope. Her pulse picked up and immediately she realized how right Mitchell had been to arrange the trip. How important it was to get away from the city, to distance herself from Hubbard, White & Willis, from Wendall Clayton's ghost.

She pushed off the crest of the mountain.

It was the best run of her life.

Suddenly there was nothing in her universe but speed and snow and the rhythm of her turns.

Speed, speed, speed . . .

Which was all she wanted. Her mouth was open slightly in the ellipse that suggests fear or sexual heights. Her teeth dried and stung in the frigid slipstream but the pain only added to her surge of abandon.

Taylor danced over moguls the way girls skip double-Dutch jump rope on playgrounds. Once, her skis left the ground and she landed as if the snow had risen timidly to stroke the bottom of the fiberglass. Trees, bushes, other skiers were a swift-ratcheting backdrop sweeping past, everyone hushed, it seemed, listening to the cutting hiss of her Rossignol.

She was sure she was hitting sixty or seventy miles an hour. Her hair was whipping her shoulders and back. She wished she'd borrowed Reece's helmet—not for safety, but to cut the wind resistance of the tangled mass of drag.

Then it was over. She brodied to a stop near the base of the run, her thighs in agony but her heart filled with a glorious rush of fear and victory.

She did four runs this way, until on the last one, on a big mogul, she lost control and had to windmill her arms to regain her balance.

It sobered her.

Okay, honey, one suicide a week is enough.

At the bottom of the mountain, she kicked out of her skis and loosened her boot clasps. A tall, thin man came up to her and said in a Germanic accent, "Hey, that was a, you know, pretty okay run. You feel maybe like another one?"

"Uh, no, not really."

"Okay, okay. Hey, how about a drink?"

"Sorry." She picked up her skis and walked toward the cabin. "I'm here with my boyfriend."

And she realized suddenly that, by God, she was.

███████

Taylor returned to find Reece in great spirits, the tiny room cluttered with papers and documents delivered by FedEx or DHL. He was on the phone but he motioned her to him and kissed her hard then resumed his conversation.

She sat on the bed, wincing as she pulled off her sweater

and stretch pants, and began massaging her thighs and calves.

It was around that time that Reece hung up the phone and stacked the files away in a corner.

When they awoke in mid-afternoon they went to several antique stores, which weren't the precious collections of cheese dishes and brass surveying instruments you find in Connecticut or New York. These were barns packed with furniture. Rows of dusty chairs and tables and dressers and pickle jars and canopy beds and armoires. Very rustic and practical and well cared for.

None of the shopkeepers seemed to expect them to buy anything and they didn't.

That night they ate in one of the half-dozen inter-changeable inns in the area, their menus virtually the same, they'd found: veal chop, steak, chicken, duck à l'orange, salmon or trout. Afterward, they had a drink in the common room in front of a huge fireplace.

After they made love that night and Reece had fallen asleep, Taylor Lockwood lay under the garden patch quilt of a hundred hexagons of cotton and felt the reassuring pres-sure of a man's thigh beside her. She smelled the cold air as it streamed through the inch-open window and gathered on the floor. She tried to forget about Wendall Clayton, about Hubbard, White & Willis, about life on the other side of the looking glass.

At 4 A.M. she finally fell asleep.

On Thursday morning Taylor was first in the lift line.

She skied her first run fast, smelling the clean electric scent of snow, the biting perfume of fireplace smoke, hear-ing the sharp hiss of her turns in the granular snow.

Today, however, the speed had none of the cleansing ef-fect that it'd had on her first day out. She felt alone, fright-ened, vulnerable. Like the first time her father made her ride her bike without training wheels. He'd put her on the tall Schwinn, aimed it down a hill and pushed. (She'd refused to scream until the wobbly front wheel hit a curb and she'd gone over the handlebars onto the sidewalk.)

She made mistakes, skied too defensively and nearly wiped out bad.

At the bottom of the mountain she loaded her skis and boots into the rental car.

No, Dad, I'm *not* getting back on the fucking horse, she thought now.

She drove to their inn and went back to the room, where Reece was taking a shower. She poured coffee from the pot he'd ordered and dropped into the musty armchair.

Thinking:

Where and for a first cause of action, Taylor Lockwood did willfully . . .

Outside she could see other skiers heading down the mountain, some fast, some timidly.

. . . and with full knowledge of the consequences, without a warrant or other license, enter the office of one Wendall Clayton, the decedent, and . . .

She sipped the coffee.

Where and for a first cause of action, Taylor Lockwood did willfully ascertain and make public certain facts about one Wendall Clayton, the decedent, that caused . . .

Taylor sat back in the chair, closed her eyes.

. . . that caused said decedent to blow his fucking brains out.

Mitchell Reece, wrapped in a towel, opened the bathroom door and, smiling with pleasant surprise, walked up to her. Kissed her on the mouth.

"Back early. You okay?"

"I don't know. Wasn't fun. Thumb still hurt?" she asked.

"A bit. I tell you I'm no good at this sort of thing. . . . I'm much better with simpleminded, safe sports. . . ." He seemed to be groping for a joke, something cute about sex probably, but he sensed that she was upset. He sat down on the bed opposite her.

"So what's up, Taylor?"

She shook her head.

"What is it?" he persisted.

"Mitchell, you know history?"

He motioned with an open palm for her to continue.

She asked, "You know what the Star Chamber was?"

"Just that it was a medieval English court. Why?"

"We learned about it in my European history course in college. It came back to me last night. The Star Chamber was a court without a jury, run by the Crown. When the king thought the regular court might decide against him he'd bring a case in the Star Chamber. You got hauled up before these special judges—the king's privy counselors. They'd pretend to have a trial but you can guess what happened. If the king wanted him guilty he was guilty. Very fast justice, very efficient."

He looked at the coffee, swirled it. He set it down without drinking any more. His face was somber.

She blurted, "Christ, Mitchell, the man is dead."

"And you think it's your fault."

A spasm of anger passed through her. Why can't he understand? "I was so stupid." Taylor looked at him briefly. Wondering how Clayton had felt lifting the gun. Had it been heavy? Had there been pain? How long had he lived after pulling the trigger? What had he seen? A burst of yellow light, a second of confusion, a wild eruption of thoughts, then nothing?

"Taylor," Reece said with measured words, "Clayton was crazy. No sane man would've stolen the note in the first place and no sane man would've killed himself if he'd been caught. You can't anticipate people like that."

She gripped his arm firmly. "But that's the point, Mitchell. You're thinking the problem is that Wendall outflanked us—that our fault was we weren't clever enough. But the *fault* was that we shouldn't've been playing the game in the first place. That firm's like Wonderland—it's got its own set of rules, which don't even make sense half the time but you never think about that because you're so deep in the place. Topsy-turvy. . . . Everything's topsy-turvy."

"What're you saying?"

"That we *should've* gone to the police. And we should've

let the chips fall wherever. So New Amsterdam would've left the firm. Well, so what? And you? You're one of the best lawyers in New York. You would've landed on your feet."

He rose and walked to the window.

Finally he said softly, "I know, I know. . . . You think I haven't been living with exactly what you're talking about?" He turned to face her. "But if I don't lay part of the blame at Clayton's feet, it undermines all my beliefs as a lawyer." He touched his chest. "It undermines all that I am. You know, this is something I'm going to have to live with too. I mean, you did what I asked you to do. But ultimately it was my decision."

So here was another aspect of Mitchell Reece—not all-powerful, not in control, not immune to pain.

She walked next to him, lowered her head onto his shoulder. His hand twined through her hair. "I'm sorry, Mitchell. This is very odd for me. It's not the sort of thing *Ms.* or *Savvy* prepares the working girl for."

He rubbed her shoulders.

"Can I ask a favor?" she said.

"Sure."

"Can we go back?"

He was surprised. "You want to leave?"

"I've had a wonderful time. But I'm in such a funky mood. I don't want to spoil our time together and I think I'd be a drag to be with."

"But I haven't learned to ski yet."

"Are you kidding? You're a graduate of the Taylor Lockwood School of Skiing Injury. You can go out now and break arms and legs all by yourself. With that kind of education there's no telling how far you can go."

"Let me see when I can get the jet."

CHAPTER THIRTY-ONE

████████ Thursday afternoon, Taylor Lockwood stood in front of the Metropolitan Museum of Art on Fifth Avenue, looking up at a brown brick apartment building across the street, about as far from the wilderness of New Hampshire as you could get, conceptually speaking.

She checked the address again and verified that she had found the right building. Inside, a solemn doorman regarded her carefully and then called upstairs to announce her.

She was approved and he nodded toward the elevator.

"Sixth floor," he said.

"Which apartment?" she asked.

He looked confused for a moment then said, "It's the whole floor."

"Oh."

She stepped into the leather-padded elevator and was slowly transported to a private entryway. She smoothed her hair, looking into a brass mirror, a huge thing. The foyer was in dark red and filled with Georgian yellow and white dovetail trim. The pictures were old English hunting scenes.

Plaster scrolls and cherubs and angels and columns were everywhere.

An ageless, unsmiling woman in a plain navy shift answered the door, asked her to wait then disappeared down the hallway. Taylor glanced through the doorway. The rooms were larger versions of the foyer. She looked back into the mirror and stared at herself, at a person who was thinner than she'd expected. Thinner and...what else? More drawn, gaunter, grimmer? She tried smiling; it didn't take.

A shadow passed across her and Mrs. Wendall Clayton stood in the doorway: a middle-aged woman, wearing the stiff, straight-cut, big-patterned clothes that people who learned style in the sixties still sometimes favor. Her straight hair was swept back and sprayed perfectly into place. Her thin face was severe. The foundation makeup had been applied thickly but her skin wasn't good and Taylor could see red patches beneath the pancake.

They shook hands and made introductions.

Taylor followed the woman into the living room. Why the hell am I doing this? she wondered suddenly. What possible point could it have?

I'm here to give you my deepest sympathy.

I'm here to say I worked with your husband.

I'm here to say that even though he's dead don't feel too bad because he tried to seduce me.

Mrs. Clayton sat upright in an uncomfortable satin wingback, Taylor in a spongy armchair.

I'm here because I helped kill your husband....

The widow asked, "Tea? Coffee?"

"No, thank you," Taylor said. And then realized that the woman's dress was red and that this was hardly a household in mourning—the room was festooned with antique Christmas decorations and there was a faint but rich scent of pine in the air. Classical Christmas music played on the stereo. Taylor looked at the woman's cocked eyebrow and her expression, which wasn't one of bitterness or sorrow. It was closer to curiosity.

"I worked with your husband, Mrs. Clayton."

"Yes."

"I just came to tell you how sorry I was."

And Taylor understood then, only at that moment, that uttering those words was all she could do. Watching this stolid, lone woman (Taylor couldn't picture her as one half of the Claytons) light a cigarette, she understood that the spirits of Donald Burdick and Vera Burdick and Messrs. Hubbard, White and Willis themselves had accompanied her here and were laying cold fingers on her lips. She could not, even here, in Clayton's home, do what she desperately wanted to do: explain.

Explain that she'd been the one who'd uncovered the terrible secrets about her husband, that she was the cause—the proximate cause, the law would say—of his death. No, there'd be no confession. Taylor knew what bound her. In this joint venture Hubbard, White & Willis had secured her soul.

"That's very kind of you." After a pause the woman asked: "Did I see you at the funeral? There were so many people."

"I wasn't there, no." Taylor eased back in the chair, uncomfortable, and crossed her arms. Wished she'd asked for coffee to keep her hands busy.

Now she looked around the room, aware of its size. The ceilings were twenty feet high. It reminded her of National Trust mansions and palaces in England. Taylor said, "He was an excellent lawyer...."

Clayton's widow said, "I suppose." She was examining a tabletop. It seemed to be a dust inspection. "But then we didn't talk much about his career."

Taylor was counting the squares in the carpet. Trying to figure out the designs. Finally: St. George and the dragon, she believed.

Beware the Jabberwock...

The widow paused. "The truth is, Ms. Lockwood, I'm a little bewildered. I don't know you—though we may have met before. But you seem genuinely upset by my husband's death and I can't quite figure out why. You're not like the

little sycophants who've come by since he died—the associates at the firm. They thought they were covering it up but I
could see through them—in their eyes you could tell that
they were amused at his death. I know they'd chuckled
about it over their beers when they were alone. Do you
know why they were here?"

Taylor was silent.

"They came because they thought word would get back
to the firm that they'd done their duty. They'd made an appearance that might earn them another point or two, get
them a step closer to being partner." She pressed out her
cigarette. "Which is so ironic, of course, because they didn't
grasp the situation at all. They should've been avoiding this
house as if it were a leper colony. If word gets back to
Burdick that young Samuel and Frederick and Douglas were
paying respects to me, well, then, my God, they're in Dutch.
At worst, they'd had the bad judgment to pick the wrong
side; at best, they were displaying an oblivion about law
firm politics.

"So you see, Ms. Lockwood, I am a little perplexed by
your sympathy call." A smile. "That sounds appropriately
Victorian, doesn't it? Sympathy call. Well, you aren't here to
toady. You aren't here to gloat. Your dress and demeanor tell
me you couldn't care less about what the Donald Burdicks
and Wendall Claytons of the world think of you. You're
clearly not one of the little malleable things he picked for
his, dare I use the euphemism, girlfriends. . . . No, you're
genuinely upset. I can see that. Well, you may have respected my husband as a lawyer and an ambitious businessman. But I doubt very much if you respected him as a
human being. And I know without a doubt that you didn't
like him."

"You had a loss in your life and I'm sorry," Taylor said
evenly. "I didn't mean anything more or less than that." She
fell silent, watching this shrewd woman light another cigarette with bony, red hands. It seemed as if the smoke that
floated out of her nose and mouth had over the years taken
with it her weight and softness.

Mrs. Clayton finally laughed. "Well, I appreciate that, Ms. Lockwood. Forgive my cynicism. I hope I haven't offended you. But don't feel sorry for me. Heavens, no. You're young. You don't have any experience with marriages of convenience."

Well, let's not go that far, Taylor thought, replaying many images: her parents' twin beds, her mother with her glass of wine sitting alone in front of the television, her father calling at midnight saying he was staying at his club. Night after night after night . . .

Clayton's widow said, "I guess you'd say our relationship wasn't even a marriage. It was a merger. His assets and mine. A certain camaraderie. Love? Was there any love between Williams Computing and RFC Industries when they consolidated? To name just one of the deals that took so much of Wendall's time . . ." She looked out over the park, spindly with branches, the residue of snow faintly surviving in shadows. "And that's the irony, you see."

"What?"

"Love—there was never any between us. And yet I'm the one he was most content with. Cold, scheming Wendall, the power broker. The master of control. But once outside of our life, he was at sea. Vulnerable. That's why he killed himself, of course. For love."

"What do you mean?" Taylor heard herself ask, her heart pounding fast.

"He killed himself for love," the widow repeated. "That's the one thing Wendall didn't understand and couldn't control. Love. Oh, how he wanted it. And as with so many beautiful, powerful people it was denied him. He was an alcoholic of love. He'd go off on his benders. With his chippies. His little sluts. And there were plenty of them—women would flock to him. A few of the men, too, I should tell you. How they all would want him!

"He'd spirit them away on carriage rides, buy them roses, have a breakfast tray put together at Le Perigord and sent to their apartments. Wendall goes a-courting. They were all disasters, of course. The girls never quite lived up

to what he wanted. The older ones . . . they turned out to be
every bit as superficial and material and cold"—she laughed
again, dropping a worm of ash in the ashtray—"as cold as I
was. Or he'd pick a young puppy, some ingenue, who'd
cling to him desperately, rearrange her life around him.
Then he'd feel the arms around his neck, dragging him
down. Someone *relying* on him. My Lord, we couldn't have
that, could we? Then he'd dump them. And back he'd come
to me. To nurse his wounds."

Taylor jumped in to steer the conversation back on
course. "What do you mean about his suicide? Killing himself for love?"

"It's the only thing that makes sense. He must've fallen
madly in love with somebody and he was sure she was the
one. When she told him no it must've devastated him."

"But the note he left said he was under pressure at work,
stress."

"Oh, he wrote that for my benefit. If he'd mentioned a
girlfriend, well, it would have embarrassed me." She
laughed. "The idea of Wendall killing himself because of
pressure? Why, he lived for pressure. He wasn't happy unless he had ten projects going at once. I've never seen him
happier than over the past few months working on the
merger, doing deals for his clients . . . and then planning the
other firm."

"What other firm?"

She looked at Taylor cautiously then pushed out her
cigarette. "I suppose it doesn't matter anymore. In case the
merger didn't go through, he was going to leave Hubbard,
White & Willis, take his boys and a couple of dozen partners and open his own firm. It was his alternative plan. I
think he almost preferred that to the merger. Because he'd
be a named partner. He always wanted to have his name on
the letterhead. Clayton, Jones & Smith, or whatever."

Another firm? Taylor wondered.

The widow resumed her examination of Central Park
flora. Then smiled. "That note . . . He could have said in the

note how unhappy he was with me as a wife. With our life together . . . But he didn't. I was very touched."

Rising, Mrs. Clayton looked at her watch. "I'd like to talk to you longer." She picked up her Dunhill cigarette case. "But I have bridge club in ten minutes."

███████

Aristocratize.

Taylor Lockwood was sitting at Wendall Clayton's desk.

It was late afternoon and a yellow-gray illumination lit the room from the pale sun over New York Harbor. The office lights were out and the door closed.

She looked at the jotting on a faded piece of foolscap.

Aristocratize.

Was that a word? Taylor glanced at the brass, the carpets, the vases, the tile painting, the wall of deal binders, the stacks of papers like the one that had held the note and tape recordings of her conversations with Mitchell Reece. The huge chair creaked as she moved.

Men of most renowned virtue . . .

Spinning around once more to face the window, she decided that, whether it was real or not, "aristocratize" certainly described the essence of Wendall Clayton.

There was no reason for her to be in the firm. Technically she was still on vacation, courtesy of Donald Burdick. She could leave at any moment, smile at Ms. Strickland and walk out of the front door with impunity. She was, in fact, due at Mitchell Reece's loft right about now. (It turned out that he could cook after all and was planning to make them a tortellini salad for dinner; he was currently baking the bread himself!) She wanted to lie in his huge bathtub, a wonderful bathtub that had claw feet, to luxuriate in the water holding a thin-stemmed glass of wine and smell him cooking whatever went into a tortellini salad.

Instead, Taylor slouched down in Clayton's chair and spun slowly in a circle, 360 degrees, once, twice, three times.

Alice spinning as she fell down the rabbit hole, Alice
buffeted on the ocean of tears, Alice arguing with the Queen
of Hearts. . . .

Off with their heads, off with their heads!

Taylor stopped spinning. She began what she'd come
here for: a detailed examination of the contents of Wendall
Clayton's desk and filing cabinets.

A half hour later, Taylor Lockwood walked slowly
downstairs to the paralegal pen. She made certain that no
one was in the cubicles surrounding hers then looked
through her address book and found the number of her favorite private eye, John Silbert Hemming.

He stopped suddenly, jolted, as he watched her slip out
of Wendall Clayton's office, looking around carefully as if
she didn't want to be seen.

Sean Lillick ducked into a darkened conference room
where Taylor Lockwood couldn't see him. It had scared the
hell out of him, as he was walking toward Clayton's office,
to see the sudden shadow appearing in the doorway. For a
split second all his chic, retro-punk East Village cynical sen-
sibilities had vanished and he'd thought: Fuck me, it's a
ghost . . .

What the hell had she been doing in there? he now
wondered.

Lillick waited until she was gone and the corridor was
empty. Then he too ducked into the dead partner's office
and locked the door behind him.

It was excellent tortellini salad—filled with all sorts of
good things only about half of which she recognized. The
bread was lopsided but Reece had propped it up in a cute
way. Whatever its shape, it tasted wonderful. He opened a
cold Pouilly-Fuissé.

They ate for ten minutes, Taylor nodding as he told her
about the impending settlement conference in Boston dur-

ing which Hanover & Stiver would transfer the bulk of the principal of the loan back to New Amsterdam. He told anecdotes about some of Lloyd Hanover's shady business dealings. Normally, she liked it when he talked about his job because, although she didn't always understand the nuances, the animation and enthusiasm that lit up his face were infectious.

Tonight, though, she was distracted.

He finally caught on that something was wrong and his voice faded. He looked concerned. But before he could question her, Taylor set her fork down with a tap. "Mitchell."

He refilled their glasses and cocked an eyebrow at her.

"There's something I have to tell you."

"Yes?" he asked cautiously, perhaps suspecting some personal confession.

"I've been looking into a few things. About Wendall Clayton."

Reece sipped his wine. Nodded.

"He didn't kill himself." Taylor picked a lopsided bit of bread crust off the table and dropped it on her plate. "He was murdered."

CHAPTER THIRTY-TWO

Mitchell Reece smiled, as if waiting for a punch line.

Then: "Why do you think that?"

"I went to see his widow," Taylor said. Then she added quickly, "Oh, I wasn't going to tell her what happened—about the note and everything. But..." She paused. "Well, you know, I'm not sure why I went. It was something I just had to do."

He said, "I hear she's a bitch."

Taylor shrugged. "She was civil enough to me. But you know what she told me? That if Wendall couldn't get the merger through he was going to start his own firm."

"What?" Reece frowned.

Nodding, she said, "He had it all planned out. I went through his desk at the firm. I found business plans, bank loan applications. He even had the firm name selected. Clayton, Stone & Samuels. He had a sample letterhead printed up and he'd been talking to a broker about space in the Equitable Building."

Reece too had put down his utensils. "But if he was ready to start his own firm it makes no sense for him to risk his career to push the merger through."

"Exactly. Stealing the note? He'd be disbarred if he got caught. And he'd probably be prosecuted." Taylor held up a finger. "Another thing. Think about the gun."

"The gun he used?"

"Right. I called my detective, my private eye, and he talked to some buddies of his at the police department. The gun he used was a .38 Smith & Wesson knockoff, made in Italy. No serial number. It's one of the most popular street guns there is. 'It's like your McDonald's of firearms' is what John said. But if you're going to kill yourself why buy an untraceable gun? You go to a sporting goods store, show a driver's license and buy a twelve-gauge shotgun."

"Or," Reece said, sitting forward, "why even shoot yourself? It's messy, unpleasant for your loved ones. I'd think you'd park your car in the garage with the engine running."

She nodded her agreement. "What I think is that somebody else stole the note and planted it in Clayton's office. Then when we found it he murdered Clayton to make it look like suicide."

"Who's the 'he'?" Reece asked.

"At first, I wondered if his widow might've done it. I mean here she was hosting a bridge party right after he died. She knew about the affairs he'd had. So she certainly had a motive."

"And she must have inherited some bucks from him."

"True. But then I got to thinking and it seems that the killer'd need to know about the firm and have access to it. Clayton's widow isn't like Vera Burdick, who's there all the time. Besides, Mrs. Clayton didn't seem that upset with all his affairs."

"Well," Reece suggested, "what about one of them? A lover? Somebody Clayton dumped?"

"Sure. That's a possibility. Or the husband or wife of

somebody he'd had an affair with. But," Taylor added, smiling, "what about some of the people we thought were suspects: Ralph Dudley. Clayton had found out about Junie and was blackmailing him."

"And Thom Sebastian. Clayton was the main reason he didn't make partner."

"He occurred to me, too. . . . And one other possibility."

Reece frowned, shaking his head.

Taylor pointed upward. "Go to the top."

"Donald Burdick?" Reece laughed. "Look, I know the motive's there. But Donald? I can't believe it. Whoever stole the note risked not only my career but risked losing a client as well—if we lost the case. There's no way Donald would've put New Amsterdam at risk."

Taylor countered, "But there *was* no risk. At the very worst, if we hadn't found the note, Donald would've sent his thief to get the note back from Clayton's office and it would've shown up on the file room floor or someplace in time for you to introduce it at trial."

Reece nodded, considering this. "And look how well Burdick covered everything up. The medical examiner, the prosecutor, the press. . . Nobody knows about the promissory note theft. And everything else—the evidence we found in Clayton's office, the real suicide note—I'm sure Burdick's shredded it by now." But then Reece shook his head. "Let's think about this. If it *is* Burdick remember that he's real tight with City Hall and Albany. We can't trust the police. We'll go to the U.S. attorney's office; I've still got friends there. I'll call them—"

"But didn't Donald call somebody in the Justice Department?" she asked. "After they found the body?"

Reece paused. "I don't remember. Yeah, I think he did."

Taylor said, "You're going to Boston tomorrow for the settlement closing. Do you know anybody in Justice up there?"

"Yeah, I do. I haven't talked to him for a while. Let's see if he's still there." He walked to his desk and found his address book and picked up the phone. But he looked at it warily.

"Bugs?" Taylor asked.

"Let's not take any chances—we'll go downstairs."

On the street they found a pay phone and Reece made a credit card call.

"Sam Latham, please. . . . Hey, Sam, Mitchell Reece."

The men apparently knew each other well and Taylor deduced from the conversation that they'd both been prosecutors in New York some years ago. After a few whatever-happened-to's, Reece told him their suspicions about Clayton's death. They made plans to meet at the U.S. attorney's office in Boston the next day, after the Hanover settlement closing. He hung up.

"He's getting his boss and an FBI agent to meet with me."

Taylor felt a huge weight lifted from her. At last the authorities were involved. This was the way the system was supposed to work.

They returned upstairs. Reece closed the front door and latched it then walked up behind her, enfolded her in his arms. She leaned her head back and slowly turned so that they were face-to-face.

He glanced at the table, where the meal sat unfinished: the exceptionally good tortellini salad, the cold wine, the sagging bread. She smiled and, with her fingertips, turned his head back to face her.

She kissed him hard.

Without a word they walked to Reece's bed.

███

So far, not so good . . .

Thom Sebastian sat back in his office chair, pushing aside the documents he'd been working on all morning, a revolving credit agreement for New Amsterdam Bank.

He should have been comfortable, should have been content. But he was troubled.

Wendall Clayton, the man who'd destroyed his chances for partnership at Hubbard, White, was gone—as dead as a shot pheasant in one of the hunting prints hanging in the partner's office.

Good.

But his life didn't really *feel* good. He had a brooding sense that his entire world was about to be torn apart. And this terrified him.

Three times he reached for the phone, hesitated, put his hands flat on his thick thighs and remained where he was.

He peeked under his blotter and saw the notes he'd gathered on Taylor Lockwood over the past ten days or so.

Taylor Lockwood . . . the sole reason that things weren't so good.

Come on, Mr. Fucking Negotiator, make a decision.

But ultimately, he knew, there was no decision at all. Because there was only one thing to do.

The problem was finding the courage to do it.

███

The next morning Reece called Taylor from Boston.

She was at her apartment; she'd decided it was safest to stay away from the firm. He called to report that the settlement had gone well. The money from the Hanover settlement had been safely wired into a New Amsterdam account and he'd endured Lloyd Hanover's relentless glare and potshots at lawyers throughout the closing.

Reece was on his way to meet with his friend in the U.S. attorney's office.

"I miss you," he said.

"Hurry home," she told him. "Let's get this behind us and go back and ski for real."

"Or," he joked, "go back and shop and eat dinner at the inns."

"I'll get you on black diamond slopes sooner or later."

"What the hell? I've still got one thumb and eight fingers left."

After some Christmas shopping Taylor stopped at a coffee shop on Sixth Avenue, around the corner from her apartment, for some lunch.

Sitting at the counter, she wondered what to get Reece for Christmas. He had all the clothes he needed. Wine was too impersonal.

Then she recalled his collection of lead soldiers.

She'd find one that was perfect for him—just one. A special one, antique, expensive. But where? Well, this was New York, the city that boasted neighborhoods devoted to special interests: the garment district, the flower district, even the sewing machine district. There was probably a cluster of stores somewhere in Midtown selling antique toys.

A man sat down next to her, a large workman in gray coveralls, wearing a baseball cap. There was something vaguely familiar about him and she wondered if he worked in her apartment building; the structure was old and there were always people renovating and repairing.

He pulled out a book and began reading.

Taylor's chicken soup came and as she was sprinkling Tabasco on it the man next to her took a sip of coffee. When he replaced the cup his elbow knocked his book to the floor. It dropped at her feet.

"Oh, sorry," he said, blushing.

"No problem," she said and bent down to retrieve the book. When she handed it to him he smiled his thanks and said, "I like this place. You come here a lot?" A trace of some accent from one of the outer boroughs.

"Some."

"With your boyfriend?" he asked, smiling, ruefully.

She nodded, and let the small lie do double duty: let him know she wasn't interested and save his ego from a flat-out rejection.

"Ah, well," he sighed and returned to his book.

When she left he was working on a double cheese-burger. He waved to her and called, "Merry Christmas."

"You too," she said.

Back at home, she pulled the phone book out from under her bed and looked up toy stores.

Well, let's start at the beginning.

As she stood to get the phone she realized she felt achy, as if a cold were coming on. Her head was hurting a bit too. She went into the bathroom to get some aspirin, swallowed them down and returned to the bedroom to start calling the stores in search of Reece's Christmas present.

Feeling tired . . .

She reclined on the bed and picked up the cordless phone.

She'd dialed the first digit when she gasped and sat up fast. A churning pain struck somewhere deep within her abdomen. Her face burst out in sweat.

"Oh, man," she whispered. Not the flu, not now. . . .

Recalling that she often got sick around Christmas when she was young. A therapist she'd seen for a while had wondered if it wasn't her dread of a holiday presided over by a domineering father.

"Oh . . ." She moaned again, pressing the skin above the pang hard with both her hands. It ceased for a moment then exploded in another eruption of agony.

Taylor stood up, adding nausea to the sensation. The room began to spin and she tried to control her fall to the parquet floor. Her head hit the dressing table and she blacked out.

When she opened her eyes she saw claws.

The Jabberwock's claws, disemboweling her, tearing her stomach, throat, the back of her mouth, shredding her flesh . . .

She squinted. No, no, they were just the claws on the legs of her bed. She—

The pain stunned her again and she moaned, a low, animal sound.

Sweat filled her eyes and ran down her nose. She wrapped her arms around herself and drew her legs up, trying to stop the pain. Every muscle hard as rubber, she tried to will the pain away but this had no effect. Then the nausea overwhelmed her and Taylor crawled to the toilet, opened the seat and held herself up on one arm while she vomited and retched for what seemed like hours.

Her hands shook, her skin was inflamed. She stared at the tiny hexagonal tiles in front of her until she fainted again. Consciousness returned and she struggled for the phone. But her muscles gave out and she dropped again to the floor. From a distant dimension she heard a thunk—the sound of her head hitting the tiles.

She understood now that she'd been poisoned.... The man at the restaurant. The workman in the coveralls and baseball cap. *He* was the one who'd stolen the note, the one who'd run them off the road, the one who'd killed Wendall Clayton.

That was why he'd seemed familiar—because she must've seen him in the firm or following her and Reece earlier. Maybe he'd overheard her conversation with John Silbert Hemming. Maybe he'd put a tap on *her* phone at the office or even in her apartment.

She—

Then the poison began to churn again and she started to retch in earnest, unable to breathe, trying to scream for help, slamming her hand on the dresser so that somebody might hear and come to her aid. Perfume bottles fell, makeup, an Alice in Wonderland snowball crashed to the floor and broke, the water and sparkles spattering her.

She began to pummel the floor—until she realized she had no feeling in her hand; it was completely numb. Taylor Lockwood began to cry.

She crawled to the phone, dialed 911.

"Police and fire emergency."

She couldn't speak. Her tongue had turned to wood.

The air was becoming thinner and thinner, sucked from the room.

The voice said, "Is anyone there? Hello? Hello? . . ."

Taylor's hands stopped working. She dropped the phone. She closed her eyes.

CHAPTER THIRTY-THREE

"What happened?" Carrie Mason asked.

The doctor was a woman in her mid-thirties. She had straight blond hair and wore no makeup except for bright blue eye shadow. The medico's badge said Dr. V. Sarravich.

The woman said, "Botulism."

"Botulism? Food poisoning?"

"I'm afraid she ate some severely tainted food."

"Is she going to be okay?"

"Botulism's much more serious than other types of food poisoning. She's unconscious, in shock. Severely dehydrated. The prognosis isn't good. We should get in touch with her family, if she has any. She lived alone and apparently the police couldn't find her address book or any next-of-kin information. We found your name and number on a card in her purse."

"I don't know where her parents live. I'll give you the name of someone who can get in touch with them. Can I see her?"

"She's in the Critical Care Unit. You can't visit now," Dr.

Sarravich said. Medical people were all so serious, the girl thought.

Carrie asked, "Is it really bad?"

She hesitated—a concession to delicacy—and said, "I'm afraid it may be fatal and even if it isn't there could be some permanent damage."

"What kind of damage?"

"Neuromuscular."

"To her hands?" Carrie asked.

"Possibly."

"But she's a musician," the paralegal said, alarmed. "A pianist."

"It's too early to tell anything at this point." A pen and paper appeared, and the doctor asked, "Now, whom should I contact?"

Carrie wrote a name and phone number. The doctor looked at the pad. "Donald Burdick. Who is he?"

"The head of the firm she works at. He can tell you everything you want to know."

███████

Taylor's eyes opened slowly. Her skin stung from the sandblasting of fever. Her vision was blurred. Her head was in a vise of fiery pressure. Her legs and arms were useless, like blocks of wood grafted to her torso. The nausea and cramps were still rampaging through her abdomen and her throat was dry as paper.

There was a young woman in a pale blue uniform making the bed next to hers.

Taylor had never been in such pain. Every breath brought pain. Every twitch was a throb of pain. She assumed that the nerves in her hands and legs had short-circuited—she couldn't move her limbs.

Taylor whispered.

No reaction from the young woman.

She screamed.

The attendant cocked her head.

She screamed again.

No reaction. Taylor closed her eyes and rested after the agonizing effort.

Several minutes later the bed was made. As the attendant walked toward the door, she glanced at Taylor.

Taylor screamed, "Poison!"

The aide leaned down. "Did you say something, honey?" Taylor smelled fruity gum on her breath and felt like gagging.

"Poison," she managed to say. "I was poisoned."

"Yes, food poisoning," the girl said and started to leave.

Taylor screamed, "I want Mitchell!"

The girl held up the watch on her pudgy wrist. "It's not midnight. It's about six."

"I want Mitchell. Please . . ."

Taylor tried fiercely to hold on to consciousness but it spilled away like a handful of sugar. She had an impression of struggling to leap out of bed and calling Mitchell in Boston but then she realized that her legs and arms had started to spasm. Then a nurse was standing over her, staring in alarm and reaching for the call button, pushing it fiercely over and over.

And then the room went black.

At 7:30 P.M. the telephone in Donald Burdick's co-op rang.

He was in the living room. He heard Vera answer it then mentally followed her footsteps as they completed a circuit that ended in the arched entrance near him. Her calm face appeared.

"Phone, Don," Vera said. "It's the doctor."

The *Wall Street Journal* crumpled in his hand. He rose and together they walked to the den.

"Yes?" he asked.

"Mr. Burdick?" a woman's matter-of-fact voice asked. "This is Dr. Vivian Sarravich again. From Manhattan General Hospital? I'm calling about Ms. Lockwood."

"Yes?"

"I'm afraid I have bad news, sir. Miss Taylor has gone into a coma. Our neurologist's opinion is that she won't be coming out of it in the near future...if at all. And if she does she's certain to have permanent brain and neuromuscular damage."

Burdick shook his head to Vera. He held the phone out a ways so that she too could hear. "It's that bad?"

"This is the most severe case of botulism I've ever seen. The infection was much greater than usual. She's had two respiratory failures. We had to put her on a ventilator. And a feeding tube, of course."

"Her family?"

"We've told them. Her parents on on their way here."

"Yes, well, thank you, Doctor. You'll keep me posted?"

"Of course. I am sorry. We did everything we could."

"I'm sure you did."

Burdick hung up and said to his wife, "She probably won't make it."

Vera gave a neutral nod and then glanced at the maid who'd silently appeared beside them. "They're here, Mrs. Burdick."

"Show them into the den, 'Nita."

███████

Donald Burdick poured port into Waterford glasses. His hands left fingerprints in a slight coating of dust on the bottle, which, he noticed, had been put up in 1963.

The year that a Democratic President had been killed.

The year he made his first million dollars.

The year that happened to be a very good one for vintage port.

He carried the glasses to the guests: Bill Stanley, Lamar Fredericks, Woody Crenshaw—all old fogies, his granddaughter might say, if kids still used that word, which of course they didn't—and three other members of the executive committee. Three young partners to whom Burdick was making a point of being kind and deferential.

Three partners who were in absolute terror at the moment—because they had been picked and polished by Wendall Clayton and then leveraged by him onto the executive committee.

The men were in Burdick's study. Outside, wet snow slapped on the leaded glass windows.

"To Hubbard, White & Willis," Burdick said. Glasses were raised but not rung together.

The Reconstruction had began swiftly. Only one of Clayton's lackeys had been fired outright—tall, young Randy Simms III, a fair-to-middlin' lawyer but one hell of a scheming nazi sycophant, Vera Burdick had observed. It had been her delightful task to transmit, through her own social network, rumors of various types of illegal scams the young partner was guilty of. By the time she was through he'd been thoroughly blackballed and was a pariah in the world of New York law and Upper East Side society.

As for the other pretty young men and women associates on Clayton's side . . . they weren't asked to leave, the theory being they'd work even harder to rid themselves of the contamination. These secessionists and collaborators were given the shaved-head treatment then kicked onto the summer outing and hiring committees.

These three Nameless were the last order of business in the Purge.

One of them said, "Your wife, Donald, is a charming lady."

Burdick smiled. They had of course met Vera before this evening though she had never served them dinner, never entertained them, never told them stories of her travels and anecdotes about her famous political friends; never, in short, grilled them like an expert interrogator.

He set the assassination-year bottle in the middle of the tea table.

He said, "Bill knows this but for the rest of you, I have some news. I'm meeting tomorrow with John Perelli. We have a problem, of course. Perelli's position is that Wendall's discussions with him suggest an implicit agreement to go forward with the merger—even though the whole firm's never approved it."

One of the Nameless nodded. Impressed that the man returned his gaze, Burdick continued, "His thinking is that we agreed to negotiate in good faith. The firm has now decided that we do not want to go forward simply because we do not want to go forward. That is *not* good faith. We have an implied contract problem. Look at Texaco and Pennzoil."

Another Nameless: "I know the law, Don." This was a little brash, as the youngster understood immediately; he continued more contritely, "I agree they'd have an argument but I think we hedged well enough so that with Wendall gone the basic deal has changed."

Vera asked bluntly, "Was Clayton's presence a condition precedent to going forward?"

Two of the Nameless blinked, hearing the charming woman nail the legal situation perfectly with one simple question.

"No."

Her husband, smiling, shrugged. "Then, I submit, we still have our problem."

The first Nameless said, "But what would they want as a remedy? Specific performance?"

Burdick decided the man was an idiot and made a mental note to give him only scut work for the rest of his time at Hubbard, White. "Of course not. The courts can't *make* us merge."

Bill Stanley said, "They want money. And what do *we* want?" When no one answered he answered himself, "Silence."

Burdick said, "No more publicity. Under any circumstances. A senior partner kills himself? Bad enough and we're going to lose clients because of that, my friend. Then a suit from Perelli? No, I want to preempt them."

Lamar Fredericks, round, bald and roasted from two weeks of golf on Antigua, said, "Preempt? You mean bribe. Cut the crap and tell us what it's going to cost."

Burdick looked at Stanley, who said to the group, "We'd pay Perelli twenty million. Up to, that is. We'll start lower, of course. Full release and agreement not to say anything to the press. If they do, liquidated damages of a double refund."

Crenshaw snorted. "What does that do to our partnership shares?"

Burdick snapped, "It'll be a cut out of operating profits. Take a calculator and figure it out yourself."

"Will they buy into it?"

Burdick said, "I'll be as persuasive as I can. The reason you're all here is that it would be an expenditure out of the ordinary course. I don't want to present it to the firm. So to authorize it we need a three-quarters vote of the executive committee."

None of them had assumed that this was solely a social dinner, of course, but it was not until this moment that they understood the total implications of the invitation. They were the swing votes and were being tested; Burdick had to know where they stood.

"So," Burdick said cheerfully, "are we all in agreement?"

This was the final exorcism of Wendall Clayton. In these three trim, handsome lawyers resided what was left of his ambitious spirit.

Was his legacy, Burdick wondered, as powerful as the man?

Gazes met. No one swallowed or shuffled. When Burdick called for the vote they each said an enthusiastic "In favor."

Burdick smiled and, when he poured more port, gripped one of them on the shoulder—welcome to the club. He was the foolish partner, the one whose professional life would be a living hell from that day on.

Then Burdick sat down in his glossy leather wingback chair and reflected on how much he despised them for not having the mettle to take Clayton's fallen standard and shove it up his—Burdick's—ass. He then grew somber. "Oh, just so you know: We have another problem, I'm afraid."

"What do you mean?" Stanley's voice was a harsh whine.

"One of the paralegals is in the hospital," Vera Burdick explained. "It's quite serious. I have a feeling she won't survive."

"Who?" a Nameless dared to ask.

"Taylor Lockwood."

"Taylor? Oh, no, not her. She's one of the best assistants I ever had on a closing. What happened?"

"Food poisoning. Nobody knows exactly how she got it."

"Should we—" one of the Nameless began to ask.

But Vera Burdick interrupted. "I'm on top of it. Don't worry."

Bill Stanley shook his head. "God, I only hope it wasn't anything we catered. Could you pass that port, Donald?"

CHAPTER THIRTY-FOUR

███████ Mitchell Reece closed his litigation bag and slid it under the seat of the shuttle from Boston as they approached La Guardia early the next morning.

Still no call from Taylor Lockwood and he hadn't been able to reach her at the firm. He'd gotten only her voice mail.

He wondered what was going on.

But as he stared at the brown and gray expanse of the Bronx beneath him his thoughts returned to Wendall Clayton's funeral, held in an Episcopalian church on Park Avenue. The minister's words came clearly to mind.

I recall one time when I happened to meet Wendall; it was a Saturday evening, late. We happened to be strolling up Madison Avenue together, he returning from the firm, I from some function at my congregation....

The minister had foresaken the pulpit and, like a talk show host, walked down into his audience.

...and we passed a few moments in idle conversation. Though we were in very different places in our lives I saw that there were striking similarities between his profession and mine.

*He voiced some concern for a young man or woman, a lawyer at
his firm, who was suffering from doubts. Wendall wanted to in-
spire this protégé to be the best lawyer they might be . . .*

Hundreds of people. Most of the partners from
Hubbard, White & Willis, many associates, many friends
had attended.

*. . . just as I in my own way deal with spiritual doubt in our
young people. . . .*

Quite a church, Reece recalled. Huge, pointy, Gothic,
solid. All the joists and beams met in perfect unison—high
in the air. It was a fitting place for an aristocratic man to be
eulogized.

Then he thought back to another death at the firm—
Linda Davidoff's. Her funeral, Reece decided, had been
much better. The church was tamer, the minister more upset. It seemed to Reece preferable to get more tears and
fewer words from men of the cloth at times of mourning.

Clayton's Upper East Side minister had been correct
about one thing, though: He and Clayton had indeed been
cut from the same bolt—noblemen and medieval clergy. In
tarot cards pentacles would be their suit. Choose this sign
for dark men of power and money.

Aggressive men.

The minister was seizing an opportunity to preach, just
as Clayton had seized a chance of his own—and had died as
a consequence of his reach.

The sudden grind and windy slam of the plane's wheels
coming down interrupted Reece's thoughts. And as he
glanced out the window, Reece decided it was ironic that he
saw below him the huge cluster of dense graveyards in
Queens—a whole city of a graveyard. He watched until it
vanished under the wing and they landed.

As he walked down the ramp toward the terminal Reece
saw his last name on a card being held up by a limo driver.

"Is that for *Mitchell* Reece?" he asked.

"Yes, sir. You have luggage?"

"Just this."

The man took his bags.

Reece gave him the address of the firm.

"We're supposed to stop someplace else, sir."

"What do you mean?"

"I'm afraid there's some kind of problem."

Reece climbed into the back of the Lincoln. "What kind of problem?"

"An emergency of some kind."

Forty minutes later the driver pulled up in front of yellow-painted doors at an annex to Manhattan General Hospital. It was deserted, except for some big blue biohazard containers and a bloody gurney sitting by itself. It seemed as if a body had just been pulled from it and hauled off to a pauper's grave.

Inside, Reece stopped at a reception desk and was directed down a long, dim corridor.

He found the basement room he sought and pushed open the door.

Gray-faced and red-eyed, Taylor Lockwood blinked in surprise at his entrance and shut off the soap opera she was watching.

She smiled. "Mitchell, it's you! Kiss me—it's not contagious—then see if you can scarf up some food. I'm starving to death."

Suck on ice," Reece said when he returned a few minutes later.

Taylor frowned.

"I asked them what you could have to eat. They said you should suck on ice."

She nodded at the IV. "Glucose. It's pure carbohydrates. I'm dying for a hamburger."

Reece gave her a Life Saver. "You look, well, awful."

"'Awful' is a compliment, considering how I did look. The nurse tells me I've recovered incredibly well."

"What happened?"

Taylor nodded. "I was stupid. I'm sure *my* phone was bugged too, either at my apartment or cubicle. I should've thought about that. Anyway, we got busted—somebody overhead us. And then at lunch yesterday this guy sits down next to me. He drops a book—I mean, *pretends* to drop a book—and when I bent down to pick it up for him I think he squirted botulism culture into my soup."

"Jesus, botulism? The most dangerous food poisoning there is."

She nodded. "I think he got it from Genneco Labs."

"Our client?"

"Yep."

"I was talking to a pathologist here. He told me Genneco does a lot of research into antitoxins—you know, like antidotes."

"So whoever killed Clayton stole some culture—or told the killer about Genneco and *he* stole it?"

She nodded.

"I was feeling a lot better last night but I called Donald and told him I was almost dead, in a coma."

"You what?"

"I wanted word to get around the firm that I was almost dead. I was afraid the killer would try again. I called and pretended I was my doctor." She gave a faint laugh. "I called my parents and told them that whatever they heard I was fine—although I have to say I was inclined to let my father stew a bit more. Carrie Mason's the only one who knows I'm okay."

Reece stroked her cheek. "Botulism...that could've killed you."

"The doctor told me that, 'luckily,' I ingested too *much* of the culture. I got sick immediately and, well, the word they used was, quote, *evacuated* most of the bacteria. Man, it was unpleasant. I'm talking Mount Saint Helens."

He hugged her hard. "We're not going to have to worry about anything like this happening again. I talked to Sam, my friend at the U.S. attorney's office, yesterday afternoon. He's coming down tomorrow with a special prosecutor from Washington. We're going to meet with him at the federal building at three—if you feel up to it."

"I'll feel up to it. Whoever's behind this . . . we're going to stop them. . . ." Her voice faded. "What's wrong, Mitchell?"

"Wrong?" His eyes were hollow and troubled. "You almost got killed. . . . I'm so sorry. If I'd known—"

She leaned forward and kissed him. "Hey, I lost those five pounds I gained at Thanksgiving and then some. Call it an early Christmas present. Now, go on, get out of here. Next time you see me I promise I won't look like Marley's ghost."

CHAPTER THIRTY-FIVE

 The girl walked sheepishly into the hospital room, hiding behind a bouquet of exotic flowers that she'd probably hand-selected from an Upper East Side florist.

"Whoa," Taylor told Carrie Mason, laughing at the massive arrangement. "Anything left in the rain forest?"

The chubby girl set the vase on the bedside table and sat in the functional gray chair near Taylor's bed, studying her carefully.

"You're looking a thousand times better, Taylor," Carrie said. "Everybody's like, ohmagod, she's dying. I wanted to tell them but I didn't. Not a soul—like you said."

Taylor gave her a rundown on her condition and thanked the girl for staying with her just after she'd been admitted.

"It's, like, no problem, Taylor. You looked . . . You were pretty sick."

Attempted murder does that to you.

"Well, I'll be getting out soon. May not eat for a week or so but it'll be good to get vertical again."

The girl avoided Taylor's eyes. She stood and arranged the flowers and it was this compulsive activity that told Taylor that she was troubled by something.

"What is it, Carrie?"

The girl paused, her back to Taylor, then sat down again. Tears were running down her cheeks. She wiped her face with the back of her fleshy hand. "I . . ."

"Go ahead. Tell me. What's the matter?"

"I think I know why Mr. Clayton killed himself. I think it was my fault."

"Your fault?" Taylor said. "What do you mean?"

"Well, okay . . . You know Sean."

One of the firm's busier spies. Taylor nodded.

"Well, what it was . . . see, last week Sean asked me out. I went over to his place. And I thought he wanted to go out with me and I was really, really excited about it. 'Cause I've had this crush on him for, like, a while. But it turned out . . . I mean, the thing was he just wanted to go through my purse."

"Why?"

"To get my log-on pass code for the firm computers. One of the operators told me he went on the system with my user name."

Taylor remembered the gum-snapping computer operator and the blank screen that should have had information about taxis and computer time and phone records. This was interesting. She nodded for the girl to continue and listened carefully.

"When I found out what he did I got totally mad. I asked him how could he do that? I mean, he way used me. Anyway he got all freaked out and apologized. But I was so mad. . . . Well, I wanted to get even with him and . . ." She again attended to the stalks of weird flowers. "And when I was in Connecticut with Mr. Clayton and you . . . Well, afterward, he came on to me, Mr. Clayton, you know and . . . well, we sort of slept together."

Taylor nodded, recalling that she'd overheard the tryst

from Clayton's den. The poor girl, suckered in by the vortex of the partner's eyes and charm.

"So, Sean found out and he had this big fight with Clayton. It was really vicious. I think Sean threatened to go to the executive committee about what happened and Clayton was afraid he'd get fired and he killed himself."

Taylor was frowning. So he and Lillick had had a fight. It had never occurred to her that *Lillick* might have killed Clayton.

Then she focused on the distraught Carrie once more. She couldn't, of course, say anything about Clayton's death but she could reassure the girl. "No, Carrie, that had nothing to do with it." A woman-to-woman smile. "Wendall Clayton slept with half the firm and he couldn't care less if anybody knew about it. Besides, I talked to Donald. I know why Clayton killed himself. I can't tell you but it had nothing to do with you or Sean."

"Really?"

"Promise."

"Despite what happened, I really kind of like him— Sean, I mean. He's weird, but underneath he's not as weird as he seems to be. We kind of patched things up. I think he likes me."

"I'm glad to hear that."

Taylor decided it was time to get out of the hospital. She feigned a yawn. "Listen, Carrie. I'm going to get some sleep now."

"Oh, sure. Feel better." Carrie hugged her. Then she asked, "Oh, one thing—do you know where the United Charities of New York general correspondence file is?"

"No idea. I never worked for them."

The girl frowned. "You didn't?"

"No. Why?"

"I was down in the pen this morning and I saw Donald Burdick's wife in your cubicle."

"Vera?"

"Yeah. She was looking through your desk. And I asked what she needed and she said she was doing a fund-raiser for the UCNY and needed the file. She thought you had it. But we couldn't find it."

"I've never checked out any of their files. Must be a mistake."

Carrie glanced at the TV and her face lit up. "Hey, look, it's *The Bold and the Beautiful....* That's my favorite! I used to love summer vacations so I could watch all the soaps. Can't do that anymore. Things sure change when you start working."

Well, that's the truth....

Taylor's eyes strayed absently to the screen, watching the actors lost in their own intrigues and desires. When she turned to the doorway to say good-bye to Carrie, the paralegal had already left.

Taylor felt uneasy. Lillick, Dudley, Sebastian, Burdick... or somebody else had tried to poison her. They might find out that she was no longer in a coma and try again. She summoned the floor nurse, who in turn managed to track down a resident. The young doctor, seeing the urgency in her eyes, reluctantly agreed to discharge her as soon as the paperwork was finished.

After he'd left, she lay back in bed and looked through her purse for her insurance card.

She found a folded sheet of paper stuck in the back of the address book.

It was the poem that Danny Stuart had given her. Linda Davidoff's poem, her suicide note. She realized that she'd never read it, which she now did.

When I Leave

By Linda Davidoff

When I leave, I'll travel light
and rise above
the panorama of my solitude.
I'll sail to you, fast and high,
weightless as the touch of night.

When I leave, I'll become a light
that shows our love in a clear, essential way
(After all, what is a soul but love?).
After all is reconciled, and the darkness
    pitched away,
I'll travel light, transported home to you
in the buoyancy of pure and peaceful flight.

Taylor Lockwood thought of Linda, the beautiful, quiet, gypsy poet. She read the lines again very slowly.

Then she read them once more.

A moment later a huge orderly appeared in the door. "Ms. Lockwood, good news: The warden called."

He grinned; she frowned, not understanding.

Then the man delivered the rest of what would be his stock joke. "It's a full pardon. You're free to go." And he maneuvered the wheelchair into the room.

■

Taylor Lockwood had learned early who the real power centers were at Hubbard, White.

One of the most powerful was a short, round-faced woman of sixty. Mrs. Bendix had used her miraculous skills at memory and association to save the butts of almost every attorney and paralegal in the firm on more than one occasion by finding obscure file folders buried among the millions of documents residing on the gray metal shelves.

She was the doyen of the firm's massive file room.

Taylor now stood over Mrs. Bendix's frothy blue hair as the woman flipped through the three-by-five cards that were her computer. Taylor silently waited for her to finish. Mrs. Bendix—even more so than a senior partner—was a person one did not interrupt. When she was through she looked up and blinked. "I was told you were in the hospital. We contributed for the flowers."

"They were lovely, Mrs. Bendix. I recovered more quickly than expected."

"They said you were almost dead."

"Modern medicine."

Mrs. Bendix was eyeing Taylor's jeans and sweatshirt critically. "This firm has a dress code. You're outfitted for sick leave, not work."

"This is a bit irregular, Mrs. Bendix. But I have a problem and you're just about the only person who can help me."

"Probably am. No need to stroke."

"I need a case."

"Which one? You've got about nine hundred current ones to chose from."

"An old case."

"In that event, the possibilities are limitless."

"Let's narrow things down. Genneco Labs. Maybe a patent—"

"Hubbard, White does not do patent work. We never have and I'm sure we never will."

"Well, how about a contract for the development of bacterial or viral cultures or antitoxins?"

"Nope."

Taylor looked at the rows and rows of file cabinets. A thought fluttered past, then settled. She asked, "Insurance issues, the storage of products, toxins, food poisoning and so on?"

"Sorry, not a bell is rung, though in 1957 we did have a cruise line as a client. I got a discount and took a trip to Bermuda. I ate pasta that disagreed with me very badly. But I digress."

In frustration, Taylor puffed air into her cheeks.

Mrs. Bendix said tantalizingly, "Since you said toxins, food poisoning and so on I assume you meant toxins, food poisonings and so on."

Taylor knew that when people like Mrs. Bendix bait you, you swallow the worm and the hook in their entirety. She said, "Maybe I was premature when I qualified myself."

"Well," the woman said, "my mind harkens back to . . ." She closed her eyes, creasing her gunmetal eye shadow, then opened them dramatically. "...Biosecurity Systems, Inc. A contract negotiation with Genneco for the purchase and installation of Genneco's new security system in Teterboro, New Jersey. Two years ago. I understand the negotiations were a nightmare."

"Security," Taylor said. "I didn't think about that."

Mrs. Bendix said, "Apparently not."

"Can you tell me if anyone checked out the files on that deal in the past few months?"

This was beyond her brain. The woman pulled the log-book out and thumbed through it quickly then held it open for Taylor to look at. Taylor nodded. "I'd like to check it out too, if you don't mind."

"Surely."

Then a frown crossed Taylor's face. "I wonder if we could just consider one more file. This might be trickier."

"I live for challenges," Mrs. Bendix replied.

CHAPTER THIRTY-SIX

The New York State Department of Social Services worked fast.

After one anonymous phone call to the police the West Side Club became the front-page feature in the evening edition of every tabloid in the New York area.

Though gentlemen did not read such newspapers Ralph Dudley made an exception this once, since the *Times* wouldn't have the story until tomorrow morning. He now sat at his desk, lit only by a single battered brass lamp and the paltry December dusk light bleeding into his office, and stared at the same article he'd already read four times. A half-dozen people were under arrest and two underage prostitutes were being placed in foster homes in upstate New York.

Good-bye Junie, Dudley thought.

He'd made one last trip to see her—just before he'd made the call to 911, which closed up the West Side Art and Photography Club forever.

"Here," he'd said, handing her a blue-backed legal document.

She'd stared at it, uncomprehending. "Like, what is it?"

"It's a court order. The marshal seized your mother's and stepfather's bank accounts and house and they've put the money into a special trust fund for you."

"I . . . Like, I don't get it."

"The money your father left you? The court took it away from your mother and they're giving it back to you. I won my petition."

"Whoa, like radical! How much is it?"

"A hundred and ninety-two thousand."

"Awesome! Can I—?"

"You can't touch it for three years, until you're eighteen."

"Or whatever," she'd added.

"And you only get it if you go to school."

"What? That's fucking bogus."

It was also untrue. There were no strings on the money once she turned eighteen, as the trust officer would undoubtedly tell her. But she'd have a few years to think about it and might just try a class or two. Junie might just succeed at school; she was, he'd concluded, more savvy than half the lawyers at Hubbard, White & Willis.

She'd hugged him and then looked at him in that coy way that, before this, would've melted him. But he'd said he had to be going. He had an important meeting—with a pay phone. He'd looked at her for a long moment then kissed her on the cheek and left.

He wondered if Junie would say anything about him. She was, of course, in a position not only to destroy the delicate balance of his career, such as it was, but also to send him to prison for the rest of his life.

These possibilities he considered with remarkable serenity, sipping coffee from a porcelain cup. He weighed the odds and decided that she would say nothing. Although she'd been badly used by life and had the dangerous edge of those who learn survival skills before maturity, Junie was nonetheless motivated by a kind of justice. She saw essential good and essential evil, assigned her loyalty accordingly and stuck by her choice.

There were few adults with that perception. Or that courage.

Also, Dudley chose to believe that the girl loved him, at least by her wary definition of that word.

Good-bye, Junie....

He now set the paper down and rocked back in his chair.

Reflecting that for once in his forty years as a lawyer he'd given up charming people and trying to win clients. Rather, he'd mastered a tiny bit of the law. In this small area of expertise he was now the best in the city: restitution of parentally converted intestate distributions (though he himself preferred to think of the subniche as "saving teenage hookers' bacon"). And he was proud of what he'd learned and done.

Still, there was one more potential problem: Taylor Lockwood knew his secret.

He picked up the phone and dialed a number he'd been calling so often over the past two days that he had it memorized.

The main operator at Manhattan General Hospital answered. He asked to speak to the floor nurse about the paralegal's condition.

They'd been reluctant to talk about details but it was clear from the tone—as well as from the gossip around the firm—that the girl was near death.

Maybe she'd died. That would take care of all the problems.

But then an orderly came on the phone. The man listened to Dudley's question and replied in a cheerful voice, "Don't you worry, sir. Your niece, Ms. Lockwood, was discharged today. She's doing fine."

An electric charge shot through him at this news. He hung up.

With Clayton dead, she was the one person who could destroy his fragile life here at the firm. She was the one risk to his budding life as a real lawyer. So much of the law deals with risk, Dudley reflected, some acceptable, some not. On which side did Taylor Lockwood fall?

He rocked back, looking out the window at the tiny sliver of New York Harbor that was visible between the two brick walls outside his office.

■■■■■

As she left the firm by the infamous back door—no longer taped open, she noticed—Taylor Lockwood was aware of someone's presence near her.

She stepped onto the sidewalk of Church Street, which at one time had been the shoreline of lower Manhattan. Now a half mile of landfill had extended the island well into the Hudson and the harbor.

Pausing, she looked behind her.

This was a quiet street, with a few bad restaurants, a girlie bar (ironically next to the rear entrance to Trinity Church) and the dingy service entrances to a number of office buildings. The street was now largely deserted.

She noticed a few businesspeople hurrying to or from one of the gyms near here and some construction workers. A number of vans were parked on the narrow street, half on the sidewalk. She had to walk around a drapery cleaning van to step into the street and hail a taxi.

Of course, there were none.

Then, in the bulbous disk of a wide-angle rearview mirror on one of the vans, she noticed a man looking her way.

She gasped.

There was nothing ambiguous about the recognition this time.

It was the man in the baseball cap, the one who'd sat next to her in the coffee shop.

The killer, the thief.

Okay. He doesn't know you saw him. You can get out of this.

Shaking her head casually, as if discouraged that there were no cabs, Taylor turned slowly back to the sidewalk.

Then instantly reversed herself and, sprinting as fast as her still-weak legs could carry her, made straight for population.

She glanced back once and saw that the man had given up any pretense—he was running after her. He reached into his coveralls and pulled out a long dark object. At first she thought it was a gun but then she realized that it was a knife or ice pick.

Still dehydrated and in severe pain from the poisoning, her muscles began to slow. Judging distances, Taylor realized that she wasn't going to make it to Broadway or one of the other heavily traveled streets before the killer reached her.

She stopped suddenly in the middle of the street and jogged down the concrete stairs to the Rector Street subway stop. This was better than the street anyway—not only would there be people on the platform but the token seller in the booth would have a hot line to the transit police. The killer wouldn't follow her here. He—

But he *was* following, grim determination—to kill her—on his face. A glance back showed that he'd picked up the speed, as if he could sense her fatigue and was moving in for the coup de grace.

"Help me!" she screamed to the startled young woman in the token booth. Three or four people scattered or ducked as Taylor vaulted the turnstile and fell hard onto the platform. One man started to help her but she raged, "Get away. No, get away!"

There were more screams behind her as the killer reached the bottom of the stairs and looked for her.

A businessman hovering nearby saw the ice pick in the hand of the killer and backed up.

Rising to her feet, she ran as fast as she could along the platform to the far exit of the subway. She heard the staticky voice of the token seller call out, "Pay your fare," as the killer jumped onto the platform and started after her.

Sprinting as best she could, she came to the end of the platform and turned to run up the stairs at the exit door.

But it was chained.

"Oh, Jesus," she cried. "No ..."

Taylor returned to the platform and saw the killer, his face emotionless, walking slowly now, studying her carefully from thirty feet away. Anticipating her escape routes.

She jumped off the platform and dropped four feet into the muck between the rails. Turning away from the killer, she began to run through the tunnel, stumbling over the slippery ties.

He was right behind her, saying nothing, not threatening her or urging her to stop. Not negotiating—there was only one thing he needed to do—kill her.

Taylor got only about twenty feet when, exhausted, she slipped on a slick piece of tie and nearly fell. By the time she regained her balance the killer had made a leaping grab and seized her by the ankle. She went down hard against the solid piece of wood.

Catching her breath, she lashed out with her other foot and caught him in the mouth or cheek with her sole—a solid blow—and he grunted and lost his grip. "Fuck you," he muttered, spitting blood.

"No, fuck you!" she screamed. And kicked again.

He dodged away from her and swung with the pick.

Taylor rolled away and he missed. But she couldn't climb to her feet; he was coming forward too fast, swinging the steel, keeping her off balance.

Finally she managed to stand but just as she was about to start running he grabbed her overcoat and pulled her legs out from under her. She tumbled again to the ground, her head bouncing hard on a tie. She rose, exhausted, to her hands and knees.

"No," she said. "Please."

The killer was up, ready to pounce. But Taylor remained motionless, on her hands and knees, stunned. "What do you want?" she gasped, breathless, spent.

Still, no answer. But why should he respond? It was clear what he wanted. She was the tiny bird that her father had hunted, she was the victim of the Queen of Hearts—off with her head, off with her head.

The weapon drawing back, its needle-sharp point aiming at her face. She lifted her head and gazed at him, piteous. "Don't, please."

But he leaned forward and lunged with the pick, aiming toward her neck.

Which is when she dropped to her belly and scrabbled backward.

She'd been feigning, remaining on all fours like an exhausted soldier, when in fact she had—somewhere—a tiny bit of strength left.

"Ah, ah, ah, ah . . ."

Taylor squinted at him, still in the position of attack, right arm extended, clutching that terrible weapon.

"Ah, ah, ah, ah . . ." The terrible moan from his throat.

In his haste to stab Taylor he'd ignored what was just beyond her body—what she'd been trying to sucker him into hitting: the electrified third rail of the subway, which held more amperage than an electric chair.

"Ah, ah, ah, ah."

There were no sparks, no crackles but every muscle in his body was vibrating.

Then blood appeared in his eyes and his sandy hair caught fire.

"Ah, ah, ah—"

Finally the muscles spasmed once and he collapsed onto the tracks, flames dancing from his collar and cuffs and head.

Taylor heard voices and the electronic sound of walkie-talkies from the Rector Street platform. She supposed it would be the transit cops or the regular NYPD.

It didn't matter. She didn't want to see them or talk to them.

She knew now that there was only one thing to do that might save her. Taylor Lockwood turned and vanished into the darkness of the tunnel.

CHAPTER THIRTY-SEVEN

"Do you mind my saying? . . . I mean, will you take it personally if I say you don't look very good?" John Silbert Hemming asked.

Taylor Lockwood said to the huge private eye, "I lost eight pounds in two days."

"Quite a diet. You should maybe write a book. I'm told you can make a lot of money doing that."

"We couldn't market it—the secret ingredient ain't so appetizing. I'm feeling better now."

They were at Miracles Pub. She was probing at a bowl of Greek chicken soup flavored with lemon. It wasn't on the menu. Dimitri's wife had made it herself. She had some trouble with the spoon—she had to keep her fingers curled; her rings tended to fall off if she didn't.

"Maybe," he joked cautiously, "you should've taken my offer to have dinner. Probably would've been better than where you ended up eating."

"You know, John, I wish I had." Then she said, "I need a favor."

Hemming, who was eating a hamburger, said, "If it's not

illegal and not dangerous and if you agree to go to the opera with me a week from Saturday at eight o'clock sharp, I'd be happy to oblige."

She considered. She said, "One out of three?"

"Which one?"

"I'd like to go to the opera."

"Oh, dear. Still, it makes me very pleased. Though nervous—considering you're balking on the other two. Now, what's the favor?" He nodded toward his plate. "This is a very good hamburger. Can I offer you some?"

She shook her head.

"Ah." He resumed eating. "Favor?" he repeated.

After a moment, she asked, "Why do people murder?"

"Temper, insanity, love and occasionally for money."

The spoon in her hand hovered over the surface of the soup, then made a soft landing on the table. She pushed the bowl away. "The favor is, I want you to get me something."

"What?"

"A gun. That kind I was telling you about—the kind without any serial numbers."

It would be near quitting time at the firm.

The end of another day at Hubbard, White & Willis.

Files being stacked away, dress shoes being replaced with Adidas and Reeboks, places in law books being marked for the night, edits being dropped in the In Box for the night word processing staff.

Four miles away Taylor Lockwood was hiding out in Mitchell Reece's loft. She was concerned that the person behind Clayton's death might figure out that she'd been responsible for the death of one hired gun and had called in a second one who was staking out her apartment right now.

She picked up the scarred gray .38 revolver that John Silbert Hemming had gotten her. She smelled it, sweet oil and wood and metal warmed by her hand. She hefted the small pistol, much heavier than she'd thought it would be.

Then she put the gun in her purse and walked unsteadily

to Mitchell Reece's kitchen, where she found a pen and one of his pads of yellow foolscap.

She wrote the note quickly—he was due home at any moment—and she didn't want him here to deter her from what she had to do.

In her scrawled handwriting Taylor promised that she'd explain everything to him later—if she wasn't killed or arrested—but she begged him to please, please stay away from the firm tonight. After all the deceit and horrors of the past two weeks she'd learned who Wendall Clayton's killer was. She'd gotten a gun and, finally, she was going to make sure that justice would be done.

CHAPTER THIRTY-EIGHT

Taylor Lockwood had never liked this room—the big conference room in the firm.

For one thing, it was always dim—a pastel room so underlit that the colors became muddy and unreal. For another, she associated it with the large meetings in which the paralegal administrator would gather her flock and give them all a rah-rah pep talk, which amounted to a plea not to quit just because the raises this year were going to be only 5 percent.

Mindless, proletariat babble.

Nonetheless, at eight o'clock in the evening, here was Taylor Lockwood, sitting in a large swivel chair at the base of the U, the chair Donald Burdick reserved for himself.

Suddenly the huge teak doors to the room opened and Mitchell Reece ran inside.

He stopped, gasping, when he saw the gun in her hand.

She looked at him with surprise. "Mitchell, what are you doing here?"

"Your note! I read the note you left. Where did you think I'd be?"

"I told you not to come. Why didn't you listen to me?"

"What're you going to do with the gun?"

She smiled absently. "It's pretty obvious, isn't it? I've got to save us."

"The U.S. attorney's coming tomorrow! Don't do this to yourself."

"The cops? The U.S. attorney?" She laughed skeptically. "And what would they do? We don't have any evidence. You and I are never going to be safe. We got run off the road, I was poisoned. I was almost stabbed to death."

"What?"

She didn't tell him about the latest assault just yet. She muttered, "It's just a matter of time until we're dead—if I don't stop things right here. Now."

"You can't just shoot somebody in cold blood."

"I'll claim self-defense. Insanity."

"The insanity defense doesn't work, Taylor. Not in cases like this."

She rubbed her eyes.

"The man who stole the note's dead."

"What?"

"The janitor or whatever he was, the one who put the poison in my food—him. He tried again. He chased me into the subway. But he got electrocuted."

"Jesus. What did the police say?"

"No." She shook her head. "I didn't go to them. It wouldn't do any good, Mitchell. They'd just hire somebody else."

"Well, who is it?" he asked. "Who's behind all this?"

She didn't answer. She glanced up, over Reece's shoulder, and said, "Turn around and find out." She hid the gun behind her back and called, "We're over here. Come on in."

Reece spun around.

A figure emerged from the dull light of the hallway into the deeper shadow of the end of the conference room. Donald Burdick, his posture perfect, like a ballroom dancer's, stepped past the doors, which swung closed with a heavy snap.

The partner called from across the room, his voice ringing dully, like a bell through fog. "Taylor, it *is* you." He nodded at Reece.

"Surprised to see I'm still alive?"

"Your call . . . it didn't make any sense. What's all this about Wendall's death?" He walked to within ten feet of them and stopped. He remained standing. "We thought you were sick."

"You mean, you *hoped* I was *dead!*" She slowly lifted the gun.

His mouth opened. He blinked. "Taylor, what are you doing with that?"

She started to speak. Her voice choked and then she cleared her throat. "I had a speech rehearsed, Donald. I forgot it. . . . But what I do know is that you hired that man to steal the note and set up Clayton's suicide. Then you had him run us off the road and try to kill me—twice."

The dapper partner gave a harsh bark of a laugh. "Are you crazy?" He looked at Mitchell for help. "What's she saying?"

Reece shook his head, gazing at Taylor with concern.

"I went through the file room logs, Donald. You checked out a file for Genneco last week. I saw your signature."

"Maybe I did. I don't remember. Genneco's my client."

"But there'd be no reason to check *this* file out. It wasn't active. As part of a contract negotiation their insurer analyzed their pathogen storage facility in New Jersey. It was basically a blueprint about how to break into the place. You checked the file out and gave the information to your hit man. He broke in, stole some botulism culture and poisoned me!"

"No, I swear I didn't."

"And when that didn't work you sent him to stab me. Well, he's *dead,* Donald. How do you like that?"

"I don't know what you're talking about." He started to turn and walk away.

"No!" Taylor cried. "Don't move." She thrust the gun toward him. The partner stumbled backward, lifting his hands helplessly.

"Taylor!" Reece shouted.

"No!" she screamed and cocked the gun. Burdick backed against the wall, his eyes huge disks of terror. Reece froze.

They stood in those positions for a long minute. Taylor stared at the gun, as if willing it to fire by itself.

"I can't," she whispered finally. "I can't do it."

The gun drooped.

Reece stepped forward slowly and took the pistol from her. He put his arm around her shoulders. "It's all right," he whispered.

"I wanted to be strong," she said. "I wanted to kill him. But I can't do it."

Burdick said to them both, "I swear I had nothing to do—"

She pulled away from Reece's arm and faced Burdick in her fury. "You may think you have the police and the mayor and everyone else in your pocket but it's not going to stop me from making sure you spend the rest of your life in jail!"

Taylor grabbed a telephone off the table.

The partner shook his head. "Taylor, whatever you think, it's not true."

She had just started dialing when a hand reached over, lifted the receiver away from her and replaced it in the cradle.

"No, Taylor...," Mitchell Reece said. He sighed and lifted the gun, the muzzle pointing at her like a single black pearl. "No," he repeated softly.

CHAPTER THIRTY-NINE

She gave a faint laugh of surprise.

Much the same sound that Mitchell Reece himself had uttered when she told him a few days ago that Clayton had been murdered. Then her smile faded and with bottomless horror in her voice she said, "What are you doing?"

His face was stone, his eyes expressionless, but the answer was clear.

"You, Mitchell?" she whispered.

Donald Burdick said, "One of you tell me what's going on here."

Reece ignored him. Still holding the gun on both of them, he walked to the door, looked outside, made sure the corridor was empty and returned. He said to her angrily, "Why the hell didn't you stop when you should have, Taylor? Why? It was all planned out so carefully. You ruined it."

Burdick, horrified, said, "Mitchell, it was you? You killed Wendall Clayton?"

Taylor's eyes closed for a brief moment. She shook her head.

Reece told her, "Wendall Clayton killed the woman I loved."

Taylor frowned then said, "Linda? Linda Davidoff!"

Reece nodded slowly.

"Oh, my God..."

After a moment Reece said, "It was all about a man and a woman. As simple as that." His eyebrows rose. "A man who'd never had time for relationships, a woman who was beautiful and creative and brilliant. Two people who'd never been in love before. Not real love. It wasn't a good combination. An ambitious, tough lawyer. Best in law school, best at the firm... The woman was a poet—shy, sensitive. Don't ask me how they became close. Opposites attract, maybe. A secret romance in a Wall Street law firm. They worked together and started going out. They fell in love. She got pregnant and they were going to get married."

A moment passed and Reece seemed to be hefting the words to select among them. Finally he continued, "Wendall was working on a case one weekend, and he needed a paralegal. Linda'd cut way back on her hours— that's when she'd stopped working for me and Sean Lillick took over. But she still worked occasionally. She did a few assignments for Wendall Clayton and he got obsessed with her. One weekend in September he found out she was at her parents' summer house in Connecticut, not far from his place. He went to see her, tried to seduce her. She called me, crying. But before I could get up there or she could get away there was a struggle and she fell into the ravine. She died. Clayton left her poem to make it look like a suicide."

"This whole thing," Taylor whispered, "it was fake. You lied about everything.... Your mother, in the hospital? You weren't going to see her at all. You were going to Scarsdale—to take flowers to Linda's grave."

Reece nodded.

The nail of Taylor's index finger touched the marble. "Oh, Mitchell, it's so fucking clear now." She looked at Burdick. "Don't you see what he's done?" She turned to face

Reece, who leaned against the dark, dried-blood-red conference table, looking gaunt and pale. "You got one of your
criminal clients from the pro bono program—what? A hit
man, a killer, a mercenary soldier? You got him to break into
your own file cabinet, steal the Hanover note and hide it in
Wendall's office. Then you had him bug your own office so
you'd look as innocent as possible. You recorded some conversations then planted the tapes with the note. You had me
track him down."

She thought for a moment. "Then, at Clayton's party, I
found the receipt from the security service: upstairs, where
you sent me to search—after you planted it there.... Finally
I found the note in Clayton's office." She laughed bitterly.
"And after the Hanover trial your hit man killed him right
away—because he couldn't very well be accused of something he hadn't done."

The lawyer made no effort to deny any of this.

She continued, "And his suicide note...It was fake,
wasn't it? Who forged it? Another criminal client?"

The associate lifted his eyebrow, conceding the accuracy
of her deduction.

She laughed bitterly, glancing at the partner.

Men of most renowned virtue...

Reece was gazing at her, impassive as a statue.

Eyes still on Reece, locked on his, Taylor said, "And
Donald was a big help, wasn't he?" She turned to the partner. "Nothing personal, Donald, but you laid a pretty damn
good smoke screen." Her hands were shaking now. The
tears started. "And as for me, well, you were keeping pretty
close tabs on your pawn. All you had to do was look across
the pillow."

A bit of emotion blossomed in his face at this—like the
first cracks in spring ice. Reece took a Kleenex from his
pocket and began rubbing the trigger guard and grip and
frame of the gun. He nodded. "You won't believe me if I tell
you that what happened between us wasn't part of the
plan."

"Bullshit! You tried to kill me!"

His eyes grew wide. "I didn't want to hurt you! You should have stopped when you were supposed to!"

Burdick said, "But Mitchell, how could you risk it? You love the law. You'd *risk* everything for this, for revenge?"

He smiled with a look as bleak as a hunting field in December. "But there *was* no risk, Donald. Don't you know me by now? I knew I'd get away with it. Every nuance was planned. Every action and reaction. Every move anticipated and guarded against. I planned this exactly the same way I plan my trials. There was no way it wouldn't work." He sighed and shook his head. "Except for you, of course, Taylor. You were the flaw. . . . Why didn't you just let it go? I killed an evil man. I did the firm—hell, I did the *world*—a favor."

"You used me!"

Donald Burdick sat heavily in a chair, his head dipping. "Oh, Mitchell, all you had to do was go to the police. Clayton would've been arrested for the girl's death."

The young lawyer gave a harsh laugh. "You think so? And what would've happened, Donald? Nothing. Any half-assed criminal lawyer could've gotten him off. There was no witness, no physical evidence. Besides, you of all people ought to know how many favors Clayton could've called in. The case wouldn't've even gotten to the grand jury."

His attention dipped for a moment to the gun. He flipped it open expertly and saw six cartridges in the cylinder. Then from his pocket he took the note that Taylor Lockwood had written to him, the note about going to confront a killer. He folded it into a tight square, stepped forward and stuffed it into her breast pocket.

She whispered, nodding at it, "I wrote my own suicide note, didn't I? I kill Donald and then myself. Oh, my God . . ."

"It's your fault," he muttered. "You should've just moved on, Taylor. You should've let Clayton stay in hell and let the rest of us get on with our business."

"My fault?" She leaned forward. "What the hell happened to you? Has it all caught up? Finally? Pushing, pushing, pushing...years and years of it. Win the case, win the goddamn case—that's all you see, all you care about! You don't know what justice is anymore. You've turned it inside out."

"Don't lecture me," he said wearily. "Don't talk to me about things you can't understand. I live with the law, I've made it a part of me."

Burdick said, "There's no way you can justify it, Mitchell. You killed a man."

Reece rubbed his eyes. After a moment, he said, "You get asked a lot why you go to law school. Did you go because you wanted to help society, to make money, to further justice? That's what people always want to know. Justice? There's so little of it in the world, so little justice in our lives. Maybe on the whole it balances out; maybe God looks down from someplace and says, 'Yeah, pretty good, I'll let it go at that.' But you know the law as well as I do, both of you. Innocent people serve time and guilty ones get off. Wendall Clayton killed Linda Davidoff and he was going to go free. I wasn't going to let that happen."

Taylor said, "The suicide note—Clayton's. 'Men of most renowned virtue...' How does it go?"

Reece said, "'Have sometimes by transgressing most truly kept the law.'"

"You meant it about you, then, not Clayton."

Reece nodded solemnly. "It's about me."

"Mitchell," Burdick whispered, "just put the gun down. We'll go to the police. If you talk to them—"

But Reece walked slowly over to Taylor. He stood two feet away. She didn't move.

"No!" Burdick shouted. "Don't worry about the police. We can forget what happened. There's no need for this to go beyond this room. There's no need...."

Reece glanced at the partner briefly but didn't speak. His whole attention was on Taylor. He touched her hair, then her cheek. He nestled the muzzle of the gun against her breast.

"I wish..." He cocked the gun. "I wish..."

Taylor wiped the thick tears. "But it's me, Mitchell. *Me*. Think about what you're going to do."

"Please, Mitchell," Burdick said. "Money, do you want money? A fresh start somewhere?"

But it was Taylor who raised her hand to silence the partner. "No. He's come too far. There's nothing more to say."

At last there were tears on Reece's face. The gun wavered and rose. For a moment it seemed to be levitating; maybe he intended to touch the chill muzzle to his own temple and pull the trigger.

But his deeper will won and he lowered the black weapon to her once more.

Alice, in this dreadful world on the other side of the looking glass, remained completely still. There was no place to go. All she could do was close her eyes, which is what she now did.

Mitchell Reece, practical as ever, held his left hand to his face to protect himself from the blast—and her spattered blood—and then he pulled the trigger.

CHAPTER FORTY

In the hushed conference room the metallic click was as loud as the gunshot would have been.

Reece's eyes flickered for a moment. He pulled the trigger three more times.

Three more clicks echoed throughout the room. His hand lowered.

"Fake," he whispered with the tone of someone observing an impossible occurrence. "It's fake?"

Taylor wiped the streaming tears from her face. "Oh, Mitchell..."

Burdick stepped forward and firmly lifted the gun away from him.

Taylor said, "The gun's real, Mitchell, but the bullets're just props." She shook her head. "All I had was speculation. I needed proof that you did it."

Reece leaned against the wall. "Oh, my God." He was staring at Taylor. "How?" he whispered. She'd never seen such shock in anyone's eyes—pure, uncomprehending astonishment.

"A lot of clues I finally put together today," she said. "What got me wondering was the poem, Linda's poem."

"Poem?"

"The one that Wendall left as her suicide note. I read it in the hospital and, you know, everybody *thought* it was a suicide note. But nobody really understood what it was about. It was a *love* poem. It wasn't about killing herself, it was about leaving solitude and loneliness and starting a new life with somebody she loved. Anybody who was going to kill herself wouldn't leave that as a suicide note. Danny Stuart, her roommate, said she wrote it just a few days before she died."

He was shaking his head. "Impossible. You couldn't make that kind of deduction, not from the suicide note back to me."

"No, of course not. It's just what put the idea in my head that maybe she didn't kill herself. But then I started to think about everything that'd happened since you'd asked me to help you find the note, everything I'd learned. I thought about you nudging me away from the other suspects and toward Clayton. I thought about what kind of strategist you were, about Clayton's womanizing, about how it would be easy for you to get a gun from one of your clients in the criminal pro bono program. Your trips to Linda's grave . . . I had my private-eye friend check out your mother. Yes, she was a paranoid schizophrenic. But she died four years ago. Oh, Mitchell, you looked me right in the eye and lied. I felt like crying when you told me about your mother!"

Still, he held her eye, not a flicker of remorse in his.

"Then," she continued, "I called the Boston U.S. attorney's office. Your friend Sam hasn't worked for them for four years. . . . You faked that call to him from the street in front of your loft, didn't you?" Her anger broke through. "You're a pretty fucking good actor, Mitchell!"

Then, calming, she continued. "Hard evidence? You yourself helped me there—that first day I met you, when you mentioned that the records in law firms reveal all kinds of information about where people've been and how they

spend their time. I went through the time sheets going back
a year and figured out exactly what happened. It's all right
there: You and Linda working together, taking time off together, logging travel time to clients on the same date, joint
meal vouchers. Then Linda's time drops and she takes sick
leave and files insurance claims because she's pregnant. And
not long after that she dies.

"Then I found the Genneco security system contract negotiation files. And, yeah, it was checked out to Donald. But
if he'd used them to get access to the botulism he sure as
hell wouldn't use his own name. Then I asked Mrs. Bendix
to find any other files Donald had supposedly checked out
recently. There was one—an insurance claim. Where a car
went off the road and looked like it was going to sink in the
reservoir in Westchester but ended up on a ledge of rock
that kept it from sinking. In exactly the same place we drove
into the reservoir that night. You needed to make it look like
Clayton was desperate enough to kill us so he'd be desperate enough to kill himself. Right? Am I right?"

Reluctantly he nodded.

"Oh, sure, a lot of people had motives to kill Clayton.
Thom Sebastian and Dudley and Sean Lillick...and
Donald here. Even Donald's wife. And probably a dozen
other people. But I decided you were wrong—when you
told me that motive is the most important thing in finding a
killer. No, the most important thing is finding the person
who has the *will* to murder. Remember your herald,
Mitchell? Preparation and will? Well, of all the people in this
firm, you were the only one I believed could actually murder someone. The way you destroyed that doctor on cross-
examination...you had a killer's heart. I could see that.

"But even then I wasn't absolutely sure. So I called
Donald earlier tonight and we arranged this little play of our
own—to find out for sure."

"You don't understand," Reece whispered desperately.
"Clayton was pure evil. There was no way to bring him to
justice otherwise. He—"

Taylor's hand flew up toward him, palm out. "Justice?"

she raged. "Justice?" She sighed and lowered her head, speaking into the microphone hidden under her collar.

"John, could you come in please?"

The door opened and John Silbert Hemming entered. Reece stared up at the huge man as he gripped Reece's arm tightly and stepped protectively between the lawyer and Taylor.

The man said to her softly, "You could have stopped earlier, before he tried to use that." Nodding at the gun. "We had enough on tape for a conviction."

She was looking into Reece's evasive eyes as she said in a whisper, "I had to know."

The handcuffs went on quickly, with a crisp, ratchety sound.

"You can't do this!" Reece muttered bitterly. "You have no legal authority. It's illegal detention and kidnapping. And that fucking tape is illegal. You'll be subject—"

"Shhhh," John Silbert Hemming said.

"—to civil liability and criminal charges, which I'll pursue on the federal and state levels. You don't know the kind of trouble—"

"Shhhh," the big man repeated, looking down at Reece ominously. The lawyer fell silent.

Seeing Reece standing in front of her, oddly defiant, even angry at what they'd done to him, she wondered if she was going to scream, or slap him, or even reach for his throat with her hands, which seemed to have the strength, more than enough, to strangle him to death.

Reece said, "Taylor, I can make you understand. If you'll just—"

"I don't want to hear anything more."

But she was speaking only to John Silbert Hemming, who nodded solemnly and escorted the lawyer out into the firm's lobby to await the police.

███████

She spent an hour giving several lengthy statements to two humorless detectives from Police Plaza. She refused a ride home from gallant John Silbert Hemming but promised that she'd call him about their opera "date," a word that she pointedly used.

"Looking forward to it," he said, ducking his head to step into the elevator car.

Taylor walked slowly back to her cubicle. She was almost there when she heard the sound of a photocopier and noticed Sean Lillick copying sheets of music on the Xerox machine near the paralegal pen. He looked up and blurted, "Taylor! You're out of the hospital? We heard you were totally sick."

"Back from the dead," she said, glancing at the music, the copying of which he was probably charging to a client.

"You're all right?"

If you only knew . . .

"I'll live."

He nodded toward the manuscript paper. "Take a look. My latest opus. It's about Wendall Clayton. I found all of these pictures and papers and things in his office the other day and I'm writing this opera about him. I'm going to project pictures on the screen and get some Shakespearean text and—"

She leaned close and shut him up with an exasperated look. "Sean, can I give you some advice?"

He looked at the music. "Oh, these're just the rough lead sheets. I'm going to arrange them later."

"I don't mean that," she whispered ominously. "Listen up: If Donald Burdick doesn't know you were Clayton's spy yet, he will in about a day or two."

He gazed at her uneasily. "What're you talking about?"

"I'm talking about this: Pack up your stuff and get out of here. I'd recommend leaving town."

"Who the hell're you to—"

"You think Clayton was vindictive, you ain't seen nothing yet. Donald'll sue your ass for every penny of the money Clayton paid you to be his weasel."

"Fuck you. What money?"

"That you've got hidden under your stinky mattress."

He blinked in shock. He started to ask how she knew this but he gave up. "I was just—"

"And one more thing. Leave Carrie Mason alone. She's too good for you."

The kid tried to look angry but mostly he was scared. He grabbed his papers and scurried off down the corridor. Taylor returned to her cubicle. She'd just sat down and begun to check phone messages when she heard someone coming up behind her. She spun around fast, alarmed.

Thom Sebastian stood in the doorway, hands stuffed in his pockets.

"Hey," he said, "only me. Mr. Party Animal. Didn't mean to spook you."

"Thom."

"I was mega-freaked when I heard you were sick. They wouldn't let me in to see you. Did you get my flowers?"

"I might have. I was pretty out of it. I couldn't read half the cards."

"Well, I was worried. I'm glad you're okay. You lost weight."

She nodded and said nothing.

A dense, awkward moment. His voice quavered as he said, "So."

"So."

He said, "Anyway, I just wanted to let you know.... Looks like I'm leaving."

"The firm?"

He nodded. "What I was telling you about, that new firm I'm starting with Bosk? It's going to happen. Tomorrow's my last day here. I've got ten associates from Hubbard, White coming with me. And a bunch of clients too. We've already got fifteen retainer agreements. St. Agnes, McMillan, New Amsterdam, RFC, a bunch of others."

Taylor laughed. "You're kidding." These were Hubbard, White's biggest clients. They represented close to one third of the firm's revenues.

Thom said, "We're going to do the same work Hubbard, White did but charge them about half. They were ready to leave anyway. Most of the presidents and CEOs I talked to said everybody here was paying too much attention to the merger and firm politics and not enough to the legal work. They said the other associates and I were the only ones who gave a shit about them."

"That's probably true."

"The funny thing is, if I'd made partner I'd be under a noncompetition agreement so I couldn't've taken any clients with me. But since I'm just an associate the firm can't stop me."

"Congratulations, Thom."

She started to turn back to her desk. But he stepped forward nervously and touched her arm. "The thing is, Taylor." He swallowed uneasily. "The thing is, I have to say something." He looked around, his eyes dark and troubled. "I've spent a lot of time..." He swallowed. "I've spent a lot of time thinking about you and checking you out. What you found in my office, my notes about you? I shouldn't've done that, I know. But I just couldn't get you out of my head."

Taylor stood up, glanced at her arm. He removed his hand from it and stepped back. "What're you saying?" she asked.

"I'm saying I learned some things about you that're a problem for me."

She looked at him steadily. "Yes?"

"I've learned that you're the sort of person I don't think I'll ever meet again. Who I think I could spend the rest of my life with." He looked away. "I guess I'm saying that I think I love you."

She was too surprised even to laugh.

He held up a pudgy hand. "I know you think I'm goofy and crude. But I don't have to be that way. I *can't* be that way at my new firm. I'm giving up the drugs. That's what I was meeting with Magaly about the night she was killed— the night you got me out of jail. I wasn't going to score any-thing—I was going to tell her I wasn't going to buy from her anymore. I was doing that for you. Then, that night at the Blue Devil, I was going to ask if you maybe wanted to go out with me—kind of, I guess, steady." He shook his head at the old-fashioned word. "I had it all planned out, what I was going to say . . . but then Magaly got shot and you had to bail me out. The whole night went to hell and I couldn't even look you in face, let alone tell you how I felt about you."

She began to speak but he took a deep breath. "No, no, no, don't say anything yet. Please, Taylor. Just think about what I said. Will you do that? I'll have the firm, I'll have money. I can give you whatever you want. If you want to go to law school, fine. You want to play music, fine. You want to have a dozen babies, fine."

"Thom."

"Please," he begged, "don't say yes and don't say no. Just think about it." He took a deep breath and seemed on the verge of tears. "Jesus, I'm the world's greatest fucking negotiator and here I am breaking all my rules. Look, everything's in there." He handed her a large white envelope.

"What is it?" she asked.

"I did kind of a deal memo."

Now, she couldn't help but laugh. "Deal memo?"

He grinned. "For us. About how we might work things out. Don't panic, we don't get to marriage until phase four."

"Phase four."

"We'll take it nice and easy. Please, just read it and let the idea sit for a while."

"I'll read it," she said.

Then, unable to resist, he threw his arms around her and hugged her hard. He retreated before she could say anything more.

Don't get too interested in her. . . . Sebastian's comment to Bosk. It was a warning from a jealous lover, not a potential killer.

Taylor lowered her face to her hands and laughed softly. Thinking: I guess it's safe to say, *What a night.*

Her desk was a mess; Vera Burdick's ransacking hadn't left it in very good shape. When she'd called Burdick about Reece earlier in the evening she'd asked him bluntly why his wife was searching through her things.

"Vera doesn't trust anybody," Burdick had said, laughing. "Samuel Lockwood's daughter? She thought for sure you were working with Clayton, helping him push the merger through—or, after he died, sabotaging me. You should consider it a compliment."

The way a fly should feel complimented that he's a spider's first choice for dinner.

Taylor noticed a blinking red light on her phone. She lifted the receiver and pressed the play button.

"Hey, counselor."

Hello, Dad.

"Listen, hope you're feeling better. 'Cause I've made some plans for us tomorrow. I get into La Guardia in the morning. How 'bout you come pick me up? I've made lunch reservations at the Four Seasons. There's somebody from Skadden I want you to meet. A senior partner. He said they're looking for people like my little overachiever. Now, get a pen: My plane gets in at—"

Click. Taylor Lockwood hit a button.

A woman's electronic voice reported: *"Your message has been deleted."*

She hung up the receiver.

Taylor pulled on her raincoat and walked through the half-lit corridors. The Slavic cleaning women in their blue uniforms moved from office to office with their wheeled carts. Taylor could hear the whine of vacuums coming from different directions. She imagined she could smell sour gunpowder, as if Reece had in fact fired real bullets from the heavy pistol. But she realized, as she passed a conference room littered with a thousand papers, that the smell was only the residue of cigar smoke. Earlier in the evening a deal had perhaps closed here. Or maybe it'd fallen apart. Or maybe negotiations had been postponed till tomorrow or the next day. In any case the participants had abandoned the room for the time being, leaving behind only the pungent aroma of tobacco as the evidence of that success or failure or uncertainty.

The police had gone. Burdick had gone. The partner would need some rest—he'd have plenty to do in the morning. More favors would have to be called in. Taylor suspected, though, that Donald Burdick and his wife would have a sizable inventory remaining.

She continued through the firm, pressed a door latch button and stepped into the lobby. The door swung closed behind her and when the elevator arrived she stepped in wearily.

Outside, Wall Street was nearly as quiet as the halls of Hubbard, White & Willis. This neighborhood was a daytime place. It worked hard and curled up to sleep early. Most of the offices were dark, the bartenders had stopped pouring drinks, cabs and cars were few.

Occasionally someone in a somber overcoat would appear from a revolving door then vanish into a limo or cab or down a subway stairwell. Where, she wondered, were they going? To one of Sebastian's clubs, to pursue some private lust like Ralph Dudley, to plot a coup like Wendall Clayton?

Or maybe just to retreat to their apartments or houses for a few hours' sleep before the grind began again tomorrow?

What a place this was, the topsy-turvy land at the bottom of the rabbit hole. . . .

But, Taylor considered, was this *her* land?

Alice's trips to Wonderland and the Looking-Glass world had, after all, been dreams and the girl had eventually wakened from them.

She couldn't, for the moment, say.

Taylor flagged down a cab, got in and gave the driver the address of her apartment building. As the dirty vehicle squealed away from the curb she slouched down in the seat, staring at the greasy Plexiglas divider.

Thank you for not smoking. 50-cent surcharge after 8 p.m.

The cab was a block away from her apartment when she leaned forward and told the driver she'd changed her mind.

Taylor Lockwood sat in the spotlight.

Dimitri twisted his curly hair and leaned over the microphone. (His habitual suspicion left when she told him,

"I'll play for free. You keep the receipts—all of them—but the tips're mine. And, Dimitri: No satin touch. Not tonight, okay?")

"Ladies and gentlemen..."

She whispered ominously, "Dimitri."

"...it is my pleasure to present Miss Taylor Lockwood at the piano."

He hit the switch controlling the faux spotlight. She smiled at the crowd and touched the keys, cold and smooth as glass, enjoying their yielding resilience as she began to play.

After half an hour Taylor looked out into the cockeyed lights, brilliant starbursts beaming at her, so bright she couldn't see the patrons. Maybe the wobbly tables were completely occupied. Or maybe the place was empty. In any event, if anyone *was* in the audience they were listening in absolute silence.

She smiled, not to them but only for herself, and swayed slowly as she played a medley of Gershwin that she herself had arranged, all revolving around *Rhapsody in Blue*. Tonight she improvised frequently, playing jazzy harmonies and clever riffs, allowing the music to carry itself, the notes soaring and regrouping, then flying to risky altitudes. But Taylor Lockwood never let go completely and was careful to alight at regular intervals on the theme; she knew how much people love the melody.

About the Author

A former journalist, folksinger and attorney, Jeffery Deaver is the international number-one bestselling author of thirty-seven novels, three collections of short stories and a non-fiction law book, and a lyricist of a country-western album. His novels have appeared on bestseller lists around the world and are sold in 150 countries and translated into twenty-five languages.

His most recent novels are *Solitude Creek*, a Kathryn Dance novel; *The October List*, a thriller told in reverse; and *The Steel Kiss*, a Lincoln Rhyme novel. For his Dance novel *XO* Deaver wrote an album of country-western songs, available on iTunes and as a CD; and before that, *Carte Blanche*, a James Bond continuation novel, a number-one international bestseller.

Deaver has been nominated for seven Edgar Awards, an Anthony, a Shamus and a Gumshoe. He was shortlisted for the ITV3 Crime Thriller Award and for the Prix Polar International 2013.

His novel *A Maiden's Grave* was made into an HBO movie, and *The Bone Collector* was a feature release from Universal Pictures, starring Denzel Washington and Angelina Jolie. Lifetime aired an adaptation of his *The Devil's Teardrop*. And, yes, the rumours are true; he did appear as a corrupt reporter on his favourite soap opera, *As the World Turns*. He was born outside Chicago and has a bachelor of journalism degree from the University of Missouri and a law degree from Fordham University.

Readers can visit his website at www.jefferydeaver.com.

JEFFERY
DEAVER

THE LESSON
OF HER DEATH

When Detective Bill Corde looks at the beautiful
face of the murdered girl in the mud, he does not
know his own life is about to turn into
a terrifyingly real nightmare.

For the girl's killer is now on the trail of Corde
and his unsuspecting family: his wife, teenage son,
and imaginative but vulnerable daughter, Sarah.
Sarah, who alone knows the identity of the killer . . .

The lesson Bill Corde is about to learn – the lesson
of her death – is an education that no one
will ever forget.

Out now in paperback and ebook.

HODDER